3e Shopper, Buyer, and Consumer Behavior

Theory, Marketing Applications, and Public Policy Implications

Third Edition

Jay D. Lindquist
Western Michigan University

M. Joseph Sirgy
Virginia Polytechnic Institute & State University

ATOMIC**dog**PUBLISHING

Cincinnati, Ohio
www.atomicdog.com

Book Team

Vice President, Publisher Steve Scoble
Developmental Editor Christine Abshire
Director of Interactive Media and Design Joe Devine
Director of Quality Assurance Tim Bair
Senior Production Coordinator Mary Monner
Quality Assurance Editor Dan Horton
Marketing Manager Mikka Baker
Web Production Editor Joyce Powers
Cover Design Zach Hicks

ISBN 1-59260-232-0

Library of Congress Control Number: 2005928584

Printed in the United States of America by Atomic Dog Publishing,
35 East Seventh Street, Fourth Floor, Cincinnati, Ohio 45202

10 9 8 7 6 5 4 3 2 1

Brief Contents

iv

Contents

v

Cases

Marketplace Boxes

Preface

As the title of this text—*Shopper, Buyer, and Consumer Behavior: Theory, Marketing Applications, and Public Policy Implications*—indicates, this book focuses on consumer decision making and behavior, with consideration of the theoretical foundations and practical marketing management implications and actions. We present some answers to the question, "Why do consumers do what they do in the marketplace when they do it?" and raise others.

This text is about a subset of behaviors—the psychology and sociology of human behavior as it relates to consumer decision making and actions. Shopping, buying, and consuming of goods and services that deliver desired benefits is a major focus of the book. In fact, we assert that people do not really buy "goods" and "services"; they buy the "benefits" that these goods and services provide. Thus, when consumers buy toothpaste, they are really buying healthy teeth and gums, or fewer trips to the dentist, or fresh breath, or a bright, sexy smile. We also deal with where goods and services may be purchased and how shoppers decide where to go. We use the word *outlet* rather than *retail store*, since people can shop and buy in many places, such as on the web, at the mall, from a catalog, at a flea market, or in a "bricks-and-mortar" store. For example, you can buy cars from dealers, homes through retailers, airline tickets on the web, and antiques at yard sales.

Understanding what benefits consumers are seeking and how they make decisions, shop, buy, and actually consume helps marketers develop and carry out more effective product/service, price, place, and promotion actions. Hence, practical marketing management implications and actions are also key ingredients in this book. As you read and study this text, you will be able to better understand your own behavior in the marketplace and, we hope, improve upon it.

Note that this field of study focuses on decision making, shopping, buying, and consuming behavior. Some students have the impression that this field only touches on shopping and buying, with the acts of consumption, possession, and/or use of a product not being key parts. In fact, coverage of consumption is often sparse in other texts. We feel that understanding consumption has major importance in the development of marketing strategies. How individuals use a particular product or service, taking advantage of its benefits, is a driving force for marketers as they develop, position, and sell what people are looking for.

The study of decision making, shopping, buying, and consuming is part of "marketing science." That is, it is a scientific field of study designed to help marketers make better decisions as they develop goods and services that deliver the benefits consumers are seeking. Motivation to buy is often driven by a desire to enjoy a certain quality of life. Study in these areas is one part "marketing science" and one part "policy science." It's about marketing and also about public policy. Public policy designed to regulate marketing should be guided by study and mastery of the various areas presented in this book. Public policy officials have to understand how people make decisions, shop, buy, and consume before determining the need for and scope of any regulation.

One final point: This text does not deal only with individual behaviors. Shoppers, buyers, consumers, and decision makers can be families and organizations. Thus, topics related to these units are also covered.

Our Objectives in Writing This Book

Our main purpose in writing this book was to address the issues just presented in a way that is direct and relevant to you—the student. That's the short answer. The longer answer is that we wrote this book to accomplish a number of objectives, specifically:

- To encourage you to take a closer look at the marketplace around you and then to consider what you have observed and experienced as you look at the theory and practical applications discussed in the text
- To offer you the chance to work through the "whys" related to consumer decision making and behavior
- To provide you with a better understanding of the causal links between consumer behavior and marketer behavior
- To establish the practical connection between what we know and understand about consumer behavior and the development of sound marketing strategy, targeting, positioning, and marketing mix decisions
- To move you to the point where you will become a more informed, efficient, and effective consumer
- To expose you to the most current thinking and research results, giving you an up-to-date perspective on what we know and understand about shopper, buyer, and consumer behavior and its public policy implications
- To train you to think like consumer researchers

The book is suitable for a variety of college students, most obviously those in business majors—particularly, marketing and advertising—as well as communications and journalism majors who are studying advertising, integrated marketing communications majors, interactive marketing majors, and other promotion-related majors. Students in the consumer sciences, retailing, and fashion merchandising also will find this text very useful, as will students in cross-functional studies of consumer behavior as a subset of human behavior. If you are a student at a four-year college or university or a two-year college, this book is written for you. The text is concise, yet thorough in its coverage. It is practical in its viewpoint, up-to-date, and "on-theory."

We have made the text friendly, interesting, and involving. The language and style are more familiar and conversational than is typical of texts on consumer behavior. There is a strong emphasis on tying your own experiences and what you see or have seen around you in the marketplace into the text's flow of topics.

Current Influences

We are in times of great change, and the text addresses some of the key issues of our day, including (1) consumer behavior in the global marketplace; (2) the changing ethnic character of North America and the resulting variety of consumer behavior patterns; (3) the Internet as a marketplace and its influence on consumer behavior and the retail landscape; (4) an increased understanding that consumers buy benefits, not simply products and services; (5) the changing makeup of the households of America and how this affects the marketplace behavior of these units; (6) the consumer behavior impact of shifting gender roles across cultures; (7) environmentally and socially responsible consumption; and (8) the increasing cry for enforcement of the "Consumer Bill of Rights." Also, the events of September 11, 2001 have impacted consumer behavior worldwide, and this impact is touched upon in a number of places in the text. All of these topics are sometimes treated separately, but in many cases, are woven throughout the fabric of the entire book because that is the reality of their impact.

What's New for This Edition

A major review of the key marketing, consumer behavior, advertising, and related scholarly journals was used to update the text, along with many other relevant magazine, newspaper, website, and selected sources. Flow diagrams are now present in all chapters to offer visual relationship presentations, thereby tying together the various sections of the chapter material for a clearer view. Additional sources are cited in a number of areas to maintain the up-to-date nature of the theory, research, and applications presented.

The following are examples of new and/or expanded topics included in this edition:

- *Chapter 1*—Skill capital and information capital, irrelevant information impact, a new section on Uber-commerce (U-commerce)

- *Chapter 3*—The new political dimensions of country of origin based on 9/11, consumer evaluative criteria and planning based on 9/11, online choice decisions

- *Chapter 4*—Expansion of material on compulsive consumption, online customer satisfaction, mere-measurement impact on customer satisfaction, marketer ethical performance and ethical cues influence on satisfaction, consumer "fandom," loyalty in e-commerce, service failure and recovery impact, dealing with angry or hostile customers

- *Chapter 5*—More recent research on self-image congruence and the influence of personality traits on consumer behavior

- *Chapter 6*—More coverage of recent research on consumer lifestyles and the psychology of relationship marketing

- *Chapter 7*—Significant expansion of the section on consumer perceptions to reinforce "old" topics and to cover new topics

- *Chapter 8*—More coverage of recent research on consumer motivation, emotions, mood, and involvement

- *Chapter 9*—More coverage of recent research on consumer beliefs, affect, attitude, and intention

- *Chapter 10*—Bilingual advertising, model beauty and trustworthiness impact, advertising spokesperson gender influence, animation speed impact on web page effectiveness, "priming" effects on web pages, fear appeals and adolescents, attention capture—visuals, text and brand elements

- *Chapter 11*—Cultural role in marketer's ethical decision making, time scarcity and time personality impact, stressed-out individuals in the marketplace

- *Chapter 12*—Cell phone manners and civility, expanded section on consumer ethnocentrism with added international focus, patriotism impact of 9/11

- *Chapter 13*—African-American male perceptions of the marketplace, selection of family-safe food products, Latino youth and television, behavior of foreign-born consumers in the U.S., Chinese children in America, Chinese-American shopping behavior, new material on "Tweens," teens and cell phones, teen deception of parents with regard to purchasing and consumption behavior, new section on Generation Y (shopping, buying and consumption behaviors), the new "youth-car" segment, seniors (net worth, Internet use, serving them on the web)

- *Chapter 14*—Luxury, luxury goods and choice behavior, "best friends" as a market segment

- *Chapter 15*—Marketplace behavior of working women with infants, men's influence on household decisions, husband-wife influence, men who shop, do's and don'ts of marketing to today's youth, consumer behavior of children in China

- *Chapter 16*—More coverage of recent research in public policy and consumer advocacy

- *Chapter 17*—More coverage of recent research related to issues of macro-consumption and quality-of-life issues

- *Chapter 18*—Identifying organization decision-makers, multigenerational technology diffusion, why new technology is not readily accepted, and the theory of innate consumer innovativeness

We also added a chapter on consumer research (Chapter 19). This chapter does not focus on traditional marketing research methods that are typically found in many of the marketing research textbooks. Instead, the chapter focuses on showing how marketing researchers can and should use models and concepts from the study of shopper, consumer, and buyer behavior to guide the formulation of the research questions, select an appropriate research design, and develop methods for data collection and measures for the research constructs.

At the end of the book, we also added a number of cases that can be used for homework assignment, in-class discussion, and group projects. Many of the cases were selected with students' interests in mind. Example cases involve Nextel cell phone service, Netflix DVD rental, and iPod MP-3 players, among many others.

Text Organization

The book is divided into five parts. Part 1 contains a single chapter, focusing on the consumer's search for benefits in the marketplace, discovering segments of like consumers, positioning products in the minds of consumers, and applying a comprehensive consumer behavior model.

Part 2 deals with the consumer as decision maker. Chapters 2 through 4 flow through the steps in the consumer decision-making process, with consumption as a separate topic added after presentation of the choice step. Chapter 2 covers problem recognition and information search, Chapter 3 discusses alternative evaluation and choice, including outlet choice, and Chapter 4 focuses on consumption and post-purchase behavior.

Part 3 focuses on the following psychological influences on consumer decision making and related topics: symbolic consumption, self-image, and personality (Chapter 5); personal values, lifestyles, psychographics, and relationships (Chapter 6); memory, learning, and perception (Chapter 7); motivation, emotion, mood, and involvement (Chapter 8); beliefs, affect, attitude, and intention (Chapter 9); and communications and persuasion (Chapter 10).

Part 4 is devoted to sociological influences on consumer decision making, with emphasis on the following topics: cultural influences: perspectives (Chapter 11); cultural influences: generalizations and cross-cultural perspectives (Chapter 12); subcultural influences (Chapter 13); social class and reference group influences (Chapter 14); and household and family influences (Chapter 15).

Part 5, the closing section of the book, addresses "special topics," including public policy and consumer advocacy (Chapter 16), consumer behavior and society (Chapter 17), organizational buying and diffusion of innovation (Chapter 18), and consumer research (Chapter 19).

The text's organization is flexible, such that after Part 1, the remaining parts can be covered in any order. Each part stands on its own and lends itself nicely to change in order. Basically, there are many "right" ways of presenting this material.

Online and in Print

Shopper, Buyer, and Consumer Behavior is available online as well as in print. The online chapters demonstrate how the interactive media components of the text enhance presentation and understanding. For example,

- Animated illustrations help to clarify concepts.
- QuickCheck interactive questions and chapter quizzes test your knowledge of various topics and provide immediate feedback.
- Clickable glossary terms provide immediate definitions of key concepts.

- Highlighting capabilities allow you to emphasize main ideas. You can also add personal notes in the margin.

- The search function allows you to quickly locate discussions of specific topics throughout the text.

You may choose to use just the online version of the text, or both the online and print versions together. This gives you the flexibility to choose which combination of resources works best for you. To assist those who use the online and print versions together, the primary heads and subheads in each chapter are numbered the same. For example, the first primary head in Chapter 1 is labeled 1-1, the second primary head in this chapter is labeled 1-2, and so on. The subheads build from the designation of their corresponding primary head: 1-1a, 1-1b, etc. This numbering system is designed to make moving between the online and print versions as seamless as possible.

Finally, next to a number of exhibits in the print version of the text, you will see the interactive exhibit icon at left. The icon indicates that this exhibit in the online version of the text is an interactive animation that is designed to apply, illustrate, or reinforce the concept.

Pedagogy

In addition to all of the interactive capabilities of the online version of the text, both the print and online versions of the book have a number of learning aids that make this text especially friendly, involving, and appealing.

- *Chapter Spotlights* open and close each chapter, highlighting key topics and simplifying review and study.

- *Marketing Management—Implications and Actions* sections at the end of major sections within chapters present suggestions for how the material could be the focus of specific marketing management actions.

- *FAQs* (frequently asked questions) throughout each chapter provoke thought with commonly asked, down-to-earth queries about consumer behavior.

- *CBites* offer tidbits of information about marketing practices, interesting research findings, and company anecdotes that bring additional life and color to the material.

- *Marketplace* and *International Marketplace* boxes offer more detailed looks at special topics. These boxes present additional examples and interesting sidelights, and generally add to the landscape of the chapter and your understanding. The international boxes focus on consumer behavior from cultures around the world. A list of the Marketplace and International Marketplace boxes begins on page xii.

- *Key Terms* in both the print and online versions of the text are highlighted and defined on first appearance. In the print version, key terms are also defined in the text margins and listed in alphabetical order at the end of each chapter. A *Glossary* at the end of the print book presents all of the definitions alphabetically. In the online version of the text, "pop-up" definitions of key terms provide you with immediate clarification of a term's meaning.

- *Review Questions* at the end of each chapter allow you to check your comprehension of the chapter's major concepts. Each chapter has ten multiple-choice review questions.

- *Team Talk* at the end of each chapter gives you realistic and engaging ways to discuss, review, apply, and comprehend chapter concepts. These are not ordinary discussion questions. They involve you in the marketplace and often in thoughts and observations about your own behavior as a consumer. You are encouraged to work through these questions as part of a group.

- *Workshops* at the end of every chapter are scenarios and projects that give you practical, manageable tasks that provide a hands-on feel for where "consumer behavior rubber meets the marketing road." Three workshops in each chapter—the Research Workshop, the Creative Workshop, and the Managerial Workshop—can be assigned as in- or out-of-class project work, or used as test assignments.

- *Notes* are provided at the end of each chapter for the convenience of the student and/or instructor. These can be used to study the entire article from which an in-chapter citation came or as the basis for further study on the topic.

Supplemental Materials

Atomic Dog is pleased to offer a robust suite of supplemental materials for instructors using its textbooks. These ancillaries include a Test Bank, PowerPoint® slides, Instructor's Manual, and Lecture Animations.

- The Test Bank for this book includes over 1,800 questions in a wide range of difficulty levels for each chapter. The Test Bank offers not only the correct answer for each question, but also a rationale or explanation for the correct answer and a reference—the location in the chapter where materials addressing the question content can be found. This Test Bank comes with ExamViewPro® software for easily creating customized or multiple versions of a test, and includes the option of editing or adding to the existing question bank.

- A full set of over 400 PowerPoint slides is available for this text. This is designed to provide instructors with comprehensive visual aids for each chapter in the book. These slides include outlines of each chapter, highlighting important terms, concepts, and discussion points.

- The Instructor's Manual for this book offers sample lesson plans, chapter outlines/important topics, key terms, teaching ideas and suggestions, suggested answers to the case discussion questions, and essay questions with suggested answers.

- Lecture Animations allow instructors to use the animations from our online editions in their own PowerPoint slide shows. These include all of the animated figures from each chapter of the text in an easy-to-use format.

Acknowledgments

The authors would like to give a special thanks to Steve Scoble, Nikki Herbst, Christine Abshire, Vickie Putman, Mary Monner, and the entire Atomic Dog Publishing Team.

About the Authors

JAY D. LINDQUIST is a consumer behaviorist and marketer (Ph.D., University of Michigan, 1973) and professor emeritus of marketing at Western Michigan University. He has published in the areas of time perceptions and use impact on consumer behavior, time in the workplace, consumer ethnocentrism, retail stores, hospital and physician image, children's attitudes toward advertising, promotional strategy, interactive marketing segmentation, use of marketing research by decision makers, and consumer decision rules applied in industrial marketing settings.

His work appears in the *Journal of the Academy of Marketing Science, Journal of Consumer Research, Journal of Retailing, Journal of Business Research, International Business Review, Journal of Managerial Psychology, Journal of Consumer Marketing, Industrial Marketing Management, Journal of Health Care Marketing, Journal of Business and Psychology, Marketing Management Journal, Journal of Promotion Management, Time & Society,* and *Journal of Hospital Marketing.* He acted as editor for a special issue on retail management for the *Journal of the Academy of Marketing Science.*

Professor Lindquist has served as the President, Vice President for Programs, Chairperson of the Board of Governors, and Director of International Programs of the Academy of Marketing Science and was selected as a Distinguished Fellow. He was also named the first recipient of the Harold and Muriel Berkman Academy of Marketing Science Distinguished Service Award. He has served in leadership roles for the Marketing Management Association, American Collegiate Retailing Association, and the American Academy of Advertising. Professor Lindquist has organized five AMS/ACRA Triennial National Retailing Conferences, the 1985 Academy of Marketing Science Conference, and the World Marketing Congresses of 2001, 2003, and 2005.

In the course of his teaching career, Professor Lindquist has taught consumer behavior, marketing research, advertising and promotion, media planning and research, direct marketing, marketing strategy, marketing principles, and product and pricing strategy.

M. JOSEPH (JOE) SIRGY is a consumer psychologist (Ph.D., University of Massachusetts, 1979), Professor of Marketing, and Virginia Real Estate Research Fellow at Virginia Polytechnic Institute and State University (Virginia Tech). He has published extensively in the area of consumer behavior, marketing communications, and macromarketing. He is the author/editor of several consumer behavior, marketing communications, and macromarketing books. He presently serves as a section editor of the *Journal of Macromarketing.* He has served the Academy of Marketing Science in many positions, dating back to the early 1980s (e.g., member of the board of governors, vice president–programs, president-elect, president, immediate past president, co-chair of several AMS conferences, conference track chairs). He is a Distinguished Fellow of the Academy.

1

The Shopper, Buyer, and Consumer in the Marketplace: Modeling the Process

Why do shoppers, buyers, and consumers do what they do in the marketplace when they do it? This is the underlying question we want to answer when we study the behaviors of each of these groups. You can't attempt to answer this question without first defining who "shoppers," "buyers," and "consumers" are and what is meant by "the marketplace," especially as we leap into the nonstore electronic and "dot com" world. Further, how do marketers attract shoppers and consumers to their offerings, and encourage them to buy? How do consumers find products and services to meet their needs? Chapter 1 lays the groundwork for exploring these and other related concepts and introduces a basic model of how buying decisions are made. In Part 2 we will explore the decision making, consumption, and post-purchase evaluation and behavior steps that shoppers, buyers, and consumers go through. Parts 3 and 4 will take us through the psychological and sociological influences experienced by shoppers, buyers, and consumers, and Part 5 will lead us through public policy and other societal influences and consequences encountered by these groups. Also in this part is a discussion of the consumer research process.

An Overview of the Foundations of Shopper, Buyer, and Consumer Behavior

For Alex and his parents, it is decision time. The university where Alex is studying has decided to go to "ubiquitous computing," which means that all students must have laptop computers in all of their classes. The classrooms have been wired to allow connection to the Internet, the library, the university, and college-based servers. Special software needed in courses such as communications, graphic design, psychology, media planning, research, anthropology, retailing, advertising, and marketing strategy will also be accessible in class. The teaching and learning possibilities will be restricted only by the imagination of the faculty and the students.

The decision Alex and his parents must make is both simple and complicated. It is simple in that a computer needs to be purchased, yet complicated because of the number of choices from among which they must choose. Alex's parents are involved because his mom uses a laptop much of the time (which means she has experience as a consumer of this type of product), and she, her husband Jack, and Alex will have to consider price limits when making their decision. Costlier laptops have more "bells and whistles," but all of the functions might not be needed. Alex needs to determine what the machine must be able to do, how much searching he and his parents are willing to engage in, how the computers will be evaluated and compared, where the final choice will be purchased, and how payment will be made. Certainly, you may think of other questions and steps that you'd be faced with if you were in this situation, but this overview paints a typical picture.

Alex and his parents will move through a distinct sequence of steps leading to the decision concerning which laptop to buy. He'll prioritize benefits he needs and compare different options, and he and his parents will make a choice. As he uses the new computer, Alex will naturally evaluate the decision he and his parents made, and what he learns and feels about it will drive future related decisions. In this chapter, we explore the process consumers go through as they move toward a purchase decision and some of the powers that influence them along the way. When searching for information, people act as shoppers. In this case Alex and one or more of his parents may do some of this shopping as they look for the "best" solution. The person among the three who actually completes the transaction will be the "buyer," regardless of the source of payment.

1-1 Shopper, Buyer, and Consumer Benefits

There is a simple premise that is central to understanding all shopper, buyer, and consumer behavior—*people do not buy products or services, they buy benefits.* That is, we make purchases not for the products themselves, but for the problems they solve or the opportunities they offer. **Consumer benefits** can be as practical as needing a key to open a door or as unusual as owning a Monet painting in order to achieve a sense of tranquility.

Shoppers are individuals who go into the marketplace through various means such as visiting stores at a mall or thumbing through catalogs or getting on the Internet. They can be "just looking" individuals or those with very definite purpose. Their objectives are tied to finding and comparing product and service offerings that will deliver the benefits they are seeking. **Buyers** are those individuals who complete the exchange transaction, acquiring the goods or services for money or credit or "frequent buyer points/miles," as examples. The shopper is often the buyer, but not always. The **consumer** is the individual who will actually use and/or possess that which is "purchased." In some cases the shopper, buyer, and consumer are one in the same, while in other cases these three roles may be acted out by two or three people. For example, playing all three roles, you could be the shopper for a pair of running shoes, actually order and pay for them on the Internet from Adidas, and then wear them as you do your morning jog.

We must also consider that in some cases there will be "influencers" involved. Such people or groups exert various levels of power over the choices a person makes in certain product categories. The variety of potential influences and "influencers" will be addressed in a number of places in the text.

Viewed from the perspective that people buy benefits, not products, it's easy to see why we, as consumers, have so many choices. Simply put, different types of people seek different benefits. The athlete who buys a brand name sports watch that keeps perfect time and works under water is looking for something very different from the person who receives an inscribed watch as an anniversary gift. In practical terms, the two watches serve an identical purpose—they both tell the time—but the other benefits they offer differ widely. Similarly, a business executive who takes her clothes to a laundry service is buying not just clean business suits but a sharp professional image. Mary, a senior citizen in the market for a new car, is looking for much more than a means of getting from point A to point B. She's buying safety, reliability, and, perhaps, a "look" that makes her feel younger than her years. In each of these cases, the benefits delivered, not the functions performed, are what the customer buys.

The **marketplace** is anywhere that a transaction can be completed. This would include such diverse situations as a visit to an Internet website, making a telephone call to a seller, mailing in an order form to a seller, buying from a street vendor, going into a retail store on the street or in a mall, having a direct seller come into your home, or attending a "garage sale."

1-1a Benefits and the Total Product Concept

Notice from the examples of the athlete, business executive, and senior citizen just described that people typically do not seek just one, but rather a bundle of benefits, some tangible and some intangible. *Tangible benefits* are those that are in some sense measurable, whereas *intangibles* are more often associated with the feelings you experience when owning and/or using a product or service. The watch keeps accurate time (tangible). Its brand name speaks to the reputation of the manufacturer (intangible). Its color, shape, and design are distinctive (tangibles). Wearing the watch reinforces the customer's self-image as an athlete (intangible). This broader view of goods and services as a sum of their benefits is known as the **total product concept.** Exhibit 1-1 shows how the total product concept works. It involves four types of benefits: a *basic core,* an *accessory ring,* a *psychological ring,* and the *time* dimensions of a product or service.

Let's consider the first three of these. The basic core of a product is the bundle of utilitarian benefits purchased. The basic core of a laptop computer, for example, consists of its design, features, memory, speed, operating system, installed software, warranty, and credit

consumer benefits Those positive factors that the consumer obtains as a result of the possession and/or use of a product or service. Tangible benefits are those that are in some sense measurable, whereas intangible benefits are based on the feelings experienced.

shopper The person who gathers information in the marketplace about products and/or services in preparation for making or recommending a choice from among them.

buyer The person who completes the marketing transaction through a purchase or other exchange either for himself/herself or another person or group of persons. In the organizational sense, a buyer is the person who purchases goods or services and may or may not be involved in the mechanics of transaction completion.

consumer The individual who actually uses and/or possesses a product or service.

marketplace Any location (store, mall, street market, etc.) or medium (by mail, by phone, on the web, etc.) in which a marketing exchange is carried out.

F A Q

To what extent are shoppers, buyers, and consumers aware that benefits, not products, are what they are after?

Total Product Concept

Every product has four components: a basic core of functional benefits, an accessory ring of added-value benefits, a psychological ring of benefits tied to consumer feelings, and the benefits of time saved or taken by the product.

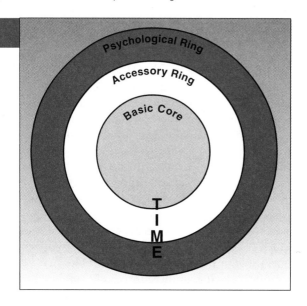

▶ **total product concept**
(see p. 3) A concept that involves four types of benefits: a basic core, an accessory ring, a psychological ring, and time. The basic core of a product is the bundle of utilitarian benefits purchased. Accessory benefits include those not directly paid for, yet received. Benefits that result from the consumer's feelings associated with the possession and/or use of a product make up the psychological ring. The fourth element is time. Everything we purchase either saves time or takes time from us, and in each case, this may be perceived as good or bad.

plan offered by the seller. Accessory benefits include such "added-value" factors as store reputation, manufacturer prestige, and convenience of location. Other benefits such as friendliness of the sales clerks, ease of parking, or quick service also fall into this category. These benefits are not perceived by the shopper, buyer, or consumer as being directly paid for, yet they are part of what is received.

Benefits that result from the consumer's feelings associated with the possession and/or use of a product make up the psychological ring. A sense of belonging derived from wearing the same brand of running shoes as your friends or driving an economical car that makes you feel thrifty are examples. Buying an innovative product in order to feel that you are ahead of the crowd is another. The advertisement in Exhibit 1-2 presents the core benefits of absorbing and eliminating odors and a spill-proof box for this Arm and Hammer product. An accessory benefit would be the reputation of this brand, and a psychological benefit could be the feelings associated with being a good homemaker because of having an odor-free home.

Every product or service is a bundle of benefits, as noted earlier. The relative importance of each benefit varies from product to product, from person to person, and from situation to situation. To a technophile, for instance, the basic core benefits of a laptop computer are of primary importance, whereas for a student looking for acceptance from peers, the psychological benefits tied to the brand name may matter more.

Notice that in Exhibit 1-1 the fourth element is *time*.[1] Perceptions of time may affect perceptions about other benefits. Everything we purchase either saves time or takes time from us. Eating at a fast-food outlet rather than an elegant restaurant saves an hour or more of time. So does shopping at a convenience store rather than at a supermarket, or through a catalog rather than at a shopping center. Remember, however, that the value of saving time depends upon the perspective of the person—to some people taking time shopping to find the perfect item is time well spent, whereas to others it is time wasted. The point is that whether a product or service "gives" time or "takes" time may be desirable or undesirable depending on the consumer's situation. Consumers may think of time and its benefits with respect to a product or service as either *literal* or *metaphoric*.[2] Literal expressions of time involve reality, are precise, objective, and unambiguous. Metaphoric time expressions go beyond the information provided, are used in the context of a situation, and often present figurative relationships. Expressions such as "time flies" or "time is money" or "this product can free up your time" are metaphoric.

Thinking about time "literally," an example would be to choose between ordering a pair of aviator sunglasses on the web and having them delivered the next day for a premium shipping-price or paying less and having the glasses in hand within two to four days. The result is a measurable amount of time saved in gaining possession of the glasses. Alternatively, you may think of time "metaphorically," deciding to buy a calculator for school

E x h i b i t 1-2

This ad for Arm and Hammer's Fridge-n-Freezer brand baking soda shows core product benefits such as "absorbs and eliminates odors that can yuck up taste" and indicates that the box is "spill-proof." What accessory and psychological ring benefits are also present but not explicitly stated?

Source: Reprinted by permission of Church & Dwight Co., Inc.

on the web rather than going to the mall or downtown to buy the same thing because you see your time as "too valuable to waste" on shopping at a "bricks and mortar" retail outlet. Here time is associated with the shopping process rather than the product itself.

Different consumers seek different benefits packages in different situations. This brings us to a second basic premise as we seek to understand shopper, buyer, and consumer behavior. Let's look at this from the consumer perspective. While we are all unique, for marketing purposes, we can often be seen as falling into groups or clusters of individuals who seek similar benefits. This is the principle behind **market segmentation,** the identification of like-minded clusters of consumers who can be expected to behave in similar ways, making similar decisions in the marketplace in similar situations.

1-1b Consumer Benefits and Market Segmentation

Marketers do not create market segments, they find them. This is a process of discovery because people in the marketplace have already "segmented themselves." The marketplace is made up of natural groupings of consumers in search of common benefits. They behave in similar ways and make similar product choices for similar reasons. Market segmentation is the study of the marketplace in order to discover viable groups of consumers who are similar or homogeneous in their approaches to choosing and/or consuming goods and services.

There are many firms that offer different options to marketers to help them find market segments and learn more about them. Examples include the Claritas PRIZM NE approach, which offers geographic and household segment information; MapInfo PSYTE, which is designed to identify market and product potential, store placement, and targeting information; the Donnelley DQI3, a database of over 220 million people in 104 million households in the U.S. that can be used to find customers who fit the demographic profile of segment members; and ESRI's Business Information Solutions' ACORN, which is

market segmentation
The identification of like-minded clusters of consumers who can be expected to behave in similar ways, making similar decisions in the marketplace in similar situations.

Marketplace 1-1

A New Way to Look at Consumer Segments in the United States

Forget yuppies, boomers, soccer moms, and dinks, and say hello to "Stressed by Lifers," "Family Limiteds," and "Renaissance Elders." The U.S. is undergoing a generational power shift from the long-dominant baby boomers to the aggressive tech-savvy Generation Xers (that is, people born between about 1961 and 1981, after the baby boomers). The latter group is driving the marketplace of the future, and according to some analysts the boomers don't want to lead the marketplace any longer.

A 2000 Monitor MindBase study by Yankelovich divides consumers into eight categories that are further refined into 32 subgroups. Marketers use such studies to provide guides to reach similar consumers with the right products and services that deliver desired benefits and to determine the types of ads they will see, hear, read, or click on.

The eight broad consumer categories found in the study are the following:

- *Up & Comer*—Upbeat, active, upwardly mobile, and childless consumers who strive to improve and expect to benefit from their skills. Corporate America loves them for their youth and money. They are likely to "tell marketers what to do; not to be told what to do," according to the study. They are seen as the biggest group of Generation X; they want to be in charge and are in position to take charge as wireless technology moves ahead.

- *Young Materialist*—Cynical, aggressive singles who think money equals happiness but often don't have a clue how to get it.

- *Stressed by Life*—Parents with limited resources and heavy responsibilities. They are often located in urban, ethnically diverse neighborhoods.

- *New Traditionalists*—People living the modern American dream. They are upscale, family oriented, progressive in values, and involved in their communities. The study author says, "The New Traditionalists will set the agenda for how the baby boomers move through the next phase of their lives."

- *Family Limiteds*—Parents totally concentrated on their families to the exclusion of all else, including social issues, self-exploration, and non-family activities and interests.

- *Detached Introverts*—The geek chic. Cut off socially by work or by choice, they're successful but lonely and turn to the web for solace.

- *Renaissance Elders*—Mature persons who are still involved in the world and enjoying life. Their deep pockets make them popular with marketers.

- *Retired from Life*—Mature, but uninvolved and somewhat sedentary persons. Many see the changing world and technology as a threat. People in this category hear marketers "knocking" but won't let them "come in."

Source: Excerpt from "Label-crazy marketers have got you pegged" by Michael McCarthy, *USA TODAY,* August 1, 2000, p. 1B.

designed to provide accurate demographic and lifestyle pictures of neighborhoods (Chapter 6 will discuss this in greater detail).

Let's look at a segmentation example. Consider a big-ticket purchase such as a college education. Not all high school students are looking for the same college experience. For some, university academic or athletic reputation is key. Some students decide to go away from their home areas to attend school, while others prefer to study nearby. Some would rather be on an inner-city campus, whereas others look for less urban locations. The decision may depend on financial aid availability. Choosing a state-supported college may be important, or going to a private school could be the main goal. Thus, college-bound students naturally split themselves into various market segments, each of which can be targeted differently by the recruiting staffs of schools wishing to attract them. Check out Marketplace 1-1, a contemporary view of how U.S. consumers are segmented. Then turn to Marketplace 1-2 for a look at the traditional senior citizen segment's desire for customized exercise equipment.

segment bounding
A method of setting conditions whereby consumers qualify or do not qualify as part of a segment. Segments are bounded on descriptors, location, and time.

Segment Bounding   A first step in understanding how a market is segmented is termed **segment bounding,** which is a means by which marketers differentiate among consumers and among market segments. Segment bounding is simply a method of setting conditions whereby consumers qualify or do not qualify as part of a segment.

First, marketers *develop a set of descriptors of consumers* likely to be seeking the benefits that the business or organization can deliver. Descriptors may be single characteristics or a combination of characteristics that consumers in the same segment share. They

Marketplace 1-2

Targeting Older Exercisers

As Americans age, they become more concerned about maintaining a healthy heart. As a result, people over 45 years old now represent the largest consumer group for aerobic exercise equipment.

The American College of Sports Medicine recommends that older people get at least one hour per week of aerobic exercise, as well as another hour of exercise to enhance muscle tone. Plain old walking is the favorite for people 55 and older and is engaged in by 26 percent of older fitness buffs. Working out on a treadmill ties for second place with the use of stationary bikes, each with 18 percent. Cross-country ski machine use accounts for 13 percent, and working out on rowing machines accounts for 11 percent. Running and jogging are favored by 3 percent of the older fitness seekers.

Marketers are responding to older users by designing exercise equipment that fits their needs and concerns. Key considerations are safety, simplicity, and sturdiness. To make bikes easier for seniors to get on and off, manufacturers have introduced recumbent models. Another trend is the inclusion of sophisticated biofeedback features that let the user monitor heart and pulse rates and the number of calories burned per hour. Treadmills have been designed with handrails that are cushioned and made of wider tubing for a better grip. Also, the treadmill platforms are getting wider and longer. Even the packaging on some equipment is targeted to seniors—manufacturers print a warning if the equipment weighs more than 70 pounds and indicate which end is the heaviest.

Source: From "Older Enthusiasts Targeted in the Exercise Rage" by Richard Halverson from *Discount Store News*, April 7, 1995. Reprinted with permission from *Discount Store News/DSN Retailing Today.*

include demographics, psychographics, benefits sought, and marketplace and consumption behavior. Exhibit 1-3 provides an overview of descriptors marketers commonly use to bound segments. Market segmentation based on each descriptor is further explored later in the text, as indicated in the exhibit. The fewer descriptors used, the easier it is to identify and locate segment members. To further simplify segment bounding, a useful rule of thumb is to use established descriptors. For example, if a target market consists of women aged 24 to 34 years, but census data is available only for 25- to 34-year-olds, it may make sense to switch to the latter, saving time and cost in finding and using existing data.

Second, marketers *bound segments to a specific geographic location.* Again, using existing geopolitical divisions rather than attempting to create new ones should be considered. The census, government agencies, and commercial data gatherers such as A.C. Nielsen are all useful sources to help bound segments according to census tracts, cities, metropolitan areas, counties, states, regions, and countries. Many also correlate geographic location with such demographics as age, income, gender, or some combination of these characteristics.

F A Q

What are the pros and cons to consumers of market segmentation?

Type	Examples
Demographics	Age, gender, education, income, marital status, occupation
Psychographics	Interests, opinions, values, and lifestyles (see Chapter 6)
Psychological influence	Personality and self-image (see Chapter 5), perception of risk (see Chapter 7), involvement (see Chapter 8), attitudes and beliefs (see Chapter 9)
Social influence	Culture (see Chapters 11 and 12), subculture (see Chapter 13), social class and reference groups (see Chapter 14), household/family (see Chapter 15)
Marketplace behavior	Recognition of needs (see Chapter 2), responses to marketing communications (see Chapter 10), responses to price, product acceptance
Consumption behavior	Consumption situation, usage rate, satisfaction, and loyalty (see Chapter 5)

E x h i b i t 1-3

Descriptors Used in Segment Bounding

International *Marketplace 1-1*

Western Products and the Russian Consumer

Marketing to the Russian consumer requires understanding the qualities and differences within this group, as well as determining which Russian consumers are most open to purchasing products from the West. Based on the divisions of Russia's purchasing population (research by D'Arcy Masius Benton & Bowles) described in the following five paragraphs, consider where and how marketers might concentrate their efforts in this country.

The largest percentages of both Russian women and men (45 and 30, respectively) belong to the division of society that historically lived off the produce of the land. These kuptsi (literally, "merchants") characteristically are interested in sturdy, practical goods and are not concerned with impressing others with labels or fripperies from the West.

Second in percentage size comes the division made up of 30 percent of Russia's women and 25 percent of Russia's men. These "Russian souls" hold little purchasing power and tend to depend on others to take the lead in trying new products and establishing value.

Third, just 10 percent of Russian women but 25 percent of Russian men make up a societal division that parallels businesspeople in the West. Confident, sophisticated, ambi-

tious, and financially able, members of this group choose purchases based on quality and value, regardless of the products' point of origin.

Fourth in population size is the group called "Cossacks," made up equally of men and women (10 percent of Russian men and 10 percent of Russian women). Members of this group hold Mother Russia close to their hearts while at the same time looking out for opportunities to raise their social and economic status. Deference to influence from the West is not seen in public, yet exists in private.

The final and smallest social division in Russia may be called "students." Made up of 5 percent of Russia's women and 10 percent of Russia's men, these lifelong learners hold a broad view of the world and its possibilities and see the West and its products as an emblem of a future without limits. Any shortage in purchasing funds is made up for in enthusiasm.

Source: Adapted from "Targeting the Russian Consumer," *Harper's Magazine,* June 1992, pp. 21–22.

International Marketplace 1-1 describes the five "psychological" segments that have been found to exist in Russia and the differences in the consumer behavior of persons in the different segments.

Third, marketers *bound segments in time* as a means of ensuring that all data gathered are relevant and up-to-date for the time of use. The objective is to state when the segment existed or will exist. Is the segment to be pursued next calendar year, next quarter, next month, or tomorrow? Time is particularly important when marketers forecast product sales, pricing, distribution availability, and the like for a year or several years into the future.

By bounding a segment, marketers describe its general characteristics, its location, and the time frame during which these factors will continue to define the segment so that consumers included in that segment can be properly pursued. However, segment bounding does not tell us whether the segment is viable. A *viable segment* is one that is distinctive and is of sufficient potential to be pursued. Determining viability is the second stage of market segmentation.

Segment Viability   Marketers use four factors to determine segment viability. First, for a segment to be viable for the marketing of a product, it must be of *sufficient size* to generate acceptable profits from sales. It doesn't matter how large or small the segment is as long as it meets this profitability criterion.

Second, a segment must be *measurable*. Marketers must be able to identify people within it and gather specific information, such as demographic and lifestyle characteristics, about them.

Third, a segment must be *clearly differentiated* from other segments. To justify treating different groups of consumers in different ways, the groups must be sufficiently unlike one another in their responses to one or more of the marketing mix variables. Do they seek different types of products? Do they respond differently to price? Do they wish the product to be available at different times and places? How do they respond as different types of promotions are offered? Answers to questions such as these determine differentiability.

Fourth, a segment must be *reachable*. Marketers must be able to deliver the product to members of the segment. This requires that both the consumer and the seller have access to distribution. Can the product be made available through retail, direct mail, the Internet, direct selling, or other media that members use? Will the product be easy for consumers to find and buy? Also, marketers must be able to deliver information about the product to members of the segment. This requires that both the consumer and the seller have access to appropriate media. Can the product be promoted through newspaper, magazine, Internet, or television advertising that members will see and respond to?

Let's use an example to show how segment viability is assessed. Company XYZ is an electronics manufacturer with an established brand name in the personal computer market. The company is considering developing a laptop computer. About 10 percent of the laptops currently sold carry high prices, and almost 40 percent are medium priced. This means that, using price as a segment descriptor, there are two distinct segments in the laptop computer market. The objectives for Company XYZ are to figure out what share of new buyers and replacement buyers in each of these two segments would consider its brand and ultimately buy it.

The company executives project that within two years the new laptop could win about one-sixth of the high-price segment or about one-fourth of the medium-price segment. This forecast allows the company to break even with a high-price laptop or to turn a profit on the medium-price laptop during the same period.

For both segments, profiles of typical individual and company purchasers are readily available, as are lists of current owners. Lists of consumers with similar characteristics can be obtained from list brokers. The latter are firms that rent names and other information on individuals to marketers who wish to offer products or services to them. This means each segment is easily measurable.

The two segments are easily differentiated, as each seeks different benefits in a laptop computer. Those willing to pay a higher price prefer a lighter computer with a large screen, long battery life, a fast processor, and ease-of-use features. The medium-price segment is willing to accept fewer of these benefits for a lower price—meaning lower development and production costs for Company XYZ.

Company XYZ already sells its PCs through retail outlets, attracting mostly medium-price buyers. This segment can easily be reached through computer magazines, the Internet, newspapers, business magazines, news magazines, television, and direct mail. Members of the medium-price segment are primarily located in major metropolitan areas throughout the United States, and contact through the media is very promising. Hence, reachability is not an issue.

The early break-even point, lower development and production costs, access to distribution, and access to promotion all indicate that the most viable segment for Company XYZ to target is the medium-price consumer.

Segmentation Strategies   Once viable segments have been identified, there are three segmentation strategies commonly used by marketers: *mass marketing, concentrated marketing,* and *differentiated marketing.*

Mass marketing, also known as *undifferentiated marketing,* is a method where segmentation is not used. The marketer offers the same product to the entire consumer population. Such a product is one that appeals to all types of consumers, regardless of such factors as age, gender, or lifestyle characteristics. A classic example is Henry Ford's introduction of one of the first production-line-built cars, the "Model T." The vehicles were identical inside and out, including the exterior color, black. Likewise, the original Coca-Cola soft drink, certain breakfast cereals, and a multitude of household products are all examples of products positioned for the mass market.

Concentrated marketing, also known as *focused* or *niche marketing*, is the selection of one market segment to pursue, even though the product may appeal to several. For reasons such as expertise and resources available, access to distribution or media, or brand image, the marketer chooses only one of several viable segments. For example, Rolls-Royce and Jaguar use concentrated marketing in selling to the higher-price end of the automobile market only.

A newer concept that is a subset of concentrated marketing is called "segments of one." Database technology, body scanning technology, and the ability of buyers and sellers to connect online mean that individualized marketing—marketing based on segments of one person—is becoming a reality. Consumers have the ability to seek out exactly the product benefits they want, and increasingly, marketers are able and willing to customize products or services. When ordering a computer from Gateway, you simply specify the combination of computer capabilities and hardware plus software needed, and the company will build and ship to suit you. There are clothing retail stores in the United States that have you come to the outlet and be body scanned in underclothing in a private dressing room. Using the results of the scan, the store is able to provide you with properly fitting garments. You may order clothing there, through their catalog, or on the web. In the future, we may all have current size and preference cards that will allow for better fit and targeting. These cards could even be scanned into the computer to complete clothing purchases on the web. In August 2004, the Ford Motor Company turned its back on the "one-size-fits-all" car philosophy when its refurbished Chicago, Illinois, South Side manufacturing plant had its first midsize car roll off the line. Eight different models on two different chassis can be made at this plant to meet rapidly changing consumer preferences in the fragmented car market. Production will shift as demand changes into the future.[3] As another example, Amazon.com compiles preference information based on each customer's history of book purchases, so when a customer logs on to the home page, appropriate "suggestions" are made for his or her next purchase.

Differentiated marketing is the selection of two or more different segments to pursue. Johnson & Johnson's baby shampoo is targeted not only to parents as a baby product but separately to adults attracted to its low-eye-irritation formula. In other cases, line extensions provide opportunities for differentiated marketing. Coca-Cola, first an undifferentiated product, is now offered in a variety of versions for different consumer tastes: Diet Coke, Diet Cherry Coke, and Caffeine Free Diet Coke are just some of them.

Exhibits 1-4 and 1-5 are advertisements in which differentiated marketing is used to appeal to multiple segments. The One-A-Day vitamins ad features different products targeted to both younger and older consumers. Further, ethnic diversity is shown among typical product purchasers, as is appeal to both genders. The UPS magazine advertisement appeals to shippers who either want early-morning delivery, by 8:30 A.M., or who will accept items delivered later in the morning, by 10:30 A.M. These are two distinct segments based on time requirements, though the service is not different.

As we see from all these examples, the marketer is not limited to a single strategy, but at different stages of a product's life cycle may even use them all, switching back and forth as market conditions change.

We are also seeing attempts to reach specific target segments with promotional messages tied to segment members' lifestyles and the media that are part of those lifestyles. The objective is to build "media communities." These communities are formed when consumers feel a radio station, magazine, or other medium is itself a reflection of their personal beliefs and helps them find their position in the world.[4] Nickelodeon and MTV were early attempts at such ad-sponsored communities on cable television. They are "lifestyle parades" that invite target audiences to media outlets—from cable to magazines, books, videotapes, and outdoor events that the owners license or control. The target audiences are relatively upscale children and young adults.

Relatively new is the idea of "segment-busters." These are products or services that marketers hope will fall between the cracks of the accepted segmentation picture and be successful in doing so. Take a look at CBite 1-1.

Countersegmentation—reducing the number of market segments served—is another common strategy. For example, by limiting the number of products offered

▶**countersegmentation**
Reducing the number of market segments served from current levels.

E x h i b i t 1-4

One-A-Day vitamins are clearly targeted to multiple groups of customers using differentiated segmentation. The message is that the product is for everyone.

Source: Courtesy of Bayer Corporation, Morristown, NJ.

E x h i b i t 1-5

UPS also targets more than one market segment, based on delivery needs.

Source: Courtesy of UPS.

and/or the level of customization in each, marketers reduce the number of segments served. Countersegmentation is apparent in the auto industry where, over a period of several years, the number of models on the market shrinks and grows in response to market conditions.

Segmentation in the Global Marketplace   Customers around the globe are different in many ways. Cultural heritage, geographic conditions, levels of technology,

---

CBite 1-1

Segment-busters in the Auto Industry

Automakers are striving en masse to come out with successful "segment-busters," the new holy grail of design. Makers of the Scion xB, Chrysler Pacifica, and Volkswagen Touareg all are hoping their cars will fall between the cracks of segmentation in order to earn this coveted new designation as a "conveyor of cool." In fact, so many cars are claiming to "bust" segments that the assortment is a segment unto itself. Nobody is more fond of the term than Chrysler, which produced the first segment bust with the minivan in 1983. Other segment-busters have followed, namely, the PT Cruiser and, in 2003, the Pacifica. Segment-busters strive to set trends but are not always successful. Though Honda Element sales are going great guns, this surfer segment-buster is appealing to an older crowd than Honda envisioned. Breaking the mold could be the key to a mini-sized success, or it could be the shortcut to becoming the next Aztek.

Source: Katherine Zachary, Eric Mayne, David Zola, and Bill Visnic, *Wards Auto World,* October 2003, Vol. 39, p. 49. Reprinted with the permission of Primedia Business Magazines & Media. Copyright © 2005. All rights reserved.

education, and a host of other often complex factors mean that the benefits consumers seek may vary widely from country to country. There are two approaches to global segmentation. First, marketers can treat each country as a separate market and seek consumer segments accordingly. This *localized* approach to segmentation means customizing one or more parts of the marketing mix for the various segments discovered in that market. Packaging cereal as a snack rather than a breakfast food for some South American markets is an example, as is producing smaller-size refrigerators for the Japanese market because of the lack of space available in homes and the reduced need for refrigeration of food products as more-frequent, smaller-quantity food shopping is the norm.

The second approach is *intermarket* segmentation. This is also called *standardization.* Here, marketers find that within different countries there are pockets of like-minded consumers whose behavior patterns in the marketplace are similar.[5] Intermarket segmentation emphasizes the similarities rather than the differences among consumers around the world, focusing on universal benefits and behaviors. Once such global market segments are identified, they can be offered standardized products that can be marketed similarly in all target nations.[6] Intermarket segmentation works better for some product classes than others.[7] It has worked well, for example, with upscale audio/video electronics products, designer clothing, upscale automobiles, PCs, blue jeans, certain alcoholic beverages, gourmet foods and ingredients, top-brand athletic equipment, and certain name-brand athletic clothing lines.

A study of twenty-seven multinational consumer product firms rates almost two-thirds as having "highly standardized" marketing programs across the nations in which they operate.[8] Consider Boss of Germany. Boss provides quality men's clothing and is positioned as such at the same price levels and in the same types of stores in all of the countries in which its goods are sold. Members of its intermarket segment find the same types of magazine advertisements appealing (see Exhibit 1-6), they expect the same fit and style,

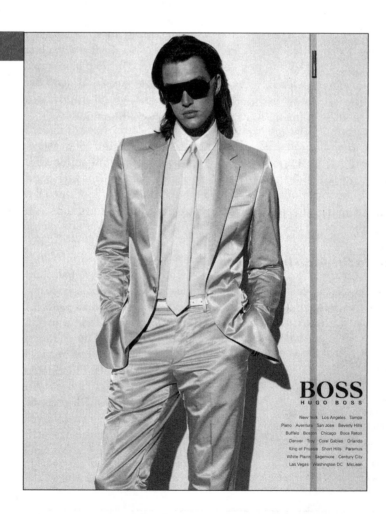

E x h i b i t 1-6

This Hugo Boss ad is typical of those found in magazines around the globe.

Source: © Peter Lindbergh.

International *Marketplace 1-2*

The Yogurt Market: Segments across Western Europe

Because competition in the global marketplace is on the rise, finding consumer segments across nations that have common buying patterns allows sellers to better target and promote their goods and services. A segmentation model was developed and tested on consumers of yogurt in eleven countries that are part of the European Union. The countries were Belgium, Denmark, France, Germany, Great Britain, Greece, Ireland, Italy, Netherlands, Portugal, and Spain. The segments were found based on consumer sociodemographics, consumption patterns, media consumption, and personality. Consumers in segment S1 tend to be older and less educated, have lower incomes and live in less urbanized areas. They visit smaller stores more often for their purchase and spend less overall on the product. They tend to listen to the radio more often, watch serials and entertainment programs on TV, and with regard to yogurt are less innovative, deal prone, and involved with the product. They also are more ethnocentric. The people in segment S2 are similar to the S1s; however, they eat yogurt as a snack more often. Members of the segment buy often but in larger stores. They respond to promotions and are less innovative and more ethnocentric. They also see yogurt as a higher involvement product than do the S1s. The S3 segment is composed of younger, more-educated consumers who have higher incomes. They use yogurt often as a snack and are relatively light users. They are more exposed to newspaper and radio advertising and are more deal prone and innovative and less ethnocentric. Segment S4 members have a sociodemographic profile similar to that of the S3s but more often live in urban areas. They spend more than any other group on yogurt and purchase more often in larger stores. They are generally less exposed to media, with the exception of the cinema.

Source: From "International Market Segmentation Based on Consumer-Product Relations" by Frenkel Ter Hofstede, Jan-Benedict E. M. Steenkamp, and Michel Wedel in *Journal of Marketing Research,* February 1999, Volume 36, pp. 10–11. Reprinted with permission from *Journal of Marketing Research,* published by the American Marketing Association.

and they look for the same level of service. Whether Boss sells its clothing in New York, Mexico City, Berlin, Hong Kong, or London, the men who come into its retail stores are very similar.[9]

In contrast, a recent a study of yogurt consumers in eleven European countries showed there were four distinctive segments across these cultures.[10] See International Marketplace 1-2 for a description of what these segments turned out to be. Global segments have also been found based on values consumers hold dear. These six segments ranged from "Strivers" to "Creatives." International Marketplace 1-3 identifies groups that surface in countries around the world. Check out CBite 1-2 for keys to intermarket segmentation success.

Shoppers may also be grouped into segments. There is a discussion of shopper segmentation with examples in Chapter 3, section 3-4a.

1-1c Consumer Benefits and Product Positioning

No matter how accurately marketers can describe a segment and understand the benefits consumers within it seek, that segment is only useful if it is a good match with the product marketed. Product **positioning** is the means through which marketers seek the right fit between a product and desired benefits. It is the placement of such things as a product, service, company, or retail outlet in the mind of the consumer. Positioning is not based solely on the benefits of the product, but on the way such benefits are perceived by consumers. A car that is perceived, for example, to be particularly safe may, in fact, be no safer than its competitors. It is the consumer's belief in or perception of its safety that makes its positioning in the market as a safe car effective.

positioning The placement of such things as a product, service, company, or retail outlet in the mind of the consumer. Position is achieved based not upon the benefits possessed alone, but on the way in which consumers perceive such benefits.

A product can be positioned for targeted segments: (1) based on perceived benefits or characteristics that point to certain benefits, (2) based on the potential consumer's perception of the product's image, (3) as something presented against the competition, or (4) by combining two or more of these methods. In Chapter 9, section 9-1a, you will find a more detailed discussion of positioning options used to change consumer beliefs about a product or service.

International *Marketplace 1-3*

Six Global Segments Based on Values

The 1997 Roper Reports Worldwide Global Consumer Survey of one thousand people in thirty-five countries found that there were six value-based segments, as follows:

- *Strivers*—This group is 23 percent of the world's adults. Strivers are slightly more likely to be men than women. They place more emphasis on material and professional goals than do members of the other groups. One in three people in developing Asia are in this group, as are about one in four in Russia and developed Asia.

- *Devouts*—This category is 22 percent of the world's adults. For Devouts, which includes more women than men, tradition and duty are very important. Devouts are most common in developing Asia and the Middle Eastern and African countries in the survey. They are least common in developed Asia and Western Europe.

- *Altruists*—This group is 18 percent of the world's adults, with a slightly higher percentage of females. Altruists are interested in social issues and the welfare of society. With a median age of 44, this group is older than the others. More Altruists live in Latin America and Russia than in the other countries.

- *Intimates*—Intimates, comprising 15 percent of the world's population, value close personal relationships and family above all else. They are almost as likely to be men as women. One in four Europeans and Americans is part of this segment, compared to just 7 percent in developing Asia.

- *Fun Seekers*—Although found disproportionately in developed Asia, this group accounts for 12 percent of the global population. Not surprisingly, Fun Seekers are the youngest group, with a male-female ratio of 54 to 46.

- *Creatives*—This group is the smallest at 10 percent worldwide. Their hallmark trait is a strong interest in education, knowledge, and technology. Creatives are more common in Latin America and Western Europe. Along with the Intimates, this group has the most balanced gender mix.

What kinds of products and services would you position against these groups in the global market? How do these groups fit with the VALS2 Lifestyle segments? See the lifestyle discussion in Chapter 6.

Source: Tom Miller, "Global Segments from 'Strivers' to 'Creatives,'" *Marketing News* (July 20, 1998), p. 11. Reprinted with permission from the American Marketing Association.

Positioning Based on Benefits or Characteristics   Marketers may position products and services based on benefits or on characteristics consumers feel will provide the benefits they seek. Maytag has been successful over the years in positioning its products as reliable. The benefits here are related to use without problems and reduced maintenance costs. The Toyota hybrid automobile Prius yields a number of benefits, two of which are good gas mileage and environmental "friendliness." Owners can experience lower costs because of the gas mileage of the car, and owners who are concerned about the environmental impact of automobiles have the benefit of feeling they are minimizing the impact while driving this car.

CBite 1-2

Intermarket Success

The characteristics successful intermarketers share include: a combination of strategic focus with geographic diversity, an emphasis on customer value, a blend of technology and closeness to the customer, a reliance on technical competence, and a mutual interdependence between the company and its employees. These strengths are not unusual; they are the same ones that bring success in domestic markets.

Source: H. Simon, "Lessons from Germany's Midsize Giants," *Harvard Business Review,* Vol. 70 (March–April 1992), pp. 115–123.

A Brand Personality Framework

Sincerity	Excitement	Competence	Sophistication	Ruggedness
Down-to-earth	Daring	Reliable	Upper-class	Outdoorsy
Honest	Spirited	Intelligent	Charming	Tough
Wholesome	Imaginative	Successful		
Cheerful	Up-to-date			

Source: Jennifer A. Aaker, "Dimensions of Brand Personality," *Journal of Marketing Research,* Vol. 34 (August 1997), p. 352. Reprinted with permission from the American Marketing Association.

Positioning Based on Image

L'Oreal hair coloring products are image-positioned as costly products that women "deserve" because they are "worth it." In reality, the image or "personality" of a brand or product, as the consumer sees it, also flow from its perceived benefits or characteristics that send signals about those benefits. This is seen as a key way to differentiate a brand in a product category.[11] **Brand personality** is thought to consist of five trait categories, namely, *sincerity, excitement, competence, sophistication,* and *ruggedness.*[12] Exhibit 1-7 shows the components of each of these five trait categories. Typical products that fit into each of the five are: sincerity—Hallmark cards; excitement—the MTV channel; competence—*The Wall Street Journal;* sophistication—Guess jeans; and ruggedness—Nike tennis shoes.

▶**brand personality**
A framework of human traits that consumers attach to products and services when they position the latter in the marketplace against other products or services; also called "brand image."

Positioning against Competitors

When positioning against competitors, marketers invite product comparison. Advertisers clearly identify the competitors or present enough clues to consumers so they can determine who the competition is. The performance of each product is compared as it relates to desirable consumer benefits. Advertising achieves competitive positioning either through direct comparison or by offering facts or imaging that is parallel to those of competitors. The objective is to achieve the same favorable position in the consumer's mind that is enjoyed by competitors, or to show superiority.

The advertisement in Exhibit 1-8 uses direct comparison. Rembrandt brand is the advertiser, and the visual cues given in the ad point to Scope brand mouthwash and what

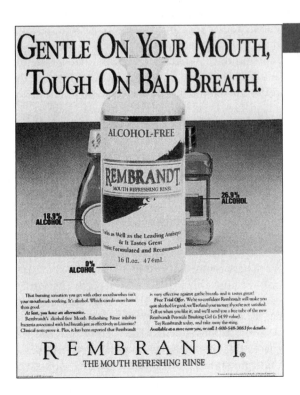

Using a "no alcohol" claim, Rembrandt is positioned against better-known brand names, Scope and another, matching other product benefits and promising this new benefit.

Source: Reprinted by permission of Den-Mat.

V8 brand vegetable juice is being positioned against orange juice, a product category, on the basis of the benefits associated with lower carbohydrates, a health issue, rather than a brand-to-brand comparison.

Source: Courtesy of Campbell Soup Company.

HALF THE CARBS OF ORANGE JUICE.

(PUT THAT IN YOUR JUICER AND SQUEEZE IT.)

100% JUICE

V8

100% VEGETABLE JUICE

V8. DRINK SMARTER.™

F A Q

Is comparative advertising a fair and honest marketing strategy? Can it backfire?

other brand as competitors? Exhibit 1-9 is an advertisement in which two product categories, rather than brands, are compared. If comparisons are made, it is important that they are accurate. A popular and effective selling strategy is to claim to offer virtually the same product at a much lower price. However, this claim rarely works well unless it is true and/or is perceived to be true by the consumer. If quality, image, and performance are not really equal or are not perceived to be so, the lower-priced product is not viewed as a good substitute. Even if very real differences do exist, if the differences are not perceived as important by the consumer, comparative claims rarely work.

Positioning Based on a Combination of Factors   Products can also be positioned based on a combination of benefits, characteristics, or image *and* competitive comparison. How is this done in the Rembrandt mouthwash ad (Exhibit 1-9)? Now take a look at the perceptual map showing comparisons of competitor positions where benefits are the dimensions in Marketplace 1-3.

Repositioning   From time to time, in response to changes in the market environment, marketers reposition products. Repositioning is difficult to achieve effectively, however, and is impossible to achieve overnight. Once the image of a product is established in the consumer's mind, he or she resists change. Repositioning involves re-educating the consumer about changes in important product, price, distribution, and/or promotional or personal selling benefits. The Mercury Cougar, first introduced as a small sporty car, was successfully repositioned as a mid-sized car, comparable to the Ford Thunderbird. Here, the segment targeted as well as the image of the car changed. The growth of the fast-food

Marketplace 1-3

Perceptual Mapping

Marketers use a method called perceptual mapping to position products against competitors. Perceptual mapping is based on the belief that when consumers think of a product category, they see it in terms of a map or grid that clusters like products or brands together. Typically, products or brands that consumers consider similar share like benefits and attributes. By understanding the perceptual maps of consumers in targeted segments, marketers can see where their products fit with others in the market. Here we see a perceptual map of pain reliever brands. Even though, as in this category, the brands may be similar in terms of chemical makeup, the way in which they are perceived is very different. Where would you place products such as Motrin Ib, Orudus, and Aleve on this perceptual map?

Sources: Robert L. Engle, "Perceptual Mapping: An Overview of an Important Marketing Tool," *Product Management* (Winter 1991), pp. 12–14; J. R. Hauser and F. S. Koppelman, "Alternative Perceptual Mapping Techniques: Relative Accuracy and Usefulness," *Journal of Marketing Research*, Vol. 16 (November 1979), pp. 495–506.

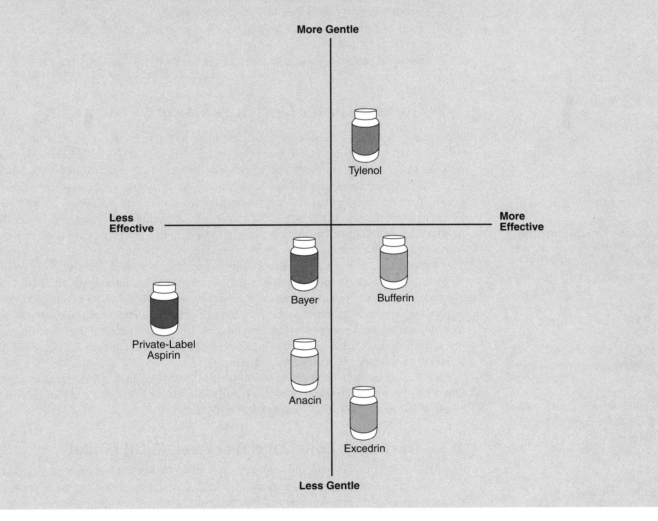

chain McDonald's can also be viewed from the perspective of repositioning. McDonald's restaurants, when first opened, were part of a chain similar to the Hot 'N' Now Hamburgers, Checkers, or Rally's of today. You parked the car and went to the window to order and pick up very-low-priced burgers, fries, and shakes. All of the outlet designs were the same. Now McDonald's offers sit-down, family restaurants with an emphasis on value at lower prices, often with a fun place for the kids to play. The menu is extensive, and the interior and exterior decor varies from restaurant to restaurant.

The rest of this chapter describes the process consumers go through as they move toward making purchase decisions. As you read, keep in mind the three premises of consumer behavior that we have explored: (1) consumers buy benefits, not products; (2) consumers naturally fall into groups that seek similar benefits in the marketplace; and (3) identifying market segments is only worthwhile if the product marketed matches the benefits consumers seek.

Marketing Management—Implications and Actions

Understanding purchasing in terms of consumer benefits helps marketers:

- Develop and promote products on the basis of benefits sought.
- Analyze products in terms of the total product concept to determine a complete picture of the benefits consumers seek and experience.
- Use segment bounding as an objective means of identifying potential market segments and analyzing the shared characteristics of members.
- Assess and compare the viability of different segments for specific products and marketing approaches.
- Position products in terms of benefits sought by targeted segments.

1-2 The Consumer Decision-Making Process

What is it that triggers consumers to be motivated to select a certain product or service? What influences them to choose one product over another when both deliver the same benefits to meet the same needs, or to choose one brand over another almost identical brand? What causes a longtime user of one brand to suddenly switch to another? And what keeps other brand users loyal, despite overtures from competing brands? To help marketers answer these and other questions central to consumer behavior, researchers have developed various **consumer decision models** that attempt to describe the processes consumers go through before, during, and after making a purchase.

A model is simply a means of describing a concept, its causes, and its effects. Models provide us with a framework for analyzing consumer behavior. By using them, we can map out each of the *causes* or **antecedents** of a particular behavior and each of its *results* or **consequences.** Viewing consumer actions in terms of cause and effect helps us, as marketers, to better anticipate consumer actions and possibly influence them. We find out, for example, not only what leads a consumer to choose one brand over another, but also what will influence that buyer's *future* purchase decisions.

Several researchers have developed models to describe consumer decision making.[13] One of the more comprehensive of these, and the one around which much of this text is based, is the Engel, Kollat, and Blackwell (EKB) model.[14]

1-2a The Engel, Kollat, and Blackwell (EKB) Model

The EKB model maps out the quite complex mix of factors that affect even the simplest of consumer decisions. A multimediation model, EKB not only shows the components of decision-making but also demonstrates the multiple relationships and interactions among the components.

Shown in Exhibit 1-10, the EKB model identifies five distinct aspects of consumer decision making. These are: (1) input, (2) information processing (3) decision process, (4) decision process variables, and (5) external influences.

Before we even consider making any purchase, we are continually subjected to *input* of all kinds. The world around us, our contact with others, our experiences, and the marketplace itself all stimulate us in some way, whether we are aware of it or not. Some of these stimuli are marketer controlled—advertising, for example. Others are not, such as our

consumer decision model A theoretical framework used to describe the processes consumers go through before, during, and after making a purchase decision. It is a means of describing a concept, its causes, and its effects. Models provide a framework for analyzing consumer behavior.

antecedents In the consumer decision model, proposed causes of certain results (or consequences).

consequences In the consumer decision model, proposed results of certain causes (or antecedents).

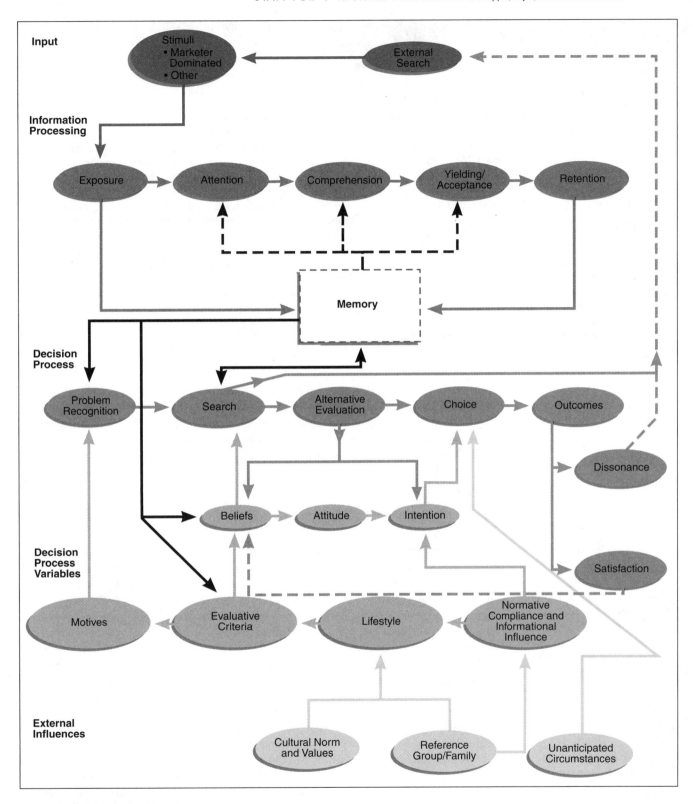

Exhibit 1-10

Engel, Kollat, and Blackwell (EKB) Model

A comprehensive model of consumer decision making, the EKB model maps out a five-step decision process during which a range of internal and external variables continually intervenes to influence the consumer before making a final purchase.

Marketplace 1-4

Stimulus and Response

Input—internal or external stimuli—is a component of the EKB model. The relationship between stimulus and response has fascinated psychologists since Pavlov first tempted his famous bell-ringing dogs. Marketers, too, recognize that, faced with a specific drive or stimulus, a consumer will give a specific response. If this response is reinforced, learning occurs. Thus, if a consumer is once successfully stimulated to buy Wrigley's gum and that action is positively reinforced, the same purchase decision will be made again and again. The dynamic between stimulus and response is particularly useful for explaining frequent, repetitive purchases, as in the category of packaged goods, where brand preference and loyalty are key.

Three types of stimuli trigger the decision process. The first type is "significative stimuli" or physical things. A consumer on a health kick and ready to change his or her eating habits evaluates food purchases in terms of such tangible aspects as fat content, serving size, and nutrition benefits. The second set of triggers is "symbolic stimuli" or representative things. The consumer considers perceived aspects of food products, such as perceived image, perceived quality, and his or her expectations of improved health. Finally, there are "social stimuli" or communications from others. The consumer talks to friends who buy health-food products or reads testimonials from peer group users.

In some instances, the stimulus and the consumer's awareness of it are very clear; in others they are not. The amount of attention the customer pays to the stimulus depends upon this stimulus ambiguity. When the stimulus is weak, a quick decision is unlikely. When it is strong, the consumer is likely to begin the decision-making process.

conversations with friends or our personal recollections. See Marketplace 1-4 about how stimulus and response work from a consumer perspective.

Once we receive input, we continually process, change, and update it. The EKB model identifies five methods of *information processing: exposure*—we see a television commercial or hear of a friend's new purchase; *attention*—we accept the information as relevant to us; *comprehension*—we attempt to find out more or really understand the information; *yielding*—we develop an attitude toward the information; for example, we believe or disbelieve it; and *retention*—we file the information away in memory for future use. (Chapter 7 describes memory, learning, and perception as they relate to consumer information processing.)

> **consumer decision process**
> The five steps suggested in the Engel, Kollat, and Blackwell (EKB) model—namely, problem or need recognition, information search, alternative evaluation, choice, and outcomes. Consumers do not go through all five steps in all situations.

The **consumer decision process,** triggered at any time during information processing, has five steps. It begins with *problem or need recognition*—we realize, for whatever reasons, that we have a problem that can be solved by making a purchase. Depending on how important that purchase is, we engage in some kind of *information search*—as simple as scanning our memories for a reminder of what product we bought in the past to solve a similar problem, or as extensive as a complete review of product information or a mall-to-mall or website-to-website shopping expedition. Once we feel we have enough information to make a good decision, *alternative evaluation* begins—we compare different solutions based on their costs and benefits. In a number of instances, information search and alternative evaluation occur at the same time. Finally, we make a *choice*—we select a specific product with specific features from a specific outlet and at a specific price that provides the benefits we are looking for. After a purchase is made, we experience the *outcome* of the decision—we use the product or service and evaluate it.

F A Q

Even after a purchase is made, why do consumers find it hard to resist the urge to keep an eye on prices, scan advertisements, and even check out competing brands?

As the EKB model shows, only two types of outcomes are possible. The first is related to satisfaction. Positive evaluation after purchase leads to satisfaction, while negative evaluation leads to dissatisfaction. Dissonance, the second possibility, actually occurs as you commit to selecting the product. It is the feeling of uncertainty that you've made the right choice. As we see from Exhibit 1-10, dissonance feeds back to start the whole process over again. If people are satisfied with a purchase, they may become "loyal." CBite 1-3 discusses the impact of price on loyalty. (Detailed discussions of the decision-making steps are found in Chapters 2–4.)

CBite 1-3
The Price of Loyalty

A survey on consumer selection of everyday products provides some interesting insights into the effect of price on brand choice during alternative evaluation. More than one out of four of us would try another brand of peanut butter if the price of our favorite brand increased by twenty cents. Around 16 percent of us would not sample a competitor's brand until the price of our brand went up by thirty cents, and 8 percent of us would stick with our brand all the way until the price difference exceeded a dollar. Half of the women who wear them would switch brands of pantyhose if the price went up by sixty cents. Around 35 percent of consumers would try another aftershave if the price went up by ninety cents.

Source: Bernice Kanner, "Standing by Their Brands—Well, Some of Them, Anyway," *Advertising Age* (February 20, 1995), p. 28.

At any or all of the five stages of the decision-making process, the consumer is subjected to a number of influences that may affect the final decision. These decision process variables are those individual qualities that make us unique as individuals and as consumers—our beliefs, attitudes, intentions, motives, and evaluative criteria along with our lifestyles, other aspects of self, and our desire to comply to certain norms of behavior. Notice from the EKB model that motives are important only during problem recognition. Different people have very different reasons to buy, thereby triggering entirely different decision-making processes. (Chapters 5–9 cover these psychological influences on consumer decision making.)

External influences are also at play during the decision-making process. The circles of social influence are as small as our immediate families or peer groups, or as large as the culture and subcultures in which we live. (Chapters 11–15 cover sociological influences on decision-making, and Chapter 10 discusses communication and persuasion.)

The EKB model is both comprehensive and easy to follow. It presents a clear pattern of decision making yet recognizes that a host of variables interact to affect the final decision. It has been successfully applied to buying situations as diverse as the purchase of automobiles and laundry detergents, with results that have aided marketers in making marketplace decisions. Do all purchases happen as a result of a specific decision process? See Marketplace 1-5 for some observations on this. What impact do you think brand recognition has on the consumer decision process? Marketplace 1-6 offers an interesting answer tied to the "Energizer Bunny."

F A Q

Why would two people with exactly the same problem seek completely different solutions?

Marketing Management—Implications and Actions

Using the EKB model helps marketers:

- Analyze every aspect of consumer decision making.
- Recognize the stage target consumers have reached in the decision-making process and find ways to aid them in further moving through it.
- Understand that decision making continues even after a sale, and take steps to encourage repeat purchasing and brand loyalty.
- Identify and classify the multiple psychological and external variables that influence purchasing of their product by target consumers.

Marketplace 1-5

Is There Really a Pattern to the Way We Make Decisions?

I t's extremely convenient for marketers to identify a process that is purported to model the way in which we make purchase decisions, but do we really go through such a sequence at all? Some say "no," questioning the validity of EKB and other decision models. Their reasoning makes sense—after all, we don't always remember what brands or even what products we buy. Even if we do remember, we don't necessarily repeat the purchase. When we know we don't have enough information to make a good decision, we often jump right in and make it anyway, with little or no information searching. And how often do we buy brands that we don't like rather than try new ones?

To explain behaviors like these, researchers conclude that not all purchases happen as the result of a rational decision process. Some occur out of necessity or lack of choice; some are derived from culturally mandated lifestyles; some are dictated by interlocked purchases (buy one item and that leads to other related item purchases); some reflect early childhood preferences or conformity to group norms; and many occur in a variety of random or superficial ways. But researchers also point out that it would be an oversimplification to characterize all purchasing behavior as either involving predecision processes or not. Some are probably hybrid strategies that can combine, say, personal recommendation with limited searching and evaluation.

As a further explanation, researchers have classified purchases into three types: purchases that involve extended problem solving where much time and energy is committed to the process, purchases that involve limited problem solving where there is some past experience and an array of known options to choose from, so less time and energy are used, and, finally, purchases that involve habitual decision making (also called automatic response behavior) where, when the problem arises, the consumer already has a product/service solution and therefore is not willing to devote much time and energy to the process. As a rule, the bigger the problem, the less experience the consumer has with solving it, the more important the purchase process is to the consumer, and the greater the risk associated with making a wrong decision—the more likely it is that a five-step decision process like that described in the EKB model will be necessary. What would be situations where an important decision could be made with either limited problem solving or habitual decision making?

Have you ever, when unable to make a decision, resorted to flipping a coin? What does this behavior say about your process of decision making? Is it consistent or inconsistent with the concept of a rational decision process?

Sources: Richard W. Olshavsky and Donald H. Granbois, "Consumer Decision Making: Fact or Fiction?" pp. 98–99; D. J. Hempel, "Search Behavior and Information Utilization in the Home Buying Process," *Marketing Involvement in the Society and the Economy* (Chicago: American Marketing Association, 1969), pp. 241–249; Roger A. Formisan, Richard W. Olshavsky, and Shelley Tapp, "Choice Strategy in a Difficult Task Environment," *Journal of Consumer Research,* Vol. 8 (March 1982), pp. 474–479; Harold H. Kassarjian, "Presidential Address, 1977: Anthropomorphism and Parsimony," in *Advances in Consumer Research,* ed. H. Keith Hunt, Vol. 5 (Ann Arbor, MI: Association for Consumer Research, 1978), pp. xii–xiv.

Marketplace 1-6

Get That Bunny!

O f the many products and marketing messages we see every day, why do some slip our minds almost immediately while others stay with us? Some marketers have proven to us that a convincing answer is brand recognition. That is, consumers cannot develop a positive attitude toward a brand without first and foremost recognizing it. An excellent example of brand recognition is the long-running and popular campaign for Energizer batteries, featuring a pink rabbit in sunglasses, the Energizer Bunny. In the midst of what turns out to be a fake advertisement for an unrelated product, a toy rabbit playing a drum suddenly pops on screen as a narrator drones, "It keeps going and going." With a smile, the consumer immediately recalls earlier commercials in the same campaign and recognizes that the advertisement is really about the long-lasting power of Energizer batteries. In the grocery store, a checkout display topped by the pink bunny not only wins attention but also reminds consumers both that it's time to stock up on batteries and that the Energizer brand lasts longer. More recently we have seen TV commercials with the bunny inside the battery with his form popping out to show he and his long-lasting power are still there, but Energizer is presenting him in a different way to the target market.

Chapter Spotlights

This chapter offers some direction toward answering a question central to marketing—why do consumers do what they do in the marketplace when they do it? Once we understand that consumers are essentially buying benefits rather than products, the question is much easier to address. The consumer's perception of benefits potentially or actually deliverable by products and services influences all marketplace decisions. With the help of decision models designed to capture consumer experiences during decision making, marketers can better understand and appropriately attempt to influence those perceptions before, during, and after a choice is made.

1. Shopper, buyer, and consumer benefits. By viewing consumers as buying benefits, not goods or services, marketers can better understand how consumer benefits drive the decision-making process, which should in turn help them steer marketing strategies.

2. The total product concept. A product offers four types of benefits to varying degrees: a basic core or functional set, an accessory ring of benefits that add value at no apparent additional charge, a psychological ring of feelings the consumer experiences as a result of the possession or use of the product, and the time saved or lost from the use of the product.

3. Market segmentation and segmentation strategies. Market segmentation is the process of examining the population to find the natural subgroups of like-minded consumers within it. Marketers use segment bounding to define market segments in terms of the characteristics of members, their location, and the time period during which these factors remain applicable. Target markets are viable if they are: (1) of sufficient size to generate an adequate level of profits, (2) measurable, (3) clearly differentiated from other segments, and (4) reachable in terms of both product distribution and media access.

There are three common segmentation methods: mass or undifferentiated marketing (one product for all), concentrated marketing (marketing to a single segment), and differentiated marketing (marketing to two or more segments). Segments as small as one consumer are also becoming increasingly possible in today's high-tech society. Intermarket segmentation is a means of segmenting global markets by identifying groups of consumers who behave in similar ways, despite differences in culture. With intermarket segmentation, standardized products and services are sold worldwide. An alternative approach for international marketers is to localize products to suit each market.

4. Positioning. Through product positioning, marketers match products to benefits sought by targeted segments of consumers. Positioning is achieved on the basis of benefits, characteristics or image, through comparison with competitors, or by a combination of both. As markets change, repositioning strategies can help marketers keep pace with shifts in the benefits consumers seek.

5. Consumer decision making. Through the use of representative models, marketers can attempt to explain why a consumer makes a purchase, why he or she chooses a certain brand, and what type of purchases that consumer will likely make in the future.

6. The Engel, Kollat, and Blackwell (EKB) model. A commonly used comprehensive model of the consumer decision landscape, the EKB model maps out a five-step decision-making process and takes into account a number of psychological, sociological, and other variables that affect the purchase decision. The model demonstrates that the decision-making process is not static, nor is it one-way—many outside influences are working that measurably affect purchase behavior.

Key Terms

antecedents (p. 18)
brand personality (p. 15)
buyer (p. 3)
consequences (p. 18)
consumer (p. 3)

consumer benefits (p. 3)
consumer decision model (p. 18)
consumer decision process (p. 20)
countersegmentation (p. 10)
marketplace (p. 3)

market segmentation (p. 5)
positioning (p. 13)
segment bounding (p. 6)
shopper (p. 3)
total product concept (p. 3)

Review Questions

Note: You can find the correct answers to these questions by taking the quiz and then submitting your answers in the Online Edition. The program will automatically score your submission. If you miss a question, the program will provide the correct answer, a rationale for the answer, and the section number in the chapter where the topic is discussed.

1. Different consumers seek _____ benefits packages in different situations.
   a. similar
   b. equal
   c. different
   d. comparable

2. The total product concept includes four types of benefits: basic core, accessory ring, psychological ring, and _____ of the product or service.
   a. price
   b. convenience
   c. availability
   d. time dimensions

3. An important concept used to differentiate among consumers and among market segments to determine if they qualify as part of a segment is called
   a. segment spanning.
   b. segment bounding.
   c. market segmentation.
   d. homogeneous segmenting.

4. A viable segment is one that is _____ and is of sufficient potential to be pursued.
   a. distinctive
   b. large
   c. qualified
   d. approachable

5. When positioning against competitors, marketers invite _____ comparison.
   a. price
   b. distribution
   c. promotion
   d. product

6. Repositioning involves re-educating the consumer about product-related changes. It is difficult to achieve because consumers
   a. change products regularly.
   b. resist change.
   c. comparison shop.
   d. are better educated today.

7. By using consumer decision-making models, we can map out the antecedents or _____ of a particular behavior.
   a. prethought
   b. planning
   c. causes
   d. information gathering

8. Consumer decision models can help answer, "What causes some buyers to remain_____ and others to suddenly switch to another product?"
   a. indecisive
   b. apathetic
   c. price shoppers
   d. loyal

9. The EKB model helps marketers to recognize the _____ that targeted consumers have reached in the consumer decision-making process.
   a. stage
   b. time
   c. loyalty level
   d. positioning

10. The consumer decision-making process has five steps: problem/need recognition,_____, alternative evaluation, choice, and outcome.
    a. problem/need analysis
    b. prealternative evaluation
    c. information search
    d. need reconstruction

Team Talk

1. Consider the statement that people do not buy goods or services, they buy benefits. What was the last clothing product or personal-care service you purchased? What were the benefits you received from it? Think about both tangible and intangible benefits.

2. Apply the total product concept to the following goods and services: buying a personal computer, renting a movie, going to a college sporting event, and buying a mountain bike. For each, identify the benefits that fit into the basic core, the accessory ring, and the psychological ring. How does time affect selection?

3. How is the restaurant marketplace in your town segmented? Describe three different restaurants in terms of consumer benefits offered. Who are the customers in each restaurant segment? How do they differ from one another? In what situations would you go to restaurants in different segments?

4. Look through the advertising section of your daily newspaper and find an advertisement for a store selling women's apparel and one for a store selling men's apparel. For each, who is the target market group for the store? What is it about the advertisement that makes you think so? Consider the headline, subheads, body copy, visuals, and overall layout and appearance of the advertisements. Are there any "mixed signals" in the advertisements, or are they totally on target?

5. Videotape a television commercial that you feel is right on target for you. Show it to team members and explain why you chose it. Consider the product, the program during which the commercial appeared, and the network. Consider the creative aspects such as the spokesperson used in the commercial, the situation represented, the music, the visuals, and the copy.

6. Review foreign periodicals in the library and find examples of intermarket segmentation. Also look for examples of imported goods or services that have been localized.

7. Members of the team should go to the Internet independently and find three websites of retailers that sell clothing targeted toward college-age women and/or men. The team should meet and mutually agree on three sites that all will evaluate. Now look at the sites as a team and come to an agreement on how each one is positioned. Why do you think each site is positioned as it is?

8. Think of an important purchase you have recently made. What triggered you to want the product? Explain as clearly as you can the thought processes and the actions you went through as you decided what to buy, which brand to choose, how much to spend, and when and where to make the purchase. How closely does your decision process resemble the five-step process described in the text?

9. On today's city and suburban highways we see more trucks or sports utility vehicles than ever before. Increasingly, they're driven by the kinds of people who just five years ago were driving sedans or station wagons. Why do you think this is so?

10. Identity theft is often mentioned in the press and on television these days. How are marketers reacting to this situation as they position their products and services?

Workshops

Research Workshop

Background

The fast-food restaurant business is an extremely competitive, crowded product category. Chains attempt to position themselves for distinct market segments. The objectives of this workshop are to determine who the target market is for each of several chains and to assess market position.

Methodology

Choose any three fast-food chains that run television commercials in your area. Videotape one commercial for each chain. Describe the target market group for the commercial as clearly as you can, explaining your conclusions.

Now watch the commercial a second time. How is the fast-food chain positioned—on key benefits, characteristics, image, or against the competition, or a combination of two or more of these? What is it about the commercial presentation that makes you think so?

To the Marketplace

What would you recommend to the executives of each of the fast-food chains to sharpen their targeting and positioning presentations on television?

Creative Workshop

Background

The total product concept is a useful means through which marketers consider all the benefits offered by a product and so develop meaningful creative strategies. The objectives of this workshop are to identify influential components of the total product of a selected college sports event and to apply them to developing creative approaches that promote attendance.

Methodology

Choose a college sports event and have team members interview up to 20 students to determine the various benefits they identify with attending such an event. Ask, for example, why they attend or do not attend. Ask about their feelings toward the sport and the team, and ask how they feel about spending their free time at sports events. Also, have respondents score the benefits in terms of their relative importance by dividing one-hundred points among the benefits identified. Classify their answers into core, accessory, psychological, and time benefits.

To the Marketplace

Compare notes to develop a list of benefits ranked by relative importance. Use the list as the basis for developing a poster that will promote attendance at games. Decide which benefits—three at most—to feature in the visuals and copy. Next, each team member should rough out an advertisement for comparison and discussion.

Managerial Workshop

Background

Your team is working with a publisher to promote a new book by Tom Peters, management guru and author of the best-selling business book *In Search of Excellence*. The objective of this workshop is to develop a strategic plan to market the new book to business executives internationally.

Methodology

Use the EKB model to sketch out the processes through which business executives buy books, mapping psychological and external influences that affect their decisions.

To the Marketplace

Prepare a rough strategic plan that reflects your research into buyer motivation, problem or need recognition, product or service search, alternative evaluation, product or service choice, and outcomes.

Notes

1. The addition of time to this model was suggested by James W. Johnson, graduate student, Western Michigan University. The application of giving time and taking time, which may be desirable or undesirable, was conceived by Jay D. Lindquist, the co-author.
2. Nancy Spears, "On the Use of Time Expressions in Promoting Product Benefits," *Journal of Advertising*, Vol. 32 (Summer 2003), pp. 33–44.
3. Kathleen Kerwin, "How would you like your Ford?" *Business Week* (August 9, 2004), p. 34.
4. Joseph Turow, "Breaking Up America: The Dark Side of Target Marketing," *American Demographics*, Vol. 19 (November 1997), pp. 51–54.
5. Ugur Yavas, Bronislaw J. Verhage, and Robert T. Green, "Global Consumer Segmentation versus Local Market Orientation: Empirical Findings," *Management International Review*, Vol. 32 (1992/93), pp. 265–272.
6. Salah Hassan and Roger Blackwell, *Global Marketing Perspectives and Cases* (Fort Worth, TX: Dryden Press, 1993), pp. 53–57; Robert D. Buzzell, "Can You Standardize Multinational Marketing?" *Harvard Business Review*, Vol. 46 (November–December 1986), pp. 102–113; "Marketers Turn Sour on Global Sales Pitch Harvard Guru Makes," *The Wall Street Journal* (May 11, 1988), p. 1.
7. S. H. Kale and D. Sudharshan, "A Strategic Approach to International Segmentation," *International Marketing Review* (Summer 1987), pp. 60–70.
8. Ralph Z. Sorenson and Ulrich E. Weichmann, "How Multinationals View Marketing Standardization," *Harvard Business Review*, Vol. 35 (May–June 1975), pp. 38–56.
9. Hassan and Blackwell, *Global Marketing Perspectives and Cases*.
10. Frenkel Ter Hofstede, Jan-Benedict E. M. Steenkamp, and Michel Wedel, "International Market Segmentation Based on Consumer-Product Relations," *Journal of Marketing Research*, Vol. 36 (February 1999), pp. 1–17.
11. Jean Halliday, "Chrysler Brings Out Brand Personalities with '97 Ads," *Advertising Age* (September 30, 1996), p. 3.
12. Jennifer L. Aaker, "Dimensions of Brand Personality," *Journal of Marketing Research*, Vol. 34 (August 1997), pp. 347–356.

13. These include the Howard and Sheth model, John Howard and Jagdish N. Sheth, *The Theory of Buyer Behavior* (New York: John Wiley and Sons, 1969), which was the first truly comprehensive model proposed, and the Nicosia model, Francesco M. Nicosia, *Consumer Decisions* (Englewood Cliffs, NJ: Prentice-Hall, 1966).

14. James P. Engel, David T. Kollat, and Roger D. Blackwell, *Consumer Behavior,* 2nd ed. (New York: Holt, Rinehart and Winston, 1973).

The Consumer as Decision Maker

Part 2 takes you step-by-step through the process consumers follow in making the decision to purchase a particular service or good. How do needs arise? How do we sift through all of the available information and options to select a product and determine how and where to buy it? In answering these questions, we also learn how we are defined by what we consume, and how we react to good and bad consumption experiences.

Problem Recognition and Information Search

Marta wants to apply for a junior year study-abroad program. She has always been interested in travel and has become tired of campus life. Her parents agree that the change will do her good and prepare her for the final year. However, they urge Marta to consider all of her options. She could take a year off and work in her uncle's travel agency. Or she could take part in a summer program. After thinking it through, Marta is sure that what she really wants is to spend the full year in another country. But she wonders where to go? She looks through dozens of brochures and talks with other students who have been abroad before. She decides to apply for an English-language program at a small, private college outside of Tokyo. The program offered there would help her if she decides on a career in the travel industry—and spending nine months in Japan will be the experience of a lifetime.

Without ever thinking of it in such terms, in looking for a study-abroad program, Marta went through the first two stages of the consumer decision process: problem (or need) recognition and information search. With every purchase we make, we do the same. And, other than with major purchases, we are rarely aware of it at all. This is particularly true during problem or need recognition. Picking up a newspaper on the way to class, renting a movie, choosing a restaurant, planning a vacation, and even major life decisions such as choosing a college all depend upon what we perceive our needs to be. Once we've decided what it is we need, we engage in some kind of search, at varying levels of intensity, for information that will help us make a choice. It is during this information search that we are most receptive to marketing information. In this chapter, we'll begin by finding out exactly what it is that makes consumers of different types and in different situations realize the need to make a purchase. We'll then see where they turn for help in seeking information to make that purchase wisely.

2-1 Consumer Decision Process Action Options

If the consumer decision process is concerned with a **high-involvement product** that has never before or has infrequently been purchased, the chances are good that all five decision process steps summarized in the EKB model in Chapter 1 will be carried out. Here, the person feels that it is essential to make the "right" decision to avoid the unpleasant consequences and risks of making one that is improper. In Chapter 8, we'll address the concept of involvement as a separate topic. Reading that material will help you put into perspective the discussions in the current chapter and the three following.

Should a person begin the five steps, a number of results are possible: (1) the person begins the process and stays with it until complete; (2) the individual starts and stops a number of times and then completes the process; (3) the individual starts and stops somewhere along the way, never finishing the process; or (4) the person starts into the process and, as a result of what is encountered during the process, returns to an earlier step. The latter may occur when the marketplace has changed significantly since the last time the consumer was in the market or when, having never shopped for such a product or service before, the consumer's perceptions about the situation are initially incorrect. What would cause a consumer to follow each of these paths? Think of reasons for doing each of these. What about the last time you purchased clothing or a piece of electronic gear or a PC or a used car? What did you do?

We'll also see that if a product or service is perceived as **low involvement** by consumers, they typically *go directly from problem recognition to choice* because they do not wish to spend time and energy in search and alternative evaluation. The decision is just not that important to them. If the individual has had some experience with the choice to be made, limited effort will be given to search and evaluation, with only a few alternatives considered. We'll talk about such *consideration sets* later in this chapter. If possible, most consumers will make most decision processes routine, giving little time and effort to them because they already know what their choice is to be. This allows them to devote time and energy to more important marketplace decisions.

2-2 Problem Recognition

Problem recognition, or need recognition, is the first of the five steps consumers take when moving through the decision process. In very simple terms, it is only when we recognize that we need something that we consider starting the process to find the product or service that will deliver the benefits to fill the need or solve the problem. Exhibit 2-1 contains a flowchart that shows the various influences on problem/need recognition.

2-2a Problem Recognition: Actual State versus Desired State

Problem recognition is a psychological process through which we evaluate the difference between our **actual state** and our **desired state**. This is a comparison of our current need or benefits state with what we would like it to be. The greater the "perceived distance" between these two, the more clearly the consumer recognizes potential need. Remember,

high-involvement product, service, or outlet (see. p. 28) Products, services, or outlets for which the consumer feels it is essential to make the "right" decision to avoid the unpleasant consequences and risks of making a decision that is improper.

low-involvement product, service, or outlet Products, services, or outlets the consumer does not see as important and for which the risks associated with an improper decision are not viewed as high.

problem recognition A psychological process through which we evaluate the difference between our actual state and our desired state. This is a comparison of our current need or benefits state with what we would like it to be. The greater the "perceived distance" between these two, the more clearly the consumer recognizes a problem or potential need.

actual state Current state of benefits the consumer enjoys from products or services used or possessed.

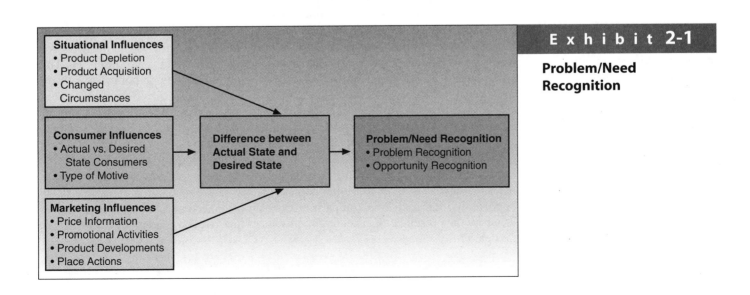

E x h i b i t 2-1

Problem/Need Recognition

Exhibit 2-2

Tylenol PM is offered as the key to a good night's sleep, relief from pain, and some peace of mind (the desired state), thereby eliminating the pain and current lack of sleep at night situation (the actual state).

Source: Courtesy of McNeil Consumer & Specialty Pharmaceuticals, a Division of McNeil-PPC.

desired state (see p. 29)
The state of benefits that the consumer wishes to enjoy from products or services used or possessed.

opportunity recognition
A variation of problem recognition. Here, the consumer is apparently completely satisfied with the current actual state. However, an option that is new or not previously known is found. The consumer does not perceive a problem but, rather, perceives an opportunity that leads to a comparison between actual state and desired state.

however, that need recognition depends upon the perception of the individual consumer. Running out of coffee or Pepsi Cola may trigger one consumer to immediately go out and buy some more because the problem is seen as urgent, while another person may simply drink a glass of water and put coffee or Pepsi on the shopping list for next Friday. The Exhibit 2-2 advertisement for Tylenol PM shows how the product can close the gap between the need to have a good night's sleep and feel refreshed and not groggy in the morning (desired state), and tossing and turning in the wee hours of the night as you worry about bills and other things (actual state). Relief from pain is also promised. This ad provides a simple visual and straightforward copy to make these points clear to the consumer.[1]

A variation of problem recognition is **opportunity recognition.** Suppose you are completely satisfied with your current computer setup. When browsing on the web, you spot an offer for additional computer memory at low cost. You begin to imagine the new programs and games you could run if you upgraded. Further, you have a friend who could help install the new memory. You decide to get the extra "gigs" for your machine. In a situation like this, the consumer does not perceive a problem but, rather, perceives an opportunity that leads to a comparison between actual state and a new desired state.[2] What are the possible influences or circumstances that create a perception of need in the first place?

2-2b **Influences on Problem Recognition**

Problem recognition can be influenced by a variety of situational, consumer, and marketing factors. These may operate singly or in combination to trigger problem recognition. These "triggers" are of interest to marketers of goods and services and are often part of the copy points included in promotional communications. "The next time you run out of laundry detergent, why not try Tide?" and a television commercial showing a man having trouble starting his lawn mower while he watches his neighbor start his Toro on the first starter cord pull are examples.

Situational Influences   Obviously, as products or services are used, consumers recognize the need to replace those that are *broken, lost, or worn out* or those for which the *contract has expired*. When the gas tank reads almost empty, the driver stops at the next gas station to fill up. When the computer runs out of paper, it's time to buy more, or if the car seems to be in the repair shop more frequently lately, maybe it's time to replace it. There is also the issue of style or color "wear out." Last year's clothing style may no longer be "in," so the consumer considers a dress, shirt, or pair of shoes to be "worn out." Can you think of other examples that could be classified as "wear outs"?

Product acquisition also leads consumers to realize new needs, as one purchase leads to another. A newlywed couple buying a house or renting an apartment quickly realizes the need to buy furniture, decorate, and stock up on household supplies before moving in. The owner of a new CD player soon finds out that this is just the beginning of a lifetime investment in compact disks.

Consumers may recognize the need for new goods and services as a result of *changed circumstances*.[3] Changes of lifestyle or environment—such as a move away from home to college, a new job, getting married, or a period of convalescence after an accident—all lead us to perceive new needs, resulting in a variety of purchases, some of which may be major.

Consumer Influences   Not all consumers respond to problems the same way. Whereas some look to existing goods and services to provide the benefits to solve their problems, others think in terms of new products.[4] Those in the first group are *actual state* consumers. They shop mostly because they realize that products presently owned require replacement or replenishment and currently available solutions are the best or acceptable answers. Those in the second group are *desired state* consumers. With a tendency to seek and recognize new product opportunities, they shop not necessarily to replace worn or lost possessions but because they enjoy the shopping experience. While shopping, they are exposed to new products, see the benefits they offer, and buy.

Motivation arousal is the sense of drive to action (motivation) a consumer experiences once a problem or need has been recognized. Different people have different motivations for buying different goods and services. Motivations—or reasons for buying—can be physiological, like hunger, or psychological, like a desire for respect.[5] Further, the personality traits of the consumer, the social environment, and various other internal and external factors also influence motives. A discussion of motivation, its meaning, and applications will be found in Chapter 8. Motivation is the driving force for action. Once a problem is recognized and the consumer intends to take action, he or she will typically have one or more motivation direction choices. What type of outcome is sought? In all cases we make choices that we hope will lead to positive benefit experiences. In general, outcome-driven motives that result in such experiences may be grouped into five types, as follows:[6]

1. The consumer makes a purchase to optimize satisfaction. We buy what we see as the "best" product or service within our economic means. This is particularly true for goods and services related to entertainment and leisure activities. Going out on a date to a fancy restaurant, taking a luxury cruise, or flying first class all maximize pleasure and are ways to optimize satisfaction. How does Marketplace 2-1 point toward optimizing satisfaction during a spring break travel experience?

motivation arousal
The sense of drive to action (motivation) a consumer experiences once a problem or need has been recognized. Calling this motive into being is arousal.

F A Q

Within the same income group, why are some people happy to drive a Honda Accord, while for others, nothing but a BMW will do?

Marketplace 2-1

Motivation and Travel

Why do people travel? As travel marketers see it, a variety of reasons can make travelers start packing their bags. People travel because they are pushed by such motives as a desire for escape or for rest and relaxation. Spring break is coming up, and all you want to do is set your books aside and head for the beach. You might even hope for a holiday romance.

This is the first stage of the decision process. Smart marketers seek to arouse motivations like these. Desires to escape, to relax, and to have fun, desires for adventure, for self-evaluation, for social prestige, and for social interactions are all motives that push people to travel.

Once motives are triggered, travelers are pulled toward specific destinations by quite a different set of factors, such as proximity to beaches or historic sites, recreation facilities, the novelty or image of a travel destination, or a special discount price.

F A Q

What qualities do these very different goods and services share: retainer fees to lawyers, self-diagnostic health kits, burial plots, and prepaid college tuition programs?

2. The consumer makes a purchase to prevent possible future problems. We often buy as a means of minimizing or eliminating negative consequences. Buyers of cars with top reliability ratings from Consumer Reports, for example, are most likely motivated by a wish to avoid breakdowns and costly repairs. Preneed purchases, such as renter's or personal liability or life insurance, also fall into this category.

3. The consumer makes a purchase to escape from a problem. Here, the motive is to avoid an existing negative situation. Obvious examples are appeals such as a getaway island vacation or a golf outing to escape from work or school pressures. Moving from one apartment to another because of continuing problems with the heating or air conditioning also is such an escape solution.

4. The consumer makes a purchase to resolve conflict. Particularly when we wish to satisfy two or more motives of different people through a single purchase, the choice is often one that resolves conflict. A woman is looking for a sporty, stylish car, while her husband thinks a car with room for the whole family would be a better purchase. Both want to please each other, and so they settle for something in between the two extremes.

5. The consumer makes a purchase to maintain satisfaction. Many purchases are made simply to maintain the status quo. Imagine, for example, that a nanny who takes care of the children for a dual-career couple resigns after several years of loyal service. The couple immediately hires another nanny to continue the same level of child care and the same lifestyle. Another example would be the action of a person who has been very pleased with the same automobile brand over the past two purchases. When it's time to replace the current car, a later model of the same brand is purchased.

Marketing Influences   Information provided by marketers may trigger problem recognition, leading the consumer to reevaluate his or her actual and desired states. *Price information,* for example, can be extremely influential. A consumer who has decided $39.95 is out of her price range for a magazine subscription may decide that the magazine is just the thing to help her with a term project when she sees a special offer at $19.95. The consumer recognizes need and moves toward the desired state. *Promotional activities* such as advertising, coupons, free offers, sweepstakes, product demonstrations, and rebates are ways in which marketers seek to influence problem recognition. *Product or service devel-*

opments, like the announcement of a breakthrough in technology or ease of use or greater product capacity and such, can trigger a consumer's reassessment of his or her actual state and desired state with respect to the product or service. The result could be that a problem is now recognized. *Place actions*—where a product that was not available can now be ordered on the web, through a catalog, or at one of the stores in town—also can trigger need recognition.

Marketing Management—Implications and Actions

Understanding problem (need) recognition, those circumstances that influence it, and the results of motivation arousal helps marketers:

- Identify what triggers consumers into problem recognition and allows for the discovery of consumer segments based on their motives for purchasing.
- Target promotional campaigns according to this segmentation.
- Provide consumers with the opportunity to recognize the need for specific brands of goods or services.
- Assist consumers as they move from actual states into desired states.
- Differentiate between those consumers who see problems and those who see opportunities—and target each accordingly.
- Identify situations in which consumers are likely to make purchases.
- Manage the elements of the marketing mix (price, product, promotion, and place) to encourage need recognition.

2-3 Information Search

Marketplace information is all around us. You walk through a shopping mall and notice the fall fashions being displayed in the windows or being worn by other shoppers. While watching your favorite program on television, you catch part of a commercial for a new brand of toothpaste. Driving to school, you hear a song on the radio from a new CD by a popular band. Even when we have no plans to make a purchase, we pick up all kinds of marketplace information almost every day through this type of incidental learning. When we do have plans to purchase, our attention to these signals is more intense. For example, you've been saving up for your first new car, and you begin to look for commercials about the brands and models you're considering. You slow down when you pass auto dealerships. You pick up brochures, notice the cars your friends are driving, and ask their opinions. Whether incidental or purposeful, the information we collect becomes the basis upon which we make future buying decisions.

There are many, many ways by which consumers can search for and find information on products. As we shall see, not all consumers look for or use information in the same ways. The way consumers search depends on what they are looking for. Fifteen percent of Americans say they want sales advice when shopping for jeans, and this share climbs to two-thirds when shopping for prescription drugs.[7] Moreover, different consumers look for differing amounts and types of information. Consumers often combine their information search with alternative evaluation, so trying to "draw the line" between the two is not always possible. As you read and study this chapter, realize that what we will cover in Chapter 3 has a natural spillover into the information search area and vice versa.

Why is it important for marketers to understand the information search process carried out by consumers? The answer is simple—so that the behavior of consumers in the marketplace can be better anticipated. If we know: (1) why consumers are searching for information, (2) where they are looking, (3) what they are looking for, and (4) how extensively they are willing to search, we can better identify potential customers and answer

F A Q

When the microwave oven was first introduced, it was not instantly adopted. Why do you think this was the case?

their information needs. In the best of situations, all the consumer needs to say is, "Here I am." The marketer should then be able to reply, "I've been waiting for you here, and I have the information you are looking for."

2-3a Types of Information Search

At different stages in the consumer decision process, we engage in different types of information search. For purchases that are very important to us, we might leave no stone unturned in looking for information to help us make the best choice. Even after we've bought something, we keep on looking to make sure the deal was a good one. For other purchases, we might simply browse through a catalog or on the web, or glance in store windows. For still others, we might not even be aware that we are conducting any search at all. Whether the consumer is conscious of it or not, search is typically an ongoing activity, occurring before, during, and even after a purchase is made.

Pre-Purchase Search   Before making purchase decisions, we engage in some kind of **pre-purchase information search.** Some searches are purposeful and deliberate. In these **directed information searches,** the consumer has a clear and conscious objective—to gather information that will help solve a specific problem. Need is already recognized, desire is already aroused, and the consumer simply requires information that will help clarify the path to purchase. For example, two to four weeks before fresh blueberries are ready for sale in Michigan, the local growers' association and individual farmers gear up for the annual influx of buyers who come to seek out the berries. There is no need for extensive advertising to attract buyers; all that is required is information on when and where the berries will be ready for picking. Through road signs and local media advertising, growers can help the consumer with his or her directed search.

Browsing is a second type of pre-purchase search. Window-shopping, thumbing through catalogs, surfing the web, and reading brochures with no immediate intent to buy are all forms of browsing. Since browsers may eventually be "converted" into purchasers, it is important for marketers to consider their needs. An eye-catching in-store display, a special offer, an attractive promotional brochure, or an exciting and inviting web page layout may be all it takes to capture their interest and turn it into intention to buy.

Accidental information search occurs when a consumer who is not looking for anything in particular is drawn to a product simply as a result of such occurrences as coming across an attractive store display, seeing a persuasive commercial, observing a person using the product, or learning of it from friends. Just as with browsers, marketers can take advantage of the purchase opportunity accidental search offers by providing eye-catching displays in windows or in stores. Further, they can seek ways to sponsor events that will keep their products in the public eye. A marathon run in support of a popular charity, a concert in the park, a free boating safety course, or an outdoor art fair are all opportunities for "accidental" exposure to goods and services.

What starts out to be accidental search may turn into browsing, and browsing may become directed search. This could occur on the same shopping trip in whatever outlet you are enjoying (catalog, shopping center, web, shopping channel on television, etc.) or it could happen later.

Post-Purchase Search   In a **post-purchase information search,** a consumer who has already made a purchase continues to gather information about his or her choice and/or evaluates other options in the marketplace. The consumer may be motivated to do so simply out of increased interest in the product category and/or the desire to stay current. This is typical among buyers of computer equipment, for example. Alternatively, the consumer may be seeking positive reinforcement that he or she made the right purchase decision. A buyer who has recently spent $30,000 on a new car may continue

pre-purchase information search A search for information made before making a purchase decision. Such searches are classified as directed, browsing, or accidental.

directed information search A type of pre-purchase search that is purposeful, having a clear and conscious objective, which is to gather information that will help solve a specific problem.

browsing information search A type of pre-purchase search where there is no immediate intent to buy.

accidental information search A form of pre-purchase search that occurs when a consumer who is not looking for any product or service acquires information as a result of such occurrences as coming across an attractive store display, seeing a persuasive commercial, observing a person using the product, or learning of it from friends.

post-purchase information search When a consumer who has already made a purchase continues to gather information about his or her choice and/or evaluates other options in the marketplace.

to compare and contrast competing models for months afterward. It is essential for marketers to understand the impact of after-purchase search both on future buying decisions by the consumer and on the influence that the buyer may have on other potential customers. Reinforcing information in advertising, brochures, and display materials must stress that the buyer has made a wise choice. This is often achieved through advertising that portrays satisfied customers who compare their purchase with other brands on the market.

Ongoing Search Engaging in **ongoing search,** consumers observe and stay current with what is happening in the marketplace and are continually open to new information. Ongoing search can occur pre-purchase, after the purchase, or both. Natural curiosity leads us to wonder what is going on in the marketplace. We're interested in new cars, new movies, new restaurants, new fashions, the latest in audio or video equipment, and new computer software programs. In fact, most of us are interested in just about anything that claims to be new.

Search behavior is not always clear-cut, and frequently the consumer undertakes a combination of some or all of the types of information searches we have discussed. Let's look at an example. Zahir visits the home of a friend who has recently bought a new, big-screen television set. Though he had (until then) been completely happy with his own TV set, Zahir starts thinking how nice it would be to have a new one with a larger picture tube or rear projection, particularly as he's planning on hosting a Super Bowl party next month. While out shopping for clothes in the mall, he looks in the window of an electronics store. He browses through sales advertisements in the Sunday newspaper. Zahir borrows a copy of *Consumer Reports* to read up on television brands. He finally visits a showroom where a salesperson helps him decide to buy a new Zenith. Even after the set is delivered, he continues to check prices, features, and screen sizes. At the Super Bowl party, he mentally compares his new Zenith with the sets that his friends own.

What types of information search has Zahir engaged in? When did they occur? At what stage do you think his decision to buy a new television set was made? When did he choose a Zenith? What important purchase have you made recently? What was your information search process like?

2-3b Internal and External Information Search

Information search can be **internal** or **external,** or it can be a combination of both. Quite simply, internal search involves no sources other than the consumer's own memory, knowledge, and experience. In external search, information can be gathered from an almost unlimited variety of sources outside the individual.

Internal Search Memory is the key component of internal search. Our first, possibly subconscious, response upon encountering a problem that may be solved in the marketplace is to scan the information stored in our memory for potential solutions.[8] Whether we are successful in finding solutions through internal search alone depends upon the availability and quality of relevant prior knowledge and experience we have in memory.

Those who are **experts** in a product or service category are consumers who have gained extensive prior knowledge through experience and training and are more likely to find the answers through internal search than are those who are **novices.**[9] The latter are consumers who have little or no prior knowledge or experience with a product or service category. For example, when it comes to buying such everyday products as breakfast cereals, bread, soft drinks, or antiperspirants, we are all "experts." Assuming satisfaction with our usual brands, we simply buy the same one when we run out. In most cases, no external search is necessary; we simply retrieve information on our current brands from memory and pick them up at the grocery store. As in this example, the greater the experience and knowledge of the product, the less need there is for external search.[10]

ongoing search Continually observing what is happening in the marketplace, looking for and being open to new information. Ongoing search can occur pre-purchase, after purchase, or both.

F A Q

Why do retailers keep an array of low-price products near the checkout counter?

internal information search Searching no sources other than the consumer's own memory, knowledge, and experience.

external information search Gathering information from a variety of sources not part of the person's own memory, knowledge, or experience.

expert Consumers who have extensive prior knowledge and experience with a product or service category.

novice Consumers who have little or no prior knowledge and experience with a product or service category.

The difference between experts and novices is important. An expert has the ability both to better store relevant information in memory and to access it efficiently. Over time, experts acquire extensive information about a particular category. They understand and usually require detailed product information, read brochures, and look at and try out products in the category whenever they come across them. Having collected all this information in memory, when they are ready to make a purchase, they can. If they choose, experts can often make decisions based on internal search alone. Alternatively, they can supplement stored information with additional information from new sources. For novices, accurate retrieval from memory is much more difficult.[11] Having little or no knowledge base with which to compare and contrast new information, the novice needs product information that is clear and to the point.

Whether internal search alone is sufficient also depends upon the quality and quantity of information already available in memory. Exhibit 2-3 summarizes the findings on how the quality and quantity of internal information affects the need for external search. For example, if past satisfaction with a particular brand is high, the consumer has little or no need for external information search. Also, if accurate data on different purchase choices is in memory, comparisons can be made without external input. On the other hand, if there are several different choices available and insufficient data in memory, there is a greater likelihood of the need for external search. What we see, in sum, is that the consumer considers the quality of information in memory storage, the quantity of information, its relevance to the problem at hand, and its timeliness (how current is the information?).

External Search   During external search, the consumer looks beyond his or her memory for new information that will aid in making the purchase decision. Information can come from personal sources such as friends, experts, or salespeople, or from impersonal sources such as advertising, in-store displays, or trade reports. As we saw in the preceding section, the inadequacy of information available in memory is one factor that motivates consumers to engage in external search. One current view of the components of external information search is that they involve the *ability to search, motivation to search, costs of search,* and *benefits of search*.[12] Let's look at a few key search considerations that have ties traceable to the underpinnings of this four-component model. They are: (1) perceived value of the search (benefits), (2) need to acquire information (benefits), (3) ease of acquiring and using information (ability), (4) confidence in decision-making ability (ability), (5) locus of control theory (benefits), (6) actual or perceived

E x h i b i t 2-3	**Factor**	**Status**	**Need for External Search**
Quality of Internal Information and the Need for External Search	Satisfaction with past experience[a]	High	None to low
	Time since last decision[a]	Long	High
	Changes in alternatives[a]	Many	High
	Problem is new[b]	Yes	High
	Quality of relevant information[c]	High	None to low
	Quantity of relevant information[c]	Sufficient	None to low

Source: [a]Geoffrey C. Kiel, *An Empirical Analysis of New Car Buyers' External Information Behavior* (School of Marketing, University of New South Wales, 1977). [b]John E. Swan, "Experimental Analysis of Predecision Information Seeking," *Journal of Marketing,* Vol. 33 (May 1969), pp. 192–197. [c]Elizabeth Cowley, "Recovering Forgotten Information: A Study in Consumer Expertise," in Chris T. Allen and Deborah R. John, eds., *Advances in Consumer Research,* Vol. 21 (Provo, UT: Association for Consumer Research, 1994), pp. 58–63.

risk (benefits), (7) costs of external search (costs), (8) type of goods/services sought (benefits/costs), and (9) characteristics of the purchase decision (benefits). Motivation to search is relevant in each of these considerations. Exhibit 2-4 shows these factors organized as situational influences, consumer influences, product influences, and purchase decision influences.

Perceived Value of the Search (Situational Influence)   When consumers consider engaging in external search, they assign some sort of value or utility to the information they hope to find. Of course, because consumers and buying situations differ widely, utility depends upon who is buying what, in what situation, and from what source. If the ratio of perceived value of an external search compared to its perceived cost is high, the consumer is likely to devote time and energy to it. The costs of external search will be discussed shortly. External search is typical for purchases the consumer considers important. For one person, this might be a major purchase, like a motorcycle, while for another it might be a favorite brand, such as Chicken of the Sea canned tuna fish. The marketer can, therefore, encourage external search by making relevant information available as quickly and painlessly as possible.

By identifying the level of importance their products or services occupy in the minds of target customers, marketers can better aid external search—by providing the right information, at the right time, and at the right place. The easier it is for potential customers to access favorable information, the more likely they are to gather it and move on to making a purchase.

Ease of Acquiring and Using Information (Situational Influence)   The easier it is to acquire relevant information, the less necessary is an extensive external search. If consumers realize that relevant information can be obtained quickly, they are unlikely to engage in a high-energy, time-consuming, external search.[13] Marketers can facilitate the acquisition of relevant—and favorable—information about their products and services through advertising, brochures, in-store displays, salespeople, and other points of contact with the consumer.

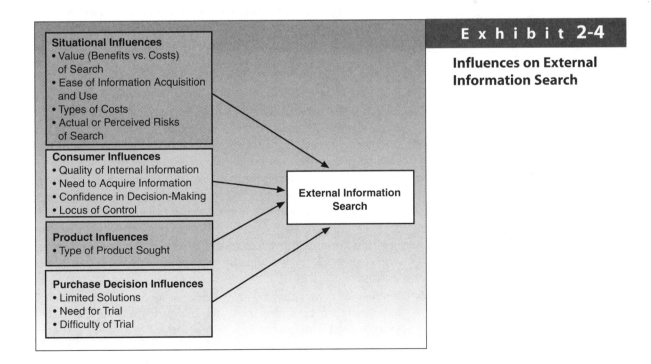

Exhibit 2-4

Influences on External Information Search

An external search is also likely to occur if the consumer has time available and feels that the information will be both easy to find and easy to understand.[14] If information acquired is difficult to absorb or use, further external searching may be limited.[15] Moira is shopping for a camcorder. In each store she visits, the salesperson inundates her with facts, figures, and a shopping bag full of support brochures that describe a mind-boggling array of choices and options. Though it was easy to acquire, the information she has will be extremely difficult and time-consuming to use. She thinks twice about gathering any more.

In addition to the issue of information overload, **information control** is also an issue. Consumers wish to have some control over what information they are exposed to, how long it will be presented to them, and what information will follow.[16] The concept of information control has been considered to be of importance for some time,[17] and it is especially significant in this time of increasing interactive data gathering and searching by consumers using the web, electronic kiosks, and other computer-assisted options. In a series of experiments related to searching for information on cameras, consumers who exercised more control were able to integrate information, remember it, and understand these inputs to their judgments at a higher level than were those consumers with less control. Surprisingly, the increase in search efficiency was not tied solely to having less information but also was enhanced by the sense of having control of the information.[18] Providing information on the web, for example, where the searching consumer can pick and choose content and its order of exposure, is very important because the consumer feels more in control.[19] In addition, to make information easy to use, the marketer must consider whether it is targeted toward experts, novices, or both, and must act accordingly.

Costs of External Search (Situational Influence)   When consumers are seeking value, they consider the benefits provided by the product or service versus the price. But the price of an item purchased is not the only cost to the consumer making the purchase. External information search costs should be considered. Consumers will weigh them along with the price to determine if an external search can be justified. What are these "costs"? The following are often identified:

1. *Financial costs.* Consumers take into account any out-of-pocket expenses incurred during the search, such as the costs of travel, parking, childcare, and meals away from home. Lost income from taking time off work is another consideration.[20]

2. *Time costs.* Depending upon the value they place upon their time, consumers make a trade-off between the desire for information about a potential purchase and the time it takes to gather that information.[21] For example, to limit the time spent, some consumers may search in fewer stores, and others may search in catalogs only.[22]

3. *Decision delay costs.* If an external search delays the purchase decision to such an extent that the consumer suffers from not being able to have and use the desired product or service, the search may be considered too costly. This is an opportunity cost.

4. *Physical costs.* Fatigue and the physical effort associated with the search process take their toll on the consumer. This is an especially important cost to older consumers and those with physical handicaps.

5. *Psychological costs.* Mental stress or anxiety arising from dealing with crowds and insensitive or unskilled salespeople, difficulty in locating products within a store or mall environment, standing in line, and finding parking all exact a cost on the searcher.[23]

6. *Information overload costs.* The gathering of too much information for the consumer to properly process during the search can cause confusion and a sense of being overwhelmed. This is another potential cost.[24]

▶information control
The level of control consumers have over what information they are exposed to, how long it will be presented to them, and what information follows.

F A Q

Why do some people who love to shop hate buying groceries?

The importance of each of these costs and its ability to dissuade consumers from engaging in external search varies from person to person, from product to product, and from situation to situation.

Information capital is information about product attributes, benefits, and prices learned by a consumer in the past that can still be used in the current situation. The greater this "capital" the lower will be the search costs. Also to be considered is **skill capital.** This is related to how to search. Consumers who have learned how to search from past experience will enjoy lower search costs, and the amount of information gathered will also be higher. Skilled consumers may consider more alternatives since there will be low search cost per alternative. Further, it has been found that consumers will direct their consumption and search activities in ways that maximize the impact of their information capital and skill capital.[25] We may also conclude that experts will typically have more information and skill capital than will novices.

Actual or Perceived Risk (Situational Influence)   Every purchase decision involves some level of risk. There are several types of risk that can discourage consumers from either making a choice or delaying the purchase decision.[26] The following are common types of risk:

1. *Functional or performance risk*. If I buy Product X, will it actually deliver the benefits it promises?
2. *Financial risk*. If I buy Product X, will I lose money? Will I find it doesn't give the anticipated value for the money? Can I find the same product for a lower price somewhere else?
3. *Psychological risk*. If I buy Product X, will owning it in any way damage my self-image, self-confidence, or ego?
4. *Social risk*. If I buy Product X, will other people think less of me because I made a socially unacceptable choice?
5. *Physiological risk*. If I buy Product X, is there potential for physical harm because I selected a product of inferior quality, one beyond my ability to use properly, or one that is poorly manufactured?
6. *Time risk*. If I buy Product X and it proves inadequate, how much of my time will I have wasted in search; or will my use of the item require more time than I had anticipated or am willing to give?
7. *Linked-decision risk*. If I buy Product X, will this result in additional purchases of other goods or services as a direct result of having selected this item?

Think of two major purchases you have made or considered recently, such as a stereo system, clothes for a special occasion, or college textbooks. What types of risk applied to each purchase decision? Were you conscious of that risk when you made the purchase? What helped you overcome the feeling of risk?

Where risk is high, the value of external search is also high for most consumers, because several types of risk can be reduced through time and effort spent in the search for information. Information search, however, is not the only choice when consumers perceive risk. Other options are to trust in well-known brands, to buy only from stores or from manufacturers with strong reputations, to believe that extra cost means extra value and buy one of the more expensive brands on the market, or to follow the recommendations of friends.

Marketers must be aware of the perceived risks that consumers attach to their products and services. Complaints, customer follow-up, or specific research results can act as guides. Product modification, proper positioning, accurate advertising copy, sales associate training, and the use of guarantees and return policies are all ways to lessen the negative impact of perceived risk on consumers.

▶**information capital**
Information about product attributes, benefits, and prices learned by a consumer in the past that can still be used in the current situation.

▶**skill capital** The amount of skill a consumer brings to a search. Consumers who have learned how to search from past experience will enjoy lower search costs, and the amount of information gathered will also be higher.

Quality of Internal Information (Consumer Influence)   "Quality" is used here to signal a broad series of considerations by the consumer made when the consumer evaluates data in memory storage. Are the data reliable and from sources including the person's own experience that are trustworthy? Next, is the quantity of the information held internally sufficient to deal with all aspects of the problem? How relevant is the information to the problem at hand? Finally, is the information in storage current enough to be useful? These four aspects point to the overall quality of what we have in our memory that could be applied to making a decision among the choices we have.

Need to Acquire Information (Consumer Influence)   It's easy to assume that consumers with limited product or category knowledge need information on which to make purchase decisions and that, therefore, they are more likely to engage in external search than are those who are experts in the product or category. Simply put, because experts know more, they need to search less. This assumption, however, is not always correct. In some cases, consumers with extensive product category knowledge (PCK) actually search more than do their novice counterparts. Because they already have an organized knowledge base and can process new information quickly and easily, experts are frequently more willing than are novices to take the time to engage in external search.[27] Their search process is efficient, and so they are able to acquire new information at lower cost and with less effort than are novices in the product category.[28] This is known as the selective search effect—because experts have extensive product category knowledge, they are able to easily identify key attributes of brands under consideration, pick and choose relevant information, and make quick decisions.[29]

Exhibit 2-5 illustrates the relationship between the amount of consumer product knowledge and the extent to which he or she actually engages in external searching.[30] The left side (low search) represents novice behavior. Novices limit their search because their knowledge base is small and they do not realize the need for information. They likely also have trouble organizing, interpreting, and prioritizing information, making the search task less productive. The right side (again, low search) shows expert behavior. Experts are able to use information in memory and judge search cues quickly. Hence, lower levels of search still produce high yields. Those in between these two extremes realize the need for information and, to varying extents, are willing to engage in external search. There are exceptions to the curve shown in Exhibit 2-5. For example, some experts engage in extensive search because of their desire to be fully informed and because of their ability to process large amounts of information efficiently.

The implications are clear. Though experts need to do little external search, marketers must be ready to bring them quickly up-to-date on product features and benefits. Novices, though their need is greater, must not be overloaded with data that they may be unable or unwilling to process. An interesting contrast in information searching is in the case of portable stereos. In one study, individuals had the opportunity to get sensory information (listen to the stereo) and written information about it. The novices relied more on written descriptions of the product, while the experts relied more on sensory information.[31] Why do you think this was the case?

Confidence in Decision-Making Ability (Consumer Influence)   A consumer's confidence in his or her decision-making ability is an important predictor of search behavior.[32] The consumer's perception of the value of external searching can be influenced in two ways by the extent to which he or she feels able to make a good decision. First, the consumer may be unsure of the ability of a product or brand to meet certain needs or solve certain problems, thus necessitating an external search for supporting information.[33] Second, the consumer may lack confidence in his or her own ability to judge a product or brand on its characteristics.[34] If a consumer feels able to accurately evaluate information about products and product attributes, external search will most likely occur. If he or she does not feel competent to do so, external search will be avoided or minimized.

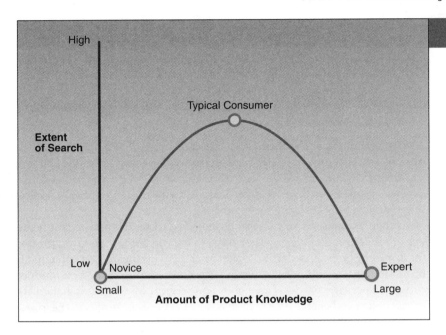

Product Knowledge and Extent of External Search
Consumers at the midpoint— those with some but limited product knowledge—are those most likely to engage in and benefit from an external search.

Source: From "The Effect of Prior Knowledge on Price Acceptability and the Type of Information Examined" by Akshay R. Rao and Wanda A. Sieben in *Journal of Consumer Research,* Vol. 19, September 1992, pp. 256–270. Copyright © 1992. Reprinted by permission of The University of Chicago Press.

E x h i b i t 2-5

An important step for marketers in assessing the consumer's level of confidence—in the potential of the brand to meet current needs and in his or her ability to judge among brands—is to determine whether the target market is made up of experts, novices, or both.

Locus of Control Theory (Consumer Influence)   Psychologists use the concept of locus of control to categorize people into two personality types: internals and externals.[35] **Externals** believe that events or outcomes are determined by forces such as luck or fate that are outside their control. Conversely, **internals** believe they are at least in part responsible for the outcomes of their actions. In general, internals tend to carry out more extensive pre-purchase external searches than do externals.[36] Internals assume responsibility for their own actions and, therefore, seek out information upon which to base decisions. Externals are more inclined to trust that the marketplace is stable, advertising is believable, and products with high sales are products of high quality and should be selected. Therefore, they see little need for external information search.

externals People who believe that events or outcomes are determined by forces such as luck or fate that are outside their control.

internals Individuals who believe they are at least in part responsible for the outcomes of their actions.

Type of Goods or Services Sought (Product Influence)   The type of goods or services sought also influences the extent to which the consumer will engage in an external search. Let's take a look at three different categories.

1. *Specialty goods and services.* Goods for which the consumer has developed strong preferences usually motivate an extensive external search. If a special brand of salsa is not available in the local grocery store, the consumer may visit two or three different stores to find it. The same could apply to the finding of a hair stylist who will be able to create a particular type of "do" that the consumer is looking for. The consumer may call a number of different shops to locate someone who has the desired skill.
2. *Shopping goods and services.* A consumer in search of a major appliance such as a refrigerator, for example, may not have settled on a specific brand but is willing to visit a number of stores or check several distributors to compare and contrast different models or brands. The search for a good car insurance supplier also would require an information search to compare policy and agent options. The time and effort devoted to these types of shopping vary by consumer.

F A Q

How might marketers go about classifying target consumers as internals and externals?

search products Goods or services for which most essential attributes and benefits can easily be evaluated prior to the purchase. This means that enough information can be found to make an informed buying decision resulting in the best product/brand being chosen.

experience products Goods and services where the evaluation cost of even the key attributes or benefits is so high that direct experience results in the lowest expenditure of time, money, cognitive effort, and other resources.

3. *Convenience goods and services.* By picking up a loaf of bread, a gallon of milk, or a six-pack of Coca-Cola at the 7-Eleven store on the way home from work, the consumer is expressing reluctance to spend time and effort on an external search. Getting a haircut or dropping off the dry cleaning on the way home from work without caring about the shops you frequent are service examples. People will generally pay more per item or unit of service simply for the convenience of this type of shopping.

A word of caution about these three classifications—the same goods or services may be categorized differently from person to person and from situation to situation. For this reason, different marketing strategies may be appropriate for each group of goods or services, depending upon the target market and marketplace conditions. Marketplace 2-2 gives some insights into searching for these different goods.

Products and services can also be classified as **search products** or **experience products.** Search products are goods or services for which most essential attributes and benefits can easily be evaluated prior to the purchase. This means that enough information can be found to make an informed buying decision resulting in the best product/brand being chosen. Experience products are goods and services where the evaluation cost of even the key attributes or benefits is so high that direct experience results in the lowest expenditure of time, money, cognitive effort and other resources. Examples of search products are clothing, jewelry, and furniture, whereas such things as books, paint, appliances, cars, food, and drugs are experience products. When considering advertising, these results suggest that ads for search products should contain more information than ads for experience products.[37]

Characteristics of the Purchase Decision (Purchase Decision Influences)   Three characteristics of the purchase decision can affect the extent of external search:

1. *Extent to which the number of possible solutions is limited.* If the acceptable characteristics of the product sought are narrowly defined, consumers are likely to accept the need for an extensive search. If such factors as brand, price, color, style, or performance limit their choices, they will expend more effort to find exactly what they want. Looking for a certain style of wooden earrings or a tie in specific colors—in both cases to complete an outfit—are examples of this.

2. *Need for trial.* If a product needs to be tried out before it is purchased, consumers are more likely to engage in external search. Selecting a dessert for an important dinner party, for example, may lead consumers to try options from different bakeries, even if it entails travel, rather than simply making a trip to the local supermarket. Remember, however, that there are instances where trial is considered essential and offered by all marketers of a product. The test-drive of a new car is a good example. In this case, the extent of the search depends on factors other than the need for trial, because nontrial is not an option for most car buyers.

3. *Difficulty of trial.* When pre-purchase trial is difficult or impossible, consumers rely upon the seller to deliver value. In these cases, the search is for a reliable, quality supplier rather than for a specific product or service. Choosing carpeting and selecting a home-remodeling contractor are examples.

The reasons why consumers engage in external searches and the factors they consider in doing so are varied and complex. What is important in the purchase of one product may be considered by the same consumer to be insignificant in the purchase of another. Similarly, different consumers and different buying situations affect the type and extent of external search. By understanding the multiple dynamics of search behavior, the marketer is better able to target the right customers, at the right time, and in the right way with relevant information that's likely to assist consumers in their purchase decisions.

Marketplace 2-2

Searching for Specialty, Shopping, and Convenience Goods

A study of durable goods purchases—refrigerators, freezers, clothes washers, and clothes dryers—showed that while for some consumers these are shopping goods, others express strong brand preferences and so consider them specialty items. In terms of the time spent shopping for them, some even treat these purchases as convenience goods. Forty-five percent of respondents spent a total of two hours shopping (convenience goods); 73 percent spent four hours or less (shopping goods). About one-third considered only one brand (specialty goods), with 84 percent considering three or fewer brands (shopping goods). Further, 37 percent visited only one store (convenience or specialty goods) and 75 percent visited three or fewer (shopping goods).

Interestingly, these results do not support the idea often expressed in retail advertising that consumers should, "come to us after you've checked elsewhere." Rather, retailers should concentrate on getting customers into their stores first, as it appears that few stores are visited by the majority of consumers. The key for marketers is to understand how the majority of the target market views the product—as a specialty, shopping, or convenience product—so that the tactics followed suit the situation.

Source: William L. Wilkie and Peter R. Dickson, "Consumer Information Search and Shopping Behavior," in Harold Kassarjian and Thomas Robertson, eds., *Perspectives in Consumer Behavior,* 4th ed. (Englewood Cliffs, NJ: Prentice-Hall, 1991), pp. 1–26.

The strategies marketers use to influence the consumer's external search are the topic of the next section.

Marketing Management—Implications and Actions

Understanding how information search occurs helps marketers:

- Provide the right information at the right time and in the right place to encourage purchasing.
- Encourage customers to feel satisfied with purchases they have already made and so repeat the purchase or recommend it to others.
- Differentiate between experts and novices, and tailor information to suit each consumer type.
- Make product information easy to find, easy to understand, and easy to use.
- Minimize both risks and costs to the consumer in making product selections.

2-4 External Search Strategy

It is important for marketers to understand the behavior of consumers as they engage in external search. By analyzing the way in which the search is conducted and the sources of marketplace information used, marketers can more effectively provide relevant product information, making the purchase decision easier.

2-4a Limiting Search Activity

Using Sets Most consumers are looking for ways to limit the amount of external search to some manageable level. One way to do this is to restrict the number of products, brands, or retail outlets about which to gather information. Hence, the concept of **sets** of options to be pursued is useful. The set of brands or retail outlets, if the latter is the focus over brand, to which the consumer has reasonable access—whether he or she is

sets Groups used to limit external search and alternative evaluation. The types include (1) universal—the group of brands or retail outlets to which the consumer has reasonable access whether aware of them or not, (2) retrieval—the group of which a person has front-of-mind awareness, (3) consideration (evoked, relevant)—all of the brands or outlets of which a person has front-of-mind awareness and that the consumer accepts as the set from among which a choice will likely be made.

aware of them or not—is called the *universal set*. With the advent of catalogs and now the Internet, this set of alternatives may be quite large. All the brands or retail outlets of which a person has front-of-mind awareness are part of what is called the *retrieval set*. This may still be a set of options that the consumer deems as too great in number. The most useful set is made up of those outlets or brands of which the consumer has front-of-mind awareness and that the consumer accepts as the group from among which a choice will likely be made. This was originally called the *evoked set*.[38] Today, the terms *relevant set* and *consideration set* are used to represent essentially the same concept.[39] Currently, "consideration set" is the most commonly used phrase when referring to this group. Marketers encourage consumers to include their brands or outlets in any search. Also, attempts are made to persuade consumers to limit the number of brands or outlets about which they seek information. The fewer alternatives the consumer investigates, the more likely that he or she will settle upon the marketer's product or brand or outlet, assuming that it is among the few. Alternative evaluation will be discussed in detail in Chapter 3. Suppose your parents offer to help you buy a new computer. Which brands come to mind immediately that you would consider purchasing? This is your consideration set of personal computers.

As the search proceeds and the consumer's information base grows, brands or outlets may be eliminated or new ones added to the set. Obviously, the ideal situation for a marketer is to position him- or herself as the sole choice for the consumer to consider. The outlet or brand name then becomes synonymous with the product category itself. To work toward this objective, marketers must be familiar with the sources consumers use to find reliable information and make sure that their brands are favorably represented there.

Irrelevant Information Impact   Consumers selectively look for information that points to the product or service as being able to deliver the desired benefits. Such information is classified as "confirming." If a marketer transmits information deemed "irrelevant" by its target market(s) through any channel, this will weaken consumer beliefs concerning the product's ability "to deliver." Consumers are looking for information that shows a product will "deliver" rather than "not deliver." They seek information that confirms beliefs about the product's ability to provide benefits. Information appears to be sorted by consumers into "confirming" or "not confirming." This grouping is then used to determine their belief in the product's or service's ability to deliver desired benefits. Examples of desired benefits found by product might include: apartment ("safe"), toothpaste ("fights cavities"), stereo system ("reliable"), computers ("fast"), mountain bikes ("sturdy"), shampoo ("high quality hair care"), and restaurant ("healthy"). Advertisers must determine desired benefits and include them in ads. Adding extra benefits that are irrelevant in consumer's eyes will lessen the stature of the products or services and make them less likely choices for purchase.[40]

2-4b Marketplace Information Sources

As Exhibit 2-6 shows, marketplace information sources are classified as either *general* or *marketer controlled* (marketer dominated). Both types of sources are further divided into those that are actively accessed *face-to-face* (including over the telephone) and those where contact is made through the *mass media* (including in-store and packaging).

General Sources   General sources are treated by consumers as being less biased. Therefore, more credibility is given to them than to those controlled by the marketer. Even so, some of the information available from general sources can be marketer generated. For example, writers, reporters, or editors for general source media may have been provided information by marketers. This may then be passed on as consumers are exposed to the information. For example, a Detroit newspaper article may include references to certain brands of automobiles based on information that was given to the writer

	General Sources	Marketer-Controlled Sources
Face-to-face	Personal influence	Salespersons
		Telemarketing
Media	General purpose	Mass advertising media
		In-store information
		In-store display
		Package labels

Marketplace Information Sources

by the manufacturer, and a bias may creep into the presentation because of it. Or a travel writer may visit a bed and breakfast at the expense of the owners and write an article about the visit in a travel magazine. He or she may feel obligated to give a positive spin to the experience.

Face-to-Face   Face-to-face general sources, "personal influence," may come from individuals such as relatives, friends, acquaintances, and others whom the consumer perceives to be expert or well informed. Sought out for advice, these types of people are important—and sometimes the only (determinant)—influences on purchase decisions. In fact, personal influence is determinant in many choice situations. Who would you go to for information and advice on multivitamin supplements: your mom, your doctor, or an advertiser? For most consumers, the doctor wins out, but mom is a close second.[41]

Looking at a series of products and services where men in our society are assumed, correctly or not, to be more expert than women (e.g., computer hardware, automobiles, sports equipment, computer software, insurance), seekers of word-of-mouth advice were either men or women, but the information sources were almost always men. Even when a woman was an informed source on these products, she was not sought out to the same degree as were male sources.[42] It is likely that, if the products or services had included day care, clothing, household items, or gifts, women would have been seen as stronger sources of expert information, as they are considered, again, correctly or not, to be more expert than men on these topics. Advertisers attempt to influence personal "expert" sources to take a stand for their particular brand with messages like, "Tell your friends about Brand X." Word-of-mouth communication among consumers, for example, may repeat advertising messages originating with the marketer. Maybe Hannah says to Allura, "You should get a Maytag dishwasher; they hardly ever need repairing." Hannah saw the commercials on television showing the "lonely Maytag repairman."

General sources can have negative as well as positive influence on consumers. If a respected personal source is disappointed with a product, he or she not only will answer negatively about it when asked but may also seek out potential customers to warn them away. Even if the marketer is aware of it, there is often nothing that can be done to control this type of information flow. In Chapter 4, we will discuss negative word-of-mouth as one of the outcomes of consumer dissatisfaction with a product, service, or retail outlet.

Mass Media   Mass media general sources include the editorial content of newspapers and magazines, books, television and radio programs, and any other information channel that reaches large segments of the buying public. Computer data sources and networks are also becoming increasingly popular. Though not controlled by marketers, such media often use public relations releases from the marketer when disseminating information. One print source that is extremely influential in buying decisions is *Consumer Reports* magazine.[43] This monthly publication rates a wide variety of products and services across a broad spectrum of attributes, including price and performance. Newspapers and magazines are also popular as information sources on a wide range of product and services categories. These print sources are not, however, typically used to make final purchase decisions. As a study of houseware purchases shows, only 12 percent to 23 percent of respondents, depending upon the product purchased, reported using print media as primary information sources.[44] A similar study found that broadcast media are primary sources of information among certain customer groups seeking information for household appliance purchases.[45]

Marketer-Controlled Sources

Face-to-Face   Face-to-face sources that are marketer controlled are those involving some level of personal contact with consumers. Marketers are in control of personal selling situations and telemarketing, for example. Trained by the retailer or the manufacturer, the in-store salesperson who explains goods or services and answers questions can be an effective and credible source of information. Knowledgeable salespeople are particularly important when the need for information is high. Pharmacists, for example, can provide vital information on health care and medication selection.[46] Similarly, in the sale of appliances, salespeople can help explain such manufacturer information as energy-use labeling, which one study found to be ineffective unless supported by additional explanation.[47] In in-home selling situations, such as the sale of cosmetics through organizations like Avon, representatives not only provide product information but also advise customers on using their purchases for the best effect. In telemarketing, contact with the customer is not literally face-to-face, but it is still personal. The distance between seller and buyer means that the communication is usually less influential than in personal selling situations.

In both personal selling and telemarketing, it is important that the marketer train those dealing with consumers and provide them with the kind of support materials that will help them match potential customers with the right choices. To be effective, this information must be both relevant and credible. It should also be appropriate for the particular selling situation in which it is to be used. These are aspects that the marketer can, to some extent, control. What is more difficult to keep track of is the skill and commitment of individual salespeople, and the consistency with which information is delivered in different selling situations.

Mass Media   The most obvious sources of marketer-controlled information are advertising and other forms of promotion through the mass media, in-store, or on the package itself. From newspaper and magazine advertising to television and radio commercials to outdoor signs to forms of specialty advertising, marketing communications are used to send relevant and favorable information directly to potential customers. The Internet is also becoming a key source for information on marketers and their product and service offerings. In Exhibit 2-7 we see a magazine ad for Expedia Brand travel agency information. The ad says "Search for: . . ." showing travel options and sending the consumer to its website, "Expedia.com."

The advantage of the mass media marketer-controlled source is that the marketer is in absolute control and can ensure that all information released is accurate and consistent. The disadvantages, however, are many. First, the marketer cannot assume that the message will be received in the way it was intended. Different people will have different interpretations of identical messages. Second, unlike personal selling situations, there is no opportunity for the consumer to ask questions or seek clarification. Third, as we will see in future chapters, people often disbelieve information provided in advertising simply because they lack faith in the good intentions of advertisers. Check out Marketplace 2-3 on page 48 to see consumer reactions to infomercials, television commercials, and magazine ads.

Through the use of in-store information, marketers seek to influence purchase decisions within the retail environment. In-store signs, special merchandise displays, in-store sampling, packaging and labeling information, and countertop brochures all offer the consumer help in the information search. A study of houseware purchases showed that at least 40 percent of buyers use information from in-store displays as part of their external search.[48] Real-time computer displays, called electronic kiosks, located in retail stores and

malls help shoppers find merchandise or stores and offer a range of related information. Providing a unique information source, some hairstyling salons today use a combination of video cameras and computers to let consumers know how different cuts, styles, and hair colors will suit them.

Package labels are a particularly important source of information at the retail level.[49] Studies show that labels are frequently read by consumers before purchase decisions are made.[50] This does not mean that labels are used or used carefully by all customers. In fact, the group for whom explicit label information specifications were primarily established by the U.S. Food and Drug Administration, those of low socioeconomic status, uses them the least.[51] This is particularly troubling when the labels carry product warnings.[52] Moreover, some labels have been found to contain so much information that they cease to be effective—shoppers suffer information overload.[53] CBite 2-1 on page 49 discusses nutrition facts on packaging.

2-4c Sources and Uses of Information in "U-Commerce"[54]

U-commerce (Uber-commerce) flows out of the hyper-networking of computers on the world stage. The network is described as having four characteristics: (1) ubiquity,

> **U-commerce (Uber-commerce)** This new view of what global commerce is becoming flows out of the hyper-networking of computers on the world stage. The network is described as having four characteristics: (1) ubiquity, (2) universality, (3) uniqueness, and (4) unison.

Marketplace 2-3

Believability of Information Sources

The table below shows the results of the Wirthlin World-wide National Quorum telephone survey of 1,007 adults residing within the continental United States. It was done on February 19–22, 1999. The margin of sampling error is plus or minus three percentage points at a 95 percent confidence level.

Source: From "Buying Influences: Consider the Source" from *The Wirthlin Report*, Vol. 9, March 1999, p. 3. Reprinted by permission of Wirthlin Worldwide.

Source	Very Believable (%)	Somewhat Believable (%)	Not at All Believable (%)
Review in *Consumer Reports*	58	37	5
Recommendation from a friend	52	42	5
News article	27	68	4
Magazine article	23	73	4
Evening network TV program	23	69	8
Radio news story	22	70	7
A seminar	22	63	12
TV talk show	17	48	33
Website on the Internet	11	60	18
Infomercial	9	48	42
Television commercial	8	71	21
Magazine ad	7	80	13
Salesperson in a store	6	73	21
Direct-mail piece	4	62	33
Celebrity endorsement	3	49	47

(2) universality, (3) uniqueness, and (4) unison. The vast network is growing, and some feel networked computers will eventually be "everywhere." Hence the term *ubiquity* is one of the network descriptors. We are already seeing low-cost embedded microprocessors and network connections being proposed to be part of all consumer durable products such as automobiles, ovens, refrigerators, and washing machines. It is suggested that they be connected to the Internet either through a wireless system in local areas and beyond or by using the electrical wiring system within a home. Examples of the beginnings of ubiquity are in such places as Nigeria, where mobile phones are being used to store cash electronically and transfer it to other phones. This was begun because there is no usable credit card system in Nigeria. Some people refer to these cell phones as "pay-as-you-go" units. Coca-Cola executives are working to find a way for cell phone users to "phone" vending machines. The call will release the containers of pop and then debit the phone. These phones become sources of information (e.g., product availability, price) and information transfer engines.

How does *universal* fit into the picture? The expectation is that in the future a person will be able to use his or her cell phone anywhere on the planet, unlike the current non-standard systems. This presents the potential for personal digital assistants (PDAs), iPODs, and laptop computers to always have access to the Internet for information searches and transactions either through a satellite or wireless global system. Hence the Internet would be available to anyone. Further, the need to have a laptop to do this is already lessening.

Information will be customized to the needs of the consumer and the situation. This is the *unique* character of U-Commerce. A person might like to have sports information, stock quotes, and international news, or the schedule of certain types of television shows

Nutrition Facts

Serving Size 2 bars (47g)
Servings Per Container 6

Amount Per Serving	Oats 'n Honey or Cinnamon		Peanut Butter	
Calories	200		200	
Calories from Fat	60		60	
	%DV*		%DV*	
Total Fat	6g	9%	6g	9%
Saturated Fat	1g	4%	1g	5%
Cholesterol	0mg	0%	0mg	0%
Sodium	170mg	7%	170mg	7%
Total Carbohydrate	35g	12%	33g	11%
Dietary Fiber	3g	11%	2g	10%
Sugars	14g		13g	
Protein	4g		5g	
Iron	6%		6%	

Not a significant source of vitamin A, vitamin C and calcium.

*Percent Daily Values are based on a 2,000 calorie diet. Your daily values may be higher or lower depending on your calorie needs:

	Calories:	2,000	2,500
Total Fat	Less than	65g	80g
Sat Fat	Less than	20g	25g
Cholesterol	Less than	300mg	300mg
Sodium	Less than	2400mg	2400mg
Total Carbohydrate		300g	375g
Dietary Fiber		25g	30g

available on a daily basis. This could be requested in video, audio, still images, or other available formats and sent to the PDA, laptop, cell phone, desk-top computer, television monitor, or the like, as needed. Another example is that when you turn on your mobile phone at Changi Airport in Singapore you immediately begin receiving messages containing hotel and taxi phone numbers and are offered reduced international calling rates. Also, in Japan, the JNAVI service enables users to enter their phone number, or street address, or even a landmark at which they are or intend to be. The service then provides information on such things as subway stations, restaurants, and shops that are within 500 meters of the location. A full color map may also be downloaded. In 2002 approximately two million hits per day were recorded, which included 50,000 map requests.

The final characteristic is *unison*, sometimes referred to as *unified*. Here all of a person's means of connectivity, PDAs, iPODs, personal computers, phones, etc., are automatically changed if any one of them is changed. Calendars, to-do lists, appointments, and other similar files of interest can be part of this synchronized approach. This can also be applied to websites and wireless application protocol (WAP) sites. Voice mail can also be available at all sites. A single interface connection point can be used.

Obviously we cannot predict when Uber-commerce will fully blossom, but bits and pieces, as already explained, are falling into place now. How will U-commerce affect potential and actual information searching by consumers?

2-4d Believability of Sources of Information on Products and Services

Consumer Reports has successfully positioned itself over time as an unbiased source of information for consumers on products and services in the United States. In a recent study, it scored the highest share (58 percent) in the "very believable" category. Next highest was "recommendation from a friend" at 52 percent in the same category. At the lowest end of the scale were "direct-mail piece" and "celebrity endorsement" at 4 percent and 3 percent, respectively.[55] Check out Marketplace 2-3 to get the rest of the story.

Marketing Management—Implications and Actions

Understanding the consumer's external search strategies helps marketers:

- Find ways to encourage consumers to include marketers' brands in their consideration sets.
- Cultivate positive and avoid negative word-of-mouth information transfer.
- Place favorable brand information in on-target media.
- Train sales staff and others in direct contact with consumers to provide timely, relevant information.
- Use advertising and other promotions as means of information dissemination.

2

Chapter Spotlights

1. Consumer decision process action options. This chapter has explored the first two steps in consumer decision making. Problem recognition triggers the process. Then consumers search internally for information to help solve the problem. If this search proves to be insufficient, then consumers weigh the costs of external search versus its value. Generally, the more relevant the information that is acquired, the clearer a consumer's needs become and the better able he or she is to evaluate different solutions. This alternative evaluation—the third step in the decision-making process—is the topic of the next chapter.

2. Problem recognition: Actual state versus desired state, and motivation arousal. Problem or need recognition results when the consumer perceives a difference between his or her actual and desired benefits state. The greater the actual or perceived difference between benefits currently enjoyed and those desired, the greater the likelihood of problem recognition. The consumer, the marketer, and the market situation all influence problem recognition.

Once the problem is framed, the consumer has to decide which type of solution he or she will seek; this will be the basis for the direction of the drive, or motivation, to do so. Motivations typically fall into one of five categories: desire to optimize satisfaction, prevent possible future problems, escape a current problem, resolve conflict, or maintain satisfaction.

3. Pre-purchase, post-purchase, and ongoing information searches. Searches for information before purchase decisions are made are of three types: directed search, browsing, or accidental search. Even after making a purchase, consumers frequently continue their information search, particularly after making an important purchase. By understanding the ways in which consumers conduct informal and formal searches, marketers can better provide the kind of information that will present their products or services in a favorable light.

4. Internal and external information searches. Consumers first scan their memories for information that will help them make purchase decisions. The amount of internal search and the level of success in carrying it out depend upon the extent to which consumers are expert in the product or service category, the quantity and quality of information in memory, and the consumer's level of satisfaction with past product or service experiences. If internal search results in insufficient information on which to base a choice, consumers may engage in external search. We reviewed the value, cost motivation, and ability dimensions of external information search.

5. Limiting search activity. We presented a discussion of universal, retrieval, and consideration sets. Consumers typically move to limit searches to the consideration set, alternatives from which they are most likely to make a final choice. Hence if a brand or outlet is to be chosen, it must be or become part of the consumer's consideration set. A key objective for marketers is to encourage consumers to include their brands in that set. Caution against including irrelevant information in communications concerning products was also presented. Such information weakens the product or service position in the eyes of the consumer, who is primarily looking for relevant and confirming information.

6. Sources of marketplace information. Information sources are either general (personal sources such as friends and opinion leaders or media sources like news editorials or buying guides) or marketer controlled (such as salespeople or advertising and promotions media). Included in this section was a discussion of "Ubercommerce," a future construct related to information transfer, availability, and use by consumers in a fully connected (networked) world. This situation will change the potential for consumer information searching and behavior while doing so. Already today we see bits and pieces of this grand design existing. We pointed out that the characteristics of U-commerce are ubiquity, universality, uniqueness, and unison.

Key Terms

accidental information search (p. 34)
actual state (p. 29)
browsing information search (p. 34)
desired state (p. 30)
directed information search (p. 34)
experience products (p. 42)
expert (p. 35)
external information search (p. 35)
externals (p. 41)
high-involvement product, service, or outlet
  (p. 29)

information capital (p. 39)
information control (p. 38)
internal information search (p. 35)
internals (p. 41)
low-involvement product, service,
  or outlet (p. 29)
motivation arousal (p. 31)
novice (p. 35)
ongoing search (p. 35)
opportunity recognition (p. 30)
post-purchase information search (p. 34)

pre-purchase information search (p. 34)
problem recognition (p. 29)
search products (p. 42)
sets (p. 43)
skill capital (p. 39)
U-commerce (Uber-commerce) (p. 47)

Review Questions

Note: You can find the correct answers to these questions by taking the quiz and then submitting your answers in the Online Edition. The program will automatically score your submission. If you miss a question, the program will provide the correct answer, a rationale for the answer, and the section number in the chapter where the topic is discussed.

1. The consumer is likely to go through all five steps in the decision process if the product or service has never been purchased before and is a _____-involvement product or service.
   a. low
   b. medium
   c. high
   d. non

2. To understand motivational arousal, the marketer needs to know that consumers make purchases to _____ satisfaction.
   a. understand
   b. optimize
   c. alleviate
   d. demonstrate

3. Which of the following is *not* a reason why consumers make purchases?
   a. to prevent possible future problems
   b. to escape from a problem
   c. to resolve conflict
   d. to strengthen relationships with other products

4. Marketers need to be aware that consumers often combine information searching with
   a. problem recognition.
   b. choice.
   c. alternative evaluations.
   d. follow-up.

5. The three types of pre-purchase searches include directed, browsing, and
   a. ongoing.
   b. manipulative.
   c. accidental.
   d. planned.

6. Expert consumers have an advantage over novice consumers in that they can both _____ and access relevant information efficiently.
   a. store
   b. collect
   c. sort
   d. apply

7. By identifying the level of importance their products or services occupy in the minds of target customers, marketers can better aid external search by providing the right information, at the right _____ and _____.
   a. price, place
   b. time, place
   c. outlet, price
   d. time, price

8. Which set is the one from which the consumer will likely make a choice?
   a. universal
   b. retrieval
   c. consideration
   d. relevant

9. *Consumer Reports* is a general type of marketplace information source called
   a. mass media.
   b. face-to-face.
   c. nonpersonal.
   d. advertising.

10. Of the following, which scored the highest in the "very believable" category of unbiased sources of marketplace information?
   a. direct mail
   b. celebrity endorsement
   c. salespeople
   d. *Consumer Reports*

Team Talk

1. Think of the last important service that you purchased. What was it? Which of the five underlying motives presented in the text caused you to make your choice? Describe the situation.

2. Think of a purchase you consider important that you made in the last year. What problem has the purchase solved for you? Answer in terms of actual versus desired state.

3. With team members, swap stories of the different information searches you have carried out. Decide whether each was a directed search, an example of browsing, or an accidental search. Which searches have been the most helpful, and which have been the most enjoyable?

4. For what two products or services have you recently been able to carry out the entire information search internally? Why did this work well for you?

5. Think of the last time you did an external search—that took more than one day to complete—for goods or services you eventually purchased. Why did you engage in an extensive external search? Describe the benefits and costs you incurred.

6. Think of the last very important product or service you purchased. What external information sources did you use? Classify them as general face-to-face, general mass media, marketer-controlled face-to-face, or marketer-controlled mass media.

7. How do you and your teammates feel about the U-commerce model as described? How do you see this affecting consumer information search strategies?

Workshops

Research Workshop

Background

Different people use different external information search approaches for the same product. The objectives of this workshop are to identify different search approaches, to attempt to understand why they are followed by consumers, and to suggest how what is learned could be practically applied.

Methodology

Find five individuals who have purchased a pair of running shoes within the past twelve months. Ask each of them to describe in detail the external search steps they went through. Compare the duration of the searches and the sources of information used. Classify the sources as to type.

To the Marketplace

Suppose you were the manufacturer of a major brand of running shoes. Assuming the five people in the study were typical of all target consumers, how would you adjust the way you make information available to potential customers?

Creative Workshop

Background

You have been hired as a creative consultant to work on a new small kitchen appliance, the Omelette Master. The product is a specially designed pan that helps make "perfect" omelets, restaurant style. The objectives of the workshop are to identify benefits that would trigger target consumers to evaluate and compare actual state and desired state and to put together some rough ideas for point-of-purchase materials.

Methodology

Have each team member conduct in-depth interviews with three consumers in an agreed-upon target market group. Find out how consumers feel about the product concept, and ask what would make them think seriously about buying an Omelette Master. Remember, you are looking for factors that might trigger problem recognition.

To the Marketplace

Develop three ideas for point-of-purchase promotional materials that would help the consumer recognize the existence of a problem that can be solved by the Omelette Master. Think in terms of the type of sales promotion activity, the actual offers, the visuals, and the copy. No point-of-purchase demonstrations may be considered.

Managerial Workshop

Background

You have been hired as the marketing product manager for a mid-size company that has developed a new advertising medium for drive-through restaurants. It is a short-range radio device that allows customers to tune to a specific radio frequency and get a full listing of the restaurant menu and specials of the day. The objectives of this workshop are to identify a problem that this new technology would help solve and to discuss how it could be marketed to drive-through restaurant owners.

Methodology

Have team members gather data from both drive-through managers and customers to determine how to present the new technology to store managers as a solution to a current problem.

To the Marketplace

Prepare a rough plan for marketing this new idea to managers of drive-through restaurants.

Notes

1. James F. Engel, Roger D. Blackwell and Paul W. Miniard, *Consumer Behavior*, 8th ed. (Fort Worth, Texas: The Dryden Press, 1995), p. 146.
2. M. Joseph Sirgy, "A Social Cognition Model of Consumer Problem Recognition," *Journal of the Academy of Marketing Science*, Vol. 15 (Winter 1987), pp. 53–61.
3. Engel, Blackwell and Miniard, p. 179.
4. Gordon C. Bruner II, "The Effect of Problem Recognition Style on Information Seeking," *Journal of the Academy of Marketing Science*, Vol. 15 Winter 1987), pp. 33–41; Gordon C. Bruner II, "Problem Recognition Styles and Search Patterns: An Empirical Investigation," *Journal of Retailing*, Vol. 62 (1986), pp. 281–297; Gordon C. Bruner II, "Recent Contributions to the Theory of Problem Recognition," in Robert F. Lusch, Gary T. Ford, Gary L. Frazier, Roy D. Howell, Charles A. Ingene, Michael Reilly and Ronald W. Stampfl, eds., *1985 AMA Educators' Proceedings* (Washington, DC: American Marketing Association, 1985), pp. 11–15.
5. John A. Howard and Lyman E. Ostland, *Buyer Behavior* (New York: Knopf, 1973).
6. Geraldine Fennell, "Motivation Research Revisited," *Journal of Advertising Research*, (June 1975), pp. 23–28; J. Paul Peter and Lawrence X. Tarpey, Sr., "A Comparative Analysis of Three Consumer Decision Strategies," *Journal of Consumer Research* (June 1975), pp. 29–37.
7. Brad Edmondson, "Five Steps Before They Buy," *Forecast*, Vol. 17 (July 1997), p. 9.
8. James R. Bettman, *An Information Processing Theory of Consumer Choice* (Reading, MA: Addison-Wesley, 1979), pp. 107–111; Gabriel J. Biehal, "Consumers' Prior Experiences in Auto Repair Choice," *Journal of Marketing*, Vol. 47 (Summer 1983), pp. 87–91; Girish N. Punj. and Richard Staelin, "A Model of Consumer Search Behavior for New Automobiles," *Journal of Consumer Research*, Vol. 9 (March 1983), pp. 366–380.
9. Mark T. Spence and Merrie Brucks, "The Moderating Effect of Problem Characteristics on Experts' and Novices' Judgments," *Journal of Marketing Research*, Vol. 34 (May 1997), pp. 233–247.
10. Punj and Staelin, "A Model of Consumer Search"; Philippe Cattin and Girish Punj, "Identifying the Characteristics of Single Retail Visits by New Automobile Buyers," in Richard P. Bagozzi and Alice M. Tybout, eds., *Advances in Consumer Research*, Vol. 9 (Ann Arbor, MI: Association for Consumer Research, 1983), pp. 383–388.
11. Elizabeth J. Cowley, "Recovering Forgotten Information: A Study in Consumer Expertise," in Curtis T. Allen and Deborah R. John, eds., *Advances in Consumer Research*, Vol. 21 (Provo, Utah: Association for Consumer Research, 1984), pp. 58–63.

12. Jeffrey B. Schmidt and Richard A. Spreng, "A Proposed Model of External Consumer Information Search," *Journal of the Academy of Marketing Science*, Vol. 24 (Summer 1996), pp. 246–256.

13. Punj and Staelin, "A Model of Consumer Search."

14. Michael L. Rothschild, "Perspectives on Involvement: Current Problems and Future Directions," in Thomas C. Kinnear, ed., *Advances in Consumer Research*, Vol. 11 (Provo, Utah: Association for Consumer Research, 1984), pp. 216–217.

15. Punj and Staelin, "A Model of Consumer Search. "

16. Dan Ariely, "Controlling Information Flow: Effects on Consumers' Decision Making and Preferences," *Journal of Consumer Research*, Vol. 27 (September 2000), pp. 233–248.

17. See James Bettman, *An Information Processing Theory*, Reading, MA: Addison Wesley, 1979; Bart A. Weitz, "Relationship Between Salesperson Performance and Understanding of Customer Decision Making," *Journal of Marketing Research*, Vol. 15 (November 1978), pp. 501–516; Peter L. Wright, "The Cognitive Process Mediating Acceptance of Advertising," *Journal of Marketing Research*, Vol. 9 (February 1973), pp. 53–62.

18. Dan Ariely, "Controlling Information Flow."

19. Michelle L. Peterman, Harper A. Roehm, Jr., and Curtis P. Haugtvedt, "An Exploratory Attribution Analysis of Attitudes Toward the World Wide Web as a Product Information Source," in Eric J. Arnould and Linda M. Scott, eds., *Advances in Consumer Research*, Vol. 26 (Provo, Utah: Association for Consumer Research, 1999), pp. 75–79.

20. Brian T. Ratchford, "The Value of Information for Selected Appliances," *Journal of Marketing Research*, Vol. 17 (February 1980), pp. 14–25.

21. Lawrence W. Felick, Robert O. Herrmann, and Rex H. Warland, "Search for Nutrition Information: Synthesis and Empirical Test," in Richard F. Bagozzi and Alice M. Tybout, eds., *Advances in Consumer Research*, Vol. 9 (Ann Arbor, MI: Association for Consumer Research, 1983), pp. 624–629.

22. Sharon E. Beatty and Scott M. Smith, "External Search Effort: An Investigation Across Several Product Categories," *Journal of Consumer Research*, Vol. 14 (June 1987), pp. 83–95.

23. Steven M. Shugan, "The Cost of Thinking," *Journal of Consumer Research*, Vol. 7 (September 1980), pp. 99–111.

24. Jacob Jacoby, "Perspectives on Information Overload," *Journal of Consumer Research*, Vol. 11 (March 1984), pp. 432–435.

25. Brian T. Ratchford, "The Economics of Consumer Knowledge," *Journal of Consumer Research*, Vol. 27 (March 2001), pp. 397–411.

26. Raymond A. Bauer, "Consumer Behavior as Risk Taking," in Robert S. Hancock, ed., *Dynamic Marketing for a Changing World* (Chicago: American Marketing Association, 1960), pp. 389–398.

27. Merrie Brucks, "The Effects of Product Class Knowledge on Information Search Behavior," *Journal of Consumer Research*, Vol. 12 (June 1985), pp. 1–16.

28. Joseph W. Alba and J. Wesley Hutchinson, "Dimensions of Consumer Expertise," *Journal of Consumer Research*, Vol. 13 (March 1987), pp. 411–424; Girish Punj and Narasimhan Srinivasan, "Influence of Expertise and Purchase Experience on the Formation of Evoked Sets," in Thomas R. Srull, ed., *Advances in Consumer Research*, Vol. 16 (Provo, Utah: Association for Consumer Research, 1989), pp. 507–514.

29. Brucks, "The Effects of Product Class Knowledge"; Joseph W. Newman and Richard Staelin, "Prepurchase Information Seeking for New Cars and Major Household Appliances,"

Journal of Marketing Research, Vol. 9 (August 1972), pp. 249–257; Narasimhan Srinivasan and Brian Ratchford, "An Empirical Test of a Model of External Search for Automobiles," *Journal of Consumer Research*, Vol. 18 (September 1991), pp. 233–242.

30. Akshay R. Rao and Wanda A. Sieben, "The Effect of Prior Knowledge on Price Acceptability and the Type of Information Examined," *Journal of Consumer Research*, Vol. 19 (September 1992), pp. 256–270.

31. Fred Selnes and Roy D. Howell, "The Effect of Product Expertise on Decision Making and Search for Written and Sensory Information," in Eric J. Arnould and Linda M. Scott, eds., *Advances in Consumer Research*, Vol. 26 (Provo, Utah: Association for Consumer Research, 1999), pp. 80–89.

32. Calvin P. Duncan and Richard W. Olshavsky, "External Search: The Role of Consumer Beliefs," *Journal of Marketing Research*, Vol. 19 (February 1982), pp. 32–43.

33. John A. Howard and Jagdish N. Sheth, *The Theory of Buyer Behavior* (New York: John Wiley and Sons, 1969).

34. Peter D. Bennett and Gilbert Harrell, "The Role of Confidence in Understanding and Predicting Buyers' Attitudes and Purchase Intentions," *Journal of Consumer Research*, Vol. 2 (September 1975), pp. 110–117; Peter W. Hermann, "The Effects of Self-Confidence and Anxiety on Information-Seeking in Consumer Risk Reduction," *Journal of Marketing Research*, Vol. 17 (May 1979), pp. 268–274.

35. Julian B. Rotter, *Social Learning and Clinical Psychology* (Englewood Cliffs, NJ: Prentice-Hall, 1954).

36. Narasimhan Srinivasan and Surinder Tikoo, "Effect of Locus of Control on Information Search Behavior," in John F. Sherry, Jr. and Brian Sternthal, eds., *Advances in Consumer Research*, Vol. 19 (Provo, Utah: Association for Consumer Research, 1992), pp. 498–504.

37. George R. Franke, Bruce A. Huhmann, and David L. Mothersbaugh, "Information Content and Consumer Readership of Print Ads: A Comparison of Search and Experience Products," *Journal of the Academy of Marketing Science*, Vol. 32 (Winter 2004), pp. 20-31.

38. Howard and Sheth, *The Theory of Buyer Behavior*; Engel, Blackwell and Miniard, *Consumer Behavior*, p. 215.

39. Engel, Blackwell and Miniard, *Consumer Behavior*, p. 215; Mark G. Weinberger and William R. Dillon, "The Effects of Unfavorable Product Rating Information," in Jerry Olson, ed., *Advances in Consumer Research*, Vol. 7 (Ann Arbor, MI: Association for Consumer Research, 1980), pp. 528–532; "Study Tracks Housewares Buying Information Sources," *Marketing News* (October 14, 1983), p. 16; "Whirlpool Corporation," in Roger D. Blackwell, James F. Engel, and W. Wayne Talarzyk, *Contemporary Cases in Consumer Behavior*, rev. ed. (Hinsdale, IL: Dryden Press, 1984), pp. 365–388.

40. Tom Meyvis and Chris Janiszewski, "Consumers' Beliefs about Product Benefits: The Effect of Obviously Irrelevant Product Information," *Journal of Consumer Research*, Vol. 28 (March 2002), pp. 618–635.

41. Rachel X. Weissman, "A New Tack for 'Natural,'" *American Demographics*, Vol. 6 (November 1998), p. 18.

42. Mary C. Gilly, John L. Graham, Mary Finley Wolfinbarger, and Laura J. Yale, "A Dyadic Study of Interpersonal Information Search," *Journal of the Academy of Marketing Science*, Vol. 26 (Spring 1998), pp. 83–100.

43. Mark C. Weinberger and William R. Dillon, "The Effects of Unfavorable Product Rating Information."

44. "Study Tracks Housewares Buying."

45. "Whirlpool Corporation."

46. "Public Goes on Strong 'Self-Medication Kick,'" *Marketing News* (June 27, 1980), p. 1.

47. John D. Claxton and C. Dennis Anderson, "Energy Information at Point of Sale: A Field Experiment," in Jerry Olson, ed., *Advances in Consumer Research,* Vol. 7 (Ann Arbor, MI: Association for Consumer Research, 1980), pp. 277–282.

48. "Study Tracks Housewares Buying."

49. Dennis L. McNeill and William L. Wilkie, "Public Policy and Consumer Information: Impact of the New Energy Label," *Journal of Consumer Research,* Vol. 6 (June 1979), pp. 1–11.

50. Kenneth C. Schneider, "Prevention of Accidental Poisoning through Package and Label Design," *Journal of Consumer Research,* Vol. 4 (September 1977), pp. 67–73.

51. James McCollough and Roger Best, "Consumer Preference for Food Label Information: A Basis for Segmentation," *Journal of Consumer Affairs,*Vol. 14 (Summer 1980), pp. 180–192.

52. Lorna Opatow, "How Consumers 'Use' Labels of OTC Drugs," *American Druggist,* Vol. 177 (March 1978), pp. 180–192.

53. Jacob Jacoby, George Szybillo, and Jacqueline Busato-Schach, "Information Acquisition Behavior in Brand Choice Situations," *Journal of Consumer Research,* Vol. 3 (March 1977), pp. 209–216.

54. Richard T. Watson, Leyland F. Pitt, Pierre Berthen, and George M. Zinkhan, "U-Commerce: Expanding the Universe of Marketing, *Journal of the Academy of Marketing Science,* Vol. 30 (Fall 2002), pp. 333–347.

55. "Buying Influences: Consider the Source," *The Wirthlin Report,* Vol. 9 (March 1999), p. 3.

Alternative Evaluation and Choice

3

Fiona and Scott are expecting their first baby. Like all new parents, they want to capture those special moments as their baby grows. Fiona would love a new digital camera, complete with zoom lens for close-ups. Though they've never used one before, they also think how nice it would be to have a camcorder. After checking their budget, Scott and Fiona think through their options. They decide that a camcorder appeals to them most, since it will let them take spontaneous shots and record every look, smile, and sound their baby makes. They review information in *Consumer Reports,* collect catalogs and brochures, and call a friend who has just bought a new instant-playback model. They fix on three brands, try them each out in the store, and decide which one they like best. The brand choice determined, there are still a number of other decisions to be made. Scott and Fiona need to decide where to buy, when to buy, and how to buy. It almost makes having the baby seem simple.

This chapter explores the next two stages of the consumer decision process—alternative evaluation and choice. In comparing the merits of buying photography equipment or a camcorder, Scott and Fiona first evaluated different product categories. They then narrowed their options to compare several camcorder brands. The final choice was made only after their alternative evaluation was complete, and it triggered a range of new decisions relating to outlet selection and shopping behavior that had to be resolved before the purchase. All of this means that each stage of the alternative evaluation and choice processes offers marketers and retailers opportunities to influence purchase decisions. Identifying and acting upon those opportunities is the topic of this chapter.

3-1 Alternative Evaluation

Alternative evaluation—the process through which we compare and contrast different solutions to the same marketplace problem— is the third step in the decision-making process. Usually occurring simultaneously with information searching, it involves comparing different products, services, retail outlets, and/or brands in order to select what best delivers the benefits we are seeking.

Alternative evaluation is not always a part of the decision process. In some cases, consumers skip this step entirely. Habitual buying patterns are a good example. Lashika looks in the refrigerator and sees that she is out of Diet Coke. The next time she is at the grocery store, she picks up another six-pack of the product. In this case, there is no alternative evaluation; Lashika relies simply on memory—she liked the product in the past and buys it again.

Now suppose that when Lashika is out of Diet Coke, she thinks of other carbonated drinks to try. This time, instead of heading straight for the Diet Coke at the grocery store, she also looks at 7-Up and Minute Maid Orange. Here, alternative evaluation precedes her decision and happens at the same time as the information search.

Next, suppose Lashika again goes to her refrigerator and discovers she is out of Diet Coke. She thinks about buying more, then about buying 7-Up or Minute Maid Orange, but this time none of these options seems appealing. She talks to a friend who always drinks Sprite and later sees a television commercial for a new brand of cola. When she's in the store, a display for Dr. Pepper catches her eye. Here, external searching leads to the gathering of information about a range of options, and this in turn results in alternative evaluation. In both of these examples, notice that Lashika is making brand comparisons—she wants to buy a product within the carbonated soft drink category and is choosing among several different brands.

Taking the example one step further, suppose Lashika decides to give up carbonated drinks altogether, perhaps for health reasons. The range of options now becomes much broader—it is a class comparison rather than a brand comparison. At a party she tries a couple of bottled fruit drinks. She sees a commercial for canned iced tea. A friend at her health club suggests she try flavored mineral water. At the grocery store, she takes her time comparing labels and prices before making a choice. Here, the information search and alternative evaluation processes lead to a reformation of the marketing problem—it's no longer that she's out of Diet Coke, but that Lashika needs a change in beverage to match her change in lifestyle.

This four-tiered example illustrates how the same recognized problem—I'm out of Diet Coke—led to four different search and alternative evaluation procedures. It progressed from simple habitual buying to a brand comparison involving minimal search and limited problem solving to a category comparison with fairly extensive problem solving. The process of alternative evaluation became increasingly complex. Exhibit 3-1 shows the flow diagram for the alternative evaluation process.

3-1a Consumer Benefits and Evaluative Criteria

In Chapter 2, we saw how consumers' consideration sets of products, services, brands, or retail outlets simplify the information search process. A brand in the consumer's consideration set jumps to mind as soon as a need to purchase arises, because members of such a set are likely candidates for purchase. Consideration set construction involves reducing the number of alternatives that the consumer will actually compare in the marketplace to a manageable size and retaining alternatives that will be easy to compare when making a final choice.[1] Also, consumers appear to create consideration sets of *heterogeneous* alternatives when 1) they don't want to miss a viable choice, 2) they see some common benefits that will make comparison easier, or 3) different groups of potential choices offer a benefits trade-off.[2] How do you think this would apply to automobiles or coffees?

Alternative evaluation involves two other types of consumer sets, as mentioned in Chapter 2. The universal set is made up of all product, service, outlet, or brand alternatives in the marketplace to which the consumer has reasonable access, whether she or he is aware of them. Of these, a retrieval set is the subset that consumers can bring up from memory.[3] The objective for marketers is to make sure that their products, services, outlets, or brands are, at a minimum, part of the latter set and so are remembered when it comes time to buy. However, the key is to be part of the consideration set.

Consumer sets are extremely important for marketers who want to attempt to influence alternative evaluation. Consumers evaluate goods and services based on the benefits offered to them. If the benefits of a brand are important to the consumer, the brand has a

> **alternative evaluation**
> (see p. 56) The process through which consumers compare and contrast different solutions (products, services, outlets, brands) to the same marketplace problem.

F A Q

Would Henry Ford's classic anecdote—that his customers could order the Model T in any color so long as it was black—work for today's marketers?

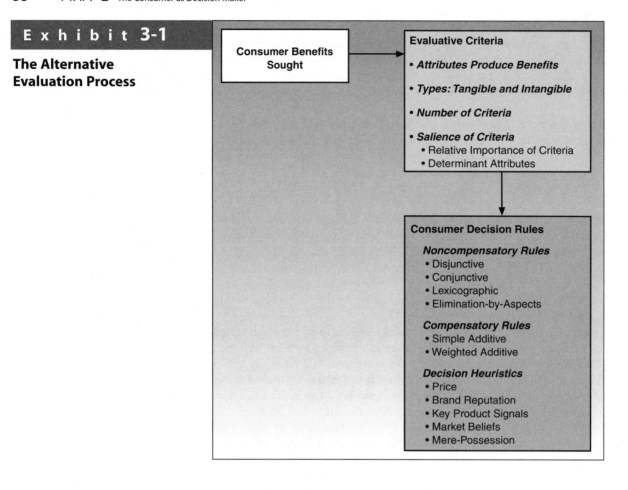

Consumer Benefits Sought

Evaluative Criteria

- *Attributes Produce Benefits*

- *Types: Tangible and Intangible*

- *Number of Criteria*

- *Salience of Criteria*
  - Relative Importance of Criteria
  - Determinant Attributes

Consumer Decision Rules

Noncompensatory Rules
- Disjunctive
- Conjunctive
- Lexicographic
- Elimination-by-Aspects

Compensatory Rules
- Simple Additive
- Weighted Additive

Decision Heuristics
- Price
- Brand Reputation
- Key Product Signals
- Market Beliefs
- Mere-Possession

good chance of becoming part of the consumer's retrieval set and, from there, becoming part of the consideration set from which a final selection is made.

To assess benefits offered by goods and services, consumers use a range of evaluative criteria. These are the means through which consumers compare product classes, brands, vendors, and so on. **Evaluative criteria** can be tangible. In that case, benefits associated with such characteristics as price, color, size, shape, and performance are compared. Intangible benefits criteria also may be considered, such as whether the perceived consumer image matches the image of the brand user or other feelings associated with ownership or use. How well a product "scores" on these tangible and intangible benefits criteria determines its chances of being part of the consumer's retrieval and/or consideration set.

Evaluative criteria vary from consumer to consumer, from product to product, and from situation to situation. Because of this, it is essential for marketers to determine which criteria consumers in the target market use in judging goods or services in various purchase situations. Only then can marketers attempt to deliver on those criteria. Check out Marketplace 3-1. To what benefits criteria do you think Peapod is appealing?

Two questions are important in understanding the use of evaluative criteria in selecting from several alternatives. First, how many criteria do consumers use during alternative evaluation? Second, what is the relative importance of each criterion?

> **evaluative criteria**
> The tangible and/or intangible benefits that consumers use to compare product classes, brands, vendors, and so on.

Number of Evaluative Criteria   Consumers typically use six or fewer evaluative criteria.[4] As a general rule, the more important the consumer considers the purchase and the more experience he or she has with the product category, the greater the number of evaluative criteria used.[5] Car buyers who see their purchases as simply a means of transportation may use price (economic benefit), trunk capacity (ability to carry more luggage on trips benefit), and reliability (less worry when traveling, less time in the repair shop inconvenience, and lower maintenance costs benefits) as evaluative criteria. On the other hand, buyers who place more importance on the cars they drive as extensions of themselves may add to these three criteria such factors as style ("the car is as youthful and exu-

Marketplace 3-1

Welcome to Peapod: Online Grocery Shopping and Delivery

Peapod, an online grocery shopping service, began as a small start-up business with only 400 households in 1989 in Evanston, Illinois, a suburb north of Chicago. It was a company looking for a way for busy people and others to no longer have to make late-night runs to the grocery store for necessities. Brothers Andrew and Thomas Parkinson began test marketing the fledgling grocery concept and performed all of the picking and packing of groceries, making deliveries in their own vehicles with the help of their families. Today it is the nation's leading Internet grocer, serving 13 U.S. markets and delivering more than 5 million orders in its 15-year history. Now owned by Royal Ahold, a food service company from The Netherlands, and working closely with Stop & Shop and Giant Foods, Peapod has revolutionized the way Americans shop for food.

"The biggest hurdle was convincing consumers they could shop online and still maintain control over the quality of their (product) picks," says Marc van Gelder, company president and CEO. "That's been Peapod's cornerstone all along. Today, customers see us for what we are: a lifestyle solution for their busy lives." He adds, "The increased use of high-speed broadband, advances in portable technologies and the growing numbers of women in the online shopping ranks are mounting forces that will spur the industry...."

Peapod serves more than 155,000 customers each year and since its acquisition in 2001 has employed a more integrated "bricks and clicks" business strategy: expanding its partnerships with Ahold U.S.A. stores (Peapod by Stop & Shop and Peapod by Giant); leveraging the buying power of Ahold to make higher-volume, lower-priced purchases; lowering distribution and transportation costs; and boosting inventory management to reduce out-of-stocks.

Peapod combines the value of a well-priced, diverse product selection with the ease of Internet shopping and delivery. It's a smart supermarket experience for customers, such as those dual-career couples stocking up on basics for their families, time-starved professionals seeking the convenience of prepared foods, people in search of natural, organic, and specialty fare, and even new mothers with a need for baby products or personal health and beauty aids. About 75 percent of Peapod's customers are women, and almost 80 percent of the people who try the service stay with it.

Peapod personal shoppers are trained to prepare quality meats and seafood and to improve the ritual of hand picking, squeezing and smelling perishables. Customers can even provide directives for some picks, for example, by selecting yellow or green bananas or thin- or thick-sliced deli meats during their shopping. Customer orders are carefully packed in bags and special temperature-controlled, crush-proof containers. The company's Stay Fresh delivery system exceeds food safety standards and maintains products at their optimum temperature and freshness, from the distribution center all the way to a customer's front door.

Customers are offered weekly specials and are notified about new items, and they are allowed to simply jot down lists of products that are immediately matched. Further, they can go to their "my lists" tab to create new shopping lists, look at old orders, or save personalized lists (like a Thanksgiving list). Products can be sorted on the Peapod list by price, nutritional content (sodium, carbohydrates, fat, cholesterol, calories, etc.), or even best-seller status. Customers can browse by store aisle format or by items or brand names. Recipes and entertaining ideas and tips are also available. Over 8,000 products are available.

Customers go to www.peapod.com, place their orders, and look for the Peapod van or the green Volkswagen "Pod Bug" at the time and day of week selected for delivery. Shopping time may be cut from two hours to just 20 minutes or less on the keyboard.

What distinctive benefits does Peapod offer to consumers? To what types of consumers, besides those named above, are such benefits important and appealing?

Sources: www.peapod.com/ourCompany and /corpinfo, August 26, 2004 and "The Grocery Cart in Your PC" by Susan Chandler, *Business Week*, September 11, 1995.

---

berant as am I"), color ("red says I'm racy"), and brand ("this brand is driven by up-and-coming young professionals, which I am").

Evaluative criteria are often used in combination, making it difficult to understand the influence of each on consumer choice. A study of alternative evaluation of women's clothing stores, for example, found that such criteria as price, quality of apparel, class of customers, merchandise displays, apparel styles, helpfulness of salespeople, and the benefits these imply were all combined in the consumer's mind into a single criterion named "exclusiveness."[6]

Interestingly, the more important the decision is to the consumer, the fewer acceptable alternatives there are. Also, each additional evaluative criterion used narrows the consumer's options to some extent.[7] For example, a fashion-conscious woman in search of the perfect pair of earrings to go with a new outfit will consider everything from the color, shape, and size to the material and weight of the different alternatives, balancing the benefits combination each delivers. The number of options that meet all her criteria is likely small.

Salience of Evaluative Criteria

By determining the relative importance or **salience** of each evaluative criterion, marketers are able to identify those characteristics most likely to influence target consumers. Goods and services can be shaped to satisfy the most salient criteria, as can the positioning of a good or service offering in the consumer's mind, and in promotional communications the most salient/important attributes and/or benefits information can become the focus of the copy and visuals presented.

Salience varies from consumer to consumer, product to product, and situation to situation. Consider, for example, "quality" as an evaluative criterion. For some products, such as paper clips or low-grade copy paper, quality hardly matters at all, whereas for others quality may be very important. In general, it is far more important in high-visibility goods, such as clothing or gifts, and for durable goods than it is for low-visibility, nondurable goods.[8]

Salience also varies from buying situation to buying situation. Copy paper that is good enough for rough drafts or letters to friends may fall too short on quality to be used for term papers, reports, or photograph printing from a computer file.

Attributes that are salient for some consumers are less important or not important at all to others. Exhibit 3-2 demonstrates how different criteria have greater or lesser salience for different consumer types. In this example, consumers planning to buy a new car are asked to distribute 100 "salience points" ("importance points") among the attributes they consider important. Remember that attributes are indicators to the consumer of certain deliverable benefits. The more important the attribute, the higher the points awarded. Consumer Type A considers five criteria to be salient, with price, style, and economy accounting for 75 percent of the total points awarded. Price (30 points) is three times as important as trunk capacity (10 points), twice as important as color (15 points), and one and one-half times as important as economy (20 points). For Consumer Type B, price and safety account for 70 percent of the points for salience. Price is the most salient criterion, and color is the least. Who do you think is a typical Type A consumer, and what types of cars would they buy? Answer the same questions for the Type B consumer. Marketers can use even simple analyses like this to identify salient evaluative criteria and to develop and market their products based on them.

Consumers on occasion treat unimportant attributes, called **trivial attributes,** as though they are critically important in their impact on product or service choice. These irrelevant or unneeded evaluative criteria affect choice because they are unique to one of the options, draw attention away from more important attributes, or dilute the effect of important attributes. In some cases, the trivial attribute acts as a "heuristic cue" that allows the consumer to forgo the more detailed evaluation process of more meaningful attributes.[9] Sometimes the results are negative, and sometimes they are positive. Whether a consumer will use trivial attributes to make the final choice seems to be a function of the product or service type, the number of choices in the set, the choice situation, and the consumer himself or herself.[10] An example of the use of a trivial attribute might be where three hair dryers all have equal power, are the same with respect to the main features a person is considering, and feature price and performance similar enough to be seen as equal. All three deliver the same benefits package. Though color is not an issue, the person is drawn to the silver dryer, even though the dryer's color is a trivial attribute. As another example, studies have found that 11- to 12-year-old children, when compared to adults, evaluate brand extensions by relying more on "surface cues" such as brand name characteristics of the new product than on "deep cues" such as the similarity of category of the new product as compared to the category of the parent product. The children in one study concerned with a new iced tea and a new toffee candy rated the extensions with the rhyming names, "Coca-Cola Gola" iced tea and "Wrigley's Higley" toffee, more positively than extensions with the non-rhyming names Coca-Cola Higley iced tea and Wrigley's Gola toffee. Adults rated both types of names similarly.[11]

---

salience The relative importance of each evaluative criterion in the alternative evaluation process.

F A Q

To what extent is price always a salient evaluative criterion?

trivial attribute An irrelevant or unneeded criterion that affects the consumer's evaluation of a product or service alternative.

F A Q

Do you agree or disagree that the surface cues used by the 11- to 12-year-olds to rate a new drink and a new kind of candy are trivial attributes?

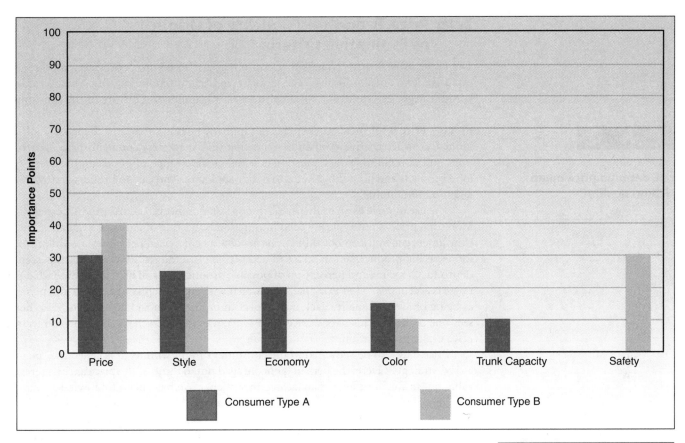

Consumer Type A   Consumer Type B

E x h i b i t 3-2

Relative Importance of Evaluative Criteria— Buying a Car

Determinant Attributes   Salient (important) attributes that have a direct influence on alternative evaluation and final choice are **determinant attributes.**[12] Though an attribute may be salient, it is not always determinant. Consider, for example, the consumer comparing three different brands of running shoes. The price, materials, and color are the same for all three, as are the perceived benefits tied to these characteristics. Though these are all salient criteria, the fact that they are the same means they are of no value to the consumer in making a choice among the three competing alternatives. The consumer must look for some other criterion, such as styling, to differentiate among the shoes. Styling, with its benefits message, becomes the determinant attribute. Particularly in the marketing of "parity" products, where major product differences do not exist, an attribute that seems very minor can become the center of an entire promotional campaign. That criterion is determinant because the competing brands are "tied" on other, more important, criteria.

Though consumers typically first use physical or psychological product benefits to judge product categories or brands, the buying situation can also affect which benefits are determinant and which are not. When and where products are used, how they are used, why they are used, by whom they are used, and with whom they are used all affect the evaluation process.[13] A consumer selecting cheese for a dinner party at which one of the guests is something of a connoisseur is likely to use country of origin, region, type, softness-hardness, and age as determinant attributes. For a casual picnic with friends, the same consumer is more likely to use price and popularity among the group as the determinant attributes. Similarly, in selecting restaurants, the consumer planning a special evening out will be seeking very different benefits as determinant criteria than the consumer who is out shopping at the mall and wants a quick snack.[14]

As we have seen, the salience of evaluative criteria varies from product to product, from situation to situation, and from consumer to consumer. Because of this, it is essential for marketers to identify benefits criteria that are salient and determinant for each market group targeted. Products and promotions can then be developed accordingly.

determinant attributes
Those evaluative criteria that have a direct influence on alternative evaluation and final alternative choice.

3-1b Price, Brand, and Country of Origin as Evaluative Criteria

The range of evaluative criteria that consumers use to compare products and brands is extensive. Two are almost always used: price and brand reputation, In certain product or service categories, country of origin also enters the evaluation picture of the consumer.

Price   Price is for most consumers, and in many buying situations, the most significant influencer in alternative evaluation. Knowing this, marketers count on price in promotions and at retail to attract consumers across a wide range of goods and services, from food products and household items to major appliances and cars to brokerage services and fast-food restaurants.

The use of price as an evaluative criterion varies, however, across product categories.[15] Moreover, price is not typically used in isolation but is one of a mix of evaluative criteria. Consumers generally do not think in terms of a specific, fixed price they are willing to pay for a specific product, but in terms of acceptable price ranges. Past purchases, perception of product benefits, and perception of possible product costs all help determine what price range is acceptable.[16] For example, for a watch with a typical mix of features and perceived as being of average quality, Jack may expect to pay between $44.95 and $59.95. When he sees one that meets his needs priced at $49.95, it falls within that range and so meets the price evaluative criterion.

Price may also be reframed in the consumer's mind with what is called the "pennies-a-day" strategy.[17] Here, the person is encouraged not to think of the price as the aggregated value but in much smaller manageable increments. We have been told by television personality Sally Struthers that for only "72 cents a day" we can feed a starving child. A certain mattress retailer in Chicago claims you can sleep on one of its beds for "10 cents a night." Also, when talking to a salesperson at an auto dealer where you are thinking about purchasing or leasing a new car, notice how he or she emphasizes the size of the monthly payment rather than the total cost of the car. Such a price reframing can influence the consumer to see a product or service as being affordable.[18]

Consumers do not always look for the lowest price or even the best price/quality ratio. Other criteria can be equally or more important than price for certain types of purchases and in certain buying situations.[19] For example, one study noted that price reductions for high-quality brands resulted in consumers switching "up" to them, yet when similar reductions were applied to low-quality items, the same level of switching "down" did not occur.[20] Quality was the overriding factor here. Further, strong national consumer product brands can successfully charge higher prices than competitors yet periodically cater to the more price-sensitive consumers with short-term price reductions. This way, national brands can attract both quality-sensitive and price-sensitive consumers.[21] In some instances, high price can, in fact, positively influence alternative evaluation—by leading consumers to attribute higher quality to a brand that carries a higher price tag.[22] Some consumers wish to pay a high price for a good or service just to be able to do so or let others know they did so.

In some situations, consumers are not even aware of the price of the goods purchased.[23] This is more common for products that are low in importance for consumers, such as household necessities like toothpaste or floor cleaners. This phenomenon is more common for consumers with money to spend than for those on extremely tight budgets.

Brand Reputation   The reputation of a brand is a second major influencer in alternative evaluation. Brand name is frequently perceived by consumers to be an indicator of product or service quality.[24] A high-quality position is important in establishing brand power, also called "brand equity," because this leads to greater brand market share and profitability in the long run.[25] This apparent brand-quality relationship is most likely tied to the perceived risks associated with a poor purchase decision. The more difficult it is for consumers to judge quality, the higher the perceived risk.[26] If consumers can rely upon brand reputation for that quality assessment, they perceive less risk. In the pharmaceutical industry, for example, marketers have been very successful in persuading consumers to pay higher prices for name-brand prescription drugs, even when generic products with identical chemical makeup are available more cheaply. The same is true of brand-name multi-vitamins. Both of these are typically perceived as high-risk purchases, probably because of the importance consumers place on good health.

Country of Origin   Country of origin, the nation where a particular product or service primarily comes from, can be an important evaluative criterion. Leather goods from Spain, computer software from the United States, china dinnerware from England, opal gemstones from Australia, and automobiles from Germany or Japan are examples of products of special quality tied to a consumer-preferred country of origin. It is not always clear where a product truly comes from, however, because of the "off shore" subcontracting of parts or manufacture of the entire item. Marketplace 3-2 offers insights on country-of-origin perceptions by consumers.

Turning attention to television sets and stereos, it's been found that people have a more positive attitude toward these products when they are assembled in the United States if U.S. parts are also used rather than if Mexican parts are used. Purchase intention for these two classes of products is similarly higher when assembly is in the United States and the product has U.S. parts than when assembly is in the United States and the parts are from Mexico.[27] Quality perception seems to be the key here.

In recent years, country of origin has taken on a political dimension not heretofore seen. For example, we find Egyptians in Cairo boycotting U.S. businesses, products, and services, and even products with ingredients from the U.S., because of American ties to Israel.[28] Similarly, we saw Americans boycotting French products, especially wines, when the French government decided not to send troops as part of the multinational force in Iraq during the war in Iraq. Some Americans even began calling French-fried potatoes "freedom fries," not wanting to even refer to the French. In some cases, access to travel for consumers has been restricted or denied because of a person's country of origin, out of potential or actual security concerns arising from the events of 9/11.

3-1c The Impact of 9/11 on Evaluative Criteria

On September 11, 2001, as you all recall, attacks by terrorists in hijacked aircraft that struck the World Trade Center Towers in New York City, the Pentagon in Washington, D.C., and a field in Pennsylvania changed the world as we know it. Those of you who travel, especially by air, have seen how added security emphasis has affected people's desire to travel. Further, the list of "safe" destinations for individuals from countries around the world has shrunk. Into the foreseeable future, personal security will continue to be of concern to us all and will likely be high on the list of key evaluative criteria along with price, brand reputation, and country of origin. Take a look at CBite 3-1 for a study report on tourist safety concerns. In Chapter 12 we'll touch on this topic again when we consider a phenomenon known as "cultural animosity."

3-1d Consumer Decision Rules

So far, we have explored different types of criteria used to aid consumers as they compare different alternatives, but for marketers to encourage consumers to make purchase decisions that favor their brands, it is essential that they understand exactly how consumers use these evaluative criteria during alternative evaluation. To this end, researchers have identified a number of consumer decision rules that govern the way in which different consumers evaluate different products and services in different buying situations.

Consumers use decision rules, either consciously or subconsciously, to help them quickly and efficiently select from among several purchase alternatives. These rules can be noncompensatory or compensatory. A **noncompensatory consumer decision rule** is one in which the weaknesses of a possible alternative are not offset by its strengths. This means that if a product does not meet certain of the consumer's requirements, it is eliminated from further consideration. In contrast, a **compensatory consumer decision rule** allows for trade-offs among strengths and weaknesses. Typically, noncompensatory rules are used to help the consumer reduce the number of choices from among which a decision will be

▶ **noncompensatory consumer decision rule**   A decision rule that does not allow for weaknesses in an alternative to be offset by its strengths. Such a rule is used to reduce the number of alternatives to be further evaluated.

▶ **compensatory consumer decision rule**   A decision rule designed to allow for trade-offs among the strengths and weaknesses of alternatives being evaluated. Typically results in a winning choice.

Marketplace 3-2

Country-of-Origin Consumer Perceptions

We live in a world of stereotypes, and we perceive different countries and the products they offer in different ways. Asked to express their thoughts on products from ten countries, one group of consumers revealed the following notions about price and quality: Japan offers high quality at a reasonable price; Korea offers low price, unfortunately matched by lower quality; products from India and Iran are not particularly high priced, but are not of particularly good quality either; in England, France, Germany, and Switzerland, the quality is high—but so is the price; the United States rates lower on quality and less favorably on price than Japan and Western Europe.

How many of these preconceptions do you share? Stereotypes like these are, of course, biased, but they do come into play as consumers seek to narrow their choices during alternative evaluation. We consider some countries to be more stylish than others. We're proud of our Italian shoes, our British shirts, and our French colognes, but would we buy cars or cellular phones made in Italy, Britain, or France? We might try to save money by buying a stereo system built in Korea, but only if the brand name is a good one. Much as we might sympathize with the efforts of Eastern European nations to build their economies, would we really

risk buying electronic equipment or cars from them, no matter how well-known the brand?

We sometimes use country of origin as a rule of thumb that helps us decide what to buy. If we know a product was made in a country that we believe delivers quality, that might be enough to drive a purchase. If it's from a country not known for high quality, country of origin can, at the very least, act as a trigger that motivates us to evaluate other alternatives more thoroughly.

Interestingly, the less consumers know about a particular product or product category, the more likely they are to use country of origin as an evaluative criterion. In a category such as personal computers, experts use characteristics like technical descriptions or reliability ratings to compare different options, whereas novices tend to use country of origin to determine which brand is best. When limited information is available, experts use country of origin, too.

Sources: Terence A. Shimp, Saeed Samiee, and Thomas J. Madden, "Countries and Their Products: A Cognitive Structure Perspective," *Journal of the Academy of Marketing Science,* Vol. 21 (Fall 1993), pp. 323–330. Maheswaran Durairaj, "Country-of-Origin as a Stereotype: Effects of Consumer Expertise and Attribute Strength and Product Evaluations," *Journal of Consumer Research,* Vol. 21 (September 1994), pp. 354–365.

made. Though a "winner" may be found, these rules are typically used to produce pools of "acceptables" and "unacceptables" from the alternatives being considered. Then, a more stringent rule is applied to the "acceptables" to find a "winner." Compensatory rules are more stringent than are noncompensatory rules, and they are used to find "winners." Gen-

---

CBite 3-1

Travel Choices and Safety Go Together

In the United States, according to a poll conducted by CIC Research, leisure travelers who once considered travel safety a low-priority concern when planning vacations now make it a high priority. This change, poll results indicate, is directly linked to the September 11, 2001, terrorist attacks. Using a rating scale where 1 equals the lowest concern for security and 10 equals the highest concern, the poll found the following to be true:

- Fifty-five percent of U.S. poll respondents rated security as one of their highest travel priorities (10 on the scale).
- Sixty-three percent of international poll respondents visiting the United States rated security as one of their highest travel priorities (10 on the scale).
- Overall, U.S. poll respondents gave security an 8.9 rating (9.6 for international visitors).
- Selection of leisure activities and accommodations, in addition to destination, were chosen with safety in mind (9 average on the scale; 10 on the scale for over 50 percent of respondents).

CIC Research, based in San Diego, conducted the poll over 12 months in Orange County, California, the location of Disneyland. More than 2,300 visitors to Orange County responded.

Source: Adapted from James Zoltak, "Poll: Safety a Main Concern in Travel Plans," *Amusement Business* 116 (March 22, 2004): 7.

E x h i b i t 3-3

Hi & Lois talk about facing too many toothpaste choices at the store.

Source: © Reprinted with special permission of King Features Syndicate.

erally speaking, noncompensatory rules are less complex than are compensatory approaches. Consumers also use a third type of decision rule, **decision heuristics.** Quite simply, these are rules of thumb or shortcuts that allow the individual to make rapid decisions on which alternative is best.

Before we discuss the different rules used, it is important to point out that the amount of cognitive effort needed to carry out the evaluation of an alternative does impact on the evaluation (see Exhibit 3-3). For example, if two alternatives are quite close in evaluation, that which takes more thought processing effort will be seen more negatively and will not be chosen over the other. However, where the more difficult alternative has a higher evaluation, it will be chosen despite the negative association.[29] This is a great lesson for marketers. It shows the importance of providing the kind of information the consumer is seeking in the desired form and depth and at the place expected by the potential purchaser. If this is done, especially when differences among choices are not great, the chance of a sale will be increased. See the discussion of external information search in Chapter 2.

> **decision heuristics** Rules of thumb or shortcuts that allow the consumer to make rapid decisions about which alternative is best.

Noncompensatory Rules   Johanna is balancing the demands of school with those of a new part-time job, her volunteer work, and a hectic social life. She decides she's in the market for a cellular phone that will help her keep on top of all her commitments. She doesn't want to spend more than $35 per month in service charges and can afford up to $100 for the phone itself. She wants reliable service and a broad calling area. After calling five different suppliers and talking with representatives, Johanna is not convinced that any of the plans offered meet all four of her evaluative criteria. She doesn't sign up with any of the plans. In this case, Johanna is using a noncompensatory rule—for her, there are no trade-offs. If a product does not meet all evaluative criteria, the consumer does not buy. We shall present four common types of noncompensatory rules: *disjunctive, conjunctive, lexicographic,* and *elimination by aspects.* After reading the material in the following sections, determine which specific type of noncompensatory rule Jill is using. In familiar purchase situations a simple noncompensatory "screening rule" might be based on brand familiarity or memory accessibility. In novel product purchase situations, particularly those that are stimulus based, consumers will likely use one or more attribute (minimum) cutoffs.[30]

Disjunctive Rule   Using the disjunctive rule, the consumer first decides which criteria are determinant and which are not, and then establishes a minimum "score" or level of benefits to be delivered on each one. Each alternative considered must meet this score on each determinant attribute to be acceptable. If more than one product meets the minimum, there is no winner and some other rule must be used to lead to a final choice.

For Johanna, service charges ($35 per month maximum) and calling area (at least statewide) are determinant attributes. She subjectively set these minimum capabilities, $35 and statewide, for acceptable phone service. Other attributes, such as the price of the phone and reliability of service, are not considered at this point. In this case, Johanna would have asked each supplier questions about the price and calling area. Those who met both would be acceptable, and those who did not would be eliminated from consideration.

Conjunctive Rule   Using the conjunctive rule, the consumer considers all evaluative criteria as determinant, and a minimum/maximum acceptable value or score is established for each one. Johanna sets the service charge maximum at $35, coverage area minimum at statewide, and maximum price of the phone at \$100, and she decides on a reliable service minimum score of 8 on a scale of 1 to 10 with 10 being best. Her establishment of a reliability score of 8 as minimum is subjective, as will be the scores she assigns to each alternative. A phone service supplier must meet each requirement on each criterion to be considered "acceptable." If she's fortunate, Johanna will find a clear winner—one supplier will meet the minimum/maximum on all four criteria, and the others will fail to do so on at least one criterion.

Authors of a recent study found that the conjunctive rule is the most often used decision model in consideration set formation for fast food outlets. The four factors used by consumers were: popularity, geographic location, cleanliness, and menu variety.[31]

Lexicographic Rule   Using the lexicographic rule, the consumer places the evaluative criteria in rank order of importance. The alternatives are then compared on the most important evaluative criterion. If one of them has a higher score (is a better choice) than any of the remaining alternatives, that one is the "winner." If two or more alternatives have the same "highest score" on the highest-ranked criterion, the consumer drops the other alternatives and goes to the second evaluative criterion following the same procedure just described. If necessary, the third criterion, the fourth, and so on are used as the basis for comparison until no more highest-score ties are found, leaving one alternative the winner. At the end of this process, it could be possible for two or more alternatives to be tied on the last evaluative criterion used for comparison. In that case there would be no winner. If this were to occur, a different rule would have to be used to find a winner among the surviving alternatives. Note that once an alternative is eliminated at any step in the process, it is no longer considered.

Suppose Johanna ranks the four criteria from most important to least in this order: service charges, calling area, price of the phone, and reliability. She gathers information from two suppliers who tie on both service charges and calling area. Next, she judges them based on price of the phone, finds them to be different, and chooses the lower-priced supplier. It is not necessary for her to consider reliability at all.

Elimination-by-Aspects Rule   Using the elimination-by-aspects rule, the consumer again ranks the evaluative criteria and also sets minimum scores that must be met on each of them. The alternatives that don't meet each minimum on one or more of the evaluative criteria are eliminated. The remaining alternatives are then compared using the same procedure as followed when applying the lexicographic rule.

Johanna looks at five potential suppliers and finds three that meet all minimum scores on all evaluative criteria. Hence, these are "acceptables." She then ranks the criteria as she did for the lexicographic example. The first two suppliers are tied and score higher than the third on her most important criterion, service charges. The third supplier is eliminated from further consideration. The two surviving suppliers tie on calling area. Next, she compares them on price of the phone. One supplier has a lower price, so this supplier is chosen.

Compensatory Rules   The drawback to using noncompensatory rules is obvious—there may be no clear winner and so the consumer is unable to make a choice between two or more acceptable alternatives. In these cases, compensatory rules are more effective, as the consumer is able to make trade-offs when comparing alternatives. If the score on one attribute is very strong, this compensates for weakness in another. We will discuss two commonly used types of compensatory rules: simple additive and weighted additive.

Simple Additive Rule   Using the simple additive rule, the consumer scores each alternative on each of the evaluative criteria. The scores typically run from 1 to 10 with 10 being the best score. A score for each alternative is determined by summing its individual evaluative criterion scores. The highest score wins. This rule assumes that all criteria are of equal importance. Should no winner be found, a different rule could be applied to the surviving alternatives or the scores for each criterion could be reevaluated.

As an example of applying the simple additive rule, suppose the XYZ Company is in the market to equip its sales representatives with cellular phones. The executives of the company are looking for low monthly rates, local-area coverage, itemized billing, and good customer service. If one supplier outscores all others, it will be chosen—even if its monthly rates are high.

Weighted Additive Rule   Using the weighted additive rule, the consumer assigns a relative weight to each evaluative criterion based on its perceived relative importance. Then the score on each evaluative criterion is multiplied by the relative weight to produce a weighted score. These weighted scores are summed for each alternative being considered, and the alternative with the highest score is the winner.

To weight each of its four evaluative criteria according to importance, XYZ Company divides up a total of 10 points as follows: monthly rates (4), calling area (2), itemized billing (1), and customer service (3). Suppliers A and B score, out of a possible 10, as follows:

	Relative Weights	Supplier A	Supplier B
Monthly rates	4	5	7
Calling area	2	8	6
Itemized billing	1	10	8
Customer service	3	9	7

When the scores are multiplied by the weights assigned to each criterion, Supplier A is the clear winner, having scored 73 points, compared to 69 for Supplier B.

	Supplier A	Supplier B
Monthly rates	20	28
Calling area	16	12
Itemized billing	10	8
Customer service	27	21
Total	73	69

Decision Heuristics   Within a typical week, a consumer may go through any number of alternative evaluation processes for a dizzying variety of products and services. Just think of the number of items in the family shopping cart at the supermarket. For each of these, some sort of evaluation was made. For most purchases, consumers either do not have the time or are unwilling to take the time or effort to evaluate every alternative available in the marketplace. While they may do so for major, high-risk, or important purchases, it's unlikely to occur during routine shopping or when looking for unimportant, uninteresting products. Instead, consumers use a range of rules of thumb, or *decision heuristics,* to help them narrow their options, eliminate alternatives, and make the best choices.[32] Price, brand reputation, key product signals, and market beliefs are all commonly used heuristics. They are mental shortcuts that help consumers reach decisions quickly and efficiently. Also, the concept of "mere-possession," though not a decision heuristic by itself, can influence brand or product choice.

Price   Price can be perceived as an indicator of quality, and consumers may often be willing to pay more for products or services they think are of better quality than the competing products or services. The rule of thumb that "higher price means higher quality" is far from reliable, however. As we saw earlier, generic drugs, identical in content to brand-name products, usually have a significantly lower price.

Brand Reputation   Some consumers use brand reputation alone to help them make certain purchase decisions. History shows us the power of brand names: a study crossing thirty product categories showed that 90 percent of brands that were the market leaders in 1930 were still leaders in the late 1980s.[33] Top brands can generate profits up to 50 percent greater than those of the second-place competitor.[34] What this indicates is that faith in dominant brands is so strong that consumers often feel brand name is the only evaluative criterion they need when choosing among alternatives.

The question of *brand line stretch* effects also needs to be addressed. An example of this would be when Marriott International opened its Courtyard by Marriott and Fairfield Inn lines. In these cases, the company did downward stretches, with Fairfield being the farthest down. In particular, the "ownership" dimension is of interest. That is, if you were a regular

F A Q

How might the country from which a product comes work as a decision heuristic?

Marketplace 3-3

True or False?

Here are just a few examples of the beliefs consumers take for granted about the marketplace. Which of these beliefs do you use as rules of thumb when you shop?

Product Beliefs

- Larger-size containers are cheaper per unit than small-size containers.
- Synthetic goods are of lower quality than those made of natural materials.
- When in doubt, go with a national brand.
- Stores that always have merchandise on sale are not really saving the customer money.
- Higher price means higher quality.

Distribution Beliefs

- Larger stores offer better prices than smaller stores.
- Specialty stores are good places to shop and find out about products, but it's cheaper to buy at a discount retailer.

Promotion Beliefs

- When you buy heavily advertised products, you are paying for the brand name and not for better quality.
- Low-quality products are usually sold through "hard sell" strategies.

Personal Selling Beliefs

- Salespeople in specialty stores are more knowledgeable than are salespeople in other outlets.
- Locally owned stores give better service.

Source: From "Consumer Market Beliefs: A Review of the Literature and an Agenda for Future Research" by Calvin P. Duncan in *Advances in Consumer Research,* Vol. 17, edited by Marvin E. Goldberg, Gerald Gorn, and Richard W. Pollay, (1990) pp. 729–735. Reprinted by permission of the Association for Consumer Research, Valdosta, GA.

---

guest with Marriott hotels, what would your opinion be of this chain when they introduced the new, lower-quality, lower-priced residences? It turns out that an owner's liking for the parent brand generally translates into more favorable responses to the brand line stretches. This occurred for both upward and downward stretches of two non-prestige brands tested, the Acura automobile and Gap clothing. It also occurred for upward stretches of two prestige brands, BMW automobiles and Calvin Klein clothing. The ownership effect did not occur for downward stretches of prestige brands, because this reduced brand exclusivity in the eyes of the prestige brand owners.[35]

Key Product Signals   In evaluating alternatives, consumers tend to rely on subtle cues or signals that imply the existence of attractive attributes. Used-car buyers, for example, may see that the interior and exterior of a car are clean and infer from this that the vehicle is mechanically sound.[36] In this way, product signals are used by the consumer to fill in missing information.[37] Understanding the power of key product signals, retailers have even scented clothing displays to attract female customers. In some supermarkets, fresh produce is periodically misted with water to act as a freshness cue for the shopper.

Market Beliefs   Consumers make certain assumptions or generalizations about the marketplace and the way it operates in order to simplify their purchase decisions. True or not, these market beliefs act as convenient shortcuts in alternative evaluation.[38] Check out the key product signals often used, rightly or wrongly, by consumers in Marketplace 3-3.

mere-possession
The concept that simply possessing a brand of a product or service can lead to preference for that brand or for that good or service over other options.

Mere-Possession   Research has shown that simply possessing a brand of a product or service, called **mere-possession,** can lead to preference for that brand or for that good or service over other options.[39] This has been found to occur "instantaneously" upon taking possession, yet it is said to be an arbitrary conclusion of the consumer. A test of a small set of restaurant choices (three) by consumers showed that when the restaurants simply offered coupons, the mere-possession effect of having the coupon actually occurred before the consumers went to the restaurant.[40]

3-1e Initial Commitment by Consumers

The third stage in the consumer decision-making process, alternative evaluation, presents a number of opportunities for marketers to attempt to influence the final purchase decision. It is during alternative evaluation that consumers first commit to a product category and then move toward selecting a specific brand or retail outlet. Often in need of help or reasons to limit their options, consumers are particularly receptive to messages from marketers during this stage. The amount of help needed depends on the extent to which their purchases are planned or unplanned, the topic of the next section.

Marketing Management—Implications and Actions

Understanding alternative evaluation helps marketers:

- Identify whether consumers are making class or brand comparisons and communicate with them accordingly.
- Find ways to get their brands into the retrieval and consideration sets of target consumers.
- Deliver on tangible and intangible benefits criteria that are perceived as important by target consumers.
- Discover determinant attributes to set their brands apart from parity competitors.
- Be aware of the implications of price decisions and set prices within acceptable ranges.
- Identify decision rules and heuristics used by consumers, and develop appropriate strategies for using that information.

3-2 Planned versus Unplanned Purchasing

So far, we have explored what happens during alternative evaluation for purchases that are consciously thought out and planned by the consumer, yet many purchase decisions are made with virtually no apparent planning at all. By categorizing purchases into those that are planned and those that are unplanned, marketers are better able to guide consumers through or encourage them to skip completely the alternative evaluation stage of decision making. See Exhibit 3-4 for an overview of the purchasing behavior factors associated with planned and unplanned purchases by consumers.

There are four types of purchase situations.[41] A **specifically planned purchase** is one in which the item and even the brand is decided before the consumer visits a store or investigates other outlet options. Enrique decides ahead of time to buy a package of Oreo cookies and does so. A **generally planned purchase** is one in which a decision is made before visiting an outlet that an item from a certain product category will be purchased. The specific item and the brand are not yet decided. A purchase is also considered generally planned if the consumer has—even without considering product purchase as a solution— given thought to solving a problem. Enrique has just finished a great mystery novel and would like to read another. He decides to go to the eBay website to find one. He does so and orders two, clicking on delivery within two to three days. A **substitute purchase** is made when a consumer switches from a specifically or generally planned item to an altogether different one. This time, Enrique drives right by 7-Eleven, where he was going to buy a package of microwave popcorn, and instead stops at Burger King for a chicken sandwich. Finally, an **unplanned purchase** is one that is made with no conscious prior consideration or need recognition. It is this type of purchase that is more likely than others to be triggered by some stimulus in the marketplace. When Enrique arrives at 7-Eleven, a display of low-priced audiotapes catches his eye, and he buys one.

3-2a Planned Purchasing Behavior

Does the fact that a consumer intends to buy really mean that he or she will go ahead and make the purchase? For marketers, understanding consumer buying intention is key to

▶**specifically planned purchase** A purchase in which the item and even the brand are decided before the consumer visits a store or investigates other outlet options.

▶**generally planned purchase** A purchase in which a decision is made before visiting a store that an item from a certain product category will be purchased.

▶**substitute purchase** A purchase in which a consumer switches from a specifically or generally planned item to an altogether different one for purchase.

▶**unplanned purchase** When consumers buy, for whatever reasons, an item that is not on a written or mental shopping list.

Planned Purchasing Behavior

Types
• Specifically Planned Purchase
• Generally Planned Purchase
• Substitute Purchase

Intention to Purchase, Purchase Probability

Intervening Variables (Anticipated or Unanticipated)
  • Change in Financial Status
  • Change in Employment Situation
  • Family or Household Size
  • Social Conditions
  • Social Norms
  • Weather Conditions
  • Deliberation

Unplanned Purchasing Behavior

Types
• Pure Impulse
• Reminder Impulse
• Suggestion Impulse
• Planned Impulse

Point-of-Sale Actions to Encourage Unplanned Purchase
• Displays
• Salespeople
• Outlet Atmosphere
• Packaging
• Multiple-Item Discounts
• Demonstrations/Samples
• Shelving Techniques
• Coupons
• Outlet Layout
• Price Reductions

Purchase

predicting and attempting to influence planned purchasing behavior. Marketers try to measure intention to buy in several ways. Many of us have participated in a research survey, for example, through which marketers evaluate how likely we are to buy their products. While consumers who report intentions to purchase actually do have higher buying rates than those who do not, measures of intention are not sufficient to predict purchase behavior accurately. Key reasons are that situations change, and plans consumers make today may not be achievable or even desirable tomorrow.

As an example, suppose that in a car-buying survey you say you'll be in the market for a new car in less than six months. Time passes and your bank account looks less healthy than you thought. You change jobs and decide to commute by train rather than by car. Or a friend saves money by leasing or by buying a used car, and you decide to do the same. All these and many other unanticipated circumstances work against the purchase. Unanticipated events can even occur right at the point of purchase—you see a competing brand on sale and buy that one instead of the brand you'd planned on. A second reason such surveys are not always reliable lies in the method of questioning itself. Suppose you tell an interviewer that you will definitely buy a new car within the next six months when what you mean is that you would like to do so. This is a wish, not a true measure of your purchase intention.[42]

More reliable than simple measures of intention is research aimed at assessing purchase probability.[43] In this type of survey, consumers indicate how strongly they believe they will follow through with their intentions. Researchers ask consumers to estimate, on a scale of 0 percent to 100 percent (with 100 being absolutely certain), the likelihood of buying a specific item during a specific time period. While unanticipated circumstances can still change the outcome, measuring purchase probability is a better predictor of actual purchase than is a measure of intention alone.

Intervention of Planned Purchases   From forming an intention to the time a purchase is made, several factors can change the consumer's plans. Examples of these **intervening variables** include changes in financial status, employment situation, family or household size, social conditions or norms, and even weather conditions. Some intervening variables are anticipated by consumers; others are not.

> **intervening variables**
> The factors that arise after intention to act in a certain way is determined and that are the causes of change in consumer choice results.

Suppose you've been saving money over the past year so that as soon as you graduate from college you'll be able to buy a good personal computer. When asked what it is you're saving for, you even know the brand of computer you'll most likely buy. Now suppose you walk out to the parking lot and your car won't start. You have it towed to the garage, and the estimated repair bill is $1,500. There is no way you can afford a new car, so you tap into your savings for the repairs, delaying the computer purchase or even deciding against it altogether. This is an example of an unanticipated circumstance acting as an intervening variable that changes the intended course of action.

Now let's suppose you've been shopping for a television set and are leaning toward a low-priced model by a name-brand manufacturer, even though you're tempted to buy a newer-model, large-screen set with surround sound. Rather than buy right away, you wait until your boss announces end-of-year bonuses. You now head to the store and pick up the surround-sound model. In this example, the intervening variable is anticipated and acts as a decisive factor that changes intention to purchase. Even when a consumer has definite plans to make a purchase, several factors can intervene to change those plans or the way in which they are carried out. Let's look at the most influential of these.

Deliberation as an Intervening Variable   Deliberation is part of both the information search and the alternative evaluation stages of the decision process. The amount of time a consumer spends thinking about a choice decision affects both the actual purchase and the timing of that purchase. Quite simply, the longer we put off making a purchase, the higher the chances that it is no longer available or that it has been replaced by a newer model. The product we eventually buy may be very different from the one we intended to buy. In some cases, the consumer ends up the loser, going without the benefits of owning the desired product during the deliberation period. Possibly when we're ready to buy, the product is sold out. In other cases, the deliberation period works in our favor when a desirable product is replaced by an even better one.

For marketers whose brand the consumer intends to purchase, there is no benefit to lengthy deliberation. Their objective should be to attempt to shorten the deliberation process or move consumers through it more efficiently. Because actual buyers—during the information search—are more likely to visit outlets than non-purchasers are, attracting potential customers to visit retail and other outlets is key. Incentives such as coupons, special sales, demonstrations, and other traffic-building techniques have proven to have such drawing power.

3-2b Unplanned Purchasing Behavior

When we enter the marketplace we carry with us a written or mental list of places to go and things to buy. When we buy items that are not on either list, for whatever reasons, the purchase is considered unplanned or made upon impulse. CBite 3-2 gives information on product categories planned and unplanned in shopping.

The bigger the shopping trip and the more items we buy, the more likely it is that some of these are impulse purchases. For the most part, these purchases are low-involvement products and products we do not routinely purchase.[44] The decision to buy is made once we are in the shopping environment, where we are most receptive to marketing stimuli. During a typical shopping trip, 63 percent of discount-store shoppers and 39 percent of department-store shoppers, for example, buy at least one unplanned item.[45]

CBite 3-2
What's on Your Shopping List, and What's Not?

What types of purchases do we plan in advance, and which do we pick up as our fancy takes us? Research done in a classic study a number of years ago across a variety of product categories provides some insights. Fifty-one percent of baby food selections are specifically planned, as are purchases of fruits and vegetables (46 percent); dairy products (43 percent); tobacco products, alcoholic beverages and mixes (42 percent); and soft drinks (41 percent). What about substitution? In these categories, it's not typical. Also, only 6 percent of detergent buyers ever substitute. Levels are even lower in snack foods (5 percent) as well as apparel, cereal, and soft drinks (4 percent). In categories like these, it's critical for marketers to get their brands into the evoked (consideration) sets of target consumers so that the brand names spring to mind, to the exclusion of all other brands, whenever a need arises.

The highest level of unplanned purchasing is in the category of magazines/newspapers—an astounding 84 percent of purchases of these printed media are unplanned. Apparel is next (71 percent), followed by snack foods (68 percent), grooming aids (65 percent), oral hygiene products (57 percent), cereal (55 percent), tobacco products (54 percent), and detergents (50 percent). Though the percentages found in this study may have shifted some in recent years, the relative positioning is likely similar today. The message for retailers in these categories is still clear—in-store promotions and point-of-purchase displays can make a real difference in triggering unplanned purchases.

Source: F. Thomas Juster, "Consumer Buying Intentions and Purchase Probability: An Experiment in Survey Design," in *Consumer Buying Intentions and Purchase Probability* (New York: Columbia University Press, 1966).

F A Q

Why do people window shop?

Types of Unplanned Purchase   Four types of unplanned purchase have been suggested.[46] *Pure impulse purchases* are those bought for the sake of novelty, a departure both from patterns of brand loyalty and from typical buying behavior. Understandably, pure impulse purchasing lessens during periods of economic recession.[47] Pure impulse purchases result from spontaneity and even from a diminished regard for decision consequences. When shopping for groceries, Janet sees a point-of-purchase display for a new perfume and picks up a bottle. She doesn't know for sure that it will suit her, but she's excited at the prospect of trying it out.

Reminder impulse purchases, though not specifically anticipated, are usually of routine products. Typically, in-store displays serve to remind consumers of existing needs. While walking down the aisle in a supermarket looking for hairspray, Janet sees bottles of shampoo. She realizes that the bottle at home is nearly empty and picks up another.

A consumer responds to a *suggestion impulse* when a product, *seen for the first time,* stimulates immediate need recognition. Janet notices a very pleasant scent as she passes a point-of-purchase display. There she finds envelopes of time-release cranberry potpourri. Though she has never thought of cranberry as an appropriate room scent and has never seen potpourri in envelopes before, she imagines the scent in her guest bedroom and purchases a few packets.

Making a *planned impulse purchase,* a consumer responds to a special incentive to buy an item considered in the past but not selected. A need may have been previously recognized, but until certain market conditions exist it is not fulfilled. Sale announcements, cents-off coupons, and other special offers all encourage planned impulse purchases. Janet has thought off and on about trying a new high-fiber cereal but always considered the price too high. At the store, she notices an on-shelf dispenser with dollar-off coupons for the cereal. Attracted both by the product and the savings, she takes a coupon and puts the cereal in her cart.

Impulse buying is probably a contributing reason for the growth of one-stop shopping. The Michigan-based chain Meijer Thrifty Acres offers everything from foodstuffs to

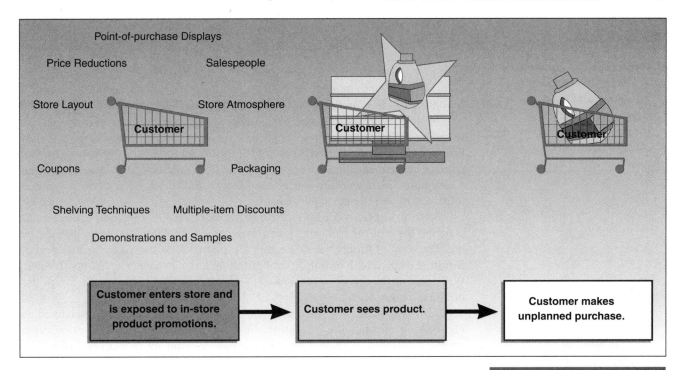

Point-of-purchase Displays

Price Reductions   Salespeople

Store Layout   Store Atmosphere

Customer   Customer   Customer

Coupons   Packaging

Shelving Techniques   Multiple-item Discounts

Demonstrations and Samples

| **Customer enters store and is exposed to in-store product promotions.** | → | **Customer sees product.** | → | **Customer makes unplanned purchase.** |

Exhibit 3-5

In-Store Influences on Unplanned Purchases

Once consumers enter an outlet, marketers and retailers enjoy a number of opportunities to encourage impulse spending. These are just some of the merchandising techniques open to them.

scrambled merchandising
A wide variety of unrelated product types offered in close proximity to one another in a single retail outlet.

CDs, tools to house plants, photo processing to television sets, goldfish to tennis shoes, and toys to camping equipment. Meijer Thrifty Acres is also an example of **scrambled merchandising,** another popular selling modality. Here, a wide variety of unrelated product types are offered in close proximity to one another in a single store. Most food supermarkets use scrambled merchandising to varying extents. Serving to make shopping easier and less time-consuming for consumers, scrambled merchandising also encourages unplanned purchasing.

Encouraging Unplanned Purchases at Point of Sale   Aware of the high levels of on-the-spot decision making, retailers provide the shopper every opportunity to buy on impulse. Exhibit 3-5 summarizes important in-store influences that encourage unplanned purchasing.

Usually found at outlet entry points, check-out positions, on shelves, and at the ends of aisles, *point-of-purchase displays* are intended to increase sales of specific items. Though their impact varies widely across product class and brand, they are generally considered effective.

Offering items at a reduced price is a powerful technique to trigger impulse purchases. In one study, while 27 percent of teenage respondents bought more unplanned beauty products because of point-of-purchase displays, 56 percent purchased them because they were on sale.[48] Typically, when price reductions end, sales return to near normal.[49] *Price reductions* boost sales in four ways. Some of us stockpile items on special offer and buy ahead based on anticipated needs. We switch brands—sometimes temporarily, sometimes permanently—to take advantage of a price cut, particularly with parity products. We try out goods from new categories, especially if the non-sale price is prohibitive. We also try out new outlets, attracted by low prices to break our shopping routines.[50]

In-store coupons trigger unplanned purchases. We pick up free tabloids at supermarket entrances to scan the coupons. As we shop, on-shelf electronic coupon dispensers catch our attention, as do manufacturers' coupons on or inside packages. Unlike coupons from magazines or free-standing inserts (FSIs) that we bring to the store with us and plan on using, in-store coupons are an incentive toward impulse purchasing.

Like price reductions, *multiple-item discounts* encourage stockpiling. Promoted through supermarket tabloids, in-store signs, or on-shelf announcements, the offers vary and can be for the same product ("four cans of soup for $2" or "buy one, get one free") or

F A Q

What types of consumers are more likely to take advantage of price deals—those with money to spend or those on tight budgets?

for related products ("buy Brand X popcorn and Brand Y canola cooking oil for that special TV treat and save $1").

The color, shape, and size of *packaging* can all catch the shopper's eye and encourage impulse purchases, as can the product name, price, and details of a special offer. If we can quickly figure out that the product we're looking at is a new hair conditioner with 30 percent more inside, plus a coupon toward the next purchase, we're likely to give it a try.

In-store demonstrations and *free samples* allow consumers new to a category or brand to try out products before they buy or see someone in the store show them how they work. Free sample-size pizza bites right out of the toaster oven are used to encourage frozen pizza sales. In department stores, the same pizza samples might be given away to show how well a new home pizza oven or toaster oven works. *Free items,* such as recipes and product information, work in the same way.

Store atmosphere—a combination of decor, music, lighting, odors, merchandise display, and the number and behavior of shoppers—can be used to trigger impulse purchasing. The scent of freshly baked bread in a supermarket draws us to the in-store bakery. A furniture display, with a complete room setting and all accessories, invites us to sit down. When we buy the chairs, we're tempted to take the matching table and the lamps that make up the display.

Store layout and the *merchandise shelving display* may encourage unplanned purchasing. Placing merchandise in high-traffic areas and using special aisle and department arrangements can increase a product's exposure—and its chances of being purchased. Shelving children's cereals down low where the kids can see them and pick them up also increases probability of purchase.

Salespeople, too, can influence unplanned purchasing. In a department store, a salesperson helps you choose a suit for job interviews. As you head toward the changing room to try it on, he brings you a shirt and tie that will go with it. As you ring up your purchases, he reminds you that you'll need matching socks, too. Suggestive selling, or cross-selling, especially when the consumer has a clear need, can be extremely effective.

Marketing Management—Implications and Actions

Understanding planned and unplanned purchasing helps marketers:

- Assess purchase probability and isolate factors likely to encourage consumers to follow through on their intentions to buy.
- Identify and seek to control variables likely to intervene with planned purchases.
- Use point-of-purchase merchandising techniques to stimulate impulse purchasing.

3-3 Choice

So far in this chapter, we have seen that, through alternative evaluation, consumers are able to limit their options and focus on preferred product categories, goods and services, or brands. Further, purchases may be either planned or unplanned, with varying levels of deliberation. The purchase decision, however, is still far from made. A surprising number and variety of considerations determine final choice. In the remainder of this chapter, we shall explore one of the most influential of these, outlet selection. Shopping behavior and shopper types will also be discussed.

3-3a Outlet Selection

Gone are the days when a single marketer or a single marketing channel enjoyed exclusive distribution of unique products. Today, the moment a new product hits the market, dozens of imitators or parity products rapidly follow. And not only are they available to us from retail stores, but they are found on the web, they grace the pages of catalogs, and they're offered through our television sets, telephones, and fax machines. No matter how specialized the product, we can choose from an ever-increasing array of outlets or distribution channels to acquire it. Outside our homes, we can visit retail stores, strip malls, discount

---

CBite 3-3
Jean Machine

"I love jeans. While most people have two or three pairs, I have twelve. In fact, my life was one long search for the perfect pair of jeans until I heard about Levi's Original Spin, which allowed me to create my very own, customized Levi's. Nirvana! And it was easy. At the Levi's store in San Francisco, I used a computer to choose the model, fabric, even the kind of fly I preferred. Then, after a full body scan in a Star-Trek–like steel chamber, it was off to the dressing room, where a sales associate brought a few pairs similar to the ones I'd requested. I tried on four or five to tweak the fit—smaller in the waist, tighter in the butt, looser in the thighs. The associate wrote up the measurements and was done. Total time: about 45 minutes. Cost: $70. Two weeks later, my jeans were in. And if I wasn't satisfied, I had 60 days to return them for a store credit or a refund, even if I'd washed them. But I won't be returning mine. They fit me like a glove."

Learn more about Original Spin on the web (www.levi.com/original_spin). For custom-made products like this one, which comes first—the outlet or the brand?

Source: Excerpt from "Jean Machine" in *Fast Company,* November 2001, pp. 52, 56. Reprinted by permission of Gruner & Jahr.

---

malls, huge indoor shopping centers, or the new "town centers." The latter are destinations that are one-third retail stores, one-third dining locations, and one-third entertainment. We can look at non-store locations such as flea markets, swap meets, auctions, or even garage sales. Increasingly, we don't even need to step outside our home or apartment. Within the home, we shop from catalogs, on our fax machine, over the telephone, by watching television shopping channels, or through a variety of sites on the Internet.

The Internet has "shaken up" the retail options picture. It has dramatically changed the way goods and services are sold and how consumers shop. We are seeing web-only "e-tailers" like Garden.com and Amazon.com, and online extensions of bricks-and-mortar retail stores like Bloomingdale's, J.C. Penney, and Wal-Mart with their Bloomingdales.com, jcpenney.com and Walmart.com sites. In the year 2000, 43 percent of people who were online made at least one purchase, and 80 percent of online buyers expected to buy more in 2001. In one survey, 60 percent of the online consumers stated that if they are not happy with a retailer's website, they are less likely to buy from the company's traditional store.[51] In the year 2002, about $53 billion was spent on the web by consumers in the United States. Women outspent men 51 percent to 49 percent. This is a dramatic shift from the women's share of 34 percent in 1998.[52]

With all these outlet choices available, the challenge for marketers is to understand exactly what drives consumer choice. Marketers need to focus on determining why, in different situations and among different consumer groups, one type of outlet is preferred over all others. Before exploring how consumers choose among outlets, however, we must first resolve another fundamental question. That is, which decision comes first and therefore drives the other—the choice of brand or the choice of outlet? Finding jeans that fit is a problem, right—especially for women? Check out CBite 3-3 for the Levi's solution.

3-3b Outlet Choice or Brand Choice, Which Comes First?

Do brands attract people to outlets, or are people first drawn to particular outlets and only then to the brands within them? Exhibit 3-6 shows the different choice paths.

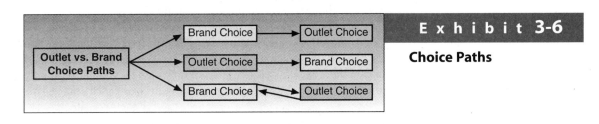

Exhibit 3-6

Choice Paths

Consider the following situations. Shirley is looking for a new pair of jeans. She knows she wants Levi Strauss, but has no outlet preference. She spots the jeans in a catalog and orders them. Maria also needs a pair of jeans. She hasn't thought much about the brand, but The Gap is her favorite clothing store. She likes the salespeople, and she always has luck finding what she wants there. Maria heads for The Gap to make her final choice. Maria's friend Mei, who likes Levi's, wants to know what else is available before she buys. She visits three local stores to try on different brands and checks prices and styles in a catalog before making her choice.

Shirley, Maria, and Mei are all faced with the same purchase decision but use very different brand and outlet choice strategies to make it. Shirley chose brand first; Maria selected outlet first; and Mei worked with both brand and outlet. By understanding these strategies and the ways in which they are used by different market segments, marketers are better able to position and promote their products and services within favored outlets. Let's take a closer look at each of the shopping strategies in the example.

F A Q

Which is easier for the shopper, choosing a brand first or choosing an outlet first?

When Brand Choice Drives Outlet Choice   When brand choice drives outlet choice, the consumer typically has a favorite brand or set of brands from which a selection will be made. His or her shopping strategy is simply to pick an outlet where the brand is available and buy the item there. There are three situations in which purchases are likely to be driven by brand choice rather than outlet choice:

1. When the consumer has no particular outlet preference or loyalty. The consumer doesn't care where the purchase is made, so long as the location is convenient and the price is right.
2. When brand loyalty is strong. A consumer who always buys the same brand of running shoes will purchase from the outlet that offers the greatest convenience and/or the best price for that brand.
3. When the consumer has sufficient product information to make the expertise of sales personnel or other outlet characteristics unimportant.

Shirley, interested only in buying Levi Strauss jeans, does not care where they can be found. She allows brand choice to drive her outlet choice.

When Outlet Choice Drives Brand Choice   Often, the consumer chooses an outlet before a brand is selected, because of faith in the outlet. The situations in which this happens are the reverse of those in which brand choice dominates:

1. Store loyalty or preference is high.
2. Brand loyalty is low.
3. The consumer has insufficient product information and, therefore, values the characteristics of the outlet—such as helpful sales staff.

Maria, heading straight to The Gap to buy jeans, favors outlet over brand choice. Exhibit 3-7, an advertisement for NAPA AutoCare Centers, emphasizes outlet over brand.

When Brand Choice and Outlet Choice Work Together   There are cases in which brand and outlet choices work together, as the consumer seeks to buy a preferred brand at an appropriate outlet. Mei's search for different brands of jeans through different outlets and outlet types illustrates this. In Exhibit 3-8, the outlet, Nordstrom, and the brand, Skechers, are presented together, inviting the consumer to consider the two in tandem. In this case, image, which we will explore in the next section, is of paramount importance. If consumers perceive a good match between the brand image, the outlet image, and their self-image, they are more likely to buy.[53]

The marketer's best strategy is to be able to have, in the eyes of the target market, the "best" brands and the "best" outlet. This means understanding the benefits various brands provide to the consumer and making them available through channels that help communicate those benefits clearly. A second challenge is to determine the type of outlet that is the best "fit" for the consumer, matching his or her self-image. Exhibit 3-9 is an overview

E x h i b i t 3-7

NAPA AutoCare Centers focus on outlet while sending some product and subtle brand signals.

Source: Courtesy of NAPA.

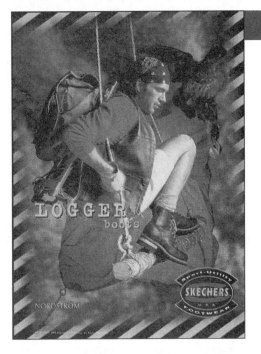

E x h i b i t 3-8

Here, the outlet Nordstrom and the brand name Skechers share equal billing, appealing, in particular, to those who consider both brand and outlet in making purchase choices.

Source: Courtesy of Skechers USA.

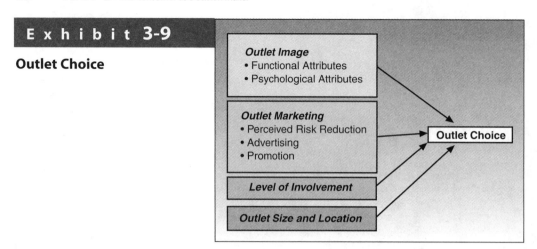

of how outlet image, outlet marketing, the consumer's level of involvement, and outlet size and location impact on outlet choice. We'll now look at each of these factors in turn.

3-3c Outlet Image

You walk into a department store with several purchases in mind. You have not shopped there before, but you know—both from local advertising and from conversations with others who shop there—that the store stocks the type of goods you're seeking. As you walk into the store, you stop dead in your tracks. Something about the place is not what you expected or is not quite right. It could be the layout, the lighting, the merchandise, the clerks, or even the other shoppers. Perhaps it is the combination of all these that makes you feel uneasy. For whatever reasons, the **retail outlet image** is wrong for you, and you turn around and leave. Later that evening while checking your mail, a new catalog catches your eye. You begin to leaf through the pages and see the same types of goods you were shopping for earlier. Yes! Here, everything looks and feels right—the catalog and the way the goods are presented in it are a perfect fit with your self-image. Self-image is discussed in Chapter 5. You might want to review the concept discussion at this time to help you understand material in the current section.

Outlet image, whether of a retail store, a catalog, a home shopping network, or even a flea market, has a great deal to do with why consumers choose to shop there. If we feel there is a good match between the image of an outlet and our own self-image, we are more likely to shop there. Image is very much in the eye of the beholder—it is what the consumer perceives it to be, and it varies from person to person.[54]

Outlet image results from a mix of functional and psychological attributes.[55] *Functional attributes* include merchandise selection, price ranges, credit policies, store layout, and other factors that can be measured to some degree and used to compare one outlet objectively with its competitors. Different functional attributes suit different types of customers and different shopping situations. While some enjoy the wide selection of a store like Office Depot, others, preferring speed and ease in shopping, find it overwhelming and would rather go to a small office supply retailer or order from a catalog.

Psychological attributes are a little more difficult to identify and compare across outlets. They include such subjective considerations as a sense of belonging, a feeling of warmth or friendliness, or a feeling of excitement. A shopper hoping to spend a few quiet moments wandering around a bookstore is at ease with a very different set of psychological attributes than the customer at a busy newsstand looking for a magazine to read on the train when traveling home after work.

Consumers form an outlet image based simultaneously on functional and psychological attributes. That image develops through the consumer's perception of just about everything associated with the outlet—things that can be put into words and those that can't.

Attributes of Outlet Image   Exhibit 3-10 lists nine key attributes that make up the image of retail outlets. Some of these can readily be classified as functional. Merchandise

retail outlet image Image or personality resulting from a mix of functional and psychological attributes of the outlet as perceived by the consumer.

F A Q

Retailers tell us we are moving into the age of the cybermall. Examples of this already are taking shape on the web. What is the image of the cybermall likely to be, and what type of consumers is it likely to attract?

**Image Attributes
at Retail Stores**

Merchandise	Quality, selection or assortment, styling or fashion, guarantees, warranties, and pricing; in service situations, merchandise offered as part of the service
Service	Service in general, salesclerk service, presence of self-service, ease of merchandise return, delivery service, phone ordering, and credit policies
Clientele	Social-class appeal, self-image congruency (fit between self-image and store image), and store personnel
Physical Facilities	Elevators, lighting, air conditioning, rest rooms, and so on; may also include store layout, shopping ease, aisle placement and width, and carpeting and architecture
Convenience	General convenience, location convenience, and parking access
Promotion	Sales promotions, advertising, displays, and symbols and colors
Store Atmosphere	Atmosphere of congeniality, customers' feelings of warmth, acceptance, or ease
Institutional Factors	Conservative versus modern projection of the store, reputation, and reliability
Post-Transaction Satisfaction	Merchandise in use, and returns and adjustments policies

Source: Jay D. Lindquist, "Meaning of Image," *Journal of Retailing,* Vol. 50 (Winter 1974–75), p. 31.

quality, selection, style, and price fit into this category, as do service, physical facilities, convenience of parking and location, the various types of sales promotions and advertising used, and some aspects of post-transaction satisfaction, especially those associated with returns and adjustments. Psychological attributes include those associated with the customer, especially social class appeal and fit of self-image with store image. Other psychological attributes include promotions tied to symbols that have meaning to the consumer; store atmosphere—the feelings the customer has based on decor, music, and lighting; institutional factors, such as an image of being modern or conservative or innovative or unpredictable and the way in which this fits with consumer self-image; and post-transaction satisfaction—feelings associated with the store and the products or services previously purchased. This mix of attributes, though presented in marketing research three decades ago, has stood the test of time. Current research has only reinforced and clarified it.[56]

In a recent study on atmosphere, "scent" and music were varied. The conditions were no music, pleasant low arousal music (slow tempo, relaxing), and high arousal music (energizing). Each of these was paired with one of the following types of scent: no scent, pleasant low arousal scent (lavender), and high arousal scent (grapefruit). It was found that matching music type and scent (e.g., pleasant low arousal music and pleasant low arousal scent) made consumers feel more positive about the shopping environment. Further, higher levels of impulse buying occurred and increased consumer satisfaction resulted from that combination.[57]

Two other factors affecting store atmosphere are customer perceptions of the number of store employees and how crowded the customers feel the store is. Both factors are tied to anticipated wait time. The greater number of employees and the less crowded the store, the less negative are customer wait expectations and the more positive is the evaluation of store atmosphere. Having to wait, for most customers, has direct negative impact.[58] This means that store managers should strive to have more sales and customer service people on the sales floor and invest in technology that will allow for efficient checkout. Kiosks that provide customer information also help with reducing wait time.

Marketplace 3-4

Invisible Images

How do consumers compare the images of marketers they cannot actually "see," such as mail, telephone, or online marketers, with those they can see, such as retail outlets and catalog marketers? Consumers were asked to compare "invisible" and "visible" marketers using a series of image scales, including safe–risky, convenient–inconvenient, extravagant–economical, fast–slow, difficult–easy, practical–impractical, unenjoyable–enjoyable, and sensible–foolish. The results indicated that women are significantly more positive than men are about catalog and store shopping, but this is not the case for other mail or telephone media. Married respondents are positive about magazine and catalog shopping, but less so about store shopping. Consumers of low socioeconomic status are less positive about magazines or catalog shopping and more positive about store shopping than are consumers of higher socioeconomic status. In general, consumers consider the images of mail- and telephone-order media to be markedly inferior to that of store or catalog shopping, particularly when it comes to perception of risk.

What all this tells us is that invisible marketers have a long way to go to create a positive outlet image in the minds of consumers. Although offers like refunds and warranties help minimize financial risk, they do not address the social and psychological risks—like wasted time and effort, embarrassment, or low self-esteem—that consumers rightly or wrongly attach to buying from invisible marketers.

Source: Robert B. Settle, Pamela L. Alreck, and Denny E. McCorkle, "Consumer Perceptions of Mail/Phone Order Shopping Media," *Journal of Direct Marketing,* Vol. 8 (Summer 1994), pp. 30–45.

F A Q

Is it possible for a retail outlet to have no image at all?

Functional and psychological attributes apply just as easily across all types and sizes of outlets. For example, the image of 7-Eleven is one of convenience. Locations depend upon population density. The stores provide fast in-and-out service for a narrow selection of frequently purchased items such as milk, bread, soft drinks, beer, snacks, magazines, and easy-to-prepare foods. Prices charged are higher than average, as a trade-off for convenience of location and speed of shopping. Now compare this with a D and W supermarket in Kalamazoo, Michigan or a supermarket in your hometown. Compare, too, the Wal-Mart discount chain stores across America with Macy's in New York or the giant Mall of America in Minneapolis/St. Paul with the elegant River Walk Mall in New Orleans or some strip mall in a town near where you live. How do these very different retailers stack up with the nine attributes in Exhibit 3-10? The same attributes are equally applicable to non-retail product and service outlets. Think how well they apply to the Lands' End, Talbots, or Popcorn Factory catalogs and the Amazon.com website. How do consumers compare the images of marketers they cannot actually "see," such as mail, telephone, or online types, with bricks-and-mortar retail outlets or catalogers? Take a look at Marketplace 3-4 for some insights.

Marketing Outlet Image The connection between outlet image and outlet choice is not clear-cut, making it difficult for marketers to predict with any accuracy how changes in image influence the choices of target consumer groups. Looking again at the nine retail store attributes in Exhibit 3-10, however, note that retailers do have some control over most, if not all, of them. By shaping these attributes, retailers can adjust outlet image to attract target customers. It is essential, however, that any attempt to refine an outlet's image does not interfere with the image already established for the outlet in the consumer's mind. As we have seen, different customer groups have different expectations of the different types of outlets available to them.[59] An image, once established, must continue to be clear and easily understood by the target consumers. It is important for marketers to look carefully at their target market and to understand the benefits sought. Only then can they effectively shape the outlet to this vision. Check out CBite 3-4 for a look at how catalogers do this.

All marketers, whatever the medium, seek to achieve a perfect fit with their target customers. From merchants selling their wares at flea markets, garage sales, or farmers' markets to high-tech marketers using home shopping channels or the Internet, all are working to match themselves with their potential customers. But just how important is outlet image in influencing the consumer's decision on whether or not to patronize it? What other considerations influence their choices? These are the topics of the next section.

CBite 3-4

A Catalog for Every Customer

Consider how well catalog marketers target different groups of customers—and even sell them identical products. Skim through the catalogs that come through your family mailbox, those addressed to your parents and grandparents as well as to you. First, look at the covers—the catalog name, the items featured, the use of models, the colors, and the layout. Then look inside. How is color used? Are the pages filled with items or does each page only feature a few? Look at the models wearing or using the products. How are they posing? What kind and style of merchandise is featured? How are the prices? These are just some of the many different signals sent to the potential customer. From the cover alone, the catalog marketer wants the consumer to recognize in just a matter of seconds that the items inside are a good "fit," in terms of tastes, lifestyle, and price.

3-3d How Consumers Choose among Outlets

As we shall see, although image is important, there are other factors that affect outlet choice. Some are directly related to the consumer, whereas others, like image, relate to the way the outlet is presented to the consumer by marketers. Beginning with image, let's look at the most powerful influencers of the consumer's choice of outlet. Though the examples we'll look at come from the traditional retail environment, keep in mind that they apply in general across all types of outlets.

Image and Outlet Choice   As we have seen, marketers can shape the image of their outlet to meet the expectations of the target market. By doing so, they are making an important assumption: that consumers are constantly searching for outlets whose image is appropriate to them. Certainly, consumers like to simplify their overall buying process as much as possible, and the use of outlet image may allow them to do so by narrowing the number of choices to be considered. But do most consumers really make a conscious effort to find an outlet whose image is a perfect fit?

Though there is no universally accepted explanation of the role of image in the process consumers go through when choosing outlets, the eight-step flowchart in Exhibit 3-11 provides a useful overview. Devised to describe retail store choice, its underlying assumptions and the steps included point to its applicability in all outlet choices. Outlet choice begins with the characteristics of the consumer, leading to recognition of needs that may be fulfilled through the purchase of products or services. Different customers, as we have seen, seek out different outlet attributes and consider some attributes more or less important than others. Their perception of such attributes creates an outlet image in the minds of consumers. A favorable image leads to a positive attitude toward the outlet. The more positive the attitude toward the outlet, the more likely the consumer is to shop there. Once the consumer actually uses the outlet, evaluation of in-store stimuli takes place, and the purchase choice is made. Notice the feedback lines in the flowchart. Information the consumer gathers while shopping and purchasing at the store is placed in memory and serves to strengthen or weaken the store's image in the mind of the consumer. After the purchase choice is made, the consumer's level of satisfaction determines whether other purchase needs are recognized.

The flowchart emphasizes the key role of outlet image in influencing final purchase choice. By using the flowchart, along with having an understanding of the characteristics of target consumer groups, marketers can develop strategies to establish the image most likely to encourage purchasing by target consumers.

Though not all researchers agree that outlet image plays a central part in predicting purchase behavior, few deny its influence. One study, for example, looked at the impact of image on the choice of hospitals by consumers who were not sent to a specific facility by their doctors. Seven of the nine image attributes identified in Exhibit 3-10 played a part,

FAQ

Do informal retail sales outlets like outdoor markets or flea markets, garage sales, swap meets, in-home shopping parties, or auctions have images? If so, how do these images differ from one another?

Exhibit 3-11

An Eight-Step Process of Outlet Selection

Developed to describe retail store selection but applicable to other outlet types, the model illustrates the role of image in driving outlet choice.

Source: From "A Path-Analytic Explanation of Retail Patronage Influences" by Kent B. Monroe and Joseph B. Guiltinan in *Journal of Consumer Research,* Vol. 2, June 1975, p. 21. Copyright © 1975. Reprinted by permission of The University of Chicago Press.

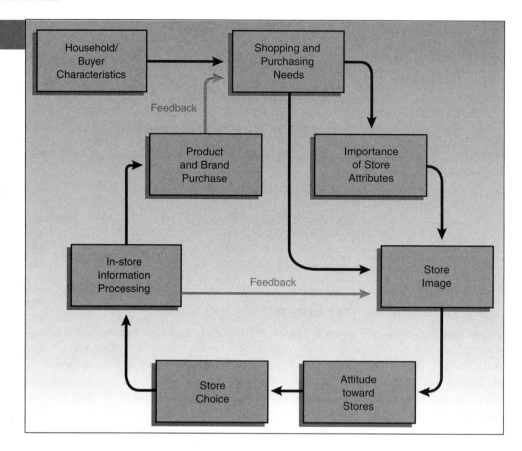

namely staff, physical facilities, clientele, experience, convenience, and institutional factors.[60]

Level of Involvement and Outlet Choice   Level of involvement—the degree to which making the right product choice is important to the consumer and the risks associated with the wrong choice are high—influences outlet choice. For products that are of low involvement to the consumer, the choice of outlet is usually of minor concern. This is true, for example, for purchases of household items. Moreover, for the type of consumer who, in general, sees shopping as a low priority, outlet is most likely a low-involvement choice. In both these situations, expertise of salespeople is far less important than, for example, ease and speed of shopping. Convenience stores, supermarkets, and fast-food restaurants all respond to a low level of involvement among consumers. In contrast, specialty stores and catalogs typically offer higher-involvement products, like gifts, clothing, or jewelry. Stores offer technical assistance or salesperson expertise to attract customers, so that the choice of outlet becomes as important as the choice of product or brand. Consider a customer in search of a Texas Instruments scientific calculator. The brand has been recommended to her by a trusted source, but she knows she will need help figuring out how the product works and determining which model to buy to meet her needs. This means that finding the right outlet—one with expert salespeople and excellent service, in addition to reasonable prices—is essential. (Involvement is covered in more detail in Chapter 8.)

Perceived Risk and Outlet Choice   As we saw in Chapter 2, perceived risk attached to making a purchase is far more complex than simply feelings about the money spent. The same is true in choosing outlets. The choice can involve the same range of perceived or actual risks discussed earlier: performance risk, financial risk, social risk, psychological risk, physiological risk, time risk, and linked-decision risk. Any one or a combination of these can cause a consumer to avoid certain outlets altogether or avoid them when looking for certain items or services.

Whether the risks are real or imagined, it is important that the marketer be aware of the different types of risks consumers associate with outlets. To minimize perceived risk, the objective for marketers and retailers should be to create an environment in which target customers can shop comfortably and with confidence.

Advertising and Outlet Choice   Retailers dominate the advertising pages of most newspapers. Why? Because newspapers are where their customers expect retailers to be. Before we go shopping, many of us scan the paper to see where the sales are or what's on special offer. The bulk of the Sunday paper is made up of all kinds of advertising—full-page display advertisements in each section, classified advertising, free-standing inserts, and coupons galore. About 40 percent of shoppers routinely use newspaper advertising to help plan their shopping trips.[61] This type of planning is widely used in grocery shopping, as consumers expose themselves to advertising to help them decide where to go, when to shop, and what to buy.[62]

It is, however, almost impossible for advertisers to measure the impact of advertising on its ability both to attract consumers to the outlet and to persuade them to buy once they get there. One study estimated that as many as 81 percent of the people drawn to a store by advertising made a purchase. Of these, 26 percent purchased the advertised item only; a further 34 percent bought the advertised item and one other; 21 percent did not buy the advertised item but purchased at least one other item. The remaining customers made no purchase.[63] Obviously, this high level of response makes a very positive statement to advertisers. Advertising increased sales of the advertised item, and there appears to have been an effect on the purchase of other goods—whether planned or unplanned—by the same customers.

Of course, not all consumers are receptive to advertising, and some find it particularly annoying in certain media. Users of the Internet, for example, are strong in their opposition to being exposed to advertising, particularly that which is not specifically targeted to them. Even in this medium, however, it has been found that consumers who have a positive attitude toward interactive (direct) marketing in general are likely to respond to advertising on the Internet, provided that it is correctly targeted to them.[64]

An important guideline in promoting an outlet is that the advertising must accurately portray the image of the outlet, its customers, and the goods and/or services offered. It should never promise more than can be delivered. Any customer who comes into the outlet in response to an advertisement must feel that the advertising "told" an accurate story.

Price and Outlet Choice   Increasingly, competing on price is a fact of retailing life. A number of factors influence the decision to cut prices, among them cost of goods to the retailer, profit margins, and competitor pricing. The question is, are we consumers getting what we think we are when a discount is offered? CBite 3-5 tells what's often really going on. The ways in which advertisers communicate price-based offers also varies. "Get $10 off your purchase of $50 worth of merchandise," "20 percent off of your next $100 purchase," "money-back mail-in rebate," and "buy four at $10 and get the fifth one free" are just some of the types of price promises retailers make.

CBite 3-5
Let the Buyer Beware

Though price offers have proven very effective in the retail environment in influencing outlet choice, marketers should be careful in their use of low price to draw customers. Today's shoppers are market-smart. They know that an advertisement promising "30 percent off" is not necessarily a terrific deal. It's a great bargain if the discount is calculated from an already-low everyday price. But, if the discount is set from an artificially high manufacturer's suggested price, consumers will not be easily taken in. A markdown of 60 percent off a manufacturer's suggested retail price of $100 is a $60 savings. But if that item typically sells for $60, the $40 sale price is only about 33 percent off. Let the buyer beware!

The last of these is particularly effective because it uses the word "free"—always a draw to price-conscious consumers. Other powerful phrases used in price-based retail advertising include "special offer," "for a short time only," and "compare our low prices." Of course, their influence varies across product and service class, from consumer to consumer, and from situation to situation.[65] Is using the phrase "regular price" good or bad for a retailer? Such price claims actually may be harmful in certain situations. It is interesting to note that when shoppers have information about competing retailers, the use of a "regular" price claim may convince them that the store's regular prices are actually higher without convincing them that sale prices are lower. In particular, it has been found that "regular" price claims should not be used for brand name shopping goods when the price is easily compared to those at other stores, unless the regular price is truly competitive. One substitute for using the "regular price" phrase is to suggest that the product be compared by using a "sold by others at $X" claim.[66] We know that factory-outlet centers focus on price. However, careful shopping when goods are on sale at regular department stores and specialty stores can often yield as good a "deal" as one might find in a bricks-and-mortar outlet mall or at an online outlet mall. In a number of cases the merchandise offered is not exactly the same as in the retailer's regular stores. It is outlet mall merchandise, not of comparable quality that appears to be the genuine goods. Also, "seconds" or irregular merchandise may also be found on occasion in these outlets.

Exhibit 3-12 is an example of an "everyday low price" advertising strategy. The Wal-Mart athletic shoes advertisement touts in-style items at "down-to-earth prices." This is a

Exhibit 3-12

This Wal-Mart ad appeals to cost-conscious family shoppers looking for everyday low prices.

Source: Reprinted by permission of Wal-Mart and Bernstein-Rein Advertising, Inc.

very strong price pitch, enhanced by the attractive photo of mom, dad, son, and daughter having fun on a Ferris wheel. The ad appeals strongly to cost-conscious family shoppers.

Outlet Size and Location and Outlet Choice

The level of outlet attraction can be measured by both outlet size and convenience of location. Of course, the importance of either varies by product, consumer, and situation. As a general rule, assuming that the sizes of two outlets offering similar merchandise are the same, most consumers will go to the one that is closer or more convenient. If both locations are equally convenient, most consumers prefer the larger outlet. There are, of course, exceptions—those who want to get in and out quickly, for example, will favor the smaller outlet. Also, some senior citizens feel overwhelmed in large shopping environments and will avoid them while turning to smaller outlets and smaller shopping centers or strip malls.

Some people are willing to travel farther than others to shop. For specialty goods, even consumers who value convenience may still go out of their way. In general, however, the smaller and more distant the outlet is from the consumer, the less attractive it is.[67] For low-involvement products, convenience goods, and minor purchases, people tend to be unwilling to travel far out of their way. For high-involvement products, they are more willing to do so.[68] How the concepts of "size" and "location" affect the choice of outlets such as catalogs or the Internet is questionable, since all of the research in this area is tied to bricks-and-mortar outlets.

What do you think about this dilemma? Take a look at CBite 3-6 for a discussion on "outshopping." This is where people shop outside of their neighborhood or simply beyond their normal range.

CBite 3-6

Outshopping

When consumers shop outside their neighborhoods, they are outshopping. Outshopping is more common for some types of purchases than for others. In general, people will go out of their way to shop for high-involvement purchases, like cars, furniture, and dress clothes. They are less willing to travel for everyday wear, sporting goods, small appliances, and food and grocery items, which are generally low-involvement products. To help persuade consumers to choose distant or less convenient locations, retailers often offer free transportation to and from stores. Outshopping is particularly popular during vacations or holiday seasons. At Christmas, parades, street decorations, and festive stores attract people from outlying areas to city centers where they can find specialty goods not available in local stores.

Source: Robert Williams, "Outshopping: Problem or Opportunity?" *Arizona Business* (October/November 1981), p. 9.

Marketing Management—Implications and Actions

Understanding consumers' outlet selection helps marketers:

- Create different strategies to attract consumers whose choices are brand driven and those whose choices are outlet driven.
- Develop an outlet image that matches the self-image of target consumers.
- Determine whether products are likely to be of high or low involvement to the consumer and develop outlets accordingly.
- Minimize the consumer's perception of risk by creating a shopping environment in which customers feel at ease.
- Develop advertising and pricing strategies that both attract consumers to an outlet and deliver on their expectations.
- Determine optimum outlet size and location based on product type, consumer type, and shopping behavior.

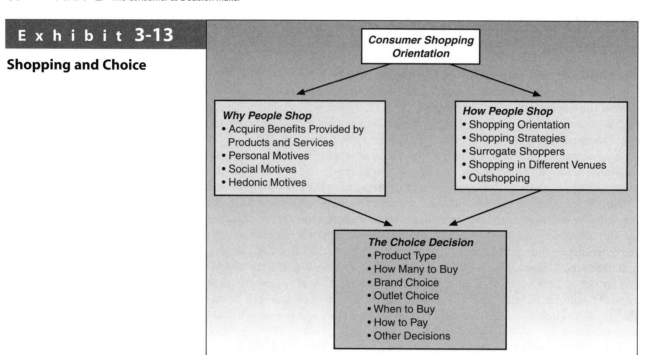

E x h i b i t 3-13

Shopping and Choice

3-4 Consumer Choice and Shopping Behavior

A simple question central to understanding all consumer behavior is, "Why do we shop?" In the rest of this chapter, we'll attempt to provide some answers by exploring the shopping process and the different factors that motivate different types of consumers toward making different shopping choices. Exhibit 3-13 provides an overview of the relationships among shopping motivation and other factors and the various decisions to be made at the time of product or service choice.

3-4a The Shopping Process

People do not shop just as a means of obtaining benefits from the desired goods and services—the motivations behind shopping behavior are far more complex than this. Shopping is not just about spending money. Among other things, it involves meeting and talking with others, exploring an out-of-home environment (in some cases), seeing new things, and learning new trends.[69] When attempting to understand why people shop, we must focus on the purchase and on the entire shopping process.[70]

Why Do We Shop? Obviously, people shop to gain information, compare alternative products, and in many cases purchase the goods or services that will deliver the benefits they are seeking. In addition, researchers have suggested the following range of other reasons why consumers shop. These are broadly categorized into **personal motives** and **social motives.**[71]

Personal motives include the tendency of people within societies to role-play. Various types of shopping are part of the role behaviors prescribed by the prevailing culture, such as the role of mother, father, homemaker, high school student, or business buyer.[72] People also shop for the sake of diversion. For some, it's a means of escape from the routines of daily life, and so it becomes recreational. Some shop as a means of self-gratification. Shopping makes them feel good about themselves, alleviating depression and providing some kind of reward. The more adventurous or innovative consumers shop in order to learn new trends or find out about new services, gadgetry, colors, product forms, and so on. They like to be informed or to keep up with fashions. Some even shop just for the physical activity it provides, shopping as a form of exercise as they pace from outlet to outlet.

personal (shopping) motives Reasons for shopping that do not relate to the selection of goods and services but are primarily focused on personal feelings, role-playing, diversion, and other related outcomes tied to the shopping experience.

social (shopping) motives These reasons for shopping are based on the desire to have social experiences outside of the home, including interactions with others.

This is particularly true in large, suburban covered malls, many of which are open to walkers outside of shopping hours. Lastly, people shop for the sake of sensory stimulation. The sights, the sounds, the colors, the products, the scents, the music—these and other sensory stimuli contribute to the appeal of shopping. It's a chance to look, touch, and experience the retail marketplace.

Social motives for shopping include the desire for social experience outside the home. The marketplaces and village squares of old have become the modern farmers' markets, shopping centers, malls, and retail shopping districts of today. As people shop, they see friends and acquaintances and have a chance to chat with them in a neutral setting. People shop to communicate with others of similar interests. In outlets selling hobby materials, home improvement items, electronic gear, or sporting goods, people with common interests make contact with one another. They have the chance to strike up conversations, swap experiences, or give and receive advice as they shop. Similarly, peer group attraction encourages shoppers. The mall, department store, sports center, and specialty store are places where shoppers go to encounter others of similar age, subculture, religion, and so on. People are frequently attracted to locations that draw their peers. A desire for status and authority is another social motivator. Some shoppers seek a master-servant relationship. As the saying goes, "The customer is always right," so some people are motivated to shop in search of the respect and deference they can obtain from sales personnel. Finally, some shop for the pleasure of bargaining. Shoppers—particularly in cultures in which bargaining is an everyday part of shopping—enjoy the bargaining process and the sense of triumph and satisfaction that accompanies a successful negotiation.

Another way to look at why shoppers are in the marketplace is to consider their *hedonic motives*. Here consumers shop for "advantage" (stimulation, adventure, and "being in another world"), "gratification" (stress relief, reduce negative mood, treat oneself), "role" (shopping for others, friends, family, etc.), "value" (looking for sales, discounts, bargains), "idea" (to keep up with trends, new fashions, see new products and innovations), and "social" reasons (shopping with friends and family, socializing while shopping, bonding while shopping).[73] Note that some of these motives were already identified in the earlier studies relating to personal and social motives. However, the hedonic view is worth considering, since it introduces some new ideas.

Suppose you do not like to shop. Is there a way around this? CBite 3-7 presents one option.

Consider such retailers as Eddie Bauer, Neiman-Marcus, Structure, Nike Town, RadioShack, Macy's, and Victoria's Secret. In what ways do they successfully apply their understanding of the motivations behind shopping to improve their retail strengths?

F A Q

Why do we typically see more women than men in grocery stores?

CBite 3-7
You Shop, I Relax

Picture this: Frazzled shoppers pack your favorite store, and the lines at the register seem endless. You, meanwhile, relax in a fitting room far from the fray as a salesperson gathers the merchandise you've requested. When you're done, your purchase is rung up while you dress. You're out the door in a flash. You are not hallucinating. These days, many stores are saving the time and sanity of customers with personal shopping services—and they're doing it at no charge. You're not even required to make a purchase. Macy's, Bloomingdale's, Nordstrom, and Saks are among the retailers that offer this perk. For fastest results, you're encouraged to be specific about style, color, and price range. If you call ahead, the store will have merchandise waiting when you arrive. Plus, your personal shopper will keep style preferences on file and call when something comes in that he or she thinks you'll like. Do you like the sound of this? What does this tell you about your shopping orientation?

Source: "Speed Shopping," *McCall's* (March 1995), p. 20.

shopping orientation
A consumer's style or way of shopping. Both feelings about shopping and actual shopping procedures come into play.

How Do We Shop?   How and why consumers shop depends on their **shopping orientation**, which is, quite simply, their style or way of shopping. It entails feelings about shopping and the shopping process as well as actual shopping behavior. One study has linked shopping orientation to lifestyle and related variables, including family or household life cycle, income level, and retail work experience.[74] All of these singly or in combination help to form shopping orientation.

Think about the way you shop. Do you plan your shopping trip route? Do you make a written or mental list of what to buy, including brands? Do you mostly shop alone? Do you go to the same stores as your parents go to or used to go to, even if there are other choices? Do you shop daily, weekly, or biweekly? Are there any ways in which you feel your shopping behavior differs from that of those around you?

As you can probably guess from the answers to these questions, it is possible to group consumers based on similarity of shopping orientation. One such classification scheme is illustrated in Exhibit 3-14. Here, shoppers are clustered into six types, each of which has a

Exhibit **3-14**	Shopper Type	Shopping Strategies
Shopper Types and Shopping Strategies	**In-Store Economizer (19%)**	Compares prices, uses unit prices, redeems coupons; shops for bargains and believes a person can save by shopping in different stores; does not believe grocery shopping is an important task, nor an opportunity to exercise or break out of the normal routine; does not plan menus; is relatively young with a large family; is well-educated; prefers stores with many price specials and quality store brands
	Apathetic or Mechanistic (9%)	Has negative attitude toward shopping; has negative feelings about the value or enjoyment of shopping, menu planning, or cooking; has a small family
	Involved Traditional (24%)	Has positive attitudes toward trying new brands, planning, comparing prices, and redeeming coupons; has positive feelings about the value or enjoyment of shopping, use of recipes, and menu planning; is older
	Economy Planner (25%)	Has positive attitudes toward using unit prices, coupons, and newspaper advertisements; compares prices; does not like to try new brands; likes to plan menus and recipes; does not like to change stores; is below average age; has the largest family size; looks for convenience; quality of store brands is important
	Homemaker (12%)	Believes brand name implies quality; plans menus; believes grocery shopping is an important task; has negative attitudes toward shopping in more than one store; is average on all demographic variables; is relatively less concerned about store advertising, deals, and friends' outlet choices
	Convenience Seeker (12%)	Has positive attitudes toward redeeming coupons but does not use unit pricing; does not like to shop in more than one store because he or she knows the layout of the present store but is willing to visit other stores to see what is new; believes brand name implies quality; has a low level of education; is very concerned with convenience in reaching or in moving through the store; has low concern for store brands

Source: From "Identifying and Analyzing Consumer Shopping Strategies" by Joseph P. Guiltinan and Kent B. Monroe in *Advances in Consumer Research*, Vol. 7, edited by Jerry C. Olsen (1980), pp. 745–748. Reprinted by permission of the Association for Consumer Research, Valdosta, GA.

Exhibit 3-15

To what shopper type or types is this Clorox brand bleach advertisement targeted?

Source: © 1994 The Clorox Company. CLOROX is a registered trademark of The Clorox Company. Used with permission.

different shopping style. *In-store economizers* tend to rely upon information searching during the actual shopping trip, especially in the store itself, while *economy planners* more often use external information sources. Though *involved traditionals* and *homemakers* can both be considered involved shoppers, the former group is the more concerned of the two with value and with social pressures. On the other hand, homemakers are more quality conscious and household-role oriented. The advertisement in Exhibit 3-15 is targeted to these two groups. *Apathetic* or *mechanistic shoppers* and *convenience seekers* tend to do less planning or budgeting than the other groups.

A study of grocery shoppers in 2004 focused on what was called *emotional drivers*. The study outcome showed nine "state-of-mind occasions" that supposedly determine grocery shopping behavior.

Consumers can be grouped into those who shop in stores only, those who shop on the Internet only, and those who cross-shop stores and the Internet. The type of product is a determining factor in shares in each of the three groups. For example, when shopping for products termed cognitive (videos, computer software, books, and music), 52 percent of the men and women shopped in stores only, 8 percent shopped on the web, and 40 percent reported shopping in both venues. Turning to sensory experiential products (apparel and apparel accessories), 68 percent shopped only in stores, 3 percent shopped on the web, and the remaining 29 percent cross-shopped.[75]

No outlet can be "all things to all shoppers." A key decision for any retailer is to identify the types of shoppers to be targeted. This decision will then direct the development of the right image for the outlet. The classifications discussed here, though simplified for our purposes, are a good starting point.

Surrogate Shoppers   Some consumers do not like to shop for certain goods or do not feel qualified to do so. These people may turn to a "surrogate shopper" to go into the marketplace to do the shopping for them. A **surrogate shopper** is a person, firm, or other entity engaged and paid by the consumer or other interested party on behalf of the consumer to make or facilitate a product or service selection decision on behalf of that consumer.[76] Such a person is expected to make a choice from among a variety of options. This distinguishes a surrogate from expert store-employed salespeople (see CBite 3-7). The latter would typically only shop the store where they are employed to find items for the customer.

> **surrogate shopper** A person, firm, or other entity engaged and paid by the consumer or other interested party on behalf of the consumer to make or facilitate a product or service selection decision on behalf of that consumer.

Let's look at a surrogate example. Yolanda, a middle manager for an industrial engineering firm, detests clothing shopping. She has a hard time finding things that fit and does not like the stress of the whole process. She also feels that she has neither the time nor the energy to do it. "Shop For You" is a surrogate shopping firm in the city. She contacts them, and a person comes to her to gather information about tastes, preferences, needs, and the like. Expenditure limits are also set. The surrogate goes into the marketplace, does the shopping, handles any exchanges or returns, and, upon satisfactory completion of the task, gets paid.

In a less formal arrangement, Richard offers to pay a college student who is a "computer whiz" to shop for and buy a new computer system. The student, Gizelle, determines what Richard needs and what he can afford. She buys the system and sets it up for him, and he pays her $100 for her time and effort. Here is a situation where the consumer does not feel qualified to shop for the goods, so someone was hired to act in his stead.

Shopping Behavior in Different Shopping Venues   Shopping center traffic primarily consists of women. In fact, about 70 percent of total store sales in these centers, also known as shopping malls, come from female shoppers. Of the total, 43 percent of sales are from working women. On the other hand, some 46 percent of American men shop in shopping centers, with the majority being under 30 years of age. Only 29 percent of female shoppers are under 30. Calvin Klein considered this and created a special sampling program for one of its colognes in a number of shopping centers rather than continuing to focus all such efforts in the traditional department store setting.[77]

People also gain benefits from the shopping center shopping process. In a study comparing how the shopping process benefits people enjoyed at shopping centers stacked up with those benefits common to catalog shopping, it turned out that catalog shoppers rated retail service contact and unusual product source benefits higher than did shopping center shoppers.[78] This points to the "sales clerk strength" winner being the catalog retailer, which may be a bit surprising to some, as these are telephone transactions. As expected, people liked being able to find more unusual items in catalogs. There were no differences in the level of entertainment/escape and product variety and assortment exposure benefits. This shows that retailers must be conscious of not just what they offer, but what shoppers feel about the benefits of shopping in different retail settings.

Check out Marketplace 3-5 for some great insights into what supermarket managers know about you as you enter their stores. This could help you better understand your shopping experience.

3-4b Choice Decisions during the Shopping Process

The process of shopping involves a number of basic decisions that are made by the consumer at the time of purchase. Of course, these vary according to the goods or services sought and from situation to situation, but they provide a useful overview of what is going on while the consumer shops. The consumer makes some or all of the following decisions while shopping:

Marketplace 3-5

What Supermarkets Know about You

Maybe you thought there was only one rule to think about in supermarket design: put milk at one end, bread at the other, and force the shopper to go the length of the place. That simplistic approach came into being a long time ago. It turns out that each inch of space is scientifically calibrated to hold only what you will buy at the highest profit margin—a layout that is the culmination of complex experiments, observational studies of the way consumers move through stores, and intricate research on the effects of lighting, color, and music.

Grocers hire professional designers to shape a store's interior—its tables, stalls, shelves (known as gondolas), and the 30,000 products typically displayed—into a landscape that lures us in, moves us deliberately about, and sends us back out the door with bulging grocery bags. These "people in the lab" say you're probably female, although increasingly you're male. You shop on average 2.2 times per week in supermarkets. A mere 31 percent of you arrive with a list, but it doesn't matter: Only one-third of your purchases are planned. The others, sometimes called "splurchases," are nearly as predictable. The vast majority of you who sample a product will purchase it, so that's why you see female senior citizen demonstrators offering tastes of cheese and crackers, new sausage links right from the frying pan, chips and dips, and the like.

The average "eye height" of a woman is fifty-nine inches; a man's is sixty-four inches. And because the best viewing angle is fifteen degrees below the horizontal, the choicest elevations on any aisle are between fifty-one and fifty-three inches off the floor. When you examine a shelf, you like to stand about four feet away. Also, experiments have shown that if the store's layout encourages you to turn your cart one direction, you will look the other way into the turn's "strong side." This a good place to put merchandise that needs moving.

On any given visit, shoppers will spend on average thirty-five to forty minutes in the store. For each minute beyond, you will spend about $2 more. If background music is slowed from a lively allegro of one hundred and eight beats per minute to sixty beats per minute, researchers report, the speed of the average cart slows, more looks are taken at the goods, and purchases soar as much as 38 percent.

Source: Adapted from "What Supermarkets Know about You" by Jack Hitt as appeared in *The New York Times Magazine,* March 10, 1996, pp. 136–138. Reprinted by permission of the author. Jack Hitt is a contributing writer for the *New York Times Magazine, Harper's Magazine,* and the public radio program "This American Life."

1. *Which product type to buy.* In certain cases, as search and alternative evaluation progress, the consumer begins to narrow down the number of specific product types from which to choose. For example, a consumer who needs equipment on which to play both CDs and DVDs may decide to buy a single component rather than two separate players.

2. *How many to buy.* The consumer decides whether to buy a single item or multiple items of the same kind. If, for example, a consumer wants to buy soft drinks, he or she can choose two large bottles, an eight-pack of plastic bottles, or a twelve-pack of cans. Promotions in the grocery store where there is a limit to the number of items at a lower price an individual consumer can buy will increase the number, on average, bought. Multiple unit offers at discount, even if the discount percentage is only 10 percent to 20 percent, also result in increased quantities purchased.[79]

3. *Which brand(s) to buy.* The consumer has already decided to buy a specific type of product or service and now chooses among brands. In the category of laundry detergents, for example, where parity products are common, the choice needs to be narrowed down to one brand.

4. *The outlet at which to purchase.* Once the type of product and the brand have been decided upon, the consumer must choose where the purchase is to be made. Alternatively, as we have seen in this chapter, the outlet may be chosen before the brand is selected. In some cases, where the product is available from only one source, there is no outlet decision. If you want to have your hair cut by your favorite stylist, there is only one place to go. Today the Internet is often the medium of choice, and the specific website becomes the outlet of choice. Marketplace 3-6 is based on two articles relating to this. One deals with reasons for online shopping at Christmas time in America, and the other explores online purchasing problems.

Marketplace 3-6

Online Choice

A study was done to determine reasons shoppers would give for shopping online during the Christmas season. Here are some key results. Five of these are related to convenience, two are tied to value, and one is an assortment reason. Can you decide which is which? Would you put these eight reasons in the same order we see here?

Stated Reasons for Online Purchasing	Share of Total Responses (%)
Save time by not going to store	70
Can shop when stores are closed	69
Avoid the holiday crowds	68
Might be able to find better prices	59
Can find products online more easily	52
Find products not available in stores	50
Easier to compare prices	47
Have gifts sent directly to recipients	36

Source: Robyn Greenspan, "E-Tailers Will See Green," *CyberAtlas* (cyberatlas.com), November 6, 2003.

Most online shopping experiences are not as positive as they could be. The Internet "promises" shopping convenience, but users do not always find this to be true. The Boston Consulting Group study "Winning the Online Consumer" found that 60 percent of online consumers maintain that if they were not satisfied with a company's web shopping site, they are less likely to purchase from that company's traditional store. This is a very interesting finding, to say the least. So what were the most frequently found problems of online purchasing?

Online Purchasing Problem	Share (%) of Online Shoppers Stating Problem Happens "Sometimes" or "Frequently"
Pages took so long to load I gave up	48
Site was so confusing that I couldn't find the product I was looking for	45
Desired product was not available/in-stock	32
System crashed (got logged off) before completion	26
Had to contact customer service	20
Product took much longer than expected to arrive	15
Returned the product	10
Site would not accept credit card	9

When people go to a site, they must understand what's being offered in less than 30 seconds. Bluefly.com, for example, delivers its positioning as soon as a consumer accesses the site with the message "The outlet store in your home" and lists the names of top designers available on the site. In addition, the total shopping experience must meet, if not exceed, the consumer's expectations in order to move the shopper from browser to first-time buyer to repeat customer.

Source: Kevin J. Clancy, "Getting Serious about Building Profitable Online Retail Brands," *Retailing Issues Newsletter,* Vol. 12 (November 2000), Texas A & M University Center for Retailing Studies, pp. 1, 4. Reprinted by permission.

5. *When to complete the transaction.* The timing of the purchase can follow immediately upon the earlier decisions or it can occur much later. A consumer might, for example, decide upon a particular make and model of car and even decide where to buy it—yet wait until he or she has money saved for the down payment.

6. *How to pay.* Deciding the method of payment—cash, check, debit card, credit card, or a store's revolving charge plan or layaway program—can affect all the other purchase decisions. As a means of saving for Christmas, for example, a consumer buys gifts as part of a layaway program—and may end up spending more because the money wasn't needed up front.

7. *Other decisions.* In addition to the preceding decisions, several others apply to certain purchases in certain situations. They include purchase of extended warranties; purchase of support items such as batteries, software, cables, etc.; payment for delivery; purchase of installation or setup of equipment or services; payment for gift-wrapping; and shipping arrangements and charges. In some cases, consumers are not able to buy related materials or services at the same source, because of the lack of availability or expense, and choose another outlet for them.

Marketing Management—Implications and Actions

Understanding shopping behavior helps marketers:

- Focus on their products or brands and on the entire consumer shopping experience.
- Better meet consumers' needs by analyzing the many different reasons we shop.
- Categorize consumers into various shopper types and develop strategies for targeting each group.
- View the shopping process as a series of linked decisions and address each one.

Chapter Spotlights

In this chapter, we explored steps three and four of the consumer decision-making process—alternative evaluation and choice. Consumers often face a number of choices in making even the simplest of purchases. By viewing them as a series of linked decisions, marketers are better able to lead consumers toward their brands and away from those of competitors.

1. Alternative evaluation. Alternative evaluation often occurs simultaneously with information search, as consumers compare and contrast different marketplace solutions to an identified problem. If necessary, the consumer first makes a class comparison of different types of products that meet the same need. This leads to a brand comparison of specific products within the same category. In some cases retail outlet alternatives are solely or jointly considered with the product or service brand decision.

2. Consumer benefits and evaluative criteria. Consumers use a range of different judgment factors or evaluative criteria when assessing purchase options. These are based on the benefits sought by the person. By understanding which criteria are used, their salience, and the extent to which they are determinant, marketers can better identify opportunities to develop and position their offerings, and present favorable information about these goods and services.

3. Consumer decision rules and heuristics. To carry out alternative evaluation, consumers consciously or unconsciously use decision rules. These are either noncompensatory—where weaknesses in one attribute are not offset by strengths in another—or compensatory, allowing trade-offs among the weak and strong points of an alternative. Consumers also use informal rules of thumb, or decision heuristics, to make quick decisions. These include price, brand name, key product signals, and market beliefs.

4. Planned versus unplanned purchasing. The key to influencing planned purchasing is having an understanding of purchase intention and the strength of the consumer's commitment to it. Several variables, including deliberation by the consumer, can delay or intervene to change plans to purchase. Planned purchases are classified as specifically planned, generally planned, or substitute purchases. Also, there are four types of unplanned purchase: pure impulse, reminder impulse, suggestion impulse, and planned impulse. Marketers, and particularly retailers who control the point of purchase, use several merchandising techniques to encourage each type of unplanned purchase.

5. Outlet selection. Almost every product need can be met through multiple channels—from traditional retail stores to direct mail to online services to shopping channels and more. The consumer's choice of outlet becomes increasingly difficult for the marketer to either predict or to influence. Sometimes outlet choice is driven by a brand decision the consumer already made. At other times, the reverse is true, or the two choices are made in tandem.

6. Outlet image. Just as brand image affects brand selection, so can outlet image influence the choice of outlet. Image is formed through the consumer's perception of a combination of functional and psychological attributes of an outlet. We identified nine key attributes that make up outlet image and saw how marketers and retailers position their outlets based on these attributes to attract consumers whose self-image and purchase situation are a good fit with the outlet image. The outlet selected is also affected by the marketing activities of the firm. These include reduction of consumer perceived risk, advertising and other promotion activities, and price. The shopper's level of involvement impacts choice as well as outlet size and location in the case of bricks-and-mortar shopping environments.

7. Consumer choice and shopping behavior. We provided an overview of several linked consumer decisions: what to buy, how many to buy, which brands to buy, which outlet to use, when to buy, how to pay, and others. Beyond the desire to acquire goods and services, consumers display a range of personal, social, and hedonic motives for shopping, each influencing shopping choices. Shopping style or orientation also influences choice. We looked at different types of shoppers as a function of the shopping strategies they followed, showing how marketers can cluster consumers into groups and design strategies that will successfully attract targeted shopper types.

Key Terms

alternative evaluation (p. 56)
compensatory consumer decision rule (p. 63)
decision heuristics (p. 65)
determinant attributes (p. 61)
evaluative criteria (p. 58)
generally planned purchase (p. 69)
intervening variables (p. 71)

mere-possession (p. 68)
noncompensatory consumer decision rule
  (p. 63)
personal shopping motives (p. 86)
retail outlet image (p. 78)
salience (p. 60)
scrambled merchandising (p. 73)

shopping orientation (p. 88)
social shopping motives (p. 86)
specifically planned purchase (p. 69)
substitute purchase (p. 69)
surrogate shopper (p. 90)
trivial attribute (p. 60)
unplanned purchase (p. 69)

Review Questions

Note: You can find the correct answers to these questions by taking the quiz and then submitting your answers in the Online Edition. The program will automatically score your submission. If you miss a question, the program will provide the correct answer, a rationale for the answer, and the section number in the chapter where the topic is discussed.

1. The process through which we compare and contrast different solutions to the same marketplace problem is called
   a. information searching.
   b. alternative evaluation.
   c. choice/selection.
   d. comparison shopping.

2. Marketers must determine the relative importance or _____ of each evaluative criterion to identify those most likely to influence consumers.
   a. contributions
   b. likelihood
   c. degree of detail
   d. salience

3. Rules of thumb that are shortcuts called _____ allow consumers to make rapid decisions regarding the best alternatives.
   a. decision heuristics
   b. fast starts
   c. compensatory decisions
   d. noncompensatory decision rules

4. Which noncompensatory rule is used to consider all evaluative criteria as determinant and to establish a minimum/maximum acceptable value or score for each one?
   a. disjunctive
   b. conjunctive
   c. elimination by aspects
   d. lexicographic

5. By using which compensatory rule does the consumer only score each alternative on each evaluative criterion and then sum the scores to determine a winner?
   a. weighted additive rule
   b. simple additive rule
   c. weighted-simple additive rule
   d. decision heuristics

6. Marketers must remember that _____ , such as changes in financial or employment status or social conditions/norms, affect decisions.
   a. intervening variables
   b. economic rules
   c. social/cultural taboos
   d. worldwide conditions

7. Outlet managers must allow for a type of unplanned purchase called a _____ impulse, where a product, seen for the first time, stimulates immediate need recognition.
   a. planned
   b. pure
   c. reminder
   d. suggestion

8. When considering where to offer a product, the marketer's best strategy is to be able to have, in the eyes of the target market, the "best" brands and the "best"
   a. price.
   b. promotion.
   c. place (outlet).
   d. coupon.

9. Consumers choose among outlets by examining image, level of involvement, and perceived risk. Other factors include advertising, price, and outlet
   a. parking and size.
   b. location and age.
   c. friendliness and convenience.
   d. size and location.

10. Robbi Jones is going on a shopping spree. Which of these is *not* a choice decision she must make?
    a. which product to buy
    b. how many of the product to buy
    c. which brands to buy
    d. how to advertise the product

Team Talk

1. What brands would be in your consideration set if you were planning to buy a new personal computer? Could your consideration set be expanded? If so, what might cause this to happen?

2. Alternative evaluation and external information search often occur simultaneously. Can you remember this being the case for a product you eventually bought within the last 12 months? Describe how search and alternative evaluation overlapped.

3. Your team is part of a student group that on weekends takes disabled children on outings to local places of interest. You are considering buying a used van to save on transportation costs. The money is to be raised from donations by students at your school. What evaluative criteria would you use in shopping for a van, and which ones would be most salient? Divide 100 salience ("importance") points among your evaluative criteria to express their relative importance. If a salesperson approached you at an auto dealership, how could he or she be most effective in moving you toward a purchase?

4. What decision rule or heuristic would you use to choose each of the following products: a tube of toothpaste; a new television set; a college/university to attend for an undergraduate degree; a hair stylist?

5. Describe three recent unplanned purchases you have made, classifying each as one of the four types explained in the text.

What factors influenced these purchases? How do they differ from recent planned purchases, both in terms of the product itself and in terms of your shopping behavior?

6. Most of us have shopped in bricks-and-mortar retail stores, and most likely we have all, at one time or another, shopped at a flea market, farmer's market, garage sale, or swap meet, or from a "for sale" bulletin board. Choose one of these options and explain why you chose to shop at this type of outlet.

7. How do level of involvement and/or perceived risk enter into the picture when you are shopping on the Internet for any of the following goods or services: a pair of roller blades; a new sweatshirt; a cell phone; car insurance?

8. In the text we explored social motives for shopping. Which of them apply to you when you are shopping under the following conditions: at the local shopping center; at an upscale department store in a downtown location; on a television shopping channel; at a convenience store; on the Internet; at the college bookstore?

9. Look over the nine grocery shopper types presented in Marketplace 3-5. Which best describes you and why? Answer these two questions based on your going for groceries to prepare a meal for three close friends who are coming over to spend the evening and watch a movie.

Workshops

Research Workshop

Background

Planned and unplanned purchasing differs from consumer to consumer, from product to product, and from situation to situation. The objectives of this workshop are to provide insights into how consumers behave when making planned and unplanned purchases and to recommend marketplace actions to induce both types of purchase.

Methodology

Have four people who generally shop alone for food items and health and beauty aids keep all of their receipt tapes and shopping lists from purchases made at supermarkets and convenience stores over a one-week period. In separate interviews, discuss the process used to select each item. Classify each purchase as planned or unplanned. Further classify the planned purchases into those that are specifically planned, generally planned, or substitute choices, and classify the unplanned purchases into pure impulse, reminder impulse, suggestion impulse, or planned impulse. Determine what share of the purchases falls into each main category and each sub-category.

How do the four people compare in terms of planned versus unplanned purchases? Are certain products more likely to be planned or unplanned? Into which subcategories do most purchases fall? What is the effect of using a shopping list on the share of unplanned purchases made? What other observations can you make from the data collected?

To the Marketplace

Prepare a list of recommendations you would make to marketers and retailers to boost sales of items that are typically planned or unplanned. Consider both in-store and out-of-store activities.

Creative Workshop

Background

The role of marketers is to communicate product benefits to target markets. As consumers evaluate alternatives, they look for information about the evaluative criteria that are important to them. The objectives of this workshop are to take known evaluative criteria, prepare a rough in-store advertisement that properly includes them, and then suggest ways in which retailers can be persuaded to display it.

Methodology

One source students interested in buying book bags typically use to gather information is the in-store poster. The evaluative criteria they use and the importance they attach to each are: price (30), capacity (25), durability (20), color (15), and brand (10). Prepare a rough draft of an in-store poster that you think will include all of these criteria, placing appropriate emphasis on each. Develop the headline and the copy along with a description of the visual layout of the poster.

To the Marketplace

How would you convince store owners to offer space in their outlets to display your poster? What incentives would you offer? Where should the poster be in the store?

Managerial Workshop

Background

Making it easier for customers coming into a retail outlet both to find information and to evaluate alternatives is an important goal for store managers. The objectives of this workshop are to gather examples of how this is done and to prepare a plan for a retail store to improve in these two areas.

Methodology

Visit five retail outlets of various types in your local marketplace. Through observation, note what steps the store management has taken to make it easier for customers to gather information on products and evaluate alternatives. Check such things as store layout and signage, special displays, posters, package arrangements on the shelf, shelf product signs, video or computer screen aids, and clerk helpfulness and knowledge. Record what you find.

To the Marketplace

Choose one of the outlets you visited and put together a plan for that store. The plan should include specific details as to how you could improve ease of customer information search and alternative evaluation.

Notes

1. Amitav Chakravarti and Chris Janiszewski, "The Influence of Macro-Level Motives on Consideration Set Composition in Novel Purchase Situations," *Journal of Consumer Research,* Vol. 30 (September 2003), pp. 244–258.
2. Ibid.
3. Frank R. Kardes, Gurumurthy Kalyanaram, Murali Chandreshekaran, and Ronald J. Dornoff, "Brand Retrieval, Consideration Set Composition, Consumer Choice, and the Pioneering Advantage," *Journal of Consumer Research,* Vol. 20 (June 1993), pp. 62–75.
4. James F. Engel, Roger D. Blackwell, and Paul W. Miniard, *Consumer Behavior,* 8th ed. (Fort Worth, TX: The Dryden Press, 1995).
5. Michael L. Rothschild and Michael J. Houston, "The Consumer Involvement Matrix: Some Preliminary Findings," in Barnett A. Greenberg and Danny N. Bellenger, eds., *Contemporary Marketing Thought* (Chicago, IL: American Marketing Association, 1977), pp. 95–98; Jay Dahl Lindquist, *Retail Store Image in the Purchase Decision Process: An Empirical Study,* unpublished doctoral dissertation (Ann Arbor, MI: The University of Michigan, 1973), p. 270.
6. Lindquist, *Retail Store Image in the Purchase Decision Process,"* p. 253.
7. Michael L. Rothschild, "Advertising Strategies for High and Low Involvement Situations," in John C. Maloney and Bernard Silverman, eds., *Attitude Research Plays for High Stakes* (Chicago, IL: American Marketing Association, 1977), pp. 74–93.
8. Gerard J. Tillis and Birger Wernerfelt, "Competitive Price and Quality under Asymmetric Information," *Marketing Science,* Vol. 6 (Summer 1987), pp. 240–253.
9. Christina L. Brown and Gregory S. Carpenter, "Why Is the Trivial Important? A Reasons-Based Account for the Effects of Trivial Attributes on Choice," *Journal of Consumer Research,* Vol. 26 (March 2000), pp. 275–385.
10. Ibid.
11. Shi Zhang and Sanjay Sood, "'Deep' and 'Surface' Cues: Brand Extension Evaluation by Children and Adults," *Journal of Consumer Research,* Vol. 29 (June 2002), pp. 129–141.
12. Mark I. Alpert, "Identification of Determinant Attributes: A Comparison of Methods," *Journal of Marketing Research,* Vol. 8 (May 1971), pp. 184–191.
13. Deborah J. MacInnis, Kent Nakamoto, and Gayathri Mani, "Cognitive Associations and Product Category Comparisons: The Role of Knowledge Structure and Content," in John F. Sherry and Brian Sternthal, eds., *Advances in Consumer Research,* Vol. 19 (Provo, UT: Association for Consumer Research, 1992), pp. 260–267.
14. Kenneth E. Miller and James L. Ginter, "An Investigation of Situational Variation in Brand Choice Behavior and Attitude," *Journal of Marketing Research,* Vol. 16 (February 1979), pp. 111–123.
15. Andre Gabor and C. W. J. Granger, "Price Sensitivity of the Consumer," *Journal of Advertising Research,* Vol. 4 (December 1964), pp. 40–44.
16. Paul M. Lane and Jay D. Lindquist, "Pricing in Times of Inflation," in N. W. Edwards, C. H. Anderson, B. J. Bergiel, and C. Jenkins, eds., *Midwest Marketing Association 1982 Proceedings* (Carbondale, IL: Midwest Marketing Association, 1982), pp. 31–36.
17. John T. Gourville, "Pennies-a-Day: The Effect of Temporal Reframing on Transaction Evaluation, *Journal of Consumer Research,* Vol. 24 (March 1998), pp. 395–408.
18. Ibid.
19. Kent B. Monroe, "Buyers' Subjective Perceptions of Price," *Journal of Marketing Research,* Vol. 10 (February 1973), pp. 70–80.
20. K. Sivakumar and S. P. Raj, "Quality Tier Competition: How Price Change Influences Brand Choice and Category Choice," *Journal of Marketing,* Vol. 61 (July 1997), pp. 71–84.
21. Ibid.
22. William B. Dodds, Kent B. Monroe, and Dhruv Grewal, "Effects of Price, Brand and Store Information on Buyers' Product Evaluations," *Journal of Marketing Research,* Vol. 28 (August 1991), pp. 307–319.
23. George Haines, "A Study of Why People Purchase New Products," in R. M. Haas, ed., *Science, Technology and Marketing* (Chicago: American Marketing Association, 1966), pp. 665–685.
24. David M. Gardner, "Is There a Generalized Price-Quality Relationship?" *Journal of Marketing Research,* Vol. 8 (May 1971), pp. 241–243; James F. Engel, D. A. Knapp, and D. E. Knapp, "Sources of Influence in the Acceptance of New Products for Self-Medication: Preliminary Findings," in R. M. Haas, ed., *Science, Technology and Marketing* (Chicago, IL: American Marketing Association, 1966), pp. 776–782.
25. Dhruv Grewal, Kent B. Monroe, and R. Krishnan, "The Effects of Price-Comparison Advertising on Buyers' Perceptions of Acquisition Value, Transaction Value, and Behavioral Intentions," *Journal of Marketing,* Vol. 62 (April 1998), pp. 46–59.

26. Raymond A. Bauer, "Consumer Behavior as Risk Taking," in Robert S. Hancock, ed., *Dynamic Marketing of a Changing World* (Chicago, IL: American Marketing Association, 1960), pp. 389–398.

27. Paul Chao, "The Moderating Effects of Country of Assembly, Country of Parts, and Country of Design on Hybrid Product Evaluations," *Journal of Advertising*, Vol. 30 (Winter 2001), pp. 67–81.

28. "Cairene Shoppers' Intifada," *The Economist*, November 4, 2000.

29. Ellen C. Garbarino and Julie A. Edell, "Cognitive Effort, Affect and Choice," *Journal of Consumer Research*, Vol. 24 (September 1997), pp. 147–158.

30. Chakravarti and Janiszewski, "The Influence of Macro-Level Motives."

31. Michel Laroche, Chankon Kim, and Takayoshi Matsui, "Which Decision Heuristics Are Used in Consideration Set Formation," *Journal of Consumer Marketing*, Vol. 20, No. 3 (2003), pp. 192–209.

32. Dennis Gensch, "A Two-Stage Disaggregate Attribute Choice Model," *Marketing Science*, Vol. 6 (Summer 1987), pp. 223–231; Peter Wright and Frederick Barbour, "Phased Decision Strategies: Sequels to Initial Screening," in Martin Starr and Milan Zeleny, eds., *Multiple Criteria Decision Making: TIMS Studies in the Management Sciences* (Amsterdam: North-Holland, 1977), pp. 91–109.

33. Richard W. Stevenson, "The Brands with Billion-Dollar Names," *The New York Times* (October 28, 1988), p. A1.

34. Ronald Alsop, "Enduring Brands Hold Their Allure by Sticking Close to Their Roots," *The Wall Street Journal*, centennial edition (1989), p. B4.

35. Amna Kirmani, Sanjay Sood, and Sheri Bridges, "The Ownership Effect in Consumer Responses to Brand Line Stretching," *Journal of Marketing*, Vol. 63 (January 1999), pp. 88–101.

36. H. Beales, M. B. Jagis, S. C. Salop, and R. Staelin, "Consumer Search and Public Policy," *Journal of Consumer Research*, Vol. 8 (June 1981), pp. 11–22.

37. Gary T. Ford and Ruth Ann Smith, "Inferential Beliefs in Consumer Evaluations: An Assessment of Alternative Processing Strategies," *Journal of Consumer Research*, Vol. 14 (December 1987), pp. 363–371; Gary L. Sullivan and Kenneth J. Berger, "An Investigation of Determinants of Cue Utilization," *Psychology and Marketing*, Vol. 4 (Spring 1987), pp. 63–74.

38. Beales et al., "Consumer Search and Public Policy."

39. Sankar Sen and Eric J. Johnson, "Mere-Possession Effects without Possession in Consumer Choice," *Journal of Consumer Research*, Vol. 24 (June 1997), pp. 105–117.

40. Ibid.

41. POPAI/*DuPont Consumer Buying Habits Study* (New York: Point-of-Purchase Advertising Institute, 1987).

42. F. Thomas Juster, "Consumer Buying Intentions and Purchase Probability: An Experiment in Survey Design," in *Consumer Buying Intentions and Purchase Probability* (New York: Columbia University Press, 1966).

43. Donald H. Branbois and Ronald P. Willett, "An Empirical Test of Probabilistic Intentions and Preference Models for Consumer Durables Purchasing," in Robert L. King, ed., *Marketing and the New Science of Planning: Proceedings of the 1968 Conference of the American Marketing Association* (Chicago: American Marketing Association, 1968), pp. 401–408.

44. David T. Kollat and Ronald P. Willett, "Is Impulse Purchasing a Useful Concept for Marketing Decisions?" *Journal of Marketing*, Vol. 51 (Spring 1987), pp. 79–83.

45. V. Kanti Prasad, "Unplanned Buying in Two Retail Settings," *Journal of Retailing*, Vol. 51 (Fall 1975), pp. 3–12.

46. Hawkins Stern, "The Significance of Impulse Buying Today," *Journal of Marketing*, Vol. 26 (April 1962), pp. 59–62.

47. *Supermarket Shoppers in a Period of Economic Uncertainty* (New York: Yankelovich, Skelly and White, Inc, 1982), p. 53.

48. "The Teen Market," *Product Marketing*, (Spring 1987), p. S–26.

49. Joe A. Dodson, Alice M. Tybout, and Brian Sternthal, "Impact of Deals and Deal Retraction on Brand Switching," *Journal of Marketing Research*, Vol. 15 (February 1978), pp. 72–81.

50. Mark M. Moriarity, "Retail Promotion Effects on Intra- and Interbrand Sales Performance," *Journal of Retailing*, Vol. 61 (Fall 1985), pp. 27–47.

51. Kevin J. Clancy, "Getting Serious about Building Profitable Online Retail Brands," *Retailing Issues Letter*, Vol. 12 (November 2000), p. 1.

52. "Indicators—Online Spending," *Time*, December 19, 1999, p. 26.

53. Dodds, Monroe, and Grewal, "Effects of Price, Brand and Store Information on Buyers' Product Evaluation."

54. J. J. Kasulis and Robert F. Lusch, "Validating the Retail Store Image Concept," *Journal of Marketing*, Vol. 45 (Fall 1981), pp. 419–435.

55. Pierre Martineau, "The Personality of the Retail Store," *Harvard Business Review*, Vol. 36 (January–February 1958), p. 47.

56. Jay D. Lindquist, "Meaning of Image," *Journal of Retailing*, Vol. 50 (Winter 1974–75), pp. 29–38; also see R. Hansen and T. Deutscher, "An Empirical Investigation of Attribute Importance in Retail Store Selection," *Journal of Retailing*, Vol. 53 (Winter 1977–78), pp. 59–73; M. R. Zimmer and L. L. Golden, "Impressions of Retail Stores," *Journal of Retailing*, Vol. 64 (Fall 1988), pp. 265–293.

57. Anna S. Mattila and Jochen Wirtz, "Congruency of Scent and Music as a Driver of In-store Evaluations and Behavior," *Journal of Retailing*, Vol. 77, No. 2 (2001), pp. 273–299.

58. Dhruv Grewal, Julie Baker, Michael Levy, and Glenn B. Voss, "The Effects of Wait Expectations and Store Atmosphere Evaluations on Patronage Intentions in Service-Intensive Retail Stores," *Journal of Retailing*, Vol. 79, No. 4, (2003) pp. 259–268.

59. James R. Lumpkin, Barnett A. Greenberg, and Jack L. Goldstucker, "Marketplace Needs of the Elderly," *Journal of Retailing*, Vol. 61 (Summer 1985), pp. 75–103.

60. Paul M. Lane and Jay D. Lindquist, "Hospital Choice: A Summary of the Key Empirical and Hypothetical Findings of the 1980's," *Journal of Health Care Marketing*, Vol. 8 (December 1988), pp. 5–20.

61. Elizabeth Hirshman and Michael K. Mills, "Sources Shoppers Use to Pick Stores," *Journal of Advertising Research*, Vol. 20 (February 1980), pp. 47–51.

62. *A Study of Consumer Response to Advertising*, National Technical Information Service, U.S. Department of Commerce (PB80–128507).

63. Ibid.

64. Raj Mehta and Eugene Sivadas, "Direct Marketing on the Internet: An Empirical Assessment of Consumer Attitudes," *Journal of Direct Marketing*, Vol. 9 (Summer 1995), pp. 21–32.

65. Edward A. Blair and E. Laird Landon, Jr., "The Effects of Reference Prices on Retail Advertisements," *Journal of Marketing*, Vol. 45 (Spring 1981), pp. 61–69; William O. Bearden, Donald R. Lichtenstein, and Jesse E. Teel, "Comparison Price, Coupon and Brand Effects on Consumer Reactions to Retail Newspaper Advertisements," *Journal of Retailing*, Vol. 60 (Summer 1984), pp. 11–34; Donald R. Lichtenstein and William O. Bearden, "Contextual Influences on Perceptions of Merchant-Supplied Reference Prices," *Journal of Consumer Research*, Vol. 16 (June 1989), pp. 55–66; Paul M. Herr, "Priming Price," *Journal of Consumer Research*, Vol. 16 (June 1989), pp. 67–75.

66. Edward A. Blair, Judy Harris, and Kent B. Monroe, "Effects of Shopping Information on Consumers' Response to Comparative Price Claims," *Journal of Retailing*, Vol. 78, No. 3 (2002), pp. 175–182.

67. C. Samuel Craig, Avijit Ghosh, and Sara McLafferty, "Models of the Retail Location Process: A Review," *Journal of Retailing*, Vol. 60 (Spring 1984), pp. 5–33; Robert Ellinger and Jay D. Lindquist, "The Gravity Model: A Study of Retail Goods Classification and Multiple Goods Shopping Effect," in Thomas Kinnear, ed., *Advances in Consumer Research*, Vol. 11 (Chicago, IL: Association for Consumer Research, 1984), pp. 391–395; Roy D. Howell and Jerry D. Rogers, "Research into Shopping Mall Choice Behavior," in Kent B. Monroe, ed., *Advances in Consumer Research*, Vol. 8 (Chicago, IL: Association for Consumer Research, 1981), pp. 671–676.

68. W. Papadopoulos, "Consumer Outshopping Research: Review and Extension," *Journal of Retailing*, Vol. 56 (Winter 1980), pp. 41–58; Robert Williams, "Outshopping: Problem or Opportunity," *Arizona Business*, (October–November 1981), pp. 8–11.

69. Robert J. Donovan and John R. Rossiter, "Store Atmosphere: An Environmental Psychology Approach," *Journal of Retailing*, Vol. 58 (Spring 1982), pp. 34–56.

70. Robert A. Westbrook and William C. Black, "A Motivation-Based Shopper Topology," *Journal of Retailing*, Vol. 61 (Spring 1985), pp. 78–102.

71. Edward M. Taylor, "Why Do People Shop?" *Journal of Marketing*, Vol. 36 (October 1972), pp. 46–59.

72. Kenneth R. Evans, Tim Christiansen, and James D. Gill, "The Impact of Social Influence and Role Expectations on Shopping Center Patronage Intentions," *Journal of the Academy of Marketing Science*, Vol. 24 (Summer 1996), pp. 208–218.

73. Mark J. Arnold and Kristy E. Reynolds, "Hedonic Shopping Motivations," *Journal of Retailing*, Vol. 79, No. 2 (2003), pp. 77–95.

74. William R. Darden and Roy D. Howell, "Socialization Effects of Retail Work Experience on Shopping Orientations," *Journal of the Academy of Marketing Science*, Vol. 15 (Fall 1987), pp. 52–63.

75. Soyeon Shim, Mary Ann Eastlick, and Sherry Lotz, "Assessing the Impact of Internet Shopping on Store Shopping," *Journal of Shopping Center Research*, Vol. 7 (Fall/Winter 2000), pp. 7–44.

76. Stanley C. Hollander and Kathleen M. Rassuli, "Shopping with Other People's Money: The Marketing Management Implications of Surrogate-Mediated Consumer Decision Making," *Journal of Marketing*, Vol. 63 (April 1999), pp. 102–118.

77. Nicole Crawford, "Shopping for Segments," *PROMO Magazine*, September 1997, pp. 77ff.

78. Jay D. Lindquist, William W. Keep, and Robert W. Dahlstrom, "Consumer Shopping Process Benefits: Shopping Centers Versus Catalogs," *Marketing Management Journal*, Vol. 10 (Spring/Summer 2000), pp. 131–141.

79. Brian Wansink, Robert J. Kent, and Stephen J. Hoch, "An Anchoring and Adjustment Model of Purchase Quantity Decisions," *Journal of Marketing Research*, Vol. 35 (February 1998), pp. 71–81.

Consumption and Post-Purchase Behavior

4

Michelle is thrilled to be invited to join a small group of friends on a four-day nature trek in the mountains. Nervous that she'll be a terrible camper, Michelle makes a number of purchases she thinks she'll need for the trip. She ends up buying far more than she expected, but feels ready for an experience of a lifetime. A month later, Michelle opens her credit card bill and frowns. It was great to spend so much time with her friends, but she now knows that camping is not her thing. The sleeping bag, though warm and cozy, was far heavier than the ones her friends had. She didn't really need a compass or a penknife—she'd bought really good ones—and her flashlight flickered on and off whenever she tried to use it. Worst of all, the brand-name hiking boots she stretched her budget to buy gave her blisters on the first day. On the bright side, Michelle loves the jacket she bought for the trip and knows she'll wear it often. She returns the compass and the penknife for store credit. She isn't as lucky with the flashlight—the store insists that she must have dropped it and tells her if she wants to take the matter any further, she'll have to contact the manufacturer. It's the last time Michelle will shop there.

At some time or other, we all have mixed feelings about the purchases we make or the places we shop. Michelle's camping experiences demonstrate, among other things, that the relationship between buyer and seller does not end with the sale. Both during and after actual consumption, the consumer's experience with and feelings toward a brand continue to develop, influencing future buying decisions. In this chapter, we explore what happens during and after consumption, looking in particular at its effect on customer satisfaction and future buying decisions.

4-1 Product and Service Consumption

Consumption, in its broadest and simplest sense, is the possession and/or use of goods and services and the benefits they deliver. The reasons for using these products and services and the ways in which we use them are, however, quite complex. Though consumption is not one of the five steps in the consumer high-involvement decision process, it is discussed

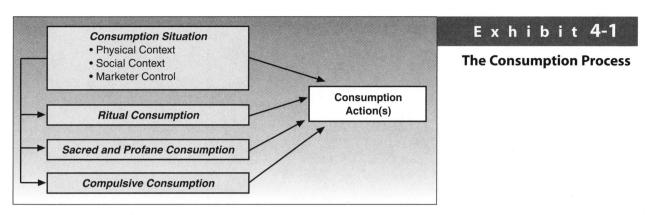

E x h i b i t 4-1

The Consumption Process

here because it impacts on post-purchase evaluation, which will be presented later in this chapter.

Consumption and lifestyle are inseparable. Quite simply, as our lifestyles change, so do the things we purchase and use. Lifestyle is discussed in depth in Chapter 6. Think of the typical **consumption set**—the mix of goods and services acquired and used—of young teenagers: games, sports gear, bubble gum, teen magazines, and pop posters. Now compare this with the consumption set as these same teenagers reach their college years: Nintendo and Sega give way to work- and study-related software packages; theme park outings are replaced by ski weekends and camping trips; and preferences for candy and sweet soft drinks wane. Other lifestyle changes—a move from a city to a rural community, a job straight out of college in a high-pressure business environment, an inheritance, or marriage—also bring with them changes in consumption sets. Sometimes the changes are immediate and obvious; other times they are so gradual that we're barely aware of them.

Consumption and the culture in which we live are also closely connected, again influencing the consumption set. In some instances, culture literally dictates consumption choices. In certain Islamic nations, for example, the type of clothing style to be worn by women is prescribed by the culture, and stores carry only those styles considered appropriate. In other instances, the influences of our culture and subculture are more subtle, impacting such things as the foods we eat and the cars we drive. Our choices are less our own than we think. The influences of culture and subculture will be presented in Chapters 11, 12, and 13. Exhibit 4-1 summarizes various components of the consumption process, including the consumption situation and ritual, sacred and profane, and compulsive consumption.

4-1a Consumption Situation

As these observations on lifestyle and culture demonstrate, given different situations, we buy and use different products. The **consumption situation** is the physical and social context in which we actually use goods and services purchased. The **physical context** is simply the time and place of consumption. Suppose you're at the ballpark watching the Red Sox against the Tigers. Hawkers are selling hot dogs, Coca-Cola, and peanuts. Usually you don't eat hot dogs, but you'll do it at the game. Why? Because it is a part of the total ballpark experience. At the New Orleans Blues and Jazz Festival, you join in the spirit of the occasion by buying and wearing a festival T-shirt. In both cases, an atypical situation leads to an atypical purchase.

In these examples, both the purchase and the situation are out of the ordinary, yet even with everyday purchases, situation affects consumer behavior. Compare how you might behave while having your hair styled by a celebrated stylist in an upscale salon with your behavior toward a local hair stylist. How would you speak and interact with each stylist? The difference in behavior arises from the difference in physical context.

The presence of others gives the consumption situation a **social context**. That is, who are you with while you are consuming a product or service? Consciously or subconsciously, we behave differently around different types of people. Having dinner with

consumption (see p. 100) The possession and/or use of goods and services and the benefits they deliver.

consumption set The mix of goods and services acquired and used by a person, household, or other group.

consumption situation The physical and social context in which we actually use goods and services purchased.

physical (consumption) context The time and place of consumption of a good or service.

social (consumption) context The presence of others when consumption occurs.

The consumption situation influences the consumer's behavior. This advertisement portrays both the physical context of consumption and a social context.

Source: Reprinted by permission of Lake of the Ozarks.

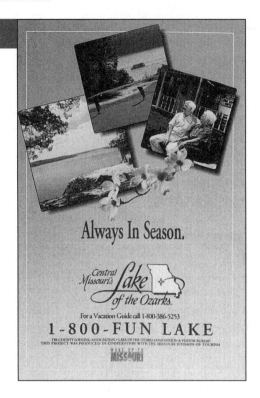

consumption episode
The set of items consumed belonging to the same event and occurring in temporal proximity.

consumption system
A bundle of goods and services that are consumed over time in multiple episodes.

family, for example, makes us act differently than we act when having dinner with new acquaintances, with colleagues, with friends who are vegetarians, or with children. In what we consume and how we consume, we are influenced by the people around us. We modify our choices and our behavior accordingly. Just think how differently you'd behave when shopping for clothes with friends than when shopping with your parents—especially if they're paying! Look at the advertisement in Exhibit 4-2 for vacations in the Lake of the Ozarks area. In what ways does the marketer use physical and social consumption contexts to appeal to the seniors market?

The concept of a **consumption episode** fits nicely with this discussion on the consumption situation. Such an episode is defined as "the set of items belonging to the same event and occurring in temporal proximity."[1] An example of this would be having an appetizer, a salad, a main course, a dessert, and a cup of coffee at the same restaurant. Going to the movies on a date and having popcorn, some M&M's, and an Orange Slice is another consumption episode. The marketer understands that these items "go together" and often will package them at a discount. Some universities put together a "family package" for a Saturday afternoon outing to watch a football game. Four tickets, four hot dogs, four Coca-Colas, and four pompoms are offered.

You can also put together a number of related consumption episodes. When done, this is called a **consumption system.** More specifically, a consumption system is defined as "a bundle of goods and services that are consumed over time in multiple episodes."[2] Of course, these goods and services are themselves bundles of benefits that the consumer is truly buying. The decision to combine episodes into a system is a matter of judgment and/or degree. What is an example of such a system? One that is very common is tied to the purchase or lease of a new car. In this case, the consumer is likely to be considering the choice of a dealer who not only will provide the car but will also be there to offer regular maintenance and repair work. Over the life of a three-year lease, for example, there may be oil changes and tire rotations done at regular intervals plus 15,000- and 30,000-mile services. In between, various problems could arise that require attention. The latter are usually covered under a warranty, so part of the lease decision will hinge on this. Certainly, people could have their oil changed at "Uncle Ed's" and other places, and tire rotations may be done cheaper at "Discount Tire." Still, the idea of purchasing a system is reasonable, and its various episode components are likely part of the "choice" decision. Later in this chapter, we'll deal with the impact of the consumption system on satisfaction.

From all these examples, it is clear that by understanding the consumption situation, marketers are better able to match their goods and services to the physical and social episodic contexts in which they are used. By positioning products on these bases, promotional messages, mood, copy, and visuals all fall in place to emphasize physical and social situations that encourage and reinforce desired behaviors. However, it is easier for marketers to influence some consumption situations than others. Consumption situations can be classified into three types according to the level of control the marketer has over them: extensive control, limited control, and no control at all.

Extensive Marketer Control   In many cases, particularly in the marketing of services, the marketer is present during consumption and can both watch and influence how it plays out. Visits to the dentist or auto mechanic, a round of golf, a horseback riding lesson, or a stay at a motel are all such situations. A restaurant proprietor, for example, can control the consumption experience of diners in several ways—the atmosphere, the type of service, and the presentation of the food can all guide the diner toward a certain type of consumption behavior and experience.

Physical attributes of the service situation also influence behavior. Location, design, decor, lighting, sounds, and cleanliness are all important. A restaurant located in a noisy shopping center, with a playground for kids, plastic tables, and bright lights, induces a very different type of behavior from customers than does a candlelit cafe with linen tablecloths and napkins, plush carpets, and soft background music. All of these physical attributes are controlled by the marketer and are selected according to the type of customers targeted and the type of consumption behavior expected from them.

Limited Marketer Control   For the types of goods and services that are usually consumed close to the place of purchase, marketers can easily see and to some extent influence the consumption situation. Outdoor vendors of ice cream, submarine sandwiches, and other snacks all offer products that are meant to be consumed on the spot. Sporting events and outdoor concerts attract marketers of this type of product, along with vendors of baseball caps, T-shirts, or sunglasses. In each of these situations, marketers have the opportunity to watch how their products are consumed and improve or promote them accordingly. They can use the knowledge gained to attract more customers.

No Marketer Control   The consumption situation for the majority of goods is away from the place of purchase. For cars, clothes, electronics, computers, books, and a host of other everyday products, the act of consumption takes place elsewhere, and the marketer has virtually no control over the situation or location in which the products are used. Rather than view the reactions of customers firsthand, marketers rely on customer feedback to determine how their products are used, how well they perform, and how closely they meet the expectations of consumers.

4-1b Ritual Consumption

A useful way of classifying certain types of consumption is through the rituals associated with them. *Rituals* are patterns of behavior tied to events that we consider important in our lives. Rituals usually have some special symbolic meaning to us, occur in a fixed or predictable sequence, and are repeated with some regularity.[3] A ritual may be as infrequent as a marriage, involving all kinds of goods and services from the purchase of an engagement ring through the honeymoon trip, or it can be as regular as a Thanksgiving Day turkey dinner, with very predictable purchases associated with it. It might even be an everyday occurrence, such as the bedtime story from Dr. Seuss for the little one each evening. Hence, **ritual consumption** is the consumption of goods and services that is tied to specific rituals.

Because rituals involve the use of goods and services, it is important for marketers to understand them and the ritualistic behaviors they give rise to. A complete discussion of rituals, ritual consumption, ritual artifacts, and ritual types is presented in Chapter 11.

F A Q

People behave differently at outdoor events—like an open-air music festival—than they behave at indoor venues. Why?

F A Q

Can marketers create rituals? Have they done so?

▶ **ritual consumption**
Consumption of goods and services that is tied to specific rituals.

4-1c Sacred and Profane Consumption

sacred consumption
Consumption that occurs during out-of-the-ordinary situations.

profane consumption
Consumption of goods or services that is part of everyday life.

desacralization What occurs when the consumer transforms objects, places, people, and events from the sacred to the profane. Sacralization is the reverse action.

sacralization What occurs when the consumer transforms objects, places, people, and events from the profane to the sacred. Desacralization is the reverse action.

Another way of classifying consumption behavior is by considering the extent to which it is typical of the consumer's everyday lifestyle. Obviously, consumption tied to holidays and rites of passage is not. These and other special events are considered **sacred consumption;** those that are a part of everyday life are considered **profane consumption.**[4] Because of its etymology, the word "sacred" has religious overtones and has traditionally been tied to objects, places, behaviors, special days, and seasons with religious meaning. Some marketers, however, give the term a much broader application, covering any objects, places, behaviors, days, or seasons that have special meanings to any individual or group of individuals.

What is quickly apparent is that, depending on the consumer and the situation, what is sacred to one will be profane to another. Moreover, as cultures and other social groups change over time, the processes of **desacralization** (losing sacred status) or **sacralization** (gaining sacred status) occur. A good example of desacralization is the consumption of souvenirs. For example, miniatures of the Statue of Liberty, once a sacred symbol in the United States, are mass-produced and sold as cheap remembrances. Similarly, the Christian cross, once used only in religious contexts, is now widely used as jewelry, on T-shirts, and in other nonreligious situations.[5] Religious holidays, too, are frequently dominated by family activities rather than religious observance. Christmas is one example. Originally, the celebration of the birth of Christ was paramount at Christmas, but today evergreen trees, giving of gifts, Santa Claus, Rudolph, and secular songs are a major part of the holiday for many people. To relive experiences that are sacred to them, people use souvenir icons. These can be photographs, videos, postcards, pieces of music, or artifacts.[6] Gift shops in the United States alone sell in excess of twenty billion such artifacts or souvenirs a year.[7]

Sacralization occurs when objects, places, people, and events are transformed from the profane to the sacred. A piece of original handwritten sheet music by Mozart, an article of clothing worn by George Washington, the footprint of the Buddha, one of Eric Clapton's guitars, and pieces of the Berlin Wall have all become sacred and, hence, of value to those who consider them such. Places become sacred when significant events occur there. Mecca (a center of the Muslim faith), Mount Vernon (George Washington's residence), Hollywood's Walk of Fame, the Louvre Museum in Paris or the Prado Museum in Madrid, the Biltmore Mansion (a Vanderbilt estate), the Bunker Hill battlefield from the Revolutionary War, the Anasazi Indian dwellings in Colorado, the site of the World Trade Center in New York City (because of the 9/11 events), and even Disneyland are examples of places that have been sacralized. Because of their power to attract visitors, such locations become industries unto themselves. In many cultures, the home is a sacred place. The refuge of the family, it is considered a reflection of family identity.[8] Marketing of goods and services to protect the home and reinforce its sacredness is a thriving business.

Throughout history, people like Abraham Lincoln, Muhammad Ali, Anne Frank, Marilyn Monroe, the Beatles, and many movie and music stars have been sacralized. Their possessions, places of birth, residences, and other objects and places associated with them have become valuable to own or visit. The product featured in Exhibit 4-3, a collector's plate, shows how rock singer Elvis Presley and all products associated with him have become sacred for certain consumer groups.

Events, too, can be sacred. Religious events or rituals, as we have seen, are an obvious example. To some people, vacation time is sacred. When they travel, they are in search of special or authentic experiences that take them out of their everyday existences.[9] Tour providers understand and market in response to this need. In sports, such events as the Olympic Games, the World Cup, the Super Bowl, the Americas Cup, the World Series, the Indianapolis 500, and the Tour de France have become sacralized by various segments around the world.

Look again at these examples of sacred and profane consumption. Think of ways in which the goods and services around you are positioned to appeal as sacred products to targeted consumers. Can you name a product that you personally have sacralized? Why did

Exhibit 4-3

Here, a collector's plate, "The King," appeals to those who have sacralized Elvis Presley. By offering products like this, the marketer supports the process of sacralization.

Source: Reprinted by permission of The Bradford Exchange and Elvis Presley Enterprises, Inc.

you do so? In some instances there is no "line" between ritual consumption and sacred consumption. Can you think of some examples when this would happen?

4-1d Compulsive Consumption

Compulsive consumption is "a response to an uncontrollable drive or desire to obtain, use, or experience a feeling, substance, or activity that leads the individual to repetitively engage in behavior that will ultimately cause harm to the individual and/or others."[10] It has been suggested that such behavior is found among consumers who come from families where one or more of the following are found: abuse of alcohol or other forms of substance abuse, physical violence, divorce, separation, or other types of emotional conflict.[11] Compulsive consumers are less concerned with the economic value or utility of their purchases than with a sense of increased self-esteem or the ability to have increased levels of interaction with other people.[12] We find this at the high school and university level in the United States. Here, young people, especially those looking to "fit in," may find themselves feeling obligated, at least at first, to smoke, use smokeless tobacco, or consume alcohol or other drugs. Take a look at Marketplace 4-1. It addresses an alcohol-related compulsive consumption problem on college and university campuses. A discussion of reference group peer pressure impact on consumer behavior will be found in Chapter 14.

There is considerable evidence that children from single-parent families have a higher propensity to engage in alcohol and substance abuse than do children from two-parent families.[13] Family structure is related to both compulsive consumption and the desire for material goods. According to one study, young adults whose parents are divorced or separated show higher levels of both of these behaviors than do young adults whose parents are together.[14] A more recent investigation did not find the same significant and positive relationship between family structure issues and compulsive buying,[15] so the jury is still out on such connections. A study of male and female shoppers in Israel showed that those who scored higher in compulsivity made more unplanned purchases and were more likely to be female. Also, compulsive buyers had lower self-esteem, a higher tendency to fantasize, and higher levels of depression, anxiety, and obsession tendency than did less compulsive buyers.[16] Compulsive consumption and its marketplace and societal implications are pursued in more depth in Chapter 17.

> **compulsive consumption**
> A response to an uncontrollable drive or desire to obtain, use, or experience a feeling, substance, or activity that leads the individual to repetitively engage in behavior that will ultimately cause harm to the individual and/or others.

Marketplace 4-1

Young Female Drinkers Compete with Male Counterparts

Citing feminism as a reason for her actions, one representative of the emerging group of U.S. women and girls aged teens to early 20s engaging in excess drinking of alcoholic beverages (defined as consuming more than four drinks in a row) hopes to take her place beside—or even outpace—the guys. For this 22-year-old woman, whom we'll call "Sarah," a major goal for her senior year in college is to "drink a guy under the table."

Common consequences of this social phenomenon include the following for this age group of women and girls:

- Alcohol poisoning
- Physical injury from falls when drunk
- Sexual assault
- Hospitalization
- Susceptibility to alcoholism

According to a 1990s study of high school–age girls and boys:

1. Girls in the current generation are four times as likely as their mothers to begin drinking by age 16.
2. Girls who begin drinking in their early teens are more likely than their male counterparts to become alcoholics.

3. Ninth-grade girls are as likely as their male counterparts to drink alcohol.
4. Over a less-than-10-year period, girls who had ranked almost 10 percentage points behind boys in binge drinking (22.4 percent to 31.4 percent, respectively) narrowed the gap to 2 percentage points.

For "Sarah" and her female cohorts, the payoff for risking the consequences of excess drinking apparently comes from winning something more important to them: impressing the guys. In "Sarah's" words, it's a "badge of honor." Her reasoning calls to question whether she has given deep thought to how taking risks as a woman solely to impress men can correspond with feminism or whether she truly understands what feminism means.

In striving to guide and protect the young, educators and government agencies—as well as parents and concerned others—face a challenge. Marketers of alcohol can join in this challenge to display their own "badge of honor." How could these groups and individuals work together and/or singly to stem this troubling tide?

Source: Adapted from Jodie Morse, "Women on a Binge," *Time,* April 1, 2002, pp. 56–61.

Marketing Management—Implications and Actions

Understanding consumption behavior helps marketers:

- Respond to changing consumer consumption sets with new products and promotions.
- Position products to match the physical and social contexts of the consumption situation.
- Develop and market products around needs triggered by consumer rituals as well as by consumer views of products as sacred or profane.

4-2 Consumption Effects on Consumer Satisfaction

As we begin the new millennium, there is likely no topic closer to the hearts of marketers than customer satisfaction. This is the case because satisfaction is the key to the long-term relationships that provide benefits to both sides of the buyer-seller equation. The number of purchase options open to consumers in almost all product and service categories continues to increase at such an alarming rate that fewer and fewer are unique or exclusive to a single marketer. Moreover, as the cost of attracting new customers escalates, it is more important than ever to keep current customers and others like them coming back for additional purchases. Increasingly, it is the consumer, not the marketer, who is in control. Exhibit 4-4 is a flowchart that shows the connections among expectations, outcomes, satisfaction level, customer characteristics, other factors, and marketer actions to promote customer satisfaction.

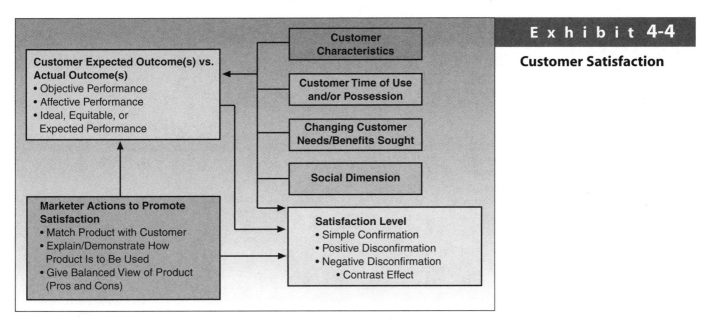

Customer Satisfaction

It is easy to see why customer satisfaction is so important. Quite simply, if we're happy with a product or service purchased, we're likely to buy it again, as well as select other products offered by the same marketer. In the best cases, we even tell our friends about the product, and they buy it, too. On the other hand, if we're not happy with a purchase, we'll not only write off that product but everything from that marketer—and we'll advise our friends to do the same. What product and service industries are consumers in America more satisfied or less satisfied with? The American Customer Satisfaction Index, the only cross-industry index of customer satisfaction in the United States, was first measured in 1994. The Retail Index in the fourth quarter of that year was 73.6 on a 100-point scale.[17] It then moved steadily down through 1997. Since that time this quarterly measure has been moving generally upward, and the Retail Index for the fourth quarter of 2003 stood at 75.0. A newly developed index for e-commerce retail began in the third quarter of 2000 at 78.0, and the latest reported data, the fourth quarter of 2003, shows a Retail Index of 84.0.[18] If you compare this to the Retail Index for commerce other than e-commerce you see that the e-commerce index is 10 points higher. Why do you think this is the case? Further, industries such as the soft drink industry and the apparel industry and organizations such as electric utilities, hospitals, and even the Internal Revenue Service are separately scored by consumers. Traditional companies continue to score well on product quality, but they are about 10 points behind e-commerce on service.[19] Check out Marketplace 4-2 for a listing of a number of satisfaction ratings.

But how do marketers, particularly those who are remote from customers and do not see the way in which their products are used, find out just how satisfied or dissatisfied customers are with the different aspects of their products? How do they go about increasing levels of satisfaction? In this section, we'll work toward answering these questions.

4-2a Satisfaction versus Dissatisfaction

As explained in Chapters 1–3, long before we make a final purchase, we build expectations about desired products and services concerning the benefits they will provide and the needs they should fulfill. The moment a product is purchased and used, we begin to judge it. The level of satisfaction or dissatisfaction we experience depends upon how well the product's performance meets our expectations.[20] That is, what is the perceived difference between expected performance, called "expectation," and actual or perceived performance, called "realization"? If a product or service performs as well as or better than expected, we're happy; if it falls short of our expectations, we're not. A finite time period

Marketplace 4-2

American Customer Satisfaction with Selected Industries

Americans' overall satisfaction with goods and services has varied up and down over the past five years. The *American Customer Satisfaction Index* is a measure of this satisfaction. The data comes from more than fifty thousand consumer surveys across more than three thousand brands from nearly two hundred companies and government agencies. Thirty-four industries are scored. Here are some selected industry scores. The maximum overall satisfaction score is 100. The following results are from the first quarter of the year 2000.

Industry	Customer Satisfaction Score
Beverages (soft drinks)	84
Consumer electronics	83
Household appliances	82
Apparel	79
Automobiles	78
Gasoline (service stations)	76
Insurance (life)	76
Athletic shoes	76

Industry	Customer Satisfaction Score
Utilities (electric service)	75
Supermarkets	74
Telecommunication (local and long-distance)	72
Personal computers	72
U.S. Postal Service	72
Hospitals	69
Motion pictures	68
Police service (central cities)	64
Broadcasting (TV network news)	64
Airlines (scheduled)	63
Internal Revenue Service (IRS)	51

The highest rating was soft drinks, with consumer electronics and household appliances very close. As you can see, the IRS had the lowest satisfaction rating at 51.

Source: From "American Customer Satisfaction Holding Steady" from *The Wirthlin Report,* Vol. 10, June 2000, p. 1. Reprinted by permission of Wirthlin Worldwide.

of possession and/or use is necessary to determine satisfaction. This could be a matter of microseconds in the case of a server at a restaurant placing food in front of you, the look or odor of which immediately repels you, or it could take three years for you to decide that the car you're driving is a brand you'll never buy again because of the amount of time it spends in the repair shop.

Satisfaction is not easily measured, for a number of reasons. First, *it means different things to different people.* While some are quick to complain about even minor shortcomings, others are more tolerant. The exact same level of performance can be judged either satisfactory or unsatisfactory, depending upon the person experiencing it and the situation in which he or she is found. Second, *one's level of satisfaction can change, for better or worse, over time.* In some situations, we know immediately if a product meets our expectations—a new pair of running shoes feels great during the first few weeks of wear. In others, it takes time to make that judgment—the same shoes wear down too quickly at the heels and are soon too uncomfortable for jogging. Third, *satisfaction can change when consumer needs and preferences change.* A product that is perfectly acceptable one month can fail to satisfy the next, as lifestyle, tastes, or needs change. Finally, there also *appears to be a "social dimension" to satisfaction.* That is, the expressed satisfaction of other relevant members of a household with the consumer's choice often adds to his or her satisfaction.[21] Researchers also found that "it was not comparison standards matched against performance perceptions that mattered most . . . what carried most weight were the meanings and emotions [of the] consumers' usage experiences.[22]

A recent review of the major findings concerning satisfaction found three general components. The first is that consumer satisfaction is primarily emotional, though sometimes cognitive. Consumers describe feelings (emotional) about their satisfaction with a product or service in a number of positive and negative ways, including "like," "love," "excited," "pleasantly surprised," "relieved," "helpless," "cheated," and "neutral." Second, the response has a particular focus, or object, such as the product, its consumption, the purchase decision, the salesperson, or the store/acquisition. Finally, the timing of the response is an issue. A product or service may be evaluated after it is chosen but before it is actually purchased. It may occur before a choice is made or even when a choice has not yet been made. An example of the latter would be when a consumer is dissatisfied with a store in another town that he or she has never patronized, because it put a local store out of business. Also since satisfaction varies over time it can only be determined at the time it is measured.[23]

An interesting finding concerning satisfaction measurement is that "merely measuring it" seems to have some impact on customers. Though the results are preliminary, an influence of such a measurement on actual customer behavior appears to occur. Those asked about satisfaction made new purchases in a shorter time period after their initial purchase than did those customers who were not asked to rate satisfaction. This persisted over several months and in some cases over a year.[24] Also, is there a relationship between how the employee feels satisfaction with the encounter with the customer and the resulting satisfaction of the customer? "Encounter satisfaction" does appear to be based on both the customer and the employee view of what happened. In a furniture company retail outlet in the Netherlands, measuring social competence and task competence of the employee from the viewpoint of the employee and the customer showed that if both felt positive there was greater customer satisfaction.[25]

Does this finding ring true to you? Would it apply in your home country? In summary, we must admit that at this time exactly what satisfaction is and how it is to be measured are not fully settled issues.

4-2b Relationship between Expectation and Satisfaction

To narrow the gap between expectations and product experience, the first step is to understand exactly what benefits consumers expect, whether they are promised by the marketer or not. In other words, the marketer must discover which requirements the product actually meets and which it does not. To do so, it is useful to classify product experiences into three types, according to the degree to which the consumer's expectations are fulfilled. This is known as **expectancy disconfirmation**.[26] That is, if realization—actual or perceived performance in terms of possession and/or use—does not match expectation, what the consumer thought would happen is not confirmed. The term "disconfirmation" is used to indicate this condition. "Confirmation" indicates a match. With *simple confirmation,* the purchase performs as expected, resulting in satisfaction. *Positive disconfirmation* occurs when performance is better than expected, leading to a higher level of satisfaction. Should the purchase fall short of expectations, a condition of *negative disconfirmation* occurs, resulting in some level of dissatisfaction. Negative disconfirmation is particularly interesting. It has been found that if there is a wide negative disparity between expectations and actual performance, customers tend to magnify this poor performance. This reaction is known as the **contrast effect**.[27] Because of the contrast effect, the level of dissatisfaction can seem out of proportion with the level of poor performance. Think of times when you have gone to a restaurant or seen a movie that friends raved about but that you did not enjoy at all. The chances are you experienced the contrast effect.

If a consumer experiences a certain level of negative disconfirmation with the performance of a particular attribute, this has a greater impact on the dissatisfaction level than the same level of positive performance of the same attribute would have on the level of satisfaction. This is referred to as an **asymmetric effect**. For example, if you expected a car to give you the feeling of being "a hip professional on the go," and as you drove it you did not have this feeling, your level of dissatisfaction would be greater than the level of satisfaction you would have experienced had the car truly made you feel like such a person. Not only does this negative experience affect your satisfaction with the choice, but it also impacts repurchase intention.[28]

Ideal, Equitable, and Expected Performance   Satisfactory performance may be placed in one of three categories. *Performance is ideal* if a purchase performs as or better than expected.[29] Suppose with a new digital "aim and shoot" camera touted for its great results, you take better pictures than ever before. In this case, ideal performance is both

expectancy disconfirmation What occurs when realization—actual or perceived performance in terms of possession and/or use of a good or service—does not match expectation; what the consumer thought would happen is not confirmed.

contrast effect   The reaction that occurs when there is a wide negative disparity between expectations and actual performance, and customers tend to magnify this poor performance.

asymmetric effect   An imbalance in level of satisfaction. For example, if a consumer experiences a certain level of negative disconfirmation with the performance of a particular product or service attribute, this has a greater impact on the dissatisfaction level than the same level of positive performance of the same attribute would have on the level of satisfaction.

moral equity The extent to which a situation is perceived by an individual to be fair, just, morally right, and acceptable to one's family.

expected and delivered. *Performance is equitable* if it is adequate for the cost and effort the consumer made to obtain the product.[30] This time, you buy an older, used camera, and though the shots are clear, there are tiny scratch marks in the top corner of every print. Still, considering the price paid, performance is fair. *Expected performance*, the lowest level of satisfactory performance, means that although the purchase works out as anticipated, it barely qualifies as satisfactory.[31] Here, you know the camera you're buying is not a particularly good one, but you take it anyway. When your first shots are poor, you're not particularly disappointed, as your expectations were low in the first place.

Obviously, all other things being equal, those who expect ideal performance are more likely to be dissatisfied. Typically, we hold purchases that are important to us or that cost more—both in terms of money and effort—to a higher performance standard than that expected of less important purchases. It is these high-involvement or high-risk products with which we are most likely to be dissatisfied, not because of their poor performance but because of our higher expectations.

Ethical Performance   What do we know about the impact of ethical cues on customer satisfaction? A measure of **moral equity** has been developed, and it includes items reflecting the extent to which a situation is perceived by an individual to be fair, just, morally right, and acceptable to one's family.[32] A study of an automobile repair situation showed that unethical cues from the service provider resulted in sharp reductions of both ethical assessments and satisfaction ratings, but those people who were exposed to an ethical auto repair shop situation did not indicate increased ethical assessments or satisfaction scores.[33] This is a result very similar to the "contrast effect" discussed earlier. This suggests to service marketers that if their everyday way of doing business is ethical there will be no increase in consumer satisfaction, since this is expected, but if they engage in unethical practices there will be a very strong negative response by customers or potential customers. Do you think that these findings could be extended to the marketing of products, political candidates, issues, and the like? Why or why not?

4-2c Relationship between Performance and Satisfaction

objective performance A measure of how well a product or service meets all functional (benefits) expectations.

affective performance A measure of how well the product or service purchased meets the emotional (benefits) expectations (feelings associated with possession and use of product or service) of the buyer.

Two aspects of performance are important to the consumer's satisfaction with the consumption experience. First, **objective performance** is service- or product-related and depends on whether the product or service meets all functional (benefits) expectations.[34] A computer system, for example, is judged on whether it processes as quickly as expected. A watch is judged on whether it keeps good time. Second, **affective performance** is consumer-related and depends on whether the purchase meets the emotional (benefits) expectations (feelings associated with possession and use of product or service) of the buyer.[35] Does my new Pearl Jam CD make me feel as though I'm at a live concert? Do these flying lessons really give me the sense of escape I thought they would? The advertisement for Allstate Life Insurance in Exhibit 4-5, inviting consumers to "Go ahead. Make a wish," promises affective performance, a feeling of security in retirement. Whereas it's usually possible to judge objective performance upon first use of a product, affective performance may take longer to evaluate.

4-2d How Marketers Can Close the Gap between Expectation and Performance

By understanding consumer expectations and the extent to which purchases satisfy them, marketers have a base from which they can work to either increase satisfaction or reduce the chances of dissatisfaction. Closing the gap between expectation and performance begins with matching product benefits to consumer needs. If there is no match or the match is poor, then there is little point in continuing the marketing effort. The product has nothing to offer targeted consumers. This is particularly true for high-risk, high-involvement products. Assuming the needs of targeted consumers and the benefits of the product are a good fit, the way in which the product is presented to the consumer has a great deal to do with the extent to which expectations are met.

This advertisement emphasizes affective performance. By inviting the consumer to "Make a wish," the marketer promises a feeling of security in retirement that can be achieved with the help of Allstate Insurance.

Source: Allstate Insurance Company.

Next, product information and communications must clearly describe not only the benefits of the product but the way in which it is to be used. The consumer should not be led to expect, for example, that an electric drill designed to penetrate wood will also go through steel plate, nor should a car that gets only eighteen miles per gallon in city driving be touted as a twenty-five-mile-per-gallon vehicle. There is a caution here. Sometimes consumers are so intent on purchasing a product or service that they only "hear the good stuff" about their prospective choice. No matter how hard the marketer works to give consumers both the pros and cons of a decision, consumers are often deaf to the cons. Later, if the consumer is dissatisfied, he or she will complain that the seller did not explain the cons, so the challenge is to obtain consumers' attention and get the message to them. This is a case of "Let the seller beware." CBite 4-1 gives a great example of going farther than expected to make sure the customer is satisfied.

CBite 4-1
Doing What's Right and Going the Extra Mile

FedEx was running two days late on a delivery of intravenous tubes for premature babies to an Asheville, North Carolina, hospital. With no hope of speeding up delivery, an employee at FedEx's Asheville station took the matter into her own hands. She found the maker of the tubes in California. Then she obtained the name of the tube manufacturer's dealer for the Southeast. The dealer put FedEx in touch with a Winston-Salem, N.C., hospital that had some of the tubes. The FedEx employee offered to buy them, but the hospital agreed to share its supply. A FedEx truck picked them up and got them to the nursery in time.

During a customer-service seminar, the FedEx managing director of strategic sales systems indicated that the employee did this without asking a manager. There really was no one to ask, so she did it on her own. He said, "That's the secret at FedEx. We create an environment where people do what's right and go that extra mile."

Source: From Jeff Sturgeon, "Companies strive to relearn art of satisfying customers," *The Roanoke Times,* April 11, 1999, pg. Bus. 1. Used by permission of *The Roanoke Times.*

> ## Marketing Management—Implications and Actions
>
> Understanding how customers determine their satisfaction or dissatisfaction in the marketplace helps marketers:
>
> - Attract repeat customers and others like them.
> - Measure and respond to levels of post-purchase satisfaction and dissatisfaction.
> - Take steps to improve objective and affective performance.
> - Develop and promote products in ways that narrow the gap between expectation and performance.

4-3 Purchase-Associated Cognitive Dissonance

▶ **purchase-associated cognitive dissonance**
The state of mind that occurs before the consumer determines whether a product or service is satisfactory. As the consumer makes a commitment to the purchase or selection of the product—in most cases, before use or possession—there is a feeling of uncertainty about whether the right choice is being made.

Purchase-associated cognitive dissonance occurs before the consumer makes a determination concerning whether a product or service is satisfactory. As he or she makes a commitment to the purchase or selection of the product—in most cases before use or possession—there is a feeling of uncertainty about whether the right choice is being made.[36] The customer may even feel physically uncomfortable or anxious about writing out the check or laying down a credit card. Hence, as soon as the consumer takes a specific mental or physical action indicating commitment, dissonance may occur. We see that, in the case of purchase-associated cognitive dissonance, the consumer does not have to have taken possession of or used the product. Therefore, there is no finite time of possession or use requirement as there was with judgment on satisfaction. Exhibit 4-6 is a flowchart showing the relationships among the factors potentially affecting the occurrence of such dissonance, and consumer and marketer attempts to reduce it.

The experience and intensity of this form of cognitive dissonance varies from customer to customer, from situation to situation, and from purchase to purchase. Here are just some of the factors that cause it.

1. *Importance of the purchase decision.* High-involvement, high-risk purchases are much more likely to result in cognitive dissonance than are low-involvement, low-risk purchases. The more we feel that it's important to make the "right" decision and/or the higher the risks associated with making the wrong decision, the more susceptible we are to such dissonance.

2. *Consumer's tendency toward anxiety.* Some consumers are naturally more anxious about all things in life than others. Anxious people are more likely to experience cognitive dissonance.

Exhibit 4-6

Purchase-Associated Cognitive Dissonance

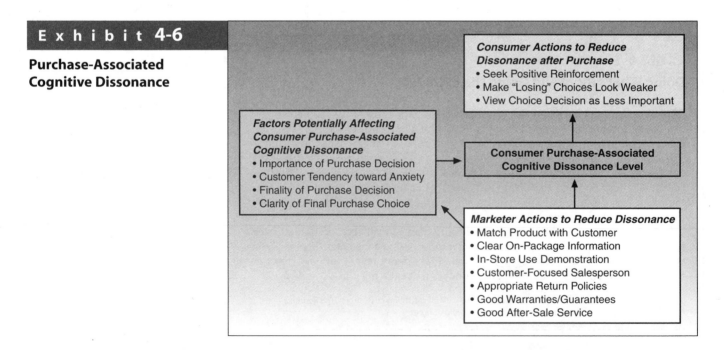

Factors Potentially Affecting Consumer Purchase-Associated Cognitive Dissonance
- Importance of Purchase Decision
- Customer Tendency toward Anxiety
- Finality of Purchase Decision
- Clarity of Final Purchase Choice

Consumer Actions to Reduce Dissonance after Purchase
- Seek Positive Reinforcement
- Make "Losing" Choices Look Weaker
- View Choice Decision as Less Important

Consumer Purchase-Associated Cognitive Dissonance Level

Marketer Actions to Reduce Dissonance
- Match Product with Customer
- Clear On-Package Information
- In-Store Use Demonstration
- Customer-Focused Salesperson
- Appropriate Return Policies
- Good Warranties/Guarantees
- Good After-Sale Service

E x h i b i t 4-7

This example of comparative advertising aims to lessen post-purchase dissonance by making all other "ordinary bandages" look weaker. Curad is presented as the best possible purchase choice.

Source: Curad ad reprinted by permission of Beiersdorf USA.

3. *Finality of the purchase decision.* The more irrevocable the decision and the longer we have to live with the product purchased, the greater the potential for cognitive dissonance.

4. *Clarity of the final purchase choice.* The more difficult the purchase choice is to make, the more likely cognitive dissonance will be experienced. If two or more purchase options are very similar, there's no clear winner and it's hard to pick the best one. In such cases we're more likely to feel uneasy, whatever the final choice.

4-3a How Consumers Attempt to Reduce Dissonance

To reduce purchase-associated cognitive dissonance, consumers first try to find ways to reinforce the desirability of the choice made. They may, for example, pay special attention to advertisements or product reviews that praise the brand chosen. Or they may look for positive information about it in *Consumer Reports* magazine if options in the product or service category have been tested. Showing new purchases to friends, hoping they will react favorably, is another positive reinforcement strategy. Second, consumers may try to make the "losing" choices look weaker in comparison to the brand they actually purchased. In Exhibit 4-7, we see an example of comparative advertising that allows consumers to do this. Third, some consumers make a conscious effort after purchase to view the choice decision as less important than they had originally thought. By trivializing the purchase decision, they increase their comfort level with the chosen brand.

4-3b How Marketers Attempt to Reduce Dissonance

The best way to reduce purchase-associated cognitive dissonance is for marketers to do everything in their power to match their products with the appropriate target consumers. That way, the set of benefits delivered fits the set of benefits sought by the customer. Matching the educational, product or service experience, financial, time, and other resources of the buyer is also critical. The product itself, its packaging, and promotional communications should all be developed with this objective in mind. As cognitive dissonance generally occurs at point of sale, well-targeted, on-package information can make a real difference. Also, return policies, warranties, in-store demonstrations, and post-purchase installation and service can all serve to increase the consumer's level of comfort with the purchase. In face-to-face selling situations, such as at retail, salespeople can be particularly influential in reducing dissonance by answering questions and providing information that diminishes the consumer's anxieties or concerns about a purchase.

F A Q

Direct-mail offers that promise money-back guarantees, no questions asked, outperform those without guarantees. Why is this?

> ### Marketing Management—Implications and Actions
>
> Understanding customer purchase-associated cognitive dissonance helps marketers:
> - Identify factors that cause customers to experience this phenomenon.
> - Reduce purchase-associated cognitive dissonance at point of purchase.

4-4 Post-Purchase Behavior

Analyzing what happens after a sale is as important as understanding what causes consumers to buy in the first place. In fact, because this is an analysis of actual rather than potential customers and purchase situations, enlightened marketers consider post-purchase behavior of primary importance in its impact on future sales. Analyzing both positive and negative post-purchase behavior is a very effective means through which goods and services can be improved, promotions better targeted, and strategies reshaped both to keep current customers and to attract new ones like them.

4-4a Positive Post-Purchase Behavior: Customer Loyalty

loyalty A consumer's feeling of commitment to a product, brand, marketer, or outlet that results in high levels of repeat purchases or visits.

The most positive outcome from achieving customer satisfaction is to gain customer loyalty. **Loyalty,** in its simplest sense, is a feeling of commitment on the part of the consumer to a product, brand, marketer, or outlet that results in high levels of repeat purchasing or outlet visiting, as appropriate. This deeply held commitment results in consistent future purchasing in spite of changes in the customer's situation and efforts by competing marketers to cause switching behavior.[37] Loyalty typically develops over time, based on positive market experiences. Exhibit 4-8 contains flowcharts showing future positive and negative customer actions based on whether he or she is satisfied with a purchase decision. Various influences that we will discuss are also included in this exhibit.

Consumer loyalty, because it takes the form of repeat purchasing, is directly linked to the formation of purchase habits. Repeat and, from there, habitual purchasing is encouraged by the consumer's experiences with products that perform as or better than expected, and through positive reinforcement by the marketer after the purchase has been made.[38] Remember that, for various reasons, consumers might always buy a particular brand, but unless there is commitment, they are not considered loyal. Being loyal would result in rejection of substitutes and a willingness to search for an outlet at which the consumer can find the desired brand. In some cases, a person might simply go without until the brand to which he or she is loyal is available. If habitual drinkers of Coca-Cola or regular drive-through customers at Burger King repeat those product experiences because each one is satisfying, these likely are loyal customers.

We should also think about what is called, "the satisfaction trap."[39] That is, just because a customer is satisfied does not make him or her loyal. For example, in the automobile industry we find 85 percent to 95 percent of buyers report being satisfied with their cars, yet only 30 percent to 40 percent repurchase the same model or from the same manufacturer.[40] What do you think would be typical causes of this lack of a direct tie between satisfaction and loyalty?

It's been suggested that loyalty formation is somewhat akin to attitude formation; the latter will be discussed in Chapter 9. Here, we talk of "loyalty phases."[41] Phase 1, *cognitive loyalty,* is loyalty based on beliefs about the brand (outlet) only. It can be formed as a result of prior or vicarious knowledge or recent experience. This is the weakest form of loyalty. In phase 2, *affective loyalty,* a liking or positive attitude toward the brand, is developed on the basis of repeated satisfying use. This type of loyalty is not easily changed. Phase 3, *conative loyalty,* may be thought of as behavioral intention loyalty or "a good intention" based on repeated episodes where positive affect toward the brand is experienced. This is considered to be a commitment to intend to buy the brand (visit the outlet), but it is more aptly a form of motivation. Finally, phase 4, *action loyalty,* occurs when the motivation in

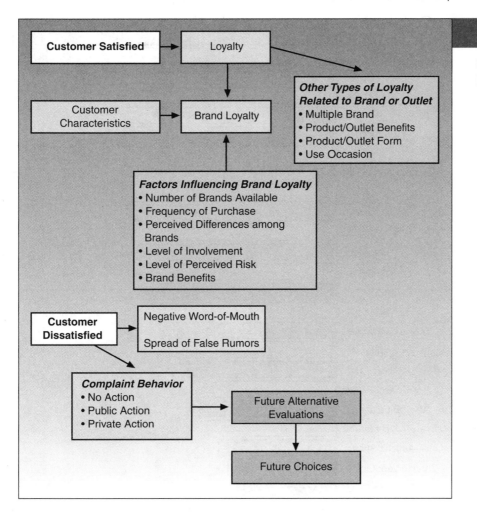

Satisfaction Impact on Future Customer Actions

phase 3 is converted to readiness to act, with the additional desire to overcome the obstacles that might prevent the act. How do think this could be applied to becoming loyal to a restaurant or a brand of athletic gear?

Brand Loyalty   Brand loyalty is more evident in some product categories than others. Exhibit 4-9 lists twenty-four product categories, showing the share of consumers who claim to be loyal to a single brand within each. We can make some useful generalizations from the list. The products that are geared to personal tastes—cigarettes, toothpaste, coffee, headache remedies, and even bath soap—achieve fairly high levels of reported loyalty. Similarly, loyalty is high in categories in which there are a few dominant brands, as in the case of camera film. Levels of loyalty are lower among products that are purchased infrequently, such as athletic shoes, batteries (almost a commodity product), jeans, auto tires, television sets, and underwear. Look at the other product types in the list. Why do you think they appear on the list where they do?

Factors Influencing Brand Loyalty   In addition to satisfaction with the purchase experience, there are several other factors that influence brand loyalty:

1. *Number of brands available.* The smaller the number of brands we have to choose from, the more likely we are to be brand loyal.[42] We already saw evidence of this in Exhibit 4-10.

2. *Frequency of purchase.* The more frequently we purchase a product, the more likely we are to be brand loyal.[43]

F A Q

Does buying the same product again and again always mean that customers are loyal to it? What else can habitual purchase mean?

Exhibit 4-9

Customer-Reported Brand Loyalty by Product Category

For a number of reasons, consumers tend to be more brand-loyal to products in some categories than others.

Source: From "Brand Loyalty Is Rarely Blind Loyalty" by Ronald Alsop from *The Wall Street Journal*, October 19, 1989, p. 132. Copyright © 1989 by Dow Jones & Co., Inc. Reproduced with permission of Dow Jones & Co., Inc. via Copyright Clearance Center.

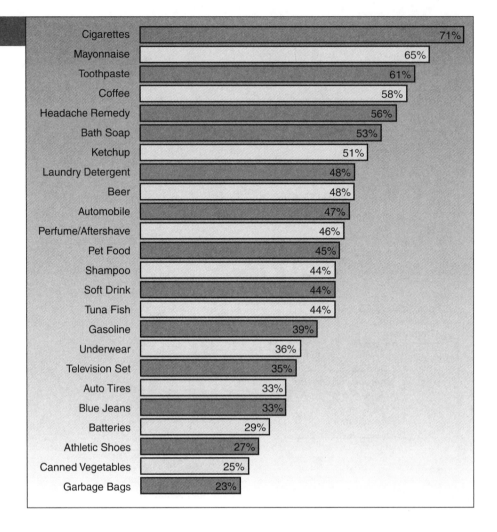

Product Category	Loyalty
Cigarettes	71%
Mayonnaise	65%
Toothpaste	61%
Coffee	58%
Headache Remedy	56%
Bath Soap	53%
Ketchup	51%
Laundry Detergent	48%
Beer	48%
Automobile	47%
Perfume/Aftershave	46%
Pet Food	45%
Shampoo	44%
Soft Drink	44%
Tuna Fish	44%
Gasoline	39%
Underwear	36%
Television Set	35%
Auto Tires	33%
Blue Jeans	33%
Batteries	29%
Athletic Shoes	27%
Canned Vegetables	25%
Garbage Bags	23%

3. *Perceived differences among brands.* If we perceive significant differences among brands, we're likely to be brand loyal. There is, however, evidence that this is not always the case. Headache remedies and shaving creams, for example, have low levels of perceived differences, yet high brand loyalty. Conversely, cola drinks, fast-food restaurants, and men's colognes have higher levels of perceived differences and lower brand loyalty.[44]

4. *Level of involvement.* We're more likely to remain loyal to brands of high-involvement products than low-involvement products. The reason is that we spend more time and energy initially to make a good decision and then stick to it.[45]

5. *Level of perceived risk.* Brand loyalty is high when the level of perceived risk associated with the the choice is high.[46]

6. *Brand benefits.* Brands that provide the benefits that best suit our needs are the strongest candidates for customer loyalty.

These six factors work singly or in combination as consumers form brand loyalties. Once achieved, however, brand loyalties do not necessarily stay the same. Many things can happen to change them. Moreover, consumers who are loyal to a particular brand during one period of their lives are not necessarily so during other periods.[47]

Brand-Loyal Consumers No matter what stage of their lives, some consumers are more brand-loyal than others. These consumers share a number of common characteristics. First, they tend to be self-confident.[48] They feel capable of making good brand choices in the marketplace and will stay with the choices they make. They tend to perceive quite high levels of risk involved in product purchase and so stand by accepted brands in order to reduce that risk.[49] As well as being brand loyal, they tend to be outlet loyal. Because they use only a limited pool of outlets, their choices are limited to the brands available there. In this way, outlet loyalty serves to regulate brand loyalty.[50]

Interestingly, children and young adults tend to be quite brand-loyal. As the customers of tomorrow, young people are courted by forward-thinking marketers. McDonald's, with its play yards and kid-size meals; Maybelline, with its bubblegum-flavored lip gloss; and L'eggs, featuring Little L'eggs tights and knee-highs, all target younger consumers. Very young children—first-graders and younger—are not noticeably brand loyal. Older children are loyal to some products but not others, and those from homes of higher socioeconomic status show more brand loyalty.[51] Their loyalty seems to develop earliest for simple, inexpensive products such as soft drinks.[52] Teens, observed to be relatively cautious, insecure consumers, look to brand names for assurances of quality.[53] As teens are particularly susceptible to peer pressure within schools, neighborhoods, and ethnic or other groups, they tend to be loyal to brand names accepted by those groups.

Consumer Devotion   In certain situations we find consumers with extremely strong connections with particular brands or outlets. They actually become "devoted" to the latter. The level of loyalty is so intense that it survives poor product performance, scandal, bad publicity, high prices, and even the absence of promotional activities. This loyalty often results in customers buying t-shirts, baseball caps, window decals for their cars, and bumper stickers to announce their connection to the brand and its trademark. Devotion such as this could be classified as the "sacralizing" of the brand or outlet (see section 4-1c). Fans of college football or basketball teams are a good example of this. Extreme devotion to sports teams and even in non-sport contexts such as the "Trekkies" (*Star Trek* television and movie series devotees) has been called **"fandom."**[54]

Loyalty to Multiple Brands, Product Benefits, Product Form, and Use Occasion   Twenty-four percent of shoppers say brand loyalty means they almost always buy the same brand within a food product category. Another 36 percent indicate they are brand loyal in some categories but will buy other brands if they get a better deal. Twenty-six percent have a preferred brand that may not be purchased on this week's shopping trip if something else is on sale or fits their budget better. The remaining 14 percent indicate they are loyal to a group of three or four brands in a category.[55]

While not loyal to a specific brand, many consumers are loyal to a group of brands that are essentially equal in their eyes. This consideration set is used as the buying selection pool. Then the consumer makes a decision based on what is happening in the marketplace. Such factors as price, coupons available, availability of the brand, and similar factors help with the current choice. Some consumers are loyal to the benefits a group of brands or a single brand offers.[56] Some are loyal, for example, to the benefits of sugar-free foods. As shown in Exhibit 4-10, the Russell Stover Company offers an extensive line of sugar-free candies in response to this type of loyalty. Others are loyal to a particular form of a product, preferring, for example, liquid detergents to powdered detergents and frozen vegetables to canned. Still others are loyal to certain product types, depending upon the occasion of use. They'll use ready-to-serve cereals for breakfast during the week, for example, but switch to preparing oatmeal in the mornings on weekends. Check out CBite 4-2, a discussion of "consumer inertia."

What this means to marketers is that brand advertising should not star the brand alone but should also emphasize key product-class benefits, characteristics, and situations of consumption. These are not new ideas, but approaches that have been neglected somewhat in recent years as marketers overemphasize the power of the brand alone. These approaches are particularly effective where loyalty, though it exists, is weak, and serves to remind the consumer of the reasons for being brand loyal.

Outlet Loyalty   As part of our discussion of outlet choice in Chapter 3, we explored the relationship between brand and outlet loyalty. We saw that while some consumers determine a preferred brand first and then go shopping for it, others first choose an outlet to which they are loyal and make purchases depending on the brands available there.

▶**"fandom"** Extreme devotion to sports teams and even in non-sport contexts such as the "Trekkies" ("Star Trek" television and movie series devotees).

Most shoppers have favorite outlets, whether retail stores, catalogs, television shopping channels, computer networks, websites, or flea markets. However, just as some of us are more brand-loyal than others, so are some consumers inclined to be outlet-loyal. Typically, they share some of the same characteristics as brand-loyal consumers: they tend to perceive a high level of risk in making purchases, and they limit the number of outlets they use.[57] Even in their chosen outlets, outlet-loyal consumers tend to shop less often than do other consumers. They are familiar with fewer stores and, not surprisingly, engage in little pre-purchase searching.[58] This low-search, low-knowledge, low-use tendency is more

CBite 4-2
Consumer Inertia

Inertia describes the behavior of consumers who alternate frequently among a set of brands. Though loyal to the brands within that set and reluctant to buy brands outside it, they consider all the brands within it to be more or less equal. These are the people who change loyalties with every price offer, coupon, or sales promotion that come their way. The best way for marketers to combat inertia is to make sure their brands get into the consideration sets of this type of consumer. If the brand name jumps to mind as soon as the consumer discovers a need within a product category, the less likely that consumer is to fall prey to enticements to switch to products offered by other marketers.

Marketplace 4-3

The Making of Outlet-Loyal Customers

Developing loyalty among customers is still the best way to guarantee the success of a business enterprise. Loyal customers, after all, provide businesses with a stable market and give rise to beneficial word-of-mouth "advertising." Marketing actions should, therefore, be attuned to the changing needs of customers, because winning customer satisfaction can be the best way to create loyalty. The following are four marketing approaches that work to build customer satisfaction and, ultimately, customer loyalty:

1. *Show sensitivity.* A couple was shopping at a major clothing retailer, and though the man was pleased with the service, the woman was being ignored. The woman sent a letter to the company explaining how she always enjoyed shopping at the store, but she felt she was not receiving the same level of service that was typically experienced by men and that more attention should be paid to the female shoppers. Within two weeks, she received a letter from the company president, a woman, which included an apology and a gift certificate for $25. Also, the woman's letter was circulated to all company store managers. Needless to say, the woman made a number of positive comments to other people about the experience.

2. *Make customers feel comfortable.* A customer purchased a laser printer from an international office supplies company with a return policy that simply stated, "If you don't like it, send it back—even if it sits in your place for a couple of months." The customer turned out not to need the printer, and the carton was never opened. Because the printer had been around for more than two months, the consumer was reluctant to try to return it in anticipation of a hassle. However, when the customer service representative was contacted, he wanted nothing more than to satisfy the request—no questions asked. The customer was made to feel comfortable about the return and certainly would go back there in the future.

3. *Do a little extra.* A consumer was looking for a TV set. There were two electronic stores within a quarter mile of his home. Store A promised to beat anybody's price, so he went to Store B first. The salesperson offered a good price and delivery at no charge. The salesperson at Store A offered to beat the price, but would have to charge extra for delivery. The cost of the two deals was "a wash," but the consumer went with Store B because of the added service offered.

4. *Listen to the customer.* A shopper went to a video store to buy a couple of films. He asked to talk to the clerk who had told him over the phone that the movies he wanted were in stock. The clerk pulled the videos out from under the counter and rang up the order. She then gave him some coupons and said that he should have purchased the films the following day, a double coupon day. He asked why she hadn't told him this before the sale, in which case he would have come in the next day. Her reply was, "Well, it's too late now. I've already rung up the order, and there is nothing I can do." The customer asked to speak to the manager, who listened to his complaint and gave him the extra coupons. By letting the customer voice his displeasure, the manager kept him as a loyal customer.

Showing sensitivity, making customers feel comfortable, doing a little extra, and listening to them can go a long way toward building solid relationships and lasting customer satisfaction.

Source: From "The Making of Loyal Customers" by Dom Del Prete in *Marketing News,* April 24, 1995, p. 6. Reprinted with permission from *Marketing News,* published by the American Marketing Association.

---

often found among consumers of lower socioeconomic status. This may imply that their outlet loyalty is a result of their limited financial means or limited outlet choices. Similarly, outlet-loyal women tend to be lower in income, less educated, and older than non-outlet-loyal women.[59] Women higher on the socioeconomic ladder see the marketplace as more diverse, with more options to choose from because they can spend the time and money to explore it. Though they may still be loyal to some outlets, in general they shop more widely for their purchases. How do marketers encourage outlet-loyal customers? Look at Marketplace 4-3 to see how this can be done.

Factors Influencing E-tailer Loyalty   Those who study e-commerce are concerned about what influences consumers to become loyal to those outlets with whom they deal electronically. This **e-loyalty** is directed toward **e-tailers** (electronic retailers; retailers on the web). A study of some 1200 online customers revealed that there are potentially seven influences at work, as follows:[60]

1. *Customization.* The ability of the e-tailer to tailor products, services, and the transactional environment to the individual customer.

▶**e-loyalty** Consumer loyalty to an electronic retailer.

▶**e-tailer** A retailer who offers goods and services on the web; also called an electronic retailer.

2. *Contact interactivity.* The dynamic nature of the engagement between the e-tailer and customer through its website, to include navigation, level of product information, and rapid response to email inquiries.

3. *Care.* The attention paid by the e-tailer to all the pre- and post-purchase customer interface activities for the current transaction and long-term relationships. Keeping the customer informed about availability of preferred products, order status, and minimal disruption in providing service (because, for instance, one can shop online at night, on weekends, during holidays, and so on) are examples of this.

4. *Community (virtual community).* An online social entity comprised of existing and potential customers, organized and maintained by the e-tailer, to aid in the exchange of opinions/information regarding products and services offered.

5. *Cultivation.* The extent to which an e-tailer provides relevant information and incentives to its customers to extend the breadth and depth of their purchases over time.

6. *Choice.* Whether the e-tailer is typically able to offer a wider range of product categories and a greater variety of products within any given category; this may also include alliances with other suppliers so that the customer can just work with a single vendor.

7. *Character.* The overall image or personality that the e-tailer projects to consumers through the use of inputs such as text, style, graphics, colors, logos, and slogans/themes on the website.

Think about your own e-tailer shopping and buying. Would you agree that these are the seven factors that you consider? If you had "100 importance points" to distribute among the seven evaluative criteria, what would be your distribution of those points? Why?

There are a number of benefits that are enjoyed by the maker of a brand name or an outlet that come from their loyal customers. Read over CBite 4-3 to see what these are. Do these ring true when you are a loyal customer?

CBite 4-3

Some Benefits of Customer Loyalty

The following are seven customer-loyalty benefits enjoyed by marketers. They provide strong incentive to keep customers coming back.

1. *Cost savings*—Loyal customers are more efficient in the way they use the seller's resources.

2. *Referrals*—Customers mention the brand (outlet) to their friends and acquaintances.

3. *Complain rather than defect*—Customers who are loyal feel that they are stakeholders in the brand (outlet); it's "theirs," so they want to fix it rather than walk away.

4. *Channel migration*—Loyal customers will buy the same brand through multiple channels, such as stores, catalogs, and online.

5. *Unaided awareness*—customers have the brand name (outlet name) on the "top of their mind."

6. *Greater awareness of brand (outlet) assets*—Customers are more aware of auxiliary benefits or "hidden assets" (free delivery, dedicated service person, perceived better value) of the brand (outlet).

7. *"Turn left rather than right"*—Customers favor the brand name (outlet) when confronted with a last-minute marketplace decision (e.g., Lowe's vs. Home Depot, Borders vs. Barnes and Noble, Amazon.com vs. BN.com).

Source: From Dennis L. Duffy, "Internal and External Factors Which Affect Customer Loyalty," *Journal of Consumer Marketing,* Vol. 20, No. 5 (2003), pp. 480–485. Reprinted by permission of Emerald.

4-4b Negative Post-Purchase Behavior

Negative post-purchase behavior (from the marketer's perspective) takes several forms, each of which can erode brand and outlet loyalty and diminish customer satisfaction. Some negative behaviors are passive—such as the lack of repeat purchases or recommendations to other consumers. Active negative behaviors are of more interest to marketers, as these are potentially damaging to the reputation and, therefore, to the future sales of the product. Refer back to Exhibit 4-9 as you read through this discussion on negative post-purchase behaviors.

The level of negative action taken by a consumer after experiencing dissatisfaction initially is influenced by what are called **recovery expectations.** These expectations are tied to customer beliefs about the level of "reparation," compensation of customer for losses produced by the service failure, that is appropriate after a failure.[61] Studies of service failures show that customer service recovery expectations are influenced by how severe the failure was, what the causes of the failure were, and customer expectations about the long-term relationship they have had and will continue to have with the service provider.[62] Existing strong customer-service organization relationships can help to shield the organization from the negative effects of failures to produce customer satisfaction. In fact, customers who expect the relationship to continue have lower service recovery expectations. This results in greater satisfaction with service performance after recovery.[63]

> **recovery expectations**
> Expectations tied to customer beliefs about the level of "reparation" (compensation of the customer for losses produced by the service failure) that is appropriate after a failure.

Negative Word-of-Mouth   Negative word-of-mouth, through which consumers express their dissatisfaction with a purchase to others, is a private action. That is, it is not an overt form of complaint, but it nevertheless influences the buying behavior of those exposed to it.[64] Negative word-of-mouth is more powerful in its effects than positive comments by customers. Three times as many people hear negative comments as hear positive ones.[65] They're also likely to pay more attention to them.[66] Think about instances when you have been turned off to a particular product or brand simply because of negative comments friends have made. Perhaps you've decided against seeing a movie, reading a book, or shopping at a certain department store as a result.

Interestingly, if the consumer perceives that the seller will respond favorably to complaints, negative word-of-mouth decreases. When sellers are responsive, consumers are more inclined to take their problems directly to the sellers rather than simply talk about them to others.[67]

Rumor   The rumor is a particularly insidious form of negative communication. Through rumors, not only negative but also untrue information about products and brands can be spread. Some rumors take hold gradually and unintentionally; others are purposely constructed and voiced to do damage.

One of the most notorious rumors about a major manufacturer involved Procter and Gamble. The word spread that, when held upside down, the beard on the man in the moon on the company logo read as the number 666, implying the company was in league with Satan. Rumor had it that a share of the company's profits was used for satanic purposes.[68] Other damaging rumors have been spread about even the most successful of companies: Bubble Yum gum supposedly contained spider eggs;[69] Entenmann's, the world's largest cake products baker, was said to be owned by Reverend Sun Myung Moon's Unification Church;[70] Gillette hair dryers were purportedly made using asbestos;[71] and McDonald's hamburgers were falsely described in one part of the United States as containing red worms.[72] Rumors like these are not only untrue but often extraordinary in their claims. Sales losses were experienced in all of these situations.

It is very important for marketers to confront the spread of false rumors quickly. This does not mean just discovering the source or beginning litigation, but initiating a positive, nondefensive public relations campaign to restore the reputation of the product or brand in the minds of the consumers.[73] The cost to organizations hurt by rumors in reestablishing positive brand images can be enormous and, although negative information eventually fades away, recovery is arduous and time-consuming. To underestimate the power of a rumor is foolhardy, regardless of how absurd that rumor appears to be.

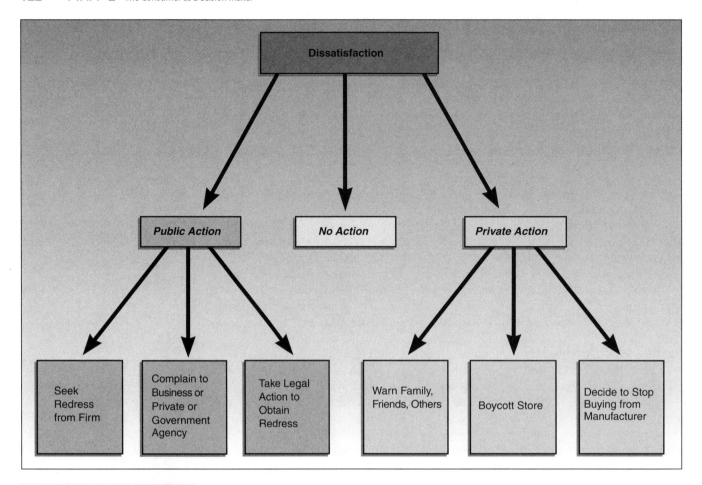

E x h i b i t 4-11

A Model of Consumer Complaint Behavior

Dissatisfied customers respond in one of three ways: no action, private action, or public action.

Source: From "Selected Determinants of Consumer Satisfaction and Complaint Reports" by William O. Bearden and Jesse E. Teel in *Journal of Marketing Research,* February 1983, Volume 20, p. 22. Reprinted with permission from *Journal of Marketing Research,* published by the American Marketing Association.

private action Dissatisfied customer action with no attempt to obtain redress; it could involve negative word-of-mouth and personal boycott of brands and outlets.

Complaint Behavior Not all consumers who are dissatisfied with the performance of a purchase take steps to remedy the situation. An average of only one in three people will do so.[74] Exhibit 4-11 shows the forms of complaint behavior people engage in. There are three paths: no action, private action, and public action. As we have seen, though **private action** involves no attempt to obtain redress, it does involve negative word-of-mouth and personal boycott of brands and outlets. **Public action** includes seeking a remedy for the problem at the purchase location or from the manufacturer, taking legal action, and complaining to groups that represent the interests of consumers, such as the Better Business Bureau, the Federal Trade Commission, or the attorney general of the state.

Why do some people complain and others not? Largely, cultural values and personal attitudes are responsible. In addition, four factors appear to influence the decision to complain.[75] First, if the purchase is important to the consumer, the likelihood of complaint increases. Price, social visibility, and the length of time the consumer will have to live with the unsatisfactory purchase all influence complaint behavior. Second, the consumer's level of knowledge of and experience with the product purchased are significant. If a consumer is knowledgeable, has purchased the product before, and feels confident of his or her ability to make a good purchase choice, complaint behavior is more likely. Moreover, if consumers have complained before, they are more prone to do it again. Third, the greater the time, energy, and financial costs of making a complaint, the less likely consumers are to do so. Lastly, if consumers perceive that complaining will lead to a positive outcome, they are more likely to pursue it.

What type of consumer complains? Frequent complainers share certain characteristics. They tend to belong to higher rather than lower socioeconomic groups and have higher-than-average levels of education.[76] Generally confident of their decision-making ability, they value a sense of individuality.[77] Despite this, they tend to blame others rather than take responsibility upon themselves for their dissatisfaction.[78] They tend to support consumerist activities, and, therefore, are quick to approach consumer advocacy groups with complaints.

By analyzing the characteristics of consumers who are most likely to complain, marketers can better avoid the reasons for those complaints and plan how best to deal with them when they do occur. Note that those engaged in consumerist activities tend to complain more. The reason is that they are particularly sensitive to products or services that can potentially harm the consumer. Obviously, the best means of avoiding complaints from these consumers is to ensure that products do deliver the benefits consumers expect.

Complaint Response by Marketers What can marketers do to regain the confidence of consumers who complain? Overall, it is essential to be sensitive to the potential for complaint. This is particularly important for high-involvement, high-risk products where the consumer has a lot at stake. Providing a swift remedy for any legitimate complaint is the best course of action. As a means of building a positive image, enlightened marketers also quickly settle certain not-legitimate complaints through, for example, "no-questions-asked" return policies. The popularity of company toll-free phone complaint numbers is evidence both of the consumer's desire to find an easy means of redress and the marketer's willingness to provide it. Another benefit of listening to consumer complaints is the opportunity it presents to find out more about product use and the extent to which products meet consumer needs. This type of unsolicited feedback can be useful in reshaping products or improving marketing communications programs.

Consumers appear to be seeking three kinds of "justice" when they complain. These are: (1) **distributive justice,** where equity in terms of settlement versus perceived costs experienced by the person is the issue; (2) **procedural justice,** which is derived from the complaint policies, procedures, and criteria used to make a decision; heavy emphasis is placed by the consumer on timeliness, responsiveness, and convenience; and (3) **interactional justice,** which has to do with the way customers are treated during the process, including such factors as politeness, interest, truthfulness, and the seller's acceptance of blame.[79] Of the three types of justice, interactional justice appears to have the greatest impact on whether customers would again buy from the seller and whether negative word-of-mouth would occur.

It is estimated that about 55 percent to 60 percent of consumer complaints are resolved in a way that leaves the customer satisfied.[80] Response rates from sellers to the complaints of customers vary across product or service categories—one study found the best responses from snack and pizza manufacturers and the worst from clothing vendors, but, for the most part, marketers want to make things right.[81] Most firms send coupons or refunds when responding to complaints that have been received through regular mail. Results across various product classes show that 56 percent to 77 percent of complaining customers are satisfied with such solutions.[82] Marketers realize that if they can show customers they care, satisfaction and intent to repurchase will increase.[83]

There also is the question of the customer's emotional state if he or she is dissatisfied. Dissatisfaction is an outcome-dependent emotion that is associated with the undesirability of an event, but not with the cause. Dissatisfied customers have a feeling of "unfulfillment," thinking about what they missed out on. They appear to make a deliberate judgment on how to act and may focus on who or what was responsible for the event.[84] In some situations the customer is angry and when complaining may say something nasty, want to get back at the organization, and want to "hurt" someone.[85] In all situations service recovery efforts on the part of the marketer must be forceful and effective. This means that part of the responsibility of the organization is to prepare workers to deal with angry customers. It is important to acknowledge what the angry customer is saying and feeling, before acting on what the customer is complaining about and resolving the problem.[86] The following marketer actions can increase the probability of customer satisfaction and thereby reduce customer complaints:

1. *Build realistic expectations about product or service performance.* The advertisement for Dermasil Lotion in Exhibit 4-12 uses a before-and-after comparison to show consumers what to expect. It is important to explain to the prospective purchaser what products and/or services will and will not do.

2. *Demonstrate or explain product use,* for example, through product documentation, illustrations, video, or pre-purchase testing.

---

public action (see p. 122) What occurs when a dissatisfied customer seeks a remedy for the problem at the purchase location or from the manufacturer, by taking legal action, or complaining to groups that represent the interests of consumers, such as the Better Business Bureau, the Federal Trade Commission, or the attorney general of the state in which the customer resides.

distributive justice When, during the complaint process, equity in terms of settlement versus perceived costs experienced by the person is the issue.

procedural justice The perceived justice that is derived from the complaint policies, procedures, and criteria used to make a decision; heavy emphasis is placed by the consumer on timeliness, responsiveness, and convenience.

interactional justice The perceived justice that has to do with the way customers are treated during the complaint settlement process, including such factors as politeness, interest, truthfulness, and the seller's acceptance of blame.

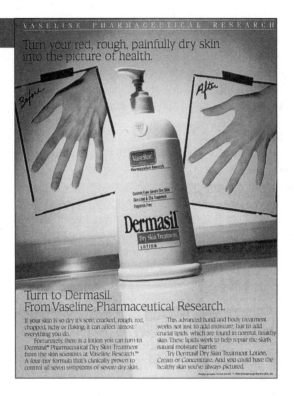

Exhibit 4-12

This before-and-after comparison appeal for Dermasil Lotion seeks to reduce the chance of consumer dissatisfaction by establishing accurate performance expectations.

Source: Courtesy of Unilever United States, Inc.

3. *Stand behind the product* by offering appropriate guarantees and warranties.

4. *Encourage customer feedback* on performance and satisfaction.

5. *Periodically make contact with customers* to show interest and thank them for their support.

These suggestions are not only good for the consumer but are sound business practices. Following such action steps will strengthen the link between marketer and customer and contribute to the building of long-term, profitable relationships. Check out CBite 4-4 to find ways to deal with customer complaints with digital systems.

CBite 4-4

Use Digital Systems to Route Customer Complaints Immediately

L istening to customers means hearing their complaints about current product shortcomings. Passing bad news from customers all the way to the product design groups, however, is surprisingly hard to do. I recommend the following approach:

1. Focus on your most unhappy customers.
2. Use technology to gather rich information on their unhappy experiences with your product and to find out what they want you to put into the product.
3. Use technology to drive the news to the right people in a hurry.

If you do these three things, you'll turn those draining bad news experiences into an exhilarating process of improving your product or service. Unhappy customers are always a concern. They're also your greatest opportunity.

Companies that invest early in digital nervous systems to capture, analyze, and capitalize on customer input will differentiate themselves from the competition. *You should examine customer complaints more often than company financials.* And your digital systems should help you convert bad news to improved products and services.

Source: From "Bill Gates' New Rules" by Bill Gates in *Time,* March 22, 1994, p. 74. Copyright © 1994 Time Inc. Reprinted by permission.

Marketing Management—Implications and Actions

Understanding post-purchase behavior helps marketers:

- Encourage brand and outlet loyalty.
- Respond promptly to dispel rumors and other negative communications.
- Offer swift redress to consumers who complain and thereby regain a positive brand or outlet image.
- Use feedback from both positive and negative post-purchase behaviors to improve products and promotions.

4-5 Product Disposition

Product consumption does not end with purchase and use. The physical product, packaging, and the promotional materials associated with it must be disposed of. **Product disposition** is the process of reselling, recycling, trashing, repairing, trading, and the like associated with the physical product, packaging, and its promotional materials when no longer perceived as useful by the consumer or marketer. This has become an increasingly important issue in a world of growing population size, limited space, limited natural resources, and high levels of manufacture. Hence, disposition is a critical part of the consumption process. Marketers have a joint responsibility with consumers to find and/or provide appropriate product disposition methods, especially if marketers wish to attract and keep environmentally conscious consumers. See Exhibit 4-13.

> **product disposition**
> The process of reselling, recycling, trashing, repairing, trading, and the like associated with the physical product, its packaging, and its promotional materials when the consumer or marketer no longer perceives the product as useful.

4-5a Role of the Consumer

Consumers have a number of options when a product is no longer of use to them. They may sell it, donate it to charity, give it away, rent it, loan it out, modify it to a new purpose or to better perform its original task, repair it, or, of course, throw it in the trash. Obviously, the type of product and the way it is consumed influence disposition options for both the product and its packaging. Household items like cereal boxes, cans, and bottles, for example, are immediately dropped in the trash or sent to a recycling center. An old lawn mower in reasonable working order is more likely to be sold at a garage sale, traded in on a new one, or donated to charity than it is to be thrown out with garbage. Empty paint cans or used engine oil can be dropped off at a hazardous waste recycling point. Computer hardware is passed on to children or friends, often more than once, or donated to charitable organizations before it's ready for memory erasure and final disposal.

There are many, many ways we can do our part to conserve resources and protect the environment. Increased awareness of efficiency ratings on cars, furnaces, refrigerators, and other appliances helps us save gasoline, electricity, natural gas, and fuel oil. Remembering to turn down the heat or air conditioning at night or when our homes are unoccupied also helps save energy. Car pooling and using public transportation cut air pollution and save gasoline. Care in disposing of chemicals limits contamination of the water

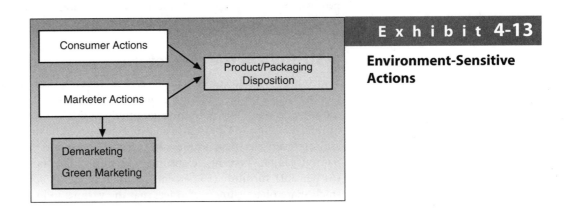

E x h i b i t 4-13

Environment-Sensitive Actions

Marketplace 4-4

Disposition of Special Possessions by Older Consumers

"I keep telling my children, 'If you want something, take it.' They say, 'Hold it.' I say, 'No.' We are reaching a point that we don't need all that we have. We need to get rid of it all. And we are. Slowly—You know, when you get to a certain stage in life, you're trying, you don't want to—But see, as you get older, we have all this stuff that we don't really use ... I go to estate sales all the time. And when I go, every time I go, I realize that I have to do something. I must get rid of what I have. It is so sad [stresses the word sad], and there are these beautiful items that are being sold—And I think of these people, and how they must have felt. They had all this, and it meant so much to them. So, every time I go, I think that's not going to happen to me ... When you have something that means something to you ... you want [your children] to have it. It should mean as much to them as it means to me." (Iris, a 78-year old married woman)

These comments are typical of older individuals. It occurs at a time of *life review*. This type of review may be brought on by such events as an illness (possibly diagnosed as terminal), death of a loved one, conversations with family members, experiences of others, a personal crisis, or norms and traditions within the family. Also, as people age, they become more accepting of their mortality, sometimes referred to as "finitude." The possessions accumulated over a lifetime now must be disposed of. Certain of these are "special possessions." The portrait of great-grandmother Juliana and the one of great-grandfather William in his Civil War uniform, the rocking chair that the person was rocked in as a baby and which now is used to rock her or his grandchild, the charcoal drawing done by mother, and a couple of

the toys played with as a child are examples of special possessions. These have bundles of meanings and often have stories attached to them. They might even be seen as sources of "symbolic immortality."

The questions of who is to get the possessions, when this is to occur, and how it will be carried out are the challenges faced by the older consumer. The "who" may be based on family traditions or cultural norms (repeat traditional pattern, same gender or bloodline, oldest child, family name, or initials), receiver congruity (most likely to appreciate, close relationship, cares about family tradition, asks first), or reciprocity (most deserving person or the original gift giver).

When the transfer should occur is also a key concern. It could be opportunistic (result of conversation, a meeting or visit with children, receiver is ready to appreciate), occur on ritual occasions (marriage, special birthday, Christmas, or other key religious celebrations), be the subject of control (to ensure object will be loved and cared for, to ensure it will not be lost, in time to avoid conflict), or be the subject of holding ("not until I die," never—"take to the grave").

Finally, the "how" of the process has to be settled. This could be a direct transfer (a gift, direct bequest) or a transfer through an intermediary (one caretaker to another, held until recipient is "ready," put someone in charge to distribute) or the item could be sold.

Source: Based on Linda L. Price, Eric J. Arnould, and Carolyn Folkman Curasi, "Older Consumers' Disposition of Special Possessions," *Journal of Consumer Research,* Vol. 27 (September 2000), pp. 179–201, with additional comments by the authors.

---

supply. Recycling of cans, bottles, plastics, cardboard, newspapers, telephone directories, engine oil, and car batteries is not just becoming the "norm," it has also been made easier for us. Curbside recycling saves us the trouble of packing up and driving used household goods to a recycling center. The price of a new car battery includes the cost of disposing of the old one. At oil-change services shops, we pay a small fee for the handling and recycling of used oil. When products are not yet ready to be trashed, we engage in lateral recycling— we give or sell them to others or trade them in for newer models. Older consumers are a special case because they are often faced with disposition and distribution of important possessions as they approach the end of their lives.[87] Marketplace 4-4 gives us some insights on this process.

4-5b Role of the Marketer

Which industries do consumers perceive as "causers," "solvers," or "neither" with regard to environmental problems in the United States? In a recent study, consumers identified the top three "causers" of environmental problems as chemicals (73 percent of respondents), oil and gasoline (64 percent), and automotive emissions (58 percent). The top three "solvers" were electrical utilities (18 percent), forest and paper products (16 percent), and natural gas (15 percent). Consumers identified the top three "neithers" as computers (61 percent), furniture (55 percent), and natural gas (53 percent).[88] What is striking is the small share of consumers who feel that the various industries are doing much about the

---

CBite 4-5

Consumer Perceptions of Industries Causing and Solving Environmental Problems

Thinking of issues involving the environment, let's talk about some specific industries. In general, do you feel the _____ industry has *caused* environmental problems, *solved* environmental problems, or neither?

Industry	Caused (%)	Solved (%)	Neither (%)
Computers	16	12	61
Natural gas	23	15	53
Electrical utilities	28	18	45
Furniture	25	7	55
Steel	46	10	36
Forest and paper products	40	16	38
Plastics	51	14	29
Nuclear power	45	14	32
Fast food	46	5	45
Automotive	58	9	30
Oil and gasoline	64	7	26
Chemicals	73	4	20

Source: From "Environmental Update" from *Research Supplement—The Wirthlin Report,* Vol. 10, November 2000, p. 1. Reprinted by permission of Wirthlin Worldwide.

---

environmental impact of their production of goods and services. Check out CBite 4-5 to see a more complete summary of the twelve industries reviewed.

Marketers encourage recycling and conservation in a variety of ways. In some cases, government regulations lead directly to environmentally responsible product development and marketing measures. Legislation governs, for example, minimum miles-per-gallon requirements for vehicles for each manufacturer in the United States in order to conserve gasoline. Regulations on the production of Freon and other fluorocarbons or the release of chemicals into the water supply are in place to protect the environment. The Environmental Protection Agency (EPA) Energy Star advertisement in Exhibit 4-14 is just one example of how this type of regulation is reflected in the promotion of products to reassure consumers that manufacturers are conscious of and responsive to environmental concerns.

In response to both pressure from regulatory bodies and consumer demand, more and more marketers are taking the initiative to attempt to reduce demand for certain goods and services and produce environmentally friendly products. The process of **demarketing** occurs when sellers attempt to reduce the demand for their goods and services. This is usually a result of environmental sensitivity and/or undersupply of their products or services. Many power companies across the country are demarketing their energy supplies to consumers. Energy rates are high during peak demand periods to discourage excessive use. Customers are encouraged to conserve energy in the home through proper insulation and the use of energy-efficient appliances.

Manufacturers use more recyclable materials in packaging—from cereal boxes to liquid detergent bottles, milk containers, and soda cans. A broad range of products across a number of categories carry the familiar symbol of the "three chasing arrows" that indicates the product or its container or shipping materials are recyclable and/or that recycled materials were used to make the packaging. Increasingly, **green marketers** send the message that their products are environmentally friendly as a means of attracting environmentally

demarketing The marketing processes sellers use to reduce the demand for their goods and services. This is usually a result of environmental sensitivity and/or undersupply of their products or services.

green marketing The development and selling of products and services that are environmentally friendly.

Green marketing is on the rise as consumers become increasingly concerned with protection of the environment.

Source: Courtesy of United States Environmental Protection Agency.

F A Q

Which is the better choice in supermarkets— reusable plastic bags or recyclable paper bags?

conscious consumers. Green is associated with the purity of the grass and trees of Mother Nature. Check out some tips on "going green" in Marketplace 4-5.

In some cases, the greening of industry has benefited marketers by lowering costs. Recycled materials, for example, are generally cheaper than new ones. But the decision to be environmentally conscious is not always an easy one for marketers to make. There frequently is a cost involved. In some cases, marketers lose sales volume as a direct result of environmental regulations or as a result of their own green marketing efforts. For example, if light bulbs are designed to last longer, saving materials and energy, the result is that fewer light bulbs are needed or sold. Similarly, in the auto industry, improvements in car efficiency led to fewer service actions and a reduction in the need for replacement parts. Again, the result was lost revenue.

Recycling itself is an industry, and the movement toward green marketing has opened up new opportunities. The rapid growth, for example, of the waste management industry in recent years is just one indicator that green manufacturing and green marketing are here to stay, transforming the ways in which products are developed, packaged, promoted, and brought to market.

Marketing Management—Implications and Actions

Understanding product disposition helps marketers:

- Make their products appeal to an increasingly environmentally conscious consumer population.
- Act responsibly to encourage safe disposition of used products through supporting both regulatory and voluntary environmental programs.
- Use green marketing strategies and claims to make products distinctive.

Marketplace 4-5

Going Green

After years of confusion over environmental marketing and the ensuing backlash from skeptical consumers, some marketers are now getting it right. They've done their homework, learned from mistakes—theirs and others'—and are now executing sophisticated green marketing strategies that really appeal to consumers. Here are some of the lessons they've learned:

1. *Green your product before you are forced to.* Start working now toward environment-related product quality, eco-labeling, and product life-cycle analysis with its potential impact on the environment.

2. *Communicate environmental aspects of products, especially recycled content.* Remember, less packaging is more, and beige is better than bleached white. Concerning recycled content, 62 percent of consumers now recognize the three "chasing arrows" (recyclable) logo.

3. *Deliver on performance and price.* Green attributes can break a tie between product offerings, but they can't make up for a second-rate product. Don't expect to fetch a premium for your greened-up product, unless meaningful benefits ensue.

4. *Dramatize environmental benefits.* Environmental benefits are often intangible and not visible to the consumer. Tell the consumer about them!

5. *Stress direct, tangible benefits.* While green attributes appeal to a growing number of consumers, the direct benefits they support, such as a lower price or greater convenience stemming from concentrated form, can attract a wider audience.

6. *Be consistent and thorough.* To overcome the skepticism of committed environmentalists toward green claims, make sure all your messages are consistently—and honestly—green.

Source: From "When It Comes to Marketing, Companies Are Finally Getting It Right" by Jacquelyn A. Ottman in *Brandweek,* April 17, 1995, p. 17.

Chapter Spotlights

In this chapter, we covered consumption and post-purchase behavior. Product use is the most reliable means through which consumers learn about brands and outlets, confirm their preferences, and make future buying decisions. The consumption and post-purchase experiences can also trigger new needs, for either the same or related products. In this way, the decision-making process begins over again.

1. Product and service consumption. Each consumer's consumption set is influenced by such factors as lifestyle and culture. Particular consumption situations are further influenced by both the physical and social contexts in which they occur. People also consume in terms of episodes. Depending upon how close they are to the act of consumption, marketers may exert extensive, limited, or no control over it.

2. Ritual, sacred, profane, and compulsive consumption. Rituals, or symbolic patterns of behavior—whether routine or linked to social, religious, or cultural events—present opportunities for marketers to position their products against the needs such rituals give rise to. Similarly, as consumers sacralize products, people, places, and events, new marketing opportunities emerge. Routine consumption, called profane, must be treated differently by marketers, as is the case with compulsive consumption.

3. Customer satisfaction and dissatisfaction. Gaining satisfaction is key to keeping customers and attracting others like them. Satisfaction depends not only on how well a purchased product or service performs, but on how closely it meets the consumer's expectations. The objective for marketers should be to close the gap between expectation and performance and thereby work toward customer satisfaction.

4. Purchase-associated cognitive dissonance. Purchase-associated cognitive dissonance occurs when consumers are not sure they have made the correct product or service choice, which results in feelings of anxiety and doubt. It is common with high-involvement, high-risk purchases. To reduce such dissonance, marketers seek to reinforce the message that the consumer's choice was a good one, particularly at the point of purchase where dissonance occurs.

5. Post-purchase behavior. Depending upon the level of customer satisfaction, post-purchase behavior is either positive or negative. Encouraging positive post-purchase behavior centers on building customer loyalty to brands, outlets, product forms, and/or product characteristics. Negative post-purchase behavior includes negative word-of-mouth, the spreading of rumors, and overt complaining, either directly to the seller or through consumer advocacy or regulatory bodies.

6. Product disposition. In a world that has finite resources to be shared and where the population is becoming increasingly environmentally conscious, safe disposition of used products and their packaging is the joint responsibility of the consumer and the marketer. By supporting conservation and environment-protection actions, the marketer stands to gain both consumer confidence and competitive advantage.

Key Terms

affective performance (p. 110)
asymmetric effect (p. 109)
compulsive consumption (p. 105)
consumption (p. 100)
consumption episode (p. 102)
consumption set (p. 101)
consumption situation (p. 101)
consumption system (p. 102)
contrast effect (p. 109)
demarketing (p. 127)
desacralization (p. 104)
distributive justice (p. 123)

e-loyalty (p. 119)
e-tailer (p. 119)
expectancy disconfirmation (p. 109)
"fandom" (p. 117)
green marketing (p. 127)
interactional justice (p. 123)
loyalty (p. 114)
moral equity (p. 110)
objective performance (p. 110)
physical (consumption) context (p. 101)
private action (p. 122)
procedural justice (p. 123)

product disposition (p. 125)
profane consumption (p. 104)
public action (p. 122)
purchase-associated cognitive dissonance
    (p. 112)
recovery expectations (p. 121)
ritual consumption (p. 103)
sacralization (p. 104)
sacred consumption (p. 104)
social (consumption) context (p. 101)

Review Questions

Note: You can find the correct answers to these questions by taking the quiz and then submitting your answers in the Online Edition. The program will automatically score your submission. If you miss a question, the program will provide the correct answer, a rationale for the answer, and the section number in the chapter where the topic is discussed.

1. In the marketing of _____ in particular, the marketer is present during consumption and can both watch and influence how consumption plays out.
  a. tangibles
  b. intangibles
  c. services
  d. exclusive items

2. The difference between sacralization and desacralization is that the former _____ sacred status.
  a. loses
  b. gains
  c. balances
  d. forfeits

3. The difference between positive disconfirmation and simple confirmation is that the former means that performance is _____ than expected.
  a. less
  b. more meaningful
  c. better
  d. more fulfilling

4. _____ performance is consumer-related and depends upon whether the purchase meets the emotional expectations of the buyer.
  a. Objective
  b. Cognitive
  c. Equitable
  d. Affective

5. The major factors that cause purchase-associated cognitive dissonance do *not* include the
  a. importance of the purchase decision.
  b. consumer's tendency toward anxiety.
  c. finality of the purchase decision.
  d. how long the item has been used or possessed.

6. Analyzing what happens after _____ is as important as understanding what causes consumers to buy in the first place.
  a. the purchase decision is made
  b. a sale
  c. the information search
  d. alternatives are evaluated

7. Brady Griggs tends to be brand loyal because the brands he chooses provide satisfaction. All of these factors can also influence Brady's choices *except*
  a. number of brands available.
  b. frequency of purchase.
  c. purchase price level.
  d. level of involvement.

8. The text discusses all of the following forms of loyalty *except* loyalty to
  a. the benefits.
  b. the salesclerks consumers trust the most.
  c. a particular form of product.
  d. product types depending upon the occasion of use.

9. The role of the marketer in product disposition may include demarketing. This response means that sellers attempt to _____ demand for their products.
  a. reduce
  b. increase
  c. maximize
  d. reposition

10. What "color" are marketers who send the message that their products are environmentally friendly?
  a. green
  b. gray
  c. brown
  d. blue

Team Talk

1. Share your experiences of two recent consumption situations in which the physical and social context clearly had an influence on your behavior.

2. Describe one routine or daily task you perform that involves ritual consumption.

3. Discuss one good or service you buy that you consider sacred or that has, in your view, become sacralized. Choose a nonreligious example.

4. Select two advertisements for different types of goods and/or services. Based on each advertisement, what are your expectations of each product? Would you characterize your expectations as ideal performance, equitable performance, or expected performance? Why?

5. Think of the most recent purchase you have made with which you felt dissatisfied. Why were you dissatisfied? What did you do about it, and what was the outcome? Before the purchase, what, if anything, could the seller have done to help prevent your dissatisfaction?

6. Describe a recent situation in which you experienced purchase-associated cognitive dissonance. How did you feel, and what steps did you or others around you take to help resolve those feelings?

7. Is there a brand or a retail outlet to which you consider yourself loyal? What makes you think you are loyal? What are the reasons for your loyalty?

8. Have you or any member of your team ever taken action when either satisfied or dissatisfied with a purchase? What was done? What was the seller's response? What did you or the other team member(s) learn from this experience?

9. How does your position on the environment influence your behavior as a consumer? Think in terms of both product selection and product and packaging disposition. Be specific.

Workshops

Research Workshop

Background

Different levels of brand loyalty for carbonated soft drinks exist within the college student population. The objectives of this workshop are to explore the concept of brand loyalty to decide whether college students are single-brand loyal, multiple-brand loyal (loyal to a consideration set of brands), loyal to product characteristics, or loyal to product form.

Methodology

In teams of three to five, gather a sample of up to thirty students. Select, if you can, full-time, undergraduate students who are drinkers of carbonated soft drinks. Include both men and women from mixed ethnic backgrounds, if possible. Next, develop a questionnaire that will identify distinguishing characteristics of respondents and that will determine purchase behavior and commitment levels to the brand or brands most often consumed. Each researcher should test the questionnaire on one or two respondents before it is administered. As a team, modify the questionnaire as necessary after comparing test results.

Gather data using the modified questionnaire. Describe students in the sample according to the extent to which they are single-brand loyal, multiple-brand loyal, loyal to product characteristics, or loyal to product form. Through what purchase and consumption behaviors is their loyalty evident? Are there any noticeable differences in responses according to gender, ethnic background, or other demographic characteristics?

To the Marketplace

Though the sample here is much too small to generalize on college student soft drink preferences, what recommendations would you make to the marketers of soft drinks to this population group?

Creative Workshop

Background

One purpose of advertising is to position the expected performance of goods or services so as to minimize customer dissatisfaction. The objectives of this workshop are to evaluate advertising in various media based on the appropriateness of performance expectation messages, and to compare advertisements across four age groups.

Methodology

Select a total of four print advertisements, television commercials (two minutes or less in length), or television infomercials. Each must be targeted to a different age group (9 to 12; 13 to 16; 25 to 34; 65 or older) and must be focused on one product class. Evaluate the advertisements in terms of the stated or implied performance expectation. Look at the copy, the headlines, the people and situations portrayed, the use of color, the music, the lighting, and other creative cues. Also consider the mood of the advertisement. Grade the advertisements according to probability of leading to customer satisfaction.

To the Marketplace

Suggest ways in which to test advertising for its potential to lead to customer dissatisfaction. Be specific. How would you improve the advertisements that scored the lowest for customer satisfaction?

Managerial Workshop

Background

This workshop explores customer satisfaction strategies by catalog marketers. The first objective is to identify strategies used by selected catalog marketers to increase customer satisfaction and reduce potential for dissatisfaction. A second objective is to determine the strengths and weaknesses of strategies and to recommend alternatives.

Methodology

Select two catalog marketers. Examine their catalogs, noticing design, layout, use of color, use of models, and product information. Carefully read all ordering instructions, methods of payment, shipping options, refund/return procedures, and back-order procedures.

Identify, describe, and evaluate actions and procedures used by each marketer that can influence customer satisfaction or dissatisfaction. Compare and contrast the strategies of each marketer. Prepare a summary of each marketer's performance in terms of customer satisfaction and dissatisfaction.

To the Marketplace

What recommendations can you offer each of the catalog marketers to either increase customer satisfaction or reduce the potential for dissatisfaction?

Notes

1. Ravi Dhar and Itamar Simonson, "Making Complementary Choices in Consumption Episodes: Highlighting Versus Balancing," *Journal of Marketing Research,* Vol. 36 (February 1999), pp. 29–44.

2. Vikas Mittal, Pankaj Kumar, and Michael Tsiros, "Attribute-Level Performance, Satisfaction, and Behavioral Intentions Over Time: A Consumption System Approach," *Journal of Marketing,* Vol. 63 (April 1999), pp. 88–101.

3. Dennis W. Rook, "The Ritual Dimension of Consumer Behavior," *Journal of Consumer Research,* Vol. 12 (December 1985), pp. 251–264; Mary A. S. Tetreault and Robert E. Kline III, "Ritual, Ritualized Behavior, and Habit: Refinements and Extensions of the Consumption Ritual Construct," in Marvin Goldberg, Gerald Gorn and Richard W. Pollay, eds., *Advances in Consumer Research,* Vol. 17 (Provo, UT: Association for Consumer Research, 1990), pp. 31–38.

4. Russell W. Belk, Melanie Wallendorf, and John F. Sherry, Jr., "The Sacred and the Profane in Consumer Behavior: Theodicy on the Odyssey," *Journal of Consumer Research,* Vol. 16 (June 1989), pp. 1–38.

5. Deborah Hofmann, "In Jewelry, Choices Sacred, Profane, Ancient and New," *The New York Times* (May 7, 1989).

6. Beverly Gordon, "The Souvenir: Messenger of the Extraordinary," *Journal of Popular Culture,* Vol. 20, No. 3 (1986), pp. 135–146.

7. Belk, Wallendorf and Sherry, "The Sacred and the Profane."

8. Gerry Pratt, "The House as an Expression of Social Worlds," in James S. Duncan, ed., *Housing and Identity: Cross-Cultural Perspectives* (London: Croom Helm, 1981), pp. 135–179.

9. Dean MacCannell, *The Tourist: A New Theory of the Leisure Class* (New York: Shocken Books, 1976).

10. Thomas C. O'Guinn and Ronald J. Faber, "Compulsive Buying: A Phenomenological Exploration," *Journal of Consumer Research,* Vol. 16 (September 1989), pp. 147–157.

11. Elizabeth C. Hirshman, "The Consciousness or Addiction: Toward a General Theory of Compulsive Consumption," *Journal of Consumer Research,* Vol. 19 (September 1992), pp. 155–179.

12. O'Guinn and Faber (1989).

13. Aric Rindfleisch, James E. Burroughs, and Frank Denton, "Family Structure, Materialism, and Compulsive Consumption," *Journal of Consumer Research,* Vol. 23 (March 1997), pp. 312–325.

14. Ibid.

15. James A. Roberts, Chris Manolis, and John Tanner, Jr., "Family Structure, Materialism, and Compulsive Buying: A Reinquiry and Extension," *Journal of the Academy of Marketing Science,* Vol. 31 (Summer 2003), pp. 300–311.

16. Aviv Shoham and Maja Makovec Brencic, "Compulsive Buying Behavior," *Journal of Consumer Marketing,* Vol. 20, No. 2 (2003), pp. 127–138.

17. "American Customer Satisfaction Holding Steady," *The Wirthlin Report,* Vol. 10 (June 2000), p. 1.

18. American Consumer Satisfaction Index website, http://www.theasci.org/fourth_quarter.htm, September 15, 2004.

19. Susan Posnak, "Customer Satisfaction Up Online," *American Demographics,* Vol. 26 (April 2004), p. 16.

20. Rolph E. Anderson, "Consumer Dissatisfaction: The Effect of Disconfirmed Expectancy on Perceived Product Performance," *Journal of Marketing Research,* Vol. 11 (February 1973), pp. 38–44.

21. Susan Fournier and David Glen Mick, "Rediscovering Satisfaction," *Journal of Marketing,* Vol. 63 (October 1999), pp. 5–23.

22. Ibid, p. 15.

23. Joan L. Giese and Joseph A. Cote, "Defining Consumer Satisfaction," *Academy of Marketing Science Review,* online at http://www.amsreview.org/amsrev/theory/giese00-01. html.

24. Utpal M. Dholakia and Vicki G. Morwitz, "The Scope and Persistence of Mere-Measurement Effects: Evidence from a Field Study of Customer Satisfaction Measurement," *Journal of Consumer Research,* Vol. 29 (September 2002), pp. 159–167.

25. Willemijn van Dolen, Joseph Lemmink, Ko de Ruyter, and Ad de Jong, "Customer-Sales Employee Encounters: A Dyadic Perspective," *Journal of Retailing,* Vol. 78, No. 4 (2002), pp. 265–279.

26. Anderson, "Consumer Dissatisfaction."

27. Ibid.

28. Vikas Mittal, William T. Ross, and Patrick M. Baldasare, "The Asymmetric Impact of Negative and Positive Attribute-Level Performance on Overall Satisfaction and Repurchase Intentions," *Journal of Marketing,* Vol. 62 (January 1998), pp. 33–47.

29. Morris B. Holbrook, "Situation-Specific Ideal Points and Usage of Multiple Dissimilar Brands," in Jagdish N. Sheth, ed., *Research in Marketing,* Vol. 7 (Greenwich, CT: JAI Press, 1984), pp. 93–112.

30. Robert B. Woodruff, Ernest R. Cadotte, and Roger L. Jenkins, "Modeling Consumer Satisfaction Using Experienced-Based Norms," *Journal of Marketing Research,* Vol. 20 (August 1983), pp. 296–304.

31. M. Leichty and Gilbert A. Churchill, Jr., "Conceptual Insights into Consumer Satisfaction with Services," in Neil Beckwith et al., eds., *Educators' Conference Proceedings* (Chicago, IL: American Marketing Association, 1979), pp. 509–515.

32. Donald P. Robin, R. Eric Reidenbach, and P. J. Forrest, "The Perceived Importance of an Ethical Issue as an Influence of the Ethical Decision-Making of Ad Managers," *Journal of Business Research*, Vol. 35 (1996), pp. 18–28.

33. James L. Thomas, Scott J. Vitell, Faye W. Gilbert, and Gregory M. Rose, "The Impact of Ethical Cues on Customer Satisfaction with Service," *Journal of Retailing*, Vol. 78, No. 3 (2002), pp. 167–173.

34. Gilbert A. Churchill, Jr. and Carol Suprenant, "An Investigation into the Determinants of Customer Satisfaction," *Journal of Marketing Research*, Vol. 19 (November 1983), pp. 491–504.

35. Laurette Dube-Rioux, "The Power of Affective Reports in Predicting Satisfaction Judgments," in Gerald A. Gorn and Richard W. Pollay, eds., *Advances in Consumer Research*, Vol. 17 (Provo, UT: Association for Consumer Research, 1990), pp. 571–576; Lalita A. Manrai and Meryl P. Gardner, "The Influences of Affect on Attributions for Product Failure," in Rebecca H. Holman and Michael R. Solomon, eds., *Advances in Consumer Research*, Vol. 18 (Provo, UT: Association for Consumer Research, 1991), pp. 249–254.

36. William H. Cunningham and M. Venkatesan, "Cognitive Dissonance and Consumer Behavior: A Review of the Evidence," *Journal of Marketing Research*, Vol. 14 (August 1976), pp. 303–308.

37. Richard L. Oliver, *Satisfaction: A Behavioral Perspective on the Consumer* (New York: McGraw-Hill, 1997).

38. Howard H. Kendler, *Basic Psychology* (New York: Appleton-Century-Crofts, 1968).

39. Frederick F. Reichfield, *The Loyalty Effect* (Boston, MA: Harvard Business School Press, 1996).

40. Richard L. Oliver, "Whence Consumer Loyalty?" *Journal of Marketing*, Vol. 63 (Special Issue 1999), pp. 33–44.

41. ———, *Satisfaction: A Behavioral Perspective on the Consumer* (New York: Irwin/McGraw-Hill, 1997).

42. Thomas Exeter, "Looking for Brand Loyalty," *American Demographics*, Vol. 10 (April 1988), p. 33.

43. Ibid.

44. H. Bruskin Associates, "New Study on Brand Loyalty," *Marketing Review*, Vol. 43, No. 9 (1988), p. 25.

45. Sharon E. Beatty, Lynn R. Kahle, and Pamela Homer, "The Involvement-Commitment Model: Theory and Implications," *Journal of Business Research*, Vol. 16 (March 1988), pp. 149–167.

46. "Brand Loyalty Beats Price in Some Product Categories," *Marketing News* (November 28, 1980), p. 1.

47. Richard E. DuWors, Jr. and George H. Haines, "Event History Analysis Measures of Brand Loyalty," *Journal of Marketing Research*, Vol. 28 (November 1990), pp. 485–493.

48. George S. Day, "A Two-Dimensional Concept of Brand Loyalty," *Journal of Advertising Research*, Vol. 9 (September 1969), pp. 29–36; James M. Carman, "Correlates of Brand Loyalty: Some Positive Results," *Journal of Marketing Research*, Vol. 7 (February 1970), pp. 67–76.

49. Ted Roselius, "Consumer Rankings of Risk Reduction Methods," *Journal of Marketing*, Vol. 35 (January 1971), pp. 56–61; Jagdish N. Sheth and M. Venkatesan, "Risk-Reduction Processes in Repetitive Consumer Behavior," *Journal of Marketing Research*, Vol. 5 (August 1968), pp. 307–311.

50. Carman, "Correlates of Brand Loyalty: Some Positive Results."

51. Lester P. Guest, "Brand Loyalty Revisited: A Twenty Year Report," *Journal of Applied Psychology*, Vol. 48 (April 1964), pp. 93–97.

52. *Advertising Age* (March 22, 1974), p. 62.

53. *Advertising Age* (January 16, 1975), p. 31; *Advertising Age* (March 22, 1974), p. 62.

54. Robert W. Pimentel and Kristy E. Reynolds, "A Model for Consumer Devotion: Affective Commitment with Proactive Sustaining Behaviors," *Academy of Marketing Science Review* (Online), http://www.amsreview.org/articles/pimentel05-2004.pdf (2004).

55. "Brand X (and Sometimes Y)," *American Demographics* (August 1997).

56. Kerry J. Smith, "If You Think They Are Dumb, Think Again, Shoppers Are Savvier Than Ever," *PROMO*, Vol. 7 (November 1994), pp. 97–101.

57. Robert D. Hisrich, Ronald J. Dornoff, and Jerome B. Kernan, "Perceived Risk in Store Selection," *Journal of Marketing Research*, Vol. 9 (November 1972), pp. 435–439; Joseph F. Dash, Leon G. Schiffman, and Conrad Berenson, "Risk and Personality Related Dimensions of Store Choice," *Journal of Marketing*, Vol. 40 (January 1976), pp. 32–39.

58. Arieh Goldman, "The Shopping Style Explanation for Store Loyalty," *Journal of Retailing*, Vol. 53 (Winter 1977–78), pp. 33–64, 94.

59. Fred D. Reynolds, William R. Darden, and Warren S. Martin, "Developing an Image of the Store-Loyal Customer," *Journal of Retailing*, Vol. 50 (Winter 1975–76), pp. 73–84.

60. Srini S. Srinivasan, Rolph Anderson, and Kishore Ponnavolu, "Customer Loyalty in E-Commerce: An Exploration of Its Antecedents and Consequences," *Journal of Retailing*, Vol. 78, No. 1 (2002), pp. 41–50.

61. Valarie A. Zeithaml, Leonard L. Berry, and A. Parasuraman, "The Nature and Determinants of Customer Expectations of Service," *Journal of the Academy of Marketing Science*, Vol. 21 (Winter 1993), pp. 1–12.

62. Richard D. Oliver and John E. Swan, "Consumer Perceptions of Interpersonal Equity and Satisfaction in Transactions: A Field Survey Approach," *Journal of Marketing*, Vol. 53 (April 1982), pp. 21–35.

63. Ronald L. Hess, Jr., Shankar Ganesan, and Noreen M. Klein, "Service Failure and Recovery: The Impact of Relationship Factors on Customer Satisfaction," *Journal of the Academy of Marketing Science*, Vol. 31 (Spring 2003), pp. 127–145.

64. Steven Brown and Richard F. Beltramini, "Consumer Complaining and Word of Mouth Activities: Field Evidence," in Thomas K. Srull, ed., *Advances in Consumer Research*, Vol. 16 (Provo, UT: Association for Consumer Research, 1989), pp. 9–16.

65. Marsha L. Richins, "Negative Word-of-Mouth by Dissatisfied Consumers: A Pilot Study," *Journal of Marketing*, Vol. 47 (Winter 1983), pp. 68–78.

66. Richard W. Mizerski, "An Attribution Explanation of the Disproportionate Influence of Unfavorable Information," *Journal of Consumer Research*, Vol. 9 (December 1982), pp. 301–310.

67. Jagdip Singh, "Voice, Exit and Negative Word-of-Mouth Behaviors: An Investigation Across Three Service Categories," *Journal of the Academy of Marketing Science,* Vol. 18, No. 1 (Winter 1990), pp. 1–15.

68. "P&G Drops Logo: Cites Satan Rumors," *The New York Times* (April 25, 1985), p. D1; "P&G Once Again Has a Devil of a Time with Rumors about Moon, Stars Logo," *The Wall Street Journal* (March 26, 1990), p. B3.

69. "Bubble Gum Maker Wants to Know How the Rumors Started," *The Wall Street Journal* (March 24, 1977), p. 1.

70. "A Puzzlement Over a Bakery Rumor," *The New York Times* (September 10, 1981), p. A16.

71. Alice M. Tybout, Bobby J. Calder, and Brian Sternthal, "Using Information Processing Theory to Design Marketing Strategies," *Journal of Marketing Research,* Vol. 18 (February 1981), pp. 73–79.

72. Ibid.

73. Susan M. Smith, Thomas J. Steele, and William H. McBroom, "Consumer Rumors and Corporate Communications: Suggestions for Forestalling and Combating Rumors," *Marketing Management Journal,* Vol. 10 (Spring/Summer 2000), pp. 97–106.

74. Jagdip Singh, "Consumer Complaint Intentions and Behavior: Definition and Taxonomical Issues," *Journal of Marketing,* Vol. 52 (January 1988), pp. 93–107.

75. Ralph L. Day, "Modeling Choices among Alternative Responses to Dissatisfaction," in Thomas C. Kinnear, ed., *Advances in Consumer Research,* Vol. 11 (Provo, UT: Association for Consumer Research, 1984), pp. 496–499.

76. Michelle N. Morganowsky and Hilda Mayer Buckley, "Complaint Behavior: Analysis by Demographics, Lifestyles and Consumer Values," in Melanie Wallendorf and Paul Anderson, eds., *Advances in Consumer Research,* Vol. 14 (Provo, UT: Association for Consumer Research, 1987), pp. 223–226.

77. Kathy J. Cobb, Gary C. Walgren, and Mary Hallowed, "Differences in Organizational Responses to Consumer Letters of Satisfaction and Dissatisfaction," in Melanie Wallendorf and Paul Anderson, eds., *Advances in Consumer Research,* Vol. 14 (Provo, UT: Association for Consumer Research, 1987), p. 227.

78. Richins, "Negative Word-of-Mouth by Dissatisfied Consumers"; Singh, "Consumer Complaint Intentions."

79. Jeffrey G. Blodgett, Donna J. Hill, and Stephen S. Tax, "The Effects of Distributive, Procedural, and Interactional Justice on Postcomplaint Behavior," *Journal of Retailing,* Vol. 73 (Summer 1997), pp. 185–210; Stephen S. Tax, Stephen W. Brown, and Murali Chandrashekaran, "Customer Evaluations of Service Complaint Experiences: Implications for Relationship Marketing," *Journal of Marketing,* Vol. 62 (April 1998), pp. 60–76.

80. Cynthia J. Grimm, "Understanding and Reaching the Consumer: A Summary of Recent Research. Part II— Complaint Response Satisfaction and Market Impact," *Mobius,* (Fall 1987), p. 18.

81. Cobb, Walgren, and Hallowed, "Differences in Organizational Responses."

82. Judy Strauss and Donna J. Hill, "Consumer Complaints by E-Mail: An Exploratory Investigation of Corporate Responses and Customer Reactions," *Journal of Interactive Marketing,* Vol. 15 (Winter 2001), pp. 63–73.

83. Denise T. Smart and Charles L. Martin, "Manufacturer Responsiveness to Consumer Correspondence: An Empirical Investigation of Consumer Perceptions," *Journal of Consumer Affairs,* Vol. 26 (Summer 1991), pp. 104–128.

84. Roger Bougie, Rik Pieters, and Marcel Zeelenberg, "Angry Customers Don't Come Back, They Get Back: The Experience and Behavioral Implications of Anger and Dissatisfaction in Services," *Journal of the Academy of Marketing Science,* Vol. 31 (Fall 2003), pp. 377–393.

85. Bougie et al., "Angry Customers."

86. T. Riley, *C.H.A.R.M. School: Lessons in Customer Hostility and Rage Management* (Santa Cruz, CA: Applied Psychology Press, 2002).

87. See Jacob Jacoby, Carol K. Berning, and Thomas F. Dietvorst, "What About Dispossession?" *Journal of Marketing,* Vol. 41 (April 1977), pp. 22–28; Melissa Martin Young, "Disposition of Possessions During Role Transitions," in Rebecca Holman and Michael Solomon, eds., *Advances in Consumer Research,* Vol. 18 (Provo, UT: Association for Consumer Research, 1991), pp. 33–39; Melissa Martin Young and Melanie Wallendorf, "Ashes to Ashes, Dust to Dust: Conceptualizing Consumer Disposition of Possessions," *American Marketing Association Winter Educators' Proceedings* (Chicago, IL: American Marketing Association, 1989), pp. 33–39.

88. "Environmental Update," *Research Supplement—The Wirthlin Report,* Vol. 10 (November 2000), p. 1.

Focusing on internal processes, we will now look closely at the emotional and cognitive forces that shape buying decisions. How do we learn about products? Why do we remember some and forget others? How does what we believe shape what we will buy and change in response to what we have bought? How does a good mood affect our shopping? When do we tend to take risks on new products? The information that flows from the marketer to the consumer and back carries a wealth of nuances that affect these and many other interactions.

Symbolic Consumption, Self-Image, and Personality

Claudine, a college sophomore, is shopping in a new department store. As she enters the store, she notices that the women's department is divided into four sections: classic, sensual, trendy, and natural. She begins wandering through the classic section—straight-line black dresses, sophisticated suits, and blazers, all with matching accessories. Claudine doesn't see herself as the Chanel No. 5 type and quickly moves on.

Next, she enters the sensual section. She's overwhelmed by colors, textures, and fragrances, by the red lipsticks, creamy moisturizers, and silky fabrics. Claudine imagines the type of woman who shops here—sexy, pampered, and self-indulgent. This is certainly not her!

She moves on to the trendy section, which is filled with new styles, unique, daring, and provocative. These are for the woman who wants to make a statement through her fashion sense and whom others try to copy. Her roommate is a little like that—she has a knack for style that Claudine sometimes envies but is not entirely comfortable with.

Just as she is about to give up, Claudine enters into the natural section, full of unbleached cottons, fresh scents, comfortable shoes, natural leather accessories. Right away, she says to herself, "This is me." Within minutes, she has worked her way through the racks, chosen a few outfits, and is on her way to the fitting rooms.[1]

As Claudine shopped for clothes, she thought not about colors and fabric but about **self-image.** That is the essence of this chapter. As we shall see, the ways in which consumers view themselves and how they feel they are viewed by others have a great deal of influence on their attitudes toward brands and on their purchase choices.

5-1 Symbolic Consumption

Symbolic consumption is the process through which consumers—on the basis of symbols—buy, consume, and dispose of products. Understanding the effects of symbols can provide important insights into consumer behavior. As we saw when Claudine shopped, most goods and services are, to some extent, symbolic and carry special meanings for both the people who use them and the people who see them. Consumers buy and use goods and services not just for their utility but for the things they represent. A great part of consumption is, therefore, symbolic—it reflects the personalities, lifestyles, and desires of consumers.

5-1a Semiotics

Research into consumption over the last decade has been dominated by **semiotics,** the study of signs and their meanings. Consumer semiotics focuses on issues such as how consumers use symbols to interpret the world, how those symbols are chosen and given meaning, and how they provide insight into certain aspects of the consumer's life.[2] Consumer semioticians study not only immediate, spontaneous consumer actions or responses, but also the reasons behind such responses. Thus, introspection, personal admission, imagination, and repressed attitudes and motives are all a part of consumer semiotics.[3]

Signs and Their Influence   Signs used by marketers to influence consumer choices are usually grouped into three categories: icons, indexes, and symbols.

Icons are visual representations of objects, persons, or events. They are clear and unambiguous; they communicate ideas to consumers exactly as the marketer intends. A print advertisement featuring a photograph of a chocolate bar with lots of peanut filling, for example, is iconic—it is designed to appeal directly to consumers who find chocolate and peanuts irresistible.

Indexes rely on some easily recognizable property of the idea they are representing, like the telltale "click" of a well-struck golf shot or the sigh of satisfaction after drinking a cold soda on a hot day. Indexes communicate something about the quality of the idea.

Symbols use learned associations between a signifier and a signified to communicate ideas. Suppose an art director chooses light blue in creating an advertisement for ice cream, believing it will generate a feeling of freshness. The color blue is the signifier in the advertisement, and the feeling of freshness is the signified. Symbols are the most powerful of signs because they can be used to induce certain states of mind or feelings in the consumer.[4] An executive suite in which brandy is served is a symbolic sign of success and achievement in the business world.

Marketplace 5-1 shows the influence of symbolic consumption on aesthetic plastic surgery. As described, cosmetic surgery symbolizes many things to many people. The symbols include improved body image, social acceptance, an act of self-completion, and a move toward a positive body image. Marketplace 5-2 describes the symbols perceived in body decoration. For example, teenagers pierce their bodies to symbolize passage from adolescence to adulthood.

The marketing implications of semiotics are significant. By paying close attention to what consumers say about and do with specific goods and services, marketers are better able to reconfigure those goods or services to maximize perceived value. Thus, semiotics assists marketers in uncovering hidden signs and meanings in consumers' experiences with their goods and services. Understanding those hidden signs and meanings allows the marketer to design effective programs that maximize consumer perceptions of the value of the marketer's good or service.

5-1b How Consumers Perceive Brands

Take a brand like Guess jeans. What is your image of the brand? Are Guess jeans high quality? Classy? Sexy? Consumers perceive brands in terms of a variety of attributes. Some are related to the tangible characteristics of the product, such as fabric, cut, or quality, while others reflect characteristics of the consumer, such as being fashionable or adventurous. How consumers perceive brands tells a great deal not only about the brand itself but also about the consumer and the consumer's self-image.

5-1c Brand Image

Brand image can be defined as the overall vision or position of a brand in the mind of the consumer. Image is a result of a combination of attributes—both tangible and intangible—perceived by the consumer about a brand. On another dimension, each attribute is either a benefit or a cost to the consumer. Starbucks coffee, for example, may be perceived as offering such tangible benefits as freshness and great taste as well as the intangible benefit

---

self-image (see p. 136) A configuration of beliefs about the self.

symbolic consumption (see p. 136) The process through which consumers—on the basis of symbols—buy, consume, and dispose of products.

semiotics The study of signs and their meanings.

icons Visual representations of objects, persons, or events.

indexes Easily recognizable properties of an idea.

symbols Learned associations between a signifier and a signified to communicate ideas.

F A Q

Why do some people like to wear logos on their clothing?

brand image An overall vision or position of a brand in the mind of the consumer.

Marketplace 5-1

Symbols and Cosmetic Surgery

A study investigated the influence of symbolic consumption on what many consider a radical purchase—aesthetic plastic surgery. The researcher started out with the following hypotheses:

1. Cosmetic surgery symbolizes improved body image. Dissatisfaction with specific physical features may motivate consumers to consider plastic surgery.

2. Cosmetic surgery symbolizes social acceptance. People may elect plastic surgery in the hope of improving their performance in key social roles.

3. Cosmetic surgery serves as an act of self-completion. Consumers believe plastic surgery will help consolidate a desired identity.

4. Cosmetic surgery symbolizes a move toward a positive body image or an escape from a negative one.

In-depth interviews with nine consumers of aesthetic plastic surgery not only supported these hypotheses but also gave rise to other symbolic properties of cosmetic surgery. One emergent theme was that plastic surgery assists in the reintegration of self. That is, given a role transition (such as a divorce), cosmetic surgery supplied some subjects with physical attributes that helped them feel more comfortable about their newly adopted roles. Another theme was that plastic surgery was viewed as an aid to further change during role transition. One subject who was recently divorced thought that nose surgery and chin implant surgery would help her feel good about herself, and she needed such self-confidence in order to return to college and succeed.

Source: Adapted from "Selves in Transition: Symbolic Consumption in Personal Rites of Passage and Identity Reconstruction" by John W. Schouten in *Journal of Consumer Research,* Vol. 17, March 1991, pp. 412–425. Copyright © 1991. Reprinted by permission of The University of Chicago Press.

of social acceptability among peers. The same consumer may perceive its costs to be not only its high price, but also the need to travel to a special outlet to buy it.

A brand image is determined by three sets of needs that are reflected in brand attributes. These are utilitarian/functional needs, experiential/aesthetic needs, and value-expressive/symbolic needs (see Exhibit 5-1).

Read CBite 5-1. The study described shows that brand image is influenced easily by one's desire to compare oneself with significant others. Thus, a brand image can be molded as a direct function of social influence.

A useful way of classifying those attributes and benefits that make up brand image is by considering the extent to which they meet three types of consumer need: utilitarian or functional need, experiential or aesthetic need, and value-expressive or symbolic need.

utilitarian or functional needs Needs that are met by products that help consumers remove or avoid problems.

Utilitarian or Functional Needs
Products that help consumers remove or avoid problems meet **utilitarian or functional needs.** A driver's-side air bag and other safety restraints, for example, help prevent injury in the event of an automobile accident.

experiential or aesthetic needs Needs that are met by products that satisfy sensory expectations.

Experiential or Aesthetic Needs
Products that satisfy sensory expectations meet **experiential or aesthetic needs.** A fine restaurant offering unique atmosphere, decor, and entertainment as well as a wonderful menu appeals directly to the senses and helps con-

Exhibit 5-1

Brand image is a function of utilitarian/functional, experiential/aesthetic, and value-expressive/symbolic attributes.

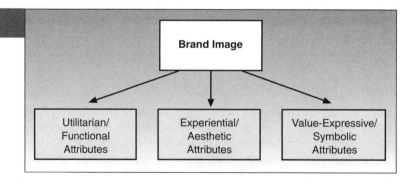

Marketplace 5-2

Body Decoration

Body decoration serves many purposes. First, body decoration separates group members from nonmembers. Why do you think many teenagers color their hair green, blue, purple, and other nontraditional colors? Could it be that they want to separate themselves from the adults?

Second, body decoration places the individual in the social organization. That is, people have rites of passage, and body decoration becomes an instrument to facilitate the rite of passage. Again, teenagers go through a rite of passage from adolescence to adulthood. Perhaps getting tattoos and piercing their bodies is symbolic of this rite of passage. Third, body decoration places the person in a gender category and enhances gender-role identification. This means that for a woman to express her womanhood, she decorates her body in ways that make others recognize her as such. A girl turning into a woman decorates her body differently. She starts wearing makeup and putting on lipstick. Doing so communicates a message to others—that she is now a woman.

Fourth, body decoration indicates desired social conduct. For example, some gay men wear an earring in the left or right ear to communicate to others their preference to meet others who are submissive versus dominant. Fifth, body decoration indicates high status or rank. For example, some people think that people who wear glasses tend to be of high rank. As a result, some people wear glasses with clear lenses to enhance their perceived rank, even though they do not have vision problems. Finally, body decoration provides a sense of security. Decorating the body with lucky charms and rabbits' feet is believed by some to protect them from the "evil eye."

Marketers of body decoration products and services can benefit from understanding the source of motivation of their customers in seeking to decorate their bodies. By understanding their customers' motivation, marketers can better develop products and services that meet the needs of their customers and promote these products and services in persuasive ways.

Source: Adapted from Ruth P. Rubinstein, "Color, Circumcision, Tattoos, and Scars," in *The Psychology of Fashion,* edited by Michael R. Solomon (Lexington, MA: Lexington Books, 1985), pp. 243–254; Peter H. Bloch and Marsha L. Richins, "'You Look 'Mahvelous': The Pursuit of Beauty and the Marketing Concept," *Psychology and Marketing,* Vol. 9 (January 1992), pp. 3–16.

sumers enjoy the entire dining experience. Recent research has focused on how retail establishments vary in the way they provide hedonic value to shoppers. Hedonic shopping value reflects an evaluation that interacting with a shopping environment is rewarding for the sake of the experience itself.[5]

Value-Expressive or Symbolic Needs   Products that help consumers express their own self-images meet **value-expressive or symbolic needs.** A young man buying his first car might go for a sports model, believing it will help project a macho image and, therefore, make him more attractive to women.[6]

Understanding the benefits associated with a given product helps the marketer develop a high-demand product and create a distinctive brand image for that product.

> **value-expressive or symbolic needs** Needs that are met by products that help consumers express their own self-images.

CBite 5-1

I'll Have What He's Having

In one study, subjects were asked to select a brand of cola. A previous study had revealed that one brand (Brand A) was preferred in blind taste tests. For this study, each subject was placed in a room with three confederates of the researcher (stooges). The stooges rated the taste of the colas in front of the subject and selected the least popular brand (Brand B). The subject was then asked to make a choice. Subjects scoring high on the measure of attention to social comparison information ended up selecting the cola that was preferred by the stooges, while those who scored low on the measure were less influenced by the confederates' cola preference and tended to select Brand A.

Source: Adapted from William O. Bearden and Randall L. Rose, "Attention to Social Comparison Information," *Journal of Consumer Research,* Vol. 16 (March 1990), pp. 461–471.

That image can be supported further by advertising focusing on easily identifiable consumer needs.

5-1d Brand-User Personality or Brand-User Image

"Be a Pepper!" rang out a successful campaign for the popular soft drink, Dr. Pepper. Being a "Pepper" meant having more confidence, being more assertive, and taking control. The marketers of Dr. Pepper created a personality around their product that appealed to the consumer's sense of fun, transmitted through innovative, creative advertising.[7] **Brand-user personality,** also known as **brand-user image,** is based on value-expressive attributes that characterize the brand.[8]

> **brand-user personality** or **brand-user image** A mental representation of a brand along value-expressive attributes.

Research studies of brand image and brand personality are enormously valuable to marketers. By gaining insight into the image consumers currently have of a brand and of brand users, marketers can, if needed, begin to reshape that image and create a new, more favorable personality for the brand. Product or service attributes that are perceived as negative are changed, and those perceived as positive are reinforced. One such study investigated the user image of mass-transit riders, finding that consumers generally viewed the typical rider of mass transit in an unfavorable light. Because of this negative perception, potential riders shied away from using the mass-transit system. A marketing campaign was developed to transform the negative user image into a more positive one.[9]

To truly understand how a brand-user image affects consumer behavior, marketers need to understand how the brand-user image interacts with consumers' self-image and whether the congruence between the brand-user image and the consumer self-image motivates purchasing.

Marketing Management—Implications and Actions

Understanding how symbols influence consumer behavior helps marketers to:
- Use semiotics research to understand consumers' relationships to product offerings.
- Use icons, indexes, and symbols to create a positive brand personality.
- Classify which of the three types of needs their products or services will best meet.

5-2 Self-Image

The consumer's self-concept plays a significant role in predicting and explaining behavior. Consumers have multiple selves, reflecting the many roles they play in their daily lives. Social psychologists talk about the multiple selves as *role identities*. A typical college student, for example, has a number of identities outside the classroom—as son or daughter, brother or sister, fraternity or sorority member, athlete, class project leader, lover, friend, and so on. Each identity is distinct and gives rise to a different set of purchase needs and purchase motivations.

Role identities, then, have enormous impact on marketplace behavior. The self-concept, however, is more complex than role identity. It encompasses not just the roles in which consumers see themselves but extends to how consumers feel they are viewed by others in each of these roles. When we make a purchase, we consider not just how the purchase suits our image of ourselves; we also consider how others will react to us once we buy, own, and use the product purchased. Through this process of reflective evaluation,[10] consumers figure out how they will be viewed in the eyes of others and create a social self—an image of how they believe others see them.

5-2a Forms of Self-Image

What is self-image? It is a configuration of beliefs related to the self. Consumer researchers define self-image in terms of the relationship between consumers and products. For example, if they own a sports car, certain consumers may see themselves as attractive and outgoing. Other consumers might see themselves as wealthy and reckless. As Exhibit 5-2 suggests, there are four major types of self-image that play a part in consumer behavior: actual self, ideal self, social self, and ideal social self.[11] Other forms of self-image discussed in consumer behavior literature include the extended self,[12] situational self,[13] expected self,[14] possible self,[15] and interdependent self;[16] however, for the sake of simplicity, we will limit the discussion to the four popular forms (actual, ideal, social, and ideal social).

Actual Self   Actual self-image is part of what psychologists refer to as the *private self*. The private self involves those images that one has of oneself about which one feels protective. "This is who I am," the person may say, or "This is not how others think of me." Actual self-image is how consumers see themselves, their personal identity. A sports car, for example, has a specific user image—consumers tend to think of the person who drives it as outgoing, attractive, even sexy. Do target consumers see themselves in this light? If so, that is their actual self-image. Perhaps, however, they see themselves as introverted, unattractive, and not very sexy. That, then, is their actual self-image.

Exhibit 5-2 further demonstrates that people are motivated to protect their personal identities. They feel uncomfortable if they catch themselves doing things that are not reflective of their true selves. This is the **self-consistency motive.** It drives people to act in ways that are in line with their actual self-images.[17]

Ideal Self   Ideal self-image, as shown in Exhibit 5-2, is also part of the private self. Ideal self-image is how consumers would like to be. A person may see himself as timid and lacking in confidence (actual self-image), yet he may not like this self-perception. He may want to become sensitive but self-assured (ideal self-image). As you may imagine, there is often a discrepancy between actual and ideal self. The ad in Exhibit 5-3 is an attempt to create an image that would be in conflict with the consumer's idealized self in retirement. The ad is directed to an older crowd who idealize youth.

▶**actual self-image**
How consumers see themselves.

▶**self-consistency motive**
The motivational tendency that drives people to act in a manner consistent with their actual self-images.

▶**ideal self-image**
How consumers would like to see themselves.

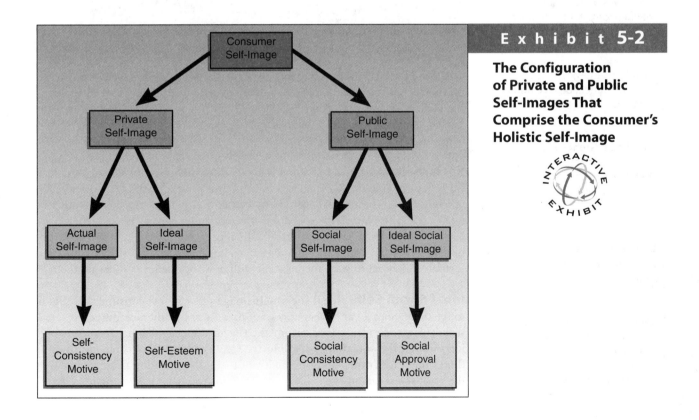

E x h i b i t 5-2

The Configuration of Private and Public Self-Images That Comprise the Consumer's Holistic Self-Image

self-esteem motive
The motivational tendency that drives people to act in a manner consistent with their ideal self-images.

social self-image
How consumers believe others see them.

social consistency motive
The motivational tendency that drives people to act in a manner consistent with their social self-images.

ideal social self-image
How consumers would like others to see them.

social approval motive
The motivational tendency that drives people to act in a manner consistent with their ideal social self-images.

The ideal self motivates behavior through what psychologists call the **self-esteem motive.** People have ideal images of themselves, and realizing these images (through the acquisition of products that are associated with them) boosts their self-esteem. That is, buying and using a product that has an image consistent with consumers' ideal self-image helps them feel good about themselves.[18]

Social Self   As shown in Exhibit 5-2, **social self-image** is linked to the public self—how we believe people think of us, and how we like people to think of us. Social self-image reflects how consumers believe others see them. A person may believe others see her as introverted and plain. This social self-image may be consistent or inconsistent with the actual and ideal self. Social self-image influences behavior through the **social consistency motive.** People are motivated to maintain an image others have of them. They feel uncomfortable if they act in ways inconsistent with how they believe others see them.[19]

Ideal Social Self   **Ideal social self-image** reflects how consumers would like others to see them. Sports car buyers may want to be seen by others as outgoing, attractive, and sexy. This is their ideal social self-image. The ideal social self-image affects people's behavior through the **social approval motive** (see Exhibit 5-2). People are motivated to do things that cause others to think highly of them. By definition, acting in ways that realize the ideal social self-image is likely to earn approval from others. Actions that are inconsistent with the ideal social self-image lead to social disapproval. Therefore, people tend to act consistently with their ideal social self-images to gain positive reactions from significant others.[20]

Consider the following statistic. Married men aged 35 to 54 without children are 130 percent more likely than other men to buy hair color to cover their gray.[21] So what is going on here? Why do men in this demographic category feel more motivated than men in other demographic categories to cover their gray hair with hair color? Perhaps their ideal social self-image is a man in their age category who doesn't have children and who looks more masculine and more like a husband than a father. This ideal social self-image is of a handsome man with youthful looks, so gray hair is out.

5-2b Self-Image Congruence

When a consumer's self-image matches brand-user image, the result is **self-image congruence.** This match or mismatch can occur with any one or more of the four types of self-concept, actual self-image, ideal self-image, social self-image, or ideal social self-image, as shown in Exhibit 5-4. A match of the brand-user image with the consumer's actual self-image is referred to as *actual self-congruity,* with ideal self-image as *ideal self-congruity,* with social self-image as *social self-congruity,* and with ideal social self-image as *ideal social self-congruity.*[22]

> **self-image congruence**
> The degree of match between the consumer's self-image (actual, ideal, social, or ideal social self-image) and the brand-user image.

Actual Self-Congruity Suppose consumers have a stereotyped image of a Porsche owner as adventurous. This is the brand-user image. Potential customers are likely to feel motivated to buy a Porsche if they have self-images that fit with this user image. Specifically, if Richard sees himself as adventurous (actual self-image), he may feel motivated to own or drive a Porsche because doing so reinforces this view of himself. He develops a favorable disposition toward the Porsche because doing so meets his need for self-consistency and allows him to be true to himself and his personal identity. This situation is referred to as **actual self-congruity** (see Exhibit 5-4). This congruity means that the brand-user image is matching with the consumer's actual self-image.

On the other hand, if Richard does not see himself as adventurous, he might feel silly owning a Porsche, saying, "This is not me," or "I don't see myself as a Porsche kind of person." These are expressions indicating that the need for self-consistency is violated. The consumer is not motivated to own or drive a Porsche because doing so would conflict with how he sees himself. In this example, Richard experiences actual self-incongruity, which means that the brand-user image is not matching with the consumer's actual self-image.

> **actual self-congruity**
> The degree of match between the consumer's actual self-image and the brand-user image.

Note a different example dealing with actual self-congruity. Consider the following statistic: In 1983, 58 percent of adults weighed more than is recommended for their height and frame size. That share stood at 63 percent in 1993.[23] Why are Americans gaining instead of losing weight? Perhaps because more Americans are accepting themselves as overweight and downplaying guilt. People are increasingly saying to themselves, "This is who and what I am, and I'm okay with it." This self-acceptance attitude motivates those of us who are overweight to buy and consume products matching our actual self-image of ourselves as being overweight. This is actual self-congruity at work. We are not motivated by our ideal but our actual self-image. We go about our daily lives acting in ways consistent with our actual self-image of being overweight. Hence, we are not motivated to change. We are learning to accept our bodies. Around 63 percent of Americans say there is too much emphasis on being thin in our society. Around 57 percent say they are eating pretty much what they want to, up from 49 percent in 1977. A statement made by Judith Langer of Langer Associates, a research firm in New York City, captures the notion of actual self-congruity well. She says, "We still revere thin, slender bodies. But more and more, I am hearing that it is OK to be myself."[24]

Marketers can persuade consumers to adopt a product or service through promotional messages designed to induce actual self-congruity. Consider, for example, the marketing of oversize clothes to overweight people. Marketers motivate overweight people to

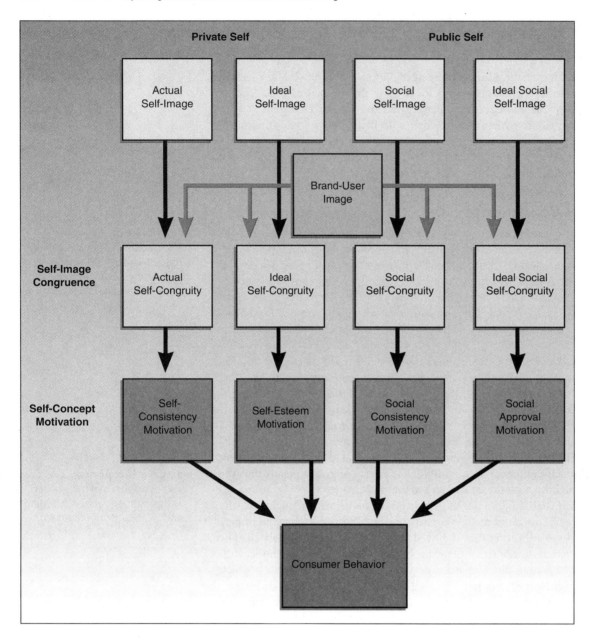

Driven to act with self-congruence, consumers will search out products and services with brand-user images congruent to their own.

consider certain designs, styles, or brands of clothes specifically designed for overweight people by employing models that overweight consumers can identify with. Marketers want overweight consumers to say, "This model is like me. The model is wearing outfit X. I like this outfit because it matches the kind of person I am." Here, consumers become motivated to adopt the advertised outfit because doing so is consistent with their actual self-image of being overweight. Purchasing and wearing such an outfit reinforces the actual self-image and thus satisfies consumers' need to act in ways consistent with their own actual self. That is, adopting the advertised outfit serves to satisfy their need for self-consistency.

Ideal Self-Congruity Some psychologists link the discrepancy between the actual and the ideal self-image to measures of self-esteem. By reducing the discrepancy, people can approach their ideal self-images and thus increase self-esteem.[25] Consider the following statistic. Seven out of ten women say that exercise enhances their self-image. This means that women exercise because they are motivated to enhance their self-esteem.[26] Exercising is a way to help them approach their ideal self-image in relation to their body shape. That is, exercise helps them reduce the discrepancy between the actual and ideal self-image. This situation reflects what we call **ideal self-congruity** (see Exhibit 5-4). The brand-user image (in this case the image of the person who is exercising as being in good shape) is matching the consumer's ideal self-image (wanting to be in good shape). Note that in this example, social psychologists would say that the women in question are motivated by self-esteem (behavior designed to get the person closer to her ideal self-image), *not* by self-consistency (behavior that reinforces one's actual self-image).

Marketers have made use of this notion by creating "fantasy advertising," designed to reduce the discrepancy and encourage consumers to buy products that would otherwise be inconsistent with their actual self-images. Perfume advertising is a good example. Typical advertisements suggest that wearing a certain fragrance will make women sexually desirable. The element of fantasy reduces the risk of actual self-incongruity and allows the consumer to focus on the product image's congruity with her ideal self-image.[27] This example shows how marketing strategy is formulated and guided by the notion of ideal self-congruity. That is, fantasy advertising motivates consumers to adopt the product because the user image of the product meets their ideal self-images. Women want to feel sexy and sexually desirable (ideal self-image). The image presented in fantasy advertising is consistent with the ideal self-image (ideal self-congruity). Therefore, buying the perfume is likely to enhance the consumer's self-esteem by realizing her ideal self-image of being sexy and sexually desirable.

CBite 5-2 shows how a pioneer brand has an advantage over follower brands because of ideal self-congruity.

Social Self-Congruity   Consider the case of "Sam," an adolescent who was considered to be a "good kid" by his parents until Sam made a new friend at school. His friend invited Sam to his home when his parents were away and introduced Sam to drugs. While driving back home, Sam crashed into a light pole. The police arrested him and charged him with driving under the influence. His license was suspended. His parents grounded him for a month. Before the month was up, Sam decided to get together with his new friend again because he felt that this friend was the only person who understood him. Sam sneaked out of the house and got into trouble again—this time with his friend's neighbors, who complained about the music being too loud and tangled with Sam. A fight broke out.

> **ideal self-congruity**
> The degree of match between the consumer's ideal self-image and the brand-user image.

CBite 5-2

The Pioneering Advantage: An Ideal Self-Congruity Explanation

A new brand that establishes a new product category is referred to as a pioneer brand. Brands like Coca-Cola, Kleenex, and Microsoft are considered pioneer brands. Pioneer brands do have a significant competitive advantage over follower brands. Professors Frank Alpert and Michael Kamins suggested that this competitive advantage might have something to do with the way consumers compare the image of the pioneer brand with their ideal self-image. A pioneering brand may be associated with valued personal traits such as authenticity, ingenuity, and trustworthiness. In many respects, consumers are likely to have an ideal self-image that includes these valued personal traits. If so, then they are most likely to experience ideal self-congruity with a pioneer brand. This ideal self-congruity motivates them to choose that brand more often than follower brands.

Source: Adapted from Frank H. Alpert and Michael A. Kamins, "Pioneer Brand Advantage and Consumer Behavior: A Conceptual Framework and Propositional Inventory," *Journal of the Academy of Marketing Science,* Vol. 22 (Summer 1994), pp. 244–253; Frank H. Alpert and Michael A. Kamins, "An Empirical Investigation of Consumer Memory, Attitude, and Perceptions Toward Pioneer and Follower Brands," *Journal of Marketing,* Vol. 59 (October 1995), pp. 34–45.

The police were summoned, and they took Sam home to his parents. They told his parents to "get Sam under control."

These two incidents provided the backdrop for Sam's parents to begin thinking of Sam as a "problem kid." Every encounter they had with him focused on the negatives. They started losing trust in him. Sam started to believe that his parents thought of him as "bad." Thus, his social self-image was changed from being a "normal kid" to being a "bad kid." Not surprisingly, Sam's irresponsible behavior got worse. His parents looked back and asked, "What happened?" Could they have prevented this from occurring? The answer is, perhaps they could have. Sam kept acting "bad" because he believed that his parents (and possibly significant others) thought of him as bad. People do things to maintain the view that others have of them. This is what the social consistency motive is all about. Sam said to himself, "If they think I am bad, I'll show them what bad really is!" So he got into more trouble to reinforce his parents' view of him. His parents might have been able to prevent the snowballing effect by maintaining a view of him that was positive. According to social consistency theory, this positive view of Sam might have saved him.

The same motive—the need for social consistency—operates in the marketplace. That is, we are all motivated by **social self-congruity,** buying products and services that reinforce our social self-images (see Exhibit 5-4). For example, if I believe that I am viewed by others as a nerd, then I'm likely to act as a nerd, and I'll buy things that nerds buy.

Marketers typically appeal to our social self-images through advertising. Consider pickup trucks, for example. Many pickup truck commercials show rugged men driving pickup trucks and hauling all kinds of things. The result of this type of advertising repetition is the creation and reinforcement of an image of the kind of people who drive pickup trucks. Marketers try to target their advertising to consumers who have a social self-image of themselves as rugged men driving pickup trucks, hauling all kinds of things in the truck. Men who believe that other people see them this way might be motivated to buy the advertised truck because doing so would satisfy their need for social consistency. Buying and driving the pickup truck would reinforce their belief that others see them and treat them as rugged men. This is part of their self-identity. Doing otherwise would be discomforting. People don't want to do things that violate their images in the eyes of others, especially significant others.

Ideal Social Self-Congruity
Consider the following statistic: 39 percent of Caucasian women believe working out helps with "being accepted by co-workers."[28] This is an example of **ideal social self-congruity.** Exercising meets the need for social approval by moving the consumer closer to her ideal social self-image, thus reducing the discrepancy between the social and ideal social self-image. It meets other women's approval because this image is currently valued by working women. Do you see how *the need for social approval* is at work in this example? This need motivates consumers to do things (including buying and consuming things) that have user images consistent with their ideal social self. The image of the woman who exercises is the kind of image that is valued and that is accepted by co-workers. Therefore, exercising is consistent with the ideal social self-image of "being accepted by co-workers." This is what ideal social self-congruity is all about (see Exhibit 5-4).

Consider the following example of an advertising campaign comparing the Pontiac Bonneville to a BMW. The commercial positions the Bonneville to appeal to drivers who would like others to see them in a BMW—as BMW types—but who want to achieve this image at a $10,000 savings by buying the lower-priced car. By likening the Bonneville to a BMW, the marketer persuades potential buyers that they will experience the same level of ideal social self-congruity. Driving the Bonneville will be consistent with how they like others to see them.

5-2c Gender Roles and Self-Image

Certain products in the marketplace are invariably perceived as men's goods, while others are perceived as women's. They are associated with gender roles or are gender typed.[29] Typical men's products might be certain models of cars, pocketknives, tool kits, shaving

---

▶ social self-congruity
The degree of match between the consumer's social self-image and the brand-user image.

▶ ideal social self-congruity
The degree of match between the consumer's ideal social self-image and the brand-user image.

cream, briefcases, whiskey, IRA accounts, or wall paint. Baby oil, hand lotion, clothes dryers, food processors, wine, long-distance phone services, and facial tissue, on the other hand, are commonly perceived as women's items.

Gender-typed products may be matched with the consumers' **gender-role orientation**—the extent to which men and women see themselves as masculine, feminine, or **androgynous** (that is, having both masculine and feminine characteristics). In the United States, masculinity is associated with such traits such as independence, toughness, aggressiveness, competitiveness, achievement, and rebelliousness, while femininity is commonly associated with tenderness, sensitivity, dependence, compliance, and cooperation. An androgynous personality type might display all of these traits.[30] The interaction between **gender-typed products** and consumers' gender role orientations influences consumer responses in the marketplace. One study has found, for example, that women who are masculine in their gender role orientation tend to prefer advertising portrayals of women in nontraditional roles. In another study, highly masculine consumers preferred ads with masculine themes (containing phrases such as "X beer has the strong, aggressive flavor that really asserts itself with good food and good company"). In contrast, highly feminine consumers preferred ads with feminine themes (containing phrases such as "Brewed with tender care, X beer is a full-bodied beer that goes down smooth").[31]

Consider the following statistic. In 1996, half of U.S. women surveyed said they wear high-heeled shoes on a daily basis. Among those who don't wear high heels every day, 55 percent say it's because the shoes hurt. Those who wear them agree that high heels cause discomfort, yet they keep wearing them. Forty-three percent of women say they've gotten blisters from high heels; 39 percent report pain in the balls of their feet; 23 percent say they get corns and calluses from high heels; and 22 percent report that they had back pain directly attributable to high heels. So why do women keep wearing them? The answer is women, like all humans, are motivated to gain approval and avoid disapproval of others. They may think that not wearing high heels will take away from their feminine look, an image they like to maintain in the eyes of others. Most importantly, wearing high heels is part of being a woman, a woman's role identity. Not wearing high heels may violate that role identity; it would go against the needs for social consistency and social approval. That is, women are motivated to behave in ways consistent with their social roles, how people perceive them to be. The message from society is "You are a woman, act like one. Wearing high heels is part of being a woman, so wear high heels."[32]

How do marketers use this information? Simple. They advertise gender-typed products such as high-heeled shoes in ways that appeal to highly feminine women—those who see themselves as feminine (actual self-image), those who like to see themselves as feminine (ideal self-image), those who think that others think of them as feminine (social self-image), and those who like others to think of them as feminine (ideal social self-image).

5-2d **Body Image**

Body image—how people view their bodies, physical selves, and appearance—is central to personal identity. Just as important to marketers is the concept of **ideal body image**—how people would like their bodies to be. Advertising for diet foods, shampoos, fashions, aerobics classes, and fitness equipment, for example, frequently compares body image and ideal body image to capture the attention of potential customers.

One consumer researcher conducted in-depth interviews with nine people who had plastic surgery to deal with body parts that were a significant source of dissatisfaction (examples include women who had facial wrinkles or noses or chins they found unattractive). This research indicated that cosmetic surgery usually occurs during role transitions, such as after a divorce. The research also indicated that plastic surgery boosts the consumer's self-esteem. Consumers of plastic surgery felt much better about themselves after surgery. Their views of themselves more closely matched their ideal and social selves.[33]

Marketplace 5-3 illustrates the conflict between how people like to see their body and how they believe they are seen by others. This conflict drives their purchasing of many products that affect their body image.

▶**gender-role orientation** The extent to which men and women see themselves as masculine, feminine, or androgynous.

▶**androgynous** Displaying both masculine and feminine characteristics.

▶**gender-typed products** Products associated with gender types—that is, masculinity and femininity.

▶**body image** How people see their bodies, physical selves, and appearance.

▶**ideal body image** How people would like their bodies to be.

Marketplace 5-3

The Socialized Body

Our culture is full of dualities. For example, the concept of mind and body is dualistic. Our culture emphasizes the virtues of the body in advertising and media. By the same token, we espouse the ideology of mind over body. Our mind is trapped in a material body. We desire to escape the body and the forces that drive it. The body changes in unwanted ways and eventually deteriorates. The mind resists the forces of nature, namely the aging process. We idealize youthfulness and the youthful body, yet we emphasize the notion that our true identities are not reflected in the bodies that house our souls.

How do we deal with this duality? We apply the mind to change the body. We correct the body to restore or maintain its youthfulness. And how do we do this? By changing our buying and consumption habits. People change their eating habits by buying and consuming less fatty products, such as eggs, meat, butter, ice cream, potato chips, and meals with fatty sauces. This duality between mind and body generates another duality in food consumption. Advertisers on the one hand advertise foods that are tempting and may "damage" the body; and, on the other hand, they advertise foods that are healthy for the body but that do not taste as good, leaving people torn between good taste and good health. They feel guilty if they go for good taste, and they feel unsatisfied if they go for good health. A paradox! A duality of sorts!

The duality of mind and body is also manifested in the duality of actual and ideal body. People feel that they don't measure up to the ideal body image propagated by society. Here is an excerpt from Angela, an 18-year-old high school senior:

> I am pretty content with my hair because I have good hair. I have good eyesight (laughs), so I don't have to wear glasses or anything that would make my face look different from what it is. In terms of bad points, well there is a lot. I got a lot of my father's features. I wish I had more of my mother's. My hands are pretty square. I have a kind of a big butt. Then I don't have that great of a stomach. I like my arms. They're not flabby, like you see a lot of people with flabby arms. I like my ankles. It sounds really stupid, but a lot of people have like these trunks and it's very unattractive. So I don't have huge fat ankles. One thing I really hate is that I have large calves, which I don't like.

Like this teen, many people express conflicts about their bodies. So what do they do to deal with this conflict? They camouflage their body flaws through clever grooming. They purge after they eat. They don't eat. They get plastic surgery. They exercise and diet. They do this not necessarily to approach the ideal body image as established by society through mass media, but to avoid the ridicule, guilt, and other forms of emotional distress that come from be treated as deviant.

Source: Adapted from "Understanding the Socialized Body: A Poststructuralist Analysis of Consumers' Self-Conceptions, Body Images and Self-Care Practices" by Craig J. Thompson and Elizabeth C. Hirschman in *Journal of Consumer Research,* Vol. 22, September 1995, pp. 139–153.

The marketing implications of the discrepancy between body image and ideal body image may be obvious. By determining the standards of attractiveness and the ideal body image of target consumers, marketers demonstrate how certain products help consumers achieve an ideal body image or reinforce actual body image. Advertising for women's blue jeans, for example, might compare shapeless, loose-fit jeans with those that accentuate a woman's contours—the ideal body image of the target audience. Wearing this brand helps consumers look and feel good.

Consumers are motivated to correct body problems that cause them to feel negative about themselves, that is, problems that deflate their self-esteem. As such, marketers of products and services dealing with enhancing the beauty (or reducing the "ugliness") of certain body parts can appeal to consumers who are dissatisfied with those body parts. They can appeal to consumers by demonstrating how the product or service reduces consumer dissatisfaction with the body part in question.

body cathexis Satisfaction with a particular physical feature or body part.

An interesting concept connected with body image is **body cathexis.** Body cathexis means that people tend to be satisfied with a particular physical feature or body part. Some like their hair, others their eyes, and others are satisfied with their height, their build, and so on. How does body cathexis affect consumer behavior? One study found that consumers who were most satisfied with their hair and eyes were more frequent users of hair conditioner, blow dryers, cologne, toothpaste, and pumice soap.[34] This finding suggests that consumers are more likely to purchase goods and services related to physical features

Marketplace 5-4

How Shoplifters See Themselves

Everyone knows that shoplifting is something to be ashamed of, right? Wrong! In a study of the problem of shoplifting, researchers examined the user image of the typical shoplifter, both among nonshoplifters and among actual shoplifters. Nonshoplifters, predictably, had a negative image of the typical shoplifter, describing them as "cowardly," "bitchy," and "criminal." Actual shoplifters, however, professed to a much more positive impression of the typical shoplifter as "brave," "pleasant," and "moral." This study recommended a marketing campaign that would change the image of the typical shoplifter in the minds of actual shoplifters and, therefore, quell the aberrant behavior of shoplifting.

Source: Adapted from M. Jeffery Kallis, Kathleen A. Krentler, and Dinoo J. Vanier, "The Value of User Image in Quelling Aberrant Consumer Behavior," *Journal of the Academy of Marketing Science,* Vol. 14 (Spring 1981), pp. 29–35.

about which they have positive feelings and fewer products related to features about which they feel less positive.

Marketers who understand body cathexis can channel their resources into targeting consumers with positive feelings about the part of the body related to their product. This is often counterintuitive, as many marketers tend to do the opposite. Think of the weight-loss industry, for example. Marketers tend to target very overweight people. If the principle of body cathexis holds true, these people feel negative about their weight and are, therefore, the people least likely to spend money on weight-loss products. Instead, marketers should target those who feel positive about their weight and want to maintain their current weight or lose just a few pounds.

Marketplace 5-4 shows that people's perception of themselves cannot be inferred from their behavior. For example, shoplifters see themselves in a more positive light than expected.

F A Q

In hair-replacement ads, would the "before" picture look as bad without the "after" picture for comparison?

Marketing Management—Implications and Actions

Understanding the concept of self-image helps marketers to:

- Create advertising to appeal to the consumer's actual, ideal, social, or ideal social self-image as appropriate.
- Position products to enhance self-image congruity.
- Respond in ways to enhance or to adjust gender typing of their products or services.
- Re-examine the positioning of body-related products in a manner consistent with consumers' body cathexis.

5-3 Personality

What is **personality?** Personality refers to an individual's response tendencies across situations and over time. For example, a consumer who buys a lot of new electronic gadgets is said to have a response tendency to adopt technological innovations. Something about his or her personality makes him or her prefer new technology. By understanding the relationship between the personality of consumers and their purchase behavior, marketers are better equipped to target and promote their products effectively. Psychologists use two common approaches in the study of personality: the state approach and the trait approach.[35]

personality An individual's response tendencies across situations and over time.

state approach to personality A method of studying personality involving studying how the whole person (all of his or her traits) affects behavior. The study focuses on one person at a time.

trait approach to personality The method of studying personality involving studying how one personality trait affects behavior. The study focuses on one trait at a time across many people.

general personality trait A trait that invariably affects an individual across a range of situations—both those that are consumption-related and those that are not.

consumption-specific personality trait A trait that affects the consumer only in situations related to consumption and does not extend its influence into nonconsumption situations.

compliance A personality trait describing a tendency to deal with anxiety by moving toward people and complying with their wishes.

aggressiveness A personality trait describing a tendency to deal with anxiety by moving against people and offending them.

detachment A personality trait describing a tendency to deal with anxiety by moving away from people and asserting one's independence.

5-3a State Approach to Personality

The **state approach to personality** advocates understanding the individual in the context of the whole. It is the study of personality that allows us to predict what a person will do in a given situation.[36] The state approach to the study of personality is a holistic process—the focus is on understanding the individual as a whole. Typically, psychologists use a variety of measurement techniques to uncover an individual's response tendencies under a variety of conditions, thus predicting how that person would respond in any given situation. This approach takes into account external influences such as family, groups, culture, and so on. The obvious limitation of the state approach for marketers is that it examines individuals, not groups or market segments; its focus is on what makes each person tick, one at a time.

5-3b Trait Approach to Personality

More useful to marketers is the understanding of personality traits—consistent tendencies to respond to a given situation in certain ways. The fundamental assumption of the **trait approach to personality** is that we all share the same traits, but they are expressed at different levels, resulting in different personalities. Researchers analyze market segments to ascertain the extent of influence of a specific personality trait or combination of traits on the behavior of consumers in that segment. For example, one study has shown that caution and deliberateness are personality traits that produce a high level of risk perception and an attitude of unwillingness to try new products.[37] When targeting segments that display this particular personality trait, marketers can develop campaigns that effectively communicate the benefits of their products and help overcome the resistance of people who share this trait.

5-3c General and Consumption-Specific Personality Traits

Consumer researchers make a distinction between general personality traits and those that are consumption-specific. A **general personality trait** is one that invariably affects an individual across a range of situations, both those that are consumption-related and those that are not. Self-confidence, shyness, and aggressiveness are all general personality traits. A **consumption-specific personality trait** affects the consumer only in situations related to consumption and does not extend its influence into nonconsumption situations. Product innovativeness is a good example—it is meaningful only in situations involving the purchase or use of new products or technological innovations.

5-3d How General Personality Traits Influence Consumer Behavior

Compliance, Aggressiveness, and Detachment   People deal with anxiety through one of three response tendencies: **compliance, aggressiveness,** or **detachment.** In response to stress, some people move consistently *toward the stressor* (the person or object generating the stress) and become dependent on that person or object. This compliance commonly results in a reluctance to make decisions in the marketplace. Purchase decisions are usually made by the person upon whom the compliant personality type is dependent. In response to stress, some people move consistently *against the stressor.* Aggressive personality types are typically critical of others, often complain, and tend to attack others verbally. In response to stress, some people move consistently *away from the stressor.* The detached personality generally likes to be left alone, withdraws from others, and finds others threatening.

One study hypothesized that compliant types show more favorable response to products designed to enhance social relationships, aggressive types are most likely to choose products with high status and success images; and detached types are most likely to respond to appeals to their independence.[38]

The marketing implication of this study dealing with compliance, aggressiveness, and detachment types of personalities shows that marketers need to realize that different products and services tend to appeal to different people as a direct function of their personalities. Marketers of products and services related to helping people create and/or maintain social relationships (such as professional societies, social clubs, and fraternities) should target and appeal to consumers with compliant personalities. Marketers of achievement, status, and power-related products and services (such as status automobiles and power boats) should target and appeal to consumers with aggressive personalities. In contrast, marketers of products related to helping people achieve independence (such as financial investment instruments and retirement communities) should target and appeal to consumers with detached personalities.

Generalized Self-Confidence

A consumer with **generalized self-confidence** is one who is comfortable making decisions. One study found a distinct relationship between brand choice and self-confidence. Generally, consumers low in self-confidence were more inclined to choose brands from highly visible manufacturers than from lesser-known companies. Similarly, consumers high in self-confidence were more willing to be first adopters of new products.[39]

Retail analysts generally consider self-confidence to be negatively related to store loyalty—the more confidence a consumer has in the marketplace, the less likely he or she will be to develop strong store loyalty because there will be less risk perceived in exploring new outlets.[40]

Marketers of technological innovations should target consumers who are self-confident because these consumers are most likely to adopt technological innovations. In contrast, marketers with highly established brand names should target and appeal to consumers with low self-confidence. These consumers would feel quite uneasy buying unknown or "unproven" products.

With respect to stores, marketers of new stores and outlets should target and appeal to consumers with high self-confidence. Conversely, marketers of stores with well-established reputations should attempt to retain their store patrons by targeting and appealing to those who have low self-confidence. These patrons are most likely to stay loyal to these stores.

> **generalized self-confidence**
> A personality trait describing a tendency to feel comfortable making decisions.

Self-Consciousness

Self-consciousness is a tendency to be keenly aware of oneself in many situations.[41] Some students, for example, become much more apprehensive than others when speaking in front of the class. Some drivers feel very ill at ease behind the wheel of a luxury car, while others are in their element.

Those characterized as being self-conscious are very sensitive to the image they communicate to others. This heightened awareness of the self makes them use products in a manner that conveys what they feel is an appropriate self-image. For example, consumer researchers have found that consumers who score high on self-consciousness tend to be more interested in clothing and are heavier users of cosmetics.[42] Other research has shown that self-consciousness plays an important role in the way consumers use touch screen self-service. Consumers who have a favorable attitude toward using touch screen self-service but who are highly self-consciousness tend to shy away from using the touch screen gadgets.[43]

If marketers know that target consumers are likely to be self-conscious when using a particular product, they should consider offering accessories or benefits that are likely to reduce social anxiety stemming from this trait. Consider a clothing boutique catering to teenagers. If we assume that teenaged girls are self-conscious, then the retailer might consider offering private fitting rooms to attract more customers.

> **self-consciousness**
> A personality trait describing a tendency to be keenly aware of oneself in many situations.

Self-Monitoring

Akin to self-consciousness, **self-monitoring** refers to the ease with which people adapt to different situations and manage the impressions they make on others. High self-monitors are adept at managing such impressions, are attuned to the demands of different situations, and adapt their behavior accordingly. Low self-monitors

> **self-monitoring**
> A personality trait describing a tendency to adapt to different situations and so manage the impressions made on others.

are sensitive to inner feelings, attitudes, and beliefs. Their behavior is mostly influenced by internal cues such as personal beliefs and values. Thus, they rarely change their behavior as a function of the situation. For example, in a social get-together of colleagues and associates who are conservative in their political disposition, a high self-monitoring person would probably express conservative opinions, while in situations involving family and friends who may be quite liberal, the same high self-monitoring individual would express liberal opinions. Thus, high self-monitors tend to express opinions and behave in a manner to create the most favorable impression in the eyes of those present. In contrast, people characterized as low in self-monitoring tend to express their same opinions and beliefs about things irrespective of the audience. In other words, they tend to express their opinions in a manner that reflects their principles rather than adapting their opinions to create the most favorable impression on the audience at hand.[44]

One study showed that high self-monitors are more influenced by image advertising than informational advertising. The reverse was true for low self-monitors.[45] A series of recent studies showed that high self-monitors tend to explain their attitudes toward advertising in social terms rather than in utilitarian terms.[46] This was most evident with multiple-function products (sunglasses, for example, serve the utilitarian purpose of providing protection from the sun as well as the social identity goal of self-expression). It was less evident with products serving predominantly utilitarian needs (an air conditioner serves the utilitarian goal of obtaining relief from the heat) or products serving social identity needs (a university flag or decal serves to show that the holder is a member of the university community).[47]

Yet another study made the distinction between two motivational states underlying self-monitoring, namely, acquisition and protection self-presentation. **Acquisition self-presentation** refers to the motivational tendency to self-monitor in situations where there is a chance for social gain or if social risk is involved (for example, telling a lie to gain approval). In contrast, **protective self-presentation** refers to the motivational tendency to self-monitor out of fear of socially adverse effects (for example, drinking at home to avoid being perceived as a drunk). The study found that consumers adopting an acquisitive self-presentation style acted more assertively in resisting sales requests, seeking information, and seeking redress than did those who adopted a protective self-presentation style.[48]

If marketers know the extent to which their target consumers tend to score high or low on self-monitoring, then they can develop more effective marketing programs. In relation to promotion, marketers should communicate with consumers high in self-monitoring using social rather than informational messages. That is, marketers should not provide much technical information about their product or service to high self-monitors. High self-monitors are more sensitive to information that affects their image—the way they present themselves to others. For example, marketers of automobiles targeting high self-monitors should promote their cars using image advertising. A typical image ad would focus on the driver and how he or she is admired by others while driving the car. Advertising to low self-monitors, on the other hand, should be informational. Talk about the roominess, the gas mileage, the power, the reliability, durability, handling, and so on.

In a context of personal selling, salespeople should assist high self-monitors who have an acquisitive self-presentation style by providing information. Don't push hard to make that sale, as it will likely backfire. When encountering high self-monitors with a protective self-presentation style, the sales person should provide selective information that shows how the purchase of the product or service is likely to preserve their good image in the eyes of their neighbors, friends, or associates.

Self-Esteem

People with high **self-esteem** feel generally positive about themselves, while those with low self-esteem don't. People low in self-esteem generally expect less of themselves and tend to avoid situations in which they may be evaluated by others. In extreme cases, they may be afraid to do things and may be riddled with conflict and anxiety.[49] Thus, low-self-esteem consumers tend to use different products and services to deal with stress and anxiety. The manufacturer of Sara Lee baked goods, for example, found

---

▶ **acquisition self-presentation** The motivational tendency to self-monitor in situations where there is chance for social gain, if social risk is involved (for example, telling a lie to gain approval).

▶ **protective self-presentation** The motivational tendency to self-monitor out of fear of socially adverse reactions from others.

▶ **self-esteem** A personality trait describing the extent to which the actual self is congruent with the ideal self. People whose actual self falls very short of their ideal self are characterized as low in self-esteem. Conversely, those whose actual self is close to their ideal self are characterized as high in self-esteem.

that consumers low in self-esteem, feeling they lacked self-control, preferred portion-controlled snack items.[50]

Viewing self-esteem as a personality trait, marketers can learn a great deal about differences in product preferences, pricing sensitivity, shopping habits, and media habits between low and high self-esteem consumers. For example, the entire industry of self-help books can benefit by targeting and appealing to people with low self-esteem. Through additional consumer research, this industry can develop a detailed profile of low self-esteem individuals in terms of the kind of self-help books most preferred, their willingness to buy these books at price, their shopping habits regarding self-help books, and their media habits. This information would be extremely helpful to marketers of self-help books in developing an effective marketing program for low self-esteem consumers.

Dogmatism

A *dogmatic* person tends to be closed-minded, seeing life in black and white terms. A *nondogmatist* is more open-minded, appreciating complexity in life and seeing it in many shades of gray. The dogmatic person has one view of reality and fits experiences and situations to that reality. For the nondogmatist, many realities are possible, and life is experienced from several perspectives. Consumer researchers have found that highly dogmatic people are generally less receptive to new or unfamiliar stimuli, such as new styles of music or new products.[51]

The marketing implication related to research on **dogmatism** is that marketers of technological innovations should target their products or services to consumers who are open-minded, or less dogmatic. Open-minded consumers are likely to express less resistance to the possibility of change or the adoption of new products than are dogmatic consumers.

> **dogmatism** A personality trait describing a tendency to be closed-minded, seeing life in terms of black and white.

Rigidity

Some people are more flexible than others in tastes and preferences. Like children who will only eat certain kinds of food, rigid people are very set in their ways. As you would expect, **rigidity** generally correlates negatively with risk-taking behavior or innovativeness.[52] That is, consumers who are rigid are not likely to engage in risk-taking activities such as riding motorcycles, climbing mountains, hang gliding, or racing.

The marketing implication here is that marketers of technological innovations, especially those innovations related to risk-taking activities, should target their products or services to consumers who are less rigid. Less-rigid consumers are likely to express less resistance to the use of products and services that involve high-risk activities.

> **rigidity** A personality trait describing a tendency to be inflexible in tastes and preferences.

Tolerance of Ambiguity

There is much ambiguity in the marketplace. Consider the purchase of a house. What constitutes a good house? A good house for one consumer may be a bad house for another. Therefore, quality in housing is said to involve a high level of ambiguity. Some people can tolerate ambiguity; others cannot. Tolerant people tend to engage more in exploratory behaviors. That is, they gather information by shopping around. One study has found that intolerant consumers perceive atypical products as "newer" than do consumers who can tolerate ambiguity. Intolerant consumers were also found to be more reluctant to buy such products.[53] Research has also uncovered a relationship between **tolerance of ambiguity** and information acquisition. Consumers who are tolerant of ambiguity are more likely to search for information as the choice task becomes more complex and as the products become more novel.[54]

There are several marketing implications related to research on tolerance of ambiguity. First, marketers of products and services that involve a high degree of ambiguity (houses, art, vacation sites and tours, etc.) should target consumers known to be tolerant of ambiguity. Second, these marketers should disseminate as much information as possible about their products and services to these consumers.

> **tolerance of ambiguity** A personality trait describing a tendency not to feel bothered by situations in which the person lacks information to guide action.

Attention to Social Comparison Information

Some consumers have a high tendency to compare themselves with others—to pay heed to social comparison information. These consumers tend to be overly aware of how others react to their behavior and are very concerned about these reactions. Thus, consumers who score high on **attention to social comparison information** are likely to change their beliefs, attitudes, and

> **attention to social comparison information** A personality trait describing a tendency to compare oneself with others—to pay heed to social comparison information.

F A Q

Why is it so embarrassing to see someone else wearing the same thing you're wearing?

behaviors toward products and brands to conform to group norms. By obtaining levels of agreement to statements such as the following, researchers measure attention to social comparison: [55]

- "It is my feeling that if everyone else in a group is behaving in a certain manner, this must be the proper way to behave."
- "I actively avoid wearing clothes that are not in style."
- "At parties, I usually try to behave in a manner that makes me fit in."

The marketing implication here is straightforward. If marketers are targeting consumers who score high on attention to social comparison information, then appropriate promotional messages can be devised. Consider the following example of a car ad targeting college students. The ad shows a student visiting a dealer showroom with a friend, and both are looking at an economy Japanese car that provides very high gas mileage. The student says to his friend, "I love this car. Lots of college students drive this kind of car. Isn't it neat?" His friend replies by saying, "Yes, I noticed that a lot of my friends drive this kind of car, too. I think this car is really cool."

optimum stimulation level (OSL) A personality trait describing a desire to explore the environment and seek stimulation.

Optimum Stimulation Level
Some people have a greater desire to explore the environment and seek stimulation than others. Psychologists refer to this individual difference factor as **optimum stimulation level (OSL)**.[56] Researchers have used this personality trait to predict consumer behavior. Studies have shown that a consumer's optimum stimulation level is related to curiosity-motivated behavior, such as variety seeking and risk taking. Specifically, consumers with a high OSL were found to generate more cognitive responses to advertising, were bored after a few repetitions of the advertising, sought more information, engaged in a higher level of variety-seeking behaviors, made riskier decisions, and gambled more than did consumers with a low OSL.[57] The marketing implication is that marketers targeting high-OSL consumers should advertise using different messages or variations of the main advertising theme. Each piece of advertising should also contain more information than the average advertisement.

state versus action orientation A personality trait in which some people have a tendency to act readily without hesitation (action-oriented), whereas others hesitate and procrastinate in taking action (state-oriented).

State versus Action Orientation
Some people are **action-oriented**—they can more easily transform their intentions into actual behaviors than state-oriented people.[58] For example, an action-oriented consumer is likely to be more decisive than a state-oriented consumer, is likely to take less time shopping around, and is quick to take action. The **state-oriented** consumer, on the other hand, is likely to waffle and waver. Researchers have found this particular personality trait helpful in predicting consumer behavior, specifically coupon usage.[59]

When target consumers are mostly action-oriented, marketers should develop campaigns to meet product trial objectives. An example might be: "By the end of the year, the campaign should increase product trial from 10 percent to 30 percent." When target consumers are mostly state-oriented, marketers should strive to develop campaigns to meet brand attitude objectives. An example might be: "By the end of the year, the campaign should increase favor toward the brand from 30 percent to 50 percent."

connectedness A personality trait describing a tendency for some people to perceive themselves as highly connected with others.

separateness A personality trait describing a tendency for some people to perceive themselves as individuals, separated from others.

Separateness versus Connectedness
Some people perceive themselves as individuals separated from others, while some tend to see themselves as highly connected with others. For example, one mother can view herself in terms of her family, while another can view herself in terms of herself separated from her family. The former is said to have a strong sense of **connectedness,** while the latter is viewed as having a strong sense of **separateness**.[60]

This personality trait is important in consumer behavior because people react differently to advertising themes having separated versus connected themes. For example, an ad about a beach resort is targeted to mothers. The ad touts the family togetherness aspect of a vacation. Here, the theme of the ad is the connectedness with family members. The ad shows a family enjoying the beach resort and then zooms in on the mother endorsing the resort, saying something like, "We're having the best vacation ever at the XYZ beach resort!"

Now contrast that ad with another that has a separateness theme. The ad focuses on a professional woman who is independent and ambitious. The ad shows her making important job-related decisions. Then it shows her at the beach resort with her husband or significant other, looking like she is enjoying herself. Her endorsement is, "I'm having a wonderful time at XYZ beach resort!"

It is likely that the first ad will appeal to women with a connectedness self-concept, whereas the second ad would appeal to women with a separateness self-concept. Thus, advertisers can do a better job targeting consumers by focusing on either connected or separate personalities, tailoring their advertising messages to the appropriate target segments. That is, if the marketer targets connected consumers, then the ads should have connected themes, and to appeal to separate consumers, advertisers should use ads with separateness themes.

Impulsiveness

Impulsiveness is a personality trait that can be described and measured using twelve adjectives: impulsive, careless, self-controlled (**reverse coded**; this occurs when a measurement item is capturing the concept being measured in the reverse manner—that is, when adding the scores pertaining to all items, the researcher has to reverse code those particular items that are reversed in meaning), extravagant, farsighted (reverse coded), responsible (reverse coded), restrained (reverse coded), easily tempted, rational (reverse coded), methodical (reverse coded), enjoys spending, and a planner (reverse coded). Subjects describe themselves using these adjectives on a scale varying from "usually would describe me" to "seldom would describe me." Consumers high on **impulsiveness** were more likely to indicate willingness to buy a sweater they did not need but liked than would those scoring low on impulsiveness. Impulsive consumers also indicated that they are willing to pay more for the sweater than were low-impulsive consumers.[61]

If marketers know that their target consumers are likely to score high on impulsiveness, then point-of-purchase displays should be used to attract those consumers. The point-of-purchase displays should be placed in high-traffic areas of the store (e.g., next to the cashier or checkout counter). The prices of these products can be set high without adversely affecting sales.

Extraversion and Neuroticism

Extraversion is part of a personality trait dealing with two polar opposites, namely extraversion and introversion. This personality trait refers to the extent to which people seek stimulation from the environment. Thus, an extravert is likely to be quite sociable and socially active. In contrast, introverts are typically loners—they like to be left alone. They feel uncomfortable in an environment full of people, noise, and things. Early research in extraversion-introversion indicates that people are born with nervous systems that vary in sensitivity to environmental stimulation. Those who have nervous systems highly sensitive to environmental stimulation tend to avoid extra stimulation because they feel overwhelmed by too much stimulation. These are introverts. Conversely, extraverts have a nervous system that lacks sensitivity to external stimulation. Thus, they seek external stimulation to achieve an adaptive level of stimulation. Research has shown that extraverts tend to experience a positive affect more often than a negative affect. **Neuroticism** is the tendency to experience too much negative affect. People referred to as "neurotics" tend to score high on measures of neuroticism.[62]

Recent research in consumer behavior has shown that extravert consumers tend to experience more positive feelings than negative feelings in response to advertising. In contrast, neurotic consumers tend to experience more negative feelings than positive ones. The study exposed subjects to two ads (on video) that had a balance of uneasy, upbeat, and warm ad content. Subjects' personalities (extraversion and neuroticism) were assessed through a self-report personality inventory. Subjects scoring high on extraversion experienced more positive feelings such as "upbeatness" and warmth, whereas subjects scoring

reverse coded When a measurement item is capturing the concept being measured in the reverse manner—that is, when adding the scores pertaining to all items, the researcher has to reverse code those particular items that are reversed in meaning.

impulsiveness A personality trait describing a tendency to act on the spur of the moment without considering the consequences of one's action.

extraversion Part of a personality trait dealing with two polar opposites, namely extraversion-introversion. This personality trait refers to the extent to which people seek stimulation from the environment. Thus, an extravert is likely to be quite sociable and socially active. In contrast, introverts are typically loners—they like to be left alone. They feel uncomfortable in an environment full of people, noise, and things.

neuroticism A personality trait describing a tendency to experience negative affect.

high on neuroticism experienced more negative feelings such as disinterest and uneasiness.[63]

The promotion implications of the research on extraversion and neuroticism are quite important. Marketers targeting extraverts should use advertising and other promotional messages that are positive. That is, the ads should contain cues that evoke feelings of upbeatness and/or warmth. Extraverts are likely to respond positively to such advertising. In contrast, advertising directed toward those scoring high on neuroticism is quite challenging because those consumers respond better to ads that evoke negative rather than positive feelings. In this case the challenge to advertisers is, can the advertised product or service be promoted effectively through inducing neurotics to experience negative feelings such as sadness, anger, and depression? Perhaps yes, although a great deal of creativity is needed here.

Consider this example. Suppose we want to advertise a political candidate running for county sheriff. The demographics of the county show that residents are poor and experience many urban problems such as high crime, low-quality education, government corruption, and so on. One can hypothesize that such an environment is likely to cause a certain amount of neuroticism among the county residents. Thus, a candidate who speaks to the plight of the poor (inducing sadness, anger, and depression) can be effective in persuading voters to cast their ballots in favor of his or her candidacy.

Need for Cognition

need for cognition
A personality trait that distinguishes people who have varying needs of thinking. Those high in need for cognition feel the urge to think most of the time. Those low in need for cognition don't like to do much thinking.

Some consumers tend to think through purchase decisions more thoroughly than others. The tendency is referred to as the **need for cognition**.[64] One study revealed that consumers who have a high need for cognition tend to be persuaded by advertising with quality arguments, whereas consumers low in need for cognition seem to be influenced by endorser attractiveness. Furthermore, it was found that high levels of advertising repetition tend to work best with consumers low in need for cognition.

Recent research has reinforced the notion that need for cognition is a strong personality factor that can explain variations in how consumers respond to advertising. Specifically, through a series of studies, it was found that consumers who are high in need for cognition tend to process arguments in advertising more extensively than do consumers low in need for cognition. This effect was found to be more vivid under the following conditions:

1. When a product evaluation goal is not made salient (important) while processing the advertising message,
2. When the advertising message is short, and
3. When the message is not necessarily counterattitudinal. That is, when the message position is not counter to the consumer's position.[65]

Marketers targeting consumers who are likely to score high on need for cognition should design their ads to generate the best quality argument possible. This means they need to focus on showing the product's (or service's) costs and benefits in relation to those of alternative products (or services) and make a case that the benefits outweigh the costs. This strategy becomes particularly important when the goal of product evaluation is not highlighted in the message, the message is short, and the message position is not counter to the audience's position. Advertising designed for consumers scoring low on need for cognition can be one-sided, image-based, and simple in message complexity.

Need for Power, Affiliation, and Achievement

need for power A personality trait describing a tendency to seek control of one's environment by influencing people and events.

People with a strong **need for power** are motivated to impact, control, or influence other people. The following statements measure a person's need for power by getting the person to agree or disagree:

- "One should enjoy being the center of attention."
- "I would like an important job where people look up to me."
- "I think I would enjoy having authority over other people."
- "I strive to gain more control over the events around me at school or work."

Business executives, teachers, psychologists, and members of the clergy tend to score high on measures of the need for power.[66]

Products can be used to draw attention to oneself. For example, college students who have a strong need for power tend to purchase prestige products such as television sets, tape recorders, stereos, radios, rugs, framed pictures, and wall hangings. Adults might use cars, wine glasses, college banners, or credit cards to gain prestige.[67] Recent research has shown that power motive incentives mediate the relationship between the strength of the power motive in consumers and their level of involvement in products such as expensive cars and interview clothes. That is, consumers with a strong need for power agreed with statements such as "I would display the assertive side of my character if I owned this expensive car" (incentive that activates the need for power and causes consumers to express involvement with the car).[68]

People with a strong **need for affiliation** are motivated to act to establish, restore, or maintain a close, warm, friendly relationship with other people. A college freshman buying greeting cards for friends back home may be motivated by a need for affiliation if he or she is trying to maintain close ties with old friends (an affiliation incentive). That person, therefore, is likely to feel emotionally involved with greeting cards. An empirical study confirmed this relationship for greeting cards.[69]

> **need for affiliation**
> A personality trait describing a tendency to be friendly with others and to establish and maintain social relationships.

People with a strong **need for achievement** are motivated to achieve excellence or to outperform others. Thus, we could hypothesize that shoppers who consider buying achievement products like calculators or computers may be highly involved with those calculators or computers if they have a strong need for achievement and if they perceive that the calculators or computers are indeed incentives for them to achieve performance excellence.[70]

> **need for achievement**
> A personality trait describing a tendency to achieve high scores on performance tasks.

Marketers targeting consumers who are likely to score high on need for power should design their ads to clearly show how the advertised product or service would lead the consumer to assert himself or herself and control the situation. Similarly, marketers targeting consumers who are likely to score high on need for affiliation should design their ads to clearly show how the advertised product or service would help the consumer enhance or maintain relationships with significant others. Marketers targeting consumers with a strong sense of the need for achievement should design their ads to clearly show how the product or service would help the consumer achieve performance excellence.

Affect Intensity   Some people consistently experience emotions with greater strength than others do when exposed to emotionally provocative situations, regardless of whether these emotions are positive or negative. These people are characterized as high on **affect intensity**.[71] Recent evidence in consumer research shows that consumers characterized as high in affect intensity tend to react more emotionally and strongly to ads with emotional appeals than do consumers low in affect intensity. The experiment producing this evidence involved emotional and nonemotional versions of an ad. Both ads started out with: "The following is a message from the Society for the Prevention of Cruelty to Children." Both ads ended with the same appeal for financial aid. The emotional ad showed a dramatic scene in which a parent is beating a child and the child is trying to run away from that terrible beating. The nonemotional ad described statistics related to child abuse. Emotional responses were recorded through eight adjectives: alarmed, angry, frightened, worried, sad, concerned, compassionate, and sympathetic.[72]

> **affect intensity** A personality trait describing a tendency to consistently experience emotions with greater strength when exposed to emotionally provocative situations, regardless of whether these emotions are positive or negative.

The results of this research showed that marketers should gauge their target consumers' levels of affect intensity, because the design of advertising can be guided by such information. If marketers know that most of their targeted consumers score high on affect intensity, then they need to design ads with this in mind. Emotional ads are typically designed with the anticipation that consumers are not likely to overreact or underreact to the emotional content of the message. However, if target consumers are expected to score high on affect intensity, then they are likely to overreact to the message. What would be the result of this overreaction? Would this overreaction deter the overall persuasiveness of the message? If so, then the emotional content of the message has to be toned down.

Conversely, if target consumers are expected to score low on affect intensity, then perhaps the emotional content of the advertising message should be toned up to generate an appropriate response from the consumers. Marketplace 5-5 describes the consumption behavior of high-affect intensity consumers—those who chase thrills.

Exhibit 5-5 on page 160 sums up general personality traits and their effects on consumer behavior.

5-3e How Consumption-Specific Personality Traits Influence Consumer Behavior

The Market Maven Type   The **market maven** consumer is the kind of consumer who has information about many kinds of products, places to shop, and other aspects of the marketplace. He or she initiates discussions with and responds to others who request product and store information. This type of consumer is measured through a series of items in which the respondent indicates agreement or disagreement. Example items are:

market maven
A marketplace-specific personality trait describing a tendency to gather information about many kinds of products, places to shop, and other aspects of the marketplace. A market maven also initiates discussions with and responds to others who request product and store information.

- "I like introducing new brands and products to my friends,"
- "I like helping people by providing them with information about many kinds of products."
- "People ask me for information about products, places to shop, or sales."

A national survey employing the market maven measure revealed that consumers believe market mavens influence the way they (consumers) make purchasing decisions. Market mavens were found to be usually aware of new products. They provide information about products to other consumers. They tend to engage in information searches such as reading *Consumer Reports* and paying close attention to advertisements. They tend to participate in various market activities such as using coupons in purchases. They enjoy shopping and use browsing to find out about new products.[73]

More recently, research has empirically reinforced the following notions about market maven consumers. Specifically, market mavens:

- Have an early awareness of new products across product categories and an awareness of specific new brands within several product categories,
- Exhibit high levels of specific information provisions to other consumers across product categories,
- Demonstrate a high level of general market information seeking through the use of diverse sources,
- Demonstrate high levels of general market interest through shopping enjoyment and attention to advertising, and
- Tend to read much direct mail advertising.[74]

The marketing implications of these research findings are clear. Marketers of new products should target these consumers. Doing so is likely to facilitate the diffusion of these new products in the marketplace. Promotional messages should be laden with information about the product, and direct mail should be considered as an effective promotional vehicle.

consumer innovativeness
A product-specific tendency on the part of consumers to be among the first to purchase new products within specific categories.

Consumer Innovativeness   **Consumer innovativeness** is the tendency on the part of consumers to be among the first to purchase new products within specific categories.[75] Consumer researchers measure innovativeness in relation to any product category by asking consumers to agree or disagree with statements such as: "In general, I am among the first in my circle of friends to buy a new brand of cola when it appears," or "If I heard that a new breakfast cereal was available in the store, I would be interested enough to buy it." This personality trait is very important for marketers of technological innovations. Diffu-

Marketplace 5-5

The Thrill Chasers and Sensation Seekers

The U.S. Bungee Association estimates that there have been seven million bungee jumps worldwide in the last ten years or so. The U.S. Parachute Association reports 130,000–150,000 people skydive every year. Besides bungee jumping and sky diving, rock climbing, mountaineering, whitewater rafting, and other high-risk sports are also on the increase. What motivates people to engage in high-risk sports? Some consumer theorists believe that there may be two kinds of people who engage in high-risk sports. We can call one group the "image boosters" and the other group the "adrenaline junkies."

The image boosters are those who want to change their social self-image with a quick fix. For example, an accountant who thinks he is viewed by his coworkers as disciplined, controlled, stable, compliant, and conservative may rebel against this social self-image. He rebels by bungee jumping off a two-story bridge. Now his coworkers see him in a new light.

The adrenaline junkies are those who cannot be happy unless they push the limits in some way. These are extreme people—they are perfectionists, and they are very professional at work, but outside their work, they are risk takers. They drive their cars fast, take undue risks in love, and live their lives in the "fast and intense lane." They like to engage in unpopular and daring activities. If the risky sport becomes popular, the thrill is gone. Risk is seen as a desirable thing. These people are deficient in MAO enzyme levels in their brain, and high-adrenaline activities are a means to elevate the MAO enzyme to normal levels. SRI International of Menlo Park, California, estimates that 12 percent of all adults are adrenaline junkies. They are likely to be between the ages of 18 and 34, of Hispanic origin, never married or engaged, and make between $40,000 and $60,000 or over $100,000. The adrenaline junkie could be either a male or female. As a matter of fact, many adrenaline junkies tend to meet other adrenaline junkies in their risky sport, fall in love, and get married. Part of the attraction of falling in love is the match with another adrenaline junkie.

Source: Adapted from "You Can Buy a Thrill: Chasing the Ultimate Rush" by Rebecca Piirto Heath in *American Demographics,* June 1997.

sion of a technological innovation starts with the innovators and eventually trickles down to other users.

Just as they would target market mavens, marketers of new products should target consumers considered high on innovativeness and expose them to their new products. Doing so is likely to facilitate the diffusion of these new products in the marketplace.

Opinion Leadership   **Opinion leadership** is a product-specific personality trait related to product expertise. That is, an opinion leader is a person who is well versed in a product category because, for example, his or her job is somewhat related to the product. Also, this expert is characterized as being motivated to "spread the word" about the product in ways that reflect his or her opinion (positive or negative). For example, a computer engineer is more likely to know much about computers and computer hardware because of his or her specialty.

Note that opinion leadership is different from the general personality trait of market maven just described. A market maven consumer is the kind of person who knows a lot about many products and shopping places and volunteers much information to others to help them in their shopping expeditions. An opinion leader, in contrast, has expertise on a specific product class and volunteers information to others in relation to that product class and only that product class. Opinion leadership has been found to play an important role in the diffusion of technological innovations.[76]

Marketers of technological innovations should target consumers considered high on opinion leadership and educate them about their new products. Doing so is likely to facilitate the diffusion of these new products in the marketplace.

Product-Specific Self-Confidence   **Product-specific self-confidence** refers to the extent to which certain consumers feel confident about making decisions with regard to a product category. For example, people who feel confident making purchase decisions about computers are high in computer self-confidence. Such consumers are more inclined

> **opinion leadership**
> A product-specific tendency to acquire, store, and communicate information to others about a particular product class.

> **product-specific self-confidence** A product-specific tendency to make decisions about the product category without doubting the effectiveness of one's decisions.

Exhibit 5-5	General Personality Traits and Their Effects on Consumer Behavior
Trait	**Effect**
Compliance	Reluctance to make decisions; preference for products designed to enhance social relationships
Aggressiveness	Preference for products with high status and success images
Detachment	Tendency to move away from stress; desire to be left alone
High generalized self-confidence	Early adopters of new products; tendency against store loyalty
Low generalized self-confidence	Preference for brands from highly visible manufacturers; tendency toward store loyalty
Self-consciousness	Tendency to use products in a manner that conveys what they feel is an appropriate self-image
Self-monitoring	Tendency to be influenced more by image advertising than by informational advertising
Low self-esteem	Preference for portion-controlled snack items because of lack of self-control
Dogmatism	Reluctance to accept new or unfamiliar products
Rigidity	Unwillingness to risk the purchase of new products
Intolerance of ambiguity	Reluctance to seek information about products; tendency to buy typical rather than atypical products
Attention to social comparison	Tendency to choose brands preferred by others
High optimum stimulation level	Tendency to respond cognitively to advertising; easily bored by repetitious advertising; tendency to seek more information about and variety in products; riskier decision maker
State versus action orientation	Action-oriented; tendency to try new products or brands
Separateness	Tendency to react positively to ads reflecting independence and individualism
Connectedness	Tendency to react positively to ads reflecting relationships and togetherness
Impulsiveness	Tendency to buy products and services driven by emotion rather than utilitarian need
Extraversion	Tendency to experience more positive than negative feelings in response to advertising
Neuroticism	Tendency to experience more negative than positive feelings in response to advertising
Need for power	Tendency to prefer products and services high on status and prestige
Need for affiliation	Tendency to prefer products and services that serve to bring people together and help with personal relationships
Need for achievement	Tendency to prefer products and services that serve to get the job done and achieve excellence in task achievement
High affect intensity	Tendency to overreact to emotional advertising
Low affect intensity	Tendency to underreact to emotional advertising
High need for cognition	Tendency to respond to advertising with quality arguments
Low need for cognition	Tendency to respond to advertising featuring attractive endorsers

to buy computers from a specialty computer store than from a department store. The converse is true for consumers low in self-confidence.[77]

Marketers of specialty products sold in specialty stores (e.g., computers sold in computer stores) should target self-confident consumers—self-confident in relation to the product in question. Promotional messages describing the benefits and costs of the product in relation to competitor products should be directed to these consumers, because they are likely to act on these messages and adopt the product in question.

Product-Specific Self-Efficacy

Consumer self-efficacy represents the consumer's belief in his or her own performance capability or competence in relation to a product category. In other words, while some consumers may feel that they are competent to perform a specific task related to a product category, others may feel incompetent to do so. With personal computers, for example, those consumers who are at ease working with PCs can be characterized as high in self-efficacy in relation to computers. Consumer researchers have shown that self-efficacy may play a significant role in resistance to and adoption of technological innovations.[78] That is, those who are high in self-efficacy in relation to a product category are more likely to adopt a technological innovation in that category than are those low in self-efficacy.

Another study has shown that the persuasive effectiveness of vivid promotional messages related to health (e.g., discouraging behavior that causes skin cancer) is dependent on self-efficacy. Vivid messages are messages communicated in graphic ways through the use of pictures, examples of situations that dramatize the point of the message, and so on. Specifically, those who believe they can follow the recommendations in the message (those with high self-efficacy) were more likely to be persuaded by vivid messages than nonvivid ones. The vividness effect was less evident for low self-efficacy subjects.[79]

Yet another study has shown that **product-specific self-efficacy** can influence how consumers process information from product manuals. The study showed that consumers who score high on self-efficacy (perception of capability of operating a product) tend to have an "overconfidence bias." That is, they tend not to read the product manual and thus increase the likelihood of injury through product misuse.[80]

> **product-specific self-efficacy**
> A product-specific tendency to perceive oneself as being highly capable and competent in the acquisition, use, and disposal of a product class.

Marketers of technological innovations should target consumers considered high on self-efficacy directly related to the product in question. A promotional campaign designed to educate these consumers about the costs and benefits of the product in relation to competitor products should be attempted. Furthermore, these promotional messages should be as graphically vivid as possible. With respect to product manuals, specific messages have to be designed to further encourage self-efficacious consumers to read them. These messages have to be particularly persuasive, because those consumers tend to skip over the manual (because of their overconfidence).

Product-Specific Subjective Knowledge Consumer subjective knowledge of a specific product is what consumers perceive they know about the product in question. For example, researchers have measured this construct using items such as the following: [81]

- "I know pretty much about (product X)."
- "I know how to judge the quality of (product X)."
- "I think I know enough about (product X) to feel pretty confident when I make a purchase."
- "Among my circle of friends, I'm one of the experts on (product X)."
- "I have heard of most of the new (product Xs) that are around."
- "I can tell if a (product X) item is worth the price or not."

In one study, consumer subjective knowledge (of wine) was found to correlate significantly and positively with measures of objective knowledge (of wine), innovativeness (in relation to wine), enduring involvement (in relation to wine), opinion leadership (in relation to wine), and consumption measures (of wine). Subjective knowledge (of wine) was also found to correlate significantly and negatively with opinion seeking (in relation to wine) and price sensitivity (in relation to wine).[82]

Coupon Proneness, Value Consciousness, and Deal Proneness Coupon **proneness** is the tendency to redeem coupons by purchasing the advertised product or service. Researchers measure coupon proneness through response to such statements as: "I enjoy clipping coupons out of the newspapers," or "When I use coupons, I feel that I am getting a good deal."[83]

> **coupon proneness**
> A marketplace-specific tendency to use coupons in the purchase of economic goods from retail outlets.

Value consciousness, on the other hand, is defined as the amount of concern the consumer has for need-satisfying properties of the product or service in relation to the price of that product or service. Researchers measure value consciousness through the consumer's

> **value consciousness**
> A marketplace-specific tendency to consider the value (both costs and benefits) of the product in the purchase of economic goods.

response to such statements as: "I am very concerned about low prices, but I am equally concerned about product quality," or "When grocery shopping, I compare the prices of different brands to be sure I get the best value for the money." Research revealed that coupon proneness and value consciousness are strong predictors of coupon redemption.[84]

> **deal proneness**
> A marketplace-specific tendency to seek the best bargain possible in shopping situations.

Deal proneness can be viewed in three ways. The first view treats deal proneness as a generalized form of "dealing" behavior that extends beyond the use of coupons to encompass a variety of "deals." These include the use of various sales promotion incentives such as cents-off deals, trading stamps, coupons, advertised sales, and the like. Thus, a deal-prone consumer usually takes advantage of any kind of deal. The second view treats deal proneness as a domain-specific construct. That is, people may have different dispositions toward different types of deals. For example, a coupon-prone consumer may not necessarily take advantage of a cents-off deal or an advertised sale. And conversely, a person who usually becomes motivated to respond to advertised sales may not be prone to use coupons. The third view treats deal-proneness as involving a propensity by consumers to take advantage of only certain kinds of deals, such as price-oriented deals or active-oriented deals.

Two studies were conducted to test these three views of deal proneness. The results support the notion that deal proneness is a domain-specific construct. That means that some consumers tend to be coupon prone, while others tend to be prone to advertised sales, while others tend to be prone to cents-off deals, and so on.[85]

Marketers who use sales promotion devises (e.g., coupons, price discounts, and sampling) should realize that there is no such thing as a universal deal-prone consumer who is likely to take advantage of whatever deal is offered. Therefore, marketers who use coupons as an important sales promotion tool should conduct further research to profile those consumer groups in terms of their size in relation to the product in question. If the research indicates that a sizable segment of the target market takes advantage of coupons, then the marketer of the product in question should use coupons as a primary method of promotion. Similar research should be conducted with other forms of sales promotion.

> **product-specific involvement**
> A product-specific tendency to feel emotionally involved in a product class.

Product-Specific Involvement

Some consumers express a great deal of **product-specific involvement**—emotional involvement in a particular product class or category. For example, sports car enthusiasts are highly involved with sports cars and all products and services related to sports cars; wine connoisseurs are highly involved with all products and services related to wine making, wine tasting, and wine bottle collecting, wine advertising, and so on. Those who are emotionally involved with a particular product class or category are likely to have a belief structure about the product that is more complex and integrated than will those who are not involved with the product. These beliefs link perceptions of the product attributes with perceptions of consequences (both functional and psychosocial) associated with product use, which in turn are further linked with more abstract goals and values of the consumer. For example, purchasing greeting cards can be described in terms of concrete attributes (such as physical store attributes, the size of the greeting card, the space to write on the card, the color of the card), abstract attributes (such as store atmosphere, convenience of the store location, selection variety of greeting cards), functional consequences (such as the communication goals of the greeting card), psychosocial consequences (such as cheering up a friend and making him or her laugh), instrumental goals (such as expressing the sender's personality), and terminal goals (such as making the sender feel happy about expressing his or her feelings toward the recipient). Thus, a consumer who is emotionally involved with the product is likely to have a means-end chain of beliefs concerning the cards that links many concrete attributes of the product with abstract attributes, functional consequences, psychosocial consequences, instrumental goals, and terminal goals.[86]

Measuring product involvement is very important for marketers because such measurement allows the segmentation of the market into those who are more and less emotionally involved with the product in question. Most marketers prefer to target those who are emotionally involved with their products. Once these consumers are identified, marketers attempt to profile them in terms of their preferences of product alternatives and models, willingness to buy the various product alternatives at various price levels, shopping habits and preferences, and media habits and preferences for obtaining information.

Research shows that promoting a product to highly involved consumers should capture how the product fits in the consumer's lifestyle, connecting the very specific, concrete attributes with abstract ones, with functional and psychosocial consequences, and with instrumental values and terminal ones, too.

Consumer Relationship Proneness

Consumer Relationship Proneness   Some consumers are inclined to engage in relationships with retailers of particular product categories. This should be differentiated from the tendency to establish and maintain relationships. The latter is related to brand or customer loyalty; the former deals with a personality trait about interpersonal interactions. Measures of this personality trait include:

- "Generally, I am someone who likes to be a regular customer of an apparel store."
- "Generally, I am someone who wants to be a steady customer of the same apparel store."
- "Generally, I am someone who is willing to go the extra mile to purchase at the same apparel store."

Research has shown that consumer relationship proneness plays a significant role in relationship quality. More specifically, consumers who are relationship prone are more likely to show higher levels of trust and commitment toward retailers than will consumers who are not relationship prone.[87]

Technology Anxiety

Technology Anxiety   **Technology anxiety** is the fear, apprehension, and hope consumers feel when they consider using or actually use computer technology. Thus, technology-anxious consumers are excessively timid in using computers and information science. They attempt to reduce the amount of time they spend using computers and even avoid computers if possible. Examples of measurement items capturing this disposition include:

> **technology anxiety** The fear, apprehension, and hope consumers feel when they consider using or actually use computer technology.

- "I have difficulty understanding most technological matters."
- "I feel apprehensive about using technology."
- "Technological terminology sounds like confusing jargon to me."
- "I hesitate to use technology for fear of making mistakes I cannot correct."

The more consumers agree with the above statements, the more likely it is that they are technology anxious. A recent study has shown that , compared to those who score low on technology anxiety, consumers who score high on technology anxiety tend to use less self-service technologies such as teleshopping, are typically less satisfied with self-service technologies, and more frequently communicate negative word-of-mouth information about self-service technologies to others. However, technology-anxious consumers who initially have a satisfying experience with self-serving technologies tend to communicate positive word-of-mouth information to others than do those low in technology anxiety.[88]

Need for Tactile Input

Need for Tactile Input   The **need for tactile input** is a tendency for certain consumers to inspect the product by exploring the product's impact, sticking, sliding, slipping, and texture. Consumers with higher levels of need for tactile input are less likely to rely exclusively on sensory inputs such as sight or hearing in evaluating a product. Examples of measurement items capturing this consumer disposition include:

> **need for tactile input** A tendency for certain consumers to inspect the product by exploring the product's impact, sticking, sliding, slipping, and texture.

- "I need to touch a product in order to evaluate its quality."
- "I need to touch a product in order to evaluate how much I like the product."
- "I feel it necessary to touch a product in order to evaluate its physical characteristics."

- "I feel it is necessary to touch a product to evaluate its quality."
- "I need to touch a product in order to create a general evaluation of it."

A recent study has provided evidence that the degree of the need for tactile input in making product evaluations plays an important role in determining the choice of shopping medium. That is, those who have a high need for tactile input tend to rely less on a shopping medium such as the Internet than do those who have a low need for tactile input. This is because the Internet does not allow consumers to inspect the product by touching it.[89]

centrality of visual product aesthetics The overall level of significance that visual aesthetics hold for a particular consumer in his or her relationships with products.

Centrality of Visual Product Aesthetics
The **centrality of visual product aesthetics** is defined as the overall level of significance that visual aesthetics holds for a particular consumer in his or her relationships with products. This individual difference factor has three related dimensions: (1) the value that consumers assign to product appearance in enhancing personal and social well being, (2) acumen or ability to recognize and evaluate product design, and (3) level of response to visual design aspects of a product.

The first dimension—the value that consumers assign to product appearance in enhancing personal and social well being—refers to the belief that beauty in products does make a significant contribution to the quality of life. Examples of items capturing this dimension include (respondents agree or disagree to the statements):

- "Owning products that have superior designs makes me feel good about myself."
- "I enjoy seeing displays of products that have superior designs."
- "A product's design is a source of pleasure for me."
- "Beautiful product designs make our world a better place to live."

The acumen or ability to recognize and evaluate product design refers to consumers' ability to make artistic judgments about the beauty of product design. Examples of items measuring this dimension include:

- "Being able to see subtle differences in product designs is one skill that I have developed over time."
- "I see things in a product's design that other people tend to pass over."
- "I have the ability to imagine how a product will fit in with designs of other things I already own."

Level of response refers to the intensity of feelings of pleasure experienced with a product that has good design. Some consumers react more intensely than do others. Consumers who experience pleasure seeing a well-designed product are motivated to purchase the product. Examples of measurement items capturing this dimension include:

- "Sometimes the way a product looks seems to reach out and grab me."
- "If a product design really 'speaks' to me, I feel that I must buy it."
- "When I see a product that has really great design, I feel a strong urge to buy it."[90]

Exhibit 5-6 sums up the effects of consumption-specific personality traits on consumer behavior.

Marketing Management—Implications and Actions

Understanding consumer personality and personality traits helps marketers to:
- Position brands to enhance their appeal to target consumers by communicating the brand benefits that match consumers' personality types.
- Modify all promotional messages as a direct function of consumers' personality and their tendency to respond to advertising content.
- Identify the extent to which consumers of the product category are coupon prone, value conscious, and deal prone, and market accordingly.

Trait	Effect	
Market maven	Tendency to gather information and coupons about a variety of products and brands, shop around for new products, and advise others about what is good and bad in the marketplace.	**E x h i b i t 5-6**
Consumer innovativeness	Tendency to adopt technological innovations	**Consumption-Specific Personality Trait Effects on Consumer Behavior**
Opinion leadership	Tendency to educate and inform others about the introduction of a new product or service that falls within the opinion leader's area of expertise	
Product-specific	Tendency to buy from specialty stores self-confidence	
Low product-specific self-efficacy	Resistance to adoption of technological innovations	
High product-specific subjective knowledge	Tendency to be innovative, emotionally involved, and buy and consume the product category	
Coupon proneness	Tendency to redeem coupons	
Value consciousness	Tendency to prefer brands having high value for the money spent	
Deal proneness	Tendency to look for deals and bargains	
Product-specific involvement	Tendency to inject meaning into the various attributes and features of a particular product or service	
Consumer relationship proneness	Tendency to engage in relationships with retailers of a particular product category	
Technology anxiety	Tendency to feel anxious when using self-serving technologies	
Need for tactile input	Tendency to need to inspect the product by touching it to evaluate the product	
Centrality of visual product aesthetics	Tendency to notice and dwell on the aesthetics aspects of product design	

Chapter Spotlights

This chapter dealt with psychological influences on consumer behavior by exploring how the differences among consumers affect the ways in which they interpret and evaluate products, and how they act in relation to them.

1. Symbolic consumption—how symbols influence consumer behavior. Symbolic consumption highlights the importance of signs and symbols in understanding the motivations behind purchase decisions. By correctly interpreting the signs that influence consumer choices, marketers can ensure that their goods, services, and advertising messages accurately address consumer motivations.

2. Brand-user image and brand-user personality. Inherent in understanding consumer motivations is the concept of brand image. Brands can be characterized in terms of the extent to which they meet three basic types of consumer need: utilitarian, experiential, and value-expressive needs. By using symbols that imply satisfaction of these needs, marketers can create effective brand images. An extension of brand image is the concept of brand user image or brand personality—how consumers perceive typical brand users. By

reflecting the way typical users are viewed by potential customers, marketers can motivate those prospects to become brand users.

3. Self-image in the marketplace. Brand user image interacts with consumers' self-concepts to determine the extent to which they favor or disfavor brands. There are four types of self-concept: actual self, ideal self, social self, and ideal social self. Congruence between brand user image and self-concept motivates consumers to favor certain brands, while lack of congruence leads to disfavor.

4. Personality and personality traits. There are two common ways to understand personality: the state approach and the trait approach. The state view advocates understanding the individual in a holistic way. The trait approach sees people as having common traits to differing degrees. There are two types of personality traits that influence consumer behavior: general personality traits and consumption-specific personality traits. By studying the personality traits of specific market segments, marketers are better equipped to develop appropriate products and services and to position them effectively.

Key Terms

acquisition self-presentation (p. 152)
actual self-congruity (p. 143)
actual self-image (p. 141)
affect intensity (p. 157)
aggressiveness (p. 150)
androgynous (p. 147)
attention to social comparison information
 (p. 153)
body cathexis (p. 148)
body image (p. 147)
brand image (p. 137)
brand-user personality or brand-user image
 (p. 140)
centrality of visual product aesthetics (p. 164)
compliance (p. 150)
connectedness (p. 154)
consumer innovativeness (p. 158)
consumption-specific personality trait (p. 150)
coupon proneness (p. 161)
deal proneness (p. 162)
detachment (p. 150)
dogmatism (p. 153)
experiential or aesthetic needs (p. 138)
extraversion (p. 155)
gender-role orientation (p. 147)

gender-typed products (p. 147)
general personality trait (p. 150)
generalized self-confidence (p. 151)
icons (p. 137)
ideal body image (p. 147)
ideal self-congruity (p. 145)
ideal self-image (p. 141)
ideal social self-congruity (p. 146)
ideal social self-image (p. 142)
impulsiveness (p. 155)
indexes (p. 137)
market maven (p. 158)
need for achievement (p. 157)
need for affiliation (p. 157)
need for cognition (p. 156)
need for power (p. 156)
need for tactile input (p. 163)
neuroticism (p. 155)
opinion leadership (p. 159)
optimum stimulation level (OSL) (p. 154)
personality (p. 149)
product-specific involvement (p. 162)
product-specific self-confidence (p. 159)
product-specific self-efficacy (p. 161)
protective self-presentation (p. 152)

reverse coded (p. 155)
rigidity (p. 153)
self-consciousness (p. 151)
self-consistency motive (p. 141)
self-esteem (p. 152)
self-esteem motive (p. 142)
self-image (p. 136)
self-image congruence (p. 143)
self-monitoring (p. 151)
semiotics (p. 137)
separateness (p. 154)
social approval motive (p. 142)
social consistency motive (p. 142)
social self-congruity (p. 146)
social self-image (p. 142)
state approach to personality (p. 150)
state versus action orientation (p. 154)
symbolic consumption (p. 136)
symbols (p. 137)
technology anxiety (p. 163)
tolerance of ambiguity (p. 153)
trait approach to personality (p. 150)
utilitarian or functional needs (p. 138)
value consciousness (p. 161)
value-expressive or symbolic needs (p. 139)

Review Questions

Note: You can find the correct answers to these questions by taking the quiz and then submitting your answers in the Online Edition. The program will automatically score your submission. If you miss a question, the program will provide the correct answer, a rationale for the answer, and the section number in the chapter where the topic is discussed.

1. Which of the following "signs" relies on some easily recognizable property of the idea it represents?
 a. icon
 b. index
 c. symbol
 d. visual portrayal

2. Monica Juarez has been conducting research on signs and their meanings for her college consumer behavior class. She is studying
 a. semiotics.
 b. symbolics.
 c. symbiosis.
 d. psychosomatics.

3. When we choose products that help us express our own self-image needs, they are called _____ or symbolic.
 a. experiential
 b. aesthetic
 c. value-expressive
 d. homogeneous

4. Brand-user image or brand-user personality is based on _____ attributes that characterize the brand.
 a. value-laden
 b. value-filled
 c. value-perceived
 d. value-expressive

5. Marketing scientists have determined that self-concept has at least four dimensions that affect consumer behavior. They are
 a. actual self, ideal self, expected self, and deserved self.
 b. actual self, ideal self, social self, and ideal social self.
 c. ideal self, social self, aspired self, and real self.
 d. real self, social self, predicted self, and desired self.

6. Which of the following drive(s) people to act in ways that are in line with their actual self-image?
 a. ideal self-image
 b. self-consistency
 c. self-esteem
 d. attitudes

7. An androgynous personality is characterized as
 a. high on feminine characteristics.
 b. high on masculine characteristics.
 c. having both feminine and masculine characteristics.
 d. having neither masculine nor feminine characteristics.

8. Central to personal identity, _____ image explains how people see their bodies, physical selves, and appearance.
   a. body
   b. personal
   c. full
   d. loyal

9. To predict what a person will do in a given situation, marketers use the _____ approach to study consumer personality.
   a. trait
   b. general personality
   c. state
   d. consumption-specific

10. Some consumers change their behavior as a function of the situation in which they find themselves. We call this
    a. self-adjustment.
    b. self-monitoring.
    c. self-esteem.
    d. self-idealism.

Team Talk

1. Are all purchases driven by self-image congruence? Can you think of any exceptions? Discuss the importance of this phenomenon with your team.

2. Are there different standards of female and male attractiveness? Discuss these standards with your team in relation to the marketing of clothing.

3. Can the principles of body cathexis be used to market things other than body-specific items? What about sport utility vehicles? Or long-distance telephone service?

4. Can you think of brands or product classes have changed their marketing in response to shifts in gender-role orientation? Can you think of any that are androgynous?

5. Discuss the personality traits in Exhibits 5-6 and 5-7. Have everyone in the team raise a hand when they feel that they rate high on a particular trait. Does your group have certain traits? Do you feel that the spread of these traits is random, or does it reflect a certain segment of society?

6. A beloved grandparent gives you a slightly used television as a Christmas present, but shortly after you get it, the television set malfunctions. What do you do? Have everyone in your team respond to this situation. How do the responses fall into the three categories of anxiety response (compliance, aggression, detachment)?

7. Watch a sitcom with your team. During the commercial breaks, take notes on the icons, indexes, and symbols used in the ads shown during the program. Afterward, compare notes. Did everyone catch the same signs?

8. Select a purchase everyone in your team has made lately. Dissect this purchase in terms of the different needs it may serve. Be sure to address all three types of needs (utilitarian, experiential, and value-expressive). Does everyone have the same need fulfillment requirements? Do the differences reflect differences in self-image?

9. Take a walk through a local department store. Note the different areas devoted to certain styles. Discuss with your team the ways in which different forms of self-image are used to establish clothing market segments.

Workshops

Research Workshop

Background

A small perfume company wants to create a niche in the market for a unique, fruit-scented oil. The objective of this workshop is to uncover inexpensive, targeted communications opportunities for marketing the new scent.

Methodology

Focus on a segment of the population, let's say young people who have a need to be seen as different from others. Develop a few representative personality measures that you can use to identify these people. Administer these measures to your classmates, and identify those who score high on the need for uniqueness items. Ask them about their preference in various men's and women's fragrances.

To the Marketplace

Identify situations in which these consumers may wear perfume or cologne, i.e., on a date, at a social get-together, in a casual setting. Make a list of places or occasions that would be effective opportunities for targeting young people who have a high need for uniqueness.

Creative Workshop

Background

You are working as a clerk in a clothing boutique that serves overweight shoppers, and the boss asks you to help develop a more positive image for the store. The objective of this workshop is to use the principles of body cathexis to reposition the store in the local market.

Methodology

Discuss with your classmates their feelings about their bodies. What aspects of their bodies do they feel positive about? Which ones do they feel negative about?

To the Marketplace

Draft a one-page proposal for creating a new image for a clothing store using the principles of body cathexis and the feedback of your classmates.

Managerial Workshop

Background

You are assigned the task of developing a new marketing program that can help Tide defend its dominant market position. The objective of this workshop is to explore how Tide is perceived by different people and what role it plays in their personal and social identities.

Methodology

Identify at least three major consumer segments that use laundry detergent. Select one consumer segment and ask yourself how these people are likely to describe Tide in terms of its brand image or brand personality. How are the same consumers likely to describe their actual, ideal, social, and ideal social selves? What needs or motives drive the purchase of Tide in these different consumer segments?

To the Marketplace

Based on your understanding of these psychological links between Tide's brand personality and the self-image of the different consumer segments, develop ideas for a new marketing communications campaign for Tide.

Notes

1. Adapted from an idea presented in "What's Your Beauty Personality?" *Redbook*, (November 1993), p. 107.

2. For an excellent article introducing the study of consumer semiotics and symbolic consumption, see David Glen Mick, "Consumer Research and Semiotics: Exploring the Morphology of Signs, Symbols, and Significance," *Journal of Consumer Research*, Vol. 13 (September 1986), pp. 196–213. For other interesting applications of symbolic consumption concepts, see Maria Piacentini and Greig Mailer, "Symbolic Consumption in Teenagers' Clothing Choices," *Journal of Consumer Behavior*, Vol. 3, (March 2004), pp. 251–263; and Morris B. Holbrook and Robert M. Schindler, "Nostalgic Bonding: Exploring the Role of Nostalgia in the Consumption Experience," *Journal of Consumer Behaviour*, Vol. 3 (December 2003), pp. 107–120.

3. Judie Lannon and Peter Cooper, "Humantistic Advertising: Cultural Perspective," *International Journal of Advertising*, Vol. 2 (1983), pp. 195–213.

4. For an overview of semiotics, see Mick, "Consumer Research and Semiotics"; for a recent application of semiotics in advertising, see Teresa J. Domzal and Jerome B. Kernan, "Leisure Advertising: Media Portrayals of the Postmodern Homo Ludens," in M. Joseph Sirgy and A. Coskun Samli, eds., *New Dimensions of Quality-of-Life/Marketing Interface* (Westport, CT: Quorum Books, 1994).

5. C. Whan Park, Bernard J. Jaworski, and Deborah J. MacInnis, "Strategic Brand Concept-Image Management," *Journal of Marketing*, Vol. 50 (October 1986), pp. 135–145.

6. Barry J. Babin and Lauri Babin, "Seeking Something Different? A Model of Schema Typicality, Consumer Affect, Purchase Intentions, and Perceived Shopping Value, *Journal of Business Research*, Vol. 54 (November 2001), pp. 89–96.

7. Joseph T. Plummer, "How Personality Makes a Difference," *Journal of Advertising Research*, Vol. 24 (January 1985), pp. 27–31.

8. Ibid.

9. Dinoo J. Vanier and Donald Sciglimpaglia, "Development and Application of the Concept of User Image: The Case of Mass Transit Ridership," *Journal of the Academy of Marketing Science*, Vol. 9 (April 1981), pp. 479–489.

10. Erving Goffman, *The Presentation of Self in Everyday Life* (Garden City, NY: Doubleday, 1959); George H. Mead, *Mind, Self and Society* (Chicago, IL: University of Chicago Press, 1934); Charles H. Cooley, *Human Nature and the Social Order* (New York: Scribner's, 1902); Michael R. Solomon, "The Role of Products as Social Stimuli: A Symbolic Interactionism Perspective," *Journal of Consumer Research*, Vol. 10 (December 1983), pp. 319–329.

11. M. Joseph Sirgy, "Self-Concept in Consumer Behavior: A Critical Review," *Journal of Consumer Research*, Vol. 9 (December 1982), pp. 287–300.

12. Russell W. Belk, "Possessions and the Extended Self," *Journal of Consumer Research*, Vol. 15 (September 1988), pp. 139–168.

13. Sirgy, "Self-Concept in Consumer Behavior."

14. Ibid.

15. Amy J. Morgan, "The Evolving Self in Consumer Behavior: Exploring Possible Selves," *Advances in Consumer Research*, Vol. 20, Leigh McAlister and Michael L. Rothschild, eds. (Provo, UT: Association for Consumer Research, 1993), pp. 311–318.

16. Harry C. Triandis, "The Self and Social Behavior in Differing Cultural Contexts," *Psychological Review*, Vol. 96 (Issue 3, 1989), pp. 506–520; H. Markus and S. Kitayama, "Culture and the Self: Implications for Cognition, Emotion, and Motivation," *Psychological Review*, Vol. 98 (1991), pp. 224–253; Naomi Mandel, "Shifting Selves and Decision Making: The Effects of Self-construal Priming on Consumer Risk-taking," *Journal of Consumer Research*, Vol. 30 (2003), pp. 30–40; Jennifer L. Aaker and Angela Y. Lee, "'I' Seek Pleasure and 'We' Avoid Pains: The Role of Self-regulatory Goals in Information Processing and Persuasion," *Journal of Consumer Research*, Vol. 28 (June 2001), pp. 33–49.

17. M. Joseph Sirgy, *Self-Congruity: Towards a Theory of Personality and Cybernetics* (New York: Praeger Publishers, 1986).

18. Ibid.

19. M. Joseph Sirgy and A. C. Samli, "A Path Analytic Model of Store Loyalty Involving Self-Concept, Store Image, Socioeconomic Status, and Geographic Loyalty," *Journal of the Academy of Marketing Science*, Vol. 13 (Summer), pp. 265–291.

20. Ibid.

21. Marcia Mogelonsky, "Covering Gray (or Brown or Blonde)," *American Demographics* (November 1996).

22. M. Joseph Sirgy, "Self-concept in Consumer Behavior: A Critical Review," *Journal of Consumer Research*, Vol. 9 (1982), pp. 287–300; M. Joseph Sirgy and A. C. Samli, "A Path Analytic Model of Store Loyalty Involving Self-image Congruence, Store Image, Geographic Loyalty, and Socio-economic Status," *Journal of the Academy of Marketing*

Science, Vol. 13 (1985), pp. 265–291; M. Joseph Sirgy, Dhruv Grewal, Tamara F. Mangleburg, Jae-Ok Park, Kye-Sung Chon, C. B. Claiborne, J. S. Johar, and Harold Berkman, "Assessing the Predictive Validity of Two Methods of Measuring Self-image Congruence," *Journal of the Academy of Marketing Science,* Vol. 25 (1997), pp. 229–241; M. Joseph Sirgy and Chenting Su, "Destination Image, Self-congruity, and Travel Behavior," *Journal of Travel Research,* Vol. 38 (2000), 340–352; M. Joseph Sirgy, "Using Self-Congruity and Ideal Congruity to Predict Purchase Motivation," *Journal of Business Research,* Vol. 13 (1985), pp. 195–206; M. Joseph Sirgy, "Self-Image/Product-Image Congruity and Consumer Decision-Making," *International Journal of Management,* Vol. 2 (December 1985), pp. 49–63; Mary K. Ericksen and M. Joseph Sirgy, "Employed Females' Clothing Preference, Self-Image Congruence, and Career Anchorage," *Journal of Applied Social Psychology,* Vol. 22 (May 1992), pp. 408–422; Mary K. Ericksen and M. Joseph Sirgy, "Achievement Motivation and Clothing Behavior of Working Women: A Self-Image Congruence Analysis," *Journal of Social Behavior and Personality,* Vol. 4 (April 1989), pp. 307–326. Sak Onkvisit and John Shaw, "Self-Concept and Image Congruence: Some Research and Managerial Issues," *Journal of Consumer Marketing,* Vol. 4 (Winter 1987), pp. 13–23; M. Joseph Sirgy, Dhruv Grewal, Tamara F. Mangleburg, Jae-Ok Park, Kye-Sung Chon, C. B. Claiborne, J. S. Johar, and Harold Berkman, "Assessing the Predictive Validity of Two Methods of Measuring Self-Image Congruence," *Journal of the Academy of Marketing Science,* Vol. 25 (Summer 1997), pp. 229–241; Kye-Sung Chon, "Self-image/Destination-image Congruity," *Annals of Tourism Research,* Vol. 19 (1992), pp. 360–362; Timothy R. Graeff, "Using Promotional Messages to Manage the Effects of Brand and Self-image on Brand Evaluations," *Journal of Consumer Marketing,* Vol. 13 (1996), pp. 4–18; Jae W. Hong and George M. Zinkhan, "Self-concept and Advertising Effectiveness: The Influence of Congruence, Conspicuousness, and Response Mode," *Psychology and Marketing,* Vol. 12 (1995), pp. 53–77; Naresh K. Malhotra, "A Scale to Measure Self-concepts, Person Concepts, and Product Concepts," *Journal of Marketing Research,* Vol. 18 (1981), pp. 456–464; Naresh K. Malhotra, "Self-concept and Product Choice: An Integrated Perspective," *Journal of Economic Psychology,* Vol. 9 (1988), pp. 1–28; Sarah Todd, "Self-concept: A Tourism Application," *Journal of Consumer Behaviour,* Vol. 1 (November 2001), pp. 184–197.

23. Chip Walker, "Fat and Happy," *American Demographics* (January 1993).

24. Ibid.

25. Harrison G. Gough, Mario Fioravanti, and Renato Lazzari, "Some Implications of Self Versus Ideal-Self Congruence on the Revised Adjective Check List," *Journal of Personality and Social Psychology,* Vol. 44, No. 6 (1983), pp. 1214–1220.

26. Deborah Bosanko, "Why Do Working Women Work Out?" *American Demographics* (February 1994).

27. Steven Jay Lynn and Judith W. Rhue, "Daydream Believers," *Psychology Today,* (September 1985), p. 14.

28. Bosanko, "Why Do Working Women Work Out?"

29. Kathleen Debevec and Easwar Iyer, "Sex Roles and Consumer Perceptions of Promotions, Products, and Self: What Do We Know and Where Should We Be Headed," in Richard J. Lutz,

ed., *Advances in Consumer Research,* Vol. 13 (Provo, UT: Association for Consumer Research, 1986), pp. 210–214.

30. Sandra L. Bem, "The Measurement of Psychological Androgyny," *Journal of Consulting and Clinical Psychology,* Vol. 42 (1974), pp. 155–162; Deborah E. S. Frable, "Sex Typing and Gender Ideology: Two Facets of the Individual's Gender Psychology That Go Together," *Journal of Personality and Social Psychology,* Vol. 56, No. 1 (1989), pp. 95–108.

31. Lynn J. Jaffe and Paul D. Berger, "Impact on Purchase Intent of Sex-Role Identity and Product Positioning," *Psychology & Marketing,* (Fall 1988), pp. 259–271; Lynn J. Jaffe, "The Unique Predictive Ability of Sex-Role Identity in Explaining Women's Response to Advertising," *Psychology and Marketing,* Vol. 11 (September/October 1994), pp. 467–482.

32. Diane Crispell, "Have High Heels, Will Limp," *American Demographics* (May 1997).

33. John Schouten, "Selves in Transition: Symbolic Consumption in Personal Rites of Passage and Identity Reconstruction," *Journal of Consumer Research,* Vol. 17 (March 1991), pp. 412–425.

34. Dennis W. Rook, "Body Cathexis and Market Segmentation," in Michael R. Solomon ed., *The Psychology of Fashion* (Lexington, MA: Lexington Books, 1985), pp. 233–241.

35. For an interesting and historical exposition of the history of personality research as it applies to consumer behavior, read the following article: Norman S. Endler and Alvin J. Rosenstein, "Evolution of the Personality Construct in Marketing and Its Applicability to Contemporary Personality Research," *Journal of Consumer Research,* Vol. 6 (Issue 1, 1997), pp. 55–66.

36. Earl E. Baughman, *Personality: The Psychological Study of the Individual,* (Englewood Cliffs, NJ: Prentice Hall, 1972), p. 9.

37. Kathryn E. A. Villani and Yoram Wind, "On Usage of 'Modified' Personality Trait Measures in Consumer Research," *Journal of Consumer Research,* Vol. 2, No. 3 (December 1975), p. 223.

38. Joel B. Cohen, "Toward an Interpersonal Theory of Consumer Behavior," in Harold H. Kassarjian and Thomas S. Robertson eds., *Perspectives in Consumer Behavior* (Glenview, IL: Scott Foresman, 1968).

39. John A. Howard and Lyman E. Ostlund, *Buyer Behavior: Theoretical and Empirical Foundations* (New York: Knopf, 1973), p. 554.

40. Joseph F. Dash, Leon G. Schiffman, and Conrad Berenson, "Risk- and Personality-Related Dimensions of Store Choice," *Journal of Marketing,* Vol. 40 (January 1976), p. 36.

41. Arnold W. Buss, *Self-Consciousness and Social Anxiety* (San Francisco, CA: W. H. Freeman, 1980).

42. Michael R. Solomon and John Schopler, "Self-Consciousness and Clothing," *Personality and Social Psychology Bulletin,* Vol. 8 (1982), pp. 508–514.

43. Pratibha A. Dabholkar and Richard P. Bagozzi, "An Attitudinal Model of Technology-Based Self-Service: Moderating Effects of Consumer Traits and Situational Factors," *Journal of the Academy of Marketing Science,* Vol. 30 (Summer 2002), pp. 184–201.

44. Mark Snyder and Steve Gangestad, "On the Nature of Self-Monitoring: Matters of Assessment Matters of Validity," *Journal of Personality and Social Psychology,* Vol. 51 (1986), pp. 125–139; for a good review of self-monitoring studies in

consumer research, see the following article: Mark Slama and Kevin Celuch, "Self-Presentation and Consumer Interaction Styles," *Journal of Business and Psychology,* Vol. 10 (Fall 1995), pp. 19–30.

45. M. Snyder and K. G. DeBono, "Appeals to Image and Claims About Quality: Understanding the Psychology of Advertising," *Journal of Personality and Social Psychology,* Vol. 49 (1985), pp. 586–597.

46. Also see Timothy R. Graeff, "Image Congruence Effects on Product Evaluations: The Role of Self-Monitoring and Public/Private Consumption," *Psychology and Marketing,* Vol. 13 (August 1996), pp. 481–499.

47. Sharon Shavitt, Tina M. Lowrey, and Sang-Pil Han, "Attitude Functions in Advertising: The Interactive Role of Products and Self-Monitoring," *Journal of Consumer Psychology,* Vol. 1 (April 1992), pp. 337–364.

48. Mark Slama and Kevin Celuch, "Self-Presentation and Consumer Interaction Styles," *Journal of Business and Psychology,* Vol. 10 (Fall 1995), pp. 19–30.

49. Roy F. Baumeister, Dianne M. Tice, and Debra G. Hutton, "Self-Presentation Motivations and Personality Differences in Self-Esteem," *Journal of Personality and Social Psychology,* Vol. 57 (September 1989), pp. 547–575.

50. Emily Yoffe, "You Are What You Buy," *Newsweek* (June 4, 1990), p. 59.

51. See literature review in P. S. Raju, "Optimum Stimulation Level: Its Relationship to Personality, Demographics and Exploratory Behavior," *Journal of Consumer Research,* Vol. 7, No. 3 (December 1980), p. 273.

52. Raju, "Optimum Stimulation Level."

53. Ibid.

54. Charles Schaninger and Donald Sciglimpaglia, "The Influence of Cognitive Personality Traits and Demographics on Consumer Information Acquisition," *Journal of Consumer Research,* Vol. 8 (September 1981), pp. 208–215.

55. William O. Bearden and Randall L. Rose, "Attention to Social Comparison Information: An Individual Difference Factor Affecting Consumer Conformity," *Journal of Consumer Research,* Vol. 16 (March 1990), pp. 461–471.

56. For a literature review of this personality trait in psychology, see Marvin Zuckerman, *Sensation Seeking: Beyond the Optimum Level of Arousal* (Hillsdale, NJ: Erlbaum, 1979).

57. Jan-Benedict E. M. Steenkemp and Hans Baumgartner, "The Role of Optimum Stimulation Level in Exploratory Consumer Behavior," *Journal of Consumer Research,* Vol. 19 (December 1992), pp. 434–448.

58. Julius Kuhl, "Motivational and Functional Helplessness: The Moderating Effect of State Versus Action Orientation," *Journal of Personality and Social Psychology,* Vol. 40 (January 1981), pp. 155–170.

59. Richard P. Bagozzi, Hans Baumgartner, and Youjae Yi, "State Versus Action Orientation and the Theory of Reasoned Action: An Application to Coupon Usage," *Journal of Consumer Research,* Vol. 18 (March 1992), pp. 505–518.

60. Cheng Lu Wang and John C. Mowen, "The Separateness-Connectedness Self-Schema: Scale Development and Application to Message Construction," *Psychology and Marketing,* Vol. 14, No. 2 (1997), pp. 185–208.

61. Radhika Puri, "Measuring and Modifying Consumer Impulsiveness: A Cost-Benefit Accessibility Framework,"

Journal of Consumer Psychology, Vol. 5 (Issue 2 1996), pp. 87–113. Michael A. Jones, Kristy E. Reynolds, Seungoog Weun, and Sharon E. Beatty, "The Product-Specific Nature of Impulse Buying Tendency," *Journal of Business Research,* Vol. 56 (July 2003), pp. 505–512.

62. Hans J. Eysenck. *The Biological Basis of Personality.* Springfield, IL: C. C. Thomas, 1967.

63. Todd A. Mooradian, "Personality and Ad-Evoked Feelings: The Case for Extraversion and Neuroticism," *Journal of the Academy of Marketing Science,* Vol. 24 (Spring 1996), pp. 99–109.

64. Curt Haugtvedt, Richard E. Petty, John T. Cacioppo, and Theresa Steidly, "Personality and Ad Effectiveness: Exploring the Utility of Need for Cognition," in Michael J. Houston, ed., *Advances in Consumer Research,* Vol. 16 (Provo, UT: Association for Consumer Research, 1988), pp. 33–36.

65. Curtis P. Haugtvedt, Richard E. Petty, and John T. Cacioppo, "Need for Cognition and Advertising: Understanding the Role of Personality Variables in Consumer Behavior," *Journal of Consumer Psychology,* Vol. 1 (March 1992), pp. 239–260.

66. D. G. Winter and A. J. Stewart, "The Power Motive." In H. London and J. Exner, eds., *Dimensions of Personality* (New York: Wiley, 1978).

67. D. G. Winter, *The Power Motive.* New York: The Free Press, 1973; D.G. Winter, "The Power Motive in Women—and Men," *Journal of Personality and Social Psychology,* Vol. 54 (1988), pp. 510–519.

68. Laura C. Schmidt and Irene Hanson Frieze, "A Mediational Model of Power, Affiliation, and Achievement Motives and Product Involvement," *Journal of Business and Psychology,* Vol. 11 (Summer 1997), pp. 425–446.

69. Ibid.

70. Ibid.

71. Randy J. Larsen and Ed Diener, "Affect Intensity as an Individual Difference Characteristic: A Review," *Journal of Research in Personality,* Vol. 21 (March 1987), pp. 1–39.

72. David J. Moore, William D. Harris, and Hong C. Chen, "Affect Intensity: An Individual Difference Response to Advertising Appeals," *Journal of Consumer Research,* Vol. 22 (September 1995), pp. 154–164.

73. Lawrence F. Feick and Linda L. Price, "The Market Maven: A Diffuser of Marketplace Information," *Journal of Marketing,* Vol. 51 (January 1987), pp. 83–97. Michel Laroche, Frank Pons, Nadia Zgolli, Marie-Cecile Cervellon, and Chankon Kim, "A Model of Consumer Response to Two Retail Sales Promotion Techniques," *Journal of Business Research,* Vol. 56 (July 2003), pp. 513–522.

74. Russell Abratt, Deon Nel, and Christo Nezer, "Role of the Market Maven in Retailing: A General Marketplace Influencer," *Journal of Business and Psychology,* Vol. 10 (Fall 1995), pp. 31–55.

75. Ronald E. Goldsmith and Charles F. Hofacker, "Measuring Consumer Innovativeness," *Journal of the Academy of Marketing Science,* Vol. 19 (Summer 1991), pp. 209–221.

76. Everett M. Rogers and David G. Cartano, "Methods of Measuring Opinion Leadership," *Public Opinion Quarterly,* Vol. 26 (Fall 1962), pp. 435–441; Charles W. King and John O. Summers, "Overlap of Opinion Leadership Across Consumer Product Categories," *Journal of Marketing Research,* Vol. 7 (February 1970), pp. 43–50.

77. Dash, Schiffman, and Berenson, "Risk- and Personality-Related Dimensions of Store Choice."

78. Pam Scholder Ellen, William O. Bearden, and Subhash Sharma, "Resistance to Technological Innovations: An Examination of the Role of Self-Efficacy and Performance Satisfaction," *Journal of the Academy of Marketing Science,* Vol. 19 (Fall 1991), pp. 296–307.

79. Lauren G. Block and Punam Anand Keller, "Effects of Self-Efficacy and Vividness on the Persuasiveness of Health Communications," *Journal of Consumer Psychology,* Vol. 6 (Issues 1, 1997), pp. 31–45.

80. Kevin G. Celuch, John A. Lust, and Linda Showers, "An Investigation of the Relationship Between Self-Efficacy and the Communication Effectiveness of Product Manuals," *Journal of Business and Psychology,* Vol. 9 (Spring 1995), pp. 241–252.

81. Leisa Reinecke Flynn and Ronald E. Goldsmith, "A Short, Reliable Measure of Subjective Knowledge," *Journal of Business Research,* Vol. 46 (September 1999), pp. 57–66.

82. Ibid.

83. For a good literature review article on coupon proneness, see Lisa Guimond, Chankon Kim, and Michel Laroche, "An Investigation of Coupon-prone Consumers: Their Reactions to Coupon Feature Manipulation," *Journal of Business Research,* Vol. 54 (November 2001), pp. 131–137.

84. Donald R. Lichtenstein, Richard G. Netemeyer, and Scot Burton, "Distinguishing Coupon Proneness from Value Consciousness," *Journal of Marketing,* Vol. 54 (July 1990), pp. 54–67.

85. Donald R. Lichtenstein, Richard G. Netemeyer, and Scot Burton, "Assessing the Domain Specificity of Deal Proneness: A Field Study," *Journal of Consumer Research,* Vol. 22 (December 1995), pp. 314–326.

86. Mark B. Houston and Beth A. Walker, "Self-Relevance and Purchase Goals: Mapping a Consumer Decision," *Journal of the Academy of Marketing Science,* Vol. 24 (Summer 1996), pp. 232–245. For recent research showing the impact of product category involvement on relationship quality, see Gaby Odekerken-Schroder, Kristof De Wulf, and Patrick Schumacher, "Strengthening Outcomes of Retailer-Consumer Relationships: The Dual Impact of Relationship Marketing Tactics and Consumer Personality," *Journal of Business Research,* Vol. 56 (March 2003), pp. 177–190.

87. Gaby Odekerken-Schroder, Kristof De Wulf, and Patrick Schumacher, "Strengthening Outcomes of Retailer-Consumer Relationships: The Dual Impact of Relationship Marketing Tactics and Consumer Personality," *Journal of Business Research,* Vol. 56 (March 2003), pp. 177–190.

88. Matthew L. Meuter, Amy L. Ostrom, Mary Jo Bitner, and Robert Roundtree, "The Influence of Technology Anxiety on Consumer Use and Experiences with Self-Service Technologies," *Journal of Business Research,* Vol. 56 (2003), pp. 899–906.

89. Alka Varma Citrin, Donald E. Stem, Eric R. Spangenberg, and Michael J. Clark, "Consumer Need for Tactile Input: An Internet Retailing Challenge," *Journal of Business Research,* Vol. 56 (2003), pp. 915–922.

90. Peter H. Bloch, Frederic F. Brunel, and Todd J. Arnold, "Individual Differences in the Centrality of Visual Product Aesthetics: Concept and Measurement," *Journal of Consumer Research,* Vol. 29 (March 2003), pp. 551–565.

Personal Values, Lifestyles, Psychographics, and Relationships

6

Yvette has always been the kind of person who likes to try out new things. Although she doesn't consider herself a computer buff, she was the first in her group of friends to go online. She told everyone she did so to help with her schoolwork, but what she enjoys most is checking her email and joining in chat groups. As soon as it came on the market, Yvette talked her parents into signing up for a pretty sophisticated telephone system—she has her own telephone line, complete with voice mail and caller ID. Yvette thinks of herself as a busy person—she's in her sophomore year at college, works irregular hours in a part-time job, belongs to an amateur drama group, and likes the feeling that her social life is full, even hectic. In fact, her life is getting so crazy that she feels she needs to buy just one more thing to help her keep everything straight—a cellular phone. Staying in constant touch with her friends is so important to her that she wants to be sure she'll never miss a call. Since many of her friends have cell phones, Yvette wants to be able to show off by having a phone with all the features she can pack onto it, from Internet access to voice dialing, video messaging, and the ability to play 3D games. Yvette's choices in telecommunications equipment reveal not only aspects of her lifestyle but also tell us about the things that are important to her. In this chapter, we explore the personal values and lifestyles of consumers and their influence on marketplace behavior. We will also explore how consumers form relationships with brands and marketing firms.

6-1 Personal Values

Personal values—enduring beliefs that specific modes of conduct or end-states of existence are preferred to other specific modes of conduct or end-states—differ from person to person. To some of us, discipline, achievement, and self-control are all-important, while others among us build our lives around values of compassion, relationships, and humanity. The values we hold dear tell a great deal not only about our personalities, but also about our preferences and behaviors as consumers.

Because personal values influence marketplace and consumption behaviors, it is obviously important for marketers to take them into account when identifying and analyzing potential market segments. The benefits sought by consumers who hold one set of values are different than those sought by consumers who hold another. Think, for instance, of the very different benefits sought in making vacation choices by those who value hedonistic experiences compared to those who are looking for unity with nature. Several methods are available to marketers to help define and measure the personal values of consumers. Most popular are the Rokeach Personal Values Scale and the List of Values (LOV).

6-1a Rokeach Personal Values Scale

Psychologist Milton Rokeach defined personal values as enduring beliefs that specific modes of conduct or end-states of existence are preferred to other specific modes of conduct or end-states.[1] Specific modes of conduct, or **instrumental values,** might be ambition, broad-mindedness, capability, cheerfulness, cleanliness, or helpfulness, among others. If enacted over time, each of these behaviors leads to desirable end-states or terminal values. **Terminal values** might be a comfortable life, a sense of accomplishment, a world at peace, or racial equality. Exhibit 6-1 lists several instrumental and terminal values held by two population groups, men and women. The higher the value in the list, the more important that value is considered by that group. Terminal values such as a world at peace, family security, and freedom are important to both groups. Men value a comfortable life more than do women, to whom salvation and forgiveness are more important. Instrumental values of honesty, ambition, responsibility, broad-mindedness, and courage are important to both men and women.

The Rokeach scale is useful in identifying market segments in terms of the personal values members hold. Once the marketer identifies values related to a particular product, it is possible to develop communications messages consistent with those values. The Rokeach scale was used, for example, in a study of deodorant consumers to identify the values of those segments most likely to prefer Right Guard over Arrid. The study revealed that those who preferred Right Guard tended to place high importance on the terminal value of mature love, a good theme for future promotions to that segment.[2]

6-1b List of Values

The **List of Values (LOV)** consists of nine dominant consumer values.[3] These are:

1. Self-fulfillment
2. Excitement
3. Sense of accomplishment
4. Self-respect
5. Sense of belonging
6. Being well respected
7. Security
8. Fun and enjoyment
9. Warm relationships with others

Consumers cluster into three groups that display different value combinations: internals, interpersonals, and externals. Internals tend to value self-fulfillment, excitement, a sense of accomplishment, and self-respect. They also seek to control their lives. When buying food, for example, they seek nutrition information and tend to buy foods that claim to be all natural. This is a means of exerting control.[4] Externals, in contrast, tend to value a sense of belonging, being well respected, and security. In making food choices, they tend to avoid all-natural claims, perhaps out of a desire to be like the rest of society. Interpersonals value fun and enjoyment and warm relationships with others.

6-1c Means-End Chain Model

The **means-end chain** model is used by marketers to link products and product benefits with personal values. It demonstrates how the physical, tangible attributes of products (means) can be psychologically linked with personal values (ends) in the minds of consumers.[5] As shown in Exhibit 6-2, the model is built around six different aspects of the product:

1. Concrete attributes
2. Abstract attributes
3. Functional consequences
4. Psychosocial consequences
5. Instrumental values
6. Terminal values

F A Q

Do our personal values change over time? If so, what makes them change?

personal values (see p. 172) Enduring beliefs that specific modes of conduct or end-states of existence are preferred to other specific modes of conduct or end-states.

instrumental values Personal values that are enduring beliefs that specific modes of conduct or end-states of existence are preferred to other specific modes of conduct or end-states. Specific modes of conduct might be ambition, broad-mindedness, capability, cheerfulness, cleanliness, or helpfulness, among others.

terminal values Personal values that are enduring beliefs that specific modes of conduct or end-states of existence, if enacted over time, lead to desirable end-states or terminal values (end-states of existence that are preferred over other end-states). Terminal values might be a comfortable life, a sense of accomplishment, a world at peace, or racial equality.

List of Values (LOV) Consists of nine dominant consumer values: self-fulfillment, excitement, sense of accomplishment, self-respect, sense of belonging, being well respected, security, fun and enjoyment, and warm relationships with others.

Exhibit 6-1	*Terminal values* in the order of their importance as perceived by most American men and women surveyed in the late 1960s and early 1970s:	
Personal Value Components Classified by Gender	**Men**	**Women**
	A world at peace	A world at peace
	Family security	Family security
	Freedom	Freedom
means-end chain (see p. 173) A cognitive map of a product in the consumer's mind that connects how the consumer perceives the product in terms of concrete attributes and how these concrete attributes are linked to abstract attributes, functional consequences, psychosocial consequences, and instrumental and terminal values.	A comfortable life	Salvation
	Happiness	Happiness
	Self-respect	Self-respect
	A sense of accomplishment	Wisdom
	Wisdom	Equality
	Equality	True friendship
	National security	A sense of accomplishment
	True friendship	National security
	Salvation	Inner harmony
	Inner harmony	A comfortable life
	Mature love	Mature love
	A world of beauty	A world of beauty
	Social recognition	Pleasure
	Pleasure	Social recognition
	An exciting life	An exciting life

Instrumental values in the order of their importance as perceived by most American men and women:	
Men	**Women**
Honesty	Honesty
Ambition	Forgiveness
Responsibility	Responsibility
Broad-mindedness	Ambition
Courage	Broad-mindedness
Ability to forgive	Courage
Helpfulness	Helpfulness
Capability	Cleanliness
Cleanliness	Ability to love
Self-control	Cheerfulness
Independence	Self-control
Cheerfulness	Capability
Politeness	Politeness
Ability to love	Independence
Intellectual ability	Obedience
Ability to be logical	Intellectual ability
Obedience	Ability to be logical
Ability to be imaginative	Ability to be imaginative

Source: Data from Milton Rokeach, *The Nature of Human Values* (New York: The Free Press, 1973), pp. 57–58.

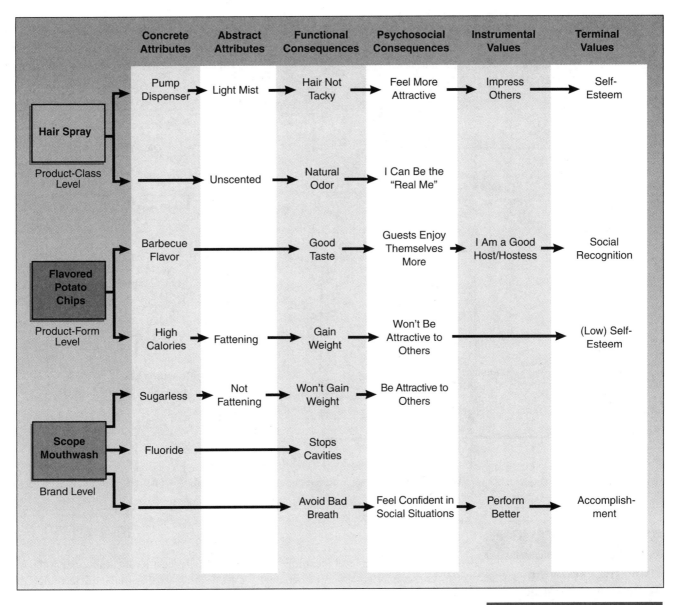

	Concrete Attributes	Abstract Attributes	Functional Consequences	Psychosocial Consequences	Instrumental Values	Terminal Values
Hair Spray Product-Class Level	Pump Dispenser	Light Mist	Hair Not Tacky	Feel More Attractive	Impress Others	Self-Esteem
		Unscented	Natural Odor	I Can Be the "Real Me"		
Flavored Potato Chips Product-Form Level	Barbecue Flavor		Good Taste	Guests Enjoy Themselves More	I Am a Good Host/Hostess	Social Recognition
	High Calories	Fattening	Gain Weight	Won't Be Attractive to Others		(Low) Self-Esteem
Scope Mouthwash Brand Level	Sugarless	Not Fattening	Won't Gain Weight	Be Attractive to Others		
	Fluoride		Stops Cavities			
			Avoid Bad Breath	Feel Confident in Social Situations	Perform Better	Accomplishment

Exhibit 6-2

Examples of Means-End Chains

Each of these three examples makes explicit connections among products and personal values.

Source: From *Consumer Behavior and Marketing Strategy* by J. Paul Peter and Jerry C. Olson, p. 103. Reprinted by permission of The McGraw-Hill Companies.

In Exhibit 6-2, we see a concrete attribute of a particular type of hair spray—it offers a pump dispenser. The concrete attribute of having a pump dispenser implies an abstract attribute that the spray achieves a light, even mist. The functional consequence of a light mist is that the spray, unlike that of competitors, does not make the user's hair tacky. Functional consequences are benefits or costs that consumers think about when they evaluate a product. Why should consumers care how their hair feels? Because it allows them to feel attractive to others, a psychosocial consequence. Psychosocial consequences are personal benefits and/or costs associated with the consumption of a product. Psychosocial consequences, at still higher levels of analysis, are linked with instrumental values. In the hair spray example, feeling attractive, a psychosocial consequence, is related to being able to impress others, an instrumental value. This, in turn, is related to the terminal value of self-esteem. Exhibit 6-2 also features two other products. How would you interpret what is going on in each case?

Laddering   The **laddering** technique is a method of analyzing means-end chains to reveal how certain goods and services are connected with personal values in the minds of consumers. It is a research technique that involves in-depth probing directed toward

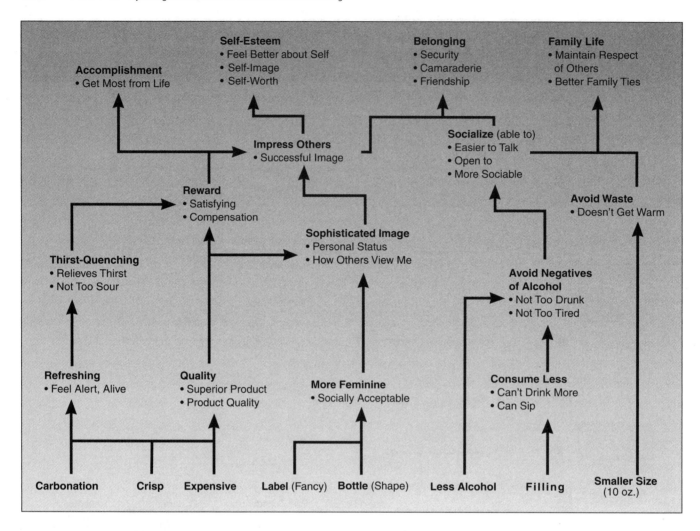

Source: From "Laddering Theory, Method, Analysis, and Interpretation" by Thomas J. Reynolds and Jonathan Gutman in *Journal of Advertising Research,* February/March 1998, p. 19. Reprinted by permission from the *Journal of Advertising Research,* © 1998, by the Advertising Research Foundation.

Exhibit 6-3

Using the Laddering Technique to Connect Products to Values

This hypothetical example demonstrates how means-end chain laddering allows a multi-layered interpretation of the relationships among product attributes and personal values.

▶**laddering** (see p. 175) A method of analyzing means-end chains to reveal how certain goods and services are connected with personal values in the minds of consumers.

uncovering higher-level meanings at both the benefit/cost level (functional and psychosocial consequences) and the personal values level (instrumental and terminal values).[6] In Exhibit 6-3 we see how attributes pertaining to wine coolers (carbonation, crisp, expensive, label, bottle, less alcohol, filling, smaller size) are connected to consequences (refreshing, thirst-quenching, more feminine, no negatives of alcohol, impress others, etc.), which in turn are connected to personal values (self-esteem, accomplishment, belonging, family life).

The marketing implications of personal values and the means-end chain model are significant. As an example, suppose the marketer of potato chips using the means-end chain model discovers that the ridges on the potato chip are linked both to positive values (being a good host and obtaining social recognition) and to negative values (being overweight and social disapproval because of physical unattractiveness). This type of analysis tells the marketer to take steps to strengthen the links with positive values and weaken those with negative ones. A new advertising campaign and the parallel development of a chip lower in fat might be answers.

Examine CBite 6-1. Many products are purchased and consumed because they are necessity items (for example, buying gas for your car). Even though they are necessity items, marketers are challenged to associate them with positive values. Marketers who are able to do this gain an extra competitive advantage over their competitors.

CBite 6-1

Accentuate the Positive

Consumers experience products in positive or negative ways. Positive products are those about which we have warm, upbeat feelings. We enjoy shopping for them and welcome new versions or spin-off products. The reverse is true for negative products. We might need them, but we don't particularly want them and certainly don't love to shop for them. Sporting goods, vacation travel, clothing, and entertainment are all positive product categories, while gasoline, auto repairs, groceries, and pest-control services are troublesome, negative products. Marketers of negative products have a special challenge: to ensure that the purchase experience is as pleasant and trouble-free as possible. Supermarkets offer free cups of hot coffee, and bookstores offer play areas for children. Pest-control advertising is usually humorous or light. Gas stations offer free car washes with fill-ups. The Shell credit card offers free gasoline based on quantities purchased over time. We still may not enjoy shopping for them or paying for them, but special efforts like these help overcome our resistance to those products toward which we have poor attitudes.

Source: Adapted from S. Widrick and Eugene Fram, "Identifying Negative Products," *Journal of Consumer Marketing,* No. 2, 1983, pp. 59–66.

Marketing Management—Implications and Actions

Understanding personal values helps marketers to:

- Identify values-based market segments. This means that markets can be segmented by values.
- Uncover positive and negative values linked to their goods or services. For example, how should a DVD be advertised? A marketer could develop a mean-end chain map showing how the perception of the concrete features of DVDs translate into consumer benefits, which in turn satisfy important needs. Such a psychological map would allow advertisers of DVDs to show how using a DVD allows consumers to experience heightened emotional involvement with the movie on the disk and how doing so satisfies their need for empathy.

6-2 Consumer Lifestyles

A direct marketer of life insurance examines demographic data on two families living side by side. In both households, the husband is 27.3 years old, finished 3.8 years of college, and earns $24,783 a year. Both households have two children and 0.6 of a dog. Based on demographics alone, both husbands are prime prospects for life insurance.

But, taking a closer look, we find that only one of these is a potential buyer. The fellow living in the solid colonial to the right conducts himself as a model of sober family devotion. His happiest moments occur when he can point his minivan home from the office early to spend an extra hour with the kids. This consumer could not be sold on a life insurance policy under $150,000 and would no sooner miss a premium due date than he would kick his 0.6 of a dog. He is definitely a hot prospect.

His neighbor, on the other hand, orders his life around a different set of priorities. He enjoys nothing more than hopping into his yellow Corvette and racing noisily off for a night on the town. His wife struggles to make ends meet because he spends most of the family income indulging his taste for expensive stereos, golf clubs, and other personal luxuries. On the brink of divorce, he is an unlikely candidate for life insurance.

Exhibit 6-4

This ad is designed to appeal to a lifestyle segment—namely, independent and successful professional women.

Source: Reprinted by permission of Nestle USA.

You're a smart,

successful, independent woman.

Stop eating like a **frat boy.**

Do something **good** for yourself.

Do something good for yourself with dishes like Shrimp & Angel Hair Pasta in a creamy seafood sauce. From Stouffer's Lean Cuisine.

It's not just lean. **IT'S CUISINE.**

Lean Cuisine.
CAFE CLASSICS
Shrimp & Angel Hair Pasta

www.LeanCuisine.com

© Nestle USA

The behavioral differences between these two prospects reflect lifestyle patterns that do not show up in demographic data, yet they predetermine the effectiveness of life insurance advertising or a visit from an insurance salesperson to each household.[7] The purpose of exploring lifestyles is to obtain more precise pictures of how consumers think and act than may be available from demographics alone. See Exhibit 6-4. This ad for Lean Cuisine is directed at independent and successful professional women. The ad appeals directly to this lifestyle segment by saying "You're a smart, successful, independent woman."

6-2a Defining Consumer Lifestyle

Lifestyle can be described using the following characteristics:

- *Lifestyle is a group phenomenon.* An individual's lifestyle is influenced by a variety of factors, including participation in social groups and relationships with significant others. A college student maintains a lifestyle dramatically different from that of a construction worker, and the lifestyle of a rebellious adolescent is far apart from that of his or her parents. These are easily explained differences. Less obvious are the divergent patterns exhibited by, say, two clerks who share office space in a corporation and earn the same salary. While one supports his family in a style compatible with his income, the other plunges into debt.

- *Lifestyle influences many aspects of behavior.* A person's lifestyle commits that individual to a certain consistency in behavior. Knowing our conduct in one aspect of life enables marketers to predict how we are likely to behave in other areas. People who prefer oil and vinegar on their salads are more inclined to attend a ballet than people who use commercial dressing. Liberals are more likely to see foreign films than people who profess to be conservative.

lifestyle A constellation of individual characteristics that reflect certain behaviors, such as participation in social groups and relationships with significant others, commitment to certain behaviors, and a central life interest, and that may vary according to sociologically relevant variables, such as age, sex, ethnicity, social class, and region, among others.

- *Lifestyle implies a central life interest.* A distinct lifestyle may be identified when some activity or interest influences other, even unrelated, activities. A person's central interest, for example, may be family, work, leisure, or religion. The upper-middle-class lifestyle, for instance, is usually regarded as education- and career-oriented.

- *Lifestyles vary according to sociologically relevant variables.* These include such determinants as age, sex, ethnicity, social class, region, and many more. The rate of social change also has a great deal to do with variation in lifestyles. The United States in the 1990s, for example, tolerated considerably more diversity than in the 1950s, when lifestyles were more homogeneous.[8]

6-2b Consumer Lifestyles and Product Constellations

A useful indicator of lifestyle is the groups of products or **product constellations** used by consumers.[9] By looking at product constellations, marketers can identify segments of consumers who tend to use the same goods and services—an indication that they share a similar lifestyle. Yuppies—young urban professionals of the 1980s and 1990s—are defined demographically as consumers aged 25 to 34 who live in the city and earn at least $30,000 per year. Yet more indicative of membership than demographics is the type of products Yuppies tend to buy. These consumers share a taste for status-laden products.[10] Their lifestyle can be defined through the following product constellation: Rolex watches, Brooks Brothers suits, New Balance running shoes, Sony Walkmans, and BMW automobiles.[11]

> **product constellation**
> Certain goods and services that go together, reflecting certain lifestyles.

Read Marketplace 6-1 for interesting illustrations of how product constellations reflect consumers' lifestyles. One example is the lifestyle of a BMW kind of a person. This person's lifestyle is likely to dictate many of his or her consumption habits, not only personal preference for a certain brand of car.

Exhibit 6-5 shows product constellations associated with different men's occupational roles. Note the differences between the professional and the blue-collar worker—the type of car driven (BMW versus Ford pickup), beverage preferences (wine versus beer), and magazines read (*Atlantic* versus *Field & Stream*). These examples give a flavor of product constellation contrasts. Each occupational role represents a potentially different consumer lifestyle that involves a different consumption pattern.

6-2c Influence of Major Life Events on Consumption-Related Lifestyles and Patronage Preferences

Recent research has shown that development and changes in patronage preferences are the result of major life events.[12] Examples of major life events include marriage, death of a spouse, birth or adoption of a child, relocation to a different place, having one's last child move out of the household, retirement, lost job/business, change of job, serious injury or illness, and community crisis or natural disaster. Major life events usually mark transitions into new roles. For example, marriage as a major life event changes the person's role from that of a single to that of either a husband or wife. Major life events affect patronage preferences both directly and indirectly (see Exhibit 6-6 on page 182). Both actual and anticipated life events create chronic or global stress on the individual, reflecting the social pressure on the individual to adjust to his or her new role. That stress makes the individual change his or her consumption-related lifestyle, which in turn influences patronage preferences (changes in one's grocery stores, clothing stores, pharmacies, restaurants, automobile service/repair shops, mail-order catalog companies, insurance companies, doctors, banks, mutual fund companies, long distance companies, and credit card issuers.). Examples of consumption-related lifestyles include:

- Went on a vacation abroad for the first time or after not going for a long time
- Took a new hobby or recreational activity
- Changed attendance of religious activities
- Changed attendance of cultural events
- Changed the amount or type of TV viewing

Marketplace 6-1

Product Constellations, Self-Image, and Product Attachment

Analyzing our product constellations reveals a great deal not only about our lifestyles but also about ourselves. We each play different roles in different aspects of our lives—as parent or child, brother or sister, student or teacher, employee or employer, and so on. As we play each role, we use different products and groups of products. These constellations make up our extended self.

There are at least four levels of extended self: individual, family, community, and group. At the individual level, we define ourselves in terms of personal possessions, such as jewelry, clothing, or cars. Consider, for example, the differences between drivers who consider themselves a "BMW kind of person" and drivers who feel most at ease behind the wheel of a pickup truck. At the family level, we define ourselves in terms of family residence and home furnishings, while at the community level, we use our neighborhood or town as extensions of our identities. At the group level, we use goods and services related to our membership within a group. A baseball hat, for example, identifies the wearer as a fan of a particular team. Convincing evidence that our personal identities are shaped by our personal possessions is the loss of self one experiences when a possession is lost. Victims of burglaries, for example, frequently state that they feel alienated, depressed, and "violated."

Consistent with the notion of the extended self is the concept of product attachment. Product attachment is the extent to which possessions are used by a consumer to maintain his or her self-concept. In other words, if we are emotionally attached to a product, we define ourselves through it. To measure product attachment, consumer researchers use statements such as:

- "Imagine for a moment someone making fun of your car. How much would you agree with the statement, 'If someone ridiculed my car, I would feel irritated'?"

- "How much do you agree with the statement, 'My car reminds me of who I am'?"

- "Picture yourself encountering someone who would like to get to know you. How much do you think you would agree with the statement, 'If I were describing myself, my car would likely be something I would mention'?"

Usually, consumers do not attach themselves to every product they own. They may not feel very attached to, say, their work clothes or television sets. They are more likely to feel attached to possessions that are socially visible—cars, name-brand clothes or shoes, or stereo equipment. The same can be said of expensive products—consumers may define themselves through the value of the house they own or the jewelry they wear. Personalized items, too, are likely to promote feelings of product attachment. Consider a person who is very involved in the design of her house. It carries her personal stamp, reflecting who she is, her tastes, her needs, and her orientation to life.

The dark side of product attachment is the inner-city headlines that tell shocking stories of violence triggered by attachment to material possessions. Teenagers have been known to fight and kill for a pair of name-brand athletic shoes. This behavior is an extreme example of the intensity of feelings people can place on certain products and the extents they are willing to go to hold onto them or steal them from others.

Sources: Adapted from Michael R. Solomon, "The Role of Products as Social Stimuli: A Symbolic Interactionism Perspective," *Journal of Consumer Research,* Vol. 10 (December 1983), pp. 319–328; M. Csikszentmihalyi and Eugene Rochberg-Halton, *The Meaning of Things: Domestic Symbols and the Self* (Cambridge, MA: Cambridge University Press, 1981); Russell W. Belk, "Possessions and the Extended Self," *Journal of Consumer Research,* Vol. 15 (September 1988), pp. 139–168; Floyd Rudmin, "Property Crime Victimization Impact on Self, on Attachment, and on Territorial Dominance," *CPA Highlights, Victims of Crime Supplement,* Vol. 9, No. 2 (1987), pp. 4–7; Deborah A. Prentice, "Psychological Correspondence of Possessions, Attitudes, and Values," *Journal of Personality and Social Psychology,* Vol. 53, No. 6 (1987), pp. 993–1002; A. Dwayne Ball and Lori H. Tasaki, "The Role and Measurement of Attachment in Consumer Behavior," *Journal of Consumer Psychology,* Vol. 1 (February 1992), pp. 155–172.

- Increased the consumption of alcoholic beverages
- Used more anti-depressants or tranquilizers than usual
- Experienced a change in social relations
- Started diet/weight control or exercise program
- Ate out a lot more times than usual
- Remodeled or refurnished home
- Received professional counseling for the first time or after not receiving it for a long time
- Made more changes than usual in key investments
- Gave more money or time than usual to charities
- Changed the amount or type of insurance coverage

Product Constellations Associated with Occupational Roles

Professional	**Attorney**	**Public Defender**
Seiko watch	Prince tennis racket	Levi's cords
Burberry raincoat	Leather briefcase	Wallaby shoes
Lacoste shirt	American Express gold card	Calvin Klein glasses
Atlantic magazine	Cadillac El Dorado	Molson beer
Brooks Brothers suit	Michelob beer	L.L. Bean shirts
Bass loafers	Vantage cigarettes/cigars	RCA VCR
Silk tie	Johnston & Murphy shoes	Volkswagen Rabbit
French wine	L.L. Bean catalog	*Esquire*
BMW	**Salesman**	**Suit Salesman**
Businessman	Farrah slacks	Zenith TV
Tiffany jewels	Budweiser beer	Oldsmobile 98
Steuben glass	Buick Skylark	Whirlpool freezer
Leather briefcase	Coca-Cola	Gillette shaver
Cross pen	McDonald's	Old Spice cologne
Cuff links	M & M's	Miller beer
Ralph Lauren shirt	Puritan gold shirts	JVC stereo
VCR	Fayva shoes	**Janitor**
Lincoln Continental	Samsonite luggage	Remington shaver
Wall Street Journal	Timex watch	Aramis cologne
Blue-Collar Worker	**Unskilled Worker**	Fruit-of-the-Loom
Schaefer beer	Chevrolet	Dial soap
AMF bowling ball	Goldstar TV	Campbell's soup
Ford pickup truck	*NY Daily News*	Coca-Cola
Levi's jeans	Hanes T-shirts	Sunkist orange soda
Marlboro cigarettes	Levi's jeans	
RCA TV	Coca-Cola	
Field & Stream	Miller beer	
Black & Decker tools	McDonald's	
McDonald's	Camel cigarettes	

Source: Michael R. Solomon and Henry Assael, "The Forest of the Trees: A Gestalt Approach to Symbolic Consumption," in Jean Umiker-Sebeck, ed., *Semiotics: New Directions in the Study of Signs for Sale* (Berlin: Mouton de Gruyter, 1987), pp. 189–218.

6-2d Psychographics

Through **psychographics**—the attempt to analyze and measure lifestyle—marketers seek to describe the human characteristics of consumers that influence their responses to market variables, that is, products, packaging, media, and so on, that demographics or socioeconomic measures alone cannot explain.[13] To obtain a psychographic profile of consumers or consumer segments, marketers examine various aspects of personality and behavior, including:[14]

- Personality traits and concept of self
- Attitudes toward product classes and toward brands
- Activities, interests, and opinions

> **psychographics** A term that consumer researchers use to describe consumers in terms of personality traits and concept of self; attitudes toward product classes and toward brands; activities, interests, and opinions; value systems; goods and services consumed; and media use patterns.

Exhibit 6-6

How Major Life Events Affect Changes in Patronage Preferences

Source: Adapted from Euehun Lee, George P. Moschis, and Anil Mathur, "A Study of Live Events and Changes in Patronage Preferences," *Journal of Business Research,* Vol. 54 (October 2001), pp. 25–38. Reprinted with permission from Elsevier.

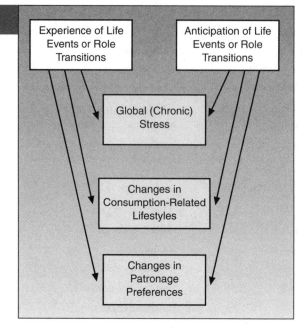

FAQ

Do research respondents necessarily tell the truth when asked about their attitudes, interests, and opinions?

- Value systems
- Goods and services consumed
- Media use patterns

Psychographics has two important marketing applications. First, analyzing consumers in terms of psychographics helps marketers identify consumer types or market segments. Exhibit 6-7 shows the results of a study of young males who drive while under the influence of alcohol. Segment profiles like these are useful in creating multiple campaigns, for instance, to promote the concept of designated drivers to each distinct segment. Second, psychographic research helps uncover attitudes, interests, and opinions (AIOs) of segment members. AIO inventories are typically developed through interviews or questionnaires in which the respondent agrees or disagrees with a series of statements. By correlating agreements, it is possible to obtain an in-depth analysis of the attitudes, interests, and opinions of targeted consumers.

Consider this example. Research into vacation travel of married women shows that 24 percent have taken trips without their families over the past two years and a similar number have stated they would like to. A psychographic profile reveals that these women tend to be well educated and have social networks independent of their husbands and families. They are mostly stay-at-home mothers who feel that vacationing with other women gives them freedom. They feel a vacation with the husband and children is not really a vacation at all, because they are still "on duty." Taking a vacation with women friends allows them to talk about marital problems, their kids, and, more importantly, their dreams. Interestingly, most of their husbands tend to venture off on their own "bubba trips," too.[15] This example serves to illustrate how much more useful psychographic information is to marketers than demographic information alone.

Marketplace 6-2 illustrates how marketers have used psychographic research in the cosmetics industry, and how this kind of research helped marketers from Clairol team up with marketers of *New Woman* magazine to address certain social issues related to women.

6-2e VALS™ Typologies

The first Values and Lifestyles (VALS™) system, developed by the Stanford Research Institute (now SRI International) in 1978, was intended as a study of human maturation but was adapted by marketers to predict consumer behavior.[16] VALS was based on people's

Four Psychographic Segments of Young Male Drivers

Segment 1: Good Timers (23%)

Heavy partyers with a macho and sensation-seeking orientation

The highest incidence of reported drinking-driving behaviors

Youngest of all segments (average age 20)

Least likely to be married (13 percent)

About half work full-time (55 percent)

About half attend school (47 percent)

Most likely to drink while driving or sitting in car (13 percent)

Most likely to drink at rock concerts (40 percent)

Most likely to drink at parties (61 percent)

Most likely to watch MTV (46 percent)

Heavy 7 P.M.–midnight radio listening (64 percent)

High preference for AOR (album-oriented rock) radio format (53 percent)

Segment 2: Well Adjusted (27%)

Most content and satisfied with their lives, with no problem behavior and average in partying and macho tendency

Next-to-the-lowest rate of reported drinking-driving behavior

Mid-range in age (average age 21)

Less likely to be married (20 percent)

About half work full-time (54 percent)

About half attend school (41 percent)

Not likely to drink while driving or sitting in car (3 percent)

Not likely to drink at rock concerts (15 percent)

Less likely to drink at parties (32 percent)

Less likely to watch MTV (35 percent)

Less 7 P.M.–midnight radio listening (51 percent)

Less preference for AOR radio format (42 percent)

Segment 3: Nerds (24%)

Generally unhappy and below average in problem behavior, partying, sensation seeking, and macho orientation

The lowest reported drinking-driving problem

Oldest of segments (average age 22)

Most likely to be married (33 percent)

About half work full-time (56 percent)

About half attend school (45 percent)

Least likely to drink while driving or sitting in car (1 percent)

Least likely to drink at rock concerts (10 percent)

Least likely to drink at parties (28 percent)

Least likely to watch MTV (27 percent)

Less 7 P.M.–midnight radio listening (51 percent)

Least preference for AOR radio format (34 percent)

Segment 4: Problem Kids (24%)

Above-average problem behavior tendency and an average profile on all other factors

Next-to-the-highest level of reported drinking-driving behavior

Mid-range in age (average age 21)

More likely to be married (30 percent)

Most work full-time (67 percent)

Fewest of any segment to attend school (25 percent)

Likely to drink while driving or sitting in car (6 percent)

Likely to drink at rock concerts (29 percent)

Likely to drink at parties (48 percent)

Less likely to watch MTV (36 percent)

Heavy 7 P.M.–midnight radio listening (57 percent)

Highest preference for AOR radio format (64 percent)

Source: Adapted from "A Lifestyle Typology to Model Young Male Drinking and Driving" by John L. Lastovika, John P. Murry, Erich A. Joachimsthalor, Guray Bhalla, and Jim Schevrich in *Journal of Consumer Research,* Volume 14, September 1987, pp. 257–263. Copyright © 1987. Reprinted by permission of The University of Chicago Press.

Marketplace 6-2

AIO Inventory in Action

Just how useful is lifestyle analysis for marketers? An example from the cosmetics industry shows how detailed a picture of target consumers it can provide.

An AIO inventory was used to investigate the lifestyles of heavy users of eye cosmetics. Demographic data revealed the typical member of this target market is young and well educated and lives in a metropolitan area. A working wife rather than a full-time homemaker, she is also a frequent purchaser of other cosmetics. She smokes, typically drives to work, and makes long-distance telephone calls. Her television tastes run to movies and talk shows. In magazines, she prefers fashion, news, and general-interest periodicals over such publications as *True Confessions*.

This demographic information told marketers quite a lot about their target consumers, but their responses to questions about attitudes, interests, and opinions gave a much clearer picture. Interested in fashion, the typical heavy user of eye cosmetics indicated that being attractive to others, especially men, formed an important part of her self-image. She was likely to fantasize about a trip around the world and to enjoy going to art galleries, to the ballet, and to parties. Her attitudes toward home were style-conscious rather than utilitarian. She liked to serve unusual dinners, did not like housework or grocery shopping, and would furnish a home for style rather than comfort.

AIOs (or Activities, Interests, and Opinions) are the key to successful cross-marketing, a strategy where two or more products or services join to reach common segments. Research into readership interests led New Woman *magazine to join forces with Clairol to launch a highly successful 1993 fundraising effort that benefited both the magazine and its readers. The key: finding a common interest in social issues among the magazine's readers and Clairol's target segment.*

Source: Richard Cross and Janet Smith, *Customer Bonding* (Chicago: NTC Business Books, Chicago, 1995).

In general, the typical heavy user of eye cosmetics could be described as a person who accepts contemporary rather than traditional ideas. She likes to think of herself as a bit of a swinger, enjoys bright splashy colors, and genuinely believes that blondes have more fun.

Source: Adapted from "Activities, Interests and Opinions" by William D. Wells and Douglas J. Tigert in *Journal of Advertising Research,* Volume 11, Number 4, August 1971, pp. 27–35. Reprinted by permission from the *Journal of Advertising Research,* © 1971, by the Advertising Research Foundation.

social values—their attitudes about abortion rights, legalization of marijuana, and military spending. After about ten years of commercial use, researchers found that the diffusion of social values over time weakened their ability to be effective predictors of consumer behavior. So in 1989, SRI International put together a team, including experts from Stanford University and UC Berkeley, to revise the VALS system. The revised system is based on psychological characteristics and demographics. Japan VALS™ is a similar consumer segmentation developed specifically for understanding Japanese consumers.

Described in Exhibit 6-8, VALS divides U.S. adult consumers into eight groups, first on the basis of primary motivation and then on the basis of resources to which they have access. Resources include such measures as income, education, energy level, and eagerness to buy. As shown in Exhibit 6-8, three motivations are possible. First, ideals-motivated people are more influenced by closely held beliefs or principles than by other motivations. Second, status-motivated people are influenced by others who are important to them, imitating their actions and opinions and seeking their approval. Third, those who are self-expression–oriented seek physical or social activity and tend to take risks. To get a feel for the VALS survey, visit http://www.sric-bi.com/VALS/.

6-2f Applying the Lifestyle Concept to Marketing

The most striking advantages of using the lifestyle concept and related research today are found in marketing plan development, media selection, creative strategy formulation, product positioning, and retail strategy development.[17]

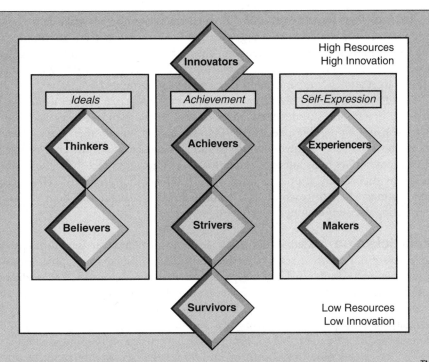

Exhibit 6-8

Characteristics of the Eight VALS Consumer Types

Motivations—ideals, achievement, or self-expression—determine both the objectives and the behaviors of consumers.

Source: SRI Consulting Business Intelligence (SRIC-BI), http://www.sric-bi.com/VALS. Reprinted by permission.

Innovators are consumers with abundant resources. They are located at the top of the VALS™ hierarchy. They are likely to be successful and sophisticated. They are open to change. They tend to be concerned with social issues. As consumers, they display discriminating tastes. That is, they buy to please themselves, not others.

Ideals-oriented Thinkers tend to be mature and are well-rounded. They are mostly satisfied with their lives. They have resources sufficient to accommodate their lifestyles. They are practical and value functionality in the goods and services they buy.

Like Thinkers, Achievers also have sufficient resources. They value their careers; they are successful in their jobs. They feel they have control over their lives. They are risk averse and value stability in life. Yet, unlike Thinkers, Achievers are status-motivated; they buy goods and services not only for their functionality but also to display status and prestige.

Unlike Thinkers and Achievers, Experiencers are younger in age. They tend to be action-oriented—they are impulsive and tend to take risks. When they have money to spend, they are likely to try new things.

Believers have fewer resources than Thinkers, Achievers, or Experiencers. They are driven by their own strong principles much like the Thinkers. As consumers, they tend to buy proven brands.

Strivers have limited resources. Strivers seek security; they seek to gain approval from significant others and avoid their disapproval. As consumers, they tend to buy goods and services that bestow status. Prestige brands of goods and services serve to gain social approval or avoid disapproval.

Much like the Strivers, Makers have limited resources. Even so, they are self-sufficient. They are motivated to express their individuality, their uniqueness as people and consumers. They have much energy and drive, and they apply this energy and drive in carrying out constructive projects with skill and precision. For example, Makers typically build their own houses, make things, and do their own repairs. In our culture, we customarily refer to a Maker as a "jack-of-all-trades." As consumers, they are very practical in their orientation. In other words, they buy things for their practicality, not for their status or prestige.

Survivors are classified at the bottom of the VALS™ hierarchy. They have minimal resources—little education, few skills, and no money. They live on a day-to-day basis, preoccupied with meeting their daily needs, and do not have the mental energy to worry about tomorrow. They typically buy goods and services that are daily essentials.

Marketing Plan Development   Because research into consumer behavior has traditionally used the methods and jargon of the behavioral sciences, communicating the results to businesses has been problematic. The marketing director confronted with a complicated research model may be skeptical. Copywriters presented with reams of statistics on their target audience are inclined to ignore the data provided.

The lifestyle concept, however, as a framework for research recommendations, offers marketing practitioners understandable portraits of people engaged in recognizable patterns of consumption. A lifestyle portrait for heavy users of men's after-shave lotion reveals not only how old users are, where they live, and what socioeconomic groups they belong to, but also describes their interests and opinions and how they feel about their daily activities. More importantly, it predicts what other products they are likely to buy and which media are most likely to reach them. This provides an unusually rich body of data to use in marketing decision making.

Media Selection   Media salespeople generally attract advertisers through accurate profile descriptions of their readers, viewers, or listeners using demographics gathered and presented either by individual media representatives or through syndicated media research resources. This type of demographic analysis provides little insight into people's attitudes and opinions. A demographic analysis of a regular *Playboy* reader may portray him as essentially the same person who savors *The Smithsonian,* but there are probably important differences in the ways these two consumers view advertising and products. Lifestyle analysis provides considerably more information about the personality characteristics, attitudes, opinions, and product-use patterns of heavy users of newspapers, magazines, and television. And consumers can be differentiated further on the basis of the types of magazines or programs they are most likely to read or watch. See Marketplace 6-3 for an example of how lifestyle research is used to develop and market a media vehicle.

Creative Strategy Formulation   In most major advertising campaigns, responsibility for communicating with consumers ultimately rests with an advertising agency's creative department. Here, research is sifted through the intuition of people who come up with a strategy or concept that will make advertising effective. During the process, lifestyle information about target consumers is helpful to creative people in three ways. First, it gives them an idea of what type of consumer will be at the other end of the communication. This is useful in choosing actors and spokespeople for the product and placing them in appropriate settings. Second, lifestyle data suggests the tone and style of language appropriate to appeal to target audiences—humorous or serious, contemporary or traditional. Third, lifestyle information indicates how the product fits into people's lives, how they feel about it, and how they may be using it to communicate things about themselves to other people.

Product Positioning   Establishing a product in a consumer's frame of reference calls for an understanding of just what that frame of reference is. Take as an example a new brand of toothpaste. A distinguishing characteristic is that it has an extra whitening ingredient. Positioning this product effectively would demand research into heavy users of toothpastes that promise sparkling white teeth, such as the competing product, Pearl Drops. If target consumers turned out to be teenagers and young singles, advertising and media strategies would probably sell sex appeal—a print campaign in *Seventeen* or *Cosmopolitan,* along with a heavy television and radio schedule. But AIO research might just as readily uncover surprising data on this group of teens, who may be attracted by more traditional values. A more appropriate advertising message would then be to emphasize the health benefits of the toothpaste.

Marketplace 6-3

Lifestyle of the Tight and Frugal

What is the lifestyle of a tightwad? A person who agrees with the following self-descriptors is defined to be frugal in consumption:

1. If you take good care of your possessions, you will definitely save money in the long run.
2. There are many things that are normally thrown away that are still quite useful.
3. Making better use of my resources makes me feel good.
4. If I can reuse an item I already have, there is no sense in buying something new.
5. I believe in being careful in how I spend my money.
6. I discipline myself to get the most from my money.
7. I am willing to wait on a purchase I want so that I can save money.
8. There are things I resist buying today so I can save for tomorrow.

Consumers who subscribe to *Tightwad Gazette* scored significantly higher on these items than do members of other populations.

Source: Adapted from "Lifestyle of the Tight and Frugal: Theory and Measurement" by John L. Lastovicka, Lance A. Bettencourt, Renee Shaw Hughner, and Ronald J. Kuntze in *Journal of Consumer Research*, Vol. 26, June 1999, pp. 85–98.

One company for which lifestyle research presented surprising results was Kentucky Fried Chicken.[18] Before lifestyle information on buyers of carry-out fried chicken was available, Kentucky Fried Chicken had been advertised as a folksy, down-home product. Research into frequent buyers revealed that typical customers were women who tended to be active, somewhat self-indulgent housewives who expressed a much more contemporary state of mind than earlier campaigns suggested. The product was repositioned accordingly in subsequent advertising, and new product developments, such as roasted chicken meals, soon followed.

Retail Strategy Development   Just as lifestyle information can be used to identify consumers who are likely to use certain goods and services, so can it point to differences in shopping behavior. An early study identified two purchasing patterns: creative and passive.[19] Creative consumers are more likely to respond to new modes of distribution than are passive consumers. They were found in the vanguard of people who first popularized innovative retail environments such as the supermarket and the shopping center.

Marketing Management—Implications and Actions

Understanding psychographics helps marketers to:

- See beyond demographics to consumers' relationships with goods and services. That is, most products and services do not lend themselves to demographic segmentation. Instead, they can be segmented using psychographics.
- Venture into cross-marketing with other products in the same constellation. Suppose you are a marketer of athletic bags. To be effective, you can target certain athletes such as basketball players, tennis players, racquetball players, etc., identifying their needs and the various products and services they use. Doing so would allow you to market your bag in conjunction with those products and services.

6-3 Relationships

The last fifteen years have witnessed an unprecedented surge of research on relationship marketing. **Relationship marketing** refers to the development of marketing strategies to enhance relationships with customers. These relationships can be with the firm's brands or with the firm at large. Relationships with brands tend to be dominant in consumer marketing (marketing of consumer goods and services), whereas relationships with the firm at large are prevalent in business-to-business marketing (marketing of products and services to organizations that, in turn, will use these products and services to serve other customers). The impetus behind relationship marketing is the recognition of a fundamental truism, namely that 80 percent of a firm's sales can be attributed to repeat business, while only 20 percent accounts for new business. Therefore, repeat business is more important than new business. Given that, marketers should develop strategies to enhance customer retention rather than focus on customer recruitment. Understanding the factors that influence customer retention led marketing scholars to focus on understanding how relationships are formed, strengthened, and dissolved. Such understanding should help enhance customer commitment to the firm and its products and services, that is, it should foster customer retention.

6-3a Relationships with Brands

Consumers establish relationships with selected brands of products and services. Susan Fournier, a marketing scholar, has used the concept of human relationship as an analogy to describe how consumers establish and maintain relationships with brands.[20] She identifies fifteen forms of relationships that consumers may have with brands. See Exhibit 6-9.

Committed Partnerships   A committed partnership is the perfect relationship characterized by long-term commitment, love, trust, and strong intimacy. The relationship persists despite periodic adversity. An example of a committed partnership between a consumer and a product would be a consumer who has a long-term relationship with his Buick (automobile brand). He has had this car for five years. The car needed expensive repairs last year, but the owner has never thought that the time has come to trade it in. He loves his Buick and will never trade it in for any other. If and when the time comes to buy another car, he will buy another Buick. Look at the iPod example in Marketplace 6-4 for an example of how the iPod can be construed as a "committed partner."

Arranged Marriages   An arranged marriage is a nonvoluntary union usually imposed by a third party. The relationship is intended to be long-term; however, feelings of affective attachment are not well developed. For example, a husband keeps using the brand of detergent that his wife used before she passed away. Thus, the marriage between the laundry brand and the husband has been "arranged" by third parties.

Marriages of Convenience   A marriage of convenience is a long-term and committed relationship in which the commitment to the marriage is not by free choice. If given a choice, this marriage would have been dissolved. The marriage persists because of environmental factors making the dissolution difficult. For example, a consumer is holding on to his car. He has had this car for the last eight years. He can't think of letting go of this car because he can't afford to buy another car. He is not emotionally attached to the car, and, if he had the means, he would trade it in without hesitation.

Courtships   Courtships are transient or interim relationships that may lead to committed relationships. They are characterized by a "sense of trial." A consumer is trying out a new line of skillet dinners—Lean Cuisine. She used to eat the Green Giant brand. She does not know whether she will stick with this brand or switch back to Green Giant. She is motivated to try Lean Cuisine to lose a few pounds.

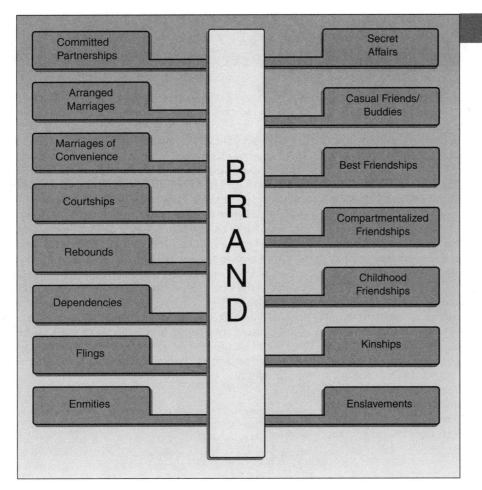

Exhibit 6-9

The Human Relations Metaphor in Action: Describing Consumers' Relationships with Brands

Rebounds A relationship on the rebound is characterized by a desire to move away from a prior or available partner. The person is not necessarily attracted to a new person. For example, a person trying to quit smoking may take up chewing gum. Thus, he establishes a relationship with a certain brand of gum to help him quit smoking.

Dependencies Dependencies are relationships characterized by obsession. At least one partner feels that the other is irreplaceable. It is an emotionally charged relationship. Separation usually results in a great deal of anxiety. There are certain products that consumers do get "addicted" to, and attempts to stop using the product may result in a great deal of anxiety. Certain pharmaceutical drugs, such as Valium, may reflect a state of dependency on the part of the consumer.

Flings A fling is a short-term relationship that is emotionally charged and is temporarily rewarding. The relationship does not lead to a commitment. For example, going on a cruise is a fling. The relationship is for that one time. It is not likely that the customer may do this again. Other examples may include flying on a Concorde jet, riding a submarine, sky diving, and using a one-time product or service.

Enmities These are relationships that are intensely involving, characterized by negative affect and motivation to avoid or inflict pain on the other. Products and services associated with negative experiences can be considered enmities. For example, a consumer was admitted to a hospital for a bronchitis problem and ended up with a staph infection. Then,

Marketplace 6-4

Cult Brands: The iPod

There are many brands out there that are "cult brands." Cult brands are not ordinary brands. They have a strong following. The users of these brands do not only use these brands, they "live" them. They use them to express their own identity and form communities around them. They are obsessed with these brands. They are passionate about their brands. They don't feel like "customers" but "product owners" and feel a high affinity and kinship with other "product owners." This social bond among product owners helps establish product communities. Product owners are not passively consuming the product; they get on the Internet and talk to one another in chat rooms about consumption experiences. The Internet is helping build product owner communities.

Consider Apple junkies. Many consumers swear by iMac computers and editing software. They would consider themselves "traitors" if they used a PC. They love their iMac, even though they may hate it, too. For example, Casey Neistate, 23, is building his filmmaking career with the company's iMac equipment. He usually leaves his apartment with an iPod plugged into his ear. Casey discovered iPod's batteries were irreplaceable and last for only 18 months. He felt furious and launched a protest website called iPod's *Dirty Secret*. Casey says that the protest was an act of love for the iPod. He loves this product so much that he cannot think of himself without it. And because of his devotion to his iPod, he felt furious about the fact that the batteries may be an obstacle between him and his iPod. This is contrary to marketing principles. Marketing textbooks assert that a dissatisfied customer is most likely to defect; in other words, dissatisfaction leads to brand switching. Not in the case of cult brands. Consumers are fiercely loyal to certain brands, even though they may have a love-hate relationship with these brands. The case of Casey and his iPod is a typical example. Casey's anti-iPod website has generated 1.4 million hits from around the world. The loyal, if sometimes nagging, community of Apple users—combined with the tremendous success of the iPod—helped the dollar value of Apple climb up to $6.9 billion.

The iPod managed to build a cultlike following. This brand is self-consciously different from its rivals. Its users are bound by a set of clearly defined values, and iPods fulfill a range of needs for iPod owners. The brand projects an aura, an attractive group identity.

Source: Adapted from Diane Brady, Robert D. Hof, Andy Reinhardt, Moon Ihlwan, Stanley Holmes, and Kerry Capell, "Cult Brands," *Business Week* (August 2004), pp. 64–67.

the hospital sends the patient a bill that he can't afford to pay. The patient takes the hospital to court. Therefore, the relationship between the hospital and that patient can be considered full of enmity.

Secret Affairs   Secret affairs are relationships that are socially tabooed. Therefore, at least one partner sneaks around to ensure that the nature of this relationship is not disclosed. An example of a secret affair is a father who subscribes to a pornographic magazine such as *Hustler*. He keeps this subscription a secret from his wife and teenage children for fear of being ostracized by his family.

Casual Friends/Buddies   Casual friendship is characterized by low emotional involvement and infrequent and sporadic use. For example, a single professional who spends very little time at home has a casual friendship with certain brands of household cleaning products. She uses the same brands repeatedly, but she is not emotionally involved with the use of these brands, nor does she feel committed to them.

Best Friendships   Best friendships are relationships based on reciprocity, mutual rewards, and common interests. Best friends are usually intimate with each other and are very trusting of each other. For example, an athlete (basketball player) may feel that his Nike basketball shoes are "his best friend." He trusts these shoes; he counts on them, and they deliver. He, in turn, treats them well. He takes care of them and tucks them away in a safe place.

Compartmentalized Friendships   Compartmentalized friends are considered as such because of the situation. They are not considered friends outside the situation. For example, people form certain friendships at work—they go out to lunch together, and they socialize at work and help each other with work-related tasks, but they don't socialize on the evenings or weekends. In the consumer arena, this may translate into a woman's relationship with a brand of perfume. She feels connected with Elizabeth Taylor's White Diamonds. That perfume does well by her when she goes out on a date. Therefore, her relationship with that brand of perfume is only relevant when she is in a dating situation.

Childhood Friendships   Childhood friendships are relationships that are infrequently engaged. Nevertheless, they are affect laden, and they remind the parties of old times. They serve to connect the person with his or her past. A consumer uses Nestle Quik chocolate powder because she used it when she was a girl.

Kinships   Kinships are nonvoluntary relationships with people associated by blood or marriage. Consumer examples include a relationship with Earl Grey English Tea. The consumer has "inherited" this relationship from his father. That was his father's favorite brand and the brand that was available at the house. The consumer eventually established a relationship with Earl Grey English Tea as he started drinking tea.

Enslavements   Enslavements are nonvoluntary unions monopolized by one partner. That partner has much power over the other in the relationship. The relationship is held hostage because the subjugated party does not have a choice to dissolve the relationship. Consumer relationships that come close to being viewed as "enslavements" include a consumer who feels stuck with his telephone company, his cable company, his power company, his gas company, and so on. Many consumers feel "enslaved" by public utilities.

6-3b Relationships with Firms

Professors R. M. Morgan and Shelby D. Hunt defined relationship marketing as "all marketing activities directed at establishing, developing, and maintaining successful relational exchanges in . . . supplier, lateral, buyer, and internal partnerships."[21] Corporate performance is determined mostly by managing relationships with various organizational stakeholders. That successful corporate performance is mostly based on establishing commitment and trust in relation to the various organizational stakeholders. Therefore, the performance of a business firm should not be judged in terms of profit or market share measures but based on measures of relationship quality with various stakeholders. Recent research has shown that relationship quality leads to customer referrals. That is, consumers who feel a certain degree of satisfaction with the firm, had more trust toward the firm, and felt committed to do future business with the firm are likely to recommend the firm to their friends, relatives, and associates.[22] Also recent research has shown that patients' trust in their physician correlates positively with the length of their relationship and satisfaction with their physician.[23]

From a marketing perspective, relationship quality refers to the extent to which the relationship between manufacturers and business customers is based on trust, satisfaction, and commitment. Research has shown that relationship quality does play an important role in repeat business. That relationship quality is positively related to vendor stratification in that high-status vendors are those characterized by high relationship quality, and low-status vendors have low relationship quality.[24]

Relationships with Corporate Firms   What is relationship quality in relation to corporate firms? How can a firm measure the quality of its relationship with consumers? Marketing communications scholars have long argued that relationship quality can be

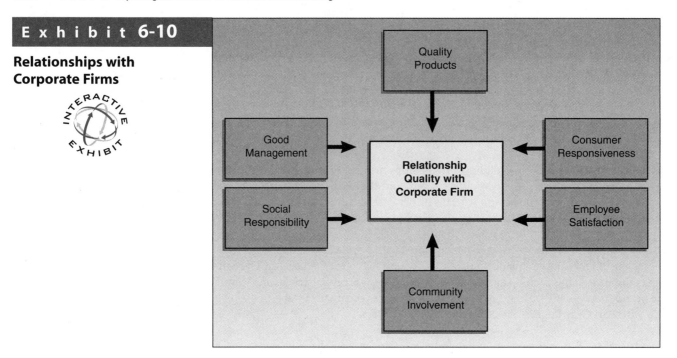

captured through what they call "corporate image." A company's corporate image can be characterized by whether it:

- produces and/or delivers good products and services,
- is well-managed,
- is guided by social concerns beyond the profit motive,
- is involved with the community,
- is responsive to consumer needs, and
- treats its employees well.[25]

Consumers who perceive a company as rating high in these six dimensions are likely to feel good about that company, remain loyal to it, and recommend the company to their network of friends, associates, and relatives. See Exhibit 6-10.

Relationships with Service Firms   What is relationship quality for service firms? How can service firms measure the quality of their relationships with their customers? Professors A. Parasuraman, Valerie A. Zeithaml, and Leonard L. Berry have long argued that relationship quality with services should be measured using five basic dimensions: tangible benefits, reliability, responsiveness, assurance, and empathy.[26] See Exhibit 6-11. In other words, relationship quality with services is a condition in which customers of the service firm perceive the firm as:

- providing tangible benefits,
- reliable in delivery of these tangible benefits,
- responsive to their (customers') needs,
- providing those tangible benefits with assurance, and
- empathic through expressions of care.

Recent research has shown that relationship quality with a service firm can be characterized by three forms of commitment to the service firm: (1) normative, (2) affective, and (3) continuance commitment. Normative commitment refers to an obligation-based attachment to the firm (i.e., customers remain with a service firm because they *ought* to—it is the right thing to do). Affective commitment refers to a desire-based attachment to the firm (i.e., customers remain with a service firm because they *want* to). Continuance com-

Exhibit 6-11

Relationships with Service Firms

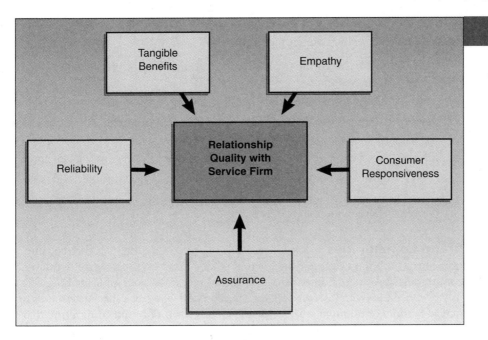

mitment refers to a cost-based attachment where the customer feels he or she has to remain with the firm because they *need* to. The results of a study involving a survey of auto-repair customers have shown that these three forms of commitment do play a significant role in predicting switching intentions. That is, the study found support for the notion that commitment to one's service provider can be obligation based (normative commitment), desire based (affective commitment), and cost based (continuance commitment). Customers stay because "I ought to" (normative commitment), "I want to" (affective commitment), and "I have to" (continuance commitment).[27]

Relationships with Internal Divisions within a Firm   Marketing is not restricted to the relationship between a firm and its customer groups that use the firm's products and services. Marketing includes the management of relationships between one part of the firm and another. In many ways, one part of the firm is responsible to meet the demands of another. For example, the research and development (R&D) department in many firms is organized to cater to the marketing department. The marketing manager asks the R&D manager to develop certain products that meet customers' specifications. Therefore, the R&D group within the firm treats the marketing group as its customers and caters to the needs and demands of the marketing staff. If so, then how does an internal division measure relationship quality with another division? Professors L. L. Stanley and J. D. Wisner developed the concept of "internal service quality" to address this issue.[28] See Exhibit 6-12. They argue that relationship quality in that context can be conceptualized and measured through communication effectiveness and management activities. For example, an internal customer can be asked to rate the extent to which the focal division communicated and worked well with the internal customer as a team to meet the needs of

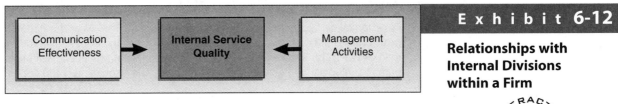

Exhibit 6-12

Relationships with Internal Divisions within a Firm

the internal customer. With respect to management activities, the internal customer can be asked the extent to which the focal division:

- held meetings between the two divisions to address and resolve issues critical to the mission of the customer,
- assembled cross-functional teams that included people within the two divisions,
- developed manuals or written training materials that can help address the customer needs,
- informally and regularly interacted with the managers of the internal customer,
- conducted orientations for new employees of the internal customer, and
- conducted interviews and surveys to better understand the needs of the internal customer division and help address those needs.

Brand Communities   Recent research has uncovered the fact that consumer relationships with brands can take the form of what consumer researchers are calling "brand communities." A brand community is a specialized, non-geographically bound community of consumers who interact with one another and who feel a special closeness to a particular brand. For example, a farmer's market is a form of brand community that brings together consumers who believe that eating fresh, nonprocessed food that is not treated with pesticides is good living. Examples of other brand communities include skydivers and owners of Harley-Davidson motorcycles (see CBite 6-2) and Jeeps.

Brand communities are characterized by three markers: (1) consciousness of kind, (2) rituals and traditions, and (3) moral responsibility. *Consciousness of kind* refers to a sense of togetherness shared by users or owners of a particular brand. Members feel that there is a special bond between them by the mere fact that they own or use that brand. Users of the MP-3 player iPod feel that they share something unique; they belong to a special group who are connected by the mere fact that they all use this particular brand of MP-3 player and feel they are different from the users of other brands. This consciousness of kind transcends geographic boundaries. The brand community is recognized as a special club. Club owners do not feel close to one another because they share that one particular brand; they feel connected by their opposition to competing brands. In other words, they have stories to tell about how "bad" the other brands are.

Brand communities also are characterized by rituals and traditions, which are essentially shared experiences with the brand. For example, the Saab community (the community of Saab car owners) has a ritual that when a Saab driver passes another Saab on the road, the custom is to flash lights and beep the horn. This ritual serves as a greeting when two members of the same brand community first make contact.

Brand communities are also marked by shared moral responsibility. Moral responsibility refers to a sense of duty to the community as a whole. This sense of duty contributes

---

CBite 6-2

Harley-Davidson: What a Following!

Harley-Davidson helps organize its owners—around 886,000 of them. The company organizes rides, training courses, social events, and charity fund-raisers. Harley-Davidson owners pore through the company magazine. They wear the Harley-branded gear; it makes them feel more like rugged individualists and outlaws when they hit the road on weekends. The company organized an event in Milwaukee to celebrate the brand's centennial, and a quarter of million Harley-Davidson owners showed up for this event.

Source: Adapted from Diane Brady, Robert D. Hof, Andy Reinhardt, Moon Ihlwan, Stanley Holmes, and Kerry Capell, "Cult Brands," *Business Week* (August 2004), p. 66.

to group cohesion. When a member of the brand community attempts to switch brands, other community members may talk him or her out of it. For example, when Mac computer users contemplate jumping ship and buying a PC, other Mac users apply pressure by making them feel that they are betraying a social cause, that they will join the ranks of traitors, and that they will "lose their soul" in the process.[29]

Marketing Management—Implications and Actions

Understanding relationships helps marketers to:

- Develop programs that can enhance consumers' loyalty and commitment to the company brand. For example, an airline company develops a frequent flier program based on the concepts of relationship marketing. The frequent flier program rewards loyalty and commitment through dividend miles.

- Develop marketing programs to enhance the quality of consumers' relationships with a corporate firm. For example, a company such as Bank of America can enhance its relationship quality with its customers by launching an aggressive campaign designed to consolidate and reinforce the perception that the bank satisfies consumers' needs, that it is socially responsible, that it treats its employees well, and so on.

- Develop marketing programs to enhance the quality of consumers' relationships with a service firm. For example, a local bank can do better by enhancing its relationships with its customers. It can do so by establishing and reinforcing programs designed to increase the bank's responsiveness to customers' needs.

Chapter Spotlights

1. Personal values. Personal values are abstract, evaluative beliefs that are considered to reflect what is and is not important to consumers. Values such as achievement, progress, family, friendship, and success influence consumer decision making. Two popular typologies, the Rokeach Personal Values Scale and the List of Values (LOV), are used to measure a range of personal values. Marketers can use such techniques as the means-end chain model and laddering to demonstrate linkages between personal values and goods and services. This information is used to position or reposition brands to enhance the likelihood of purchase.

2. Consumer lifestyles. Studying consumer lifestyles provides richer insights into the ways consumers think and act than can be obtained from demographic data. By understanding the lifestyle of a particular segment, marketers can identify product constellations likely to appeal to that segment.

3. Psychographics. Psychographic research both identifies consumer segments and explores the activities, interests, and opinions (AIOs) of those segments. To predict consumer behavior, marketers use a comprehensive typology of values and lifestyles (VALS 2) that describes consumers as belonging to eight different lifestyle groups. The result is a rich body of data for use in marketing decision making, media selection, and creative strategy development.

4. Relationships. Consumers have relationships with brands and firms. Relationships with brands can be described using the metaphor of human relationships. Thus, relationships with brands can be described in terms of committed partnerships, arranged marriages, marriages of convenience, courtships, rebounds, dependencies, flings, enmities, secret affairs, casual friends and buddies, best friends, compartmentalized friendships, childhood friendships, kinships, and enslavements. Consumers also have relationships with firms. Business customers have relationships with manufacturing firms, and the quality of these relationships is determined by the degree of satisfaction with past transactions with that firm, the trust that the customer has established in that firm, and the commitment the customer feels toward the firm.

Key Terms

instrumental values (p. 173)
laddering (p. 175)
lifestyle (p. 178)
List of Values (LOV) (p. 173)

means-end chain (p. 173)
personal values (p. 172)
product constellation (p. 179)
psychographics (p. 181)

relationship marketing (p. 188)
terminal values (p. 173)

Review Questions

Note: You can find the correct answers to these questions by taking the quiz and then submitting your answers in the Online Edition. The program will automatically score your submission. If you miss a question, the program will provide the correct answer, a rationale for the answer, and the section number in the chapter where the topic is discussed.

1. The List of Values (LOV) does *not* include
   a. security.
   b. self-fulfillment.
   c. sense of individuality.
   d. fun and enjoyment.

2. The means-end chain model is built around all of these different aspects of a product *except*
   a. terminal values.
   b. instrumental values.
   c. functional consequences.
   d. physiological consequences.

3. All of the following describe lifestyle *except*
   a. group phenomenon.
   b. influences many aspects of behavior.
   c. implies a central life interest.
   d. varies according to physiologically relevant variables.

4. By studying product constellations that consumers use, marketers can identify segments of consumers who tend to use _____ goods and services.
   a. the same
   b. complementary
   c. substitute
   d. competing

5. Lifestyle research helps uncover attitudes, interests, and
   a. desires.
   b. wants.
   c. opinions.
   d. needs.

6. VALS divides people into eight groups based on motivations and
   a. demographic profiles.
   b. AIO statements.
   c. social-self studies.
   d. the basis of resources to which they have access.

7. Application of the lifestyle concept to marketing is useful in all of the following ways *except*
   a. marketing plan development.
   b. media timing.
   c. creative strategy formulation.
   d. product positioning.

8. Positioning a product in a consumer's mind calls for first establishing an understanding of the consumer's
   a. buying habits.
   b. physiological makeup.
   c. frame of reference.
   d. brand loyalties.

9. Consumers establish relationships with selected brands and
   a. promotions.
   b. firms.
   c. price ranges.
   d. distribution points.

10. The existence of the need to build relationships with service firms means that consumers see the firms as being all of the following *except*
    a. sympathetic.
    b. providers of tangible benefits.
    c. reliable in delivery of tangible benefits.
    d. responsive to their needs.

Team Talk

1. List three personal values you hold. How are these reflected in recent purchases you have made? Do they influence your choice of retail outlet?

2. Using Exhibit 6-2, sketch out a probable means-end chain model for one of the following products: caller ID phone service, fat-free frozen yogurt, or Sega computer games.

3. Select two print advertisements you feel are developed around the lifestyle concept. What has the marketer tried to achieve, and how successful is the attempt, in your opinion?

4. Take a list of the eight VALS categories to a bookstore or newsstand. Match each type to a magazine. Explain your choices.

5. Do consumers have a relationship with their cellular phones? Describe this relationship using human relationship metaphors.

6. Customer satisfaction, trust, and commitment are very important in relationship marketing. What is relationship marketing? What is relationship quality? How can airline companies (e.g., United Airlines) develop programs to enhance customer satisfaction, trust, and commitment?

Workshops

Research Workshop

Background

The catalog business is so diverse that there seems to be a catalog not just for every product type but also for every possible consumer type. The objective of this workshop is to evaluate several consumer direct-mail catalogs in terms of the personal values and lifestyle characteristics of consumers to whom they are targeted.

Methodology

In small groups, select three or four consumer catalogs you feel are directed toward different consumer types. Taking into account the products and the way in which they are presented as well as the creative elements of the catalog, describe the lifestyles and values of potential consumers.

To the Marketplace

Make a list of recommendations to each catalog marketer to improve its appeal to the lifestyle segment targeted.

Creative Workshop

Background

VALS provides a useful framework through which marketers can classify consumers based on psychological characteristics. The objective of this workshop is to use lifestyle analysis to develop outdoor advertising aimed at dissuading those most likely to drink and drive to mend their ways over a holiday season.

Methodology

Using AIO inventories and VALS, analyze the lifestyles of members of the community to identify those most likely to drink and drive. Consider, in particular, their attitudes towards drinking. Create a profile of the group identified.

To the Marketplace

Create rough drafts—visuals, headlines, and copy—for an outdoor advertising program that alerts commuters to the dangers of drinking and driving and encourages them to take advantage of public transportation during the holiday season.

Managerial Workshop

Background

This workshop is designed to help you sharpen your marketing decision-making skills by applying some of the concepts discussed in this chapter. The objectives are to identify an innovation currently being promoted that is not targeting college students. Make a re-positioning decision based on your understanding of the concept of lifestyle in this chapter as applied to a college student population.

Methodology

Find a magazine advertisement or a television commercial for a new product such as a portable electronic gadget that allows people to read electronic books. Cut out and mount the advertisement or make a copy of the commercial. Considering both the message and the medium, decide on and describe the intended target market for the advertisement or commercial. Assess how the marketer has positioned the product in terms of lifestyle in relation to the targeted audience.

To the Marketplace

What would you do differently in your advertising to re-position the product for a college student population? Consider the current advertising, your assessment of the type of innovation, and the way you can capture the lifestyle of college students to identify the most persuasive message.

Notes

1. Milton Rokeach, *The Nature of Human Values* (New York: The Free Press, 1973).
2. Robert E. Pitts and Arch G. Woodside, "Personal Influences on Consumer Product Class and Brand Preferences," *Journal of Social Psychology*, Vol. 58, pp. 193–198.
3. Lynn R. Kahle, Sharon Beatty, and Pamela Homer, "Alternative Measurement Approaches to Consumer Values: The List of Values (LOV) and Values and Lifestyle (VALS)," *Journal of Consumer Research*, Vol. 13 (December 1986), pp. 405–409; Thomas P. Novak and Bruce MacEvoy, "On Comparing Alternative Segmentation Schemes: The List of Values (LOV) and Values and Life Styles (VALS)," *Journal of Consumer Research*, Vol. 17 (June 1990), pp. 105–109.
4. Novak and MacEvoy, "On Comparison Alternative Segmentation Schemes"; for a more recent application of the LOV segmentation scheme, see Wagner A. Kamakura and Thomas P. Novak, "Value-System Segmentation," *Journal of Consumer Research*, Vol. 19 (June 1992), pp. 119–132.
5. Jonathan Gutman, "A Means-End Chain Model Based on Consumer Categorization Processes," *Journal of Marketing* (Spring 1982), pp. 60–72.
6. Thomas J. Reynolds and Jonathon Gutman, "Laddering Theory, Method, Analysis, and Interpretation," *Journal of Advertising Research*, Vol. 28 (February–March 1988), pp. 11–31.
7. Christopher Gilson, *How the Right Demographics Can Help You Find the Wrong Consumers* (Chris Gilson Inc., 1980).
8. Harold W. Berkman and Christopher C. Gilson, "Consumer Lifestyles and Market Segmentation," *Journal of the Academy of Marketing Science*, Vol. 2, No. 1 (Winter 1974); Joseph T. Plummer, "The Concept and Application of Lifestyle Segmentation," *Journal of Marketing*, Vol. 38 (January 1974).
9. Michael R. Solomon, "Mapping Product Constellations: A Social Categorization Approach to Symbolic Consumption," *Psychology & Marketing*, Vol. 5, No. 3 (1988), pp. 233–258.
10. Howard W. Comb and McRae C. Banks, "Marketing to Yuppies," *SMA Advances Management Journal* (Summer 1987), p. 52; Russell W. Belk, "Yuppies as Arbiters of the Emerging Consumption Style," in Richard J. Lutz, ed., *Advances in Consumer Research*, Vol. 13 (Provo, UT: Association for Consumer Research, 1986), pp. 514–519.
11. Michael R. Solomon and Bruce Buchanan, "A Role-Theoretic Approach to Product Symbolism: Mapping a Consumption Constellation," *Journal of Business Research*, Vol. 22 (March 1991), pp. 95–110.
12. Emanuel Demby, "Psychographics and Whence It Came," in William D. Wells, ed., *Lifestyle and Psychographics* (Chicago, IL: American Marketing Association, 1974), p. 13.

13. Euehun Lee, George P. Moschis, and Anil Mathur, "A Study of Live Events and Changes in Patronage Preferences," *Journal of Business Research*, Vol. 54 (October 2001), pp. 25-38.

14. Jerry Wind and Paul Green, "Some Conceptual, Measurement, and Analytical Problems in Lifestyle Research," in William D. Wells, ed., *Lifestyle and Psychographics* (Chicago, IL: American Marketing Association, 1974), p. 13.

15. Eleena De Lisser, "Women Shed Family Baggage on Trips," *The Wall Street Journal* (February 9, 1996), pp. B1, B8.

16. Arnold Mitchell, "Styles in the American Bullring," *Across the Board*, Vol. 20, No. 3 (March 1983), pp. 45–54.

17. Berkman and Gilson, "Consumer Lifestyles and Market Segmentation."

18. Joseph T. Plummer, "Lifestyle and Advertising: Case Studies" Paper given at the 54th Annual International Marketing Conference, American Marketing Association, 1966.

19. Emanuel Demby, "Going Beyond Demographics to Find the Creative Consumer," paper presented at Market Research Section, American Marketing Association, New York Chapter (June 1967).

20. Susan Fournier, "Consumers and Their Brands: Developing Relationship Theory in Consumer Research," *Journal of Consumer Research*, Vol. 24 (March 1998), pp. 343–373.

21. R. M. Morgan and Shelby D. Hunt, "The Commitment-Trust Theory of Relationship Marketing," *Journal of Marketing*, 58 (7, 1994), pp. 20–38.

22. Peter C. Verhoef, Philip Hans Franses, and Janny C. Hoekstra, "The Effect of Relational Constructs on Customer Referrals and Number of Services Purchased from a Multiservice Provider: Does Age of Relationship Matter?" *Journal of the Academy of Marketing Science*, Vol. 30 (Summer 2002), pp. 202–216.

23. Birgit Leisen and Michael R. Hyman, "Antecedents and Consequences of Trust in a Service Provider: The Case of Primary Care Physicians," *Journal of Business Research*, Vol. 57 (2004), pp. 990–999.

24. Michael J. Dorsch, Scott R. Swanson, and Scott W. Kelly, "The Role of Relationship Quality in the Stratification of Vendors as Perceived by Customers," *Journal of the Academy of Marketing Science*, Vol. 26 (Spring 1999), pp. 128–142; James C. Anderson, "Relationship in Business Markets: Exchange Episodes, Value Creation, and Their Empirical Assessment," *Journal of the Academy of Marketing Science*, Vol. 23 (4, 1995), pp. 346–350; Lawrence A. Crosby and Nancy Stephens, "Effects of Relationship Marketing on Satisfaction, Retention, and Prices in the Life Insurance Industry," *Journal of Marketing Research*, Vol. 24 (November 1987), pp. 404–411;

Robert F. Dwyer, Paul H. Schurr, and Sejo Oh, "Developing Buyer-Seller Relationships," *Journal of Marketing*, Vol. 51 (April 1987), pp. 11–27; Shankar Ganeson, "Determinants of Long-Term Orientation in Buyer-Seller Relationships," *Journal of Marketing*, Vol. 58 (April 1994), pp. 1–19; Gregory T. Gundlach, Ravi S. Achrol, and John T. Mentzer, "The Structure of Commitment in Exchange," *Journal of Marketing*, Vol. 59 (January 1995), pp. 78–92; Robert F. Lusch and James R. Brown, "Interdependency, Contracting, and Relational Behavior in Marketing Channels," *Journal of Marketing*, Vol. 60 (October 1996), pp. 19–38; Christine Moorman, Rohit Desphande, and Gerald Zeltman, "Factors Affecting Trust in Market Research Relationships," *Journal of Marketing*, Vol. 57 (January 1993), pp. 81–101; Jagdish N. Sheth and Arun Sharma, "Supplier Relationships: Emerging Issues and Challenges," *Industrial Marketing Management*, Vol. 26 (1997), pp. 91–100; C. B. Bhattacharya and Sankar Sen, "Consumer-company Identification: A Framework for Understanding Consumers' Relationships with Companies," *Journal of Marketing*, Vol. 67 (April 2003), pp. 76-90.

25. R. Javalgi, M. Taylor, E. Lampan, "Awareness of Sponsorship and Corporate Image: An Empirical Investigation," *Journal of Advertising*, Vol. 23 (4, 1994), pp. 47–58.

26. A. Parasuraman, Valerie A. Zeithaml, and Leonard L. Berry, "SERVQUAL: A Multiple-Item Scale for measuring Consumer Perceptions of Service Quality," *Journal of Retailing*, Vol. 64 (1, 1988), pp. 12–40; A. Parasuraman, Valerie A. Zeithaml, and Leonard L. Berry, "Refinement and Re-Assessment of the SERVQUAL Scale," *Journal of Retailing*, Vol. 67 (4, 1991), pp. 420–450; A. Parasuraman, Valerie A. Zeithaml, and Leonard L. Berry, "A Conceptual Model of Service Quality and Its Implications for Future Research," *Journal of Marketing*, Vol. 49 (Fall 1995), pp. 41–50.

27. Harvir S. Bansal, P. Gregory Irving, and Shirley F. Taylor, "A Three-Component Model of Customer Commitment to Service Providers," *Journal of the Academy of Marketing Science*, Vol. 32 (Summer 2004), pp. 234–250.

28. L. L. Stanley and J. D. Wisner, "Internal Service Quality in Purchasing: An Empirical Study," *International Journal of Purchasing and Materials Management*, Vol. 34 (Summer 1998), pp. 50–60.

29. Albert M. Muniz, Jr. and Thomas C. O'Guinn, "Brand Community," *Journal of Consumer Research*, Vol. 27 (2001), pp. 412-432; James H. McAlexander, John W. Schouten, and Harold F. Koening, "Building Brand Community," *Journal of Marketing*, Vol. 66 (January 2002), pp. 38–55.

Memory, Learning, and Perception

One night during finals week, Jeff studies so long in his library carrel that he can't *blink* without a throbbing pain in his temples. It's the fluorescent lights, he thinks, giving him instant brain strain. He stumbles from the library, squinting, to the student union pharmacy aisles (more fluorescents—argh!) in search of a pain reliever.

He ponders the rows of little boxes. Okay, there's new stuff like Aleve. Old stuff like Bayer. Old new stuff like Tylenol. He grabs the Tylenol. This seems like the one. But why, he wonders, is this the one he picks up?

Oh yeah. Last night there was an ad for Tylenol with a woman doing aerobics just a few days after knee surgery. He remembers being impressed by that. If it's strong enough for that kind of pain, it should be fine for his organic-chem-cramming brain strain.

Consumers are, first and foremost, individuals. As individuals, consumers display a virtually infinite variety of buying behaviors because they think, remember, learn, and perceive the world differently. To influence the ways in which consumers behave in the marketplace, marketers must first understand how every aspect of their behavior is influenced by how they process new information in memory, learn new behaviors, and perceive marketplace stimuli.

7-1 Memory

Marketing information is not processed in a vacuum but in the context of previous knowledge and experience stored in memory. Our memory of past experiences with products is the single most influential factor in our future responses to marketing information about those products. This body of previous knowledge and experience makes each of us unique as consumers. Because none of us share exactly the same product memories, no two consumers are likely to respond in exactly the same way to new marketing information.

In making purchase decisions, we use two sources of product information. First, from the external environment, we receive packaging, labels, point-of-purchase displays, prices, and other pieces of relevant marketing information. Second, and more importantly, memory provides us with details of past experiences, family preferences, word-of-mouth communications, and memorable advertising. As we shop, marketers reach out to us through the use of coupons, displays, and special offers. But memory, a quiet yet persistent voice in the background, reminds us of the brands we like that might be missing from the displays but available on the shelf. It is these brands, imprinted on our memories, that we are likely to choose.[1]

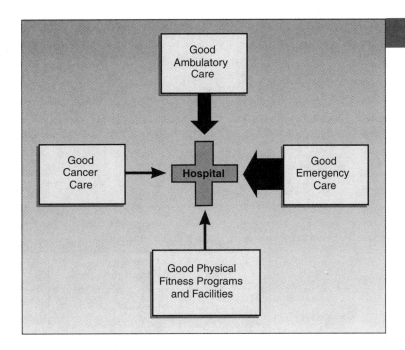

Exhibit 7-1

An Associative Network of Knowledge for a Hospital

Each piece of knowledge about the hospital in memory is represented by a node connected to other concepts by links. Links may be strong or weak, reflected by the thickness of the arrows in the exhibit. Moreover, the links differ with each individual consumer.

Psychologists believe that information is organized in memory in terms of an **associative network** in which each concept in memory, a **node,** is connected to other concepts by **links.** As Exhibit 7-1 shows, you may remember a variety of facts about a regional hospital, for example, its excellent emergency and ambulatory care, the physical fitness programs, and its specialization in cancer services. The hospital and each of these pieces of information about it (nodes) are linked in a special way in memory. Links may be strong, or they may be weak. The link between the hospital and emergency care as shown by the thickness of the arrows in Exhibit 7-1, for example, is stronger than the link with physical fitness programs, reflecting the strength of the consumer's impressions regarding the hospital.[2]

Alongside associative networks, information is also organized in memory around different types of episodes or events, such as shopping trips, coffee breaks, and so on. Consumers store information in terms of scripts—each individual may have a restaurant script, a script related to buying clothes, or a script related to the use of credit cards. Storing episodes and scripts allows the organization of information in memory in such a way that it can be easily retrieved when needed in appropriate situations.

Now that we know how information is structured in memory, we can begin to explore how it is captured, processed, and stored through these associative networks and scripts.

7-1a How Information Is Captured and Stored in Memory

Cognitive psychologists believe there are three processing areas in memory, namely, sensory, short-term, and long-term memory. These are shown in Exhibit 7-2. The operative word is "believe," because we don't really know how many processing areas there are.

Sensory Memory   When information first enters the brain, it is captured by **sensory memory,** where it may register as little more than a sensation and may last for only fractions of a second. Processing is shallow: The consumer simply registers a fleeting sensation of color, contour, size, or shape, for example. The information capacity of sensory memory is extremely limited, as sensations are constantly replaced by other sensory experiences.

Short-Term Memory   Transmitted from sensory memory, information is first analyzed and assigned meaning in **short-term memory.** Although it may last in short-term memory for less than a minute, it can be rehearsed (repeated) to retain its meaning. The capacity of short-term memory is limited to a finite number of chunks (units of memory), each of which stores information and gives it meaning.

▶**associative network**
A system of beliefs organized in memory.

▶**nodes** and **links** In the context of an associative network, concepts involved in beliefs are nodes that are connected to other nodes through links.

▶**sensory memory** That part of the brain that captures information when it first enters the brain. The information may register as little more than a sensation and may last for only fractions of a second.

▶**short-term memory** The part of the brain that analyzes the information from sensory memory and assigns meaning to the information.

Memory Processes

In theory, there are three processing areas in memory: sensory memory, short-term memory, and long-term memory.

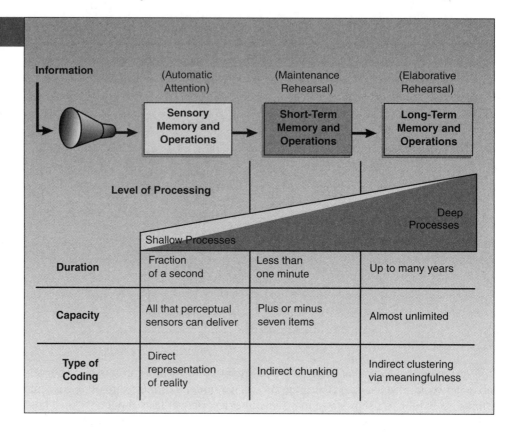

	(Automatic Attention)	(Maintenance Rehearsal)	(Elaborative Rehearsal)
Information →	**Sensory Memory and Operations**	**Short-Term Memory and Operations**	**Long-Term Memory and Operations**
Duration	Fraction of a second	Less than one minute	Up to many years
Capacity	All that perceptual sensors can deliver	Plus or minus seven items	Almost unlimited
Type of Coding	Direct representation of reality	Indirect chunking	Indirect clustering via meaningfulness

Level of Processing — Shallow Processes / Deep Processes

long-term memory Information that is rehearsed in short-term memory and transmitted to long-term memory, where it is stored for a long time and can be retrieved as needed.

retention The amount of material previously learned that is remembered.

Why can I remember my second-grade teacher's name but not what I ate for lunch two days ago?

Long-Term Memory Information rehearsed in short-term memory is transmitted to **long-term memory,** where it is stored for a long time and can be retrieved as needed. The information capacity of long-term memory is thought to be unlimited.

All information appears to flow through these three types of memory. The depth of processing varies according to the importance of the information to the individual.[3] Information decays quite rapidly in sensory and short-term memory but may not decay at all in long-term memory.

Marketplace 7-1 shows how marketers use frequent ad exposures to penetrate consumers' memories—sensory, short-term, and long-term.

7-1b How Information Is Retained in Memory

Retention can be defined as the amount of material previously learned that is remembered. The opposite is forgetting, a loss in retention of material previously learned. Needless to say, not all learned material is remembered.

People tend to forget information over time. This is due to a process psychologists call retroactive inhibition. New sensations and learning interfere with information already stored in long-term memory, which is eventually lost or forgotten. Conversely, stored data can interfere with new information so that it is not processed.

Memory is selective, and retention varies according to a number of factors. These factors can be organized into two broad categories: those related to incoming information and those related to the person receiving the information (see Exhibit 7-3).

How Retention Is Influenced by Incoming Information There are five major factors that affect the retention of product information in memory: repetition, relevance, competing information, completeness of information, and time.

Repetition Most forgetting occurs almost immediately after learning, but repetition or rehearsal of information increases the chances of retention. Repetition strengthens the consumer's beliefs regarding incoming information. Because an advertisement shown

Marketplace 7-1

If at First You Don't Succeed, Try, Try Again

The first time Shonda looks at an advertisement, she does not see it. The second time, she does not notice it. The third time, she is conscious of its existence. The fourth time, she faintly remembers having seen it before. The fifth time, she reads it. The sixth time, she turns up her nose at it. The seventh time, she reads it through and says, "Oh, brother." The eighth time, she says, "Here's that confounded thing again." The ninth time, she wonders if it amounts to anything. The tenth time, she thinks she will ask her neighbor if he has tried it. The eleventh time, she wonders how the advertiser makes it pay. The twelfth time, she thinks perhaps it is worth something. The thirteenth time, she thinks it must be a good thing. The fourteenth time, she remembers that she has wanted such a thing for a long time. The fifteenth time, she is tantalized because she cannot afford to buy it. The sixteenth time, she thinks she will buy it sometime. The seventeenth time, she makes a memorandum of it. The eighteenth time, she swears at her poverty. The nineteenth time, she counts her money carefully. The twentieth time she sees it, Shonda buys the article.

Source: Adapted from H. E. Krugman, "An Application of Learning Theory to TV Copy Testing," *Public Opinion Quarterly,* Vol. 26 (1962), pp. 626–634.

once is not likely to be as well remembered as one that is shown several times,[4] it makes sense for marketers to communicate with target customers by repeating messages frequently.

Even with commercials people say they dislike, the greater the frequency, the better the message is remembered. A campaign for Charmin bathroom tissue featuring Mr. Whipple warning customers not to "squeeze the Charmin" was reportedly unpopular with viewers. Even so, the brand's market share increased dramatically through sheer repetition of the commercial.[5]

There is, however, a point of diminishing retention—advertisements repeated too frequently lose their effectiveness. Thus, campaigns comprising several variations upon a central theme tend to be stronger than simple repetitions of a single advertisement.[6] Excessive repetition can even have a negative impact—consumers tune out messages observed too frequently or are irritated by tiresome repetition. One study found that the point at which repetition loses effectiveness varies according to the advertising or product in question.[7] The more creative or the more on target the advertisement, the less repetition is necessary to drive its message home.

Research has also found that, given the same level of repetition, a lengthy, complex message will be forgotten more readily than a shorter, less complicated one. Lengthy, complex messages must, therefore, be repeated more frequently to ensure the same degree of retention as short, simple ones.

Relevance   Retention is greater when new information fits into the array of data or stimuli that the consumer considers relevant to the situation at hand. Because of its relevance,

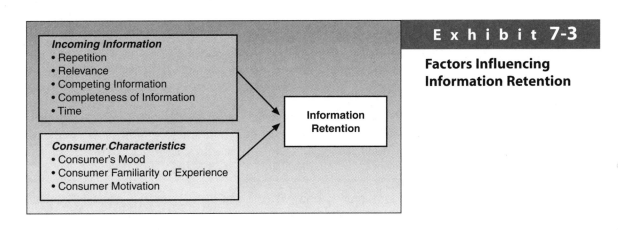

E x h i b i t 7-3

Factors Influencing Information Retention

Incoming Information
• Repetition
• Relevance
• Competing Information
• Completeness of Information
• Time

Information Retention

Consumer Characteristics
• Consumer's Mood
• Consumer Familiarity or Experience
• Consumer Motivation

> ### CBite 7-1
> #### No Time for Browsing
>
> Shorter messages are the key to effective television direct-response advertising. In one study, two commercials invited viewers to join a book club. As an incentive to join, the first commercial offered three specific books for a dollar. The second asked the viewer to choose from several books shown. Although both were aired the same number of times, the first commercial was more successful. The "choice" message in the second commercial was complicated and probably required additional repetition to gain the same retention as the "no choice" message in the first.
>
> *Source:* Adapted from Doubleday Advertising Company, 1977.

information is likely to be processed in memory at deeper levels. Hence, advertisements that are well targeted and contain copy and situations appropriate to their target audiences are likely to be considered meaningful by the consumers and are, therefore, better remembered.[8] They fit easily into the consumers' frame of reference and are perceived as appropriate and familiar.

Competing Information   Forgetting occurs because of interference—a previously learned message is forgotten when new learning occurs. For example, consumers constantly bombarded with fast-food advertising are not likely to remember a particular advertisement for a particular restaurant. New information interferes with the retention of old.[9]

Commercial clutter is particularly prevalent in television advertising. As sixty-second segments are broken down into thirty- and fifteen-second messages, the problem escalates. To overcome clutter, advertisers look for creative messages that are particularly relevant to target customers and, therefore, stand out and are remembered. Another option is to explore less cluttered media vehicles that reach target consumers. CBite 7-1 shows how marketers conduct research to identify aspects of direct-response ads that influence consumers' retention of information.

Completeness of Information   The Zeigarnik effect states that if a message is not complete, people will attempt to retain it for the purpose of future completion.[10] In the late 1980s, Post Grape-Nuts ran a commercial split into two parts. The first part was aired at the beginning of a commercial break. The spokesperson set out to prove that Grape-Nuts always stay crunchy by pouring milk over a bowl of the cereal. The commercial was interrupted and continued at the end of the commercial break to show that the cereal was still crunchy. The advertiser kept the audience interested by providing incomplete information. Viewers were primed to retain the original message at least until it was completed at the end of the commercial break and, more likely, long afterwards. The end result was increased retention.

Time   Forgetting occurs as a logarithmic function of the time elapsed since the information was learned. If two associations are of equal strength, the older one (in elapsed time) will lose strength more slowly during the same space of time. Thus, it is important for marketers to follow up or repeat advertising early after the launch of a campaign. Consumers are more likely to forget large pieces of the message early in the campaign.

How Retention Is Influenced by the Information Recipient   Three important factors affecting retention of information in memory are the consumer's mood, the consumer's level of familiarity or experience with a product or service, and the consumer's motivation to remember.

Consumer's Mood   Recent evidence suggests that a positive mood enhances the encoding of information in memory. For example, several studies have shown that brand names

Exhibit 7-4

The Catfish Institute wants you to think about the product's attributes rather than its less-than-attractive whiskers—an attempt to force consumers to process information to overcome possible negative preconceptions (consumer familiarity or experience).

Source: Courtesy of The Catfish Institute.

were better recalled when consumers learned these names when they were in a positive rather than a neutral mood.[11]

Consumer Familiarity or Experience   Product familiarity affects retention in two ways. First, consumers who are familiar with a product category are more likely to remember new information about new or existing brands than are those consumers less familiar with the category. This is because experienced consumers are better able to process new product information at deeper levels than are those with limited background knowledge. For example, an advertisement for a specific personal computer is more likely to be remembered by consumers who are knowledgeable about computers than by those who are not.[12] Marketers are thus advised to segment consumers into two groups: those with good product knowledge and those without. When targeting less-knowledgeable consumers, the primary goal should be to educate them about the product category. Only once they become familiar with the category should brand messages dominate.

The second way familiarity influences retention is the effect it has on the way information is organized in memory. One way consumers analyze information is in terms of product attributes and their benefits (attribute-based information processing). If a consumer shopping for a new car, for example, is concerned about safety, he or she is likely to process such information as availability of airbags or antilock brakes in such a way that it is accessed easily whenever he or she thinks about safety.[13] The Catfish Institute ad in Exhibit 7-4 is an attempt to force the consumer to process product attributes to overcome possible negative preconceptions.

Another way in which consumers organize information is in terms of brand names (brand-based information processing).[14] Research has shown that the more a consumer knows about a product category, the more likely the information is to be processed by brand name rather than by attributes or benefits.[15]

It is important for marketers to understand attribute-based versus brand-based processing in order to target consumers who have different levels of product or brand familiarity with appropriate messages. Less-experienced consumers need to know about the attributes of a product and how it will help them meet their goals. Experienced consumers already know this and instead need information about the brand, showing how well it stacks up against its competitors. Marketplace 7-2 shows an interesting case study in which

Marketplace 7-2

A Change of Diaper Branding

When Dundee Mills acquired the Chix line of baby products from Johnson & Johnson, it faced a serious marketing problem. One of the conditions of the sale was that the Chix brand name had to revert to Johnson & Johnson in five years: Thus, the new owners would have to effect the change from the Chix brand to the Dundee brand while still retaining the loyalty of customers and retailers.

The strategy adopted by Dundee Mills was to make the change in a series of steps to be completed under the five-year threshold. First, a new package was introduced that featured the old brand name, Chix, in large letters, just like the former design, but added the words "by Dundee" in small letters under the familiar brand name. In the next step, the package emphasis was reversed. "Chix" was in small letters, and "by Dundee" was in large type. Dundee thus became the most visible graphic element but without overpowering the Chix identification. In the final step, "Chix" was entirely eliminated, and "Dundee" became the brand's new—and only—name. According to Herbert M. Myers, one of the graphics consultants, this strategy of gradual change in small increments "provided a virtually unnoticed changeover from a 50-year-old brand name to an unfamiliar one with no adverse market reaction."

Source: Adapted from "Three-Step Name Change Lets Firm Retain Brand Loyalty" in *Marketing News,* August 17, 1984, p. 3. Reprinted with permission from *Marketing News,* published by the American Marketing Association.

marketers used the principle of consumers' familiarity in retention to change the name of a brand without suffering loss in brand sales.

Consumer Motivation   Research has shown that consumers who are motivated to process information are likely to do so at deeper levels of memory and to retain it longer and more accurately than those who are not motivated to do so.[16] That is, the consumer's motivational state at the time of exposure to new information influences the level of retention. Psychologists make a distinction between incidental learning and directed learning.[17] Incidental learning occurs when the consumer does not actively participate in information processing. Directed learning occurs when consumers consciously process information in a goal-directed manner.

Related to directed learning is the concept of goal-directed encoding. Consumers who categorize or "file" incoming information in memory in relation to important goals are more likely than others to remember this information.[18] For example, two consumers are shopping separately for cars, gathering information about alternatives. The first consumer has some very specific goals in mind. She is looking for an economy car that is also safe to drive. The second consumer has not yet articulated what he is looking for. Both visit several dealers and take home brochures. They also look at newspaper advertisements and talk to family and friends. Who is likely to remember more of the information gathered? Because the first consumer organized information around specific goals, she is most likely to remember it accurately.

7-1c How Information Is Retrieved from Memory

The fact that information is available in memory does not necessarily mean that the consumer is able to retrieve or recall it. Moreover, even when it is retrieved, the information is not always a perfect match with that originally stored. Several factors affect how information is pulled up from memory and reconstructed by the consumer: retrieval cues, interference from competing cues, and the consumer's state of mind (see Exhibit 7-5).

Retrieval Cues   A popular commercial for Life cereal from Quaker Oats featured the character Mikey. For several years, Quaker Oats printed a scene from one of the commercials in the lower right-hand corner of its cereal boxes. The image served as a retrieval cue, prompting consumers to remember the advertising. As another example, Campbell Soup Company reported a sales increase of 15 percent when point-of-purchase displays were

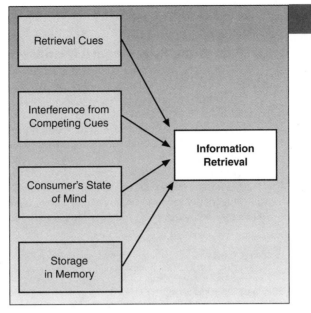

Exhibit 7-5

Factors Influencing Information Retrieval

directly related to television advertising, prompting recall.[19] As both examples demonstrate, to retrieve information from memory, consumers have to use or be exposed to retrieval cues.

Information **retrieval** is determined mostly by the particular retrieval cues available at the time.[20] Retrieval cues can be either self-generated or externally generated. To retrieve, say, a brand name, a consumer may try to reconstruct the situation in which the product was last seen or used. The cue is self-generated. If the consumer, however, sees a picture of a celebrity spokesperson on a package and thus recalls an advertisement, the cue is externally generated.

retrieval The consumer's ability to recognize or recall product or service information previously retained in memory.

Interference from Competing Cues   Imagine a supermarket shopper examining four different brands of toothpaste on the shelf. In front of one of the brands is a large point-of-purchase display featuring a popular character used in the brand's television advertising. The consumer picks up a tube, drops it into his or her shopping cart, and moves on without giving a thought to advertising he or she may have seen for the other three brands on the shelf. This is an example of interference. The point-of-purchase display pushes the brand into short-term memory, interfering with the retrieval of information on all other brands. Marketers can increase the salience of their brand through cues that inhibit the consumer's ability to recall information on competing brands from memory.[21]

Consumer's State of Mind   Research has long indicated that information retrieval may depend on how well the consumer's state of mind at the time of retrieval matches his or her state of mind at the time information was originally processed. That is, a consumer is more likely to recall product information if his or her mood or level of interest is similar to that of the environment in which the information was first learned. Suppose a consumer first sees a car at an auto show where it is displayed in an environment vibrant with rock music and psychedelic lights. An advertisement that matches the energetic mood of the auto show is far more likely to help that consumer remember seeing the car than one that does not.

Storage in Memory   Research has shown that recall of numerical coded information (e.g., an ad highlighting the fact that the car gets "36" miles per gallon) is better than verbal information (e.g., an ad highlighting the fact that the car gets "good" gas mileage).[22] To help understand how information stored as either numerical or verbal information in memory affects retrieval, we have to make the distinction between two concepts, namely

---

CBite 7-2

The Pioneering Advantage: A Memory-Based Explanation

Pioneer brands (a new brand that establishes a new product category) like Coca-Cola, Kleenex, and Microsoft have a significant competitive advantage over follower brands. This competitive advantage may have something to do with the way consumers process, store, and retrieve information about pioneering brands relative to follower brands. Because of the novelty associated with pioneer brands, consumers may elaborate more on the first brand they experience in a product category. Thus, the pioneer brand becomes more accessible in consumer memory and is therefore easily retrieved into a consumer's consideration or evoked set. Having a pioneer brand more accessible in memory and easily retrieved increases the chances that the pioneer brand will be selected more frequently than follower brands.

Sources: Frank R. Kardes, Gurumurthy Kalyanaram, Murali Chandrashekaran, and Ronald J. Dornoff, "Brand Retrieval, Consideration Set Composition, Consumer Choice, and Pioneering Advantage," *Journal of Consumer Research*, Vol. 20 (June 1993), pp. 62–75. Ronald W. Niedrich and Scott D. Swain, "The Influence of Pioneer Status and Experience Order on Consumer Brand Preference: A Mediated-Effects Model," *Journal of the Academy of Marketing Science*, Vol. 31 (Fall 2003), pp. 468–480.

▶ **surface-level processing**
Storage of information as is, without analysis of its meaning.

▶ **meaning-level processing**
Storage of the meaning of the information, not the "raw" information per se.

surface-level processing and meaning-level processing.[23] **Surface-level processing** refers to storing information as is, without analyzing its meaning. For example, an ad touting a car generating 50 miles per gallon may be stored in memory as "Car X gets 50 miles per gallon." In contrast, **meaning-level processing** stores the meaning of the information, not the "raw" information *per se*. Let's go back to the car ad example in which the ad highlights the fact that the car gets 50 miles per gallon. Here, the consumer may process the meaning of "50 miles per gallon" as "superior in gas economy," and the meaning ("superior in gas economy") is stored rather than the raw data ("50 miles per gallon"). Cognitive psychologists refer to the distinction between surface- versus meaning-level processing as "sensory versus semantic processing." Storing information at the surface level makes the retrieval of this information faster than that of information stored at a meaning level. Although storing information at the surface level is likely to generate faster consumer recognition, researchers caution that consumers may make errors in product judgments by relying on surface-level processing. Consumers should be encouraged to process advertising information meaningfully, and as such they may be able to better use this information in making product selection decisions—decisions guided by accurate and meaningful information. CBite 7-2 shows how a pioneer brand has an advantage over follower brands because of memory factors.

7-1d How Memory Can Be "Artificially" Reconstructed

Psychologists have discovered that sometimes when recently generated images become accessible in mind, people forget the source and retain the new images, overshadowing images from the past. For example, suppose that a woman undergoes hypnotherapy. Her hypnotherapist, through the power of suggestion, induces her to imagine that she was sexually molested by her father. It is likely that the newly created images overshadow the real childhood memories of what happened. Psychologists refer to this memory phenomenon as "imagination inflation."[24] Imagination inflation also can occur with consumer post-experiences overshadowed by advertising messages.[25] Take, for example, a television commercial showing a wonderfully delicious pizza with fresh toppings and a person eating it and expressing a great deal of pleasure. Let's say this is a Pizza Hut commercial. The consumer has had a bad experience with Pizza Hut on his last visit. The pizza was not that tasty. It didn't have enough cheese, the toppings were sparse, and the pizza was kind of dry.

The television commercial is likely to overshadow this negative memory. The memory created by the advertisement may feel veridical ("real") to the consumer and is likely to be more accessible than the memory of the last experience.

Furthermore, research has uncovered the fact that message repetition may cause consumers to reconstruct memory biased by the repeated message. That is, repeated claims contribute to increased belief in those claims. Consumer researchers have named this effect the "truth effect."[26] Elderly consumers were found to be more susceptible to the truth-inflating effect of repetition than were the young.[27]

Marketing Management—Implications and Actions

Understanding memory helps marketers:

- Provide information that consumers will retain.
- Decide how much repetition of product information is needed.
- Develop packaging, advertising, or display cues to assist in memory retrieval.

7-2 Learning

How consumers learn about and develop habits regarding goods and services is the next step in applying what is retained in memory. Consumer researchers have treated the topic of consumer learning from three theoretical viewpoints: probability theory, behavior analysis, and cognitive theory.

7-2a Probability Theory

Probability theory treats learning as the formation of habits. Formed and changed through experience with products or services, habits are particularly important to marketers. Once buying habits are formed, product or brand loyalties can develop, leading consumers to consistently choose a particular product, a particular brand, a particular supplier, or a particular retail store.

> **probability theory** A theory of learning that treats learning as the formation of habits by examining the person's history of behaviors.

Strength of habit depends upon the amount of reinforcement it receives. As Thorndike's Law of Effect states:

> When a connection is accompanied by a satisfying state of affairs, its strength is increased [and] the probability of its recurrence is greater. Inversely, when the connection is accompanied by an annoying state of affairs, its strength is reduced or weakened . . . [a]n organism tends to repeat that which has previously been satisfying and avoid that which has been dissatisfying.[28]

In consumer decision making, this suggests that the person who buys an Oldsmobile every two years does so because that brand continues to satisfy his or her needs. Habits are formed as a result of constant reinforcement and explain a variety of consumer behaviors, including brand loyalty, brand acceptance, and brand switching.

To predict the formation of buying habits, consumer researchers have developed stochastic or probability models. A probability measure rests on the idea that a buyer's previous (and particularly most recent) purchasing behavior will determine future behavior. Numerous models have been designed to quantify this relationship and have been applied to the study of brand loyalty, brand acceptance, brand switching, and new product forecasting.

Brand Loyalty   In an early application of probability models to consumer behavior, studies conducted on the purchase of frozen orange juice found that frequent purchasers are the consumers who will most probably develop brand loyalties. Conversely, the greater the time interval between purchases, the smaller the probability that the same brand will be purchased. With this type of low-involvement product, purchasers do not form brand loyalties strong enough to negate the possibility of brand switching.[29]

UPS targets entrepreneurs who are current users of other shipping services. The goal of the ad is to induce brand switching.

Source: Courtesy of UPS.

Brand Acceptance

Probability models are used to measure brand acceptance by investigating the behavior of consumers who are trying a new or existing brand for the first time. In general, high-volume users of a product are more difficult to win over to a new brand (once they have tried it) than are average users. However, buyers who tend toward brand loyalty are more likely to accept a new brand once they have tried it.[30] This information is particularly valuable to marketers of new products who are seeking an indication of probable future performance. It is also useful for monitoring the strength of existing brands to predict future sales.[31] Recent research has shown that brand loyalty can be positively influenced by loyalty rewards program membership (e.g., a frequent flier miles program run by a major airlines).[32] These programs can be thought of as positive reinforcement in learning theory.

Brand Switching

Because certain attributes of brand loyalty are predictable, it stands to reason that brand switching can also be predicted. Research into the soft-drink choices of students and secretaries over a three-week period revealed substantial brand switching in the soft-drink market; thus the brand-loyalty factor is well below average. The three brands achieving the largest market share were fairly close in preference but substantially higher than the brands gaining smaller shares. The variance in shares among the three majors is an indication of substantial switching.[33]

The UPS ad in Exhibit 7-6 is designed to induce brand switching. The ad targets entrepreneurs who have not used UPS in the past, perhaps having used some other shipping company. The ad appeals to these people and induces them to switch to UPS because of the great benefits associated with the UPS e-logistics system. Remember, brand switching is the converse of brand loyalty.

New Product Forecasting

One study using a probability model of first-purchaser activity was able to forecast new subscriptions to cable television. Observing data from subscriptions for cable installations over a ten-year period, the study authors noted that the market was rapidly reaching saturation. Researchers contended that an earlier forecast based on initial new-user data would have provided a reasonably good forecast of peak sales four years before the event.[34]

I. Some Applications of Respondent Conditioning Principles		

E x h i b i t 7-7

Applications of the Behavior Modification Principles in Marketing

A. Conditioning Responses to New Stimuli

Unconditioned or Previously Conditioned Stimulus	*Conditioned Stimulus*	*Example*
Patriotic events or music	A product or person	Patriotic music as background in political commercial

B. Use of Familiar Stimuli to Elicit Responses

Conditioned Stimulus	*Conditioned Response(s)*	*Example*
Familiar music	Relaxation, excitement, goodwill	Christmas music in retail store
Familiar social cues	Excitement, attention, anxiety	Sirens sounding or telephones ringing in a commercial

II. Some Applications of Operant Conditioning Principles		

A. Rewards for Desired Behavior (Continuous Schedules)

Desired Behavior	*Reward Given Following Behavior*
Product purchase	Trading stamps, cash bonus or rebate, prizes, coupons

B. Rewards for Desired Behavior (Partial Schedules)

Desired Behavior	*Reward Given (Sometimes)*
Product purchase	Prize for every second, or third, etc., purchase

C. Shaping

Approximation of Desired Response	*Consequence Following Approximation*	*Final Response Desired*
Opening a charge account	Prizes, etc., for opening account	Expenditure of funds
Trip to point-of-purchase	Entertainment at store	Purchase of products
Entry into store	Door prize	Purchase of products
Product trial	Free product and/or some bonus for using	Purchase of products

D. Discriminative Stimuli

Desired Behavior	*Reward Signal*	*Example*
Entry into store	Store signs	50%-off sale

Source: From "A Behavior Modification Perspective on Marketing" by Walter R. Nord and J. Paul Peter in *Journal of Marketing,* Spring 1980, Volume 44, p. 42. Reprinted with permission from *Journal of Marketing,* published by the American Marketing Association.

7-2b Behavior Analysis

The relationship between marketers and consumers in the marketplace often resembles a negotiation. As with any relationship, the terms on which the exchange takes place can involve many different forms of offers, counteroffers, rewards, and punishments. It may seem that marketers hold all the cards, because it is their intention to change the consumer's behavior, but the consumer always holds the trump card: choice.

Behavior analysis focuses on how learning can be modified through incentives and offers, counteroffers, and other forms of rewards and punishments. Exhibit 7-7 offers a compilation of behavior modification principles (BMPs).

> **behavior analysis** A theory of learning that focuses on how learning can be modified through incentives and offers, counteroffers, and other forms of rewards and punishments.

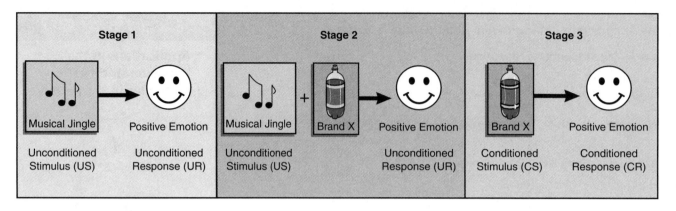

Stage 1	Stage 2	Stage 3
Musical Jingle → Positive Emotion	Musical Jingle + Brand X → Positive Emotion	Brand X → Positive Emotion
Unconditioned Stimulus (US) Unconditioned Response (UR)	Unconditioned Stimulus (US) Unconditioned Response (UR)	Conditioned Stimulus (CS) Conditioned Response (CR)

Exhibit 7-8

Classical Conditioning

Note how positive feelings are transferred from the jingle to the product.

INTERACTIVE EXHIBIT

▶ **classical or respondent conditioning** Conditioning based on the simple premise that learning results from a relationship between stimulus and response.

7-2c Classical Conditioning

Classical or **respondent conditioning** is based on the simple premise that learning results from a relationship between stimulus and response. This was first demonstrated by Russian physiologist Ivan Pavlov and his famous salivating dogs. Simply, Pavlov noted that when meat is placed in a dog's mouth, saliva begins to flow as a natural and automatic behavior—an unconditioned response. An unconditioned stimulus—such as the ringing of a bell—by itself creates no reason for a dog to salivate. But if the bell is rung immediately before each feeding, before long the ringing alone is sufficient to make the dog salivate. A relationship is established between the bell and the food so that the response the dog originally made to the food is now made to the bell. Here, a conditioned stimulus—the ringing bell before each feeding—results in a conditioned response—salivation.

Initially, we might believe that buying behaviors cannot be conditioned in this way because they are voluntary—there are no unconditioned stimuli that automatically produce them. But a closer analysis suggests that respondent conditioning may be responsible for some consumer actions. Researchers have pointed out that "when a new product for which people have neutral feelings is repeatedly advertised during exciting sports events, it is possible for the product to eventually generate excitement on its own, solely through the repeated pairing with the exciting events."[35]

Consider the following experiment. In a lab setting, two groups of subjects are asked how much they would be willing to pay for a television set. A credit card is placed on the table in front of the first group, but not the second. Members of the first group indicate they would be willing to pay around $137 for the television set; the second group would pay only $67. In this example, the credit card is a conditioned stimulus because it is paired with spending and the positive feelings that often occur from the purchase of a product. The purchase of the television at higher price levels by the first group can thus be viewed as a conditioned response.[36] Exhibit 7-8 summarizes how classical or respondent conditioning works to influence brand choices.

Recent research has explained how conditioned stimuli have predictive value for the consumer. That is, conditioned stimuli allow consumers to anticipate consequences of a purchase behavior (the ringing bell told Pavlov's dogs that food was on its way). Given a conditioned stimulus, then, consumers focus their attention in order to experience positive consequences or to help them avoid negative ones.[37] A consumer who loves Chinese food walks past a restaurant and is greeted by the delicious aroma of Szechuan cuisine (a conditioned stimulus). Captivated by the odor, he or she imagines (or predicts) how the food might taste and steps into the restaurant for a meal (conditioned response).[38]

Conditioned stimuli have the power to influence even neutral stimuli, thus making them conditioned, too. The pairing of a popular celebrity, for example, with a particular product can make consumers want that product whenever they see the celebrity. This concept is known as higher-order conditioning.

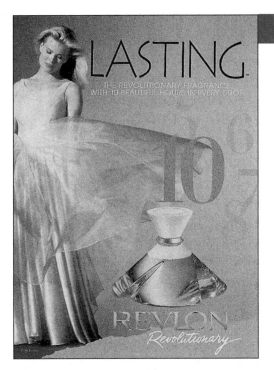

Exhibit 7-9

Revlon employs the strong unconditioned stimuli of sensuality and romance to sell its Lasting perfume.

Source: Courtesy of Revlon.

Strength of the Unconditioned Stimulus   The stronger the unconditioned stimulus, the stronger the conditioning: Pavlov's dogs were more likely to respond to a loud, distinctive bell than to a lulled ring.[39] Marketers should, then, choose unconditioned stimuli that are clear and strong with which to pair their products. Compare the stimulus of a desire for adventure with the desire for rest and relaxation. Both elicit positive, unconditioned responses, but, particularly with younger audiences, the first is likely to be stronger than the second. Examine the advertisement in Exhibit 7–9 for Revlon's Lasting perfume. It successfully pairs the brand with very strong unconditioned stimuli: sensuality and romantic feelings.

Number of Pairings   In some cases, as many as thirty pairings may be necessary before consumers are conditioned to show a preference for a given brand.[40] For the advertiser, this means message repetition: High exposure frequency will pair the unconditioned stimulus with the advertised brand more effectively than will low exposure frequency.

Forward Versus Backward Versus Simultaneous Conditioning   **Forward conditioning** occurs when the conditioned stimulus is presented first, followed by the unconditioned stimulus. **Backward conditioning** occurs when the unconditioned stimulus is presented first, followed by the conditioned stimulus. Simultaneous conditioning occurs when the conditioned and unconditioned stimuli are presented at the same time. Consumer researchers have evidence that forward conditioning is more effective than backward or simultaneous conditioning.[41] Consider the following example. As the soundtrack for a new advertisement, you choose a piece of music that is popular among target consumers. Would you play this music before, during, or after you present the product? Because forward conditioning is most effective, the music (unconditioned stimulus) should come after the product presentation (conditioned stimulus).

New Versus Existing Products   Conditioning can be more effective for new brands because no associations between the brand and attributes have been formed. Therefore, new conditioning does not interfere with old. As a result, marketers are advised to limit the use of classical conditioning techniques to new products and brands.

forward conditioning
The type of conditioning that occurs when the conditioned stimulus is presented first, followed by the unconditioned stimulus.

backward conditioning
Occurs when the unconditioned stimulus is presented first, followed by the conditioned stimulus.

Exhibit 7-10

Häagen-Dazs wants you to think of their ice cream as "one of life's purest pleasures," or "the ultimate personal indulgence."

Source: Reprinted by permission of Ice Cream Partners USA, LLC. Copyright © 2001 HDIP, Inc.

7-2d Operant Conditioning

▶**operant** or **instrumental conditioning** The process in which the frequency of occurrence of a bit of behavior is modified by the consequences of the behavior.

Operant or **instrumental conditioning** is "a process in which the frequency of occurrence of a bit of behavior is modified by the consequences of the behavior."[42] Much consumer behavior results from operant conditioning. From choosing a brand of coffee from a supermarket shelf to selecting a restaurant to making a telephone call, frequency of behavior is conditioned by the extent of reinforcement associated with that behavior. Researchers have repeatedly found that operant conditioning is especially relevant to low-involvement purchases. Behavior is most easily modified when little thought is necessary for adequate decision making.[43] For example, Mary regularly travels on business, and she enjoys that part of her job. The Häagen-Dazs ice cream ad (Exhibit 7-10) shows Mary eating Häagen-Dazs in a pleasurable situation—that is, during business travel. Business travel reinforces her eating of this brand of ice cream. This is what reinforcement is about. Mary is likely to continue ordering and eating this brand of ice cream in the future, thus reinforcing the probability of future purchases.

Rewards and Punishments   What distinguishes operant conditioning from classical conditioning is the principle of reward and punishment. In operant conditioning, a specific behavior results in a specific consequence. Behavior modification is reinforced or rewarded by a positive consequence and punished by a negative one.

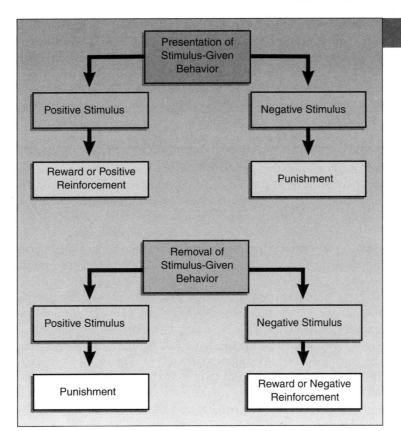

Various Forms of Rewards and Punishments

Both positive and negative stimuli can have a dual role in shaping behavior, depending on their presentation or removal.

The various forms of rewards and punishments are summarized in Exhibit 7-11. Rewards can take two forms. A positive stimulus can be presented following a behavior (a shopper enters a store and is given a Coke), or a negative stimulus can be removed following a behavior (a person finds out that he lost ten pounds after eating less fat for the last two months). Both are rewards, but one is related to the application of a positive stimulus and the other to the removal of a negative stimulus.

Similarly, there are two forms of punishment. A negative stimulus can be presented following a behavior (a consumer experiences a product malfunction after purchase), or a positive stimulus can be removed following a behavior (a traveler's special hotel privileges are taken away because he or she did not spend enough nights in the hotel over the previous twelve months). Both are punishments, but one is related to the application of a negative stimulus and the other to the removal of a positive stimulus.

How Rewards and Punishments Influence Consumer Behavior
Three characteristics of rewards and punishments influence consumer behavior: schedule, shaping, and quality and quantity.[44]

Reward and Punishment Schedule A **reinforcement schedule** is a schedule of rewards or punishments used for learning. In operant learning, reinforcements or punishments do not have to be continuous in order to be effective—that is, not every correct response needs to be rewarded nor every incorrect one punished for learning to occur. An **intermittent reinforcement** schedule, however, is necessary—at least some responses have to be rewarded or punished on a fairly regular basis. Like a gambler at a Las Vegas slot machine who keeps playing because coins do fall out from time to time, consumer behavior needs to be reinforced by intermittent rewards. The most efficient use of reinforcement in operant learning is to begin with **continuous reinforcement** so that the response will occur frequently, then switch to intermittent reinforcement to keep the desired response from being extinguished.

▶**reinforcement schedule**
A schedule of rewards or punishments used for learning.

▶**intermittent reinforcement**
The use of rewards and punishments on a fairly regular basis.

▶**continuous reinforcement**
A schedule of rewards and punishments that reflects the situation in which every correct response is rewarded and every incorrect one is punished.

There is evidence to suggest that where there is no competition, reinforcement is just as effective when it occurs sporadically as when it occurs on a regular basis. In a competitive marketplace, however, regular reinforcement has its benefits. In fact, sporadic reinforcement may even be perceived by the consumer as punishment when it doesn't occur rather than as a reward when it does.[45]

Rewards and punishments are most effective when they take place at the same time as the desired behavior. That is, an immediate reinforcer is more effective than a delayed one. An offer of a free drinking glass with the purchase of a hamburger will sell far more burgers if the consumer gets the glass immediately, rather than receiving a coupon that must be mailed in to get the glass—a procedure that can take weeks and requires additional initiative on the part of the consumer. As stated in one study, "When the premium arrives, it may strongly reinforce the behavior of opening one's mailbox rather than the behavior of making multiple purchases of the product."[46]

shaping A form of operant conditioning in which consumers are gradually trained to produce a desired response. Behavior is reinforced or punished until it approximates more and more closely the response ultimately desired.

Shaping Responses through Rewards and Punishments   **Shaping** is a form of operant conditioning in which consumers are gradually trained to produce a desired response. Behavior is reinforced or punished until it approximates more and more closely the response ultimately desired.[47] A form of consumer shaping popular among marketers is the offer of free or reduced-price trials. For example, new readers are offered a three-month subscription to *The New York Times* at a bargain rate. Over time, the consumers gradually adjust their daily routines to allow time for reading the paper, thus experiencing the paper's own reinforcing properties. Daily reading of the *Times* becomes a habit that continues even when the consumer has to pay full price. Other uses of the shaping principle include the use of coupons, free samples, and other trial offers. The consumer is induced to make repeat purchases and, after this behavior is established, the stimulus is withdrawn.[48]

Quality and Quantity of Rewards and Punishments   By manipulating the quantity and quality of reinforcers and punishers, marketers can attempt to influence consumer behavior. For example, increasing the monetary incentive of a rebate is likely to attract more buyers. Providing better premiums as rewards for frequent purchases may also make a difference, as anyone who has cashed in a frequent-flyer award knows. One way to ensure that the reinforcer is of high quality is to match the consumer situation with the most effective type of reinforcer. Applying the most effective reinforcer or punisher in a situation is necessary for effective marketing.

7-2e Generalization

When a new stimulus is similar to one previously learned, consumers are likely to respond to it in the same way as to the old one. And the more the new stimulus resembles the earlier one, the stronger the response. This tendency to respond in similar ways to similar stimuli is known as **generalization.** It is because of generalization that buyers shift purchase responses from one brand to a new one that is similar.[49] This is why, for example, some marketers have found it effective to imitate the packaging of market leaders, thereby increasing their own market share.

generalization The tendency to respond in similar ways to similar stimuli. When a new stimulus is similar to one previously learned, consumers are likely to respond to it in the same way as to the old one. And the more the new stimulus resembles the earlier one, the stronger the response.

Exhibit 7-12 demonstrates the gradient of generalization—a measure of the tendency of consumers to switch brands. In the exhibit, B_0 is the original brand choice. B_1, B_2, B_3, B_4, and B_5 are brands that are progressively less similar to B_0. D_1 represents one level of consumer desire or drive for a product or service, and D_2 a higher level. As drive increases, the gradient of generalization also increases. In other words, the more a consumer feels the need to buy a certain product, the greater his or her tendency will be to choose a brand similar to the one he or she ordinarily uses if the latter is not readily available.

The relationships that occur because of generalization have two implications. First, an advertiser building up drive for a product must be careful not to create a desire for just the generic product—the desire must be for the specific brand. In an advertisement that induces thirst for ginger ale, for example, the marketer of Canada Dry wants to make consumers crave that brand, not ginger ale in general. Second, to take advantage of the gener-

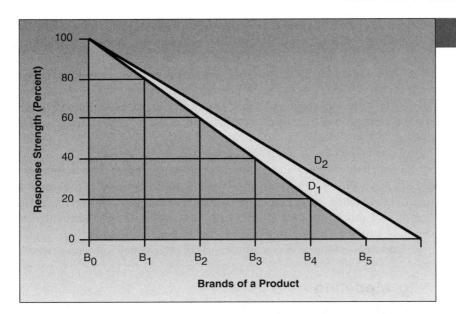

E x h i b i t **7-12**

Gradient of Generalization

This graph measures the tendency of consumers to switch brands. The more a consumer feels the need to buy a certain product, the greater the tendency to generalize across brands.

Source: John A. Howard, *Marketing Theory* (Boston, MA: Allyn & Bacon, 1965), p. 109.

alization principle, a company's product should be readily available. If it is not, the buyer is apt to settle for a similar brand to avoid both the delay and inconvenience of looking elsewhere for the preferred brand.[50]

In many cases, generalization is an unwanted variable in consumption. Marketers want their specific brand—not the generic product—to be the drive reinforcer. Sometimes, however, generalization is a marketing goal. In family branding, for example, a marketer may display a well-known name prominently on every product in a line. Birds Eye's use of its name and logo on each of a broad range of products is a case in point. In using family branding, the marketer hopes consumers considering a new product will associate it favorably with the quality standards of familiar products in the line.

Procter & Gamble uses an opposite strategy—product differentiation. The objective here is to provide a different brand for almost every conceivable consumer need and so lock out competitors from entering the entire product category. For example, Procter & Gamble markets several brands of toilet tissue. White Cloud is promoted for its softness; Charmin is aimed at the premium market, offering both softness and fluffiness at a premium price; and a recently tested brand, Certain, is lotion-treated to appeal to consumers for whom the product's cleaning effectiveness is a primary concern. Thus, various combinations of benefits appeal to several different market segments. The competition that Procter & Gamble encourages among its own brands helps reach the broadest possible market without actually cannibalizing its own products.

7-2f Discrimination

In psychology, **discrimination** training involves teaching a person who instinctively responds identically to two stimuli to respond to each differently. The person is conditioned to react to one stimulus while extinguishing the other.[51] Marketers use consumer discrimination to convince people that one brand of aspirin is more effective than another, that Kellogg's corn flakes taste better than competitors' brands, or that Xerox stock is a better investment than IBM. Discrimination is, then, a process through which consumers restrict their range of responses and attach themselves to a particular brand. The extent to which consumers are able to differentiate one brand from another is mostly influenced by three factors: product differentiation, brand image, and product familiarity. Consumers are likely to distinguish one brand from another when the products are effectively differentiated, that is, when there are perceived differences in costs and/or benefits among them. Consumers are also likely to distinguish a brand from that of competitors when the image of the brand is both positive and strong. Lastly, consumers who are familiar with the product category are likely to differentiate easily among different brands.

discrimination Learning to respond to two similar stimuli differently.

When product differences are easily recognizable, such as those between a Chevrolet Corvette and a Toyota Celica, it is relatively easy for consumers to discriminate. But when products are generically equal and undifferentiated, as is the case in any competitive or parity category, the challenge is to encourage consumers to perceive one brand as different from the others. This is achieved through product positioning, a strategy of establishing a "place" for a product in the consumer's frame of reference that differentiates it from others in the same category. Thus Excedrin became "the extra-strength pain reliever" to distinguish it from simple aspirin. In the soft-drink category, 7-Up is positioned as the "uncola" to emphasize its uniqueness in the soft-drinks market.

Research on cigarette and cola consumption has shown that consumers do not usually detect significant differences from one brand of a given product to another. The presence of brand labels does affect taste perception in that users express preference for "their" brands over others on the basis of "taste." Thus, both external factors (such as color or design of labels, packaging, and advertising) and internal factors (such as mental set, past experience, self-esteem, and risk reduction) are interrelated in brand perception.[52]

7-2g Modeling

modeling The process through which an individual learns a behavior by observing the behavior of others and the consequences of this behavior.

Modeling is the process through which an individual learns a behavior by observing the behavior of others and the consequences of this behavior.[53] Several factors affect the extent to which consumers emulate a model's marketplace behavior.[54]

Characteristics of the Model   Research has shown that modeling behavior is enhanced if the model is perceived to be physically attractive, credible, or successful.[55]

Characteristics of the Modeled Behavior   The likelihood of modeling is enhanced if the model is perceived to be in a realistic situation doing realistic things, such as overcoming difficulties and then succeeding. Also, the likelihood of modeling is enhanced if the sequence of the modeled behavior is vividly detailed.[56]

Characteristics of the Observers   Identification with the model is an important factor influencing emulation. Furthermore, people who are dependent and/or lack self-esteem are particularly prone to emulate the behavior of successful models. People who highly value the consequences of the model's behavior are also likely to imitate it.[57]

Characteristics of the Modeled Behavior Consequences   A person is more likely to emulate a model if he or she perceives that the model's actions have led to positive consequences for him or her. In other words, if the model is rewarded and observers see that outcome, the observers are likely to emulate the model, anticipating that they will be rewarded similarly.[58]

7-2h Cognitive Theory

cognitive theory An alternative to behavior analysis that emphasizes the thinking rather than the doing aspects of learning.

Cognitive theory is an alternative to behavior analysis that emphasizes the thinking rather than the doing aspects of learning. Consumer researchers believe that consumers learn mostly from experience with marketplace objects and events. As shown in Exhibit 7-13, cognitive theory involves a four-stage process: formulation of hypotheses, exposure, encoding, and integration.[59]

During hypotheses formulation, the consumer generates specific testable assumptions about products or brands. Suppose Brenda takes Brand X headache remedy. It does nothing to relieve her pain, and she wonders why. She develops hypotheses to account for its failure. Perhaps it's not strong enough for very severe headaches. Perhaps her headache is of the kind that requires a different brand. Perhaps there is no brand powerful enough to take the headache away.

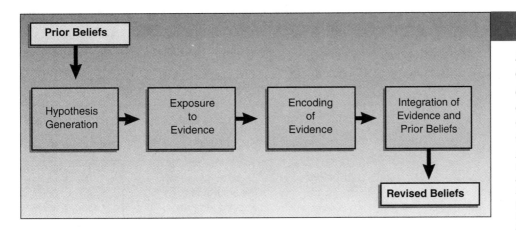

E x h i b i t 7-13

A Cognitive Model of Consumer Learning

Consumers learn mostly from experience with marketplace objects and events. The learning occurs as a four-stage process.

Source: From "Managing What Consumers Learn from Experience" by Stephen J. Hoch and John Deighton in *Journal of Marketing,* April 1989, Volume 53, p. 3. Reprinted with permission from *Journal of Marketing,* published by the American Marketing Association.

Next, Brenda tests each hypothesis about a product or brand. This exposure to evidence may be passive or active. She may evaluate information about Brand X if and when it is presented to her (passive observation), or she may check up on Brand X, looking up its performance record in *Consumer Reports* or talking to her doctor (active information seeking).

As the result of exposure to evidence, Brenda now has more information about a product or brand. By encoding the evidence, she attempts to make sense of that information by categorizing it to fit the hypotheses she made earlier. Perhaps she has found out more about the type of headache Brand X is formulated to relieve. Perhaps her doctor has introduced her to another brand that is stronger.

Once new information is gathered, it is assimilated with Brenda's earlier assumptions about a product or brand. Through integration of new information with earlier hypotheses, Brenda forms certain beliefs. If new information supports her earlier hypothesis, that hypothesis now becomes a belief. If she finds evidence that Brand X was formulated for mild headaches only, she believes that it is not a strong enough brand for her headaches.

How Consumers Turn Hypotheses into Beliefs   The cognitive theory model suggests that there are three important moderators that affect how consumers process information from hypothesis generation to integration of evidence with prior beliefs. These are demonstrated in Exhibit 7-14.

Familiarity with a product or service affects consumer learning by making the consumer less likely to be influenced by new or conflicting information in the marketplace. Ambiguity affects learning, too. When experience is clear (low in ambiguity), the consumer learns fast and information in the marketplace plays only a secondary role. This is because the consumer relies more on prior experience than on new information. If experience is unclear (high in ambiguity), however, information in the marketplace becomes a primary source of influence. Marketers can help reduce ambiguity by providing information that encourages desirable beliefs about a brand and weakens others. Motivation affects the generation of hypotheses by the consumer. The more motivated the consumer, the more hypotheses are likely to be generated and the more likely the consumer is to seek out information about the brand. Moreover, consumers who are motivated to learn are less likely to rely on advertising as evidence to test their hypotheses about different brands.[60]

The Value of Cognitive Theory to Marketers   Cognitive theory is increasingly used by marketers to develop marketing strategy. In this section, we'll explore two examples of marketing strategies developed from cognitive theory. Exhibits 7-15 and 7-16 summarize

Exhibit 7-14				
Consumer Readiness to Learn from Experience	**How Motivated Are Consumers to Learn?**	**What Do Consumers Already Know?**	**How Much Can Experience Teach?**	
			Little (High Ambiguity)	*A Lot* (Low Ambiguity)
	Highly Motivated	*Unfamiliar*	Learning is most susceptible to management.	Learning is spontaneous, rapid, and difficult to manage.
		Familiar	Formation of "superstitious" beliefs is possible. Existing beliefs inhibit "suggestibility."	
	Weakly Motivated	*Unfamiliar*	Learning is slow to start and difficult to sustain but is susceptible to management.	Learning is difficult to initiate and, once started, is difficult to manage.
		Familiar	Complacency inhibits initiation of learning, so experience is unresponsive to management.	

Source: From "Managing What Consumers Learn from Experience" by Stephen J. Hoch and John Deighton in *Journal of Marketing,* April 1989, Volume 53, p. 11. Reprinted with permission from *Journal of Marketing,* published by the American Marketing Association.

the implications of the cognitive theory model for marketers of two different types of brands: market leaders (top dogs) and brands with little or no market share (underdogs).

Strategies for Marketing Top Dogs   Three key strategies for top dogs are reinforcement, blocking, and explaining.

- *Reinforcement* If target consumers are unfamiliar with a product category yet are highly motivated to learn, communications that reinforce the brand work well for top-dog marketers. Ryder Trucks, for example, tells consumers that they have three choices when it comes to home removals: "Pay someone else an arm and a leg; borrow your brother-in-law's truck; or Ryder." The advertising message reinforces the strength of the Ryder name by blocking the consumer from evoking any other brand than Ryder, thus keeping competitors from being considered.

  Top-dog marketers can also reinforce their brands by influencing the attributes that target consumers consider when making a brand choice. For example, a leading brand of cereal that repeatedly states "provides the recommended daily allowances of eight important vitamins and minerals" is prompting consumers to evaluate all brands of cereal based on their vitamin and mineral content.

E x h i b i t **7-15**

Top Dog Strategies

How Motivated Are Consumers to Learn?	What Do Consumers Already Know?	How Much Can Experience Teach?	
		Little (High Ambiguity)	*A Lot (Low Ambiguity)*
Highly Motivated	*Unfamiliar*	Reinforce the agenda.	Explain the experience.
	Familiar	Block exposure to evidence.	
Weakly Motivated	*Unfamiliar*	When consumer motivation is low, inertia works to the top dog's advantage. Strategies designed for the highly motivated consumer are also appropriate here, though implementation should be easier.	
	Familiar		

Source: From "Managing What Consumers Learn from Experience" by Stephen J. Hoch and John Deighton in *Journal of Marketing,* April 1989, Volume 53, p. 12. Reprinted with permission from *Journal of Marketing,* published by the American Marketing Association.

E x h i b i t **7-16**

Underdog Strategies

How Motivated Are Consumers to Learn?	What Do Consumers Already Know?	How Much Can Experience Teach?	
		Little (High Ambiguity)	*A Lot (Low Ambiguity)*
Highly Motivated	*Unfamiliar*	When the consumer *wants* to learn, natural curiosity works to the underdog's advantage. Strategies designed for the weakly motivated consumer are also appropriate here.	
	Familiar		
Weakly Motivated	*Unfamiliar*	Disrupt the agenda.	Facilitate trial.
	Familiar	Do everything.	

Source: From "Managing What Consumers Learn from Experience" by Stephen J. Hoch and John Deighton in *Journal of Marketing,* April 1989, Volume 53, p. 11. Reprinted with permission from *Journal of Marketing,* published by the American Marketing Association.

Another means of reinforcement is to explain to consumers the differences between the brand advertised and its competitors in terms that make the marketer's brand the obvious best choice. In a campaign for Bufferin pain reliever, celebrity Angela Lansbury explains that Bufferin is unique because it's the only medication that has "buffers" to prevent stomach upset.

- *Blocking* When consumers are both motivated to learn and are already familiar with the product and its various competitors, blocking the consumer's exposure to evidence is a powerful strategy. AT&T used it to combat competition with the simple statement, "Why change if you are happy with what you have?" This effectively dissuaded consumers from questioning their current telephone service or from checking out competitors. Another way to block exposure to evidence is to derogate competitors' messages. Recently, a number of cellular providers have launched TV and radio commercials in which they show a typical service provider offering poor service, while they tout that they provide excellent service.

- *Explaining* When consumers are highly motivated to learn and their experience with the brand is not necessarily ambiguous, explaining the brand is an effective top-dog strategy. In a campaign for Perdue Chicken, for example, Mr. Perdue himself explains that the reason his chicken tastes particularly good is that they are fed an especially healthy diet.

Strategies for Marketing Underdogs   For the underdog, the best advice might be to try a little of everything in order to win attention away from the market leaders and competing brands. Consumers may be happy with the brand they already use and need a reason to switch to a less familiar alternative. Comparative advertising or refutational advertising—messages that discount the claims of competitors—may be particularly effective. Also consider the strategies of disruption and trial facilitation.

- *Disruption* If consumers are familiar with the brand but unmotivated to try it— perhaps because of loyalty to a competitor—an effective underdog strategy is to disrupt the consumer's feeling of security with his or her current brand. This may be done by offering consumers incentives to reevaluate their brand choices by searching and comparing. Lee Iacocca, as spokesperson for Chrysler, did just this in an advertising campaign that stated "We challenge you to compare."

- *Facilitating trial* When consumers are unmotivated to learn, experience may be the best teacher. Advertising should make it easy and pleasurable for consumers to try out the product. Underdogs can offer free samples and free trial periods or simply design advertising that invites the consumer to try out the brand, such as Pepsi's campaign with the slogan "Try it and let your taste decide."

Marketing Management—Implications and Actions

Understanding how consumers learn helps marketers:

- Foster brand loyalty and reduce brand switching.
- Position the good or service as a reward, not a punishment.
- Use modeling to increase acceptance of new products.
- Develop targeted strategies for top-dog or underdog positions

---

7-3 Perception

What makes a consumer prefer one brand of instant coffee over another? The leading brands are all very much alike in taste and convenience, and theoretically one brand should be perfectly substitutable for another. Yet studies reveal that some households always buy the same brand.[61] What are the distinguishing features these consumers perceive between their preferred brands and the others on the market?

Brand image, pricing, and risk avoidance are all aspects of consumer perception. The way a product or service is perceived is intricately tied to the share of market it gains and the consumers it attracts. Understanding perception and the factors determining how consumers view products and services is central to effective marketing.

For our purposes, we may define perception as the way in which an individual gathers, processes, and interprets information from the environment. Consumer perception can be approached from three vantage points. First, perception can be understood through its relation to sensory modalities, that is, the effects of the five senses on the way in which products are perceived. Second, Gestalt psychology looks at how consumers perceive information within and as part of the context in which it is presented. Gestalt theory is particularly useful in making decisions related to advertising and packaging. Third, consumer interpretations of perceptions add an abstract dimension to the study of perception. Interpretation involves such intangibles as brand image, risk, and attribution in the way consumers perceive products.

7-3a Sensory Perception

The five senses—sight, sound, smell, touch, and taste—govern **sensory perception.** Sensory perception focuses on specific attributes of a product or service and how these attributes are understood and ultimately evaluated by consumers. For example, sensory perception of a personal computer includes the tactile feel of the keys on the keyboard, the view of the monitor, and the sounds emitted from the computer when it is in operation.

Factors Affecting Sensory Perception   Sensory perception is affected by two major sets of factors—stimulus factors and individual response factors (see Exhibit 7-17).

Stimulus Factors   Sensory cues are such attributes as color, shape, and size for visual cues; tempo and pitch for aural cues; sweet, bitter, and floral for olfactory cues; and soft, coarse, and silky for tactile cues. Color is a powerful cue in visual perception, long recognized by marketers in their use of color in product design, packaging, promotion, and store decor. Color can affect consumers' experience with a product in a variety of ways. The packaging of coffee, for example, is traditionally brown, thus reinforcing the product and its attributes.[62]

Music can be a powerful aural cue in advertising. Perception researchers have explored the relationship between the technical properties of music—tempo, pitch, and so on—with emotional responses, finding that certain types of music can induce a range of emotions, from solemnity, to dignity, to triviality, to gaiety.[63] Jingles are a powerful awareness-creation tool for advertisers who want a certain tune to be associated, through repetition, with a certain product or service.

> **sensory perception**
> Perception governed by the five senses—sight, sound, smell, touch, and taste. Sensory perception focuses on specific attributes of a product or service and how these attributes are understood and ultimately evaluated by consumers.

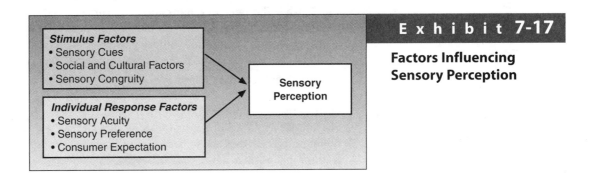

Stimulus Factors
- Sensory Cues
- Social and Cultural Factors
- Sensory Congruity

Individual Response Factors
- Sensory Acuity
- Sensory Preference
- Consumer Expectation

Sensory Perception

E x h i b i t **7-17**

Factors Influencing Sensory Perception

Perceptions of smell are greatly influenced by cultural and social factors. As one consumer researcher points out, odors are "more than experiences dallying with the chemical composition of substances. . . . Odors involve emotional and other conditioned responses which may be too varied and diverse to catalog."[64] Through the use of scent strips in the promotion of fragrances in print media, marketers hope to evoke emotional responses. In the future, products such as coffee, chocolates, or room deodorizers may all be promoted with the aid of scent strips.

Perceptions of taste are, of course, all-important in food marketing. When consumers complained that rice cakes tasted like Styrofoam, Quaker Oats developed and promoted a rice cake that tasted like buttered popcorn with significant sales results.[65]

Perceptions of the textures of clothing, car upholstery, hand lotion, and carpets occur through the sense of touch. But, as with odors and tastes, our responses are to a large extent conditioned. Manufacturers of fabric softeners and synthetic fibers cater to our learned responses because interpretation of tactile stimuli varies according to individual and social learning. In the United States, a soft bed sheet is considered desirable, whereas in other countries a coarse cotton sheet is preferable.[66]

Lighting also plays an important role in sensory perception. For example, display lighting, a component of store atmospherics, does affect consumer behavior. In one study, shoppers examined and handled significantly more items under "bright" lighting conditions than under "soft" lighting conditions. This finding signifies that the brightness of lighting does affect the level of arousal in shoppers.[67] Another study showed that shoppers spent significantly more time at "lit displays" than "nonlit" ones.[68]

Sensory congruity is the extent to which one sensory cue for a product is perceived to be consistent with its other sensory cues. Imagine a men's winter suit that is pink in color. The color certainly is not culturally congruent with other aspects of the outfit. Because of its visual incongruity, consumers are likely to evaluate the suit negatively. Congruity also influences scent reactions. That is, a pleasant scent may not elicit a positive mood when that scent is mismatched with other features of the product. For example, a floral scent (positive ambient scent) is unlikely to induce a positive response at a motorcycle dealership, because the scent does not match other image characteristics of the dealership.[69]

Individual Response Factors There are three important individual response factors affecting sensory perception: sensory acuity, sensory preferences, and consumer expectations.

- *Sensory acuity* Different people tend to have different capacities to recognize and differentiate among certain sensory cues. In scent acuity, for example, research has uncovered that women consistently out-perform men in their ability to identify odors. Other factors such as age, illness, and smoking can lessen scent acuity.

- *Sensory preferences* The perception and evaluation of a given sensory product feature are likely to be influenced by consumers' preferences. For example, in olfactory perception, research suggests that while people tend to agree on what smells are "dreadful" (decaying vegetation, spoiled milk, and skunk secretions), it is not so obvious what smells are desirable. However, floral scents tend to be consistently viewed as pleasant across cultures and individuals. Children dislike oily smells, while the smell of onions and chives are enjoyed most by young adults. One cannot predict odor preference on the basis of personal temperament, but introverts are generally more receptive to unusual odors than are extroverts. Males are more predictable in their odor preferences than are females.

- *Consumer expectation* Expectations affect how certain product features are likely to be perceived and evaluated. For example, consumers expect a product's visual characteristics to appear in certain ways—such as stereo components with a matte black finish. If the stereo's visual features violate these expectations, such as a finish of lime-green enamel, consumers are not likely to perceive the stereo's product features in a positive light.

7-3b Gestalt Theory of Perception

The five senses play an integral part in human comprehension and interpretation of experience. Beyond this, however, the processes through which we organize sensations demand a higher level of perception, known as the **Gestalt principle,** which can be stated simply as the whole adds up to more than the sum of its parts. Gestalt theorists contend that a whole object cannot be perceived simply by adding up our perceptions of its parts. Some of the parts may, in fact, become unobservable when combined with other parts. For example, the sensations of "brownness," "smoothness," "fizziness," "coolness," and "wetness" all add up into the meaningful unit, "I have a glass of cola in my hand." Gestalt theory holds that we perceive form above all else. This is useful in understanding how individuals process perceptual data into meaningful wholes. Think of the different versions of the McDonald's theme tune, "We Love to See You Smile." In some commercials, it's fast and bouncy; in others, it's a slow ballad. Sometimes the tune is sung by a single vocalist, sometimes by a group, and sometimes it's played as an instrumental. But whatever form it takes, it is easily recognizable and consumers immediately link it with McDonald's. In Gestalt terms, the form we perceive remains constant even though some specific features of it change.

Because lower-order variables—color, single tones, and the like—can change without affecting our perception of form, the determinants of overall form must be based on higher-order variables. Foremost among these is the principle of figure and ground. To illustrate this principle, let's focus on one form of perception: vision. Any contour divides stimulation of the eye into two regions, and the shape of both cannot be perceived simultaneously. At a given moment, only one shape is seen. That is the figure. That shape appears to be interposed between viewer and some indeterminate backdrop, the ground.[70] As shown in Exhibit 7-18, perception of form is a process determined by the ability to distinguish figure from ground.

To understand how this translates into the perception of marketing communications, consider a point-of-purchase display designed to distract customers from competitive items at retail. The most effective point-of-purchase materials are those that use colors and shapes in an arresting way not typically found in the surrounding environment. Also, if the display is large, actually moves or creates the illusion of motion, or is separated from other displays either physically or through some means of bracketing (for example, using color borders around a product display), it is more effective.

Factors Influencing Gestalt Perception   Stimulus factors are the physical, chemical, electromagnetic, and other observable characteristics of the person, object, or situation perceived. Individual response factors are determinants of perception within the perceiver—the consumer (see Exhibit 7-19).

Stimulus Factors   Stimulus factors affecting consumer sensory perception include color, contrast, size, intensity, movement, position, isolation, and repeated exposure.

- *Color and contrast*   Although a color print or television advertisement generally captures greater attention than one in black and white, it loses impact when seen in the context of other color advertisements. The principle of contrast suggests that, in

> **Gestalt principle**
> The processes through which we organize the sensations that play an integral part in human comprehension and interpretation of experience and that demand a higher level of perception beyond the five senses.

Exhibit 7-18

Distinguishing Figure and Ground

Does your eye alternate between the two shapes here?

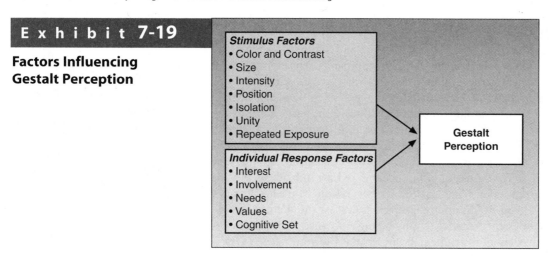

E x h i b i t 7-19

Factors Influencing Gestalt Perception

a full-color context, a black-and-white advertisement is more likely to be noticed. Color perception involves subjective judgments. While fluorescent colors may gain attention, they may also cause irritation. Some products seem to have very limited ranges of acceptable color. Would you wash your hands with jet-black soap? Our perception of body cleanliness traditionally demands white or pastel colors, although new soap products in brown and green are gaining acceptance today. Shampoos, on the other hand, have always come in deep and varied colors.

- *Size* Large sizes tend to attract greater attention than small, but the ratio of size increase to attention gained is not a simple one. The larger an object is, the greater any enlargement must be to be perceived. The amount of size increase needed for its perception is proportionately related to the initial size of the stimulus. Exhibit 7-20 demonstrates how positioning large numerals in white space attracts attention.

- *Intensity* Intensity has to do with the strength of a stimulus, for example, the loudness of sounds or brightness of colors. More attention is usually gained as intensity increases. As with size, however, doubling the intensity of a stimulus does not double the attention given to it. There is only a fractional increase in attention.

- *Position* Position is one of the most interesting determinants of sensory perception. When a written language runs left to right down the page, as English does, the upper half of a page gets more attention than the lower half, the left-hand side more than the right. However, languages with different movement, such as Arabic or Japanese, give perceptual emphasis to other portions of a page.[71]

- *Isolation* Centering a small object in a virtually blank page draws the eye to it immediately. One television advertisement for an antacid began with a tiny rotating white sphere in a dark space—a dramatic use of the isolation principle.

- *Unity* Unity refers to the extent parts of a display (e.g., the visual components) connect in a meaningful way. Gestalt psychologists explain unity in terms of what they call figural goodness or "pragnanz." The Gestalt laws of proximity (i.e., elements that are closest to one another form a group), similarity (i.e., elements that are similar form a group), and common density (i.e., parts of a figure that have a common density form units) are ways to achieve unity.[72] One study conducted by consumer researchers instructed subjects to examine color photographs of living-room furniture. Some sets of furniture were consistent in style (i.e., all contemporary or all traditional); others were a random mix of styles. The consumer researchers found that aesthetic response was positively related to perceived unity of style (i.e., a consistent style). The greater the consistency of styles, the greater the perception of "beauty" of the furniture.[73]

E x h i b i t 7-20

Positioning the large numeral in white space gets this message across simply and quickly.

Source: Reprinted by permission of the American Red Cross and The Advertising Council.

- **Repeated exposure** Repeated exposure to the stimulus tends to increase liking towards the stimulus, up to a point. A recent study has found that the influence of repeated exposure to a product may be dependent on the level of complexity of the product design. The study has manipulated the level of complexity of clothing styles and asked consumers about their liking of the different designs. Consumers' preferences for visually complex product designs tend to increase with repeated exposures.[74]

- **Individual Response Factors** Factors unique to the individual perceiving the product or service play a vital role in Gestalt perception. Internal response factors cannot, however, be gauged with the same accuracy as stimulus factors. The physiological capacity to respond can be measured, but interest, attention, needs, memory, experiences, values, and cognitive sets are less quantifiable.

- **Interest** Interest varies from individual to individual. We can, however, make generalizations about similarities among groups. Women, for example, tend to be more easily stimulated than men by pictures of babies and children. Level of interest also influences brand perception. A Honda owner is more likely to notice Honda advertising than Yamaha advertising. Consumers tend to pay less attention to advertisements for lesser-known brands than for popular, widely distributed ones.

- **Involvement** Involvement is an indicator of how important something is to a person. The higher the level of involvement with a product or service, the more likely the consumer is to be attentive to its features and to interpret those features in a meaningful way. In contrast, consumers who are not involved are not likely to make the effort to understand product stimuli.[75] A recent study has shown that consumers use the dress code of sales people to make inferences about service quality and purchase intention. Specifically, consumers who noticed employees dressing professionally made inferences that the quality of the service is high and made decisions to purchase again from the same service establishment. Consumers who did not notice how sales people were dressed made no such inferences. What is interesting about this finding is the fact that consumers who were less involved made those inferences more often than did consumers who were more involved.

This is due to the fact that consumers who are more involved are likely to use more substantial cues to make inferences about service quality such as the service provider's promptness, responsiveness, and care in service delivery.[76]

- *Needs* Internal needs do, within certain limits, affect perception. Because of internal needs, a teenage girl in American society is likely to overestimate the good effects of cosmetic products. Because of cultural pressures, she is influenced by a need to appear attractive to others. Similarly, advertisements for Marlboro cigarettes cater to many men's needs to display signs of virility.

- *Values* Related to values is the theory of perceptual defense, which posits that individuals block out perceptions that, for various psychological or sociopsychological reasons, are repugnant to them. For instance, certain people with strong beliefs can "block out" alcohol or cigarette ads.[77]

- *Cognitive set* The cognitive set is the map one makes of one's world, through which certain skills, experiences, needs, values, and goals are elevated and others lowered. This map takes into account the individual's physical and mental capabilities and sociocultural background and environment. One person's view of New York may be composed of a law office on Park Avenue, the theater, French restaurants, tennis courts, Bloomingdale's, and exclusive Sutton Place. Another's may be composed of an apartment in Spanish Harlem, the Iglesia Pentecostal church, and a tiny groceria.

A person's cognitive set underlies all perception and influences the selectivity of perception—how the same objective event can be perceived very differently by different observers. In the game of Chinese Whispers, children whisper a message from one to another. The last child repeats the message out loud, and, invariably, it bears little resemblance to the original message. The message is distorted by each child's perception.

7-3c How Consumers Interpret Perceptions

A consumer is moved to select a given product from among a group of alternatives not so much by the product's intrinsic qualities as by his or her perception of those qualities. The consumer interprets those perceptions through filters of individual needs, desires, and personality characteristics, as well as a host of situational factors. How consumers interpret their own perceptions about products can be examined in several areas: consumer categorization, consumer attributions, product/service quality, price perception, perceived value, and risk perception/risk reduction.

Consumer Categorization   **Categorization** is the psychological process through which a consumer compares the perception of a product with a mental representation of that product in memory. Given that there is a match between the perception and the mental representation, the consumer classifies the perceived product as representative of the product category in memory. Mei is given a glass of wine at a dinner party. Considering herself to be a connoisseur, she tries to figure out the vintage. Is it sweet or dry? Heavy or fruity? French or Italian? Can she take a guess at the vineyard?

Categorization can be analytic or nonanalytic. In **analytic categorization,** the perceived product has to conform to a set of necessary attributes before it can be put into a certain category.[78] Ariel may, for example, think of beer as having the following attributes: it is alcoholic, it has a certain color and taste, and it has distinctive foam. Presented with a new brand that is nonalcoholic, he is not likely to categorize it as beer at all. Since the product is missing the essential attribute of being alcoholic, he is likely to categorize it simply as a beverage, not as a beer.

Whereas in analytic categorization the consumer classifies a product by analyzing specific features, in **nonanalytic categorization,** he or she focuses on the entire pattern of features in a holistic manner.[79] If the overall impression fits the category, the product is accepted; if not, it is rejected. Therefore, presented with a nonalcoholic beverage that had the taste, fizz, color, and aroma of beer, Jeffery would add the beverage to his beer category.

FAQ

Is everyone's cognitive set the same size?

▶**categorization**
The psychological process through which a consumer compares the perception of a product with a mental representation of that product in memory.

▶**analytic categorization**
Having the perceived product conform to a set of necessary attributes before it can be put into a certain category.

▶**nonanalytic categorization**
The process by which the consumer classifies a product by focusing on the entire pattern of features in a holistic manner, whereas in analytic categorization the consumer classifies a product by analyzing specific features.

There are two other ways that consumers categorize brands in their memories, namely abstraction versus exemplar. An **abstraction** or prototype of the product is formed in memory by focusing on the product's important features and forming a category that associate those features in relation to the product. Suppose that a consumer encounters several food processor models that are different in terms of features such as number of blades, motor size, and bowl capacity. The abstraction model suggests that the consumer will construct a "composite" food processor that averages important attributes across different brands. For example, the consumer may form a prototype food processor that has five blades, a heavy-duty motor, and a 2.5-quart bowl. In contrast, an **exemplar** is the use of a particular brand that represents most other brands. In relation to food processors, the exemplar model suggests that the consumer may focus on an individual food processor (e.g., Cuisinart, Sunbeam, etc.) and use that brand to describe most other brands of food processors.[80]

The implications of categorization are important, particularly for marketers of new products or innovations. Presented with an innovative product for the first time, consumers are likely to try to assign it to a product category based on their knowledge of similar items. Correct categorization will help consumers accept the innovation, but improper categorization will lead them to shy away from it. By understanding how new products are categorized in the minds of target consumers, marketers can select strategies that lead to correct categorization.

Prototypicality Much research in consumer behavior has shown that shoppers enter the patronage process with expectations regarding what makes up a specific type of store, and that the knowledge about the store is processed holistically in the form of cognitive categorization mechanisms. In other words, shoppers have schemas in their mind representing prototypical stores (e.g., an image of what a good fashion clothing boutique is all about), and they compare that prototypical store image to a store they may evaluate in a shopping situation. If the store is perceived as matching the prototypical store image, then the shoppers evaluate the store positively; and conversely, if the store is perceived as not matching the prototype, they may evaluate the store negatively. For example, research has shown that consumers evaluate fast-food restaurants against prototypes. The psychological contrast between an actual restaurant and the prototype affects consumer attitudes toward the restaurant. Specifically, consumers have more favorable attitudes for fast-food restaurants high in typicality (matching the fast-food restaurant prototype) than restaurants low in typicality.[81]

Consumer Attributions **Attribution** is the process through which people connect events and behavior with causes. Consumers seek explanations for marketplace events, and the way they come up with answers affects how they feel toward related products, services, brands, and firms. For example, a salesperson at Sears is trying to help a shopper who is looking at a Kenmore washing machine. The salesperson compliments the customer for looking nice wearing a colorful outfit. The way the shopper interprets this complement may affect how she may feel about the salesperson, Sears, and the Kenmore brand. If she interprets the compliment as lacking in sincerity, then she may develop an unfavorable attitude. Conversely, believing that the compliment is sincere may make the shopper feel much better about the brand. This cause-and-effect association can be critical to marketers. Attribution can take three forms: product/service perception, self-perception, and person perception.[82]

Product/Service Perception A consumer buys a new camera, and within three months the film advance mechanism snaps. To understand the cause of the product failure, he or she tests such hypotheses as: Did I buy an inferior brand? Was the camera already faulty when I bought it? Do all the cameras this company manufactures have the same problem? These are **product/service perceptions**—the inferences consumers make about products/services, attributing their performance to specific qualities or features. How consumers attribute product failures affects the intensity of dissatisfaction consumers feel toward the brand. Specifically, if consumers attribute failure to inherent characteristics of the brand

abstraction A process in which concrete attributes of a product are associated with more meaningful aspects to the consumer.

exemplar A cognition used to classify incoming perceptions to attribute meaning to these perceptions.

attribution The process through which people connect events and behavior with causes. This cause-and-effect association can be critical to marketers. Attribution can take three forms: *product perception, self-perception,* and *person perception.*

product/service perception A form of mental inference (or attribution) that consumers make about products or services, attributing product or service performance to specific qualities or features.

(internal attribution), then the dissatisfaction is likely to be strong. In contrast, attributing the product failure to situational factors having little to do with the brand (external attribution) may lead to less dissatisfaction. For example, a Toyota Corolla car owner is experiencing car trouble (let's say transmission and clutch problems). If he infers that the reason for the car trouble is that he bought a lemon (internal attribution), then his feelings toward the Toyota Corolla are likely to be very negative. However, if he attributes the car problems to the rough road conditions and the way he abuses the car, then he may not feel that bad about the car. This is an external attribution.

Psychologists refer to this phenomenon as *attribution theory*. Specifically, the extent to which consumers make internal versus external attribution is referred to as the *attribution locus of control*. Attributions are characterized by two other dimensions, namely stability and controllability. *Attributions of stability* given product/service failure refer to the extent to which the consumer attributes the cause of the product or service failure to a one-time event versus a "stable" event—an event that does seem to vary over time, that occurs frequently, or that is permanent. In contrast, *attributions of controllability* given product/service failure refer to the extent to which the consumer attributes the cause of product or service failure to events that could have been controlled by the firm versus those that could not have been controlled.

A recent experiment illustrates the effects of attributions of stability and controllability on consumer behavior. The experiment involved consumers reacting to various situations involving an order of a moderately priced steak in a restaurant. The scenario described the study participant as ordering a steak dinner cooked medium, but the steak was not prepared that way. Respondents who made unstable attributions felt less dissatisfied with the service than did those who made stable attributions. That is, consumers who considered the bad steak to be a "one-time fluke" do not feel as bad about the restaurant as did those who felt that poor steak preparation was common at that restaurant.

With respect to attributions of controllability, the expectation was that subjects who make uncontrollable attributions are likely to be less dissatisfied with the service than those who make controllable attributions. That is, consumers who considered the serving of the bad steak to be a situation that could not have been controlled (e.g., too busy in the kitchen) would not feel as bad about the restaurant as would those who feel that this occurrence could have been controlled. However, the hypothesis pertaining to attributions of controllability was not supported by the data.[83]

Self-Perception A consumer makes a donation to a charity without really knowing much about the cause it serves. He or she later asks: Do I really believe it was a deserving cause? Did I make the donation because my friend was watching? The causes to which consumers attribute their own behavior are a dimension of their **self-perception.** Research has shown that brand attitude and preference is influenced by self-perceptions. In other words, if a consumer perceives herself as using a specific brand, she will infer that she must like it.

Person Perception A salesperson approaches a customer in a shoe store and praises the features of Adidas sneakers. The customer thinks: Why is this salesperson trying to sell me Adidas sneakers instead of a cheaper pair? Is it because he is likely to make more money selling Adidas than other brands? Is it because the Adidas brand really is better? **Person perceptions** are the inferences consumers make about the reasons behind the actions of others. Person perception can affect source credibility. In the case of the salesperson, if the consumer interprets the salesperson's action as having an ulterior motive, then the salesperson becomes less credible, and of course less persuasive. Psychologists refer to this phenomenon as the *discounting principle*. Discounting occurs when the consumer making the attribution decides that external pressures are provoking the salesperson to act that way—that is, the act is not a true reflection of the quality of Adidas shoes.

In contrast, suppose the salesperson does something unexpected. The salesperson asserts that he gets an extra bonus trying to get his customers to buy Reebok shoes, not Adidas, but that he truly believes that Adidas shoes are the best. Here the consumer is likely to believe the salesperson and may end up buying Adidas shoes. What happened here, psychologically speaking, is that the consumer has augmented the weight of the salesperson

self-perception A form of mental inference (or attribution) in which consumers attribute their own behavior, such as the purchase of a brand, as reflecting their preference for that brand.

person perception A form of mental inference (or attribution) consumers make about the reasons behind the actions of others.

recommendation for Adidas. Psychologists refer to this phenomenon as the *augmentation principle*.[84]

Consumers also have a tendency to make a *fundamental attribution error* in person perception. In other words, consumers are biased to attribute behaviors to people, not the situation. They explain the behavior of people by attributing a personal characteristic motivating the person to engage in the observed action. They are less likely to explain the behavior by attributing it to external factors that made the person do it. For example, suppose a salesperson is having a bad day because his boss reprimanded him for being late that day. The salesperson's mood suffers. He does not greet a customer who walks in the show room. He then approaches the customer and asks if he can help, but the approach seems cold. When the customer decides to ask questions, the salesperson responds, but not in an enthusiastic way. The customer in this situation forms the impression that the salesperson is aloof, unfriendly, and incompetent. The customer does not know that the salesperson is in a bad mood because his boss reprimanded him. It is easy for the customer to attribute the salesperson's behavior to personality characteristics rather than situational factors. This is what the fundamental attribution error is all about.[85]

Researchers have recently documented the effects of a *positivity bias* in the way consumers make attributions about service providers. When consumers have little experience with a service, positive information about a single employee leads to inferences that the firm's other employees are similarly positive. In contrast, negative information does not lead to inferences that the firm's other employees are similarly negative.[86]

Perceptions of Product/Service Quality   Perceived product/service quality is a perceptual outcome generated from processing product or service features that lead the consumer to make inferences about the quality of that product or service. Typically, a measure of product or service quality involves a self-report questionnaire in which the consumer is asked to rate the quality of the product or services on a nine-point semantic differential scale (poor/excellent, inferior/superior, low standards/high standards).[87] Typical dimensions of perceived quality of durable goods include ease of use, versatility, durability, serviceability, performance, and prestige. *Ease of use* refers to how easily the product can be used by the customer; the easier the use of the product, the higher the perception of quality. *Versatility* refers to added product features that distinguish the product from its stripped-down version. Thus, a versatile product is a product that goes beyond its basic model. *Durability* refers to the extent to which the product has longevity. *Serviceability* refers to the extent to which consumers feel the product is easy to repair. *Performance* refers to how well the product does what it is supposed to do. *Prestige* refers to the extent to which the ownership of the product bestows status on the owner.[88] See Exhibit 7-21.

With respect to service quality, consumer researchers generally have adopted one of two conceptualizations. The first is the "Nordic" perspective, so-called because it was developed by Norwegian scholars, and it defines the dimensions of service quality in global terms as consisting of functional and technical quality.[89] *Functional quality* represents how the service is delivered; that is, it defines customers' perceptions of the interactions that take place during service delivery. For example, a consumer gets a haircut. His perception of the functional quality of this service is the quality of the interaction with the hair stylist, the person who took the appointment, and the person who processed payment. *Technical quality* reflects the outcome of the service act, or what the customer receives in the service encounter. Going back to the hair salon example, technical quality is the quality of the haircut.

The second conceptualization, the "American" perspective, uses terms that describe service encounter characteristics such as reliability, responsiveness, empathy, assurance, and tangibles.[90] Using the hair salon as the context, *reliability* means receiving the same haircut time and time again. *Responsiveness* means that the hair stylists and other service personnel at the hair salon are attentive to the needs of their customers. *Empathy* means that the service personnel can understand the customer's feelings or attitude toward the service experience. *Assurance* means that the service provider guarantees that the customer will be satisfied with the outcome of the service. *Tangibles* refer to evidence of the outcome

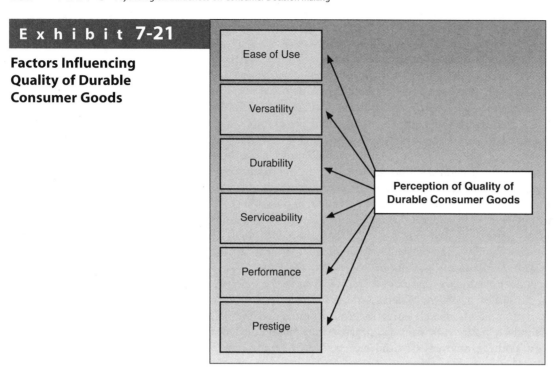

E x h i b i t　7-21

Factors Influencing Quality of Durable Consumer Goods

of the service. In the context of the hair salon, having a good haircut is tangible evidence of the quality of the service.

Recent research construed service quality based on the customer's evaluation of three dimensions of the service encounter: (1) the customer-employee interaction, (2) the service environment, and (3) the outcome.[91] Each of the primary dimensions of service quality (interaction, environment, and outcome) has three subdimensions. Customers aggregate their evaluations of the subdimensions to form their perceptions of the service provider's performance on each of the three primary dimensions. Those perceptions then lead to an overall service quality perception (see Exhibit 7-22).

In regard to the *customer-employee interaction dimension*, the research indicates that three distinct factors constitute customer perceptions of interaction quality. These are the

E x h i b i t　7-22

Factors Influencing Perception of Quality of Service

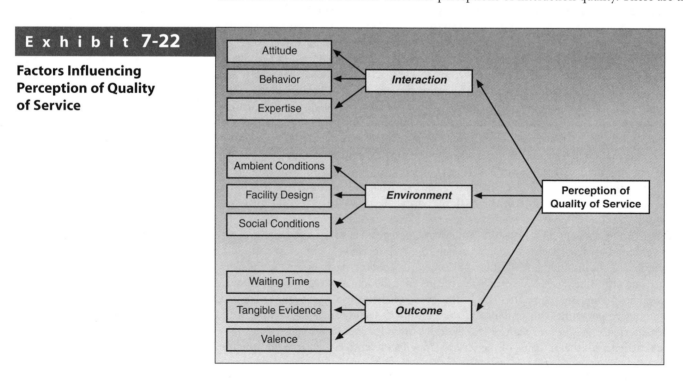

attitude, behaviors, and expertise of the service personnel. Consider the following comment from a consumer: "The staff was friendly [attitude] and knowledgeable [expertise], and I was greeted as soon as I walked in the door [behavior]."

The second dimension of service quality is the *service environment*. The service environment is made up of three subdimensions: ambient conditions, facility design, and social factors. *Ambient conditions* refer to nonvisual aspects, such as temperature, scent, and music. *Facility design* refers to the layout or architecture of the environment and can be either practical or visually pleasing or some combination of the two. *Social conditions* refer to the number and type of people in the service setting as well as their behaviors. For example, an unruly crowd can exert a negative influence on the perception of service quality; and, similarly, the disturbance caused by a crying baby can affect consumers' attitudes toward service.

The final dimension of service quality is the *outcome*. Outcome is what the customer is left with when the service job is done. Thus, the service outcome should contribute to service quality perceptions. Service outcome is influenced by three factors. One is *waiting time*. In most cases, consumers feel negative about the service outcome if they had to wait for a long time, and many feel positive if the service was provided in a timely manner. Another influence on service outcome perceptions is *tangible elements* that the service produces. Customers use any tangible evidence of the service outcome as a proxy for judging performance. In the context of the hair salon example, the customer may say "I like XYZ Salon because they give me the hair style I want." *Valence* is the third factor influencing outcome. That is, valence captures and groups those aspects that cause customers to believe the service outcome is good or bad, regardless of their evaluation of any other aspect of the experience. Using the sample of the hair salon, the customer may say, "The experience I receive visiting Hair Salon XYZ is wonderful."

A product (or a service) perceived to be of high quality tends to contribute to consumer satisfaction toward the product (service).[92] However, recent research has shown that consumer satisfaction may be a factor in how consumers perceive quality, too.[93] Some consumers are cognitively oriented (they tend to evaluate a product or service by thinking about the costs and benefits of the product or service). For these consumers, they first evaluate the features of the product or service and arrive at a perception of quality. This perception of quality guides their feelings of satisfaction with the product or service. In contrast, other consumers are affectively oriented. For these people, their satisfaction or dissatisfaction with the product or service biases their perception of quality. In other words, their perception of product (or service) quality is mostly determined by how they feel about the product (service) to begin with.

Risk Perception/Risk Reduction

Risk perception/risk reduction is a perceptual process and behavior outcomes generated from the perception of risk in the purchase of a product or service. Specifically, the model says that consumers see risk in what they purchase and act to reduce that risk. The risk they see (perceived risk) involves two components: severity of consequences and the uncertainty related to those consequences (see Exhibit 7-23).[94] For example, consumers, when offered a deal from a travel company to vacation in a fancy hotel at an island resort, may see risks such as:

▶ **risk perception/risk reduction** A perceptual process and behavior outcomes generated from the perception of risk in the purchase of a product or service.

- The hotel may not be as nice as it appears in the brochure.
- They will be charged excessively for making telephone calls at the hotel.
- The meals provided will be disappointing.
- They may get sick from food or water during the trip.
- The meals provided by the hotel may be unsatisfactory.
- There may be political unrest or military trouble during the holiday.
- The tour operator will go bankrupt.
- There may be a natural disaster (such as an earthquake) during the holiday.
- The tour guide may quit the tour operator company during the holiday.
- The tour representative guide will not participate in such activities as windsurfing or scuba diving.[95]

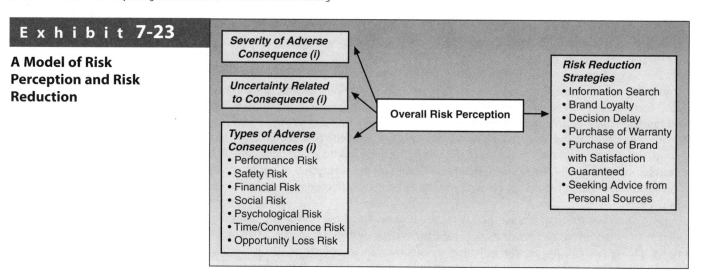

Exhibit 7-23

A Model of Risk Perception and Risk Reduction

Each of the above is a risk attribute, and each has two components: severity of the consequence and probability of the consequence. The severity of the consequence reflects the fact that each of the risk attributes varies in consumers' perceptions of how bad each consequence is. For example, if we examine the risk attributes above, research has shown that most consumers feel that "the hotel may not be as nice as it appears in the brochure" is more severe compared to "the tour representative guide will not participate in such activities as windsurfing or scuba diving." Therefore, these risk attributes vary in the severity of the perceived consequence. Furthermore, these risk attributes vary in their level of uncertainty. For example, one consumer may believe that "the hotel may not be as nice as it appears in the brochure" is the least uncertain, whereas "the tour representative guide will not participate in such activities as windsurfing or scuba diving" is most uncertain. Therefore, the consumer perceives risk in relation to each risk attribute, and this risk perception is a composite of the severity of the consequence and the level of uncertainty associated with that consequence. Overall risk perception is, then, a summative composite of all these risk perceptions (multiply each severity of consequence with its corresponding level of uncertainty of each risk attribute and then sum across all attributes).

Traditionally, consumer researchers have classified types of risk perception into seven major categories:

1. Performance risk (the possibility that the product will not perform as expected),
2. Financial risk (the possibility that money will be wasted on a failed product),
3. Physical risk (the possibility that the consumer or others may be physically injured by the product),
4. Social risk (the possibility that significant others will express their disapproval at the consumer having purchased a failed product),
5. Psychological risk (the possibility that the consumer himself or herself will feel guilty for having purchased a failed product),
6. Time and convenience risk (the possibility that the consumer may waste valuable time and energy to purchase a failed product), and
7. Opportunity loss risk (the possibility that the consumer may waste the opportunity to buy a better product).[96]

Risk reduction strategies are behaviors consumers engage in an attempt to reduce their perception of risk in purchase situations. Using the example of the travel company offering a vacation deal in a hotel at an island resort, the following risk-reducing strategies were identified:[97]

• Reading independent travel reviews on the hotel and island.
• Visiting the tour operator or travel agency personally.

- Taking a similar holiday from a tour operator with whom the consumer has dealt previously.

- Reading travel brochures on the resort and hotel.

- Purchasing such travel items as electrical adapters and comfortable shoes.

- Asking family or friends for advice.

- Asking travel agent representatives for advice.

- Purchasing travel insurance recommended by the tour operator.

- Asking a person knowledgeable about the destination site.

- Waiting to pay for the holiday until the last minute, except for the required booking deposit.

- Watching a television program about the destination site.

- Watching any travel program about holiday traveling.

- Studying the language of the host country.

These are behaviors designed to reduce the perception of risk in the purchase of the holiday/hotel package deal. Specifically, some of these behaviors are designed to reduce the severity of the consequence (if it occurs). Examples include "purchasing some kind of travel insurance" and "purchasing such travel items as electrical adapters and comfortable shoes." Other risk-reducing behaviors are designed to reduce the level of uncertainty associated with the negative consequence. Examples include "reading independent travel reviews on the hotel and island" and "visiting the tour operator or travel agency personally." For more information on risk perception/risk reduction, see section 2-3b in Chapter 2.

Perception of Switching Costs Recent research using consumers of credit cards and long-distance telephone companies has shown that the perception of switching costs (that is, the costs of switching long-distance service providers) does play a significant role in a consumer's intention to stay with his or her incumbent service provider. That is, consumers perceiving greater switching costs tend to continue using the service provider they are already doing business with.[98] Switching costs were classified as procedural, financial, and relational (see Exhibit 7-24).

Price Perception Consumers evaluate whether the price tag of a specific brand is high or low as a function of comparing that price with an internal price or what consumer

---

Exhibit 7-24

The Effect of Perceived Switching Costs on the Intention to Stay with the Incumbent Provider

- *Procedural switching costs* are costs related to consumers' perceptions of time and effort expenditure. These may include *economic risk costs* ("I worry that the service offered by other service providers won't work as well as expected."), *evaluation costs* ("I cannot afford the time to get the information to fully evaluate other service providers."), *learning costs* ("Learning to use the features offered by the new service provider as well as I use my service would take time."), and *set-up costs* ("It takes time to go through the steps of switching to a new service provider.").

- *Financial switching costs* are losses of financially quantifiable resources. These may include *benefits lost* ("Switching to a new service provider would mean losing or replacing points, credits, services, and so on that I have accumulated with my service provider.") and *financial loss* ("Switching to a new service provider would involve some up-front costs such as setup fees, membership fees, deposits, etc.").

- *Relational switching costs* involve psychological or emotional discomfort due to the loss of identity and the breaking of social bonds. These may include *personal relationship loss costs* ("I would miss working with the people at my service provider if I switched providers.") and *brand relationship loss costs* ("I like the public image my service provider has.").

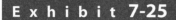

Exhibit 7-25

Applying Social Judgment Theory to Understand Price Perceptions.

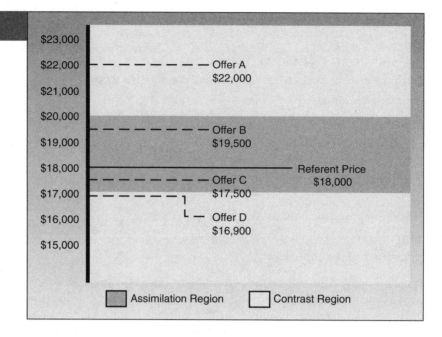

behavior researchers refer to as *referent price.* Suppose that a consumer is shopping for a Honda Civic. She has seen a number of television commercials saying that now you can buy a Honda Civic for $18,000 (basic sticker price). Consider the following scenarios:

- **Scenario A:** She goes to a Honda dealer and, after talking with a salesperson, she finds that the actual price tag is $22,000. How is she likely to perceive that price tag? She perceives that price as unacceptable because it is significantly higher than the advertised price (the price she expected, her internal or referent price).

- **Scenario B:** Suppose that instead of an offer of $22,000, the same dealer offers her essentially the same car for $19,500. She perceives the price tag of $19,500 as acceptable.

- **Scenario C:** Suppose that the offer is $17,500 or $500 less than what she expected. She perceives $17,500 price tag as acceptable because it is essentially what she expected.

- **Scenario D:** Here, the offer is $16,900 or $1,100 less than the advertised price. She perceives this price is a "bargain."

Refer to Exhibit 7-25 to understand why this consumer perceived these different price tags in these different scenarios as unacceptable, acceptable, and bargain, respectively. There is a theory in psychology called the **social judgment theory.** This theory states that people attribute meaning to incoming information by matching this information to a mental category or referent. This matching process is characterized as involving two regions—one called the assimilation region and the other called contrast region. The assimilation region is the area around the referent in which the incoming information is categorized as similar to that referent. The contrast region is the area in which the incoming information is categorized as different from the referent. Now let us apply the concepts of assimilation and contrast region to understand how consumers perceive certain prices as "acceptable," "unacceptable," and "bargain." The consumer expects to buy the Honda Civic for $18,000. This is the consumer's referent price. Around that referent price there is a region of assimilation. This region is within $17,000 and $20,000. That is, any offer between $17,000 and $20,000 is likely to be perceived to be about the same as what is expected—the referent price. Therefore, offers B and C are considered to be acceptable because they fall within the region of assimilation—they are the same as what the consumer expected to begin with. The consumer went to the dealer expecting that price

social judgment theory
The theory that states that people attribute meaning to incoming information by matching this information to a mental category or referent. This matching process is characterized as involving two regions—one called the assimilation region and the other called the contrast region. The assimilation region is the area around the referent in which the incoming information is categorized as similar to that referent. The contrast region is the area in which the incoming information is categorized as different from the referent.

(because this is what was advertised) and was ready to buy the Honda Civic for that price. However, offer A ($22,000) was categorized as outside the assimilation region. Offer A fell into the contrast region, making the consumer experience what psychologists call a "contrast effect." The consumer felt that the offer in scenario A was different from what she expected and, therefore, felt it was "unacceptable." Offer D, on the other hand, was also perceived to be different from the referent price because it fell into the contrast region. However, here the consumer felt that this offer was a bargain because it was perceived to be significantly different and below what she should pay.[99]

The concepts of assimilation and contrast are important, not only in helping us understand how consumers perceive prices, but also in conducting consumer research to measure the size of the assimilation region around a particular referent price. If consumers are likely to reject a certain offer from a marketer because it is "different" from what they expected, then the marketer needs to know what the consumers' referent price is and above and below what price threshold they are likely to perceive an offer different from the referent price. Knowing the consumers' referent price and the scope of the assimilation region should help marketers make acceptable offers to consumers and possibly offers that can be perceived as bargains.

Having learned something about how prices are perceived and evaluated in relation to a referent price, let's turn our attention to the concept of referent price and see if we can understand it better. Where does this reference price come from? How is it formed? Consumer researchers have shown that a referent price is influenced by:

- Aspiration price (or the price desired by the consumer),
- Previously paid price (or the price the consumer remembers having paid last),
- Fair price (or the price the consumer thinks is fair for the benefits received),
- Recalled price (or the price the consumer recalls from memory),
- Reservation price (or the price used to reserve the product),
- Expected price (or price the consumer expects),
- Expected future price (or the price the consumer expects the product to climb to in the near future),
- Normal market price (or the average price across a variety of brands in the same product category),
- Highest and lowest prices (or the highest price and lowest price recalled), and
- Contextual price (or the price many consumers have paid).[100]

In other words, a referent price used in price perception is a belief about what the price should be, which in turn is influenced by any combination of the aforementioned factors—aspiration price, previously paid price, and so on.

Perceived Value   Perceived value refers to perceptions of trade-off between product benefits (e.g., product quality) and monetary sacrifice. Some scholars think that perceived value is a perception of trade-off between product benefits and product costs. That is, not only monetary sacrifice (money paid for the product) is included in the mental trade-off but also other costs such as the consumer's effort in seeking suitable alternatives and the effort in information gathering about alternative brands. Therefore, we can think of the consumer-perceived value of a particular brand to be a cognitive "ratio" of perceived benefits over perceived costs (see Exhibit 7-26), that is:[101]

> **perceived value** Perceptions of trade-off between product benefits (e.g., product quality) and monetary sacrifice.

$$\text{Perceived value} = \text{perceived benefits} / \text{perceived costs}$$

For example, let's say that a consumer is shopping for an economy car. She is considering two options: a Honda Civic and a Hyundai. She perceives the Honda Civic to be more expensive than the Hyundai, but she also perceives that the Honda Civic has a more established reputation than does the Hyundai. Also, there is a Honda dealer in the same

Exhibit 7-26

Perceived Value

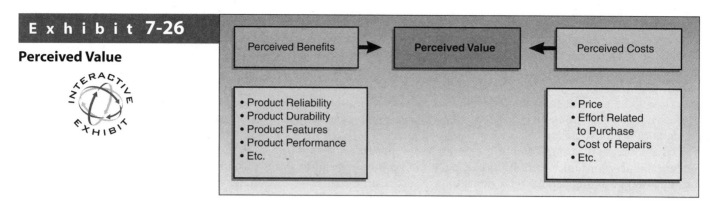

town, but she has to travel to the neighboring town (approximately thirty miles away) to get to the Hyundai dealer. To her, the trade-off pertaining to the Honda Civic seems to outweigh the trade-off for the Hyundai. That is, she thinks that the Honda Civic is a better value than the Hyundai.

Recent research has applied the concept of perceived value to predict the effectiveness of loyalty or frequency programs. These programs reward customers as a direct function of their purchase frequency; examples are frequent flier miles programs, hotel loyalty programs in which the customer gets a free stay at the hotel after a number of purchased room nights, and fast food restaurants that give customers a free meal after they accumulate a designated number of reward points. The research points to the fact that value perception does play a significant role in both program loyalty as well as brand loyalty. In other words, customers who perceive value in a product offer are likely to remain loyal to the brand and participate actively in a loyalty program.[102]

country image An image in the mind of most consumers that signals an association between a specific product or service and a country.

Country Image **Country image** is a concept that marketing scholars have classified into three categories: (1) overall country image, (2) aggregate product country image, and (3) specific product country image. *Overall country image* is the total of all beliefs that a consumer has about a particular country. *Aggregate product country image* is the entire cognitive "feel" associated with a particular country's products—the perception of overall quality of the products from that particular country. *Specific product country image* is the overall perception consumers form of a specific product category from a particular country.

As an example of the three categories of country image, Turkish consumers may have mixed feelings about the U.S. in various respects. The overall image of the U.S. is both good and bad; it may be perceived as good in relation to its stance against terrorism and bad in relation to its treatment of Muslims. The same Turkish consumers may perceive that U.S. products are generally of high quality. This would be the aggregate product country image. In contrast, the same Turkish consumers may perceive American computers as being of the highest quality. This would be an example of a specific product country image.[103]

The effect of country image (specific product country image) on product evaluation has been noted in relation to durable goods, more so than nondurables. The country-image effect on product evaluation has been explained as follows. Country-image perceptions influence product evaluations through a halo effect. When consumers do not have much information about a particular brand, they use their image of the country to generate inferential beliefs about the brand. For example, Turkish consumers may know little about Dell computers; however, they perceive that computers made in the U.S.A. tend to be of high quality. Therefore, they make an inference that Dell computers are of high quality too. This is called the *halo effect*.[104] For more information on country image, see section 3-1b in Chapter 3.

Perception of a Pioneer Brand A pioneer brand is a brand that is first to sell in the market in a product category. For example, Kleenex was a pioneer brand because the Kleenex brand was first to establish a presence in the market for tissue paper. It is well recognized by marketing scientists that a pioneer brand has a competitive advantage over follower brands. That advantage lies in the way consumers *perceive* the pioneer brand. In the context of a new product category, consumers are initially unsure about how attributes contribute to product quality, so the new entrant brand determines quality. That is, it sets the standard for quality. When follower brands enter the market, they are perceived in relation to the pioneer brand. If consumers were to perceive the follower brands as not too distinct from the pioneer brand, then they view the follower brands as "me too brands." A "me too brand" is typically perceived unfavorably compared to the pioneer brand. This explanation of the advantage of pioneer brand has come to be known in marketing circles as the *prototypicality* explanation of pioneer brands.[105]

Marketing Management—Implications and Actions

Understanding consumer perceptions helps marketers:

- Manage sensory factors to appropriately influence consumers.
- Make the principles of Gestalt theory work in the product's favor.
- Work within the consumer's needs to categorize products.
- Communicate product or service features in ways to help develop perceptions of product or service quality.
- Identify consumers' perception of risk in the purchase of a product or service and help consumers reduce the perception of risk through risk reduction strategies.
- Identify consumer referent prices and estimate at what higher price levels consumers are likely to perceive certain offers as unacceptable and at what lower levels consumers perceive bargains.

Chapter Spotlights

This chapter explores the aspects of memory, learning, and perception and how they impact critical consumption decisions such as brand loyalty, new product acceptance, and product categorization.

1. How consumers accept, retain, and retrieve market information from memory. Consumer memory can be viewed as an associative network in which an endless array of concepts or nodes are linked to each other, forming the consumer's beliefs about products and services. It is thought that there are three types of memory through which all product information flows—sensory, short-term, and long-term. Sensory memory produces simple signals or sensations that are then organized and given meaning in short-term memory. The signals or sensations and their associated meanings are then transferred into long-term memory for permanent storage and retrieval. Accurate retention of information in memory depends upon such factors as repetition, relevance, competing information, and the passage of time. Accuracy of retrieval from memory is influenced by the availability of retrieval cues, the presence of competing retrieval cues, and the consumer's state of mind.

2. Predicting brand choices through probability theory. Probability theory treats learning as the formation of habits that can be strengthened, weakened, or changed by marketplace stimuli. Through the use of probability models, marketers can predict buyer behavior in such areas as brand loyalty, brand acceptance, brand switching, and new product acceptance.

3. The relationship between learning processes and marketplace behavior. From a behavior analysis perspective, consumer learning involves five theoretical concepts. First, classical conditioning posits that consumers learn to respond to marketplace stimuli when those stimuli are associated or paired with stimuli that serve specific goals or needs of the consumer. Second, operant conditioning involves the use of rewards and/or punishments to shape consumer behavior. Third, the concept of generalization suggests the use of familiar cues to educate consumers about new products and brands. Fourth, discrimination theory demonstrates how marketers can educate consumers about the differentiating features or benefits of their products or brands. Last, modeling involves the use of live characters to encourage consumers to emulate a desired marketplace behavior.

4. How consumers learn from experiences in the marketplace. Consumers learn about products and brands through a four-stage process: formulation of hypotheses regarding the product or brand, exposure to evidence to support or refute such hypotheses, encoding of that evidence, and eventual integration of the evidence with earlier assumptions to form beliefs about the product or brand. How a consumer advances through these learning stages is dependent upon the consumer's product familiarity, the ambiguity of the product experience, and the consumer's motivation to learn. Based on these factors, marketers can develop strategies that optimize consumer learning for particular types of products or brands in particular situations.

5. How brand preferences are influenced by consumers' perceptions.   By understanding how sensory perception works through the five senses, marketers can develop products, packaging, and promotions that make a desirable impact on the senses, thus motivating consumers to buy. The Gestalt theory of perception holds that consumers perceive the overall form of a product, not its individual features. For marketers, this means that the way in which factors such as color, contrast, size, intensity, position, and isolation work together can affect how a product is ultimately perceived. Moreover, the consumer's own level of interest and involvement, needs, values, and cognition also influence perception. Consumers interpret perceptions of a product's attributes through filters of personal needs, desires, fears, and a host of other individual and situational factors. Because of this, marketers can attempt to influence

perceptions in order to differentiate otherwise identical products in the minds of consumers.

6. How consumers use and interpret perceptions to categorize products.   The way in which consumers categorize products—particularly new products or innovations—in memory can influence their success in the marketplace. By understanding analytic and nonanalytic categorization, marketers can select market strategies that help consumers understand, accurately remember, and ultimately prefer their brands over those of competitors.

7. How consumers connect marketplace events and behavior with causes.   To control the inferences consumers make about products, marketers must understand the motivations behind them, the marketplace information on which they are based, and the beliefs underlying them.

Key Terms

abstraction (p. 229)
analytic categorization (p. 228)
associative network (p. 201)
attribution (p. 229)
backward conditioning (p. 213)
behavior analysis (p. 211)
categorization (p. 228)
classical or respondent conditioning (p. 212)
cognitive theory (p. 218)
continuous reinforcement (p. 215)
country image (p. 238)
discrimination (p. 217)
exemplar (p. 229)

forward conditioning (p. 213)
generalization (p. 216)
Gestalt principle (p. 225)
intermittent reinforcement (p. 215)
long-term memory (p. 202)
meaning-level processing (p. 208)
modeling (p. 218)
nodes and links (p. 201)
nonanalytic categorization (p. 228)
operant or instrumental conditioning (p. 214)
perceived value (p. 237)
person perception (p. 230)
probability theory (p. 209)

product/service perception (p. 229)
reinforcement schedule (p. 215)
retention (p. 202)
retrieval (p. 207)
risk perception/risk reduction (p. 233)
self-perception (p. 230)
sensory memory (p. 201)
sensory perception (p. 223)
shaping (p. 216)
short-term memory (p. 201)
social judgment theory (p. 236)
surface-level processing (p. 208)

Review Questions

Note: You can find the correct answers to these questions by taking the quiz and then submitting your answers in the Online Edition. The program will automatically score your submission. If you miss a question, the program will provide the correct answer, a rationale for the answer, and the section number in the chapter where the topic is discussed.

1. Psychologists believe that information in memory is organized in terms of
   a. nodes.
   b. associative networks.
   c. scripts.
   d. linear flowcharts.

2. Marketers must move perceptions from sensory memory in consumers' minds to short-term and _____ memory.
   a. relevant
   b. conscious
   c. long-term
   d. subconscious

3. For marketers to send appropriate messages, they must understand the difference between attribute-based and _____ -based processing.
   a. brand
   b. outlet
   c. product
   d. service

4. Brand switching _____ be predicted.
   a. cannot
   b. can
   c. always will
   d. need not

5. In some cases, as many as _____ pairings of brand and unconditioned stimuli may be necessary for a consumer to show preference for a given brand.
   a. 20
   b. 25
   c. 30
   d. 35

6. A shopper enters a store and is given a one-dollar bill. This positive stimulus or reward is called _____ conditioning.
   a. classical
   b. reward
   c. Pavlovian
   d. operant.

7. Rewards and punishments are most effective when they take place at the same time as the
   a. purchase.
   b. desired behavior.
   c. cognitive dissonance.
   d. opinion leader's approval.

8. The five senses govern
   a. stimulus factors.
   b. perception.
   c. sensory perception.
   d. sensory acuity.

9. Students of consumer behavior know that stimulus factors that affect consumer sensory perception include all of the following *except*
   a. color.
   b. contrast.
   c. belonging.
   d. size.

10. Consumers are moved to select a given product by their _____ of the product's intrinsic qualities.
    a. perception
    b. association
    c. knowledge
    d. reinforcement

Team Talk

1. Your team is assigned to promote a new over-the-counter drug that reduces nicotine cravings. The objective of the advertising campaign is to generate brand awareness so that after one year, 70 percent of smokers who want to quit are aware of the availability of the product. Your job as part of the account team is to report on the cognitive principles of memory and retention and factors affecting memorability that may be relevant to the campaign.

2. You are the marketing manager of a national coffee brand that is losing market share. Design a sales promotion campaign that has at its core the concepts of memory and retrieval and the factors affecting retrieval.

3. Find a piece of print advertising for either a fragrance for women or a cologne for men. Analyze the advertisement using the principles of classical (respondent) conditioning. Is the advertisement effective? Explain your answer using the theory of classical conditioning.

4. You have a family friend who runs a local pizzeria. He tells you that the business is in trouble and may go under. Sales have been down for the last three months, and over that period the pizzeria netted a loss of $7,000. Use the principles of operant conditioning to create a campaign to save the business.

5. The Vice President of Student Affairs at your college approaches the marketing club to assist in developing a promotional campaign to encourage students to practice safe sex in order to decrease the incidence of AIDS on campus. Design a promotion campaign guided by the principle of modeling.

6. Suppose you are part of the advertising/marketing team working on the AT&T account. The primary campaign objective is to convince current and previous customers that AT&T is not more expensive than the competition and that it offers better service. Use the four-stage cognitive model of consumer learning to design a campaign strategy for AT&T.

7. Think of your favorite restaurant. Analyze the ambience of the restaurant by focusing on its visual features (interior decor, lighting, seat arrangement), auditory features (the type and loudness of music, customer noise), olfactory features (food aromas), and tactile features (tablecloths, napkins, seat upholstery). How are customers' sensory perceptions likely to affect their overall image of the restaurant?

8. You are the marketing manager assigned to a new product, a brand of chewing gum that also works in lieu of toothpaste. Should the product be positioned as a new brand of chewing gum or as an innovative product that replaces toothpaste? The marketing implications are significant. Use the principles of categorization to help you develop the most effective positioning for the product.

9. Imagine that you work for an advocacy organization for the homeless. You are assigned to work with a team to develop a fund-raising communication campaign. You realize that a key reason that people are reluctant to make donations to aid this cause is the negative attributions society at large makes about the homeless. Apply selected attribution principles to the development of the fund-raising campaign.

Workshops

Research Workshop

Background

Smokebreakers, an on-campus service, plans to offer group sessions in smoking cessation behavior. The objective of this workshop is to discover what behavior modification techniques are most effective with different groups of people.

Methodology

Conduct a literature search on behavior modification in relation to smoking cessation. Identify the key behavior modification methods used. With respect to each behavior modification method, identify the conditions under which the technique is most effective.

To the Marketplace

What behavior modification techniques do you think would be most effective on college students? Which ones should Smokebreakers offer as the subjects of seminars, and why?

Creative Workshop

Background

You have been appointed head of Students for Less Cluttered TV, a special-interest group with the objective of discouraging pointless commercial repetition. The objective of this workshop is to refine an advertising message so that less repetition is needed.

Methodology

Pick a commercial that seems to you to lack a good persuasive message and to rely totally on repetition to be effective. Redevelop the commercial so that it will be more effective and less objectionable to the viewer. In redoing the commercial, be sure to use the same product advantage stressed in the original commercial.

To the Marketplace

Present a storyboard of the commercial to your team and discuss the improvements you have made.

Managerial Workshop

Background

You are preparing to address an audience of sales clerks from a chain of retail appliance stores on effective sales strategies for your high-quality, high-price television model. The objective of this workshop is to develop strategies to enhance sales.

Methodology

Use cognitive theory to develop a set of recommendations to help sales clerks communicate the benefits of the product to prospective customers. You may use either top dog or underdog strategies.

To the Marketplace

Write and deliver a one-page speech to the sales force.

Notes

1. Eric J. Johnson and J. Edward Russo, "The Organization of Product Information in Memory Identified by Recall Times," in H. Keith Hunt, ed., *Advances in Consumer Research,* Vol. 5 (Chicago. IL: Association for Consumer Research, 1978), pp. 79–86.
2. James Bettman, "Memory Factors in Consumer Choice: A Review," *Journal of Marketing,* Vol. 43 (Spring 1979), pp. 37–53.
3. Lyle E. Bourne, Roger L. Dominowski, and Elizabeth F. Loftus, *Cognitive Processes* (Englewood Cliffs, NJ: Prentice-Hall, 1979).
4. Adapted from Herman Ebbinghaus, *Memory* (Teachers College, Columbia University, 1913); D. O. Hebb, *The Organization of Behavior* (New York: Wiley, 1949); Carl I. Hovland, Irving L. Janis, and Harold H. Kelly, *Communication and Persuasion* (New Haven, CT: Yale University Press, 1953).
5. James F. Donius, "Campaign Simulation via Multiple Exposure On-Air Copy Testing," *Journal of Advertising Research,* Vol. 23 (April–May 1983), pp. 30–38.
6. Leo Bogart, *Strategy in Advertising* (New York: Harcourt, Brace and World, 1967).
7. John B. Stewart, *Repetitive Advertising in Newspapers* (Cambridge, MA: Harvard University Press, 1964).
8. Ebbinghaus, *Memory;* Hebb, *The Organization of Behavior;* Hovland et al., *Communication and Persuasion.*
9. Ibid.
10. Charles Osgood, *Method and Theory in Experimental Psychology* (New York: Oxford University Press, 1964).
11. Angela Y. Lee and Brian Sternthal, "The Effects of Positive Mood on Memory," *Journal of Consumer Research,* Vol. 26 (September 1999), pp. 115–127.
12. Ebbinghaus, *Memory;* Hebb, *The Organization of Behavior,* Hovland et al., *Communication and Persuasion.*
13. Cynthia Huffman and Michael J. Houston, "Goal-Oriented Experiences and Development of Knowledge," *Journal of Consumer Research,* Vol. 20 (September 1993), pp. 190–207.
14. Johnson and Russo, "The Organization of Product Information in Memory Identified by Recall Times."
15. Eric J. Johnson and J. Edward Russo, "Product Familiarity and Learning of New Information," *Journal of Consumer Research,* Vol. 11 (June 1984), pp. 542–576.
16. Gabriel Biehal and Dipankar Chakravarti, "Information-Presentation Format and Learning Goals as Determinants of Consumers' Memory Retrieval and Choice Processes," *Journal of Consumer Research,* Vol. 8 (March 1982), pp. 431–441. For an insightful and interesting analysis of how shoppers use retrieval cues guided by shoppers' motives, see Arch G. Woodside and Randolph J. Trappey III, "Learning Why Customers Shop at Less Convenient Stores," *Journal of Business Research,* Vol. 54 (November 2001), pp. 151–159.
17. Barry McLaughlin, "Intentional and Incidental Learning in Human Subjects: The Role of Instructions to Learn and Motivation," *Psychological Bulletin,* Vol. 63 (May 1965), pp. 359–376.
18. Huffman and Houston, "Goal-Oriented Experiences."
19. Kevin Lane Keller, "Memory Factors in Advertising: The Effect of Advertising Retrieval Cues on Brand Evaluations," *Journal of Consumer Research,* Vol. 14 (December 1987), pp. 316–333; Joseph O. Eastlack, Jr., "How to Get More Bang for Your Television Bucks," *Journal of Consumer Marketing,* Vol. 1 (1984), pp. 25–34.
20. John G. Lynch, Jr., and Thomas K. Srull, "Memory and Attentional Factors in Consumer Choice: Concepts and

Research Methods," *Journal of Consumer Research,* Vol. 9 (June 1982), pp. 18–37; Lauren G. Block and Vicki G. Morwitz, "Shopping Lists as an External Memory Aid for Grocery Shopping: Influences on List Writing and List Fulfillment," *Journal of Consumer Psychology,* Vol. 8, No. 4 (1999), pp. 343–376.

21. Joseph W. Alba and Amitava Chattopadhyay, "Effects of Context and Part-Category Cues on Recall of Competing Brands," *Journal of Marketing Research,* Vol. 22 (August 1985), pp. 340–349; Joseph W. Alba and Amitava Chattopadhyay, "Salience Effects in Brand Recall," *Journal of Marketing Research,* Vol. 23 (November 1986), pp. 363–369; Anand Kumar and Shanker Krishnan, "Memory Interference in Advertising: A Replication and Extension," *Journal of Consumer Research,* Vol. 30 (2004), pp. 602–612; Robert D. Jewell and H. Rao Unnava, "When Competitive Interference can be Beneficial," *Journal of Consumer Research,* Vol. 30 (2003), pp. 283–293.

22. Peter Dickson, "The Impact of Case Enriching and Statistical Information on Consumer Judgments," *Journal of Consumer Research,* Vol. 8 (March 1982), pp. 398–406; Valerie Zeithaml, "Consumer Response to In-Store Price in Information Environments," *Journal of Consumer Research,* Vol. 8 (March 1982), pp. 357–369.

23. Terry L. Childers and Madhubalan Viswanathan, "Representation of Numerical and Verbal Product Information in Consumer Memory," *Journal of Business Research,* Vol. 47 (February 2000), pp. 109–120.

24. Maryanne Garry, Charles G. Manning, Elizabeth F. Loftus, and Steven J. Sherman, "Imagination Inflation: Imagining a Childhood Event Inflates Confidence That It Occurred," *Psychonomic Bulletin and Review,* Vol. 3 (1996), pp. 208–214.

25. Kathryn A. Braun, "Postexperience Advertising Effects on Consumer Memory," *Journal of Consumer Research,* Vol. 25 (March 1999), pp. 319–334.

26. Scott A. Hawkins and Stephen J. Hoch, "Low Involvement Learning: Memory without Evaluation," *Journal of Consumer Research,* Vol. 19 (September 1992), pp. 212–225.

27. Sharmistha Law, Scott A. Hawkins, and Fergus I. M. Craik, "Repetition-Induced Belief in the Elderly: Rehabilitating Age-Related Memory Deficits," *Journal of Consumer Research,* Vol. 25 (September 1998), pp. 91–107.

28. Howard L. Kingsley and Ralph Garry, *The Nature and Conditions of Learning* (Englewood Cliffs, NJ: Prentice-Hall, 1957).

29. Alfred A. Kuehn, "Consumer Brand Choice As a Learning Process," *Journal of Advertising Research,* Vol. 2 (December 1962), pp. 10–17.

30. David A. Aaker, "A Measure of Brand Acceptance," *Journal of Marketing Research,* Vol. 9 (May 1972), pp. 160–167.

31. Aaker, "A Measure of Brand Acceptance," p. 167

32. Ruth N. Bolton, P. K. Kannan, and Matthew D. Bramlett, "Implications of Loyalty Program Membership and Service Experiences for Customer Retention and Value," *Journal of the Academy of Marketing Science,* Vol. 28 (Winter 2000), pp. 95–108.

33. Frank M. Bass, "The Theory of Stochastic Preference and Brand Switching," *Journal of Marketing Research,* Vol. 11 (February 1974), pp. 1–20.

34. Wellesley Dodds, "An Application of the Bass Model in Long-Term New Product Forecasting," *Journal of Marketing Research,* Vol. 10 (August 1973), pp. 308–311.

35. Walter R. Nord and J. Paul Peter, "A Behavior Modification Perspective on Marketing," *Journal of Marketing,* Vol. 44, No. 2 (Spring 1980), p. 37.

36. Richard A. Feinberg, "Credit Cards as Spending Facilitating Stimuli: A Conditioning Explanation," *Journal of Consumer Research,* Vol. 13 (December 1986), pp. 348–356; Terence A. Shimp and Margaret P. Moody, "In Search of a Theoretical Explanation for the Credit Card Effect," *Journal of Business Research,* Vol. 48 (April 2000), pp. 17–23.

37. Chris Janiszewski and Luk Warlop, "The Influence of Classical Conditioning Procedures on Subsequent Attention to the Conditioned Brand," *Journal of Consumer Research,* Vol. 20 (September 1993), pp. 171–189.

38. Chris Allen and Thomas Madden, "A Closer Look at Classical Conditioning," *Journal of Consumer Research,* Vol. 12 (December 1985), pp. 301–315; Francis K. McSweeney and Calvin Bierley, "Recent Developments in Classical Conditioning," *Journal of Consumer Research,* Vol. 11 (September 1984), pp. 619–631.

39. McSweeney and Bierley, "Recent Developments in Classical Conditioning."

40. James J. Kellaris and Anthony D. Cox, "The Effects of Background Music in Advertising: A Reassessment," *Journal of Consumer Research,* Vol. 16 (June 1989), pp. 113–118.

41. McSweeney and Bierley, "Recent Developments in Classical Conditioning"; Elenora W. Stuart, Terence A. Shimp, and Randall W. Engle, "Classical Conditioning of Consumer Attitudes: Four Experiments in an Advertising Context," *Journal of Consumer Research,* Vol. 14 (December 1987), pp. 334–349.

42. David S. Austin and James M. Johnson, *Explaining Behavior* (Encino, CA: Dickenson, 1974).

43. H. H. Kassarjian, "Anthropomorphism and Parsimony," in H. Keith Hunt, ed., *Advances in Consumer Research,* Vol. V (Ann Arbor: Association of Consumer Research, 1978), pp. xiii–xiv.

44. Foxall, "The Consumer Situation."

45. Michael L. Rothschild and William C. Gaidis, "Behavioral Learning Theory: Its Relevance to Marketing and Promotions," *Journal of Marketing,* Vol. 45, No. 2 (Spring 1981), pp. 71–73.

46. Rothschild and Gaidis, "Behavioral Learning Theory," p. 73. For a recent and insightful study dealing with the use of reward to establish and strengthen relationship quality, see Gaby Odekerken-Schroder, Kristof De Wulf, and Patrick Schumacher, "Strengthening Outcomes of Retailer-Consumer Relationships: The Dual Impact of Relationship Marketing Tactics and Consumer Personality," *Journal of Business Research,* Vol. 56 (March 2003), pp. 177–190.

47. B. F. Skinner, *The Behavior of Organisms: An Experimental Analysis* (New York: Appleton-Century-Crofts, 1966).

48. Rothschild and Gaidis, "Behavioral Learning Theory," p. 71.

49. John Howard, *Marketing Theory* (Boston: Allyn and Bacon, 1965), p. 109.

50. Ibid.

51. Austin and Johnson, *Explaining Behavior,* p. 69.

52. James H. Myers and William H. Reynolds, *Consumer Behavior in Marketing and Marketing Management* (Boston: Houghton Mifflin, 1976), pp. 16–19.

53. Nord and Peter, "A Behavior Modification Perspective on Marketing."

54. Rothschild and Gaidis, "Behavioral Learning Theory."

55. Michael J. Baker and Gilbert A. Churchill, Jr., "The Impact of Physically Attractive Models on Advertising Evaluations," *Journal of Marketing Research*, Vol. 14 (November 1977), pp. 538–555; "Models' Clothing Speaks to Advertising Market: Study," *Marketing News*, (November 22, 1985), p. 16; Lynn R. Kahle and Pamela M. Homer, "Physical Attractiveness of the Celebrity Endorser: A Social Adaptation Perspective," *Journal of Consumer Research*, Vol. 12 (March 1985), pp. 954–961.

56. Charles C. Manz and Henry P. Sims, "Vicarious Learning: The Influence of Modeling on Organizational Behavior," *Academy of Management Review*, Vol. 6 (January 1981), pp. 105–113.

57. Albert Bandura, *Social Learning Theory* (Englewood Cliffs, NJ: Prentice Hall, 1977).

58. Ibid.

59. Stephen J. Hoch and John Deighton, "Managing What Consumers Learn from Experience," *Journal of Marketing*, Vol. 53 (April 1989), pp. 1–21.

60. Hoch and Deighton, "Managing What Consumers Learn from Experience."

61. Cynthia Fraser and John W. Bradford, "Competitive Market Structure Analysis," *Journal of Consumer Research*, Vol. 10, No. 1 (June 1983), pp. 15–31.

62. Ronald Alsop, "Color Grows More Important in Catching Consumers' Eyes," *The Wall Street Journal*, (November 29, 1984), p. 37; Kelly Costigan, "How Color Goes to Your Head," *Science Digest*, Vol. 24, No. 1 (December 1984); Brad Edmondson, "The Color Purple," *American Demographics*, Vol. 24 (June 1987); Bernice Kanner, "Color Schemes," *New York* (April 3, 1989), pp. 22–23; Israel Abramov, "An Analysis of Personal Color Analysis," in Michael R. Solomon ed., *The Psychology of Fashion* (Lexington, MA: Lexington Books, 1985), pp. 212–223; Barry J. Babin, David M. Hardesty, and Tracy A. Suter, "Color and Shopping Intentions: The Intervening Effect of Price Fairness and Perceived Affect," *Journal of Business Research*, Vol. 56 (July 2003), pp. 541–552; Daniel Milotic, "The Impact of Fragrance on Consumer Choice," *Journal of Consumer Behaviour*, Vol. 2 (December 2003), pp. 179–190.

63. Lage Wedin, "A Multidimensional Study of Perceptual-Emotional Qualities in Music," *Scandinavian Journal of Psychology*, Vol. 13, No. 4 (1972), pp. 241ff. For research on background music and store evaluations, see Laurette Dube and Sylvie Morin, "Background Music Pleasure and Store Evaluation: Intensity Effects and Psychological Mechanisms," *Journal of Business Research*, Vol. 54 (November 2001), pp. 107–113. For research on the effect of background music on the effectiveness of in-store selling, see Jean-Charles Chebat, Claire Gelinas Chebat, and Dominique Vaillant, "Environmental Background Music and In-store Selling," *Journal of Business Research*, Vol. 54 (November 2001), pp. 115–123.

64. Richard I. Doty, "The Role of Olfaction in Man: Sense or Nonsense?" in S. Howard Bartley, ed., *Perception in Everyday Life* (New York: Harper and Row, 1972), p. 143; Jean-Charles Chebat and Richard Michon, "Impact of Ambient Odors on Mall Shoppers' Emotion, Cognition, and Spending: A Test of Competitive Causal Theories," *Journal of Business Research*, Vol. 56 (July 2003), pp. 529–540.

65. Eben Shapiro, "The People Who Are Putting Taste Back on the Table," *The New York Times* (July 22, 1990), p. F5.

66. Joann Peck and Terry L. Childers, "Individual Differences in Haptic Information Processing: The 'Need for Touch' Scale," *Journal of Consumer Research*, Vol. 30 (2003), pp. 430–440.

67. C. S. Areni and D. Kim, "The Influence of In-store Lighting on Consumer Examination of Merchandise in a Wine Store," *International Journal of Research in Marketing*, Vol. 11 (1994), pp. 117–125.

68. Teresa A. Summers and Paulette R. Herbert, "Shedding Some Light on Store Atmospherics: Influence of Illumination on Consumer Behavior," *Journal of Business Research*, Vol. 54 (November 2001), pp. 145–150.

69. Charles S. Gulas and Peter H. Bloch, "Right Under Our Noses: Ambient Scent and Consumer Responses," *Journal of Business and Psychology* (in press); Doty, "The Role of Olfaction in Man," pp. 159–161.

70. Julian E. Hochber, Perception (Englewood Cliffs, NJ: Prentice-Hall, 1964).

71. "Are Color Television Commercials Worth the Extra Cost?" (New York: Association of Color Advertisers, Inc., 1966).

72. Kurt Koffka, *Principles of Gestalt Psychology* (New York: Harcourt, Brace, 1935).

73. Stephen S. Bell, Morris B. Holbrook, and Michael R. Solomon, "Combining Esthetic and Social Value to Explain Preferences in Product Styles With the Incorporation of Personality and Ensemble Effects," *Journal of Social Behavior and Personality*, Vol. 6, No. 6 (1991), pp. 243–273; also see other studies involving unity with other products such as clothing styles, telephones, and refrigerators: Sharron J. Lennon, "Effects of Clothing Attractiveness on Perceptions," *Home Economics Research Journal*, Vol. 18, No. 3 (1990), pp. 303–310; Robert W. Veryzer, Jr., and J. Wesley Hutchinson, "The Influence of Unity and Prototypicality on Aesthetic Responses to New Product Designs," *Journal of Consumer Research*, Vol. 24 (March 1998), pp. 374–394. See also the following article on online retailing atmospherics: Sevgin A. Eroglu, Karen A. Machleit, and Lenita M. Davi, "Atmospheric Qualities of Online Retailing: A Conceptual Model and Implications," *Journal of Business Research*, Vol. 54 (November 2001), pp. 177–184.

74. Dena Cox and Anthony D. Cox, "Beyond First Impressions: The Effects of Repeated Exposure on Consumer Liking of Visually Complex and Simple Product Designs," *Journal of the Academy of Marketing Science*, Vol. 30 (Spring 2002), pp. 119–130.

75. Anthony G. Greenwald and Clark Leavitt, "Audience Involvement in Advertising: Four Levels," *Journal of Consumer Research*, Vol. 11, No. 1 (June 1984), pp. 483–491.

76. Myers and Reynolds, *Consumer Behavior in Marketing and Marketing Management*, p. 12ff.

77. Chris Y. Shao, Julie Baker, and Judy A. Wagner, "The Effects of Appropriateness of Service Contact Personnel Dress on Customer Expectations of Service Quality and Purchase Intention: The Moderating Influences of Involvement and Gender," *Journal of Business Research*, Vol. 57 (2004), pp. 1164–1176.

78. Joel B. Cohen and K. Basu, "Alternative Models of Categorization: Toward a Contingent Processing Framework," *Journal of Consumer Research*, Vol. 13 (1987), pp. 455–472.

79. Kunal Basu, "Consumers' Categorization Processes: An Examination With Two Alternative Methodological Paradigms," *Journal of Consumer Psychology,* Vol. 2 (1993), pp. 97–121.

80. For an excellent article on how consumers categorize brands and the marketing implications of consumer categorization, see Girish Punj and Junyean Moon, "Positioning Options for Achieving Brand Association: A Psychological Categorization Framework," *Journal of Business Research,* Vol. 55 (April 2002), pp. 275–283.

81. J. C. Ward, M. J. Bitner, and J. Barnes, "Measuring the Protypicality and Meaning of Retail Environment," *Journal of Retailing,* Vol. 68 (Summer 1992), pp. 194–220. For a more recent study involving prototypicality, see Barry J. Babin and Laurie Babin, "Seeking Something Different? A Model of Schema Typicality, Consumer Affect, Purchase Intentions, and Perceived Shopping Value," *Journal of Business Research,* Vol. 54 (November 2001), pp. 89–96.

82. Richard W. Mizerski, Linda L. Golden, and Jerome B. Kernan, "The Attribution Process in Consumer Decision Making," *Journal of Consumer Research,* Vol. 6 (September 1979), pp. 123–140; Valerie S. Folkes, "Recent Attribution Research in Consumer Behavior: A Review and New Directions," *Journal of Consumer Research,* Vol. 14 (March 1988), pp. 548–568.

83. "Ronald L. Hess Jr., Shankar Ganesan, and Noreen M. Klein, "Service Failure and Recovery: The Impact of Relationship Factors on Consumer Satisfaction," *Journal of the Academy of Marketing Science,* Vol. 31 (Spring 2003), pp. 127–145. Also see Karen A. Machleit and Susan Powell Mantel, "Emotional Response and Shopping Satisfaction: Moderating Effects of Shopper Attributions," *Journal of Business Research,* Vol. 54 (November 2001), pp. 97–106; Rajiv Vaidyanathan, and Praveen Aggarwal, "Who Is the Fairest of Them All? An Attributional Approach to Price Fairness Perceptions," *Journal of Business Research,* Vol. 56 (June 3003), pp. 453–463.

84. John R. O'Malley, Jr. "Consumer Attributions of Product Failures to Channel Members," in *Advances in Consumer Research,* Vol. 23, Kim Corfman and John Lynch, eds. (Provo, UT: Association for Consumer Research, 1996, pp. 342–345.

85. Robert Baer, "Overestimating Salesperson Truthfulness: The Fundamental Attribution Error," in *Advances in Consumer Research,* Vol. 17, Marvin Goldberg et al., eds. (Provo, UT: Association for Consumer Research, 1990), pp. 501–507.

86. Valerie S. Folkes and Vanessa M. Patrick, "The Positivity Effect in Perceptions of Services: Seen One, Seen Them All?" *Journal of Consumer Research,* Vol. 30 (2003), pp. 125–135.

87. Jerry B. Gotlieb, Dhruv Grewal, and S. W. Brown, "Consumer Satisfaction and Perceived Quality: Complementary or Divergent Constructs?" *Journal of Applied Psychology,* Vol. 79, No. 6 (1994), pp. 875–885. For an excellent article on the measurement of service quality, refer to Robert F. Hurley and Hooman Estelami, "Alternative Indexes for Monitoring Customer Perceptions of Service Quality: A Comparative Evaluation in a Retail Context," *Journal of the Academy of Marketing Science,* Vol. 26 (Summer 1998), pp. 209–221. Also, we recommend the following article: Valerie A. Zeithaml, "Service Quality, Profitability, and the Economic Worth of Customers: What We Know and What We Need to Learn," *Journal of the Academy of Marketing Science,* Vol. 28 (Winter 2000), pp. 67–85; David A. Garvin, "Competing on the Eight Dimensions of Quality," *Harvard Business Review,* 65 (November–December 1987), pp. 241–243; Merrie Brucks, Valerie A. Zeithaml, and Gillian Naylor, "Price and Brand Name as Indicators of Quality Dimensions for Consumer Durables," *Journal of the Academy of Marketing Science,* Vol. 28 (Summer 2000), pp. 359–374.

88. Ibid.

89. Christian Gronroos, *Strategic Management and Marketing in the Service Sector.* Helsingfors: Swedish School of Economics and Racine-Administration (1982); Christian Gronroos, "A Service Quality Model and Its Marketing Implications," *European Journal of Marketing,* Vol. 18 (1984), pp. 36–44; Christian Gronroos, *Service Management and Marketing: Managing the Moments in Truth in Service Competition.* Lexington, MA: Lexington Books (1990).

90. Emin Babakus and Gregory W. Boiler, "An Empirical Assessment of the SERVQUAL Scale," *Journal of Business Research,* Vol. 24 (1992), pp. 253–268; James M. Carman, "Consumer Perceptions of Service Quality: An Assessment of the SERVQUAL Dimensions," *Journal of Retailing,* Vol. 66 (1990), pp. 33–55; James M. Carman, "Patient Perceptions of Service Quality: Combining the Dimensions," *Journal of Services Marketing,* Vol. 14 (2000), pp. 337–352; Albert Caruana, Michael T. Ewing, and B. Ramaseshan, "Assessment of the Three-Column Format SERVQUAL: An Experimental Approach," *Journal of Business Research,* Vol. 49 (2000), pp. 57–65; Alison M. Dean, "The Applicability of SERVQUAL in Different Health Care Settings," *Health Marketing Quarterly,* Vol. 16 (1999), pp.1–15; Srinivas Durvasula, Steven Lysonski, and Subhash C. Mehta, "Testing the SERVQUAL Scale in the Business-to-Business Sector: The Case of the Ocean Freight Shipping Service," *Journal of Services Marketing,* Vol. 13 (1999), pp. 132–148; Scott W. Kelley and L. W. Turley, "Consumer Perceptions of Service Quality Attributes at Sporting Events," *Journal of Business Research,* Vol. 54 (November 2001), pp. 161–166.

91. Michael K. Brady and J. Joseph Cronin, Jr., "Some New Thoughts on Conceptualizing Perceive Service Quality: A Hierarchical Approach," *Journal of Marketing,* Vol. 65 (2001), pp. 34–50.

92. Ibid.

93. Pratibha Dabholkar, "A Contingency Framework for Predicting Causality Between Consumer Satisfaction and Service Quality," in *Advances for Consumer Research,* Vol. 22 (Provo, UT: Association for Consumer Research, 1995), pp. 101–106.

94. R. A. Bauer, "Consumer Behavior as Risk Taking," in *Risk Taking and Information Handling in Consumer Behavior,* D. F. Cox, ed., Harvard University Press, Cambridge, MA, pp. 23–43.

95. Vincent-Wayne Mitchell, Fiona Davies, Luiz Moutinho, and Vassiliades Vasso, "Using Neural Networks to Understand Service Risk in the Holiday Product," *Journal of Business Research,* Vol. 46 (October 1999), pp. 167–180.

96. F. J. Dash, L. G. Schiffman, and C. Berenson, "Risk- and Personality-related Dimensions of Store Choice," *Journal of Marketing,* Vol. 40 (January 1976), pp. 32–39; R. D. Hirsch, R. J. Doronoff, and J. B. Kernan, "Perceived Risk in Store Selection," *Journal of Marketing Research,* Vol. 9 (November 1972), pp. 435–439; V. K. Prasad, "Socioeconomic Product Risk and Patronage Preferences of Retail Shoppers," *Journal of*

Marketing, Vol. 39 (July 1975), pp. 42–47; V. -W. Mitchell, "Re-conceptualizing Consumer Store Image Processing Using Perceived Risk," *Journal of Business Research,* Vol. 54 (November 2001), pp. 167–172; Sandra M. Forsyth and Bo Shi, "Consumer Patronage and Risk Perceptions in Internet Shopping," *Journal of Business Research,* Vol. 56 (2003), pp. 867–875; Olivier Brunel and Paul Emmanuel Pichon, "Food-related Risk-reduction Strategies: Purchasing and Consumption Processes," *Journal of Consumer Psychology,* Vol. 3 (2004), pp. 360–374.

97. Ibid.

98. Thomas A. Burnham, Judy K. Frels, and Vijay Mahajan, "Consumer Switching Costs: A Typology, Antecedents, and Consequences," *Journal of the Academy of Marketing Science,* Vol. 31 (Spring 2003), pp. 109–126.

99. Kent B. Monroe, "Buyers' Subjective Perceptions of Price," *Journal of Marketing Research,* Vol. 10 (February 1973), pp. 70–80: Muzafer Sherif and Carl Hovland, *Social Judgment: Assimilation and Contrast Effects in Communication and Attitude Change* (New Haven, CT: Yale University Press, 1961); Abhijit Biswas, Elizabeth J. Wilson, and Jane W. Licata, "Reference Pricing Studies in Marketing: A Synthesis of Research Results," *Journal of Business Research,* Vol. 27 (1993), pp. 239–256; Bruce L. Alford and Brian T. Engelland, "Advertised Reference Price Effects on Consumer Price Estimates, Value Perception, and Search Intention," *Journal of Business Research,* Vol. 48, (May 2000), pp. 93–100; Chris Janiszweski and Donald R. Lichtenstein, "A Range Theory Account of Price Perception," *Journal of Consumer Research,* Vol. 25 (March 1999), pp. 353–368; Chezy Ofir, "Reexamining Latitude of Price Acceptability and Price Thresholds: Predicting Basic Reaction to Price," *Journal of Consumer Research,* Vol. 30 (2004), pp. 612–622.

100. R. Chandrashekaran, "The Implications of Individual Differences in Reference Price Utilization for Designing Effective Price Communications," Journal of Business research, Vol. 53 (2001), pp. 85-91.

101. Dhruv Grewal, Kent B. Monroe, and R. Krishnan, "The Effects of Price-Comparison Advertising on Buyers' Perceptions of Acquisition Value, Transaction Value, and Behavioral Intentions," *Journal of Marketing,* Vol. 62 (April 1998), pp. 45–69; Akshay R. Rao and Kent B. Monroe, "The Effect of Price, Brand Name, and Store Name on Buyers' Perceptions of Product Quality: An Integrative Review," *Journal of Marketing Research,* Vol. 26 (August 1989), pp. 351–357; Valerie Zeithaml, "Consumer Perceptions of Price, Quality, and Value: A Mean-End Model and Synthesis of Evidence," *Journal of Marketing,* Vol. 52, (July 1988), pp. 2–22; R. Kenneth Teas and Sanjeev Agarwal, "The Effects of Extrinsic Product Cues on Consumers' Perceptions of Quality, Sacrifice, and Value," *Journal of the Academy of Marketing Science,* Vol. 28 (Spring 2000), pp. 278–290.

102. Youjae Yi and Hoseong Jeon, "Effects of Loyalty Programs on Value Perception, Program Loyalty, and Brand Loyalty," *Journal of the Academy of Marketing Science,* Vol. 31 (Summer 2003), pp. 229–240.

103. Ming-Huei Hsieh, Shan-Ling Pan, and Rudy Setiono, "Product-, Corporate-, and Country-Image Dimensions and Purchase Behavior: A Multicountry Analysis," *Journal of the Academy of Marketing Science,* Vol. 32 (Summer 2004), pp. 251–270; Koert van Ittersum, Math J. J. M. Candel, and Matthew T. G. Meulenberg, "The Influence of the Image of a Product's Region of Origin on Product Evaluation," *Journal of Business Research,* Vol. 56 (March 2003), pp. 215–226; Louis A. Heslop, Nicolas Papadopoulos, Melissa Dowdles, Marjorie Wall, and Deborah Compeau, "Who Controls the Purse Strings: A Study of Consumers and Retail Buyers' Reactions in an America's FTA Environment," *Journal* of Business Research, Vol. 57 (2004), pp. 1177–1188.

104. C. Min Han, "Country Image: Halo or Summary Construct?" *Journal of Marketing Research,* Vol. 26 (May 1989), pp. 222–229.

105. Gregory S. Carpenter and Kent Nakamoto, "Consumer Preference Formation and Pioneering Advantage," *Journal of Marketing Research,* Vol. 26 (August 1989), pp. 285–298.

Motivation, Emotion, Mood, and Involvement

Johnny is on the track team in high school. Doing well on the track team is important to him. His classmates respect him for his athletic performance. The girls admire him for his good looks. Most importantly, he believes that doing well on the school's track team may help him obtain an athletic scholarship for college.

Whatever Johnny buys and consumes nowadays seems related to his activities on the track. For example, every food item he buys and consumes is related to his performance on the track team. Look at the Power Bar ad shown in Exhibit 8-1. The ad says, "In my experience, it takes a lot more than two wheels to cross the finish line." The ad is emphasizing the fact that Power Bar is a nutritional snack that can provide sufficient energy to athletes to allow them to "cross the finish line." The ad appeals to athletes like Johnny who want to perform at their very best and need to eat something that can give them the extra boost. The ad appeals to a product need. Athletes like Johnny who are exposed to this ad are likely to become motivated to purchase and consume Power Bars to satisfy their need to help them "cross the finish line."

Consumer motivation is one of the driving forces of consumer behavior. Consumers buy and use products because they are motivated by the need or desire to do so. The key objective of marketing and marketing communications is to motivate consumers to prefer and purchase one product or brand over another.

Tied to motivation is the concept of affective states. Simply stated, affective states are emotions, feelings, and moods that are connected with a purchase decision and that can motivate the consumer to buy. In this chapter, we'll discuss the concepts of motives, emotions, mood, and involvement to show how marketers should account for these concepts when developing strategies.

8-1 Consumer Motivation

Consumer motivation is the drive to satisfy needs and wants, both physiological and psychological, through the purchase and use of products and services. Some motives are simple—we need food, water, warmth, and shelter in order to survive. Others are more complex, such as the yearning for love or the desire for status and admiration.

An impelling and compelling force behind most marketplace behaviors, consumer motivation can be viewed as a process through which needs are satisfied. The process has five stages, as demonstrated in Exhibit 8-2. It begins with a latent need, such

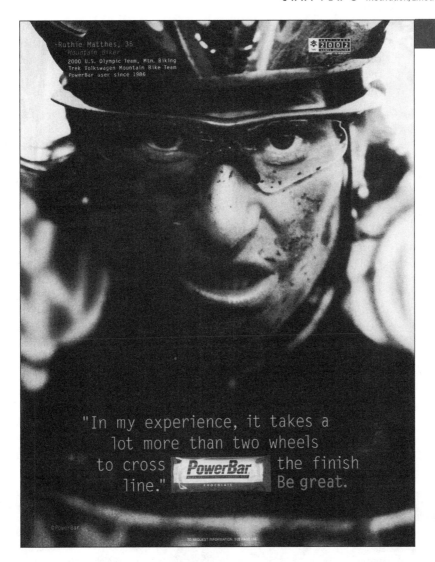

The Power Bar ad appeals to athletes' need to "cross the finish line."

Source: Copyright John Huet 2001. Reprinted by permission of Marilyn Cadenbach Associates.

▶**consumer motivation**
(see p. 248) The drive to satisfy needs and wants, both physiological and psychological, through the purchase and use of products and services.

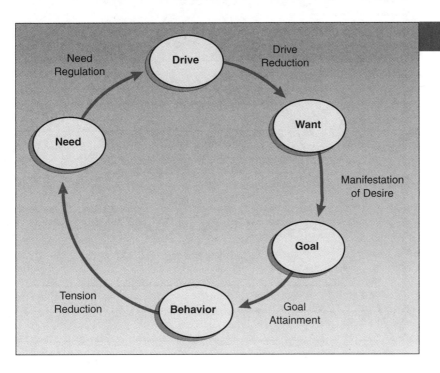

Motivation as a Process

Motivation moves consumers from latent need through stages of increasing specificity to the behavior that satisfies the need.

as hunger. Once the need is recognized, we feel a drive to reduce it. You realize you are hungry and start thinking about lunch options. Need translates into want or desire—you crave pizza. Desire is manifested into a specific goal as you look in the Yellow Pages for alternative pizza restaurants and decide on Pizza Hut. That goal is achieved through a behavior that satisfies the original need and thus reduces tension—you sit down in Pizza Hut and order a large pepperoni pizza.[1]

8-1a Using Behavior Models to Explain Motivation

To understand how the concept of motivation applies to marketing, let's begin by looking at three key behavior models or classification schemes that explain the process of motivation and predict how consumers will behave in response to it.

Maslow's Hierarchy of Needs   Psychologist Abraham Maslow described motivation as a means of satisfying human needs. As summarized in Exhibit 8-3, Maslow explained personal growth through the identification and satisfaction of a **hierarchy of needs,** from the basics of food and shelter to sophisticated psychological desires.[2]

At the base of the pyramid are physiological needs—basic physical needs such as food and water, and biological needs such as sleep, exercise, and the drive for sex. Once these needs are partially or fully met, we begin to yearn for safety—protection from danger, security, and reliable order and routine in daily affairs. From safety evolves a need for love and belonging—the desire to give and receive affection and to be accepted as one who belongs as part of a family or group. Once accepted into the group, we begin to crave esteem or status—the desire for self-respect and the respect of others, as well as the need to feel competent, confident, important, and appreciated. As needs become more abstract and sophisticated, we desire self-actualization—the need to realize our own potential, to achieve our dreams and ambitions. As the desire for self-actualization grows more potent, it evolves into a more specific hunger for knowledge and understanding—the search for

hierarchy of needs
As described by Maslow, a hierarchy of human needs— from the basics of food and shelter to sophisticated psychological desires—the identification and satisfaction of which motivate human growth.

Exhibit 8-3

Maslow's Hierarchy of Needs

As each need is satisfied, beginning with the basics of food and shelter, human needs move to the emotional desires and finally to sophisticated psychological needs.

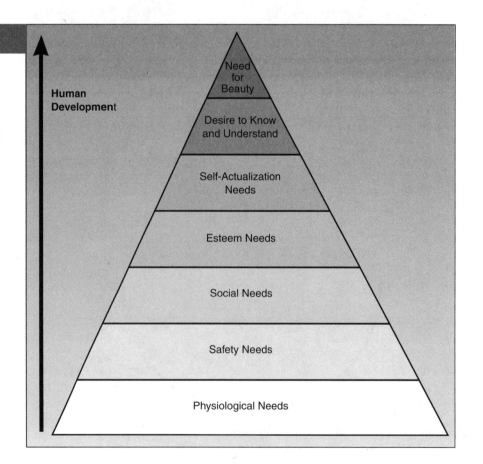

Consumption Motives	Examples	
1. Power-masculinity-virility	Power tools, hot rods, coffee, red meat, heavy shoes, razor	E x h i b i t **8-4**
2. Security	Ice cream, home baking, hospital care	**Dichter's Major Consumption Motives**
3. Eroticism	Sweets, gloves, red convertible sports car	
4. Moral purity/cleanliness	Soap, cotton fabric, household cleaning chemicals, oatmeal	
5. Social acceptance	Ice cream, coffee, toys	
6. Individuality	Gourmet food, foreign cars	
7. Status	Scotch whiskey, fashionable clothes, luxury cars	
8. Femininity	Cakes, cookies, dolls, silk	
9. Reward	Candy, ice cream, cigarettes, alcohol	
10. Mastery over environment	Kitchen appliances, powerboats, sporting goods	
11. Disalienation	Home decoration, morning radio	
12. Magic-mastery	Drinking soup when sick	

meaning and analyses of self and environment. Lastly comes the most refined need of all, that for beauty.

Maslow believed that these motivating forces operate more or less sequentially. That is, as needs at one level are partially or fully satisfied, those at the next are felt more intensely. Lower-level needs must be met or partially met if higher-level needs are to emerge. Although no level of need may ever be completely satisfied, as satisfaction at one level increases, the need at the next level becomes a stronger and stronger motivator.

Dichter's Major Consumption Motives   Ernest Dichter's model of consumption motives stems from a 1950s study he conducted on behalf of Procter & Gamble into the consumer needs motivating the purchase of Ivory soap. Dichter concluded that bathing as a cleansing ritual has a symbolic appeal among consumers, signifying purification from the taints of the world. He related the use of soap to a need for spiritual purity. On the basis of this research, Dichter steered the development of an extremely successful advertising campaign.[3]

According to Dichter, product consumption is driven by twelve key motives.[4] Exhibit 8-4 demonstrates how each of these motivations translates into different purchase choices.

Sheth's Consumer Motives   Developed as a classification scheme to predict consumer decisions in travel, Jagdish Sheth's consumer needs model applies equally well to most other products and services. Sheth isolated five dimensions of motivation, each oriented to the achievement of specific goals.[5] The functional motive involves the utility of a product or service or the function it performs. The aesthetic/emotional motive is met by the appearance or attractiveness of a product or service. The social motive is reflected in the status or esteem value of a product or service. The situational motive is triggered by an unexpected benefit of a product or service, such as discounted price or immediate availability. The curiosity motive is simply the interest aroused by a product or service. Exhibit 8-5 provides examples of each motive, with a resulting consumption action.

Marketers can use Sheth's model to predict brand choices by consumers. A study of cigarette smoking found that aesthetic/emotional motives dominate in the decision of whether or not to smoke. People associate such criteria as feeling intelligent, feeling confident, and/or feeling safe with the decision to smoke. The choice between filtered and nonfiltered cigarettes, however, is governed by both functional and social motives. Consumers consider both taste (functional) and referent groups with whom they identify (social). Choice of

	Motives	Examples
E x h i b i t 8-5		
Sheth's Consumer Motives	1. Functional	Purchase of a car because of its gas mileage, reliability, roominess, safety, etc.
	2. Aesthetic/emotional	Purchase of a car because of its style, color, shape, etc.
	3. Social	Purchase of a car because it has an image reflecting a reference group
	4. Situational	Purchase of a car because it was heavily discounted
	5. Curiosity	Purchase of a car because it is a new experience

brand is the result of social motives. Specifically, Marlboro smokers associate their brand with "men," "cowboys," "outdoorsmen," and "blue-collar workers." Virginia Slims smokers associate their brand with "women," "sophisticated women," and "rich people."

The three models—Maslow, Dichter, and Sheth—all describe the needs that drive consumer behavior. Their comprehensiveness allows consumer researchers and marketers to explain and predict almost any conceivable motive influencing consumer actions.

8-1b How Consumer Motivation Affects Marketplace Behavior

The motives described by Maslow, Dichter, and Sheth affect several types of consumer behavior, most importantly consumer decision making, consumer conflict resolution, and consumption patterns.

Influence on Consumer Decision Making   In making product and service decisions, consumers move through a sequence of choices, as shown in Exhibit 8-6. First, the consumer selects a generic category of goods or services. A would-be tourist, for example, decides to travel rather than stay home to watch the Super Bowl. Second, the consumer makes a modal choice. For the tourist, this involves choosing between air or rail travel. Finally, the consumer makes a specific choice. Once the decision is made to fly, the choice is made between, say, Delta and United Airlines. In each of these three decisions, the consumer is swayed toward or away from different alternatives by the strength or weakness of

E x h i b i t 8-6

The Effects of Consumers' Needs on Decision Making

Consumers' needs affect every stage of the choice sequence. One need—curiosity, for instance— may affect category selection, while another—functional, perhaps—may affect modal choice, and yet a third may influence the specific choice.

INTERACTIVE EXHIBIT

Consumers' Needs:
• Functional
• Aesthetic/Emotional
• Social
• Situational
• Curiosity

Select a generic category. → Make a modal choice. → Make a specific choice.

Consumer Decision Making

different motives. The choice of airline might, for example, boil down to the lowest fare. The decision is mostly dictated by a functional motive—the need to save money.[6]

Influence on Consumer Conflict Resolution   Any two or more motives can be activated at the same time, pulling the consumer in different directions. Shonda sees a wonderful dress at the department store and is very tempted to buy it. Her budget, however, will not allow it. While buying the dress would satisfy her need to look and feel good, it frustrates her need to be financially responsible and avoid getting into debt. Pulled in two directions, she experiences conflict and seeks ways in which to resolve it. In this section, we will explore how motives are activated and how conflicts are resolved in the marketplace.

As a form of goal-seeking behavior, motivation usually involves one of three forms of conflict.

Approach-Approach Conflict   In an **approach-approach conflict,** the individual faces a dilemma of choosing between or among alternatives—or approaches—that seem equally attractive. Miya, a single woman, has $1,000 saved for a winter vacation and plans a trip to Club Med in Guadalupe, Mexico, to enjoy a relaxing week in the sun. As much as the vacation itself, she is looking forward to returning home to Milwaukee with a good tan and the envy of her colleagues. A friend calls and invites Miya to join her for a week at Winter Carnival in Quebec, Canada. Miya loves to ski, so the two alternatives are equally attractive. How will she decide? Travel marketers know that consumers have so many options that difficult choices are inevitable. "It's Better in the Bahamas" and "The U.S. Virgin Islands: We have the best weather in the Caribbean" are examples of competing campaigns to help consumers resolve approach-approach conflicts.

approach-approach conflict
A situation in which the consumer faces a dilemma of choosing between or among alternatives—or approaches—that seem equally attractive.

Approach-Avoidance Conflict   In an **approach-avoidance conflict,** the same goal has both positive and negative characteristics. Many families would love to own a powerboat. It means freedom, fun on the water, a chance to entertain and impress friends, and a welcome escape from workaday life. But powerboats, as anyone who has one knows, can also be a virtually endless drain on family finances. Fuel and maintenance costs, insurance, docking fees, and expensive repairs all add up to a high financial risk. The consumer who returns from a boat show armed with brochures, ready to choose between models, will most likely experience approach-avoidance conflict as soon as friends who own boats and other sobering information sources are consulted. To overcome approach-avoidance conflict, powerboat marketing typically stresses dependability, easy maintenance, and fuel economy.

approach-avoidance conflict
A situation in which the same goal has both positive and negative characteristics.

F A Q

Is conflict the basis of all decision making?

Avoidance-Avoidance Conflict   A particularly daunting marketing task is to resolve the type of conflict no consumer likes—an **avoidance-avoidance conflict,** which involves choosing between two undesirable alternatives. Buying a new set of tires is very expensive. But if the alternative is to keep a set of old tires and risk hydroplaning on the highway in a rainstorm, most consumers will choose the lesser of two evils and make the investment in fresh treads. Tire manufacturers recognize avoidance-avoidance conflict and market their strengths to overcome the consumer's natural resistance through ads like that in Exhibit 8-7, featuring product information about quality ("Goodyear—serious technology") and assurance of safety and security ("Goodyear—freedom from worry").

avoidance-avoidance conflict
A situation in which the consumer faces two negative alternatives.

Influence on Consumption Patterns   Motives, once activated, shape resulting behaviors. The need for achievement affects such behaviors as performing well on the job or in school; the need for power affects such behaviors as competing for a management position; the need for affiliation affects such behaviors as being pleasant to others in order to gain their friendship.

Several studies have revealed the influence of consumer motives on actual marketplace behavior.[7] One recent study measured health motivation using a self-report inventory with items such as: "I try to prevent health problems before I feel any symptoms," "I

am concerned about health hazards and try to take action to prevent them," and "I try to protect myself against health hazards I hear about." Health-related behaviors have also been measured using self-report inventories related to dieting (eating a well-balanced diet, reducing sodium intake, cutting back on snacks and treats), stress-related behaviors (getting enough rest and sleep, reducing anxiety, maintaining a balance between work and play), and consumption of tobacco and alcohol, among others.

Although many consumption behaviors can be directly related to obvious motives, others involve a web of different motivations. A recent study investigated the various and complex motives behind high-risk leisure activities.[8] The study revealed that people who engage in activities such as skydiving, mountain climbing, scuba diving, and hang gliding tend to be motivated differently at different stages of the activity. First, motives for getting started include curiosity, thrill seeking, social compliance, and a desire for adventure. As one skydiver puts it:

> There were twenty of us. One guy goes, "Man, I've always wanted to skydive. Why don't we do that this weekend?" And we were like, "Yeah, sure," in one ear and out the other. Well, this guy organized the whole trip. I was so excited. It was something I would never pursue on my own. Five of us went, three guys and two girls. I can say one thing. It helped out a lot having them with me. I would never have done that by myself.[9]

Second, motives for sticking with the activity include efficacy (a desire to develop technical skill for both personal satisfaction and social status), the creation of a new self-identity, group camaraderie (a need to develop and reinforce interpersonal bonds), and heightened experience (a desire for intense emotional experience).

While a crooked Christmas tree is not at the top of everyone's gripe list, many consumers, presented with a solution, will opt to seek the desired state of having a straighter evergreen under which to put presents.

Third, motives for increased involvement include **flow** (a need for intense experience with thrill and excitement), communitas (a need for a sense of community), and phatic community (a need for a special means of communication or language that helps the bonding process and that excludes those who do not share the experience).[10]

flow Motivation experienced when the skills involved in the achievement task match the consumer's skills level.

8-1c How Marketers Can Trigger Consumer Motives

Marketers can trigger consumer motives by inducing need recognition, triggering motivation through need-benefit segmentation, and triggering subconscious motivation.

Inducing Need Recognition   To activate consumer motives and thus guide marketplace behavior, the marketer must steer the consumer from an actual state to a desired state. Take, for example, the ad in Exhibit 8-8 for a Christmas tree stand. Many families have struggled to straighten a crooked pine tree in a traditional stand. The actual state is frustration; the desired state is to have a lovely, straight tree. The advertisement induces need recognition—consumers realize they need the advertised tree stand to avoid the annual yuletide hassle.

Marketplace 8-1 describes an interesting debate in macromarketing. The debate centers on the question of whether marketers create consumer needs for the purpose of selling their products. Read the article to find out what the answer is.

F A Q

Can anything be marketed without reference to a desired state?

Triggering Motivation through Need-Benefit Segmentation   By understanding consumer motivations, marketers can better target goods and services to meet the needs of specific market segments. They can emphasize benefits that satisfy recognizable needs. A tire manufacturer, for example, might advertise in *Modern Maturity* that its radial tire is blowout-proof, satisfying the need of older consumers for safety and security. Advertised in *Playboy*, the same tire can be offered with racy white lettering to appeal to consumers eager to project a young, sporty image, satisfying the need for esteem. Look back at the Goodyear ad in Exhibit 8-7. What need segment is this ad addressing?

Marketplace 8-2 describes a typology of shopping motives for mail-order purchases—that is, consumers buy from catalogs for a variety of reasons. What are those reasons? Marketplace 8-3 describes another typology of shopping motives for online grocery purchases. For cross reference material on shopper types, see Exhibit 3-15 and Marketplace 3-5.

Marketplace 8-1

Do Marketers Create Needs?

Needs drive consumers to set and meet goals through specific kinds of purchasing behavior. Can needs be created by advertising? Is it advertising that raises the question in people's minds as to whether they are driving the wrong car, wearing the wrong sports shoes, or using the wrong brand of laundry detergent? Does advertising inspire the desire for a getaway vacation, a rich dessert, or a remodeled kitchen? Not really. Because the basic need to be liked and respected or to live comfortably is already there, as part of our culture and as part of the consumer's psychological makeup. Advertising simply highlights these needs in the consumer's mind by presenting goods and services that promise to satisfy them.

From another perspective, however, people blame advertising for "making them" buy things they had hardly given thought to before. The tremendously successful AT&T campaign, "Reach Out and Touch Someone," makes this point. Prior to the campaign, most people thought about long-distance telephone service in terms of functional needs—calls are made to relay information, set up appointments, and make plans. The campaign injected other psychological needs into the use of long distance: By using the telephone to keep in touch, customers expressed and experienced love, friendship, and a sense of belonging. Although all this may have at some level motivated people to call long distance, the campaign strengthened these associations, played them up, and made them central to the use of long-distance telephone services. Judge for yourself. Did AT&T create a need? What other instances can you think of?

Marketplace 8-2

Shopping Motives for Mail Catalog Shopping

What are the motives that drive people to shop for products through mail catalogs? Recent research has uncovered that these motives can be classified into the following eleven major dimensions:

- *Perceived value.* People shop using mail catalogs because they get good value for their money, they buy high-quality products, and they buy dependable products.

- *Convenience.* People shop using mail catalogs because they feel that they can find what they want in the least time, they save time and effort searching, and they can shop whenever they want.

- *Economic utility.* People shop using mail catalogs because they can comparison shop, they can find real bargains, and they can shop "carefully."

- *Home environment.* People shop using mail catalogs because they can shop in the comfort, safety, and privacy of their home.

- *Merchandise assortment.* People shop using mail catalogs because they can buy the latest styles, access many brands, and access a wide selection of goods.

- *Order services.* People shop using mail catalogs because they can easily order through a toll-free number and use credit services.

- *Company clientele.* People shop using mail catalogs because friends know, like, and recommend the company.

- *Information services.* People shop using mail catalogs because the salespeople who answer the phone are courteous, helpful, and eager to please.

- *Salesperson interaction.* People shop using mail catalogs because they like to talk with the salesperson who answers the phone and negotiate a lower price.

- *Company responsiveness.* People shop using mail catalogs because they feel that it is easy to return purchases and that the company is friendly to its customers.

- *Company reputation.* People shop using mail catalogs because they feel they are doing business with a well-known company, a company that has been in business for a long time, and a company they can trust.

Source: Adapted from "Shopping Motives for Mail Catalog Shopping" by Mary Ann Eastlick and Richard A. Feinberg in *Journal of Business Research,* Volume 45, July 1999, pp. 281–290.

Marketplace 8-3

Online Grocery Shopping Types

Research has shown that shoppers who purchase groceries online can be characterized as belonging to one of the following four motivational groups:

1. *The convenience shopper.* This type of shopper is motivated by the prospects of overall online shopping convenience.

2. *The variety seeker.* This type of shopper, although somewhat motivated by online shopping convenience, is driven by variety seeking.

3. *The balanced buyer.* This type of shopper is motivated by both online shopping convenience and variety seeking.

4. *The store-oriented shopper.* These shoppers are motivated by the desire for immediate possession of goods and social interaction. Of course these shoppers exhibit the least propensity to do much of their grocery shopping online. They prefer to shop for groceries at their neighborhood grocery store.

Source: Adapted from "A Typology of Online Shoppers, Based on Shopping Motivations" by Andrew J. Rohm and Vanitha Swaminathan in *Journal of Business Research,* Volume 57, July 2004, pp. 748–757.

Triggering Subconscious Motivation   Many purchases reveal subconscious motivations. For instance, the use of cigars and cigarettes is connected to such hidden motives as oral and sexual gratification. Similarly, some consumers view sports cars as symbols of virility.[11]

Can marketers sell anything—no matter how trivial or useless the product or service? Of course, they can do so by associating the offering with important consumer needs or motives. The question then becomes: Is it ethical to do so? Read Marketplace 8-4 to provoke some thought.

Marketing Management—Implications and Actions

Understanding consumer motivation helps marketers:

- Know which underlying needs motivate consumption.
- Reduce the conflict that can hamper consumer decision making.
- Target marketing images to consumers' subconscious motivations.
- Trigger motivation through need-benefit actions.

8-2 Emotions

Emotions are affective responses that reflect the activation of deep-seated and value-laden beliefs within the consumer. An example might be "robbery is wrong." The evocation of a belief generates a corresponding emotion, and different emotions are triggered by different beliefs. Consumers who deeply believe that robbery is wrong are likely to exhibit the emotive response of anger once they discover their house has been burgled. Conversely, consumers who believe that ownership of property is of low importance will have a very different emotional response.[12]

> **emotions** Affective responses that reflect the activation of deep-seated and value-laden beliefs within the consumer.

8-2a How Consumers Experience Emotions

People purchase and use products and services in order to experience certain emotional states or to achieve emotional goals. We use products to create fantasies, to gain feelings

Marketplace 8-4

The Art of Selling Nothing

Taking the famous "nonproduct" of the 1970s, the Pet Rock, one step further, two advertising executives in 1984 created a product that perhaps set the all-time record for nothingness: the canned alien. As the Pet Rock did, the canned alien came with a story: The students of Mung, a totally dark and airless planet many light years away, were eager to visit other parts of the galaxy, so Mungians established a student exchange program. Because their students could not survive in our hostile environment, they were sealed in tin cans and delivered to earth by the Canned Alien Placement Service of Clemmons, North Carolina. The cans were stamped with the legend: "Do not puncture this can! Alien will die and disappear without a trace."

The can came in a small windowed box that also contained an "Alien Care Booklet," which was droll—and needed to be because that was the sizzle for which consumers paid. If, despite all the warnings, the host opened the can, the only thing he found was the "Last Will and Testament" of the alien student he had just "killed."

Although some may think this product was a hoax, the implications may not be so simple. Did the product satisfy any needs? If so, what needs? Could the product be said to have any value as a direct result of need satisfaction? Sit down with your mood ring and ponder the deeper implications.

Source: Adapted from "The Art of Selling Nothing" by Philip H. Dougherty from *The New York Times,* July 9, 1984, p. D9. Copyright © 1984 by The New York Times Co. Reprinted by permission.

through the senses, and to obtain emotional arousal.[13] Certain products have little functional value and are purchased purely for their ability to arouse emotions. The purchase of a diamond ring, for example, symbolizes love and permanence. We go to movies, rock concerts, the theater, or sporting events for the emotional experiences they bring to us. Consumers experience emotions through a cognitive appraisal process. For example, gratitude, as an emotion, is triggered by having a consumer appraise a marketplace event as a pleasant, moderately certain, fair circumstance. The consumer infers the success condition to be caused by the firm or personnel in the firm, and the consumer is not assuming personal responsibility for the pleasant event.[14] See Exhibit 8-9.

CBite 8-1 on page 260 illustrates how consumers' purchases of leisure products and services are guided by emotionality.

Emotions and Post-purchase Evaluation   Emotions play an important role in determining the extent of satisfaction or dissatisfaction with purchased products or services. A purchaser who subsequently experiences positive emotions such as joy and pleasant surprise is likely to be satisfied with the product purchased. Conversely, of course, if the consumer experiences negative emotions such as distress or anger, the result is dissatisfaction.[15]

In one study, new car owners were asked about their feelings regarding the cars they had just purchased. The study revealed that pleasant surprise and interest were associated with consumer satisfaction whereas, as one would expect, disgust, contempt, guilt, and sadness were predictive of dissatisfaction.[16]

A recent study has demonstrated that anger toward a service provider and dissatisfaction are distinct emotional reactions. Anger is associated with appraising an event as harmful and frustrating. It is typically directed at another person, a firm, or at oneself. People associate anger with feelings "as if they would explode." Typical thoughts include "thinking of violence towards others." An action tendency of anger may be for someone to "feel like behaving aggressively." An example of an action related to anger is "saying something nasty." In contrast, dissatisfaction is a "distress" emotion that occurs when an event is perceived to be unpleasant or obstructive to achieving one's goals. It is an undifferentiated and general emotion. Cognitions of negative disconfirmation, underfulfillment of needs, and inequity are associated with dissatisfaction. In a study involving a survey of consumer

Consumer Emotion	Key Marketplace Appraisals
Love	Pleasant, certain, fair marketplace event; no obstacles and no anticipated effort on the part of the consumer; responsibility and control of the pleasant event lies with the firm or personnel within the firm (not with the consumer)
Happiness	Pleasant, certain, fair marketplace event; no obstacles and no anticipated effort on the part of the consumer; responsibility for the pleasant event, in part, lies with the consumer
Pride	Pleasant, certain, extremely fair marketplace event; responsibility for the pleasant event is attributed to the self (consumer) for the most part and modestly to the firm (or personnel within the firm)
Gratitude	Pleasant, moderately certain, fair marketplace event; responsibility for the pleasant event is attributed to the firm or personnel within the firm, and very little to the self (consumer)
Fear	Unpleasant, highly uncertain marketplace event; the event requires consumer attention and effort to address modest obstacle
Anger	Unpleasant, highly unfair marketplace event with an obstacle to overcome; responsibility for the unpleasant event is attributed to the firm or the personnel within the firm, not the self (consumer)
Sadness	Unpleasant, uncertain, moderately unfair marketplace event; consumer believes that s/he could have exercised control over the situation; blames self
Guilt	Unpleasant marketplace event; the consumer blames himself/herself for the event (moderately strong perceived obstacle); consumer does not blame the firm or the firm's personnel
Uneasiness	Unpleasant, uncertain marketplace event involving a high amount of anticipated effort
Embarrassment	Unpleasant marketplace event involving an obstacle; responsibility is attributed to neither self nor firm

Consumers' emotions are triggered by their cognitive appraisals of marketplace events.

Source: Adapted from Julie A. Ruth, Frederic F. Brunel, and Cele C. Otnes, "Linking Thoughts to Feelings: Investigating Cognitive Appraisals and Consumption Emotions in a Mixed-Emotions Context," *Journal of the Academy of Marketing Science,* Vol. 30 (Winter 2002), pp. 44–58.

experiences with service organizations, anger was found to be affected by consumer dissatisfaction rather than the other way around. In turn, both consumer dissatisfaction and anger played a significant role in consumers complaining about the service provider, switching to another service provider, and engaging in negative word-of-mouth communication about the service provider.[17] For additional discussion of post-purchase evaluation, see section 4-4b in Chapter 4.

Emotions and Communication   Emotions play a mediating role in consumer responses to advertising.[18] This is demonstrated in Exhibit 8-10. Specifically, communication cues can evoke emotional responses such as pleasure or displeasure, which in turn affect consumers' attitudes toward the advertising. Attitude toward the advertising, in turn, influences attitude toward the advertised brand.[19]

Advertising can also induce such feelings as anger, fear, sexual desire, and surprise, albeit at relatively low levels. Moreover, these feelings, experienced as a direct result of advertising, affect beliefs, knowledge, and behavior.[20] Many advertisements are designed with a very specific emotional appeal in mind. They aim to arouse a range of emotions from humor, to desire, to guilt, to nostalgia, and so on.

Exhibit 8-10

The Mediating Effect of Emotions on Communication Cues and Attitude toward the Brand

Emotional responses evoked by advertising may, in turn, affect consumers' attitudes toward the advertised brand. This theory has been used to argue against the use of fear ads that may generate negative feelings.

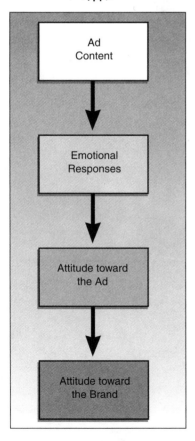

8-2b How Emotional States Are Induced

Psychologists have long recognized that people have little control over the affective system. Affective responses to environmental cues are immediate and automatic. Take color as an environmental stimulus, for example. People respond immediately to certain colors without even knowing why. Some respond more strongly than others, influencing their like or dislike of products simply on account of their color.[21]

A recent study showed that emotions (positive and negative affect) can be induced by perceptions of salespersons' unethical behavior. Specifically, the research has shown that consumers respond with negative affect when they notice a salesperson behaving opportunistically. Perceptions of violations of moral contracts also were found to induce a negative affect. For example, consumers expect a salesperson at a car dealer to act in ways considered to be amoral. By the same token, consumers do not expect insurance agents to act opportunistically. If they run into a situation in which an insurance agent is perceived to act not in the best interest of the consumer, the consumer is likely to experience negative affect, which in turn leads to the decision not to do more business with that insurance agent.[22] For additional discussion of moral equity, see section 4-2b in Chapter 4.

Behavior and Emotions   Although we have little influence over the triggering of emotions, we can exert some control through our behavior. By acting in certain ways, we can experience outcomes that yield desirable affective reactions in particular situations. For example, a consumer who feels insulted when ignored by a salesperson in a retail environment can complain to the store manager. Complaining generates a feeling of satisfaction. In a crowded store, customers might feel frustrated because they have to fight the crowds to find the right product or get assistance and wait in long lines to pay. To exert control, they can leave crowded stores and shop in less crowded ones. This behavior allows them to control emotions by reducing the experience of negative feelings and enhancing the likelihood of experiencing positive ones.[23]

Specific Emotions   The following are examples of specific emotions and how they are involved in marketplace behavior:

Anger   Anger can be elicited by showing characters in an advertisement insulting each other, showing characters deliberately blocking important goals, or showing characters treating each other unfairly.[24] Advertisements for Save the Children, like the one in Exhibit 8-11, show children struggling for survival. People seeing the advertisements are likely to feel angry because the children depicted in it are suffering through no fault of their own, either through natural disaster or perhaps governmental or parental neglect. The advertiser uses anger to motivate people to take action.

Fear is elicited by two important factors: the unfavorableness of the consequences given a certain situation and the likelihood that these unfavorable consequences will occur.[25] In other words, for a fear appeal to work effectively, the advertisement must provide evidence—implicit or explicit—that an unfavorable consequence is likely. The Fit for a Kid ad in Exhibit 8-12 elicits fear by suggesting to parents that their children's safety depends on buckling their children securely while driving. By eliciting fear, the advertiser hopes to get parents to respond in a certain way, specifically to ensure that children are properly secured in the car.

Humor   The sheer volume of advertisements that use humor is testimony to the perceived power of humor in motivating consumers to action. Consider the television commercials that won at the International Advertising Festival in 2001. Every year the International Advertising Festival selects the best television commercials at a celebration in Cannes, France. The 2001 jury gave the top honor to Cliff Freeman & Partners' hilarious campaign for Fox Sports. The campaign involves showing sports coverage from different regions of the world. For example, in one spot, Fox Sports showed an unusual sport practiced in India. Two men in a ring surrounded by cheering spectators wail on one another with huge clubs. The unique aspect of this sport—and what many people found hilarious—is that the two men clubbing one another are blindfolded. In another spot, a man is shown diving off a cliff in Turkey. The judges' numerical scores are superimposed on the screen. The catch is there is no water. The divers land with a thud on a dusty flat. Funny!

Warmth   Warmth is a positive, mild, yet volatile emotion involving physiological arousal. It is usually precipitated by experiencing relationships that involve love, family, or friendships.[26] One study has shown that warmth in advertising can be induced through commercials that use creative approaches such as sentimentality, or themes involving family and friends.[27] Another study found that warmth can be induced through commercials involving affectionate couples, warm relationships, mother-child interactions, and appealing characters such as Pillsbury's "soft and cuddly" Doughboy.

Flow   Flow is an experiential state that is desirable, an optimal state of arousal that occurs when an individual engages in a challenging task that matches or exceeds his or her skills related to that task. A person experiencing flow is characterized in terms of complete attention devoted to the task at hand, loss of self-consciousness, feelings of control over the action and the environment, momentary loss of anxiety and constraint, and significant feelings of pleasure. Consider the following situations in which some people may experience flow: Playing a chess tournament, parachute jumping, white-water rafting, mountain climbing, and playing an excellent game of tennis.[28]

Consumer researchers have suggested that some consumers may experience flow while shopping on the Internet. For example, one study has shown that consumers who reach the state of flow while shopping on the Internet may get so wrapped up in browsing that they miss the opportunity to complete the transaction.[29] Much research is underway to examine the effects of flow on Internet buying. The following relationships were proposed for future testing:

- *When perceived risks are high, browsing is facilitated by a longer and more intense flow state.* This occurs because when consumers experience flow they become more engrossed in browsing.

- *When perceived risks are high, one-time purchases are facilitated by a longer and less intense flow state.* This occurs because the flow state facilitates browsing and decreases the perception of risk. Decreased perception of risk facilitates the likelihood of purchase. However, this may occur only if the flow state is not too intense. Otherwise, intense flow distracts from purchase.

- *When perceived risks are high, repeat purchases are facilitated by a shorter and more intense flow state.* In this situation, consumers who experience flow may feel more positive about the brand they have previously purchased and contemplate repurchase. Doing so reduces the perception of risk and facilitates purchase of a repeat product. However, a longer flow may distract from repeat purchase.[30]

Desire   Consumer desire is essentially the motivating force behind much of consumption. Desire is different than consumer needs in that desire is a strong emotion that motivates consumers to want to consume a particular product or service. Desire is an emotion that is both discomforting and pleasurable. Consider the following idiomatic expressions used to describe this emotional state: burn with desire, pierced by desire, sick with desire, tortured by desire, ache with desire, tormented by desire, possessed by desire, seized by desire, ravished by desire, overcome by desire, mad or crazy with desire, blinded with desire, enveloped or enchanted by desire, and so on. Consider how one consumer expressed his desire for a Honda car: "I wanted this car so bad I could taste it! I could hardly function throughout the day because I would make myself sick thinking about the Honda and how bad I wanted it."

Desire involves a quest for otherness, sociality, danger, and inaccessibility. The *quest for otherness* refers to the feeling that consuming the product in question is likely to provide escape; it promises a transformation of sorts. Desire is usually embedded in the past. It is expressed in feelings of longing: "I always wanted a cabin. When I was a little girl, Nanni and Poppi had a cabin in the mountains. . . ."

The desire for *sociality* means that the source of desire for consuming an object lies with people and interpersonal interactions with others. That is, consumers desire to consume objects because these objects bring them close to other people: "Over time, my desire to own a mountain bike greatly increased as my friends went on hiking trips . . . ."

Acting on a desire sometimes feels like the action is *dangerous* and may be out of control. The desire is unpredictable, uncontrolled, and irrational. Desire is associated with fantasies: "I live a proper life during the week, like normal people. I want a crazy life on the weekend . . . The crazy nightlife breaks that monotony. . . ." With respect to *inaccessibility,* we desire objects that we cannot readily have. The more difficult to acquire a product the more our desire for that product intensifies.[31]

Consumer researchers developed the "warmth monitor," an instrument to measure the extent of warmth people feel when viewing commercials.[32] The measure is based on self-report and is continuous and concurrent. That is, subjects express the degree of warmth they feel about different scenes in the commercial instantly and continuously, one scene after another. The subject moves a pencil down a paper while viewing the commercial, moving it to the left and right to reflect how warm his or her feelings are at any given time.

Marketing Management—Implications and Actions

Understanding emotions helps marketers:

- Know what emotions consumers may experience in relation to specific goods or services.
- Trigger emotional states that will lead to brand preference, purchase, and customer satisfaction.

8-3 Mood

A couple shopping at a mall for a new stereo begins to argue about an unrelated event that occurred earlier in the day as they walk into an electronics store. As they are greeted by a salesperson, they turn their attention to the various stereos on display. However, both are still visibly upset by the argument. Their mood affects the shopping experience, and they leave the store without making a purchase. CBite 8-2 describes a study that shows how mood, involvement, and the quality of the shopping experience have an impact on shopping behavior.

A **mood** is an affective state that is general and pervasive.[33] Moods are much less intense than emotions. Whereas consumers may be aware of their emotions, they are much less conscious of moods and the effect moods have on marketplace behavior.

As shown in Exhibit 8-13, consumer moods are induced in three different marketplace settings: service encounters, point-of-purchase stimuli, and communications. These mood states, in turn, influence consumer recall of products and services, evaluation of

> ▶**mood** An affective state that is general and pervasive. Moods are much less intense than emotions.

CBite 8-2
Mood and Involvement

A recent retail study showed that consumer mood, involvement, and perception of the quality of the shopping experience interact in influencing future shopping behavior (or the intention to repeat the experience). Involved shoppers were found to magnify their evaluations of the shopping experience. That is, involved shoppers in good moods evaluated good experiences as still better and bad shopping experiences as even worse than did noninvolved shoppers.

Source: William R. Swinyard, "The Effects of Mood, Involvement, and Quality of Store Experience on Shopping Intentions," *Journal of Consumer Research,* Vol. 20 (September 1993), pp. 271–280.

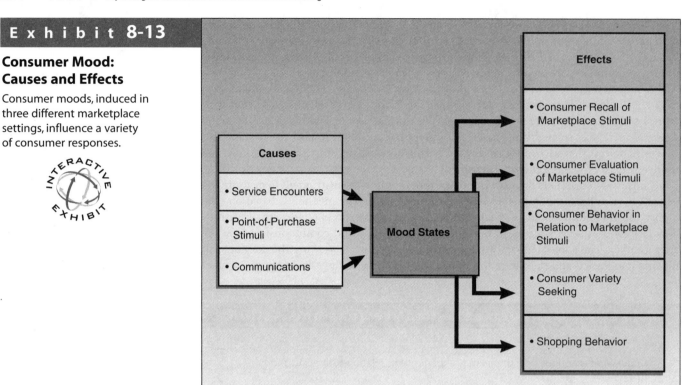

**Consumer Mood:
Causes and Effects**

Consumer moods, induced in
three different marketplace
settings, influence a variety
of consumer responses.

INTERACTIVE EXHIBIT

products and services, and other marketplace behavior. It is this effect that spurs retailers
to devote a great deal of attention to the layout, lighting, design, and staffing of outlets.

8-3a Effects of Mood on Consumer Recall

Recall can be affected by the consumer's mood at the time of exposure to marketplace
stimuli and at the time of retrieving information from memory. Specifically, if a consumer
is in a positive mood at the time of initial exposure, he or she is likely to encode the information about that stimulus along with cues related to the positive mood. Hence, to retrieve
the information accurately, the consumer has to also retrieve the positive cues. At point-
of-purchase, marketers provide cues to help consumers recall certain brands, thereby
increasing the probability of purchase. However, if the cues do not induce the same mood
that was generated at the time of initial exposure to the stimulus, consumers may fail to
retrieve the desired information.[34]

8-3b Effects of Mood on Consumer Evaluation

Mood states bias product evaluation. Specifically, consumers in a negative mood state are
more likely to make negative product evaluations than positive ones. The converse is also
true. The impact of mood on product evaluation is particularly important to packaged-
goods marketers, because it demonstrates that negative evaluations of brands may be
a result of retail conditions. Packaged-goods marketers thus have to work with retail
management to ensure that target consumers experience positive mood states in the retail
environment.[35]

Recent studies were able to empirically demonstrate that positive/negative affect influences brand evaluations. Specifically, study results showed that positive affect increased the
extremity of the brand's evaluative implications (i.e., its scale value) rather than the importance (or weight) consumers attached to it. That is, the more a consumer rated a brand on
any evaluative criteria as *very positive*, the more likely the consumer was to end up expressing preference for that brand. [36]

8-3c Effects of Mood on Consumer Behavior

Moods influence a host of consumer behaviors. For example, one study found that children who generate happy thoughts contribute the most to a charity, while children who generate sad thoughts contribute the least.[37] Also, a positive mood encourages consumers to seek variety, increasing their willingness to try new things.[38] A recent study showed that some 10 percent of the population shops while they are in a negative mood. Negative mood seems to reduce shoppers' desire to search, to exert themselves, and to make long-term plans. Shoppers who are in bad mood make "feel-good purchases" and seem to be interested in trying new products and new activities. Perhaps buying these new products and engaging in these new activities are ways these shoppers try to make themselves feel better.[39]

8-3d Inducing Positive Mood States

Marketers have several opportunities to induce positive moods in consumers, from service encounters to point-of-purchase contact to marketing communications. In service encounters, marketers can induce positive moods through aspects of transaction mechanics, service personnel, and physical setting. For example, if Jill is offered help the moment she walks in the store and is able to find what she needs quickly and easily, she is likely to be in a positive mood and may buy more. Customers linger in stores with a pleasant ambience, increasing the probability of purchase.[40]

In marketing communications, both the media and the message can positively or negatively influence the consumer's mood. For example, viewers watching a news report on famine conditions overseas or child abuse at home are probably in a negative mood state and are, therefore, unlikely to respond well to a commercial for luxury items following the report. Media placement should always consider the consumer's probable mood state. Several aspects of the message itself can also affect the consumer's mood: the advertising claim, the use of pictures, the use of emotional music, the graphics, the design features, and so on.[41]

Marketing Management—Implications and Actions

Understanding moods helps marketers:

- Provide mood cues to aid in consumer information retrieval.
- Create positive mood states in retail or other purchase settings.

8-4 Involvement

Consumer researchers characterize some consumers as being more involved in products and shopping than others. A consumer who is highly involved with a product is likely to want to know a lot about it prior to purchase and so reads brochures thoroughly, compares brands and models available at different outlets, asks questions, and looks for recommendations. **Involvement** is a heightened state of awareness that motivates consumers to seek out, attend to, and think about product information prior to purchase.

There are two types of involvement: situational and enduring.[42] Involvement is induced by factors related to the consumer, the product, or the purchase situation. Involvement affects a variety of consumer behaviors, such as information search, information processing, and information transmission. In this section, we will explore both situational and enduring involvement and their causes and effects.

involvement A heightened state of awareness that motivates consumers to seek out, attend to, and think about product information prior to purchase.

8-4a Situational versus Enduring Involvement

Situational involvement refers to the feelings a consumer experiences in a particular situation when he or she thinks about a particular product. Situational involvement is specific to a product or situation and is temporary. Enduring involvement reflects feelings experienced toward a product category that are persistent over time and across different situations. Honeymooners renting a Porsche for their trip are highly involved in the choice, but their involvement does not last. Contrast this with Max, whose hobby is car racing. His involvement endures over time and affects his responses in any situation related to pre-purchase, purchase, and post-purchase of sports cars. In the first example, involvement is triggered by a special situation; in the second, it comes from and is part of the consumer and so endures. The distinction between situational and enduring involvement is important, because when marketers measure involvement, they examine the extent to which it can be induced by the product or selling situation. Marketers then work to control products or selling situations depending on the type of involvement with which they are faced.[43]

8-4b Effects of Consumer Involvement

When consumers become involved with a product, they process product-related information more readily. This information is processed deeply and is, therefore, retained for a longer duration. Consumers engage in cognitive elaboration (or think deeply about the product), become emotionally aroused, and tend to engage in extended problem solving and word-of-mouth communications.[44] These consequences fall into three categories: information search, information processing, and information transmission. See Exhibit 8-14.

Information Search   Highly involved consumers tend to search for information and shop around more than do consumers with low involvement. For example, a consumer who is highly involved with PCs and is thinking about buying one is likely to gather information about alternative models to figure out the advantages and disadvantages of each. The more involved consumers are with a product, the more likely they are to seek information about the product category and the various alternatives within that category.

Also, when highly involved consumers seek out information, they do so through a variety of information-seeking behaviors. One such behavior is to shop around. They visit a number of retail outlets to gather information and examine and compare alternatives. Highly involved consumers do much more shopping around than do consumers with low involvement.

To attract highly involved consumers, marketers need to make information easily accessible. They also must provide adequate opportunity for highly involved consumers to visit retail outlets and obtain help from salespeople. These consumers should be encouraged by retailers to come in and browse and to compare alternative models in their attempts to meet information needs.

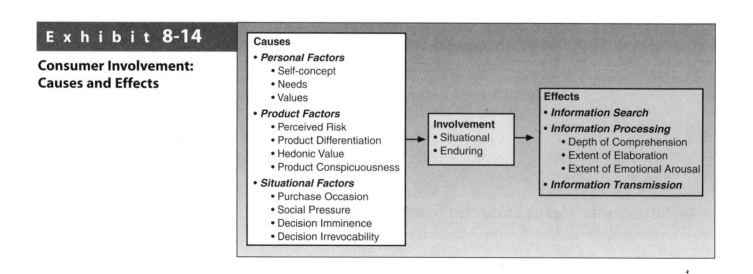

E x h i b i t 8-14

**Consumer Involvement:
Causes and Effects**

Causes
- *Personal Factors*
  - Self-concept
  - Needs
  - Values
- *Product Factors*
  - Perceived Risk
  - Product Differentiation
  - Hedonic Value
  - Product Conspicuousness
- *Situational Factors*
  - Purchase Occasion
  - Social Pressure
  - Decision Imminence
  - Decision Irrevocability

Involvement
- Situational
- Enduring

Effects
- *Information Search*
- *Information Processing*
  - Depth of Comprehension
  - Extent of Elaboration
  - Extent of Emotional Arousal
- *Information Transmission*

Information Processing   By "information processing" we mean the amount of information consumers consider, the depth of attempted comprehension, the extent of cognitive elaboration, and the extent of emotional arousal.

Depth of Comprehension   Highly involved consumers tend to process product information at deeper levels of comprehension than do consumers with low involvement. Suppose we're marketing a pharmaceutical product to hospitals. Physicians are likely to be much more involved with this type of product than are hospital purchasing agents, and they are, therefore, more likely to respond positively to detailed brochures outlining the benefits of the product and how it should be used. Moreover, this information is likely to be retained for a long period of time by physicians, while it will be soon forgotten by purchasing agents. Marketers targeting highly involved consumers need only provide cues to help the consumers retrieve information from memory; those targeting consumers with low involvement should make the necessary information as accessible as possible at the time of choice and purchase.

Extent of Elaboration   Highly involved consumers tend to do much more thinking about product choices than do consumers with low involvement. The cognitive elaboration of highly involved consumers involves support argumentation and/or counterargumentation. That is, highly involved consumers tend to generate cognitive responses either in support of the product information provided by the marketer or against the information.

Let's look at the example of marketing a new drug. Suppose the drug, although effective, has significant negative side effects. Physicians are likely to give this a great deal of thought before deciding whether or not to prescribe the drug to patients. To ensure that physicians generate positive thoughts, the marketer has to provide a quality argument that the drug's benefits outweigh its negative side effects. If the argument is not well informed and is not persuasive, it is likely to produce negative thoughts, resulting in an unfavorable attitude toward the drug.

Extent of Emotional Arousal   Highly involved consumers tend to be more emotionally aroused than consumers with low involvement. Their cognitive elaboration can change evaluations of advertisements. In other words, consumers who are highly involved are likely to react more strongly to product-related information than are low-involved consumers. This can work for or against marketers, because any information interpreted negatively is likely to be exaggerated many times over, causing the consumers to reject the product.[45]

Information Transmission   Information transmission is the extent to which highly involved consumers transmit information about the product to others. This is usually done through word-of-mouth communication. Consumer researchers have shown that highly involved consumers tend to talk about the product to others much more often than do consumers with low involvement. Satisfied consumers who are highly involved are likely to speak favorably about the product to others, while those who are dissatisfied tend to speak unfavorably. Therefore, marketers catering to highly involved consumers should make every attempt to enhance consumer satisfaction and decrease dissatisfaction.

8-4c Causes of Consumer Involvement

Involvement is increased when there is congruence of the personal, product, and situational factors that influence consumer involvement. Let us now look at these factors in more detail.

Personal Factors   Three personal factors influence the extent of consumer involvement in a product or service: **self-concept** (that is, a consumer's perception of his or her own personal identity, including the private and public self, and the actual and ideal self)

F A Q

Does any product benefit from word-of-mouth more than movies?

▶**self-concept** Consumers' perceptions of their own personal identity—their private and public self, their actual and ideal self.

needs, and values. The more a product's image, the value symbolism inherent in it, and the needs it serves are congruent with the consumer's self-image, values, and needs, the more likely the consumer is to feel involved with it.[46] Advocates of environmentalism, for example, share a certain self-image, certain values, and certain needs. They tend to consume a constellation of products and services that reflect this aspect of their lifestyle. Casual clothes, mountain bikes, solar power, membership in Greenpeace, and health food are typical products they consume, and they are likely to be highly involved in the purchase of these items.

Product Factors   The greater the perceived risk in the purchase of a good or service, the greater the consumer involvement.[47] It is likely that consumers will feel more involved in the purchase of their cars than in the purchase of their toothpaste—it is in many respects a much riskier purchase.

Product differentiation affects involvement, too. The more alternatives there are to choose from, the greater consumer involvement.[48] This may be due to the fact that consumers feel variety means greater risk. The hedonic value of a product or service also influences involvement. Some products are a greater source of pleasure to the consumer than are others. Coffee, for example, has a high level of hedonic value compared to, say, household cleaners, and involvement is, therefore, higher.

Involvement increases with product conspicuousness. Because consumers care how they are viewed by others, any product that is socially visible or that is consumed in public demands high involvement. Driving a red Porsche is a highly conspicuous activity—most people can't help looking at the car as it speeds by, making all kinds of assumptions about the driver.

Situational Factors   The situation in which a product is bought or used can generate emotional involvement. The reason for purchase or *purchase occasion* affects involvement. For example, buying a pair of socks for yourself is far less involving than buying a gift for a close friend.[49] **Social pressure** can also significantly increase involvement. You're likely to be much more self-conscious about the products and brands you look at when shopping with friends than when shopping alone.[50]

Decision imminence, or the need to make a fast decision, also influences involvement. A consumer who needs a new washing machine and sees a one-day-only sale at an appliance retailer doesn't have the time to shop around and compare different brands and prices. The imminence of the decision heightens involvement.

Decision irrevocability can also increase involvement if, once a decision is made, it can't be undone. Perhaps the retailer doesn't accept returns on sale items, or the postage cost for returning catalog purchases is prohibitive. Situations in which consumers realize that their purchase decisions are irrevocable heighten involvement.

In sum, involvement can come from outside the individual, as with situational involvement, or from within the individual, as with enduring involvement. It can be induced by a host of personal-, product-, and situation-related factors, many of which can be controlled by the marketer. Involvement affects the ways in which consumers seek, process, and transmit information to others.

8-4d Consumer Behavior Models Based on Involvement

Marketers use four key consumer behavior models to aid in strategic decision making, particularly in marketing communications: the low-involvement learning model, the learn-feel-do hierarchy model, the level of message processing model, and the product versus brand involvement model.

Low-Involvement Learning Model   Low-involvement products are typically those that are low in risk, perhaps by virtue of being inexpensive, and that are frequently

> **social pressure** Influence over purchase decisions coming from significant others such as friends, parents, relatives, and associates.

> **decision imminence** The state in which an imminent decision is present; an imminent decision is one that the consumer expects to make in the very near future.

> **decision irrevocability** The state in which a decision will be irrevocable; an irrevocable decision is one that once made cannot be undone.

and repeatedly used by consumers. Hand soap is a good example. Television advertising about such products follows the principle of **low-involvement learning.** Without actually trying to change consumer attitudes first, attempts are made to replace old brand perceptions with new beliefs about the product.[51] Thus, advertisers can facilitate learning about a product that will result in a viewer's trying it—without attempting the complicated business of attitude change. (Typically, with high-involvement products, marketers use advertising to try to change consumers' attitudes and thus lead them to purchase. With low-involvement products, attitude barely comes into consideration.)

One way to accomplish low-involvement learning is through positioning—associating the product with a particular need in the consumer's frame of reference. For example, "the hand soap for the whole family" is not so abrasive as to turn a woman's hands red or so perfumed as to make a man feel effeminate.

Learn-Feel-Do Hierarchy
Some purchase decisions demand a great deal of thought; others are dominated by feelings. Some are made through force of habit; others are made consciously. The **learn-feel-do hierarchy** is a simple matrix that attributes consumer choices to information (learn), attitude (feel), and behavior (do) issues. Shown in Exhibit 8-15, the matrix has four quadrants, each specifying a major advertising goal: to be informative, to be affective, to be habit forming, or to promote self-satisfaction. Thinking and feeling are represented as a continuum—some decisions involve one or the other, and many involve elements of both. Over time, there is movement from thinking toward feeling. High and low importance are also shown on a continuum, and over time importance can diminish.

High Involvement/High Thinking   Consumers buying goods and services in this quadrant have a high need for information, both because of the importance of the product and the thinking issues related to it. Major purchases such as cars, houses, and furnishings qualify, along with almost any new product that needs initially to convey its function, price, and availability. The strategy model is learn → feel → do: Marketers provide salient information to build consumers' attitudinal acceptance and lead to purchase.

High Involvement/High Feeling   This product decision is involving, but information is less important than feeling in inducing purchase. Typical purchases tied to self-esteem would include jewelry, cosmetics, and apparel. The strategy model is feel → learn → do: Marketers provide emotional appeals that encourage consumers to find out more about the product or service and ultimately lead to purchase.

Low Involvement/Low Thinking   This product decision requires minimal involvement or thought, tending to result from habitual buying. Most food and staple packaged goods belong here. Over time, almost any product can fall into this category. Information, to the extent that it plays a role, consists of any point of difference from competitors that the marketer can meaningfully exploit. Brand loyalty may result simply from habit, but it's quite likely most consumers have several acceptable brands. The strategy model is do → learn → feel. It suggests that simply inducing trial through coupons or free samples can generate subsequent purchase more readily than can product information.

Low Involvement/Low Feeling   This product decision is triggered primarily by the need to satisfy personal tastes, many of which are influenced by self-image. Cigarettes, liquor, candy, and movies all fall into this category, along with such products as beer and soft drinks. Group influences are often apparent in the purchase of these items. The strategy model is do → feel → learn. The consumer is reacting to social pressures or to situations—loyalty will be hard to hold or short-lived.

The learn-feel-do hierarchy helps marketers choose appropriate strategies for different types of products.

low-involvement learning
The situation in which consumers replace old brand perceptions with new beliefs about the product without the mediation effects of brand attitude.

learn-feel-do hierarchy
A simple matrix that attributes consumer choices to information (learn), attitude (feel), and behavior (do) issues.

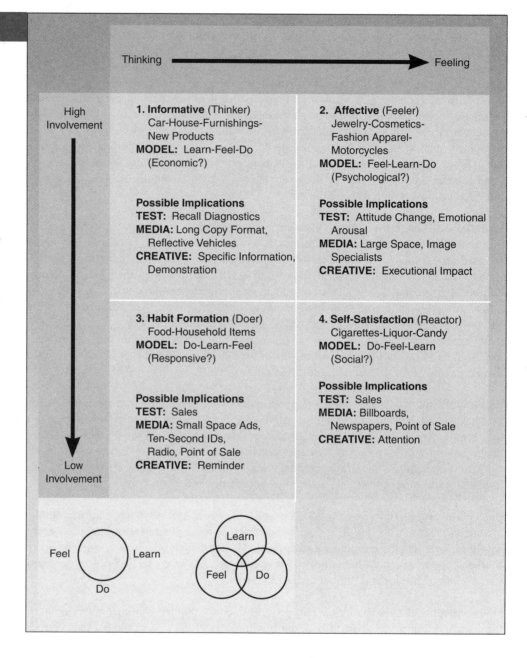

Exhibit 8-15

The Learn-Feel-Do Hierarchy

This simple matrix attributes consumer choices to information (learn), attitude (feel), and behavior (do) issues. Thinking and feeling are represented as a continuum—some decisions involve one or the other, and many involve elements of both.

Source: Adapted from "The Consumer Mind: How to Tailor Ad Strategies" by Richard Vaughn. Reprinted with permission from the June 9, 1980 issue of *Advertising Age.* Copyright, Crain Communications Inc. 1980.

Level of Message Processing Model   Consumer research suggests there are four levels of involvement that affect consumer attention to advertising: preattention, focal attention, comprehension, and elaboration. As shown in Exhibit 8-16, each calls for a different level of message processing. Preattention demands only limited processing—the consumer simply registers familiarity or significance. Focal attention hones in on the message source and usually involves such basic information as product name or use. Through comprehension, the message is analyzed for content. Through elaboration, the content of the message is integrated with other information in memory to form concepts or beliefs.[52]

An advertisement that is successful in making the consumer feel involved with the advertised product is one that induces elaboration. To capture attention, the message first has to be easily understood, that is, it has to be meaningful to its audience. More specifically, the audience has to understand the message as intended by the advertiser. Finally, the consumer should not merely process the message and understand it but should integrate

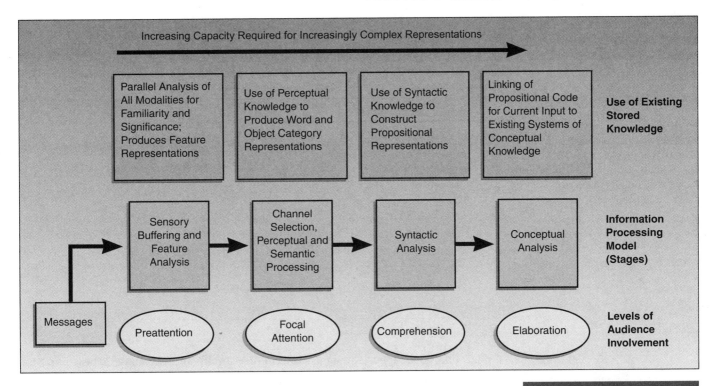

Increasing Capacity Required for Increasingly Complex Representations

| Parallel Analysis of All Modalities for Familiarity and Significance; Produces Feature Representations | Use of Perceptual Knowledge to Produce Word and Object Category Representations | Use of Syntactic Knowledge to Construct Propositional Representations | Linking of Propositional Code for Current Input to Existing Systems of Conceptual Knowledge | **Use of Existing Stored Knowledge** |

| Sensory Buffering and Feature Analysis | Channel Selection, Perceptual and Semantic Processing | Syntactic Analysis | Conceptual Analysis | **Information Processing Model (Stages)** |

| Messages | Preattention | Focal Attention | Comprehension | Elaboration | **Levels of Audience Involvement** |

E x h i b i t 8-16

The Level of Message Processing Model

Four levels of involvement affect consumer attention to advertising: preattention, focal attention, comprehension, and elaboration, each calling for different levels of message processing.

Source: Adapted from "Audience Involvement in Advertising: Four Levels" by Anthony G. Greenwald and Clark Leavitt in *Journal of Consumer Research,* Vol. 11, June 1984, p. 585. Copyright © 1984. Reprinted by permission of The University of Chicago Press.

it into his or her belief system. The message thus alters the consumer's cognitive structure, as he or she learns something that is both new and meaningful.

Product versus Brand Involvement Model   Consumers may be highly involved with a product category but may not necessarily be involved with a given brand in that category. Teenagers may like sports cars but may not know a great deal about the Ford Mustang, for example. As shown in Exhibit 8-17, consumers can be segmented into four consumer types according to their involvement with either a product category or with a particular brand.[53]

Brand Loyalists   These consumers are highly involved with both the product category and with particular brands. Beer drinkers, for example, are typically brand loyal. To keep customers, marketers should develop advertising that reinforces brand loyalty. It should be both informational and emotional. Because loyal consumers have a high level of involvement with both the product category and the brand, they are likely to be receptive to both types of appeals.

Information Seekers   These shoppers are highly involved with a product category but may not have a preferred brand. They are likely to seek information to help them decide which brand is best. For this segment, informational advertising is more effective than emotional appeals. These consumers are more likely to search out information even if it is not offered by marketers. The best advertisements provide detailed information about the brand's benefits, with evidence that supports the advertiser's claims.

Routine Brand Buyers   These consumers are not highly involved with the product category but may be involved with a particular brand within that category. A consumer who doesn't eat out often, for example, may patronize the same restaurant every time he or she does eat out. Routine brand buyers do not necessarily look for the "best" brand. They have low emotional attachment with the product category and care only about their preferred

F A Q

Why are toothpaste users so brand loyal?

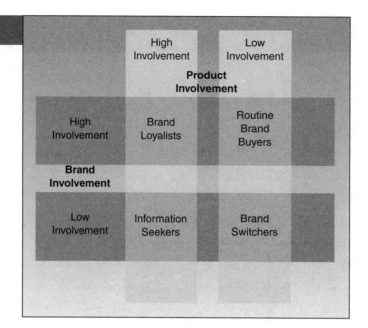

Exhibit 8-17

The Product versus Brand Involvement Model

Consumers can be segmented into four consumer types according to their involvement with either a product category or with a particular brand.

Source: Adapted from Peter Cushing and Melody Douglas-Tate, "The Effect of People/Product Relationships on Advertising Processing," in Linda Alwitt and Andrew P. Mitchell, eds., *Psychological Processes and Advertising Effects* (Hillsdale, NJ: Lawrence Erlbaum, 1985), pp. 241–259.

brand. Emotional appeals designed to reinforce loyalty and encourage repeat purchase work best with routine brand buyers.

Brand Switchers   Switchers are neither involved with the product category nor with the brand. They do not look for a "best" brand and have no emotional attachment to either the category or any brand within it. They typically respond to price. Economic appeals work well with brand switchers, particularly messages that emphasize savings and value for money.

Marketing Management—Implications and Actions

Understanding consumer involvement helps marketers:

- Know when to adjust the selling environment to reinforce situational involvement.
- Know what sort of marketing information is needed for the typical level of consumer involvement.
- Assess product factors that influence involvement.

Chapter Spotlights

This chapter covered four aspects of human psychology that have significant impact on consumer decision making and marketplace behavior: motivation, emotion, mood, and involvement.

1. How human needs motivate consumers to buy. We explored three classification schemes of human motivations. First, Maslow's hierarchy of needs theory explains personal growth as a progression from basic survival needs to sophisticated psychological desires. Second, Dichter's major consumption motives model describes subconscious motives that can be triggered by marketers through product symbolism. Third, Sheth's consumer needs model classifies motivations into five types, each oriented to the achievement of specific goals.

2. What specific motives play a role in marketplace behavior. We explained how motivations influence three aspects of behavior. First, consumer motives can shape the sequence of choices consumers make in reaching final purchase decisions. Second, behavior can be influenced by conflicting motivations, the resolution of which is achieved through consumer purchases. Third, motivations influence consumption patterns as consumers seek to satisfy needs or avoid unfavorable consequences. Marketers apply their understanding of motivational states to induce motives that increase the probability of purchase. This can be achieved through market segmentation based on consumer needs and through the exploration of subconscious or hidden motives.

3. How marketers can elicit specific emotions to sell products and services. Marketers can trigger desired emotional states in consumers through advertising that appeals directly to such emotions as anger, fear, humor, or warmth. Understanding the psychology of emotions is imperative in creating such marketing appeals.

4. How moods affect consumption patterns. The consumer's mood state has a significant impact on his or her ability to recall product information or evaluate brands, and on actual marketplace behavior. Marketers must attempt to trigger positive mood states in service encounters, at point-of-purchase, and through communications.

5. How consumer involvement with products and services changes the effects of marketing information. Situational and enduring involvement both influence every aspect of the decision-making process from information search, to information processing, to information transmission in the marketplace. Consumer involvement with marketplace stimuli is determined by a host of personal, product, and situational factors. We explored such models as low-involvement learning, the learn-feel-do hierarchy, and level of message processing. We also explained how product category involvement differs from brand involvement and reviewed appropriate strategies for increasing each.

Key Terms

approach-approach conflict (p. 253)
approach-avoidance conflict (p. 253)
avoidance-avoidance conflict (p. 253)
consumer motivation (p. 248)
decision imminence (p. 268)

decision irrevocability (p. 268)
emotions (p. 257)
flow (p. 255)
hierarchy of needs (p. 250)
involvement (p. 265)

learn-feel-do hierarchy (p. 269)
low-involvement learning (p. 269)
mood (p. 263)
self-concept (p. 267)
social pressure (p. 268)

Review Questions

Note: You can find the correct answers to these questions by taking the quiz and then submitting your answers in the Online Edition. The program will automatically score your submission. If you miss a question, the program will provide the correct answer, a rationale for the answer, and the section number in the chapter where the topic is discussed.

1. Marketers can use Jagdish Sheth's model to predict consumer
   a. needs.
   b. brand choices.
   c. interaction.
   d. usage patterns.

2. The three models—Maslow, Dichter, and Sheth—all describe the _____ that drive consumer _____.
   a. needs, complaints
   b. behaviors, needs
   c. needs, behaviors
   d. relationships, purchases

3. Sometimes, a shopper in a store must choose among alternatives that seem equally attractive, which is called an
   a. approach-avoidance conflict.
   b. approach-approach conflict.
   c. avoidance-avoidance approach.
   d. approach-avoidance situation.

4. Marketers can trigger consumer motivation by inducing _____ recognition.
   a. need
   b. subconscious
   c. conscious
   d. subliminal

5. Humor has been shown to _____ consumers into action.
   a. laugh
   b. motivate
   c. thwart
   d. manipulate

6. New products such as cars, houses, and furnishings are high involvement/thinking type products. They reflect the _____ hierarchy of effects.
   a. learn-feel-do
   b. feel-learn-do
   c. do-learn-feel
   d. do-feel-learn

7. Moods are much less intense than
   a. fears.
   b. emotions.
   c. traumas.
   d. detachment.

8. What type of involvement reflects feelings over time?
   a. situational
   b. enduring
   c. temporary
   d. invoked

9. The greater the perceived _____ in the purchase of a good or service, the greater consumer involvement.
   a. cost
   b. price
   c. need
   d. risk

10. The learn-feel-do hierarchy attributes consumer choices to information, _____, and behavior.
   a. attitude
   b. willingness
   c. intention
   d. emotions

Team Talk

1. Do irrational needs exist? Discuss your answer.

2. Select an advertisement designed to appeal to specific consumer motives. How does the advertiser succeed—or fail—at appealing to those motives? Consider Maslow's hierarchy of needs.

3. Select an advertisement you think appeals to hidden motives, as described by Dichter. Apply Dichter's motivational research techniques to uncover the hidden motives to which the advertiser is appealing.

4. Of the three needs systems—Maslow's, Dichter's, and Sheth's—which do you find the most plausible? Why?

5. Obviously consumers feel emotions in regard to purchases or product experiences. Are these emotions something marketers can or should attempt to influence?

6. Discuss the psychology of fear as an emotion. How can fear be induced? Using the psychology of fear, design an advertisement that aims to curb the spread of AIDS by encouraging people to practice safe sex.

7. You are hired to redesign the interior of a local family restaurant. Consider the psychology of mood states that would induce a positive mood in walk-in customers.

8. How can a marketer take advantage of consumers' situational involvement in developing promotional strategies?

9. Your cousin, the Star Trek fanatic, asks you to help her market a Jean-Luc Picard baseball hat she's designed. How would you market this to an enduring involvement segment? To a situational involvement segment?

Workshops

Research Workshop

Background

The objective of this workshop is to explore motivations behind alcohol consumption. As a college student aware of the social problems associated with drinking by college students, you have decided to start up a service called Alcohol Breakers to help students give up the habit.

Methodology

Conduct a literature search in the area of behavior modification in relation to drinking cessation. You may need the assistance of the office of student affairs, student clubs, fraternities/sororities, the university police, the town police, and available support programs in the community.

To the Marketplace

Decide which motivational techniques will be most effective on the student population. Identify all motives that lead students to drink. For each motive identified, list a product, service, and/or program to neutralize the source of motivation.

Creative Workshop

Background

The objective of this workshop is to find the best emotional positioning for a health care organization. You are marketing director of a company that owns and operates several health care centers, including a women's health care center, a center for home care, a pediatrics practice, and a cancer treatment center. You are assigned to develop a corporate image campaign to get community residents to feel good about the company.

Methodology

You realize that emotions are central to the campaign. You need to get community residents to feel warmth and trust and to care about the company. Make some notes about typical emotions related to each of the company's four health services.

To the Marketplace

From your notes, generate a series of rough sketches for advertisements that will induce feelings of warmth, trust, and caring toward the health care company.

Managerial Workshop

Background

The objective of this workshop is to relate involvement to marketing communication decisions. As marketing manager of an electronics store, you are preparing an advertising plan for the forthcoming year. You realize that understanding the psychology of involvement is extremely important in planning both the creative and media aspects of the campaign.

Methodology

Apply the learn-feel-do model in your development of the advertising plan. Be sure to establish which quadrant of the matrix (Exhibit 8-16) is most applicable.

To the Marketplace

Draft a two-page plan showing explicitly how the model is applied to creative and media decisions.

Notes

1. Johan Arndt, "How Broad Should the Marketing Concept Be?" *Journal of Marketing*, Vol. 42 (January 1978), pp. 101–103.

2. Abraham H. Maslow, *Motivation and Personality*, 2nd ed. (New York: Harper and Row, 1970).

3. Marianne Paskowski, "Psycho-Marketing," *Industrial Marketing* (July 1981), p. 44.

4. Jeffrey F. Durgee, "Interpreting Dichter's Interpretations: An Analysis of Consumption Symbolism in the Handbook of Consumer Motivations," in Hanne Hartvig-Larsen, David Glen Mick, and Christian Alstead, eds., *Marketing and Semiotics: Selected Papers from the Copenhagen Symposium* (Copenhagen, Denmark, 1991).

5. W. Fred van Raaij and Kassaye Wandwossen, "Motivation-Need Theories and Consumer Behavior," in H. Keith Hunt, ed., *Advances in Consumer Research*, Vol. V (Chicago, IL: Association for Consumer Research, 1978), pp. 590–595.

6. van Raaij, "Motivation-Need Theories and Consumer Behavior," p. 593.

7. Christine Moorman and Erika Matulich, "A Model of Consumers' Preventative Health Behaviors: The Role of Health Motivation and Health Ability," *Journal of Consumer Research*, Vol. 20 (September 1993), pp. 208–228.

8. Richard L. Celsi, Randal L. Rose, and Thomas W. Leigh, "An Exploration of High-Risk Leisure Consumption through Skydiving," *Journal of Consumer Research*, Vol. 20 (June 1993), pp. 1–23.

9. Celsi et al., "An Exploration of High-Risk Leisure," p. 10.

10. Compare this study to a more recent study: Aviv Shoham, Gregory M. Rose, and Lynn R. Kahle, "Practitioners of Risk Sports: A Quantitative Examination," *Journal of Business Research*, Vol. 47 (March 2000), pp. 237–251.

11. Ernest Dichter, *Handbook of Consumer Motivations* (New York: McGraw-Hill, 1964).

12. For an excellent article integrating much of the consumer behavior literature on emotions, see: Richard P. Bagozzi, Mahesh Gopinath, and Prashanth U. Nyer, "The Role of Emotions in Marketing," *Journal of the Academy of Marketing Science*, Vol. 27 (Spring 1999), pp. 184–206.

13. Morris Holbrook and Elizabeth Hirschman, "The Experiential Aspects of Consumption: Consumer Fantasies, Feelings, and Fun," *Journal of Consumer Research*, Vol. 9 (September 1982), pp. 132–140.

14. Julie A. Ruth, Frederic F. Brunel, and Cele C. Otnes, "Linking Thoughts to Feelings: Investigating Cognitive Appraisals and Consumption Emotions in a Mixed-Emotions Context," *Journal of the Academy of Marketing Science*, Vol. 30 (Winter 2002), pp. 44–58.

15. Haim Mano and Richard L. Oliver, "Assessing the Dimensionality and Structure of the Consumption Experience: Evaluation, Feeling, and Satisfaction," *Journal of Consumer Research*, Vol. 20 (December 1994), pp. 451–466. Amy K. Smith and Ruth N. Bolton, "The Effect of Customers' Emotional Responses to Service Failures on Their Recovery Effort Evaluations and Satisfaction Judgments," *Journal of the Academy of Marketing Science*, Vol. 30 (Winter 2002), pp. 5–23.

16. Robert A. Westbrook and Richard L. Oliver, "The Dimensionality and Consumption Emotion Patterns and Consumer Satisfaction," *Journal of Consumer Research*, Vol. 18 (June 1991), pp. 84–91; Richard L. Oliver, "Cognitive, Affective, and Attribute Bases of the Satisfaction Response," *Journal of Consumer Research*, Vol. 20 (December 1993), pp. 418–430. For recent research showing how emotions affect future purchase intentions, see Barry J. Babin, Mitch Griffin, and James S. Boles, "Buyer Reactions to Ethical Beliefs in the Retail Environment," *Journal of Business Research*, Vol. 57 (2004), pp. 1155–1163.

17. Roger Bougie, Rik Pieters, and Marcel Zeelenberg, "Angry Customers Don't Come Back, They Get Back: The Experience and Behavioral Implications of Anger and Dissatisfaction in Services," *Journal of the Academy of Marketing Science*, Vol. 31 (Fall 2003), pp. 377-393.

18. Morris B. Holbrook and Rajeev Batra, "Assessing the Role of Emotions as Mediators of Consumer Responses to Advertising," *Journal of Consumer Research*, Vol. 14 (December 1987), pp. 404–417.

19. The findings were further reinforced by the following study: Julie A. Edell and Marian Chapman Burke, "The Power of Feelings in Understanding Advertising Effects," *Journal of Consumer Research*, Vol. 14 (December 1987), pp. 421–433.

20. Chris Allen, Karen Machleit, and Susan Marine, "On Assessing the Emotionality of Advertising Via Izard's Differential Emotions Scale," in Michael Houston, ed., *Advances in Consumer Research*, Vol. 15 (Provo, UT: Association for Consumer Research, 1988), pp. 226–231.

21. Carrol E. Izard, Jerome Kagan, and Robert B. Zajonc, eds., *Emotions, Cognition, and Behavior* (New York: Cambridge University Press, 1984).

22. Barry J. Babin, Mitch Griffin, and James S. Boles, "Buyer Reactions to Ethical Beliefs in the Retail Environment," *Journal of Business Research*, Vol. 57 (2004), pp. 1155–1163.

23. Michael K. Hui and John E. G. Bateson, "Perceived Control and the Effects of Crowding and Consumer Choice on the Service Experience," *Journal of Consumer Research*, Vol. 18 (September 1991), pp. 174–184; Rik G. M. Pieters and W. Fred van Raaij, "Functions and Management of Affect: Application to Economic Behavior," *Journal of Economic Psychology*, Vol. 9 (1988), pp. 251–282.

24. Deborah MacInnis and Robert Westbrook, "The Relationship between Executional Cues and Emotional Response to Advertising," Working Paper, Series 27, Department of Marketing, University of Arizona, Tucson, AZ, October 1987.

25. R. W. Rogers and R. Mewborn, "Fear Appeals and Attitude Change: Effects of a Threat's Noxiousness, Probability of Occurrence, and the Efficacy of Coping Responses," *Journal of Personality and Social Psychology*, Vol. 34 (1976), pp. 54–61.

26. David A. Aaker, Douglas M. Stayman, and Michael R. Hagerty, "Warmth in Advertising: Measurement, Impact, and Sequence Effects," *Journal of Consumer Research*, Vol. 12 (March 1986), pp. 365–381.

27. David A. Aaker and Donald E. Ruzzone, "Viewer Perceptions of Prime-Time Television Advertising," *Journal of Advertising Research*, Vol. 21 (October 1981), pp. 15–23.

28. M. Csikszentmihalyi, *Beyond Boredom and Anxiety*, San Francisco, CA: Jossey-Bass, 1975, 1977; M. Csikszentmihalyi, *Flow: The Psychology of Optimal Experience*, New York: Harper & Row, 1990.

29. Sandelands, J. "Effects of Work and Play Signals on Task Evaluation," *Journal of Applied Social Psychology,* Vol. 18 (1988), pp. 1032–1048.

30. Donnavieve N. Smith and K. Sivakumar, "Flow and Internet Shopping Behavior: A Conceptual Model and Research Propositions," *Journal of Business Research,* Vol. 57 (2004), pp. 1199–1208.

31. Russell W. Belk, Guliz Ger, and Soren Askegaard, "The Fire of Desire: A Multisited Inquiry into Consumer Passion," *Journal of Consumer Research,* Vol. 30 (December 2003), pp. 326–351.

32. Mary Jane Sclinger, "A Profile of Responses to Commercials," *Journal of Advertising Research,* Vol. 19 (1979), pp. 37–46.

33. Meryl Paula Gardner, "Mood States and Consumer Behavior: A Critical Review," *Journal of Consumer Research,* Vol. 12 (December 1985), pp. 281–300.

34. Ibid.

35. Ibid; Michael J. Barone, Paul W. Miniard, and Jean B. Romeo, "The Influence of Positive Mood on Brand Extension Evaluations," *Journal of Consumer Research,* Vol. 26 (March 2000), pp. 386–400; Rajagopal and Julie R. Irwin, "Walking the Hedonic Product Treadmill: Default Contrast and Mood-based Assimilation in Judgments of Predicted Happiness with a Target Product," *Journal of Consumer Research,* Vol. 28 (December 2001), pp. 355–368.

36. Rashmi Adaval, "How Good Gets Better and Bad Gets Worse: Understanding the Impact of Affect on Evaluations of Known Brands," *Journal of Consumer Research,* Vol. 30 (2003), pp. 352–360.

37. Bert Moore, Bill Underwood, and D. L. Rosenhan, "Affect and Altruism," *Developmental Psychology,* Vol. 8 (1973), pp. 99–104.

38. Barbara E. Kahn and Alice M. Isen, "The Influence of Positive Affect on Variety Seeking among Safe, Enjoyable Products," *Journal of Consumer Research,* Vol. 20 (September 1993), pp. 271–280.

39. Sarah Maxwell and Arthur Kover, "Negative Affect: The Dark Side of Retailing," *Journal of Business Research,* Vol. 56 (July 2003), pp. 553–559.

40. Gardner, "Mood States and Consumer Behavior."

41. Ibid.; Michaelle Ann Cameron, Julie Baker, Mark Peterson, and Karin Braunsberger, "The Effects of Music, Wait-length Evaluation, and Mood on a Low-cost Wait Experience," *Journal of Business Research,* Vol. 56 (2003), pp. 421–430.

42. Peter H. Bloch and Marsha L. Richins, "A Theoretical Model for the Study of Product Importance Perceptions," *Journal of Marketing,* Vol. 47 (1983), pp. 69–81.

43. Marsha L. Richins, Peter H. Bloch, and Edward F. McQuarri, "How Enduring and Situational Involvement Combine to Create Involvement Responses," *Journal of Consumer Psychology,* Vol. 1 (1992), pp. 143–153; for measures of enduring involvement see: John L. Lastovicka and David M.

Gardner, "Components of Involvement," in J. C. Maloney and B. Silverman, eds., *Attitude Research Plays for High Stakes* (Chicago, IL: American Marketing Association, 1979), pp. 53–73; Mark B. Traylor and W. Benoy Joseph, "Measuring Consumer Involvement with Products: Developing a General Scale," *Psychology and Marketing,* Vol. 1 (Summer 1984), pp. 65–77; Gilles Laurent and Jean-Noel Kapferer, "Measuring Consumer Involvement Profiles," *Journal of Marketing Research,* Vol. 22 (February 1985), pp. 41–53; Judith L. Zaichowsky, "Measuring the Involvement Construct," *Journal of Consumer Research,* Vol. 12 (December 1985), pp. 341–352; Peter H. Bloch, Daniel L. Sherrell, and Nancy M. Ridgeway, "Consumer Search: An Extended Framework," *Journal of Consumer Research,* Vol. 13 (June 1986), pp. 119–126.

44. Carolyn Costley, "Meta Analysis of Involvement Research," in Michael Houston, ed., *Advances in Consumer Research,* Vol. XV (Provo, UT: Association for Consumer Research, 1988), pp. 554–562; Robin A. Coutler, Linda L. Price, and Lawrence Feick, "Rethinking the Origins of Involvement and Brand Commitment," Journal of Consumer research, Vol. 30 (September 2003), pp. 151–169.

45. David M. Sanbonmatsu and Frank R. Kadres, "The Effects of Physiological Arousal on Information Processing and Persuasion," *Journal of Consumer Research,* Vol. 15 (December 1988), pp. 379–385.

46. M. Joseph Sirgy, "Self-Concept in Consumer Behavior: A Critical Review," *Journal of Consumer Research,* Vol. 9 (December 1982), pp. 287–300.

47. Raymond A. Bauer, "Consumer Behavior as Risk Taking," in *Dynamic Marketing for a Changing World* (Chicago, IL: American Marketing Association), p. 389.

48. Laurent and Kapfrer, "Measuring Consumer Involvement Profiles."

49. Russell W. Belk, "Effects of Gift-Giving Involvement on Gift Selection Strategies," in Andrew Mitchell, ed., *Advances in Consumer Research,* Vol. 9 (Ann Arbor, MI: Association for Consumer Research, 1981), pp. 408–411.

50. Zaichkowsky, "Measuring the Involvement Construct."

51. John L. Lastovicka and David M. Gardner, "Low Involvement versus High Involvement Cognitive Structures," in H. Keith Hunt, ed., *Advances in Consumer Research,* Vol. 5, (Chicago, IL: Association for Consumer Research, 1978), pp. 82–91.

52. Anthony G. Greenwald and Clark Leavitt, "Audience Involvement in Advertising: Four Levels," *Journal of Consumer Research,* Vol. 11, No. 1 (June 1984), pp. 483–491.

53. Peter Cushing and Melody Douglas-Tate, "The Effect of People/Product Relationships on Advertising Processing," in Linda Alwitt and Andrew A. Mitchell eds., *Psychological Processes and Advertising Effects* (Hillsdale, NJ: Lawrence Erlbaum, 1985), pp. 241–259.

Beliefs, Affect, Attitude, and Intention

Mary, a student on a limited budget, wants to buy a camera to take on vacation to Mexico. Because her brother is a professional photographer, she believes that single lens reflex cameras are better than automatics—they're more versatile and the picture quality is better. Besides, Mary has always thought of herself as "artistic." Yet when she checks out prices at a specialty camera store, Mary is shocked to discover how much a good brand will cost—and she's secretly worried that she may not be able to use it properly. On the way out of the store, she slips a couple of brochures on popular automatics into her purse. Reading the literature and talking the purchase over with her brother, Mary is soon persuaded that a good automatic may be the best choice. True, she won't look like a professional, but automatics are compact and easy to use, and the picture quality can be surprisingly good. Her mind made up, Mary heads for her favorite department store to buy a top-of-the-line auto-focus Minolta. As she enters the camera department, she sees a display for a new model Pentax on sale that seems to do all the things the Minolta can. She picks it up and heads toward the sales desk.

Mary's choice of camera, the price she pays, and the outlet at which she buys it all say a great deal about her attitudes. From her early dismissal of automatics, believing them inferior, her attitudes slowly change—particularly toward price and quality. Although she goes to the store intending to buy one brand, a last-minute change of heart—again with price in mind—leads her to another. In this chapter, we explore consumer attitude in terms of the three components that led to Mary's final purchase decision: beliefs (a cognitive component), affect (an emotive component), and intention (a behavioral component).

9-1 Beliefs: The Cognitive Component of Consumer Attitude

A consumer **belief** is a psychological association between a product or brand and an attribute or feature of that product or brand. Beliefs are cognitive (based on knowledge) as opposed to affective (based on feelings). Whether they are true or not, consumers link certain attributes with certain products, accepting them as facts: Diet Pepsi is low in calories and sodium; Volvo cars are safe; or Reebok shoes are aerodynamic. The stronger the association of features or attributes with the product or brand, the stronger the consumer's belief. Exhibit 9-1 demonstrates how these cognitive brand associations work.

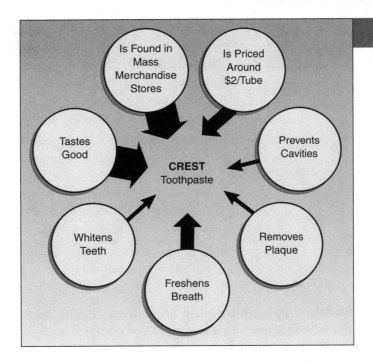

A Hypothetical Belief Structure for Crest Toothpaste

Some brand associations are stronger than others, as indicated by the thickness of the connecting arrows. Some are so strong that they are accepted as facts and, as such, are extremely influential in marketplace decisions.

As we saw in Chapter 7, it is in terms of brand associations that brands are organized in the consumer's memory. *Brand equity* is a measure of the strength of those associations in the marketplace. The stronger a brand is, the more readily it is retrieved from memory, the more likely it is to be purchased, and, in most cases, the higher the level of continuing loyalty it experiences.[1] Marketplace 9-1 shows how brand equity is typically measured.

▶**belief** (see p. 278) A psychological association between a product or brand and an attribute or feature of that product or brand.

9-1a Strategies to Change Consumer Beliefs

It is through positioning brands in the minds of consumers that marketers attempt to establish or change consumer beliefs about them. Marketers use the positioning strategies we will discuss, singly or in combination, to create brand beliefs, strengthen positive beliefs, or weaken and eliminate negative beliefs, thereby increasing brand equity and market share.

Exhibit 9-2 shows the many types of brand associations that contribute to brand equity. By manipulating brand associations, marketers can develop strategies that impact consumer beliefs as a means of increasing brand equity.

Positioning by Product Attributes   The simplest and most common way of positioning products is through association of specific attributes with a brand. Some marketers aim to make their products synonymous with, for example, performance attributes that make consumers buy. Hewlett Packard's Laser Jet printer promises excellent-resolution computer printouts, and Viva paper towels offer high absorbency.[2]

Marketplace 9-2 on page 281 illustrates how many brands try to position themselves by product attributes that help differentiate them from private labels commonly found in chain supermarkets. CBite 9-1 on page 281 warns that positioning by too many product attributes may backfire. Read on.

Positioning by Consumer Benefits   As we saw in Chapter 1 (section 1-1, "Shopper, Buyer, and Consumer Benefits"), marketers attempt to influence consumer beliefs about brands by associating them with important consumer benefits. A brand of shampoo with natural protein (an attribute) is positioned to highlight the fact that it's the only shampoo that will not damage hair, no matter how frequently it is used (a benefit). A computer with touch-screen entry (an attribute) attracts consumers looking for ease of use (a benefit).[3]

F A Q

Which are more powerful—positive beliefs or negative beliefs?

Marketplace 9-1

Measuring Brand Equity

Brand Loyalty

- I consider myself to be loyal to X.
- X would be my first choice.
- I will not buy other brands if X is available at the store.

Perceived Quality

- The likely quality of X is extremely high.
- The likelihood that X would be functional is very high.

Brand Awareness/Associations

- I can recognize X among other competing brands.
- I am aware of X.
- Some characteristics of X come to my mind quickly.
- I can quickly recall the symbol or logo of X.
- I have difficult imagining X in my mind. (reversed scored)

Source: Adapted from Boonghee Yoo and Naveen Donthu, "Developing and Validating a Multidimensional Consumer-based Brand Equity Scale," *Journal of Business Research,* Vol. 52 (April 2001), pp. 1–14.

Positioning by Intangible Attributes   Product quality, technological leadership, and value for money are all intangibles—nonfunctional factors or bundles of factors the consumer associates with a brand. Car advertising typically relies on the power of intangibles to build brand equity. Ford, for example, in its advertising across all makes and models, attempts to persuade consumers to associate the brand with high quality.[4]

In an interesting study of consumer beliefs, subjects were shown two brands of cameras described in terms of intangible attributes—one was technically sophisticated and the other easy to use. Detailed information was provided clearly showing that the easy-to-use brand was, in fact, technically superior. When asked to recollect each brand two days later, subjects simply remembered one as easy to use and the other as technically sophisticated. They recalled not the detailed specifications they had read, but the advertising claims, demonstrating the power of intangible attributes to influence consumer beliefs.[5]

E x h i b i t 9-2

Brand Associations

Multiple brand associations—all of which, to varying extents, can be manipulated by marketers to increase market share—contribute to a brand's equity.

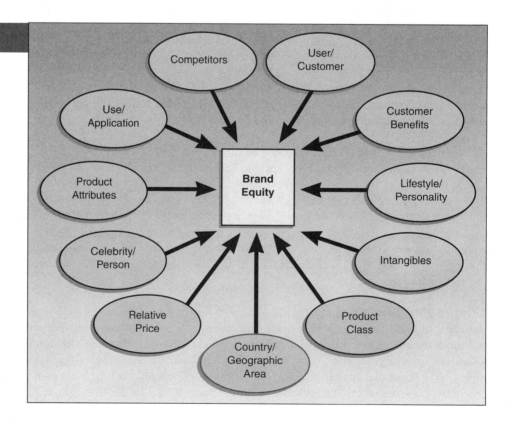

Marketplace 9-2

Brands Fight Back against Private Labels

Private-label brands—brands owned by retailers that match features, benefits, and often the quality of market leaders—are nibbling away at the equity of established brands. These products are offered at lower prices and are prominently displayed by the retailers that own them. Consumers can't see the differences between them and the name brands they once preferred. Here is an action checklist for marketers to win back brand equity and market shares.

- Make sure the brand more than delivers on its promises and that benefits are conveyed to the consumer through marketing efforts.

- Reduce the product portfolio, weeding out marginal brands and selecting only those with the greatest potential of becoming power brands.

- Choose between selling name-brand products and the sideline of manufacturing and supplying private-label products to retailers. It may be lucrative, but in the long run, it undermines the power of brands.

- Close the price gap between name brands and private labels to the point where consumers can afford to remain loyal to the name brand.

- Become the brand that performs better than anything else in meeting a specific consumer need.

- Avoid product proliferation by reversing the decline in research and development spending and

Even strong brands have certain limitations: the better known the brand, the tighter the image—which limits its use in new product categories but can provide a powerful base for line extensions close to home. The Campbell Soup Company has added scores of successful new products to its established line of canned soups, but Colgate's brand name did not travel well when it attempted to enter the food market.

Source: Adapted from George Gruenwald, *New Product Development,* 2nd ed. (Chicago, IL: NTC Business Books), 1992, p. 32.

redirecting effort toward new brand features and market entries that will build categories rather than merely win a few more fractions of share.

- Be a "high-value marketer," balancing the lowest cost with the highest quality.

- In all marketing communications, emphasize and constantly reiterate the best-value positioning.

- Use brand-building advertising to sustain a brand's perceived value in the minds of consumers.

- Build relationships with customers, possibly through interactive media, to counter the bond between consumer and retailer.

Source: Adapted from "Brands Fight Back against Private Labels" in *Marketing News,* January 16, 1995, p. 8. Reprinted with permission from *Marketing News,* published by the American Marketing Association.

Positioning by Price   Consumers associate certain brands with a particular price or price range. Price, particularly price relative to that of competitors, influences the way we retrieve brand information from memory. We have very different expectations when entering Kmart than when walking into Saks Fifth Avenue. Consider how hotel chains are perceived. Budget hotels such as Motel 6, Econolodge, and Days Inn are positioned as low in price—and in quality. Mid-range hotels, such as Courtyard, Ramada, and Holiday Inn, offer reasonable quality but good value for the money. Luxury hotels like Marriott, Hyatt Regency, and Embassy Suites promise high quality, but at a high price.[6]

CBite 9-1

Information OVERLOAD

Presenting too many different attributes to the consumer can undermine attitude change. One study found that when consumers were exposed to a range of possible financial consequences associated with purchasing a solar water heater, they were less likely to change their previously held beliefs. This is probably a result of information overload.

Source: Adapted from Scott A. Neslin and Gert Assmus, "Consumer Response to Information That Presents a Range of Possible Performance Levels for a New Product," *Journal of Consumer Affairs,* Vol. 17 (Summer 1983), pp. 81–105.

In all kinds of weather, on all kinds of roads, you're well equipped

for outdoor adventure when you drive the new Subaru Outback L.L.Bean

Edition. Like every Outback, the L.L.Bean Edition comes with

full-time All-Wheel Drive, so you can be surefooted in the trickiest

terrain. But the L.L.Bean Edition also sports a new 6-cylinder

engine, so you have more power than ever to go where you want

INTRODUCING THE LATEST ALL-WEATHER GEAR FROM L.L.BEAN.

to go and do what you want to do. And with signature features like

leather-trimmed seats and a mahogany and leather steering wheel by

Momo, you can weather the great outdoors in classic L.L.Bean style.

Visit us at www.subaru.com, call 1-800-WANT-AWD or stop in for a

test-drive. Because this gear from L.L.Bean   **OUTBACK**

can only be found at your local Subaru dealer.   L.L.Bean EDITION

SUBARU
The Beauty of All Wheel Drive

Exhibit 9-3

Subaru uses celebrities to connect the celebrity's personality and values to its products.

Source: Reprinted by permission of Subaru of America, Inc.

FAQ

What happens to brand equity when celebrity endorsers act in ways that are inconsistent with the values people expect them to represent?

Positioning by Application   Consumers associate particular uses or applications with different brands. By discovering the most common use of a product, marketers position brands to gain market share. Campbell's soup has been positioned primarily as a lunchtime product and Gatorade as the drink for athletes, particularly in the summertime. One study indicated as many as nine use-contexts for coffee: it is a drink to start the day, a break between meals, a break with friends, a lunch or supper drink, an after-dinner drink with guests, a means of relaxation, a way to keep awake, or a weekend indulgence. [7]

Positioning by Brand User   Related to the concept of ideal self-image is the association of a particular kind of user with a brand. Nike, for example, typically associates athletic types, often celebrities, with its products. Cover Girl cosmetics features wholesome, healthy looking women in its advertising. Canada Dry positions itself as the soft drink for adults, leaving Coke and Pepsi for the youth market. [8]

Positioning by Celebrity Recognition   We perceive celebrities in terms of their personalities and the values they represent. Through celebrity recognition, marketers associate brands with a celebrity endorser and so connect the celebrity's personality and values with them. Consumers ultimately respond to the brand in the same positive way in which they respond to the celebrity. The success of the Subaru Outback can clearly be attributed to the enormous popularity of its spokesperson, Paul Hogan, the Australian actor who starred in the movie *Crocodile Dundee*, pictured in Exhibit 9-3. [9]

Positioning by Brand Personality   Several successful campaigns have manufactured a "personality" with which to associate brands. A classic example is Betty Crocker baked goods. Betty Crocker has built market share by associating its brand with a personality that comes across as traditional, honest, dependable, friendly, and caring. In a long and enduring rivalry, Coke is associated with a strong, family-oriented, all-American image, whereas Pepsi is positioned as exciting, innovative, fast-growing, and somewhat brash and pushy. [10]

Positioning by Product Category   Marketers create identities for brands through strong association with a particular, sometimes unexpected, product category. The most obvious example is the positioning of 7-Up soft drink as the "uncola"—the logical alternative to colas but with a better taste. Caress hand soap is set apart from competitors in the soap category by association with bath oil.[11] Arm & Hammer goes from strength to strength—from baking soda to toothpaste to detergent.

Positioning by Association with Competitors

Marketers can purposely associate their brands with competitors in order to share the consumer perceptions enjoyed by market leaders. A market follower tries to capitalize on the well-established image of the market leader, hoping this will persuade consumers to make positive inferences about its product. A well-known and well-executed example of this strategy was the campaign for Avis rental cars: "We're number two, but we try harder." The message here is that although Hertz is number one in car rentals, Avis is a very close second—and offers superior customer service.[12]

Positioning by Country or Geographic Area

Brands can be associated with a particular country or geographic locale with a reputation for quality.[13] Japan, for example, is associated with high-quality cars and electronic goods, France with perfumes and fashion, Italy with shoes and leather goods, Germany with high-quality beer and cars, and Russia with vodka and fur coats. In recent years, following the political climate, "Made in America" has become a powerful positioning statement.

Products are positioned using combinations of all of these strategies. Crest toothpaste, for example, has fluoride—an attribute. It fights cavities—a benefit in which consumers believe. It offers high quality—an intangible attribute. It's competitively priced. It works best when used three times a day, after each meal—a specific application. It's popular with families—both a brand user and personality association. It has been associated with celebrities—Bill Cosby uses it. It's made in the United States—a country-of-origin association. CBite 9-2 shows the world's 10 most valuable brands. These brands have high levels of brand equity. In other words, consumers recognize the brand names and also have strong and positive images of the brands (associations with benefits, attributes, etc.). These strong and positively valenced associations reflect brand equity.

CBite 9-2
The World's 10 Most Valuable Brands

Rank	Brand	2004 Brand Value (Billions)	Rank	Brand	2004 Brand Value (Billions)
1	Coca-Cola	$67.39	6	Disney	27.11
2	Microsoft	61.37	7	McDonald's	25.00
3	IBM	53.79	8	Nokia	24.04
4	GE	44.11	9	Toyota	22.67
5	Intel	33.50	10	Marlboro	22.13

Source: Interbrand Corp., J. P. Chase & Co., Citigroup, Morgan Stanley.

The method used to rank brands by *Business Week* is as follows. The first step is to estimate what percentage of a company's revenues can be credited to a brand (the brand may be almost the entire company, as in McDonald's, or just a portion, as in Marlboro). The second step involves estimating five years of earnings and sales for the brand. The third step is to deduct operating costs, taxes, and a charge for the capital employed to arrive at the intangible earnings (the portion of earning from intangibles such as patents and customer convenience that is due to the brand). Finally, the brand's strength is assessed. Factors in estimating a brand's strength include market leadership, stability, and global reach. Brand strength is used to determine the risk profile of the earnings forecasts. That is, it is used as a discount rate, which is applied to brand earnings to get a net present value.

Source: Adapted from: Diane Brady, Robert D. Hof, Andy Reinhardt, Moon Ihlwan, Stanley Holmes, and Kerry Capell, "Cult Brands," Business Week (August 2004), pp. 64–68.

> ### Marketing Management—Implications and Actions
>
> Understanding consumer beliefs helps marketers:
> - Change the way in which consumers think about brands.
> - Strengthen associations between their brands and positive attributes.
> - Develop positioning strategies that increase brand equity and market share.

9-2 Affect: The Emotive Component of Attitude

affect The way in which we feel in response to marketplace stimuli, such as brands. Unlike belief, affect is emotive rather than cognitive in nature. It results not just from our knowledge of marketplace stimuli but from our evaluation of them. In other words, affect is made up of beliefs, plus the way in which we feel about or evaluate those beliefs.

Whether we are conscious of it or not, our purchase decisions are continually influenced by our affective responses. **Affect** is the way in which we feel in response to marketplace stimuli such as brands. Unlike belief, affect is emotive rather than cognitive in nature. It results not just from our knowledge of marketplace stimuli but from our evaluation of them. In other words, affect is made up of beliefs plus the way we feel about or evaluate those beliefs.[14]

Every piece of new information we collect about a product category or about a brand has the potential to change our affective responses. Advertisements, magazine articles, salespeople, the advice of friends, and the purchase setting itself all help shape the way we feel about brands in the marketplace, encouraging or discouraging purchase. From the brands we choose, to the price we pay, to the outlet at which we shop, our affective responses influence each stage of the purchase decision.

Our affective responses can be very general or very specific. We might, for example, display general feelings toward an entire product class—"I hate shopping for clothes," or toward a brand—"Corn flakes is the best breakfast cereal for children." In other cases, affect is limited to a specific purchase experience—"I didn't care for the service at Denny's this morning—it was slow." Exhibit 9-4 illustrates various levels of specificity in affective responses to marketplace stimuli.

Several studies have explored the affective component of attitude, resulting in the development of a number of conceptual models that explain its influence on marketplace behavior. Three attitude models incorporating a variety of market factors dominate:[15]

> **FAQ**
>
> **Do consumers really care enough about brands to have feelings about them?**

1. Functional theory of attitude
2. The Fishbein model
3. Belief-importance model

A fourth model—cognitive dissonance theory—was covered in Chapter 4 (section 4-4), where we discussed post-purchase behavior.

9-2a Functional Theory of Attitude

functional theory of attitude Attitude toward a product based on four functions: adjustment, ego defense, value expression, and application of prior knowledge.

Affective responses help consumers reach purchase decisions in four ways: adjustment, ego defense, value expression, and application of prior knowledge, all of which will be discussed in this section.[16] The **functional theory of attitude** recommends that marketers seek to influence affective responses by creating messages that appeal to consumers on the basis of one or more of these four types of responses.

E x h i b i t 9-4	**Level of Specificity of a Product**	**Example**
Levels of Specificity of Affect	Product class	Car
	Product form	Economy cars
	Brand	Honda Accord
	Model	The Honda Accord LXi
	Brand/model/situation	The Honda Accord LXi at the Honda dealer in town

International *Marketplace 9-1*

Different Cultures, Different Attitudes

Advertisers from Mojo Australia, sent on behalf of the Australian government's export program to educate the Taiwanese about Australian food, ended up getting some culinary culture shock treatment themselves. They were treated to a local delicacy that taught them much about Taiwanese tastes. Swallow's spit, a clear, syrupy drink with brown flecks, is made from fungus found in selected top-quality bird's nests. The drink is rich in protein and has numerous vitamins, amino acids, and trace elements, and the Taiwanese believe its ingredients are capable of restoring equilibrium and are beneficial to the nerves, lungs, and skin.

This is just one example of how attitudes that are clearly understood in one culture can mean something else entirely in another. While Westerners generally don't turn to food for its healing attributes, foods with purported pharmaceutical properties are a natural part of life in Taiwan.

On returning to Australia, Mojo turned its new knowledge of the Taiwanese market to its advantage. The Mojo team, rather than emphasizing product purity and fastidious processing techniques—messages that are popular with Japanese and American food marketers—skewed its campaign to an image of warmer, more natural, even friendlier Australian products. At the same time, Mojo tapped in to the Taiwanese desire for food that draws strength from its natural origins. The campaign ran for four months, resulting in a 95 percent increase in consumer awareness of Australian foods and a 50 percent sales increase.

Source: Adapted from "Mojo Cultivates Taste for Aussie Food Campaign," *Advertising Age*, January 2, 1995.

International Marketplace 9-1 shows how attitudes toward products may vary significantly across cultures. This may be due to the emphasis of different "functions" in different cultures.

Adjustment   **Adjustment** is the tendency to develop affective responses that lead most efficiently toward perceived rewards and avoid most conveniently any perceived punishments. A freshman whose family loves to ski takes up snowboarding in order to join in trips to the slopes with new friends on campus. It soon becomes her favorite winter sport. A consumer who learns he has a heart condition starts using less salt and avoids foods with high sodium content.

Marketers can encourage adjustment to better suit their products to changing consumer needs or aspirations. A marketer of fitness equipment targets consumers who dislike strenuous exercise. To overcome reluctance, the marketer emphasizes ease of use, limited time commitments, and fast results. The objective is to change affective responses from "Exercising is difficult and takes up too much time" to "Exercise can be easy and can fit in with my schedule." Exhibit 9-5 shows a product ad that offers a strong argument to overcome consumer reluctance toward healthy food (eating tomato products to minimize the risk of certain cancers) by showing how Campbell's tomato soups are "M'm! M'm! Good!"

adjustment The tendency to develop affective responses that lead the consumer to purchase a product or service because this product or service leads to gaining certain rewards and avoiding certain punishments.

Ego Defense   **Ego defense** is a means through which we try to realize personal goals and images. To protect our self-image, we might, for example, develop positive attitudes toward such self-enhancement products as fashions, grooming aids, impressive cars, and other outward signs of attractiveness or confidence. Another aspect of ego-defense is our tendency to respond critically toward others who display signs of shortcomings or weaknesses we are reluctant to admit we share.

Affective responses that result from ego defense are difficult to change. One strategy that works is advertising that promises to remove obstacles to the consumer's goals or positive self-image. A commercial for breath fresheners in which a young woman is worried that she has bad breath can reinforce ego defense by offering a way to ward off the threat of public embarrassment.

ego defense The tendency to develop affective responses that lead the consumer to purchase a product or service because this product or service leads to the attainment of personal goals and images.

Value Expression   Through **value expression**, consumers display their own values to the external world. Concern for the environment, for example, is expressed in buying a

value expression The concept that an attitude can serve to express a person's values. For example, buying a hybrid car may express the buyer's values related to environmentalism.

bicycle, using cold water for laundry, bundling the Sunday paper off to the recycling center, recycling aluminum cans, or buying soda in returnable bottles. The Ford ad in Exhibit 9-6 shows that cars can express the consumer's environmental concern.

Application of Prior Knowledge   Knowledge has both positive and negative effects on affective response. It can, for example, lead to stereotyping—prior knowledge of one brand of fat-free frozen yogurt is a shortcut to "knowing" just what to expect of other brands. Knowledge can also serve as an information filter that makes it easier to sort out which messages we will pay attention to and which we will ignore. It provides us with a unique frame of reference through which to observe and understand the marketplace around us. Knowledge leads Cara to have confidence that she prefers denim to lace. She doesn't have to re-examine her values, habits, and lifestyle each time she shops for clothes.

Marketers can overcome negative affective responses that result from prior knowledge by presenting the consumer with new information that creates dissonance among previously held attitudes. Dominic has never considered buying a personal computer because he thinks of them as difficult to use and expensive. He is now exposed to information that convinces him otherwise—new models are easy to use, and the cost is falling all the time. His affective response to computers changes, despite his earlier knowledge of them.

Measuring attitudes is not that straightforward. The functional theory of attitudes helps consumer researchers to ask the right questions about consumer preferences for certain products and brands. CBite 9-3 illustrates this point clearly.

Exhibit 9-6

Ford knows that consumers like their purchases, especially major ones, to express their values, even environmental concern.

Source: Courtesy Ford Motor Company.

9-2b The Fishbein Model

The **Fishbein model** directly relates consumer beliefs with affective response. Affective response to a brand is made up of two factors: the strength or weakness of a consumer's beliefs about that brand and its attributes and the consumer's evaluation of or feelings toward those attributes.[17] The Fishbein model recommends that marketers create messages that change beliefs in order to change affective responses.

> **Fishbein model** A model that directly relates consumer beliefs with affective response. Affective response to a brand is made up of two factors: the strength or weakness of a consumer's beliefs about that brand and its attributes and the consumer's evaluation of or feelings toward those attributes.

CBite 9-3

Asking about Attitudes

One of the thorniest problems in attitude measurement concerns the phrasing of statements or questions so that they do not affect the subject's responses. To a simple question like "Do you like orange soda?" for example, two people—one who drinks it every day, the other who last tasted it five years ago—might both answer "Sure," making an attitude survey meaningless. Even a more open-ended question like "What kinds of soda do you like?" raises problems. The trouble is that few of us are likely to remember all the sodas we like. Even if we buy and drink orange soda often, the likeliest response is "Coke" or "Pepsi," because these heavily advertised brands are usually the first to come to mind. The best solution is to offer alternative choices:
What kinds of soda do you like?

1. Cola
2. Root beer
3. Orange
4. Grape
5. Cream

This mode of questioning lets the consumer focus evenly on specific items.

Exhibit 9-7

Fishbein Model

According to the model, consumer beliefs are linked to affective response: If beliefs are strong and favorable, affective response is positive.

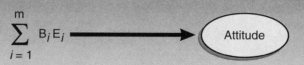

$$\sum_{i=1}^{m} B_i E_i \longrightarrow \text{Attitude}$$

B_i — Belief about the extent to which the product has attribute (benefit or cost) i.

E_i — Evaluation of attribute i.

Consumer researchers use a simple formula to represent the model:

$$A = \sum_{i=1}^{m} B_i E_i$$

where

$A =$ attitude toward a brand
$B_i =$ belief that the brand possesses attribute i
$E_i =$ evaluation or desirability of attribute i
$i =$ attribute $1, 2, \ldots m$

The formula is demonstrated in Exhibit 9-7.

Here is an example of how it works. A radio station is planning an advertising campaign but first wishes to find out how listeners feel about four key attributes.

Attribute (*i*)	B_i	E_i	$B_i \times E_i$
Plays lots of music	+3	+3	+9
Plays lots of commercials	+3	−3	−9
Gives news updates	+1	+1	+1
Has interesting DJs	+2	+3	+6
Sum			**+7**

In this example, each attribute is scored according to consumer responses to product-related questions, measured upon a scale as follows:

Do you believe that Radio WXYZ plays lots of music?

Yes   +3 +2 +1 0 −1 −2 −3   No

Evaluation weights are assigned as follows:

How appealing is it to you when a radio station plays lots of music?

Very appealing   +3 +2 +1 0 −1 −2 −3   Not appealing

The first column measures the belief strength (B_i) of the radio station's target listeners. They strongly believe (+3) that the radio station plays lots of music and plays lots of commercials. They moderately believe (+1) that the station gives news updates, and they believe moderately to strongly (+2) that the station has interesting DJs. The second column measures evaluation weights (E_i) assigned by target listeners. The attribute "plays lots of music" is highly desirable (+3), while the attribute "plays lots of commercials" is highly undesirable (−3). The attribute "gives news updates" is moderately desirable (+1), while the attribute "has interesting DJs" is highly desirable (+3).

Column 3, the sum of $B_i \times E_i$, reveals the radio station's strengths and weaknesses as perceived by target listeners. The station may decide to capitalize on its strengths by playing even more music and eliminate weaknesses by decreasing the frequency of commercial interruptions (possibly by presenting blocks of commercials rather than dispersing them intermittently throughout the programming) and either replacing DJs or helping them better address the interests of the target audience. Having made these changes, marketers can attract new listeners by promoting new strengths.

Using the Fishbein Model to Change Affective Responses   The Fishbein model suggests three strategies through which marketers can adjust affective responses:[18]

1. *Change B_i.* Marketers can communicate to consumers that the brand no longer has a negative attribute consumers believe it to have or possesses a positive attribute of which they are unaware. The message "Cadillac gets good mileage" is a good example. The objective is to adjust consumers' perception of one or more attributes. Moreover, providing negative information has greater impact than positive information. This is because negative information is still a novelty for most consumers, who most commonly encounter it in the form of corrective advertising demanded by regulatory agencies to make up for fraudulent claims.[19] However, in political advertising the use of negative information is common.

2. *Change E_i.* Marketers can convince consumers to reassess their evaluation of a particular attribute of a brand. Whereas in most cases consumers would automatically consider "bad taste" to be a negative attribute, the marketers of Listerine have persuaded their target market that it is a good quality for its product to possess. Overall, changing E_i is less effective in altering consumer attitudes than is changing B_i.

3. *Add a new B_i/E_i combination.* Marketers can introduce a new, often unexpected, attribute to increase the overall attractiveness of their brand. Magnavox does this by promoting a color television that automatically adjusts itself to changes in room lighting.

The Fishbein model allows marketers to identify the extent to which consumers believe that a product has certain features and the extent to which those features are considered appealing. The conclusions from surveys based on the model provide marketers with information that allows them to develop positioning strategies that strengthen positive responses and overcome negative ones. The Fishbein model is particularly useful for the development of public service campaigns, for which competitive analysis is usually not a factor.

F A Q

Do consumers ever really forget negative attitudes toward brands?

9-2c The Belief-Importance Model

Whereas the Fishbein model analyzes brands in isolation, the **belief-importance model** allows marketers to compare affective responses toward competing brands. We each have an evoked set of brands—a list of brands we consider prior to making a decision. The final selection is made only after we evaluate the desirability of each brand according to the same set of attributes. The following formula represents the belief-importance model:

$$A_o = \sum_{i=1}^{m} B_{io}I_i$$

where

A_o = attitude toward brand (*o*)

B_{io} = belief that brand (*o*) does well or poorly when its attribute (*i*) is compared with those of competitors

I_i = importance of attribute (*i*) in selecting a brand

i = attribute 1, 2, . . . m

The formula is demonstrated in Exhibit 9-8.

belief-importance model
A model that compares affective responses toward competing brands. We each have an evoked set of brands—a list of brands we consider prior to making a decision. The final selection is made only after we evaluate the desirability of each brand according to the same set of attributes.

Exhibit 9-8

Belief-Importance Model

This model evaluates beliefs about brand attributes in terms of their importance to the consumer, allowing for comparison across brands.

$$\sum_{i=1}^{m} B_{io} I_i \longrightarrow \text{Preference}$$

B_{io} — Belief that brand *(o)* does well or poorly when its attribute *(i)* is compared with those of competitors

I_i — Importance of attribute *(i)* in selecting a brand

Here is an example of how the formula works. Three brands of athletic shoes score as follows on ten attributes (note that all the numbers here are hypothetical):

Attribute (*i*)	Importance (*I_i*)	Belief (*B_io*)		
		Reebok	*Nike*	*Asahi*
Price	20	−2	−1	+2
Shock absorbency	10	+3	+5	+1
Durability	15	+2	+3	+1
Color/style	15	+2	+4	+5
Comfort	20	+4	+4	+4
Arch support	10	+3	+2	+1
Fastener	2	+2	+2	+2
Material	2	+3	+3	+3
Specialty performance	5	+4	+5	+3
Country of manufacture	1	+3	+3	−2
Sum	*100*	*193*	*273*	*253*

In this example, a constant sum scale is used to express importance. Here, 100 "importance points" are distributed among the attributes based on their perceived relative importance. The more points awarded, the more important is the attribute. Beliefs are rated as follows:

Excellent +5 +4 +3 +2 +1 0 −1 −2 −3 −4 −5 **Terrible**

In the example, Nike rates highest (+273), followed by Asahi (+253), then Reebok (+193). The marketer of Asahi can see from the belief-importance model that, in comparison to competitors, consumers perceive the brand's weaknesses as country of manufacture (−2), shock absorbency (+1), durability (+1), and arch support (+1). However, an analysis of importance weights (I_i) assigned by consumers shows that these weaknesses are not considered equally important. Of all of these attributes, durability matters most (15%) and should, therefore, be the focus of product improvements and future promotions.[20] Asahi's strengths are color/style (+5) and comfort (+4). Both attributes are considered to be important by consumers (15% and 20%, respectively). Future promotions should also emphasize, therefore, the appealing colors and styles and the comfort of Asahi.[21]

The strength of the belief-importance model is its ability to measure affective responses toward a brand compared to others, making it extremely useful in the development of competitive strategies or competitive positioning statements.

9-3 Intention: The Behavior Component of Consumer Attitude

Intention is the behavior component of attitude. As we have seen, affect is a general, emotive response to brands, reflecting the consumer's overall disposition. It is often no more than a general feeling of like or dislike. As such, it is not closely linked to actual purchase.[22] **Behavioral intention** describes attitude not toward a brand but toward brand purchase and, as such, is a far better predictor of behavior than either beliefs or affective responses.

Consider the results of a study reported in CBite 9-4 about the link between attitude and behavior. We do not always do as we say.

Suppose Saturn discovers that, although college students display positive beliefs and affective responses toward its cars as fairly priced and reliable, few have any real plans to purchase. They feel insurance and upkeep costs will be high, and Saturn doesn't have quite the right image to impress their friends. The strategic implication here is that marketing has to be directed toward the factors that affect attitude toward brand purchase rather than beliefs or affective response—assurance that insurance and upkeep costs are low and an image campaign to popularize the brand within the college community. Two behavioral models seek to explain the psychology of consumer intention and its connection with purchase:

1. The theory of reasoned action
2. The theory of trying

behavioral intention
The behavior component of attitude. Behavioral intention describes attitude not toward a brand but toward brand purchase and, as such, is a far better predictor of behavior than either beliefs or affective responses.

9-3a The Theory of Reasoned Action

The **theory of reasoned action** states that behavior is a direct result of intention. Particularly with planned purchases, as we saw in Chapter 3 (section 3-2a), and even with impulse purchases, we buy only after we have formed an intention to do so.

There are two factors involved in behavioral intention: attitude toward an act and subjective norm.

theory of reasoned action
The theory that states that behavior is a direct result of intention. Particularly with planned purchases, and even with impulse purchases, we buy only after we have formed an intention to do so. Two factors are involved in behavioral intention: attitude toward an act and subjective norm.

CBite 9-4
Do We Always Do As We Say?

Only 60 percent of people who say they intend to buy a car actually do so within a year. And of those who do not intend to buy, 17 percent end up driving home in a new car.

Source: Cited in Kenneth A. Longman, "Promises, Promises," in L. Adler and L. Crespi, eds., *Attitude Research on the Rocks* (Chicago, IL: American Marketing Association, 1986), pp. 28–37.

Attitude toward the Act   The consumer's **attitude toward the act** of purchasing a particular brand is expressed by consumer researchers as A_{act}. It is the sum of the consumer's belief strengths in consequences that will result from a purchase and the evaluation weight assigned to each of those consequences. The formula is as follows:

$$A_{act} = \sum_{i=1}^{m} B_i E_i$$

where

$\quad B_i\ $ = belief that performance of a certain behavior—brand purchase—leads to an anticipated outcome

$\quad E_i\ $ = evaluation of an anticipated outcome, either a positive benefit or avoidance of a negative consequence

$\quad i\ $ = anticipated outcome $1, 2, \ldots m$

Here's an example of how the formula works. Jerry, a high school student, is considering using the wages from his summer job to buy a Dell personal computer. He thinks about all the possible consequences of the purchase: He'll be able to type school reports at home with relative ease (B_1); he'll be able to incorporate graphics into his work (B_2); and he'll have access to email (B_3). Jerry allocates a different evaluation weight to each of these possible outcomes (E_i): It is very desirable for him to submit well-typed reports (E_1), but he is less excited about using graphics (E_2) and isn't sure he'll need email at all (E_3). Jerry's overall A_{act}—or attitude toward—the purchase of a Dell PC is determined by his beliefs (B_i) about all these possible outcomes and his evaluations of these outcomes (E_i).

Subjective Norm   **Subjective norm** is our perception of what other people think we should do with respect to a certain behavior, such as a brand purchase.[23] Suppose that Jerry feels pressured into buying a Dell PC because he is involved with several group projects. Or perhaps Jerry's friends and basketball teammates consider the Dell PC the best computer available, and he wants to impress them with his choice. These external influences make up the subjective norm.

Subjective norm is determined by both normative beliefs and motivation to comply with those beliefs. A **normative belief** is the perceived expectation that significant others think the consumer should or should not behave in a certain way (buy the brand). **Motivation to comply** is the extent to which the consumer considers the possible opinions of significant others when forming an intent to purchase.[24] This is expressed as follows:

$$SN = \sum_{j=1}^{n} NB_j MC_j$$

where

$\quad SN\ $ = subjective norm—the motivation toward an act as determined by the influence of significant others

$\quad NB_j\ $ = normative beliefs—belief that significant others (j) expect the consumer to engage in an action

$\quad MC_j\ $ = motivation to comply—the extent to which the consumer is motivated to realize the expectations of significant others (j)

$\quad j\ $ = significant other $1, 2, \ldots n$

The expectations of Jerry's teammates and his friends constitute a normative belief. Jerry's desire to meet those expectations through the purchase of a Dell PC constitutes his motivation to comply.

Combining A_{act} and Subjective Norm   Combining attitude toward an act and subjective norm, the following formula represents the theory of reasoned action:

$$B = f(BI) = f[(A_{act})w_1 + (SN)w_2]$$

where

$$
\begin{aligned}
B &= \text{overt behavior, i.e., brand purchase} \\
BI &= \text{behavioral intention or purchase intention} \\
A_{act} &= \text{attitude toward purchase of brand} \\
SN &= \text{subjective norm} \\
w_1 \text{ and } w_2 &= \text{empirically determined evaluation weights}
\end{aligned}
$$

The formula states that purchase of a given product is determined by intention to purchase that product, which, in turn, is determined by the attitude toward the purchase of the product and the subjective norms associated with the purchase. The formula is demonstrated in Exhibit 9-9.

Here is an example of how the formula works.[25, 26]

Alicia is considering buying a CD player and wants to select a brand that will impress her friends, her roommate, and her parents. As she comes closer to the purchase, the opinions of the salesperson are also important to her. All these people are salient referents influencing her purchase. In selecting a CD player, Alicia is looking for sound quality, the latest in technological features, and value for money. These are the salient attributes that will influence the purchase.

As one of several respondents to a survey on intentions to purchase CD players, Alicia is first asked to express her A_{act} through using a specific measurement scale by responding to such items as:

"Describe how you feel about buying Brand X CD player."

Good   + 3 +2 +1 0 −1 −2 −3   Bad

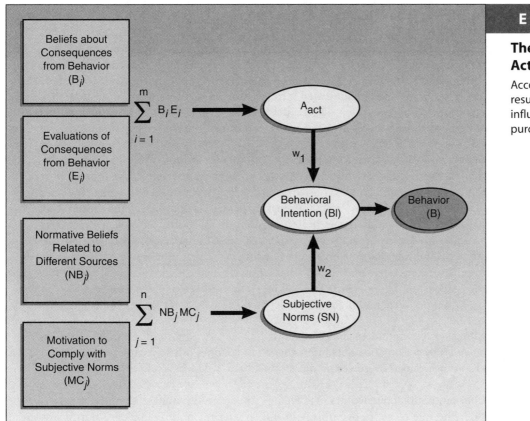

Theory of Reasoned Action

According to the model, purchase results from intention to purchase, influenced by attitudes toward purchase and subjective norms.

Alicia's response registered on this scale provides a numerical expression of her A_{act}. Second, Alicia's evaluation (E_i) of salient attributes is measured using the same scale:

"Describe the degree to which it is desirable for you to have the latest technological features in any CD player you buy."

Good   +3 +2 +1   0   –1 –2 –3   Bad

Third, Alicia's cognitive beliefs (B_i) with respect to salient attributes are measured using a similar scale:

"Describe the extent to which you think you would get the latest in technological features if you bought Brand X CD player."

Very possible   +3 +2 +1   0   –1 –2 –3   Impossible

Fourth, Alicia's normative beliefs are measured with respect to her salient referents (NB_j):

"Describe the extent to which you think your close friends would approve if you buy Brand X CD player."

Highly approve   +3 +2 +1   0   –1 –2 –3   Highly disapprove

Fifth, Alicia's motivation to comply with salient referents (MC_j) are measured using the following scale:

"How motivated are you to go along with what your close friends think about the CD player?"

Highly motivated   +3 +2 +1   0   –1 –2 –3   Not motivated at all

Lastly, Alicia's behavioral intention (BI) is measured using a similar scale:

"How likely are you to buy Brand X CD player?"

Very likely   +3 +2 +1   0   –1 –2 –3   Very unlikely

Applying the Theory of Reasoned Action to Change Consumer Intentions

The theory of reasoned action is a powerful model frequently used by marketers to describe and predict the determinants of purchase intention and behavior. The model guides the marketer to identify those attributes most important in causing consumers to develop positive (or negative) attitudes toward the purchase of a product. Those attributes can then be manipulated through product development and through marketing communications programs. The model also allows marketers to identify and, therefore, attempt to adjust sources of social pressure and their possible role in intention formation.

Changing Attitude toward Purchase   To influence attitude toward brand purchase, the marketer must first determine which attributes (or consequences) are most important to the consumer. This can be achieved by analyzing the evaluation weights (E_i) consumers assign each attribute. Obviously, the marketer should primarily seek to reinforce those that are most positive and change those that are most negative. Second, the marketer must examine the belief strengths (B_i) associated with the selected attributes. Do the belief strengths indicate that consumers are not convinced that purchasing the brand will result in positive consequences? If so, the marketing challenge is clear: Persuade consumers that the purchase and use of the brand will result in positive consequences.

Suppose Alicia and other respondents in the CD player survey indicate that they do not believe that purchasing Brand X will allow them to experience high-quality sound. Moreover, all respondents rate sound quality as a very important attribute. Again, the challenge is clear: Convince consumers that Brand X does offer a high level of sound quality, even if it means re-engineering the product.

Changing Subjective Norms   To change intention to purchase, the marketer must consider the role of subjective norms in influencing intention. Subjective norms are social influence factors. Consumers may decide to buy the brand, not necessarily because of its intrinsic features or tangible benefits, but because they seek to gain the approval or avoid the disapproval of significant others. .

Now suppose Alicia and other respondents in the CD player survey indicate that their intention to purchase Brand X CD player is heavily influenced by the possible reactions of close friends to the purchase. A promotional campaign that shows friends using and recommending Brand X would most likely influence the consumer's intention to purchase.

9-3b **The Theory of Trying**

A serious limitation of the theory of reasoned action is that it cannot be used to predict behavior in situations in which consumption takes place over an extended period of time. It cannot, for example, help us predict the consumption of a yard service, a cooking class, or a diet program, where consumption is spread over a number of weeks or months. Although the model allows us to predict whether a specific consumer is likely to purchase or sign up for services like these, it fails to predict the extent to which the consumer is likely to continue with those services.

The **theory of trying** was designed to address this limitation by exploring consumption behavior rather than buying behavior.[27] The model is demonstrated in Exhibit 9-10.

Saving for retirement is a difficult task. We sometimes try and try again. Marketers have designed programs and services that help consumers to try and succeed. An example is the START program described in Marketplace 9-3.

Here is an example of how the theory of trying model works. Jade is trying to lose weight and is thinking of signing up for an aerobic exercise program. According to the theory of trying, the intensity of her attempt to lose weight through aerobic exercise can be predicted by the following three factors:

1. Intention to try
2. Frequency of past trying
3. Recency of past trying

As one of several respondents in a weight-loss survey, Jade is asked about her **intention to try** to lose weight through such measures as:

> **"I presently intend to try to lose weight by doing aerobics during the next week."**
>
> **Very likely   +3 +2 +1 0 –1 –2 –3   Very unlikely**

Next, Jade is asked about her previous weight-loss attempts—the past frequency of trying. The more a person has tried to achieve a goal in the past, the more likely that person is to try again. The principle here is that past behavior is a good predictor of future behavior. The survey might contain the following statement and responses:

> **"In the past I have tried to lose weight through aerobics."**
>
> 1 = **very many times**
> 2 = **many times**
> 3 = **several times**
> 4 = **a couple of times**
> 5 = **once**
> 6 = **not at all**

Jade is now questioned about the recency of her past attempts to lose weight. The more recent the past trying experience, the higher the individual's motivation to try again. The survey may contain the following question:

> **"Have you tried to lose weight through aerobic exercise during the past three months?"**
>
> **Yes/No**

Now let's us look at those factors that can predict Jade's intention to try to lose weight. Intention to try is determined by three factors: frequency of trying (as discussed above), social norms toward trying, and attitude toward trying.

Social norms toward trying include the extent to which Jade thinks that others expect her to try to lose weight. A typical measure is:

theory of trying The theory designed to predict consumption behavior rather than buying behavior. According to the theory of trying, the intensity of an attempt to consume a product can be predicted by intention to try, frequency of past trying, and recency of past trying.

intention to try The plan to engage in action, which is motivated by frequency of past trying, social norms toward trying, and attitude toward trying.

social norms toward trying The extent to which the consumer thinks that others expect him or her to try to engage in the consumption act in question.

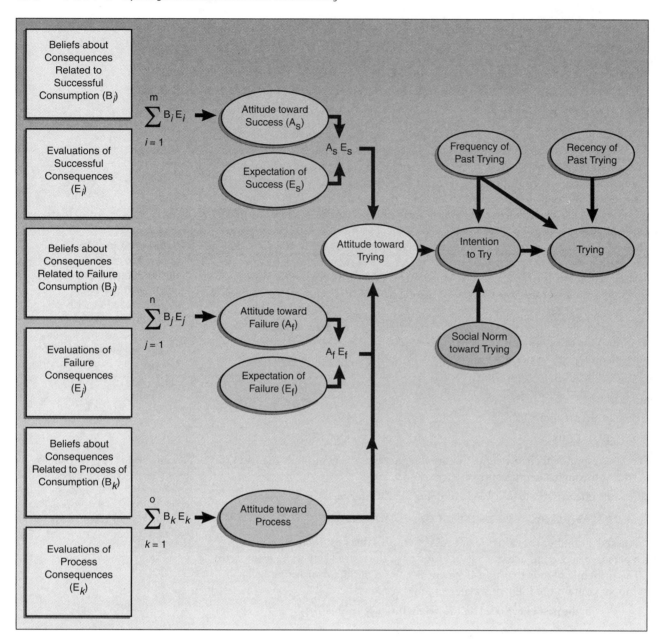

Exhibit 9-10

Theory of Trying

This model explains actual consumption behavior. Used to analyze consumption of services that are used over time, it provides insight into the building of long-term customer relationships.

"Most people who are important to me think that I should try to lose weight through aerobic exercise next week."

Very likely +3 +2 +1 0 −1 −2 −3 Very unlikely

Jade's attitude toward trying is her general disposition toward her attempts to lose weight. We would measure her attitude toward trying as follows:

"All things considered, I think of trying to lose weight through aerobics during the next week as _____."

Good +3 +2 +1 0 −1 −2 −3 Bad

Attitude toward trying can be further broken down into three specific types of attitudes and expectations:

1. Attitude toward success together with expectation of success
2. Attitude toward failure together with expectation of failure
3. Attitude toward the process

Marketplace 9-3

The START Program

Retirement is a mounting concern for today's baby boomer population. Many baby boomers are alarmed by downsizing trends; they are worried that they may not be able to count on Social Security in retirement. The START program was designed to deal with this concern. The program—which stands for Spend Today And Retire Tomorrow—takes a percentage of every purchase a consumer makes with a participating firm and deposits that money into a tax-deferred annuity. The specific contributions are: 1 percent of the first $1,000 spent with START companies each year, 3 percent of the next $1,000, and 6 percent of annual purchases totaling more than $2,000. These contributions are funded by the participating firms.

START, based in Herndon, Virginia, helps participating companies in three ways. It recruits new customers for the participating companies. It encourages existing customers to increase their use of the products of the participating companies. It also helps create loyal customers. Examples of

It is relatively expensive for companies to attract new customers and inexpensive to retain current ones. Programs like START help marketers maximize both of these critical goals.

Source: David A. Aaker, *Managing Brand Equity* (New York: The Free Press, 1995), p. 19.

participating companies are MCI, Hertz, Spiegel, Paul Frederick Shirt Co., and Nautilus. All companies are guaranteed exclusivity in their industry category. This means, for example, that MCI doesn't have to worry about Sprint taking away its customers. Therefore, the program offers consumers a major incentive to invest toward retirement by restricting their purchases to those products offered by the participating companies.

Source: Adapted from Shari Caudron, "Brand Loyalty: Can It Be Revived?" *Industry Week* (April 5, 1993), p. 11 (3).

Attitude toward success is the extent to which Jade would feel good, given that she tries to lose weight and succeeds. A scale like the following would measure this factor:

> **"The thought of succeeding at losing weight through aerobics during the next week is _____."**

> **Pleasant +3 +2 +1 0 −1 −2 −3 Unpleasant**

Expectation of success is the extent to which Jade anticipates her success in losing weight. The following would assess this factor:

> **"Assuming I try to lose weight during the next week, it is _____ that I actually would succeed."**

> **Very likely +3 +2 +1 0 −1 −2 −3 Very unlikely**

Attitude toward failure is the extent to which Jade would feel bad, given that she tries to lose weight and fails. This might be assessed with the following scale:

> **"The thought of failing if I try to lose weight through aerobics during the next week is _____:"**

> **Pleasant +3 +2 +1 0 −1 −2 −3 Unpleasant**

Expectation of failure is the extent to which Jade anticipates her failure to lose weight: The following scale might be used:

> **"Assuming I try to lose weight during the next week, it is _____ that I actually would fail."**

> **Very likely +3 +2 +1 0 −1 −2 −3 Very unlikely**

Attitude toward the process involves the consumer's feelings toward the actions necessary in order to consume a product. Jade may have to call the exercise studio in advance to make reservations; she may need to make babysitting arrangements; and she may have to be there fifteen minutes before the class begins in order to find a parking place and change clothes. To measure her attitude toward the process, Jade might be asked, for example:

attitude toward success The extent to which the consumer would feel good, given that he or she tries to consume the product in question and succeeds in goal attainment.

expectation of success The extent to which the consumer anticipates that he or she will be successful in goal attainment, given the consumption of the product.

attitude toward failure The extent to which the consumer would feel bad, given that he or she tries to consume the product and fails to attain the desired goal.

expectation of failure The extent to which the consumer anticipates that he or she will fail in goal attainment, given the consumption of the product.

attitude toward the process Involves the consumer's feelings toward the actions necessary in order to consume a product.

"The process I have to go through in order to participate in the aerobics class is _____."

Pleasant +3 +2 +1 0 –1 –2 –3 Unpleasant

Lastly, beliefs about consequences determine the consumer's attitude toward both the successful consumption of products and the consumer's evaluation of that consumption as successful. Jade's beliefs about the consequences should she successfully lose weight can be measured by her responses to the following:

"If I succeed in losing weight, I will look good."

"If I succeed in losing weight, I will feel good about myself."

"If I succeed in losing weight, others will admire me."

Very likely +3 +2 +1 0 –1 –2 –3 Very unlikely

The consumer's evaluation of successful consequences is the extent to which he or she values those consequences. For example, Jade may value highly the consequence that she'll feel good about herself if she succeeds. She might not care very much at all about others admiring her for her success. Similarly, beliefs about consequences determine the consumer's attitude toward both the failure to consume products and the consumer's evaluation of the lack of consumption as failure.

The consumer's evaluation of the consequences of failure is the extent to which he or she feels bad about the costs of failure. Jade may feel bad that others might think of her as a failure if she doesn't lose weight, whereas other respondents might evaluate this consequence less negatively.

Beliefs about consequences also help determine attitude toward the process and the consumer's evaluation of those consequences. Jade's concerns about calling for reservations, making babysitting arrangements, and finding the time to park and change all have consequences, and all are evaluated in the decision of whether or not to take an aerobics class.

Applying the Theory of Trying to Change Consumption Behavior   The value of the theory of trying is its focus on consumption behavior rather than purchase behavior. Understanding consumption behavior is very important to marketers who seek to establish and maintain long-term relationships with customers. To do this, marketers have to go beyond controlling the purchase act and seek to encourage, support, and reward the consumption act.

Suppose you are the marketing manager of Jade's fitness center. The center has recently opened, and the initial join-up campaign has been very successful. However, it would be a mistake to think that because you've succeeded in selling an optimum number of memberships the center is a hit. Its long-term success depends upon maintaining the loyalty of members. To achieve this, you first need to understand how members use the center. The theory of trying can help you identify the factors that influence its use.

Through the model, you find out that several members have no intention to try to lose weight through the fitness programs you offer. They feel this way because they have a negative attitude toward the process of trying. Specifically, this negative attitude results from their belief that they will have to make babysitting arrangements in order to come to the center regularly. The solution is now obvious: Try to offer babysitting services at the fitness center. Suppose you next find out that finding parking at the center is negatively evaluated, and this plays a significant role in your members' overall negative attitude toward the process of taking aerobics classes. The marketing solution is to improve access to parking facilities. Exhibit 9-11 shows how Louis Kemp Seafood tried to overcome consumer reluctance to cook seafood dishes at home by, among other things, offering a simple recipe.

The theory of trying is used by marketers to predict consumption behavior, particularly of products whose consumption is spread over a long time period. Exercise programs, counseling programs, and drug rehabilitation programs are all good examples, as their success in satisfying consumers can only be assessed over time. By providing the means through which marketers can measure and predict the extent to which consumers are willing to try a program, the theory of trying model helps in the development of the types of services that are likely to result in long-term customer satisfaction.

Louis Kemp Seafood used a humorous ad campaign to address consumer fears about seafood preparation, even offering a simple recipe to raise consumers' expectations of success.

Marketing Management—Implications and Actions

Understanding consumer intention helps marketers:

- Encourage consumers to change how they behave toward brands.
- Apply the theory of reasoned action to identify and promote salient attributes and subjective norms that move consumers toward purchase.
- Apply the theory of trying to encourage long-term consumption behavior and repeat purchase.

9-4 Attitude-Behavior Consistency

As we have seen, a positive attitude toward a product and even a positive attitude toward product purchase does not necessarily mean that a consumer will buy.[28] **Attitude-behavior consistency**—the extent to which attitude leads to purchase—is determined by a variety of consumer, situational, and measurement factors, as summarized in Exhibit 9-12. Each of these factors has strategic implications for marketers.[29]

▶ **attitude-behavior consistency** Refers to the extent to which attitude leads to purchase.

9-4a Consumer Influences

The relationship between attitude and behavior is influenced by the consumer at four levels. First, the consumer's access to resources—whether he or she has money to buy—is a determining factor, regardless of how positive attitudes toward a brand are. Excellent advertising and top-rated brand attitude are worthless if the target consumer can't afford the product. Marketers of high-cost products, like cars, need to be particularly sensitive to the consumer's bottom line. Installment programs, long-term financing, reduced interest rates, and delayed payment incentives are all strategies intended to overcome the obstacle of limited consumer resources.

Second, the consumer's past experiences with a brand are important. Attitudes formed through personal experience are stronger and more predictive of future buying behavior than are those formed through advertising.[30] The lesson for marketers is that

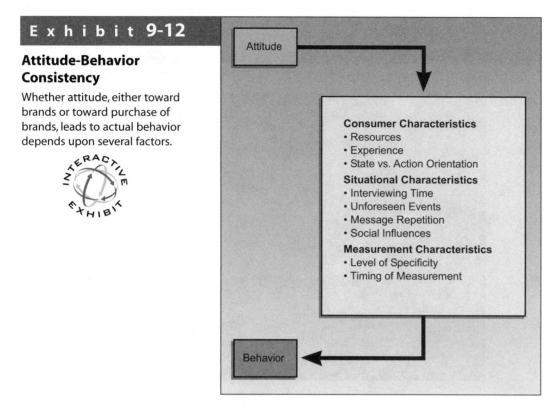

Attitude-Behavior Consistency

Whether attitude, either toward brands or toward purchase of brands, leads to actual behavior depends upon several factors.

F A Q

Do state-oriented consumers ever make impulsive purchases?

brand advertising alone will not lead to purchase. It needs to be supported by product trials or similar incentives through which the target consumer experiences the brand directly.

Third, consumer orientation influences purchase. Some consumers are action-oriented, others are state-oriented. Action-oriented consumers are those who are always ready to act. State-oriented consumers, though they may feel motivated to act, are not likely to do so quickly. A state-oriented consumer who expresses a liking for a brand and says he or she intends to buy is less likely to follow through than is an action-oriented consumer, who does so without much hesitation.[31]

9-4b Situational Influences

Three situational factors influence the relationship between attitude and behavior. First, the time passed between a consumer developing a positive attitude toward brand purchase and the actual opportunity to buy is important. As explained in Chapter 3 (section 3-2a, "Planned Purchasing Behavior"), the more time that intervenes, the more unforeseen events can occur to change attitude. Unforeseen events—such as shortage of money or negative opinions of others—can occur even without the passage of time. Attitude toward purchase can change, for example, between the time a consumer enters and leaves a store. In one study, consumers were asked on entering an appliance store what they intended to buy. Of those who specified a brand, only 20 percent left with it.[32] Another recent study has shown that attitude toward touch screen self-service and intention to use this self-service is dependent on perceived waiting time. That is, in spite of the fact that consumers have a favorable attitude toward the use of touch screen self-service, they would not plan to do so if they perceive that they will have to wait a while to do this.[33]

Second, given a high level of message repetition, attitude toward a brand can translate into brand purchase.[34] Brand attitude is likely to be held with more confidence and is likely to influence purchase behavior if the advertising message that generates it is repeated frequently.

Third, social influence is a strong factor affecting the extent to which brand attitude translates into brand purchase. For example, subjective norms can, as we have seen, change

E x h i b i t 9-13

Code West Footwear uses a social influence approach to affect consumers' attitudes toward the brand.

attitude. Suppose a consumer likes a particular brand of computer but realizes that his or her boss doesn't think highly of it. Because of this social pressure, the consumer is not likely to buy. A successful campaign by Burger King effectively used peer-group influence. Targeted to teenagers, the campaign showed three young people making fun of McDonald's "fried" burgers. The message was that to gain the admiration of their friends, teenagers should eat at Burger King, not McDonald's. A similar peer group approach is used by Code West footwear in Exhibit 9-13.

9-4c **Measurement Factors**

The relationship between intention and behavior is influenced by the level of specificity of measurement. Attitude can predict behavior only if it is measured with a high level of specificity. Look again at Exhibit 9-4 to see how attitudes can be measured at various levels of specificity. If researchers can assess consumers' attitudes toward purchasing the 1995 Honda Accord LXi from a specific dealership, they are better able to predict purchase behavior of the car than if attitudes simply toward the brand, Honda Accord, are measured.

When consumers are asked about their attitudes, the **timing of measurement** is also important.[35] On Friday, Marilyn is asked about her attitude toward buying milk. She indicates a favorable attitude and an intention to buy, as she usually buys a gallon every Saturday morning when she does her weekly grocery shopping. If she is asked on Sunday instead of Friday her answer is likely to be "no."

timing of measurement
A concept that helps us understand why a consumer's expression of an attitude toward a product (or service) is sometimes different from their actual purchase. That is, when people are surveyed and indicate a positive attitude toward a product (or service), yet they end up purchasing a different product or service. The timing of measurement is one factor that explains this discrepancy—the more time that lapses between the attitude survey and the observed purchase behavior, the greater the probability of other intervening factors coming into play and changing the consumer's attitude toward the product (or service).

Marketing Management—Implications and Actions

Understanding attitude-behavior consistency helps marketers:
- Link attitude to behavior and so assess the likelihood of purchase.
- Target the types of consumers most likely to follow through on their intentions.
- Encourage follow-through of planned purchases.

Chapter Spotlights

This chapter explored consumer attitudes, how they develop, and how they can be influenced by marketers. We analyzed attitude in terms of three components: beliefs (cognitive), affect (emotive), and intention (behavioral).

1. Beliefs. Beliefs are the cognitive component of consumer attitude. Positive brand associations enhance brand equity and are achieved through a number of positioning strategies. Through brand associations, marketers establish and influence favorable beliefs about a brand and unfavorable beliefs about competitors.

2. Affect. Affect is the emotive component of consumer attitude. Three research models describe the determinants of affective response. The functional theory of attitude explains that consumers buy as a result of one of four psychological functions: adjustment, ego defense, value expression, and application of prior knowledge. The Fishbein model relates consumer beliefs and evaluations to affective response: If beliefs are strong and desirable, affective

responses are positive. The belief-importance model analyzes affective responses across competing brands.

3. Intention. Intention is the behavioral component of consumer attitude. Two research models demonstrate the relationship between intention to purchase and actual purchase and consumption. The theory of reasoned action explains purchase behavior as a direct result of intention, influenced by attitudes toward purchase and by subjective norms. The theory of trying explains actual consumption behavior of purchasers. It provides insight into the establishment and maintenance of long-term relationships with consumers.

4. Attitude-behavior consistency. The extent to which attitude leads to purchase is determined by a variety of consumer, situational, and measurement factors. Each of these can be affected by marketer actions.

Key Terms

adjustment (p. 285)
affect (p. 284)
attitude-behavior consistency (p. 299)
attitude toward the act (p. 292)
attitude toward failure (p. 297)
attitude toward the process (p. 297)
attitude toward success (p. 296)
behavioral intention (p. 291)

belief (p. 278)
belief-importance model (p. 289)
ego defense (p. 285)
expectation of failure (p. 297)
expectation of success (p. 297)
Fishbein model (p. 287)
functional theory of attitude (p. 284)
intention to try (p. 295)

motivation to comply (p. 292)
normative beliefs (p. 292)
social norms toward trying (p. 295)
subjective norm (p. 292)
theory of reasoned action (p. 291)
theory of trying (p. 295)
timing of measurement (p. 301)
value expression (p. 285)

Review Questions

Note: You can find the correct answers to these questions by taking the quiz and then submitting your answers in the Online Edition. The program will automatically score your submission. If you miss a question, the program will provide the correct answer, a rationale for the answer, and the section number in the chapter where the topic is discussed.

1. Which of the following is *not* a positioning strategy explained in your text?
   a. by product attributes
   b. by consumer benefits
   c. by intangible attributes
   d. by manufacturer name

2. Which of the following is *not* a positioning strategy explained in your text?
   a. by price
   b. by government approval
   c. by application
   d. by brand user

3. Savvy marketers know that _____ is a means through which we try to realize personal goals and images.
   a. ego defense
   b. the id
   c. self-image
   d. self-actualization

4. An advantage of the belief-importance model is that it allows marketers to compare affective responses toward competing
   a. prices.
   b. promotion.
   c. brands.
   d. outlets.

5. To influence attitude toward brand purchase, the marketer must first determine which attributes or _____ are most important to the consumer.
   a. intangibles
   b. consequences
   c. tangibles
   d. evoked sets

6. The theory of trying was designed to address _____ behavior rather than _____ behavior.
   a. consumption, buying
   b. buying, consumption
   c. consumption, cognizant
   d. buying, research

7. The theory of trying can help us identify the factors that influence a product's
   a. resale value.
   b. usefulness.
   c. use.
   d. disposition.

8. It is very useful to know that consumer orientation influences purchase. Some consumers are action oriented, while others are _____ oriented.
   a. state
   b. society
   c. internally
   d. externally

9. Consumer attitudes are also based on the _____ of measurement.
   a. timing
   b. cost
   c. experience
   d. type

10. Action-oriented consumers are always ready to
   a. take suggestions.
   b. explain a product's use to a friend.
   c. act.
   d. rely on advertising to influence them.

Team Talk

1. Take two minutes for each member of your team to write down his or her beliefs on: the soft-drinks category, Nike athletic shoes, and Kentucky Fried Chicken restaurants. Compare notes and explain each of your beliefs. Explore how these beliefs were formed.

2. Your team is working on a campaign for an on-campus childcare center, the objective of which is to create brand associations that will ensure a long-term positive image. Design a campaign strategy that will build brand equity.

3. Are some products or brands more likely to stir affective responses than others? Talk about your feelings toward fashions, cosmetics, computers, fast food, Disney World, Ivory liquid soap, Levi's jeans, and Hershey's Chocolate Kisses. To what extent do you think your affective responses are a result of advertising?

4. Using the belief-importance model, analyze two or three of the classes you are planning to sign up for in your next academic year. First, list the attributes of each. Next, decide

the importance of those attributes in making your class selections. Next, decide how well you believe the classes will compare on each attribute. Does this exercise help you make your class selections? How might each department increase its enrollments?

5. Talk about recent purchases you have made, both major and minor. Did subjective norms influence your decision?

6. Your team is working with a drug and alcohol rehabilitation center that is experiencing high dropout rates among college students. Apply the theory of trying to find out why students are leaving the center before their treatment is complete, and prepare a plan to reverse this trend.

7. Describe a purchase situation in which you changed your intention to buy a product. Perhaps you bought an alternate brand, spent the money on something entirely different, or didn't buy anything at all. What factors made your behavior inconsistent with your earlier attitudes?

Workshops

Research Workshop

Background

Do pets like the same flavors their owners enjoy? The objective of this workshop is to measure the extent to which this attitude is held by dog lovers and make recommendations for flavors in a new line of dog foods, Dogourmet.

Methodology

Select a sample of at least five dog owners and ask them to rate the following flavors in the order they would be most likely to buy them for their pets, based on their attitudes toward their dogs' tastes: beef; liver; chicken; cheese; filet mignon; cheeseburger; bacon; and fried chicken. (Of these, the first three are established pet-food flavors.)

To the Marketplace

On the basis of your findings, make a list of recommendations for the Dogourmet line. What does this exercise suggest about dog owners' attitudes toward their pets?

Creative Workshop

Background

Cuisinart, the high-end manufacturer of food processors, invites your team to compete in a college contest to create comparative advertising for its product. The objective of this workshop is to develop advertising that encourages positive affective responses to Cuisinart that may ultimately result in purchase.

Methodology

Apply the belief-importance model to compare Cuisinart with competing food processor brands. Visit a department store or review catalogs or advertising to find out all you can about the product category, the attributes of each of the top brands, and the type of promotions and communications messages used. Talk to family and friends about the features and benefits most likely to appeal to them. Identify those attributes of Cuisinart and other brands that are most important to consumers.

To the Marketplace

Develop a proposal for the new campaign. Include an analysis of the attributes of both Cuisinart and its leading competitors and a rough sketch of your comparative advertisement.

Managerial Workshop

Background

The dean's office asks your team to help combat the popularity of "research services" on campus that sell term papers to students to meet course requirements. The objective of this workshop is to recommend a communications program that will alter students' attitudes toward academic achievement and toward cheating.

Methodology

Use one or more of the models in the chapter that you feel are appropriate to the task of evaluating students' attitudes toward the use of research services and toward cheating.

To the Marketplace

Provide an analysis of students' attitudes and create a list of recommendations for a communications campaign that will dissuade students from using research services.

Notes

1. David A. Aaker, *Managing Brand Equity: Capitalizing on the Value of a Brand Name* (New York: The Free Press, 1991); Leonard L. Berry, "Cultivating Service Brand Equity," *Journal of the Academy of Marketing Science,* Vol. 28 (Winter 2000), pp. 128–137; Girish N. Punj and Clayton L. Hillyer, "A Cognitive Model of Customer-Based Brand Equity for Frequently Purchased Products: Conceptual Framework and Empirical Results," *Journal of Consumer Psychology,* Vol. 14 (2004), pp. 124-134.

2. Aaker, *Managing Brand Equity,* pp. 114–115.

3. Aaker, *Managing Brand Equity,* p. 120; Stuart Agres, *Emotion in Advertising: An Agency's View* (The Masschalk Company, 1986).

4. Aaker, *Managing Brand Equity,* p. 116.

5. Joseph W. Alba and J. Wesley Hutchinson, "Dimensions of Consumer Expertise," *Journal of Consumer Research,* Vol. 13 (March 1987), pp. 411–454.

6. Aaker, *Managing Brand Equity,* pp. 120–122; Agres, *Emotion in Advertising.*

7. Aaker, *Managing Brand Equity,* pp. 122–123; Glen L. Urban, Philip L. Johnson, and John R. Hauser, "Testing Competitive Market Structures," *Marketing Science,* Vol. 3 (Spring 1984), pp. 83–112.

8. Aaker, *Managing Brand Equity,* pp. 123–124.

9. Aaker, *Managing Brand Equity,* p. 125; Tom Murray, "The Wind at Nike's Back," *Adweek's Marketing Week* (March 27, 1986), pp. 28–31.

10. Aaker, *Managing Brand Equity,* p. 126; Roger Enrico, *The Other Guy Blinked* (New York: Bantam Books, 1986).

11. Aaker, *Managing Brand Equity,* p. 127.

12. Ibid.

13. Aaker, *Managing Brand Equity,* pp. 128–129; C. Min Han and Vern Terpstra, "Country-of-Origin Effects for Uni-National and Bi-National Products," *Journal of International Business Studies,* Vol. 19 (Summer 1988), p. 242; N. G. Papadopoulos, L. A. Heslop, F. Graby, and G. Avlonitis, "Does Country-of-Origin Matter?" Working Paper, Marketing Science Institute, 1989.

14. A recent study made the distinction between affect and attitude in that affective responses can play an important role in the formation of attitude. See H. Onur Bodur, David Brinberg, and Eloise Coupey, "Belief, Affect, and Attitude: Alternative Models of the Determinants of Attitude," *Journal of Consumer Psychology,* Vol. 9 (1, 2000), pp. 17–28. Also see John Kim, Jee-Su Lim, and Mukesh Bhargava, "The Role of Affect in Attitude Formation: A Classical Conditioning Approach," *Journal of the Academy of Marketing Science,* Vol. 26 (Spring 1998), pp. 143–152.

15. For a review of multiattribute attitude models, see Richard J. Lutz and James R. Bettman, "Multiattribute Attitude Models: A Bicentennial Review," in Arch G. Woodside, Jagdish N. Sheth, and Peter D. Bennett, eds., *Consumer and Industrial Buying Behavior* (New York: North-Holland, 1977), pp. 137–149; William L. Wilkie and Edgar A. Pessemier, "Issues in Marketing's Use of Multiattribute Attribute Models," *Journal of Marketing Research,* Vol. 10 (November 1973), pp. 428–441.

16. Daniel Katz, "The Functional Approach to the Study of Attitudes," *Public Opinion Quarterly,* Vol. 24 (1960), pp. 163–204; Sharon Shavitt, "The Role of Attitude Objects in Attitude Functions," *Journal of Experimental Social Psychology,* Vol. 26 (1990), pp. 124–148; J. S. Johar and M. Joseph Sirgy, "Value Expressive Versus Utilitarian Appeals: When and Why to Use Which Appeal," *Journal of Advertising,* Vol. 20 (September 1991), pp. 23–34; Ann E. Schlosser, "Applying the Functional Theory of Attitudes to Understanding the Influence of Store Atmosphere on Store Inferences," *Journal of Consumer Psychology,* Vol. 7, No. 4 (1998), pp. 345–370.

17. Martin Fishbein, "An Investigation of the Relationship between Beliefs about an Object and the Attitude Toward That Object," *Human Relations,* Vol. 16 (1963), pp. 233–240.

18. Richard J. Lutz, "Changing Brand Attitudes Through Modification of Cognitive Structure," *Journal of Consumer Research,* Vol. 1 (March 1975), pp. 49–59.

19. Ibid.

20. Harold H. Boyd, Jr., Michael L. Ray, and Edward C. Strong, "An Attitudinal Framework for Advertising Strategy," *Journal of Marketing,* Vol. 36 (April 1972), pp. 25–30.

21. Ibid.

22. Martin Fishbein, "An Overview of the Attitude Construct," in G. B. Hafer, ed., *Look Back, A Look Ahead* (Chicago, IL: American Marketing Association, 1980), p. 3.

23. Martin Fishbein and Icek Ajzen, *Belief, Attitude, Intention, and Behavior: An Introduction to Theory and Research* (Reading, MA: Addison-Wesley, 1975).

24. Robert E. Burnkrant and Thomas A. Page, Jr., "The Structure and Antecedents of the Normative and Attitudinal Components of Fishbein's Theory of Reasoned Action," *Journal of Experimental Social Psychology,* Vol. 24 (January 1988), pp. 66–87; Martin Fishbein and Icek Ajzen, "On Construct Validity: A Critique of Miniard and Cohen's Paper," *Journal of Experimental Social Psychology,* Vol. 17 (May 1981), pp. 340–350; Paul W. Miniard and Joel B. Cohen, "An Examination of the Fishbein-Ajzen Behavioral Intention Models, Concepts, and Measures," *Journal of Experimental Social Psychology,* Vol. 17 (May 1981), pp. 309–339. Richard

G. Netemeyer and William O. Bearden, "A Comparative Analysis of Two Models of Behavioral Intention," *Journal of the Academy of Marketing Science,* Vol. 20 (Winter 1992), pp. 49–59; Richard L. Oliver and William O. Bearden, "Crossover Effects in the Theory of Reasoned Action," *Journal of Consumer Research,* Vol. 12 (December 1985), pp. 324–340; Michael J. Ryan, "Behavioral Intention Formation: The Interdependence of Attitudinal and Social Influence Variables," *Journal of Consumer Research,* Vol. 9 (December 1982), pp. 263–278; Blair H. Sheppard, Jon Hartwick, and Paul Warshaw, "The Theory of Reasoned Action: A Meta Analysis of Past Research with Recommendations and Modifications for Future Research," *Journal of Consumer Research,* Vol. 15 (December 1988), pp. 325–343; Terence Shimp and Alican Kavas, "The Theory of Reasoned Action Applied to Coupon Usage," *Journal of Consumer Research,* Vol. 11 (December 1984), pp. 795–809; Yingjiao Xu, Teresa A. Summers, and Bonnie D. Belleau, "Who Buys American Alligator? Predicting Purchase Intention of a Controversial Product," *Journal of Business Research,* Vol. 57 (2004), pp. 1189–1198.

25. The example is adapted from a study conducted by Netemeyer and Bearden, "A Comparative Analysis of Two Models of Behavioral Intention."

26. It should be noted that the theory of reasoned action has been further developed into what is now called "theory of planned action." The key difference between the two theories is that the theory of planned action extends the theory of reasoned action by adding another predictor of behavioral intention. The theory of reasoned action predicts behavioral intention through attitude toward the act and subjective norms. The theory of planned action predicts behavioral intention through attitude toward the act, subjective norms, and perceived behavioral control. Perceived behavioral control is defined as the person's belief as to how easy or difficult the performance of the behavior is likely to be. For an excellent review and discussion of the theory of planned action and the many studies conducted to test this theory, the student is referred to: Art Sahni Notani, "Moderators of Perceived Behavioral Control's Predictiveness in the Theory of Planned Behavior: A Meta-Analysis," *Journal of Consumer Psychology,* Vol. 7 (3, 1998), pp. 247–271.

27. Richard P. Bagozzi and Paul R. Warshaw, "Trying to Consume," *Journal of Consumer Research,* Vol. 17 (September 1990), pp. 127–140.

28. Icek Ajzen and Martin Fishbein, "Attitude-Behavior Relations: A Theoretical Analysis and Review of Empirical Research," *Psychological Bulletin,* Vol. 84 (September 1977), pp. 888–918.

29. For research on attitude-behavior consistency, see Donald H. Granbois and John O. Summers, "Primary and Secondary Validity of Consumer Purchase Probabilities," *Journal of Consumer Research,* Vol. 1 (March 1975), pp. 31–38; Paul W. Miniard, Carl Obermiller, and Thomas J. Page, Jr., "A Further Assessment of Measurement Influences on the Intention-Behavior Relationship," *Journal of Marketing Research,* Vol. 20 (May 1983), pp. 206–212; David J. Reibstein, "The Prediction of Individual Probabilities of Brand Choice," *Journal of Consumer Research,* Vol. 5 (December 1978), pp. 163–168; Paul R. Warshaw, "Predicting Purchase and Other Behaviors from General and Contextually Specific Intentions," *Journal of Marketing Research,* Vol. 17 (February 1980), pp. 26–33.

30. Russell H. Fazio, Martha C. Powell, and Carol J. Williams, "The Role of Attitude Accessibility in the Attitude-to-Behavior Process," *Journal of Consumer Research,* Vol. 16 (December 1989), pp. 280–288. Robert E. Smith and William R. Swinyard, "Attitude-Behavior Consistency: The Impact of Product Trial Versus Advertising," *Journal of Marketing Research,* Vol. 20 (August 1983), pp. 257–267.

31. Julius Kuhl, "Action vs. State Orientation as a Mediator between Motivation and Action," in W. Hacker et al., *Cognitive and Motivational Aspects of Action* (Amsterdam: North-Holland, 1982), pp. 67–85.

32. Kenneth A. Longman, "Promises, Promises," in L. Adler and L. Crespi, eds., *Attitude Research on the Rocks* (Chicago, IL: American Marketing Association, 1986), pp. 28–37.

33. Pratibha A. Dabholkar and Richard P. Bagozzi, "An Attitudinal Model of Technology-Based Self-Service: Moderating Effects of Consumer Traits and Situational Factors," Journal of the Academy of Marketing Science, Vol. 30 (Summer 2002), pp. 184–201.

34. Ida E. Berger and Andrew A. Mitchell, "The Effect of Advertising on Attitude Accessibility, Attitude Confidence, and Attitude-Behavior Relationship," *Journal of Consumer Research,* Vol. 16 (December 1989), pp. 269–279.

35. H. Shanker Krishnan and Robert E. Smith, "The Relative Endurance of Attitudes, Confidence, and Attitude-Behavior Consistency," *Journal of Consumer Psychology,* Vol. 7, No. 3 (1998), pp. 273–298.

Communication and Persuasion

Fran hates grocery shopping. When she hears about a new online computer shopping service, she is elated. Ordering groceries by computer for home delivery sounds like a dream come true. This way, Fran thinks, she can avoid the barrage of sales and coupons and special offers that can make shopping so tiring and confusing. However, Fran soon finds that the wild frontier of computer shopping holds several surprises.

On her first trip to the cybermarket, Fran gets lost. It takes her awhile to realize that she was used to walking the aisles of the store and picking up whatever caught her eye. She relied on labels, shelf tags, and special displays to remind her of things she might need. The terrible truth dawns on her: She misses the advertising.

Fortunately, Fran eventually discovers the websites, home pages, shopping services, and online catalogs that offer her all the product information she needs, and she is soon buying almost everything through her computer, and paying with her credit and debit cards, or even virtual money.

In some ways, we can all relate to Fran. As Fran finds, marketing communication is a complex entity. In this chapter, we will look at marketing communication and also explore the qualities of good advertisements that save them from joining the sea of collective clutter that often drowns today's consumers.

Advertising and other forms of marketing communication surround us. Whether we realize it or not, we eat, drink, and sleep advertising. And most forms of marketing communication are subtle—much of the time we are not even aware of them or that we are acting in response to them. Yet as we shall discover, our complex relationship with advertising can be seen as we skim through magazines, channel surf, pass billboards, or sort through our mail. It is not as simple as it seems. To appreciate the complexity of the marketing communications process, we will look at communications from the perspective of the multitude of decisions that are made during its creation, its execution, and its delivery. Exhibit 10-1 is a flowchart showing the elements of the advertising decision process that impact on the communications process.

If you look at the various communications effects models presented in section 10-2 you will note that consumers move through a series of stages from not being aware of a product or service to actual purchase. Message content,

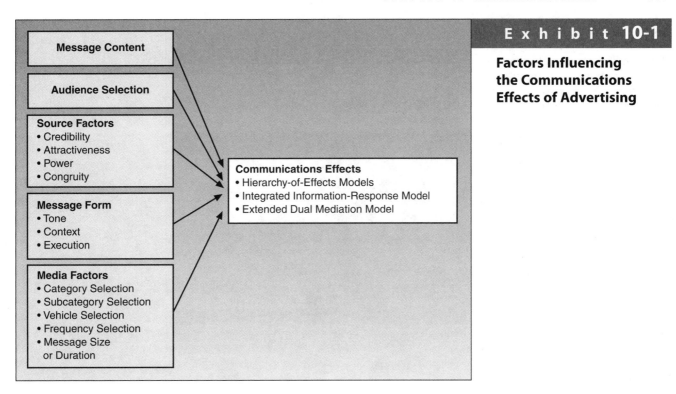

audience selection, message source factors, the form of the message and media factors will singly and in combination contribute to the consumer's position on these hierarchies and help move them through the process toward purchase.

10-1 Content and Audience Decisions

Message content and audience selection decisions cannot be made in a vacuum. Marketers must rely heavily on consumer research into decision processes, consumer involvement, and other aspects of the marketing environment that can be influenced by a well-crafted message. Only through such research can we thoroughly understand the needs and motivations of targeted consumers and predict how they will respond to different advertising approaches.

10-1a Message Content

The message is the central component of any piece of marketing communications. An effective message tells a great deal not only about the brand advertised but also about its target audience, its competitors, and the marketer's brand strategy.

The message can communicate a number of important pieces of information to target consumers, including product benefits, price, and availability. Different messages emphasize one or more of these. Advertising for established market leaders, such as the ad for SUN-MAID in Exhibit 10-2, usually does not mention price at all but concentrates on benefits that reinforce brand image. Retail advertising, on the other hand, particularly in food categories, emphasizes price and location almost exclusively.

Message content flows directly from product positioning. Only through positioning research are marketers able to decide exactly which aspects of the brand are most likely to persuade target consumers to buy. Pepsi, for example, discovered that its target market of teenagers and young adults could be motivated by a frequent purchase plan that rewarded high-volume consumers with free logo-marked clothing and sporting goods. This discovery led to the creation of the Pepsi website shown in Exhibit 10-3.

This ad for Sun-Maid emphasizes brand image but also points out the energy and natural foods benefits that are part of the image.

Source: Courtesy of Sun-Maid Growers of California.

Pepsi motivates consumers in its target market by offering premiums as a reward for purchase.

Source: Courtesy of Pepsi-Cola Company.

CIGNA insurance targets women at one particular lifestage, namely pre- and post-pregnancy.

Source: Courtesy of Graciela Iturbide.

10-1b Audience Selection

Message content cannot be determined without a detailed profile of the targeted market, the message audience for whom it must be tailored. To communicate effectively with consumers and stimulate response, marketers must not only understand who these consumers are but must also find out what they already know or feel about the brand and how likely they are to process new information about it. An interesting study of Latinos (Puerto Ricans, Mexicans, and Cubans) who were bilingual in English and Spanish found that if the visual component(s) in an advertisement closely matched the written text, conceptual processing was increased in English, considered the "second language." Also, in this situation recall of the ad was higher than if there was a poor match between the visuals and the advertising text.[1] This reinforces the general proposition that visuals and copy in advertising must go hand-in-hand.

The first step in audience selection is consumer research to find viable market segments. Once target segments are selected, the next step is to find out more about the consumers within them. This includes their media habits (the channels through which consumers can be most easily and most effectively reached), message effectiveness (the extent to which consumers respond favorably to certain types of messages), and source effectiveness (the extent to which consumers respond favorably to the spokesperson). Exhibit 10-4 is an example of unique and effective targeting. Here, CIGNA reaches a specific target market—women whose healthcare needs center around pre- and post-pregnancy. As we will see later in the chapter, effective targeting leads to a highly motivated target group that will be more inclined to process the ad's message.

10-2 Communication Effects

To work effectively, communications must meet objectives set by the marketer. That is, the marketer must be able to shape and predict the effects of the communication on targeted customers. Communication effect or desired response is the most complex element of marketing communications. Different advertising and/or campaigns are designed to generate different effects, depending upon the audience and product positioning. The desired response may be increased awareness, brand acceptance, brand preference, brand trial, or brand adoption. It may involve one or more of these marketing objectives. Long-running campaigns often progress through each stage, ending in product purchase.

10-2a Hierarchy-of-Effects Models

> **hierarchy of effects** Refers to a sequence of cognitive, affective, and conative responses consumers experience in relation to exposure to marketing communication messages.

To describe message effects, researchers have developed a series of models that explain different levels of consumer response to advertising. These are known as **hierarchy of effects** models. Consumer researchers have used hierarchy-of-effects models to attempt to explain how marketing communication influences the responses of target consumers. The first model, developed as early as the 1890s and still in widespread use, is the AIDA model.[2] The AIDA model suggests there are four steps to motivate a consumer to purchase. The marketer must create *attention*, capture *interest*, stimulate *desire*, and invoke *action*.

That is, first, the message has to be exciting enough to win consumers' notice and draw them in. Unless it gains attention and interest, the message will not be processed and will, therefore, not be remembered by its target audience. Next, the message must move consumers in some way and create in them a desire for the product advertised. Finally, the message has to encourage consumer motivation to act upon this desire and translate it into a product purchase.

A more complex model, built around the psychology that underlies consumer purchases, is a variation of that proposed by Lavidge and Steiner, illustrated in Exhibit 10-5.[3] It breaks down effects into five sequential stages: awareness, acceptance, preference, buying intention, and trial or purchase. To be successful, advertising must have as its objective the causation of one or more of these five effects on target consumers. The choice depends upon the brand's current market position and the way in which the brand and the product category are perceived by the target audience. CBite 10-1 is about a series of video ads on the web that point out the consequences of the use of illegal drugs. These 30 "spots" target different people at different stages of the hierarchy-of-effects model. Also targeted are nonusers concerning their responsibility to help friends and family members who are users.

Exhibit 10-5

The Hierarchy-of-Effects Model

This model, a simplified version of the Lavidge and Steiner model, has fewer steps and is most popular with marketers today.

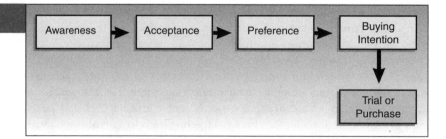

CBite 10-1

Anti-Drug Ads on the Web Targeted at Users and Friends or Family of Users

L et's go to freevibe.com. Here are a series of great television ads that each run for 30 seconds and can be viewed with Real Player or QuickTime on your computer. Here's the message: "You've seen our ads over the years. Love 'em or hate 'em, they're designed to get people thinking about the consequences of doing drugs. Is someone more likely to get taken advantage of sexually while doing drugs? Would someone be more likely to crash into an innocent pedestrian because they were driving under the influence of drugs? Accidents. Crime. Car Crashes. Depression. Murder. Arrest. Jail. All these words seem to be associated with drug use. All negative consequences. Watch the ads and decide for yourself."

The ads feature teens and adults showing consequences of drug use and in some cases focus on the responsibility of friends to talk to drug-using friends and relatives. The ads are hard-hitting, to the point, and set up to reach multiple audiences. They feature people with a variety of ethnic backgrounds and some are in Spanish. Viewers are also encouraged to submit their own anti-drug ads for possible inclusion at the site.

Go to www.whatsyourantidrug.com/ads.asp. Do you think that these ads are effective? Which ones were your favorites? Where along the hierarchy-of-effects model do you think they are focused? Are they tied to more than one model position?

Source: http://www.whatsyourantidrug.com/ads.asp, November 22, 2004.

Awareness Gaining attention for a brand and getting its name known are prerequisites for inducing positive consumer response. There is a strong relationship between awareness of a brand and preference for that brand among consumers as well as eventual intent to purchase.[4]

In 1984, Beatrice embarked on an awareness campaign to call attention to the fact that the conglomerate owned a number of familiar brands, from Jensen stereo, to Max Factor cosmetics, to Tropicana orange juice, to Orville Redenbacher popcorn. The campaign, "You've known us all along," was supported by the repackaging of several products to include a red stripe prominently displaying the name Beatrice. There was no attempt to sell specific products; the objective was simply to promote awareness of Beatrice as the company linking a diverse range of quality brands.

Acceptance A brand achieves consumer acceptance only when it comes to mind as a viable choice whenever a consumer thinks of the product category to which it belongs. That is, an accepted brand is one of the few in the consumer's evoked or consideration set. For example, while the state of Florida has been considered a vacation haven for the elderly, it has not enjoyed widespread acceptance among younger, upscale travelers. A new advertising campaign attempts to add Florida to the consideration set of these vacationers, along with such glamorous destinations as Acapulco and Monte Carlo.

Some recent research in persuasion shows that people tend to accept advertising appeals unless these individuals are specifically motivated to be looking for and resisting what appears to be manipulative intent on the part of the advertiser.[5]

Preference Once a consumer is aware of and has accepted a brand, the next step for marketers is to make the brand the one most preferred in the consumer's consideration set. California almond growers have sponsored a long-running preference campaign, illustrated in Exhibit 10-6. The desired effect on consumers is a clear preference for almonds as a nutritious snack over other types of non-nutritious snack food.

Buying Intention and Trial or Purchase An advertisement creates intention to buy if it brings consumers to a point just short of actual purchase. Although intent to buy does not always result in immediate purchase, it does reinforce acceptance and preference

California almond growers emphasize the nutritious value of almonds as snack food.

Source: Reprinted by permission of the Almond Board.

and is, therefore, likely to lead to a future purchase. Promotional messages through which marketers can most readily measure intent to buy and product trial are those that ask for some kind of action, such as use of a cents-off coupon to purchase the product.

Midas, in addition to using national television campaigns to build awareness of its auto services, runs local newspaper advertising with an incentive offer to coax customers to come in for repairs. Retail advertising typically encourages immediate trial or purchase. Limited-time-only offers and newspaper advertising focusing on special prices are common. Banks offer incentives to bring in customers to open new accounts. Direct response advertising, like the Coldwater Creek ad in Exhibit 10-7, asks for immediate orders or purchases. In this ad, notice that a $15 price off will be given on any order of $75 or more if the purchase is made by a certain date. Both the 800-number and the website are listed for customers to take advantage of this offer.

Note that in each of the previous examples, different levels in the hierarchy apply in high- and low-involvement decisions. Awareness alone may be all that's required to persuade consumers to pick up a snack cake from 7-Eleven, while higher-order responses are involved in higher-risk decisions, such as choosing new household appliances.

10-2b Integrated Information-Response Model

Illustrated in Exhibit 10-8, the **integrated information-response model** is more effective than the hierarchy-of-effects models described so far and is able to capture a diverse range of consumer responses.

The model shows that, in making purchase decisions, consumers combine information from marketing communications with information from direct product experience. Fur-

▶**integrated information-response model** A marketing communications model that shows that, in making purchase decisions, consumers combine information from marketing communications with information from direct product experience.

Exhibit 10-7

In this ad, Coldwater Creek offers a price-off opportunity if the customer acts by a certain date. This is a good example of a direct response ad.

Source: Kim Puluti, Photographer. Used by permission of Aspenwood Advertising and Coldwater Creek.

ther, it illustrates that different levels of the hierarchy may affect cognitive, affective, or behavior components in the decision process. These can be thought of as the "thinking," "feeling," and "doing" components of behavior. Moreover, the process is not always bottom-to-top in sequence. In some decisions, the thinking, feeling, and doing components occur in different orders. The model in Exhibit 10-8 shows several different patterns of consumer response.

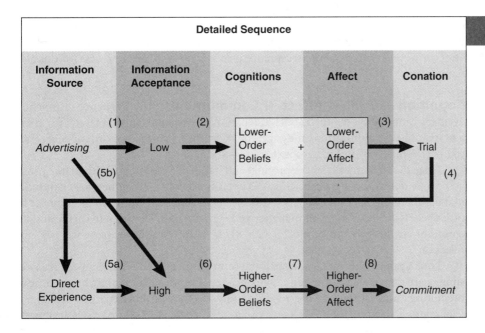

Exhibit 10-8

The Integrated Information-Response Model

Information alone can form lower-order beliefs in consumers, but only direct experience can form higher-order beliefs.

Source: Adapted from "Information Response Models: An Integrated Approach" by Robert E. Smith and William R. Swinyard in *Journal of Marketing,* Winter 1982, Volume 46, p. 85. Reprinted with permission from *Journal of Marketing,* published by the American Marketing Association.

Welch's makes a compelling argument for its white grape juice, a message that will resonate among the target audience—parents of young children.

Source: Courtesy of Welch Foods Inc., Concord, MA.

Cognition → Affect → Commitment The simplest, though not the most plausible, pattern is that the consumer sees an advertisement, immediately accepts the information it communicates (path 5b), and forms higher-order beliefs (path 6), leading to higher-order affect (path 7) and commitment (path 8). To achieve this effect, an advertisement needs to be very convincing and must be targeted to a very receptive audience. The advertisement for Welch's white grape juice in Exhibit 10-9 is a good example, combining a compelling argument with a high level of need among target consumers. Targeted to parents of young children who are concerned about their children's diets, the advertisement relies upon immediate acceptance that white grape juice is more easily digested (path 5b), translating into a strong belief that drinking the juice will make the child healthier (path 6). The information in the advertisement is particularly convincing as it comes from a credible source, the medical journal *Pediatrics.* Believing the medical evidence provided, consumers should develop a strong positive attitude toward white grape juice (path 7), leading them to purchase the product repeatedly (path 8). However, no matter how compelling the message, consumers typically do not run out and buy products immediately after seeing an advertisement. Acceptance is much too complex a process for this always to happen.

Cognition → Trial → Affect → Commitment This sequence of psychological events is captured by the full model, the path with the solid arrow. Following exposure to a marketing communications message, the consumer forms lower-order beliefs and affect (path 2), which may induce product trial (path 3).

Once the consumer tries the product and has direct experience with it, he or she either accepts or rejects the message claims. Acceptance serves to strengthen lower-order beliefs, making them higher-order beliefs (path 6). Upon activation from memory, these higher-order beliefs are likely to result in higher-order affect (path 7), which in turn translates into commitment toward the product (path 8) or, if the product experience was negative, rejection.

Look again at the Welch's advertisement in Exhibit 10-9. What happens if target consumers are skeptical about medical evidence reported in *Pediatrics?* At best, the advertisement might interest them in the possible good effects of the juice (paths 1 and 2). Product trial might help strengthen this lower-order affect (path 3). As time passes and parents see their children enjoying good or improved health, they may attribute it in part to the white grape juice (path 4), and their belief in its benefits is thus strengthened (paths 5a and 6). With continued use, the juice is accepted as a means of maintaining good childhood health and is purchased repeatedly (paths 7 and 8).

Cognition → Trial → Trial → Trial   Although the model shows a transition between trial and direct experience that leads to the formation of higher-order beliefs and affect, consumers do not always behave in this way. The consumer may, for example, consistently switch brands and never form a strong preference for any one brand. In this case, trial after trial may never lead to commitment. Returning once more to the Welch's advertisement in Exhibit 10-9, what happens if target consumers give their child the juice to drink but do not observe significant improvements in the child's health or physical well-being? This direct experience makes them unlikely to accept the information in the advertisement or to form beliefs in the benefits of the juice. At best, they will form lower-order beliefs (paths 1 and 2) sufficient to make them try the juice again (path 3). More likely, they will try out other juices or brands (path 3) until they find one they feel yields the desired results.

Using the Integrated Information-Response Model   The integrated information-response model helps marketers set specific goals that are directly related to the model components. Depending upon the different information-response patterns encountered, marketers can decide which of these goals to emphasize. For pattern 1 (cognition → affect → commitment), the marketing communication objective is to inform and educate consumers about the product and its benefits. The message should be tailored to match that pattern; that is, it should be highly informational with credible supportive arguments.

In contrast, pattern 2 (cognition → trial → affect → commitment) indicates that consumers are not likely to form a positive attitude toward the brand or become committed to it unless they try it first. Hence, the goal of the advertisement should be to induce trial. This pattern is typical with low-involvement products.

Pattern 3 (cognition → trial → trial → trial) is the most problematic. The marketer has multiple goals: to reinforce initial beliefs about the brand's attributes and benefits, strengthen positive attitude toward the brand, and reinforce commitment.

10-2c The Extended Dual Mediation Model

Illustrated in Exhibit 10-10, the dual mediation model (DMM) comprises four constructs: ad cognitions (Cad), attitude toward the ad (Aad), brand cognition (Cb), and attitude toward the brand (Ab).[6] The **extended dual mediation model** further connects affect (Aff) to the basic model.[7] The model argues that an audience exposed to an ad reacts to the ad emotionally. That is, something about the ad triggers a feeling or an affective reaction (e.g., anger, joy, laughter, sadness, envy). This feeling (Aff) plays an important role in influencing thoughts about the ad (Cad) as well as the attitude toward the ad (Aad). By the same token, the attitude toward the ad (Aad) is further influenced by the kind of thoughts generated about the ad (Cad). The thoughts about the ad (Cad) as well the attitude toward the ad (Aad) in turn influence the formation or change of the audience's thoughts about the brand (Cb) and the attitude toward the brand (Ab). Attitude toward the brand, finally, plays a significant role in the formation of the intention to purchase that brand (PI).

Go back and look at the ad in Exhibit 9-13. The picture is a woman who likes to lead her life, is anti-establishment, and is attractive looking. Suppose that an audience of high school and college-age women is exposed to this ad. Perhaps the gut reaction this audience may experience looking at this ad is "freedom," "asserting one's self," and "sexy." These feelings (Aff) may get that audience to examine this ad closely and think about the ad and the brand being advertised. The audience may think about what it means being "anti-establishment" and the lifestyle of a woman who is of the anti-establishment type (Cad). They may think about the brand of shoes—Code West Footwear—being advertised (Cb). The thoughts triggered about the ad (Cad) are likely to generate thoughts about the brand

F A Q

Is one response pattern the most preferable?

▶**extended dual mediation model**   A marketing communications model that argues that an audience exposed to an ad reacts to the ad emotionally and that this feeling influences thoughts about the ad, as well as the attitude toward the ad. In turn, both the thoughts about and the attitude toward the ad influence the formation or change of the audience's thoughts about the brand and the attitude toward the brand.

E x h i b i t 10-10

The Extended Dual Mediation Model

Key: Aff = Affect; Cad = Cognitions toward the ad; Aad = Attitude toward the ad; Cb = Cognitions toward the brand; Ab = Attitude toward the brand; PI = Purchase intentions

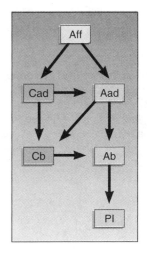

(Cb): "Do women who are anti-establishment wear these kinds of shoes?" "What kind of lifestyle and dress code go with the anti-establishment type?" If these thoughts lead to other thoughts such as, "I am the anti-establishment type" (Cad), then it is likely that the audience will form a favorable attitude toward the ad (Aad). If additional thoughts such as, "I like the looks of the shoes that reflect an anti-establishment image" occur, then it is likely that the audience will form a positive attitude toward this brand of footwear (Ab). This positive attitude toward the Code West Footwear (Ab) is likely to motivate the audience to purchase that brand in the right shopping situation. In other words, the positive attitude toward Code West Footwear is likely to lead to the formation of an intention to purchase that brand (PI) when the opportunity arises.

Using the Extended Dual Mediation Model   Marketers use the extended dual mediation model by developing ads that trigger a key emotion. This feeling (Aff) is then responsible for getting the audience to think about the ad. The ad cues have to be designed in such a way to get the audience to generate positive thoughts about the ad (Cad). These thoughts are extremely important because they set the stage for everything else. These thoughts (Cad) lead the audience to form a positive attitude toward the ad at large (Aad) and further motivate the audience to think positively about the advertised brand (Cb). A positive attitude toward the ad motivates the audience to think positively about the brand. Again, positive thoughts about the brand (Cb) as well as a positive attitude toward the ad (Aad) are responsible for the formation of a positive attitude toward the brand (Ab), which in turn leads to the formation of a purchase intention (PI)—the ultimate goal of the advertisement.

Marketing Management—Implications and Actions

Understanding communication effects helps marketers:

- Construct precise communications goals.
- Use messages to move consumers through the hierarchy of effects toward purchase.
- Adjust message effects to match their positioning goals.

10-3 Source Factors

The source—the individual delivering the communications message—may be a celebrity or spokesperson in an advertisement, a clerk in a retail environment, or a salesperson in a personal selling situation. The persuasiveness of the message is influenced by a variety of factors related to the source of the message (i.e., the communicator)—source credibility, source attractiveness, the power of the source, and source congruity.

10-3a Source Credibility

source credibility Perception by the target audience that a source has the knowledge, skill, or experience related to the product or service promoted and that the source is objective and trustworthy.

A source is credible if perceived by the target audience as having knowledge, skill, or experience related to the product or service promoted. Moreover, a credible source must be trusted by its audience to provide product information that is objective. These two components—expertise and trustworthiness—are essential to **source credibility.** The greater the expertise of the source, the greater the potential persuasiveness of the message. Similarly, the honesty and integrity of the source enhance message effectiveness.

Source credibility affects consumer persuasion through the process of internalization. People are motivated to search for opinions and beliefs, whether about issues or about goods and services. If they consider such opinions "correct," they are adopted or internalized. Hence, through credible spokespersons who come across as expert and/or trustworthy, marketers can encourage consumers to adopt desired opinions about their brands.[8]

It was recently found that source trustworthiness was not related to advertising female model attractiveness. That is, model beauty may not be related to beliefs about her willingness to give valid information. Also, though highly attractive models are well suited in ads for "enhancing, attractiveness-relevant" products such as lipstick or earrings, they are not more effective than normally attractive models in ads for "problem-solving" items such as acne covering or treatment products.[9]

Celebrities seem to project trust and expertise for "hedonic services." These are services that are more personal, fun, experiential, pleasurable, and/or value-expressive to the consumer. This does not appear to be the case if the service is more utilitarian. In a comparison between a restaurant ad and a bank ad, actor Harrison Ford was viewed as more trustworthy and expert when acting as spokesperson for the restaurant when compared to a waiter or a customer. The reverse was true when Ford, a bank teller, and a customer spoke on behalf of the bank. Here the latter two were scored as more trustworthy and expert.[10] Trust seems to be an important factor in personal selling. For example, recent research has shown that trusting a car salesperson makes quite a bit of difference in a consumer's decision to repurchase from the same car dealership.[11] The study also revealed that perceptions of trust results from:

- the use of low-selling ("soft sell") tactics,
- the perception that the salesperson is competent,
- the perception that the service is of high quality, and
- the perception that the car manufacturer cares about its customers.

10-3b **Source Attractiveness**

Research has shown that sources considered attractive by target audiences are more persuasive than those that are unattractive. Experts explain the effect of **source attractiveness** through the psychological process of identification.

Identification with Actual Self　**Identification with actual self** is when consumers identify with a source, seeing similarities between that source and the way they perceive themselves. They feel "This spokesperson is very much like me; I can understand where he or she is coming from." This source similarity[12] is particularly influential if consumers can be led to identify with sources on matters that are important to them. The woman in the advertisement for arthritis medicine in Exhibit 10-11 is an effective spokesperson because she reminds potential consumers of themselves—she shares the concerns of other arthritis sufferers in managing their pain.

> **source attractiveness** Refers to the audience perception of the source (communicator) as being physically attractive.

> **identification with actual self** Consumer identification with a source, seeing similarities between that source and the way the consumer perceives himself or herself.

E x h i b i t　10-11

Potential consumers will identify with the woman in this ad, a result of source similarity.

Source: Reprinted by permission of Del Labs.

Celebrity power is at work here as Hillary Duff, a young television and movie star, shows how milk provides essential nutrients that allow young women to "shop and not drop."

Source: Used by permission of Lowe and National Fluid Milk Processor Promotion Board.

identification with ideal self Consumer identification with a source, seeing similarities between that source and the way the consumer would like himself or herself to be. Marketers achieve consumer identification with ideal self through the use of either popular celebrities or attractive models.

Identification with Ideal Self Identification with ideal self is when consumers identify with a source, seeing similarities between that source and the way they would like themselves to be. Marketers achieve consumer identification with ideal self through either the use of popular celebrities or attractive models. Celebrities are effective because they appeal to the consumer's ideal self-image. Consumers feel they want to become "stars"—to be affluent and always in the spotlight. They admire celebrities because celebrities belong to a special referent group whom they idealize.[13] Research shows that the use of celebrities increases the power of advertisements to win attention, increases recall, and enhances product preference.[14] Hillary Duff, a popular television and movie actress, has become a celebrity with particular appeal to preteen and teenage girls. These girls love to shop "until they drop." The ad shown in Exhibit 10-12 is one of the "got milk" series. It shows the tie between the essential nutrients provided in milk and the energy needed to "shop and not drop." However, marketers should always bear in mind that negative publicity for a celebrity spokesperson can directly impact the performance of the brand.

The use of decorative and physically attractive models in advertising also contributes to the consumer's favorable evaluation of the message. Research has shown that models are particularly effective if they are gender appropriate and relevant to the product promoted.[15] Though models work well in advertising fashion and beauty aids, they are less effective in communicating serious issues such as, for example, threats to the environment. Credible sources, such as ecologists, may work better for those messages.

10-3c Source Power

Consumers perceive communicators as having different types of **source power.** Communicators perceived as having authority, such as doctors in health-care advertising and police representatives in public service campaigns, induce compliance. Here, consumers feel motivated to comply with the "demands" of the communicator because the source is perceived (consciously or subconsciously) as able to administer positive or negative sanctions to them. The power of a source to persuade depends on three factors: perceived control, perceived concern, and perceived scrutiny.[16]

> **source power** The different kinds of power that consumers perceive communicators as having.

Perceived Control   **Perceived control** is the consumer's perception that the source is able to administer rewards and/or punishments if the consumer does not comply with the message demand. Consider the following situation. A small poultry farm routinely buys a food additive to reduce molting from a farm supplies company, the only supplier of the popular product. A salesperson from the supplier calls on the farm aggressively selling a new product, a lighting device that increases egg production.

> **perceived control** Consumer perception that the source is able to administer rewards and/or punishments if the consumer does not comply with the message demand.

Although the farmer is not convinced that he needs the new product, he worries that if he fails to buy it, his supply of the antimolting additive will be jeopardized. He thinks the salesperson may punish him by delaying his next order or by increasing the price. Although this example is of a highly unethical business practice, it illustrates how perceived control by the communicator can increase persuasiveness.

Perceived Concern   **Perceived concern** is the consumer's perception that the source cares whether or not the consumer complies. Continuing the previous example, the poultry farm operator, knowing that the salesperson works on commission, perceives a high level of concern. Not buying the lighting device would mean loss of commission for the salesperson.

> **perceived concern** Consumer perception that the source cares whether or not the consumer complies.

Perceived Scrutiny   **Perceived scrutiny** is the consumer's perception that the source is able to know whether the consumer complied or not. Suppose the poultry farm operator, knowing that the salesperson is due to transfer territories, promises to order the device within the month. Noncompliance is easier because he thinks the salesperson will not check on the order.

> **perceived scrutiny** Consumer perception that the source is able to know whether the consumer complied or not.

Although source power in marketing communications can be effective in the short term, its persuasiveness diminishes if it is overused. In the 1980s, Procter & Gamble (P&G) used source power strategies to obtain shelf space for its brands at retail outlets. The result was a negative company image among retailers, who felt that P&G and its sales force were pressuring them into pushing P&G products. To correct this situation and appease retailers, P&G developed a conciliatory set of procedures and policies for sales representatives.[17]

10-3d Source Congruity

Source congruity refers to the extent to which a celebrity who endorses a brand has characteristics that match the brand attributes. For example, Clint Eastwood is perceived to be "rugged" by most people. If he endorses a brand of watches that may be characterized as "rugged," then you can say that there is congruity between the source and the brand. Such congruity plays an important role in advertising effectiveness.[18]

> **source congruity** The extent to which a celebrity who endorses a brand has characteristics that match the brand attributes.

Recent research has shown that source congruity plays a more important role in advertising persuasion when consumers are likely to elaborate on the advertised product. Suppose consumer subjects are presented with an ad in which Clint Eastwood is endorsing a "rugged" watch. These subjects are then asked, "How good do you think this product is?" These subjects are likely to think about the message, the brand attributes, and the source communicating the message. The fact that Clint Eastwood has an image of ruggedness that matches the image of the watch helps convince the subjects that the watch is made for rugged people. If they perceive themselves as rugged too, they are likely to be most disposed to the purchase of the advertised watch. In other words, when consumers are in a situation to think about the product and its attributes (high issue-relevant elaboration), source congruity is more likely to play a key role in advertising persuasion than when consumers do not think about the product attributes (low elaboration).[19]

It has been found that the gender of a spokesperson and/or the announcer in a television commercial has impact on consumer perceptions of the effectiveness of the presenter. If the product is gender-neutral, men and women as spokespersons or announcers were judged equally effective as presenters. For female-gender-imaged products a female spokesperson or announcer was seen as more effective than a male. The evaluation of the ad was also more positive in this situation. However, for male-gender-imaged products the sex of the presenter had no impact on the evaluation of the commercial. This points to the need for advertisers to select females as presenters for female-gender-imaged products.[20]

Marketing Management—Implications and Actions
Understanding source factors helps marketers:
• Choose either actual or ideal self-identification to enhance product positioning and message acceptance.
• Adjust source power to levels appropriate to the communication goal.

10-4 Message Form

Just as message content is important in persuasion, so too is message form. How the message is said—its tone, its context, and its execution—have enormous impact on the processing of message content and, thus, on overall communication effectiveness.

10-4a Message Tone

message tone The emotional versus factual appeal of a message.

Message tone refers to the emotional versus factual appeal of a message. In this section, we'll discuss the distinction between emotional and factual appeals and various forms of emotional appeal.

factual versus emotional appeals The tone of a message or the way in which it appeals to consumers can be either factual or emotional. A factual tone appeals to the consumer's thinking processes and focuses on informational reasons to buy, whereas an emotional tone appeals to feelings.

Factual Versus Emotional Appeals **Factual versus emotional appeals** is a decision involving whether the tone of a message or the way in which the message appeals to consumers should be either factual or emotional. A factual tone appeals to the consumer's thinking processes, whereas an emotional tone appeals to feelings. Factual messages focus on informational reasons to buy. This is the central route to attitude change—attitudes change as a direct response to the physical attributes or benefits of the products as processed through the consumer's cognitive faculties. In contrast, emotional appeals take a peripheral route to attitude change. The consumer does not respond to the pros and cons of the product by making a cognitive decision but responds instead to the feelings the message arouses.

elaboration likelihood A marketing communications model that argues that there are two routes to persuasion—central and peripheral. The central route is a process of attitude change as a direct response to the physical attributes or benefits of the products as processed through the consumer's cognitive faculties. In contrast, the peripheral route to persuasion reflects the processing of emotional appeals. The consumer does not respond to the pros and cons of the product by making a cognitive decision but responds instead to the feelings the message arouses.

The **elaboration likelihood** model in Exhibit 10-13 illustrates the two routes to message persuasion. Given central route processing, factual messages are likely to be effective. Messages are remembered because they contain quality arguments, substantiated by convincing evidence. Given peripheral route processing, emotional appeals may make a positive impact—by making the consumer feel good, for example. However, the impression these messages make is temporary and can be easily forgotten or changed by competitive messages.

Two conditions affect elaboration likelihood—motivation and ability. Consumers are likely to process cognitively—think about—a message if they are motivated to do so and if they are able to clearly distinguish among the product benefits it promises. If consumers are not motivated to process the message and are not able to distinguish its merits, they are more likely to absorb it peripherally than centrally. Thus, given a highly motivated audience of consumers who are willing to expend cognitive effort to process marketing

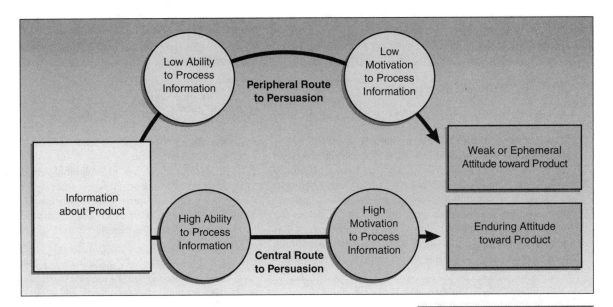

E x h i b i t 10-13

**The Elaboration
Likelihood Model**

Factual messages are effective for central route processing, while emotional messages have more impact for peripheral route processing.

information, factual messages work best. Low motivation and low cognitive ability mean emotional appeals will be more effective. Motivation to process the message depends upon the following three factors: message relevance, need for cognition, and purchase responsibility.[21]

Message Relevance   What is the **message relevance** to the consumer? Suppose an engineer who uses various kinds of computer software in her work sees an advertisement for a new software package. Because it might help her advance in her career, this consumer is likely to be motivated to process a factual message about the product. Contrast the homemaker who uses the computer for little more than paying bills and personal correspondence. If persuaded to buy the product at all, this consumer is more likely to respond to an emotional rather than a factual appeal.

Need for Cognition   Does the consumer have a high need for cognition? Continuing the previous example, the homemaker may be motivated to process a factual message if she is the type of person who is curious about computers in general and, therefore, has a high need to know and understand.

Purchase Responsibility   Who has **purchase responsibility?** Does the consumer feel that he or she is ultimately responsible for making an effective decision? Suppose an organization decides to purchase new computer software to automate its outdated accounting system. An employee assigned to evaluate different programs will obviously feel responsible for the decision and will, therefore, examine relevant information very closely and respond well to factual appeals. If the responsibility is diffused among several employees or to a committee, motivation to process factual messages weakens. The lack of personal responsibility leads to peripheral processing, through which emotional appeals are likely to be more effective.

Marketplace 10-1 discusses an interesting topic in the psychology of advertising—namely, subliminal advertising. Much of the scientific evidence of studies of subliminal advertising suggests that it does not work.

Message Processing   Three other factors influence the ability to process messages: distraction, message pace, and product familiarity or experience.

Distraction   A **distraction** is anything that pulls the consumer's attention away from the content of a factual message and lessens the message's ability to communicate effectively.

message relevance
The extent to which the marketing communications message is perceived to be personally relevant to the consumer.

purchase responsibility
The extent to which the audience of a marketing communications message feels responsible in making a purchase decision.

distraction Anything that pulls the consumer's attention away from the content of a factual message and lessens the message's ability to communicate effectively.

Marketplace 10-1

Subliminal Advertising

Subliminal perception is usually defined as a stimulus processed below threshold so that it is imperceptible. The threshold of a particular stimulus is the dividing line between the intensity level at which that stimulus registers awareness or non-awareness. In practical terms, it is usually measured as that stimulus value that is correctly detected 50 percent of the time. Research in psychophysics has documented behavioral effects of stimuli that fall below the threshold. Also, research from social psychologists has shown that, under some circumstances, unattended stimuli can be processed to a degree that is sufficient to elicit a sub-

---

The American Marketing Association, in its definition of subliminal advertising, notes that "There is no scientific evidence to indicate that this approach is effective communication and, if there were convincing evidence of effectiveness, the approach would likely be prohibited as a deceptive business practice."

Source: *Dictionary of Marketing Terms*, Peter D. Bennett, ed. (Chicago, IL: NTC Business Books, 1994), pp. 277–278.

---

sequent affective reaction (i.e., like/dislike) without their being recognized as having been previously encountered. In other words, affective reactions can occur without extensive perceptual cognitive encoding.

Although the concept of subliminal perception is acknowledged by some in the scientific community, its effectiveness in advertising remains largely undemonstrated. After reviewing much evidence in both psychology and marketing, one consumer research study concluded:

> subliminal directives have not been shown to have the power ascribed to them . . . In general, the literature on subliminal perception shows that the most clearly documented effects are obtained only in highly contrived and artificial situations. These effects, when present, are brief and of small magnitude. The result is perhaps best construed as an epiphenomenon, a subtle and fleeting by-product of the complexities of human cognitive activity. These processes have no apparent relevance to the goals of advertising.

Source: R. B. Zajonc, "Feeling and Thinking: Preferences Need No Inferences," *American Psychologist*, Vol. 35, No. 2 (1980), pp. 151–175.

F A Q

Don't consumers feel responsible for all of their purchases?

message pace How fast or slow a message is presented to an audience in the context of a media vehicle.

product familiarity The extent to which the consumer is experienced with the product in question.

priming A preliminary presentation of visual or copy information that places a product or service into a category based on type or benefits. This is offered before the target member is exposed to the ad itself.

Loud background music in a television commercial, for example, can distract viewers from processing the finer details of the argument made in the message.

Message Pace   It takes time for consumers to process detailed factual messages accurately. Such media channels as television and radio are typically less effective than print simply because they do not always provide the consumer with ample time to process factual messages. The **message pace** or speed of such messages is often too great.

Animation speed on the web has been explored to determine optimum animation speed. The concern is that an overdose of animation speed may result in negative perceptions of the site. It was found that if the advertiser presented sequential information aiming to generate positive impressions of the product, the initial web page should have faster animation speed. The following page should provide slow animation speed to be most effective. On the other hand, if the advertiser wishes to generate a high degree of arousal the sequence should be reversed, with slow animation first, followed by fast animation.[22]

Product Familiarity or Experience   Consumers who already have **product familiarity** with the product advertised are more likely to be able to process factual messages about it than are those who do not have this familiarity. Therefore, emotional appeals work better than factual appeals with new products or with new consumer segments.

Priming   In order to affect message processing by directing attention, some preliminary presentation of visual or copy information that places the product or service into a category, known as **priming,** may be carried out to help the consumer in his or her evaluation of it. Priming could also be tied to certain features or benefits that the advertiser would like the consumer to focus on. In a test of advertising background "wallpaper" on the web, feature priming was carried out on cars and sofas. The participating consumers were made up of "experts" and "novices." The wallpaper background for cars was red and orange flame-like (a safety feature prime) and green with small dollar signs (a price prime). The wallpaper for the sofa ads was a blue background with fluffy clouds (a comfort prime) and

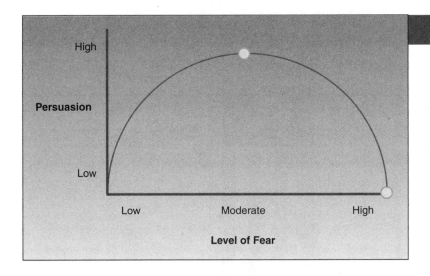

Exhibit 10-14

The Relationship between Fear Intensity and Persuasion

Persuasion through fear is most effective at moderate intensity. High levels of fear may cause consumers to block out the message.

a green background with imbedded pennies (a price prime). The primes affected the novices. They looked at more safety, comfort, and price features based on matching wallpaper. Experts on the other hand looked at both primed and unprimed features regardless of the wallpaper used on the website. The background wallpaper makes the feature more salient for the novices, whereas the experts, having more product knowledge and experience, already know what features are important.[23]

Emotional Appeals   The use of **emotional appeals** depends largely upon the positioning of the product or service promoted. Emotional appeals run the gamut from fear to humor to sex to romance to anger to nostalgia. Let's take a look at some of the most effective and most familiar emotional appeals in marketing communications.

▶ **emotional appeal** A message that reflects certain emotions, such as fear, humor, sex, romance, anger, and nostalgia.

Fear Appeals   Recent research has shown that while scare tactics are not the best persuasive advertising tool, **fear appeals** can be effective in certain situations and with certain types of consumers. As Exhibit 10-14 shows, the relationship between fear and persuasion is curvilinear. This means that with either very low or very high levels of fear within a marketing message, persuasion is low. At a moderate intensity, however, persuasion through fear is effective. Fear has facilitating effects: It attracts attention to the message, arouses interest, and motivates consumers to take action to resolve problems. Thus, increasing the level of fear in a message from low to moderate usually results in increased persuasion. However, high levels of fear have an inhibiting effect: Consumers emotionally block or tune out the message.[24] The public service advertisement in Exhibit 10-15 is an example of a low-intensity fear message.

▶ **fear appeal** A message communicated to an audience through the use of fear—that is, the message is designed to arouse fear in the audience.

One study, implying a connection between antismoking advertisements that use fear as a persuader and a concurrent national drop in smoking, concluded that high fear appeals, usually regarded as counterproductive, can be particularly effective with people who are "low in anxiety and high in self-esteem, who exhibit coping behavior, who normally find the topic or category of low relevance, and who normally see themselves as having low vulnerability to the threat in the fear message."[25]

In another study that was related to antismoking advertising targeted on adolescents it was found that fear appeals relating to the dangers that others face from "second hand smoke" and those suggesting that smoking is a barrier to achieving maturity, independence, life savvy, physical attractiveness, and being "cool" were affective in motivating young people to stop smoking or not start. Few adolescents felt vulnerable to any health risks, so such fear appeals did not work.[26] Product users are more likely to be persuaded by low-level than by high-level fear appeals. Conversely, nonusers are more likely to be persuaded by high-level rather than low-level fear appeals.[27] An audience of smokers is likely to act very defensively to graphic, high-intensity fear advertisements. Feeling threatened, the smoker is likely to disparage, disbelieve, and ultimately reject the message as implausible.

F A Q

How do marketers measure fear intensity in an ad?

Exhibit 10-15

This low-intensity fear appeal works by showing a negative consequence of not voting.

Source: Courtesy of Federal Voting Assistance Program, Department of Defense, Pentagon.

SINCE ONLY 60% OF AMERICANS VOTE*, WILL THIS BE THE KIND OF FLAG WE WAVE?

REGISTER AND VOTE

In contrast, an audience of nonsmokers may be motivated to process the message and is likely to be convinced of the dangers of smoking.

humor appeal A message communicated to an audience through the use of humor—that is, the message is designed to arouse humor in the audience.

Humor Appeals   **Humor appeals** in advertising have long been controversial. Whereas some campaigns have been unquestionably successful, others have either fallen flat or have entertained consumers at the expense of persuading them. Exhibit 10-16 shows the results of the rather limited research that has been conducted into the use of humor in marketing communications.

As the most powerful characteristic of humor is its ability to attract and hold the attention of consumers, humor appeals work best in cluttered media environments. Humor appeals effectively penetrate the clutter. The Purina ad shown in Exhibit 10-17 on page 326 uses an arresting visual image to make a point different from other dog food ads. Studies have also shown that humor appeals work best with consumers of higher intelligence and education as these ads typically demand a fairly sophisticated level of comprehension.

sex appeal A message communicated to an audience through the use of sex—that is, the message is designed to arouse sexual excitement in the audience.

Sex Appeals   Research shows that **sex appeals,** such as nudity, in advertising are generally not effective. They result in low product recall, low evaluation of advertising appeal, and poor product/marketer perceptions. At best, overt sex appeals are effective only with products that are directly related to sex. This does not, however, mean that sex appeals do not work. Less overt sex appeals, used judiciously, can be extremely effective.[28]

Both male and female audiences pay attention to the use of attractive models in advertising, particularly when those models are of the opposite sex.[29] One study analyzed the sexual content of magazine advertising between 1964 and 1984. The percentage of advertisements with sexual content did not increase over the twenty-year period, but the types of sexual portrayals did. Specifically, sexual portrayals became more explicit, that is, with greater use of visual than verbal sexual cues. Also, the study showed that female models are more typically used in sexual portrayals than are male models.[30]

To be effective, sex appeals must result in positive brand name recall. One study found that nonsexual illustrations are more effective in producing brand name recall than are sexual illustrations. This response becomes more pronounced with the passage of time. Moreover, individuals already favorable to the use of sex appeals in advertising recall a greater number of correct brand names than do those who do not favor the use of sex appeals.[31]

Pluses	Minuses	**Exhibit 10-16**
Attracts attention Humorous ads can often cut through clutter.	**Too much repetition** Overexposure dramatically reduces the attention-getting factor. If a humorous commercial relies on an unexpected punch line, for example, the effect is lost with the second exposure.	**The Effects of Humor in Marketing Communications**
Positively distracts the audience Distracts consumers from creating counterarguments, yielding an increase in persuasion.		
Enhances source credibility A previously unidentified source may be perceived to have greater attributes of character when the advertisement delivers humorous rather than serious communication.	**Hampers comprehension** If the execution unduly complicates a selling story or rests on "borrowed" interest remote from the product, comprehension may be reduced.	
Reinforces arguments Humorous advertising may be superior to serious advertising, as it induces long-term support argumentation.	**Is not necessarily more effective** Though humor can be persuasive, the effect is at best no greater than that of serious appeals.	
Increases audience interest in consuming the advertised product Humor serves to heighten involvement.	**Decreases recall** Humorous ads may significantly decrease recall of product uses and benefits.	
Reduces irritation toward advertising in consumers Many consumers feel advertising is an intrusion. Humor advertising, because it is seen as a form of entertainment, counters these negative feelings to some extent.		

Sources: Brian Sternthal and C. Samuel Craig, "Humor in Advertising," *Journal of Marketing,* Vol. 37 (October 1973), p. 17; David M. Gardner, "The Distraction Hypothesis in Marketing," *Journal of Marketing Research,* Vol. 10 (December 6, 1970); G. Brunner, "A Further Experimental Study of Satire as Persuasion," in Sternthal and Craig, "Humor in Advertising;" T. J. Madden, "Humor in Advertising: An Experimental Analysis," Working paper No. 83-27, University of Massachusetts (1984); C. P. Duncan, and J. Nelson, "Effects of Humor in a Radio Advertising Experiment," *Journal of Advertising,* Vol. 14, No. 2 (1985), pp. 33–40; H. B. Lammers, L. Leibowitz, G. E. leymore, and J. E. Hennessey, "Immediate and Delayed Effects of Humor on Cognitive Responses to Advertising Stimuli: A Trace Consolidation Approach," *Journal of Business Research* (1985).

The article in CBite 10-2 argues that sex is commonly used in advertising nowadays, despite the growing awareness of sexism and its adverse social effects. Students of marketing should understand that many social critics of marketing have deemed the use of sex appeal in advertising as unethical.

In another study, consumers themselves judged the inherent sexual connotations of various advertisements, evaluating such factors as degree of nudity, realism, romantic content, sexual overtones in printed words, and sexual arousal. Researchers observed that suggestiveness of copy is rather uniformly noticed by women but not by men. Moreover, men are less inclined than women to report awareness of nudity, although different groups of men can be segmented on the basis of their responses to sexual themes in advertising.[32]

These findings tend to discredit the traditional view that sexual appeals work best with male audiences. Suggestive copy might be used more effectively in advertising to women, while nudity seems to be barely noticed by a significant number of male consumers.

Ego-Focused Versus Other-Focused Emotional Appeals   Recent research has made the distinction between ego-focused emotional appeals and other-focused appeals.[33] **Ego-focused emotional appeals** are messages that arouse certain kinds of emotions such as pride, happiness, frustration, and anger. These emotions are characterized as reflective of an "independent self." These emotions relate to the person as an autonomous individual.

▶**ego-focused emotional appeals** Messages that arouse certain kinds of emotions, such as pride, happiness, frustration, and anger. These emotions are characterized as reflective of an "independent self" and relate to the person as an autonomous individual.

Purina found a funny and meaningful visual to express the misery caused by different dog foods. It is both attention-getting and relevant.

Source: Reproduced by permission of Carl Furuta Studio, Inc., Los Angeles, CA.

Sudden changes in your dog's diet can lead to stomach discomfort.

By suddenly introducing your dog to a new diet, you could be treating him to a stomach ache. The fact is, a consistent diet of one nutritionally complete and balanced food is actually better for dogs. And that's why you can feel good about feeding your dog Purina® Dog Chow® brand dog food each and every day. With all the taste and nutrition dogs need. Because, after all, dogs never get sick of good nutrition.

Purina® Dog Chow® Every Day.

---

other-focused appeals
Messages that arouse emotions such as empathy, peacefulness, indebtedness, and shame, which reflect an "interdependent self." These emotions tend to be associated with others, such as family, friends, co-workers, etc.

The focus is on the individual apart from a social group. In contrast, **other-focused appeals**—messages that arouse emotions such as empathy, peacefulness, indebtedness, and shame—reflect an "interdependent self." These emotions tend to be associated with others such as family, friends, co-workers, etc.

The research has shown that ego-focused appeals tend to be more persuasive (than other-focused appeals) for an audience characterized as being from an individualistic culture. Conversely, other-focused appeals tend to be more persuasive (than ego-focused appeals) for an audience characterized as being from a collectivistic culture. Individualism-

---

CBite 10-2

Sex Seems Here to Stay

If you believe that sex still sells, you are not alone. There is plenty of sexuality bopping around, and anyone who can scoop some up is determined to sell it—or rather, sell with it.

The use of masculine sex appeals in recent ads reflects even a broadening of sexual imagery available to advertisers today. It seems that one result of women's strides toward equality is to objectify men, as men have long objectified women. Now advertisers can use both men's and women's sexuality to sell products.

Many think it would be ideal if everyone just stopped using sex to sell products. However, change, if it ever comes, will come slowly. For one thing, most of the people in power (and indeed consumers, too) still have an enduring weakness for nice legs and other sundry parts. For another, any one corporation will be reluctant to stop using sexual appeals for fear that it will leave their unquestionable power as an advantage in the hands of competitors.

Source: From "Sex Still Sells (Or Does It?)" by Brian Lowry. Reprinted with permission from the March 17, 1986 issue of *Advertising Age.* Copyright, Crain Communications Inc. 1986.

Marketplace 10-2

Muzak by Satellite Offers Ads in Supermarkets

The folks at Muzak have long brought you those bland background tunes in elevators and dentists' offices. Now Muzak is jumping into in-store advertising. With its satellite receivers in thousands of supermarkets nationwide, Muzak hopes to cash in as consumer product makers and retailers try harder than ever to nail customers right where they spend money.

With Muzak, advertisers can get very specific. Say you want to push your brand of refried beans in Latino markets. Muzak can broadcast your message in Spanish to grocery stores in Latin communities in California, Texas, and Florida. If you want to advertise snow shovels in November, Muzak can send your ads only to stores located in snowy regions. Clusters of three twenty-second ads fit snugly between eight minutes of classical, light rock, or hiphop music. Product sales show positive effects, indicating that shoppers are really listening.

Source: "Hear the Muzak, Buy the Ketchup" by Dori Jones Yang and Joan Warner, reprinted from the June 28, 1993 issue of *Business Week* by special permission, copyright © 1993 by The McGraw-Hill Companies, Inc.

collectivism is a cultural factor that refers to the extent to which people in a country (e.g., the United States, Japan, Korea, Germany) tend to see themselves as independent or interdependent. For example, much research has shown that people in the United States and Germany tend to be "individualistic." That means they value personal achievements and focus on personal growth. In contrast, people in Japan, Korea, and China tend to be "collectivistic." Collectivistic people tend to value affiliation with others, being part of a group such as a family, an extended family, a community, or the like, with value placed on the collective. See the discussion in Chapter 12, section 12-2c, that deals with individualistic versus collectivistic cultures.

10-4b Message Context

Message context includes any cues imbedded in the message by the marketer. These may be as simple as choice of background music, setting or location, or use of artifacts or furnishings. All have an effect on message tone. One of the most popular contextual cues is the use of background music to influence audiences.

Use of Music   Music works through classical conditioning, by encouraging consumers to associate positive feelings aroused by the music with the advertised product. Classical conditioning was covered in detail in section 7-2c in Chapter 7. One study, conducted to demonstrate the effect of music on choice behavior, showed that hearing liked or disliked music while being exposed to a product can directly affect product preferences.[34] That is, hearing liked music can enhance preference for the advertised product, whereas hearing disliked music may decrease preference. The same study demonstrated that music is most effective in non-decision-making situations. Specifically, the positive effects of music are stronger in advertisements that do not ask for an immediate purchase but are intended instead to enhance the image of a brand. Marketplace 10-2 describes how marketers have successfully used music in the promotion of their products and services.

10-4c Message Execution

Message execution is the combination of strategies through which the message is implemented. Execution strategies are as many and as varied as there are creative people in the advertising business. Here are just a few of the most commonly used strategies in today's advertising.

Use of Implicit versus Explicit Conclusions   In advertisements with **implicit conclusions,** the outcome or desired response is not boldly stated but rather is left to the consumer to infer. When the outcome is spelled out clearly, the advertisement has an **explicit conclusion.** However, explicit conclusions are not the most effective in all cases.[35]

> **message execution**
> The combination of strategies through which a message is implemented.

> **implicit versus explicit conclusion**   In advertisements with implicit conclusions, the outcome or desired response is not boldly stated but rather is left to the consumer to infer. When the outcome is spelled out clearly, the advertisement has an explicit conclusion.

There are two effects best achieved through implicit conclusions. They are subtle persuasion and consumer involvement.

Subtle Persuasion   When the conclusion is too explicit, consumers may experience reactance—feeling overly pressured or threatened by the advertiser, they respond by doing the opposite of the advertiser's desired behavior. In aggressive, hard-sell situations, this boomerang effect is common, with the result that the message backfires. In many car dealerships, for example, the hard sell is giving way to customer-oriented and information-based selling for just that reason. Reactance is much less likely to occur with **subtle persuasion**—when the persuasion attempt is subtle and the conclusion implicit.

Consumer Involvement   The more motivated consumers are to process an advertising message (**consumer involvement**), the more effective implicit conclusions can be. If the consumer has a specific problem that the message promises to solve, he or she is more likely to make the effort to understand, process, and recall the message. Peter, for example, who has dental problems and has been warned by his dentist that he should use a particular type of toothpaste, is highly motivated to process a subtle message and draw his own conclusions from it. In contrast, a consumer who is less emotionally involved with the product and does not really know or care much about the special ingredients of different types of toothpaste is less likely to make the same effort.[36]

Use of Self-Reference

Self-reference messages speak directly to the consumer, making the advertisement seem particularly relevant to the consumer's own situation. In advertisements to discourage drinking and driving, images of road accidents are accompanied by an announcer's warning, "Don't let this happen to you." Self-reference enhances message recall because we remember information relevant to our own situations.[37]

Use of Factual versus Evaluative Information

One way to look at the information contained in advertising messages is that it is either **factual**—logical and verifiable descriptions of tangible product features—or, **evaluative**—emotional, subjective impressions of intangible aspects of the product.[38] The ad in Exhibit 10-18 attempts to show that Kmart encourages its employees to be respectful, fair, and professional to one another and to Kmart patrons.

Although an advertisement may contain both factual and evaluative information, a study that manipulated factual/evaluative content in advertisements for three different products found that factual copy elicited fewer counterarguments and more support arguments from consumers.[39] The current trend is toward using evaluative claims as substitutes for factual claims. One reason is that it is difficult to clearly differentiate brands of parity products through factual claims because competing brands can make identical claims. Evaluative claims can better establish distinct brand images. A second reason is that factual claims are typically subjected to close scrutiny by government regulatory agencies, requiring an expensive process of claim substantiation by the advertiser.[40]

This raises the concern that the increasing tendency to rely on evaluative claims makes advertising more likely to be misleading. Consumers often process evaluative claims as if they were factual assertions, filling in the gaps in logic with their own hypotheses. Consumers, for example, who read a car advertisement that claims its newest model offers "the standard of luxury," tend to fill in their own definitions of luxury and view the product accordingly. Some take the claim simply to mean that the car is comfortable; others infer that it is more luxurious than any other on the market; still others assume that it offers more luxury features than others in its price class. Some even interpret the claim as fact, believing it to describe tangible attributes they consider to be luxury features, such as leather seats or cruise control.

Use of Comparative Messages

A **comparative message** is one in which the product is compared directly with a competing product in terms of one or more product features. An advertisement for antacid, for example, that claims it matches the ability of a leading competitor to bring fast relief uses a comparative message strategy.[41]

▸ subtle persuasion
The attempt to persuade the audience without being overt about the motive to persuade.

▸ consumer involvement
The extent to which the audience is motivated to process the message.

▸ self-reference   Messages that speak directly to the consumer, making the advertisement seem particularly relevant to the consumer's personal situation.

▸ factual versus evaluative information   Factual information in an ad is a logical and verifiable description of tangible product features. In contrast, evaluative information is an emotional, subjective impression of intangible aspects of the product.

F A Q

Isn't some form of self-reference present in all forms of marketing communication?

▸ comparative message
A message in which the product is compared directly with a competing product in terms of one or more product features.

E x h i b i t 10-18

This ad uses an emotional image of care—Kmart employees caring for one another and caring for Kmart's customers, too.

Source: Reprinted by permission of Kmart Corporation.

One disadvantage of comparative messages is that they invite counterargument by the consumer.[42] An ad comparing Tylenol and Excedrin, for instance, could make consumers evaluate their satisfaction with Tylenol and leave them less likely than ever to switch brands. Therefore, comparison ads require a brand to operate from a very strong position of certainty that the claims made are accurate and can be easily proven.

They can, however, be very effective for nonmarket leaders who use them to bridge the perceived distance between their products and those of top-selling competitors.[43] The rice-milk product in Exhibit 10-19 is a comparative ad that uses mock-ups of competitors' packages to highlight the fact that Rice Dream is the original and best brand in the category.

When Does Comparative Advertising Work Best?   Comparative information in marketing communications is most effective in inducing attitude change under the following conditions:

1. When the message uses factual rather than evaluative information.[44] This is because factual information reduces the counterargument by consumers that is a typical response to comparative messages.

2. When promoting a new rather than an established brand.[45] This is because comparative messages are usually more informative than are noncomparative messages and hence are more effective for new product introductions. The new brand benefits through association with the established brand.

3. When the message is communicated through a credible rather than a noncredible source.[46] Comparative advertising is particularly likely to be evaluated by consumers for its credibility or believability. Thus, a comparative message that lacks credibility is unlikely to be persuasive. Source credibility enhances the persuasiveness of comparative advertising over and beyond noncomparative advertising.

Marketplace 10-3 shows how comparative advertising fared over the years and how effective it is in real life.

E x h i b i t 10-19

This Rice Dream ad addresses the increased competition in its category, stressing its superiority by indirect comparison.

Source: Reprinted by permission of Imagine Foods.

message evidence
Information that substantiates product claims.

Use of Message Evidence

Message evidence—information that substantiates claims—plays an important role in message acceptance.[47] Consider, for example, the claim, "Two Tums antacid tablets a day can help prevent osteoporosis." Unless consumers are told why—because "Tums are jam-packed with calcium"—they are not likely to accept the validity of the message. Moreover, any evidence provided to support a message claim must have a warrant—it must be logically connected with the claim. These three properties—message claim, message evidence, and message warrant—work together to make the advertisement persuasive. For example,

- *Message claim:* Two Tums tablets a day can help prevent osteoporosis.
- *Message evidence:* Tums is jam-packed with calcium.
- *Message warrant:* Calcium is one of the best defenses against the pain and frailty that result from osteoporosis.

A message designed to present evidence substantiating claims of product benefits is likely to be effective only if consumers are involved with the product category. Those who are not involved with the product are not likely to expend the cognitive effort it takes to process the evidence information in the advertisement. If, for example, the consumer is not particularly concerned about the onset of osteoporosis, the Tums advertisement is unlikely to be effective.

mystery advertising
A message designed to arouse a sense of mystery and therefore involve the audience in message processing.

Use of Mystery Advertising

Mystery advertising can be effective in enhancing brand awareness by producing a strong association in memory between the brand and product category.[48] A Seiko ad used the strategy very successfully. A series of interviewees were asked to describe an unidentified object. Viewers were drawn in as they tried to figure out what it was that was being described. Only at the end was the mystery object—a Seiko watch—identified.

Use of Narratives

Consider looking at two travel brochures. One brochure structures the information about the vacation in a narrative, describing the sequence of events that would occur (day one, day two, etc.). The second brochure structures the information about the vacation in a list form (describing the major attraction features and benefits).

Marketplace 10-3

Thumbs Up for Comparative Ads

Coke vs. Pepsi, Ford vs. Chevy, MCI Worldcom vs. AT&T vs. Verizon, and Pringles vs. Stax. Comparative advertising has played a big role in many battles for market share, but with debatable success. However, a recent study claims comparative TV spots with a brand-differentiating message improve the odds of achieving superior persuasion scores. Comparative advertising was found to be most effective when it involved indirect comparative claims made by new products.

"Direct" comparisons involve identifying a competitor by name, while "indirect" doesn't identify the competitor but uses language such as "better than the leading brand." The study was also divided between established products and new products, because new products do better than established brands in persuasion scores.

The results indicated that new products fare very well in both indirect and noncomparative brand differentiating advertising, 45 percent and 40 percent above the norm, respectively. But when new products use direct comparison advertising, the rate of percentage superiority drops to 28 percent. Overall, ads containing direct and indirect comparisons with a brand-differentiating message scored 21 percent higher than the norm for all ads in persuasion. Ads that used brand differentiation but no comparisons scored 18 percent higher than the norm.

Source: From "New Ammo for Comparative Ads" by Leah Rickard. Reprinted with permission from the February 14, 1994 issue of *Advertising Age*. Copyright, Crain Communications Inc. 1994.

Which brochure do you think is likely to be persuasive? Research in consumer psychology has shown that the **message narrative** form of communications is more persuasive than other forms. This is because much of the social information we acquire in daily life is transmitted to us in a narrative form. We tend to organize information in memory better in narrative than other forms and use this information more effectively to make judgments and decisions.[49]

> **message narrative**
> A message that is communicated in a narrative form—describing the sequence of events that would occur.

Marketing Management—Implications and Actions

Understanding message form helps marketers:

- Select appropriate emotional appeals.
- Create contexts that will enhance message processing.
- Use comparative advertising effectively.

10-5 Media Factors

Marketers conduct research to determine the media use habits of their target consumers. Typical research items used to measure consumers' media habits are shown in Exhibit 10-20. Consumers receive most promotional messages through mass communications media, largely newspapers, magazines, radio, television, billboards, and transit advertising. Targeted media, such as direct mail, telemarketing, the Internet, and in-store advertising are also widely used. Personal contacts, such as sales personnel or word-of-mouth, also serve as channels for marketing communications.

The subject of interpersonal forms of marketing communications is covered in greater detail in Part 4, as part of the sociological influence on consumer behavior. For our purposes in this chapter, we will explore message media from the perspective of mass media or targeted media channels. Typically, marketers make a series of decisions in placing marketing communications in mass media. They must select a media category, a subcategory (if any), a message vehicle, a frequency of message dissemination, and a size or duration for the message.

Exhibit 10-20

Survey Items Commonly Used to Measure Consumers' Media Habits

Using survey items like these, advertisers can make decisions about category, subcategory, and vehicle choice.

When Do You Usually Listen to and/or Watch TV?

	Radio		TV	
Times	Weekday	Weekend	Weekday	Weekend
6:00 A.M. to 10:00 A.M.	○	○	○	○
10:00 A.M. to 3:00 P.M.	○	○	○	○
3:00 P.M. to 7:00 P.M.	○	○	○	○
7:00 P.M. to midnight	○	○	○	○
Midnight to 6:00 A.M.	○	○	○	○

Which Stations Do You Listen to for News, Sports, or Entertainment?

	Weekday	Weekend
Radio Station A	○	○
Radio Station B	○	○
Radio Station C	○	○

What Radio Format Do You Usually Listen to?

○ Adult contemporary	○ Top 40	○ Religious
○ Beautiful music	○ Ethnic	○ Variety
○ Big band	○ Educational	○ Rock
○ Classical	○ Oldies	○ Country
○ Talk	○ Jazz	○ Soft rock
○ Progressive	○ News	○ Urban contemporary

What Kind of TV Programs Do You Usually Watch?

M–F Daytime	M–F Evening
○ "Good Morning America"/"Today Show"	○ Game shows
○ Situation comedies	○ Newscasts
○ Game shows	○ Situation comedies
○ Serials	○ Police/detective/action/adventure

10-5a Media Category Selection

The major media categories are television, radio, magazines, newspapers, billboards, transit advertising, direct mail, telemarketing, in-store advertising, and the Internet. Effective selection depends upon understanding targeted consumers and their media-use habits. Consumer research is the means through which marketers match the profiles of targeted consumers to the media categories to which those consumers are most likely to be exposed and to which they are most likely to respond favorably.

As an example, one study created a profile of consumers who are heavy television viewers, linking their television viewing habits to their purchasing preferences.[50] It found that men who are heavy television viewers tend to be older, have a lower level of education, are of lower or middle socioeconomic status, follow conventional rules of social behavior, and feel generally secure. They are conservative as shoppers, favoring popular brands and well-known manufacturers. Women who are heavy viewers are characterized as conventional, quite rigid, and intolerant of social change. They are also older, have a lower level

Prime Time   *Late Evening*

- ○ Movies
- ○ Situation comedies
- ○ Serialized dramas
- ○ Detective/police dramas
- ○ Reality television shows
- ○ News magazine shows

- ○ Newscasts
- ○ "Tonight Show"
- ○ Movies
- ○ Situational comedies
- ○ Detective/police dramas
- ○ Comedy/variety shows

Do You Usually Watch Sports on TV? If Yes, Which Do You Watch Most Often?

- ○ College football
- ○ Baseball's champion series
- ○ World Series
- ○ NFL "Monday Night Football"
- ○ NFL regular season

- ○ AFC playoffs
- ○ NFC playoffs
- ○ AFC championship game
- ○ NFC championship game
- ○ Super Bowl

Do You Usually Watch Any of the Following Cable Channels?

- ○ ESPN
- ○ WTBS
- ○ CNN
- ○ USA
- ○ CBN

- ○ MTV
- ○ Lifetime
- ○ Nickelodeon
- ○ FNN
- ○ The Weather Channel

Do You Usually Read the Newspaper?

- ○ Daily
- ○ Weekend

If You Usually Read the Newspaper, Which Sections Do You Read Closely?

- ○ Local news
- ○ National news
- ○ Weather
- ○ Sports
- ○ Business

- ○ Editorials
- ○ Classified
- ○ Travel
- ○ Comics
- ○ Arts and entertainment

of education, and are of lower socioeconomic status. As shoppers, they find reassurance in familiar brand names and take pride in their ability to hunt down bargains. Exhibit 10-20 shows a typical questionnaire for media habits.

10-5b Subcategory Selection

Each media category is made up of several subcategories. Television, for example, is made up of several different types of programming during which marketers can advertise—movies, situation comedies, talk shows, mysteries, musical programs, national news, local news, news magazine programs, sports shows, travel shows, and others. As you can see in Exhibit 10-20, one of the major functions of a media survey is to uncover the subcategory preferences of targeted groups. Before placing advertising within a subcategory, marketers examine the consumer profile of that subcategory's users. Exhibit 10-20 is an example of how important profiles resulting from consumer research help steer subcategory selection.

One study contrasted people who rate fantasy/comedy shows as their favorite programs with people who prefer late-night talk shows.[51] Fantasy/comedy enthusiasts were found to be less affluent and less educated. They tend to have a strong traditional/conservative orientation, expressed through their concerns about religion, youth, drugs, and social permissiveness. They are committed to television to the exclusion of print media or outside activities. They reveal a price-conscious, bargain-seeking approach to purchase decisions but a willingness to pay extra for nationally advertised brands. In contrast, talk show viewers feel a need for excitement in their lives. They show a strong interest in fashion and personal appearance. Interested in new products, they seek out and share information about product innovation.

Also, there are many syndicated sources of research information on general media audiences and in some cases audiences for specific media vehicles (subcategories). Examples are Arbitron data for radio audiences including programming and time slots, similar information for television audiences found in Nielsen data, and more general media information provided in Marketing Research Incorporated (MRI) reports.

10-5c Media Vehicle Selection

In evaluating specific media vehicles, marketers use three criteria: reach, cost per thousand, and editorial content.

> **reach** The media concept that describes the extent to which messages inserted in certain media vehicles will be exposed to the audience.

Reach Media vehicles may be selected on the basis of their **reach,** or the maximum exposure they can provide to the target audience. For example, from the media habits survey, marketers can compute the reach of specific media vehicles, such as *Family Circle* magazine or the television show "Good Morning America." The question to be answered is, what percentage of the target market will be reached or potentially reached by these media? Research has shown that the presence of a returning network show right before a new prime time television show or a returning network show right after it will significantly reduce the error in forecasting the reach of a new prime time television program.[52]

> **cost per thousand (CPM)** A media concept that describes the dollar cost to reach a thousand consumers.

Cost per Thousand Another way to select media vehicles is on the basis of their cost in relation to their reach. The measurement used is **cost per thousand (CPM).** Using the "Good Morning America" show as an example, a marketer may compute the CPM as:

$$CPM = \frac{\$\text{ cost of 30-sec commercial} \times 1{,}000}{\text{Number of targeted consumers reached}}$$

or

$$CPM_{\text{Good Morning America}} = \frac{\$70{,}000 \times 1{,}000}{12{,}000{,}000} = \$5.83$$

That is, the marketer pays $5.83 to reach 1,000 target consumers through "Good Morning America."

> **editorial content** The topics usually covered in a certain communication medium. Media planners study the editorial content of various media to match products with media.

Editorial Content Vehicles may also be selected based upon their **editorial content.** The marketer wants to choose media with content that appeals to the target audience and is also consistent with the advertising message and its execution. The same message for a fast-food restaurant, for example, may be viewed very differently when in the middle of a science-fiction program as opposed to in the middle of a local news show.[53] The point here is that the medium or the media vehicle is actually part of the message. Therefore the marketer wants to control the context in which the message is received.

10-5d Media Frequency Selection

> **frequency** A media concept that refers to the number of message exposures generated by a particular media schedule.

The **frequency** of an advertisement is the number of times consumers are potentially exposed to it. In print advertising, frequency means the number of advertising placements; in radio and television, it means the number of times a commercial is aired. So how often is often enough? There is no straightforward answer to this question. Also, advertisers must realize that what is purchased is potential exposure. If you run the advertisement in a magazine in six different issues, there is no assurance that subscribers will read all of the issues, or see all of the ads. In fact some subscribers may not even see the message at all across the six issues. Even if they see the ads, there is no guarantee that they will get the message or associate it with the brand. Furthermore, even if they get this far there is no guarantee that they will buy the product. Still, getting exposure is the key, since no progress can be made without it, as shown in the integrated information-response model (Exhibit 10-8).

Industry experts recommend that, in general, around three actual exposures within a purchase cycle are about adequate. Three exposures should lead to or maintain the desired level of brand awareness.[54] The first exposure elicits a "What of it?" response. On the second exposure, the audience engages the message and determines if it is relevant and convincing. The third exposure acts as a reminder or reinforcer. An effective exposure would be one where the target person understands the message and is able to tie it to the product and brand. Of course, to generate three effective exposures, marketers have to make more, perhaps many more, than three ad placements in the selected media. However, the number of exposures necessary will vary from product to product, from situation to situation, and from consumer to consumer. Not even being addressed here are the impact of the quality of the creative side of the advertising and appropriate media selections on the number of effective exposures needed to "do the job."

Furthermore, advertising experts advise that higher levels of frequency may be warranted under the following conditions: if the message is new or complex, if the message tone is highly emotional rather than factual, if the product or service represents a low level of risk, or if target consumers are not likely to be cognitively involved in message processing.[55]

Traditional wisdom holds that, regardless of competitor activity, there is an ideal frequency for every advertising campaign that will produce the desired level of brand awareness or intent to purchase. However, a concept known as "share of messages seen" challenges this view by comparing the advertised brand's frequency with the frequency of all competitive brands. In this way, marketers can measure the relative frequency with which advertisements are seen by heavy, medium, and light viewers. Very heavy television viewers, for example, may see ten times as much advertising as will light viewers during the same seven-day period, and so for a particular advertisement to make an impact on this group, it needs to be aired with greater frequency.

A recent study suggests that repetition of the same ad induces somewhat greater processing of its content when the advertised brand is unfamiliar to the target market than when a familiar brand is involved. However we also see consumers having more negative thoughts about the unfamiliar brand. This in turn leads to ad "wear out" more quickly than with ads for familiar brands.[56]

10-5e Selection of Message Size or Duration

What is the relationship between the **message size** of a print advertisement or the **duration** of a television or radio commercial and their impact upon consumers? In fact, consumer research findings have been contradictory. One study, for example, found that a half-page direct-response advertisement produced 70 percent as many coupon redemptions as a full-page advertisement.[57] However, more recent research into direct response advertisements for considered-purchase products indicated that larger (full-page) advertisements drew disproportionately greater responses.

Another study, this time into the duration of television commercials, showed that since thirty-second commercials were introduced in 1965, there has been a significant decline in the ability of viewers to recall advertised brands. For example, in 1965, 15 percent of respondents were able to recall correctly the brand advertised in the last commercial they saw before being surveyed by telephone, whereas in 1981, the figure had dropped by more than half, to 7 percent.[58] The study suggests that the continuing and increasing proliferation of commercials has undermined, and will continue to undermine, the impact of any individual commercial.

When over 3,600 consumers participated in a study where they were each shown a subset of 1,363 print ads using an infrared eye-tracking approach, it was found that the visual (pictorial) element was superior in capturing attention independent of its size. The text element best captures attention in proportion to its surface size. Finally, the brand

F A Q

Can it ever be a good strategy to overexpose a message?

▶ **message size or duration** The size of an ad in a print medium (measured in column inches and page dimensions) and the duration or length of an ad in other media (for example, a 15-second spot, a 30-second spot, or a 60-second spot).

element transfers attention to either the visual or text element of the ad. This shows that advertisers would be ill advised to maximize the surface size of the pictorial element in a print ad regardless of its content in order to maximize attention to the entire ad.[59]

Marketing Management—Implications and Actions

Understanding media factors helps marketers:

- Select media vehicles appropriate to the target market.
- Choose vehicles with cost-effective reach.
- Make strategic frequency choices.

Chapter Spotlights

This chapter demonstrated the application of consumer research to marketing communications by providing a framework through which decisions can be made. Those decisions cover six key areas: message content, message audience, message effects, message source, message form, and message media.

1. Content and audience decisions. The claim the message makes depends upon the positioning of the product, its target audience, its competitive environment, and the marketer's brand strategy. The effectiveness of the message depends on how well it reaches the consumers to whom it is directed. This necessitates not only identification of potential market segments through demographic, psychographic, geographic, and product research, but also detailed information on the media habits of the targeted segments, the extent to which certain types of messages affect them, and the types of spokespeople to whom they typically respond well.

2. Communication effects. Several research models are available through which marketers can predict the likely responses of targeted audiences to specific messages. These include the AIDA model, the Lavidge and Steiner model, and the comprehensive integrated information-response model. By understanding the likely outcomes of different types of messages, advertisers can select strategies to stimulate desired responses.

3. Source factors. Marketers are very careful in selecting the spokesperson for a message, paying special attention to such influential factors as source credibility, source attractiveness, and source power.

4. Message form. Message tone, message context, and message execution are the three elements of message form. The tone can be factual, appealing to the consumer's cognitive processes, or emotional, appealing to such feelings as fear, humor, or sex. The context is the environment in which the message is communicated—the locale, the use of music or sound effects. The execution involves myriad tactics, from the use of implicit or explicit conclusions, to self-referencing, to factual or evaluative information, to comparative information, to support evidence, to mystery.

5. Media factors. Finally, the marketer has to determine the most effective channels to carry the message. To do so, it is necessary to profile the media habits of the target consumers. By figuring out the consumers' media habits, the marketer places the message in channels to reach them in the most cost-efficient and effective manner possible. To do so, the marketer makes a series of media choices, all of which are aided by consumer research: selecting media categories and subcategories, media vehicles, media frequency, and media size or duration.

Key Terms

comparative message (p. 328)
consumer involvement (p. 328)
cost per thousand (CPM) (p. 334)
distraction (p. 321)
editorial content (p. 334)
ego-focused emotional appeals (p. 325)
elaboration likelihood (p. 320)
emotional appeal (p. 323)
extended dual mediation model (p. 315)
factual versus emotional appeals (p. 320)
factual versus evaluative information (p. 328)
fear appeal (p. 323)
frequency (p. 334)
hierarchy of effects (p. 310)
humor appeal (p. 324)

identification with actual self (p. 317)
identification with ideal self (p. 318)
implicit versus explicit conclusion (p. 327)
integrated information-response model
 (p. 312)
message evidence (p. 330)
message execution (p. 327)
message narrative (p. 331)
message pace (p. 322)
message relevance (p. 321)
message size or duration (p. 335)
message tone (p. 320)
mystery advertising (p. 330)
other-focused appeals (p. 326)
perceived concern (p. 319)

perceived control (p. 319)
perceived scrutiny (p. 319)
priming (p. 322)
product familiarity (p. 322)
purchase responsibility (p. 321)
reach (p. 334)
self-reference (p. 328)
sex appeal (p. 324)
source attractiveness (p. 317)
source congruity (p. 319)
source credibility (p. 316)
source power (p. 319)
subtle persuasion (p. 328)

Review Questions

Note: You can find the correct answers to these questions by taking the quiz and then submitting your answers in the Online Edition. The program will automatically score your submission. If you miss a question, the program will provide the correct answer, a rationale for the answer, and the section number in the chapter where the topic is discussed.

1. Message content cannot be determined without a detailed profile of the
   a. media source.
   b. targeted market.
   c. media manager.
   d. subcultures.

2. After awareness and acceptance, the marketer builds brand
   a. preference.
   b. insistence.
   c. loyalty.
   d. purchase.

3. The integrated information-response model combines information from marketing communications with information from direct product
   a. substitutes.
   b. users.
   c. intentions.
   d. experience.

4. The extended dual mediation model posits that the audience reacts to an ad by experiencing
   a. a response.
   b. a thought process.
   c. an emotion.
   d. an action.

5. The power of a source depends on three factors: perceived scrutiny, perceived control, and perceived
   a. concern.
   b. authority.
   c. credibility.
   d. knowledge.

6. Recent research has shown that source congruity plays a more important role in advertising persuasion when consumers are likely to
   a. try the product.
   b. compare with competitive products.
   c. believe it is credible.
   d. elaborate on the advertised product.

7. Two conditions affect elaboration likelihood—motivation and
   a. knowledge.
   b. ability.
   c. prior usage.
   d. brand preference.

8. Print media generally allow more time for the consumer to process factual messages than do television and radio. We call this message
   a. cognition.
   b. appeals.
   c. pace.
   d. relevance.

9. Each media category is made up of several
   a. subcategories.
   b. forms.
   c. criteria.
   d. media sources.

10. In evaluating specific media vehicles, marketers use reach, editorial content, and
    a. discounts.
    b. seasonal availability.
    c. cost per thousand or CPM.
    d. cost per hundred or CPH.

Team Talk

1. Make a list of all the ads you see in one day. Be as thorough as you can. (Warning: This can be exhausting!) For each item, be prepared to explain whether you are an appropriate target audience for the message.

2. What does awareness mean as an outcome of an advertising campaign for Levi's jeans? What if the outcomes were to be acceptance or preference?

3. If you were working on a very established brand like Tide, how would you use the integrated information-response model to set the communications objectives for the brand? How does your answer change if the product is changed to New Tide with baking soda?

4. Who is the most credible spokesperson you've seen on television in the past month? Who is the least credible? Defend your choices.

5. Think of an instance in which your consumer choice was influenced by source power. Do you think this factor affects more business purchases or more consumer purchases? Why?

6. Consider the element of responsibility in the elaboration likelihood model. How has responsibility changed a recent buying decision you have made?

7. You are creating a campaign for Royal Caribbean Cruises. What media vehicles would you choose? Explain your decision with reference to your target market, positioning, and communication objectives.

Workshops

Research Workshop

Background

The objective of this workshop is to uncover preferred media choices for marketing a movie. You are the West Coast research director of Paragon Pictures. You are assigned to develop testing materials and instruments that can be applied to the college student market.

Methodology

Because Paragon prefers inexpensive campaigns that generate a lot of word-of-mouth communication, conduct a focus group of five fellow students about their impressions of a current movie playing near campus. Probe for their sources of information. Which have the most effective reach? Which have the most authority?

To the Marketplace

Write a one-page report on the focus group results, recommending the most cost-effective promotional methods for Paragon to use for the film you selected.

Creative Workshop

Background

The objective of this workshop is to consider message effect in designing an ad campaign. As marketing director for Educational Systems Corporation, you are responsible for providing supporting materials for a sales force that visits elementary, junior high, and high school teachers to sell audiovisual materials such as films, cassettes, and filmstrips.

Methodology

Because there are so many teachers in the country and you have so few sales representatives, you consider launching the company's first-ever advertising campaign to support the sales effort. You get approval to run a series of three full-page ads in a national teachers' magazine. Given the type of sales being made, you decide to emphasize source credibility and consumer responsibility in your message.

To the Marketplace

Create mock-ups for the three print ads that will run in the teachers' magazine.

Managerial Workshop

Background

The objective of this workshop is to practice audience targeting and media selection. You are the owner/manager of a domestic-help service in Los Angeles that supplies weekly cleaning people, special help for parties, and live-in domestic servants. You are in a position to expand your market base.

Methodology

Define the characteristics of the target market and then devise a promotional scheme to reach them. Your tactics might include advertising in local papers, introductory price reductions on selected services, flier distribution in selected neighborhoods or apartment buildings, or a cooperative venture with a fellow entrepreneur, such as a caterer or florist who wants to reach approximately the same customers.

To the Marketplace

Working with a limited budget, plan a promotion that will reach potential clients and let them know about the superior quality of your services.

Notes

1. David Luna and Laura A. Peracchio, "Moderators of Language Effects in Advertising to Bilinguals: A Psycholinguistic Approach," *Journal of Consumer Research,* Vol. 28 (September 2001), pp. 284–295.

2. Ivan L. Preston and Esther Thomson, "The Expanded Association Model: Keeping the Hierarchy Concept Alive," *Journal of Advertising Research,* Vol. 24 (February/March 1984), p. 29.

3. Preston and Thomson, "The Expanded Association Model," p. 60.

4. Arch G. Woodside and Elizabeth J. Wilson, "Effects of Consumer Awareness of Brand Advertising on Preference," *Journal of Advertising Research,* Vol. 25 (August/September, 1985), pp. 41–48; Wayne D. Hoyer and Stephen P. Brown, "Effects of Brand Awareness on Choice for a Common Repeat Purchase Product," *Journal of Consumer Research,* Vol. 17 (1990), pp. 141–148; Emma K. Macdonald and Byron M. Sharp, "Brand Awareness Effects on Consumer Decision Making for a Common, Repeat Purchase Product," *Journal of Business Research,* Vol. 48 (April 2000), pp. 5–15.

5. Brad Sagarin, Serna Sherman, Robert Cialdini, and William Rice, "Dispelling the Illusion of Invulnerability: The Motivations and Mechanisms of Resistance to Persuasion," *Journal of Personality and Social Psychology,* Vol. 83, No. 3 (2002), pp. 526–541.

6. Richard J. Lutz, "Affective and Cognitive Antecedents of Attitude Toward the Ad: A Conceptual Framework," in *Psychological Processes and Advertising Effects,* Linda Alwitt and Andrew Mitchell, eds., Erlbaum, Hillsdale, NJ. 1985, pp. 45–63; Stephen P. Brown and Douglas M. Stayman, "Antecedents and Consequences of Attitude Toward the Ad: A Meta-Analysis," *Journal of Consumer Research,* Vol. 19 (June 1992), pp. 34–51.

7. Keith S. Coutler and Girish Punj, "Influence of Viewing Context on the Determinants of Attitude toward the Ad and the Brand," *Journal of Business Research,* Vol. 45, (May 1999), pp. 47–58.

8. Brian Sternthal, Lynn Phillips, and Ruby Dholakia, "The Persuasive Effect of Source Credibility: A Situational Analysis," *Public Opinion Quarterly,* Vol. 42 (Fall 1978), pp. 285–314; Brian Sternthal, Ruby Dholakia, and Clark Leavitt, "The Persuasive Effects of Source Credibility: Tests of Cognitive Responses," *Journal of Consumer Research,* Vol. 4 (March 1978), pp. 252–260; Robert R. Harmon and Kenneth A. Coney, "The Persuasive Effects of Source Credibility in Buy and Lease Situations," *Journal of Marketing Research,* Vol. 19 (May 1982), pp. 255–260.

9. Amanda B. Bower and Stacy Landreth, "Is Beauty Best? Highly versus Normally Attractive Models in Advertising," *Journal of Advertising,* Vol. 30 (Spring 2001), pp. 1–12.

10. Marla R. Stafford, Thomas F. Stafford, and Ellen Day, "A Contingency Approach: The Effects of Spokesperson Type and Service Type on Service Advertising Perceptions," *Journal of Advertising*, Vol. 31 (Summer 2002), pp. 17–35.

11. Mary Susan Kennedy, Linda K. Ferrell, and Debbie Thorne LeClair, "Consumers' Trust of Salesperson and Manufacturer: An Empirical Study," *Journal of Business Research*, Vol. 51 (January 2001), pp. 73–86.

12. J. Mills and J. Jellison, "Effect on Opinion Change of Similarity Between Communication and the Audience He Addresses," *Journal of Personality and Social Psychology*, Vol. 9 (1969), pp. 153–156; Arch G. Woodside and J. William Davenport, Jr., "The Effect of Salesman Similarity and Expertise on Consumer Purchasing Behavior" *Journal of Marketing Research*, Vol. 11 (May 1974), pp. 198–202.

13. John C. Mowen and Stephen W. Brown, "On Explaining and Predicting the Effectiveness of Celebrity Endorsers," in Kent B. Monroe, ed., *Advances in Consumer Research*, Vol. 8 (Ann Arbor, MI: Association for Consumer Research, 1981), pp. 437–441.

14. Jane Sasseem, "Consumer Sports, Jocks Run Faster, Jump Higher, and Sell Better," *Madison Avenue* (January 1984), pp. 92–98; David Ogilvy and Joel Raphaelson, "Research on Advertising Techniques That Work—and Don't Work," *Harvard Business Review*, Vol. 60 (July/August 1982), pp. 14–15; Strafford P. Sherman, "When You Wish Upon a Star," *Fortune* (August 19, 1985), pp. 66–73; "Business Celebrities," *Business Week* (June 23, 1986), pp. 100–107.

15. Robert W. Chestnut, C. C. LaChance, and A. Lubitz, "The Decorative Female Model: Sexual Stimuli and the Recognition of the Advertisements," *Journal of Advertising*, Vol. 6 (Fall 1977), pp. 11–14; Leonard N. Reid and Lawrence C. Soley, "Decorative Models and Readership of Magazine Ads," *Journal of Advertising Research*, Vol. 23 (April/May 1983), pp. 27–34; W. B. Joseph, "The Credibility of Physically Attractive Communicators," *Journal of Advertising*, Vol. 11 (1982), pp. 13–23; M. J. Baker and Gilbert A. Churchill, Jr., "The Impact of Physically Attractive Models on Advertising Evaluations," *Journal of Marketing Research*, Vol. 14 (November 1977), pp. 538–555.

16. Herbert C. Kelman, "Processes of Opinion Change," *Public Opinion Quarterly*, Vol. 25 (Spring 1961), pp. 57–78.

17. "Why P&G Wants a Mellower Image," *Business Week* (June 7, 1982), p. 60.

18. M. A. Kamins, "An Investigation into the 'Match-up Hypothesis' in Celebrity Advertising: When Beauty May Be Skin Deep," *Journal of Advertising*, Vol. 19 (1990), pp. 4–13.

19. Amna Kirmani and Baba Shiv, "Effects of Source Congruity on Brand Attitudes and Beliefs: The Moderating Role of Issue-Relevant Elaboration," *Journal of Consumer Psychology*, Vol. 7, No. 1 (1998), pp. 25–47.

20. Thomas W. Whipple and Mary K. McManamon, "Implications of Using Male and Female Voices in Commercials: An Exploratory Study," *Journal of Advertising*, Vol. 31 (Summer 2002), pp. 79–91.

21. Richard E. Petty, John T. Cacioppo, and David Schumann, "Central and Peripheral Routes to Advertising Effectiveness: The Moderating Role of Involvement," *Journal of Consumer Research*, Vol. 10 (1983), pp. 135–146; Scott B. MacKenzie and Richard A. Spreng, "How Does Motivation Moderate the Impact of Central and Peripheral Processing on Brand Attitudes and Intentions," *Journal of Consumer Research*, Vol. 18 (March 1992), pp. 519–529; J. Craig Andrews and Terence A. Shimp, "Effects of Involvement, Argument Strength, and Source Characteristics on Central and Peripheral Processing of Advertising," *Psychology and Marketing*, Vol. 7 (Fall 1990), pp. 197–214; Paul W. Miniard, Deepak Sirdeshmukh, and Daniel E. Innis, "Peripheral Persuasion and Brand Choice," *Journal of Consumer Research*, Vol. 19 (September 1992), pp. 226–239; Michael J. Dotson and Eva M. Hyatt, "Religious Symbols as Peripheral Cues in Advertising: A Replication of the Elaboration Likelihood Model," *Journal of Business Research*, Vol. 48 (April 2000), pp. 63–68.

22. S. Shyam Sundar and Sriram Kalyanaraman, "Arousal, Memory, and Impression-Formation Effects of Animation Speed in Web Advertising," *Journal of Advertising*, Vol. 33 (Spring 2004), pp. 7–17.

23. Naomi Mandel and Eric J. Johnson, "When Web Pages Influence Choice: Effects of Visual Primes on Experts and Novices," *Journal of Consumer Research*, Vol. 29 (September 2002), pp. 235–245.

24. Michael L. Ray and William L. Wilkie, "Fear: The Potential of an Appeal Neglected by Marketing," *Journal of Marketing*, Vol. 34 (January 1970), pp. 54–62.

25. Ibid.

26. Cornelia Pechmann, Gung zhi Zhao, Marvin E. Goldberg, and Ellen Thomas Reibling, "What to Convey in Antismoking Advertisements for Adolescents: The Use of Protection Motivation Theory to Identify Effective Message Themes," *Journal of Marketing*, Vol. 67 (April 2003), pp. 1–18.

27. Ray and Wilkie, "Fear: The Potential of an Appeal."

28. D. Richmond and T. P. Hartman, "Sex Appeal in Advertising," *Journal of Advertising Research*, Vol. 22, No. 5 (1982), pp. 53–61.

29. A. E. Courtney and T. W. Whipple, *Sex Stereotyping in Advertising: An Annotated Bibliography*. (Cambridge, MA: Marketing Science Institute, Research Program, 1980).

30. Lawrence Soley and Gary Kurzbard, "Sex in Advertising: A Comparison of 1964 and 1984 Magazine Advertisements," *Journal of Advertising*, Vol. 15, No. 3 (1986), pp. 46–54.

31. Major Steadman, "How Sexy Illustrations Affect Brand Recall," *Journal of Advertising*, Vol. 9, No. 1 (Winter 1980), pp. 15–19.

32. Bruce J. Morrison and Richard C. Sherman, "Who Responds to Sex in Advertising?" *Journal of Advertising Research*, Vol. 12, No. 2 (1972), pp. 15–19. Also see Deborah K. Johnson and Kay Satow, "Consumers' Reactions to Sex in Commercials," in H. Keith Hunt, ed., *Advances in Consumer Research*, Vol. V (Ann Arbor, MI: Association for Consumer Research, 1978), pp. 411–414.

33. Jennifer L. Aakers and Patti Williams, "Empathy versus Pride: The Influence of Emotional Appeals Across Cultures," *Journal of Consumer Research*, Vol. 25 (December 1998), pp. 241–261.

34. Gerald J. Gorn, "The Effects of Music in Advertising on Choice Behavior: A Classical Conditioning Approach," *Journal of Marketing*, Vol. 46 (Winter 1982), pp. 94–101.

35. Frank R. Kardes, "Spontaneous Inference Processes in Advertising: The Effects of Conclusion Omission and Involvement on Persuasion," *Journal of Consumer Research*, Vol. 15 (September 1988), pp. 225–234.

36. Alan G. Sawyer and Daniel J. Howard, "Effects of Omitting Conclusions in Advertisements to Involved and Uninvolved Audiences," *Journal of Marketing Research*, Vol. 28 (November 1991), pp. 467–474; Michael Ahearne, Thomas Gruen, and M. Kim Saxton, "When the Product is Complex, Does the Advertisement's Conclusion Matter?" *Journal of Business Research*, Vol. 48 (April 2000), pp. 55–62.

37. P. Brown, J. M. Canaan, and G. R. Potts, "The Self-Reference Effect with Imagery Encoding," *Journal of Personality and Social Psychology*, Vol. 51 (1986), pp. 897–906; Kathleen Debevec and Jean B. Romeo, "Self-Referent Processing in Perceptions of Verbal and Visual Commercial Information," *Journal of Consumer Psychology*, Vol. 1 (1992); pp. 83–102.

38. Morris B. Holbrook, "Beyond Attitude Structure: Toward the Informational Determinants of Attitude," *Journal of Marketing Research*, Vol. 15 (November 1971), pp. 545–556.

39. Julie A. Edell and Richard Staelin, "The Information Processing of Pictures in Print Advertisement," *Journal of Consumer Research*, Vol. 10, No. 1 (June 1983), pp. 45–61.

40. Terence A. Shimp and Ivan L. Preston, "Deceptive and Nondeceptive Consequences of Evaluative Advertising," *Journal of Marketing*, Vol. 45, No. 1 (Winter 1981), pp. 22–32.

41. Easwar S. Iyer, "The Influence of Verbal Content and Relative Newness on Effectiveness of Comparative Advertising," *Journal of Advertising*, Vol. 17, No. 3 (1988), pp. 15–21.

42. See the following references: George F. Belch, "An Examination of Comparative and Noncomparative Television Commercials: The Effects of Claim Variation and Repetition on Cognitive Response and Message Acceptance," *Journal of Marketing Research*, Vol. 18, No. 3 (1981), pp. 33–49; William R. Swinyard, "The Interaction Between Comparative Advertising and Copy Claim Variation," *Journal of Marketing Research*, Vol. 18, No. 2 (1981), pp. 175–186.

43. Michael Etger and Stephen Goodwin (1982), "One-Sided Versus Two-Sided Comparative Message Appeals for New Introductions," *Journal of Consumer Research*, Vol. 8 (March 1982), pp. 460–465.

44. Easwar S. Iyer, "The Influence of Verbal Content and Relative Newness on the Effectiveness of Comparative Advertising."

45. Ibid.

46. Jerry B. Gottlieb and Dan Sarel, "Comparative Advertising Effectiveness: The Role of Involvement and Source Credibility," *Journal of Advertising*, Vol. 20, No. 1 (1991), pp. 38–45.

47. Munch, Boller, & Swasy, "The Effect of Argument Structure."

48. Russell H. Fazio, Paul M. Herr, and Martha C. Powell, "On the Development and Strength of Category-Brand Associations in Memory: The Case of Mystery Ads," *Journal of Consumer Psychology*, Vol. 1 (1992), pp. 1–13.

49. Rashmi Adaval and Robert S. Wyer, Jr., "The Role of Narratives in Consumer Information Processing," *Journal of Consumer Psychology*, Vol. 7, No. 3 (1998), pp. 207–245.

50. Jesse E. Teel, William O. Bearden, and Richard M. Durand, "Psychographics of Radio and Television Audiences," *Journal of Advertising Research*, Vol. 19, No. 2 (April 1979), pp. 53–56.

51. Douglas J. Tigert, "Are Television Audiences Really Different?" Paper presented at the 54th International Marketing Congress, American Marketing Association, San Francisco, April 1971.

52. Philip M. Napoli, "The Unpredictable Audience: An Exploratory Analysis of Forecasting Error for New Prime Time Network Television Programs," *Journal of Advertising*, Vol. 30 (Summer 2001), pp. 53–60.

53. George E. Belch and Michael A. Belch, *Introduction to Advertising and Promotion*, 3rd ed. (Chicago, IL: Richard D. Irwin, 1995), p. 338.

54. Michael J. Naples, *Effective Frequency: The Relationship Between Frequency and Advertising Effectiveness* (New York: Association of National Advertisers, 1979), p. 79; Herbert E. Krugman, "What Makes Advertising Effective?" *Harvard Business Review*, Vol. 53 (March/April 1975), pp. 96–103.

55. David A. Aaker, Rajeev Batra, and John G. Myers, *Advertising Management*, 4th ed. (Englewood Cliffs, NJ: Prentice-Hall 1971), pp. 488–490.

56. Margaret C. Campbell and Kevin L. Keller, "Brand Familiarity and Advertising Repetition Effects," *Journal of Consumer Research*, Vol. 30 (September 2003), pp. 292–304.

57. Julian L. Simon, "The General Pattern of Response to Different Amounts of Advertising," in *The Management of Advertising* (Englewood Cliffs, NJ: Prentice-Hall, 1971).

58. Leo Bogart and Charles Lehman, "The Case of the 30-Second Commercial," *Journal of Advertising Research*, Vol. 23, No. 1 (February/March 1983), pp. 11–19.

59. Rik Pieters and Michel Wedel, "Attention Capture and Transfer in Advertising: Brand, Pictorial, and Text-Size Effects," *Journal of Marketing*, Vol. 68 (April 2004), pp. 36–50.

Part

4

Sociological Influences on Consumer Decision Making

Humans are to a great extent "social animals." Being such, we are sensitive to the values, behaviors, and beliefs of the people around us. It follows that our behavior as consumers is affected. There are levels of influence. That of which we are least aware, which is more subtle and yet is in almost every corner of our lives and therefore more pervasive, is *culture.* And as we move across subculture/co-culture, social class, reference groups, and family/households, the level of influence seems to become both less subtle and less pervasive—more "in your face."

In the case of culture, it is often not until we travel to another nation that "culture shock" calls us to the reality of the subtlety and pervasiveness of its influence. Social influence is in a narrower corner of your life and very apparent at the family or household level, which are closest to you. Parents, other family members, and those to whom you are not related but share living space attempt to shape you from the time of birth throughout your life, depending on your relationships with them. The amount of influence felt and its form will vary from person to person and situation to situation. In the largest sense, everyone is part of a culture.

As people migrate to other nations, cultures migrate, too, and become subcultures/co-cultures, flavoring the fabric of their new land. Examples such as Chinese and Indian enclaves can be found across the globe. Consumers also are part of subcultures/ co-cultures based on ethnic background, national origin, religion, age, or some other common life factor. Social class structures are found to some extent in all nations. Some class groups are quite similar across continents, as with the upper-middle classes of the Americas, Europe, and Asia. Subcultural/co-cultural groups also have their own social class system at work in their lives. We are also influenced at work, at play, and in social settings by reference groups. These are groups to which we belong or that we aspire to join. Professional, neighborhood, social, hobby, political, or activity groups are examples. Each of these levels of social influence from culture to family/household will be explored in turn over the next five chapters.

The managers of today and tomorrow will have to become increasingly aware of the changing global picture, whether they wish to export or import goods or services. Personal education on the differences and similarities among cultures of interest and a willingness to interact and partner with individuals in other nations will be essential for successful delivery of the benefits being sought overseas and across borders. And the same will be true when searching for suppliers of goods and services to be imported.

We'll begin the sociological influences discussion with a look at culture in Chapters 11 and 12. In Chapter 11, cultural perspectives, including the definition and the nature of an array of cultural components, will be presented. In Chapter 12, cultural generalizations, including cross-cultural perspectives and a look at the American culture, will be explored.

Chapter 13 is devoted to subcultural, sometimes called co-cultural, influences on consumer behavior in the marketplace. In Chapter 14 we explore the influences of social class and reference groups, and Chapter 15 is concerned with household and family influences.

Cultural Influences: Perspectives

11

It's International Culture Awareness Week on campus, and Don and Arla are taking part in a cross-cultural experience evening. They are to play a young married couple in Xlavia. Sent to separate rooms to change, they quickly read up on country customs, from dress to gender roles to family values to religious beliefs to shopping practices.

Arla, covered head to toe in an all-black, loose-fitting garment, enters a mock marketplace. Don appears dressed as usual, in slacks and a short-sleeved sport shirt. Looking at each other, they already feel out of touch. Don joins the men, leaving Arla with the other women to take care of the shopping. Arla bargains with sellers for every purchase. Cheaper brands tend to sell out fast, so it's important to be first in line. Even so, the older women are always waited on, while the younger women, like Arla, must wait patiently. Men are rarely seen in the market, unless the purchase is out of the ordinary, when it is the man who decides what to buy and how much to spend.

The experiences of Don and Arla during International Culture Awareness Week raise interesting questions not only about the culture they explored but also about their own environment. In this chapter, we'll look at the influence of culture not only on our buying decisions, but on the norms, customs, mores, conventions, sanctions, values, beliefs, and rituals that lead to those decisions. Cultural influences are with us in what we say, do, think, believe, and even dream. Yet we are rarely aware that they even exist. Like the water through which a fish swims, culture is essential for survival, yet most of the time we don't even perceive that we are in its midst.

11-1 Definition of Culture

Culture is defined as patterns of values, beliefs, and learned behavior that are held in common and transmitted by the members of any given society.[1] Notice that these are organized or regularized approaches to the way all or a major share of the people think about life issues and act within their society. And this is passed on over time in both formal and informal ways within the culture. It may be seen as some sort of cognitive map that we use to relate to our environment and to other people within it. Each culture has its own map that helps its members interpret the world around them.

Our native culture is the most pervasive, yet most subtle, influence on our behavior as consumers. It's in almost every corner of our lives, and yet we are the least aware of it as a level of social influence. Hence, we are not always conscious of the specific ways in which it affects our lives. In fact, that is why when you travel to another country for the first time you may experience "culture shock," those most disturbing senses of anxiety, displacement, and possibly fear. Those of you reading this text and studying in a land not your own have most likely felt this or are feeling this right now. In sum, culture is a powerful force in the lives of people in all nations, and it affects their daily decisions both in and out of the marketplace.

Understanding culture is important in marketing internationally. Culture influences the benefits sought and, therefore, the products and services needed to deliver these benefits. Because of the differences in culture, those goods and services needed in one society may be of little or no value in another. The daily behaviors and the lifestyles of consumers, prescribed by the culture, are what shape benefits sought. In Los Angeles and Chicago, for example, people tend to live in the suburbs and come to the city by car. The needs are for automobiles, gasoline, highways, and parking facilities. In London, where using public transportation is the norm, Underground ("Tube") stations, busses, taxis, and related facilities are needed. On the waterways of Venice, boats and bridges help people get around, and in Ho Chi Minh City, Vietnam, commuters rely heavily on bicycles and motor scooters. Not just consumer needs but also their preferences, even for the most basic products, vary widely among cultures. Colgate-Palmolive Company offers its bath and hand soaps in seven different fragrances and three different shapes across the 43 countries in which they are sold.[2] *Cosmopolitan* magazine is printed in about 30 international editions with varying editorial content in about one dozen languages.[3] Buying a car in one culture may differ from the same experience in another. In the United States, we typically visit dealerships and negotiate the price with the sellers, and we are on the lookout for special sales. In Germany, this type of deal shopping is not possible. Price reductions are allowed by the government only twice a year. These price cuts cannot exceed three percent.[4] Because of the regulations within the culture, the car buying/selling experience is quite different there. In sum, both marketing strategies and integrated marketing communications strategies must be tailored to each country in which a marketer is active.[5] Having said this, let's return to a look at the nature of culture.

11-2 Nature of Culture—Components

Though different cultures reveal a broad spectrum of diversity in what each expects of its members, all have the same central purpose: They exist to meet the common needs of the people.[6] Within every culture, survival of the group is the top priority. The collective good is far more important than the individual's. Hence, as a culture evolves it develops means of protecting the group. Social structures, formal laws, common language, myths, customs, rituals, and symbols are examples of those things that aim to ensure the culture's continued existence and its progress. In the same way, norms of behavior are established, and those who comply are rewarded while those who do not are punished through various types of sanctions. Values also are adopted over time that act as underpinnings for the culture. Exhibit 11-1 is a summary of these components.

11-2a Norms

All societal units establish rules of behavior for members. These rules, called norms, provide guidance regarding acceptable and unacceptable behavior. Likely these norms are determined by the majority of the group and ensure a certain stability and preservation of its existence.[7] There are exceptions to this, where power in a culture may be in the hands of a few and these people dictate how the culture is to function and what norms are to be followed. Norms may be classified as either enacted or crescive.[8] **Enacted norms** may be viewed as explicit rules, easily recognized by people inside and outside of the social unit. In some cases, these enacted norms are laws. For example, in Malta divorce is against the law. This enacted norm stems from the strength of the Roman Catholic Church in the society. In Sweden, divorce is more acceptable to the culture and has legal standing. **Crescive norms** are learned and practiced by members of a social unit but may not be readily recognized by nonmembers. Cultural members formally and informally learn what are called

► **culture** (see p. 344) Patterns of values, beliefs, and learned behavior that are held in common and transmitted by the members of any given society.

F A Q

What is culture shock?

E x h i b i t 11-1

Components of Culture

Norms

Customs

Mores

Conventions

Sanctions

Values

Beliefs
- Religion
- Myths

Rituals

► **enacted norms** Norms that may be viewed as explicit rules, easily recognized by people inside and outside of the social unit.

► **crescive norms** Norms that are learned and practiced by members of a social unit but that nonmembers may not readily recognize.

customs Behaviors that have lasted over time and are often passed down in the family setting. Examples are gender roles and special family celebrations and traditions.

mores A set of standards for values and behaviors that are considered "morally right."

conventions Those practices tied to the conduct of everyday life in various settings in a culture.

sanctions A negative action taken by members of the culture when a person acts contrary to norms, mores, customs, or conventions.

"customs," "mores," and "conventions" through their socialization into the society. (A detailed discussion on socialization is offered in section 11-3c.) Hence, people "know" what is acceptable and unacceptable and take for granted that others within the society do also.

11-2b Customs

Customs are behaviors that have lasted over time and are often passed down in the family setting. Gender roles, holiday or religious celebrations, and the types of ceremonies carried out within a society are examples. Examples of occasions celebrated with ceremonies would include birth, coming-of-age, marriage, and burial/cremation.

11-2c Mores

The **mores,** pronounced "more-ays," of a culture most often are tied to the moral standards of a culture. Societies have practices, commonly referred to as "taboos," that are forbidden among its members. Marriage to close family members is forbidden in many nations today, including the United States. Yet, in the nineteenth century, marriages within the royal family in the Hawaiian Islands were acceptable. The members of the culture set the standards for what is "morally right" and expect compliance. Violation may lead to sanctions by other members of the society.

The marketplace also brings new challenges in ethical decision making. As we find ourselves increasingly trading in a multicultural world of marketing, the compatibility of ethical values across borders is becoming more important. This means that marketers must ask what the role of culture is in influencing individual and organizational ethical decision-making practices. Religion can enter the picture in that trading with a person of the same religion or whose country is dominantly of the same religion requires certain ethical practices while trading with a person not of the same religion or from a country not dominated by the same religion is dealt with by using a different set of ethical standards. Certain general practices such as payment of "bribes" or "influence money or gifts" are common in many countries but are seen as unethical (also illegal) in other countries. Hence marketers are faced with choosing to trade or not based on their moral perceptions, evaluating the situation, making judgments as to what should or should not be done, determining their intention to behave, their actual behavior, and finally evaluating the consequences of their behavior.[9] Do you believe that "when in Rome do as the Romans do" is the correct ethical approach, or do you feel that you should not trade or market when your personal ethical standards will be breached?

11-2d Conventions

Those practices tied to the conduct of everyday life in various settings are **conventions.** Foods to be served in certain settings, appropriate clothing to be worn, the way a house should be furnished and how the grounds are to appear, how to entertain guests and family, and how respect is shown within a family or in business and other settings are typical areas where conventions are needed for the culture to function smoothly. For example, in Japan, a younger person is to show respect to one who is older. Yet, in the buyer-seller relationship in business, the seller must always show respect to the buyer, even if the seller is older. Conventions have been established for business gift giving. Exhibit 11-2 contains some examples of how this works in different cultures.

Check out International Marketplace 11-1 to better understand how Chinese consumers operate in their native land.

11-2e Sanctions

When members of a culture do not conform to the norms, customs, mores, or conventions of the society, they may be "sanctioned." **Sanctions** are negative actions on the parts of members of the culture and may be in the form of avoidance, shunning, or banning, where individuals are not allowed to participate in various activities. For example, an athlete could be banned from athletic competition because of the use of a performance-enhancing drug

Business Gift Giving around the Globe

Europe

Letter openers, scissors, and knives are symbols of the cutting of relationships; hence, they are considered unacceptable. Gourmet food items, quality chocolates, good wines, and other alcoholic beverages are fine choices. The French appreciate art prints, books, and recorded music. Always enclose a handwritten note on a blank card, never your business card.

Latin America

Soccer-related gifts are good choices, as are those that may be used by the family. Family orientation is very strong. Baseball memorabilia are also good choices. If you wish to give a leather gift, only offer the highest quality, because some of the world's best leather comes from Brazil, Argentina, and Uruguay. Avoid knives and related cutting items for the same reasons as in Europe. Good-quality corporate gifts are on target, but avoid those that imply U.S. superiority, such as technological gadgets. Remember, business relationships are seen as personal relationships.

China, Taiwan, Hong Kong, Korea, and Singapore

Gifts are to be from your company to the recipient's company and should be offered to the lead person. Expect your gift to be turned down once or twice out of politeness. You should also decline any gift offered once and then accept with thanks. Small gifts are exchanged at the first meeting to signify the hope that the relationship will last. Gifts tied to the occasion—from your hometown, state or country, or the business you work for— are highly regarded. Always wrap gifts; however, combinations of black and white for gifts or wrapping are not appropriate. In China, wrapping with red paper means good luck. Never use red ink, because funeral notices are written using this color. Never give foreign currency or commemorative coins. Because the wolf symbolizes cruelty and greed, never give gifts with a wolf on them. Clocks are thought to predict death—so don't give them either. In Hong Kong, the numbers eight and nine are positive because they are associated with "prosperity" and "eternity," respectively. Three is also a lucky number. There is a "gift continuum" in Hong Kong ranging from people who have the most intimate relationships with the giver, called "yihhei," to second-tier friends' bonds, named "renqing." Additionally, in the business context, "guanxi" ties, or networks of connections, businesses, and influencers, affect gift giving. The distinction between insiders and outsiders is important, because access to goods, services, and people is often blocked to outsiders. Proper gift giving helps move people from being outsiders to being insiders. The whole point of a gift relationship in Hong Kong is to eventually balance social relationships, show sentiment, and maintain "face."

Japan

Business gifts are often exchanged at the first meeting, but allow the other person to start the giving. Your gift should be given in private unless you have one for everyone present. The gift may not be opened in front of you. If you are asked to open a gift, do so. Wrapping is very important in Japan, almost an art form. If you wrap the item yourself, never use ribbons or bows. The color and texture of the wrapping paper can tell the type and value of the gift. Avoid brightly colored paper. Purchase tinted rice paper in the country, and wrap the gift there. Customs agents will unwrap all packages as you enter the country. Remember to include a personal note on a plain card with the gift. Designer-brand crystal, fountain pens, clothing accessories, and the like are good choices. Pens are always appreciated. Fountain pens with black ink, never blue ink, in plastic or lacquer finishes are preferred.

Australia

Australia is a place where most Americans will likely feel at home. The people are quite informal and not impressed with shows of power or rank. They do not typically give gifts in business settings. However, as in most cultures, if you are invited to a dinner in a home, bring a small gift. Chocolates, wine, flowers, folk art from home, or an illustrated book from your home area or state are good choices. If you wish to give preserved food, it must be in a bottle or can because if it is not Australian, customs will not allow it into the country.

Source: Do's and Taboos around the World, A Guide to International Behavior, 2nd ed. (New York: John Wiley and Sons, 1990); Joy Aanamma, "Gift Giving in Hong Kong and the Continuum of Social Ties," *Journal of Consumer Research,* Vol. 28 (September 2001), pp. 239–256.

International *Marketplace 11-1*

Marketing to China's Consumers the *Guo Qing* Way

For much of the Western world, consumption is a matter of routine. But for the Chinese, a quarter of the world's population, it is a novel, pleasurable, and important part of the day. About 80 percent of income is spent pursuing it. Those who wish to share in the China market, however, may do so only by adapting to *guo qing*, the Chinese way. A Communist Party directive makes this clear: "Western cultures and ideas should be adopted only if they fit *guo qing*. Good ideas applicable in China should be promoted; corrupted and inapplicable ideas should be discarded." What is "politically correct" in China opens doors, what is not closes them.

Confucian philosophy pervades Chinese culture and is a part of *guo qing*. Its characteristics include semi-isolation, self-sufficiency, and a strong bias toward obedience and against upward feedback and horizontal learning and sharing. When communicating, Westerners careful about honoring *guo qing* are advised to use official or senior channels. In advertising, for example, the accepted media for official pronouncements—newspapers, television, and radio—are the safest choices. In less-prosperous times, Chinese consumers worked to acquire four status symbols: bicycles, watches, sewing machines, and radios. But wealth has spread, especially in the big cities. The Chinese are now saving money to purchase six *da jian*, or "big things": VCRs, televisions, washing machines, cameras, refrigerators, and electric fans.

How can Rado sell thousands of $1,000 watches in China, where per capita income hovers around $600? How can people afford a KFC fried chicken dinner costing the equivalent of a day's wages? By living in small apartments, renting for as little as $3 per month, using little heat in winter, and little hot water, Chinese families save enough to buy modest luxuries and even more expensive da jian.

Source: Philip R. Cateora, *International Marketing,* 9th ed. (Burr Ridge, IL: Richard D. Irwin, 1996), p. 261.

Tired of low quality, Chinese consumers have a high regard for Western products. Locally brewed Carlsberg beer and imported Carlsberg beer are sold side by side, but the import commands a 20 percent to 50 percent premium in price. Shoppers crowding Chinese stores are often "just looking." The Chinese saying, "Never make a purchase until you have compared in three shops," is part of *guo qing*. Browsing and window-shopping are favorite weekend pastimes, and the Beijing Lufthansa Shopping Center, a department store, has recorded 120,000 visitors in a single day.

Source: Rick Yan, "To Reach China's Consumers, Adapt to *Guo Qing,*" *Harvard Business Review,* Vol. 72 (September–October 1994), pp. 66–74.

F A Q

In your culture, are people sanctioned for what they wear?

---

instrumental values
Personal values that are enduring beliefs that specific modes of conduct or end-states of existence are preferred to other specific modes of conduct or end-states. Specific modes of conduct might be ambition, broad-mindedness, capability, cheerfulness, cleanliness, or helpfulness, among others.

found to be morally unacceptable. Or, a person not of the dominant religion in a country could be treated unfairly in the marketplace because he or she is not "of the faith." Cultures deal with nonconformists in a variety of ways.

11-2f Values

In Chapter 6 (section 6-1), we discussed personal values. Such values have been defined as enduring beliefs that specific modes of conduct or end-states of existence are preferred to other specific modes of conduct or end-states.[10] Hence, we see individuals behaving in such a way as to help them attain a certain characteristic (e.g., wisdom, self-respect, or happiness) in their lives. This applies to cultures where certain behaviors of its members bring desired end results to the society at large. Modes of conduct in order to obtain certain end-states are called **instrumental values,** and the end-states toward which a person is moving are called **terminal values.**[11] One culture may place very high value on living in peace and may achieve this by being militarily stronger than others. Military preparedness as a mode of conduct is the path followed. Another country may place a similar value on living in peace but may follow the path of neutrality in all situations and not even maintain military units of any consequence.

We value the attitudes, beliefs, and behaviors of individuals based on the contributions they make to the general well-being of the culture. As an example, in the United States one hundred years ago, people placed high value on having large families and on immigration as a means of building a labor force and ensuring continued growth. Today, smaller families, emphasis on education, and conservation of resources are some of the modes of conduct carried out to strengthen the culture.

Identifying Cultural Values   What are the values that could be considered when studying a culture and comparing it to others? Two viewpoints, the Rokeach Personal Values Scale and the List of Values, were presented in Chapter 6. Review sections 6-1a and 6-1b and consider how the application of these two approaches could be used to compare culture value systems.

The Rokeach scale is useful in identifying how culturally relevant instrumental and terminal values shape demand for goods and services by nations, economic blocks of nations, and market segments within countries. Once the marketer identifies values being expressed by particular products or services or in certain situations such as shopping, it is possible to develop positioning strategies and communications messages consistent with the values. In a shopping behavior exploratory study of the Rokeach eighteen-item instrumental value list in China (Beijing and Shanghai), only ten of the values showed to be applicable.[12]

11-2g Beliefs in a Culture

What the members of a culture believe has its roots in a number of sources. Here we will explore two areas, namely religion and myth. In the case of religion, we see the origins of belief structures being tied to religious doctrines, traditions, and laws of the church. In the case of myths, these stories reflect beliefs and values and in some cases suggest their origins—and are often used to teach about these things.

Religion   Cultures are also shaped by the underlying religious philosophies of the people. There are cases where a "national religion" is recognized and impacts on the value systems, beliefs, behaviors, and even the laws. Countries such as Iran and Saudi Arabia are greatly influenced by Islamic law. We find the influence of Roman Catholic Church doctrine on the values, behaviors, and even the laws in Malta, Spain, and Italy, while in the Netherlands and Sweden very little religion-specific influence is seen. Thailand is approximately 95 percent Buddhist, and the teachings of this faith are evident throughout the culture. Some national cultures experience religious conflict, such as in Northern Ireland (Roman Catholics and Protestants), in Malaysia (Muslims and other religions), and among the emerging countries of the former Yugoslavia (Christian and Muslim).

What products and services are acceptable within the culture, how they are to be positioned, to whom they should be targeted, and what sorts of promotional communications are acceptable all must be understood by those who wish to market there. Food, clothing, entertainment (e.g., books, movies, videos, music, theater, dance), appliances, farm machinery, and other product or service classes can be affected. Understanding how religion does or does not impact on the marketplace is an essential part of success.

Myths   A **myth** is a story or fable that reflects important values shared by members of a culture, and it is used to teach one or more of these values. Usually the stories have a person, an idea, or an event as their central focus and may contain recognizable symbols. Some time after the temple at Stonehenge on the Salisbury Plain in England was constructed, one of the myths that spread was that a tribe of giants had been helped by the gods to cut, transport, and erect the great stone columns and lentils. In America there are stories about George Washington admitting to cutting down a cherry tree and saying, "I cannot tell a lie," and about Abraham Lincoln ("Honest Abe") walking many miles back to a store to return the copper penny that he had been given erroneously in change. There are also myths embodied in the stories of Horatio Alger that relate to the idea of going "from poverty to riches." These are examples of the religious underpinnings of a culture, the importance of honesty, and the potential to succeed in a free "classless" nation.

Myths appear to serve four functions: **metaphysical** (guides to the origin of existence), **cosmological** (the components of the universe are part of a single whole), **sociological** (clues to the social code of a culture), and **psychological** (guides to appropriate personal conduct).[13] Myths often have opposing forces within them, for example, good versus evil or technology versus nature. This is called **binary opposition**.[14] An example of the latter are claims made that "natural" vitamins are better than those made in the laboratory from synthetic materials—a myth where nature is seen as positive and technology as negative.

terminal values (see p. 348) Personal values that are enduring beliefs that specific modes of conduct or end-states of existence, if enacted over time, lead to desirable end-states or terminal values (end-states of existence that are preferred over other end-states). Terminal values might be a comfortable life, a sense of accomplishment, a world at peace, or racial equality.

myth   A story or fable that reflects important values shared by members of a culture and that is used to teach one or more of these values.

metaphysical myth   A myth that functions as a guide to the origin of existence.

cosmological myth   A myth that functions as a way to show that the components of the universe are part of a single whole.

sociological myth   A myth that functions to provide clues to the social code of a culture.

psychological myth   A myth that functions as a guide to appropriate personal conduct.

binary opposition   Occurs in a myth when conflicting options are offered—for example, good versus evil or technology versus nature.

Marketplace 11-1

The Mountain Man Myth: Seeking the Primitive in the United States

The "Man of the Mountain" is also referred to as a "buckskinner." Persons who wish to take on this lifestyle of the past appear to believe that living as the mountain men of old did is desirable and a worthy goal. Hence, people accomplish this move back in time by dressing, behaving, and espousing the values and attitudes of these primitive people. It has been suggested that individuals look for passion, power, transcendence, and freedom in the primitive existence—primarily because people are unable to find these qualities in urban life today. Also, people's work life is often not really satisfactory, so they seek to live with more meaning through the work and play of the myth of the mountain man.

Living simply in nature as the buckskinners of old did is not really "natural," nor is it inexpensive. As authors Russell W. Belk and Janeen A. Costa note, "Equipment is costly. A basic canvas tepee and lodge poles can run $1,000; other period tents begin at several hundred dollars ...a mountain man may spend $500 for a buffalo robe, $120 (commercially tanned) to $1,000 (more desirable brain-tanned) for buckskin leggings or trousers, and over $100 for a pair of beaded moccasins or other suitable footwear. Women may spend several hundred dollars or more for an Indian dress.... A fire grate, tripod, and basic cooking and eating utensils cost ... $150. Muzzle-loading rifles and shooting equipment run from several hundred to several thousands of dollars. Knives and tomahawks ...can cost hundreds of dollars.... A calico shirt, leather belt and hat add ... $100 or more. And these are only the barest of necessities. Beadwork, spears, tables, cupboards, water barrels, necklaces, and other accessories are always attractive additions."

At gathering places (rendezvous) there are traders' rows where items can be bought. Some mountain men and women save money by hunting elk and deer in season, tanning the hides, and making their own clothing, a difficult and time-consuming task. Most spend years putting together their gear yet have a sense that there is always need for something new. When interviewed, a mountain man named "Many Tequilas" stated, "... [in the beginning] one buffalo robe and that was it. Now it takes a ton-and-a-half truck just to haul the stuff."

People following this myth are substituting the desire to have the artifacts of the mountain man for the latest electronics, a status car, and other symbols of today's modern lifestyle. They work to develop a sense of community by creating an "alternative reality." Bonding occurs as the buckskinners act out life in an imaginary time and place. There are invented traditions, and those people who accurately play the roles and know the history are held in highest regard. Activities include flint and steel fire making, horsemanship, hide tanning, bead and quill work, music making, tall-tale telling, knife and tomahawk throwing, archery, and the like. Classes are held, and books are available.

Source: From "The Mountain Man Myth: A Contemporary Consuming Fantasy" by Russell W. Belk and Janeen A. Costa from *Journal of Consumer Research*, Vol. 25, December 1998, pp. 218–240. Copyright © 1998. Reprinted by permission of The University of Chicago Press.

Myths relating to the marketplace are one type of many that appear in popular culture. There are positive myths about elves that may be found in children's fables, for example the elves that made fine shoes at night as the poor cobbler slept. Today, Keebler brand has fostered the myth through advertising that their cookies and crackers are made by friendly elves that bake the goods while living in a hollow tree. A margarine manufacturer uses the brand name, "I Can't Believe It's Not Butter," creating a myth that its product tastes exactly like butter. And "underdog" myths are commonly found in the marketplace. The underdog winning out over the stronger opponent is illustrated by Avis Rent-a-Car. The theme used a few years ago stated that Avis was "No. 2" and, therefore, tried harder and was now better. Check out Marketplace 11-1 to explore "The Mountain Man Myth."

We've discussed customs, mores, conventions, and sanctions, each of which has a behavior component. Rituals involve patterned behavior, as did some of these.

11-2h Rituals in a Culture

Definition   A useful way of classifying certain types of behavior and consumption within a culture is through the rituals associated with them. **Rituals** are patterns of behavior tied to events that we consider important in our lives. Rituals usually have three characteristics. They have some special symbolic meaning to us, occur in a fixed or predictable sequence, and are repeated with some regularity.[15]

ritual A pattern of behavior tied to an event that we consider important in our lives.

**Ritual Dimensions
of Consumer Behavior**

Primary Behavior Source	Ritual Type	Examples
Cosmology	Religious	Baptism, marriage, meditation, religious holidays
Cultural values	Rites-of-passage	Graduation, marriage
	Cultural	Festivals, secular holidays, Super Bowl, business gift giving*
Group learning	Civic	Parades, trials, elections
	Group	Fraternity/sorority initiation, office luncheons, business negotiations
	Family	Mealtimes, bedtimes, Father's/Mother's Day, Christmas
Individual aims and emotions	Personal	Household rituals, grooming
	Gift giving*	Special events, thanks, love expressions, business relationships

Source: From "The Ritual Dimensions of Consumer Behavior" by Dennis W. Rook in *Journal of Consumer Research,* Vol. 12, December 1985, pp. 251–252. Copyright © 1985. Reprinted by permission of The University of Chicago Press.

*Authors' additions

Types   Ritual types are summarized in Exhibit 11-3 and are grouped by cosmology, cultural values, group learning, and individual aims and emotions.[16] A ritual may be as infrequent as a marriage, involving all kinds of goods and services from the purchase of an engagement ring through the honeymoon trip, or it can be as regular as a Thanksgiving Day turkey dinner, with very predictable purchases. It can even be an everyday occurrence, such as mom or dad reading the bedtime story from Dr. Seuss for the little one each evening. Note the broad spectrum of experiences and actions that are ritualistic. They range from shared rituals that sweep across the entire culture to others that are uniquely personal. Consider, too, the types of purchases associated with each. Let's look at some ritual examples.

Rites-of-Passage Rituals   Rituals associated with significant milestones in a person's life, known as rites of passage, exist in every culture and often are an important part of its history. Rituals accompany every rite of passage, from birth to coming of age to college entry and graduation to marriage to death. As an example of the latter, the great pyramids of Egypt and the artifacts found within them were connected to the transition at death from "earth life" to an "after life." Modern-day funerals—be they the pyres of India, the riderless horse at the funeral of Presidents Abraham Lincoln and John F. Kennedy, an all-night wake, or a graveside service—are also tied to this rite of passage. In all of these cases, specific steps have been carried out, and many goods and services were necessary to support the activity.

Holiday Rituals   Rituals around the world are often associated with holidays, both religious and secular. Bastille Day in France, O-Sho-Gatsu in Japan, Ramadan in Islamic nations, Thanksgiving Day in the United States, Cinco de Mayo in Mexico, and the Chinese New Year are just some examples. All of these have special traditions and artifacts associated with them.

During holidays, as we break away from our everyday routines, our behavior, our emotional state, even our perspective on life changes. This means that not only the products we buy, but also the spirit in which we purchase and use them changes from the normal. "Happy Easter from Hershey's Kisses," says the advertisement in Exhibit 11-4. A product that is available all year is presented in such a way as to tie it to a holiday ritual and so evoke a special ritualistic feeling leading to a ritualistic purchase.

Here, a product that is available all year is marketed in special ways to appeal to those observing holiday rituals. Hershey's Kisses are wrapped in pastel colors of Easter to help fit into the holiday consumption ritual.

Source: Courtesy of Hersheys.

HAPPY EASTER FROM HERSHEY'S KISSES.

Gift Giving   Gift giving has already been touched upon as governed by the rules of convention in various cultural business settings. Some of the following comments elaborate on that discussion. Gift-giving rituals in other than business situations also deserve exploration.

Gift-giving rituals are of interest to marketers. Sales over the Christmas season in countries with Christian populations are important to merchants. In the United States, for example, this season can make or break those manufacturing or selling toys. The same is true for candy marketers at Halloween or Valentine's Day, or for bridal boutiques in the run-up to the summer wedding season. Virtually any product can be promoted as a gift— as long as the marketer realizes that there is a unique dimension to gift buying. It is about building relationships with others. There are three stages to gift giving: gestation, presentation, and reformulation (see Exhibit 11-5).[17]

First, during *gestation,* we're motivated to buy a gift. This motivation may be "structural." That is, it's prescribed by the prevailing culture. Special events such as birthdays and weddings are examples. It may be "emergent," as with a spontaneous gift to a friend or romantic partner. Marketers can attempt to trigger both types of motivation with messages that encourage us not only to give gifts but to think of their products and/or brands as good choices. Examples include a festive Christmas catalog, a direct mail piece offering a selection of products as great gifts for school graduates, an in-store display of Halloween treats, or a television commercial featuring a special tenth wedding anniversary diamond bracelet.

Second, during *presentation,* we give or exchange gifts—and see how well our gifts are received. We give not just to please others but to please ourselves, so the response says a lot not just about the appropriateness of the gift, but about our relationship with the recipient. As marketers position their products as perfect gifts for specific occasions, we're more likely to buy.

Third, during *reformulation,* the bonds with the recipient are adjusted based on the new relationship that exists after we present the gift and evaluate the response. Where there's a good match between the gift and the receiver, the bond is strengthened. Images of happy children opening packages, of gifts given in romantic settings, and of a worker impressed with a thoughtful gift from the boss are all means through which marketers seek to provide this type of positive reinforcement.

Gift giving is not always a happy experience. Sometimes we give gifts not because we want to but because we feel we have to. Perhaps the gift is part of a ritual, like sending cards on Father's Day. Or perhaps the "reciprocity norm" is at work—we've received a gift and feel that one of equal value is due in return. Various cultures have varying reciprocity

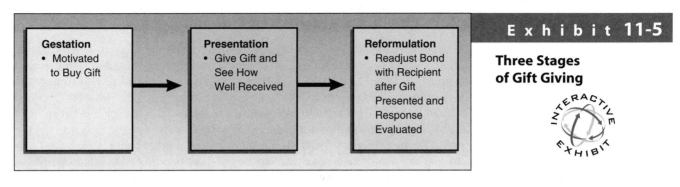

norms of action in different settings. Gift giving can become a chore rather than a means of relationship building. To overcome the negative attitudes that are implicit in this type of gift giving, it is important that marketers so position and distribute their products that the choice of an appropriate gift can be made easier and less time-consuming for the giver. To this end, gift catalog marketers frequently categorize their products into groupings such as "Gift Ideas for Secretary's Day" or "Gifts Under $10."[18]

Ritual Artifacts   Because rituals involve the use of goods and services, it is important for marketers to understand them and the ritualistic behaviors they give rise to. **Ritual artifacts** are those objects needed in order for rituals to be carried out successfully. Given a ritual situation, almost anything can be considered a ritual artifact: floats for the Rose Parade, that special book of short bedtime stories, a unity candle for a wedding, last year's Christmas tree trunk that becomes this year's Yule log, the menorah that has been in the family for five generations, the sashes worn for a fraternity initiation, or even the yearly purchase of new slippers for Dad on Father's Day. For the more unusual rituals and particularly those tied to religious or festive occasions, the marketing of artifacts is quite a specialized business. It depends on understanding the history of the ritual, the type of consumers who follow it, its time frame and frequency, the ritual steps it involves, and, of course, the range of goods needed for it to be carried out successfully. Research may be as simple as observation, or it may go deeper, requiring an examination of the motivations of consumers involved in rituals and the feelings they associate with ritual artifact selection.

▶ **ritual artifacts** Those objects needed in order for rituals to be carried out successfully.

Ritual Scripts   When rituals are carried out, scripts are often followed. *Scripts* are specific procedures that include the sequence of ritual steps and the necessary artifacts. Trace the wedding process from presentation of the engagement ring, to the selection of a wedding dress and tuxedo rental, to the rehearsal dinner, to the decoration of the place for the wedding and reception, to the scattering of rice (or birdseed) on the married couple as they leave for the reception, to the various toasts at the reception, the tossing of the bouquet, the dance with Dad, and the honeymoon. It's as though a checklist was being followed, and in some cases it is.

Marketing Management—Implications and Actions

Identifying the components of a culture helps marketers:

- Analyze the impact of norms, customs, mores, conventions, and sanctions within a culture to determine appropriate product and service offerings.
- Understand the value structure of a society and how consumers use products and services to produce value-related benefits.
- Recognize the key religious and mythological factors in a culture's belief system so as to offer only those services and products that fit.
- Position appropriate products and services against the various ritual behaviors of the members of a society.

11-3 The "Languages" of Culture

When looking across cultures, "language" beyond words must be considered. Certainly the meaning of words and the translation of product descriptions, brands, tag lines (campaign theme phrases like "Coke Is It" or company slogans such as Prudential Insurance's "Get a Piece of the Rock") and the like must be carefully considered. But what do certain colors mean, how do time concepts fit into the culture, what about the space between individuals and their gestures and postures, and what symbols are acceptable or avoided by the culture? If we are planning to offer products or services in other cultures, we must be careful and sensitive about the way we use "languages" in positioning and communicating about them. The languages to be explored here are words, colors, time, space, distance and gestures, symbols, friendship, and agreements (see Exhibit 11-6).

11-3a Words

When Coca-Cola was first introduced in mainland China, the product name sounded like "kou-ke-kou-la," which in Chinese was interpreted to mean "a thirsty mouth and a mouth of candle wax." This was disastrous considering the importance of product brand names to the people. The company changed the phonetic translation to "ke-kou-ke-le," which means "a joyful taste and happiness." The response was overwhelming to the soft drink with its new brand name translation. Revlon was translated as "lu-hua-nong," meaning "the fragrance of the flowers covered with morning dew"—a very positive image.[19] When General Motors wished to use the phrase "Body by Fisher" in Belgium, the translation into Flemish was "Corpse by Fisher," and when Pepsico attempted to translate "Pepsi Brings You Back to Life" into Chinese, the result was "Pepsi Brings Your Ancestors Back from the Grave," and the Germans thought it meant "come back from the dead."[20]

11-3b Colors

Colors send messages that vary across cultures. Although in the United States death notices typically use the color black as a border, in many African nations and in China announcements use the color white. Red is a very positive color in Argentina and Denmark, and in China it means good luck. Yet, as noted earlier, red ink when used to write a letter or note is associated with death notices in China. Red is a negative color in Nigeria and Germany. It's a feminine color in China and masculine in France and Britain. In Southeast Asia, death and mourning are indicated by the use of light blue. The use of bright colors is very popular among the cultures of the Caribbean, Mexico, and Central America, but Northern Europeans prefer more subdued tones, especially for clothing.

In developing products and packaging, choosing the "right" colors is often a critical decision. When Canada Dry used red as the dominant color on its sugar-free ginger ale container, sales were disappointing. Red was found to be associated with cola soft drinks. The redesigned container was green and white, and the response was a dramatic increase in sales.[21] Colors also move in and out of fashion. Clothing, automobiles, household appliances, electronics, and other items must be in the "in" colors to be accepted. For example, in the 1960s and early 1970s, electronic audio components all had a dark wood finish as part of the outer shell. In the later 1970s and 1980s, silver was the color of choice, and as the products were being designed for the 1990s, a black matte finish was "in." As we move into the 21st century the black matte finish is still popular, but we are seeing television set cabinets in brushed silver, especially the high-definition ready sets. Marketers must determine on a culture-by-culture basis what colors are appropriate in what situations for the various target markets being served.

11-3c Time

Time is in every aspect of social life spanning individual, group, and cultural levels.[22] Individuals experience *self-time* in the memories, perceptions, and future expectations of their everyday lives. *Interaction time* with others often occurs in informal settings, such as in the household or other social settings. *Institutional time* happens in highly structured settings,

E x h i b i t   11-6

"Languages" of Culture

Words	Gestures
Colors	Symbols
Time	Friendships
Space	Agreements
Distance	

such as organizations, schools, and the workplace.[23] Members of different cultures view and interact with time in different ways, and it has been suggested that classifying cultures on the basis of how time is woven into the fabric of the society is possible.[24] Persons, household units, organizations, institutions, and cultures likely form **time personalities** that are based on their use of a variety of **time styles.**

Time styles may be classified into groups such as approaches to time, orientation, and activity level.[25] Time processing also is part of this. **Approaches to time** are related to the issues and assumptions used in discussing and thinking about time. Although there is no universal agreement on the list of approaches, five will be presented here. They are (1) *economic*—time as a fixed resource, time as money, time allocation;[26] (2) *socio-cultural*—how a person views time based on cultural socialization, for example, what does punctuality mean to the society?[27] (3) *psychological*—subjective perceptions of time, awareness, speed, duration, value;[28] consumers also differ on their sense of time scarcity, always perceptually experiencing various levels of time surplus or shortage;[29] Some individuals always feel a sense of time shortage, and others always feel they are in time surplus. This is part of their psychological time makeup. People can feel a sense of time shortage and therefore be "stressed" based on external factors. In Australia a study was done on persons who were in a relationship, and the most common factors were that extra child care duties made men (not women) more stressed, extra housework made women (not men) more stressed, and having a stressed-out partner stressed men and women.[30] When looking at such men and women in Australia, Germany, South Korea, and the United States, researchers found that the percent of women feeling stressed was always greater than the percent of their male partners. The female-to-male "stressed" ratios were 42% to 38% in Germany, 55% to 45% in Australia, 84% to 78% in South Korea, and 90% to 83% in the U.S.; (4) *measurement*—hours, days, months, years, seasons, punctuality, synchronization, quality;[31] and (5) *physiological*—biological clock effects on periods of sleep, alertness, mood, and performance.[32]

A culture's sociocultural approach would likely impact how an individual's mix of economic, psychological, and measurement approaches affect his or her time personality. For example, within the society time might have little value (economic); it might be perceived to move rather slowly (psychological) and be measured more by the seasons than by daily or hourly increments (measurement). A person's socialization within the culture would be focused in these directions.

A person's perception of the importance of the past, present, or future is called his or her **time orientation.**[33] Statements such as "Things were better in the old days" or "What are the latest clothing styles or the newest movie or this year's hot car" or "Things will be a lot better in the future than they have ever been" are typical of persons of these three orientations. The ways values, behaviors, and the like are affected by orientation drives consumer behavior. Consumers with strong past orientation buy "oldies but goodies" music, drive vintage cars, and collect memorabilia from their past, such as old radios from the 1930s and 1940s, seats from Comiskey Park (the old Chicago White Sox stadium), and 78 rpm phonograph records. In a study comparing Malaysian and American students, both groups felt positively about the future and that things would be better—this was before the 1998 crisis in the Far East. However, the Malaysians identified more with the past than did the Americans.[34] Also, consumers may have short-term ("immediate"), intermediate, or long-term ("extended") emphasis within their past, present, or future orientations as suggested in the Temporal Orientation Horizon Matrix theory (TOHM).[35] Though specific time bounding is not offered, the authors define *immediate* as near at hand, rapid, abrupt, direct, and/or instantaneous; *intermediate* is said to be bounded, bordered, or surrounded at some "distance" from immediate; and *extended* is defined as unbounded and elongated.[36]

Although consumers may generally find themselves in one of the nine time orientation-horizon positions, their behavior will show some variation based on the current situation in which they find themselves. The *Lao gu dong* of mainland China, "old people," or "antique people" fifty years of age and older, show much intermediate past orientation. They accept "what they have" as being "all there is." They experienced World War II, the civil war, the looting of the national treasures, the loss of loved ones to Taiwan, and the "New China" under Chairman Mao Tse-tung and his successors. They do not expect to

time personality
Can be identified for persons, household units, organizations, institutions, and cultures, and is based on their use of a variety of time styles.

time styles The building blocks of time personality that tentatively consist of approaches to time, time orientation, activity level, and time processing.

time approaches (approaches to time) Related to the issues and assumptions used in discussing and thinking about time. The approaches are economic, sociocultural, psychological, measurement, and physiological.

time orientation A person's perception of the importance of the past, present, or future in his or her life. Individuals see past, present, and future as either short-term (immediate), intermediate, or long-term (extended).

have many goods or services and simply wish to rest. To this consuming segment, only the necessities of life are of any importance. They have little focus on the future, and focus on the present just to keep going.[37] In Chapter 12 we will discuss the "Confucian Dynamic," which is a dimension used to compare cultures. On the positive side of this dimension, we find cultures that are future-oriented; on the negative side are those that are past-oriented. Please see that discussion as a supplement to this section.[38] Where are you most of the time on the TOHM? How does this affect your behavior as a consumer?

Recently there has been renewed interest in the concept of **time activity level,** which is related to the number of activities people do in the same time block. Are consumers more comfortable doing one thing during a clock block of time, called *monochronic* behavior, or would they rather do two or more things at a time, named *polychronic* behavior?[39] Persons who are monochronic, "monochrons," prefer to concentrate on one activity at a time and lean more toward strict planning, time allocation, and prioritization than do "polychrons."[40] People have either a monochronic or polychronic tendency. They do not act one way or the other in all situations. Measuring this "tendency" will be touched on shortly.

Monochrons are more likely to offer their "undivided" attention to television commercials than are polychrons, who often are engaged in some other activity while watching. Perhaps greater detail embedded in the audio portion of the message rather than the visual would better capture the polychron. Reading a newspaper or magazine when eating or traveling by public transportation or working out is common. Media redesign—larger print, easily held in one hand, easy page turning—could help. Accessories such as reading stands and keyboard or TV attachments for exercise equipment fit this behavior. Single-handed eating while driving or traveling or working opens the door for improved product container and storage designs. What about chairs with writing arms for people in waiting rooms or beepers given to people so that they can continue running errands rather than sitting there? Today supermarkets offer prepared hot foods or complete sets of meal items to satisfy the need to prepare dinner, accomplish errands, and possibly pick up the kids from day care on a single trip. We see people using drive-through dry cleaners, 24-hour pharmacies, automatic teller machines, and even catalog shopping while engaged in some other behavior. Polychrons may be willing to spend more to do more simultaneously. Cell phones, laptop computers, pagers, and the like add cost but allow for multiple activity.[41]

How do we know whether a person has a monochronic or polychronic tendency overall? The Polychronic Attitude Index (PAI) is a way to do this.[42] Four scales are presented. People are asked to indicate how strongly they agree with the following four statements:

1. I do not like to juggle several activities at the same time.
2. People should not try to do many things at once.
3. When I sit down at my desk, I work at one project at a time.
4. I am comfortable doing several things at the same time.

Those who score higher in agreement with doing one thing at a time show a monochronic tendency, and a polychronic tendency results in a lower score. Later research has shown that dropping item number 3 (because of its desk tie) gives better results, because the test is then no longer associated with a specific location.[43] A more recent measurement approach produced a regression equation for predicting tendency. Compared to monochrons, polychrons in the study were less upset with schedule changes, did not think it was fun to do one thing at a time, did less detailed planning, felt they performed better under pressure, found it easier to organize activities, changed activities during the day more frequently, felt they reached their daily goals more often, and were less likely to put things off until later.[44] More recently work is being pursued on polychronic-monochronic tendency exploring scales that go beyond the PAI and contrasting men and women. The findings show that though men and women do not differ in their positions along the tendency continuum, the questions used to position them are different.[45]

People should not confuse multitasking with high polychronic tendency. In the latter case people not only engage in multiple simultaneous activity, but they do this voluntarily, having very positive feelings about such behavior, whereas multitaskers sometimes feel forced to perform in this manner or simply see it as required in order to get things done.

▶ **time activity level** A measure of whether consumers are more comfortable doing one thing during a clock block of time, called monochronic behavior, or more comfortable doing two or more things at a time, named polychronic behavior. Monochrons are persons who are monochronic, and polychrons are those who are polychronic.

F A Q

Do you think you are a polychron or a monochron in your college life?

The cultures of the Mediterranean world have been classified as polychronic and as having a slower pace of life than the cultures of Northwestern Europe and the United States, which have been identified as monochronic.[46] Are you monochronic or polychronic? How do you think this tendency affects your grocery shopping behavior, buying audio-video components, shopping for a pair of shoes, or doing Christmas or other holiday shopping?

The fourth time style is called time processing. People, organizations, and cultures can be governed in general by three different **time processing methods**.[47] The first of these is variously called *ribbon, linear, linear separable,* or *economic* time processing. Here, time is broken into discrete units with a clearly defined past, present, and future. Time is seen to have economic value, and the expression "time is money" fits here. Time is processed this way in most businesses, in developed countries, and in certain developing countries.

Procedural time is a second processing approach. Things are started when all preparations have been completed and continue until the activity is done. When all of the people or resources have been gathered, activity begins. When all tasks have been accomplished, it ends. The Hopi Indians of America use the phrase "everything in its own time" to characterize this way to process time. The idea of a "natural" time for all things also reflects this. Tribal and ritual cultures from around the globe are likely to process time this way.

Finally we speak of *circular* or *cyclical* time processing. People and cultures follow some rhythmic pattern that has a regular beginning and end. This may be daily, weekly, or yearly. It could be tied to such anchor points as occur on a religious, lunar, or secular calendar; the seasons of the year; the biweekly paycheck; daytime versus night time or weekdays versus the weekend. Here, the individual views time in terms of a repetitive cycle. Developing and agrarian societies often follow this path. For example, the Swahili people come from the coasts of Kenya and Tanzania in Africa. The language they speak today is called Swahili and is a mixture of Bantu and Arabic. Swahili has become the common language for all tribes living in East Africa; about 20 million speak this language as either a first or second tongue. In these cultures, clock time begins each day when the sun rises, and each of the numbers on the clock is then shifted by six hours. Hence, if we say in English that it is 7:30 in the morning, one would say in Swahili, "saa moja na nusu asubuhi." Here, "saa" means "time," "moja" means "one," "nusu" for "half" and "asubuhi" represents "before noon" or "morning." When it is 2:00 in the afternoon, the time in Swahili is "saa nane mchana." This means "8:00 in the afternoon." Because Kenya lies on the equator, the length of each day is the same throughout the year. The people count on this regularity to govern their days and nights. For example, the sun rises each day at 6:00 a.m., and this dawn event is a reliable sign that it is time to awaken.

The predominant time personality of a nation will, at a minimum, be the combination of approaches to time, orientation, activity level, and processing approach. If you wish to market goods and services in another culture, it is essential to understand the time personality of the target market group or groups you wish to serve and to what extent this will impact on benefits sought and marketing mix expectations.

> **time processing methods**
> Tied to time flow and, in some cases, time value. The three types are (1) ribbon, linear, linear separable, or economic; (2) procedural; and (3) circular or cyclical time.

11-3d Space, Distance, and Gestures

Appropriate or comfortable space and distance for members of one culture is different from those of members of another. People feel comfortable in smaller work and living spaces in Hong Kong, Japan, India, or Honduras. Acceptable personal space requirements are much smaller than in Australia or the United States. And the need for privacy is not the same. These varying situations are the result of population density, tradition, per capita wealth, and other factors. There is direct "space available" impact on the number and sizes of the goods that may be owned by members of the culture. Hence, marketers wishing to sell products must be aware of this. One American manufacturer attempted to sell refrigerators in Japan and assumed that the standard large size bought by most consumers in the United States would suit the Japanese market. The sales record was very poor. Because the vast majority of homes in the islands were very small, the refrigerator was not suitable. Further, it used more electricity than the smaller units and was more costly to operate. Also not considered was that Japanese shop more often for food and do not use refrigeration to the extent that Northern Europeans, Americans, and Canadians do. Failure of the product to sell was tied to space availability and these other factors.

F A Q

Are space and distance really issues in the United States?

The typical distance between individuals in various settings is not the same in all cultures. Personal space or appropriate space comes into play. For example, in Germany, Austria, Sweden, or the Netherlands, acceptable distances between individuals in a business or personal conversation are greater than in the United States or Australia. And in parallel situations in such places as Spain, Italy, Portugal, India, or Brazil, the comfortable distance is less. Distances also vary on the basis of gender, status, or relationship. Actual physical contact between individuals must also be considered. This means that when advertising products or services, the distances portrayed among the models shown is an essential consideration so as not to offend.

Gestures, postures, or body positions also vary in their meaning. These must be considered in actual marketplace situations and in the visual parts of advertising, the construction of store displays, and in catalogs where models are used. Let's consider some gesture examples. In the United States, a grabbing or sweeping arm motion toward the body is a signal to come closer whereas in Peru this means "money" or "pay me." The same motion in the Netherlands implies that someone is stealing or "getting away with something." In Europe, waving the whole hand back and forth can mean "no," while in South America it can mean, "come here." In Greece, especially if the hand is waved close to another's face, the person feels threatened. Thumbs up means "okay" in most parts of the world but is a rude gesture in Australia. A finger circle with the thumb touching the first finger is the "okay" sign in the United States and many other places, yet it is impolite in Russia and Greece; it means "money" in Japan and "worthless" or "zero" in southern France. Finally, a head nod in most countries means "yes," but it is "no" in Greece and Bulgaria.[48] In Japan, businessmen put more emphasis on nonverbal communication than on talking with one another or with foreign persons. This is called *ishin-denshin* and is carried out by generally avoiding direct eye contact with the other person. This is an example of a crescive norm that was discussed in section 11-2a. The Japanese look upon verbal contact alone as too simplistic. Business people from the United States, however, rely heavily on verbal communication and direct questioning. Missed communication and the offense felt on both sides may lead to unsatisfactory results.[49]

11-3e Symbols

In Chapter 5, we discussed the concept of "semiotics," which had to do with the meaning of things or what message people were receiving from the signs they were exposed to. One of the types of signs presented was called the *symbol*. People learn that certain things called "signifiers" send certain meanings. Signifiers are also called symbols. For example, is there a specific town, suburb, or section of a city near you where very affluent people live? When the name of the area is mentioned, what comes to people's minds? What are the messages being sent by the driver of a Rolls-Royce Silver Cloud, a Chevrolet Corvette, or a Dodge Neon? Symbols of the U.S. culture include the bald eagle and the stars and stripes of the national flag. The Statue of Liberty is also a national symbol. Symbols known around the world for some of the great cities are the Eiffel Tower of Paris, the Coliseum of Rome, the Kremlin in Moscow, the Palace in Beijing, and the Tower of London. Words and colors, as mentioned earlier, also have symbolism within a culture. Animals, flowers, and fruits also can become cultural symbols. The great bear of Russia, the bulldog of England, the dragon of China, the chrysanthemum symbolizing the royal throne in Japan, and the pineapple as a sign of hospitality in a number of cultures are a few examples. Check out CBite 11-1 for more insight on cultural symbols.

11-3f Friendship and Agreements

The meaning of *friendship* varies across cultures. A person's status within a culture, the amount of power he or she yields, and the respect given to that person may be tied to the personal friendships he or she has cultivated. Consumers may be attracted to certain outlets and to select particular service suppliers based on friendship. This factor can be more

---

CBite 11-1
Symbols of Culture

The use of cultural symbolism in advertising is just one means through which marketers attempt to tune into and keep pace with the cultures in which they work. Virtually all advertising and product packaging uses some form of expressive symbolism as a means of delivering a desired message to and eliciting a specific response from consumers within a culture. Expressive symbols can be used, for example, to make a product seem prestigious, exotic, practical, or inexpensive, or to reflect any characteristic desired by and accepted by the culture into which it is sold. Symbols can persuade the consumer that the product can bestow some special, culturally desirable advantage—that is, the products can make us beautiful, healthy, popular, powerful, or anything else we wish to be. They carry connotative meanings that are subject to interpretation. The Prudential Company, for example, uses the symbol of the Rock of Gibraltar to connote strength, stability, and dependability.

---

important than price and quality to the consumer. In countries such as those in the Middle East and in India, friendship is more important as it relates to business than it is in the United States.[50] To do business in China, you must know somebody "on the inside." You must practice *Guanxi*, which means making "powerful friendships." It requires making government employee connections and other special friendships, and networking. The focus should not be on your product or service and how good it is but rather on getting to know key people and their families.[51]

Do the members of a society put *agreements* together on the basis of accepted moral practices and customs in business and other arenas, or are they more prone to be legalistic? In the Middle East, there is a long history of business customs that governs how people come to an agreement. In the United States, such agreements mostly have to be in writing and must meet appropriate legal standards. It's rare that agreement by "handshake" is enough because of problems with trust. In the Middle East, personal trust is the key.[52] An example of a shopper-seller behavior custom is that of arriving at a fair price for a consumer item in Turkey. Suppose you are at the Grand Bazaar in Istanbul looking for a carpet. You find what you want. The price negotiation you are about to begin is viewed as both an economic and social exchange. The seller starts too high, and the shopper begins too low. After going back and forth with offers and counter offers tied to product quality and the seller's ability to support his family and your lack of funds, you arrive at a place that is about 70 percent of the starting price. Both know that this is the "right" price, and the agreement is struck. You and the seller are equally happy with the outcome.

Marketing Management—Implications and Actions

Using the knowledge and understanding of the broad variety of "languages" within a culture helps marketers:

- Design, produce, deliver, and position products and services that will be acceptable to culture members.
- Take steps to produce more effective and culturally acceptable advertising messages, presentations, and campaigns.
- Analyze and find ways to work within the time perceptions, procedures, and constraints of the society as exchanges are carried out.
- Understand the importance of friendships and the mechanics of putting together agreements with trading partners in different cultures.

11-4 The Impact of Government and Laws on a Culture

The way a country is governed and the laws that are on the books and enforced can affect consumer behavior and access to goods and services. In countries where there are totalitarian forms of government, people are very restricted in what they can do as consumers, and the kinds of goods and services available are tightly controlled. Some governments are very deeply tied to certain religious beliefs; again the consumer is restricted in what he or she can find in the marketplace and consume. In many countries in the Americas, Europe, or Eastern Asia, for example, almost all types of goods and services desired are available. Marketers operating in the international arena must be very informed on governmental style and its effects on consumers.

Laws and regulations also may act as trade barriers or serve to ease the path to the consumer. Tariffs, quotas, banned goods and services, special domestic business and agricultural protection, and protected minerals, animals, or plants are examples. Liquor and/or cigarettes may be taxed at a high rate, as they are in the United States and parts of Europe. Advertising for certain products may be banned, as is the case with cigarettes on television and radio in the United States. Advertising for either cigarettes or liquor is not allowed in much of Europe.[53] In some cases, regulations or laws vary within the country so that marketers are faced with different situations. For example, in most locations in Germany there is little or no special tax on disposable packaging. Yet after McDonald's had opened a fast food restaurant in one town, the city council passed a very high tax on such packaging, forcing the company to threaten to shut down because of the potential profit impact.

A government agency can also decide how strictly to enforce the law. A number of years ago, the government of one European country decided to reduce the flow of an Asian nation's consumer electronics products in retaliation for similar action by that nation. The law allowed customs agents to inspect every single package—which was not traditionally done. In this case, the letter of the law was followed, and all packages were opened on the docks, severely restricting the flow onto store shelves. As a result, the manufacturers and the Asian nation's government came to a new, more balanced agreement with their European trading partner.

There also are cases where certain industries, utilities, transportation systems, medical systems, and parts or all of the mass communications media are controlled by the government. This restricts choices for consumers, reduces competition, and closes or restricts market entry by firms inside and outside of the country. In the case of the mass media, government control may affect the type of advertising that is acceptable, how it is placed in the media, what its content can be, and the like. In some cases, commercial advertising may even be banned.

Marketing Management—Implications and Actions

Understanding the government position and the various trade laws and regulations in a culture will help marketers:

- Determine what steps to take to bring product and service offerings into the culture.
- Analyze the true costs of doing business in a society.
- Recognize market and advertising restrictions and opportunities that are present in a culture.

---

material artifacts The record of physical items that were part of a culture historically or are in existence in today's society.

11-5 Material Artifacts

The physical items that were part of a culture historically or are in existence in today's society are called **material artifacts.** As you are reading this, stop for a moment and look around you at the design, contents, and view tied to the room in which you are reading—

the furniture, the paintings/prints/photographs, the telephone, the light fixtures, the windows, the electrical sockets, the clothing you are wearing, glasses or contact lenses you're reading with, the buildings you see outside, the parking lot, the cars—and we could go on. The sum total of such helps tell the story of your culture.

A culture is made up of material characteristics and nonmaterial characteristics. Material characteristics or artifacts, as noted earlier, are the tangible evidence of the everyday life of the society: clothing; tools; hunting, farming, or computer equipment; buildings; cars; furnishings; and so on. Whether we look at civilizations dating back two million years, today's societies around the globe, or our own culture, artifacts are critical in piecing together a picture of a society and understanding what it would be like to be one of its members. Material artifacts help frame the stories of the pharaohs of Egypt; the people of the caves of France; the war lords of China, Korea, and Japan; the Cossacks of Russia; the Roaring '20s in America and Europe; and the people living in towns and cities in the nations of the world today. The items and the benefits that people need to live, raise children, work, worship, play, and associate with one another are the focus of marketing activity the world over. Obviously, the goods produced and marketed within a culture are all artifacts created in response to the needs of its members. Understanding a culture and trading successfully with its members requires a good grasp of the material environment of the society.

The nonmaterial or intangible characteristics of a culture relate to its values, norms, and beliefs. Nonmaterial characteristics tell us a great deal about the lifestyles of members, their artistic expressions, their religious beliefs, and their philosophies of life. By living in the culture, reading its literature, and appreciating its art forms we can learn about, for example, the values members place on education, family, community, and other threads in the fabric of the culture.

Both tangible and intangible characteristics of a culture are evident in the erosions and accretions of that culture. **Erosions** are the "tracks" or "wearing away" or "removals" left behind by past cultures. The wagon wheel tracks worn into the stone as pathways through the Rocky Mountains in the United States are evidence of the pioneer travelers of the 1800s. The tunnels bored through mountains to allow for auto and railroad traffic are signs of erosion, as is the carving of the presidents out of Mount Rushmore in South Dakota. **Accretions** are those things that are added to the natural environment by a culture or that have accumulated over time. Examples include ancient campsites in the valley of the Great Rift in Africa, the Eiffel Tower in Paris, the Coliseum in Rome, abandoned drive-in theaters, the "ghost towns" of the Old West, waste sites converted into covered hills, or urban graffiti.

We draw important conclusions about a culture from its artifacts, and the American culture is no exception. If we were to bury a time capsule for archaeologists of the year 5000 to find, it might contain such diverse elements as a recording of the CBS Evening News; the latest model Ford Taurus; a laptop computer; copies of the *Encyclopedia Britannica*, *People* magazine, *National Geographic*, and *The Wall Street Journal*; a CD of the top ten hit songs of the year; a sweatshirt with a university logo on it; a DVD of the best movie of the year; a pair of roller blades; a Pulitzer prize-winning play; and a mixture of items that we use in our everyday lives. Looking at the contents of the capsule, citizens of the future could make some fairly accurate generalizations about our lifestyles, behavior, and even our norms and values. Certainly, there would also be clues as to our consumption patterns. For instance, the presence of art and literary works would indicate that the culture had reached a point of affluence able to support endeavors not directly related to survival.

Certain material artifacts have special meaning to a culture, and this may be tied to specific rituals, conventions, customs, or myths that we discussed earlier in the chapter. One example is the small evergreen tree that may be seen growing wild in the forest that becomes transformed in its meaning when decorated as a "Christmas tree" in some Christian societies. Common candles are burned for light in some cultures and for "atmosphere" in others. The lighting of a candle by members of both families at a wedding ceremony transforms this tallow into a culturally significant "unity candle." Diamonds have become associated with the commitment to marry in a number of European countries and the United States.

▶ **erosions (cultural erosions)** The "tracks" or "wearing away" or "removals" left behind by past cultures. Both tangible and intangible characteristics of a culture may be evidenced by erosions.

▶ **accretions (cultural accretions)** Those things that are added to the natural environment by members of a culture or that have accumulated over time. Both tangible and intangible characteristics of a culture may be evidenced by accretions.

> ### Marketing Management—Implications and Actions
>
> Understanding the meaning of current and historical material artifacts within a culture helps marketers:
>
> - Show proper respect for trading partners' cultural heritage when introducing new products and services so as to properly fit into the fabric of the society.
> - Know how certain material artifacts fit into the rituals, conventions, customs, etc. of the culture and take steps to develop positioning and promote products and services that are not in conflict with these.

11-6 Consumer Products and Cultural Meanings

Consumer goods and services play a number of roles in the lives of consumers based on the perceived benefits of the items. One view of roles is that these are transmitters of cultural meaning. Values, norms, beliefs, mores, conventions, rituals, symbols, and the like give meaning to a culture. They are often reflected in the consumer goods of the society. We've already touched on these and other areas that characterize a culture but have not presented a framework for sending and carrying cultural meanings. Exhibit 11-7 shows the potential linkages between the culture and consumer goods, as well as consumer goods and the individual consumer.[54] Note that cultural meaning is found in the culture itself ("culturally constituted world"), the consumer goods, and the individual consumer having the products.

Advertising and fashion not only carry values, norms, or beliefs but also play a significant role in modeling culturally meaningful behavior. The advertising showing a mother or father choosing an automobile or van that provides maximum safety for their children, or the ad depicting the family gathered around the Thanksgiving table enjoying a traditional turkey dinner, or the ad showing the family sharing in a daughter's graduation from high school and giving her a computer as she heads for college are examples, as are the ads depicting the young woman or man on the way up in the business world or the retired couple doing volunteer work in elementary school classrooms. In all of these cases, products and services are being sold that tie to the cultural values, beliefs, and behaviors being featured.

The "fashion system" is a phrase that is much broader than clothing. It includes newspapers, magazines, television shows, radio shows, and the people who inhabit them, the current opinion leaders, and the various subcultural or fringe groups of individuals. What is culturally appropriate in the way of lifestyle, clothing, possessions, and behaviors? See the differences when you look at *Vanity Fair* or *People* magazine or watch *CSI, Days of Our Lives,* or MTV on television. What meanings are attached to the goods shown and used in these settings?

Such meanings are then transferred to individual consumers through the possession and/or use of the products. The meanings are understood by others and attached to the person. How do you think the concept of "brand-user image," which we discussed in Chapter 5, ties into cultural meaning? We've also already explored ritual behavior in this chapter. We see from Exhibit 11-7 that cultural meaning is attached to individual consumers through the use of products in *possession, exchange, grooming,* and *divestment* rituals. In sum, clothing, food, the exterior and interior of people's homes, and the type of transportation used are examples of the media that people use to tell the story of the cultural world in which they live.[55]

Exhibit 11-7

Cultural Meaning Communication Paths

McCraken refers to the "culturally constituted world," "consumer goods," and "individual consumers" as "instruments of meaning." The connecting paths—"advertising/fashion system," "fashion system," "possession ritual," "exchange ritual," "grooming ritual," and "divestment ritual"—are labeled "instrument meaning transfers."

Source: Grant McCraken, "Culture and Consumption: A Theoretical Account of the Structure and Movement of the Cultural Meaning of Consumer Goods," *Journal of Consumer Research,* Vol. 13 (June 1986), pp. 71–84.

	Culturally Constituted World		
Advertising/Fashion System		Fashion System	
Possession Ritual	Exchange Ritual	Grooming Ritual	Divestment Ritual
Individual Consumers			

Chapter Spotlights

Humans are, to a great extent, "social animals." Being such, we are sensitive to the values, behaviors, and beliefs of the people around us. It follows that our behavior as consumers is affected. There are levels of influence. That of which we are least aware, which is more *subtle*, and yet is in almost every corner of our lives, more *pervasive*, is culture. The intercultural nature of global business demands that to be successful we must understand the definition of culture and its many components and their impacts.

1. Definition of culture. Culture is defined as patterns of values, beliefs, and learned behaviors that are held in common and transmitted by the members of any given society.

2. Nature of culture—components. There are many dimensions that must be considered when attempting to characterize a culture. Norms, customs, mores, conventions, sanctions, values, beliefs, and rituals are characteristics of cultures that help us understand the people and their ways.

3. The languages of culture. Messages from and about cultures come from many different "language" sources, including words, colors, time, space, distance and gestures, symbols, and the meanings of friendships and agreements.

4. The impact of government and laws on a culture. Cultures must also be classified based on type of government and the laws of the society. These dictate the level of acceptability of goods and services types and their free flow in the culture, making certain cultural markets more viable than others.

5. The material artifacts of a culture. Material artifacts reflect a culture in many ways, such as the availability and cost of utilities, the need for individual space, the level of technology, and consumers' ties to the past. These and other conclusions based on artifacts help point to what will and will not fit the society.

6. Consumer products/services and their cultural meanings. Understanding the meanings of consumer products and services also is essential as marketers frame up potential offerings. There are advertising and fashion components tied to possession, exchange, grooming, and divestiture rituals in a culture.

Key Terms

accretions (cultural accretions) (p. 361)
binary opposition (p. 349)
conventions (p. 346)
cosmological myth (p. 349)
crescive norms (p. 345)
culture (p. 344)
customs (p. 346)
enacted norms (p. 345)
erosions (cultural erosions) (p. 361)

instrumental values (p. 348)
material artifacts (p. 360)
metaphysical myth (p. 349)
mores (p. 346)
myth (p. 349)
psychological myth (p. 349)
ritual (p. 350)
ritual artifacts (p. 353)
sanctions (p. 346)

sociological myth (p. 349)
terminal values (p. 348)
time activity level (p. 356)
time approaches (approaches to time) (p. 355)
time orientation (p. 355)
time personality (p. 355)
time processing methods (p. 357)
time styles (p. 355)

Review Questions

Note: You can find the correct answers to these questions by taking the quiz and then submitting your answers in the Online Edition. The program will automatically score your submission. If you miss a question, the program will provide the correct answer, a rationale for the answer, and the section number in the chapter where the topic is discussed.

1. Which of the following factors is *not* a part of the definition of culture?
   a. patterns of values
   b. learned behavior
   c. beliefs
   d. nonmaterial benefits

2. All cultures have the same
   a. central set of values.
   b. central theme.
   c. central purpose.
   d. central core of beliefs.

3. The end states of conduct toward which a person is moving are called
   a. terminal values.
   b. instrumental values.
   c. sanctions.
   d. cultural values.

4. Marketers must determine on a _____ basis what colors are appropriate in what situations for the markets being served.
   a. cost
   b. straight extension
   c. culture-by-culture
   d. consumer

5. Laws and regulations may serve to either ease the path to the consumer or act as
   a. inhibitors.
   b. trade barriers.
   c. sources of commerce.
   d. trade partners.

6. When government controls some of the marketing, commerce, and infrastructure, which of the following may occur?
   a. restriction of consumer choices
   b. increase in competition
   c. increase in market entry by other firms
   d. unrestricted types of media use

7. Physical items that were or are part of a culture historically are called
   a. mementos.
   b. artifacts.
   c. remnants.
   d. keepsakes.

8. Erosions are the _____ left behind by past cultures.
   a. tracks
   b. wearing away
   c. removals
   d. all of the above

9. Marketers have learned that the fashion system is much broader than
   a. clothing.
   b. what is fashionable.
   c. material items.
   d. what is "in."

10. Values, norms, beliefs, mores, conventions, rituals, and symbols are often reflected in the consumer _____ of a society.
    a. thoughts
    b. subcultures
    c. goods
    d. advertising

Team Talk

1. Share your experiences of culture shock that resulted from either visits outside your country or at home. What did these experiences teach you about the culture in which you live?

2. How do the mores you live by affect your selection of clothing to wear to school, on a date, or at the beach?

3. Identify one routine or daily task you perform that involves ritual consumption. What are three ritual artifacts that you use to do this?

4. In the language of time section there was a discussion of monochronic and polychronic behavior. Included was the four-item PAI scale. Score yourself from "5" (strongly agree) to "1" (strongly disagree) on each of the four statements.

You'll have to reverse this scoring on item 4. The higher your score, the more monochronic you are. This is a general measure. Are you more monochronic (16–20), neither (10–14), or more polychronic (4–8)? What specific behavior as a consumer is affected by your time use position?

5. Symbols within a culture have special meaning to its member. Look at the symbols around you and identify one that represents each of the following: masculinity, femininity, power, warmth, dependability, and security. Why does each symbol you chose match the characteristic you listed?

6. What are the cultural meanings of cosmetics in our society? What are the cultural meanings of automobiles?

Workshops

Research Workshop

Background

Cultures can be compared on the basis of values, beliefs, and behavior patterns of their members. The objectives of this workshop are to compare students from different cultures on a series of values and beliefs, to explore reasons for the differences and similarities, and to determine how these influence new product introductions within the culture.

Methodology

Have each team member interview between five and ten students from other countries, both male and female. Questions should cover the importance of family ties and their influence on values, behavior, and the role of women. Analyze and compare responses across both cultures and genders.

To the Marketplace

Select one product you think would have potential in one of the countries represented by your study participants. In light of your research, how would you introduce, distribute, and promote it?

Creative Workshop

Background

This workshop is a continuation of the preceding Research Workshop. The data gathered are used to create headlines and copy for two print advertisements, newspaper and magazine, for the product selected.

Methodology

Use your analysis from the Research Workshop to summarize the values, beliefs, and behaviors of consumers to whom your advertisement should appeal. Write a headline and no more than fifty words of copy for each of the two print advertisements that introduce the selected product to consumers within the targeted culture. You may also use artwork to support the message. Show your completed work to respondents from the targeted culture whom you interviewed for their reactions. Improve your work according to their responses.

To the Marketplace

Develop a set of guidelines that you could give to companies or advertising agencies working within other cultures, particularly the culture you targeted.

Managerial Workshop

Background

In a marketplace that is increasingly global, developing and marketing products within and across cultures is key to business survival. The objective of this workshop is to better understand marketing opportunities and restrictions in a specific country for new product introductions.

Methodology

Interview three to five students from the same foreign culture. First, identify domestic goods or services that respondents feel would have potential in their country. Then review their comments and select a specific product or service. Next, re-interview each respondent asking why he or she sees potential in the product, and how it would best be promoted and sold. Summarize your findings after reviewing them once more with respondents.

To the Marketplace

Describe your target market, the proposed positioning of the selected product, and your decisions on each of the marketing mix variables (product, price, promotion, and distribution).

Notes

1. Adapted from Ralph Linton, *The Cultural Background of Personality* (New York: Appleton-Century-Crofts, 1945).

2. Elana Hudak, "Global Branding and Segmentation: Are They Interdependent?" *Journal of Consumer Marketing,* Vol. 5 (Summer 1988), pp. 27–34.

3. Suzanne Cassidy, "Defining the Cosmo Girl: Check Out the Passport," *The New York Times* (October 12, 1992), p. D8.

4. D. Nance, "When in Rome (Marketing and Advertising a Product Internationally)," *Marketing* (January 31, 1993), p. 50.

5. "Top Global Markets," (Special Report) *Advertising Age* (March 21, 1994), supplement *Advertising Age International.*

6. George P. Murdock, "Uniformities in Culture," *American Sociological Review,* Vol. 5 (1940), pp. 361–367.

7. Marvin E. Shaw, *Group Dynamics* (New York: McGraw-Hill, 1971).

8. George J. McCall and J. L. Simmons, *Social Psychology: A Sociological Approach* (New York: The Free Press, 1982).

9. Katharina J. Smka, "Culture's Role in Marketers' Ethical Decision-Making: An Integrated Theoretical Framework," *Academy of Marketing Science Review* (Online) (2004), www.amsreview.org/articles/smka01-2004.pdf.

10. Milton Rokeach, *The Nature of Human Values* (New York: The Free Press, 1973).

11. Ibid.

12. Zhengyuan Wang and C. P. Rao, "Personal Values and Shopping Behavior: A Structural Equation Test of the RVS in China," in *Advances in Consumer Research,* Vol. 22, Frank R. Kardes and Mita Sujan, eds. (Provo, UT: Association for Consumer Research, 1995), pp. 373–380.

13. Joseph Campbell, *Myths, Dreams and Religion* (E. P. Dutton, 1970).

14. Claude Levi-Strauss, *Structural Anthropology* (Harmondsworth, U.K.: Peregrine, 1977).

15. Dennis W. Rook, "The Ritual Dimension of Consumer Behavior," *Journal of Consumer Research,* Vol. 12 (December 1985), pp. 251–264; Mary A. S. Tetreault and Robert E. Kleine III, "Ritual, Realized Behavior, and Habit: Refinements and Extensions of the Consumption Ritual Construct," in Marvin Goldberg, Gerald Gorn, and Richard W. Pollay, eds., *Advances in Consumer Research,* Vol. 17 (Provo, UT: Association for Consumer Research, 1990), pp. 31–38.

16. Rook, "The Ritual Dimension."

17. John F. Sherry, Jr., "Gift Giving in Anthropological Perspective," *Journal of Consumer Research,* Vol. 10 (September 1983), pp. 157–168.

18. John F. Sherry, Jr., "Gift Giving in Anthropological Perspective," *Journal of Consumer Research,* Vol. 10 (September 1983), pp. 157–168; John F. Sherry, Jr., Mary Ann McGrath, and Sidney J. Levy, "The Dark Side of the Gift," *Journal of Business Research,* Vol. 28 (November 1993), pp. 224–245; and Daniel Coleman, "What's Under the Tree? Clues to a Relationship," *The New York Times* (December 19, 1989), p. C1.

19. Rick Yan, "To Reach China's Consumers, Adapt to *Guo Qing,*" *Harvard Business Review,* Vol. 72 (September–October 1994), pp. 66–74.

20. Linda S. Coleman, Ernest F. Cooke, and Chandra M. Kochunny, "What Is Meant by Global Marketing?" in Jon M. Hawes and George B. Glisan, eds., *Developments in Marketing Science,* Vol. 10 (Akron, OH: Academy of Marketing Science, 1987), p. 178.

21. R. Alsop, "Color Grows More Important in Catching Consumers' Eyes," *The Wall Street Journal,* (November 29, 1989), p. B1.

22. David J. Lewis and Andrew J. Weigert, "The Structures and Meanings of Social Time," *Social Forces,* Vol. 60 (1981), pp. 432–461.

23. Carol Felker Kaufman, Paul M. Lane, and Jay D. Lindquist, "Time Congruity in the Organization: A Proposed Quality-of-Life Framework," *Journal of Business and Psychology,* Vol. 6 (Fall 1991), pp. 79–106.

24. Gilles Pronovost, "Introduction: Time in a Sociological and Historical Perspective," *International Social Science Journal,* Vol. 107, (1986), pp. 5–18; Edward T. Hall, *The Silent Language,* (Garden City, NY: Doubleday, 1959); Robert Levine and Ellen Wolff, "Social Time: The Heartbeat of Culture," *Psychology Today,* Vol. 19 (March 1985), pp. 29–35; Jay D. Lindquist and Paul M. Lane, "A Cross-Cultural View of Time: Summary of Empirical and Hypothetical Evidence," in Eric H. Shaw and Chou How Wee, eds., *Proceedings of the Fourth Bi-Annual World Marketing Congress,* Vol. 4 (Boca Raton, FL: The Academy of Marketing Science, 1989), pp. 110–118; and Alexander Szalai, *The Use of Time* (The Hague: Mouton, 1972).

25. Kaufman, Lane, and Lindquist, "Time Congruity in the Organization."

26. William J. Baumol, "Income and Substitution Effects in the Linder Theorem," *Quarterly Journal of Economics,* Vol. 37 (1973), pp. 629–633; Gary Becker, "A Theory of the Allocation of Time," *The Economic Journal,* Vol. 75 (1965), pp. 493–517; and Jacquelyn B. Schreiber and Barbara A. Gutek, "Some Time Dimensions of Work: Measurement of an Underlying Aspect of Organization Culture," *Journal of Applied Psychology,* Vol. 72 (1987), pp. 642–650.

27. Hall, *The Hidden Dimension;* Robert V. Levine, "The Pace of Life Across Cultures," in Joseph E. McGrath, ed., *The Social Psychology of Time* (Sage Publications, 1897), pp. 39–60; Pronovost, "Introduction: Time in a Sociological and Historical Perspective;" and E. Zerubavel, *Hidden Rhythms: Schedules and Calendars in Social Life* (Chicago, IL: University of Chicago Press, 1981).

28. Barbara Gross, "Time Scarcity: Interdisciplinary Perspectives and Implications for Consumer Behavior," in Jagdish N. Sheth and Elizabeth C. Hirschman, eds., *Research in Consumer Behavior* (Greenwich, CT: JAI Press, Inc., 1987), pp. 1–54; Douglass K. Hawes, "Leisure and Consumer Behavior," *Journal of the Academy of Marketing Science,* Vol. 7 (1979), pp. 391–403; Elizabeth C. Hirschman, "Theoretical

Perspectives of Time Use: Implications for Consumer Behavior Research," in Jagdish N. Sheth and Elizabeth C. Hirschman, eds., *Research in Consumer Behavior,* Vol. 2 (Greenwich, CT: JAI Press, Inc., 1987), pp. 55–81; and Robert Settle, Pamela C. Alreck and John W. Glasheen, "Individual Time Orientation and Consumer Life Style," in H. Keith Hunt, ed., *Advances in Consumer Research,* Vol. 4 (Ann Arbor, MI: Association for Consumer Research, 1977), pp. 315–319.

29. Carol Kaufman-Scarborough and Jay D. Lindquist, "Understanding the Experience of Time Scarcity, Linking Consumer Time-Personality and Marketplace Behavior," *Time & Society,* Vol. 12, No. 2/3 (2003), pp. 349–370.

30. Adele Horin and Bonnie Malkin, "Slaves to the Clock and Not Happy—That's a Bit Rich," *The Sydney Morning Herald,* March 7, 2003, pp. 1, 8.

31. Sigmund Gronmo, "Concepts of Time: Some Implications for Consumer Research," in Thomas K. Shrull, ed., *Advances in Consumer Research,* Vol. 16 (Ann Arbor, MI: Association for Consumer Research, 1989),pp. 339–345; Paul M. Lane and Jay D. Lindquist, "What is Time: An Empirical Exploratory Investigation," in Jon M. Hawes and John Thanopoulos, eds., *Developments in Marketing Science,* Vol. 12 (Akron, OH: Academy of Marketing Science, 1989), pp. 93–98; Levine, "The Pace of Life across Cultures"; and Zerubavel, *Hidden Rhythms.*

32. Richard M. Coleman, *Wide Awake at 3 A.M.: By Choice or By Chance?* (New York: W. H. Freeman and Co., 1986); Karl C. Hamner, "Experimental Evidence for the Biological Clock," in J. T. Fraser, ed., *The Voices of Time* (Amherst, MA: The University of Massachusetts Press, 1981), pp. 281–295; and Hudson Hoagland, "Some Biochemical Considerations of Time," in J. T. Fraser, pp. 312–329.

33. T. J. Cottle, *Perceiving Time: A Psychological Investigation of Men and Women* (New York: John Wiley and Sons, Inc., 1976); T. K. Das, "Strategic Planning and Individual Temporal Orientation," *Strategic Management Journal,* Vol. 8 (1987), pp. 203–209; and M. Iutcovich et al., "Time Perception: A Case Study of a Developing Nation," *Sociological Focus* (1979), pp. 71–85.

34. Jay D. Lindquist, Paul M. Lane, and Carol F. Kaufman, "Psychological Time Perspective Differences: A Look at Young Malaysians and Americans Using the FAST Scale," in M. Joseph Sirgy, Kenneth D. Bahn, and Tunc Erem, eds., *Proceedings of the Sixth Bi-Annual World Marketing Congress,* Vol. 6 (Blacksburg, VA: The Academy of Marketing Science, 1993), pp. 412–416.

35. Paul M. Lane and Carol F. Kaufman, "Using Time in Strategic Marketing," in Michael J. Baker, ed., *Perspectives on Marketing Management* (New York: John Wiley and Sons, Inc., 1993) and Paul M. Lane and Jay D. Lindquist, "The Three Temporal Heads of the Chinese Dragon: Facing Past, Present and Future Simultaneously," in Charles H. Noble, ed., *Developments in Marketing Science,* Vol. 22 (Chestnut Hill, MA: Academy of Marketing Science, 1999), pp. 271–276.

36. Lane and Lindquist, "The Three Temporal Heads of the Chinese Dragon."

37. Ibid.

38. Michael H. Bond et al., "Chinese Values and the Search for Culture-Free Dimensions of Culture," *Journal of Cross-Cultural Psychology,* Vol. 18 (June 1987), pp. 143–164.

39. Allen C. Bluedorn, Carol F. Kaufman, and Paul M. Lane, "How Many Things Do You Like to Do at Once? An Introduction to Monochronic and Polychronic Time," *The Academy of Management Executive,* Vol. 6 (November 1992), pp. 17–26; Hall, *The Dance of Life*; Hall, *The Silent Language;* Edgar H. Schein, *Organizational Culture and Leadership* (San Francisco: Jossey-Bass Publishers, 1985); Carol F. Kaufman, Paul M. Lane, and Jay D. Lindquist, "Exploring More than 24 Hours a Day: A Preliminary Investigation of Polychronic Time Use," *Journal of Consumer Research,* Vol. 18 (December 1991), pp. 392–401; Kaufman, Lane, and Lindquist, "Time Congruity in the Organization"; and Paul M. Lane, Carol F. Kaufman, and Jay D. Lindquist, "More Than 24 Hours a Day," in Terry Childers, et al., eds., *Marketing Theory and Practice* (St. Petersburg, FL: American Marketing Association, 1989), pp. 123–130.

40. Carol Kaufman-Scarborough and Jay D. Lindquist, "Time Management and Polychronicity: Comparisons, Contrasts, and Insights for the Workplace," *Journal of Managerial Psychology,* Vol. 14, No. 3/4 (1999), pp. 288–312.

41. Kaufman, Lane, and Lindquist, "Exploring More than 24 Hours a Day."

42. Ibid.

43. Carol Kaufman-Scarborough and Jay D. Lindquist, "The Polychronic Attitude Index: Refinement and Preliminary Consumer Marketplace Behavior Applications," in Anil Menon and Arun Sharma, eds., *Marketing and Applications,* Vol. 10 (Chicago, IL: American Marketing Association, 1999), pp. 151–157.

44. Kaufman-Scarborough and Lindquist, "Time Management and Polychronicity."

45. Jay D. Lindquist and Carol Kaufman-Scarborough, "Polychronic Tendency Analysis: A New Approach to Understanding Women's Shopping Behaviors," *Journal of Consumer Marketing,* Vol. 21 (May 2004), pp. 332-342; Jay D. Lindquist and Carol Kaufman-Scarborough, "Polychronic Tendency Models: A Gender Contrast Study," *Proceedings of the Eleventh Biennial World Marketing Congress,* Vol. 11, Session 6.6, ed. by Jeffrey Lewin (Coral Gables, FL: Academy of Marketing Science 2003), CD-ROM.

46. Edward T. Hall, *The Dance of Life;* R. V. Levine and K. Bartlett, "Pace of Life, Punctuality, and Coronary Heart Disease in Six Countries," *Journal of Cross-Cultural Psychology,* Vol. 15, pp. 233–255 and Thomas E. Slocombe and Allen C. Bluedorn, "Organizational Behavior Implications of the Congruence Between Preferred Polychronicity and Experienced Work-Unit Polychronicity," *Journal of Organizational Behavior,* Vol. 20 (1999), pp. 75–99.

47. Lindquist and Lane, "A Cross-Cultural View of Time."

48. Roger E. Axtell, *Do's and Taboos around the World,* 3rd ed. (White Plains, NY: The Benjamin Co., Inc., 1993), pp. 45–49.

49. Linda M. Delene, Martin A. Meloche, and Rosemary Wheatley, "The Influence of Cultural Values and the Marketing of Banking Services," in Ajay K. Manrai and H. Lee Meadow, eds., *Proceedings of the Ninth Biennial World Marketing Congress* (Coral Gables, FL: Academy of Marketing Science, 1999), pp. 424–432; Alain Genestre, Paul Herbig, and Alan T. Shao, "What Does Marketing Really Mean to the Japanese?" *Marketing Intelligence and Planning,* Vol. 3, No. 9 (1995), pp. 16–27; and Rex Shelley, *Culture Shock! Japan* (Portland, OR: Graphic Arts Publishing Center, 1995).

50. Edward T. Hall and Mildred R. Hall, *Understanding Cultural Differences* (Yarmouth, ME: Intercultural Press, 1990).

51. Ian P. Murphy, "It Takes *Guanxi* to do Business in China," *Marketing News* (October 21, 1996), p. 12.

52. Ibid.

53. "Selling in Europe: Borders Fade," *The New York Times* (May 31, 1990).

54. Grant McCraken, "Culture and Consumption: A Theoretical Account of the Structure and Movement of Cultural Meaning of Consumer Goods," *Journal of Consumer Research,* Vol. 13 (June 1986), pp. 71–84.

55. Ibid.

Cultural Influences: Generalizations and Cross-Cultural Perspectives

In class, Professor Dahl asks, "Is there a best country in the world?" Carlos replies that Brazil is the best country in the world; Jasmine thinks the same way about China; Sven likewise looks upon Sweden as the best place; Rajan puts India first; Hiroshi says it's Japan that is the best; Katrina knows that Germany is tops on the planet; and Rosemary feels the same about the United States. Each of these people thinks that his or her homeland is superior. In fact, the initial position taken by each is that his or her country should be the standard by which all others are judged. After more discussion, this conclusion loses favor, and most people decide that each culture has its own way and should be seen in its own separate context. But how do we do this? The students suggested that there surely must be some way to compare cultures on factors that are found in most of them. This would open the door to meaningful cultural exchanges and the marketing of goods and services around the globe. Professor Dahl was bringing home to his students a significant point when he raised the question of "best country." The initial reaction from members of the class showed strong feelings of "ethnocentrism," a very strong bias toward their own countries. After hearing this from a number of classmates, the students were likely becoming more realistic and informed, and they probably came to a more culturally relativistic position. These topics will be addressed later in the chapter.

The chapter will begin with an exploration of a number of culture generalizations dealing with the wide-ranging impact of culture, its functions, how it is learned, and how it changes. We'll also look at the impact of the natural environment on a culture. Then cultural rejection will be touched on. In our discussion of cross-cultural perspectives, the question of whether there is a global culture will be considered, and how cultures are compared on six often-used dimensions will be explored. Finally, there will be a brief discussion of the U.S. culture, primarily based on traditional and emergent values.

12-1 Culture Generalizations

When generalizing about culture and its nature, certain observations can be made. Culture is pervasive, functional, learned/shared, dynamic, and environmentally dependent. Exhibit 12-1 is a summary of the generalizations that we can make about culture. Each of these generalizations will then be discussed in turn.

12-1a Culture Is Pervasive

We've already touched on the concept of pervasiveness as it applies to each of the circles of social influence. In fact, it was seen to be the most pervasive of the five circles. When we say that culture is pervasive, this means that it is in almost every corner of people's lives. In Chapter 11 we discussed its input into the values, beliefs, rituals, customs, mores, conventions, myths, and the like of the members of society. People understand how things are and how they are to be to varying degrees in different cultures. As a reflection of this variability, cultures are referred to as either high or low in **context,** based on their communication style.[1] A *high-context* style is where the communication has most of the information in either the physical way it's presented or the person receiving it already knows the meaning. This is where the rules, values, beliefs, and such of the culture are well known by all and there is little explanation needed for its members. In *low-context* cultures, the knowledge of the ins and outs of the society is not as widespread, and guidance on the "why's" and "how's" of the culture are needed. Here, the communications themselves contain much information. Germany is a low-context culture where there is a focus on getting the message across using specific terms and concepts. Germans appear to outsiders to be impersonal, distant, and detail oriented and to not care for emotional gestures.[2] The high-context Koreans practice *nunchi*, which means "eye-measure"—an emotion- and situation-based communication approach. Here, nonverbal cues such as facial expressions send important signals about attitudes and feelings. People often speak about a topic by describing things about it rather than always directly discussing it [3]

12-1b Culture Is Functional

The ways of a culture evolve over time and do so to bring about its survival and advancement. The culture acts to do such things as preserve necessary skills, pass on essential knowledge, unify the people, provide order, maintain security, set the course for social relationships within the society, aid in communication, establish leadership and governance patterns, and bring new persons into the society. To carry out each of these functions, individuals, organizations, and resources are combined as needed. We also expect that this combining will be done according to the rules of the society.

The marketing of goods and services to support cultural functions provides many opportunities. Look around at your own culture and identify any one of its functions. What are some of the products and services needed to support this cultural function? Don't constrain yourself to purely business applications. Think also about social services or environmental, educational, or governmental organizations. How does the marketer fit into this picture?

12-1c Culture Is Learned/Shared

We are not born with the values, beliefs, behaviors, and the like that we need to know and understand to properly live in our culture. These are passed on to us. Other members of the society share their knowledge and skills with us. These can be formal or informal learning experiences. And we also learn through observation. No matter how different we feel we are or even try to be from each other, our cultural heritage seeps into our lives. The process of learning one's own culture is called **enculturation.** If a person wishes to learn about the ways of a foreign culture, he or she goes through a process of **acculturation.** Acculturation may occur informally as one interacts with cultural members, reads, observes, and participates. Or it might also be done formally where instructional sessions are attended. Those who wish to market goods and services effectively in a foreign culture will find that acculturation will be necessary in most situations. Exceptions would be where products or services fit in as they do in the "selling" culture.

Enculturation and acculturation are forms of socialization. **Socialization** is defined as a process through which we strive to acquire the characteristic ways of behaving, the

---

Exhibit 12-1

Cultural Generalization Components

Culture Is
• Pervasive
• Functional
• Learned/shared
• Dynamic
• Environmentally dependent
• Natural resource dependent

context (cultural context) May be high or low in a culture. A high-context culture is one in which the rules, values, beliefs, and such of the culture are well known by all, and there is little explanation needed for its members. In low-context cultures, the knowledge of the ins and outs of the society is not as widespread, and guidance on the "why's" and "how's" of the culture is needed.

FAQ

Is America a low-context or high-context culture? Why?

enculturation The process of learning one's own culture.

acculturation The process whereby people learn about the ways of a culture foreign to their own.

socialization The process through which we strive to acquire the characteristic ways of behaving in accordance with the values, norms, and attitudes of the social unit of which we are a part.

E x h i b i t 12-2

Socialization

Socialization Types
· Enculturation
· Acculturation

Socialization Influences
· Family
· Religion
· Education
· Mass media

values, norms, and attitudes of the social unit of which we are a part.[4] There is no standard pattern of how socialization works within cultures nor of how it influences consumption. However, understanding socialization helps marketers think more clearly about the types of goods and services best suited to particular cultures and about how these can be offered in the most appealing way.

Beginning practically at birth, individuals may be trained to play their assigned roles correctly within the prevailing culture. At different stages of life, different forces influence the socialization process. The most important of these are *family, education,* and, in many cultures, *religion.* Increasingly important in highly developed societies, particularly because of their direct influence on consumption choices, are the *mass media* (see Exhibit 12-2).

Influence of Family on Socialization   An important aspect of socialization is the learning of role behavior through family interaction. As children, we begin to develop our personalities and self-images through comparison and contrast with others in our immediate families. If Mom and Dad work together in raising the children, we'll probably think this is the way family life should be and bring up our own children the same way. Conversely, if violent talk or behavior is an everyday part of our childhood, we have the potential to become abusive parents ourselves. Gender roles, values, and lifestyle are all first learned through family experience and are likely to have a relatively permanent influence on behavior throughout life. Suppose in one family, for example, the children, both boys and girls, play baseball with Dad, see him in the kitchen cooking, and help both Mom and Dad with the yard work. Consider how different their outlook on life is likely to be from that of the children of a divorced couple, an autocratic father, or an abusive family.

The family is the learning center for an endless stream of attitudes, behaviors, and skills that the child carries through life. Family experience also serves as an interpreter of the world. Through it, parents help children understand and clarify the many different socialization maps that they receive outside the home. Think of situations in your own childhood in which you discovered behaviors that differed from your family's way of doing things. What did you do to better understand what you observed?

The key to the socialization of children is to establish an atmosphere in which they are motivated to learn culturally patterned behaviors. An important part of this is the setting up, either consciously or subconsciously, of a reward system. Typically, good, culturally acceptable behavior within a family is rewarded with a sense of belonging, approval, and love. A child shares a favorite toy with a sibling and is praised by an adult who sees this generosity. The lesson learned is that if I share, I will receive approval and love. The reward, particularly as the child grows older, can also be material. To teach a teenager the value of saving money, her parents reward her by matching the amount she saves from her allowance to help her buy that first used car.

Family influence seems to be weakening in many parts of the world. In America, this has been attributed to a variety of factors, some of which exist in other nations today: the increasing number of single-parent households; dual-income families where both parents work and have less time to spend with children; the decline in multigeneration households; the increased amount of time children spend in school and school-related activities; and, a frequent complaint, the hours children spend in front of the television instead of engaging in family conversation and interaction. However, television viewing among children in the United States has been declining. In 1998, it was the lowest since the 1970s. Most likely some of this viewing time has been shifted to computer use for games and other activities.

Families and Consumption   Family influence in socialization carries over to product choices made by children as they grow up. If the family likes to camp out and has a garage full of tents, sleeping bags, camp stoves, lanterns, and backpacks, children, as they reach adulthood, are likely to have the same types of products and even purchase the same brands as their parents. If Tide laundry detergent is the family favorite, this preference is easily passed on to the next generation. The same can be said for brands of toothpaste, running shoes, golf clubs, preferred restaurants, and favorite stores. Of course, not all consumption patterns will be passed to the next generation, but the potential for this to happen is great.

Look into your own consumption choices. Are there products and services that you now use that match those of your family? Are there others that you purposely avoid, perhaps as a means of breaking away from family ties?

F A Q

Does your family influence what you buy?

Influence of Religion on Socialization   The passing on of culturally accepted beliefs, values, norms, and behaviors through socialization is most pronounced in those cultures in which religion is a dominant force. The leaders of most organized religions take strong positions on the beliefs members are expected to accept, the values and norms they should incorporate into their lives, and the behavior they should exhibit. In strict religious cultures, such as the Islamic culture of Iran, religion is a part of all aspects of life, from family to education to the workplace to government. Only those goods and services that are acceptable in the faith can be legally marketed. In Thailand, where 95 percent of the population is Buddhist, all men are expected to enter a monastery for some period in their lifetime.

In the United States, there are more than 250 different religions, religious denominations, and sects, each with its own code of behavior. Many accept—though to differing extents—the mainstream way of life, including the tenet that work and material reward, if put to proper use, are desirable.[5] For example, a person from a strict, conservative-religious background may view expensive clothing, flashy cars, or the use of credit cards as symbols of a materialistic approach to life that is inconsistent with the laws of God. Other religious groups are more tolerant of this type of materialism. There appears to be a lessening of the socializing influence of organized religious groups in the United States. In particular, the "main line" Protestant churches (Methodists, Lutherans, Presbyterians, and the like) have been experiencing membership declines. The Catholic Church has been growing in the United States, mainly because of the increase in the Hispanic-American population maintaining socialization effects within this group. For small sectors of the culture, New Age and oriental religions are socializing influences. There is also growth among those with no religious affiliation and worshipers classed as "fundamentalist."

Religion and Consumption   The kind of religious training, or lack of it, that we receive during socialization affects our behavior as consumers. Religious practice may dictate the use of some goods and services or prohibit the consumption of others. The Amish do not buy automobiles, but they create demand for plow horses, wagons, and carriages; Mormons do not consume coffee, tea, alcohol, or tobacco products; orthodox Jews buy kosher food products; and Muslim women wear clothing that reinforces the religious value of modesty. These are all examples of direct religious influence on product selection.

Influence of Education on Socialization   The formative years of most children's lives are spent in school. In the United States, the 13 years from elementary through high school require students to spend six to eight hours a day, five days a week, wholly under the socializing influence of teachers and peers. College degrees and graduate work extend the schooling period even further. Hence, educational institutions are a major socialization influence in the lives of the members of the culture. Understanding this, there is a growing trend in the United States in favor of increased parental choice in the schools to which their children are sent. Through school, growing minds are exposed to a tremendous range of people, beliefs, values, and viewpoints that are not a part of their family socialization. Filled with conflicting views, the world becomes a much less consistent place as children grow. This is even more pronounced in the college years, as students spend more and more time away from their families. An interesting assertion by one scholar is that American universities provide students with vast amounts of knowledge and information but seem to be failing in delivering exposure to the values and ethical principles found in the literature of philosophy and other disciplines.[6] A greater number of individuals in the United States are receiving more formal education. This has produced a more highly educated and demanding consumer population, causing marketers to be more sensitive to the needs, suggestions, and complaints of shoppers and buyers.

Turning to Japan, we see students in elementary and junior high going to school five and one half days a week all year round. A typical ninth grader may leave for school at 7:30 A.M. and return home at 5:00 P.M., eat dinner at 6:00 P.M., go to "cram school" from 7:00 to 10:00 P.M., study from 10:00 P.M. to 2:00 A.M. and then sleep. If he or she does well, admission to a good high school is assured, and this opens the door for education at a top university. The Japanese system is not presently designed to promote individualism, originality, or creativity. There is much emphasis on memorizing the wisdom of others. There is almost no violence within the schools, and the drop-out rate is almost nonexistent. Upon graduation from college, students enter a six-day workweek consisting of twelve- to fifteen-hour days. Decision making is very slow, and there are many middle managers in companies, making it challenging to foreign nationals who wish to trade with Japan.

Education and Consumption   Socialization through educational institutions influences consumption in several ways. Interaction with teachers, for example, may lead to more informed choices in the marketplace. A teacher's guidance on appropriate food choices; basic medical and dental care; reproductive health; concern for the environment; and the problems associated with drugs, alcohol, and tobacco products all encourage certain marketplace behaviors. Influenced by their peers, students may make entirely different choices, affecting everything from brands and styles of clothing and entertainment options to serious lifestyle decisions, such as use of drugs or sexual behavior.

Of special interest to marketers is socialization in elementary and high school—two other settings where life-long consumption habits often begin. How advertising is understood and accepted and how it influences children are of particular interest to marketers. One study in the United States compared attitudes toward advertising among third- and sixth-grade public school students of low and high socioeconomic backgrounds.[7] Among third-graders, lower-status students saw advertising as more truthful and less biased than did their higher-status peers. Among sixth-graders, the differences between the two groups were no longer pronounced. From this we might infer that at eight years of age, children primarily reflect the positions of their families, the most important socialization influence they have encountered to that point in their lives. From third to sixth grade, school becomes a stronger socialization influence in certain areas of the child's life. In the situation here, two different socioeconomic groups came to share common views on the truthfulness and bias of advertising.

Influence of Mass Media on Socialization   The mass media are those communications options with which large shares of the population have contact on a regular basis. Television, newspapers, magazines, radio, computer networks like Prodigy and the Internet, billboards, and advertising on transportation vehicles are prime examples. These media provide a wide variety of programs and/or advertising that intentionally or unintentionally have the potential to socialize the people exposed to them. Mass media socialization appears to continue throughout a person's life.[8]

Considering television, what people watch appears to influence their perceptions of the material world. An example relates to soap opera watching in the United States. Heavy viewers observing the behaviors and possessions that were associated with an affluent lifestyle on these programs gave higher estimates of how often these behaviors and possessions occur in real life than did light viewers of such shows.[9]

The children's television show "Barney" is intentionally scripted by its production team to be a potentially socializing influence on youngsters. Parents are looking for children's shows that provide this opportunity. Hence, some parents love the program, as it helps them teach toddlers their ABCs, how to count, and the fundamentals of the English language. Just as importantly, the show introduces and reinforces positive values and behaviors in the very young. They are taught such principles as love, sharing, tolerance,

F A Q

Do mass media mirror the culture, or do they shape it?

E x h i b i t 12-3

The message here is that to be athletic is culturally desirable, and so is drinking Gatorade.

Source: Quaker Oats Company.

respect, kindness, and sensitivity to others. The show is designed to help children learn social skills. Its range of characters crosses ethnic lines and exposes children to lifestyles different from their own.

Similarly, public service advertising through the mass media seeks to provide positive behavior models and reinforce socially acceptable values and beliefs. Through campaigns against drinking and driving, or informational advertising on the spread of AIDS, young people, in particular, are taught socially acceptable behavior. The ongoing "Just Say No" campaign that urges young people not to accept offers of drugs is a good example of the mass media reinforcing a positive attitude that may not be considered popular among peer groups.

Mass Media and Consumption   All mass media advertising is, to a varying extent, an attempt by marketers to associate their goods or services with positive or popular lifestyles, behaviors, or attitudes. Fashion products, beauty aids, cars, soft drinks, and foods are all promoted in such a way as to make them seem socially "right" for the target market. The most successful actually become symbols of socialization and acceptance. Pepsi Cola and Reebok shoes, for example, are strongly associated with the youth culture.

The situations and behaviors portrayed in advertising are also socialization cues. Look for the cues built into the advertisement in Exhibit 12-3. What does this advertisement say about the culture of its target market?

How do teenage girls in America ("teenyboppers") and Japan ("ti-ni-boppa-zu") compare themselves to the female models found in advertising? American girls actively do this and use the models as a way to determine and meet cultural beauty standards. Those most likely to do this are high in public self-consciousness and have low self-esteem and high satisfaction with appearance. Though one would expect more conformity from the Japanese girls based on the traditions of that nation, this was not the case. Very few follow the American teenager approach. Those that do use the media for social comparison show high public self-consciousness.[10]

F A Q

Does public service advertising work?

> ### Marketing Management—Implications and Actions
>
> Knowing and understanding how people are socialized into a country's culture helps marketers:
>
> - Develop and position products and services that provide benefits related to learning cultural ways and gaining acceptance in the culture.
> - Identify the socializing power of families over product class and brand selection to help position and promote products and services in appropriate family situations.
> - Determine appropriate products and services to be offered based upon acceptable religious parameters within the culture.
> - Identify appropriate mass media outlets for promoting goods and services within the society, and where appropriate, engage in communication to aid in the positive socialization of members of the culture.

E x h i b i t 12-4

Culture Is Dynamic

Cultural Change Influences

· Technology
· Cultural diffusion
· Natural events
· Political events
· Conflict events

12-1d Culture Is Dynamic

Whether viewed nationally or internationally, an important characteristic of culture is that it undergoes constant change. As a culture changes, the needs and behaviors of consumers shift. Because people within a culture must be able to adapt in order to survive, cultural change is an ongoing, if sometimes uneven, process. Major factors that contribute to the process are *technology, cultural diffusion,* and *natural, political, and conflict events.* Exhibit 12-4 summarizes the factors than can influence cultural change.

The Influence of Technology   Advances in technology rarely have the power, on their own, to change a culture. A society develops and accepts advances in technology only when there is a clear need. Technological developments, therefore, gain acceptance only because cultural norms and values have *already* changed or are changing. Frozen foods and microwave ovens, although the technologies behind them had been around for some time, became popular in the United States only when homemakers were quite ready to place more emphasis on convenience and less on the merits of home cooking. Drive-in, fast-food franchises like McDonald's, Burger King, Taco Bell, and Kentucky Fried Chicken have become national institutions because of increased population mobility and the premium we place upon saving time.

Although it cannot alter the fabric of the culture, technology can accelerate changes in values and behavior. As a prime example, the reason the birth control pill drew near instant acceptance by some segments of the population was that it was introduced during a period when sexual attitudes became more permissive and smaller families became the norm. Then, into the decades of the 1980s and 1990s stormed the fear of AIDS. Primarily transmitted through sexual activity, its rapid spread around the globe has caused many to re-examine their sexual practices and so minimize their chances of becoming infected with the virus. The disease has also created the need for a range of new products and services including expanded hospice and home care for terminally ill patients, techniques for purifying donor blood supplies, and a host of drugs for treatment. Also, condoms, once marketed primarily as a birth-control product, achieved a new positioning as a protection against sexually transmitted disease.

What this means for marketers is that the innovations most likely to be successful are not necessarily unique products but are more often those that are closely in sync with cultural change. We can see this in the design of automobiles in the United States over the past two decades. In that time frame, there has been an increased call for reduced pollution, lower gasoline consumption, and increased passenger safety. Reducing pollution spawned catalytic converters and engines that generally run more efficiently. Following legislation calling for average mileage performance to increase, lighter-weight, smaller cars became available. Air bags, antilock brake systems, and better side-impact protection are results of the push for safer transportation. And now standardization of child safety seats is occurring. CBite 12-1 tells the story of how technology seems to be impacting the civility of product owners in the U.S. We would likely find citizens of other cultures in many places around the world having related problems.

CBite 12-1

The Cell Phone's Impact on Manners and Civility

Are you ever annoyed by cell phones ringing in a restaurant, or at the movies, or as you are shopping in a store? Are you sick of drivers involved in accidents or cutting you off while on their cell phone? What about the crude language people use in public on their phones? Almost half of Americans in a study conducted in 2001 say they often see people using their cell phones in a loud or annoying way in public. Interestingly, 17 percent of all cell phone owners admit that they do this. Urban residents are more likely to have experienced this behavior than are people in rural areas. This is not to say that cell phones have not been a boon to the American society, but likely no one anticipated the negative impact on civility and manners that this technology would have.

Source: Melanie Shortman, "Rude Awakening," *American Demographics* (July/August 2002), p. 18. Copyright © 2002 Crain Communications, Inc. Reprinted with permission.

The Influence of Cultural Diffusion **Cultural diffusion** occurs when people in one culture become exposed to the people and/or ways of another culture. For example, the introduction of rock music—with its electric guitars, its loud, driving beat, and the youth lifestyles and fashions associated with it—into such diverse places as Russia, Singapore, Taiwan, France, and Japan has had enormous and long-lasting impact on young people in each of these countries. Rock music has drawn them away from the music of their own cultures and also from previous paths of behavior and traditional values. The popularity of Levi Strauss jeans almost the world over has not only changed fashions for both men and women but has also influenced lifestyles and behavior patterns. The technologies of jet travel, computer chips, and satellite communications have produced incredible demand for goods and services across cultures around the globe. Another very significant example of cultural diffusion is the exchange that has occurred between East and West since World War II. Japan has emerged as a model of Western technology and marketing expertise, while the United States has developed a healthy respect for Japanese management techniques, and has adopted sushi bars and the fashions of designer Issey Miyake.

> **cultural diffusion** Occurs when people in one culture are exposed to people and/or ways of another culture, and this exposure begins to change the culture.

The western influence on the place of women in the Japanese culture is reflected in magazine advertising. Traditionally, women were more negatively portrayed in Japanese magazine advertising, but by the early 1990s both male and female central ad models were being shown in a positive way. Also, in the past women had been associated with low-priced products more often than men. However, male central figures were used more often for low-priced products and women more often for high-priced items in the 1990s ads.[11]

The Influence of Natural, Political, and Conflict Events Natural events that occur on the planet can be gradual climatic changes (the moving southward of the desert in Africa, long-term drought, long-term overabundance of rain), or the dwindling of food supply not related to climate (overfishing, overhunting, or resource exploitation through destruction of the forests, wetlands, etc.), or natural disasters (earthquakes, tsunamis, volcanic eruptions, hurricanes, and the like). Such occurrences can force populations to move; rebuild; change clothing, shelter, and food consumption patterns; change priorities; and adapt as necessary to ensure survival of the culture.

Political events such as the communization of the Soviet Union and Eastern Europe after World War II drastically affected the availability of consumer goods and services and changed expectation levels and lifestyles. The socialization of the Scandinavian countries through the elective process greatly affected who would supply services to consumers, and the burdensome tax structure greatly impacted disposable income.

Wars among nations result in the acquisition of territory and natural, human, and capital resources. However, such hostilities can also result in cultural diffusion and the artificial combining of cultures by the victors, as was the case in World Wars I and II. Internal changes can also occur, as in America during World War II. In this period, the bulk of the working male population went to war. Women who had primarily lived the roles of homemaker and child-rearer were needed to work in most of the nonmilitary sectors of society. They did many of the traditionally male jobs, which permanently changed both the society's and women's views of what they could do and be. There was cultural confusion when the men returned home, but the course had been set. This was a watershed moment for women's role definition in the U.S. culture. And today women do everything from driving bulldozers on construction projects to serving as judges on the U.S. Supreme Court. Civil war can also bring great change, as happened in China, Cuba, and Afghanistan, for example. Political and/or religious ideologies in these countries brought great change to the consumers and marketplaces.

Marketing Management—Implications and Actions

Understanding the forces that change a culture helps marketers:

- Realize when a society is ready to accept new technology and the changes it will bring and develop products, services, and transition-easing procedures to help the marketplace and consumers make the change.
- Take steps to introduce products and services to key segments of the culture so that cultural diffusion can occur.
- Understand the implications of political and conflict events on a culture and the resultant changes in benefits sought by consumers so that appropriate products and services may be offered.
- Use their strengths in a nonprofit sense to come to the aid of the victims of natural disasters and also offer for-profit goods and services to help populations cope with the situation.

12-1e Culture Is Environmentally Dependent

Cultures are also influenced by the geographic locations in which they exist and the natural resources they possess. The general weather patterns including temperatures, precipitation and humidity, length of days, hours of sunlight, and the like affect a broad spectrum of cultural factors. The topography also impacts culture. Does the society exist in a mountainous area or in the midst of a flat plain? Is it in a tropical forest, a jungle, or on the rolling dunes of the desert? Is it on a group of islands in the Pacific Ocean or in the midst of a land mass thousands of miles from the sea? Finally, altitude is a factor. Think of cultures living near sea level versus those that exist above 10,000 feet in the Andes Mountains of South America. Basics such as transportation methods, food supply and preparation, clothing needs, and forms of shelter will often vary dramatically across the environments mentioned. Because of the variations of consumer behavior in these situations, marketing activities to provide the benefits needed by consumers will also be diverse.

12-1f Culture Is Dependent upon Natural Resources

Natural resource availability and the ability to take advantage of these resources also enable or constrain a culture. Great oil resources in the Middle East have had dramatic impact on the cultures involved. Oil has been recovered and shipped around the world. Revenues have been used to raise education standards, improve roads, build facilities, and allow for the purchase of goods and services at quality and quantity levels not possible before the oil opportunity was recognized and exploited. Availability of timber, minerals, precious metals and gems, water, arable land, and harvest potential from the sea, to name a few, act as opportunities or challenges to a culture.

12-1g Rejection of the Culture

Through socialization, people learn about values, beliefs, norms, and behaviors appropriate to their cultural settings. Family, education, religion, and the mass media all contribute to the process, influencing goods and service selection and consumption. Sometimes, however, socialization backfires. Rather than allowing the culture to shape our beliefs and behavior, we react against it.

Culture rejection is most common during periods of political, social, economic, or technological change. People or groups of people discover that their values are no longer in harmony with those of the culture that surrounds them. Willingly or unwillingly, they break away from the cultural standards that once were not questioned. There are four paths people take in response to this feeling of being "out of sync" with their culture: *hedonism, etherealization, search for community,* and *activism.*

Hedonism   *Hedonism* develops when old norms and values lose meaning but no new society-wide norms arise to take their place. In response, people turn in on themselves and elevate their own good feelings to the highest position in their value hierarchy. They may, for example, espouse sexual freedom, join a political movement, go into therapy, use mood-altering drugs, jog, or become obsessed with body building or their own financial gain.

Etherealization   *Etherealization* occurs when people lose faith in the ability of their society to provide the things they want, or when they have so many material possessions that property begins to lose its meaning. Values shift to put emphasis on beauty, on the natural order, or on spirituality. People choose to buy natural foods, take up creative hobbies, go hiking or backpacking, or join religious groups. There is a shift away from viewing goods as items of value to viewing goods as symbols. One result of this break from cultural standards is the opening of markets for different types of products. An example is the popularity of goods made from recycled and recyclable materials. Similarly, to attract environment-conscious etherealists, marketers use promotions that focus on conservation or protection of endangered species.

Search for Community   When people feel that the dominant culture does not support their values, they sometimes seek to form a community with other people of similar inclinations. Communes and support groups arise. A group of divorced fathers offers moral support. A group of women traders on Wall Street offers networking opportunities and career counseling. In cities, neighborhoods develop as centers for individuals whose values differ from those of society at large. Members try to support each other, perhaps by purchasing products made or sold by others in the same community. As these various groups form, their needs for meeting spaces, dining choices, and other social activities are identified and catered to by marketers. A market for special products—such as T-shirts, coffee mugs, and other imprinted merchandise—that identify people as members of a group might also arise.

Activism   Some people who do not share the dominant values of their society turn to *activism* in order to change societal norms. Joining organizations such as Greenpeace, the Rainbow Coalition, or the Libertarian Party, they seek the opportunity to express their values and to persuade the culture at large to accept them. An excellent example of the attitudes of an activist group becoming those of the norm is what is happening in the United States as a result of antismoking campaigns. We are fast becoming a smoke-free society, as public buildings, workplaces, restaurants, factories, and airlines ban tobacco smoking. The overall result of the antismoking actions is that domestic sales of cigars and cigarettes have been affected, and the choices of consumers who smoke have narrowed. Even so, we are experiencing a dramatic increase in cigar smoking in some parts of America.

12-2 Cross-Cultural Perspectives

In this section, we'll begin by commenting on the concept of a global culture, asking ourselves whether this is a myth or reality. Next, how consumers view their own culture as compared to others and what impact this may have on their willingness to import goods and services will be touched on (see Exhibit 12-5). Six values dimensions, beyond those discussed earlier in the chapter, for measuring one culture against another will round out this section.

> ▶ **culture rejection**
> The breaking away from the ways of one's culture that may cause people to follow one of four paths: hedonism, etherealization, search for community, or activism.

E x h i b i t 12-5

Global Culture

Consumers' Cultural View
· Ethnocentrism
· Consumer ethnocentricity
· Cultural animosity
· Cultural relativism

International *Marketplace 12-1*

The Myth of the European Consumer

There were an estimated 460 million car-buying, clothes-washing, grocery-shopping consumers in the European Economic Community in 2004. Relatively affluent, they buy more brand-name items than people in any other part of the world. And thanks to the European Union (EU), it has never been easier to sell and distribute products to them. To many marketers, single-market Europe represents opportunity as never before.

Talk to the executives of any large consumer goods company, such as Lever Bros., Procter & Gamble, or Quaker Oats, and they'll eagerly tell of their pan-European marketing strategies. After all, it makes sense economically to create stand-alone Euro-brands by standardizing products, packaging, and advertising. Why sell Detergent A in England, Detergent B in Germany, and Detergent C in Spain, when Detergent X might work equally well in all three places? But while developing a "one-size-fits-all" European brand name is one thing, finding the "one-size-fits-all" European consumer is another.

Differences in tastes, habits, language, culture, climate, and income influence purchasing decisions a great deal. Europeans are bound by tradition as to the foods they eat, the way they conduct business, and the way they shop. Though Europeans may be brand conscious, 99 percent of those brands are still national, if not strictly local, in their appeal. What it all comes down to is that consumers do not consider themselves to be "European." They are Italian, German, Spanish, English, French . . . and prefer to be treated as such.

Source: Adapted from "The Myth of the European Consumer," *Industry Week,* Vol. 243 (February 21, 1994), pp. 28–30 ff.

12-2a Is There a Global Culture?

When we speak of the world as getting smaller, we are obviously talking in terms of speed of travel and communications. Though all people have much in common as human beings, there still are many differences in cultures as we move from nation to nation. We can conclude that the suggestion that a global culture exists today is a myth. Today we are already seeing nations in Europe, North America, the Asian Pacific Rim, and other regions of the world coming together to form economic trading blocks. Although this action brings together cultures with some similarity, these cultures are not homogeneous. We've already presented information and examples across a number of cultures looking at certain characteristics that bring the "difference" point home. But how are cultures compared with one another, how are they grouped, how are they better understood from marketing and consumer behavior perspectives? Obviously, comparisons can be made on any or all of the factors that have already been touched upon in Chapter 11 (section 11-2, "Nature of Culture—Components"): norms, customs, mores, conventions, sanctions, values, beliefs, rituals, the languages of culture, government and laws, material artifacts, and consumer products and cultural meanings. Also, cross-cultural views tied to how socialization occurs; level of diversity within the culture; natural, political, and conflict events impacts; and the natural environment in which the culture exists could be considered. Other variables need attention beyond these. How do consumers see their own culture as compared to others? How could cross-cultural analysis be carried out in a broader values context? It's time to look at these questions.

Check out International Marketplace 12-1. Here you'll see that the idea of a global culture is not supported even across the European community.

12-2b The Consumers' Cultural View

ethnocentrism The act of viewing one's own culture as better or even superior to others. This may result in judging other cultures by such standards.

People have a natural tendency to view their own culture as better than or even superior to others. This is called **ethnocentrism.** People who are very ethnocentric see their culture as the center of everything and even judge other cultures by their standards. Ethnocentrism serves a useful function in that people who see their own normative system as fundamentally correct will be motivated to abide by it.[12] It is, however, obviously a dangerous position for marketers of goods and services to adopt if they seek to truly understand or influence consumer behavior in other cultures that have different values, beliefs, and behaviors.

Consumer ethnocentricity is an economic form of ethnocentrism. It flows from the consumer's love and concern for her or his own country and the harmful economic impact of importing goods from other nations. Developed and tested in the United States and a number of other nations, the CETSCALE measures consumer ethnocentricity. Scores on this scale are inversely related to consumer willingness to buy imported goods, perceptions of quality of such goods, cultural openness, education, and income.[13] In fact, those who are strong consumer ethnocentrists see buying foreign goods as not just an economic issue but also a moral one. They will even buy inferior goods made in their own country when better offerings are available from other places because it is seen as immoral not to do so.[14] In a study of ten products ranging from medicine (most necessary) to personal computers (less necessary) to liquor (even less necessary) to golf clubs (least necessary) as viewed by Korean consumers, it was found that the more a product was rated as unnecessary, the greater the ethnocentric impact on importing it.[15]

The CETSCALE was tested in Soviet Armenia, using the native language, after the breakup of the Soviet Union. It was found that those who participated in the study were as consumer ethnocentric as the Koreans and more so than Americans.[16] The scale was also tested in the Czech Republic, Hungary, and Poland. Here CETSCALE in its 10-item form did not work well. A good-fitting scale using only five questions worked well in Hungary, a six-question scale was best in Poland, and a scale using seven questions worked best in the Czech Republic. The scales that worked not only differed in number of questions but also in question type; there were only two questions (one patriotism based and one economic impact based) common across all three scales.[17]

One of the problems with comparing CETSCALE scores without adjustment across cultures is what is called "extreme response style." This is the tendency for culture members to either cluster answers near the center of a response scale or to scatter them more widely across the choice positions.[18] For example, in one study Hispanic Americans used more of the scale than did non-Hispanic Americans, yet in another study American college students used more of the scale than did Korean college students.[19] This means that comparisons of scores must be adjusted for this tendency to give a clearer picture of similarities and differences. Exhibit 12-6 shows the results of a study of British consumers. They were asked what the first choice of country of origin would be for eight product categories. Notice how consumer-ethnocentric the people in the sample were. Only in the category of "TV Sets," where Japan was selected, did they choose any other country than their own more often as number one. In five out of eight product categories the British selected their homeland at a level of about 58 percent or more as first choice. This reported behavior shows a strong consumer ethnocentric tendency.[20]

A related concept is **cultural animosity.** This is the situation where the people in one nation have a very strong aversion, in some cases bordering on hatred, to the people of

> **consumer ethnocentricity**
> An economic form of ethnocentrism. It is based on the consumer's love and concern for his or her own country and the perceived harmful economic impact of importing goods from other nations. Strong consumer ethnocentrists see buying foreign goods as not just an economic issue but also a moral one.

> **cultural animosity**
> A situation in which the people in one nation have a very strong aversion to (in some cases, bordering on hatred) the people of another country. This is based on very negative historical experiences—the results of war, economics, religious or ethnic discrimination, and the like.

E x h i b i t **12-6**			**Country of Origin Preferences—The British Consumer View**				
Origin Country vs. Product	**Cars**	**Food Products**	**TV Sets**	**Toiletries**	**Fashion Wear**	**Toys**	**Do-It-Yourself Tools**	**Furniture**
Britain	48.5	74.9	23.5	57.7	46.9	70.4	72.4	66.1
United States	1.6	3.2	2.3	7.7	5.5	14.3	4.2	2.1
France	4.3	8.8	0.2	29.5	17.6	0.7	0.0	5.5
Germany	32.9	0.9	6.6	0.5	1.6	6.0	18.5	8.5
Japan	5.8	0.2	67.2	0.2	0.0	7.2	4.2	0.9
Italy	4.9	11.1	0.0	3.9	27.9	0.2	0.5	12.2

Source: George Balabanis and Adamantios Diamantopoulos, "Domestic Country Bias, Country-of-Origin Effects, and Consumer Ethnocentrism: A Multidimensional Unfolding Approach," *Journal of the Academy of Marketing Science,* Vol. 32 (Winter 2004), pp. 80–95.

Note: The numbers are percentages of British consumers by product category whose first choice was the country listed. For example, 48.5 percent of the British consumers in the research sample said that Britain was their first country of choice origin for cars.

International *Marketplace 12-2*

The Latin American Consumer Market

The Latin American market, with its bustling cities like Caracas, Sao Paulo, Mexico City, Rio de Janeiro, and Buenos Aires, represents a huge and dynamic consumer economy that is being reshaped by new technologies and media. In 2004 Brazil was the largest country in Latin America, with an estimated 168 million people. Mexico had 105 million; Argentina 39 million; and Venezuela 25 million. Latin Americans enjoy a dynamic consumer economy. Young populations and large households promise even greater future growth. Yet no matter how appealing statistics make it, the Latin American market is by no means an easy one to enter. It exists in a state of constant flux, both in terms of the fabric of the culture and the buying patterns of its members.

Like the United States, Latin America is struggling to integrate traditional values with new ideas and attitudes. Only half of Latin Americans recently surveyed are optimistic about the institutions of marriage and family. At the same time, however, the most popular leisure-time activities are family based, as are the types of products purchased. In the urban settings in Mexico and Argentina, large shares of the population have television sets, VCRs, washing machines, water heaters, and telephones. Other popular products include clock radios, CD players, and cable television, and automobile ownership is on the rise.

Despite people's familiarity with many of the same consumer goods, striking differences between the United States and its southern neighbors can create stumbling blocks for unwary marketers. Some are related to social class and income differences. Others, such as resistance to money-back guarantees, seem cultural. Brand names mean less to Latin Americans, where finding the best price is all-important. While a "Made in the USA" label connotes product superiority in casual clothing, it means much less in the realm of health and beauty aids. And when it comes to beer, Latin Americans uniformly prefer the local brews. In shopping, while giants like Wal-Mart are reshaping Latin America's shopping habits, traditional channels, including markets and street fairs, still dominate. Low price and convenient location are the only priorities.

There appear to be three ways to position products in emerging Latin American markets. First, some products offer opportunities across income groups and national boundaries. Moderately priced clothing is one such category. Second, some products are to be targeted within certain income groups, again across borders. Consumers who are college educated, have high incomes, and are in professional or white-collar occupations are more likely than average to buy second cars, second homes, and high-tech devices such as personal computers and CD players. Third, Latin America offers niche opportunities defined by taste. In the health and beauty aids category, for example, U.S. and French products are evenly rated among the general population in Mexico.

Source: Ignacio Galceran and Jon Berry, "A New World of Consumers," *American Demographics,* Vol. 17 (March 1995), pp. 26, 28–30, 32, 33.

---

another country.[21] Often this is based on very negative historical experiences—the results of war, economics, religious or ethnic discrimination, and the like. One example is the Chinese view of Japan and Japanese products. In this case, both war animosity and economic animosity toward Japan is present. People's Republic of China consumers' animosity toward Japan was found to negatively affect their willingness to buy Japanese goods even though the quality ratings of the goods were very high.[22] Such barriers to trade in many places around the globe will likely persist for long periods of time. This points to the need to measure both consumer ethnocentricity and cultural animosity in certain situations.

cultural relativism When a person views or judges any behavior, value, or norm within its own social and cultural setting.

Cultural relativism is where a person views or judges any behavior, value, or norm within its own social and cultural setting. Practicing cultural relativism, marketers, to put it simply, follow that old adage, "When in Rome, do as the Romans do." Hence, as marketers consider the types of products or services that could successfully be offered in another nation, they must look to that culture to point the way rather than to "know what is best" based on the standards of their own culture. When the values, norms, and behaviors of the members of the culture are not in line with those that the marketer wishes to acknowledge, he or she must decide either to carry on trade in line with the former or not trade profitably within the culture. Global thinking and sensitivity are the keys to marketing success.

Look at International Marketplace 12-2. What are the bases suggested for comparing consumers in various parts of Latin America? How is this different from the key values approach discussed in section 12-2c? Which is better?

12-2c Cultural Comparison—A Key Values Approach

In Chapter 11 we discussed the importance of values as a basis for comparing cultures (see section 11-2f). Hofstede proposed another approach to cross-cultural value measurement, and it has been applied more extensively. It is based on five dimensions of cultural values, sometimes called value orientations.[23] These values are: individualism versus collectivism, masculinity versus femininity, high versus low power distance, high versus low uncertainly avoidance, and abstract versus associative thinking.[24] A sixth dimension has been suggested. It is the *Confucian Dynamic.* Exhibit 12-7 summarizes six ways that cultures may be compared that are commonly used.

Individualism versus Collectivism Cultures If members of a culture put their own advancement and welfare ahead of these same factors for the groups and institutions of their culture, and their culture as a whole, this is an **individualistic culture.** In such societies, people are personally focused, have loose connections with others, and place their interests and goals above those of other individuals and the groups to which they belong. Equality, freedom, the uniqueness of the individual, and personal enjoyment are important, and competition leading to becoming "Number 1" is common and encouraged. The development of the "private self" is encouraged. Countries such as the Netherlands, Australia, England, Denmark, Sweden, Italy, France, and the United States are higher on the individualistic scale.[25] In a **collectivistic culture,** people put the good of others, the groups they belong to, and the society as a whole above their own good. Self-discipline is important, and individuals basically accept where they are in life. Competition on a group basis is acceptable but not encouraged. There is less need for equality and freedom, and ways to protect the groups to which one belongs are sought after. Here, the development of the "collective self" is fostered. Countries scoring higher on collectivism include Mexico, Panama, Chile, Venezuela, Ethiopia, Kenya, Zambia, Egypt, Taiwan, Hong Kong, South Korea, Indonesia, Thailand, Pakistan, Turkey, Portugal, Greece, and Russia.[26]

In individualistic cultures, consumers are less likely to be influenced by their peers or reference groups. Choosing products that focus on their personal self-image, that will give personal pleasure and allow them to express themselves freely will be on target. Products and services that will contribute to their skills and knowledge improvement and professional advancement will also be demanded. Easy acquisition and financing of purchases will be needed, and promotion should be focused on individual benefits. A wide variety of choices is needed to allow for individual expression. In a collectivist society, "fitting in" is important, so products and services that reference groups demand are needed. Pleasure, skills development, and knowledge acquisition in group settings are also to be a focus for offerings. Choice variety is not a necessary consideration, and promotion should be in the context of the consumer being part of various groups.

A study of advertising in men's and women's magazines revealed that individualism was featured in the main message strategy in 80 percent of the South Korean ads and in 92 percent of the U.S. ads. However, 15 percent of the Korean magazine ads had collectivist main message strategies, while only 1 percent of the U.S. ads did.[27] This is somewhat in line with the more collectivist position of Korea as found in earlier research and definitely matches the strong U.S. position on individualism.

Masculinity versus Femininity Cultures Cultures may also be judged on how the roles of men and women are differentiated and how publicly or privately segregated the two genders are one from another. Role differentiation in various settings, from within the home to within the culture at large, are assessed. Societies are classed as "masculine" if male roles are considered superior to those of the female and "feminine" if the reverse is true. In a **masculine culture,** high value is placed on such things as monetary gain, material possessions, competition, being successful, and being assertive and aggressive. The **feminine culture** sets value on nurturing, the family, quality of life, social responsibility, environmental quality, and the like over attaining wealth, possessions, and professional success. Some cultures are very masculine, leading to strict gender segregation and very

▶**individualistic culture** A society in which members put their personal advancement and welfare ahead of that for other groups, institutions, and the culture as a whole.

▶**collectivistic culture** A culture in which people put the good of others, the groups they belong to, and the society as a whole above their own.

▶**masculine culture** A society in which male roles are considered superior to female roles.

▶**feminine culture** A society in which female roles are considered superior to male roles.

F A Q

Is the United States really becoming less masculine?

restrictive behavior norms, especially for females. Women must wear certain "chaste" clothing, not leave the home unless in the presence of a male relative, and worship in a separate part of the religious building from men, and in social gatherings they are in a separate area from the men. The value of a male child may be greater than that of a female, and male members of a family may actually have the traditional right of life or death over the female members.

As the prescribed roles for men and women vary across cultures, their behavior as consumers will also. In the U.S. culture, generally the society has become less masculine over the past thirty years, and the roles of men and women have in many cases become more blurred. As a result, we see both genders shopping for groceries, buying automobiles, buying equipment for competitive sports participation, purchasing items for children, preparing meals, doing the laundry, and handling other tasks traditionally carried out by members of only one gender or the other. In Japan, we find a masculine society that is slowly changing. Women still have the primary responsibility for running the home and raising the children, while the husband is the leader and primary "bread winner." However, women are becoming more educated and are beginning to move in the business world, though they are still viewed as somewhat inferior to men. Most Islamic countries are masculine, which is in line with religious teachings and the principle of patriarchy. Afghanistan until the recent past was an example of a very masculine culture. Here, women were almost totally restricted to the home, had less academic education than their male peers, and lived according to very clearly defined roles. You can see that how a culture fits on the masculine-feminine spectrum will have direct impact on male and female goods and services demands and how consumers function in the marketplace.

High versus Low Power Distance Cultures

power distance   The level of social inequality that exists in a society and how willing members are to accept authority at all levels. High power distance means high social inequality.

Power distance within a culture is tied to the level of social inequality that exists and how willing members of society are to accept authority at all levels. This includes accepting authority at the family level, in social settings, at work, from government agencies, and the like. Very *high power distance* cultures are those where the difference in power between the most and least powerful individuals or groups is great. Caste systems and strictly observed social class systems are typical of high power distance societies. Great gulfs in such things as wealth, land, education, income, access to health care, job opportunities, political power, and privilege are typical. In high power distance cultures, there are strict vertical relationships. Here, subordinates in any situation from the home to the work place or in social settings must maintain appropriate "distance" from superiors in conversation and demeanor. People seek power and ways to increase their power as a source of satisfaction.[28] Countries with higher power distance include Venezuela, Guatemala, El Salvador, Saudi Arabia, Iraq, Egypt, India, Malaysia, Japan, and the Philippines.

In *low power distance* cultures, relationships are more informal across social levels, more equality is found among all people, and authority is more often shared. Countries with lower power distance include Australia, New Zealand, England, Germany, Sweden, Netherlands, Switzerland, Israel, Canada, and the United States. Consumer market segments will be more diverse in low power distance cultures. Spending power and the variety of benefits sought underlie this. Demand for high-quality goods is also be more widespread, and middle and upper-middle class segments exist in these cultures. In high power distance societies, large markets for necessities and basic housing and foodstuffs will be found among the "have-nots." Social or status brand images will sell well to those higher on the social ladder because such consumers are highly motivated by affiliation and status norms.[29] Likely a greater number of narrow upscale markets for goods and services will be present.

High versus Low Uncertainty Avoidance Cultures

uncertainty avoidance   The willingness of the members of a society to accept ambiguity and uncertainty.

Cultural acceptance levels of ambiguity are indications of the culture's level of **uncertainty avoidance.** *High uncertainty avoidance* (a "certainty culture") is found in societies that have routinized behavior patterns, many rules and regulations, and low tolerance for new ideas or new ways to do things. Persons in such societies tend to go to their families and others important to them to obtain advice, security, guidance, and comfort. They are more prone to stress and tend to be more openly emotional, anxious, or aggressive, and they are hard workers.[30]

Low uncertainty avoidance (an "uncertainly culture") exists in cultures where people "go with the flow." They don't have a strong desire to control their destiny and have a sense that what is to come will be. They are said to be relieved, confident, rational, and retired. Behavior patterns as individuals and consumers are more fluid and reactive, and new ideas and new ways are more easily accepted, partly because people in these cultures are more willing to accept personal risks.[31]

Selling goods and services to consumers in certainty cultures requires highly reliable offerings with excellent guarantees. Old standbys from reputable firms are winners. Buying from firms with whom consumers have a long-standing relationship is also likely to happen. Brands whose images are tied to risk aversion, problem solving, and prevention will do well.[32] The German and other Northern European cultures fit this mold, as does Japan.[33] Members of low uncertainty avoidance societies are also looking for good products with good warranties, but they are willing to consider products or services new on the market. Sensory brand images tied to variety, novelty, and sensory gratification are potentially strong choices.[34] Consumers from low uncertainty avoidance societies are more apt to take a chance if something looks good to them. People in North America, Southern Europe, and the Mediterranean world are more likely living in uncertainty cultures.[35]

Abstract versus Associative Thinking Cultures

Cultures where members are logical thinkers (also called "Greek thinkers" or "Western thinkers") interested in the principle of cause and effect are classified as **abstract thinking cultures.** Products and services are seen as good benefits-deliverers purely because of their inherent characteristics. Face-to-face communication is preferred. Members of such societies are willing and eager to make changes and to try new things, including new products and services. "If you build it, they will come," as was said in the movie *Field of Dreams*, seems to apply to such cultures if the offering is a logical addition to the fabric of the nation.

> **abstract thinking cultures**
> Those societies whose members are logical thinkers, interested in the principle of cause and effect.

In **associative thinking cultures,** the culture's connections or associations with people, celebrities, and events impact on the importance of things. Consumer products or services tied to such people or events acquire value. Thinking that a baseball bat that matches those of great hitters is better than one not tied to a special player—whether it's the correct length and weight for you or not—is an example of this. Associative thinking societies also see connections with God or gods, supernatural or mystic beings, events or places to various life events. Communication through the mass media is acceptable rather than the need for face-to-face contact. Thinking within the culture is not always logical as people come to conclusions about persons, events, products and services, and the like. Hence, promotional messages based on sound logic will not always be persuasive. The context in which something is said or how a product is offered is important. These cultures resist change and product or service innovation.

> **associative thinking cultures**
> Those societies in which connections or associations with people, celebrities, and events impact on the importance of things.

You would expect that the advertising of a nation should reflect in some way the value structure of the culture. A preliminary study looking at this was conducted across the eleven nations originally studied by Hofstede.[36] A set of forty-two commonly accepted advertising appeals was correlated with country scores on individualism, uncertainty avoidance, power distance, and masculinity.[37] In the business magazines studied, the conclusion reached was that appeals in advertising and cultural values often are related in a nonrandom way. Variation in advertising for the same products—in this case office equipment, financial services, clothing and accessories, and travel services—across societies was easily seen. Hence, studying advertising will point toward the value structure of a culture. And knowing the value structure of a society can aid in proper selection of appeals to reach target consumers or business decision makers.

The Confucian Dynamic Impact on Cultures

Although Hofstede's original scheme continues to be applied, a new dimension for cross-cultural comparison has been proposed, based on a twenty-two-country study done in the late 1980s. It was a factor that was interpreted to contain many Confucian-like values.[38] Confucius was a Chinese philosopher who lived from 551–479 B.C. He taught love for one's fellows, that children

> **▶Confucian Dynamic**
> A cultural comparative measure. At the positive end of the Confucian Dynamic scale are such values as persistence, hard work, thrift, shame, and regard for relationships that indicate a future-oriented, dynamic mentality. At the negative end are values indicating a static mentality. They are tied to the present and the past and include "face," reciprocity, and tradition.

should be dutiful to elders, and the ideal of the superior man. At the positive end of the **Confucian Dynamic** scale are such values as persistence, hard work, thrift, shame, and regard for relationships that indicate a future-oriented, dynamic mentality. At the negative end are values indicating a static mentality. They are tied to the present and the past and include "face," reciprocity, and tradition. Such values encourage people to stay within known and accepted societal boundaries.[39] This dimension is not only found in cultures with a history of Confucian influence. Brazil is one of the highest scoring countries, and Germany, the Netherlands, and Sweden are in the middle. Countries one would expect to be at the top—Hong Kong, Taiwan, Japan, and South Korea—are indeed there. Societies low on the scale are West Africa, Canada, and Pakistan. The Confucian Dynamic is referred to as "long-term versus short-term orientation."[40] Work ethic, on the positive side of the scale, is seen as one of the major reasons for Japan's success in the automobile marketplace. A Honda executive is purported to have said, "We are very different from the rest of the world. Our only natural resource is the hard work of our people."[41] Confucianism was made the primary mode of thought in Japan several centuries ago. Face, on the negative end of the scale, is found everywhere on the globe to some extent. When a person feels disgraced based on insults, rude behavior, criticism, and questions of their ability leveled by others, their "face" is being threatened. "Saving face" has to do with holding on to one's status and dignity. "Giving face" means that people are allowed to retain theirs. Executives from mainland China are extremely concerned about face, more so than executives from Hong Kong or the United States. In the area of new product development, being on the positive side of the Confucian Dynamic points to the encouragement of face, whereas the reverse is true if a culture is on the negative side.[42]

Marketing Management—Implications and Actions

Knowing and understanding the key values approach will help globally focused marketers:

- Assess the differences and similarities of cultures and the resultant patterns of benefits sought by society members.
- Use their grasp of how cultures measure up on the six key values to properly identify consumer segments within and across societies.
- Develop and market appropriate products and services that reflect culture positions on the six values.

12-3 Culture in the United States

The words "American culture" carry many meanings. The United States is seen by some as the most highly developed consumer society in the world, yet critics have accused the people of the United States of having no culture at all. The broad mix of co-cultures residing in this country with their diversity of contributions probably is part of what leads to this view. The United States does not have the history of China, or even Europe. It's a culture that is only a bit over two centuries old. Those living in this nation bring a host of varying traditions from their cultures of origin over which is being spread the developing national culture.

As outsiders may observe, American culture is in many ways relatively standardized and homogeneous. We're all exposed to the same communications media, use the same standard brands, and enjoy the same kinds of possessions. But American society is also characterized by its considerable diversity. Behavior, values, and norms differ from one geographic region to another and among ethnic, national, and religious groups. Within each, cultural characteristics are further affected by such factors as age, marital status, education, occupation, and income level. (These co-cultural influences and others are discussed in Chapter 13.)

The U.S. culture may be analyzed by examining the same characteristics discussed in section 11-2, "Nature of Culture—Components," section 12-1, "Culture Generalizations," and section 12-2, "Cross-Cultural Perspectives." In fact, comments have already been made on several factors as comparisons between the United States and a number of other cultures were made. In this section, we'll look at other variables that may be used to characterize U.S. society.

In every culture, a normative system of values and rules emerges to govern everyday conduct. Because of its diversity and the contradictions this gives rise to, a normative system of American culture is extremely difficult to describe. However, the following traits of the American people should ring true: the practice of democracy and faith in democracy; belief in the equality of all people as a fact and as a right; disregard for the indisputable nature of the law and belief instead in direct action to resolve issues; practicality; prosperity; material well-being; Puritanism; uniformity; and conformity.[43] We might add to this list deeply held beliefs in freedom, self-reliance, and independence, along with a sometimes tempered sensitivity toward the environment and a high regard for quality of life. Capitalism is the accepted way, and people in the United States place much stock in efficiency. Informality characterizes the lifestyle more than formality. Being healthy is also important to a good share of the population. More traditional values also are acting in the lives of certain segments of the population, especially among older consumers. We also see an array of emerging values in the U.S. culture and in the civilizations of the West.

Americans are great sports fans, and college football is one of the most popular places for fans to be on a Saturday afternoon in the fall. Mediamark Research took a look at football fans and developed the "Fan Index" and the "Attendance Index," relating these to the purchase and ownership of selected consumer products. CBite 12-2 summarizes some of their findings.

As part of the U.S. culture we take pride in the products and services we use, often assuming they are for the most part American originals. Check out Marketplace 12-1 for a more realistic classic view that is still true today.

F A Q

What is "pop culture"?

CBite 12-2

Completed Passes

The college football game attendance profile shows young (18–35), monied ($40,000 per year and up), educated (at least some college) fans . The index values for consumers who attended college football games in the past year and were purchasers and/or owners of various products is indicated below. An index of 100 would be average for all consumers, so numbers greater than 100 would be above the average. For example, the index of 122 for imported cars indicates that the college football fans who attended a game last year are 22 percent above average in this category.

Source: "Eleven & Goal," *American Demographics* (October 2003), p. 20. Copyright © 2003 Crain Communications, Inc. Reprinted with permission.

Product	Index	Product	Index
Cars		**Sports Equipment**	
Domestic	100	Mountain bike	184
Imported	122	Downhill skis	209
Durables		Golf clubs	244
Hot tub/spa	155	Hockey equipment	248
Rechargeable flashlight	123		
Washer/dryer	140		
Kitchen/Cooking			
Espresso/cappuccino maker	141		

Marketplace 12-1

A Typical Consumer

As an illustration of how cultural diffusion has influenced our society, here are a few minutes in the typical morning of a middle-class American commuter, Josh.

Breakfast is over, and Josh gets ready to go to work. As it looks like rain, he puts on a coat made from rubber fibers, discovered by the ancient Mexicans, and takes an umbrella invented in India. At the train station, he pauses for a moment to buy a newspaper, paying for it with coins invented in ancient Lydia. He reads the news of the day, imprinted in characters invented by the ancient Semites, by a process invented in Germany, upon a material invented in China. As Josh scans the latest editorial pointing out the dire results of accepting foreign ideas, he thinks thankfully to himself in an Indo-European language that he is 100 percent (decimal system invented by the Greeks) American (from Amerigo Vespucci, Italian geographer and seafarer).

Source: Adapted from Ralph Linton, "One Hundred Percent American," *The American Mercury,* Vol. 40 (April 1937).

12-3a Traditional American Values and Consumption

No summary of values basic to traditional American culture can be complete, and, of course, there will always be exceptions. Exhibit 12-8 on pages 388–389, however, lists several traditional values that hold sway to varying degrees today and describes the consumer behaviors each gives rise to.[44] The point in time where these values were pinpointed was ten to fifteen years after World War II. It was the calm before the Vietnam War, the civil rights movement, the women's liberation movement, and the science and technology explosion. Active mastery of the environment, emphasis on manipulation over contemplation, openness of the society, rationalism, need for orderliness, universalism, horizontal over vertical relationships, and the individual as more important than the group were characterizing factors. It is important for marketers to understand these characteristics in order to develop products and messages that do not cause dissonance with the mind-set of the typical consumer who may be still tied to these traditional values.

Have you heard of the "consumption ethic"? Check out Marketplace 12-2 to see what it is all about. Do you think it is tied to the American value structure? If so, how?

12-3b Emergent American Values and Consumption

American culture is constantly undergoing change, and though still strong, traditional patterns are being modified by insistent new, emergent values, each of which influences consumption patterns. Exhibit 12-9 on pages 390–391 looks at several of these values and describes their effects on consumer behavior: shifting away from materialism toward quality of life and concerns for the environment, placing more emphasis on leisure over work, living for today rather than postponing something, resisting change but seeing it as more inevitable, exhibiting a higher risk tolerance in life, moving away from mastering the environment to nurturing/preserving it. Though individualism is still strong, there is movement toward collectivism and placing a high value on children and their education; though there is still strong faith in youth and education, experience and wisdom are gaining ground, and the society is becoming less masculine oriented. To some extent, these changing values mirror the general change of values projected in the late 1980s for "Western Civilization." Exhibit 12-10 on page 392 is a selective summary of these values. Note the effects on family life, gender roles, quality of life, work, self-orientation, growth acceptance, and the rise of technology in our lives.

The terrorist attack that occurred on September 11, 2001, has had a lingering effect on values and behaviors in the U.S. One of the outcomes was a strong increase in patriotism. In 2002 it was reported that the profiles of patriotism in consumers were as follows: women are likely to be more patriotic than men, and older people more patriotic than

Marketplace 12-2

The Consumption Ethic

Consider how profoundly marketing has influenced American technology, education, and values. The bulk of our technological know-how is employed in developing goods and services that people want to buy. Our educational system is geared toward preparing individuals to be productive members of an affluent society—as citizens, workers, and consumers. And the cultural values we learn are most often aligned with the goals of a marketing economy: rewarding performance with material payoffs and defining lifestyles through patterns of consumption. Television, the most prevalent communications medium, exists mostly through commercial sponsorship, and thus places heavy emphasis on selling advertised products, services, and lifestyles. Even though cable and satellite television have opened the door for premium channels paid for by the viewer alone, commercial sponsorship is still the norm.

The spirit of affluent consumption surrounds almost every American cultural rite. Weddings, funerals, and bar mitzvahs all create industries that costume and cater to the participants as lavishly as they desire or can afford. Political candidates use market segmentation and other marketplace strategies to identify and attract voters. Religious groups and charitable organizations employ advertising agencies to steer fund-raising campaigns. Even young children understand the consumption ethic that underlies their choices of toys and clothing. The consumption ethic is now so prevalent in almost all aspects of life in the United States that some observers claim that it has replaced the older Protestant work ethic that was once the foundation of the American value system. Do you think we have gone too far?

The effects of marketing on the cultures of developing nations offer an interesting tangent to this argument. Critics claim that sophisticated tobacco industry promotions in developing nations entice people who cannot afford the necessities of life to spend money on a luxury, and a life-threatening one at that. At the heart of this issue is a concern about individual liberty. If marketing practices are limited, does it infringe on the rights of free individuals to make choices?

Source: Philip R. Cateora, *International Marketing,* 9th edition (Burr Ridge, IL: Richard D. Irwin, 1996), p. 739.

young. It was found that retired and less educated consumers are the most likely to be influenced by patriotic advertising. The unemployed are also more likely to support a patriotic spirit in advertising, perhaps because some lost their jobs as a result of the terrorists' actions.[45]

People in the United States have enormous confidence in technology and science as a source of knowledge and solutions to the problems of today and tomorrow. They believe in the ability of technology to make life continually more comfortable, more secure, and more pleasurable and are persuaded that medical science will find cures for cancer, AIDS, and other devastating diseases in the near future. The same advances in technology that allowed America to put people on the moon will lead to new sources of energy, ending fears of the destruction of the environment. Further, there is confidence that the technical proficiency of the society will even allow for conversion of readily available substances into food, thus saving what many perceive as an overpopulated world from starvation.

When looking at what was happening as we moved into the current century in the United States, we see that these emerging values and beliefs accurately reflected the reality of the times. It has especially been noticeable among young adults—you who are reading this text right now and others already in the mainstream of the culture. Successful marketers have been sensitive to the changing value-behavior landscape. Product development, positioning, benefits delivered, and the way communications are carried out must continue to reflect the current situation with chosen target markets.

The fact that our values are changing further complicates analysis of the United States. The rate of change continues to accelerate, driven by the country's increasing ethnic diversity, changing gender roles, and the erosion of the stability of the traditional family unit. The society is at a point of transition between traditional American values and a new emergent value system, each of which influences consumption in different ways. However, as was the case with the September 11, 2001, terrorist attack on America, a radical shift in values can occur. The consequences of this event were significant shifts toward the traditional American values of family, faith in institutions, hero worship, and patriotism.

F A Q

How has "9/11" affected you as a consumer?

Exhibit 12-8	**Traditional Value**	**Influence on Consumer Behavior**
Ritual Dimensions of Consumer Behavior 	1. American culture is organized around the attempt to *actively master* rather than *passively accept*. This tendency reveals itself through a positive encouragement of our desires, a stress on the positive nature of power, an approval of egocentrism, and other characteristics through which we assert ourselves.	Americans are interested in the performance aspects of goods and services. What is the product for? What can it do? Americans are compelled to find out how tasks can be better accomplished or mastered through using specialized products. Precision, ease of operation, safety, and speed are all important. Advertising appeals echo this desire Americans have to solve problems: "Drain clogged? Use Liquid-Plumr," or "Tide's in, dirt's out." In tests of advertising, headlines beginning with "How to . . ." outperform headlines without this problem-solving claim.
	2. American culture is more concerned with the external world of things and events, with the palpable and immediate, than with the inner experience of meaning and effect. The emphasis is more on *manipulation* than on *contemplation*.	Receptive to products that enable them to take control, American consumers would rather see a movie than read the book on which it is based. For the same reason, more people subscribe to *Reader's Digest,* a magazine that offers short versions of articles from many other magazines, than to *Discovery Magazine,* which presents more lengthy, original articles on a narrower range of topics.
	3. American culture tends to be *open* rather than *closed*. It emphasizes change, flux, movement; its central personality types are adaptive, accessible, outgoing, and assimilative.	Americans are willing to be innovative in trying new goods and services. Open to new ideas and willing to adapt, American consumers are treated to a staggering array of new products every year. These range from parity items based on other products already on the market to true innovations, such as the technology behind cellular digital picture telephones, personal digital assistants, and iPods. The novelty of a new product is often enough to attract consumers; whether the item will become established depends on whether it lives up to expectations. Comet Cleanser, a long-standing brand, still retains a large market share by reintroducing a "new and improved Comet" at regular intervals.
	4. American culture places its primary faith in *rationalism* as opposed to *traditionalism*. It de-emphasizes the past, is oriented strongly to the future, and does not accept things just because they have been done before.	Americans, though willing to accept new products, must be convinced that they offer useful benefits. Marketing appeals that use argument or reason are generally more effective than are those that count on such emotive responses as nostalgia or even those that are based upon past performance.

Traditional Value	Influence on Consumer Behavior
5. American culture prefers *orderliness* above the *unsystematic* and is accepting of transitory experiences.	Americans, especially those who identify with the upper-middle class, express a need for goods and services that bring order to their existence. This trait has two manifestations. First, it is reflected in a preoccupation with neatness and cleanliness. American consumers buy enormous quantities of deodorants, soaps, cleansers, and other goods for every cleaning or hygiene need imaginable. Some say this behavior is a result of "brainwashing" by advertisers. But the fact that these products were developed in the first place suggests that our acculturation process had already created the need for them. The marketing system has simply responded to that need and reinforces the desirability of cleanliness. Second, a need for security is manifest in the desire of Americans that the future will continue as predictably as the present, that they will be able to provide for their families, educate their children, and save for retirement. To meet these needs, industries offering insurance, savings facilities, and long-term investment opportunities flourish.
6. American culture is *universalistic* rather than *particularistic*. Rules should apply to all, rather than to selective groups only.	*The universalistic nature of American culture dictates equal standards for all.* People feel they have a right to certain products—a car and a home of their own, for example—and will stretch their budgets to buy them, whether they can afford them or not.
7. American culture values *horizontal* interpersonal relationships above *vertical* relationships: peer relations, not superior-subordinate relations, equality rather than hierarchy.	Americans use consumption as a means of conforming in varying degrees to the behavior of others. Most people in the United States elect to live in housing that is relatively standardized, wear clothing styles that fall within generally accepted norms, and structure other aspects of their lifestyles according to standards adopted by their peers.
8. American culture emphasizes *individual* personality rather than *group* identity and responsibility.	While Americans strive for some measure of conformity, they also aspire to buy products that reflect a level of individual achievement. Most consumers wish to assert themselves by sending signals that reflect their aspirations. They use symbols of position, status, wealth, and group identification, thus showing others that they are—in their own eyes—successful. Americans are quick to note small differences among products—in style, design, or packaging—that they use to differentiate themselves from others.

Source: Robin M. Williams, Jr., *American Society: A Sociological Interpretation* (New York: Knopf, 1960), pp. 469–470.

Exhibit 12-9	Emergent Value	Influence on Consumer Behavior
Emergent American Values and Consumer Behaviors 	1. American culture is shifting away from overt materialism. This is evidenced by a concern for the environment, increased interest in conservation and recycling, and an overall search for quality of life.	Consumers are limiting both the quantity and type of products they are willing to acquire. They are reducing consumption in order to enjoy what they see as a less complicated life and in order to share more fairly the world's resources. Goods and services that help them do so are increasingly appealing.
	2. American culture is increasingly emphasizing leisure over the traditional value of hard work. People weigh the joy of time devoted to family, hobbies, exercise, and various other self-fulfilling activities against the rewards and stresses of work.	In record numbers, consumers are attracted to leisure activities as they attend theme parks, watch rented movies with friends and family, fish, hunt, sail, ski, camp, eat out in restaurants, go to aerobics classes, take college courses for fun, and much more.
	3. American culture encourages a belief in living for today. Rather than the traditional value of postponing self-gratification or saving for a rainy day, consumers are willing to spend now for instant fulfillment.	Advertising, particularly through such mass media as television and newspapers, offers all kinds of products, while ease of purchasing through credit cards and actual no interest/pay later schemes allows delayed payments. Retail advertising attracts consumers with appeals that delay payments for six or even twelve months. Of course, in the mid-1990s, sluggish retail sales due to low economic and employment indicators also contributed to the appeal of deferred payments.
	4. American culture is becoming more resistant to change. Acceptance of change, once characteristic of the American culture, is becoming less prevalent.	A return to older products and the values they represent is evident. Music of the 1940s, 1950s, 1960s, 1970s, and 1980s, for example, is enjoying a resurgence of popularity, with many pieces becoming available on compact disk. Volkswagen reintroduced a new version of its popular Beetle model from the 1950s and the 1960s.
	5. American culture increasingly is becoming more tolerant of risk. This is most likely explained by the lower level of consumer confidence in the economy, threats of terrorism, corporate downsizing trends, and other issues. Americans are coming to realize that security in all areas of life is not as feasible as it once was.	No longer believing in job security, people look for ways to prepare for the future through savings, pension plans, and insurance. College education plans begin when children are in infancy because of the expected high costs. Physical security is another concern, as home protection systems, smoke detectors, and car alarms become commonplace. In recent years, car manufacturers have included alarms as standard equipment on more expensive models and have offered them as options on lower-priced vehicles.

Emergent Value	**Influence on Consumer Behavior**
6. American culture supports the preservation of the environment. Rather than master their environment, today's consumers are more inclined to admire it.	The desire to behave in environmentally as well as socially responsible ways is reflected in the rising popularity of national parks, nature preserves, and campgrounds. The demand for homes away from the stresses of city living signals a desire to get back in touch with nature. The popularity of organizations dedicated to preserving nature, protecting endangered species, and recycling consumer products is a further example of this fundamental change in attitudes.
7. American culture increasingly supports the need to work collectively to solve problems. Though the spirit of individualism is still strong, today's consumers tend to place greater value on teamwork.	The increased popularity of networking groups, counseling groups, fitness clubs, and other groups in which people of like interests and with like concerns get together reflects the desire for cooperation. As well as services that support group activities, this translates into appeal for the types of products that reflect group interests—T-shirts that indicate club membership are a good example.
8. American culture places high value on children and childhood experiences. Education is particularly important, and parents increasingly try to expose their children to a variety of sports, to travel, and to societies outside their neighborhoods.	Several goods and services contribute to increasing options for children, including a range of activities outside school—music, nature, computer classes, and more. Social programs, such as Head Start, aim to offer the same opportunities to less-privileged families. The continuing popularity of more traditional clubs and organizations—scouting, boys' and girls' clubs, Big Brothers and Big Sisters, for example—also demonstrates this critical value.
9. American culture increasingly de-emphasizes the traditional faith in youth and education as opposed to age and wisdom. As the majority population ages and people live longer, healthier lives, they continue to contribute to the society.	The financial strength of many of today's seniors means they constitute large markets, particularly for such goods and services as recreation, sporting goods, entertainment, and health care.
10. American culture favors equal opportunities for women. Traditionally a masculine-oriented society, as are the societies from which its heritage derives, today's culture supports the changing of both domestic and workplace roles.	Buying decisions that were once male- or female-dominated are increasingly made jointly or made by both sexes. Women are no longer restricted to the grocery store while men make decisions on major purchases. As work, child care, and household responsibilities are shared, so are purchase decisions that accompany them.

E x h i b i t **12-10**	**Traditional Values**	**Emerging Values**
Shifting Values in Western Civilization	Traditional family life	Alternative family options
	Traditional gender roles	Blurring of gender roles
	High standard of living	Quality of life
	Live to work	Work to live
	General definition of success	Individual definition of success
	Faith in industry and institutions	Faith in self
	Self-denial	Self-fulfillment
	Hero worship	Love of ideas
	Patriotism	Nationalism less important
	Expansionism	Pluralism
	Industrialism	Information/service growth
	Receptive to technology	Oriented to technology
	Unparalleled growth	Growth within bounds

Source: "Changing Values" originally published in the January–February 1989 issue of *The Futurist.* Used with permission from World Future Society, 7910 Woodmont Avenue, Suite 450, Bethesda, Maryland 20814. Telephone: 301/656-8274; Fax: 301/951-0394; http://www.wfs.org.

Marketing Management—Implications and Actions

Understanding traditional American values and keeping track of the changing value scene will help marketers:

- Determine which value structure matches various target markets' views and lifestyles in America.
- Develop and market goods and services properly fitting the societal value structure of specific consumer target groups.
- Position products and services on either traditional or emerging American values.

Chapter Spotlights

As noted earlier, we are sensitive to the values, behaviors, and beliefs of the people around us, and our behavior as consumers is affected. The global nature of many businesses today points toward the need not only to understand our own culture and its influences, but also to appreciate the differences and similarities within and among nations and their peoples around the world.

1. Culture generalizations. In a broad context we can say that culture is pervasive, functional, and learned/shared. People learn about their own cultures through the process of enculturation and about other cultures through acculturation. Socialization is a term used to include both of these. Its key influences are the family, education, religion, and mass media, each of which also affects consumption choices. Culture is also dynamic, and it changes based on such things as technology, cultural diffusion, and the influence of natural, political, and conflict events. Further, cultures are shaped by the environment of the geographic location in which they exist. If very displeased with circumstances, people may reject their cultures by engaging in behaviors such as hedonism, etherealization, a search for community, or activism.

2. Cross-cultural perspectives. Although people around the globe have much in common as human beings, the suggestion that a global culture exists does not ring true. We note that members of some cultures are ethnocentric, thinking that theirs is the best way and judging other cultures by their own. In fact, they may be consumer ethnocentric, meaning that they do not desire to buy goods and services produced in other cultures. At the extreme, societal members may exhibit cultural animosity toward certain other nations vowing to never deal with them as consumers. In other cultures, we find individuals who think in terms of cultural relativism, where foreign societies are judged in their own situational context—not being compared by the domestic cultural rod. Although we had already used a number of variables to show how cultures could be compared, six often-used key variables were offered, namely, individualism versus collectivism, masculinity versus femininity, power distance, uncertainty avoidance, abstract versus associative thinking, and the Confucian Dynamic.

3. Culture in the United States. The American culture is less homogenous today when compared to just fifty years ago. The culture can be analyzed by considering its traditional values, which are still of importance in influencing consumption patterns. The emergent values in the United States are also playing a significant role as we see an increasing emphasis on quality of life rather than materi-alism, leisure rather than work, hedonism rather than Puritanism, conservation and preservation rather than mastery of the environment, interdependence rather than independence, age and wisdom rather than youth and education, and equality of the sexes rather than strict male/female roles.

Key Terms

abstract thinking cultures (p. 383)
acculturation (p. 369)
associative thinking cultures (p. 383)
collectivistic culture (p. 381)
Confucian Dynamic (p. 384)
consumer ethnocentricity (p. 379)
context (cultural context) (p. 369)

cultural animosity (p. 379)
cultural diffusion (p. 375)
cultural relativism (p. 380)
culture rejection (p. 377)
enculturation (p. 369)
ethnocentrism (p. 378)
feminine culture (p. 381)

individualistic culture (p. 381)
masculine culture (p. 381)
power distance (p. 382)
socialization (p. 369)
uncertainty avoidance (p. 382)

Review Questions

Note: You can find the correct answers to these questions by taking the quiz and then submitting your answers in the Online Edition. The program will automatically score your submission. If you miss a question, the program will provide the correct answer, a rationale for the answer, and the section number in the chapter where the topic is discussed.

1. The marketing of goods and services to support cultural functions provides
   a. no opportunities.
   b. few opportunities.
   c. adequate opportunities.
   d. many opportunities.

2. Culture is encoded in us through
   a. learning.
   b. sharing.
   c. learning and sharing.
   d. socialization.

3. The most important influence on consumption is
   a. our culture.
   b. the family.
   c. the government.
   d. peer groups.

4. _____ institutions are major socializing influences in our lives.
   a. Medical
   b. Social
   c. Educational
   d. Governmental

5. People have a natural tendency to view their own culture as better or even superior to others. This is called
   a. pride.
   b. patriotism.
   c. loyalty.
   d. ethnocentrism.

6. People in one nation may have a strong aversion to people and products of other nations. This is called
   a. cultural animosity.
   b. cultural relativism.
   c. ethnocentricity.
   d. relativistic hatred.

7. Cultures may also be judged on how the roles of _____ are differentiated and how they are publicly or privately segregated.
   a. children and adults
   b. men and women
   c. teens and adults
   d. teens and the elderly

8. High uncertainty avoidance is found in societies that have
   a. routinized behavioral patterns.
   b. many rules and regulations.
   c. low tolerance for new ideas or ways to do things.
   d. all of the above.

9. American culture is constantly undergoing
   a. trade surpluses.
   b. change.
   c. unstable governments at all levels.
   d. enculturation.

10. The need to reinforce _____ values still exists in America.
    a. expensive tastes in
    b. perceived
    c. traditional
    d. high

Team Talk

1. We say that culture is "functional." Think about your shopping behavior and describe one way in which the functional nature of the culture helps you as you shop.

2. In what ways are communications technologies influencing lifestyle, beliefs, values, and other aspects of culture? How do they influence consumption of goods and services?

3. Socialization is the way in which a culture is passed on to new members. Compare how you, in one aspect of life, have been socialized by the family in which you were raised and the education you have received. Consider value patterns, beliefs, and behaviors. Has the mass media affected your socialization?

4. Have you ever wanted to break away from cultural standards and done so? Which of these paths did you follow: hedonism, etherealization, search for community, or activism?

5. Suppose that you were asked to explain the American culture to a student from another country. What would you say? Describe it in terms of its traditional or emergent values.

Workshops

Research Workshop

Background

Consumer product choices in the marketplace may be affected by the value socialization that occurred within the family. That is, certain products may be chosen or rejected on the basis of the value structure taught in the family. The objective of this study is to determine in which three product classes such socializing influence was the strongest.

Methodology

Each team member should interview eight to ten other students. Each student in the sample should be asked to identify two choice product classes and one rejection product class that were heavily influenced by the values taught within his or her family. Then each respondent should be asked to identify the value(s) tied to each choice or rejection class. Identify the choice product class most commonly mentioned and the rejection product class most commonly mentioned. Summarize the results.

To the Marketplace

Determine the most commonly identified choice product class. How could the producers of such goods position them in the marketplace from a "values" standpoint that would be in line with the culture?

Creative Workshop

Background

Considering the results found in the Research Workshop, what would a consumer-integrated marketing communications strategy be like? Provide suggestions for the advertising part of the strategy.

Methodology

Review the positioning information, look at the research comments to find copy points (what is to be said to the consumer target market), and construct a magazine print ad with the "values" orientation that is appropriate. Remember that consumers buy benefits, so the advertisement must in some way show the benefits tied to the product.

To the Marketplace

After constructing the ad, show it to about ten other students. Ask them what the ad "says" to them about the values of the target market. How successful were you in advertising the product in the "values" sense?

Managerial Workshop

Background

Take the results of the Research Workshop and, assuming that you are a retailer (store, catalog, TV shopping channel, Internet—choose one), develop a marketing strategy tied to the findings for the most mentioned choice product class.

Methodology

Identify and describe your target market(s). Develop a retail marketing strategy involving the 4 Ps (Chapter 1), concentrating on the store or catalog or TV shopping channel or Internet method of selling and distribution. Prepare a two- to three-page write-up.

To the Marketplace

Present your strategy in a class setting, get reactions, and revise it as necessary. If you were going to implement your revised strategy, what would be the practical limitations you would face?

Notes

1. Edward T. Hall, *Beyond Culture* (Garden City, NJ: Anchor Press/Doubleday, 1976), pp. 85–103.
2. Paul A. Hebig, *Handbook of Cross-Cultural Marketing* (New York: The International Business Press (Haworth), 1997), pp. 59–60.
3. Myung-Seok Park, *Communication Styles in Two Different Cultures: Korean and American* (Seoul, Korea: Han Shin Publishing Company, 1994).
4. S. Stryker, "The Interactional and Situational Approaches," in H. T. Christensen, ed., *Handbook of Marriage and Family* (Chicago, IL: Rand McNally, 1964).
5. Milton Yinger, "Religious Pluralism in America," in J. M. Yinger, ed., *Sociology Looks at Religion* (New York: Macmillan, 1963).
6. Allen Bloom, *The Closing of the American Mind* (New York: Simon and Schuster, 1987).
7. Jay D. Lindquist, "Does Social Class Influence Children's Attitudes toward Advertising on Television and Radio and in Children's Magazines?" in Howard S. Gitlow and Edward W. Wheatley, eds., *Developments in Marketing Science*, Vol. 2 (Coral Gables, FL: Academy of Marketing Science, 1979), p. 36.
8. Thomas O'Guinn and L. J. Shrum, "The Role of Television in the Construction of Consumer Reality," *Journal of Consumer Research*, Vol. 23 (March 1997), pp. 278–294.
9. Ibid.
10. Nancy J. Nentl and Catherine A. Luther, "Ti-Ni-Boppa-Zu vs. Teenyboppers: Cross Cultural Social Comparison," in Gary B. Wilcox, ed., *Proceedings of the 1996 Conference of the American Academy of Advertising* (Austin, TX: The University of Texas, 1996), p. 40.
11. John B. Ford, Patricia Kramer Voli, Earl D. Honeycutt, Jr., and Susan L. Casey, "Gender Role Portrayals in Japanese Advertising: A Magazine Content Analysis," *Journal of Advertising*, Vol. 27 (Spring 1998), pp. 113–124.
12. Rick Yan, "To Reach China's Consumers, Adapt to *Guo Qing*," *Harvard Business Review*, Vol. 72 (September–October 1994), pp. 66–72; Subhash Sharma, Terrence A. Shimp, and Jeongshin Shin, "Consumer Ethnocentrism: A Test of Antecedents and Moderators," *Journal of the Academy of Marketing Science*, Vol. 23 (Winter 1995), pp. 26–37.
13. Terence A. Shimp and Subhash Sharma, "Consumer Ethnocentrism: Construction and Validation of the CETSCALE," *Journal of Marketing Research*, Vol. 24 (August 1987), pp. 280–289; Richard Netemeyer, Srinivas Durvasula, and Donald Lichtenstein, "A Cross-National Assessment of the Reliability and Validity of the CETSCALE," *Journal of Marketing Research*, Vol. 28 (August 1991), pp. 320–327.
14. Sharma, Shimp, and Shin, " Consumer Ethnocentrism"; Terence A. Shimp and Subhash Sharma, "Consumer Ethnocentrism: Construction."
15. Sharma, Shimp, and Shin, "Consumer Ethnocentrism."
16. Richard E. Plank and Jay D. Lindquist, "Exploring the CETSCALE in Soviet Armenia," in Ajay Manrai and H. Lee Meadow, eds., *Proceedings of the Ninth Biennial World Marketing Congress* (Coral Gables, Florida: Academy of Marketing Science, 1999), pp. 113–118.
17. Jay D. Lindquist, Irena Vida, Richard E. Plank, and Ann Fairhurst, "The Modified CETSCALE: Validity Tests in the Czech Republic, Hungary, and Poland," *International Business Review*, Vol. 10 (2001), pp. 505–516.
18. Ki-Taek Chun, John B. Campbell, and Jong Hae Yoo, "Extreme Response Style in Cross-Cultural Research," *Journal of Cross-Cultural Psychology*, Vol. 5 (December 1974), pp. 465–480.
19. Chun, Campbell, and Yoo, "Extreme Response Style," and C. Harry Hui and Harry C. Tirandis, "Effects of Culture and Response Format on Extreme Response Style," *Journal of Cross-Cultural Psychology*, Vol. 20 (September 1989), pp. 296–309.
20. George Balabanis and Adamantios Diamantopoulos, "Domestic Country Bias, Country-of-Origin Effects, and Consumer Ethnocentrism: A Multidimensional Unfolding Approach," *Journal of the Academy of Marketing Science*, Vol. 32 (Winter 2004), pp. 80–95.
21. Jill Gabrielle Klein, Richard Ettenson, and Marlene D. Morris, "The Animosity Model of Foreign Product Purchase: An Empirical Test in the People's Republic of China," *Journal of Marketing*, Vol. 62 (January 1998), pp. 89–100.
22. Ibid.
23. Geert Hofstede, *Culture's Consequences: International Differences in Work-Related Values* (Beverly Hills, CA: Sage Publications, 1980); Geert Hofstede and Michael H. Bond, "Hofstede's Culture Dimensions: An Independent Validation Using Rokeach's Value Survey," *Journal of Cross-Cultural Psychology*, Vol. 15 (December 1984), pp. 417–433; also see Laura M. Milner, Dale Fodness, and Mark W. Speece, "Hofstede's Research on Cross-Cultural Work-Related Values: Implications for Consumer Behavior," in W. Fred van Raaij and Gary J. Ramossy, eds., *European Advances in Consumer Research* (Amsterdam: Association for Consumer Research, 1993), pp. 70–76.
24. Geert Hofstede, *Culture's Consequences.*
25. Harry C. Triandis, "The Self and Social Behavior in Differing Cultural Contexts," *Psychological Review*, Vol. 96 (July 1989), p. 506; Harry C. Triandis, Robert Bontempo, Marcelo J. Villareal, Masaaki Asai, and Nydia Lucca, "Individualism and Collectivism: Cross-Cultural Perspectives on Self-Ingroup Relationships," *Journal of Personality and Social Psychology*, Vol. 54 (February 1988), p. 323; Jennifer L. Aaker and Durairaj Maheswaran, "The Effect of Cultural Orientation on Persuasion," *Journal of Consumer Research*, Vol. 24 (December 1997), pp. 315–328.
26. Ibid.
27. Joyce M. Wolburg and Hoh Kim, "Messages of Individualism and Collectivism in Korean and American Magazine Advertising: A Cross Cultural Study of Values," in Darrel D. Muehling, ed., *The Proceedings of the 1998 Conference of the American Academy of Advertising* (Pullman, WA: American Academy of Advertising, 1998), pp. 147–154.
28. Martin S. Roth, "The Effects of Culture and Socioeconomics on the Performance of Global Brand Image Strategies," *Journal of Marketing Research*, Vol. 32 (May 1995), pp. 163–175.

29. Ibid.

30. Mohammed A. Rawwas, David Strutton, and Lester W. Johnson, "An Exploratory Investigation of the Ethical Values of American and Australian Consumers: Direct Marketing Implications," *Journal of Direct Marketing*, Vol. 10 (Autumn 1996), pp. 52–63.

31. Ibid.

32. Roth, "The Effects of Culture and Socioeconomics."

33. Rawwas, Strutton and Johnson, "An Exploratory Investigation."

34. Roth, "The Effects of Culture and Socioeconomics."

35. Rawwas, Strutton, and Johnson, "An Exploratory Investigation."

36. Nancy D. Albers-Miller and Betsy D. Gelb, "Business Advertising Appeals as a Mirror of Cultural Dimensions: A Study of Eleven Countries," *Journal of Advertising*, Vol. 25 (Winter 1996), pp. 57–70; Geert Hofstede, *Culture's Consequences.*

37. Richard W. Pollay, "Measuring the Cultural Values Manifest in Advertising," in James H. Leigh and Claude R. Martin, Jr., eds., *Current Issues and Research in Advertising* (Ann Arbor, MI: Graduate School of Business, Division of Research, University of Michigan, 1983), pp. 72–92.

38. Michael H. Bond et al., "Chinese Values and the Search for Culture-Free Dimensions of Culture"; and Cheryl Nakata and K. Sivakumar, "National Culture and New Product Development: An Integrative Review," *Journal of Marketing*, Vol. 60 (January 1996), pp. 61–72.

39. Geert Hofstede, "Management Scientists are Human," *Management Science*, Vol. 40 (January 1994), pp. 1, 4–13; Geert Hofstede and Michael H. Bond, "Hofstede's Culture Dimensions."

40. Hofstede, "Management Scientists are Human."

41. Thomas J. Peters and Robert H. Waterman, Jr., *In Search of Excellence: Lessons from America's Best-Run Companies* (New York: Harper and Row, Publishers, 1982), p. 39.

42. Nakata and Sivakumar, "National Culture and New Product Development."

43. Lee Coleman, "What Is An American: A Study of Alleged American Traits," *Social Forces*, Vol. 19, No. 4 (1941).

44. Robin M. Williams, Jr., *American Society: A Sociological Interpretation* (New York: Knopf, 1960), pp. 469–470.

45. Alison S. Wellner, "The Perils of Patriotism," *American Demographics* (September 2002), pp. 49–51.

Subcultural Influences

Tomas is running for president of the student government association at his university. His first step is to take a look at the student body to identify who they are, where they come from, and what benefits they expect to get from their student government group. He finds that the students are primarily from the United States, are mostly in his age group, are single, and are typically Caucasian, Latino, and African American. But, as he takes a harder look at the people on campus, he sees students from sixty or so different countries and from all the continents. Tomas, a Latino himself, had not really "looked around" the campus before and was caught off guard by the diversity he found. In the evening, the campus looks somewhat different. Many of the night students are older, full-time working people, often with families, who are completing degrees a little at a time. The day students are in the full swing of things, but the night students are "commuters" who feel little attachment to the alma mater. The university is only a small part of their busy lives. Actually, almost half of the day students are working from twenty to forty hours a week, and this has caused them to be less attached.

Tomas quickly realizes that his research has just scratched the surface. The student body is made up of people who all have different expectations of the student government that represents them. Some are more politically active, expect a strong voice at the university, and see student government as the answer. At the other extreme are the night commuters who see little or no value in student government and really don't care what it does. In light of the subcultural differences based on nationality, ethnicity, and age as starters, how he should proceed is not a simple matter. Tomas' task is to try to find what these groups have in common in their student government expectations. The answer might be "not much."

Tomas discovered that the student body consists of people from several subcultures, each having different attitudes and behaviors. Subcultures are diverse and interconnected. Based on such demographics as nationality, age, religion, income level, and marital status, we each belong to several subcultures that overlap and interweave, shaping both our outlook on life and our behavior as consumers. In this chapter, we will analyze four major subcultural classifications—nationality, age, geographic region, and religion—and explore ways in which these are helpful to marketers in determining how the larger population is segmented.

13-1 Subculture and Society

A **subculture** is any cultural patterning that preserves important features of the dominant society but provides for values, norms, and behaviors of its own. Marketers use subcultural classification of consumers to help determine goods and services needed. All nations around the globe are made up of various subcultures. It is essential that marketers realize this. When someone says, "We're going to sell to the German market," it is obvious that he or she does not understand the diversity of groups that are within the borders of that land. This single view of the nation is very uninformed.

Subcultures are typically based on a number of factors taken singly or in combination. Some of the more obvious foundations for subcultural variation are: (1) *nationality* (Tahitian, Swedish, Mexican, Japanese), (2) *ethnicity* (Basque, Croatian, Georgian, Zulu, Cajun), (3) *age* (teens, Generation Xers and Yers, baby boomers, seniors), (4) *geographic region* (Dixie, Nile valley, the Ruhr, Cappadocia), and (5) *religion* (Confucianist, Muslim, Jewish, Amish, Catholic). Less obvious are subcultures based on gender, family or household type, occupation, community type, or income level. Individual consumers typically belong to multiple subcultures. Although our strongest affiliation may be to our nationality, for example, age, religion, and several other subcultural influences are likely working to affect both our attitudes and behaviors as consumers.

The benefits consumers seek in the marketplace vary from subculture to subculture. It is this diversity that leads marketers to develop different mixes of products and to promote them in different ways. Where products are sold, how information about them is disseminated, and the way in which consumers are treated by marketers also flow from subcultural expectations. Because it is another central issue to consider in understanding consumer behavior, subcultural influences deserve special attention by marketers as they target and serve consumers. See Exhibit 13-1 for a list of key factors in determining subcultural membership.

13-1a Who Belongs to What Subculture?

Assigning individuals to subcultural groups is complex and arbitrary. Three considerations are particularly important.[1] First, since no two consumers or the ways in which they behave are exactly alike, subcultural classifications are possible only through *generalizations*. It's where we think and say, "All Swedes are like that," or "All teenagers are the same," or "You know what they say about senior citizens." This means that classification is unavoidably arbitrary. Second, because our *self-perceptions* are key to determining whether or not we even belong to subcultural groups, such perceptions must be addressed before any classification is made. If a person does not see himself or herself as a Midwesterner or Catholic or Asian American, he or she will not act as such and should not be classified into the subculture. Third, only if we *feel it is important to identify with the subcultural groups* to which we are assigned is it useful to make such classifications. In other words, it is not just our subcultural identity that influences marketplace behavior, but how important that identity is to us in our lives. Those who identify closely with a subcultural group are more strongly affected by the consumption patterns and marketplace shopping and buying behaviors of the group than are those who do not. Historically, marketers classified people without proper consideration being given to these three elements. Hence, targeting was occasionally off track.

The largest and most common subcultural groupings are those based on nationality or ethnicity, age, geographic region, and religion (see Exhibit 13-2). These and other subcultural groupings, singly and in combination, are useful foundations for discovering market segment, targeting selected groups, positioning goods and services, and developing communications and distribution strategies.

▶**subculture** Any cultural patterning that preserves important features of the dominant society but provides for values, norms, and behaviors of its own.

F A Q

Why do you think the word *co-culture* is being increasingly substituted for subculture in the United States today?

E x h i b i t 13-1

Determining Subculture Membership

Who Belongs to What Subculture?

· Generalization
· Self-perception
· Importance of identification with the subculture

E x h i b i t 13-2

Bases for Subculture

· Nationality and/or ethnicity
· Age
· Geographic region
· Religion

> ### Marketing Management—Implications and Actions
>
> Understanding subcultures helps marketers:
> - Classify market segments according to identification with subcultural groups.
> - Evaluate how identification with one or more subculture influences attitudes and behavior.
> - Develop product mixes, marketing strategies, and promotions that appeal to targeted groups.

13-2 Subcultures Based on Nationality and Ethnicity

In some countries, where the population is almost entirely made up of people from a single ethnic background, nationality and ethnicity are essentially the same. As the twenty-first century begins, however, this has become the exception rather than the rule. Increasingly, as in the United States, nations around the world are composed of multiple ethnic groups or sets of individuals who share similar traits and customs derived from the culture into which they were born.

Today, the chances are small that countries—or even regions within them—are made up of populations of a single race. Even in nations like Japan, where obtaining citizenship is difficult for those who do not have a direct blood connection with the dominant ethnic group, subcultures exist. Over history, boundaries between countries have moved back and forth—often as a result of war—without regard to the effects upon the cultures of people living within them. The result is that people who share virtually the same ethnic background may live on opposite sides of national borders. This means that they often have more in common with each other than with the citizens of the country in which they reside. At the other extreme, members of some ethnic and/or nationality groups are scattered worldwide. Ireland has sent a steady stream of emigrants to the United States since the nineteenth century. Turkish nationals moved to Germany and Algerians to France after World War II. People of Jewish heritage are scattered the world over.

When people from the same nation immigrate to a new country, they typically initially live close to one another. Despite differences in social class, education, and even religion, their nationality draws them together. However, as the number of immigrants becomes large enough, people again begin to separate into their traditional subcultural groups, though perhaps the subcultural divisions are not quite as rigid as they were in the "old country." This means that nationality is a constantly changing rather than a permanent subcultural influence. As it changes, so, too, do the attitudes and behaviors of its consumers in the marketplace.

Ethnicity is a way that people are grouped across nationalities and regions such as "Hispanics" or "Asians" and these designations are typically based on similarities in language, region of origin, or visual observable distinctions (skin color, hair color and texture, facial structure, etc.). Ethnicity and ethnic identity are not the same. Ethnicity is an objective description, whereas ethnic identity is more subjective and often is a self-designation indicating a person's commitment to a specific group. The assumption of *subjective ethnicity* is that this better reflects the internal beliefs of a person's cultural reality, how they see themselves ethnically, whereas *objective ethnicity* is the external or observable evaluation of a person's cultural position by others.[2]

13-2a How Nationality-Based Subcultures Develop

Nationality and ethnic groups maintain subsocieties within the larger culture in order to serve their members in three important ways:[3]

1. *To provide a source of psychological group identification.* Members gain a sense of identity and intimacy from association with people they feel are similar to them.

2. *To offer a patterned network of groups and institutions supportive of the subculture.* Through schools, religious institutions, clubs, shops, restaurants, and organizations,

members who wish to can maintain primary relationships with others in the subculture throughout almost all aspects of their life experiences.

3. *To serve as a frame of reference through which to evaluate the dominant culture.* Members use a knowledge and understanding of the culture of their country of origin to which they compare and evaluate the values and norms of the host society. Through this type of cultural pluralism, members retain, to varying extents, their cultural heritage. The subculture nurtures a supportive environment that serves as the training ground for new arrivals, as an interpreter of the "new land," and as a way to strengthen and preserve what is different and important to the nationality-based subcultural group.

There are two theories that explain how ethnic and/or national subcultural identity is either lost or preserved as its members move into a new society. The **theory of assimilation** maintains that ethnic and/or nationality groups lose their customs and traits over time and gradually adopt behaviors, lifestyles, and purchasing habits associated with the dominant culture in which they live.[4] Because of occupational and geographic mobility, exposure to the mass media, intermarriage, religion, and a host of other influences, identities slowly erode. This pattern is thought to be true of many of the early immigrant groups who came to the United States. The Irish, Germans, and Swedes are good examples. As individuals become assimilated they begin to select more goods and services that are common to the mainstream culture—and fewer tied to their national or ethnic subculture. With successive generations, assimilation slowly closes the gap between the prevailing culture and the ethnicity-based subculture.

Some subcultures are having second thoughts about being assimilated. See CBite 13-1 to get some reactions. In Australia, many second-generation immigrants feel they are caught in the middle. They no longer see themselves as part of their parents' culture, and they are not accepted by the Anglo-Australians, yet they want to be part of the mainstream of the society. They are Australian-educated children who are part of one of the world's most multicultural societies. Australia has absorbed almost 6 million people as immigrants since 1945, and in 1996 a bit over 40 percent of the population indicated that they were first- or second-generation migrants. As with many nationality and ethnic subcultural groups in America, the majority live in major metropolitan areas in Australia. Religion is also shifting in the society. For example, between 1991 and 1996 in New South Wales, people identifying themselves as Buddhist increased by 40 percent and Muslim by 31 percent. Australian society is quite diverse now, and this means that " the suburban corner store, run by Koreans, stocks Turkish bread and chili sauce, or that schoolgirls in head scarves join the netball competition, or a Canto pop star sells out an entertainment center."[5] What impact do you see this having on the marketplace in Australia?

The **theory of mobilization** holds that ethnic identification is preserved from one generation to the next through family traditions and the formal teaching of language,

> ▶ **assimilation (theory of)**
> The process whereby ethnic and/or nationality groups lose their customs and traits over time and gradually adopt behaviors, lifestyles, and purchasing habits associated with the dominant culture in which they live.

> ▶ **mobilization (theory of)**
> The process whereby ethnic identification is preserved from one generation to the next through family traditions and the formal teaching of language, religion, and other cultural values within the subculture.

CBite 13-1

No More Melting Pot?

Once proud of being part of the "melting pot"—an integrated American culture— some national subcultures are reacting against assimilation. This is evidenced in increased ethnic consciousness among Polish, Italian, African, Hispanic, Chinese, and other immigrant groups. Ethnic-based civil rights groups are just one sign of the trend. Culturally focused theater and arts groups are another, along with the increasing number of television programs predominantly featuring minority families and groups, and the growth of magazines and newspapers targeting specific nationality- or ethnic-based subcultural groups.

Source: Milton M. Gordon, *Assimilation in American Life* (New York: Oxford University Press, 1964).

religion, and other cultural values within the subculture.[6] Japanese Americans, many fluent in Japanese and proficient in Japanese cultural ways as a result of early training in special schools, are an example. If a group works to hold on to its ethnic or national identity, the behavior of members as consumers within the new culture changes little. They buy the same foods, wear the same clothes, and decorate their homes in the ways of the national culture.

13-2b Nationality/Ethnicity-Based Subcultures in the United States

We have selected three nationality/ethnicity-based subcultural groups for discussion: African Americans, Hispanic Americans, and Asian and Pacific Island Americans. The first two groups were chosen because they currently account for a bit over one-fourth of the U.S. population. Although African Americans were the largest minority, in 2003 their share was surpassed by the Latino community, which now is the largest minority group in the U.S. The Asian and Pacific Island Americans are the third-largest nationality-based subculture. As you read, think of other nationality-based subcultures that are smaller or that are newcomers to the United States. Consider, in particular, the extent to which they are assimilated into or are mobilized within the larger culture. Exhibit 13-3 summarizes the nationality and/or ethnicity-based subcultures that we will discuss.

13-2c African-American Subculture

Exhibit 13-4 provides an overview of the African-American population of the United States. About one in eight Americans belongs to the African-American subculture. Almost all were born in the United States. Note that the number of people with college degrees is one-half of that of the majority population. African Americans are, on average, a younger population with very high numbers living in cities, especially major metro areas. The after-tax (discretionary) income of this group was $646 billion in 2002. They spent an estimated $270 billion in that year, ranking the group as the ninth-largest economy in the world. African-American women typically earn about one-half of the total.[7] Approximately 33 percent of African-American families in 2003 had an annual income of $50,000 or more. All this adds up to a very significant market segment.

As more marketers from within and outside the African-American subculture target its members, it is important to appreciate that the group is far from homogeneous—within it there is enormous diversity. As with any population, people and their attitudes and behaviors differ greatly based upon such factors as education, urban/rural residence,

E x h i b i t 13-3

Nationality and/or Ethnicity Subcultures

· African American
· Hispanic American (Latino)
· Asian and Pacific Island American
· Chinese American

E x h i b i t 13-4

Descriptors of the African-American Population

Total population (2003)	37,099,000
Share of the U.S. population	12.8%
Share who are native-born Americans (2000)	93.1%
Share of adults with college degrees (2000)	14.3%
Share with high school diplomas or some college (2000)	52.3%
Share living in the South (2000)	54.8%
Share living in metro area, central city (1999)	55.1%
Share under age 18 (2003)	30.6%
Share of married couples, five or more children (1999)	20%
Share of families with $50,000 or more income (2003)	32.5%

Source: Jesse McKinnon and Karen Humes, "The Black Population in the United States," *Current Population Reports* (U.S. Census Bureau, U.S. Department of Commerce, March 1999); U.S. Census Bureau, *Statistical Abstract of the United States: 2004–2005* (124th Edition) Washington, DC, 2004.

and religion. Age and gender are also at work to further divide the population into potentially viable segments.

The African-American subculture derives from a history of deprivation and adjustment to prejudice and discrimination. Heavily concentrated geographically, African Americans have long suffered inequities in education, employment, and income opportunities. Members of this subculture continue to experience "marketplace discrimination." The latter is differential treatment in the marketplace based on group membership rather than individual differences. In a study of black males, they reported encountering: being perceived as "not having enough money to buy," as a potential "shoplifter," as a "threat," and as having "low status" by store owners in the marketplace. Further, they were often followed around or watched closely by employees. This level of surveillance was perceived as much higher than that typical of other patrons. Even higher-status African-American males had such experiences. Also, black men report that they sometimes dress differently to fit in when they go shopping. Goods and services providers should be aware of black customers' sensitivity to surveillance techniques and the assumptions of potential wrongdoing. At the individual customer-clerk interaction level there could be a need for sensitivity training. Also, straightforward claims of a firm's commitment to anti-discrimination are needed.[8]

There is evidence that African Americans share the consumption values of the dominant culture. Despite lower socioeconomic status, they often attempt to pursue the same lifestyle as that of the dominant culture. To some extent, African Americans make different buying decisions simply because they may have less money to spend. But this is only a partial explanation of their purchasing behavior. Just as with any subculture, African Americans purchase products to fulfill self-esteem or status needs, or as a means of asserting cultural identity. Several factors affect the types of goods and services purchased, the types of outlets used, and the methods of communication that are most persuasive. We'll address these topics next.

Marketplace Behavior   Let's begin by looking at African-American shopping behavior. In the U.S. the percentage of all consumers naming department stores as a place they spend the most money slipped from 15 percent in 2000 to 11 percent in 2003.[9] Further, price has become the primary reason for people to shop in department stores. In 2000, 23 percent of consumers reported being driven by price, and by 2003 the share had climbed to 38 percent. In 2003, 18 percent of African Americans stated that department stores were where they spent the most money. These statistics indicate that this group is moving opposite to the current trend. However, mass merchandisers were the most popular venue for blacks, with 34 percent of African Americans preferring them. In third place in 2003 were the mid-line stores, at 13 percent, as locations where blacks spent their money. Tied for fourth and fifth place were specialty stores and power retailers at 9 percent each.

African Americans and Hispanics combined account for between 25 and 30 percent of all department store sales.[10] When African Americans were asked why they made a purchase from a particular store of any type, rather than some other store, 35 percent indicated price was the reason, 28 percent said selection, and 20 percent indicated convenience or location. These were the top three reasons for whites and Hispanic Americans as well.[11] African Americans are shifting their purchasing from discounters in two directions. A good share of their soft goods, especially apparel, purchasing is being moved to department stores, and hard goods shopping is shifting to the power retailers such as Toys r Us, Best Buy, and Bed, Bath & Beyond.[12]

Other findings related to African Americans as shoppers are: 25 percent do not like to shop alone, 43 percent enjoy shopping even if they don't buy anything, 47 percent go shopping only when absolutely necessary, 34 percent make spur-of-the-moment decisions when shopping, 44 percent plan far ahead when intending to buy expensive items, 28 percent would rather shop at a local store than a national chain, and 34 percent are willing to travel to shop at a favorite store.[13] When asked how often they used a credit card in a 30-day period, black consumers were lowest in all frequencies measured at 28 percent for 1 to 5 uses (highest, Asian Americans at 49 percent), 9 percent for 6 to 19 uses (highest, Asian Americans at 27 percent), and 2 percent for 20 or more uses (highest, Asian Americans at 12 percent).[14]

F A Q

Is there a white subculture in the United States?

African Americans are generally the most fashion-conscious when compared to the majority white population, Asian Americans, and Latinos. The share that indicated that they like to keep up with changes in trends and fashions was 34 percent compared to a range of 25 to 28 percent among the other three segments. Only 12 percent say they buy what they think their neighbors will approve of; one in five say they like to impress people with their lifestyle.[15]

Across most product categories, African-American consumers are more likely than average to buy items based on direct mail advertising. Further, 32 percent have made a purchase in the past year over the phone or by mail order, but only 14 percent (one-half of the majority population rate and about one-third of the Asian-American rate) purchased anything in the past year on the Internet.[16] Between August 2000 and September 2001, Internet use among African Americans increased at an annual rate of 33 percent to a total of 18.5 million users. Viewing this from a household perspective, 50 percent were online in 2002, and by the end of 2005 approximately 63 percent were online. It is estimated that by 2006 about 66 percent of African Americans will have access to the Internet, while the majority white population's access rate will be 78 percent.[17]

This subculture has a strong belief that technology can bring value to their everyday lives. Technology is perceived as giving mobility to the group. They feel confident in their ability to learn to use and acquire new technological tools. However, about three out of four African Americans believe that the negative side of technology is that it makes it easier for government agencies to spy on them.[18] We addressed the surveillance concerns of blacks earlier. This subculture describes themselves as "early adopters," with 42 percent saying they are the first to own a new product. Further, 72 percent report keeping up with the latest technologies, and 46 percent say they act as product advisors for their friends. However, actual ownership rates lag those of other user groups. It is likely that those African Americans who are technology owners see this as a status symbol.[19]

When considering the purchase of a home, the African-American consumer is more pessimistic than his or her white or Latino counterparts. When asked if they think they have home buying opportunities equal to the rest of the U.S. population, 86 percent of whites agree that they do, 74 percent of Latinos agree, but only 55 percent of African Americans agree.[20] Certainly, after finding a home at the right price, size, and location, other characteristics come into play. In a recent survey among black home buyers the top five ranked amenities considered, in order, were: a laundry room, a linen closet, exterior lighting, an exhaust fan, and a separate dining room. Other features of importance were a separate shower enclosure, ceiling fans, a deck in the rear of the house, a patio at the rear of the house, and a walk-in pantry. The majority prefer to have four or more bedrooms in their homes because of larger immediate families and because some live with members of their extended family. In response to this, some home builders are offering custom plans that include more bedrooms and larger areas in the house, especially dining rooms and family rooms, that are more in line with the needs of African-American households.[21]

The African-American subculture is much less likely than other groups to travel on vacation or to take a trip abroad. When they do travel outside the United States, African Americans head for places that are "color and language comfortable." The Caribbean is a popular destination. Most travel takes place in summer, and tour packages are the rule rather than the exception for travel outside the United States. African Americans spend proportionately as much of their incomes on recreation and leisure products as do whites.

The African-American population represents about 12 percent of the total households with televisions in the U.S. Half of this segment is under 30 years of age. As a group they watch significantly more television than does the general population. In the fourth quarter of 2002, for example, they watched on average 76.8 hours per week, almost 11 hours per day, whereas the general public average was 53.1 hours per week, between 7 and 8 hours per day. During the overnight period their viewing rates were 151 percent more than that of the general public. They were watching 74 percent more during late night, 54 percent more in daytime, and 12 percent more during prime time. They are strongly drawn to minority television programs, with only two of their top ten prime time shows being among the top ten majority population shows.[22] Check out CBite 13-2 for insights on how advertisers are showing more respect for the history and traditions of this subculture.

CBite 13-2
A Tradition of Respect

African Americans are generally more receptive to advertising appeals than are white consumers. Campaigns that have been particularly successful with African Americans share as common characteristics a respect for the history and traditions of the subculture and an acknowledgment of its contribution not only to its own advancement, but also to the progress of the nation. Coca-Cola, for example, ran a "Share the Dream" scholarship sweepstakes focusing on the vision of Dr. Martin Luther King, Jr. McDonald's initiated a Black History Makers of Tomorrow program for African-American teens; the theme was "McDonald's Believes Making Black History Is Not Just a Thing of the Past." Burger King saluted the African-American children who were part of the struggle for equal education in Kansas in 1951.

Attitudes toward Brands   Researchers have long believed that African Americans are more brand loyal than are members of the dominant culture, yet we find that 20 percent of consumers in this subculture report "changing brands often," while white majority consumers indicate that 17 percent of their number change brands often. This shows that the two groups are very close in their level of brand loyalty based purely on brand-switching, with blacks actually showing less loyalty.[23]

Although African-American consumers at all income levels are sensitive to price, they also consider status when making purchase decisions, favoring socially visible products. Status concerns increase with income level.

Women and African Americans appear to be the most prone to purchase premium food products. These are foods that are produced using fewer or no chemicals and are lower in fat content. This is based on a study of shoppers' concern levels relating to the use of pesticides, the potential for salmonella in food that can result in food poisoning, and high fat content. "High concern" for pesticide contamination was expressed by African Americans compared to whites (83.7 percent versus 73.5 percent), salmonella in the food (84.3 percent versus 74.1 percent), and fat content (83.3 percent versus 77.1 percent). Concern across all population subcultures increases with age, reflecting greater perceived vulnerability. In a parallel study it was found that white males were least concerned, black males and white females had similar concern levels, and black females had the greatest concern with the state of the food supply. Concern was not related to income or education. The study authors' conclusion is that all classes and groups of consumers prefer foods marketed as being "natural" or "organic" and/or having "reduced fat." Marketing and labeling of food products may be of increased importance to shoppers in the future as they increasingly try to determine the safety levels of the products on the shelf or at the markets.[24]

What this points to is that it is essential for marketers targeting the African-American community to determine whether or not members will respond to product position and promotion strategies that are based upon brands. Use of a brand strategy, for example, would probably depend upon such considerations as product type, the level of status associated with it, and the socioeconomic position of the specific group targeted within the subculture. Also, marketers must become increasingly aware of the African-American female consumer's wariness of the safety of the food supply and take positive steps to assure its purity and to properly communicate with this shopping segment.

Marketing to African Americans   In recent years, more and more marketers have actively focused on the African-American subculture. As the size of the population increases, this is likely to continue and intensify. Before we look at examples, there are two overriding behaviors that marketers must incorporate in their strategies and tactics in order to target the subculture successfully. First, *being shown respect within the marketplace* is very important to African Americans. Second, *they must feel a sense of acceptance.*[25] As the competition to attract the African-American consumer increases, outlets will be patronized and purchases made only if these two conditions are met.

CBite 13-3
Unwilling Targets?

The African-American community and other advocacy groups have reacted against companies that purposely target the subculture with products that, though legal, are considered harmful. The R. J. Reynolds Tobacco Company withdrew its cigarette brand, "Uptown," from the marketplace because its niche marketing strategy targeting the African-American market was not viewed as socially responsible. Similarly, public protests by a religious leader in the Chicago area were counted among the reasons that G. Heileman Brewing Company did not go ahead with plans to introduce PowerMaster, a high-alcohol content malt liquor that was to be positioned to appeal to the low-income, inner-city black population.

Several major marketers aggressively target the African-American subculture. For example, J.C. Penney offers in-store "Authentic African" boutiques, stocking traditional African clothing, accessories, and housewares. Hasbro, Mattel, and Tyco are among the toy manufacturers producing and selling "ethnically correct" dolls, attempting to reach African-American children under age 10. Mattel's Shani—a Swahili name meaning "marvelous"—Nicelle, and Asha have hairstyles, skin tones, and bone structures that mirror variations among African-American women.[26] Kmart's ethnically sensitive campaign, "Looking Good," emphasizes clothing lines targeted to African Americans. South DeKalb Mall in Atlanta, positioned as an "Afrocentric" retail center and promoted largely through media that target African Americans, runs in-mall events and entertainment likely to appeal to the subculture, including live jazz music and African dance.

When African Americans seek subculture-specific products, they use media targeted to the subculture. These include magazines, newspapers, and radio and television stations owned and operated by members of the subculture. They watch significantly more television than the average U.S. household, as pointed out earlier, and watch many television programs featuring African-American actors and dealing with the life and times of their subculture in the U.S. Across all media, African-American consumers seem to favor equal-opportunity advertisers and those showing a willingness to identify with the problems of their communities.

CBite 13-3 addresses an ethical question concerning targeting this subculture. Check it out.

13-2d Hispanic-American Subculture

The diversity of the Hispanic American, sometimes referred to as the Hispanic or Latino, subculture points to the need for marketers to take great care in targeting its members. According to the U.S. census, in 2002, a total of 67 percent of Latino households were originally Mexican, 14.3 percent were of Central and South American origin, 8.6 percent were Puerto Rican, 3.7 percent were Cuban, and 6.5 percent were "Other Hispanic."[27] Exhibit 13-5 provides an overview of some of the population descriptors of the Hispanic-American subculture.

In 2002, the discretionary (after tax) income of Latinos was approximately $581 billion.[28] The median income of this subculture in 2002 was a bit less than three-quarters of the white median income in the United States.[29] This lower level has been influenced in part by high rates of immigration of low-income families. Exhibit 13-5 shows that in 2002, 32.4 percent of Hispanic-American families had incomes of at least $50,000. We would expect further increases in affluence. For every age group there continues to be a higher birth rate than among non-Latino women.[30] In fact, having children appears to be a very significant event in Latino family life.

Family size may also be influenced by the high membership in the Roman Catholic Church of the Hispanic-American population.

Descriptors of the Hispanic-American Population

Total population (2003)	39,899,000
Share of U.S. population (2003)	13.7%
Share of population arrived since 1981 (est.)	35%
Share of adults with college degrees (2000)	10.5%
Share with high school diplomas or some college (2000)	37.7%
Share living in the West and South (2000)	43.5% and 32.8%
Share living in metro area, central city (2000)	46.4%
Share under age 18 (2003)	34.1%
Share of family households, five or more members (2003)	23%
Share of families with $50,000 or more income (2002)	32.4%

There is variation among the Mexican, Cuban, South and Central American, and Puerto Rican groups. For example, Cubans are more likely to have higher levels of formal education than are members of the other three populations. Mexican-origin citizens have the lowest levels of formal education. The pattern for income in 2001 was slightly different, with Central and South Americans being the highest, followed closely by Cubans, with Mexicans and Puerto Ricans being near equal in the third and fourth positions, respectively. In 2001, about one-fourth of Puerto Rican families were below the poverty line, as were one-fifth of Mexicans, 15 percent of the families from Central and South America, and 13 percent of Cuban families.

Sources: Melissa Therrien and Roberto R. Ramirez, "The Hispanic Population in the United States," *Current Population Reports* (U.S. Census Bureau, U.S. Department of Commerce, March 2000); U.S. Census Bureau, *Statistical Abstract of the United States: 2004–2005* (124th ed.), Washington, D.C., 2004.

Historically, Latinos traditionally thought of themselves as Latino or Hispanic first and as Americans second.[31] However, there is an increasing move toward acculturation. This includes new emphasis on being bilingual. The number one preschool show on commercial television in 2003 was "Dora the Explorer." This is a series about a young bilingual Latina that has a special connection with Hispanic families because Dora represents a positive character who is a strong example of acculturation. She speaks Spanish and English and shows pride in her Latino background, making it an integral part of her everyday life.[32] A large share of Hispanic Americans say that the Spanish language is a very important feature of their culture, with two-thirds opting to speak Spanish at home and about 20 percent not speaking English at all.[33] Many segments of the Latino subculture fervently celebrate the holidays of their native countries—such as Cinco de Mayo and Puerto Rican Independence Day—in addition to traditional U.S. holidays.

Hispanic Americans tend to marry within the subculture, with 82 percent of Latino wives having Latino husbands and 85 percent of Latino husbands having Latino wives.[34] Dominant values tend to be traditional and conservative, including respect for elders, commitment to family, and male dominance.[35]

As indicated in Exhibit 13-5, the median age of members of the Latino American subculture is relatively low. Larger family sizes bring the median down, but even the adult population group is younger overall.[36] The Mexican population is the youngest, followed by the Puerto Rican group. The oldest of the major subgroups is the Cuban-American segment. This is mainly attributed to the number of older political refugees who entered the United States versus the much younger pools from other Latin countries.[37] Marketplace 13-1 offers insights into the subculture of poverty that crosses lines among African Americans, Latinos, and Native Americans. Take a look.

Marketplace Behavior Hispanic Americans come from a wide range of cultural backgrounds and value systems, influencing their attitudes and behavior in the marketplace. They are a diverse group, bound together by threads of language and cultural

Marketplace 13-1

A Subculture of Poverty

About one in five families in the United States lives at the poverty level. This "subculture of poverty" overlaps considerably with the African-American subculture, and with such ethnic groups as the Chicanos and Puerto Ricans, and with a subset of the elderly. It also includes Native Americans and migrant farm workers. Regionally, the South has the highest proportion of poor people in the nation. Almost all live in rural areas or in large inner cities.

The poor are characterized by a lack of participation in the institutions of the larger society; a family structure marked by the absence of childhood as a prolonged, protected state; a strong predisposition to authoritarianism; a lack of privacy; and—above all—an individual feeling of inferiority and helplessness. Among the factors perpetuating this subculture are limited educational opportunities coupled with low motivation to learn, discrimination, and a determination on the part of most Americans to keep the poor at a physical distance.

People living below the poverty line spend a significant share of their income on necessities, such as food, shelter, and medical care. They spend less on transportation and clothing relative to their income, and about the same proportion on recreation, personal care, and household equipment. A surprisingly large percentage of income is spent on durables, such as television sets, automatic clothes washers, radios, and kitchen items. These figures seem understandable when one considers the desire to be part of the mainstream middle-income lifestyle seen on television, the easy credit offered by merchants, and the disproportionate number of young families among the poor making their first appliance purchases. While the poor almost always buy appliances new, they tend to buy used cars. More than 80 percent use credit and installment buying, and the ratio of debt to annual income is approximately twice as high as in higher-income households.

The poor have fewer shopping outlets to choose from than do people in higher-income brackets, and credit costs are often higher. Further, merchandise offered is not always of a quality comparable to that found in higher-income areas. Lacking confidence to make good marketplace decisions, the poor tend to rely on merchants or relatives for purchase information, to use stores that are close by, and to fail to deliberate and compare prices before making purchases. The poor also tend to disregard free or reduced-rate programs provided for them. Understanding social issues is central to selling to low-income consumers. Marketers must make a trade-off between the level of profits anticipated and the financial and social costs of operating safely and in the best interests of the market served. One basic problem is distribution, that is, making sure that products are safely delivered to retail outlets and consumers. Because of theft and security problems and the high insurance and operating costs that come along with them, it is difficult to encourage retailers to operate in high-risk neighborhoods, and often, higher-than-average prices result.

Sources: U. S. Census Bureau, *Statistical Abstract of the United States:2004–2005* (124th ed.), Washington, D.C., 2004; Oscar Lewis, *La Vida* (New York: Random House, 1966); Henry O. Pruden, F. Kelly Shuptrine, and Douglas S. Longman, "A Measure of Alienation from the Marketplace," *Journal of the Academy of Marketing Science,* Vol. 4, No. 4 (Winter 1974); Louise G. Richards, "Consumer Practices of the Poor," in Lola M. Ireland, ed., *Low Income Life Styles,* U.S. Department of Health, Education and Welfare Administration: Division of Research (Washington, D.C.: U.S. Government Printing Office, 1969); David Caplovitz, *The Poor Pay More* (New York: Free Press, 1963); Leonard L. Berry and Paul J. Soloman, "Generalizing about Low-Income Food Shoppers: A Word of Caution," *Journal of Retailing,* Vol. 47, No. 2 (Summer 1971); Arieh Goldman, "Do Lower-Income Shoppers Have a More Restricted Shopping Scope?" *Journal of Marketing,* Vol. 40, No. 1 (1976); U.S. Bureau of Labor Statistics, *A Study of Food Stores Located in Low- and Higher-Income Areas of Six Large Cities* (Washington, D.C.: U.S. Government Printing Office, 1966).

---

bodega A small general store in a Latino-American neighborhood that serves as a popular gathering place for local residents.

heritage. Some have a recent history in the United States, while others have been here for generations.

They generally prefer to shop in smaller stores. **Bodegas**—neighborhood general stores that serve as gathering places—are very popular. Here, they most likely know the salespeople or owners, and the shopping experience becomes social, rather than purely a business exchange. In fact, the bodega was found to serve an important role in maintaining Latin culture.[38] Latinos are loyal to retail outlets owned by members of the subculture and to stores with Spanish-speaking salespeople.[39] Hispanic Americans do a lot of shopping in other retail outlets. When asked at which stores or companies they spent the most money in 2003, 32 percent said mass merchants, 25 percent said mid-line stores, and 15 percent indicated department stores. Only 5 percent stated they spent the most at power retailers. The 2 percent reporting the most spent on the Internet matched the African-American share. The white Internet share was 3 percent.[40]

When Latinos were asked where they had shopped at least once in the past three months, 48 percent said department stores and 57 percent indicated discounters. This discounter percentage is below that of whites (60 percent) and higher than that of blacks (50 percent).[41] When asked why they chose to make a purchase at a particular store or outlet rather than some other, 40 percent of Latinos indicated that price was the reason, 27 percent said selection, and 19 percent said convenience or location. These three reasons matched those of African Americans in order of importance. However, the Hispanic-American price emphasis was higher than that of blacks.[42]

When shopping, only 12 percent of Latinos indicate that they buy what they think their neighbors will approve of, 27 percent like to keep up with changes in trends and fashions, 25 percent prefer to shop with friends, 42 percent enjoy shopping even if they don't buy anything, 54 percent say they only go shopping when they absolutely need something, and 37 percent make spur-of-the-moment purchases.[43] Hispanics prefer to shop more with family than any other minority segment or the majority group. Thirty-six percent report this, and 30 percent say they like shopping with their children. One-fourth said that kids have a significant impact on the brands that are purchased. Further, Hispanic Americans are twice as likely as whites to go out of their way to find new stores (13 percent versus 7 percent), As noted earlier in the bodega discussion, 26 percent would rather shop at a local store than a national chain.[44]

When asked how many times in the past 30 days they had used a credit card, 39 percent said 1–5 times, 15 percent indicated 6–19 times, and 5 percent reported 20 or more uses. These shares of card use frequency are lower than whites or Asian Americans and higher than for African Americans. Regarding purchasing by phone or mail order or on the Internet, as reported by Latinos, in the past year 29 percent had made a purchase by phone or direct mail and 20 percent had bought something on the Internet. The Internet purchase share was less than that of Asian Americans or whites and higher than that of African Americans.[45]

Thirty-nine percent of Hispanic Americans stated that they are very likely to buy new technology products or services. However, though they see technology as desirable, Latinos are more likely to see it as inaccessible, possibly caused by language and product development barriers. It is reported that 71 percent say that technology provides access to information and enhances their lives. We also find that 52 percent say they've felt taken advantage of by "technical support" people. They prefer to buy components rather than bundles of items. Ninety-two percent report that warranties are very important to them when buying technology, and 85 percent are looking for items that are easy to repair. Portability is also important.[46]

Hispanic Americans are much more optimistic that African Americans when looking at their opportunities to become home buyers. Three out of four feel their chances to buy are equal to the rest of the population, whereas you will recall that only 55 percent of blacks felt that way in a July 2004 study.[47] The majority of Latinos prefer a home with four or more bedrooms, since in a number of cases they live with their extended family. Hispanic homeowners may have parents, grandparents, or even cousins living with them. In the first generation some Hispanic-American families tend to have large extended families who they want to live with them. After a generation or two they tend to live in more traditional family homes. They also often buy homes from the same contractors, being very loyal. Home builders have developed special plans to fit the needs of the Latino home-buying population, including larger areas, especially in the dining room and the family room. The most important features of a new home are laundry room, dining room, exterior lighting, linen closet, and walk-in pantry.[48]

Attitudes toward Brands   Latinos are very brand loyal. A Yankelovich study reported that 82 percent of respondents stick with preferred brands, compared to 57 percent of the general population.[49] They also are drawn to recognizable traditional brands.[50] This suggests that speedy introduction of new products and services is an essential competitive strategy. For the most part, Hispanic-American consumers feel that brand-name products are of high quality, and they therefore avoid generic items. Further, they will try new brands only if they are dissatisfied with the ones presently being used or if they are indifferent to them.

Products that are made in America are generally perceived to be of high quality, even though the general U.S. population may believe otherwise.[51] This is particularly true with regard to such products as cars, consumer electronics, cameras, and wine.

CBite 13-4
Latino Youth in United States Rock On

According to a 2002 study commissioned by Cultural Access, Latino youth in the United States are experiencing a cultural shift evidenced by new preferences in music, entertainment, and the language in which they choose to converse with friends. For 14-to-24-year-old Latinos, traditional Spanish music is giving way to rock 'n' roll (roquera), particularly hip-hop; Telemundo to MTV; and Spanish to English. Details of the study include the following:

- Only 13 percent of respondents in Los Angeles call themselves traditionalists, while most respondents consider themselves part of the American mainstream.

- More than a third of respondents in Los Angeles consider themselves part of the hip-hop culture.

- Respondents are twice as likely to watch English-language TV (favorite programs include *Friends* and *The Simpsons*) and listen to English-language radio than they are to watch Spanish TV or listen to Spanish radio. (In Los Angeles, English-language alternative radio station KROQ, which is geared toward youth, says that 40 percent of its listener base is comprised of Latinos.)

- In a ratio of 5 to 1, English-language newspapers are preferred over those written in Spanish.

- For more than 90 percent of respondents, English is the language of choice when speaking with friends.

The study, conducted in New York City and Los Angeles, concluded that, while most Latino youth are proud of their heritage and frequently speak Spanish in their homes, marketers to this demographic should be aware of its changes and design their strategies accordingly.

Source: Adapted from Joel Kotkin, "Los Roqueros: Latinos Like MTV, Not Telemundo," *Wall Street Journal,* November 13, 2002, p. D10.

Marketing to Hispanic Americans   When marketing to the Latino-American subculture, it is essential to remember that the community is not homogeneous. Differences arising from country of origin, history of experience in the United States, demographics, social class, and an array of other factors mean that market segmentation is vital.

The majority of Latinos use Spanish-language media for product information, though this is changing as the move to acculturation continues. Traditionally about 65 percent listen to Spanish-language radio, and 80 percent watch Spanish-language television. Twenty percent read Spanish-language magazines, and about 40 percent read Spanish-language newspapers. These shares will become smaller into the future especially among second and third generation Latinos.[52] The majority of television viewing time is devoted to Spanish-language channels and/or programming. Understanding the prevalence of the Spanish language, advertising agencies are increasingly using Latino media specialists to help with media planning. Latino youths, however are shifting toward the cultural mainstream in their increased use of English and their media choices. See CBite 13-4 to get an idea of what's happening.

Consumers who identify strongly with the Hispanic-American subculture have positive attitudes toward advertising and are likely to believe that advertising presents helpful and honest information about goods and services. To be effective, however, advertising must be in the Spanish language. Exhibit 13-6, however, is in English. This ad is a corporate expression of commitment to diversity and shows a successful General Electric executive who is a Latina. It is targeted toward both upwardly mobile Hispanic Americans and other members of the Latino subculture.

Local promotions can be very successful among Latinos. Special promotional activities associated with events such as Cinco de Mayo in Los Angeles, Calle Ocho in Miami, and the Hispanic Day Parade in Chicago or Puerto Rican Day Parade in New York are likely sound opportunities.[53] Coupons are used by almost two-thirds of the Latino population. However, Latino consumers receive far fewer coupons per year compared to the national aver-

General Electric sends a message of commitment to diversity with focus on the Hispanic-American population.

Source: Courtesy of General Electric.

age. Even though some claim that coupons are seen negatively, perceived as equivalent to food stamps by Hispanic Americans, the high percentage of users shows that promotion through coupons can be effective. In one study, however, 93 percent of the consumers interviewed indicated that the bodega at which they shopped either did not accept coupons or that consumers did not know if coupons were accepted, so there are mixed signals.[54]

Sweepstakes have also proven to be a successful sales promotion device. However, in conducting sweepstakes, sensitivity to cultural norms is essential. A Los Angeles retail store sponsoring a sweepstakes in which the prize was a trip for two to Disneyland was disappointed with the low participation level. Reminded of the strong family orientation of the Latino community, the sponsor changed the prize to a family trip, and participation increased significantly.[55] In CBite 13-5 you'll see where improper use of the Spanish language in advertising can spell trouble for the advertiser. Check it out.

We already indicated that a large share of Latinos have migrated to America in the recent past. According to the 2000 census over 31 million people living in this nation were foreign born. In 1990 the number was about 20 million. This is an increase of 57 percent, while during the same time the U.S. population grew by 9.3 percent. The top five countries of birth for members of the foreign-born population in 2000 were Mexico (9.2 million), China (1.5 million), Philippines (1.4 million), India (1 million), and Vietnam (1 million).[56] This is an interesting finding when one sees that the ratio of foreign-born consumers grew over six times as fast as native population growth in the decade of the 1990s. What are the marketplace implications for this, especially if this ratio stays positive in favor of the foreign-born? The next section of the text takes a look at Asian Americans and Pacific Island Americans.

13-2e Asian- and Pacific Island-American Subcultures

The Asian-American and Pacific Island-American subcultures consist of 29 distinct groups, each with its own languages or dialects, values, and customs. The main nationality groups in 2000 were: Chinese (23.8 percent), Filipino (18.1 percent), Asian Indian and Pakistani (16.4 percent), Vietnamese (11 percent), Korean (10.5 percent), (Japanese 7.8 percent), and Pacific Island Americans (4 percent).[57] In 2003, Asian and Pacific Island Americans numbered 12.4 million. This was 4.3 percent of the total population of the United States.[58] This is expected to grow to 15 million to 20 million as we move further into the twenty-first century. A very large share live in urban areas, though more members of this diverse subculture are moving to the suburbs of the larger cities they had traditionally settled. In 2003, 34.6 percent lived in California, where six of the top ten Asian-American centers are.[59] In Hawaii, the Asian share is a bit less than two-thirds of the population.

Asian and Pacific Islander Americans are more likely to be affluent—defined as having incomes of $50,000 per year or above—than any other ethnic group, including the white majority . In 1999, about 59 percent of Asian- and Pacific-Islander married couple families met the $50,000 level versus 58 percent of white households. The median income for Asians in the U.S. was $51,908, and that of the white population was $44,687. The Hawaiian and other Pacific Islander Americans were at $42,717.[60]

Chinese Americans   Let's look at the Chinese-American subculture, because it is the largest of the Asian subgroups. This segment of the subculture has a median income near the top of the Asian-American subculture. The Chinese-American economy is built on immigrant capital, hard work, and strong family ties. The use of informal loan clubs and the practice of hiring from within are common, as members of the community seek to help those who are part of their own ethnic group. Ninety-seven percent of this group consider themselves Chinese, American Chinese, or Chinese American rather than American. Nine out of ten believe that it is important to pass along the Cantonese or Mandarin language to their children.

Asian Americans tend to be conservative and family oriented, upholding traditional male/female roles.[61] They value education as the best way to achieve social acceptance and financial stability and security. Chinese-American children spend two to three times as much time on homework as do their peers, and family life on school nights centers around it. A way designed to preserve their cultural roots is to send their children to Chinese school on Saturdays besides having them attend regular schools on weekdays.[62] All members of the Chinese community expect to be educated and work toward this goal. A college degree is considered essential, with graduate-level education preferred.[63] Although many members of the Asian and Pacific subculture feel pressure to conform to expected models and roles, others report a need to express their individuality.[64]

Marketplace Behavior   Because the Asian-American and Pacific Island subculture is made up of some 29 nationality groups with different cultural histories and customs, very little specific information has been published to help us understand the marketplace behavior of members or their attitudes toward brands. The following observations, however, provide some insight and serve as a starting point for discussion or for further research.

As a whole, Asian and Pacific Island Americans are cost-conscious and very brand loyal.[65] Steinway and Sons, the piano manufacturer, found that Asian Americans value brand names, education, and musical culture and targeted its promotions accordingly. In the 1990s, about 15 percent of all Steinway piano sales in North America were made to this group.

The various subgroups of the Asian subculture shop mostly within their communities. When they go outside of the community, they have favorite stores, particularly supermarkets that offer ethnic food specialties and ingredients, and are willing to travel to reach them.[66] In California, for example, Safeway and Lucky Stores have successfully focused on products geared for this population group. A recent study suggests that price sensitivity and shopping practices of Chinese Americans are substantially different from those of mainstream Americans. Chinese use multiple senses when examining unpackaged foods and do so far more than do mainstream American shoppers. They also inspect more items and take much more time to shop. Also found was that Chinese supermarkets in America have substantially lower prices across many food products when compared to similar mainstream American stores. These lower prices range from 37 percent lower for packaged goods of the same brand and size to more than 100 percent lower for meats and seafood of the same type and description. This shows how price conscious these consumers are for such private consumption goods. However, when shopping for public consumption goods, especially gifts, they are more status conscious and less frugal. It is likely that social gift-giving reciprocity social norms contribute to the latter shopping behavior.[67]

Marketing to Asian and Pacific Island Americans   One of the greatest challenges for marketers is to overcome language and other barriers that separate the Asian and Pacific Island subculture from the rest of the population. The Skechers ad in Exhibit 13-7 features an Asian-American woman, an African-American man, and two white male models. This shows nice product fit across these diverse target groups.

When seeking marketing information, each subgroup often looks for media vehicles that use its native language. In both northern and southern California there are Asian-language television stations. In California there are Chinese and Japanese language newspapers, and others in various Asian languages. There also is a radio station in San Francisco with a significant share of its programming in languages other than English, mostly a variety of Asian languages.

In response to the diversity of cultures grouped within the Asian-American and Pacific Island subculture, the agricultural products division of Anheuser Busch has successfully developed not one but eight different varieties of California-grown rice, each aimed at satisfying the individual tastes of a different subgroup.[68] The marketing of cosmetics to Asian women presents some real problems in America. Check out how one female entrepreneur found a solution. It's discussed in Marketplace 13-2 on page 415.

The celebration of Asian-oriented national holidays has proven to offer good opportunities for marketers. Asian-Pacific Heritage Month (The Philippines), Harvest Celebration (Korea), Chinese New Year, and Grandparent's Day (Japan) are examples. The U.S. Post Office very successfully targeted Chinese Americans for its express mail and money transfer services during the celebration of the Chinese New Year in 1993. The language used was Mandarin.

The most effective advertising to Chinese Americans reflects traditional family values. One taboo is the display of physical contact between people of the opposite sex. Sexual innuendo and public displays of emotion are also in poor taste.[69]

Exhibit 13-7

Skechers takes the diversity of its various Asian-American and other markets very seriously, showing models representing some of these groups.

Source: Courtesy of Skechers USA.

This overview of the extremely diverse Asian and Pacific Island subcultures is necessarily brief because of the lack of published information on all groups other than the Chinese. These limited insights do, however, give a flavor of the challenges faced by marketers focusing on the Asian subculture.

Marketing Management—Implications and Actions

Understanding nationality-based subcultures helps marketers:

- Respond to changes in behavior and attitude as subcultures are assimilated into the larger culture or mobilized into the larger culture.
- Identify the types of products most likely to appeal to each subculture.
- Use media channels most frequently used by each group and promotions designed to appeal to them.

13-3 Subcultures Based on Age

Can you remember how you thought, felt, and acted when you were in fifth or sixth grade, maybe 10, 11, or 12 years of age? How did you feel about your parents, your friends, clothes, cosmetics, hairstyles, music, shopping, and life in general? What happened when you entered your teen years and you were in high school? How did you feel about relationships, about going to college, about working, and about your future? How do you

Marketplace 13-2

Cosmetics for Asian Women

Susan Yee is at home in a store. She's spent her whole career in retailing and loves just to be a consumer. But Yee also finds that shopping as an Asian woman in the United States can be frustrating, especially at cosmetics counters. Even with the wide palette of foundations and eye shadows offered by the big manufacturers, she can't find the shades that would highlight the yellow undertones of her complexion. Her five sisters and many friends have the same problem.

She and one of her sisters decided to make and sell their own cosmetics. The result is the Zhen line that they started in the mid-1990s. Zhen is pronounced "jen" and is Chinese for the word "genuine." Its makeup and skin care products are sold primarily through the company's twelve-page catalog. Two branches of Nordstrom's near Seattle also sell the cosmetics. Yee knew that her company, which is primarily family owned, had a market that many other companies weren't serving.

"I don't think anyone has targeted the Asian consumer. I had perfect demographics, and I didn't think any of those companies tried to get my money," Yee says. "The Asian consumer has a lot of power they don't realize," she went on.

While Zhen's customers are mostly Asian, Yee says white women who have a sallow complexion and black women also buy from the company. The big companies have two failings, according to Yee. They don't supply Asian women with the right colors, particularly in foundations, and they don't know how to work with Asian faces. "They don't know what to do with your eye, because there is no crease ... I'm never going to have a crease in my eye, so what can I do to make my eyes look better?"

The typical Zhen customer is 20 to 40 years old, working, and is a person "who wants a quality product and may not feel comfortable in a drugstore environment or doesn't feel like the quality is there," Yee says. "Within the Asian community, we've already made a name for ourselves. Someone will wake up, but we were here first, and we understand the Asian consumer," she says.

Source: From "Cosmetics Line Designed for Asian Women" by Joyce M. Rosenberg in *Marketing News*, October 21, 1996, p. 15. Reprinted by permission of American Marketing Association.

---

imagine your behavior will change when you enter the workplace, get married, buy a house, have children? Do you expect to be more like or more unlike your parents? How have your feelings, your behavior, and your actions as a consumer changed over the years?

Marketers see age as one of the most viable ways that the population is segmented. Perhaps more than any other cultural or societal factor, age affects almost all marketplace behavior. In this section, we will look at selected age subcultures: preteens, teens, Generation Yers, Generation Xers, baby boomers, and seniors. As you read, keep in mind that the attitudes and shopping, buying, and consumption behaviors of each group are also subject to the influences of the other subcultures, social class, reference groups, and family or household to which individuals belong. Look at Exhibit 13-8 for an overview of the age subcultures we'll be taking about.

13-3a **Preteens**

Parents control children's spending until age 3, when spending choices are first permitted.[70] In 1991, children aged 4 to 12 controlled close to $14.4 billion in spending. Of this, less than half came from allowances and about a fifth from earnings for performing household chores. About one-sixth came in the form of parental gifts and 8 percent as gifts from others. The remainder, about 10 percent, was from part-time work outside the home.[71] In 1991 boys received an average of $8.87 per week and girls $7.66.

In addition to their own income, children influence adult spending, particularly in such categories as snacks, toys, electronic gadgets, clothes, and hobby supplies. It has been estimated that they currently have some influence on about $132 billion in consumer spending in the United States. In 2004 the estimated spending of American 8- to 14-year-olds was $38 billion. Almost $25 billion was the 12- to 14-year-olds' share, which works out to $1,972 per youth. The 8- to 11-year-olds spent about $780 each for a total of $13 billion.[72]

On average, children spend about 40 percent of their total income on high-cost items, such as jewelry, video games, and running shoes that parents are unwilling to purchase for

E x h i b i t 13-8

Age Subcultures

- Preteens
- Teens
- Generation Y
- Generation X
- Baby boomers
- Seniors

them. Also, cosmetics designed for preteen girls are very popular. Barbie Lip Sweets lipstick is a good example of this.

In addition, parents encourage children to join plans to help save for their future education. Girls save more than boys, 43 percent compared to 38 percent. In recent years, banks have increasingly offered savings programs directed at children. For example, the First National Bank of Pulaski, Tennessee, recently offered its Moola-Moola savings club to children up to 12 years of age. A fuzzy monster named Moola-Moola visited area schools, encouraging youngsters to open savings accounts.[73]

Marketplace Behavior   No matter how much parents deny the fact, children are very often key influencers of family purchases. From candy, snacks, and food choices to toys and clothing, parents fight a never-ending battle not to give in to their requests—and frequently lose. Preteens influence purchases in approximately 60 product categories. Many of these preteens are the children of baby boomers, making them one of the fastest-growing age segments in the United States.[74] Even with products that children do not necessarily use and are uninterested in, like laundry detergents, they sometimes have a voice. As a result of television advertising, in particular, they almost subconsciously build a level of product awareness that they pass on to their parents.[75] Moreover, in today's society, where both parents often work, one of the household responsibilities that some children take on is shopping for food and other necessities. Hence, many children become shoppers at an early age as they begin to select products for the household.

Research shows that children rather than parents typically select the stores in which they spend their own money. About one-third of spending is at discount stores such as Kmart, Wal-Mart, and Target. A quarter is in shopping malls, mostly in clothing stores and video arcades. The remainder is dispersed. Of this, more than 10 percent is spent at toy stores.

Marketing to Preteens   Firms such as the McDonald's fast-food chain correctly see today's preteens as the adults of tomorrow. By appealing to preteens, marketers build brand preference at a very early age, hoping that when these young people move through their teen years and into adulthood they will bring their kids to "Mickey D's" for food and fun.[76]

McDonald's is just one of the many marketers attempting to build longevity into their brands by targeting children, both selling to them today and encouraging them to stay with the brands into the future. Examples include General Mills with Yoplait Trix Lowfat—a yogurt product with colored layers, Banquet Kid Cuisine frozen dinners, and Procter & Gamble with Pert shampoos—targeted directly to this group. In 1992, computer giant Macintosh introduced Performa, a computer designed specifically for preteens. Interestingly, the advertising strategy behind the product targeted parents rather than children.

The "five rules of thumb" for food marketers who wish to sell to preteens are found in Marketplace 13-3. Take a look.

The medium of choice for preteens is television. Children's programming dominates late afternoon and weekend television, particularly Saturday mornings. Cable and satellite television has meant the proliferation of programs specifically targeted to this group. In young children, learning is improved when audiovisual formats are used, pointing to the power of television as an information and advertising medium with this age group.[77] Of course, as we will discuss later, marketers must also be aware that there is much parental and governmental scrutiny of television ads aimed at children and preteens. We have seen a recent dramatic rise in children and teens (K–12 school ages) using the Internet. In the year 2000, 5.6 million of them used the Internet at home, 4.1 million at school, 1 million at a friend/neighbor/relative's home, and about one-half million at the library.[78] The use of this medium will certainly continue to grow in the future and offers the opportunity to marketers to present the benefits of their products to segments within this group.

Other media vehicles have arrived on the scene that specifically target preteens. For example, two new magazines, *Disney Adventures* and *Sports Illustrated for Kids,* are succeeding in reaching this group. Another magazine, *Kidsmarts* by Lipton Company, is

Marketplace 13-3

Food for Thought

Here are five rules of thumb for food marketers on developing new food products for children.

1. *Learn to see food the way kids do.* Forget the pyramid of nutritional food groups. As far as kids are concerned, there are four basic food groups: hand food, noisy food, fast food, and funny food.

2. *What might have been outrageous when you were a kid must be far wackier today.* Note the noodle dinosaurs, noodle Teenage Mutant Ninja Turtles, and dinosaur-studded vegetable soup. Captain Crunch looks awfully tame next to maple syrup-flavored waffle cereal. The once-shocking marshmallows in breakfast cereal must now have spangles on them and come in more fluorescent colors.

3. *If it can't be found in nature, it's good to eat.* Chocolate should always be where it is not supposed to be, as in Count Chocula or Cocoa Pebbles, two cold breakfast cereals. Fruit must be pureed, dried, rolled up like paper, and wrapped in plastic and foil. Good-for-you grains must be processed with candy flavors and cookies.

Here are some products aimed at kids that didn't survive. Do you remember any of these? Hagar the Horrible Cola. Batman Crazy Foam. I Hate Beets. Yabba Dabba Dew. Some successes: Jell-O Jigglers, Honey Nut Cheerios, Crayola Markers.

4. *The more purple, the better.* Children prefer food that you can see from a distance, for example, colored microwave popcorn, multi-hued strips of dried fruit, Oreos with red or green cream fillings, and iridescent liquids in ghoul-faced bottles.

5. *Food should talk to kids, not parents.* Ads always stress fun, not nutritional value. The creepy or candy aspects of foods touch their mischievous hearts. And good ads will speak their language: "If you tried blending 7 Natural Fruits (a drink), you'd make a mess, and Mom would have a cow."

Source: "From Soup to Purple Dinosaur Nuts" by Blayne Cutler from *American Demographics*, Vol. 14, October 1992, pp. 48–49. Reprinted by permission of the author. Blayne Cutler is a physician and writer living near Providence, Rhode Island. She worked as a senior editor for *American Demographics* magazine when this article was first published.

designed to appeal to latchkey kids, a group that is growing in numbers as it becomes increasingly common for both parents to work outside the home. The magazine seeks to help children and their parents learn how to have a more secure and productive time at home alone after school. Within the magazine are coupons and advertisements for Lipton products that appeal to young people.

The youngsters that range from 8 to 14 years of age are often referred to as "Tweens." Check out CBite 13-6 for some research observations on the funds they spend and control in the marketplace, whether brand loyalty applies to them, if they should be targeted in the traditional way, what does "Tween Speak" have to do with it, and how "avatars" are part of their lives.

13-3b Teens

From 1980 to 1990, there was an 18-percent decline in the number of young people aged 14 to 17 in the United States. This number dropped another 30 percent from 1990 to 2000. The 2000 total was 5.7 million, or 6 percent of the population. Forecasters indicate that growth will be almost flat through 2010, when teens will number 16.8 million.[79] In some geographic regions, or "teen towns," the number of teens is well above the national average. In Zavala County, Texas, just 43 miles north of the Mexican border, almost one in eleven of the predominantly Latino residents is a teenager. Most counties with high percentages of teens are low-income and rural, with high proportions of minority populations. However, Utah, with its large Mormon families, has the greatest share of teenagers. In the Deep South, and especially in Mississippi, the proportions are also high. Teens are scarce in larger cities. On Manhattan Island, New York, only 3.4 percent of residents are teens.[80]

Teens have been segmented into seven groups, based on psychographic (lifestyle) profiles. Although this segmentation scheme is more humorous than scientific, it does provide insight into potential marketplace behavior and preferences.[81]

CBite 13-6

Children's Influence on Brand Choice: Tweens, Brand Loyalty, and Avatars

The average child in America, Australia, and the United Kingdom sees between 20,000 and 40,000 television commercials each year, and 60 percent of these youngsters spend more time watching TV each year than they spend in school. Children's spending has roughly doubled every 10 years over the past 30 years. In 2004 the "Tween" (8- to 14-year-olds) segment in the 11 countries studied was estimated to control or influence $1.18 trillion. The countries included America, Australia, the U.K., Germany, and the Northern European nations. The study also revealed that the children had developed highly persuasive skills to assure that expenditures in the marketplace would go their way. A related study of some 14 countries involving 15,000 kids showed that in up to 80 percent of all brand choices Tweens control the final decision. This even applied to automobiles, where 60 percent of all Tweens had "substantial" influence. In a third study it was estimated that brand loyalty can be influenced from around age two when babies begin to form mental images of corporate logos and mascots. Children as young as three years old can recognize brand logos. It was also found that brands targeted on teens need to be accessible "24/7" at such places as websites and chat rooms.

Tweens are characterized by "fish streaming," similar to the way fish move in schools or at least in the same direction because of the current of the water in which they are swimming. Marketers, therefore, should not target single Tweens but should think in terms of several individuals. This is because Tweens are interlinked through various communications media and they decide direction jointly. This approach determines brand preferences and market trends. The idea of individual consumer (Tween) brand or store loyalty does not appear to exist anymore. If the group decides to boycott, the individual Tween could not be able to buck this action. Marketers must also be aware of "Tween Speak," the "language" used by this group when communicating. We see chat rooms, simultaneous message systems, email, and multimedia message systems all supporting the creation and sustaining of the new global language that includes icons, illustrations, abbreviations, and phrases in totally new ways.

Traditionally, a rule in marketing was to identify your target and pursue it. However, even this is an "iffy" proposition with the Tweens. Why? The average player in RealQuest has 2.3 personalities, or in the language of the virtual world, 2.3 "avatars." These are the different names and personalities that players use. In essence, they are playing different characters. Research has shown that 36 percent of all Tweens have two or more avatars, and seven percent of the world's Tween population have up to 10 avatars. Also, 46 percent of all Chinese Tweens use up to three avatars in daily life, and that share is 37 percent for American Tweens. Only 10 percent of Japanese kids have up to three avatars, and these are primarily tied to games. Tweens have great spending potential and spending control, but they must be approached in different ways and in different media than in the past.

Sources: Martin Lindstrom, "Branding Is No Longer 'Child's Play'," *Journal of Consumer Marketing,* Vol. 21, No. 3 (2004), pp. 175–182; James U. McNeal, *Kids as Customers* (Lexington, MA: Lexington Books, 1992).

1. *Jarheads:* athletes with short hair
2. *Nerds or geeks:* computer wizards with plastic pocket pencil holders, sure to outearn their classmates
3. *Prepsters or bushies:* conservative dressers and thinkers
4. *Surfer dudes:* casual dressers—oversized T-shirts are popular—with equally casual attitudes
5. *Heavy metal rockers/punks:* rebels
6. *Study gerkins:* studious types, headed for Ivy League PhDs
7. *Bohos:* bohemians who are "into" poetry and dress in black

Marketplace Behavior   Teens are significant purchasers of clothing, cars, CD players, television sets, cell telephones, video games, and home computers. In a survey of cell phone-owning teens in the 35 largest markets in America, it was found that two-thirds of these teens have some form of mobile data services. Online gaming has the best potential to jump ahead of camera phones, and Jay-Z ring tones are the next "must-have" for teens. Teens also account for double-digit subscriber percentage rates for four of the top six carriers in the U.S.: 16.7 percent of Sprint/Virgin, 14.4 percent of T-Mobile, 13 percent of Cingular, and 12.5 percent of AT&T.[82] One in seven teens owns stocks or bonds. Teens also do a large share of family grocery shopping—more than half of girls and a quarter of boys. Nearly 60 percent of teens who grocery shop help make up the shopping list, and 40 percent are involved in brand selection. Because brand loyalties often are formed during teen years, this involvement is very significant for marketers.

In a 2000 study of Israeli youth it was found that they are "responsible and influential" consumers. About 25 percent of Israeli teens have access to a credit card, with the world average being about 13 percent. Also about 25 percent are brand conscious regarding the products they use and the clothes they wear.[83]

Recent research has shed some light on teenage consumption behaviors that their parents may not approve of, as one way these youths assert their independence. Such behaviors may lead teens to attempt to deceive their parents about purchases. This "dark side" of teenage consumption may involve alcohol, tobacco, drugs, age-forbidden computer games and movies, certain types of music, and pornography. Deception is typically viewed as teens' lack of disclosure to their parents about spending and purchasing behaviors that they believe parents would find objectionable. It may include acts of omission, hiding of information, and lying. In this study more than 73 percent of the sample group reported that they engage in deception.[84]

Did you ever engage in purchase or consumption deception of your parents when you were a teen? What products or services were involved? What is it about the way products are marketed in the marketplace that causes such behavior?

Marketing to Teens   A strong characteristic of teenagers is a preoccupation with appearance. During the teenage years, young people are seeking a sense of identity, and so the way in which they appear to others is important to them and drives their behavior in the marketplace. This is particularly noticeable in choices of such personal goods and services as clothing, cosmetics, hairstyling, and hair-care items.

Another characteristic of teenagers is their openness to new ideas and new products. Across all age groups, they are the most willing to experiment. Although teenagers are great samplers, brand loyalty does begin to take hold as they approach 18 years of age.[85] Marketers target teens with such products as telephones, video games, television sets, stereo systems, movies, and video rentals. Teens typically see between two and three movies a month and are heavy FM radio listeners.

In both theme and presentation, teen advertising is easy to spot. It typically involves social or sports settings, featuring carefree young people enjoying interaction with each other and with the advertised product. Knowing that teens watch an average of five hours a week of MTV, marketers are adopting techniques learned there. Commercials frequently use the theme of teenage rebellion, teaming it with contemporary music, vivid colors, and unusual visuals. PepsiCo, both with Pepsi and Mountain Dew, creates the type of advertising that appeals to teens, a major consumer of its products. Kodak appeals to teenage girls with advertisements that present taking and looking at photographs as a fun, social activity—and Kodak is there to help make it happen. The 900 series of Real Jeans by Levi Strauss was designed and positioned specifically to appeal to teens, reached primarily through television advertising and teen magazines.

Teenage boys are also drawn to the new computer-generated (CG or 3D) animated motion picture features such as Shrek and Shrek II. This computer-literate generation is attracted by the big screen images and the technology behind them. Also the type of "bathroom" humor included makes the films seem "cool" to teens.[86]

Teens are avid television viewers, and prime-time programming typically centers on their interests. This means that shows featuring families with teens are always popular choices for those marketing teen products. Particularly for girls, magazines are also a powerful medium. Advertising in *Seventeen, Details, Sassy,* and *YM* is sure to catch the eyes of teenagers. Interestingly, products advertised are not limited to those typically targeted to the teen market but increasingly include general items such as food products. This speaks not only to the influence of teens on household purchases but also to the attempts by marketers to instill lifelong brand loyalties from an early age.

13-3c Young Adults—Generation Y

The group known as Generation Y, which numbers 70 to 80 million individuals, is nearly twice the size of Generation X. Though exact birth year boundaries are not universally accepted, we are typically talking about persons born between 1978 and 1988 who in 2005 were between 17 and 25 years old. Besides being currently called Generation Y they are also identified by some as "New Millennials," "Generation Next," the "Digital Generation," and "Echo Boomers" (children or grandchildren of the baby boomers). This group in size alone is destined to be the most formidable in American history. At its peak it will pass the baby boomers in numbers and between now and 2010 will grow at twice the rate of the general population. In 2010 it is forecasted to be about 29 percent of the population. This generation is described as autonomous and showing disdain for authority. It is diverse, interactive (in an electronic communications sense), edgy, smart, and optimistic. The older Yers are traditionalists and are known for their volunteerism and spiritualism.

Check out CBite 13-7 for some insights into the typical 21-year-old Yer. This sector of the population is saving to buy a home; they want to marry, buy a house, and seek a balance between family and work. They have never endured really difficult economic times, and their tolerance for risk is quite high when compared to those Americans who lived through the depression of the 1930s. They will also be inheriting the wealth of their baby boomer parents.[87]

Generation Y women seem to be focused on creating a new, more mature approach to adulthood combining career and home. This applies whether they are married or not and whether they are mothers or not. They are looking to be part traditional, part modern, part practical, and part whimsical, and desire to combine work and leisure in a more blended fashion centered on the home.[88] America's 53 million-strong "Mom Market" will soon see a major demographic shift as the Gen Y women enter into their prime "baby-making" years with their unique parenting approach. Motherhood is a key component on young women's checklist, but as noted earlier, they will be seeking to balance their lives differently than their mothers and grandmothers did. According to a recent study, time will be a priority. In fact 80 percent of the respondents said that in the families they form one parent will stay home with the kids, whether this means interrupting a career or working out of a home office. They also expect to be more involved with their kids than their parents were. Further, they don't feel they need to be everything and everywhere at once; they'll take on motherhood as one of many roles they intend to carry out over their lives.[89]

Generation Y is ethnically mixed in America, with minorities making up about 34 percent of this subgroup. The largest minority group of Generation Y in 2010 will be Latino American. They will account for 17 percent of Gen Yers.[90]

Marketplace Behavior   Currently the estimated consumer expenditure of Generation Y is $735 billion. This group has now taken over as the "merchants of cool" from their Generation X predecessors. Even MTV, once synonymous with Generation X, holds little appeal for its original audience. And according to AT&T executives, Gen Yers are clearly "early adopters" (of innovations).[91] These individuals have much higher expectations of the marketplace and what it offers. They tend to be more "picky."[92] Price and value are very important to this generation, especially with new cars. The average price of a car sold to buyers under 24 years of age is $15,000, with most of these being used cars. A youth car is a cheap car. They are looking for less risky auto buys along with low ownership costs.[93] Also, Gen Y students' shopping and spending on fashion items, including apparel, accessories, and footwear, is on the rise and grew 3.4 percent from 2003 to 2004, when it reached $1447 per student.[94]

CBite 13-7

The 21-Year-Old Generation Yer: Some Observations

Today's 21-year-olds were born in 1984. They are part of Generation Y, one of the most-studied groups of young adults ever. Turning 21 signals the end of youth and the beginning of adult responsibilities, which can be a scary prospect. It is also the age at which many people graduate from college and begin looking for their first "real" job.

About 4 million Americans turn 21 each year, and this is not expected to change in the next decade. However, the impact felt by the economy is likely to increase, and these people's purchasing behavior is likely to change.

At 21, men have a slight numerical advantage, because there are about 105 men for every 100 women, but after age 30 there are more women than men, and this continues at every age from then on. From age 18 to 21, there are 5 percent more men than women, but 20 percent more women are enrolled in college than men. On their 21st birthday, 1 in 4 men are full-time in college, compared to 1 in 3 women.

What are the implications of these statistics for marketers of higher education? What strategies should they follow as they attempt to shape shopping, selecting (buying), and consumer behavior toward their services?

Source: Peter Francese, "Ahead of the Next Wave—Generation Y," *American Demographics,* September 2003. Copyright © 2003 Crain Communications, Inc. Reprinted with permission.

Marketing to Gen Yers   It was indicated earlier that Gen Yers are price and value conscious, expect a lot from the offerings in the marketplace, and are therefore "picky." They are also consumers who will try new products and services because they are less risk-averse. As such, this group has proven to be a great target for such "extreme sports" as sky-diving, bungee jumping, rock climbing, snowboarding and skate boarding, BMX, and in-line skating. All of these activities generate varying rates of adrenaline and the rush that goes with it. Also, a lot of these are solo sports allowing people to express their individuality and match it against others. Many marketers of the places where these sports can be pursued, the gear necessary to participate, and in some cases the training support needed are out there already and appealing to the Gen Y group.

> **F A Q**
>
> **How do the Generation Yers fit into the picture?**

Toyota Motor Company introduced its *Scion* automobile in 2003 specifically targeted on Gen Y buyers. The car was first introduced in California and has been a success. These cars sell for under $20,000 new. Interestingly the car received 158 complaints for every 100 cars. The industry average on new cars is 119 for every 100. The gripes were relatively minor, not issues worth recall. They included rattles, wind noise, air conditioners that don't cool fast enough, heaters that aren't hot enough, and insufficient power. This result reinforces the notion of high expectations and "pickiness" of Gen Yers.[95]

The 16- to 24-year-olds in America buy 850,000 cars a year, and the estimate is that by the year 2010 there will be 63 million of these young people driving. Hyundai Motor Company's *Accent,* selling at $10,000 and the *Elantra* at $13,000 have the youngest buyers of any on the market at age 24. Besides low prices there are warranties of 5 years or 60,000 miles overall with 100,000 miles on engines and transmissions. This meets the low cost and less risk criteria of the Gen Y consumer. Hyundai hopes that over time these buyers will "move up" as their income situation improves.[96]

How do marketers make contact with these buyers? Audi of America, American Honda Motor Company, and Kia Motors used concert tours. BMW of North America is reaching out to go-kart racers as young as 15, using a Formula One racing school, and Ford Motor Company found that its "American Idol" sponsorship was a key way to reach this target. The Honda Civic tour was in its fourth year in 2004, this time with the band "Dashboard Confessional." Audi of America kicked off an online contest at www.neverfollow.com where visitors were asked to "mash-up" two of David Bowie's songs into one to win an Audi TT coupe—the winners had to be at least 13 years of age.[97]

Gen Y gets most of its information from broadcast and other electronic media. Hence, television, radio, the Internet, email, and other emerging technologies are high on the list of sources. About 39 percent of Generation Y reads newspapers on a weekday. By 2010 we know that this generation will make up about 29 percent of the adult population. This readership level compares to 58 percent of baby boomers. Unless Gen Y reads at a much higher level the forecast is that it will remain below 50 percent through the year 2010. What newspapers have begun to do is to think "across platforms" to reach this generation. Newspapers are a more trusted source than the Internet, but more than 80 percent of teens and other Gen Yers have Internet access. Content is also an issue, and newspapers are beginning to consult teens to find new ways to offer Gen Y content.

In 2004, *el diario/La PRENSA,* the largest Spanish-language daily in the Northeast, teamed up with the lifestyle magazine *Urban LATINO* to deliver a selection of entertainment and news in a monthly bilingual section called *Urban Sofrito.* This is targeted on young Latinos, 18–34. They can read about anything that has to do with being Latino and bicultural. This is also targeted on the new generation of Latino immigrants. Language turns out not to be an issue for the Gen Y Latinos; content is the key.[98] How do you think newspapers will have to change to reach the diverse Gen Y audiences in America?

13-3d Generation X

Members of Generation X, as they were named in a 1991 novel by Douglas Coupland, are the approximately 45 million people born in the United States between 1965 and 1977.[99] They have also been labeled "baby busters," "slackers," and the "13th Generation." This 11-year span was the lowest birthrate period in the United States in the twentieth century. Generation Xers account for about $125 billion in spending annually. However, increasingly cynical about their economic future, they don't see themselves as having the same opportunity to succeed as their parents, the baby boom generation. Distrustful of marketing and promotion, they feel as though the marketing establishment cares little for them because the baby boomers, teens, and preteens bring so much more buying power to the table. This distrust may be exacerbated by the knowledge, real or imagined, that most advertising is still created by members of the baby boomer generation, who sometimes present negative stereotypes or caricatures of Xers in advertising. When Xers were asked how older generations viewed them, their most frequent responses were "lazy," "confused," and "unfocused." Yet they saw themselves as "ambitious," "determined," and "independent."[100] Check out Marketplace 13-4 for a discussion of the cohort approach to "X-ers," "Boomers," and "Matures."

Generation Xers look for a balance between work and leisure and do not wish to pay the price that earlier generations did. They perceive that people in the past lived to work instead of working to live and do not intend to do so themselves. A value set of Gen X is that family comes first and career second, and home and work success do not negate one another.[101] The Xers are committed to success and causes, in fact they "crave success American-style."[102] Generation Xers enjoy seeing ordinary people rise to the top, admiring such personalities as Bill Gates, founder of Microsoft; Matt Groening, the creator of the television series *The Simpsons;* and Ross Perot, who shook up the political establishment in 1992. In fact, about one-fifth of Xers voted for Perot.[103]

Close to their parents, Xers tend to live at home. Nearly half do so into their late twenties. Although this choice is not always caused by economic necessity, even after they move out on their own, about three-quarters receive some financial help from their parents.[104] They marry later in life, often after completing their education, and delay having children. They hope that these behaviors will up their chances for a lasting marriage—and the odds are in their favor. Also, they don't just want a "place to crash"—they want a comfortable home that reflects their tastes and styles.[105]

Women Xers do not question the achievements of the female boomers in gaining sexual equality, but they do ask if the price was too high. Boomer women were willing to sacrifice home and family to achieve success. Generation Xers want to give their children what they personally missed and are not willing to compromise this for job progress. In terms of sexuality, Xers grew up in a time when AIDS was a reality, moving them to be cautious and yet compassionate.

Marketplace 13-4

Generational Group Segments: It's More Than Age

Yankelovich Partners, Inc. has specialized in research on "generational marketing" for many years. One-on-one interviews and lengthy follow-up surveys with thousands of consumers of all ages are done each year for their annual report on consumer behavior called the *Yankelovich Monitor*. In 1997, two partners of the firm published a book on generational marketing titled *Rocking the Ages*. The authors, Ann Clurman and J. Walker Smith, see America as divided into three groups: "Matures," a cohort including everyone from World War I doughboys to the Silent Generation; "Baby Boomers"; and "Gen(eration) X."

When interviewed, Smith stated, "Age is composed of two things: lifestage (lifecycle) and cohort. If you only look at age as lifestage, you end up not quite getting it right. That's where generational marketing enters the picture." Cohorts, groups of people born during certain time spans, are seen as "products" of the life experiences of their times. For example, Matures interpret the marketplace in terms of the Great Depression of the 1930s; World War II with its economic, cultural, and social changes; the Cold War and threats of the nuclear age; and the emergence of suburbia and the like.

Baby boomers do not seem to understand Gen Xers because of their different life experiences. Boomers always felt that the world could be fixed, and they were the ones to do it, whereas the Gen Xers did not see that the world could be fixed. Xers are more competitive than originally thought and far more materially driven than boomers, and they are more realistic about what the future will be for them. Boomers were rule breakers when younger. In their self-absorbed focus on self-gratification, they challenged all the old taboos. Boomers are part of a cohort that never experienced world war, lived in a time of great abundance, were

the flower-power, free-love, rock-and-roll generation, and were more educated than any previous group. They also lived in the time of civil rights focus, the end of "Jim Crow," the birth of air travel and television, and environmental sensitivity.

Matures are living longer and will continue to be an important market segment. Life spans are now in the mid to upper 70s. Matures are active and often affluent. However, because they are living longer today, some worry about having saved enough to cover their lifetime and are more cautious in their spending patterns. This also flows from their experience in the Depression of the 1930s.

Beginning in the late 1990s and continuing into the current century, the Xers will be in the process of household formation and the buying this brings about. But, in terms of buying power, they are likely to be faced with a struggle to get the attention of marketers. Because there are about 78 million boomers and 70 to 80 million "echo boomers" (Gen Yers) , the 46 million Xers will be dwarfed economically throughout their lifetimes. The real importance of the Xers is cultural. This is the "leading edge" generation. The style of the World Wide Web is Xer, though this is changing as the Yers exert their influence. Also, boomers are often seen copying the fashion styles of the Xers. That's something the Matures never did when the boomers were young.

When asked about the changing face of America, Smith replied, "I really think generational distinctions will wash out in the next decade (late '90s and early 2000s) because of the kind of pluralistic, diverse society that is emerging. It will be more a question of relating to people's peer networks than their generational cohort."

Source: From "Generational Marketing" by Kevin T. Higgins in *Marketing Management*, Fall 1998, pp. 6–9. Reprinted by permission of American Marketing Association.

Marketplace Behavior   Generation Xers experience a sense of alienation and disconnection from the traditional American values that are characterized by family orientation, success on the job, security, reasonable income, good housing, and material possessions. Their tastes in fashion (a "grunge" look, with baggy or ripped jeans and Doc Marten-style boots), music preferences (Arrested Development, Ice-T, Nirvana), and media entertainment (MTV, *Beavis and Butt-Head, The Simpsons*) all reflect this reluctance to accept the conventional American dream.[106]

Generation Xers are not drawn to the type of advertising that attracts other age groups. They typically dislike advertising that uses a lot of hype, tries to make something out of the unimportant, or that takes itself too seriously. It is likely that this generation has its own ability to resist media in general. Although they display a sense of practicality when making marketplace decisions, there are certain goods and service choices that are tempered by sensitivity to such issues as drug and alcohol abuse and the environment.

Generation Xers feel a need to stay in control, explaining their liking for communications equipment, such as beepers, email systems, faxes, answering machines, portable phones, and hand-held electronic office/calendar assistants. Because many come from homes in which both parents worked, Xers shopped as children and teens for the family and, therefore, are experienced in product evaluation and choice. When living with their parents as adults, they frequently become household decision makers, helping their parents choose such major purchases as electronic equipment, cars, and computers. They also are often involved in hiring household help and home contractors.

Marketing to Generation Xers   Generation X was the first to experience a "globalized childhood," the first to grow up with computers, and the first to play video games, and their adolescent sexuality was shaped by MTV and the threat of AIDS. They are the first to experience mass divorce and the complex issues of the post-nuclear family.[107] Since this generation was the first with many working parents it became a true "latch key" cohort. This type of childhood has helped them become consumers at the earliest age in American history. Therefore, it has affected their approach to the marketplace in many ways. Generation Xers buy products for their practicality, not for the status or esteem they bring. This means that marketing strategies used to sell expensive cars, watches, or clothing to the baby boomers are unlikely to work well on Xers. Products like economy cars, practical furniture, functional clothes, family entertainment equipment, household items, and home office equipment are more attractive to this segment. IBM successfully targeted Xers—selling personal computers to college students with its "Get Real" campaign, clearly sending the message that IBM computers are not just for businesses. Also the Dodge Neon, a fun, stylish, yet economically practical car, has been successfully positioned against this market.

As noted earlier, Generation Xers dislike advertising that hypes up products, perhaps as a reaction to information overload. Overstatement, hypocrisy, and self-importance in advertising all work against the seller. Also, Xers dislike telemarketing because it is generally uninvited and intrusive. Nike, aware of this resistance to hard-sell approaches, focuses instead on an "attitude" when targeting this segment. The "Just Do It" campaign of the 1990s appealed to Xers' desire for self-improvement based on a "no excuses" desire to get on with it.

13-3e Baby Boomers

Baby boomers, born between 1946 and 1964, have now at least reached their forties, and some are into their late fifties. The number of baby boomers is approximately 78 million.[108] Total income is over $1 trillion, increasing at a rate of about 10 percent per year, while income of the rest of the population of the United States is increasing by only 5 percent per year. Boomers have more discretionary income than other age groups, and, in general, they buy more and save less. They have a high level of education; a little less than half are college graduates. Baby boomers are less likely to marry than are members of previous generations, and when they marry, in two out of three cases, both husband and wife remain in the workforce. Boomers are health conscious, and exercise and diet are important to them. They are the generation most likely to cut back on cigarette smoking, stronger alcoholic drinks, and coffee.

There are two distinct boomer segments. The older group, in their 50s, grew up in a time when it was easier to find a job and hold it, buy a home, educate children, and enjoy a relatively high standard of living. The downsizing trends of recent years are the first time these boomers had real concerns about job security and advancement. This group is now "middle-aged" to "early senior," stable, married, and family oriented. Although earlier in life they were avid consumers, their purchasing has slowed down. Caught between growing children and aging parents, they perceive both a time and financial squeeze.

The younger boomers are now in their early to late 40s and are more likely to suffer from limited job opportunities and security. Like the older boomers, they are less likely to marry than previous generations, and when they do wed, their families are smaller.

The "yuppies"—young, upwardly mobile professionals, a term coined in the late 1970s—are a subset of the boomers. Affluent in the 1980s, these individuals made up about 5 percent of the adult population. Growing older, they are now jokingly referred to as "muppies"—middle-aged urban professionals—or "grumpies"—grown-up urban mature professionals. As this group ages, however, they think of themselves less and less as being old. No generation prior to this group seems to have "prolonged adolescence" as has

Exhibit 13-9

Concern for the environment is strong in baby boomers.

Source: Reprinted by permission of Earth Share.

the boomers. According to appearances, attitudes, and their medical charts, this certainly is the "youngest older generation in history."[109]

Baby boomers will continue to be the largest consumer group in the United States through about the year 2010, when they will be overtaken by the Gen Y "echo boomers," their children and grandchildren. In the near future, target marketing to the group, as its members become older and their needs become more predictable, will continue to be important.

Marketplace Behavior   The fall of the Berlin Wall and with it the turmoil experienced in Eastern Europe, the end of apartheid in South Africa, the changing roles of women in the American marketplace, the increased sense of the importance of diversity, awareness of threats to the global environment, and the worldwide economic downturn of the 1980s and at the turn of the century have all had a severe impact on the baby boomers. This affects their behavior as consumers in that they are becoming markedly less materialistic in outlook and, therefore, less likely to purchase new possessions. Concern for the environment and for "quality of life" for themselves and their children is acted out in their product and service selections (see Exhibit 13-9). Having created demand for quality products at reasonable prices, they shop both in specialty stores in search of quality and at discount outlets in search of value for money.

This does not mean that all boomers have radically changed their ways. There are still many who purchase status brands, use their credit cards extensively, and express their concern for health in the purchase of expensive exercise equipment and health-club memberships. Both men and women still keep up with fashions, in clothing, jewelry, cars, and—the latest trend—home theater equipment.

Marketing to Baby Boomers   The marketing of nostalgia works well, especially with the older boomers. Music and memorabilia from the 1960s are excellent items. Older boomers also like to watch reruns of popular television shows from the 1960s and 1970s, so offering related goods or advertising general goods during this type of programming are sound ideas. Similarly, radio stations that play music from the 1950s, 1960s, and 1970s appeal to both older and younger boomers.

Levi Strauss and other manufacturers, aware that it was the boomer generation that made jeans so popular, now offer varying styles, including "relaxed-fit" jeans—for boomers approaching middle age. Other products have also changed to meet the changing needs of aging boomers—bifocal eyeglasses are just one example. Older boomers represent a strong market for family-oriented products and for products used by their teenage and college-age children.

13-3f Seniors

The fastest growing segment of the U.S. population is the senior subculture. People over 65 numbered approximately 36 million in the year 2003, and the first of the baby boomers will turn 65 in 2011. By 2010 it is estimated that there will be 50 million people over 65, and this number will grow to an estimated 70 million by 2030, when 1 in 5 people will be over 65 in America.[110]

A long-held stereotype of seniors is that they live in poverty and spend what little money they have on health care. The poverty rate among seniors has dropped from 35 percent in 1960 to 10.2 percent in 2002. Although it is true that people over 65 have lower household incomes than their younger counterparts, this perception fails to take into account several factors. After-tax per capita income of seniors is above average. Seniors have twice the income of their children, and they control 70 percent of the net worth of all U.S. households, about $7 trillion.[111] Those who are homeowners have typically paid off their mortgages, and their living expenses are comparatively low. Households are small, and their need for new purchases is limited. Use of senior discounts limits their expenditures even further. In addition, for some, these are peak earning years, as they draw a pension from their former jobs and work part-time at new ones.[112] Undoubtedly, those over 65 experience more health problems than younger population groups; 8.7 percent of those 65 to 74 need much in-home (activities of daily living—"ADL") care, and this jumps to 28.7 percent for those 75 and older. Only 5 percent live in institutions.[113] One of the common problems of seniors is hearing loss. Hearing aids are targeted primarily to this population segment. Batteries are needed to power these products, and the Duracell battery ad in Exhibit 13-10 is right on target. Notice the emphasis on easy battery replacement because of the lessened manipulative skills of seniors.

With an annual purchasing power estimated at over $200 billion, a high level of per capita assets combined with a willingness to spend make seniors an important consumer group.

Marketplace Behavior   Seniors enjoy convenience in the marketplace. They also appreciate their leisure time. Looking for ways to slow down the aging process, seniors feel good about eating foods that are more nutritional, and those who can, try to exercise regularly. With the easing of the financial obligations of the past, seniors generally feel positive about spending more on themselves.

The self-image of seniors, particularly those in good health, is that they are younger than their years. Hence, attitudes toward travel, recreation, clothing choices, and hairstyles are geared to their perceived rather than their actual age. Many 65-year-olds have the same approach to life, attitudes, and behaviors as those 15 years their junior.[114] They dislike being classified as seniors or described as "in their golden years."

Although, based on experience in the marketplace, seniors tend to be brand loyal, they are also open to trying new products or brands if given good reasons to do so. Shopping is still a popular activity for those in good health who are mobile and have money to spend. Because of today's advances in medicine and nutrition and their own concern with health and fitness, many seniors are physically much more active than members of earlier generations and more able to enjoy their leisure time.

How do seniors spend their discretionary income? We see them at fitness centers. They drive a disproportionate share of the larger luxury cars. Other products and services in demand are nutritional foods, educational opportunities (Elderhostels, for example), vitamins, retirement financial planning, and pharmaceuticals. For those who are less physically able, the demand for personal shoppers has increased, along with the popularity of

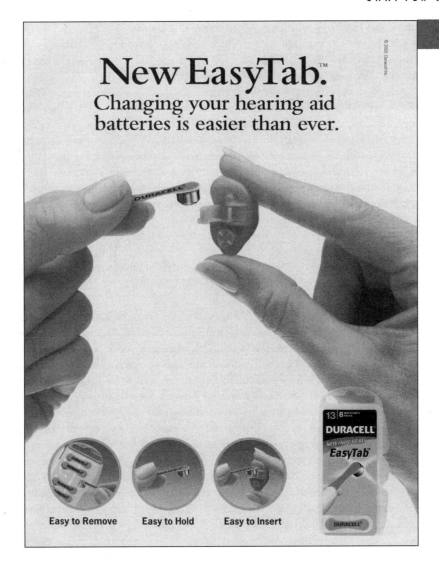

Exhibit 13-10

Duracell targets easy-to-insert hearing aid batteries to seniors.

Source: Courtesy of Duracell Batteries.

home delivery. In-home health care and senior residence facilities are also increasingly popular, along with temporary and long-term home nursing care.

Marketing to Seniors   Marketers segment seniors on the bases of age, activity level, health, and mobility. Here are four key segments:

1. Young-elderly, aged 65 to 74, who are relatively active and healthy
2. Young-elderly, aged 65 to 74, who are in poor health or disabled
3. Older-elderly, aged 75 and over, who are relatively active and healthy
4. Older-elderly, aged 75 and over, who are in poor health or disabled.[115]

Examples of products targeted to these segments singly or in combination are cross-country skis, athletic walking shoes, and more strenuous travel destinations (Segments 1, 3) and board games, puzzles, and paperback novels (Segments 2, 4).

According to the 2000 census, nearly 60 percent of the elderly do not have chronic health problems. Of those who do, women are more likely to have mobility or self-care problems than are older men.[116] Interestingly, concern over the possibility of becoming disabled influences current spending decisions. As today's seniors were children of the Great Depression of the 1930s, perhaps memories of poverty haunt them as they make decisions in the marketplace.

As noted earlier, it is important for marketers to think of this subculture not in terms of their actual age but of their **perceived age.** The elderly do not want to be reminded by

▶ **perceived age** The age a person sees himself or herself to be. This is usually younger than a person's chronological age.

marketers that they are older and, in many cases, alone. The Gerber Company learned this lesson when it attempted to introduce Singles, a ready-to-eat dinner targeted to seniors who live alone. One of the reasons for its failure was that the name reminded them that, in fact, they often did eat alone—not a happy situation.

In terms of geography, seniors with disabilities are clustered in the southeastern United States, while the Midwest contains a slower-growing group of more healthy and active seniors. Further, the suburbs of larger cities are becoming havens for the retired, who must move from homes in neighborhoods in which they have spent the best part of their lives.[117]

It is common practice for marketers to make special efforts to attract older consumers. Price promotions are frequently the tool they use. Many retail outlets offer seniors double-coupon values one day a week. Others offer senior discounts during off-peak hours for such services as haircuts and hairstyling. Special rates for seniors are common in transportation and travel services. Advertising in *Modern Maturity* magazine, Buick ran a coupon for $400 off the price of a new car. Why? Seniors own well over 50 percent of all Buicks.

A special consideration in advertising to this group is that many seniors suffer weakening sight and hearing. This is why marketers favor advertisements with low word counts; large type size; simple language; clear diction; bright, clear visuals; and action that gains and holds attention.[118]

Because seniors watch a lot of television, this is an effective advertising medium, provided programming choices are appropriate. Also, the American Association of Retired Persons (AARP) has 25 million members, and each receives *Modern Maturity* magazine monthly, another good choice. Seniors can also be reached at an increasing rate through the Internet. In 2000 they accounted for only 4 percent of Internet users; this jumped to 16 percent in 2002 and by 2004 it was 48 percent. Seniors see the Internet as helping them reconnect with others by email and providing mental stimulation. They also do research on health topics and medical and social services. Nearly three quarters of senior Internet users in a recent study reported they used it to find health information. Seniors also use the Internet to do research on specific subjects, for reading the news and about current events, to research vacation and travel information, and to check the weather.[119]

There are several things marketers can do to better and more effectively serve the senior market on the Internet. They can: (1) focus on making websites more user-friendly (site menus, point and click), (2) educate the senior market on the benefits of being online (easy access to loved ones and needed information), (3) minimize the perceived differences between virtual and real world transactions (make websites more high touch through voice chatting and three-dimensional images), and (4) diminish the problems of using the Internet for those seniors with vision or arthritic problems (promote larger keyboards and magnified computer screens).[120]

Marketing Management—Implications and Actions

Understanding subcultures based on age helps marketers:

- Follow the changing needs of consumers as they age.
- Match their products to the age groups most likely to buy them.
- Make media and message decisions based on marketplace behavior of targeted age groups.

13-4 Subcultures Based on Geographic Region

Regional subcultures can be as small as neighborhoods within a city or as large as the geopolitical divisions of the Northeast, the Midwest, the South, and the West. People living in different regions perceive themselves in different ways. In general, when cultural change occurs, it is likely to be first noticed in New York and California. Thus, marketers treat these two regions individually, each having its own special subcultural patterns. Californians and New Yorkers see themselves as innovators, leading fashion and entertainment trends. New York remains the communications center for television and the publishing and advertising industries. California has been described as a weather vane for the nation at large—what happens on the West Coast, politically, socially, and in the popular culture, gradually sweeps over the rest of the United States. In recent years, trends in conservative politics, condominium apartment living, the appeal of imported cars, and the Walt Disney entertainment expansion support this theory.

Between the two coasts, each geographic area has its own ethos and personality. The West and Southwest retain an aura of the American frontier, rugged and individualistic. The Midwest is still considered the heartland of America, where people are reputed to be conservative in terms of religion, politics, social integration, and even new-product innovation. New Englanders regard themselves as shrewd consumers. They are protective of the natural beauty of the region and resent intrusions by tourists, sports enthusiasts, summer residents, and real estate developers. The South, traditionally afflicted by high levels of poverty and perceived as tradition bound, has been growing and becoming more urbanized. Compared to the North, attachment to a local community is more common in the South; religious practices are more strongly denominational; and family and church are more influential than are schools or mass media.[121]

Regional differences have been tied to the nationality, ethnic background, or religion of the original settlers in a region. The Swedish and Norwegians who settled in Minnesota and North Dakota brought certain cultural values and behaviors with them, and even today these patterns are evident. The same can be said for the Irish in Boston, the Italians in New York and Chicago, the Chinese in San Francisco, the French in Louisiana, and the Cubans in Miami. In addition to the attitudes and behaviors of the regional culture, individuals carry with them the customs, traditions, values, and behaviors of their national or religious heritage. Any attempt to market to them based on region must be tempered by an understanding of other subcultural influences to which they have been exposed.

13-4a Marketplace Behavior

While some behavioral characteristics of people in different regions may seem stereotypical, real differences do exist in consumption patterns. In beverage preferences, for example, in New England, birch beer and cream soda are high-demand soft drinks, yet these beverages are virtually unheard of in most of the South, though cream soda is quite popular in New Orleans. Even coffee drinking varies according to region. Responding to regional preferences, Maxwell House promotes a stronger, darker coffee blend in the West than in the East.[122] And at the Cafe du Monde in New Orleans, your coffee will be blended with chicory, giving it a stronger flavor.

Some differences attributed to regional subcultures disappear as people enjoy greater mobility and exposure to mass communications. Others, such as occupation, religion, and family, are more likely to persist over time.

13-4b Marketing to Region-Based Subcultures

Certain products are needed, not needed, or have to be modified for different regions, if only because of climate, altitude, or terrain. Climate conditions such as humidity, rainfall, temperatures, amount of sunshine, length of seasons, and the like must be considered. The demand for electric razors among people in the bayou country of Louisiana—especially for consumers without air conditioning—is lower than average across the United States because of high humidity. Sun block creams and sunglasses are needed more in Florida and Arizona than in Maine and New Hampshire. The styles of winter clothing purchased by residents of northern Minnesota or Anchorage, Alaska, are not found in stores in Key Largo, Florida.

The atmospheric pressure is directly a function of the altitude of a location. This especially bears on food preparation because of its relation to temperatures at which water boils and chemical reactions occur. For example, the Betty Crocker cake mix that comes out almost perfect every time at sea level in Bear, Delaware, will be a failure if the instructions are followed as printed in Denver, Colorado, the Mile High City.

F A Q

Does the weather affect the mood of consumers and, therefore, their buying habits?

The terrain may also be a factor. Think of the differences in what goods and services people need living in the mountainous regions of Peru, or the plains of South Dakota, or in the hill country of Kentucky, or in the marshlands of the coasts of the Carolinas. How would you see the behavior of consumers affected in these areas, just in terms of everyday needs for goods and services?

Remember, too, that there are regions within regions. Regional subcultures can be found within cities, especially large metropolitan areas such as Los Angeles, New York, Toronto, Miami, Chicago, and San Francisco. Here, neighborhoods have formed on the basis of nationality, ethnicity, religion, or some combination of each. Within them, the language may be other than English, and the stores may be stocked with products peculiar to the subcultural group.

Marketing Management—Implications and Actions

Understanding subcultures based on region helps marketers:

- Find different approaches to marketing the same products in different regions.
- Take into account other subcultural influences—particularly nationality, age, and religion—when analyzing consumer attitudes and behaviors within regions.
- Identify the best regions to introduce new products and promotions.

13-5 Subcultures Based on Religion

For many religious groups, beliefs are a major influence on marketplace behavior, determining everything from acceptable dress to food and beverage consumption patterns to entertainment options. However, it is difficult, and often a mistake, to make generalizations about a population group based upon the religion it professes. The Protestant religions, for example, run the full spectrum from conservative to liberal; some are in favor of traditional family structure while others embrace alternative lifestyles and gender roles. Nationality also makes a difference—the values and behaviors of African-American or Korean Protestants and Hispanic-American Catholics are not the same as their traditional American counterparts. In America and Canada in 2003 there were 2,630 groups identified as religions.[123]

For a number of religious groups, religious calendars influence product selection, affecting food, clothing, beverages, and entertainment choices. During Lent, for example, Roman Catholics are restricted in their food choices. Religious events or seasons can also offer special opportunities. Ramadan, Christmas, Passover, and Advent, for example, are all times when consumers buy special products.

Geographic concentrations of religious sects are also important to marketers. The Amish in northeast Indiana, the Black Muslims in Chicago, the Jewish people in New York City, the Confucianists in San Francisco, the Catholics in Boston, the Mormons in Utah, and the Quakers in parts of Pennsylvania all affect distribution and sales patterns.

13-5a Marketplace Behavior

In order to explore attitudes and behaviors influenced by religious belief, let's begin by looking at just two of the many religious groups in the United States and the characteristics that make them distinct. Think how these aspects of the lifestyles of the members of each group influence their marketplace behavior. Consider other religious groups with which you are familiar in the same way.

There are large concentrations of Mormons in California and Utah. Those who follow the tenets of their faith do not drink alcohol, coffee, or tea. Some avoid any drink that contains caffeine, believing it to be forbidden by the religion. Further, smoking or the use of tobacco is prohibited. Having larger families also is part of the lifestyle of the group.

Muslim women wear clothing that covers them from head to toe, so that the body is not exposed. The religion imposes food and alcohol restrictions. Further, the roles of men and women are clearly defined. The society is patriarchal. Men and women are often separated, even during social functions.

These two examples illustrate that members of distinct religious sects have attitudes, behaviors, and lifestyles that set them apart from the majority population. Not in all religious groups, however, are these differences so apparent. Across the very broad spectrum of people who profess to be Protestant, Catholic, Muslim, or Jewish, for instance, we find a wide variety of attitudes and behaviors. Some parallel the mainstream of the majority culture, whereas others diverge to varying degrees.

13-5b Marketing to Religion-Based Subcultures

Though it is by no means always the case that consumers within a religious group will patronize the businesses of other members, this certainly happens. It is particularly common in instances where the observance of the religion creates demand for particular products that are available almost exclusively through companies or individuals who are members of the religion. The array of goods purchased to celebrate the Jewish holiday of Yom Kippur is a good example.

For most goods and services, however, members are able and willing to purchase from outsiders. Even so, those marketing to religion-based subcultures are wise to evaluate both the opportunities and the restrictions under which they must operate. As we saw earlier, those who are members of the targeted group are most likely to be successful, having both understanding and goodwill on their side. A guiding rule is to be sensitive to the attitudes, behaviors, and lifestyles of members. This means stepping inside the culture and finding out how members view themselves and their daily lives. Effective advertising will identify needs and desires that are real to the religious group targeted and offer benefits that are readily acceptable into their lifestyle.

Media choice, too, depends upon sensitivity to lifestyle and behavior patterns. For most mainstream groups, religious television or radio programming is a natural choice, assuming the product advertised is appropriate to the audience. An alternative approach is to use general family-oriented media, such as family programming on television, but to tailor the message to appeal to people with specific religious beliefs or values.

Marketing Management—Implications and Actions

Understanding subcultures based on religion helps marketers:

- Remain sensitive to the ways in which their products are perceived by religious groups.
- Seek opportunities in marketing products needed for the observance of religious rituals.

Chapter Spotlights

Subcultures can be viewed as minicultural groups within the larger social fabric of a nation. Through subcultures, people preserve a common set of values, beliefs, and attitudes. No individual is influenced by a single subculture alone, but by the many subcultures of which he or she is a part or comes in contact with.

1. Subculture and society. Subculture is any cultural patterning that preserves important features of the dominant society but provides for values, beliefs, norms, and behaviors of its own. Subcultures exist to provide a source of psychological group identification, to offer a support network, and to serve as a frame of reference for evaluating the dominant culture. Although subcultural classifications are arbitrary, they are useful as a means of identifying segments in the larger population that are made up of consumers with similar lifestyles, attitudes, and behavioral patterns. Common classifications are those based on nationality and ethnicity, age, geographic region, and religion. Individual consumers belong not to a single subcultural group, but to several, each influencing marketplace decisions.

2. Subcultures based on nationality and ethnicity. The United States is home to people from many cultures, each with its own history, customs, attitudes, and acceptable behavior patterns. While some have essentially become part of the dominant culture (assimilation), others have preserved a separate identity from generation to generation (mobilization). The three largest nationality-based subcultures in the United States are African Americans,

Latino Americans, and Asian and Pacific Island Americans. Combined, these three groups are rapidly becoming a majority. Each can be further divided into subcultural groups and, therefore, must not be treated as a homogeneous market segment.

3. Subcultures based on age. We reviewed five classifications of the population by age: preteens, teens, Gen Yers, Gen Xers, baby boomers, and seniors. Within each group, age influences purchase choices and buying habits. Age is just one influencer of behavior and works alongside other subcultural influences.

4. Subcultures based on geographic region. Climate, altitude, and terrain are the most obvious regional influences on marketplace behavior. It is also useful to look at region-based subcultures alongside nationality-based or religion-based subcultures, as members of the same ethnic group or religion tend to settle close to one another.

5. Subcultures based on religion. To varying extents, members of different religions exhibit differences in values, dress, use of technology, food and beverage choices, and several other consumption patterns. Religion combined with nationality and ethnicity is a particularly useful predictor of marketplace behavior. Not all people who profess a certain religion behave in the same way, and awareness of diversity within the subculture is important. Essential to effective marketing to religion-based subcultures is the need to be sensitive to the values and beliefs of members.

Key Terms

assimilation (theory of) (p. 401)   mobilization (theory of) (p. 401)   subculture (p. 399)
bodega (p. 408)   perceived age (p. 427)

Review Questions

Note: You can find the correct answers to these questions by taking the quiz and then submitting your answers in the Online Edition. The program will automatically score your submission. If you miss a question, the program will provide the correct answer, a rationale for the answer, and the section number in the chapter where the topic is discussed.

1. _____ leads marketers to develop different marketing mixes.
   a. Homogeneity
   b. Diversity
   c. Attitude
   d. Behavior

2. Assigning individuals to subcultural groups is complex and
   a. arbitrary.
   b. quantifiable.
   c. unique.
   d. distinguishable.

3. Nationality and ethnicity are essentially the same when the population is almost entirely made up of people from a single
   a. religion.
   b. race.
   c. country.
   d. ethnic background.

4. Nationality is a _____ subcultural influence.
   a. constantly changing
   b. constant
   c. minor
   d. fixed

5. On average, children spend about ____ percent of their total income on things other than high-cost items that parents are unwilling to purchase for them.
   a. 20
   b. 40
   c. 60
   d. 80

6. Teens known as prepsters or bushies are described as conservative
   a. students and shoppers.
   b. thinkers and writers.
   c. shoppers and readers.
   d. dressers and thinkers.

7. Some products are needed or not needed or must be modified for different regions because of climate, terrain, or
   a. rainfall.
   b. altitude.
   c. tendency to have natural disasters.
   d. plants and animals.

8. Real differences in regional _____ patterns do exist.
   a. consumption
   b. disposable income
   c. religious
   d. political

9. For a number of religious groups, religious calendars influence
   a. positioning.
   b. repositioning.
   c. product selection.
   d. abstinence from certain products.

10. Media choice depends upon sensitivity to lifestyle and _____ patterns.
    a. attitude
    b. behavior
    c. consumption
    d. self-image

Team Talk

1. Identify any two subcultural groups to which you belong that have influence over your attitudes, values, beliefs, and/or behaviors. How do each of these affect your consumer behavior?

2. Talk to a friend or make contact with a person who is from a different nationality or ethnic subculture than you. Ask how his or her nationality or ethnic background affects clothing, recorded music, and movie rental choices. Compare this with your own choices of the same three product classes.

3. We described seven classifications of teenagers, from Jarheads to Bohos. Did you belong to any of these groups in high school? Which were you closest to? How about other people in your class?

4. Consider the location of your hometown. Describe three distinctive marketplace behaviors of hometown consumers that are a result of their geographic location.

5. Talk to a friend who is a relatively devout member of a particular religious sect or denomination, other than your own. Ask that person to describe three ways in which religious beliefs affect his or her behavior as a consumer.

Workshops

Research Workshop

Background

By the time seniors reach age 65 they have a self-image that is fifteen years younger than their chronological age. The objective of this workshop is to see whether magazine advertising for goods or services typically used by men or women 65 or older is geared to chronological or to perceived age.

Methodology

Choose a magazine that contains advertising for products typically used by men or women 65 or older, or for general products that are positioned to appeal to seniors. Select four advertisements and analyze them in terms of headline, copy, visuals, models, and situation portrayed. Evaluate each as to whether it focuses on chronological or perceived age.

To the Marketplace

What changes, if any, would you make to the advertisements so that they would have greater appeal on the basis of perceived age?

Creative Workshop

Background

The same product type is often sold different ways to different target market groups. A good example is cosmetics. The objectives of this workshop are to develop separate creative approaches that can be used to sell cosmetics to women of different ages.

Methodology

Develop appropriate positioning strategies for teenagers, Generation X-ers, baby boomers, and seniors for a cosmetic product of your choice. Rough out three print advertisements for a magazine of your choosing. Each of the three ads should be targeted on a different one of the three age groups. For each advertisement, you will need headlines, copy, visuals, models, and a situation in which the product is being used.

To the Marketplace

Show your roughs to six women, two from each group. Ask which are on target and why. Modify your advertisements in light of any comments made.

Managerial Workshop

Background

You are planning to open a casual clothing store that targets teenagers in your college town. You want teens to feel comfortable in the store and enjoy shopping there. The objective of this workshop is to develop guidelines for store layout, atmosphere (decor, music, and lighting), type and brands of merchandise, variety, price range, and in-store clerk behavior.

Methodology

Put together two focus groups, one made up of six teenage girls and one made up of six teenage boys. Conduct the focus groups separately, gathering information to help you develop operational guidelines. Either record the sessions or take notes.

To the Marketplace

Develop a description of the new store that meets all the required criteria.

Notes

1. Elizabeth Hirshman, "Black Ethnicity and Innovative Communication," *Journal of the Academy of Marketing Science,* Vol. 8 (Spring 1980), pp. 100–119.

2. Ronald Cohen, "Ethnicity: Problem and Focus in Anthropology," *Annual Review of Anthropology,* Vol. 7 (1978), pp. 379–403; Elizabeth C. Hirschman, "American Jewish Ethnicity, Its Relationship to Some Selected Aspects of Consumer Behavior," *Journal of Marketing,* Vol. 45 (Summer 1981), pp. 102–110; Michael Minor, "Comparing the Hispanic and Non-Hispanic Markets: How Different Are They?", *Journal of Services Marketing,* Vol. 6, No. 2 (1992), pp. 29–32; Ed Chung and Eileen Fischer, "It's Who You Know: Intracultural Differences in Ethnic Product Consumption," *Journal of Consumer Marketing,* Vol. 16, No. 5 (1999), pp. 147–170; Jonathan F. Zaff, Ronald L Blount, Layli Phillips, and Lindsey Cohen, "The Role of Ethnic Identity and Self-Construal in Coping among African American and Caucasian American Seventh Graders: An Exploratory Analysis of Within-Group Variance," *Adolescence,* Vol. 37, No. 148 (2002), pp. 751–774.

3. Milton M. Gordon, "The Subsociety and the Subculture," in D. O. Arnold, ed., *Sociology of Subcultures* (Berkeley, CA: Glendessary Press, 1970).

4. Nathan Glazer, *Beyond the Melting Pot* (Cambridge, MA: Harvard University Press, 1964).

5. Diana Bagnall, "The Other Australians," *The Bulletin* (August 7, 2001), pp. 18–19.

6. Glaser, *Beyond the Melting Pot.*

7. Rebecca Gardyn, "Race, Ethnicity and the Way We Shop," *American Demographics,* Vol. 25 (February 2003), pp. 30–33.

8. Crockett, Grier, and Williams, "Coping with Marketplace Discrimination: An Exploration of the Experiences of Black Men," *Academy of Marketing Science Review,* Vol. 2003, p. 1.

9. "Department Stores Appeal to a New Demographic Base," *Chain Store Age,* Vol. 80 (Feb 2004), p. 68.

10. Ibid.

11. Ibid.

12. "Market Shift Impacts Sales," *Chain Store Age,* Vol. 79 (June 2003), p. 19.

13. Gardyn, "Race, Ethnicity, and the Way We Shop."

14. Ibid.

15. Ibid.

16. Ibid.

17. Alan Hughes, "Narrowing the Divide," *Black Enterprise,* Vol. 32 (May 2002), p. 26.

18. Sean Wargo, "Consumers to Watch," *Dealerscope,* Vol. 46 (February 2004), p. 20.

19. Ibid.

20. Malik Singleton, "Home Improvement," *Black Enterprise,* Vol. 35 (November 2004), p. 34.

21. Lindsay Grant, "Consumers' Preferences Vary," *Professional Builder,* Vol. 69 (July 2004), p. 85.

22. Becky Ebencamp, "The Amazing Ratings Race," *Brandweek,* Vol. 44 (May 5, 2003), p. 18.

23. Gardyn, "Race, Ethnicity and the Way We Shop."

24. Andrew Knight and Rex Warland, "The Relationship Between Sociodemographics and Concern About Food Safety Issues," *Journal of Consumer Affairs,* Vol. 38 (Summer 2004), pp. 107–120; James Flynn, Paul Slovic, and C. K. Mertz, "Gender, Race, and Perception of Environmental Health Risks," *Risk Analysis,* Vol. 14 (No. 6 1994), pp. 1101–1108.

25. Eugene Morris, "The Difference in Black and White," *American Demographics,* Vol. 15 (January 1993), pp. 44–49.

26. Cyndee Miller, "Toy Companies Release 'Ethnically Correct' Dolls," *Marketing News* (September 30, 1991), pp. 1–2.

27. U.S. Census Bureau, *Statistical Abstract of the United States:* 2004–2005 (124th ed.), Washington D.C., 2004.

28. Gardyn, "Race, Ethnicity and the Way We Shop."

29. *Statistical Abstract of the United States:* 2004–2005 (2004).

30. Stuart Livingston, "Marketing to the Hispanic-American Community," *The Journal of Business Strategy,* Vol. 13 (March/April 1992), pp. 54–57.

31. "Spanish Spending Power Growing Dramatically but Consumers Retain Special Characteristics," *Television/Radio Age,* Vol. 32 (December 1984), p. A4.

32. Herb Scannell, "The Hispanic Tipping Point," *Broadcasting & Cable,* Vol. 133 (October 27, 2003), p. 48.

33. "Publishers Shout Over the Din," *Advertising Age* (February 12, 1990), p. S 12.

34. Gary Berman, "The Hispanic Market: Getting Down to Cases," *Sales and Marketing Management,* Vol. 54 (October 1991), pp. 65–74.

35. "Cultural Differences Offer Rewards," *Advertising Age* (April 7, 1990), p. S-20.

36. U.S. Census Bureau, *Statistical Abstract of the United States:* 2004–2005.

37. F. Linden, "Latin Beat," *Across the Board* (June 1991), pp. 9–16.

38. Carol J. Kaufman and Sigfredo A. Hernandez, "The Role of the Bodega in a U.S. Puerto Rican Community," *Journal of Retailing,* Vol. 67 (Winter 1991), pp. 375–396.

39. Danny Bellenger and Humberto Valencia, "Understanding the Hispanic Market," *Business Horizons* (May–June 1982), pp. 47–50; Joel Saegert, Robert J. Hoover, and Marye T. Hilger, "Characteristics of Mexican American Consumers," *Journal of Consumer Research,* Vol. 12 (June 1985), pp. 104–109.

40. "Department Stores Appeal to a New Demographic Base."

41. Gardyn, "Race, Ethnicity and the Way We Shop."

42. "Department Stores Appeal to a New Demographic Base."

43. Gardyn, "Race, Ethnicity and the Way We Shop."

44. Ibid.

45. Ibid.

46. Wargo, "Consumers to Watch."

47. Singleton, "Home Improvement."

48. Grant, "Consumers' Preferences Vary."

49. Lynn Adkins, "New Strategies to Sell Hispanics," *Dunn's Business Monthly,* Vol. 122 (July 1983), pp. 64–69.

50. "Market Shift Impacts Sales."

51. *Successful Marketing to U.S. Hispanics and Asians.*

52. Elaine Santoro, "Hispanics Are Hot," *Direct Marketing,* (October 1991), pp. 28–32.

53. Stacy Vollmers and Ronald E. Goldsmith, "Hispanic-American Consumers and Ethnic Marketing," in Donald L. Thompson, ed., *Proceedings of the 1993 Atlantic Marketing Association Conference* (Atlantic Marketing Association), pp. 46–50.

54. Carol J. Kaufman and Sigfredo A. Hernandez, "Barriers to Coupon Use: A View from the Bodega," *Journal of Advertising Research,* Vol. 30 (October/November 1990), pp. 18–25.

55. Frank DiGiacomo, "Doing the Right Thing," *Marketing and Media Decisions,* Vol. 25 (June 1990), pp. 25–32.

56. Sandra Yin, "Home and Away," *American Demographics,* Vol. 26 (March 2004), p. 15.

57. U.S. Census Bureau, *Statistical Abstract of the United States:* 2004–2005.

58. Ibid.

59. Ibid.

60. Ibid.

61. "Marketers Target the New Majority," *Promo: The Sourcebook,* 1994, pp. 171–172.

62. David Ackerman and Gerard Tillis, "Can Culture Affect Prices?: A Cross-Cultural Study of Shopping and Retail Prices," *Journal of Retailing,* Vol. 77, No. 1 (2001), pp. 57–82.

63. "Asian-Americans Find Struggles, Success in US," *Milwaukee Journal* (April 12, 1992), pp. 27–29.

64. Ibid.

65. "Marketers Target the New Majority."

66. "The Far East Isn't So Far Anymore," *Progressive Grocer,* Vol. 70 (June 1991), pp. 35–38.

67. Ackerman and Tillis, "Can Culture Affect Prices?"

68. "Suddenly, Asian-Americans Are a Marketer's Dream," *Business Week* (June 17, 1991), pp. 54–55.

69. "The Far East Isn't So Far Anymore."

70. James U. McNeal, "The Littlest Shoppers," *American Demographics,* Vol. 14 (October 1992), pp. 48–53.

71. James U. McNeal, "Growing Up in the Market," *American Demographics,* Vol. 14 (October 1992), pp. 46–50.

72. David G. Kennedy, "Coming of Age in Consumerdom," *American Demographics,* Vol. 26 (April 2004), p. 14.

73. McNeal, "Growing Up in the Market."

74. "They May Be Small, But They Spend Big," *Adweek* (February 10, 1992), p. 12.

75. McNeal, "The Littlest Shoppers."

76. "Children Come of Age as Consumers," *Marketing News* (December 4, 1987), p. 8.

77. Laura A. Peracchio, "How Do Young Children Learn to Be Consumers? A Script-Processing Approach," *Journal of Consumer Research,* Vol. 18 (March 1992), pp. 425–440.

78. "American Internet User Survey," FIND/SVP and Grunwald Associates, 2000.

79. Tessa Romita, "Teens Are All That," *Business 2.0,* (January 2, 2001).

80. William Dunn, "Hanging Out with American Youth," *American Demographics,* Vol. 14 (February 1992), pp. 24–35.

81. Ibid.

82. Jason Meyers, "Game Theory, Teen-Style," *American Demographics,* Vol. 26 (May 2004), p. 10.

83. Aviv Shoham and Vassilis Dalakas, "Family Consumer Decision Making in Israel: The Role of Teens and Parents," *Journal of Consumer Marketing,* Vol. 20, No. 3 (2003), pp. 238–251.

84. Terry Bristol and Tamara F. Mangleburg, "Not Telling the Whole Story: Teen Deception in Purchasing," *Journal of the Academy of Marketing Science,* Vol. 33 (Winter 2005), pp. 75–95.

85. "The Teen Dream," *Mediaweek* (July 22, 1991), p. 27.

86. Jess Cagle, "The *Ice Age* Cometh," *Time,* (April 1, 2002), p. 64.

87. "Emerging Markets: Prepare for Generation Y Customers," *Cendant Media Center,* http://www.cendant.com/media/ trends_information/trends_information.cgi (December 28, 2004).

88. "Farther Along the X Axis," *American Demographics,* Vol. 26 (May 2004), pp. 21–24.

89. Becky Ebenkamp, "Mothers of Reinvention," *Brandweek,* Vol. 45 (March 8, 2004), p. 25.

90. Edna Negron, "Why Gen Y? Newspapers Have Three Years to Get It Right," http://www.mediamanagementcenter.org/ news/GenY/genY.htm (December 28, 2004).

91. Joan Engerbretson, "Odd Gen Out, " *American Demographics,* Vol. 26 (May 2004), pp. 14–17.

92. Christopher Palmer, "Toyota's Youth Models are Having Growing Pains," *Business Week,* Issue 3885 (May 31, 2004), p. 32.

93. David Welch, "Not Your Father's . . . Whatever: What Does Gen Y Want in a Car? To Automakers' Surprise, It's Price and Value," *Business Week,* Issue 3874 (March 15, 2004), p. 82.

94. "Generation Y Spending on the Rise," *DSN Retailing Today,* Vol. 43 (May 3, 2004), p. 39.

95. Palmer, "Toyota's Youth Models."

96. Welch, "Not Your Father's."

97. Jean Halliday, "Automakers Mix It Up Chasing Young Buyers," *Advertising Age,* Vol. 75, Issue 16 (April 19, 2004), p. 4.

98. Negron, "Why Gen Y?"

99. Bob Losyk, "Generation X," *The Futurist* (March/April 1997), p. 39.

100. Margot Hornblower, "Great Xpectations," *Time* (June 9, 1997), p. 60.

101. "Farther Along the X Axis."

102. Ibid.

103. Hornblower, "Great Xpectations," p. 58.

104. Karen Ritchie, "Marketing to Generation X," *American Demographics,* Vol. 17 (April 1995), pp. 34–39.

105. Ibid.

106. Laura Zinn, "Move Over Boomers," *Business Week* (December 14, 1992), p. 7.

107. "Farther along the X Axis."

108. "Billions of Boomers," *American Demographics,* Vol. 14 (March 1992), p. 6.

109. Roger Rosenblatt, "Come Together," *Modern Maturity,* Vol. 39 (January/February 1996), p. 33.

110. Jacqueline K. Eastman and Rajesh Iyer, "The Elderly's Uses and Attitudes toward the Internet," *Journal of Consumer Marketing,* Vol. 21, No.3 (2004), pp. 208–220; U.S. Census Bureau, *Statistical Abstract of the United States:* 2004–2005.

111. Betsy D. Gelb, "Discovering the 65+ Consumer," *Business Horizons,* Vol. 25 (May–June 1982), pp. 42–46.

112. U.S. Census Bureau, *Statistical Abstract of the United States:* 2004–2005; "Research Dispels Myths About Elderly," *Marketing News* (May 25, 1984), p. 5.

113. Lois Underhill and Franchellie Caldwell, "What Age Do You Feel: Age Prescription Study," *Journal of Consumer Marketing,* Vol. 10 (Summer 1983), pp. 18–27.

114. Diane Crispell and William H. Frey, "American Maturity," *American Demographics,* Vol. 15 (March 1993), pp. 31–42.

115. Ibid.

116. U.S. Census Bureau, *Statistical Abstract of the United States:* 2004–2005.

117. J. Ward, "Advertisers Slow to Catch Age Wave," *Advertising Age* (May 23, 1989), p. S1.

118. Eastman and Iyer, "The Elderly's Uses and Attitudes toward the Internet."

119. P. J. Trocchia and S. Janda, "A Phenomenological Investigation of Internet Usage among Older Individuals," *Journal of Consumer Marketing,* Vol. 17, No. 7 (2000), pp. 605–616.

120. Ibid.

121. John S. Reed, *The Enduring South: Subcultural Persistence in Mass Society* (Lexington, MA: D.C Heath, Inc., 1972).

122. William T. Tucker, *The Social Context of Economic Behavior* (New York: Holt, Rinehart and Winston, 1964).

123. "Author: America has 2,630 Religions and Counting," http://www.cnn.com/2003/US/01/31/counting.religions.ap/ index.html.

Social Class and Reference Group Influences

14

George is not looking forward to his ten-year high school reunion. He loved high school and was a popular student, but his life has not gone as planned since then. He was born into a lower-middle class family and lived that life as he moved on to college. He dropped out of college with one semester to go to get married. He finished up by going to school at night. George took a job in the big city, and the family moved while his wife, Sharon, was pregnant with their first child. He began making good money, and as he moved into the life of an accountant, he also moved into the upper-middle class. He and his wife began to live like the other members of the firm. Six years, two kids, and too many changes in each other found George and his wife unhappy in their marriage, so they called it quits. Sharon moved back to their hometown and started at the junior college, intending to become a dental technician. George's accounting career was sliding downhill, too. He hated the long hours and constantly worried about making partner. He also faced up to the fact that he had put his career above everything, including his family. Finally, the stress was too much and he quit. Since then, he's worked as a bookkeeper at a retail store and as an assistant manager of a burger joint. He is now in training to run a paving machine for the road construction company owned by his brother. He's behind on child-support payments and lives from paycheck to paycheck with no real plans for the future.

His brother convinced George to attend his high school reunion, thinking it would raise his spirits. George got a haircut for the occasion (he was wearing it long like the other guys on the road crew) and bought a new jacket, a designer brand he can't really afford. He also borrowed his brother's car, a new Saab—after all, he doesn't want everyone thinking he's a failure.

George's life since high school led him up the social class ladder, and now he's actually dropped down the ladder to a position below where his parents are. Although he is unlikely to express it in such terms, his unease in attending his class reunion is based on his fears that he no longer neatly fits in. Most of the kids he hung out with were lower-middle class. Others know he was a successful accountant and expect he'll move comfortably with the upper-middle class group at the reunion. Some of the others at the reunion also work with him now and will expect him to hang with them and behave the way they do. "Unease" is likely a mild word for the way George knows he'll feel.

In this chapter, we will first explore aspects of social class with special attention to its effects on marketplace behavior. The last portion of the chapter will be devoted to understanding what reference groups are and how they influence consumer behavior. It is part of human nature that we seek out people similar to ourselves. We are more comfortable with them than with those not like us.

14-1 Social Class

Class systems are, and always have been, a fact of life. While in the truest sense all people are equal as human beings, differences in skills, achievements, birth family, wealth, and many other aspects of life set people apart from one another. Almost every society can be viewed in terms of social class—the groupings of people who, based on characteristics that are appropriate for the culture or subculture, cluster together. A more restrictive approach is the "caste system," which will also be discussed.

14-1a Defining Social Class

A very simple way to characterize social class is, "birds of a feather flock together." People feel most comfortable when they are with others who are, in general, much like themselves in behavior, values, occupation group, wealth, and the like. The basic unit of a social class scheme is not the individual but the family or household. Members of a household share many characteristics—home, income, even values—that influence their relationships with outsiders. If members of a large group of families are approximately equal to one another and differentiated from other families, they constitute a social class.[1] Children, at least initially, assume the social classes of their families. Of course, as they grow, their education, occupations, income, and many other factors associated with social class and its attendant lifestyle can change this.

An aspect of social class of special interest to marketers is its relationship to status. In fact, the American Marketing Association defines **social class** in terms of status: *a status hierarchy by which groups and individuals are classified on the basis of esteem and prestige.* If social class is connected to such benefits as esteem and prestige, it is obviously important for marketers to understand how social class influences purchases, the means through which consumers express or reflect these benefits.

As we saw in the last chapter, every society is made up of several sub-/co-cultures. Frequently, these have social class structures of their own. Members of nationality-based subcultures may bring with them the class systems of their native countries. Ethnic groups similarly have class structures that do not always mesh with that of the "mainstream" culture of the United States. Also, sub-/co-cultural groups that are not part of the mainstream, and that are possibly discriminated against by the dominant cultural group, will naturally devise their own spoken or unspoken social class structure.

The impact of social class on a person's life is important for marketers to understand. The different lifestyles of social classes lead to different benefits being sought. Therefore, the products and services needed to deliver these benefits are varied. Where are the points of impact? The answer affects many parts of an individual's life from birth to death. Will you be born or not? That is, what is the difference in number of children in a family, religion not counted? Generally, the lower the social class, the larger the number of children. Regardless of background, as people move up the social class ladder, family size decreases. What activities will youngsters participate in: tennis, bowling, sailing, chess, basketball, cricket, gymnastics, dance, hunting, hiking, swimming? Will they go to public or private schools, and which ones? Will they go to college? Will it be public or private; will it be the Ivy League, the leading state school, or some other choice? Will they travel overseas to nations where language and culture are truly different from those in their native land? What kind of profession will they pursue? Whom will they marry? What will their funeral be like? Will it be simple or elaborate; will it be sedate or filled with vocal and other emotional expressions of grief? These are just a few of the key questions about people that give clues to their social class. Social class is another way that the marketplace segments itself.

> **social class** A status hierarchy by which groups and individuals are classified on the basis of esteem and prestige.

F A Q

Is it possible to achieve a classless society?

E x h i b i t 14-1

Social Class Membership

Membership Factors
· Occupation
· Income source
· Possessions
· Associations
· Level of influence

Social Class Assignment
· Reputational approach
· Subjective approach
· Objective approach
· Single-item index
· Multiple-item index

14-1b Social Class Membership

What are the characteristics of a person's life that help us determine where they fit on the social class ladder? Members of the same class tend to share common values, beliefs, and behaviors that—more than simple demographics—unite them. There is no universal agreement on the exact factors to use. This is logical because the society and the sub-/co-cultures within it may differ in what is important in determining a person's class position. We'll look at five factors that can be used in the mainstream U.S. class system. Other factors may be added or some deleted depending on the approach to measurement. The factors we present are *occupation, source of income, possessions, associations with others,* and *level of influence* (see Exhibit 14-1).

Occupation   What a person does for a living is one of the most telling indicators of social class. This is because occupation largely dictates other signs of class membership, such as income, personal associations, and status. Many people even consider occupation as synonymous with class membership. We think of accountants as part of the upper-middle class, owners of small stores as typically lower-middle class, welders as part of the blue-collar working class, and day laborers as members of the lower-lower class. Within each occupation, we make further class assumptions based on performance level. We see a top salesperson with a large corporation as in the upper reaches of the middle class, whereas a more average performer has a lower social status. Think of other instances in which people within the same occupation are not of the same social class.

Exhibit 14-2 provides a comparison of class membership according to occupation in the United States and Japan. Despite differences in culture and lifestyle, notice how similar the class assignments are. Occupation has an impact on membership in the African-American social class structure. See Marketplace 14-1 to explore this and other dimensions of this subcultural social class system.

Income Source   Level of income is not by itself a good indicator of class. The auto assembly-line worker, a lawyer fresh out of school, and a retiree living off investments may have the same income, but this does not mean they belong to the same class. Their occupations, investments and the like—the sources of that income—set them apart. Similarly, the professional athlete who earns $10 million a year or the rock singer who earns $20 million is probably not in the same social class as the physician who makes just $250,000. Actual income level affects ability to pay, but social class shapes the "tastes" of consumers. More than 60 percent of the members of the upper class report that money makes them feel secure, independent, comfortable, and free. Only 24 percent report that it brings happiness, and 20 percent say that it gives one status.[2] Check out Marketplace 14-2 to see how income within classes affects those with more than average and those with less.

E x h i b i t 14-2

Social Stratification by Occupation: United States vs. Japan

	Social Class Position Rank Order		
Occupation	United States	Japan
Managers	1	1
Nonmanual workers	2	4
Employers	3	
5+ employees		2
1–4 employees		5
Self-employed	4	6
First-line supervisors	5	3
Manual workers	6	7

Source: Melvin L. Kohn, Atushi Naoi, and Carrie Schoenbach, "Position in the Class Structure and Psychological Functioning in the United States, Japan and Poland," *American Journal of Sociology,* Vol. 95 (January 1990), pp. 964–1008.

Marketplace 14-1

African-American Social Class Structure

Based on occupation and income, there are three primary class divisions in the African-American subculture: a capitalist class, a middle class, and a working class.

Capitalist Class

- *Old Black Capitalist:* Waning in size and influence, members own businesses started before the civil rights era. With strong ties to the black community, the clientele is mostly African-American.
- *New Black Capitalist:* Emerging in the late 1960s and early 1970s, members of this small group run businesses that are not tied to the black community but depend to some extent on white clientele, general corporate structure, and government subcontracts. Well-educated black entrepreneurs, these capitalists are less community conscious than are old black capitalists.

Middle Class

- *Old Black Middle Class:* Dating back to the Civil War, members earn their living through ownership and operation of smaller businesses and service firms or are professionals, such as doctors and lawyers.
- *New Black Middle Class:* Members are educated or have specialist training or skills. Typically not self-

employed, they include scientists, engineers, professors, technicians, professional athletes, and entertainers. Income is high in comparison to the rest of the African-American population.

Black Working Class

- *Primary:* This upper group includes all white-collar workers, including teachers, low-level managers, health technicians, construction workers, and some production workers. Members are educated, have stable family situations, are employed, and have relatively high wages, good working conditions, and advancement opportunities.
- *Secondary:* Members work in more labor-intensive, low-prestige occupations and/or are in industries with less stable employment. Typical occupations include laborers, food service workers, housekeepers, nursing aids, janitors, stock handlers, and retail sales clerks.
- *Marginalized:* Members include those who are involuntarily without full-time employment, those on welfare, and those on the poverty line.

Source: From *Race, Class and Conservatism* by Thomas D. Boston. Copyright © 1988. Reprinted by permission of the author.

Marketplace 14-2

Money and Class

While money has a primary influence on lifestyle—if we have more we can choose to spend more—it does not dictate social class. Winning the jackpot in Las Vegas is not a ticket to the higher classes, nor does filing bankruptcy lead to demotion.

Within each social class there are three income divisions: the overprivileged, who have money to excess; the average, with neither excess nor deficient funds; and the underprivileged, with deficient funds. Even though the overprivileged may lead more affluent lifestyles, their values and behaviors tend to remain class bound, and they generally do not, like the Las Vegas winner, achieve a higher social status as a result of their income.

People perceive their wealth in different ways. Discretionary income is subjective—it's not how much money we have but how much we feel we have that influences spend-

ing. In other words, perceived level of income directly influences level of spending. This is particularly true with nonessentials. Consumers within a social class may have the same after-tax and after-essentials income. Yet some perceive the money they have left over as available for spending, while others are much more frugal. Older people, for example, particularly those who remember living through the Great Depression and World War II, consider themselves to have less discretionary income than those who grew up in the 1960s. More than actual income, which most people keep secret, subjective discretionary income is visible—we can see it in the marketplace choices people make, the possessions they have, and the services they use.

Source: From "Subjective Discretionary Income" by T. C. O'Guinn and William D. Wells in *Marketing Research,* March 1989, pp. 32–41. Reprinted by permission of American Marketing Association.

Exhibit 14-3

The Living-Room Scale

Begin with a score of 100. For each of the following in your living room (or those of friends or acquaintances), add or subtract points as indicated. Then ascertain social class according to the table at the end.

Hardwood floor	+4	Any display of "collectibles"	–4
Parquet floor	+8	Transparent plastic covers on furniture	–6
Stone floor	+4	Furniture upholstered with any metallic threads	–3
Vinyl floor	–6		
Wall-to-wall carpet	+2	Cellophane on any lampshade	–4
Working fireplace	+4		
New oriental rug or carpet	–2 (each)	No ashtrays	–2
Worn oriental rug or carpet	+5 (each)	Refrigerator, washing machine, or clothes dryer in living room	–6
Threadbare rug or carpet	+8 (each)		
Ceiling ten feet or higher	+6	Motorcycle	–10
Original paintings by internationally recognized practitioners	+8 (each)	Periodicals visible, laid out flat	
		National Enquirer	–6
Original drawings, prints, or lithographs by internationally recognized practitioners	+5 (each)	*Popular Mechanics*	–5
		Reader's Digest	–3
		National Geographic	–2
Reproductions of any Picasso painting, print, or anything	–2 (each)	*Smithsonian*	–1
		Scientific American	–1
Original paintings, drawings, or prints by family members	–4 (each)	*New Yorker*	+1
		Town and Country	+2
Windows curtained, rods and draw cords	+5	*New York Review of Books*	+5
Windows, curtained, no rods or draw cords	+2	*Times Literary Supplement* (London)	+5
Genuine Tiffany lamp	+3	*Paris Match*	+6
Reproduction Tiffany Lamp	–4	*Hudson Review*	+8
Any work of art depicting cowboys	–3	Each family photograph (black and white)	–2
"Professional" oil portrait of any member of the household	–3	Each family photograph (color)	–3

Possessions Consumption choices, driven by the resulting lifestyle, are a particularly useful indicator of social class.[3] For example, the purchase of foreign luxury cars and membership in exclusive country and tennis clubs are clearly indicative of one class, while owning minivans and participating in bowling leagues is indicative of another. Through analysis of personal possessions, sometimes called "artifacts," marketers can gain a picture of not only the class to which individuals belong, but the strength of their identification with that class. Quantity and quality of possessions should be evaluated, with quality likely being the deciding factor. The type and number of homes a person has and their location are typically accurate reflections of social class. So are home furnishings and appliances and clothing. Exhibit 14-3 invites you to analyze the contents of your living room or that of your parents as a means of finding out to which social class you belong. In the broader context, almost every item you buy and/or service you use speaks to your class membership.

Look at the sophisticated approach to the design of a bathroom tub presented in Exhibit 14-4 and the room setting in which it is set. Notice the uncluttered look of the

Each family photograph (black and white or color) in sterling silver frame	+3	Wall unit with built-in TV, stereo, etc.	−4	
Potted citrus tree with miniature fruit growing	+8	On coffee table, container of matchbooks from funny or anomalous places	+1	
Potted palm tree	+5	Works of sculpture (original, and not made by householder or any family member)	+4 (each)	
Bowling-ball carrier	−6			
Fishbowl or aquarium	−4	Works of sculpture made by householder or any family member	−5 (each)	
Fringe on any upholstered furniture	−4			
Identifiable Naugahyde aping anything customarily made in leather	−3	Every item alluding specifically to the United Kingdom	+1	
Any item exhibiting words in an ancient or modern foreign language (Spanish excluded)	+7	Any item alluding, even remotely, to Tutankhamen	−4	
Wooden venetian blinds	−2	Each framed certificate, diploma, or testimonial	−2	
Metal venetian blinds	−4	Each "laminated" ditto	−3	
Tabletop obelisk of marble, glass, etc.	+9	Each item with a "tortoise-shell" finish, if only made of Formica	+1	
No periodicals visible	−5	Each "Eames chair"	−2	
Fewer than five pictures on walls	−5	Anything displaying the name or initials of anyone in the household	−4	
Pieces of furniture over 50 years old	+2 (each)			
Bookcase(s) full of books	+7	Curved moldings visible anywhere in the room	+5	
Any leather bindings more than 75 years old	+6	**Calculating the Score**		
Bookcase(s) partially full of books	+5	245 and above	Upper class	
Overflow of books stacked on floor, chairs, etc.	+6	185–245	Upper middle	
		100–185	Middle class	
Hutch bookcase ("wall system") displaying plates, pots, porcelain figurines, etc., but no books	−4	50–100	Upper lower	
		Below 50	Lower lower	

Source: Paul Fussell, Class (New York: Summit Books, 1983), pp. 190–192.

bathroom and the use of Shaker furniture concepts. What clues does the advertisement copy give to the social class targeted and the lifestyles of potential customers?

Keep in mind, however, that possessions alone do not give a complete picture of class. Nor is that picture always accurate. The kitchen purchases, for example, of a prosperous working-class family and of an upper-middle-class family may be identical. But even when identical brands are chosen, those selections result from very different values, thought processes, and decisions.

Associations Consumption patterns and interaction networks are intimately linked; people spend their leisure time with others who share their tastes and recreational activities, and they learn new tastes from those with whom they associate.[4] Interactions with friends and relatives vary according to class membership. So do the kinds of people we associate with at school or at work. Most of us date and marry within our social class.

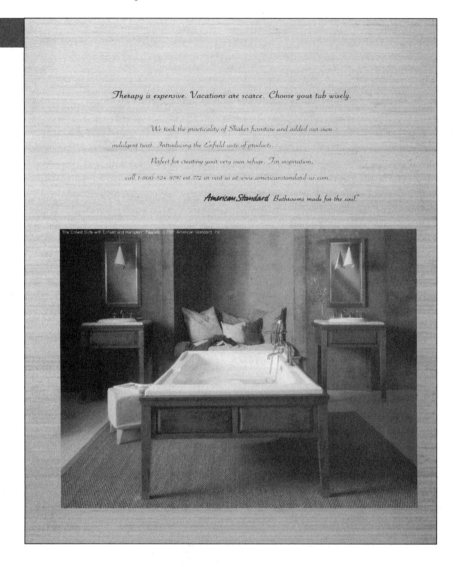

Therapy is expensive. Vacations are scarce. Choose your tub wisely.

We took the practicality of Shaker furniture and added our own indulgent twist. Introducing the Enfield suite of products.

Perfect for creating your very own refuge. For inspiration, call 1-800-524-9797 ext.772 or visit us at www.americanstandard-us.com.

American Standard *Bathrooms made for the soul.*

▶ **class consciousness**
A person's sense of belonging to a certain social class.

Further, our **class consciousness**—our sense of belonging to a particular class—is reinforced by the people with whom we associate. Consider the class consciousness of a mechanic who wins $50 million in the California lottery. Even if he buys the garage at which he works, hires a manager, and retires to Beverly Hills, will his neighbors treat him as a member of the upper class? Will he even be able to change class? The answer is probably not—his class consciousness and the society will hold him back.

Level of Influence   Class rank and influence go hand in hand. Membership in a higher class generally leads to greater influence within the workplace, organizations, and society as a whole. In complex societies like that of the United States, those who perform coordinating functions wield the most influence. These are people who oversee groups of others and manage their joint efforts toward accomplishing tasks. State senators, corporate officers, and student representatives all carry out coordinating roles, each with a different level of influence. The more responsibility a person has, the greater the influence generally given her or him. People who are higher on the social class "ladder" are often shown deference by those lower in social class. This occurs because of the expectation that persons of higher station have the skills to do well if given a position of influence. Of course, this may or may not prove to be the case.

Coordination leads to influence because the coordinator's actions partly control the behavior of those for whom he or she is directly responsible, as well as those who look to the coordinator for guidance. Influence is a large part of the class rank of people in the communications industry and politics, because they have the power to change, directly or indirectly, the attitudes and behavior patterns of other groups.[5]

14-1c Assigning Individuals to Social Classes

The five indicators we have reviewed—occupation, source of income, possessions, associations, and level of influence—though useful, are not always used directly to establish an individual's class status. It is difficult to categorize individuals on the basis of class. One reason for this is that we're simply not comfortable assigning ourselves, much less others, to social classes. In fact, the very concept of class violates the principle of equality on which democratic societies are founded. Because of its value as a means of segmentation, however, marketers find it useful to use social class to define the larger population. The most commonly used methods of assigning individuals to social classes are the *reputational, subjective,* and *objective* approaches.

Reputational Approach Using the *reputational approach,* respondents are asked to report the social class of others within their communities, rating only those people they feel comfortable assessing. Usually they are provided with a list of classes from which to choose and a list of descriptors typical of people within each class. The reputational approach is based on analyzing the perceptions of respondents. It not only results in individual social class placements but also gives an overview of the class structure within the community as perceived by respondents.

Subjective Approach The *subjective approach* requires respondents to report what they think their own social class is.[6] Again, perception is the key. Predictably, the subjective approach leads many people to place themselves as "middle class."

Objective Approaches Unlike the reputational and subjective methods, *objective approaches* rely on measurable data to establish social classification. Using the objective approach, a researcher first establishes a framework for measuring. He or she may use a single variable ("single-item measure") or two or more variables ("multiple-item measure"). The range of scores possible is determined. Then people of known social class are scored. These scores are used as comparison points. As people respond to the measuring scales, their scores determine social class position. Although these methods are referred to as objective, the scales used to measure a particular variable may be subjective in design and in scoring. For example, how would you develop a way to measure occupation to determine social class?

Single-Item Measures The most popular single-item measure, also called an index, is occupation. Despite its utility, the occupation index does not account for differentials in job performance. The occupation index, for example, would group all small business people together in the middle class. Yet there are obvious distinctions between the entrepreneur who is barely making ends meet, the owner of a thriving local business, and the owner of a regional chain of businesses. They may better be assigned to the lower-middle class, the upper-middle class, and the lower-upper class. The living-room scale described in Exhibit 14-3 is another example of a single-item measure.

Multiple-Item Measures While most researchers recognize that a combination of factors is important in determining social class, there is no universal agreement on how this should be done. Popular multiple-item measures, however, use various combinations of occupation, possessions, education, source of income, type of house, area of residence, and even power, status, and culture.[7] Exhibit 14-5 illustrates a multiple-item measure from the 1980s and 1990s using education, occupation, area of residence, and family income. Each is assigned almost equal weight, and the sum of the scores leads to assignment of the subject to one of four class groupings. Another multiple-item measure that is still being used, though published in 1958, is the Hollingshead and Redlich two-factor index of social class.

F A Q

Which is more important in marketing—a person's actual social class or perceived social class?

Exhibit 14-5

Multiple-Item Measure of Social Class

The Computerized Status Index (CSI) is a quantitative measure of social class. Shown here is one page in an interview protocol used for field collection of data, ratings, and coding for a CSI. In this particular version, occupation is weighted double when computing the total score. When a respondent is not married, education is given a double weight along with occupation. Status interpretation of the total score for conventional married couples, with male household head between 35 and 64 years of age, would run this way:

Upper American	37 to 53
Middle Class	24 to 36
Working Class	13 to 23
Lower American	4 to 12

Example of a Computerized Status Index (CSI)

Interviewer circles code numbers which best fit the respondent and family.

Age   Respondent's age _____   Spouse's age _____

Education	Respondent	Respondent's Spouse
Grammar school (8 years or less)	1	1
Some high school (9 to 11 years)	2	2
Graduated high school (12 years)	3	3
Some post-high school (business, nursing, technical, 1 year college)	4	4
Two or three years of college—possible Associate of Arts degree	5	5
Graduated four-year college (BA/BS)	7	7
Master's or five-year professional degree	8	8
PhD or six-/seven-year professional degree	9	9

Occupation Prestige Level of Household Head (Interviewer's Judgment)

(Respondent's description—as for previous occupation if retired,
    or if R. is widow, ask husband's:_____)

Chronically unemployed—"day" laborers, unskilled; on welfare	0
Steadily employed but in marginal, semiskilled jobs	1
Assembly-line workers, bus/truck drivers, police/firefighters, carpenters	2
Skilled craftsmen, small contractors, factory foremen, office workers	3
Owners of very small firms, technicians, salespeople, civil servants	4
Middle managers, teachers, social workers, lesser professionals	5
Lesser corporate officials, owners of middle-sized businesses, professionals	7
Top corporate executives, "leaders" in the professional world, "rich" business owners	9

Area of Residence (Interviewer's Impressions)

Slum area: people on relief, common laborers	1
Strictly working class: not slummy but some very poor housing	2
Predominantly blue-collar with some office workers	3
Predominantly white-collar with some well-paid blue collar	4
Better white-collar area: not many executives, but hardly any blue-collar either	5
Excellent area: professionals and well-paid managers	7
"Wealthy" or "society"-type neighborhoods	9

Total score_____

Total Family Income Per Year

Under $5,000	1	$20,000 to $24,999	5	
$5,000 to $9,999	2	$25,000 to $34,999	6	
$10,000 to $14,999	3	$35,000 to $49,999	7	
$15,000 to $19,999	4	$50,000 and over	8	Estimated status_____

(Interviewer's estimate: _____ and explanation: _____)

R's Marital Status

Married _____ Divorced/Separated _____ Widowed _____ Single _____ (CODE:____)

Source: From "The Continuing Significance of Social Class on Marketing" by Richard P. Coleman in *Journal of Consumer Research,* Vol. 10, December 1983, pp. 267, 276–277. Copyright © 1983. Reprinted by permission of The University of Chicago Press.

CBite 14-1

A New Divide between Haves and Have-Nots?

There is a troubling aspect to the emerging information age. In an era in which success is increasingly identified with the ability to use computers and gain access to cyberspace, does technology only widen the gap between rich and poor; educated and uneducated; blacks, whites, and Latinos? Access to new technology breaks down along traditional class lines. Wealthy and upper-middle-class families in 2003 formed the bulk of the approximately 62 percent of households that own computers. About one-third of all household with incomes under $20,000 have computers. This jumps to about 85 percent for households with incomes of $50,000 to $100,000 and is over 90 percent for households over $100,000. Internet access for Asian Americans is at 76 percent, and it's 61 percent for whites, 48 percent for African Americans, and 47 percent for Latinos in the U.S. We find that wealthier school districts tend to have equipment that is unavailable to poorer ones, and schools in the more affluent suburbs have twice as many computers per student as their less well-funded urban counterparts. At least seven million homes, most of them poor, do not even have the telephone lines that could provide basic access. All this disparity comes to a head in this statistic: A working person who is able to use a computer earns 15 percent more than someone in a similar job who cannot. Those people who do not have online access will most likely be the "have-nots" in our social structure.

Source: Adapted from Suneel Ratan, "A New Divide between Haves and Have-Nots?" *Time,* Vol. 145 (Spring 1995), pp. 25–26; U.S. Census Bureau, *Statistical Abstract of the United States: 2004–2005* (124th ed.), Washington, D.C., 2004.

The two factors are occupation and education. The occupations range from "higher executive, major professional," which is assigned a value of "1," to "never employed," which is valued "8." Education scores run from "1," which is "post college," to "7," which is "some grammar (elementary) school." A person's occupation score is multiplied by 7 and the education score by 4, and the results are summed. People are then assigned to one of five social classes based on their score.[8] The five classes are upper, upper-middle, middle, working, and lower. We'll discuss class structures a bit later in the chapter.

A study in the late 1990s used geodemographics (GDs) to determine dominant social classes within mail ZIP codes. For each geo-unit, the GD system contains such information as the census profiles of the people, housing structures, businesses, roads, and highways. The data comes from the U.S. Bureau of Census, Department of Transportation, and commercial vendors specializing in financial, media, and consumer panel data. The first assumption is that people living in the same neighborhood are more likely to have similar characteristics than families chosen at random from other locations. The second assumption is that neighborhoods are defined based on household characteristics. Neighborhood residents would likely have similar consumption patterns. Hence by using the GD approach, social class groups can be found.[9]

Some argue that the gap between those in the upper reaches of the social class system in the United States and those lower on the ladder is widening on the basis of access to cyberspace. Take a look at CBite 14-1 for a brief discussion on this.

Marketing Management—Implications and Actions

Understanding social class helps marketers:

- Identify population groups with similar characteristics, lifestyles, and consumption patterns.
- Apply the reputational, objective, and subjective approaches to assign consumers or groups of consumers to social classes and create appeals targeted to them.

14-2 Social Class in the United States

To illustrate how social class systems work, we'll look closely at the majority, or "mainstream," population of the United States. Keep in mind that our society is becoming more diverse and, therefore, the concept of mainstream will gradually lose its relevance. There is no universally accepted social class system in the United States, and where the "lines are drawn between classes" is also not clear. The concept of social class is based on perceptions and approximations in the United States, other nations, and subcultures within nations.

14-2a A Five-Class Hierarchy

A hierarchy of classes in the United States was first proposed through a detailed portrait of "Yankee City," a hypothetical small New England community.[10] Despite changes in the makeup of our society, which today is far less homogeneous, Yankee City still provides what is considered a reasonably definitive classification system. A later analysis, known as "Peninsula People," conducted in the late 1950s and early 1960s, confirmed a very similar social structure, dividing the population into five classes.[11] Because the Peninsula People model is based on a mix that still reflects the composition of the United States, we will use it to provide an overview of key social groupings. We will then explore lifestyles, attitudes, and behaviors of people within these groupings. Exhibit 14-6 gives an overview of the social class system used here along with an indication of which classes constitute the "quality market" and the "mass market."

Upper Class   The upper classes are often educated at Ivy League and other traditionally elite schools, making schools attended one useful indicator of membership. Members at the top of this group ("upper-upper" class) lean toward inconspicuous consumption, often paying others, known as surrogates, to shop and acquire possessions for them. In some cases, merchants bring goods or service proposals directly to the consumer. Often, the reasons for this distance between the consumer and the marketplace are concerns for personal and family security and a desire for privacy. This is particularly true for well-known or easily recognized members of the class. This class doesn't buy to impress, and its members tend to be conservative consumers, frequently driving automobiles for 10 years and wearing older suits. They spend more on services than goods because many possessions are passed on from generation to generation. They live luxuriously and work to keep inherited wealth within their social class.[12] The upper group within this class may be descendents of the great industrial families of the late 1800s and early 1900s, may be able to trace their roots to the royal families of Europe, or may be connected to the earliest families in our history. The upper group is the *only true national class* in America, and members can be identified as being in this category.

Exhibit 14-6	A Modification of the Five Class System
Social Class in the United States	Upper class
	Upper-upper class
	Lower-upper class
	Middle class
	Upper-middle class
	Lower-middle class
	Lower class
	Upper-lower class
	Lower-lower class
	Underclass
	Quality market = Lower-upper class + Upper-middle class
	Mass market = Lower-middle class + Upper-lower class

The lower portion of the upper class ("lower-upper" class) may be identified as people whose fortunes were made in their lifetimes or their parents'. There is a tendency for such people to be more conspicuous in their consumption, buying to impress, because of the "new money" situation in which they find themselves. They buy expensive cars, large estates, and expensive jewelry to show wealth and status. Also purchased are expensive furnishings, collectables, artwork, and tailor-made clothing. They expect quality, one-of-a-kind items and excellent service. They spend on services that save time such as cleaning and cooking, and they hire maids, chauffeurs, nannies, and nurses. They look to be visible and seek out high-prestige occupations, often in politics or higher education. People of this class eat out less, but their home-cooked meals are made from the finest foods and good wines are consumed.[13] If the wealth is preserved and appropriate steps are taken to hold position, the children or grandchildren of these people may move to the upper-upper class.

Upper-Middle Class   Members of the upper-middle class are typically professionals, independent business-people, or corporate executives. Usually graduates of state universities, they tend to focus on education and career, and are particularly interested in their children's education. The upper-middle class has been described as organization prone, enjoying membership in professional societies, civic groups, and social clubs. Religion is regarded as a social experience as well as—and sometimes rather than—a spiritual one. This class is key in the preservation of the traditional arts in the society. They work to support the symphonies, the ballet, the opera, the theater, and other similar cultural expressions.

Members of the upper-middle class exert more influence on the marketplace than their limited numbers suggest. These are the upscale families to whom many marketers gear products and promotions. Consumers in the lower-upper and upper-middle classes constitute the **quality market.**

> **quality market** Consumers in the lower-upper and upper-middle classes.

There are those in this class whose incomes exceed $100,000 but who find this does not guarantee them an "easy life." See CBite 14-2 to check out their "woes." As is to be expected, the members of the quality market purchase luxury goods at a disproportionately higher rate than individuals lower on the class ladder. However, with more individuals with discretionary income, even in the lower-middle class, luxury goods and service companies are reaching out to the "mass affluent" segment. This is made up of the upper-middle and lower-middle class targets. In fact the idea of "new luxury" goods and services is being suggested. These new luxury items range in price from a $4 cup of Starbuck's brew to a $6 Tuscan chicken sandwich at Panera to a $26,000 Mercedes CLK automobile. Such products allow less affluent consumers to move up to higher levels of quality, taste, and aspiration.[14] So, what does "luxury" mean to different people? See Marketplace 14-3 for some answers. In another study, when affluent consumers were asked what motivated them to make luxury purchases even in poor economic times their top six answers were: (1) to buy things I know will last, (2) for my well-being, (3) to enjoy my favorite brands, (4) to feel good about myself, (5) to indulge myself, and (6) to express myself.[15] Notice how four of these six dealt with "myself's."

CBite 14-2
Struggling to Stay on Top—of the Middle Class

There was a time when "comfortably off" meant comfortable, but no more. In the current U.S. economic climate, earners with household incomes in the $100,000 range are pressured to trade personal time and relaxation for increased work hours and responsibility in order to maintain a shaky grip on the ladder of upper-middle class success. Costs for above-average housing, children's college educations, retirement planning, and other parts of the "good life" demand priority over sitting back and enjoying the position they have attained.

Source: Adapted from "Upper-Middle Class Woes" by Joseph Spiers in *Fortune,* December 27, 1993, p. 80.

Marketplace 14-3

What Is Luxury Anyway?

When consumers were asked what association certain adjectives had with their concept of what luxury was some interesting results were found when comparing African Americans, Hispanic Americans, and whites. See Exhibit 1 as some observations are made. White consumers are more likely to define "luxury" as something "prestigious" or "exclusive" than are African Americans or Latinos. However, the latter consumer groups are almost twice as likely as whites to define luxury as "trendy" or "fashionable." Notice

also that whites and Hispanics view luxury goods as more comforting, relaxing, and pampering than do African Americans. What dilemma does this difference in luxury perception present to marketers of luxury goods who wish to offer the same luxury product to the three segments? What else do you see in Exhibit 1 that has implications for positioning?

Sources: American Demographics' E-Poll; Rebecca Gardyn, "Oh, the Good Life," *American Demographics* (November 2002), p. 32. Copyright © 2002 Crain Communications, Inc. Reprinted with permission.

Exhibit 1

Which of the Following Adjectives Do You Associate with the Term "Luxury"?

Adjectives/Segments	African Americans (%)	Hispanics (%)	Whites (%)
Glamorous/classic/elegant	69	66	72
Comforting/relaxing/pampering	38	51	58
Status symbol/exclusive/prestigious	43	41	53
Wasteful/unnecessary/extravagant	32	14	23
Trendy/fashionable/"in"	30	33	18
Flashy/gaudy/elitist	*	31	16
Practical/quality/enduring	*	*	18

*Sample size too small. Note that columns do not sum to 100 percent because more than one answer was allowed.

In recent times, Wal-Mart executives have recognized that they have a number of customers with high income that take pride in being a "smart shopper." In 2001 many of the 178 stores opened were in well-off suburbs in America. These stores included grocery sections comparable to those of a supermarket, with gourmet desserts and fresh herbs to attract these upscale shoppers. Also added were pricier items such as big-screen television sets, digital cameras, and glamorous cookware.[16]

Lower-Middle Class Members of the lower-middle class include salespeople, clerical workers, supervisors, schoolteachers, construction contractors, and the owners of small retail stores. As you can see, this group is predominantly white collar. They typically own tract homes in the suburbs or comparable accommodations in older, well-kept urban neighborhoods. They are more traditional than people in the upper-middle class. A high school diploma is considered the educational standard, although some members have two- or four-year college degrees. Lower-middle class families profess deep concern for morals, religion, and the Protestant work ethic.

Upper-Lower Class Members of the upper-lower class are skilled and semiskilled blue-collar workers. Many aspire to raise their social position and that of their children. Some members are identified as "overprivileged," earning more than most blue-collar workers, but spending money in traditional lower-middle-class patterns.[17] They drive larger cars and own more home appliances than their neighbors. They do not typically travel on vacations outside of the United States, Canada, or the Caribbean. Their home often "becomes their castle." With considerable spending power today, the upper-lower class is the most populous market in the United States, being a bit larger than the lower-middle class, and is an increasingly attractive segment to marketers. The lower-middle and upper-lower classes constitute the **mass market,** which accounts for 60 percent to 70 percent of the population.

Lower-Lower Class   Occupying the lowest position in the class hierarchy are lower blue-collar workers, the unemployed, families on welfare, and unskilled laborers. Members of this class live in substandard housing, often in rundown neighborhoods or slums. Researchers describe members of the lower-lower class as victims of "cultural deficiency," geared to an essentially middle-class frame of reference by the mass media, but thwarted in their attempts to acquire such a lifestyle. Consequently, the lower-lower class is marked by despair, anger, and apathy. Marketers have traditionally paid little attention to this group, although there are signs that this may be changing. Retailers and developers have banded together to open stylish, high-quality retail outlets in underserved urban areas. The centers strive for the open, bright appearance common to suburban shopping centers while offering guarded entrances and extra security lighting. The tenants are a mix of minority-owned businesses and respectable, mid-level retailers like Walgreen's drugstores and Goldblatt's department stores.

Though based on generalizations and, to some extent, stereotypes, this five-class system does provide a useful means of classifying the larger population. As shown in Exhibit 14-7, two similar classification schemes—one a six-class system and one a seven-class system—suggest a further division within the lower-lower class. These individuals are identified as the **"underclass."** People who are on welfare, not regularly employed, poverty-stricken, lacking in education, or employed in very low-paying, menial jobs fit into this category. Members tend to live either in the most depressed of rural circumstances or in the "battle zones" of cities.

14-2b Class Systems in Other Cultures

The United States class system has a large middle class with significant shares of the population in upper and lower classes. Japan has an even larger middle class, certainly the lion's share of the population, with a small part of the population in the upper class and a somewhat larger share in the lower class. The socialist model in Scandinavian countries also has a large middle class with almost equal higher class and lower class groups. The dominant class among the Latin American countries is the lower class, with decreasing numbers of individuals as class level increases. The shape of this society is similar to a pyramid. In India, the two top classes are part of what is termed a "caste system" and small compared to the working class. In a caste system whatever caste a person is born into cannot be changed in their lifetime. Hence they must experience the positive or negative consequences. And there is a significant share of the poor, in some cases members of the "untouchable" caste, at the bottom of the scale.[18] There are increasing examples of people even in the "untouchable" caste in India who are now rising to positions in the society reserved historically for only those who are higher on the caste ladder.

14-3 Values, Attitudes, and Lifestyles across Social Classes

Although lifestyle, along with the values and attitudes that shape it, is probably the best indicator of social class, it is extremely difficult to analyze. However, as we saw in Chapter 6 (section 6-2d, "VALS™ Typologies"), such frameworks as VALS™ provide insight into values, attitudes, and lifestyles and their influence on consumption patterns. The following observations provide an overview of values, attitudes, and lifestyles and the ways in which they reflect the social classes we have discussed.

14-3a Values

Social class is an important source of beliefs, values, and behaviors. Individuals are taught class values primarily through their associations with family, friends, and neighbors in school and in the workplace.[19] Attitude toward education is a good example of the

mass market Consumers in the lower-middle and upper-lower classes.

underclass People who are on welfare, not regularly employed, poverty-stricken, lacking in education, or employed in very low-paying, menial jobs.

E x h i b i t 14-7	**The Gilbert-Kahl New Synthesis Class Structure**[a]	**The Coleman-Rainwater Social Standing Class Hierarchy**[b]
Distribution of Social Classes: Two Approaches	A situations model from political theory and sociological analysis	A reputational, behavioral view in the community study tradition

The Gilbert-Kahl New Synthesis Class Structure[a]

A situations model from political theory and sociological analysis

Upper Americans

The Capitalist Class (1%) Their investment decisions shape the national economy; income mostly from assets, earned/inherited; prestige university connections

Upper-Middle Class (14%) Upper managers, professionals, middle-level businesspeople; college-educated; family income ideally runs nearly twice the national average

Middle Americans

Middle Class (33%) Middle-level white collar, top-level blue-collar; education past high school typical; income somewhat above the national average

Working Class (32%) Middle-level blue collar, lower-level white-collar; income runs slightly below the national average; education is also slightly below

Marginal and Lower Americans

The Working Poor (11–12%) Below mainstream America in living standard, but above the poverty line; low-paid service workers, operatives; some high school education

The Underclass (8–9%) Depend primarily on welfare system for sustenance; living standard below poverty line; not regularly employed; lack schooling

The Coleman-Rainwater Social Standing Class Hierarchy[b]

A reputational, behavioral view in the community study tradition

Upper Americans

Upper Upper (0.3%) The "capital-S society" world of inherited wealth, aristocratic names

Lower Upper (1.2%) The newer social elite, drawn from current professionals, corporate leadership

Upper Middle (12.5%) The rest of college-graduated managers and professionals; lifestyle centers on private clubs, causes, and the arts

Middle Americans

Middle Class (32%) Average-pay white-collar workers and their blue-collar friends; live on "better side of town," try to "do the proper things"

Working Class (38%) Average-pay blue-collar workers; lead "working-class lifestyle" whatever the income, school background, and job

Lower Americans

"A Lower Group of People but Not the Lowest" (9%) Working, not on welfare; living standard is just above poverty; behavior judged "crude," "trashy"

"Real Lower Lower" (7%) On welfare, visibly poverty-stricken; usually out of work (or have "the dirtiest jobs"); "bums," "common criminals"

Source: Richard P. Coleman, "The Continuing Significance of Social Class on Marketing," *Journal of Consumer Research,* Vol. 10 (December 1983), p. 267.

[a]Abstracted from Dennis Gilbert and Joseph A. Kahl, "The American Class Structure: A Synthesis," in *The American Class Structure: A New Synthesis* (Homewood, IL: The Dorsey Press, 1982).

[b]This condensation of the Coleman-Rainwater view is drawn from Chapters 8, 9, and 10 of Richard P. Coleman and Lee P. Rainwater, with Kent A. McClelland, *Social Standing in America: New Dimensions of Class* (New York: Basic Books, 1978).

difference between classes. Members of the lower classes tend to view it as less valuable than do members of the middle class. Members of the lower classes are more apt than other groups to seek immediate gratification. The strength of appeals like "buy now, pay later" among the lower classes is evidence of this. They also depend on luck for opportunities, which probably explains the popularity of state lotteries.

In contrast, members of the middle class tend to believe that they can govern their own destinies and are less averse to risk. In addition, morality and respectability are important to the middle class. They seek success by applying those values to their work and to their lives in general. Unlike the lower class, who tend to feel trapped and may not take pride in the work they do, members of the middle class feel they can achieve more and have a greater feeling of accomplishment and pride. As individuals progress up the social scale, they develop a stronger sense of self and potential for personal achievement. They also feel a strong commitment to participate.

Marketplace 14-4

Giving across Social Class

Americans gave $177 billion to charitable organizations in 2001. Less than one percent ($1.25 billion) of that was tied to the attack on September 11 of that year. In the eight recession years since 1971, there were only slight declines in giving. Regardless of income, age, education, race, or ethnicity, most Americans give back to their communities. High rates of charitable giving and volunteerism have remained relatively steady over the past 15 years.

Who gives of their time, money, or both? While most give to charity, those who give only money differ in both attitude and demographics from those who give only time. Those who do both and those who do not give at all also have different demographics. A July 2002 survey of more than 6,000 adults, conducted by CauseWorks, part of the Porter Novelli public relations firm, divides Americans into four segments.

Actives: Givers of Time and Money

Americans who give time and money to at least one cause are the largest group (39 percent) of the U.S. population. They are more likely to be women than men (55 percent to 45 percent) and are the most educated of all four segments (40 percent with at least a bachelor's degree). Actives are also more likely to be members of a racial or an ethnic minority group (30 percent are nonwhite).

Sponsors: Givers of Money

Those who donate only money represent a quarter of the total population. Half of them live in urban areas, and about a third have at least a college degree. Among all the seg-ments, they are the most likely to be white and married, and a third of them have household incomes of $75,000 or more. Like Actives, they are most likely to donate their money to feeding the hungry, health research, and helping the poor.

Advocates: Givers of Time

People who volunteer their time but do not give money to charity represent just 8 percent of the total population. These Americans are more likely to be women than men (57 percent to 43 percent), and a quarter of them are single. Like Actives this group is racially and ethnically diverse (30 percent are nonwhite), and they have the lowest household income of all segments (68 percent earn less than $50,000). Advocates are most likely to volunteer time for educational causes.

Inactives: Non-givers

Those who donate neither time nor money represent about a quarter (28 percent) of the U.S. population. They, like Advocates, tend to have lower household incomes (66 percent earn less than $50,000) than members of the other segments, and 4 in 10 have a high school education or less. Americans in this group are the least likely to be married (27 percent are single) and the most likely to be living alone.

What do you see as the social class overlay for these four charitable giving/non-giving segments? Should social class enter into appeals from non-profit charitable causes asking for money and/or time?

Source: "Generosity and Income," *American Demographics* (December 2002/January 2003), p. 47. Copyright © 2003 Crain Communications, Inc. Reprinted with permission.

Part of the value system crossing social class lines is charitable giving of money and time. Americans have always been generous givers, even in tougher economic times. This was evident before and after the 9/11 terrorist attack. Marketplace 14-4 presents some interesting findings and suggests a four-group classification of givers.

14-3b Attitudes and Self-Perceptions

Upper-middle-class husbands and wives have positive attitudes toward functioning as teams. Women tend to demand much of themselves. They feel they should work hard at child rearing and at self-development, both professional and intellectual. Those with youngsters attempt to develop bright, active, precocious children, and to look for goods and services that will enhance their success as parents.

Lower-middle-class parents are more likely to emphasize control and conformity in raising their children and to place greater value on teaching them standards of politeness, order, and cleanliness. Working-class mothers express a strong need to enjoy and interact with their children, while fathers remain fairly distant, particularly from young children.

Lower-class women usually say that they dress to please themselves; lower-middle-class women are more concerned with what other women think of their clothing; and upper-middle-class women tend to dress for themselves, their husbands, other women, and other men. Lower-class families maintain the least adventurous social boundaries, preferring to socialize with relatives. They are more prone to spend vacations staying at

F A Q

Is it possible for a married couple who have exactly the same lifestyle to belong to different social classes?

This ad positions the X-Type Jaguar with upper-middle-class couples.

Source: Reprinted by permission of Jaguar.

home, visiting relatives, or letting the husband take off by himself, than are upper-middle-class people, who spend vacations as nuclear family groups.

In terms of self-perception, lower-class women appear to understand their bodies least of any class and maintain a sense of taboo about them. Higher-class women take more pride in their bodies and consider themselves fastidious. Upper-middle-class women are less involved with such products as deodorants because they feel less anxiety about offending others. They express the most personal pride and self-esteem in grooming, while lower-middle-class women respond to social motives and general self-consciousness.

Upper-middle-class men see themselves as clean, fastidious, and well groomed and relate these traits to career success. Masculine know-how is defined as sophistication about business, restaurants, travel, and so on. The advertisement in Exhibit 14-8 is targeted to upper-middle couples. The X-Type Jaguar is a symbol of class reinforcement or a feeling of "arrival" in that class. Notice the very clean look that leads to an impression of an upper-middle-class style. The advertisement was placed in *GQ* magazine, targeted to exactly this group.

Lower-middle-class men find masculine identity in being good fathers and building a solid home life. They are characterized as serious, rather depressed, fearful of being displaced by lower-class members, and concerned that their children get a good education to achieve upward mobility.

Men in this group are the most traditional in matters of clothing and grooming and appear most resistant to innovative fashions. The ad for Gillette M3POWER in Exhibit 14-9 is targeted on men from working- through upper-middle-class. It appeals to these

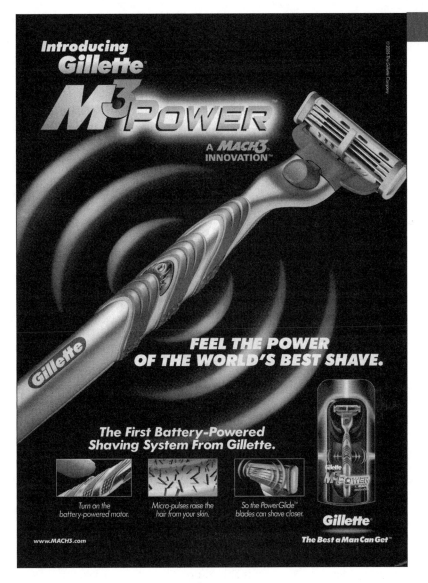

This M3POWER razor ad is targeting working-class through upper-middle-class men.

Source: Reprinted by permission of The Gillette Company.

men as a modern twist on the traditional way to shave. Also notice the three visuals in the ad explaining how the razor works. This is a direct appeal to the lower-class share of the target group who "want to know" such details. Working-class men see themselves as steadfast and reliable, earning decent livings for their families. They value manual adroitness and physical skills, and they make the most of their leisure time, with a high percentage participating in recreational sports. They are inclined to feel that life uses them up faster than it does males from other social strata.

14-3c Lifestyles

Lower-class women wake up earlier in the morning and feel they can get by with less sleep. A chronic dilemma of the working-class household is the conflict between the tendency to stay up to watch television and the need to rise earlier than those who keep normal office hours. Middle-class homemakers tend to manage their housework, to plan ahead, and to feel mastery over chores and their life schedules. Working-class women, by contrast, are more likely to use that old maxim "a woman's work is never done."

At higher status levels, more time is spent out of the home, and more hours are devoted to expressive activities such as reading, art, music, aerobics, or serving the community. Time-management patterns also vary by social class. Lower-middle-class people eat earlier and spend less time at the dinner table than do members of the upper-middle class. They also spend more time watching television.

Obviously, across classes, the types of sports and recreation activities vary widely, as do other interests and pastimes, reflecting lifestyle differences. Certainly, more extravagant lifestyles are not available to members of the lower social classes because they do not have the resources to pursue them.

Marketing Management—Implications and Actions

Understanding the U.S. social class system helps marketers:

- Identify consumer characteristics that result from class influences.
- Create products, services, and promotional appeals based on the attitudes, values, or lifestyles of targeted class members.

14-4 Social Class and Marketplace Behavior

Because of the many and varied influences it has on marketplace behavior, social class is a particularly useful means through which marketers can identify segments of consumers and target them. Class influences not just the products people buy but also the media through which they find out about them, the type of communications they respond to, their choice of outlets, and the manner in which they buy.

14-4a Influence on Media Use

F A Q

Is prime-time advertising aimed at a particular class? How about advertising during daytime or late-night talk shows?

Media are approached and used in different ways by different class groups.[20] Concerning print media, lower-class people are less likely to subscribe to newspapers than are members of the middle class. When they do subscribe, they tend to favor morning papers over evening editions when such choices are available. The reverse is true of the middle class. Choice of magazine is likely tied to education and reading ability, along with length and complexity of editorial content. Lower-middle-class readers identify with *Reader's Digest* and *Ladies Home Journal,* while those of the upper-middle class prefer *Time, Sports Illustrated, The New Yorker,* and *The Saturday Review.*[21] The image of *Reader's Digest,* offering condensed versions of longer works applicable to middle America, is right on target for the lower-middle class. *The New Yorker* and *The Saturday Review* are definitely more upscale in content and cultural positioning, appealing to college-educated professionals in the upper-middle class. Magazines appealing to the luxury market include *Departures, Travel + Leisure, Food & Wine, Architectural Digest,* and *Bon Appetit.*

Turning to the television media, members of the upper class and upper-middle class are more interested in current events and drama, whereas as one moves lower on the class scale soap operas and situation comedies are more popular.[22] Music preferences are most influenced by a person's age; however, social class differences have been found. A study across nine different types of radio programming found no differences among the upper and upper-middle class households. Middle and working class households also do not differ in listening behavior. It was found that the upper classes tuned in more to all news programs, and the dominant listening groups to country music were the middle and working classes. Only in the urban contemporary (Rap) style of music did the lower class stand out, with a share of households four times as large as any other social class group.[23] As might also be expected, lower-class families spend more time in front of the television set than their middle-class counterparts.[24] Lower-class consumers are more responsive to audiovisual forms of communication, possibly because of their lower educational backgrounds. The lower class is generally a more action-oriented and physical group; therefore, less time is spent reading print media. Reaching the lower-middle class and the lower classes is best done through television commercials.

14-4b Influence on Advertising Acceptance

The symbolic nature of advertising is important when considering its effect on different social classes. Lower-status consumers are more receptive to advertising that depicts activ-

ity, ongoing work and life, expressions of energy, and solutions to practical problems in daily life and social relationships. They also prefer advertising with a strong visual component.

Upper-middle-class people generally are more critical of advertising, suspicious of emotional appeals, and skeptical of claims. They tend to feel insulted by the straightforward and literal selling approaches aimed at lower-class groups. What seems to appeal to upper-middle-class tastes are advertisements that address consumers as individuals, that are witty, sophisticated, or stylish, and that offer objects and symbols related to status and self-expressive pursuits.[25] One way to properly target advertising on the right social class is to follow the GD approach mentioned earlier. The publishers of *Time* and *Newsweek* magazines have hundreds of regional editions of the same issue with ads that vary based upon the social class targets they are attempting to reach. The advertisement in Exhibit 14-10 is an example of typical appeals to perceptions of sophistication and style. What other aspects of this advertisement for the Ebel 1911 watch give clues to the targeted class?

14-4c Influence on Shopping and Choice Behavior

Shopping behavior and its link to social class are complex issues. Rather than explore it in depth here, we offer a few general observations that alert you to some of the patterns of behavior through which we can identify consumers from different class groups and so, as marketers, better target them. In general, lower-class women are the most "impulsive" about shopping and the least organized. They often shop in order to get out of the house and prefer retail stores where they can find easy credit and a friendly reception.[26]

Lower-middle-class women work harder at shopping, display anxiety about making decisions in the marketplace, and consider the entire process full of uncertainties. They are determined to find the "best buys" for their money and are more likely than other groups to comparison shop. Upper-middle-class women manage their shopping excursions more purposefully than do women of lower status. They gather more product information in advance, spend more time researching outlets, and cover a wider geographic territory in their shopping. They also shop more frequently than other groups, preferring stores with pleasant environments.[27]

Outlet Choice

Social class very much determines where people shop. Lower-class women often feel that they are punished for shopping in high-status stores. "The clerks treat you like a crumb," grumbled one shopper. After trying to attract the attention of a salesperson, another woman bitterly complained that she was "loftily" told, "We thought you were a clerk."[28] Although the same products and brands may appeal to members of different social classes, the places and the methods through which they feel comfortable purchasing them differ.

Department stores have distinct images, and consumers shop at stores that seem most appropriate to their social standing. Although a store may attract customers from more than one social class, once the consumer is in the store, shopping patterns differ among classes.[29] An upper-middle-class shopper may fight the crowds at a discount store for low-visibility products, such as home appliances. He or she will not, however, buy high-visibility products like jewelry there. Lower-status shoppers may find themselves in elite stores such as Neiman Marcus, Bloomingdale's, or Marshall Field's to buy gifts rather than to make routine purchases.

The image of a store can be shaped to reflect the customers it wishes to attract. One successful marketer of low-cost appliances in the New York area appeared in commercials wearing a hard hat, shouting that the "way-below retail" prices in his store were available "only to union members and their families." Note that stores with a lower-class image can be just as successful or more successful than those that cater to the elite. Wal-Mart, for example, proves that class appeal has nothing to do with profits! Yet lately the chain has been opening selected new stores at locations and with merchandise that appeal to the upper-middle class "smart shopper." Have you ever entered a retail store and had the feeling you were in the "wrong place"? Why did you feel this way? What did you do?

Use of Coupons

Upper-lower-class women are likely to respond to promotions offering coupons or other special inducements. Such appeals make them feel shrewd and economical. Lower-middle-class women may feel the same attraction but are more inclined to question their need for the product offered. These women wish to feel sensible about offers and promotions. Upper-middle-class women also tend to reject coupons more often, perhaps sensing their appeal to the lower classes. They also have difficulty in recognizing the promotional appeal as useful because the premium or savings is viewed as insignificant. Free trial product samples and in-store taste tests tend to work better, offering a direct benefit without hassle or requiring extra effort from this time-poor group.

Use of Credit Cards

In the past, members of the lower classes tended to use credit cards for installment buying while upper-class shoppers used them for convenience. Upper-class purchasers were inclined to use their cards for luxury items, travel, or restaurant meals, whereas lower-class users bought durables or essentials with them.[30] Today, we are seeing a broadening of the use of credit cards across class sectors. People now buy groceries and other items with credit cards. This will probably lead to more of the upper-middle and upper classes using cards for purchasing staple goods.

The introduction of dollar credits toward the purchase of new cars (the GM Credit Card) and, especially, cards that offer air miles based on the level of every purchase have widened the appeal and use of credit cards. This type of promotion influences the use of credit cards by the middle class in particular. New kinds of cards, such as "smart cards" and direct-debit cards, enable people from all social classes to use noncash transactions for an expanding array of goods and services.

Purchasing Hard Goods   People express class membership when they buy automobiles, furniture, and appliances. Members of the upper class prefer traditional home furnishings, while those with an eye toward upward mobility often select expensive contemporary furnishings.[31] Lower-class homemakers tend to express themselves through home appliances rather than through more typical self-expressive items such as clothing.[32] Marketers understand these situations and position their products accordingly through advertising.

Leisure Choices   Not surprisingly, choice of leisure activities varies with class membership. The following pursuits were generally engaged in less by people lower on the social class ladder than those higher up: aerobic exercise, health club participation, jogging, playing golf, swimming, playing tennis, weight lifting, going to the movies, subscribing to cable, visiting a museum, photography, barbecuing, and entertaining at home. In most instances the upper and upper-middle classes were similar and the middle and working classes were similar in participation levels. Members of the middle and working classes were similar to and higher than members of the other classes in frequency of going camping, fishing, and hunting.[33] Hence, goods and services that support the various classes in their chosen leisure pursuits must be positioned in the proper media and with the right creative approaches.

Time is also a factor in leisure preferences. Most activities enjoyed by middle- and upper-class people are less time-consuming than lower-class choices, so we see higher involvement in such activities as aerobics, going to the health club, swimming, and playing tennis by members of the middle and upper classes, whereas we noted earlier that camping, fishing, and hunting, more time-consuming pursuits, were more popular with middle and working class individuals.[34]

Two-Tier Social Class Marketing in the United States   In the United States, the upper-lower and lower-middle classes are no longer growing in numbers or purchasing power as they have traditionally. Since the early 1980s, the wealthiest fifth of the population has had income growth of 21 percent, while wages for the bottom 60 percent are almost unchanged. The 1990s saw a widening of the gap to a point only matched by that at the end of World War II. Hence, marketers are finding that the successful strategy is the high-low class approach known as "Tiffany/Wal-Mart." That is, go after the lower end of the social class ladder and the upper end.[35] Downscale denim jeans and upscale denim jeans are selling. At Gap's Banana Republic, jeans sell for $58; in Gap's Old Navy, the price is $22—and both types are moving. The $4 restaurant meal is doing well, as is the $50 meal. It's the $20 repast that's in trouble. Retailers Tiffany and Wal-Mart are doing well, while middle-of-the-road sellers such as J.C. Penney are having to work harder to keep up. Marketers are honing their skills to better serve one or both ends of the social class spectrum. The mass market group of upper-lower- and lower-middle-class customers is no longer the key segment to pursue.

Marketing Management—Implications and Actions

Understanding the relationship between social class and marketplace behavior helps marketers:

- Use the media most popular and the appeals most persuasive with targeted class groups.
- Match the type of outlet and the shopping process to the type of consumer targeted.

14-5 Reference Group Types and Influences

We all know from personal experience that influential people in our lives help us shape our buying decisions. This is particularly true for high-visibility products, such as the cars we drive, the clothes we wear, and the restaurants we choose. It is natural to feel that if we

**Reference Group and
Social Influence**

This exhibit summarizes the
connections between social
groups and consumer attitudes,
values, beliefs, and behavior.

Type of Group
• Membership
• Primary/Secondary
• Formal/Informal
• Aspirational
• Dissociative

Influence Types
• Role Setting
• Information Source
• Normative
• Self Value-Expressive

Socialization   Roles   Norms

Social Power
• Reward
• Coercive
• Expert
• Referrent

Price of Conformity   Rewards for Conformity

Consumer

Attitudes, Values, Beliefs, Behavior, Opinions

make poor choices, others will think less of us. Similarly, if we make good choices, we may earn their respect and even their envy. As we shall see, however, we are not always conscious of the social influences that affect our purchase decisions. They are often so subtle they go unnoticed.

No matter how little we say or even feel we care about what others think of our style of dress, our tastes in music, or the many other purchase choices we make, few—if any—of us are untouched by the influences of those around us. In the rest of this chapter, we shall see just how pervasive are the effects of the attitudes and opinions of others—our reference groups—on our marketplace behavior.

A **reference group** is the group whose perspective an individual takes on in forming values, beliefs, attitudes, opinions, and overt behaviors. Reference groups influence consumer behavior in two ways. First, they set levels of aspiration, offering cues as to what lifestyle and related purchasing patterns we should strive to achieve. Second, they help define the actual items/services considered acceptable for displaying those aspirations—the kind of housing, clothing, or car, for example, deemed appropriate for a member of the group.[36] Exhibit 14-11 provides an overview of reference group influences and the ways in which they affect behavior. This is a useful point of reference as you read the remainder of the chapter.

> **reference group** The group whose perspective an individual takes on in forming values, beliefs, attitudes, opinions, and overt behaviors.

14-5a Social Norms and Conformity

A **social norm** is any rule of behavior for meeting societal expectations. All members of a group must adhere to the *normative system* established for that group. To enforce normative systems, groups tend to exert *conformity pressures*, direct or indirect, on their members. Such pressures are actions taken to encourage or force members to act, think, and/or express themselves in certain ways. A college peer group may find one member's choice of clothing unacceptable and subject that member to ridicule until the accepted dress code is adopted. Or a church group whose tenets include a ban on the use of electricity may bring considerable pressure to bear on a member discovered using an electrical drill in the home of a nonmember. An example of the different ways people conform is touched on in CBite 14-3. Check it out.

> **social norm** Any rule of behavior for meeting societal (group) expectations.

CBite 14-3
Follow My Leader

Social psychologists have empirically proven the existence of conformity pressure. In one study, members of small groups were asked to identify the direction of movement of a light in a dark room. While the light did not, in fact, move at all, because of conformity pressure, group members shared the same perception of movement. In a second study, individual subjects who were members of small groups were asked to compare lengths of various lines. Other members of the group attempted to influence their judgments by calling out wrong answers. Even when answers were obviously in error, individual subjects would accept the group judgments and call out the wrong answers themselves.

Sources: Muzafer Sherif, "Group Influences upon the Formation of Norms and Attitudes," in Eleanor Maccoby, ed., *Readings in Social Psychology* (New York: Holt, Rinehart and Winston, 1958), pp. 219–232; Solomon E. Asch, "Effects of Group Pressure upon the Modification and Distortion of Judgments," in Maccoby, *Social Psychology*, pp. 174–183.

Such conformity pressure is familiar to us all. Those who seem to feel the most pressure to conform are newcomers to a group who are attempting to establish themselves as legitimate members. Those who fill group leadership roles also are more prone to conform as a way of reinforcing group standards. If a person has recently joined a professional club on campus and the members all play softball on Saturday mornings, he or she will typically go out and buy a team hat and show up at each game. Group leaders will likely attend or participate every week—and wear a team hat. Group members who are in neither of these camps have fewer reasons to comply, and their behavior is more deviant. In general, the more important a group is in our lives, the greater our desire to accept and conform to its norms.

What is going on here is simply expressed by **Homan's equation**.[37] The difference between the price we pay for conformity (loss of freedoms, time commitment, financial commitment, etc.) and the rewards obtained for doing so (levels of acceptance, advancement within the group, prestige gained, etc.) determines for each of us whether we will conform to group expectations and to what extent. For example, if being accepted by the group you work with on your new job is really important to you, and the group goes to a certain restaurant after work on Fridays, you go too. You go even if you'd rather go home, kick off your shoes, grab some Chinese take-out food, and watch a video. You see the trade-off as worthwhile.

Aware of the desire to conform, marketers typically offer products that are a visible statement of that conformity. Moreover, by showing their products within a group setting and being used by people typical of the group, advertising plays on the consumer's desire to conform.

Homan's equation
The difference between the price we pay for conformity (loss of freedoms, time commitment, financial commitment, etc.) and the rewards obtained for doing so (levels of acceptance, advancement within the group, prestige gained, etc.). This determines for each of us whether we will conform to group expectations and to what extent.

14-5b Reference Group Types

Reference groups are classed as primary or secondary. A **primary reference group** is one with which the individual has frequent face-to-face contact and in which members are close-knit. Families, households, study groups, work teams, roommates, and fishing pals are all primary groups.[38] Members exert considerable influence on each other, including marketplace influence, simply because they are significant in each other's lives. Suppose you have a small group of friends with whom you bicycle five times a week. You are thinking about buying a new racing bike, and three members of your group think a Schwinn is the best choice. To strengthen your position in the group, you feel compelled to buy that brand.

A **secondary reference group** is one in which interaction with other members is less frequent. Professional organizations, church congregations, large social clubs, and alumni associations are examples. The power to influence is far less than with primary groups and,

primary reference group
The group with which the individual has frequent face-to-face contact and in which members are close-knit.

secondary reference group
The group in which interaction with other members is less frequent than in a primary group situation.

CBite 14-4
Celebrity Cliques

The "Brat Pack," of the 1980s was a group of Hollywood actors at the beginning of their careers who were constantly together in the spotlight. It included Emilio Estevez, Anthony Michael Hall, Rob Lowe, Andrew McCarthy, Demi Moore, Judd Nelson, Molly Ringwald, and Ally Sheedy. Today this clique is no longer together, and a number of them have gone on to enjoy great film careers. More recently, another celebrity clique surrounding Leo DiCaprio was formed. This "posse," as they were known, included Tobey Maguire, Lukas Haas, and R. D. Robb, among others. As informal as these groups sound, what do you think were the requirements for membership? What other celebrity cliques do you know of?

---

therefore, the desire to buy items such as sweatshirts or caps that signify membership is much weaker. Secondary groups are often made up, however, of several smaller primary groups. Although you may not want to buy a keepsake photograph taken at a college alumni reunion, you may do so if you attend with your roommates who are also in the photograph.

Reference groups are also either formal or informal. A **formal group** is one in which there is some sort of structure and, in some cases, for which there are specific membership requirements. To join a civic club you may have to make a formal application, be voted in, and pay dues. To join a professional club, you may have to meet educational requirements. If the club runs regularly scheduled luncheons each month, you are likely to be obligated to attend, particularly if the club is both formal and primary. **Informal groups** are those that have no special membership or attendance requirements other than common interests. Walking clubs, reading groups, and mother-and-toddler play groups are typical examples. Although they may be primary, the groups do not have rigid schedules or rules. Take a look at CBite 14-4 for examples of Hollywood informal groups.

The reference groups we have looked at so far—primary, secondary, formal, and informal—are all membership groups. A **membership group** is one to which a person currently belongs. A group that a person would like to be part of, but to which she or he does not currently or may never belong is known as an **aspirational group.** Here, individuals may attempt to emulate group members by taking on the "cloak of membership," that is, by dressing, acting, and even thinking the way they perceive members do. Classifying consumers according to aspirational groups allows marketers to create special appeals. Think of the products or services endorsed by athletic or entertainment superstars. Such products are positioned to appeal to people who want to be like their hero.

Some reference groups are dissociative. **Dissociative groups** are those that individuals avoid or deny connections with. Examples would include a political party with which a person would never wish to be connected, an ethnic group, the Neo-Nazi party, or the "skinheads." Hence, clothing, music, and entertainment options tied to the dissociative group are avoided. Marketers should take care to avoid identification of their products with groups considered dissociative among target audiences.

14-5c Reference Group Influences

There are several ways of viewing reference group influence. Let's take a detailed look at the most important ones.

Reference Groups as Part of the Socialization Process
As we saw in Chapter 12 (section 12-1c, "Culture Is Learned/Shared"), it is through the process of socialization that we learn the norms, appropriate behavior patterns, and values of a society or of a group within it. As part of a reference group, we may be socialized by observing "correct" group behavior and emulating it. Some groups formally teach new members about these things. As part of a reference group, we may be the ones to pass on appropriate role behav-

---

formal group A group in which there is some sort of structure, and in some cases, for which there are specific membership requirements.

informal group A group in which there are no special membership or attendance requirements other than common interests.

membership group The group to which a person currently belongs.

aspirational group A group that a person would like to be part of but to which he or she does not currently or may never belong.

dissociative group A group that individuals avoid or deny connections with.

ior and values. Often, the latter are reflected in purchase choices, and marketers attempt to position their products and services appropriately. Retailers, for example, may advertise the type of shoes most popular with college students as a means of showing freshmen the styles that will help them fit in on campus, thus accelerating socialization. It is among adolescents that reference groups exert the strongest socializing influence, affecting a number of choices of "visible" products such as ice skates, snow skis, and high-performance bicycles.[39]

Reference Groups as Setters of Roles   Roles are behavior patterns that people are expected to carry out based on the positions they hold within groups. Members of the group expect certain behaviors and feel the need to conform to them. A woman who carries out the role of president of a local charity may oversee the organization of various activities, participate as a speaker at fund-raising events, and interact with sponsors at dinner parties and on outings. At the same time, as a family member, she may perform the role of parent, nurturing, supporting, and disciplining her children. Within the family, she is also wife, sister, and daughter, and plays those roles accordingly. In other areas of her life, she is an environmental activist and chairperson of her local college alumni association chapter. In each case, both she and other members of the groups in which she participates have expectations about what she should do. It is up to her to decide her level of conformity.

By understanding reference group membership in terms of roles set and played, marketers can offer goods and services to support those roles. Continuing with the same example, the woman is likely to respond well to advertisements for day planners or calendars that will help her keep track of appointments. As a parent and caregiver, she may be in the market for a minivan to ferry her children to school and to extracurricular activities and to take her parents to doctors' appointments.

Sometimes roles are in conflict, with each reference group having a different set of behavior expectations. In these cases, the dominance of the reference group and the individual's self-concept determine behavior. It is likely that Homan's equation is at work.

Reference Groups as Information Sources   When a reference group is used as an information source, individuals obtain and use all types of information from group members. Information is gathered verbally or in writing from the group or by direct demonstration, instruction, or observation of group members. Members become authoritative sources for all kinds of information. Obviously, some members rely more heavily than others on the information available. If the source is seen as trustworthy and the information itself is relevant to the problem at hand and is perceived as reliable, it is a more dominant influence. Also, one member of the group, the leader, for example, may be perceived as a more reliable source than others and will be, therefore, more influential. Suppose a new member of a cycling club asks questions about the best equipment and accessories to buy. Tim, a particularly authoritative or knowledgeable member, will likely be the most influential information source.

Information may be disseminated within the reference group in several ways. The group may pass on information to all members through a newsletter or group meeting, for example. An individual member may request information from co-members or authoritative members. Information may also be transmitted among members unintentionally or informally.

Reference Groups as Normative Influences   We noted earlier that groups have normative systems. Members of the group are influenced by the system. Individuals act in ways that will meet the normative system expectations of the group. The reward for this conforming behavior is increased group acceptance. If norms are not accepted or acted on, rewards may be withheld or sanctions imposed.

Consider the clothing choices of teenage and even preteen children in the United States, where there is great emphasis on choosing acceptable brands, no matter what the expense. Young people who do not or cannot afford to wear the brands considered correct by their peer groups are often treated adversely. This type of peer pressure has created serious problems in the public school system that mixes students from a wide variety of socioeconomic backgrounds. Students from disadvantaged families are expected to "measure up," causing hardship in school and even at home, where pressure is exerted on parents to provide costly clothing, shoes, and accessories.

A person may also be part of an on-campus religious or community action group. The normative system of values and behaviors may be such that members become more honest and caring in their dealings with all people and are rewarded with the support of other group members.

Reference Groups as an Expression of Self-Value   Reference groups can also draw people to them because these organizations have the values, beliefs, attitudes, images, and lifestyles that match. Individuals tend to join groups whose characteristics are in line with their own or groups with whom they wish to become more identified.

Suppose members of a reference group are involved in the community, work on Habitat for Humanity projects, give generously to causes for the homeless, drive economical cars, shop in lower-price-point clothing stores, and attend church regularly. They feel they are helping the community and managing their own resources responsibly. You join such a group because that's the way you are. Your self-image matches those of the others. Members of another group focus on developing professional skills, attitudes, and behaviors. Guest speakers are brought in and field trips are taken regularly so members can gain a better understanding of the business world. They learn how to "dress for success," construct a résumé, and interview well. On Friday nights, members get together informally for fun, darts, and pizza. These are "your kind of people," so you become an active member.

By contrasting these two groups in terms of values, beliefs, attitudes, self-image, and lifestyle, we gain a very clear picture of the way in which membership of reference groups serves as an expression of the self. Products and services are used by people in reference groups to express "who they are." Marketers understand this and position products against these targets, showing use in typical reference group situations.

Do you think that two people can be a reference group? What about best friends? Take a look at CBite 14-5 and then answer.

14-5d   Conformity Pressure and Marketplace Behavior

Conforming behavior is expected to some degree in all social groups. But how do we discover what a group's normative system is? How are we encouraged to conform to it? Many

---

CBite 14-5

Best Friends—Is This a Viable Reference Group Market Segment?

Two young women met in 1990 when they were on the swim team in high school. They both attended the same university, where they met two guys who were also best friends. Both couples married and now live just a few miles from each other in the suburbs of a big city. They see each other at least once a week and talk on the phone even more often. This type of a friendship is not so rare. A recent survey done by Market Facts for *American Demographics* showed that the typical American has known his or her best friend for 14 years, and more than half of us (55 percent) still give our best friend a call at least once a week. Best friends are often near in age and in similar lifecycle stages (see Chapter 15); less than half are of similar financial condition. How do they stay in touch? Almost a quarter (23 percent) call their best friend on a daily basis. Women are more likely to do this than men (27 percent to 20 percent), and young adults more likely than older folks to stay in touch by phone. Young adults are also more likely to email or instant message their friends. Interestingly, the majority of Americans (91 percent) say they would go on vacation with their best friend.

What products or services do marketers offer today that are targeted on best friends? What are some others that could be offered? Do you think that pursuing best friends as a segment can work?

Source: Rebecca Gardyn, "Friends Forever," *American Demographics* (October 2002), pp. 12–13. Copyright © 2002 Crain Communications, Inc. Reprinted with permission.

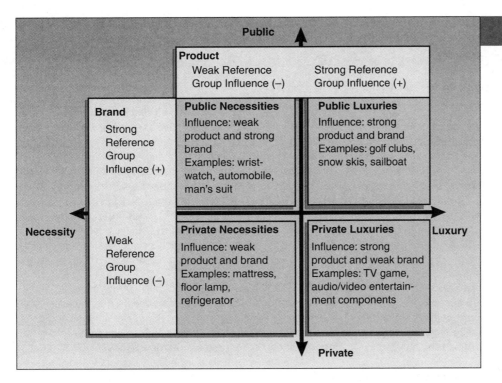

Ex h i b i t **14-12**

Group Influence, Product Visibility, and Level of Necessity

The exhibit shows the relationship between group influence and four types of products: visible and essential, private and essential, visible and nonessential, and private and nonessential.

Source: From "Reference Group Influence on Product and Brand Purchase Decisions" by William O. Bearden and Michael J. Etzel in *Journal of Consumer Research*, Vol. 9, No. 2, September 1982, p. 185. Copyright © 1982. Reprinted by permission of The University of Chicago Press.

norms are both observed and adopted passively, with no conscious effort to either learn or teach them. Group interaction and discussion is the common active means through which norms are communicated. Interaction is also more influential in effecting attitude change than is passive learning.[40] This is evident in the effectiveness of infomercials as a form of persuasive communication. These program-length television commercials usually combine dissemination of detailed product information with a sales pitch. Infomercials are designed to sell goods and services through product presentation, opinions offered by an expert, and, most importantly, interviews with a group of satisfied customers—a reference group—telling of their positive experiences with the product. If the potential customer sees himself or herself as a group fit, he or she is more likely to respond positively to the offer.

The influence of reference groups on marketplace decisions varies. Overall, groups tend to be more influential on product decisions than they are on either brand or outlet choices.[41] The type of product also has a bearing on the extent to which consumers are subject to conformity pressure when purchasing it. Purchases of such items as cars, cigarettes, and aftershave lotion are influenced by conformity pressure.[42]

It has been suggested that reference group influence on both product and brand decisions is dependent upon two types of *conspicuousness*. The first is conspicuousness based on exclusivity, which primarily affects product decisions. For example, bikers are noted for black leather jackets. You are a biker, so you own one. The second is conspicuousness associated with the individual, primarily affecting brand decisions. All of your close friends have running shoes, yet each chooses his or her personal brand. As an expression of your "fit" with the group, you have running shoes. The brand you wear is New Balance, your "allowed" personal expression. Also, as we see in Exhibit 14-12, group influence on choice depends upon whether a product is privately or publicly consumed (its *visibility*) and whether it is classified as a necessary or a luxury (its *level of necessity*). Group influence is greatest for products and brands that are luxuries and highly visible. Golf clubs are a good example. Here, the consumer generally feels that the brand chosen and the price paid reflect commitment to the group with whom the game is played. At the opposite end of the scale, nonvisible, nonluxury purchases such as bed mattresses are barely subject to group influence at all.

Pressure to conform can backfire. Individuals may react against the pressure they feel is being exerted on them, making purchase decisions that assert their individuality or that

Marketplace 14-5

What to Do If You Don't Want to Follow the Crowd

Young adults in college feel a lot of pressure to fit in. Most feel lost if they have little social contact with fellow students. One way to have social contact is to follow the crowd—as long as it's the "right" crowd. However, students sometimes find themselves with a group of student "friends" who expect them to conform to beliefs, values, and/or behaviors that they don't feel good about. So what can be done to deal with these situations?

As a college student, there are simple questions you can ask yourself and certain things you can do to have good friends and stay on the path you wish to follow. It's not always easy to take a stand for yourself, but who else is going to do it for you? Remember, you're at school to become a shepherd, not a sheep—to become a leader not a follower. To put it another way, you should be seeking to become a star that generates light on your own, rather than a moon or planet that rotates about others and only reflects their light.

Are your friends helping you to progress as a person, providing positive reinforcement in your academic, social, professional, and other parts of your life? Do they accept you as you are? If not, you're with the wrong group.

Find another group or groups to be a part of. Develop a group of friends who make you feel comfortable and who bring positive light into your life. You might start by finding just one friend who is "on the same page" as you are. This may be someone in a class who first becomes a study mate and then becomes more.

But, how do you deal with situations when they arise? One way is to have ready answers for negative or uncomfortable questions or situations with which you might be faced. When you are asked to join in, have a good reply. Practice such replies in advance so you won't get caught off-guard. Think of the most likely situations and be prepared to deal with them. By the way, if you refuse to do something or simply say "no" to your peers, your statements must be clear and direct and given with conviction. Don't be "wishy-washy." Don't apologize for refusing to act. Remember—your position is right for you, regardless of what others say or feel about it. It's also important to have some positive comment to clarify your position. For example, "No, I don't care for another drink, I'm my own designated driver."

You should work on feeling good about yourself. Make a list of your good qualities and look it over frequently, especially when things around you are a bit dark. After all, you should be your own best friend. This will make it easier for you to be a good friend to others and to find friends for yourself.

Take a stand with your friends and others when they are put in situations they are trying to avoid. This will give them the sense of support they need to act. Also, asking a lot of "why" questions of those trying to move you or someone else in the wrong direction often puts you into a more powerful position in the exchange.

The keys in trying to avoid "caving in" to the wrong kind of peer pressure are: (1) having a strong sense of your own personal worth, (2) knowing the principles that drive your life so you know what is right or wrong for you, and (3) being prepared in advance so that taking action and speaking out will be easier. Having a "buddy" who will stand with you is also a great help.

---

are purposely rebellious. The young mother who is told repeatedly that using cloth diapers will make her a better mother rejects them in favor of disposables. A college baseball player whose teammates try to pressure him into wearing a team cap off the field wears a cowboy hat in defiance. Do you find yourself having problems "fighting" against peer pressures to think and act certain ways? Look at Marketplace 14-5 for some great suggestions.

14-6 Social Power

Psychologists have viewed the influence that social groups exert in the lives of members in terms of various forms of power, specifically power of reward, coercive power, expert power, and referent power.[43]

14-6a Power of Reward

Similar to normative influence, *power of reward* is tied to the anticipation of praise, approval, public recognition, status, special privileges, and even monetary gain from a peer group. The greater the ability of the group to provide desired rewards, the greater the influence on behavior, beliefs, and values of members. It is important, however, that rewards are desirable. Only if rewards such as respect and status matter to us do we modify our behavior—drive a certain model car or dress in a certain style—in order to gain them.

14-6b Coercive Power

Rather than a reward for good behavior, *coercive power* is the means through which a reference group may discourage unacceptable behavior or failure to conform. Unless members express certain values, for example, they risk disapproval, ostracism, or even ejection from the group. A good example of coercive power at work in the marketplace is the selling of goods through "product parties," at which the host or hostess, a company representative, demonstrates and sells goods to friends and acquaintances, the peer group. This type of selling works based on coercive power—guests feel obliged to make at least one purchase, whether it is needed or not—in order to avoid disappointing the host or feeling ill at ease as other group members buy. Further, knowing that the host is compensated depending upon the volume sold at the party, guests are under an even greater sense of obligation or coercion to buy.

14-6c Expert Power

Individual members within a social group may exert *expert power* over others based upon the experience or knowledge they possess. This type of informational power attracts new members and keeps them within the group. Cherise joins a coin-collecting club explicitly to learn more about early Roman coins. She selects the club because she knows that one of the members is an expert in the field. She begins to assemble her own collection and increasingly relies on this person for advice. She continues as a member as long as that help is available and she still appreciates it. Tran is a member of an informal group of business associates. He finds out that another member, Lee, is an expert on electronic, hand-held planners. Tran seeks out opportunities to meet with the group and talk to Lee in order to ask for advice. Tran buys the planner Lee recommended. He then does not meet as often because the expert power is no longer needed.

14-6d Referent Power

The closer the match between the individual's beliefs, values, attitudes, behavior, and self-image and those of the reference group, the greater the *referent power* of the group. Referent power is more pervasive when the cognitive structure of the individual is similar to the cognitive structure of the group, resulting in stronger identification with the members of the group. Desire to belong also is stronger. Referent power was explored extensively earlier in the chapter, in Section 14-5c, which discussed self-value expression, a similar concept.

Marketing Management—Implications and Actions

Understanding reference group influence helps marketers:

- Identify the reference groups most likely to influence targeted consumers and the type of pressure they are likely to exert.
- Appeal to consumers on the basis of their identification with or desire to be associated with respected social groups.
- Identify the type of power groups have over members or aspiring members.

Chapter Spotlights

1. Social class and class membership. Social class is a status hierarchy by which groups and individuals are classified on the basis of esteem and prestige. The basic unit of a social class is the family or household. Five factors that are used singly or in combination to determine a person's social class are occupation, sources of income, possessions, associations or interactions with others, and level of influence. The three methods of assigning individuals to social classes are: the reputational, the subjective, and the objective approaches.

2. Social class in the United States. The majority of the U.S. population can be divided into five class categories: upper, upper-middle, lower-middle, upper-lower, and lower-lower. Minority populations develop their own class structures, especially if excluded from the majority structure. The quality market is composed of the lower-upper class and the upper-middle class. The mass market is a combination of the lower-middle and upper-lower classes.

3. Values, attitudes, and lifestyles across social classes. Membership in social classes can be recognized through the values, attitudes, self-perceptions, and lifestyles of individuals and the extent to which these match class groups. Tied to class, each of these influences purchase decisions and purchase behavior.

4. Social class and marketplace behavior. Social class influences all marketplace behavior, from product and brand choices to spending patterns to outlet choice to symbolic consumption. Marketers also find class an effective media selection aid. Acceptance of advertising varies from class to class, with clear distinctions in the type and style of advertisement effective for each class group. In terms of shopping behavior, consumers from different social classes make different decisions on products purchased, as well as manner of shopping, use of coupons, and use of credit cards.

5. Reference group types and influences. Groups exert various types of direct or indirect pressure to get members to conform to expected behaviors, values, attitudes, and lifestyles. Reference groups can be viewed as part of the socialization process, as setters of roles, sources of information, normative influences, and reflectors of self-value. These reference groups may be primary, where there is frequent face-to-face contact, or secondary, where contact is limited. They can be formal, with set structures, practices, and membership requirements, or informal. Reference groups may also be aspirational, attracting individuals who wish to emulate members, or dissociative, groups which individuals avoid.

6. Social power. There are four types of social power that influence individual behavior, values, attitudes, lifestyles, and, of course, purchase decisions. These are power of reward, coercive power, expert power, and referent power.

Key Terms

aspirational group (p. 460)
class consciousness (p. 442)
dissociative group (p. 460)
formal group (p. 460)
Homan's equation (p. 459)

informal group (p. 460)
mass market (p. 449)
membership group (p. 460)
primary reference group (p. 459)
quality market (p. 447)

reference group (p. 458)
secondary reference group (p. 459)
social class (p. 437)
social norm (p. 458)
underclass (p. 449)

Review Questions

Note: You can find the correct answers to these questions by taking the quiz and then submitting your answers in the Online Edition. The program will automatically score your submission. If you miss a question, the program will provide the correct answer, a rationale for the answer, and the section number in the chapter where the topic is discussed.

1. Occupation largely dictates other signs of
   a. social unrest.
   b. equality.
   c. lifestyles.
   d. class membership.

2. Consumption choices, driven by the resulting _____, are a particularly useful indicator of social class.
   a. attitude
   b. lifestyle
   c. behavior
   d. interests

3. Salespeople, clerical workers, supervisors, and the owners of small retail stores typically belong to the _____ class.
   a. upper
   b. lower-upper
   c. upper-middle
   d. lower-middle

4. The _____ class is the most populous in America today.
   a. upper-lower
   b. upper-middle
   c. middle-lower
   d. lower-middle

5. _____ is probably the best indicator of social class.
   a. Income
   b. Lifestyle
   c. Stage in the life cycle
   d. AIO

6. Which class watches more television than the middle class?
   a. lower class
   b. upper class
   c. upper-middle class
   d. lower-middle class

7. Shopping behavior and its link to social class are_____ issues.
   a. simple
   b. predictable
   c. complex
   d. not priority

8. A reference group
  a. sets the levels of aspiration.
  b. helps define acceptable products/services to buy.
  c. is too complex for the scope of this discussion.
  d. both *a* and *b*.

9. When individuals within a social group can exert power over others based upon the experience or knowledge they possess, we say they have _____ power.
  a. reward
  b. coercive
  c. expert
  d. referent

10. Only if rewards matter to us do we _____ our behavior to conform.
  a. think about
  b. modify
  c. continue
  d. seek others' approval of

Team Talk

1. Identify three occupations you feel are of high social prestige, three of average prestige, and three of low prestige. Explain why each one falls in the category selected. List all nine in rank order, and compare the list with other team members. Discuss differences and similarities.

2. In terms of the five-class system, what is your social class? To what class do your parents belong? Is there a difference between your parents' social class and yours? If so, why?

3. What is happening to the social class structure in the United States? Support your observations.

4. Consider the way your parents live. How do you think their social class affects their spending patterns for food, shelter, and clothing? Give specific examples of spending in these three areas. Why do you consider these selections as indicators of the social class of your parents?

5. Are your print media (newspaper and magazine) choices in line with your social class? Why or why not?

6. For which product categories do you think social class works well as a method of marketing segmentation? Identify three goods and three service categories, and explain your choices.

7. Identify and describe a reference group in your life that has strong influence on you. How does the group influence you in general? How does the group influence your behavior as a consumer?

8. Is there a reference group to which you belong even though you don't agree with some of its norms? Describe the situation and your reasons for conforming.

9. Have you recently been subject to any of the four forms of social power presented in this chapter when making a purchase? What type of social power influenced you? Describe its effect on your choice.

Workshops

Research Workshop

Background

Minority subcultures often develop their own social class systems or continue to follow the class structure of their native land. The objectives of this workshop are to determine the social class structure of a minority population group and to suggest marketing-mix actions for targeting a social class within the group.

Methodology

Interview five members of a minority group. Ask them to describe the class system within their subculture, identifying how many classes there are and describing typical members. Solicit a general description of the transportation, leisure activities, home appliances, and restaurant choices associated with each class.

To the Marketplace

Based on what you have learned, choose any one of the social classes that you find and discuss the marketing mix you would recommend for one product from the four categories discussed in the interviews.

Creative Workshop

Background

Marketers use reference group influence strategy to segment markets and position products. The objectives of this workshop are to analyze appeals to group influences and develop a checklist for producing new, on-target advertisements.

Methodology

Select four magazine advertisements for products in the same category that you feel focus on reference group influences. Identify characteristics that lead you to believe they have a reference group appeal.

To the Marketplace

Organize your observations and provide a Creative Characteristics Checklist that can be used by advertisers to target the reference group selected.

Managerial Workshop

Background

Members of the upper-middle class constitute part of what is called the quality market. The objectives of this workshop are to choose a product category appropriate to upper-middle-class consumers and develop a catalog concept for it.

Methodology

Choose a product category popular with the upper-middle class. Collect a number of catalogs appropriate to the class. Analyze them in terms of writing styles, photography, paper stock, cover, type, use of models, number of products per page, and use of color. What do all of these factors say to you about good catalog design?

To the Marketplace

Outline a catalog development strategy for the product category selected that takes into account the factors you have identified.

Notes

1. Joseph A. Kahl, *The American Class Structure* (New York: Holt, Rinehart and Winston, 1967).
2. Linda P. Morton, "Upper or Elite Class," *Public Relations Quarterly*, Vol. 49 (Winter 2004), pp. 30–32.
3. Sidney J. Levy, "Social Class and Consumer Behavior," in John A. Howard and Lynn E. Ostlund, eds., *Buyer Behavior* (New York: Knopf, 1973).
4. Kahl, *The American Class Structure*.
5. W. Lloyd Warner, as cited in Kahl, *The American Class Structure*.
6. Arun K. Jain, "A Method for Investigating and Representing Implicit Class Theory," *Journal of Consumer Research*, Vol. 2 (June 1974), p. 53; Richard Centers, *The Psychology of Social Classes* (Princeton, NJ: Princeton University Press, 1949).
7. W. Lloyd Warner, Marchia Meeker, and Kenneth Eels, *Social Class in America* (Chicago, IL: Social Science Research Associates, 1949); A. B. Hollingshead, *Elmtown's Youth* (New York: John Wiley and Sons, 1949); James M. Carman, *The Application of Social Class in Market Segmentation* (Berkeley, CA: Institute of Business and Economic Research, 1965); Richard P. Coleman, "The Continuing Significance of Social Class on Marketing," *Journal of Consumer Research*, Vol. 10 (December 1983), pp. 267–277; Louis V. Dominguez and Albert L. Page, "Stratification in Consumer Behavior: A Reexamination," *Journal of the Academy of Marketing Science*, Vol. 9 (Summer 1981), pp. 250–271.
8. Eugene Sivadas, George Mathew, and David Curry, "A Preliminary Examination of the Continuing Significance of Social Class to Marketing: A Geodemographic Replication," *Journal of Consumer Marketing*, Vol. 14, No. 6 (1997), pp. 463–479.
9. Ibid.
10. W. Lloyd Warner et al., *Social Class in America*.
11. Harold M. Hodges, "Peninsula People: Social Stratification in a Metropolitan Complex," in W. Clayton Lang, ed., *Permanence and Change in Social Class* (Cambridge, MA: Schenkman, 1968); *Hodges, Underdogs and Middle Americans*, 2nd ed. (Morningside, NJ: General Learning Press, 1976).
12. Linda P. Morton, "Upper or Elite Class."
13. Ibid.
14. Rebecca Gardyn, "Oh, The Good Life," *American Demographics*, (November 2002), pp. 31–34.
15. "Hot Buttons in a Chilly Economy," *Advertising Age*, March 11, 2002, p. S-2.
16. "Rich folks like bargains, too, Wal-Mart marketers find," *The Roanoke Times*, February 24, 2002, p. A12.
17. Richard P. Coleman and Bernice L. Neugarten, *Social Status in the City* (San Francisco: Jossey-Bass, 1971).
18. Marieke K. de Mooij and Warren Keegan, *Advertising Worldwide* (Englewood Cliffs, NJ: Prentice-Hall, 1991), p. 96.
19. James E. Fisher, "Social Class and Consumer Behavior: The Relevance of Class and Status," in Melanie Wallendorf and Peter Anderson, eds., *Advances in Consumer Research*, Vol. 14 (Provo, UT: Association for Consumer Research, 1987), pp. 492–496.
20. Levy, "Social Class and Consumer Behavior."
21. Hodges, "Peninsula People."
22. Sivadas et al., "A Preliminary Examination of the Continuing Significance of Social Class."
23. Ibid.
24. Levy, "Social Class and Consumer Behavior."
25. Ibid.
26. Ibid.
27. S. Dawson, B. Stern, and T. Gillpatrick, "An Empirical Update and Extension of Patronage Behavior across the Social Class Hierarchy," in Marvin E. Goldberg, Gerald Gorn, and Richard W. Pollay, eds., *Advances in Consumer Research*, Vol. 17 (Provo, UT: Association for Consumer Research, 1990), pp. 833–838.
28. Pierre Martineau, "Social Classes and Spending Behavior," *Journal of Marketing*, Vol. 23 (October 1958), pp. 121–130.
29. V. Kanti Prasad, "Socioeconomic Product Risk and Patronage Preferences of Retail Shoppers," *Journal of Marketing*, Vol. 39 (July 1975), pp. 42–47.
30. John W. Slocum, Jr. and H. Lee Meadow, "Social Class and Income as Indicators of Consumer Credit Behavior," *Journal of Marketing*, Vol. 34 (April 1970), pp. 69–74.
31. Edward O. Laumann and James S. House, "Living Room Styles: The Patterning of Material Artifacts in a Modern Urban Community," *Sociology and Social Research*, Vol. 54, No. 3 (April 1970), pp. 321–342.
32. Montrose S. Sommers, "The Use of Product Symbolism to Differentiate Social Strata," *University of Houston Business Review*, Vol. 11 (Fall 1964), pp. 1–102.
33. Sivadas et al., "A Preliminary Examination of the Continuing Influence of Social Class."
34. Ibid.
35. David Leonhardt, "Two-Tier Marketing," *Business Week* (March 17, 1997), pp. 82–87.
36. Francis S. Bourne, "Group Influence in Marketing and Public Relations," in Resis Likert and Samuel P. Hayes, eds., *Some Applications of Behavioral Research* (Paris: UNESCO, 1957).
37. George Homans, *The Human Group* (New York: Harcourt, Brace and World, 1950).
38. Ibid.
39. Scott Ward, "Consumer Socialization," in Harold H. Kassarjian and Thomas S. Robertson, eds., *Perspectives in Consumer Behavior* (Glenview, IL: Scott, Foresman and Co., 1981), pp. 380–396; Gwen Rae Bachmann, Deborah Roedder John, and Akshay R. Rao, "Children's Susceptibility to Peer Group Pressure: An Exploratory Investigation," in Leigh McAlister and Michael L. Rothschild, eds., *Advances in Consumer Research*, Vol. 20 (Provo, UT: Association for Consumer Research, 1992), pp. 463–468.
40. Kurt Lewin, "Group Decision and Social Change," in Eleanor Maccoby, ed., *Readings in Social Psychology* (New York: Holt, Rinehart and Winston, 1958), pp. 197–211.
41. William Whyte, "The Web of Words of Mouth," *Fortune* (November 1954), pp. 140–143; James E. Stafford, "Effects of Group Influence on Consumer Brand Preferences," *Journal of Marketing Research*, Vol. 3 (February 1966), pp. 68–75.
42. Robert E. Witt, "Informal Social Group Influence on Consumer Brand Choice," *Journal of Marketing Research*, Vol. 7 (November 1970).
43. John R. French and Bertram Raven, "The Bases of Social Power," in D. Cartwright, ed., *Studies in Social Power* (Ann Arbor, MI: Institute for Social Research, 1959), pp. 150–167.

Household and Family Influences

Sean, a new Beta Mu pledge, is in charge of a committee evaluating new food service providers for the fraternity house. He realizes that it's impossible to make everyone happy. Four guys are on vegetarian diets; one keeps strictly kosher; the athletes want high-protein diets; and everybody wants a different schedule of meals. On top of that, the budget is really tight, and Jesse keeps mentioning his aunt who wants to start a catering business. Then Sean's mother calls. Unable to stop himself, he vents his frustration over the food service decision:

"Well," she says, "it sounds like last year's vacation."

"Mom, it's not like that at all."

"If I remember correctly, you wanted to go backpacking in Montana; your sister was screaming for Disney World; your father wanted to be near the ocean and a golf course; and I kept saying, 'As long as there are crafts nearby, I'm fine.'"

"And we ended up going to the Wisconsin Dells."

"Right. Don't let that happen to you. Pick the one that makes the most of your fraternity brothers happy. I'm sure you can negotiate with the companies to get a better deal for the house."

"I'm not so sure. We may be dining in the Dells before I get through with this decision."

Families and other household units purchase widely different products to meet widely different needs. There is, however, an important similarity in their consumption patterns—they buy as groups, not as individuals. In this chapter, we will explore the mechanisms of group purchasing.

Like individual consumers, families and households follow a decision-making process that takes them through the five stages we have examined in part 2 of the text—problem solving, information search, alternative evaluation, choice, and post-purchase evaluation. Because more than one person is involved in the process, however, the dynamics of decision making are complicated by the different roles of each member of the group at each stage of the decision process. Also, their personalities, lifestyles, behavior patterns, and relationships with each other all influence the process and the final outcome. By understanding family and household consumer behavior, marketers are better equipped to target these groups and to facilitate decision making.

15-1 The Household as a Consumption Unit

In the past several decades, the family as an institution has been changing rapidly, and marketers have struggled to keep up. The supposedly "typical" family—complete with a working father, a homemaking mother, a minivan, a dog, and 2.3 children—has been on the wane in America. Single-parent households, childless couples, and smaller families are just some of the fundamental changes in makeup that we see today. This has resulted in enormous changes in the marketplace and the retail scene. Convenience stores and convenience foods flourish; teenage children often do the grocery shopping; and many women who work spend more money on clothes to wear to the office than they spend on home decorating. These examples are just the tip of the iceberg.

The family remains, however, the single most significant and enduring influence on all consumer behavior. Most of us cherish early memories of purchases made with family members: making a trip to the local car dealership, choosing a new television set, and sitting around the kitchen table working on vacation plans. These and many more purchase decisions made as a family unit continue to affect our consumption into adulthood. We buy the same breakfast cereals for our children that we loved ourselves. We automatically pick from supermarket shelves the same laundry detergent our mothers trusted. Conversely, we try to break away from parental influences through the fashions we wear or the cars we drive. See Exhibit 15-1 as a summary of family types, trends in families and households, and economic and gender role impact on the ability to shop, buy, and otherwise behave as a consumer in the marketplace.

As our primary and earliest frame of reference, the family is one of the key forces in determining the kind of socialization we receive. It helps shape our norms and values and provides us with a sense of identity within the sea of cultures, subcultures, and social classes around us. The family is also the principal source of individual personality development, governing such variables as early learning environment, birth order differences, and role acceptance, all of which affect our lifestyles and our buying behavior.

The **consanguine family** or **family of orientation** is the family into which we are born or adopted, while the family formed by marriage is the **conjugal family** or **family of procreation.**[1] In the United States, the extended family with its grandparents, aunts, uncles, or cousins has, over the years, been replaced as the most common mode of living by the nuclear family. A typical nuclear family consists of a mom, dad, and children. Because there are only two adult members in the nuclear unit, each is reliant upon the other for cooperation in solving family problems. When serious tensions exist between them, their

▶**consanguine family** or **family of orientation** The family into which a person is born or into which a person is adopted.

▶**conjugal family** or **family of procreation** The family formed by marriage.

Family Types

· Consanguine/orientation

· Conjugal/procreation

Key Trends Affecting Families and Other Households

· Lower birth rates

· Smaller families

· People marrying later in life

· People deciding not to marry

Economic and Gender Role Impact on Shopping, Buying, and Consuming Unit Behavior

· Two-income families

· Working women

· Single women heading families

· Gender roles

E x h i b i t 15-1

Family Types, Key Trends Affecting Families and Other Households, and Economic and Gender Role Impact on Shopping, Buying, and Consuming Unit Behavior

decision-making ability as responsible family members is severely impaired. And in times of accelerated social change, they may often be unable to draw on personal experience in handling family problems caused by changing norms and behavior.[2]

Families most often function as groups, whether they are large multigenerational households or simple husband-and-wife teams. As a primary group, the family is characterized by frequent face-to-face contact and cooperation, which are fundamental in forming the social nature and ideas of the individual.[3] Relationships within families are usually marked by mutual commitment, intimacy, and affection. Each family is a social unit that defines the roles of its members and, to varying extents, dictates and shapes their current and future behavior.

15-1a Composition of Families and Households

household A group of individuals living together in any dwelling, no matter what the relationships are among the people.

The U.S. Census Bureau defines a **household** as any group of individuals living in a dwelling, no matter what the relationships are among the people. Under this broad definition, a household can be made up of a traditionally structured family, a single person, two or more roommates, or any other combination of people. As a result of the rapid changes in family composition, the Census Bureau developed three new categories of family members for its 1990 survey: natural-born or adopted child, foster child, and unmarried partner (either opposite or same sex).[4] According to the 2000 census, the share of all households that are traditional "married-with-children" families has increased by 5.7 percent over the 1990 total. This is a reversal of a trend that in the 1970s showed a 3.3 percent decline and declined 1.8 percent in the 1980s. This stronger-than-expected showing can be attributed in large measure to the population growth of immigrant Asians and Hispanic Americans, and to the lifestyle choices of Generation Xers, who have entered their household-forming years. In fact, more than one-third of Latino and Asian households are married-with-children couples. On the other hand only 16 percent of African-American and about 23 percent of white households fit this mold. In the 1990s the total of all married couples' share of households shrank by 2.1 percent to 23.5 percent;[5] families with children decreased from 25 percent to 20 percent of all families.[6]

Changing demographics over time tell us a great deal about shifts in the family unit and resulting consumption patterns. Exhibit 15-2 summarizes changes in the makeup of households from 1980 through 2000. The 1990 census figures reveal that the number of households in the United States grew 17 percent to 93.9 million, outpacing the growth rate of the total population. By the year 2000, this number was 110.1 million, 18 percent higher than the 1990 figure. The projection for 2010 is about 117.7 million households. Average household size dropped to 2.6 persons in 1990, from 2.8 in 1980, and is still shrinking.[7]

The number of nontraditional families is on the increase in the United States. Typical are those headed by a single parent who in most cases is a woman. There are nonfamily households, headed by unmarried people. The 1990 census showed that some 23 million Americans lived alone, up 91 percent for women and 156 percent for men since 1970.[8] The total for the 2000 count was 27.2 million, and the projection for 2010 is 31.2 million persons in the United States to be living alone, with the ratio of women to men continuing at about 1.5 to 1. These singles, plus college students and young adults living with their parents, make up a huge market with annual earning power that was near $800 billion in 2000.

15-1b Trends in Family Composition

Three important trends have had a major impact on family composition. First, *lower birth rates have led to smaller families* for the majority white population. This has resulted in a significant shift in consumption patterns, as these families typically enjoy more discretionary income. Lower birth rates are not the case for Latino-American and African-American families and others who for religious or other reasons have larger families.

Second, *people are marrying later or are not marrying at all.* The median age of first marriage is 23.6 for women and 25.8 for men. Increasing numbers of Americans never marry. In 2003, 33 percent of men aged 30 to 34 had never married, compared to 9 percent in 1970; for women aged 30 to 34, in 2003, 22.7 percent had never married, compared to 6 percent in 1970.[9] Deferred marriage has changed marketplace behavior as couples

	2000		1990		1980	
	Households (1,000's)	Percent	Households (1,000's)	Percent	Households (1,000's)	Percent
All households	110,140	100	93,920	100	80,467	100
Families	77,705	70.6	66,542	70.8	59,190	73.6
Married couples	60,969	55.4	52,837	56.3	48,990	60.9
Without children	31,365	28.5	28,315	30.1	24,210	30.1
With children under 18	24,286	22.1	24,522	26.1	42,780	30.8
Nonfamilies	32,434	29.4	27,378	29.2	21,277	26.4
Men living alone	10,898	9.9	9,119	9.7	7,075	8.8
Women living alone	16,278	14.8	13,759	14.7	11,127	13.8
Other	5,258	4.8	4,500	4.8	3,075	3.8

Sources: Judith Waldrop and Thomas Exeter, "What the 1990 Census Will Show," *American Demographics,* January 1990; from Joe Schwartz, "Family Traditions: Although Radically Changed, the American Family Is As Strong As Ever," *American Demographics,* March 1987, p. 9.

E x h i b i t 15-2

Changes in American Family and Nonfamily Households

have children later in life. These trends have continued into the current century. Formal educational attainment appears to be an important factor in deciding who marries whom. One study found that while today there is some intermarriage at the middle of the educational spectrum, there is extreme polarization at the highest and lowest ends. In the year 2000, for instance, 94 percent of married high school dropouts were wed to someone who was either a high school dropout themselves or had only a high school diploma. Further, 69 percent of married adults with advanced degrees were wed to someone with at least a bachelor's degree. Less than one percent of the most highly educated had a spouse who did not complete high school. This matching of men and women with similar educational levels called *homogamy.* This is not new, but there have been slight increases over the past few decades.[10] Because of the tie that education often has with social class, one would expect that the spouses would approach the marketplace in a similar fashion.

Third, *high first marriage and even higher second marriage divorce rates* means more families are headed by single women which affects both family income level (usually lowering it) and consumption patterns.[11]

These transitions away from the traditional household structure mean that the positioning and promotion of goods and services to appeal to traditional families is no longer as effective as it once was. Increasingly, successful marketing strategies are those that can capture nontraditional families and nonfamily households, too. Some people feel that their pets should be counted as family members. Check out CBite 15-1 for the pet-lover's view.

F A Q

If there are so many of them, why aren't more nontraditional families shown in advertising?

CBite 15-1

A Populace of Pets

Try to tell animal lovers that their beloved pets do not count as members of the family, and they will soon set you straight. Households in the United States own 51 million dogs, 52 million cats, 14 million birds, 95 million fish, and 9 million other animals. The French, too, are passionate about their pets, and more households own cats and dogs than have children. Brigitte Bardot, the French actress, is the country's leading animal advocate. Her television show about animals pulled 17 percent of the national audience, compared to 5 percent for children's shows.

Sources: Clinton R. Sanders, "The Animal 'Other': Self Definition, Social Identity, and Companion Animals," in Marvin E. Goldberg, Gerald Gorn, and Richard W. Pollay, eds., *Advances in Consumer Research* (Provo, UT: Association for Consumer Research, 1989); Youssef M. Ibrahim, "French Love for Animals: Too Fervent?" *The New York Times,* February 2, 1990, p. A5.

Exhibit 15-3

Percentage of Women in the U.S. Workforce Working Part- or Full-Time, 1950–1999

The percentage of working women in the United States rose sharply after World War II; then it began a very slow rise from 1980 to the present.

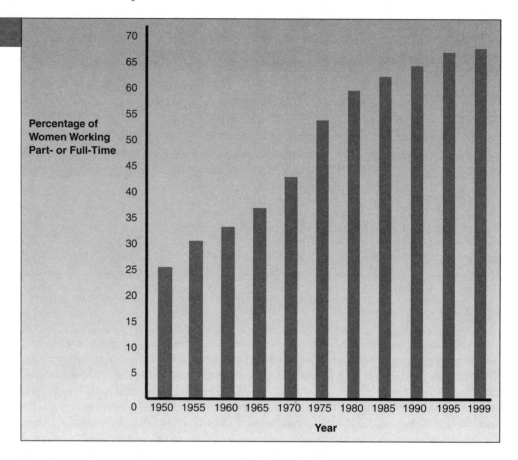

15-1c Economic and Gender Role Impact on Households

Two other important factors that have affected the consumption behavior of families and households are the increase in the number of two-income families and changing gender roles.

Two-Income Families   As shown in Exhibit 15-3, one of the most dramatic changes in the United States since the mid-1940s is the steady increase in the number of women in the workforce. In 1999, the number was 65 million. In 1950, only 26 percent of married women worked part- or full-time; by 1990, the figure was over 60 percent. In 1999, 52 percent of married working women contributed more than 50 percent of the family income. In 2003 59.8 percent of young women with preschool children were working outside the home, up from 30 percent in 1970.[12] The number of mothers in the work force with infant children has been tracked since 1976. Over the years this share has grown, and it peaked at 59 percent in 1998. By the year 2000 it had dropped to 55 percent. The women who have been taking time off are typically older mothers (30–44 years of age), married women living with their husbands, and women with at least one year of college. There was no significant decline among young mothers (under age 30), and there were slight increases among African-American mothers and those who did not graduate high school. In the United States in 2003, 74.8 percent of women from 20 to 54 years of age were working. Considering women 16 years of age and older who work, 61.9 percent of African Americans do so, as do 59.2 percent of whites and 55.9 percent of Latinos.[13] As noted earlier, the majority of working wives are in full-time rather than part-time employment, and their earnings are a significant contribution to total family income.

Two-income couples are an important target market. As well as an increase in the sharing of household activities such as cooking and shopping, these couples also typically share decisions on how to spend the higher level of discretionary income they enjoy.[14] Their lifestyles and consumption patterns differ from those of single-earner families. More interested in convenience than price, they spend more on themselves and their children.

Heavy consumers of such services as child care, cleaning, party planning, and beauty treatments, they are responsive to retail outlets that provide time-saving devices like home delivery, check-cashing, and store charge cards.[15] Understandably, women who work full-time tend to use such services as child care and restaurants more frequently than do women who work part-time.[16]

Does the fact that wives work mean that two-income families spend more? Not necessarily. A study comparing expenditures of single- and dual-earner households within the same income bracket found that there was no real difference in expenditure patterns. Even over a 12-year period, no clear differences were discernable. The study conclusion was that income, not single versus dual earning capacity, is the best predictor of spending patterns.[17]

Working Women in Two-Income Families   Working women can be divided into two broad categories: *career women* and *just-a-job women.* Career women have a median age of 36, 60 percent are married, and 50 percent have children under 18. More than half are college graduates, and many have professional or managerial jobs. As consumers, they plan ahead, tend to be brand loyal, and are likely to have credit cards. They are good consumers of such products as freeze-dried coffee, natural cereals, travel, and cars.[18] Just-a-job women also have a median age of 36 but tend to cluster at the upper and lower ends of the age scale. Their families generally have lower incomes than the families of career women. As consumers, just-a-job women are experimental, responsive to promotions, concerned about saving money when they shop, and relatively impulsive.

Recognizing the distinction between career and just-a-job women helps marketers develop different appeals for working women. Career women, for example, are more likely than just-a-job women to respond to price-quality promotions. Although both are working wives, pricing and promotion affect them very differently. A marketer of, let's say, a high-priced breakfast cereal might emphasize taste, quality, and health benefits in promoting to career women. Just-a-job women are more likely to respond positively to the same product when price promotions, such as coupons, are offered.

Single Women Heading Families   In 1998, there were 13 million single-parent families in the United States headed by women. That is, no husband was present. Fourteen percent of all white families are in this category. This share climbs to 24 percent among Hispanic-American families and to 42 percent for African-American families. In most situations, these families do not have the same income levels as families where the husband is present. There is a very strong demand for child care, though in many cases, members of the extended family provide this. Also, children participate at an earlier age and to a greater extent in shopping for themselves and the family. The woman is involved in both traditional female-dominant decisions and nontraditional male-dominant decisions and, therefore, is targeted by marketers to reflect this situation.

Gender Roles   Closely related to the growth in two-income families is the impact of the changing roles of men and women in the United States. Fewer and fewer activities, including purchase activities, are viewed in our culture to be exclusively appropriate to one gender. By the 1980s women were buying cars, attending seminars in assertiveness, and participating in active sports, and making their own investment decisions heretofore unknown in America.[19] Likewise, men were beginning to take more responsibility for housework, spending more time on child care, and becoming stronger consumers of fashion and grooming products. This **androgyny** is a gender role state where the individual experiences or acts out a blurring of gender roles, not favoring the male or female role. See Marketplace 15-1 for a look at papa's new role. Persons in this situation are of interest to marketers. It opens the door to new products, such as women's sports bras, seminars for women on basic auto maintenance and road emergencies, and classes for men on infant child care. New markets for existing products have been found as well. Kitchen equipment, for example, can be effectively advertised in men's magazines.

This blurring of roles also affects the pattern of decision making within the family. Car buying and investment decisions are more often shared rather than being the domain of the husband alone, as they were traditionally.[20] Despite increasing awareness of and belief

▶**androgyny** A gender role state where the individual experiences or acts out a blurring of gender roles, not favoring the male or female role.

Marketplace 15-1

Papa's Gotta Brand New Role

Three years after the men's movement entered the nation's consciousness, the sensitive, nurturing man invaded advertising. Whether selling beds, information services, household products, or hamburgers, companies as diverse as Thomasville Furniture Industries, SBC/Ameritech, Procter & Gamble Co., McDonald's Corp., and others began depicting dads in nurturing roles, cuddling infants, or worrying about baby's health.

It's as if fathers were suddenly unshackled from the chains of emotional reserve and set free to change diapers, take temperatures, and otherwise care for their offspring in advertising, both print and television. Such public displays of nurturing by men would have been rare just a few years earlier, but changes in the American family structure forced many fathers to become more involved with the rearing of small children.

Procter & Gamble portrayed men with babies and toddlers in ads for Zest and Ivory soaps; Johnson & Johnson showed a father washing a baby's hair and cuddling him after bath time. A McDonald's TV spot featured a father feeding his baby, and a Fruit of the Loom commercial showed a man toilet training his toddler son.

The shift in advertising portrayals can be traced to popular culture as well. The hit movie *Mrs. Doubtfire* featured a divorced father so desperate to be with his children that he dresses in drag to become their housekeeper. And the men's movement, made popular by books such as Robert Bly's best-selling tome, *Iron John,* helped crush old taboos and stereotypes.

Sources: Mathew Batstone, "Male Misgivings," *Marketing* (October 20, 1994), p. 20; Laura Zinn, "Real Men Buy Paper Towels, Too," *Business Week* (November 9, 1992), p. 75.

in equality between the sexes, in practice, gender roles within the household have been slow to change. Women still spend two to three times more time on housework and child-rearing activities than their husbands do. Men, on the other hand, spend fifteen hours more per week on leisure activities than their wives do.[21] Women are still mostly responsible for encouraging kinship within the extended family by maintaining family rituals and family ties. It is women, for example, who typically send letters and greetings cards, organize family get-togethers, and keep in touch by telephone. They also constitute the larger market for those goods and services that support family relationships.

Marketing Management—Implications and Actions

Understanding that the family or household functions as a consumption unit helps marketers:

- More clearly target the needs of smaller family households, those where adults have delayed marriage, single adults, and single adult head-of-household units.
- Properly target product and service offerings to the members of the household based on the gender roles being played out.

15-2 Family Lifecycle Influences on Consumption Patterns

family lifecycle (or life stage)
A person's position in life based on such demographic factors as his or her age, marital status, presence of children, ages of children, working status (working, receiving government financial assistance, or retired), and survivor status (retired and widowed or single).

What kinds of products are purchased and consumed by what types of families and households? To answer this question, we must first understand that just as individual consumers and their buying habits differ from person to person and from situation to situation, each family or household has similar variations. Several factors influence the ways in which they spend. Most important among them are **family lifecycle (or life stage)** position, reference group, social class, subculture, and culture. These influences, except family lifecycle, are discussed in chapters 11 through 14. Let's turn our attention to family lifecycle. As people find themselves in various positions in the lifecycle such as single, married, married with children, or widowed, their needs change. Hence, different mixes or types of products or services are required to allow them to properly function.

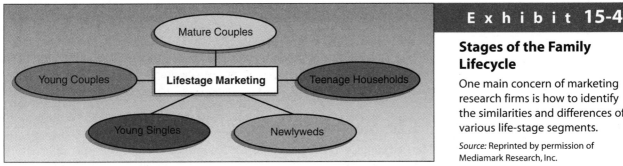

Exhibit 15-4

Stages of the Family Lifecycle

One main concern of marketing research firms is how to identify the similarities and differences of various life-stage segments.

Source: Reprinted by permission of Mediamark Research, Inc.

One approach to this breaks the family lifecycle, as shown in Exhibit 15-4, into five clear stages: young singles, newlyweds, young couples, households with teens, and mature couples. A comparison of such demographic factors as age, marital status, presence of children, ages of children, working status (working, receiving government financial assistance, or retired), and survivor status (retired and widowed or single) provides valuable insights into consumption patterns. The following sections will discuss the findings of a 1990 study that uses the five life stages for such a comparison.[22]

15-2a Young Singles

Young singles between 18 and 24 represent 7.8 percent of all adults in the United States. The majority live with parents; a minority, one in four, live with roommates. These consumers are much more likely than other adults to buy snack foods, cookies, and ice cream. They share, to some degree, grocery-shopping chores. They tend to buy more staples such as bread, butter, canned soup, spaghetti sauce, laundry detergent, and facial tissue than does the average adult. They also consume more beer, ale, wine, and spirit coolers. Discretionary income is spent mostly on entertainment, movies, records, tapes, compact discs, sports and recreation equipment, and shoes. Ownership of motorcycles by this group is 15 percent above average. Young singles tend to be heavy magazine readers and television viewers. The programming they prefer is late-night talk/variety, weekend professional basketball, situation comedy, and prime time. The focus of these individuals is primarily on themselves.

15-2b Newlyweds

The newlywed market is made up of 5.16 million people who have been married one year or less. The largest segment—43 percent—is 25 to 34 years old. Newlyweds 35 years and over own their own homes and tend to buy such household furnishings as sofas, wall units, wall-to-wall carpeting, dining room furniture, kitchen and cooking appliances, and table settings, including fine china. Younger and older newlyweds buy basic furnishings, linens, and cooking appliances at much higher rates than the general adult population. Newlyweds are cognizant of the needs of each other and often work together to select goods and services that reflect this. Joint decision making on goods and services is common. Older newlyweds may bring children into the marriage, and this will impact on consumption patterns of the family depending on the ages and genders of the kids.

15-2c Young Couples without Children

Young couples, aged 30 to 39, married without children, number 3.89 million people. In the 1980s and 1990s such couples were called "yuppies." These consumers are mostly highly educated professionals, earning $50,000 a year or more, who live mostly in cities or suburbs. As one would expect, young couples without children, whether in professional or other jobs, spend more time and money entertaining friends or relatives at home, going to bars or nightclubs, dancing, and dining out than do such couples with children. They consume above-average quantities of distilled spirits and bottled water. They own two cars in many cases, and the more affluent buy new rather than used. The yuppie group is more likely than other adults to travel overseas, purchase fine china and crystal, invest in collections of antiques and art, and remodel their homes. Not big investors, they prefer to spend rather than save. The professional young couples frequently read magazines and watch less television than do young singles. Their favorite programs are weekend baseball, weekend professional basketball, and news specials.

15-2d Married Couples with Children

Married couples with children are divided into two groups with very different lifestyles—dual-earner couples and other married couples (typically a working husband and a homemaker wife). Dual-earner couples make more money than other married couples, they have less free time, and their home life is often more hectic. The ages of the children directly impact on the consumption patterns of the family. Having preschool children brings the need for day care, baby foods, early child development learning materials, and such. When the children enter grade school, there are needs such as school clothing, sports equipment, skill lessons (dance, music, sports, etc.), youth group activity support, and peer-influenced clothing and music. Having preteens in the family also impacts on product and service need changes. What would be some of these changes? The distinction between the two groups is reflected in popular television shows.[23] Which current shows on TV do you think are targeted to these two different types of families?

15-2e Households with Teenagers

Totaling 30.6 million people, households with teenagers have a family income of $30,000, more than 24 percent above the average. In the majority of households, both spouses are employed. Households with teenagers tend to buy more than the average quantities of brownie and cookie mixes, ice cream, ice milk and sherbet, snack cakes, salty snacks, frozen pizza, and pizza mixes. They typically own cars, motorcycles, recreational vehicles, audio equipment, records, tapes, and compact discs. Television viewing includes late-night movies, drama, early morning news, and weekend sports.

15-2f Mature Couples

Mature couples, between 40 and 54 years old, are 7.2 million strong. They earn $60,000 per year and up. In many cases, both spouses are working. In one out of four households, a son or daughter works, too. Mature couples have grown children, leaving them with empty minivans and full pockets. They tend to invest more than the other groups in financial products and vacation or weekend homes. Mature couples watch golf, feature films, prime time, and news specials on television.

Knowing what types of products and services are needed by individuals and households that are in various stages in the family lifecycle helps marketers to better target them. This is another way that the marketplace "segments itself." Check out Marketplace 15-2, which deals with another view of life-stage marketing.

Marketing Management—Implications and Actions

Understanding how a person or household unit fits into the family lifecycle picture helps marketers:

- Develop and offer products and services that deliver the benefits needed for individuals and households across the lifecycle spectrum—from unmarried adult through retired solitary survivor.
- Adjust goods and services to fit the needs of older adults who find themselves in positions in the lifecycle at an older-than-typical age.

Marketplace 15-2

Life-Stage Marketing Gets Serious

Many marketers believe that recent developments in demographic and sales data, in combination with some simple predictor variables, can very nearly predict what products any household will buy. This new concept was first noticeable in the 1990s with the advent of "life event" mailing lists. These lists enabled direct marketers to contact a household shortly after the occurrence of major events such as a birth, marriage, car or home purchase, or graduation.

Take a look at the table to see how marketers, with only a few simple variables, can greatly increase their ability to target products and services at receptive market segments.

In addition to life stages, many marketers use information on consumer life events, such as marriages, births, and deaths, to target segments with relevant product and service information.

Life-Stage Segment: New, Unmarried Households

Predicting Variables:
Income $0–$24,999

Head of household age 18–24

Unmarried

Renters

No children present

Relevant Products and Services:
Credit

Basic household supplies/furnishings

Consumer electronics

Appliances

Career clothes/materials

Life-Stage Segment: Upscale, Married, New Children

Predicting Variables:
Income $75,000+

Head of household age 35–44

Married

Homeowners

Children present, age 0–5

Relevant Products and Services:
Insurance

Financial planning

Toys

Education plans

Vehicles with high safety ratings

Home entertainment products

Cameras, film, etc.

Life-Stage Segment: Pre-retired, Upscale, Empty Nesters

Predicting Variables:
Income $75,000+

Head of household age 50–64

Married, widowed, divorced (three distinct subsegments)

Homeowners or renters (two additional subsegments)

No children present, only one or two adults present

Relevant Products and Services:
Remodeling services

Real estate services

Travel services/equipment/clothes

Retirement planning

Health care planning

Upscale vehicles

Recreational items: golf, tennis, sailing, etc.

Household Decisions and Sources of Power in Household Marketplace Decisions

Husband-Wife Household Decision Types
· Husband-dominant
· Wife-dominant
· Autonomic
· Syncratic
Sources of Power in Household Marketplace Decisions
· Power earned
· Power taken
· Power given
· "Society says"
· Marketplace value

autonomic family decision making Decision making in which husband and wife independently make the same type of decision, each doing it about one-half of the time.

syncratic family decision making Decision making that husband and wife share.

15-3 Roles of Household Members in the Consumer Decision Process

15-3a Husband-Wife Decisions

As a consumption unit, the family or household functions like any other group with problems to solve and decisions to make. Exhibit 15-5 gives an overview of the various approaches to marketplace decision making within the family and how husbands and wives get the power to act on their own or together. Each member plays a role, some more active than others. To varying degrees, all family members, including children, are involved. The husband-wife relationship is, however, of key importance to marketers. It is important to consider "husband" and "wife" in a context beyond the traditional view. That is, in any family or household setting whether traditional (e.g., heterosexual couple, legally married, common law married) or nontraditional (e.g., homosexual couple, unrelated same or mixed gender group, etc.), individuals may choose or be given the role of "wife" or "husband." As they play this role out, their marketplace behavior is as though they were such a person regardless of gender, legal standing, or household situation. In order to target their messages effectively, marketers must identify the primary source of influence and the decision maker in each purchase decision the husband-wife team makes. To help them achieve this, researchers have divided purchase decisions into four categories.[24]

1. Husband-dominant family decision making
2. Wife-dominant family decision making
3. **Autonomic family decision making** (husband and wife independently make the same decision, each doing it about one-half the time; e.g., one picks the movie rental this week and the other picks next week)
4. **Syncratic family decision making** (both husband and wife share in the decision)

Certainly other members of the family or household may have varying degrees of influence on the decisions made. We'll look at children as a separate case shortly.

15-3b Sources of Power in Household Marketplace Decisions

How is it decided that a certain person in the family or household will be responsible for making all decisions on certain types of products or services used by the unit or individuals? The power to make such decisions may come in a number of different ways. Power may be *earned*. Here, the person has shown over time that he or she is very good at making such decisions, and the members of the household agree that he or she should continue to do so. A person can *take* the power. In such cases, the power is wrestled from the rest of the people in the household. They simply give in to the assertive or aggressive behavior of the "taker." On occasion, power is simply *given* to one of the members. "Why don't you make the decision, George?" says wife Ann, and the kids agree. In this case, no one else may want to do it, and George says, "Okay."

In various settings from neighborhood groups to the church, the region of the country, or the culture in general, *"society says"* who should make such decisions. Among your parents' close friends, the "woman of the house" always does the shopping and makes the decisions on groceries, so your mom accedes to that society's wishes and does this. Finally, *marketplace value* can be the source of decision power. Here, levels of income and/or wealth of the adult members of the family are considered. The person bringing the most financial strength to the household is given the right to make decisions. He or she may decide to defer to someone else but is seen as having the right of first refusal. Mom brings in $80,000 a year as a retail store manager, and Dad earns $50,000 as a high school teacher. Mom is the one to decide, if she chooses to do so. There have been attempts to put a marketplace value on the work done by the homemaker who is not working full-time outside the home setting, but to date this has not been successfully done. Hence, marketplace value seems to still hinge on actual salary and/or wealth.

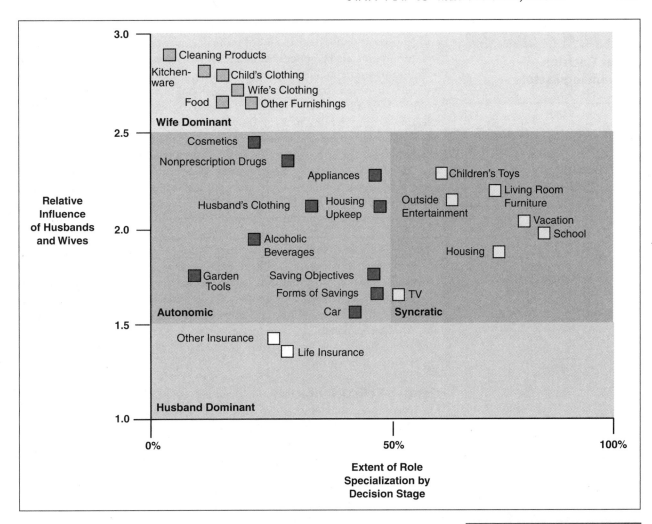

E x h i b i t 15-6

Role of Specialization in Family Decision Making

Compare the placement of husband's clothing and wife's clothing. How would you explain their positions?

Source: From "Perception of Marital Roles in Decision Processes" by Harry L. Davis and Benny P. Rigaux in *Journal of Consumer Research,* Vol. 1, June 1974, p. 57. Copyright © 1974. Reprinted by permission of The University of Chicago Press.

15-3c Other Decision-Influencing Factors

Researchers have identified three additional factors that can help marketers predict how certain decisions are made within a household or family. These are: type of product or service, gender-role orientation, and decision type.

Product Type   As shown in Exhibit 15-6, product and service purchases such as schools, vacations, outside entertainment, living room furniture, and housing result largely from syncratic decisions. As noted earlier, this is where there is a sharing among household members. Autonomic decisions govern the purchase of products such as garden tools and alcoholic beverages. In the 1970s and 1980s, wives were dominant in the purchase of cleaning products, kitchenware, children's clothing, wife's clothing, and food. Husbands dominated such decisions as life insurance, savings, and purchase of cars and garden tools. By the 1990s, men had increased their purchasing share of household groceries to one-fourth and 80 percent of men were found to do some major food shopping every month.[25] These distinctions are, of course, fluid. More recent studies have provided additional information related to product type decisions between husband and wife. For example according to Simmons Research data released by Interep's Research Division, 73 percent of adult women say men influence their household product purchasing decisions, yet only 9 percent of these women indicated that men influence those decisions "a lot." Concerning food purchases 13 percent of women said that men's influence is a lot. In the realm of durable goods, women are less likely to say men have any influence at all. For furniture, women reported men had a lot of influence in only 12 percent of the cases, and men's influence was 13 percent for major appliances. But in one area men's opinions still seem to carry a

E x h i b i t 15-7

Other Decision-Influencing Factors

- Product type
- Gender-role orientation
- Type of decision

lot of weight: cars. About half of the women say they listen to men when it comes to cars, and 20 percent said men had a lot of influence over their automobile purchases.[26]

Among married respondents in a recent study, both men and women agree that the wife is more influential in selecting a restaurant, deciding which brand of clothing to buy, and deciding where to shop. Women also pick out breakfast cereal, although 29 percent say children have a lot of influence. Both sexes recognize that husbands take the lead when selecting a computer or a new car, though 58 percent of husbands say that their wife has a lot of influence on car choice. Both spouses feel that they have an equal say in choosing vacation destinations or which television program to watch.[27]

In the spring of 2001 it was found by Mediamark Research, Inc. that men were the principal purchaser of items like groceries and children's clothing in 21 percent of all households. This points to the need for advertisers to consider this gender finding as a call to reconsider some of the messages being sent and the advertising media vehicles used to carry it. In particular packaged goods marketers should be considering men in their target array.[28] Exhibit 15-7 summarizes the three "other" decision-influencing factors.

Why are there differences in the ways husbands and wives make decisions across different products? One explanation is gender-role stereotypes. Many products and services are gender-typed. That is, they are perceived within the society as being primarily either men's or women's items. CBite 15-2 shows how things are done in Saudi Arabia. Check it out. Another explanation is product experience. Some products tend to be more likely used by husbands than by wives, and vice versa. Each exerts more influence over purchasing products they know best.[29]

Gender-Role Orientation   One step beyond gender typing is the concept of gender-role orientation. Some husbands feel and act more masculine than others, displaying such characteristics as physical strength, forcefulness, and aggression. Similarly, some wives overtly display such feminine characteristics as passivity, nurturing, kindness, and expressiveness. Also, within single-gender families and households, gender roles may be the reverse of what is typical in the culture at large. This parallels the earlier discussion on playing the husband or wife role.

Families with a less traditional gender-role orientation have a greater tendency to engage in joint decision making. Also, in such situations we find men making traditional female decisions like those associated with household cleaning products or new curtains for the bedroom. Women may have responsibility for gassing the cars, managing all auto maintenance, and painting the outside of the house. In the more traditional setting, husbands who are masculine in orientation are likely to exert more influence over masculine-typed product purchases. Similarly, wives who are feminine in orientation are likely to exert more influence over decisions on products that are feminine-typed. In the early 1990s the organization of the family in the U.S. was showing signs of shifting from "command," where one person dominated, to "negotiation" for family decision making. This shift is continuing today. Furthermore, the two-income situation in families increased the

---

CBite 15-2

Buying the Family Car

Let's look at family buying from a different cultural perspective. A 1994 study of upscale Saudi households found that although husbands allow their wives free reign over most household buying decisions, they exert a great deal of influence on the amount the family spends on big-ticket items. This is particularly true in car buying, where husbands exert the major influence in all decisions related to the purchase. What does this example tell you about household consumption patterns in Saudi Arabia and the challenges for marketers targeting households in that country?

Source: Ugur Yavas, Emin Babakus, and Nejdet Delener, "Family Purchasing Roles in Saudi Arabia: Perspective from Saudi Wives," *Journal of Business Research*, Vol. 31 (September 1994), pp. 75–86.

status and options for women. These two situations have generated increased uncertainty about gender roles and responsibilities between the adults in the household unit.[30]

Gender-role orientation guides marketers in their assessment of the extent to which their products are perceived as masculine or feminine and which orientation the majority of their target consumers have.

Type of Decision   As we have seen in earlier chapters, before making a purchase, consumers go through three major decision stages: problem recognition, information search, and alternative evaluation. The influence of husband versus wife may vary with each stage of the decision process. We'll discuss this as a separate topic shortly. As the family moves toward final purchase of important products and services, the decision typically becomes increasingly a syncratic one.[31]

Looking again at Exhibit 15-6, we see that syncratic decisions are most common for purchases like vacations, television sets, upholstery, living room furniture, carpet/area rugs, and family cars. More recently there has been research indicating that husbands continue to have more influence than wives in all phases of the decision process for television sets, automobiles, and insurance, and wives continue in their influence strength in all stages of the decision process for household appliances, furniture, and food. Both partners influence the vacation choice decision; however, wives have less influence in the problem recognition, information search, and alternative evaluation and more influence on the final choice. There is equality of influence on how much time and money to spend on vacation and when to go, but wives have more influence on where to go and where to stay (hotels, campgrounds, etc.)[32] The marketing implications are twofold. First, decisions made during information search tend to be autonomic. If the marketing objective is to disseminate information, then marketers should use media targeted specifically at either the wife or the husband, not at both. Second, as evaluation of product features occurs closer to final purchase, these must reflect the evaluation criteria of both husbands and wives. See CBite 15-3 for more on who makes family choices.

15-3d Children's Influence on Decisions

Most researchers—and most parents—agree that children influence family purchase decisions, often to alarming degrees. It was estimated that in 2000, U.S. children 12 years of age and under influenced $500 billion in family purchases, up from $188 billion in 1997.[33] This includes a substantial influence over parental decision making. Preadolescent children ages 4 to 12 spent $2.2 billion in 1968, $17.1 billion in 1994, and over $40 billion in

---

CBite 15-3
Who Makes the Family Choices?

A study of choice of professional services—such as lawyers, dentists, pharmacists, physicians, and insurance agents—found that whereas husbands dominate the selection of insurance agents, wives typically select pharmacists. Choice of family physician is wife-dominant in some families and husband-dominant in others, with a relatively low degree of joint decision making. Marketers of professional services should target primary decision makers accordingly.

Despite changing gender roles, for the most part women spend more time in the kitchen and on related purchases than do their husbands. Despite time constraints, particularly among women who work full-time, many women still feel that it is their responsibility to make sure that the family is well fed and derive satisfaction from this.

Sources: Keith J. Kelly, "Despite Full Plate, Homemakers Still Like Making Meal," *Advertising Age* (October 10, 1994), p. 30; Jack J. Kasulis and Marie Adele Hughes, "Husband-Wife Influence in Selecting a Family Professional," *Journal of the Academy of Marketing Science,* Vol. 12 (Spring 1984), pp. 115–127; Elaine Sherman and Nejdet Delener, "The Impact of Demographics on Household Personal Computer Purchasing Decisions," *Journal of the Academy of Marketing Science,* Vol. 15 (Summer 1987), pp. 25–32.

E x h i b i t 15-8

**Children's Influence
on Decisions**

· Children's persuasion
  tactics
· Product type
· Personal resources
· Age
· Mother's child
  centeredness/attitude
  toward TV ads
· Family communications
  environment
· Parental style

2002. This number is expected to exceed $51.8 billion by 2006. Older children, those 12 to 19, spent an estimated $155 billion of their own money in 2001.[34] As every parent knows, children often have more than an equal say in what goes into the shopping cart at the supermarket each week. Inspired by television advertising and peer pressure among school friends, children will plead, whine, and bargain with their parents to get what they want.[35] See Exhibit 15-8 for an overview of children's influence factors. CBite 15-4 gives us information on how kids wield influence.

Adolescents have a number of strategies that they use in interacting with their parents when participating in family decision making.[36] They "bargain," trying to create agreement based on mutual gain and mutually satisfactory outcomes.[37] They "persuade," convincing opposing family members to resolve the conflict in the teen's favor.[38] They may use "emotion-laden" tactics including crying, withdrawing, pouting, anger, or giving the silent treatment to family members in order to get their way.[39] They may "directly ask" or "explain a need or want."[40] Teens also use the "expert" strategy where they have been taught by a parent to make certain decisions and then ask to be allowed to make them.[41] Adolescents may be refused influence because the parents use what is called a "legitimate" strategy. That is, the parents, because of their position in the family, may exercise the right of refusal.[42]

It should be noted that many marketers as well as social critics and marketing ethicists have deemed advertising directly to children to be unethical. Young children are especially vulnerable to marketing messages and often cannot effectively distinguish between advertising messages and program content. The banning of cartoon images such as "Joe Camel" from cigarette advertising is a good example. To market in an ethical manner, marketers have to start out with a product that enhances the well-being of children. Marketers can use consumer behavior research to improve product design, to make it more appealing, to price the product, to distribute the product through channels accessible to families with children, and to promote the product more to the parents than the children. In Marketplace 15-3 you'll find a series of ideas that marketers should consider when pursuing youth segments.

Now let's turn to the factors that have been found to impact children's degree of influence in family decision making. Obviously, it is important for marketers to understand this so as to target effectively. Several factors help predict the influence of children on family purchases. Chief among them are type of product, children's personal resources, age of the children, mother's child-centeredness and attitude toward television or advertising, family communication environment, and parental style.[43]

Product Type   Children frequently accompany parents to supermarkets and influence grocery shopping and brand choices to varying extents, depending upon the product purchased. As an obvious example, they are much more interested in cereal than in detergent purchases.[44] Children also influence decisions on which car to buy as well as the selection of CD players, cameras, radios, and other home entertainment appliances.[45] The greatest

---

CBite 15-4
Kids Wield Big Influence

Everybody knows kids tell their parents what to buy them, but a Simmons Kids Study confirmed that they care most about sneakers. The 1993 study of 2,000 6-to-14-year-olds and their parents, from Simmons Market Research Bureau, New York, revealed that 45.2 percent of kids influence the choice of sneaker brands bought for them; 38.6 percent help decide what kind of jeans they buy; 38 percent pick shirts; 34 percent choose casual pants; and 32.8 percent select sweats. Girls are more brand conscious than boys.

Source: Gary Levin, "Kids' Influence in Purchase Decisions," *Advertising Age* (January 10, 1994), p. 22.

Marketplace 15-3

The Do's and Don'ts of Marketing to Today's Youth

1. *Don't generalize your message* and think you can reach the entire youth market. Kids under the age of seven have very active imaginations and are easily captivated by fantasy. After that, reality takes center stage. By twelve, becoming independent is top priority.

2. *Know your audience* and their language. Don't rely solely on research. Speak to kids yourself, read what they read, watch what they watch. Go out and meet your target audience where they play and shop, and in school and at home.

3. *Expect the unexpected.* Things change fast in a kid's world. What's in this week can be out the next, so be prepared to respond quickly.

4. *Do think globally.* Today's youth have as much in common with their peers in another country as they do with their neighbor down the street. They cross borders easily, and so should your message.

5. *Kids love learning new things* as long as it seems like fun. Don't be afraid to present them with new information, but do present it in a fun format.

6. *Kids love to teach their parents.* Empower kids with knowledge and they'll bring your message home.

7. *Kids have a natural tendency to want to belong.* When you reach them in a group setting, in clubs or at school, your message will have special impact. That's why kids respond so favorably to marketers' offers to join kids' clubs.

8. *Security, love, and constancy.* All kids still have those basic needs. Appeal to them with a message that will make them feel safe and secure.

9. *Don't sugarcoat your message.* Violence, the environment, abuse, and AIDS are real issues for today's youth. They care about the world they are going to inherit.

10. *Don't talk down* to young people. That's the fastest way to get them to stop listening.

11. *Kids think they are immortal.* They don't understand the concept of risk, so do be careful with your message.

12. *Kids aren't just short adults.* Don't assume that what appeals to you will appeal to them.

Source: "The Do's and Don'ts of Marketing to Today's Youth," *Promo* (July 1997), p. 47. Reprinted with the permission of Primedia Business Magazines and Media. Copyright © 1997. All rights reserved.

number of influence attempts and the highest incidence of parental yielding occur, predictably, in the product categories of breakfast cereal, snack food, candy and soft drinks, and games and toys.[46]

Adolescents perceive that their parents think their influence is strongest in the following purchases: *child-minor items* (clothes, shoes, movies, and calculators), followed by *child-major items* (personal stereos, bicycles), *family-major items* (cars, stereos, houses, television sets, vacations), and *family-minor items* (juice, toothpaste, ketchup, shampoo, breakfast cereal, and soft drinks).[47] Teens are the "biggest wave yet" in population groups. Read all about it in Marketplace 15-4.

Children's Personal Resources   Children's personal resources include the child's income, employment status, school grades, birth order, the presence or absence of siblings (with first-born and only children having more birth status resources), and parents' love and confidence. The more personal resources the child has, the greater his or her influence in family purchase decisions.[48]

Children's Age   Children's influence attempts tend to increase with age, and mothers are more willing to yield to such as children grow older.[49] This is perhaps because of the fact that older children have greater cognitive ability than younger children. Older children also have more experience with products and have learned more about consumer roles. From this, they improve in their ability to make more "responsible" decisions in the eyes of their parents. Also, they are much more likely to be consulted by parents in major purchase decisions, such as the family vacation, than are their younger siblings. Teens, in particular, as they take on more household responsibilities, exert stronger influence over buying decisions. With dual-income families and nontraditional households on the increase, this is even more pronounced. In the early 1990s, a staggering 50 percent of children in the United States lived in nontraditional households.

Marketplace 15-4

Teens: Here Comes the Biggest Wave Yet

While society has been fixated on the vast, aging cohort of the baby boomers, the ranks of teenagers have started to grow again. It began in 1992, when the U.S. teen population inched up by 70,000, ending the 15-year decline produced by the baby bust. By the time this bulge peaks at around 30.8 million in 2010, it will top the previous high-water mark set by the baby boomers in 1976 by more than 900,000.

But it won't be like old times. These teens are different. Here are some of the earmarks of the new generation of teens.

- *Multiculturalism:* Diversity is an established part of the teen environment; one in three belongs to a minority, as opposed to one in four in the total population.

- *Early maturity:* Teens are exposed to very adult problems at an early age, from crime to AIDS, to homelessness, to problems in the environment. Many teens must fend for themselves. One in four households with kids is headed by a single parent.

- *Responsibility:* Between marital splits and working parents, teens are responsible for far more decisions

Despite the fact that the next boomer generation will be marked by early maturity, marketers can expect them to be known by their choice of amusement, as the first boomers were known for disco and in-line skates. What will the next boom generation find or invent to entertain themselves?

than any other postwar generation. They do the shopping and the laundry and make dinner.

To lure teen customers, many companies are practicing "relationship marketing." Polydor Records runs an online bulletin board to keep in touch with teens. It has also launched a newsletter, *Bark,* written by and for teens, with a circulation of 9,000. The PolyGram division views *Bark* as a way to keep its finger on the pulse of teen culture. Polydor president Davitt Sigerson, 36, says it's vital that he connects with teens: as people grow older, they stay loyal to music "that resonates when they were young."

Source: "Teens: Here Comes the Biggest Wave Yet" by Laura Zinn reprinted from the April 11, 1994 issue of *Business Week* by special permission, copyright © 1994 by The McGraw-Hill Companies, Inc.

F A Q

Would kids be more likely to eat high-fiber cereals if they came with toys in the box?

socio-oriented communication
Communication characterized by harmony, pleasant social interactions and cohesiveness, and avoidance of conflict and controversy.

concept-oriented communication
Communication based on individual thought and analysis.

Mother's Child-Centeredness and Attitude toward Television or Advertising   One study of mothers' choices in cereals reported that mothers who were more child-centered did not give in to their child's preferences as much as did mothers who were less child-centered. This seeming contradiction was explained by the mothers' concern for nutritional needs that they did not feel were adequately met by their children's favorites—presweetened cereals.[50]

A second study found that mothers who restricted their children's television-viewing behavior were less likely to yield to influence attempts. Having less favorable attitudes toward advertising, they were more inclined to stand firm against their children's demands.[51] Therefore, if marketers wish to reach mothers who are child-centered and/or who restrict their children's television viewing, they should target the mothers, not the children, because the extent of the child's influence on the mother is likely to be minimal.

Family Communication Environment   There are two styles of communication within families. **Socio-oriented communication** is characterized by harmony, pleasant social interactions and cohesiveness, and avoidance of conflict and controversy. In contrast, **concept-oriented communication** reflects individual thought and analysis. Children in socio-oriented families have limited influence on purchases and are expected to go along with parents' decisions. Those from concept-oriented families exert greater influence, as they are encouraged to think and evaluate options on their own, even if it leads to conflict and controversy.[52] The communication environment is important to marketers when targeting families. If the marketer knows that targeted families are likely to engage in socio-oriented communication, advertising can be designed to appeal to this tendency. A commercial for a new minivan, for example, might create an atmosphere in which families are openly affectionate and emotionally supportive. The same product promoted to families who value concept-oriented communication might be presented in terms of the minivan's functional features, such as capacity and miles per gallon. A more recent study

---

CBite 15-5
A New View of Parental Communications Patterns

There is a new theory about family communications environments that is worth looking at. Four types are suggested:

1. *Consensual families* Here parents emphasize both socio- and concept-orientation; children are encouraged to explore the world around them and to form their own opinions.
2. *Laissez-faire families* Parents emphasize neither of the two communication dimensions, and there is little communication between parents and children
3. *Protective families* Parents stress obedience and social harmony and are not concerned with conceptual matters
4. *Pluralistic families* The stress is on concept-orientation dimensions and respect for one's interests and those of others; children are encouraged to discuss ideas openly without fear of punishment.

In summary, laissez-faire families are low on both concept- and socio-orientation; protective families are low on concept-orientation and high on socio-orientation; pluralistic families are high on concept-orientations and low on socio-orientation; and consensual families are high on both orientations.

How do you think each of these family types would impact on the influence of their children on various product and service selections for themselves or the family?

Source: Albert Caruana and Rosella Vassallo, "Children's Perceptions of Their Influence over Purchases: The Role of Parental Communications Patterns," *Journal of Consumer Marketing*, Vol. 20, No.1 (2003), pp. 55–66.

---

presents four types of families that may employ neither of these communications methods or both or some combination. See CBite 15-5.

Parental Style   There are three primary styles of parenting—*authoritarian, authoritative*, and *permissive*. **Authoritarian parents** restrict their children's activities and are not nurturing. **Authoritative parents** also set limits, but they are nurturing. **Permissive parents** are nurturing, but they do not set restrictions. The influence of children tends to be highest in families with permissive parents, followed by families with authoritative parents, and it is low in families with authoritarian parents.[53] The implications for marketers targeting families of each type are obvious. Consider the marketer of breakfast cereal who has targeted a segment in which the parents are mostly permissive. A television commercial can be developed showing a mother with her child shopping at a supermarket. In the cereal aisle, a favorite cartoon character leaps from the box of a favorite brand and invites the child to taste the cereal. The parent, without even checking the list of ingredients, responds immediately to the child's squeals of delight and throws a box into the shopping cart. This style of advertising is very unlikely to work with authoritarian or authoritative parents, who are far less likely to indulge the child's preferences in food choices.

International Marketplace 15-1 gives some insight into the role of children in the family in China along with their family marketplace decision-making influence.

authoritarian parents
Parents who restrict their children's activities and are not nurturing.

authoritative parents
Parents who set limits on their children's activities but are nurturing.

permissive parents Parents who are nurturing but do not set restrictions on their children's activities.

15-3e Roles of Family/Household Members at Each Stage in the Decision Process

So far, we have explained family and household decision making by exploring the different types of families, income effects, impact of gender roles, children's influences, and family lifecycle position. Another equally valid perspective is to examine the individual roles of family members at each stage of the purchase decision-making process, from problem recognition to information search to alternative evaluation to choice to post-purchase evaluation. As we shall see, at each of these distinct stages, different family members may exert very different influences.

International *Marketplace 15-1*

Consumer Behavior of Chinese Children

China has the largest population of children in the world with 300,000,000 under age 15. On the streets of Beijing, Shanghai, or Guangzhou we see many McDonald's, Pizza Huts, KFCs, Starbucks, Baskin-Robbins, and Dunkin' Donuts retail operations targeted on these kids. There are independent stores selling all kinds of western brands such as Kleenex, Disney, Coca-Cola, Kraft, Kellogg's, M&M's, Barbie gear, and Lego items—all targeting China's kids and parents. Hardly any of these retail and producer brands were in China prior to the 1990s and certainly not targeting children. Ethan Allen, the upscale furniture retailer, is opening a store in Tianjin, one hour east of Beijing, that will target families and their children with a section of the store set aside for children.

In 2003, 95 percent of families with one child insisted that the child be educated, trained in a trade, schooled in English, and employable. There is also a very strong desire on the part of the vast majority of Chinese families that the child be a male. When this is the case, it means that the male child can have anything he wants to make him happy, healthy, smart, and able to accomplish these goals. By the 1990s the Chinese family had to a great extent become a "filiarchy," where the child is in charge of what goes on in the household, including its consumer behavior.

If the only child is a girl, her grandparents, who believe in large families, will feel sorry for her and shower her with gifts and money. Her parents will demand that she somehow learn to earn money for them. This means that she must also be educated, and her ego will shift back and forth between shame (for not being a male) and success-seeking to achieve equality with males.

Both boys and girls become knowing consumers before they are in third grade as a result of up to five visits a week to the marketplace, and an average of 17 hours a week watching television, their number one source of new product information.

Chinese children save at a rate of about 36 percent of their income, though this rate is declining. Further, on an annual basis 7- to 11-year-olds are spending just over 800 yuan or about $100 each. The shares of main purchases made with their own money are school items (35%), snack items (28%), play items including music tapes, CDs, and sporting goods (20%), clothing (10%), and toiletries that are mostly skin care (7%).

Source: James U. McNeal and Chyon-Hua Yeh, "Consumer Behavior of Chinese Children: 1995–2002," *Journal of Consumer Marketing,* Vol. 20, No. 6 (2003), pp. 542–554.

Family members often assume varying roles across the five stages of the decision cycle. An individual could play all five roles simultaneously, or a number of family members could be involved at each stage.

1. *Problem recognition.* One or more family members assume the role of the initiator, recognizing the need for a product or service and making a case for its purchase. Sonia, a mother of two children, dreams about a get-away ski trip with her husband, Teo. They've both been working overtime and need a break from the daily routine and from their teenage children—who are due for a stay with their grandparents, in any case. Sonia recognizes the problem, and Teo agrees.

2. *Information search.* Sonia and Teo both decide to do a bit of information seeking, gathering information about alternative locations. At the same time, a search influencer, Bob, who is a friend of Teo's and an avid skier, attempts to get the couple to focus the information search on specific locations. He also has a favorite travel agent to recommend. Teo stops to see the travel agent on his way home from work. He talks to her and picks up a few skiing brochures. Sonia and Teo both engage in information search. He talks to a friend and a travel agent and picks up brochures. Sonia talks to her dad, doing both information search and looking at a possible location.

3. *Alternative evaluation and choice.* Teo brings home the brochures and tells Sonia what he found out. Sonia calls her dad, and he reminisces about his skiing days at Big Sky, Montana, and her mother gets on the phone and lets Sonia know the dates she'll be able to take care of the children. Sonia and Teo decide to stay right on the hill at Big Sky, and Teo agrees to set things up through the travel agent he met with earlier to make reservations. Sonia and Teo jointly evaluated alternatives and jointly made the choice. Teo completed the transaction.

4. *Consumption and post-purchase evaluation.* Sonia and Teo bring home photographs and rave about their trip. They had such a great time that they are thinking about going back next year. The children complain that their grandparents didn't let them watch their favorite television programs, and Sonia's parents lecture her on bringing up teenagers. All of these family experiences will influence plans for the next vacation the family takes. It looks like Sonia and Teo will need to weigh the overall satisfaction of the family unit as they think again about doing this next year. Teo and Sonia "consumed" the vacation and experienced satisfaction with it, but the experience of other family members was not as satisfactory.

By predicting who plays which role at each of these five stages of the decision-making process, marketers are better equipped to target and design effective products and services to deliver desired benefits and communications. Marital roles are particularly important predictors of purchase decision making within the family. One study explored marital roles in 25 household decisions at three decision stages: problem recognition, information search, and choice. The results suggested that husbands become the more dominant influence for most products as the decision stage progresses from problem recognition to information search. The patterns of influence shift and equalize during information search and final purchase.[54] This implies that marketers should target husbands with messages designed to satisfy the need for information and wives with messages designed to trigger problem recognition. Messages intended to assist in the final purchase decision should be targeted to both husbands and wives.

Marketing Management—Implications and Actions

Understanding the roles and influences of individual members of a household or family on the unit's buying processes helps marketers:

- Determine who will make the final decision on various products or services that are purchased for the unit.
- Assess the level of influence of children in a family on various product and service choice decisions.

Chapter Spotlights

Families and households make purchase decisions in groups. Just as individual consumers make their way through a decision cycle, so do groups, starting with problem recognition and leading to final purchase and evaluation. The challenge for marketers is to identify which member or members of the group influence the purchase decision at each stage of the cycle.

1. The household as a consumption unit. While the family remains the most pervasive influence on all consumer behavior, its makeup has changed dramatically over recent decades. Single parents, childless couples, and nonfamily households force marketers to rethink the ways in which they target household buyers. In addition, the increase in two-income families and changing gender roles have transformed the ways household purchase decisions are made and by whom.

2. Family lifecycle influences on consumption patterns. The stage of the members of the household in the family lifecycle—from young singles, to newlyweds, to young couples, to households with teenagers, to mature couples—dictates the type of purchases made

and the kinds of promotions to which the household is most likely to respond.

3. Roles of household members in the consumer decision process. Depending upon such factors as product type, gender-role orientation, and stage in the decision process, husbands and wives play varying roles in family purchase decisions. Marketers can better support consumers in making sound product and service selections by understanding which decisions are husband- or wife-dominant, which are autonomic, and which are syncratic.

Targeted by television advertising and influenced by peer pressure among school friends, children frequently exert various levels of influence over family purchase decisions. The extent of their influence varies according to product type, children's resources, their age, family communication environment, and parental style. Understanding how children affect decision making, marketers can target promotions accordingly. Each household or family member may play no part or one or more roles at each stage of the purchase decision process. Marketers identify such roles in order to target individual consumers who dominate family or household purchases.

Key Terms

androgyny (p. 475)
authoritarian parents (p. 487)
authoritative parents (p. 487)
autonomic family decision making (p. 480)
concept-oriented communication (p. 486)

conjugal family or family
   of procreation (p. 471)
consanguine family or family
   of orientation (p. 471)
family lifecycle (or life stage) (p. 476)

household (p. 472)
permissive parents (p. 487)
socio-oriented communication (p. 486)
syncratic family decision making (p. 480)

Review Questions

Note: You can find the correct answers to these questions by taking the quiz and then submitting your answers in the Online Edition. The program will automatically score your submission. If you miss a question, the program will provide the correct answer, a rationale for the answer, and the section number in the chapter where the topic is discussed.

1. A family formed by marriage is known as the family of procreation or the
   a. consanguine family.
   b. nuclear family.
   c. conjugal family.
   d. lineage.

2. In America today, the extended family has been largely replaced by the nuclear family, consisting of
   a. mom, dad, children.
   b. mom, dad, children, grandparents.
   c. mom, dad, children, grandchildren.
   d. mom, dad, children, aunts, and uncles.

3. An important trend in family lifestyle today is that lower birthrates have led to _____ families.
   a. fewer
   b. older
   c. smaller
   d. more mixed

4. Marketers know that first- and second-marriage divorce rates in the United States are
   a. lower today.
   b. higher today.
   c. about the same as they have always been.
   d. of little significance to marketing.

5. Two-income couples typically are more concerned with convenience than price and spend _____ on themselves as compared to single parents.
   a. less
   b. about the same
   c. more
   d. a variable amount

6. Which of the following is *not* an important factor that influences family and household consumption patterns?
   a. family lifecycle position
   b. reference group
   c. social class
   d. choice of recreation

7. Three additional factors used to predict how certain decisions are made within a family or household include gender-role orientation, product or service, and decision
   a. type.
   b. order.
   c. timing.
   d. deferral.

8. Children's influence on family purchases tends to _____ with age.
   a. decrease
   b. remain about the same
   c. increase
   d. increase and then decrease

9. It is possible that an individual could play all five roles simultaneously in the decision-making process for the family.
   a. true
   b. false
   c. It is difficult to determine.
   d. The question is irrelevant.

10. Messages intended to assist in the final purchase decision should be targeted to
    a. mothers.
    b. fathers.
    c. all of the children.
    d. both mothers and fathers.

Team Talk

1. What is your image of the type of household your parents grew up in? How does this compare with the households of people you know today? How do you think the changes you identify came about?

2. Why do you think we don't see more advertising that features nontraditional family settings?

3. As we have seen, family lifecycle influences family purchases. With your teammates, describe your earliest memories of the place you first lived, the house you lived in, and the products

your family consumed. How did family consumption patterns change as you progressed through school and into college?

4. Within your family, who usually makes decisions concerning the following purchases and why? Cars? Family vacations? Clothes? Food?

5. How did your marketplace decision influence level change in your household from the time you were a youngster to being a preteen to your teen years? Give a couple of specific examples in each case.

Workshops

Research Workshop

Background

The Dynamic Electric Company has just perfected a major new product, the Dynamic S72, a television system consisting of a 72-inch home-movie screen and a projection module priced several thousand dollars less than similar sets on the market. The purchase of expensive home goods often requires an appeal to more than one household member. The objectives of this workshop are to determine which family members have participated in which steps in the decision process on a purchase made in the past that they see as comparable, how they participated, and what benefits of this new TV system each member would focus on as they worked toward a final family decision.

Methodology

The CEO of Dynamic Electric wants a research questionnaire that can be used to identify family member participation in light of the objectives stated above. The questionnaire should be brief yet get the necessary information. Also, it is to be administered separately to husbands and wives while both are at home but not together at time of questioning. Design this questionnaire, and explain the process you would use to put together the group of couples to study and how to administer the survey form.

To the Marketplace

Have each member of the team find five couples using the sampling method you devised. Gather the information separately from each of the two people in the couples selected. Based on the objectives, what did you learn from the study?

Creative Workshop

Background

The information gathered about family participation and important benefits found in the research workshop is to be the basis for constructing two rough magazine print ad concepts. The two ads are to appeal separately to different persons in the family who would participate in the S72 decision.

Methodology

Look at the research results and identify who the targets are to be and what should be "said" in the ads in terms of words and situations. Also, if people are to be featured in one or both of the ads, who should these people be, and how will you identify their family roles? What are the two settings (situations) to be portrayed in the ads?

To the Marketplace

Rough out the two magazine ads. Each should have a headline and appropriate copy and visuals to communicate what you determined was to be "said." Identify the magazines where these ads should be run. Why did you choose these magazines?

Management Workshop

Background

The objectives of this workshop are to determine how to position the S72 in the minds of the family members who would participate in the decision process and in what types of retail outlet the system should be sold.

Methodology

This task follows from the research workshop and requires that the latter be carried out before attempting to meet the objectives of this management workshop. Review the data gathered from the study. Recall from Chapter 1 (section 1-1c, "Consumer Benefits and Product Positioning") that positioning may be based on product image, benefits, attributes, or versus the competition. Choose the positioning method, and identify the specific information from the research that will be used.

To the Marketplace

Write positioning statements for two of the family members who would participate in the decision process on this product. Having done this, explain specifically what steps the company should follow to successfully position the product. What types of retail outlets should be used to sell this product? If you wish to name specific retailers, that's fine, too.

Notes

1. Leonard Broome and Philip Selznick, *Sociology* (New York: Harper and Row, 1973).
2. Eugene Litwak and J. Figueira, "Technological Innovation and Theoretical Functions of Primary Groups and Bureaucratic Structures," *American Journal of Sociology*, Vol. 73 (January 1967), pp. 468–481.
3. Charles Horton Cooley, *Social Organization* (New York: Scribner's, 1909), p. 23.
4. Martha Farnsworth Riche, "Somebody's Baby," *American Demographics* (February 1988), p. 10.
5. William H. Frey, "Married with Children," *American Demographics* (March 2003), p. 18.
6. Cheryl Russell, "Throw Out the Script," *American Demographics* (September 1990), p. 2.
7. Judith Waldrop and Thomas Exter, "What the 1990 Census Will Show," *American Demographics* (January 1990), p. 27.
8. Laura Zinn, Heather Keets, and James B. Treece, "Home Alone—With $660 Billion," *Business Week*, (July 29, 1991), pp. 76–77; Blayne Cutler, "Single and Settled," *American Demographics* (May 1991), p. 10.
9. U.S. Census Bureau, *Statistical Abstract of the United States: 2004–2005* (124th ed.), Washington, D.C., 2004; Martha Farnsworth Riche, "The Postmarital Society," *American Demographics* (November 1988), pp. 22–26, 60.
10. Rebecca Gardyn, "The Mating Game," *American Demographics* (July/August 2002), p.34
11. Riche, "The Postmarital Society."
12. Michael D. Reilly, "Working Wives and Convenience Consumption," *Journal of Consumer Research*, Vol. 8 (March 1982), pp. 407–418; Charles M. Schaninger and Chris T. Allen, "Wife's Occupational Status as a Consumer Behavior Construct," *Journal of Consumer Research*, Vol. 7 (September 1981), pp. 189–196; Charles B. Weinberg and Russell S. Winer, "Working Wives and Major Family Expenditures: Replication and Extension," *Journal of Consumer Research*, Vol. 9 (September 1983), pp. 259–263.
13. U.S. Census Bureau, *Statistical Abstract of the United States*, 2004; Rifka Rosenwein, "The Baby Sabbatical," *American Demographics* (February 2002), p. 37.

14. Ronald D. Michman, "The Double Income Family: A New Market Target," *Business Horizons,* Vol. 23 (August 1980), pp. 31–37.

15. M. L. Roberts, L. J. Kirshbaum, and L. R. Cooper, "Two-Income Shoppers," *American Demographics* (March 1984), pp. 38–41.

16. Horacio Soberon-Ferrer and Rachel Dardis, "Determinants of Household Expenditures for Services," *Journal of Consumer Research,* Vol. 17 (March 1991), pp. 385–397.

17. Rose M. Rubin, Bobye J. Riney, and David J. Molina, "Expenditure Pattern Differences Between One-Earner and Dual-Earner Households: 1972–73 and 1984," *Journal of Consumer Research,* Vol. 16 (June 1990), pp. 43–52.

18. Rena Batros, *The Moving Target: What Every Marketer Should Know about Women* (New York: The Free Press, 1982).

19. "Androgyny Is a Fad, but Women Are Adopting Some Male Characteristics," *Marketing News* (May 25, 1984), pp. 3–5.

20. "Changes Found in Attitudes, Shopping Behavior of U.S.'s Two-Income Couples," *Marketing News* (October 28, 1983), p. 3.

21. John Skow, "The Myth of Male Housework: For Women, Toil Looms from Sun to Sun," *Time* (August 7, 1989), p. 62.

22. *Lifestage Marketing* (New York: Mediamark Research, Inc., 1990).

23. Martha Farnsworth Riche, "The Future of the Family," *American Demographics* (March 1991), pp. 44–46.

24. Harry L. Davis and Benny P. Rigaux, "Perception of Marital Roles in Decision Processes," *Journal of Consumer Research,* Vol. 1 (June 1974), p. 57.

25. Ibid; Robert M. Cosenza, "Family Decision Making Decision Dominance Structure Analysis—An Extension," *Journal of the Academy of Marketing Science,* Vol. 13 (Winter 1985), pp. 91–103. Note that study was conducted in the early to mid 1970s; L. Zinn, "Real Men Buy Paper Towels, Too," *Business Week,* (November 9, 1992), pp. 75–77.

26. Matthew Klein, "Mars, Venus and Shopping," *Forecast* (September 1998), www.demographics.com/publications/fc/98.

27. "Buying Influences: Consider the Source," *The Wirthlin Report,* Vol. 9 (March 1999), p. 3.

28. John Fetto, "Guys Who Shop," *American Demographics* (November 2002), p. 16.

29. Gary L. Sullivan and P. J. O'Connor, "The Family Purchase Decision Process: A Cross-Cultural Review and Framework for Research," *Journal of Business and Economics* (Fall 1988), p. 43.

30. William Qualls, "Household Decision Behavior: The Impact of Husbands' and Wives' Sex Role Orientation," *Journal of Consumer Research,* Vol. 13 (September 1987), pp. 264–279; C. Clulow, "New Families? Changes in Societies and Family Relationships," *Sexual and Marital Therapy,* Vol. 8, No. 3 (1993), pp. 269–273.

31. Davis and Rigaux, "Perception of Marital Roles in the Decision Process."

32. Mandy Putnam and William R. Davidson, *Family Purchasing Behavior II: Family Roles by Product Category* (Columbus, OH: Management Horizons, Inc., 1987); Michael A. Belch and Laura A. Willis, "Family Decisions at the Turn of the Century: Has the Changing Structure of Households Impacted the Family Decision Making Process?" *Journal of Consumer Behaviour,* Vol. 2 (December 2002), pp. 111–124.

33. Center for a New American Dream, "Just the Facts about Advertising and Marketing to Children." Available at: www.newdream.org/campaign/kids/facts.html (2002).

34. Ibid.

35. Leslie Isler, Edward T. Popper, and Scott Ward, "Children's Purchase Requests and Parental Responses: Results from a Diary Study," *Journal of Advertising Research,* Vol. 27 (October/November 1987), pp. 28–39.

36. Kay M. Palan and Robert E. Wilkes, "Adolescent-Parent Interaction in Family Decision Making," *Journal of Consumer Research,* Vol. 24 (September 1997), pp. 159–169.

37. Toni Falbo and Letitia Anne Peplau, "Power Strategies in Intimate Relationships," *Journal of Personality and Social Psychology,* Vol. 38 (1980), pp. 618–628.

38. Ibid.

39. Ibid and Rosann L. Spiro, "Persuasion in Family Decision-Making," *Journal of Consumer Research,* Vol. 9 (March 1983), pp. 393–402.

40. Palan and Wilkes, "Adolescent-Parent Interaction."

41. Ibid.

42. John R. P. French and Bertram Raven, "The Bases of Social Power," in *Studies in Social Power,* Dorwin Cartwright, ed. (Ann Arbor, MI: Research Center for Group Dynamics, Institute for Social Research, University of Michigan, 1959), pp. 150–167.

43. Thamuria F. Mangleburg, "Children's Influence in Purchase Decisions: A Review and Critique," in Marvin E. Goldberg et al., eds., *Advances in Consumer Research,* Vol. 17 (Provo, UT: Association for Consumer Research, 1990), pp. 813–825; Thamuria F. Mangleburg, "A Socialization Model of Children's Perceived Purchase Influence: Family Type, Hierarchy, and Parenting Practices," Doctoral dissertation, Virginia Polytechnic Institute and State University, Blacksburg, VA, 1992.

44. William D. Wells, "Children as Consumers," in J. W. Newman, ed., *On Knowing the Consumer* (New York: Wiley, 1966).

45. B. Wirkstriim, *Konsumentens Markesval* (Gothenburg, Sweden: Gothenburg School of Economics and Business Administration Publications, 1965).

46. Scott Ward and Daniel B. Wackman, "Children's Purchase Influence Attempts and Parental Yielding," *Journal of Marketing Research,* Vol. 9 (August 1972), pp. 316–319.

47. Chankon Kim, Hanjoon Lee, and Katherine Hall, "A Study of Adolescents' Power, Influence Strategy, and Influence on Family Purchase Decisions," in Terry L. Childers et al., eds., *1991 AMA Winter Educators' Proceedings* (Chicago: American Marketing Association, 1991), pp. 37–45.

48. Ellen Foxman, Partriya Tansuhaj, and Karen Ekstrom, "Adolescents' Influence in Family Purchase Decisions: A Socialization Perspective," *Journal of Business Research,* Vol. 18 (Second Issue 1989), pp. 159–172.

49. Ibid; see review by Mangleburg, "Children's Influence in Purchase Decisions."

50. Lewis A. Berey and Richard W. Pollay, "The Influencing Role of the Child in Family Decision Making," *Journal of Marketing Research,* Vol. 5 (February 1968), pp. 70–72.

51. Ward and Wackman, "Children's Purchase Influence Attempts and Parental Yielding."

52. George P. Moschis, "The Role of Family Communication in Consumer Socialization of Children and Adolescents," *Journal of Consumer Research*, Vol. 11 (March 1985), pp. 898–913.

53. Les Carlson and Sanford Grossbart, "Parental Style and Consumer Socialization of Children," *Journal of Consumer*

Research, Vol. 15 (June 1988), pp. 77–94; Les Carlson, Russell N. Laczniak, and Ann Walsh, "Socializing Children about Television: An Integenerational Study," *Journal of the Academy of Marketing Science*, Vol. 29 (Summer 2001), pp. 276–288.

54. Davis and Rigaux, "Perception of Marital Roles in Decision Processes."

This section contains special topics in the study of consumer behavior. One chapter deals with the relationship between consumers and public policy. New products and marketing practices sometimes require the creation of new policies, laws, and regulations. At the same time, new legal requirements can sometimes spur the creation of new goods and services. The protection and advocacy of consumer rights, explored in Chapter 16, has become a very active part of governmental activity and legislation. Some aspects of the consumer culture, however, cannot be easily regulated. Chapter 17 explores the dark side of consumer societies—shoplifting, compulsive consumption, materialism—and the "quality of life" principle as a guide for marketing ethics. Chapter 18 covers other special topics related to organizational buying behavior and diffusion of technological innovations.

Public Policy and Consumer Advocacy

16

Jeff was in the market for a cheap used car. Seeing an ad for five almost-new Pontiacs with less than 5,000 miles on them, Jeff arrived at the dealership early on the day of the sale but found no cars answering that description. The closest was a Pontiac Bonneville with 18,000 miles. The sales agent urged him to make a decision right away or this one would be snapped up, too. After an unpleasant hour of negotiating price, Jeff signed on the dotted line for what he discovered later was an exorbitant interest rate.

After a few weeks, Jeff began to feel uneasy about the car. He'd been told the car was in tip-top shape, but the brakes didn't feel right. His mechanic advised him that all four pads needed to be replaced—a $200 job. After a few calls to the dealership where no one would give him straight answers, Jeff got in touch with a consumer advocacy group specializing in retail fraud. In addition, Jeff wrote to the local paper and to Pontiac complaining about the dealership's treatment of him.

To what extent was the dealership to blame for the problems Jeff experienced with his new car? Was he purposely misled into buying a lemon? Or was he simply expecting too much from what was, after all, a used car? Central to understanding the regulation of marketing and media practices is a need to understand the rights of consumers. It is from this perspective, as presented in the "Consumer Bill of Rights" presented in the section 16-1a, that we address public policies that regulate marketing activities and the work of consumer advocacy groups to protect the consumer from questionable practices.

16-1 Regulation of Marketing Practices

Marketing in cyberspace, traveling the information superhighway . . . surfing the Internet…consumers and marketers have a love affair with computer communications networks. Millions of people are logged on to commercial networks, and thousands more are signing up every day.[1] But not all is rosy in cyberspace. Consider the case of Stratton Oakmont, Inc., an investment bank falsely accused of fraud by a Prodigy user who accessed a popular electronic bulletin board, Money Talk. Stratton fought back by filing a $200 million libel suit not only against the user but also against the carrier, Prodigy. Prodigy removed the bulletin message from the network. Take another example. An entrepreneurial couple who opened and ran an adult-only bulletin board were accused of offering pornography over the information highway and were convicted on obscenity charges. These cases and others raise some interesting questions about the regulation of marketing practices and marketing media. Should computer information networks be accessible to marketers? What if their messages infringe on consumer rights? Who should decide the type of information that can or cannot be delivered? Should consumers be protected from potentially harmful information? If so, how and by whom should information providers be regulated?

Businesses have traditionally responded to questions like these on the basis of the principle of "let the buyer beware"—the responsibility has been on the consumer to make wise purchase choices. Yet progress on both the public policy and consumer advocacy fronts is reversing this axiom, putting that responsibility with the marketer—"let the seller beware." From new product development, to product liability, to quality standards, to pricing policies, to advertising claims, all marketing practices are open to scrutiny. And increasingly, in most product categories and media—even the still emerging information superhighway—consumers are able to ask questions and demand change.

On the front line of defense against inappropriate behavior by marketers is a battalion of active consumer advocacy groups that use an armory of strategies from gentle persuasion to open litigation to ensure that consumers keep the upper hand in dealings with marketing organizations. Not only must marketers make sure to abide by state and government regulations, they must act in socially responsible ways to protect consumers. By enhancing consumers' quality of life, marketers can establish long-term relationships with consumers, which in turn influence long-term profitability. Note the abbreviated speech by Jim Guest, president of the Consumer Union, in Marketplace 16-1. He addresses the importance of consumer advocacy in today's society.

16-1a The "Consumer Bill of Rights"

The purpose of public policies that regulate marketing activities is to protect the rights of consumers. The **"Consumer Bill of Rights"** in the United States describes those rights as:[2]

1. The right to be informed
2. The right to safety
3. The right to redress
4. The right to choose
5. The right to a healthful environment
6. The right to privacy

In the remainder of the chapter, we explore each of these rights, the public policies through which they are protected, and the efforts of consumer advocacy groups to uncover unfair practices and provide recourse to consumers whose rights have been abused.

> **"Consumer Bill of Rights"**
> Laws designed to protect consumers from unfair and unjust marketing practices. Specifically, these laws protect the right to be informed, the right to safety, the right to redress, the right to choose, the right to a healthful environment, and the right to privacy.

Marketing Management—Implications and Actions

Understanding the range and purpose of regulation of marketing practice helps marketers:

- Ensure that their marketing activities are both legal and socially responsible.
- Make continual improvements to their products that benefit consumers and offer competitive advantages.
- Build long-term customer satisfaction.

16-2 Right to Be Informed

The consumer's **right to be informed** is the right to be "protected against fraudulent, deceitful, or grossly misleading information, advertising, labeling, or other practices, and to be given the facts he [or she] needs to make an informed choice."[3] This means that marketers are responsible for providing complete and unambiguous information on which we can base purchase decisions. Marketing communications that include misinformation, including exaggeration or distortion of facts, are an infringement of the right to be informed.

> **right to be informed**
> The consumer's right to be protected against fraudulent, deceitful, or grossly misleading information, advertising, labeling, or other practices, and to be given the facts he or she needs to make an informed choice.

Marketplace 16-1

Excerpts from a Speech by the President of the Consumer Union

Today I'd like to share some thoughts with you on the state of consumers and the consumer movement. The need and the opportunity for us in the consumer movement to make a much-needed impact has been underscored by the spate of high-profile abuses recently in the marketplace:

- the Ford-Firestone debacle,
- the California energy crisis with its manipulation of the power supply, soaring energy bills, and rolling blackouts,
- the failures in telecommunications after business interests persuaded Congress to deregulate the industry with misleading claims that it would be good for consumers,
- the lapses in airline security and public health protection that caught all of us unaware on September 11 and afterward,
- and now, of course, the scandal of Enron and the Arthur Andersen accounting firm, and more to come.

These breaches of consumer welfare and the public trust have sent shock waves through the American public. They demonstrate all too clearly the need for consumer watchdogs and for strong, vigilant oversight of the marketplace. And that requires the kind of research and expertise on consumer matters that only consumer advocacy groups and government consumer protection agencies can provide. I see five overarching lessons.

Lesson 1: The consumer movement is absolutely essential in pressing for a fair and just marketplace for all consumers, and we've made a huge impact.

Lesson 2: In markets where corporations lack effective incentives to regulate their own conduct responsibly—or where health, safety, and other special concerns are at issue—we need effective public oversight.

Lesson 3: There are serious holes in our product safety net and consumer protection infrastructure. We must give public watchdog agencies the resources, authority, and public support to be effective.

Lesson 4: Recognizing that too many consumers still cannot afford the basic necessities of life, the consumer movement should intensify the fight for affordable goods and services, fair financial practices, and a society in which all Americans have a fair chance at a decent living. For those without that chance, government must provide.

Lesson 5: We in America must curb wasteful overconsumption that threatens the environment before it's too late.

To summarize: For our system to work, we need strong public watchdogs, which include both government agencies and the consumer movement itself. We need to make investing in an effective consumer protection infrastructure a national priority, and we need to consider how this infrastructure can be improved and modernized. We need to help families meet their basic needs, and beat back predatory financial practices, so consumers will be able to live in dignity and save for the future. And we need to do more to curb wasteful overconsumption practices that threaten the environment.

We who work on consumers issues and in the consumer movement face a time of both crisis and opportunity. Our economic system has delivered goods and services in abundance, often at competitive and affordable prices, and, in many ways, it performs remarkably well. But the problems I've identified here today are serious and real. Just as men are not angels, corporations won't regulate themselves. We shouldn't expect them to.

It's a long agenda that those of us in the consumer movement have before us. We have an enormous opportunity to make fundamental, enduring improvements in the welfare of consumers here and around the world.

Source: Adapted from Jim Guest, "Colston E. Warne Lecture: Consumers and Consumerism in America Today," *Journal of Consumer Affairs,* Vol. 36 (2002), pp. 139–150.

▶**Federal Trade Commission (FTC)** The U.S. government body responsible for protecting the consumer's right to be informed. The FTC regulates truth in marketing, which covers deceptive advertising, false advertising claims, mail-order fraud, retail sales fraud, retail credit contracts, and door-to-door sales. The FTC also sets and enforces packaging and labeling policies.

The **Federal Trade Commission (FTC)** is the U.S. government body responsible for ensuring that the right to be informed is protected.[4] The FTC regulates truth in marketing, which covers deceptive advertising, false advertising claims, mail-order fraud, retail sales fraud, retail credit contracts, and door-to-door sales. Packaging and labeling policies are also set and enforced by the FTC. The items marked with an [I] in Exhibit 16-7 (see section 16-3) are selected consumer protection laws related to the consumer's right to be informed. The purpose of each is to equip consumers with information that will allow them to select the best-quality products possible at the best possible price.

Marketplace 16-2 is an interesting exposition on how the pharmaceutical industry goes about providing information to consumers in drug advertising. Pharmaceutical companies do so to ensure that consumers' right to be informed is not violated. However, read on. Providing the right information to consumers can be a challenging task!

Marketplace 16-2

Drug Advertising: A Prescription for Controversy

In the past, prescription drug manufacturers typically marketed only to physicians. This is changing, as more and more advertisements target consumers directly in the hope they will request a particular drug from their doctors. All told, drug makers spend some $200 million a year to advertise about a dozen prescription products.

But neither marketers nor consumer advocates are happy with the way such advertising is regulated. Regulations created to apply to the traditional advertising of prescription drugs to physicians are now made to apply to the new wave of consumer advertisements. The Food and Drug Administration (FDA) rules that any advertisement for a named prescription drug must include a brief summary—long lists of product data, typically a full page in tiny type of "medicalese" that consumers have little hope of understanding. The advertising must also clearly indicate potential hazards as well as limits. Consumer advocates claim that this format allows drug makers to hide vital information on product dangers in text no one reads. Marketers don't like the format either, because it hobbles their efforts to reach consumers by adding unnecessary marketing costs.

There's no consensus about how to improve the regulation of drug makers' advertisements. Some critics say the brief summary should be shortened or eliminated. Others argue that consumers should get more information, such as clearer caveats in the text of an advertisement. Activists

The brief summary rule was developed for ads aimed at doctors and was extended to cover consumer ads as well. The basic requirement is that if a drug and its use are identified, the marketer must provide the brief summary. If the ad discusses a disease or condition, but no specific drug is mentioned, the requirement is waived. Thus, ads for hay fever or baldness that simply say, "See your doctor!" do not have to present the brief summary.

want the FDA to ban direct-to-consumer advertising altogether until tighter standards are set.

Amid all the cacophony, some well-balanced advertisements do get produced. Johnson & Johnson Inc.'s Ortho unit, for instance, worked with the FDA for much of a year to develop a print advertisement for birth-control pills that both industry officials and regulators cite as a model. It lists in the main copy such cons as the risk of smokers on the pill suffering heart attacks, along with such pros as the pill's potential for protecting against ovarian cancer.

Source: Adapted from "Drug Ads: A Prescription for Controversy" by Joseph Weber and John Carey reprinted from January 18, 1993 issue of *Business Week* by special permission, copyright © 1993 by The McGraw-Hill Companies, Inc.

Marketplace 16-3 describes how many consumers are deceived by marketers' use of reference prices and the semantic cues they use to describe the reference price. Marketplace 16-3 also describes the FTC's position on this issue, and how this position changed overtime. Also see CBite 3-5 (Let the Buyer Beware), which deals with true discounts versus those tied to a manufacturer's suggested retail price.

16-2a Advertising Substantiation

The FTC has ruled that companies that make claims about a product's safety, performance, efficacy, quality, or comparative price must provide tests, studies, or other data to support their claims. The goals of this **advertising substantiation** program are to give consumers enough information to facilitate rational decision making, and to enhance competition by allowing companies to challenge the advertising claims of competitors.[5] By leveling the competitive playing field, advertising substantiation ensures that consumers are able to buy quality goods at appropriate prices. To comply, marketers are obligated to make proof of their claims accessible to the public. Regulators have developed guidelines that help them examine claims and detect misinformation or exaggeration. Offenders are subject to legal action.

16-2b Corrective Advertising

The FTC has the power to compel marketers to correct wrongful beliefs consumers form about a product as a result of deceptive advertising. The classic example is the campaign that ran for decades claiming that Listerine mouthwash could prevent or lessen the severity of colds and sore throats. Ordered by the FTC to develop a **corrective advertising** program designed to change consumers' beliefs in these unproven claims, the marketers of

F A Q

If advertising claims are subject to regulation, why are local newspapers, in particular, full of ads that make exaggerated, if not misleading, claims?

▶ **advertising substantiation**
An FTC-developed program that says that companies that make claims about a product's safety, performance, efficacy, quality, or comparative price must provide tests, studies, or other data to support their claims.

▶ **corrective advertising**
An FTC-developed program that compels marketers to correct wrongful beliefs consumers form about a product as a result of deceptive advertising.

Marketplace 16-3

The Use of Reference Price Claims in Advertising and the FTC's Position

Advertisers often use words such as "Regular Price," "Manufacturer's Suggested List Price," and "Compare At" to label price offerings. This information about reference price is designed to provide consumers with a higher price as a point of reference to enhance consumers' perceptions of value. This type of information may mislead the consumer. Exaggerating a reference price may deny consumers the benefits of the bargain they thought they were getting.

Furthermore, the use of different words to express the reference price leads to different interpretations, as it is unlikely that all consumers evaluate or interpret price comparisons the same. For example, "Compare At" may not have the same meaning for consumers as "Manufacturer's Suggested Price." Such words may inform or deceive the consumer, depending on how consumers interpret them. The courts have determined that if a statement in an ad lends itself to more than one interpretation by an average consumer, then one of those interpretations may be considered deceptive.

Reference price advertising claims were challenged on a regular basis by the FTC during the 1950s and 1960s, but less so in the 1970s. The FTC provided Guides (advice, not law) against Deceptive Pricing in 1958 and revised the

guides in 1964. Beginning in 1984, the FTC determined that if around 20 to 25 percent of the audience is misled by an ad, then the ad may be declared illegally misleading. Later in 1984, the FTC changed this standard to question whether the hypothetical reasonable consumer (rather than simply the audience) is misled. This approach now forced the FTC to empirically substantiate when a "reasonable consumer" would interpret an ad in a misleading way, and thus, evidence of actual consumer interpretations is important in making these determinations.

Sources: Adapted from: Larry D Compeau, Joan Lindsey-Mullikin, Dhruv Grewal, and Ross D Petty, "Consumers' Interpretations of the Semantic Phrases Found in Reference Price Advertisements," *Journal of Consumer Affairs,* Vol. 38 (Summer 2004), pp. 178–188: Larry D. Compeau and Dhruv Grewal, "Comparative Price Advertising: An Integrative Review," *Journal of Public Policy & Marketing,* Vol. 17 (1998), pp. 257–273; Dhruv Grewal and Larry D. Compeau, "Comparative Price Advertising: Informative or Deceptive?" *Journal of Public Policy & Marketing,* Vol. 11 (1992), pp. 52–62; Ross D. Petty, *The Impact of Advertising Law on Business and Public Policy* (Westport, CT: Quorum Books, 1992); Ross D. Petty and Robert J. Kopp, "Advertising Challenges: A Strategic Framework and Current Review," *Journal of Advertising Research,* Vol. 35 (1995), pp. 41–55; Larry D Compeau, Dhruv Grewal, and Rajesh Chandrashekaran, "Bits, Briefs, and Applications: Comparative Price Advertising: Believe it or Not," *Journal of Consumer Affairs,* Vol. 36 (Winter 2002), pp. 284–295.

Listerine spent in excess of $10 million to do so, mostly through television advertising.[6] Even so, subsequent studies showed that the campaign changed overall consumer beliefs about the product by only 20 percent, significantly less than expected.[7]

Exposed to corrective advertising, we usually react in one of the following ways.[8] Sometimes we believe the new information with which we're presented and change our attitude toward or perception of the advertised brand accordingly. Other times we don't accept the new information and hold on to earlier beliefs. Sometimes, while we don't accept the new information, we're curious about the discrepancy and seek further information for clarification. And there are times when we simply become confused and uncomfortable, not knowing what to believe.

At its best, corrective advertising is based upon consumer behavior research. Only by understanding the types of false beliefs consumers hold about a product and how they were formed can we begin to change those beliefs. Message testing, through which sample groups of consumers are exposed to different corrective messages and changes in their beliefs are measured, is the research technique most commonly used to develop effective corrective advertising campaigns. Despite such efforts, however, experts agree that although corrective advertising works, it is not usually powerful enough to remedy problems of advertising deception.[9]

F A Q

Should advertising of unsafe or harmful products like cigarettes and alcohol be banned altogether?

16-2c Information Disclosure

The FTC mandates the use of warning labels on several products and their supporting advertising. Alcoholic beverages are a good example.[10] Advertisements typically warn of the dangers of consuming alcohol during pregnancy; the addictive qualities of alcohol; and the risk of throat, stomach, and prostrate cancer and diseases of the liver and heart resulting from alcohol consumption.[11]

Of all consumer complaints relating to **information disclosure,** truth in advertising is most frequently criticized. Exhibit 16-1 describes several categories of deceptive

▶**information disclosure**
An FTC-developed program that mandates the use of warning labels on several products and their supporting advertising.

Category	Deceptive Claim
	E x h i b i t 16-1

Categories of Deceptive Claims

Category	Deceptive Claim
Objective Claim	A standard for comparison exists against which the claim may be compared to determine if it is deceptive or not. Example: A Poly-Grip commercial that claimed denture wearers could eat foods such as corn on the cob or apples without fear of their dentures loosening. In reality, the front teeth of many dentures are for cosmetic purposes only. Poly-Grip would not be effective for these types of dentures.
Subjective or Opinion Claim	This type of claim is difficult to prove false because trade "puffery" or valuative claims are allowed. The Federal Trade Commission's position is that advertisements that claim certain products are "the best" are not usually taken seriously by the average consumer.
Implied Claim	This claim involves the overall impression the consumer has concerning a product or service, apart from the literal advertising text, or "deception by innuendo." Example: In 1962, a television commercial was shown whose purpose was to display the superiority of Libby plate glass over plain glass. In fact, plate glass does possess many attributes that ordinary glass does not. However, as a means of demonstrating this notion, the commercial showed an outdoor scene filmed from the inside of two car windows—the windows representing each of the two forms of glass. From the inside of the "ordinary glass," viewers saw a distorted scene. The view through the "plate glass" window pictured a perfect view. In actuality, the "ordinary glass" scene had been filmed through a window smeared with Vaseline, and the "plate glass" scene had been filmed out of a rolled-down window.
The Claim with Two Meanings	If an advertisement has two meanings, one of which is false, then the entire ad is considered deceptive. Example: In an advertisement from the National Commission on Egg Nutrition that encouraged individuals to eat eggs, the FTC issued a cease-and-desist order that prevented the commercial from containing the statement, "There is no scientific evidence that eating eggs increases the risk of . . . heart disease." The commission decided that research in this area still provided mixed results such that the claim should not be made.
The Unsubstantiated Claim	Affirmative claims for a product that are not reasonably supported. Example: "Miracle" weight-loss products, cosmetics that claim to retard aging or remove wrinkles.
Evaluating the Sufficiency of Information	An advertisement can be deemed deceptive if it fails to disclose relevant facts or conditions. Example: Fresh Horizons was a bread that was positioned as having a high fiber content. However, the packaging and advertising did not disclose that the source of the fiber was tree pulp.

Source: Based on Dorothy Cohen, "Protecting Consumers from Unfairness and Deception," in Paul N. Bloom, ed., *Consumerism and Beyond: Research Perspectives on the Future Social Environment* (Cambridge, MA: Marketing Science Institute, 1982), pp. 68–74.

claims.[12] Particularly alarming, roughly 60 percent of consumers believe that less than half the advertisements they see are informative and honest.[13]

A 2001 study demonstrated that education level and warning vocabulary affect consumer reactions to warnings. Consumers who did not complete high school were not able to comprehend warnings with difficult vocabulary as well as warnings with simple words.

Product Warnings

The FTC has instructed cigarette and alcohol marketers to label their products with warnings like this one to ensure that consumers are better informed about the purchase and consumption of these products.

> **SURGEON GENERAL'S WARNING:**
> Cigarette Smoke Contains Carbon Monoxide.

They perceived products that carry warnings with simple words as safer than products labeled with difficult words warnings. Furthermore, consumers with more education were found to have more negative attitudes toward warnings with difficult words than warnings with simple words. This suggests that marketers should use simple language on warning labels.[14]

Information disclosure works best when guided by consumer research. By tailoring information messages to consumers most likely to benefit from them, marketers can significantly increase the likelihood that those consumers will make an informed decision on using or not using the product. Remember that the purpose of information disclosure is not directly to discourage consumers from using products that have potentially harmful consequences, but to provide them with the means to make an informed decision on the use of those products. Warnings on cigarettes, like the one in Exhibit 16-2, for example, do not tell pregnant women not to smoke but ensure they are cognizant of the risks of cigarette smoking to unborn children.

16-2d Unit Pricing

unit pricing An FTC-developed program that says that retailers must provide consumers with two prices for every packaged goods item: the price per package and the price per unit of measure. The goal is to allow consumers to make value comparisons among products and package sizes.

The FTC has ruled that retailers must provide consumers with two prices for every packaged goods item: the price per package and the price per unit of measure. The goal is to allow consumers to make value comparisons among products and package sizes. Research has allowed several insights into the use and benefits of **unit pricing**.[15]

Awareness   A majority of consumers are familiar with unit pricing, although awareness increases the more it is promoted. At least 50 percent of consumers understand what unit pricing means, with higher awareness among better-educated, middle-income, young, white shoppers.

Consumer Use   Those who are unaware of unit pricing do not use it in item selection. About half of those who are aware of it actually take advantage of unit pricing. Demographically, users tend to fit the profile of affluent, young, white shoppers.

Influence on Purchase Behavior   Using unit pricing saves consumers money. Brand, package size, and store switching are common among consumers who use unit pricing. Public policy and consumer advocacy groups should educate those who do not use unit pricing on how they can save money by applying unit pricing to brand, package size, and outlet selection.

16-2e Product Labeling

product labeling An FTC-developed program that mandates labeling on most food products to indicate appropriate product warnings, use-by dates, and nutritional values.

Consumers increasingly report concern over inadequate and misleading **product labeling** on food products. Federal law mandates labeling on most food products to indicate appropriate product warnings, use-by dates, and nutritional values.[16] Whereas consumer response to warnings and use-by dates has been minimal, nutrition labels, such as the one in Exhibit 16-3, are very popular. Several studies have measured various aspects of consumer response to the policy.

Awareness   In a test conducted by food-store chains, about 26 percent of consumers were aware of nutrition labeling, and 16 percent understood them.[17] Awareness increased with promotion and was positively related to income and education. To further improve awareness, public policy and consumer advocacy groups should aim to inform consumers, particularly those from lower income brackets and with less formal education, of the benefits of nutrition labeling.

E x h i b i t **16-3**

Nutrition Facts/Datos De Nutricion
Serving Size/Tamaño por Ración 2 cookies/2 galletas (25g)
Servings Per Container/Raciones por Envase 6

Amount Per Serving/Cantidad por Ración

Calories/Calorias 130	Calories from Fat/Calorias de Grasa 50

	% Daily Value*/% Valor Diario*
Total Fat/Grasa Total 6g	**9%**
Saturated Fat/Grasa Saturada 3.5g	**17%**
Cholesterol/Colesterol 5mg	**2%**
Sodium/Sodio 50mg	**2%**
Total Carbohydrate/Carbohidrato Total 17g	**6%**
Dietary Fiber/Fibra Dietetica 1g	**4%**
Sugars/Azúcares 9g	
Protein/Proteinas 2g	

Vitamin/Vitamina A 0% • Vitamin/Vitamina C 0% • Calcium/Calcio 0% • Iron/Hierro 0%

Nutrition Labels
Uniform nutrition labels enable consumers to make important dietary distinctions between similar products.

Consumer Use   Early research showed that among consumers who understood the nutrition labeling program, 59 percent used the labels in purchasing. Both comprehension and use of nutrition information increased with program duration. More recent studies have shown fewer positive results.[18] It is evident, however, that the better designed nutrition notices are, the more likely they are to be used. Specifically, when nutrition information is presented in such a way that it arouses interest, for example, by pointing out health benefits, consumers are more likely to use the labels in decision making.[19] Because of this, public policy groups should work closely with marketers to ensure that labels are designed in such a way as to attract attention and enhance the likelihood of use.

Nonuse Benefits   Even consumers who do not use labels agree that nutrition information increases confidence in the food industry, that use of labels indicates a greater concern on the part of the marketer for consumer welfare and consumer education, and that consumers have the right to know the nutrition value of food products on the market. This finding is significant, because it shows that nutrition labeling offers a public relations advantage to marketers in that it enhances overall corporate image.

Influence on Purchase Behavior   Studies by the Food and Drug Administration (FDA) indicate that consumers are more likely to select packages with nutrition labeling over nonlabeled items. Also, consumers prefer detailed nutrition labels, particularly those that express nutrition values as a percentage of FDA Recommended Daily Allowances.[20] This confirms a further advantage to marketers of properly labeling their products—it increases the likelihood of purchase.

CBite 16-1 illustrates the use of labels on raw meat. Do you think that the information on the label is likely to influence consumers' safe handling of meat products?

16-2f Disclosure of Interest Rate Provisions

The 1968 Truth-in-Lending Act was enacted to give consumers information on credit terms to help them seek favorable interest rates. Most significantly, the law requires that lenders **disclose interest rate provisions** in a way that informs consumers of the actual rate of interest—expressed, for example, as 18 percent per year rather than as a monthly rate of 1.5 percent. Studies into disclosure of interest rates have reported the information that follows.[21]

Awareness   Both awareness of disclosure and knowledge of interest rates increased after the Truth-in-Lending Act was passed. Although the increase was evident across all income groups, consumers in the higher brackets were best informed. Consumer credit knowledge is, however, still inadequate: Almost half the borrowers surveyed in one study either over- or underestimated their interest payments by 50 percent or more. Other

disclosure of interest rate provisions Disclosure required by the 1968 Truth-in-Lending Act, which was enacted to give consumers information on credit terms to help them seek favorable interest rates. Most significantly, the law requires that lenders inform consumers of the actual rate of interest—expressed, for example, as 18 percent per year rather than as a monthly rate of 1.5 percent.

CBite 16-1

Labels on Raw Meat

F ollowing the efforts of consumer advocates, raw meat and poultry sold in grocery stores and to cafeterias and restaurants must be prominently labeled with instructions on safe handling and cooking. The label's message: "Some animal products may contain bacteria that could cause illness if the product is mishandled or cooked improperly." Advocates are now pushing to make the label even more specific. It should instruct consumers to cook meat until it "is no longer pink and has an internal temperature of 160 degrees."

Source: Adapted from Anita Manning, "Consumer Labels to Appear on Raw Meat," *USA Today* (August 12, 1993), p. 1.

---

research found that consumers have only a gross awareness of the ranking of different types of lenders according to cost (such as banks versus commercial finance companies). A large proportion of consumers are unaware of current interest rates for home mortgages, automobiles, and revolving credit at department stores. Moreover, consumers are, on the whole, less concerned with interest rates than with the size of monthly payments. These findings point to a need for public policy and consumer advocacy groups to educate consumers about credit and about evaluating lenders based on the cost of paying interest.

Credit Search Behavior   Although there is evidence that more consumers seek out credit alternatives since passage of the Truth-in-Lending Act, more than 75 percent still seek credit from only one financing institution. Not surprisingly, interest rate knowledge and search behavior are positively related to education and income and to the size of the loan sought.[22] These findings show that public policy and consumer advocacy groups should encourage consumers, especially less-educated consumers in lower income brackets, to shop around for a lender.

16-2g Consumer Advocacy and the Right to Be Informed

To support the efforts of policy makers and to protect consumer rights in areas they fail to address, consumer advocacy groups are active in the battle to keep the consumer well informed. There are five important ways in which they work to protect the consumer's right to accurate, complete, and timely information.

First, advocacy groups work to improve the decision-making skills of consumers. The better informed we are, the better we can make rational purchase decisions and so obtain the best possible product at the best possible price.[23] To improve decision-making skills, advocacy groups have sought to teach consumers how to assess the true cost of a purchase—not just its selling price, but the time and energy needed to buy it.[24] Advocacy researchers have also suggested ways in which consumers can take advantage of retail price variability by staying informed of price changes and buying only when the price is right. This consumer efficiency teaches consumers to take the time to seek out products with acceptable levels of quality, compare prices over time, and be ready to take advantage of special sales or discounts when they occur. The *Pueblo* website advertised in Exhibit 16-4 helps consumers with information about investing for retirement, getting federal benefits, raising healthy children, and buying surplus government surplus.

Second, advocacy groups are on the alert for cases of deceptive advertising. Although some campaigns are blatantly deceptive, in others, intention to deceive is difficult to spot. A campaign consumers fail to interpret correctly, for example, is not necessarily deceptive.[25] Advocacy groups have sought to develop research methods to identify both blatantly false claims and claims that are false through implication.[26] A good example is the expansion implication—an advertiser implies a level of performance that is not or cannot be

E x h i b i t 16-4

Websites like *Pueblo* are one source of information about consumption decisions that are sometimes confusing.

achieved in reality. Suppose a cigarette manufacturer advertises its brand as lower in tar than competitors. Although this may be true, the manufacturer fails to disclose that the brand is not low in tar at all.[27] By exposing consumers to potentially misleading advertisements and examining the frequency with which they agree with false claims made or implied, advocacy researchers can measure the extent to which claims are deceptive.[28] Researchers can also compare consumer responses to advertisements that make or imply false claims with those that don't.[29]

Third, advocacy groups work to identify and address consumer information problems. They analyze the type and quality of information provided to consumers and make recommendations to manufacturers on improving that information to better serve consumers. Exhibit 16-5 provides examples of typical information problems and the recommendations consumer advocacy groups may suggest to correct them.

Fourth, advocacy groups design product information programs that make specific and objective information available to consumers so that they can make better-informed choices. This is achieved through print and broadcast advertising, labeling guidelines, dissemination of information at point of purchase, programs to make product information easier to find and use, and the introduction of info-aid supers—superimposed disclaimers or messages qualifying televised advertising claims.[30]

Fifth, advocacy groups exert pressure on marketers to provide accurate and complete information about the costs and benefits of their goods and services. One popular group is the Center for Science in the Public Interest (CSPI). With a charter to disclose deceptive advertising and marketing practices, CSPI has taken on such industry giants as Kellogg's and Quaker Oats.[31] Exhibit 16-6 shows how some companies use extra information wisely.

E x h i b i t 16-5   Strategies to Address Consumer Information Problems

Problem	Recommendation
The marketer provides misleading information by advertising its products as "better" than competing brands.	Spell out exactly how the product is superior, using explicit metrics or standards so that the consumer can judge comparative claims objectively.
The marketer advertises that its product provides a certain benefit, implying uniqueness.	Provide comparative product information acknowledging that most competing brands offer the same benefit, some at an even lower price.
An advertisement focuses exclusively on the benefits of a product.	Disclose both positive and negative product information, such as negative side effects of pharmaceutical products.
Customer satisfaction is low at retail because of high-pressure selling.	Allow a "cooling-off period" during which customers can nullify transactions.
Customer satisfaction is low in professional services.	Meet and exceed minimum quality standards.
Accusations of price fixing are made.	Keep up-to-date with appropriate antitrust laws.
The marketer targets customers who have insufficient expertise to judge its product. For example, an insurance salesperson sells a policy to a consumer who knows little about insurance and does not know what to look for in a good policy.	Provide information that educates consumers about the product category so that they are able to make an objective choice.
A supplier targets consumers with insufficient expertise to judge effectively. For example, an auto repair shop charges for unnecessary repairs.	Provide information that educates consumers about the need for and the costs of services so that they are able to reject unnecessary charges.
The marketer of credence products, such as enrollment in a trade school, fails to provide information on the intrinsic or extrinsic features of the goods or services sold.	Provide information that educates consumers about the credence product so they can better evaluate it.

Source: Adapted from "A Decision Model for Prioritizing and Addressing Consumer Information Problems" reprinted with permission from *Journal of Public Policy and Marketing,* published by the American Marketing Association, Paul N. Bloom, Vol. 8, 1989, pp. 161–180.

E x h i b i t 16-6

Savvy companies like Pepsi can make the availability of extra information a marketing plus.

Source: Courtesy of Pepsi-Cola Company.

Marketing Management—Implications and Actions

Respecting the consumer's right to information helps marketers:

- Ensure that their own advertising—as well as that of competitors—makes honest claims that can be proven.
- Use the provision of information that benefits consumers as a competitive advantage.
- Win the confidence—and repeat purchases—of selective, well-informed consumers.

16-3 Right to Safety

Established under the 1972 Consumer Product Safety Act, the **Consumer Product Safety Commission (CPSC)** protects the consumer's **right to safety** in the United States. Three other federal agencies also monitor aspects of product safety: the FTC regulates advertising claims related to product safety; the Traffic Safety Administration (TSA) ensures that automobile manufacturers adhere to safety standards and remedy safety defects; and the FDA oversees safety issues in food and drug-related products.

Exhibit 16-7 summarizes laws and public policies—marked with an [S]—directly related to product safety. The items marked with an [I] are selected consumer protection laws related to the consumer's right to be informed.

16-3a Product Quality and Safety

Dissatisfaction usually results when the products we buy fail to work well or do not represent good value for money. Generally, the more expensive the product, the higher the level of dissatisfaction, but quality is a concern across all product categories. Even that family favorite, the hot dog, has long been criticized by parents and consumer groups as a product of minimal nutritional value, manufactured with little or no quality control. Quality is an issue of growing concern in the service sector, too, particularly in the retail and hospitality industries and in the management of public transportation.

Product safety is a sensitive issue in several categories, particularly children's toys, drugs, automobiles, household appliances, and such seemingly harmless packaged goods as cosmetics. Although manufacturers and service providers develop their own safety procedures, this is often not enough. As an example, product liability lawsuits have charged that both Ford Motor Company and General Motors continued to market "problem" car models after their own internal testing procedures had identified deadly hazards to drivers.[32]

A further problem is that consumers do not always respond as hoped to product safety legislation. A 1994 study investigated the impact of driver-side airbags on the number of personal injury and collision claims filed, with disturbing results. Personal injury claims were significantly higher for cars equipped with airbags than for those with seat belts only. The study concluded that airbags and other mandated safety devices may encourage driver carelessness, thus negating the legislative intent of safety policies.[33] To some extent, public safety campaigns aimed at consumer education can help, particularly when accidents result not from product design defects but from consumer misuse.[34] Campaigns promoting the use of seat belts have been particularly effective. In the area of cigarette consumption, however, tax increases have proved to be a more effective deterrent.[35] Alternatively, safety products could be marketed and promoted, as is done with the carbon monoxide detector featured in Exhibit 16-8 on page 509.

Marketers have both a social and an ethical responsibility to ensure that their products can be safely consumed and that packaging can be disposed of by consumers and nonconsumers who come into contact with them. Consumer behavior research helps marketers identify and correct potential safety hazards that can arise during and after consumption.

> ▶**Consumer Product Safety Commission (CPSC)** The commission established under the 1972 Consumer Product Safety Act that protects the consumer's right to safety in the United States. Three other federal agencies also monitor aspects of product safety: the Federal Trade Commission (FTC) regulates advertising claims related to product safety; the Traffic Safety Administration (TSA) ensures that automobile manufacturers adhere to safety standards and remedy safety defects; and the Food and Drug Administration (FDA) oversees safety issues in food and drug-related products.

> ▶**right to safety** The consumer's right to have several U.S. federal agencies monitor aspects of product quality and safety, both through safety legislation and consumer education campaigns. One consideration in the setting of policies is the extent to which consumers are willing to sacrifice such benefits as low price for improved quality or safety.

F A Q

Should we be prepared to pay more if we want extra-safe products?

Exhibit 16-7

Selected Federal Consumer Protection Laws

Pure Food and Drug Act (1906) [S]	Prohibits adulteration and misbranding of foods and drugs sold in interstate commerce
Food, Drug, and Cosmetic Act (1938) [S]	Prohibits adulteration and sale of foods, drugs, cosmetics, or therapeutic devices that may endanger public health; allows the Food and Drug Administration (FDA) to set standards and guidelines
Wool Products Labeling Act (1940) [I]	Protects producers, manufacturers, distributors, and consumers from undisclosed substitutes and mixtures in all types of manufactured wool products
Fur Products Labeling Act (1951) [I]	Protects consumers and others against misbranding, false advertising, and false invoicing of furs and fur products
Flammable Fabrics Act (1953) [S]	Prohibits interstate transportation of dangerously flammable wearing apparel and fabrics
Automobile Information Disclosure Act (1958) [I]	Requires automobile manufacturers to post suggested retail prices on all new passenger vehicles
Textile Fiber Products Identification Act (1958) [I]	Guards producers and consumers against misbranding and false advertising of fiber content of textile fiber products
Cigarette Labeling Act (1965) [I]	Requires cigarette manufacturers to label cigarettes as hazardous to health
Fair Packaging and Labeling Act (1966) [I]	Declares unfair or deceptive packaging or labeling of certain consumer commodities illegal
Child Protection Act (1966) [S]	Excludes sale of potentially harmful toys; allows the FDA to remove dangerous products from the market
Truth in Lending Act (1968)	Requires full disclosure of all finance charges on consumer credit agreements and in advertisements of credit to allow consumers to be better informed regarding their credit purchases
Child Protection and Toy Safety Act (1969) [S]	Protects children from toys and other products that contain thermal, electrical, or mechanical hazards
Fair Credit Reporting Act (1970) [I]	Ensures that credit reports will contain only accurate, relevant, and recent information and will be confidential unless requested for an appropriate reason by a proper party
Consumer Product Safety Act (1972) [S]	Created an independent agency to protect consumers from unreasonable risk of injury arising from consumer products; agency is empowered to set safety standards
Magnuson-Moss Warranty Improvement Act (1975) [I]	Provides for minimum disclosure standards and defines minimum content standards for written warranties; allows the Federal Trade Commission to prescribe interpretive rules and policy statements regarding unfair or deceptive practices

Source: William M. Pride and O. C. Ferrell, *Marketing: Basic Concepts and Decisions,* 4th ed. (Boston: Houghton Mifflin, 1985), 481.

16-3b Consumer Advocacy and the Right to Safety

Consumer research into safety issues is the most important activity of consumer advocacy groups. It involves working with government agencies to collect data relating to product safety and interviewing consumers who claim injury from unsafe products. Interviewing consumers is particularly important as it helps distinguish problems related to product defects from problems arising from consumer misuse. If actual defects are the cause, advocacy groups look to the manufacturer for recourse. Where safety problems result from misuse, communications programs that educate consumers on proper product use are the

Marketplace 16-4

Blowing Smoke

Although some consumers may wish for a complete ban on cigarettes, few believe it's ever likely to happen. The U.S. Surgeon General's office has long labeled cigarettes dangerous, but it has had no real muscle to curb their use. However, the tide may be turning. The U.S. Food and Drug Administration has repeatedly threatened to regulate the nicotine in cigarettes in the same way that it regulates drugs. The agency has shrewdly used the threat of an out-and-out ban to prod Congress into passing a round of curbs that hurt the tobacco industry, which indeed took place in the last few years.

Two developments prompted the FDA to take action. One was the disclosure in several lawsuits of internal industry documents that show tobacco companies regard nicotine as a drug. Equally important is a changed political climate swirling around tobacco. The industry has been reeling from a spate of state and local laws that prohibit smoking in public areas.

Predictably, cigarette makers are counterattacking. Not only is the FDA on shaky legal ground, they say, but new regulations would take away people's "right to make individual choices," argues a spokeswoman for RJR Nabisco Inc.'s tobacco unit.

Sorry, RJR, but it's time for action. The statistics are just too grim. More than 430,000 Americans die each year of tobacco-related causes. The annual cost: $68 billion in health-care expenses and lost productivity, estimates the Congressional Office of Technology Assessment. That's more than the $46.7 billion Americans spend on tobacco.

Source: Adapted from "It's Time for Regulators to Stop Blowing Smoke" by John Carey reprinted from March 14, 1994 issue of *Business Week* by special permission, copyright © 1994 by The McGraw-Hill Companies, Inc.

Exhibit 16-8

Products are designed and marketed to meet consumers' need for safety.

Source: Reprinted by permission of Aim Safety.

answer. Marketplace 16-4 describes the case of tobacco. Although this article was published in 1994, the saga continues.

Although several federal and state agencies oversee product safety through laws and public policies, consumer advocacy groups also have a role to play. There is much evidence of their social marketing efforts. For example, to encourage the wearing of seat belts, advocacy groups have used such strategies as reward programs, emotional appeals like the one in Exhibit 16-9, and appeals from opinion leaders to reduce auto fatalities and injuries resulting from failure to use seat belts.[36]

Exhibit 16-9

Consumer advocacy groups use informational marketing to highlight the advantages of certain consumer behaviors.

Source: Courtesy of U.S. Department of Transportation and the Ad Council.

As another example, social marketing messages with psychosocial themes that deglamorize smoking have proven effective in encouraging consumers to quit smoking, particularly younger smokers. After receiving such messages, youths are more immune to commercial cigarette advertising.[37] Research has shown that warning labels used in cigarette packaging and advertising fail to draw the consumer's attention to the dangers of smoking. Consumers are more likely to be influenced by pictorial representations.[38]

Several nonprofit organizations are dedicated to dealing with the immense social problem of drinking and driving, which causes at least 25,000 highway fatalities and 900,000 injuries per year.[39] Researchers have segmented drinkers into four distinct types, depending upon their lifestyles, and have applied different social marketing strategies to combat drinking and driving in each group. These may include consumer education, social pressure, and economic incentives and disincentives as rewards and punishments.[40]

CBite 16-2 raises the question of whether consumers are willing to pay for the additional costs of safety features on their own. The answer is: not likely.

CBite 16-2

The Price of Safety

How much are we willing to pay for safe products? One consideration in the setting of safety and quality policies is the extent to which consumers are willing to sacrifice price or other product benefits. The United States Product Safety Commission, for example, estimated in the late 1970s that a mandatory safety requirement stipulating that all consumer apparel must meet minimum flame-resistant standards would force a price increase of 25 percent, reduce the wash-and-wear properties of certain garments, diminish choices of fabric, and cut back on a variety of styling. These are not sacrifices that most of us will make willingly.

Source: Stephen C. Bruner, "Assessing the Impact of Increased Product Safety on Consumer Utility," in H. Keith Hunt, ed., *Advances in Consumer Research, Proceedings of the Eighth Annual Conference on Consumer Behavior,* 1978, Vol. V, pp. 186–193.

Marketing Management—Implications and Actions

Respecting the consumer's right to safety helps marketers:

- Take steps to create safe products and so protect themselves from liability.
- Develop communications programs that educate consumers on proper product use.

16-4 Right to Redress

The **right to redress**—to be heard—is the right to complain and express grievances about product failure. Once we find products unsatisfactory, what can we do about it? Although many products carry warranties, compensation is usually limited to exchanges or refunds. The consumer is not compensated for the time and energy it takes to return a product or for other losses resulting from its failure. When a new refrigerator breaks down and its contents spoil, ruining plans for a dinner party, a service call the following day offers little consolation.[41]

When deception or fraud is involved, the only recourse open to consumers may be litigation. This is not, however, a viable option for those without the funds, the education, or the energy to take a manufacturer to court. Even a successful lawsuit may only result in an order to cease and desist deceptive practices, without making restitution to those consumers who have already been exploited.

For these reasons, consumers have a low level of confidence that their grievances will be handled in a satisfactory way by manufacturers.[42] Marketers who wish to increase consumer confidence in their products can do so by ensuring that warranty policies are honored and by listening carefully to consumer complaints and grievances. Not only does a well-handled complaint have promotional value, but it also can provide invaluable feedback on product performance. Moreover, a well-designed warranty can invite dissatisfied customers to express their grievances in a format that the marketer can easily interpret and share with other departments within the company in order to improve product or service quality.[43]

> **right to redress**
> The consumer's right to complain and express grievances about product failure.

> **F A Q**
>
> **Should there be limits on consumer litigation against manufacturers to prevent frivolous lawsuits?**

16-4a Consumer Advocacy and the Right to Redress

Consumer advocacy groups protect the consumer's right to be heard by expressing grievances and taking legal action against offenders on behalf of consumers. An example is litigation against manufacturers of silicone breast implants. Consumer research is vital in collecting and analyzing evidence to prove whether marketers are at fault or not.

Marketing Management—Implications and Actions

Respecting the consumer's right to redress helps marketers:

- Handle complaints—both those that are well founded and those that are not—in a timely, professional manner that regains the confidence of customers.
- Use negative consumer feedback to improve goods and services.
- Develop and honor warranty policies that reduce the consumer's perception of risk in making purchases.

16-5 Right to Choose

According to the "Consumer Bill of Rights," "Consumers have the right to assured access, whenever possible, to a variety of products at competitive prices. In those industries in which competition is not workable, government regulation is substituted to assure satisfactory quality and service at fair prices."[44] The **right to choose** discourages monopolies and encourages fair competition. Monopoly restricts choice and, in extreme cases, forces

> **right to choose**
> The consumer's right to assured access, whenever possible, to a variety of products at competitive prices. In those industries in which competition is not workable, government regulation is substituted to assure satisfactory quality and service at fair prices. The intent here is to discourage monopolies and encourage fair competition. Monopoly restricts choice and, in extreme cases, forces consumers to accept questionable quality and/or high prices. Competition typically motivates marketers to offer improved quality and fair pricing.

Marketplace 16-5

Homeopathic Medicine: Cure-All or Consumer Risk?

As a young American studying medicine at Germany's Heidelberg University, Dr. Alan Shackelford became alarmed when his 4-year-old daughter developed recurrent ear and sinus infections that antibiotics didn't control. After watching her nighttime fits of coughing and vomiting, Shackelford tried a 200-year-old European remedy: microscopic doses of plant extract. The infections quickly vanished.

Homeopathic medicines like this are based on the theory that "like cures like." Natural substances that cause certain symptoms allegedly cure those symptoms when given in tiny doses. Like old-time medicine men, homeopaths claim they can cure or prevent almost anything, even cancer. However, for the vast majority of doctors and researchers, homeopathic medicines are about as scientific as the witches' brew in *Macbeth*. No one can explain how they work or even if they do. Yet there is essentially no government regulation of them. They require no prescription and usually cost less than rival medicines. Many traditional physicians are pushing for government regulation. Their argument is that homeopathy can lead patients to neglect proven treatment.

Do homeopathic medicines present an opportunity or a risk to consumers? What consumer rights would their regulation support or violate?

Source: Adapted from "Take Two Eyes of Newt and Call Me in the Morning" by Stewart Toy, Mike McNamee, and Ruth Pearson reprinted from March 28, 1994 issue of *Business Week* by special permission, copyright © 1994 by The McGraw-Hill Companies, Inc.

Sherman Act / Robinson-Patman Act Antitrust law designed to protect the consumer's right to choose. In those industries in which competition is not workable, government regulation is substituted to assure satisfactory quality and service at fair prices. The intent here is to discourage monopolies and encourage fair competition. Monopoly restricts choice and, in extreme cases, forces consumers to accept questionable quality and/or high prices. Competition typically motivates marketers to offer improved quality and fair pricing.

consumers to accept questionable quality and/or high prices. Competition typically motivates marketers to offer improved quality and fair pricing. The breakup of AT&T's monopoly in the telecommunications industry, for example, led to the fostering of competition, as companies like MCI and Sprint entered the long-distance market. Antitrust legislation, such as the **Sherman Act** and the **Robinson-Patman Act** were designed to protect the consumer's right to choose.[45]

Marketplace 16-5 presents an interesting case that exemplifies consumers' right to choose. Some say that homeopathic medicine is good; others disagree. Should consumers be given the freedom to choose between traditional medicine and homeopathic medicine?

Of particular note is the power of antitrust laws to regulate price conspiracy or the collusion on price by competitive organizations. As well as charges levied against the airline and oil industries that attract the attention of the media, the Justice Department routinely investigates less public cases, such as an investigation into fifty-five private schools that allegedly engaged in price-fixing.[46] Marketplace 16-6 illustrates a price discrimination suit in the pharmacy retail market. Marketplace 16-7 discusses possible antitrust behaviors stemming from relationship marketing (the kind of marketing that focuses on establishing strategic alliances with suppliers, distributors, and customers).

16-5a Consumer Advocacy and the Right to Choose

To make an effective case against marketers that have monopolistic control within their markets, the government or consumer advocacy groups must show that consumers are not able to exercise their right to choose. Many antitrust cases are under way. In recent years, Microsoft has been the subject of many legal actions claiming that its business practices have the result, or even the intent, of hampering competition in the computer software industry.

F A Q

When a company develops a truly innovative product, should it be protected from copycat products by competitors?

Marketing Management—Implications and Actions

Respecting the consumer's right to choose helps marketers:

- Improve the quality of their products in the spirit of healthy competition.
- Develop and communicate product benefits that are important to the consumer as a means of differentiation.

Marketplace 16-6

Price Discrimination

The prescription-drug market is subdivided by drug manufacturers into six main categories: government (veterans and state hospitals), hospitals, HMOs (owned by insurance companies and considered to be nonprofit entities by manufacturers), mail-order, chain store pharmacies, and independent pharmacies. These six categories are considered different classes of trade by drug manufacturers and, therefore, receive different discounts. This is why you can purchase prescriptions cheaper through the mail. It isn't because HMOs and mail-order houses can dispense prescriptions cheaper; it's because they're allowed to purchase drugs cheaper—a lot cheaper. And these purchases aren't always based on volume. Major manufacturers need to do away with tier pricing so all providers purchase at the same price.

Rite Aid Corp., nine other chains, and ten independents have filed suit against seven big drugmakers. Their claim: the manufacturers' discounts amount to illegal price discrimination. On the surface, it seems hard for the drug companies to justify the often huge disparities in prices. Schering-Plough Corp., for instance, charges hospitals just $2.03 for one hundred tablets of its potassium supplement, K-Dur, while retail pharmacies pay $27.31—a 1,245-percent markup. Most drugmakers won't discuss their prices or the suit, which they're fighting.

The pharmacies face an uphill battle with their litigation—both politically and practically. For starters, drugmakers grant price breaks because they have no other

Contrary to popular belief, discriminatory pricing can be legal under certain conditions. In general, price discrimination restrictions do not apply to services and apply only to those commodities involved in interstate commerce, sold in the same market, and not representing different levels of perceived quality. In practice, most price differentials actually serve to intensify competition and make markets more efficient. Think of lower prices for children and senior citizens, "ladies nights," volume discounts, and lower medical fees for the indigent as examples.

Source: Michael H. Morris and Gene Morris, *Market Oriented Pricing* (New York: Quorum Books, 1990), p. 154.

choice. HMOs and hospitals can choose the drugs they want to stock, and so pit manufacturers against one another to win bargains. Retail pharmacies have to stock nearly everything or lose customers to a store around the corner. What's more, pressure from HMOs, hospitals, and mail-order buyers, which account for more than 30 percent of the U.S. drug sales, helps keep prices down—and reformers won't want that to change.

The retail pharmacies also have a tough legal case to prove. Drugmakers can argue they have to offer such breaks to HMOs or lose business. They don't face the same risk with retail pharmacies. Indeed, the Federal Trade Commission has already found no fault with the drug manufacturers' differential pricing.

Sources: Adapted from George Mauney, "Guarantee That Consumers Can Choose Their Pharmacy," *Roanoke Times* (May 28, 1994), p. A9; and Joseph Weber, "Can a 1,245% Markup on Drugs Really Be Legal?" *Business Week* (November 1, 1993), p. 34.

Marketplace 16-7

Antitrust Implications of Relationship Marketing

Recently, a number of marketing scholars have raised the issue that relationship marketing may violate antitrust laws. This violation may occur because relationship marketing undercuts competition. The spirit of relationship marketing encourages firms to foster intense relationships with key trading partners. It prompts firms to integrate vertically in the context of the channel of distribution (e.g., manufacturers merging or acquiring wholesalers and retailers). It induces firms to collaborate with competitors.

Relationship marketing activities that lead to price collusion—resulting in restraining competition—are illegal (in violation of the Sherman Act). Relationship marketing activities that lead to mergers resulting in lessened competition in the marketplace are illegal (in violation of the Clayton Act). In many cases, relationship marketing results in the creation of barriers to entry, that is, obstacles erected to discourage new companies from establishing a presence in an industry. This is also illegal according to antitrust laws.

Although antitrust laws apply equally to all business firms, small firms rarely have the resources or power to restrict trade or reduce the power of competition substantially. Hence, the controversy applies essentially to large firms or oligopolistic industries (industries that are highly dominated by a small handful of competitors such as in the automobile industry or the telecommunication industry). Marketing scholars recommend that, to avoid violating the law, business executives must scrutinize new-market-dominating mergers, business-to-business online exchanges, tying agreements, and price discriminations. Consider what has happened recently in the telecommunications industry. Sprint has merged with Nextel, and AT&T Wireless with Cingular. Are these mergers good or bad for consumer well-being? The jury is still out.

Source: Adapted from Renee J. Fontenot and Michael R. Hyman, "The Antitrust Implications of Relationship Marketing," *Journal of Business Research*, Vol. 57 (November 2004), pp. 1211–1221.

right to a healthful environment The consumer's right to have legislation that protects public health in the areas of hazardous waste control, toxic substance control, and safe drinking water programs.

Environmental Protection Agency (EPA) The agency that sets and regulates polices to protect the environment.

Superfund Amendments and Reauthorization Act The 1986 act that authorizes appropriations for the EPA Hazardous Substance Response Trust Fund program to charge violators and to clean up hazardous waste sites.

Emergency Response Act The 1986 act that amends the Toxic Substances Control Act to require the EPA to develop regulations pertaining to inspections and development of plans to manage asbestos.

Safe Drinking Water Act Amendment The 1986 act that authorizes appropriations for and revision of EPA safe drinking water programs.

F A Q

Which is more important: the right of nonsmokers to a healthful environment or smokers' rights?

16-6 Right to a Healthful Environment

U.S. legislation protects consumers' **right to a healthful environment,** especially in the areas of hazardous waste control, toxic substance control, and safe drinking water programs. Environmental pollution is of rising concern in industrialized nations. Manufacturing processes and by-products can do lasting damage to both the environment and public health.[47] The **Environmental Protection Agency (EPA)** sets and regulates polices to protect the environment. Examples of legislation include the following:[48]

1. The U.S. 1986 **Superfund Amendments and Reauthorization Act** extends and amends the 1980 Comprehensive Environmental Response Compensation and Liability Act. It authorizes appropriations for the EPA Hazardous Substance Response Trust Fund program to charge violators and to clean up hazardous waste sites.

2. The U.S. 1986 **Emergency Response Act** amends the Toxic Substances Control Act of 1976 to require the EPA to develop regulations pertaining to inspections and development of plans to manage asbestos. The 1988 Toxic Substance Control Act Amendment provides companies with more time to develop and implement asbestos removal from schools.

3. The U.S. 1986 **Safe Drinking Water Act Amendment** authorizes appropriations for and revision of EPA safe drinking water programs.

The study of consumer behavior is central to developing programs to protect the public from pollution and from toxic substances in the environment. This is because the first step in designing such legislation is to determine those aspects of current legislation with which consumers are dissatisfied and those aspects of any proposed legislation they are likely to support.

16-6a Consumer Advocacy and the Right to a Healthful Environment

As Exhibit 16-10 suggests, there are opportunities for consumer advocacy groups to take action on a broad range of environmental issues, among them waste control and recycling, concern for wildlife and the biosphere, environmental labeling, concern for health, and energy awareness.[49]

The Department of Energy (DOE) has a long history of encouraging and funding social marketing campaigns to motivate conservation behaviors.[50] Some programs curtail energy use, for example, by encouraging consumers to wash clothes in cold water, turn the thermostat down in winter and up in summer, and drive less or carpool. Other programs encourage maintenance behaviors, such as changing motor oil regularly and getting regular car tune-ups, checking for plumbing leaks, and turning out lights. Still other programs encourage efficiency behaviors, like buying fuel-efficient cars and energy-efficient appliances, and installing thermal pane windows.[51]

Marketplace 16-8 on page 516 illustrates the case of genetically altered foods and consumers' right to know. Do consumers have the right to know when their food is genetically modified? Do consumers have the right to safe food? Do consumers have the right to a healthful environment?

CBite 16-3 illustrates an interesting point—that even if a product is safer and more environmentally friendly than competitor products, consumers may not buy the better product. Consumer behavior is complex and cannot be easily predicted by product quality and safety concerns alone.

A variety of social marketing strategies enhances the development of consumer behaviors consistent with environmental protection. First, the use of continuous reinforcement and reminders can encourage long-term conservation behavior.[52] Second, using opinion leaders and word-of-mouth communications can provide consumers with role models of energy-responsible behaviors to emulate.[53] Third, campaigns that

Environmental Issues Addressed by Consumer Advocacy Groups

To protect consumers, there is an advocacy group for every issue. Here is just a sampling of environmental concerns.

Concern for Waste

Waste control

Green space conservation

Resource conservation

Landfills

Recycling

Waste disposal/reduction

Energy conservation/efficiency

Concern for Wildlife

Wildlife preservation

Habitat protection

Wilderness protection

Deforestation

Species preservation

Desertification

Ecosystem preservation

Trade in rare species

Concern for the Biosphere

Biosphere protection

Resource depletion

Toxic waste

Ozone depletion

Greenhouse effect

Concern for Health

Water protection

Air pollution

Human health protection

Citizen education

Energy Awareness

Clean energy

Rain forest preservation

Alternative energy sources

Energy conservation

Automobiles

Water pollution

Concern for Environmental Technology

Biotechnology

Composting

Community economic development

Safe technology

Interest in Popular Issues

Environmental labeling

Citizen education

Overpopulation

Citizen participation

Climate change

Soil pollution/erosion

Source: Adapted from Mary R. Zimmer, Thomas F. Stafford, and Marla Royne Stafford, "Green Issues: Dimensions of Environmental Concern," *Journal of Business Research,* Vol. 30 (May 1994), pp. 63–74.

CBite 16-3

Big on Image, Not on Sales

We believe in natural products, so why aren't we buying them? A survey of attitudes toward natural products found that their image is almost impeccable, a promising picture for future growth. Yet sales just don't back up that promise. For example, while 43 percent of respondents thought free-range chicken was better than conventional chicken, a mere 6 percent actually bought it. Similarly, while 53 percent gave organic fruits and vegetables the thumbs up, only 19 percent put their money down for it. The survey also found people with higher education and incomes think natural products are better. For example, 55 percent of college graduates compared with 40 percent of non-high-school graduates say natural cereal is better. Also, 56 percent of those with household incomes of more than $50,000 think natural cereal is better, compared with only 45 percent of those with incomes of under $15,000.

Source: Adapted from "Natural Products Score Big on Image" by Leah Rickard reprinted with permission from the August 8, 1994 issue of *Advertising Age.* Copyright © 1994 Crain Communications, Inc.

Marketplace 16-8

Consumer Rights and Bio-Engineering

Food growers and processors introduce well over one hundred new plant varieties each year. Through sometimes minor and sometimes noticeable genetic changes, agronomic modifications both improve farm performance and increase consumer choice in the produce department. Super sweet corn, brocco-flower, and several new pepper varieties are recent examples of fresh market products with enhanced consumer appeal. Processors are also looking to alternative crops for food ingredients. The search for nutritionally superior oils with higher degrees of unsaturation, for example, has led to new products such as canola oil that benefit consumer health.

According to supporters of genetically developed foods, consumers don't have to worry about the safety of the food they eat because other people do. Safety assessment is a critical part of the development process. Whether it is a new variety of carrot or a gourmet pasta sauce, the food industry works hard to ensure that products are safe. Consumers in the United States can confidently choose from a vast array of packaged and fresh market food products throughout the year.

With genetic engineering, scientists have a tool with the potential to benefit consumers and producers. New varieties of crops cut pesticide use. New foods last longer and can be processed more easily. However, the potential benefits of genetic engineering also carry with them potential risks. New varieties may carry allergens that humans have never been exposed to. The nutritional value of a long-lasting tomato, for instance, may be diminished as it waits to be eaten. And many consumers want, and all consumers deserve, to know the origin of the foods that they serve their families.

The Food and Drug Administration (FDA) classifies the bioengineering of genetically engineered foods as a continuation of traditional produce-breeding techniques that growers have successfully used for centuries. This means they are classified as "Generally Recognized As Safe," or

---

Critics of genetically engineered foods have noted that many consumers have religious or ethical beliefs that would compel them to avoid foods developed with animal genes. The FDA and industry advocates argue that this is unscientific and cannot be a basis for labeling requirements. Does the consumer's right to know outweigh all other concerns? Would expanded label requirements constitute a burden on producers and potentially block the development of new and beneficial foods?

GRAS, a classification designed to allow approval of foods that have been consumed for decades and even centuries without apparent ill effect.

This policy is founded on a fundamental flaw, however, because genetic engineering is not merely a refinement of previous breeding techniques. We don't have the wisdom of centuries of hindsight with genetically engineered foods. Tomatoes with flounder proteins or corn with firefly genes have never been part of the human diet. We don't know, therefore, what the health effects of these new products might be. The FDA itself has noted that potential risks from genetic engineering include new toxicants, unexpected effects, and reduced effectiveness of antibiotics. Although the FDA has developed a flow chart for companies to consider as they develop bio-engineered products, the agency allows companies to simply decide for themselves if a food presents a risk.

Although the FDA has considered a labeling requirement for genetically engineered food, no action has been taken yet on any labeling requirements. The current approach is plainly inadequate; it is bad for consumers, growers, and for the nascent biotech industry.

Source: Adapted from "Genetically Developed Foods: Are Existing Regulations Inadequate?" by Dominic Madigan and Alan Goldhammer in *At Home with Consumers,* Volume 14, August 1993. Reprinted by permission of Direct Selling Education Foundation.

---

encourage behaviors consistent with consumers' ecological values and attitudes can motivate consumers to put their beliefs into action through environmentally responsible behavior.[54] Those who value environmental protection, for example, are likely to respond well to appeals to recycle waste.[55] Fourth, market segmentation techniques can help social marketers develop different strategies for groups of consumers with different attitudes toward environmental protection.[56] Fifth, boycotting of companies that violate the environment exerts pressure upon the violators to mend their ways, particularly when media coverage and consumer support are strong. A boycott against Burger King in the United States protested the use of veal products from animals raised in inhumane conditions. Another, against Dow Chemical Corp., protested its marketing of herbicides that were environmentally harmful.[57] Exhibit 16-11 illustrates how government and industry cooperate to ensure that electronic goods are energy efficient.

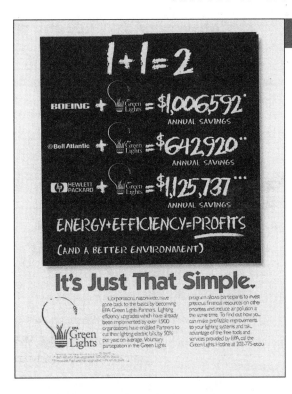

E x h i b i t 16-11

Where the environment is concerned, government and industry must often cooperate to find common ground beneficial to all interests, such as energy-efficient electronic goods.

Source: Courtesy of U.S. Environmental Protection Agency.

Marketing Management—Implications and Actions

Respecting the consumer's right to a healthful environment helps marketers:

- Use sensitivity to environmental issues as a competitive benefit.
- Develop technologies that benefit the environment and promise long-term profitability.
- Develop a corporate image that is in sync with the consumer's concern for the environment.

16-7 Right to Privacy

The consumer's **right to privacy** is an issue of increasing urgency that gained momentum through the 1990s.[58] The application of sophisticated database technology to business has led to alarming increases in the amount of information businesses are able to obtain about individual consumers. Insurance companies, for example, have health records on nine out of ten working Americans. There are 1,200 credit bureaus in the United States that keep records on almost every adult in the country. Marketers commonly develop detailed profiles of their customers and potential customers based on their own records of transactions and transactions with other institutions. More than 20,000 such lists are sold or leased to any and every business imaginable to reach specified consumer populations. American Express is reported to maintain weekly profiles of every one of its credit holders. The profiles are so detailed that they involve four hundred and ten attributes, from age, sex, and income, to the particulars of specific purchases.

Four out of five consumers report that they value their privacy and believe it should be protected by law. Congress passed the first privacy act, the **Fair Credit Reporting Act,** in 1970. It requires credit reporting agencies to notify consumers and supply information on adverse decisions made about them. The **Privacy Act** of 1974 applies broader record-keeping restrictions to U.S. government agencies. The 1984 **Cable Communications Act** mandates cable companies to disclose to their subscribers any information collected about them, the reason for its collection, how long it will be retained, and who might use it and under what conditions.[59]

right to privacy
The consumer's right to be left alone. Four out of five consumers report that they value their privacy and believe it should be protected by law. Business does not have the right to collect information about consumers to establish detailed profiles about their lives and shopping habits.

Fair Credit Reporting Act
The first privacy act, passed by Congress in 1970, which requires credit reporting agencies to notify consumers and supply information on adverse decisions made about them.

Privacy Act The 1974 act that applies broader record-keeping restrictions to U.S. government agencies.

Cable Communications Act
The 1984 act that mandates cable companies to disclose to their subscribers any information collected about them, the reason for its collection, how long it will be retained, and who might use it and under what conditions.

16-7a **Consumer Advocacy and the Right to Privacy**

The main activity of consumer advocacy groups that promote the consumer's right to privacy is consumer education. For example, in the area of direct marketing, advocates educate consumers about the benefits offered by this medium—convenience, fast service, broad selection, and more. They also educate consumers on the ways in which they can minimize invasion of privacy—by having their names removed from mailing and telemarketing lists, for example.[60]

Marketing Management—Implications and Actions

Respecting the consumer's right to privacy helps marketers:

- Limit marketing costs by targeting only those consumers who welcome their product information.
- Protect their customers from well-informed competitors.

Chapter Spotlights

This chapter highlights consumer issues central to the development of marketing strategies that both meet regulatory requirements and are sensitive to social concerns. Together, regulatory bodies and consumer advocacy groups police marketing practices to ensure the protection of consumer rights. Moreover, by building quality and safety standards into manufacturing processes and by espousing socially responsible marketing strategies, companies can better establish long-term relationships with consumers and so ensure long-term profitability.

1. Regulation of marketing practices. The provisions of the "Consumer Bill of Rights," supported by legislation and by the actions of consumer advocacy groups, serve to protect consumers in the six areas explored in the chapter.

2. Right to information. Regulated by the U.S. Federal Trade Commission, the consumer's right to be informed ensures truth in marketing and advertising, unit pricing, product labeling, disclosure of interest rates, and more.

3. Right to safety. Several U.S. federal agencies monitor aspects of product quality and safety, both through safety legislation and

consumer education campaigns. One consideration in the setting of policies is the extent to which consumers are willing to sacrifice such benefits as low price for improved quality or safety.

4. Right to redress. The right to redress is the right of consumers to express grievances and seek recourse when products are found unsatisfactory. Through the use of warranties and by having a system in place to answer consumer complaints, marketers can both improve quality and increase consumer confidence.

5. Right to choose. U.S. antitrust legislation protects consumers against monopolistic practices or price collusion that limit their right to choose.

6. Right to a healthful environment. U.S. legislation protects public health in the areas of hazardous waste control, toxic substance control, and safe drinking water programs.

7. Right to privacy. In the age of information, consumer privacy is a controversial issue. Legislation protects U.S. consumers in such areas as personal data collection and credit reporting.

Key Terms

advertising substantiation (p. 499)
Cable Communications Act (p. 517)
"Consumer Bill of Rights" (p. 497)
Consumer Product Safety Commission (CPSC) (p. 507)
corrective advertising (p. 499)
disclosure of interest rate provisions (p. 503)
Emergency Response Act (p. 514)
Environmental Protection Agency (EPA) (p. 514)

Fair Credit Reporting Act (p. 517)
Federal Trade Commission (FTC) (p. 498)
information disclosure (p. 500)
Privacy Act (p. 517)
product labeling (p. 502)
right to a healthful environment (p. 514)
right to be informed (p. 497)
right to choose (p. 511)
right to privacy (p. 517)
right to redress (p. 511)

right to safety (p. 507)
Robinson-Patman Act (p. 512)
Safe Drinking Water Act Amendment (p. 514)
Sherman Act (p. 512)
Superfund Amendments and Reauthorization Act (p. 514)
unit pricing (p. 502)

Review Questions

Note: You can find the correct answers to these questions by taking the quiz and then submitting your answers in the Online Edition. The program will automatically score your submission. If you miss a question, the program will provide the correct answer, a rationale for the answer, and the section number in the chapter where the topic is discussed.

1. Today, the axiom "let the _____ beware" still holds true.
   a. buyer
   b. seller
   c. marketer
   d. manufacturer

2. The Federal Trade Commission may require companies to furnish tests, other data, or _____ to properly inform the buying public.
   a. studies
   b. samples of products
   c. legal compliance
   d. warranties

3. The Federal Trade Commission has ruled that retailers must provide consumers with two prices: the price per package and the _____ price.
   a. total
   b. refund
   c. unit
   d. variable

4. Consumer reporting on inadequate and misleading labeling on food products is
   a. decreasing.
   b. constant.
   c. increasing.
   d. collected on a limited scale.

5. Consumers do not always _____ as hoped to product safety legislation.
   a. write congressmen
   b. respond
   c. comply
   d. care about

6. Consumers have a _____ level of confidence that manufacturers will handle their grievances in a satisfactory way.
   a. very high
   b. high
   c. medium
   d. low

7. The intent of right to choose legislation is to discourage _____ and encourage _____.
   a. fair competition, monopolies
   b. monopolies, fair competition
   c. unfair pricing, fair competition
   d. monopolies, fair labeling

8. Antitrust laws attempt to regulate price conspiracy and
   a. collusion.
   b. discrimination.
   c. loss leaders.
   d. ceiling prices.

9. The U.S. 1986 Safe Drinking Water Act called for a revision of safe drinking water programs and for
   a. stricter legislation.
   b. more lax legislation.
   c. appropriations.
   d. more control of water coming in from Canada and Mexico.

10. What percent of consumers report that they value their privacy and believe it should be protected by law?
    a. 20
    b. 40
    c. 60
    d. 80

Team Talk

1. Discuss past experiences in which you feel your rights may have been violated by marketers. What steps should the marketer have taken to protect your rights? What recourse, if any, did you take? What recourse could you have taken?

2. Look through your local newspapers for examples of advertising that could be considered deceptive. To what extent and in what ways are the ads deceptive? How might you verify your suspicions?

3. Should marketers be held responsible for injuries to consumers who engage in inherently dangerous activities, such as skydiving, extreme skiing, or stock-car racing? Discuss.

4. The airline industry has eliminated the commission of 10 percent once paid to travel agents upon the sale of tickets. Commissions are now capped at $50 per ticket. Travel agents feel that they now have no choice but to charge customers for ticketing services that were previously provided free of charge. Do you think there is any merit in charges from agents that airline companies conspired to fix prices and that this is anticompetitive? Are the rights of consumers violated in any way?

5. In a team made up of smokers and nonsmokers, argue the case for and against permitting smoking in such public areas as shopping malls, airports, and sports stadiums. How would you go about investigating the effects of a no-smoking policy on consumers?

6. How do you handle telephone calls to your home from telemarketing representatives? What is your attitude toward such calls? Do you have the same attitude toward "junk mail"?

Workshops

Research Workshop

Background

The Student Action Committee, of which you are a member, has litter control on its agenda. Some members are in favor of banning nonreturnable bottles, the most visible litter problem on campus. Others argue that outlawing a popular form of packaging will not solve the fundamental consumer behavior problem of which littering is a symptom. The objective of this workshop is to investigate the impact of a ban on nonreturnable bottles both on students' perception of the litter problem and on their right to choose.

Methodology

Develop arguments both for and against the ban in fifty words or less. Based on this, devise a short questionnaire aimed at discovering how strongly students feel about the litter problem, the contribution made to it by nonreturnable bottles, and their freedom to choose to buy drinks in nonreturnable bottles. Administer the questionnaire to at least twenty-five people at the student union or another heavily trafficked area.

To the Marketplace

Based on the attitudes indicated by your sample, make a recommendation either for or against banning nonreturnable bottles. If you recommend against the ban, what other options, suggested by the study, are feasible for the committee?

Creative Workshop

Background

Your team has been hired by Babyworld, manufacturers of baby furniture and accessories, to develop a communications program that will convince safety advocates and consumers that its folding playpen is safe. The product had been cited the previous year as potentially unsafe by Consumers Union and has since been completely redesigned. The objective of this workshop is to identify key product benefits that convincingly argue the safety of the redesigned product.

Methodology

Familiarize yourself with the different playpens on the market. Choose one that, for the purpose of this assignment, will be the Babyworld product. List key product benefits and assume that some of these are improvements over the previous model. Compare with competing brands to identify strengths and weaknesses. Sketch out themes for the campaign that both address the issue of poor safety in the past and prove improved performance.

To the Marketplace

Along with a final campaign concept including visuals, headline, and copy, present a list of recommendations to Babyworld to overcome the negative publicity from Consumers Union. Consider, for example, media recommendations, press releases, speeches and other public relations activities, and offers of seminars or information on safety for new parents.

Managerial Workshop

Background

As a member of the town board, you receive a request from a group of residents to pass an ordinance prohibiting home sales solicitations, which, the request claims, violate the right to privacy. Another group opposes the ordinance on the grounds that it restricts the right to information and the right to choose. A third group, representing nonprofits who solicit door-to-door on behalf of charities, also objects. Your job is to help the town board decide on the course of action that is in the best interests of its residents. The objective of this workshop is to help you explore the options open to consumers, advocates, and marketers when one or more of the rights of individuals conflict.

Methodology

Make a list of pros and cons of home solicitations from the viewpoint of the consumer. Use this as a starting point to explore the effects of the proposed ordinance on the consumer's right to privacy, right to information, and right to choose.

To the Marketplace

Make recommendations to the board on the type of research needed before a decision can be made, and suggest ways in which the research should be conducted.

Notes

1. Catherine Yang, "Flamed with a Lawsuit: Will Courts Set Limits on the Freedom of Cyberspeech?" *Business Week* (February 6, 1995), p. 70.
2. "The Consumer Bill of Rights," in *Consumer Advisory Council, First Report* (Washington, DC: U.S. Government Printing Office, 1963).
3. Ibid.
4. David M. Gardner, "Deception in Advertising: A Conceptual Approach," *Journal of Marketing*, Vol. 39 (January 1975), pp. 40–46; Joe L. Welch, *Marketing Law* (Tulsa, OK: PPC Books, 1980).
5. John S. Healey and Harold H. Kassarjian, "Advertising Substantiation and Advertising Response: A Content Analysis of Magazine Advertisements," *Journal of Marketing*, Vol. 47 (Winter 1983), pp. 107–117; Dorothy Cohen, "The FTC's Advertising Substantiation Program," *Journal of Marketing*, Vol. 44, (Winter 1980), pp. 26–35.
6. Gary M. Armstrong, Metin N. Gurol, and Frederick A. Russ, "A Longitudinal Evaluation of the Listerine Corrective Advertising," *Journal of Public Policy and Marketing*, Vol. 2, (1983), pp. 16–28.
7. Gary M. Armstrong, Metin N. Gurol, and Frederick A. Russ, "Detecting and Correcting Deceptive Advertising," *Journal of Consumer Research*, Vol. 6, (December 1979), pp. 237–246; Richard W. Mizerski, Neil K. Allison, and Stephen Calvert, "A Controlled Field Study of Corrective Advertising Using Multiple Exposures and a Commercial Medium," *Journal of Marketing Research*, Vol. 17, (August 1979), pp. 341–348.
8. J. C. Maloney, "Curiosity Versus Disbelief in Advertising," *Journal of Advertising Research*, Vol. 2 (June 1962), pp. 2–8, as cited in Debra L. Scammon, "Expectancy-Discrepant Information: Does Format Influence Effects?" in H. Keith Hunt, ed., *Advances in Consumer Research*, Vol. 5 (Ann Arbor, MI: Association for Consumer Research, 1978), pp. 145–150.

9. William L. Wilkie, Denis L. McNeill, and Michael B. Mazis, "Marketing's 'Scarlet Letter': The Theory and Practice of Corrective Advertising," *Journal of Marketing*, Vol. 48 (Spring 1984), pp. 11–31.

10. Joseph P. Kennedy, Sensible Advertising and Family Education Act, 102nd Congress, H. Doc. 4493 (Washington, DC: U.S. Government Printing Office, 1990).

11. Todd Barlow and Michael S. Wogalter, "Alcoholic Beverage Warnings in Magazine and Television Advertisements," *Journal of Consumer Research*, Vol. 20 (June 1993), pp. 147–156.

12. Dorothy Cohen, "Protecting Consumers from Unfairness and Deception," in Paul N. Bloom, ed., *Consumerism and Beyond: Research Perspectives on the Future Social Environment* (Cambridge, MA: Marketing Science Institute, 1982), pp. 68–74; for additional literature on the use of misinformation, anti-factual information, and puffery, see the following articles: Avery M. Abernethy and George R. Franke, "The Information Content of Advertising: A MetaAnalysis," Journal of Advertising, Vol. 25 (Summer 1996), pp. 1–17; Ivan L. Preston, "Puffery and Other 'Loophole' Claims: How the Law's 'Don't Ask, Don't Tell' Policy Condones Fraudulent Falsity in Advertising," *Journal of Law and Commerce*, Vol. 18 (Fall 1998), pp. 49–114; Ivan L. Preston, "A Problem Ignored: Dilution and Negation of Consumer Information by Antifactual Content," *Journal of Consumer Affairs*, Vol. 36 (2002), pp. 263–284.

13. "The Public is Wary of Ads," *Business Week* (January 29, 1972), p. 69.

14. Elzbieta Lepkowska-White and Amy L Parsons, "Comprehension of Warnings and Resulting Attitudes," *Journal of Consumer Affairs*, Vol. 35 (Winter 2001), pp. 278–295.

15. Roger Kerin and Michael Harvey, "Consumer Legislation: A Proactive or Reactive Response to Consumerism?" *Journal of the Academy of Marketing Science*, Vol. 2, No. 4 (Fall 1974), pp. 582–592; George S. Day, "Assessing the Effects of Information Disclosure Requirements," *Journal of Marketing*, Vol. 40 (April 1976), p. 46; Kenneth C. Manning, David E. Sprott, and Anthony D. Miyazaki, "Unit Price usage Knowledge: Conceptualization and Empirical Assessment," *Journal of Business Research*, Vol. 56 (May 2003), pp. 367–377.

16. Thomas J. Miller, "Food Advertising and Health Claims: Everything You Read Is Not Always Good for You," *Journal of State Government*, Vol. 62 (May/June 1989), pp. 107–110. For an article dealing with labeling issues in the power and electricity industry, see Brian Roe, Mario F. Teisl, Huaping Rong, and Alan S. Levy, "Characteristics of Consumer-preferred Labeling Policies: Experimental Evidence from Price and Environmental Disclosure for Deregulated Electricity Services," *Journal of Consumer Affairs*, Vol. 35 (2001), pp. 1–26.

17. Alan S. Levy, Odonna Matthews, Marilyn Stephenson, Janet E. Tenney, and Raymond E. Scuker, "The Impact of a Nutrition Information Program on Food Purchases," *Journal of Public Policy and Marketing*, Vol. 4 (1985), pp. 1–13; J. Edward Russo, Richard Staelin, Catherine A. Nolan, Gary J. Russell, and Barbara L. Metcalf, "Nutrition Information in the Supermarket," *Journal of Consumer Research*, Vol. 13 (June 1986), pp. 48–70; Scot Burton, Judith A. Garretson, and Anne M. Velliquette, "Implications of Accurate Usage of Nutrition Facts Panel Information for Food Product Evaluations and Purchase Intentions," *Journal of the Academy of Marketing Science*, Vol. 27 (Fall 1999), 470–480; Fuan Li, Paul W. Miniard, and Michael J. Barone, "The Facilitating Influence of Consumer Knowledge on the Effectiveness of Daily Value Reference Information," *Journal of the Academy of Marketing Science*, Vol. 28 (Summer 2000), pp. 425–436.

18. Ibid.

19. Christine Moorman, "The Effects of Stimulus and Consumer Characteristics on the Utilization of Nutrition Information," *Journal of Consumer Research*, Vol. 17 (December 1990), pp. 362–374. For more recent studies dealing with the use of nutrition labels, see Rodolfo M. Mayga, Jr., "Nutritional Knowledge, Gender, and Food Label Use," *Journal of Consumer Affairs*, Vol. 34 (Summer 2000), pp. 97–113; Judith A. Garretson and Scot Burton, "Effects of Nutrition Facts Panel Values, Nutrition Claims, and Health Claims on Consumer Attitudes, Perceptions of Disease-related Risks, and Trust," *Journal of Public Policy & Marketing*, Vol. 19 (Fall 2000), pp. 213–228. See also J. Craig Andrews, Richard G. Netemeyer, and Scot Burton, "Consumer Generalization of Nutrient Content Claims in Advertising," *Journal of Marketing*, Vol. 62 (October 1998), pp. 62–75; Scot Burton and Abhijit Biswas, "Preliminary Assessment of Changes in Labels Required by the Nutrition Labeling and Education Act of 1990," *Journal of Consumer Affairs*, Vol. 27 (Summer 1993), pp. 127–44; Judith A. Garretson, and Anne M. Velliquette, "Implications of Consumers' Utilization of Nutrition Facts, Label Information on Food Product Evaluations and Purchase Intentions," *Journal of the Academy of Marketing Science*, Vol. 27 (Fall 1999), pp. 470–80; Siva K. Balasubramanian and Catherine Cole, "Consumers' Search and Use of Nutrition Information: The Challenge and Promise of the Nutrition Labeling and Education Act," *Journal of Marketing*, Vol. 66 (July 2002), pp. 112–128.

20. Kerin and Harvey, "Consumer Legislation: A Proactive or Reactive Response to Consumerism?"; Day, "Assessing the Effects of Information Disclosure Requirements."

21. Day, "Assessing the Effects of Information Disclosure Requirements."

22. Kerin and Harvey, "Consumer Legislation: A Proactive or Reactive Response to Consumerism?"

23. E. Scott Maynes, "An Information Decider Evaluation of Sources of Consumer Information," in Robert N. Mayer, ed., *Enhancing Consumer Choice: Proceedings of the Second International Conference on Research in the Consumer Interest* (Columbia, MO: American Council on Consumer Interests, ©1991), pp. 491–514.

24. E. Scott Maynes, *Decision Making for Consumers* (New York: Macmillan, 1976).

25. Ivan L. Preston and Jeff I. Richards, "The Relationship of Miscomprehension to Deceptiveness in FTC Cases," in Richard J. Lutz, ed., *Advances in Consumer Research*, Vol. 13 (Provo, UT: Association for Consumer Research, 1986), pp. 138–142.

26. Armstrong, Gurol, and Russ, "Detecting and Correcting Deceptive Advertising"; Frederic L. Barbour and David M. Gardner, "Deceptive Advertising: A Practical Approach to Measurement," *Journal of Advertising*, Vol. 11 (January 1982), 21–30; J. Edward Russo, Barbara L. Metcalf, and Debra Stephens, "Identifying Misleading Advertising," *Journal of Consumer Research*, Vol. 8 (September 1981), pp. 119–131.

27. Ivan L. Preston, "The FTC's Handling of Puffery and Other Selling Claims Made 'By Implication,'" *Journal of Business Research,* Vol. 5 (June 1977), pp. 155–181.

28. Jacob Jacoby and Constance Small, "The FDA Approach to Defining Misleading Advertising," *Journal of Marketing,* Vol. 39 (October 1975), pp. 65–68.

29. Raymond R. Burke, Wayne S. DeSarbo, Richard L. Oliver, and Thomas S. Robertson, "Deception by Implication: An Experimental Investigation," *Journal of Consumer Research,* Vol. 14 (March 1988), pp. 483–494.

30. R. Bruce Hutton, Dennis I. McNeill, and William L. Wilkie, "Some Issues Designing Consumer Information Studies in Public Policy," H. Keith Hunt, ed., *Advances in Consumer Research* (Ann Arbor, MI: Association for Consumer Research, 1978), pp. 131–136; J. Edward Russo and France Leclerc, "Characteristics of Successful Product Information Programs," *Journal of Social Issues,* Vol. 47, No. 1 (1991), pp. 73–92; Lalita A. Manrai, Ajay K. Manrai, and Noel Murray, "Comprehension of Info-Aid Supers in Television Advertising for Social Ideas: Implications for Public Policy," *Journal of Business Research,* Vol. 30 (May 1994), pp. 75–84.

31. N. Craig Smith and John A. Quelch eds., *Ethics in Marketing* (Homewood, IL: Irwin, 1993), p. 638.

32. N. Craig Smith and John A. Quelch, "Suzuki Samurai: The Roll-Over Crisis," in N. Craig Smith and John A. Quelch, eds., *Ethics in Marketing* (Homewood, IL: Irwin, 1993), pp. 196–218; Patrick Wright, *On a Clear Day You Can See General Motors* (Wright, self-published, 1979).

33. Steven P. Peterson and George E. Hoffer, "The Impact of Airbag Adoption on Relative Personal Injury and Absolute Collision Insurance Claims," *Journal of Consumer Research,* Vol. 20 (March 1994), pp. 657–662.

34. Richard Staelin and David Pittle, "Consumer Product Safety: A Discussion Paper," American Marketing Association Consumerism Workshop Monograph (Chicago, IL: American Marketing Association, 1977).

35. George R. Franke, "U.S. Cigarette Demand, 1961–1990: Econometric Issues, Evidence, and Implications," *Journal of Business Research,* Vol. 30 (May 1994), pp. 33–41.

36. E. Scott Geller, "Seat Belt Psychology," *Psychology Today* (May 1985), pp. 12–13.

37. Cornelia Pechmann and S. Ratneshwar, "The Effects of Antismoking and Cigarette Advertising on Young Adolescents' Perceptions of Peers Who Smoke," *Journal of Consumer Research,* Vol. 21 (September 1994), pp. 236–251.

38. Bhalla and Lastovicka, "The Impact of Changing Cigarette Warning Message Content and Format."

39. National Accident Sampling System (Washington, DC: Government Printing Office, 1982), p. 14.

40. Laurel Hudson and Paul N. Bloom, "Potential Consumer Research Contributions to Combating Drinking and Driving Problems," in Thomas C. Kinnear, ed., *Advances in Consumer Research,* Vol. 11, (Provo, UT: Association for Consumer Research, 1984), pp. 676–681.

41. John S. Berens, "Consumer Costs in Product Failure," *MSU Business Topics,* Vol. 19 (Spring 1971), p. 28.

42. Hiram C. Barksdale and William R. Darden, "Consumer Attitudes toward Marketing and Consumerism," *Journal of Marketing,* Vol. 36 (October 1972), pp. 28–35.

43. C. L. Kendall and Frederick A. Russ, "Warranty and Complaint Policies: An Opportunity for Marketing Management," *Journal of Marketing,* Vol. 39, No. 2 (April 1975), p. 36.

44. "The Consumer Bill of Rights."

45. Richard A. Posner, *Antitrust Law: An Economic Perspective* (Chicago, IL: University of Chicago Press, 1976); F. M. Scherer, *Industrial Market Structure and Economic Performance,* 2nd ed., (Chicago, IL: Rand McNally, 1980).

46. Gwendolyn K. Ortmeyer, "Ethical Issues in Pricing," in N. Craig Smith and John Quelch, eds., *Ethics in Marketing* (Homewood, IL: Irwin, 1993), pp. 389–404.

47. "Special Report: The Greenhouse Effect," *Newsweek* (July 11, 1988), pp. 16–23.

48. John R. Nevin, "Consumer Protection Legislation: Evolution, Structure, and Prognosis," Working Paper, University of Wisconsin–Madison, WI, August 1989.

49. Mary R. Zimmer, Thomas F. Stafford, and Marla Royne Stafford, "Green Issues: Dimensions of Environmental Concern," *Journal of Business Research,* Vol. 30 (May 1994), pp. 63–74.

50. Pam Schodler Ellen, "Do We Know What We Need to Know? Objective and Subjective Knowledge Effects on Pro-Ecological Behaviors," *Journal of Business Research,* Vol. 30 (May 1994), pp. 43–52.

51. Russell Belk, John Painter, and Richard Semenik, "Preferred Solutions to the Energy Crisis as a Function of Causal Attributions," *Journal of Consumer Research,* Vol. 8 (December 1981), pp. 306–312.

52. R. Bruce Hutton and Dennis L. McNeill, "The Value of Incentives in Stimulating Energy Conservation," *Journal of Consumer Research,* Vol. 8 (December 1981), pp. 291–298.

53. Michael L. Rothschild, "Providing Reinforcers for Environmentally Unconcerned Consumers," in Kent B. Monroe, ed., *Advances in Consumer Research,* Vol. 8 (Ann Arbor, MI: Association for Consumer Research, 1981), pp. 642–643.

54. John A. McCarty and L. J. Shrum, "Recycling of Solid Wastes: Personal Values, Value Orientations, and Attitudes about Recycling as Antecedents of Recycling Behavior," *Journal of Business Research,* Vol. 30 (May 1994), pp. 53–62; Abhijit Biswas, Jane W Licata, Daryl McKee, Chris Pullig, and Christopher Daughtridge, "The Recycling Cycle: An Empirical Examination of Consumer Waste Recycling and Recycling Shopping Behaviors," *Journal of Public Policy & Marketing,* Vol. 19 (Spring 2000), pp. 93–105.

55. Examples of measures used to identify ecologically-concerned consumers include: Thomas C. Kinnear and James R. Taylor, "The Effect of Ecological Concern on Brand Perceptions," *Journal of Marketing Research,* Vol. 10, No. 2 (May 1973), pp. 191–197; Thomas C. Kinnear, James R. Taylor, and Ahmed Sadrudin, "Ecological Concerned Consumers: Who Are They?" *Journal of Marketing,* Vol. 38, No. 2 (April 1974), pp. 20–24; Dorothy Leonard-Barton, "Voluntary Simplicity Lifestyles and Energy Conservation," *Journal of Consumer Research,* Vol. 8, No. 3 (December 1981), pp. 243–252; Avraham Shama, "The Voluntary Simplicity Consumer," *Journal of Consumer Marketing,* Vol. 2, No. 4 (1985), pp. 57–63.

56. Bronislaw J. Verhage, Lee D. Dahringer, and Edward W. Cundiff, "Will a Global Marketing Strategy Work? An Energy Conservation Perspective," *Journal of the Academy of Marketing Science,* Vol. 17 (Spring 1989), pp. 129–136.

57. Dennis E. Garrett, "The Effectiveness of Marketing Policy Boycotts: Environmental Opposition to Marketing," *Journal of Marketing,* Vol. 51 (April 1987), pp. 46–57; Jill Gabrielle Klein, N. Craig Smith, and Andrew John, "Why We Boycott: Consumer Motivations for Boycott Participation," *Journal of Marketing,* Vol. 68 (July 2004), pp. 92–105.

58. Les Dlabay, "Focus on . . . U.S. Office of Consumer Affairs," *American Council on Consumer Interests Newsletter,* Vol. 39 (March 1990), pp. 3–4.

59. Mary Gardiner Jones, "Privacy: A Significant Marketing Issue for the 1990s," *Journal of Public Policy and Marketing,* Vol. 10 (Spring 1991), pp. 133–148.

60. James E. Johnson, "Is Direct Marketing an Invasion of Privacy?" *Sales and Marketing Management in Canada,* Vol. 30 (March 1989), pp. 18–22. Cathy Goodwin, "Privacy: Recognition of a Consumer Right," *Journal of Public Policy and Marketing,* Vol. 10 (Spring 1991), pp. 149–166. For studies dealing with privacy issues online, see Anthony D. Miyazaki and Ana Fernandez, "Consumer Perceptions of Privacy and Security Risks for Online Shopping," *Journal of Consumer Affairs,* Vol. 35 (Summer 2001), pp. 27–45; Eve M. Caudill and Patrick E. Murphy, "Consumer Online Privacy: Legal and Ethical Issues," *Journal of Public Policy & Marketing,* Vol. 19 (Spring 2000), pp.7–19; Ellen R. Foxman and Paula Kilcoyne, "Information Technology, Marketing Practice, and Consumer Privacy: Ethical Issues," *Journal of Public Policy & Marketing,* Vol. 12 (Spring 1993), pp. 106–119; Jonathan W. Palmer, Joseph P Bailey, and Samer Faraj, "The Role of Intermediaries in the Development of Trust on the WWW: The Use and Prominence of Trusted Third Parties and Privacy Statements," *Journal of Computer-Mediated Communication,* Vol. 5 (March 2000), http://www.ascusc.org/jcmc/volS/issue3/palmer.html; Kim Bartel Sheehan, and Mariea Grubbs Hoy, "Dimensions of Privacy Concern among Online Consumers," *Journal of Public Policy & Marketing,* Vol. 19 (Spring 2000), pp. 62–73.; George R. Milne and Andrew J. Rohm, "Consumer Privacy and Name Removal Across Direct Marketing Channels: Exploring Opt-in and Opt-out Alternatives," *Journal of Public Policy & Marketing,* Vol. 19 (Fall 2000), pp. 238–250: Ross D. Petty, "Marketing Without Consent: Consumer Choice and Costs, Privacy, and Public Policy," *Journal of Public Policy & Marketing,* Vol. 19 (Spring 2000), pp. 42–54; Perry 6, "Who Wants Privacy Protection, and What Do They Want?" *Journal of Consumer Behaviour,* Vol. 12 (September 2002), pp. 80–91.

Consumer Behavior and Society

17

At the end of the fall semester of her freshman year, Jackie was upset to find out that her room-mate, Diana, had applied for a room change. When she confronted Diana, who she considered a friend, she was shocked to hear a flood of complaints. Diana felt that Jackie was too bossy and self-centered. Their common area was full of Jackie's computer, stereo, and exercise bike, which Jackie rarely let Diana use. Jackie was forever borrowing Diana's things. Diana's most stinging criticism was that Jackie was "just too materialistic."

All through Christmas break, Jackie thought about what Diana had said. Sure, she liked to shop. She was ambitious and often talked of "getting ahead." But did that make her a bad person? Even though she thought Diana had been unfair, Jackie decided to make a special effort to get along better with her new roommate. She'd keep her stuff in her part of the room and respect her roommate's privacy. She'd talk less about herself and find out more about her roommate's interests. She'd even try to be more generous with some of her things.

Materialism, a by-product of living in a consumer society, is just one of the social ills we'll look at in this chapter. We begin by exploring how consumer societies develop and the ways in which marketers influence their progress. To follow our discussion of regulatory issues and consumer rights in the previous chapter, we'll also find out how marketers, as responsible members of society, regulate their own practices.

17-1 The Consumer Society

We've all heard stories of the good old days, when life was simple, families and relationships mattered, and all was right with the world. Our grandparents claim they barely recognize the world we live in today. Life is complex. Crime statistics in the inner cities are alarmingly high. Divorce and single parenthood are becoming more the norm than the exception. Parents work and spend too little time with their children. The television becomes a baby-sitter, and advertising tempts young and old alike with the promise of happiness through purchase. As our grandparents would view it, society is in poor shape, and social ills are worse than they ever experienced.

Social critics hold the consumer society at least partly responsible. Economic development and the materialism that goes along with it have been paired with personal alienation that, in turn, is linked to social malaise. In this section, we'll explore aspects of macroconsumption—both the positives and the negatives—that have influenced the shaping of culture in developed countries and the way we live. In doing so, we'll look at the role of the marketer within society and, in particular, the ways in which marketing activities accelerate the development of a consumer society.

17-1a Development of a Consumer Culture

A **consumer culture** is one in which a high level of economic development is reflected in a high level of consumption of goods and services by a majority of its members—macroconsumption. Consumer societies have developed at different paces and in different ways throughout the world. Macromarketers have systematically detailed a number of factors that commonly influence their development.[1] These are summarized in Exhibit 17-1.

External Facilitating Factors A consumer society is likely to develop within a culture if that culture has the six technical characteristics listed in Exhibit 17-1. A prerequisite is an abundant supply of goods and services. As the economy begins to meet demand with supply, shortages become less common and steady production is possible. As people gain economic freedom, they are increasingly motivated to work and so reap the rewards of labor. Thus, production capabilities grow. The number and variety of mass marketing institutions grow, as advertising agencies, marketing research firms, mass merchandise retail outlets, and channel intermediaries arise as a result of increased production. Communications and transportation technologies develop as improved road, rail, air, and sea networks move manufactured goods from factories to consumer outlets. Advances in advertising media allow businesses more and more options, from newspapers, magazines, transit advertising, and outdoor bulletin boards to radio and television to direct mail and telemarketing. Innovations open new markets as businesses adapt their goods and services to the changing needs of consumers.

Certain economic factors also facilitate the development of a consumer society. Increased wealth and purchasing power provide consumers with the ability to purchase goods and services, thus accelerating economic development. Diffusion of wealth through the populace increases demand. Growth of marketing and promotion industries further increases consumption by stimulating demand.

External Socioenvironmental Factors Economic development and the development of a consumer society cannot occur without favorable environmental conditions. The faster the rate of urbanization, the greater the likelihood of economic development. When people concentrate in cities, economic activity accelerates. As they become urbanized, people are less self-sufficient. They no longer make their own clothes, build their own homes, or make household items. Instead, they buy everything they need from businesses. In turn, they gain economic power through employment—by offering specialty skills to business. Geographic mobility also affects the development of a consumer society. Labor specialization is a necessity in highly developed economies and, as a result, relocation is common as people move from job to job. Most likely, as people move away from homes and families to follow job opportunities, the interdependence of family members weakens. Symptomatic of a consumer society, people place greater value on material possessions than on the families and relationships from which they have become distanced.

Similarly, with favorable cultural or societal values, the development of a consumer society is accelerated. A strong work ethic motivates people to work and so enhance their purchasing power. Economic power leads to the rise of materialism, as people earn the money to spend on more and more consumer items. Relaxation of sumptuary laws—laws that grant power to the police to regulate behaviors that offend the personal and religious beliefs of the community—allows the opportunity for macroconsumption to increase. The most obvious example of sumptuary laws restricting consumerism is the policing of women's dress codes in Saudi Arabia, where clothes that reveal skin are taboo. The existence of a class structure in which most citizens belong to—or see themselves as belonging to—an economically self-sufficient middle class accelerates macroconsumption. In contrast, in developing countries the majority population is part of a lower class, living at poverty levels. In consumer societies, people believe in the myth of progress—progress

consumer culture A culture in which a high level of economic development is reflected in a high level of consumption of goods and services by a majority of culture members—a state of macroconsumption.

F A Q

Is the development of consumer societies negative or positive? What are the trade-offs?

<table>
<tr><td>

E x h i b i t 17-1

Factors Influencing the Development of a Consumer Society

</td></tr>
</table>

External Facilitating Factors

Technical Factors
Supply of goods and services
Growth of production capabilities
Growth of mass marketing institutions
Growth of communications and transportation technologies
Growth of advertising media
Innovation

Economic Factors
Increased wealth and purchasing power
Increased diffusion of wealth and purchasing power
Growth of marketing and promotion

External Socioenvironmental Factors

Physical Environment
Population density—urbanization
Decline of self-sufficiency
Urban anonymity
Geographic mobility

Changes in Societal (Collective) Values
Decline of the work ethic
Rise in materialism
Decline of sumptuary laws
Nature or absence of class structure
Myth of progress

Internal Motivational Factors

Desire for Possessions

Desire for Status
Desire to show status
Desire to emulate people of status

Desire for Affiliation and to Communicate Affiliation
Reference and aspiration groups
Opinion leadership

Perceptions of Abundance

Source: Adapted from Kathleen M. Rassuli and Stanley C. Hollander, "Desire-Induced, Innate, Insatiable?" *Journal of Macromarketing,* Vol. 6 (Fall 1986), pp. 4–24.

F A Q

Does the development of a consumer society mean that a culture is advancing?

measured primarily in economic terms as people strive to achieve a higher standard of living. International Marketplace 17-1 shows how consumer culture is related to advertising. Consumer culture evolves with its advertising.

Internal Motivational Factors   The development of a consumer society is predicated on the assumption that people are economically motivated. This means that people desire possessions, viewing them as a means to signify status. Possessions are also a means through which people can emulate others who have status. People have desire or a sense of

International *Marketplace 17-1*

Advertising and the Development of Consumer Societies

Hand in hand with a country's economic growth comes the development of a consumer society. At first, that society reflects utilitarian values—people buy only the essentials. As the economy develops, hedonistic values come to the fore. People buy not out of need but for the pleasure of ownership.

The style of advertising used reflects a country's stage of development. Within a utilitarian society, for example, an advertisement for a refrigerator is likely to focus exclusively on price and performance. Within a hedonistic society, appearance, special features, and other aspects that communicate status are likely to be the center of the advertisement.

A comparison of advertising from Hong Kong, the People's Republic of China, and Taiwan showed some marked differences. In Hong Kong, advertising stressed hedonistic values with a focus on having. In the People's Republic of China, utilitarian appeals with a focus on being were prevalent. Taiwanese advertising fell between the two extremes.

Source: David K. Tse, Russell W. Belk, and Nan Zhou, "Becoming a Consumer Society: A Longitudinal and Cross-Cultural Content Analysis of Print Ads from Hong Kong, the People's Republic of China, and Taiwan," *Journal of Consumer Research,* Vol. 15 (March 1989), pp. 457–472.

affiliation with others, particularly with those they perceive as superior, as signified through their possessions. People in a consumer society perceive abundance as positive. They believe that their needs and desires can be met through acquiring goods and services.

Within a consumer society, culture changes at a rapid rate as a result of the myriad factors we have explored. Hand in hand with economic development, the emergence of a consumer society fuels further development by providing a ready market for all that the advanced economy produces. There is, however, a downside to economic development of which policy makers and marketers are aware. We pay a price in social ills for accelerated economic growth. We shall return to this topic later in the chapter. Exhibit 17-2 illustrates how Russia's consumer culture is growing rapidly.

Exhibit **17-2**

Russia is experiencing the explosive growth of a consumer culture. In this fertile environment, creative marketing can make Mars' products like Snickers wildly popular.

Source: peterblakely.com

17-1b Marketing and the Development of the Consumer Culture

It is clear just from scanning the list of factors in Exhibit 17-1 that marketing and advertising are particularly influential in speeding the development of a consumer society. Marketers not only supply products, but they encourage the demand for them by making them culturally desirable. As we explored in more detail in Chapter 11 (section 11-3e, "Symbols"), marketers achieve this largely through the use of cultural symbolism. Exhibit 17-3 describes the types of symbols that advertisers purposely associate with their products, thus investing them with the cultural desirability of those symbols. Through the use of symbols, marketers tell us that certain characteristics—power, youth, and beauty, for example—are culturally desirable. The associations marketers make between their products and these cultural characteristics affect not only the consumption of those products, but also our perception of the culture at large. An excellent example of how symbols work is the success of the long-running campaign for Nike shoes featuring the serious-minded athlete. The marketers of Nike shoes have managed successful promotion campaigns by associating the product with characteristics admired within the culture, such as competition, hard work, athletics, and winning.

Exhibit 17-3		
Categories of Cultural Meaning for Material Objects	**Ancestral Totem**	This category of symbols describes the significance of objects valued as statements of ethnicity or kinship. Examples of ethnicity symbols include a sari, a prayer shawl, a set of bagpipes, and a framed portrait of Martin Luther King. Examples of kinship symbols include a bronzed baby shoe, a grandmother's china cup, and old family photographs.
	Social Status Communication	Material objects can signal belonging or division. Examples include a white lab coat, an expensive briefcase, a tube of lipstick, flashy earrings, or a red Corvette.
	Interpersonal Medium	Material objects can signify social observances. Examples include flowers and clothes to signal shared rejoicing or mourning dress to share sorrow.
	Self-Expression	Material objects may reflect the development of the ideal self. Examples include medical books, a college diploma, a tennis trophy, or an exercise machine.
	Utility	Material objects can be valued strictly for the useful function they serve. Examples include an iron used to press clothes, a stapler used to bind sheets of paper together, or a telephone used to communicate with others.
	Pleasure-Giving	Material objects can be used in ways to provide pleasure to the user. Hence, the symbols associated with these products are related to pleasure-giving. Examples include drinking brandy after dinner, smoking a pipe, and using a whirlpool tub.
	Experiential Memoir	Material objects such as mementos can also be used to remember the past. Examples include a photo album, travel souvenirs, or a child's first drawings.
	Transcendence	Material objects can be used to transcend the limits of one's own existence. Examples include a Greenpeace bumper sticker, a collection of crystals, or a rosary.

Source: Adapted from "The Role of Marketing Processes in Creating Cultural Meaning" by Marye Tharp and Linda Scott from *Journal of Macromarketing,* Vol. 10, Fall 1990, pp. 47–60.

International *Marketplace 17-2*

How Others View Us

As the first and probably the strongest consumer culture in the world, how is the American culture perceived? Those Muslims who are fundamentalists all over the world see Levi's jeans, Hollywood movies, and popular music as signs of a cultural invasion of their society by the United States and are up in arms to fight it. American brands invade their landscape as fast-food chains like McDonald's, Burger King, Taco Bell, and Pizza Hut set up in major cities and in smaller towns. From cigarettes to cereals to computers, American brands are infiltrating the Muslim landscape.

The people of Mexico, too, see often unwelcome influences creeping into their culture, where the best-selling piñata figure is not of the traditional burro, but of American cartoon character Bart Simpson. American football—and the consumption that surrounds it—has been exported to Russia, where the Russian Association of American Football has launched its own Super Bowl. In Japan, where American brands enjoy enormous popularity, consumers rejected a specially designed Japanese Barbie doll introduced by Mattel. The doe-eyed Japanese beauty was turned down in favor of the original American Barbie.

What positive and negative impressions of the American culture do these and other examples give to consumers in other nations?

Sources: Adapted from Morley Safer, "60 Minutes," November 6, 1994; Tim Padgett, "The Gringos Are Coming," *Newsweek* (November 30, 1992), p. 55; William E. Schmidt, "West Sets Up Store and the Russians Are Seduced," *The New York Times* (September 27, 1991), p. A4; David Kilburn and Julie Skur Hill, "Western Barbie," *Advertising Age* (October 7, 1991), p. 40; John F. Sherry, Jr. and Eduardo G. Camargo, "'May Your Life Be Marvelous:' English Language Labeling and the Semiotics of Japanese Promotion," *Journal of Consumer Research*, Vol. 14 (September 1987), pp. 174–188.

It is important for marketers to understand the effects of advertising on the development of the consumer culture because, through both the creation of products and their affiliation with cultural symbols, they contribute to the subtle changes that over time transform the culture we live in. Those changes are not always positive. Consider, for example, advertising for a product like premium whiskey. To build sales to professional businesspeople, the marketer decides to associate the product with such images as success and aggressive competitiveness. From a micromarketing perspective, by exulting these characteristics, the marketer simply hopes to sell more whiskey. From a macromarketing perspective, however, the potential effects on consumers and on the culture in which we live are much more complex. The advertising promotes behavior that is potentially dysfunctional and presents whiskey as culturally desirable. It encourages the development of cultural values and behaviors that are not always—as in this example—in the best interest of society at large. In the remainder of the chapter, we will explore those social ills that are indirectly related to marketing. Understanding how their actions potentially contribute to social malaise may help marketers make decisions that result in the selling of their products in a socially responsible manner. International Marketplace 17-2 describes how non-Americans all over the world view America's consumer culture.

17-1c The Effect of Consumption on the Quality of Life

There is much evidence that suggests consumers in higher income brackets own more material possessions than those in lower brackets. Material possessions (e.g., a house, a car, and furnishings) do play an important role in the quality of life. Ownership of economic goods enhances subjective well-being.[2] Quality-of-life researchers typically treat subjective well-being as an indicator of quality of life. For example, in a large-scale study, satisfaction with life was found to increase with income. Life satisfaction also was found to be positively related to the possession of products such as new home entertainment equipment and financial instruments.[3] Those who have new home entertainment centers (have more financial investments) seem to be happier with their lives than those who do not have the home entertainment centers (have no financial investments). Furthermore, shopping enjoyment was positively related to life satisfaction. That is, those who are more satisfied with their lives report higher levels of shopping enjoyment than do those less satisfied with their lives.[4]

In another study, consumer researchers have found that satisfaction with material possessions tends to contribute to overall life satisfaction, but only for materialistic people. This is because materialistic people tend to value material possessions and place much importance in the significance of material possessions and wealth in life. As such, any satisfaction in the material life domain spills over to other life domains affecting one's overall feelings about life. Thus, for the highly materialistic, satisfaction with material possessions plays an important role in subjective well-being. By the same token, dissatisfaction with material possessions makes these people feel miserable about their lives. Satisfaction with material possessions in this study was measured as a composite of satisfaction with the following material items: house/condo, consumer electronics, furniture and appliances, auto vehicles, clothing/accessories and jewelry, and savings and investment.[5]

17-1d Green Consumers

There are many consumers who are very conscientious about doing the right thing when it comes to protecting the environment. They conserve their consumption of electricity and water, they recycle, they buy environmentally friendly products, and they dispose of used products in ways that are least damaging to the environment. We call these consumers **"green consumers."**

> **"green consumers"**
> Consumers who are very conscientious about doing the right thing when it comes to protecting the environment.

Much research has been done to profile green consumers. This is what we know about them. There is much evidence suggesting that males tend to have higher and better knowledge about green issues than females. However, females tend to exhibit both higher concern and participate more frequently in various types of green activities. Also, some research suggested that married men tend to be more green than nonmarried consumers. Green consumers tend to be part of large families—that is, the more children in the family the more the family members are likely to have greater knowledge about environmental issues, and the more likely they are to express concern about environmental quality and participate in green activities. Green consumers tend to be more educated than non-green consumers. They tend to have higher socio-economic status than non-green consumers.[6] See Chapter 4, section 4-5, for a related discussion on green consumers.

Marketing is important because it plays an important role in enhancing people's quality of life. The danger lies in the abuses of consumption, not in consumption and not in the marketing of products or services. Of course, marketing can be accused of being the catalyst of overconsumption. We will discuss this issue in some detail in the next section.

Marketing Management—Implications and Actions

Understanding how consumer societies develop helps marketers:

- Anticipate social or cultural trends that offer opportunities for new products or promotions.
- Use cultural symbolism to associate products with positive cultural values.
- Appreciate the macro- as well as the microeffects of marketing actions.
- Understand the socio-demographic profile of green consumers and how to appeal to them.

17-2 The Dark Side of the Consumer Society

Economic development is not without its negatives. Critics point to many social ills that are the direct or indirect result of macroconsumption, from the disintegration of the family and family values to increased crime, drug abuse, addiction, vandalism, product tampering, and even terrorism. The result is a general social malaise that defies the improved standard of living that economic development promised to help us achieve. In this section, we will examine some of these social ills and review the research that links them to the emergence of the consumer society. The topics we'll cover include the rise of materialism, addictive or compulsive consumption, and shoplifting.

17-2a **Materialism**

We live in a material world. This means that we allow material goods to play an important role in our lives—we are materialistic. **Materialism** is the extent to which we measure our self-worth by our external assets and possessions rather than by other intrinsic characteristics.[7] Why is it that material possessions are important to us? Consumer researchers have suggested several reasons.

1. *Material possessions reflect self-worth.* Material wealth is an expression of our perception of our value in society. Hence, we are motivated to acquire possessions in order to achieve status and esteem.[8] If there is a significant gap between the possessions we wish to acquire and the ones we currently have, the result is dissatisfaction, leading to a negative perception of self-worth.

2. *Material possessions reward societal contributions.* According to the capitalist or meritocratic view, affluence and materialism reflect individual contributions to society. Those who become affluent have made greater contributions to society, and affluence is a symbol of that achievement.[9] Although affluence is not itself a bad thing, some feel it is a symbol that has become separated from its referent— achievement—and has become empty of meaning.

3. *Material possessions lead to control.* According to Marxist and neo-Marxist thinkers (that is, those who follow the teachings of Karl Marx), the motivation to acquire material possessions is rooted in a desire for control. In this system of thought, affluence is seen as a vehicle of social and political power.[10]

4. *Material possessions help us achieve secular immortality.* Secular immortality is social prominence that continues after death. It is usually achieved through philanthropic deeds or donations of publicly noted possessions, such as art collections or buildings.[11] A more typical means through which consumers achieve secular immortality is the pursuit of wealth in order to bequeath it to others who will then honor the memory of the giver.

5. *Acquiring material possessions is encouraged within certain religions.* Particularly in the United States, commercialism and consumption have become allied with religion. The acquisition of wealth has been sacralized by certain fundamentalist Christian sects, spilling over to other segments of society. Consumption has, in extreme cases, become a religion in which wealth and material possessions are venerated.[12]

6. *Material possessions are a route to happiness.* Advertising and other promotion efforts constantly tell consumers that they should be dissatisfied with what they have, promising happiness if they buy and use new products. Told that happiness is just around the corner and can be attained by buying this or that product, consumers become increasingly materialistic.[13] Recent research has shown: (1) that television commercial viewership may influence the development of materialism in countries such as the United States but less so in other countries such as China, Australia, Canada, and Turkey; (2) that materialism is a factor in negative evaluations of one's standard of living and economic well-being; that is, those who are highly materialistic tend to feel unhappy with their standard of living and income; and (3) that this dissatisfaction with one's standard of living and income contributes to dissatisfaction with life in general.[14]

The Materialistic Personality   Three personality traits are common to materialistic people.[15] First is envy. Materialistic people covet the possessions of others, be they objects, experiences, or relationships. Envious people are materialistic because envy drives them to acquire possessions, especially from others. They are likely to agree with the following statements:

- I am bothered when I see people who buy anything they want.
- There are certain people I would like to trade places with.
- When friends have things I cannot afford, it bothers me.
- I don't seem to get what is coming to me.

materialism The extent to which we regard material goods as important to the overall quality of life. To be materialistic is to measure our self-worth by our external assets and possessions, rather than by other intrinsic characteristics.

F A Q

If we live in a consumer society, is it possible not to be materialistic?

CBite 17-1

How Materialistic Are You?

Decide how materialistic you are by rating the extent to which you agree with the following statements on a scale of one to five. The higher your score, the more important material possessions are to you.

- I admire people who own expensive homes, cars, and clothes.
- Some of the most important achievements in life include acquiring material possessions.
- I like to own things that impress people.
- Buying things gives me a lot of pleasure.
- I like a lot of luxury in my life.
- I'd be happier if I could afford to buy more things.

Source: Adapted from Marsha L. Richins and Scott Dawson, "A Consumer Values Orientation for Materialism and Its Measurement: Scale Development and Validation," *Journal of Consumer Research,* Vol. 20 (December 1992), pp. 303–316.

F A Q

Is there a positive side to materialism?

The second characteristic of the materialistic personality is "nongenerousness." Materialistic people are unwilling to give or share possessions. They are likely to agree with the following statements:

- I don't like to lend things, even to good friends.
- I don't like to have anyone in my home when I'm not there.

Third, materialistic people are possessive. Seeking ownership and control, they are typically overly concerned about loss of possessions. They save objects of all kinds, from souvenirs and photographs to paintings, sculpture, and other symbols of wealth and affluence. They are likely to agree with the following statements:

- I tend to hang on to things I should probably throw out.
- I get very upset if something is stolen from me, even if it has little monetary value.
- I worry about people taking my possessions.

As we see, the picture consumer researchers paint of materialism is very negative. Materialism is considered a social ill precisely because people who are materialistic are seen as not making valuable contributions to the betterment of society. A negative outcome of the development of a consumer society, macroconsumption, and the advertising and marketing activities associated with it dispose people to materialistic characteristics that negatively influence society in general.[16] Find out how materialistic you are by taking the test in CBite 17-1.

17-2b Addictive or Compulsive Consumption

From harmless cravings for chocolate or ice cream to addiction to the caffeine in coffee or cola, to dependency on cigarettes, alcohol, or drugs, almost any consumer product can be addictive. Gambling at the racetrack or at slot machines and watching too much television are also compulsive behaviors.

Addictive or **compulsive consumption** is consumption behavior that is beyond the control of the consumer. Often acting out of tension, anxiety, depression, or boredom, a compulsive person seeks immediate gratification of needs or desires, no matter how short-lived and no matter how deeply that behavior is regretted afterwards.[17] Cross addiction is a common phenomenon. A person who is compulsive is likely to have more than one addiction, indicating that addictive behavior has psychological causes.[18]

There are two types of compulsive consumers: distressed compulsives and sociopathic compulsives. Distressed compulsive consumers are characterized by feelings of self-doubt,

addictive or compulsive consumption Consumption that is beyond the control of the consumer. Often acting out of tension, anxiety, depression, or boredom, a compulsive person seeks immediate gratification of needs or desires, no matter how short-lived and no matter how deeply that behavior is regretted afterward.

incompetence, and personal inadequacy. Incapable of managing stress and anxiety through internal means, they resort to external methods, such as shopping, overeating, exercising, taking drugs, and sexual promiscuity. In contrast, sociopathic compulsive consumers are driven by strong impulsive desires. They tend to be sensation seekers and do not feel remorse or guilt over their actions.[19]

There is some evidence to suggest that family structure plays a significant role in the propagation of addictive or compulsive buying. Specifically, one study has found that adolescents from divorced families are more likely to engage in compulsive shopping than those from non-divorced families.[20] That is, adolescents seem to deal with the stress of divorce through shopping. For a related discussion on addictive consumption, see Marketplace 4-1 (in Chapter 4), which is about alcohol-related compulsive consumption on college and university campuses.

Shopping itself is an increasingly common addiction in consumer societies. People who buy compulsively tend to be compulsive in many things they do. They have low self-esteem and tend to be prone to fantasy. Frequently, they are motivated to buy not by the product acquired but by the buying process itself. Consequences of compulsive buying include stress and frustration, loss of one's sense of control, financial debt, and ensuing domestic problems.[21]

Compulsive behavior, as a negative outcome of the development of a consumer society, makes certain demands upon marketers who wish to be socially responsible. Marketers must take care that programs designed to build frequency of purchase do not lead to compulsive actions on the part of users. Frequency programs within shopping malls, for example, that reward shoppers for repeat purchases can have the negative effect of encouraging compulsive shopping behavior, which, in turn, leads to extreme overspending. Consumer research can help by providing marketers with the means to create consumer profiles of those with addictive shopping tendencies and thus avoid targeting advertising and promotion to them.

17-2c **Shoplifting and Consumer Cheating**

Shoplifting is pervasive, particularly in the United States and Europe.[22] Not only does it hurt retailers, but shoplifting also takes its toll on all consumers—we pay higher prices in the long term because of markups to cover losses from retail theft.[23]

Contrary to common belief, shoplifting is not the domain of the underprivileged or of professional thieves. Instead, shoplifters are often middle- or high-income people who steal either for the thrill of it or because of deep-rooted psychological problems.[24] There are two types of shoplifting: shoplifting by acquisition (taking merchandise from a store without paying, switching price tags) and shoplifting by disposition (returning products to the store after they have been used or damaged by the consumer). Shoplifters commonly try to justify their behavior in one of several ways:[25]

- Denial of responsibility—by claiming that the temptation was too great and beyond control
- Denial of injury—by insisting that despite shoplifting, retailers make profits
- Denial of victim—by blaming the store for setting unreasonable prices
- Condemning the condemners—by claiming that if stores are lax enough to make shoplifting possible, they deserve what they get
- Appealing to higher loyalties—by claiming shoplifting was necessary in order to survive and provide for families

Thirty-seven percent of all adolescents have admitted to shoplifting at least once over a twelve-month period. The reasons? Temptation (the appeal of store merchandise); the ability to rationalize or deny the act as theft ("the store won't even miss it . . ." or "this store robs people through its outrageous prices . . ."); and low perceived risk ("I won't be caught").[26]

Shoplifting is endemic to the consumer society, costing retailers millions of dollars each year and hurting consumers both in terms of the prices paid for products and in

F A Q

Because addiction to shopping increases purchasing, why should marketers take steps to discourage it?

shoplifting The act of taking goods from retail stores without paying for them at the cashier or checkout stand.

The prevention of shoplifting is a big business for retailers. Are there ways in which a change in marketing practices could be as effective as a Sensormatic gate in reducing shoplifting?

Source: Reprinted by permission.

STOP SHOPLIFTING. CALL SENSORMATIC.

OVER 100,000 STORES WORLDWIDE ARE USING SENSORMATIC SOLUTIONS

CALL 1 800 368-7262

Sensormatic
WORLD LEADER IN ELECTRONIC SECURITY

---

terms of its negative effects on societal values. It is estimated that about 4 in 10 people have stolen from a store at some time in their lives and that most theft goes unreported.[27] Retailers invest heavily in containing theft, and the literature on shoplifting demonstrates the importance of managing opportunistic behavior of shoppers.[28] Consumer research can help marketers and retailers combat the problem by providing the means to understand and to change attitudes toward shoplifting. Alternatively, security devices such as Sensormatic (see Exhibit 17-4) are marketed to help alleviate shoplifting.

Consumer cheating is also pervasive. For example, many service firms are unwilling to provide service guarantees because of consumer cheating. Many consumers engage in opportunistic behaviors. An example of consumer cheating (besides shoplifting) would be the purchase of goods with the intention of using them for some time and then returning the goods for a full refund. A consumer buys a video camcorder for use on a vacation. When he returns from the vacation, he returns the camcorder, claiming that it didn't perform as expected, and demands a full refund.[29]

What cause consumers to cheat? One recent study found that consumers who are least likely to cheat are those who intend to patronize a firm again, are highly satisfied with the service, are high self-monitors (high self-monitors tend to manage their public presentation by assessing the social situation and adjusting their presentation of self to meet the demands of the situation), have high levels of morality, and have low levels of Machiavellianism (Machiavellians are people who do not have an affective attachment with others; they lack concern for conventional morality; and they manipulate others for their own interests).[30]

Materialism, compulsive behavior, shoplifting, and consumer cheating are just some of the costs the consumer society exacts from us that are more closely related to marketing activities. They represent just a tiny portion of social ills that the consumer society engenders. Marketplace 17-1 provides more detail about the magnitude of the shoplifting problem and how retailers are dealing with it.

What we have discussed so far is the tip of an iceberg. There are many other types of consumer misbehavior. A recent study classified consumer misbehavior into five major categories: (1) consumer misbehavior directed against marketer employees (e.g., customers physically or verbally abusing employees, and customers willfully disobeying store rules), (2) consumer misbehavior directed against the firm (e.g., shoplifting, fraudulent

consumer cheating
Examples of consumer cheating (besides shoplifting) include the purchase of goods with the intention of using them for some time and then returning the goods for a full refund.

Marketplace 17-1

Sticky Fingers

In the 1990s retailers were losing approximately $15 billion a year in costs related to shoplifting and employee theft. Shrinkage—losses to theft, paperwork errors, and the like—in 1992 was estimated at 1.88 percent of sales, up from 1.79 percent just two years before.

Retail analysts attribute the increase to a number of factors. First, to keep a lid on costs, many retailers have cut back on sales staffs, leaving fewer workers to supervise customers and other employees. Second, wages in the industry have remained low while the use of part-timers has risen—leading to lower employee loyalty and higher theft. Third, financial instability or breakneck growth only exacerbates a retailer's potential for theft problems. Finally, the increase is partly attributed to criminal activity from gangs and organized theft rings.

How are retailers dealing with the situation? Many stores are installing inventory tracking systems. Others are adding surveillance systems. Still others are using special software programs to help loss-prevention managers track employee purchases, price overrides, and refunds.

Source: Adapted from "Sticky Fingers Are Rifling through Retail" by Wendy Zellner reprinted from March 28, 1994 issue of *Business Week* by special permission, copyright © 1994 by The McGraw-Hill Companies, Inc.

returns, switching or altering price tags, coupon misredemptions, use of forged or stolen tickets, and copyright theft), (3) consumer misbehavior directed against other consumers (e.g., jumping queues and illegitimate use of express or "cash only" checkout lines), (4) consumer misbehavior directed against the firm's financial assets (e.g., defrauding retail cashiers, failing to report billing errors, false or questionable claims of injury at the firm's premises, bad check passing, credit card fraud, loan fraud, fraudulent assertions to avoid payment, warranty frauds, insurance frauds, computer-based consumer crime, and rumor generation against the firm), and (5) consumer misbehavior against the firm's physical or electronic premises (e.g., destructive theft acts, vandalism, arson, database theft, and the spreading of computer viruses).

The same study advanced several macro-level explanations to account for consumer misbehaviors. These are unfulfilled aspirations, deviant thrill-seeking, absence of moral constraints, differential associations, pathological socialization, provocative situational factors, and calculating opportunism.

The *unfulfilled aspirations* explanation for consumer misbehavior states that consumer misbehavior is determined by the discrepancy between widely held consumption goals (e.g., everyone has a nice house and automobile, everyone travels overseas on vacations, and so on) and reality. Some consumers resort to misconduct in the marketplace as a means to realize their unfulfilled aspiration, given that they cannot achieve these goals through legitimate means. An example is a teen male shoplifting a pair of "cool sneakers" because "everyone has a pair like them" and he doesn't have the money to pay for them.

The *deviant thrill-seeking* explanation states that some consumers engage in misconduct in the marketplace because misconduct is a thrilling experience. The thrilling experience defies basic and moral norms; thus, consumers lash out at traditional institutions and customs.

The *absence of moral constraints* explanation asserts that some consumers do not have the moral disposition to restrain their misconduct in the marketplace. These consumers do not perceive that certain misbehaviors are unethical. For example, some consumers lacking moral restraints may perceive that returning a product for a refund after using it (while not having any intention to purchase the product in the first place—they purchased the product to use it for this one occasion only) is not unethical.

The *differential association* explanation refers to norms related to group initiation. Specifically, consumer misbehavior may be a rule of initiation to a street gang. Therefore, it can be construed as consumer socialization that is perverse.

According to the *pathological socialization* explanation, some consumers misbehave because they do not have any sympathy or empathy for large firms. Thus, they do not hesitate to victimize large firms compared to small firms. Large firms are impersonal entities with no human-like qualities to them. In contrast, small firms have a human face.

The *provocative situational factors* explanation directs us to account for consumer misbehavior by looking at environmental factors such as crowding in stores, lack of heat in theatres, or enticing displays. These conditions provoke misbehavior as a way to lash back at them.

Finally, according to the *calculating opportunism* explanation, some consumers are more opportunistic than others. Opportunistic consumers calculate their expected benefits and costs based on self-interest. If the misbehavior is perceived to be associated with more benefits than costs, the consumer engages in that misbehavior. Thus, misbehavior in the marketplace is a rational process based on the service to the self, i.e., the consumer.[31]

Marketing Management—Implications and Actions
Understanding the social ills that come with macroconsumption helps marketers:
• Avoid advertising messages that encourage negative personal dispositions or encourage dysfunctional behaviors.
• Take steps to avoid targeting directly those consumers prone to compulsive behaviors.
• Discourage retail theft and other antisocial behaviors by attempting to change attitudes toward those behaviors.

17-3 Social Responsibility and Marketing

So far in this chapter, we have explored the social problems associated with macroconsumption and marketing activities. In Chapter 16, we looked at ways in which public policy and consumer advocacy groups work to contain those problems by protecting the rights of consumers in the marketplace. Here, we will look at ways in which marketers themselves can police their own behavior by acting in accordance with a standard of ethics. We will also see how this kind of social responsibility in marketing benefits not only the buyer but also the seller.

17-3a Consumer Sovereignty

consumer sovereignty
The situation in which consumers' interests dominate producers' interests. If consumers are accurately informed about quality and price of optional brands, then they can reward producers who develop high-quality products at lower prices. Thus, consumers have clout by exercising their economic votes—that is, the contents of their pocketbooks.

producer sovereignty
The situation in which producers' interests dominate consumers' interests. The opposite of consumer sovereignty.

Much of the American economic system is based on the concept of **consumer sovereignty** as advocated by eighteenth-century Scottish philosopher and economist Adam Smith. Consumer sovereignty is also the foundation of marketing ethics.[32] Early marketing practice was guided by what economists have called **"producer sovereignty."** That is, producers' interests dominated consumers' interests. Consumers were assumed to make the right decisions based on the notion "let the buyer beware." That is, consumers should be cautious and not trust producers. However, the consumer and environmental movements have shifted the burden onto the producer. State and federal regulations have forced producers to "shape up or ship out." The attitude shifted to using the wisdom of consumers to help regulate the economic enterprise. If consumers are accurately informed about quality and price of optional brands, then they can reward producers who develop high-quality products at lower prices by buying their products and punish producers who market low-quality products at high prices by not buying their products. Thus, consumers have clout by exercising their economic votes, i.e., the contents of their pocketbooks.

Economists realize that for consumers to make decisions to buy the best-quality product at the lowest prices, consumers have to have accurate information and choice among brands in the marketplace. This means that state and federal laws have to be created to ensure that (1) consumers are better informed about the costs and benefits of alternative brands, and (2) there is competition among producers of the product. For example, the American antitrust laws are designed to ensure that producers do compete among themselves and do so fairly. Also, Federal Trade Commission regulations were created to ensure that consumers receive accurate information from advertisers.

Recently the concept of consumer sovereignty has come under attack.[33] Consumer researchers have argued that consumer sovereignty in an increasingly high-tech world is more fiction than fact. They demonstrate how the principle of consumer sovereignty that governs the societal impact of economic competition is not valid. The world of "high tech" has changed consumers' opportunity, ability, and motivation to make wise decisions that help them to select the best-quality product at the lowest price. The same world has created changes in the producers' opportunity, ability, and motivation to compete against other producers. Producers, for the most part, develop strategies to avoid competition rather than engage in competition.

Let us focus on the consumer side of the equation (rather than the producer side). The argument is that in a high-tech world, consumers cannot be expected to make rational decisions by selecting the best-quality high-tech product at the lowest price. This is said to be the case because consumers do not have the *opportunity* to do so, they do not have the *ability* to do so, and they do not have the *motivation* to do so. Let us examine these factors in greater detail.

Opportunity   Most consumers cannot easily identify most of the brands in a product category, because consumers do not rely on the Internet to identify all possible brands. They do not buy consumer buyer guides. They simply go to their neighborhood department stores, discount stores, or electronic stores. What they see at these stores is what they think are the alternative brands. Most consumers do not have easy access to product and brand information. Information about quality and price of all alternative brands is not easy to find, and most consumers do not expend the time and effort to find this information.

Ability   Consumers cannot easily inspect competing brands, even if they have information about the brands. It takes a technological expert to understand the technical language used to describe the various features of the optional brands. Consumers do not have the technical know-how to compare the advantages and disadvantages of optional brands. Not only do consumers lack the knowledge and background to evaluate quality and price of high-tech products, but they also lack the information-processing capacity to make decisions about quality. In many cases, to evaluate high-tech gadgets one has to apply evaluation techniques that are done by computers, not humans, because the evaluation can be quite complex.

Motivation   Consumers' motivation to make utilitarian decisions is diminishing in an ever-increasing world of "high tech." Much research on consumer behavior has shown that consumers make purchase decisions of high-tech products motivated by symbolic rather than utilitarian needs. For example, a person may be motivated to buy a computer not because of what the computer can do for him (that is, helping him do things with less effort and more speed) but because of social pressures. Buying a computer helps the person be accepted as being modern. A consumer not doing so runs the risk of being viewed as being from the "Stone Age." Thus, consumers who are motivated to purchase computers for symbolic rather than utilitarian goals are not likely to do comparison shopping to buy the best quality computer at the lowest price. Furthermore, there is much evidence suggesting that consumers tend to minimize cognitive effort in making shopping decisions. They rely on heuristics such as brand name and reputation from the advertising they see to help them make purchase decisions. Consumers who are not motivated to compare the various brands and examine the costs and benefits of each cannot be trusted to make "wise" purchase decisions. Remember, a "wise" decision here is the kind of decision that produces a purchase of a high-quality/low-price brand.

17-3b **Ethics in Marketing**

Ethics in marketing is particularly important because, as we have seen, many of the things that marketers do affect society at large and its development. Although a single action by a single marketer may be lawful, the aggregate effects of the combined marketing actions of many marketers can have long-term adverse effects on society. Government regulation controls only certain aspects of marketing activity and is effective only when the abuser is caught. Ethics can do much more by persuading marketers to be responsible for their own actions.

F A Q

Why should marketers bother with ethics? Isn't it enough to obey the law?

Marketplace 17-2

Teen Smoking and Social Responsibility

A 1994 poll demonstrated that in the American public's mind, the connection between cigarette advertising and teen smoking has already been made. Sixty-eight percent of consumers believe cigarette advertisements influence children and teens to smoke. A whopping 66 percent of the total—and 60 percent of smokers—believe some cigarette advertisements are especially designed to appeal to young people. And two-thirds of consumers—including almost half of all smokers—want the U.S. government to impose greater restrictions on cigarette advertising. For 53 percent, that means a total ban.

The Tobacco Institute questions the effectiveness of a cigarette advertising ban. In Europe, where there have been bans in effect, consumption of cigarettes is increasing. Philip Morris USA asserted that a ban is not necessary because, according to government statistics, smoking incidence among kids is going down.

The growing antitobacco trend is likely to influence U.S. legislation that would shift jurisdiction over tobacco marketing from the Federal Trade Commission to the Food and Drug Administration, a shift that would effectively bring an end to tobacco marketing. Also, there is a push in the U.S. Congress to attach to health-care legislation a provision to deny tobacco advertising expenditures as a business deduction.

Which of the eight ethics tests do, or should, tobacco marketers apply to their activities, particularly with regard to the public's perception of teen smoking?

Source: Adapted from "Teen Smoking and Ads Linked" by Steven W. Colford and Ira Teinowitz reprinted with permission from the February 21, 1994 issue of *Advertising Age.* Copyright, Crain Communications Inc., 1994.

---

legal test A test that marketers use to recognize whether an action is ethical and does not violate the law. By becoming familiar with all laws, rules, and regulations governing their industry and its marketing practices, marketers respect the legal rights of consumers.

duty of fidelity An ethics concept regarding the promise to remain faithful to contracts, to keep promises, and to tell the truth.

duty of gratitude The ethics concept that states that the marketer owes and should express gratitude to consumers for their transactions.

duty of justice The ethics concept that states that the marketer is obligated to distribute rewards based upon merits.

duty of nonmaleficence The ethics concept that states that the marketer is obligated to do no harm to consumers.

Through the following eight tests, marketers can judge the extent to which their actions toward consumers are both lawful and ethical. These tests are a popular and very useful guide to ethical marketing practices.[34]

1. *The* **legal test**. Ethical marketers do all they can to ensure their activities do not violate the law. By becoming familiar with all laws, rules and regulations governing their industry and its marketing practices, they respect the legal rights of consumers.

2. *The duties test.* Ethical marketers owe five duties to consumers:

   - **Duty of fidelity.** The promise to remain faithful to contracts, to keep promises, and to tell the truth. A retailer who breaks a promise to service a product promptly and at no cost when a consumer returns it for repair fails the duty of fidelity test.

   - **Duty of gratitude.** The marketer owes and should express gratitude to consumers for their transactions. The retailer who treats customers well up until the purchase is made but is disrespectful once money has passed hands fails this test.

   - **Duty of justice.** The marketer is obligated to distribute rewards based upon merits. An example of a violation is the marketer who refuses to honor a coupon or a price-off offer to a minority consumer because of race.

   - **Duty of nonmaleficence.** The marketer is obligated to do no harm to consumers. A toy manufacturer who knowingly markets a hazardous product breaks this ethical code.

   - **Duty of beneficence.** The marketer should, if possible, take actions to improve the lives of consumers. Suppose a pharmaceutical company knows that a new ingredient in its drug is likely to be more beneficial than the one currently used. Although the new formula costs more to produce and, therefore, is less profitable than the existing product, the marketer has a duty to consumers to provide it.

3. *The* **special obligations test.** Marketers should consider any special obligations peculiar to their industry. Examples include the duty of pharmaceutical firms to produce safe products and the duty of alcoholic beverage marketers to promote responsible drinking. Marketplace 17-2 describes an ethics case that was widely cited in marketing—that of tobacco advertising. Apply the ethics tests discussed here to

Marketplace 17-3

Is There a Relationship between Customer Satisfaction, Employee Satisfaction, and Profitability?

Many businesspeople feel that everything they do in business has to relate to the bottom line, namely, making a profit. So when "do-gooders" prompt businesses to do more for customers and employees, business people ask why. They say, "Show me evidence that spending money on programs that make customers and employees happier will result in higher company profits." A recent study has provided such evidence. Professors Kenneth Bernhardt and Naveen Donthu from Georgia State University with Professor Pamela Kennett from the University of South Alabama have conducted a longitudinal analysis of customer/employee satisfaction and company profit for a national chain of fast-food restaurants. A total of 342,308 consumers and 3,009 employees were surveyed, and twelve months of profitability measures were analyzed. The study has shown that at any given point in time, customer satisfaction (as well as employee satisfaction) responses were not correlated significantly with measures of company prof-

itability. However, over time, positive changes in customer satisfaction were shown to lead to increases in company profitability. Furthermore, the data show that customer satisfaction is correlated positively and significantly with employee satisfaction. That is, restaurants that report having happy customers also report having happy employees, and vice versa.

Based on the study findings, the authors advised management to exercise patience in evaluating the impact of customer and employee satisfaction programs. Investing in such programs may not provide a quick return on investment. The effects of these programs are real, but they take time.

Source: Adapted from Kenneth L. Bernhardt, Naveen Donthu, and Pamela A. Kennett, "A Longitudinal Analysis of Satisfaction and Profitability," *Journal of Business Research,* Vol. 47 (February 2000), pp. 161–171.

---

help you arrive at your own conclusion about the ethical stance of the tobacco companies and their past advertising campaigns.

4. *The* **motives test.** This test asks marketers to examine the intentions of their actions to ensure that they keep the good of the consumer in mind. A marketer who intentionally produces and promotes a product that will harm minority consumers, for example, acts out of prejudice and, therefore, breaks this code.

5. *The* **consequences test.** Ethical marketers consider both the positive and negative potential consequences of their actions, with the intent of providing as many positive consequences as possible for both parties.

6. *The* **utilitarian test.** The responsible marketer considers all alternative actions and their potential benefits to consumers before making marketing decisions. A chemical-agriculture firm develops a drug that controls disease among dairy cattle. In pricing the product, the marketer has two alternatives: a high price that will maximize profits but is affordable only to large-scale farming operations, or a lower price with narrower profit margins that will make the drug available to all farming operations. According to the utilitarian test, the second alternative is more ethical. Why should business firms try hard to meet the needs of both their customers and employees? Read Marketplace 17-3 for a possible answer.

7. *The* **rights test.** The responsible marketer ensures that marketing actions do not infringe upon consumer rights, as protected by the "Consumer Bill of Rights." These include the right to information, the right to safety, the right to redress, the right to choose, the right to a healthful environment, and the right to privacy. A marketer who knowingly does harm by selling an unsafe product yet refuses to compensate consumers for the damage done violates both the right to safety and the right to redress.

8. *The* **justice test.** The responsible marketer avoids marketing actions that damage the well-being of targeted consumers. A tobacco company that targets an underprivileged class such as black youths or youths in developing countries makes a bad situation worse and thus violates the justice test.

Marketers can ensure that their policies and programs are socially responsible by subjecting them to these eight ethical tests. If a policy or program fails any of these tests, it must be reassessed and redesigned to make it ethically responsive.

duty of beneficence
(see p. 538) The ethics concept that states that the marketer should, if possible, take actions to improve the lives of consumers.

special obligations test
(see p. 538) The ethics concept that states that marketers should consider any special obligations peculiar to their industry.

motives test The ethics concept that states that marketers should examine the intentions of their actions to ensure that they keep the good of the consumer in mind.

consequences test
The ethics concept that states that ethical marketers consider both the positive and negative potential consequences of their actions, with the intent of providing as many positive consequences as possible for both parties.

utilitarian test (see p. 539)
The ethics concept that states that responsible marketers consider all alternative actions and their potential benefits to consumers before making marketing decisions.

rights test (see p. 539)
The ethics concept that states that responsible marketers ensure that marketing actions do not infringe upon consumer rights, as protected by the "Consumer Bill of Rights." These include the right to information, the right to safety, the right to redress, the right to choose, the right to a healthful environment, and the right to privacy.

justice test (see p. 539)
The ethics concept that states that the responsible marketer avoids marketing actions that damage the well-being of targeted consumers.

quality-of-life marketing
A movement within marketing thought and practice that guides marketers to seek the best interests of consumers and other publics without damaging the organization's financial health, restricting its growth, or otherwise harming its stakeholders.

17-3c Quality-of-Life Marketing

In addition to the ethics test, researchers have developed the quality-of-life (QOL) concept as a tool with which to further encourage the application of ethics in marketing activities. The key marketing objective of increasing short-term profitability sometimes falls in conflict with the marketing ethicist's objective of protecting the consumer. It is this need for short-term profitability that drives marketers, often unknowingly, into socially irresponsible marketing practices. **Quality-of-life marketing** seeks to resolve the conflict by guiding marketers to seek the best interests of consumers and other publics without damaging the organization's financial health, restricting its growth, or otherwise harming its stakeholders. In essence, the QOL concept has two goals: first, to guide the development of products that enhance the well-being of targeted consumers; second, to guide the marketing of those products effectively and efficiently in ways that minimize negative effects on consumers and other publics while generating long-term profits.

The QOL concept helps marketers analyze the impact of marketing actions on consumers and on organizational objectives so that they can make better judgments about the overall effectiveness of those strategies. As Exhibit 17-5 shows, this analysis is conducted on each of the four parts of the marketing mix, or the Four Ps—product, price, place (distribution), and promotion.[35]

Product Objectives   Marketers applying the QOL concept to product strategies should first consider how their product can enhance the well-being of targeted consumers. Let's use as an example the diet pill industry, frequently criticized as a clear violator of marketing ethics. A manufacturer of diet pills should seek long-term health benefits for its target market. This means not only ensuring that the drug itself is safe, is beneficial, and has no negative side effects, but also that it is used correctly by target consumers, perhaps as part of a diet and exercise regimen.

Second, the marketer should consider the impact of the product on publics other than its target consumers. Tobacco is the obvious example. Cigarette smoking not only harms smokers but also nonsmokers who inhale tobacco smoke passively. According to the QOL principle, tobacco marketers have a social responsibility to reduce negative side effects not only on their target audience but also on the nonsmoking public.

In setting product objectives, therefore, marketers must not only develop risk-reducing strategies for their target audiences, but also identify other segments likely to be exposed to their products. The QOL principle also dictates that good product design takes into account potential adverse product effects on the environment. Therefore, product design has to be sustainable. Marketplace 17-4 describes sustainable product design scenarios.

Exhibit 17-5

Quality-of-Life Marketing

Applying the quality-of-life concept helps marketers make socially responsible decisions on each element of the marketing mix.

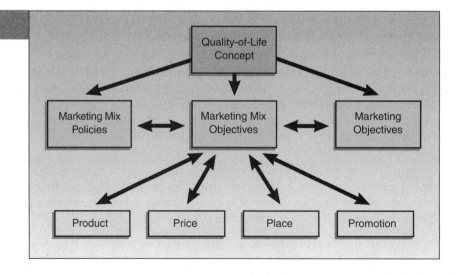

Marketplace 17-4

Sustainable Product Design Scenarios

Professors Donald Fuller and Jacquelyn Ottman describe sustainable product design in terms of a continuum. One end of the continuum is eco-redesign, the middle of the continuum is eco-innovations, and the other end of the continuum is sustainable technology innovations. *Eco-redesign* involves modifying present product designs to lessen the environmental damage of products when they are consumed and disposed. Professors Fuller and Ottman characterize eco-redesign as a short-term, low functional-change, low-risk approach to make minor adjusts in the product design to abide by environmental regulations. For example, security systems in door-locking devices could use metal keys and mechanical deadbolts made from recycled materials.

Eco-innovations, on the other hand, are not "business as usual." Eco-innovations tend to be longer-term solutions to creating product design that have minimal adverse impact on the environment. Here, the firm shifts to an available, but very different, alternative technology. Continuing the security systems example, eco-innovations may entail the use of programmable plastic key cards and electronic locks.

In contrast, *sustainable technology innovations* utilize emerging, radical technologies. In regard to security systems, a hypothetical technology considered sustainable may be the use of a fingerprint-activated touch pad that triggers a computerized locking mechanism. Fuller and Ottman argue that sustainable product design may have the following advantages:

- Lower production costs,
- Reduced short-term regulatory compliance costs,
- Reduced long-term environmental liability costs,
- Better estimates of profitability when using full-cost accounting methods that include waste and environmental costs,
- A hedge against costly future environmental regulations,
- Meeting of required environmental mandates such as ISO 1400 certification, and
- Enhanced corporate image.

Source: Adapted from Donald A. Fuller and Jacquelyn A. Ottman, "Moderating Unintended Pollution: The Role of Sustainable Product Design," *Journal of Business Research*, Vol. 57 (November 2004), pp. 1231–1238.

Price Objectives   The QOL principle dictates that to be socially responsible, marketers must set prices that target consumers can reasonably afford—the product is not beneficial to consumers if the price places it beyond their reach. Suppose a pharmaceutical company discovers a drug that can control the spread of AIDS. Even though some sectors of the public may be willing to pay an exorbitant price for the product, marketers who apply the QOL principle will price it to be affordable to as many people infected with the virus as possible.

Place Objectives   In setting distribution strategies, the marketer must research all channels used by target customers and through which they will be ensured access to post-purchase service. Suppose that through a consumer behavior study, a marketer of diet pills finds that target consumers are likely to benefit most if the drug is administered through a network of health providers at the community level. This is because consumers get the best and safest results if the pills are part of a managed eating program that provides guidance and support. Even though profits may be maximized by offering the pills at retail, the QOL principle favors limiting its distribution to health-care networks. Studying the effects of various channels of distribution on the well-being of consumers guides the marketer to select channels most likely to deliver maximal long-term benefits to target consumers.

Does the Body Shop practice quality-of-life marketing? Read International Marketplace 17-3 and judge for yourself.

Promotion Objectives   Marketers can better serve the consumer through conducting research that identifies how target consumers select among product alternatives and the evaluation criteria they use. Understanding this, marketers can then develop campaigns that effectively educate target consumers about long-term benefits of their products in a manner that is consistent with both the needs and value system of the targeted segment. The marketer of diet pills selects as its target market consumers whose extreme obesity prevents them from exercising to lose weight. Within this group, research reveals that

International *Marketplace 17-3*

Quality of Life at the Body Shop

For the Body Shop, less is more. An aversion to lavish packaging, a refusal to advertise, and a loudly proclaimed commitment to social causes are part of the company's image.

The Body Shop's personality has been shaped by the larger-than-life image of CEO Anita Roddick and the publicity she encourages as she travels in Africa, Asia, and Latin America foraging for indigenous secrets she can incorporate into Body Shop products. Significantly, by raising a wide range of social and environmental issues, the Body Shop targets and speaks to specific consumers who buy personal-care products at 1,136 stores in forty-five countries. The typical customer is a 29-year-old female who is likely to be interested in the retailer's philosophy and practices, including its aversion to selling products tested on animals, its in-store petitions aimed at protecting endangered species, and its attempts to assist developing countries through business partnerships.

Despite the boom in natural personal-care products, Body Shop managers say its corporate philosophy allows the chain to continue to distinguish itself. "A lot of our cus-

The Body Shop, led by flamboyant CEO Anita Roddick, places good corporate values on an equal level with profits. Will more companies follow the Body Shop's lead?

tomers shop with us because they share those same values," said Angela Bawtree, the Body Shop's head of investor relations. "It's not simply a question of buying a bubble bath." The Body Shop is expanding rapidly, opening one hundred and fifty stores a year, mostly in the United States, Japan, and Europe. In a recent report, NatWest Securities expressed "confidence that the international growth potential [over 2,000 stores in the year 2000] cannot only be realized, but also translated into healthy profits," and up to 20 percent annual growth in five years.

Source: Adapted from "Body Shop Marches to Its Own Drummer" by Charles Siler, reprinted with permission from the October 10, 1994 issue of *Advertising Age.* Copyright, Crain Communications Inc., 1994.

motives for taking the pills vary. Some take pills to make themselves more attractive, some to improve their health, and some to avoid being ostracized by others. By targeting each of these three segments with messages that promise benefits that match their motives, marketers can effectively educate each group about the long-term benefits of using the product and, at the same time, maximize sales. Note that promotion guided by the QOL concept emphasizes education, not persuasion. That is, the objective is to inform target consumers of product benefits through quality argument and presentation of evidence rather than through, say, emotional appeals.

Following the QOL concept further, marketers should deliver their messages through media that are beneficial to society in general and avoid those that are harmful, such as television programs that undermine positive societal values, that promote violence, or that reinforce negative stereotypes. Quality-of-life marketing promotes ethical marketing practices that enhance consumer well-being and do not adversely affect other publics. Consumer behavior research is central to effective QOL marketing. It is the means through which marketers identify consumer segments that are likely to use the product in ways that are beneficial to themselves and that are not harmful to others. In addition, consumer research can guide pricing, distribution, and promotion decisions that are congruent with QOL objectives. International Marketplace 17-4 illustrates the case of Novo Nordisk and its quality-of-life marketing program.

Marketing Management—Implications and Actions

Understanding social responsibility helps marketers:

- Use ethics tests to regulate their marketing practices.
- Apply the quality-of-life concept to ensure that each aspect of their marketing efforts favors the best interests of consumers.
- Use commitment to the well-being of consumers as a competitive strength, building goodwill and long-term customer satisfaction.

International *Marketplace 17-4*

Novo Nordisk's Mean Green Machine

Novo Nordisk is an excellent example of a company that turned responsible marketing practices into a gold mine. This $2 billion company emerged as a pioneer in "green chemistry"—finding more benign substitutes for synthetic chemicals. Decades before many rivals, Novo saw that synthetic chemicals would be attacked for harming the environment and that natural substances could perform many of the tasks chemicals traditionally do—acting as solvents or flavor enhancers, for instance—with less cost to the environment. Enzymes—natural catalysts that can speed up a chemical reaction without being consumed in the process—are biodegradable. And because they work best in mild conditions, they can require up to one-third less energy to use than many synthetic chemicals do. Novo has developed more than forty industrial enzymes for everything from stonewashing jeans to ripening apples more quickly. For example, in the soil of an Indonesian Monkey Temple, Novo unearthed an enzyme that is now widely used by soft-drink suppliers to change starch into sugar. In a pile of leaves at a Copenhagen cemetery, a researcher picked up a bug that produces an enzyme that can be used in detergents to help remove protein stains.

A heightened interest in "sustainable development"—the idea that future economic health depends on cutting pollution and using fewer natural resources—is fueling a conversion to greener alternatives by chemical makers such as DuPont, Dow, and South San Francisco's Genencor International. The business, which in the 1990s was growing by 10 percent to 15 percent a year and commanding premium prices for novel products, is a promising area for future growth.

Source: Adapted from "Novo Nordisk's Mean Green Machine" by Julia Flynn, Zachary Schiller, John Carey, and Ruth Coxeter reprinted from the November 14, 1994 issue of *Business Week* by special permission, copyright © 1994 by The McGraw-Hill Companies, Inc.

Chapter Spotlights

This chapter dealt with societal issues that affect both consumer behavior and marketing practices. By viewing the marketplace as a consumer society that has developed in tandem with economic growth, we see both the positive and negative effects of macroconsumption on the individual and on the culture at large.

Economic growth, the world over, is inextricably linked to the development of macroconsumption. Accelerated manufacturing creates products and, through employment, provides the means for people to buy them. The two feed upon each other, and the result is that the prevailing culture changes to accommodate macroconsumption. Several factors—technical, economic, environmental, and individual—contribute to the development of a consumer society.

1. Consumer culture. Goods and services have taken such a strong hold in the lives of consumers that any culture can be characterized by the consumption habits of its members. Advertising, by associating products with symbols that are part of the culture, has the power to influence how that culture develops, affecting the ways in which people behave, the things they desire, and the way they would like to live. Because of this, marketers contribute to the development of cultural values and behaviors that are not always in the best interests of the culture at large.

2. Materialism. The consumer society encourages materialism—the acquisition of possessions through which people measure their worth and that of others. Materialism, though desirable for marketers whose objective is to sell more goods and services, is not beneficial to the culture at large as it encourages characteristics and behaviors that do little to improve society.

3. Addictive or compulsive consumption. Consumerism encourages addictive behavior toward or involving advertised products. Of most relevance to marketers and retailers is the increasing number of instances of addiction to the process of shopping itself.

4. Shoplifting and consumer cheating. Particularly important to retailers, shoplifting also exacts costs on the consumer—we all pay more when prices rise to cover losses from shoplifting, and we all suffer the moral consequences of a society that condones shoplifting. Consumer research can help change consumer attitudes toward shoplifting by providing insight into the reasons people shoplift and designing programs to dissuade them from doing so.

5. Social responsibility and marketing. In addition to the efforts of public policy and consumer advocacy groups, marketers can regulate their own actions by understanding and applying ethical practices. A range of self-regulatory tests and the quality-of-life concept serve to help marketers identify and correct marketing actions that can have negative consequences for society.

Key Terms

addictive or compulsive consumption (p. 532)
consequences test (p. 539)
consumer cheating (p. 534)
consumer culture (p. 525)
consumer sovereignty (p. 536)
duty of beneficence (p. 538)
duty of fidelity (p. 538)

duty of gratitude (p. 538)
duty of justice (p. 538)
duty of nonmaleficence (p. 538)
"green consumers" (p. 530)
justice test (p. 539)
legal test (p. 538)
materialism (p. 531)

motives test (p. 539)
producer sovereignty (p. 536)
quality-of-life marketing (p. 540)
rights test (p. 539)
shoplifting (p. 533)
special obligations test (p. 538)
utilitarian test (p. 539)

Review Questions

Note: You can find the correct answers to these questions by taking the quiz and then submitting your answers in the Online Edition. The program will automatically score your submission. If you miss a question, the program will provide the correct answer, a rationale for the answer, and the section number in the chapter where the topic is discussed.

1. As people gain economic freedom, production capabilities
   a. grow.
   b. stagnate.
   c. decline.
   d. remain fairly constant.

2. The development of a consumer society is accelerated with favorable cultural or
   a. population growth.
   b. democratic trends.
   c. societal values.
   d. national consumer legislation.

3. Satisfaction with material possessions tends to contribute most to overall life satisfaction for
   a. materialistic people.
   b. everyone.
   c. the affluent.
   d. baby boomers.

4. Many believe that material possessions are a route to a state of
   a. happiness.
   b. bliss.
   c. respect.
   d. upward mobility.

5. Nongenerous personalities don't like to lend things to other people. Nongenerous people are
   a. materialistic.
   b. affluent.
   c. individualistic.
   d. ethnocentric.

6. Shopping itself is an increasingly common _____ in consumer societies.
   a. addiction
   b. problem
   c. social rite
   d. group ceremony

7. Shoplifters commonly try to justify their behavior by denying responsibility, claiming injury, and claiming
   a. a lack of money.
   b. it is a habit.
   c. they lack sanity.
   d. they are victims.

8. Many argue that we cannot select the best high-tech product because we lack the opportunity, motivation, and
   a. money.
   b. stores in our area.
   c. ability.
   d. websites.

9. Marketers applying the quality-of-life concept to product strategies should first consider how their products can enhance the _____ of targeted consumers.
   a. satisfaction
   b. quality level
   c. well-being
   d. positioning

10. Quality-of-life marketing promotes practices that do not _____ affect other publics.
   a. adversely
   b. normally
   c. financially
   d. economically

Team Talk

1. Within your own life, what evidence do you see of the accelerated development of the consumer society within the last twenty years? Consider the lifestyle you follow, the possessions you have, and the media you use as compared to those of your parents or grandparents.

2. Choose a specific product—soft drinks, cigarettes, fast food, or vacation travel, for example. Research and discuss ways in which the product itself, the way in which it is used, and the marketing activities that support it have changed over the last decade. What does this tell you about changes in the consumer culture? To what do you attribute those changes?

3. Talk with students who come from another country. Find out their impressions of the supply and demand of goods and services, the rate of growth of the marketing industry, the level of materialism, and the degree of urbanization in their country. Would you judge the country selected to be a consumer society?

4. Discuss the pros and cons of a consumer society. Consider such factors as the level of employment, the marketplace, the natural environment, the economy, and the quality of life.

5. Among people you know, which gender group do you consider more materialistic? Which age group, religious group, socio-economic group, or social/political group is most materialistic? How materialistic are today's business undergraduates?

6. Have members of your team ever engaged in antisocial behaviors, such as shoplifting, vandalism, or drug use? Share your experiences, explaining why you were attracted to them and how you feel you can dissuade others from engaging in them.

7. Businesses have a responsibility to employees and shareholders to increase profits. If social responsibility conflicts with this, which is more important? Gather examples and discuss.

8. RJR Nabisco launched advertisements that showed its cartoon character Joe Camel flanked by girl camels, provoking charges that the company was trying to lure young men to smoke. Meanwhile, RJR signed actor Danny Glover to star in public-service advertising that discouraged underage smoking. What do these two marketing activities tell us about advertising symbolism and about marketing ethics?

Workshops

Research Workshop

Background

When taken to extremes, materialism is a negative social influence. The objective of this workshop is to conduct a study to find out whether advertising in women's magazines encourages materialism and to make recommendations on responsible marketing actions.

Methodology

Collect up to ten issues of each of two consumer magazines targeting women, such as *Glamour, Cosmopolitan, McCall's,* or *Redbook.* Based on the definition of materialism used in this chapter, isolate cues and symbols in the advertisements that appeal to materialistic values. Randomly select five advertisements from each issue of the two selected magazines and record the number of materialistic cues or symbols you find. Compare the frequency of materialistic cues and symbols from the two magazines.

To the Marketplace

Interpret your findings, categorizing each materialistic cue or symbol according to the effect it is likely to have on readers. Make a list of recommendations for marketers targeting the readership of each magazine for avoiding overt materialistic messages.

Creative Workshop

Background

Shoplifting hurts not just the retailer but also all consumers in the form of higher prices. The objective of this workshop is to develop in-store posters that discourage this antisocial behavior.

Methodology

Based on your understanding of the psychology of shoplifting, write a profile of the type of consumer to whom the posters should be tar-geted. Develop three alternative sketches and headlines that you feel discourage shoplifting. Provide a brief rationale for each.

To the Marketplace

Visit retail outlets on campus and within your local community and seek advice on which advertising concept works best. Refine the strongest concept into a poster, complete with visuals, headline, and copy.

Managerial Workshop

Background

As marketing director of a small pharmaceutical company that specializes in vitamin supplements, you have been criticized for using "hard-sell" strategies to increase sales. The objective of this workshop is to develop a checklist that will help you ensure that future promotions are socially responsible.

Methodology

Seek out information and examples of advertising from marketers of vitamin supplements. Analyze their marketing activities in terms of product, price, distribution, and promotion. Identify the extent to which each strategy is socially responsible.

To the Marketplace

Create a list of questionable practices and, where possible, suggest alternate strategies that are potentially as cost-effective and will result in similar levels of sales and increased levels of customer satisfaction.

Notes

1. Kathleen M. Rassuli and Stanley C. Hollander, "Desire-Induced, Innate, Insatiable?" *Journal of Macromarketing,* Vol. 6 (Fall 1986), pp. 4–24.

2. Ed Diener, Jeff Horwitz, and Robert A. Emmons, "Happiness of the Very Wealthy," *Social Indicators Research,* Vol. 16 (1985), pp. 263–274; Robin A. Douthitt, Maurice MacDonald, and Randolph Mullis, "The Relationship Between Measures of Subjective and Economic Well-Being: A New Look," *Social Indicators Research,* Vol. 26 (1992), pp. 407–422; Richard A. Easterlin, "Does Economic Growth Improve the Human Lot? Some Empirical Evidence," In *Nations and Households in Economic Growth,* edited by Paul A. David and Melvin W. Redder (New York: Academic Press, 1974, pp. 89–121); Randolph Mullis, "Measures of Economic Well-Being as Predictors of Psychological Well-Being," *Social Indicators Research,* Vol. 26 (1992), pp. 119–135.

3. R. S. Oropesa, "Consumer Possessions, Consumer Passions, and Subjective Well-Being," *Sociological Forum,* Vol. 10, No. 2 (1995), pp. 215–244.

4. Ibid; for an interesting and insightful analysis of the effects of the availability of too many brand options on consumers, see David Glen Mick, Susan M. Broniarczyk, and Jonathan Haidt, "Choose, Choose, Choose, Choose, Choose, Choose Choose: Emerging and Prospective Research on the Deleterious Effects of Living in Consumer Hyperchoice," *Journal of Business Ethics,* Vol. 52 (June 2004), pp. 207–211.

5. M. Joseph Sirgy, Dong-Jin Lee, Val Larsen, and Newell Wright, "Satisfaction with Material Possessions and General Well-Being: The Role of Materialism," *Journal of Consumer Satisfaction, Dissatisfaction and Complaining Behavior,* Vol. 11 (1998), pp. 103–118.

6. For an excellent and comprehensive review of the literature on the socio-demographic profile of green consumers, see Adamantios Diamantopoulos, Bodo B. Schlegelmich, Rudolf R. Sinkoves, and Greg M. Bohlen, "Can Socio-demographics Still Play a Role in Profiling Green Consumers? A Review of the Evidence and an Empirical Investigation," *Journal of Business Research,* Vol. 56 (2003), pp. 465–480.

7. For a comprehensive review of the literature on materialism, see the following article: Val Larsen, M. Joseph Sirgy, and Newell D. Wright, "Materialism: The Construct, Measures, Antecedents, and Consequences," *Academy of Marketing Studies Journal,* Vol. 3, No. 2 (1999), pp. 75–107.

8. Gianfranco Poggi, *Calvinism and the Capitalist Spirit* (Amherst, MA: University of Massachusetts Press, 1983); Gordon Marshall, *In Search of the Spirit of Capitalism* (London: Hutchinson, 1982).

9. S. N. Eisenstadt, *The Protestant Ethic and Modernization* (New York: Basic Books, 1968).

10. Raymond Williams, *Marxism and Literature* (Oxford, England: Oxford University Press, 1977).

11. Elizabeth C. Hirschman, "Secular Immortality and the American Ideology of Affluence," *Journal of Consumer Research,* Vol. 17 (June 1990), pp. 31–42; W. L. Warner, Marcia Meeker, and Kenneth Eells, *Social Class in America* (Chicago, IL: Science Research Associates, 1949).

12. Thomas O. O'Guinn and Russell W. Belk, "Heaven on Earth: Consumption at Heritage Village, USA," *Journal of Consumer Research,* Vol. 16 (September 1989), pp. 227–238.

13. M. Joseph Sirgy et al. "Does TV Viewership Propagate Materialism, Dissatisfaction with Standard of Living and Life: A Cross-Cultural Study," *Journal of Advertising,* in press.

14. M. Joseph Sirgy, Dong-Jin Lee, Rustan Kosenko, H. Lee Meadow, Don Rahtz, Muris Cicic, Guang Xi Jin, Duygun Yarsuvat, David L. Blenkhorn, and Newell Wright, "Does Television Viewership Play a Role in the Perception of Quality of Life?" *Journal of Advertising,* Vol. 27 (Spring 1998), pp. 125–142.

15. Russell W. Belk, "Materialism: Trait Aspects of Living in the Material World," *Journal of Consumer Research,* Vol. 12 (December 1985), pp. 265–281. For a recent review of materialism measures, see Marsha L. Richins, "The Material Values Scale: Measurement Properties and Development of a Short Form," *Journal of Consumer Research,* Vol. 31 (2004), pp. 209–220.

16. For an interesting psychological theory that explains why materialistic people tend to be less happy with life than nonmaterialistic people, see the following article: M. Joseph Sirgy, "Materialism and Quality of Life," *Social Indicators Research,* Vol. 43 (1998), 227–260. Also, see Aric Rindfleisch and James E. Burroughs, "Terrifying Thoughts, Terrible Materialism? Contemplations on a Terror Management Account of Materialism and Consumer Behavior," *Journal of Consumer Psychology,* Vol. 14 (2004), 219–230; Jamie Arndt, Sheldon Solomon, Tim Kasser, and Kennon M. Sheldon, "The Urge to Splurge Revisited: Further Reflections on Applying Terror Management Theory to Materialism and Consumer Behavior," *Journal of Consumer Psychology,* Vol. 14 (2004), pp. 225–235.

17. Georgia Witkin, "The Shopping Fix," *Health,* Vol. 73 (May 1988); Rajaan Natataajan and Brent G. Goff, "Manifestations of Compulsiveness in the Consumer-Marketplace Domain," *Psychology and Marketing,* Vol. 9 (January 1992), pp. 31–44.

18. Jean Seligmann, "Taking Life One Night at a Time; Sex Addicts Seek Help," *Newsweek* (July 20, 1987), p. 48.

19. Stephen J. Hoch and George F. Loewenstein, "Time-Inconsistent Preferences and Consumer Self-Control," *Journal of Consumer Research,* Vol. 17 (March 1991), pp. 492–507; Elizabeth C. Hirschman, "The Consciousness of Addiction: Toward a General Theory of Compulsive Consumption," *Journal of Consumer Research,* Vol. 19 (September 1992), pp. 155–179.

20. Aric Rindfleisch, James E. Burroughs, and Frank Denton, "Family Structure, Materialism, and Compulsive Consumption," *Journal of Consumer Research,* Vol. 23 (March 1997), pp. 312–325. Also see James A. Roberts, Chris Manolis, and John F. Tanner, Jr. "Family Structure, Materialism, and Compulsive Buying: A Reinquiry and Extension," *Journal of the Academy of Marketing Science,* Vol. 31 (Summer 2003), pp. 300–311.

21. Thomas C. O'Guinn and Ronald J. Faber, "Compulsive Buying: A Phenomenological Exploration," *Journal of Consumer Research,* Vol. 16 (September 1989), pp. 147–157; for a more recent article summarizing research on compulsive buying, see John C. Mowen and Nancy Spears, "Understanding Compulsive Buying among College Students," *Journal of Consumer Psychology,* Vol. 8 (4, 1999), 407–430: James A. Roberts and Eli Jones, "Money Attitudes, Credit Card Use, and Compulsive Buying Among American

College Students," *Journal of Consumer Affairs,* Vol. 35 (2001), pp. 213–240; Hyokjin Kwak, George M. Zinkhan, and Joseph R. Dominick, "The Moderating Role of Gender and Compulsive Buying Tendencies in the Cultivation Effects of TV Shows and TV Advertising: A Cross-Cultural Study Between the U.S. and South Korea," *Media Psychology,* Vol. 4 (2002), pp.77–111; Hyokjin Kwak, George M. Zinkhan, and Melvin R Crask, "Diagnostic Screener for Compulsive Buying: Applications to the USA and South Korea," *Journal of Consumer Affairs,* Vol. 37 (Summer 2003), pp. 161–171.

22. Catherine A. Cole, "Deterrence and Consumer Fraud," *Journal of Retailing,* Vol. 65 (Spring 1989), pp. 107–120.

23. "Shoplifting: Bess Myerson's Arrest Highlights a Multibillion-Dollar Problem that Many Stores Won't Talk About," *Life* (August 1988), p. 32.

24. Stephen J. Grove, Scott J. Vitell, and David Strutton, "Non-Normative Consumer Behavior and the Techniques of Neutralization," in Terry Childers et al., eds., *Marketing Theory and Practice* (1989 AMA Winter Educators' Conference, Chicago, IL: American Marketing Association, 1989), pp. 131–135.

25. David Strutton, Scott J. Vitell, and Lou E. Pelton, "How Consumers May Justify Inappropriate Behavior in Market Settings: An Application on the Techniques of Neutralization," *Journal of Business Research,* Vol. 30 (July 1994), pp. 253–260.

26. Dena Cox, Anthony D. Cox, and George P. Moschis, "When Consumer Behavior Goes Bad: An Investigation of Adolescent Shoplifting," *Journal of Consumer Research,* Vol. 17 (September 1990), pp. 149–159.

27. Jeffery M. Kallis and Dinoo J. Vanier, "Consumer Shoplifting: Orientations and Deterrents," *Journal of Criminal Justice,* Vol. 13 (Issue 5 1985), pp. 459-473.

28. Catherine A. Cole, "Deterrence and Customer Fraud," Journal of Retailing, Vol. 65 (Spring 1989), pp. 107–120. Anthony D. Cox, Dean Cox, Ronald D. Anderson, and George P. Moschis, "Social Influences on Adolescent Shoplifting—Theory, Evidence, and Implications for the Retail Industry," *Journal of Retailing,* Vol. 69 (Summer 1993), pp. 234–246; Michele Tonglet, "Consumer Misbehaviour: An Exploratory Study of Shoplifting," *Journal of Consumer Behaviour,* Vol. 1 (June 2002), pp. 336–355.

29. Wujin Chu, Eitan Gerstner, and James D. Hess, "Managing Dissatisfaction: How to Decrease Customer Opportunism by Partial Refunds," *Journal of Service Research,* Vol. 1 (Issue 2 1998), pp. 140–155. Tracey Longo, "At Stores, Many Unhappy Returns," *Kiplinger's Personal Finance Magazine,* Vol. 20 (1995), pp. 239–255; James A. Muncy and Jacqueline K. Eastman, "Materialism and Consumer Ethics: An Exploratory Study," *Journal of Business Ethics,* Vol. 17 (1998), pp. 137–145; James A. Muncy and Scott J. Vitell, "Consumer Ethics: An Empirical Investigation of the Ethical Beliefs of the Final Consumer," *Journal of Business Research,* Vol. 24 (1992), pp. 297–311; Scott J. Vitell, James R. Lumpkin, and Mohammed Y. A. Rawwas, "Consumer Ethics: An Investigation of the Ethical Beliefs of Elderly Consumers," *Journal of Business Ethics,* Vol. 10 (1991), pp. 365–375; Scott J. Vitell and James Muncy, "Consumer Ethics: An Empirical Investigation of Factors Influencing Judgments of the Final Consumer," *Journal of Business Ethics,* Vol. 11 (1992),

pp. 585–597; Johannes Brinkmann, "Looking at Consumer Behavior in a Moral Perspective," *Journal of Business Ethics,* Vol. 51 (2004), pp. 129–141.

30. Jochen Wirtz and Doreen Kum, "Consumer Cheating on Service Guarantees," *Journal of the Academy of Marketing Science,* Vol. 32 (Spring 2004), pp. 159–175; for studies dealing with consumer cheating across cultures, see the following articles: Jamal Al-Khatib, Scott J. Vitell, and Mohammed Y. A. Rawwas, "Consumer Ethics: A Cross-cultural Investigation," *European Journal of Marketing,* Vol. 31 (1997), pp. 750–767; Robert W. Armstrong and Jill Sweeney, "Industry Type, Culture, Mode of Entry and Perceptions of International Marketing Ethics Problems: A Cross-cultural Comparison," *Journal of Business Ethics,* Vol. 13 (1994), pp. 775–785; David J. Burns and John T. Brady, "Retail Ethics as Appraised by Future Business Personnel in Malaysia and the United States," *Journal of Consumer Affairs,* Vol. 30 (1996), pp. 195–217; Michael Jay Polonsky, Pedro Quelhas Brito, Jorge Pinto, Nicola Higgs-Kleyn, "Consumer Ethics in the European Union: A Comparison of Northern and Southern Views," *Journal of Business Ethics,* Vol. 31 (2001), pp. 117–130; Mohammed Y. A. Rawwas, "Consumer Ethics: An Empirical Investigation of the Ethical Beliefs of Austrian Consumers," *Journal of Business Ethics,* Vol. 15 (1996), pp. 1009–1019; Mohammed Y. A. Rawwas, "Culture, Personality and Morality: A Typology of International Consumers' Ethical Beliefs," *International Marketing Review,* Vol. 18 (2001), pp. 188–209; Mohammed Y. A. Rawwas, Gordon Patzer, and Michael Klassen, "Consumer Ethics in Cross Cultural Settings," *European Journal of Marketing,* 29 (1995), pp. 62–78.

31. R. A. Fullerton and G. Punj, "Repercussion of Promoting an Ideology of Consumption: Consumer Misbehavior," *Journal of Business Research,* Vol. 57 (November 2004), pp. 1239–1249.

32. N. Craig Smith, "Marketing Strategies for the Ethics Era," *Sloan Management Review,* Vol. 60 (Summer 1995), pp. 85–97.

33. M. Joseph Sirgy and Chenting Su, "The Ethics of Consumer Sovereignty in an Age of High Tech," *Journal of Business Ethics,* Vol. 28 (2000), pp. 1–14; E Scott Maynes, "Marketing-One Consumer Disaster," *Journal of Consumer Affairs,* Vol. 37 (2003), pp. 196–207; E. Scott Maynes and Terje Assutn, "Informational Imperfections in Local Consumer Markets: Empirical Findings and Policy Implications," *Journal of Consumer Affairs,* Vol. 6 (1982), pp.62–87; E. Scott Maynes, James N. Morgan, Weston Vivian, and Greg J. Duncan, "The Local Consumer Information System: An Institution-To-Be?" *Journal of Consumer Affairs,* Vol. 11 (1977), pp. 17–33

34. Gene R. Laczniak, "Framework for Analyzing Marketing Ethics," *Journal of Macromarketing,* Vol. 3 (Spring 1983), pp. 7–18.

35. This section draws heavily on two papers: M. Joseph Sirgy, "Strategic Marketing Planning Guided by the Quality-of-Life (QOL) Concept," *Journal of Business Ethics,* Vol. 15 (March 1996), pp. 241–259; M. Joseph Sirgy and Dong-Jin Lee, "Setting Socially Responsible Marketing Objectives: A Quality-of-Life (QOL) Approach," *European Journal of Marketing,* Vol. 30 (Spring 1996), pp. 20–34.

Organizational Buying and Diffusion of Innovation

18

Dean Relande is dean of the school of engineering at a southeastern university. The school of engineering has been expanding rapidly. The student body and faculty have doubled in the last decade, and the school has been running out of space. The state agency overseeing the budget for higher education has given in—finally—and agreed to fund the development of a new building for the school. Dean Relande is ecstatic when he first hears the news. He calls his assistant dean, Martha Delozier, and says, "Marty, we need to put together a building committee to oversee the development of this project. I need you to chair this committee, and I need a faculty representative from each of the five departments."

The committee's first meeting lasts for two full hours. At the end of the meeting, Assistant Dean Delozier tells her colleagues, "This committee will have lots of decisions to make. Free up at least a couple of hours a week for the next six months to take care of tasks and responsibilities related to this project. Our work on this committee is just beginning."

This chapter addresses organizational buying. We will discuss many of the procedures and processes organizations go through in their purchase of products and services. Organizational buying is more complex than individual and family buying. Understanding the psychology and sociology of organization buying helps business-to-business marketers with many decisions, from target marketing to marketing communications.

Families, households, and organizations purchase widely different products to meet widely different needs. There is, however, an important similarity in their consumption patterns—they buy as groups, not as individuals. In this chapter, we will explore the mechanisms of organizational purchasing and how consumers buy technological innovations. We will also look at the ways in which innovations are diffused into the marketplace, describing the types of consumers who adopt them, their characteristics, and their lifestyles.

18-1 Organizational Buying

Organizational buying decisions, like household purchases, are made by groups of individuals working together to solve common problems and meet shared goals. The organizational buyer buys for or on behalf of a group, whether in the purchase of materials for manufacturing firms or in the purchase of goods or services for such institutions as schools or hospitals. Organizational buying is different from both individual and household buying in that demand is derived not from the desire to satisfy personal wants or needs, but from economic considerations.[1]

Unlike consumer goods, industrial products need not always appeal to aesthetic tastes, and their purchase is not directly motivated by psychological needs. They are bought only to help organizations manufacture, distribute, or sell goods or services in order to improve their economic and competitive positions. Rarely bought on impulse, organizational purchases are subject to a series of checks and balances in both price and quality that are non-existent in most personal or household buying situations.[2]

Having said this, organizations move, like individuals, through a decision cycle from problem recognition to choice. Let's now take a look at the organizational decision-making process, noting its similarities to and differences from the consumer decision cycle.

18-1a **The Decision Cycle in Organizational Buying**

The **decision cycle** in organizational buying can be viewed as a sequential process, beginning with the identification of a need within the organization and progressing through the actual receipt and use of the products purchased. It can be broken down into the steps seen in Exhibit 18-1.

> **decision cycle** A sequential process, beginning with the identification of a need within the organization and progressing through the actual receipt and use of the products purchased.

Understanding that organizations go through a specific decision-making process allows marketers of business- or manufacturing-related goods and services to develop programs designed to influence each of the various stages of that process. If a marketer knows, for example, that a customer is about to establish purchasing specifications, he or she can provide useful technical information or offer advice on industry standards and other factors that may affect the formulation of those specifications.[3]

Of the eleven-step process, steps eight to eleven are usually considered to be the most important, and in the sections that follow, we will explore them more fully. It is during these stages that specific vendors are closely examined and their performance evaluated. Note that the last two stages occur post-purchase. Because repeat purchasing is the key to survival in the business-to-business area, analysis of post-purchase performance is critical.

Evaluating Alternative Vendors   The most important stage of the process, because it leads directly to the actual purchase decision, is evaluation by the organizational buyer (or buying team) of alternative vendors. A study involving a survey of purchasing agents in forty-five countries arrived at a long list of criteria used in evaluating suppliers:[4]

- Overall reputation of the supplier
- Financing terms
- Supplier's flexibility in adjusting to the company's needs
- Experience with the supplier in analogous situations
- Technical services offered
- Confidence in salespeople
- Convenience in placing orders
- Reliability of the product or service
- Price
- Technical specifications
- Ease of operation or use
- Preferences of the principal user of the product
- Training offered by the supplier
- Training time required
- Reliability of delivery date promised
- Ease of maintenance
- Sales service expected after date of purchase

E x h i b i t 18-1

The Organizational Buying Decision Cycle

1. Identify need.	Apple Computers has identified a need—to improve its advertising as a means of increasing sales.
2. Establish purchasing objectives and specifications.	The objective is clear—to hire an agency that can create advertising that will spur sales of Apple computers. Specifications are many—experience in handling major national accounts, expertise in the computer industry, reputation for creativity, track record of improving sales through advertising, marketing research capabilities, and location reasonably close to Apple headquarters.
3. Obtain technical data.	Next, qualitative specifications are translated into technical data so that the company has an objective means through which to compare candidate agencies. For example, having marketing research capabilities may in some agencies mean running an in-agency research department, while in others it means subcontracting out to a research firm.
4. Determine quantities to be purchased.	In determining quantities to be purchased, Apple decides how many and which of its accounts the new agency will handle.
5. Negotiate price.	Next, Apple determines the optimum method and terms of agency compensation.
6. Schedule delivery time.	Although more obviously applicable to manufacturing firms than to service industries like advertising, steps six and seven, delivery time and delivery method, help Apple determine the kinds of schedule and approval and delivery processes the new agency will be expected to maintain.
7. Specify delivery method and routing.	
8. Evaluate alternative vendors.	Next, in evaluating vendors, Apple considers the strengths and weaknesses of alternative agencies based on its original specifications, the number of accounts to be assumed, price, and schedule.
9. Select vendor.	Once alternative agencies have been evaluated, the successful agency is selected. Even after the agency has been hired and begins work, the decision process continues.
10. Adjust and settle complaint.	Apple and the agency enter a period of adjustment during which a working relationship is established and problems are resolved.
11. Conduct post-purchase appraisal.	Finally, a post-purchase appraisal completes the decision process as Apple reviews the agency's performance, particularly in terms of its objective of increasing sales through advertising. If this objective has not been achieved or Apple is dissatisfied with the agency's performance, the decision cycle loops back to step one, and a new needs analysis begins.

Source: Ronald H. Gorman, "Role Conception and Purchasing Behavior," *Journal of Purchasing,* 7 (February 1971), p. 67.

Although this list is not complete, it indicates that many factors influence the choice of a vendor and, therefore, the ultimate purchase. If marketers can successfully predict which of the evaluation criteria each customer rates most highly and is most likely to use, they can better position themselves as the optimum supplier and so increase the likelihood of being selected.

The evaluation criteria in vendor selection can be divided into two groups: product criteria and emotional criteria.

Product Criteria   New task decisions—initial purchase decisions based on little or limited prior buying experience—are influenced by:[5]

1. Product specifications
2. Price limits
3. Delivery conditions
4. Service terms and requirements
5. Method and terms of payment
6. Order routine and quantities
7. Acceptable supplier characteristics
8. Selected supplier characteristics

Vendors soliciting business from an organization for which vendor selection is a new task need to convince the customer that they can meet organizational requirements on each of these eight criteria. Besides new task decisions, four other types of buying situations use variations of these criteria in vendor selection.[6] The four buying situations range from the routine, where several criteria may be skipped, to the complex, where other factors may complicate the selection.

1. **Routine decisions** involve frequently ordered and used products, such as office supplies. There is no training needed in the use of such products.
2. **Procedural purchases** involve products or services that require training, such as accounting information systems.
3. **Performance purchases** are those in which vendors solve technical problems. Examples are photocopy machines and image setters.
4. **Political decisions** involve major capital outlay, such as high-cost medical equipment purchased by a hospital. In political purchases, multiple departments compete for the same funds.

Exhibit 18-2 shows the results of a study on the influence of the buying situation on evaluation criteria used in organizational buying decisions. By identifying which of the four buying situations applies, marketers can create programs that emphasize attributes likely to influence buyers in each situation. As we can see, price and reliability of delivery are very important in routine orders. Attributes associated with minimizing training difficulties (technical service, ease of use, and training offered) are important in vendor selection for procedural purchases. In making performance purchases, buyers rely heavily on attributes that facilitate judgments on whether the vendor and its product can do the job (reputation, flexibility, reliability data, technical service, and reliability of delivery). In making political purchases, attributes such as price, reputation, product reliability data, and reliability of delivery are important, particularly where intergroup conflict is an issue. Note that in Exhibit 18-2, reliability of delivery is consistently rated as highly important across all four buying situations. Obviously, this is because delayed deliveries can have a negative impact on the organization's overall productivity.

Emotional Criteria   It is important to remember that even the most routine of organizational purchases is influenced by people. Even in organizational buying situations, individuals seek, to some extent, to meet personal goals or satisfy personal needs. Some choose suppliers based solely upon reputation, wishing to reduce the risk of error. Others attempt to impress management by selecting the supplier who asks the lowest price. Most people, to varying extents, consider the impressions their purchase decisions make on co-workers. As an example, recognizing emotional influences on organizational decisions, the 3M ad in Exhibit 18-3 shows the user how many ways the product can enhance his or her job performance and even make the user "look good." Even when selling industrial products as impersonal as electronic switches or relay systems, emotional motivations come into play. Buyers might, for example, be influenced by the high-tech qualities of a product, believing that by choosing a sophisticated technology, they are assured of impressing co-workers with their forward-planning.[7]

new task decisions Initial purchase decisions based on little or limited prior buying experience.

routine decisions Decisions that involve frequently ordered and used products, such as office supplies. No training is needed in the use of such products.

procedural purchases Purchases that involve products or services that require training, such as accounting information systems.

performance purchases Purchases in which vendors solve technical problems. Examples are photocopy machines and image setters.

political decisions Decisions that involve major capital outlay, such as high-cost medical equipment purchased by a hospital. In political purchases, multiple departments compete for the same funds.

Exhibit 18-2   Factors Influencing Choice in Different Buying Situations

Attribute	Product Type							
	Routine Order		Procedural Problem		Performance Problem		Political Problem	
	Mean	Rank	Mean	Rank	Mean	Rank	Mean	Rank
1. Reputation	4.84*	4	5.33	7	5.29	5	5.53	2
	(1.09)		(0.80)		(0.82)		(0.69)	
2. Financing	4.51	9	4.07	16	3.91	16	4.91	13
	(1.39)		(1.29)		(1.31)		(1.24)	
3. Flexibility	5.07	3	5.40	5	5.42	2	5.51	5
	(1.12)		(0.62)		(0.62)		(0.59)	
4. Past experience	4.71	6	4.93	13	5.07	9	5.04	10
	(0.94)		(0.86)		(0.69)		(0.93)	
5. Technical service	4.36	12	5.53	1	5.38	3	5.40	7
	(1.28)		(0.66)		(0.89)		(0.62)	
6. Confidence in salespeople	3.96	14	4.73	15	4.42	15	4.58	16
	(1.35)		(1.23)		(1.20)		(1.20)	
7. Convenience in ordering	3.80	15	3.73	17	3.71	17	4.08	17
	(1.32)		(1.29)		(1.34)		(1.24)	
8. Reliability data	4.47	11	5.16	11	5.33	4	5.53	3
	(1.24)		(1.07)		(0.67)		(0.59)	
9. Price	5.60	2	5.29	8	5.18	8	5.56	1
	(0.62)		(0.70)		(0.94)		(0.69)	
10. Technical	4.73	5	5.22	9	5.27	6	5.42	6
	(1.25)		(0.67)		(0.69)		(0.72)	
11. Ease of use	4.51	10	5.53	2	5.24	7	5.18	8
	(1.29)		(0.59)		(0.80)		(0.83)	
12. Preference of user	4.00	13	4.76	14	4.53	13	4.84	14
	(1.19)		(1.11)		(1.14)		(0.90)	
13. Training offered	3.22	16	5.42	3	4.73	12	5.00	11
	(1.18)		(0.87)		(1.19)		(0.83)	
14. Training required	3.22	17	5.11	12	4.44	14	4.69	15
	(1.22)		(1.23)		(1.22)		(1.02)	
15. Reliability of delivery	5.64	1	5.42	4	5.44	1	5.53	4
	(0.53)		(0.72)		(0.66)		(0.69)	
16. Maintenance	4.60	8	5.20	10	4.82	11	5.00	12
	(1.05)		(0.69)		(0.96)		(0.74)	
17. Sales service	4.64	7	5.36	6	5.07	10	5.09	9
	(1.25)		(0.77)		(0.84)		(0.70)	
Product Type Mean	**4.46**		**5.07**		**4.09**		**5.11**	

Source: From "Difference in Attitude Importance for Different Industrial Products" reprinted with permission from *Journal of Marketing,* published by the American Marketing Association, Donald R. Lehmann and John O'Shaughnessy, April 1974, p. 39.

*Mean (standard deviation).

There are other, subtle criteria that affect buying decisions, most notably the ethically suspect arrangement of buyer-seller reciprocity. In reciprocal agreements, a supplier may be asked to buy its customer's product in order to guarantee a purchase of its supplies from that customer.[8]

Does intuition fit into the organizational decision-making picture? See CBite 18-1 for how this seems to be a factor among advertising, marketing, and marketing research professionals.

Post-Purchase Evaluation   Post-purchase satisfaction is of primary importance for marketers selling to organizations. Once a decision is made and implemented, post-purchase evaluation is the single most important factor influencing subsequent purchasing decisions. Whether or not rebuys take place depends largely on the actual performance of the product and on the way customer complaints and requests are handled. Marketers selling to organizational customers use a variety of strategies to ensure post-purchase satisfaction, ranging from performance warranties to free service for the life of the product.

Post-purchase satisfaction is likely to lead to a straight rebuy, which in all probability will be made individually. Dissatisfaction is likely to force the organization to seek new vendors, which entails either a modified rebuy or a new task decision. New tasks and modified rebuys are typically decided upon by more than one individual within the organization.[9]

The Effect of Supplier Reliability and Benevolence   Recent research has shown that reliability and benevolence play an important role in customer satisfaction and intentions to

CBite 18-1

Using Intuition as a Decision-Making Strategy

Have you heard the "little voice" inside your head or had that "funny feeling" in your stomach when making a decision? These events seem to affect the decision-making outcomes for executives in advertising, marketing, and marketing research. In a study done in the mid-1990s, 89 percent of the respondents said they frequently used intuition to guide some part of their decision making. Apparently in their fast-paced, continually downsizing, and urgent business world they don't have the time they had in the past to gather and analyze all of the data needed to support every decision. Compared to similar research done in the mid-1980s, and probably due to the often right-brain nature of these businesses, we see intuition being used more by these executives than those in other organizations. People in top management were more prone to do this than middle managers. It looks like the higher a person is on the ladder of success, the greater the use of intuition.

Contrary to previous research, the gender skew toward females using more intuition than males was reversed in the mid-1990s, with males using intuition a higher percentage of the time than their female peers in the decision-making process. If a person uses intuition for less than 50 percent of their decisions, then this mode is not the driver. In that case it is likely that a good deal of data is being used.

Do you think it is wrong or right for an executive in an organizational decision setting to use intuition?

Source: Thomas R. Keen, "What's Your Intuitive Decision-maker Quotient?" *Marketing News* (October 21, 1996), p. 6. Reprinted with permission from the American Marketing Association.

---

supplier reliability
The supplier's ability to keep a promise (for example, ability to deliver according to contract, provision of enough and relevant information, trust in provided information, and trustworthiness of supplier).

supplier benevolence
A perceived willingness of the supplier to behave in a way that benefits the interest of both parties in the relationship (for example, willingness to support the customer if the environment causes changes, consideration of the customer's welfare when making important decisions, responding with understanding when problems arise, consideration of how future decisions and actions will affect the customer, and dependable support on things that are important to the customer).

do repeat business.[10] **Supplier reliability** is defined as the supplier's ability to keep a promise (e.g., ability to deliver according to contract, provision of enough and relevant information, trust in provided information, and trustworthiness of supplier). **Supplier benevolence** is defined as a perceived willingness of the supplier to behave in a way that benefits the interest of both parties in the relationship (e.g., willingness to support the customer if the environment causes changes, consideration of the customer's welfare when making important decisions, responding with understanding when problems arise, consideration of how future decisions and actions will affect the customer, and dependable support on things that are important to the customer).

The Effect of Supplier Market Orientation   Supplier market orientation refers to the perception of the customer that the supplier has policies and programs in place to serve customers in a manner better than that of the supplier's competitors. For example, a supplier is said to have a high level of market orientation if its customers perceive that the supplier:

- has routine or regular measures of customer service,
- develops products and services based on good market and customer information,
- knows its competitors well,
- has a good sense of the value the customer places on products and services,
- is more customer focused than its competitors,
- competes primarily based on product or service differentiation,
- believes the customer's interest should always come first, and
- believes its business exists primarily to serve its customers.[11]

Recent research has shown that the supplier's market orientation plays an important role in enhancing customer satisfaction, heightens perceptions of trust of the supplier, increases commitment to the supplier, and furthers feelings of cooperation with the supplier.[12]

In organizational buying, then, the key stages of the decision-making process are vendor selection and post-purchase evaluation. As we have seen, in different buying situations, organizations use different criteria to help them make these important decisions. By identifying the buying situation of the organization, marketers are better able to influence vendor selection and to ensure post-purchase satisfaction.

Vendor Stratification   **Vendor stratification** occurs when many customers in highly competitive markets stratify vendors and develop what is known in business-to-business purchasing as "preferred supplier programs." Vendors are rated according to criteria related to relationship quality. Thus, a cumulative set of customer experiences with the company's vendors provides a basis from which to rank the vendors. Many customers rank vendors based on the vendors' history of supplying high-quality products at low prices.[13]

18-1b **Identifying Organizational Decision Makers**

Unlike the majority of consumer purchases, the decisions behind organizational buying are made or at least influenced by more than one individual. In this respect, organizational decision making resembles family or household behavior. While some companies make decisions with very little group communication, others consult members of various company departments—the **buying center**—before major purchase decisions are made. A typical buying center is composed of a purchasing manager and representatives of appropriate departments, selected on the basis of expertise or experience with the product to be purchased.

One study of one hundred and fifty-one organizational purchase decisions provides insight into the types of individuals within organizations who are most likely to be influential within a buying center.[14] Influencers are likely to be those who have expert power—those who are perceived by other members to be knowledgeable about the product to be purchased. Also influential are those who are perceived to have reward power—the ability to provide or withhold material or nonmaterial resources to or from members of the group. Expert power is most often manifested in buying centers that are large, that are not under tight deadlines, and in which in-fighting between members is common. In contrast, reward power is found in buying centers that are small, under time pressures, and not characterized by in-fighting.

Individual versus Joint Decisions   Three sets of factors affect the extent to which organizational purchases result from individual or joint decisions: type of purchase, type of organization, and type of buying situation. See Exhibit 18-4 for a summary outline of these factors.

Type of Purchase   There are three basic purchase types:

1. *Straight rebuy.* The simplest and most routine of all purchasing transactions is a **straight rebuy.** The buyer simply repeats or reorders a prior purchase from the same supplier. There is virtually no information search, as there is no need to identify alternative suppliers or brands. The purchase decision is usually made individually, most likely by a purchasing agent.

> **vendor stratification** What occurs when many customers in highly competitive markets stratify vendors and develop what is known in business-to-business purchasing as "preferred supplier programs." Vendors are rated according to criteria related to relationship quality. Thus, a cumulative set of customer experiences with the company's vendors provides a basis from which to rank the vendors.

> **buying center** Essentially, a committee put together to make a purchase decision. The committee is usually composed of members of several organizational units selected on the basis of expertise or experience with the product to be purchased and includes the purchasing manager.

> **straight rebuy** A purchase decision typically determined by post-purchase satisfaction. The customer tries a new product. The customer is satisfied with its performance. The customer buys it again.

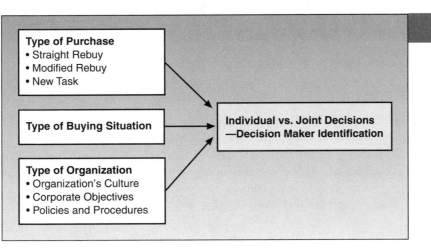

E x h i b i t 18-4

Identifying Organizational Decision Makers for Individual versus Joint Decisions

modified rebuy Similar to a straight rebuy, with modifications. Although the customer is happy with the product (and therefore re-orders it), the customer makes modifications to the order based on his or her experience with the product.

2. *Modified rebuy.* In a **modified rebuy,** either product specifications or supplier suitability have changed, necessitating information search and evaluation of vendors. If, for example, a vendor goes out of business or is unable to keep up with increased demand, a modified rebuy is necessary. Modified rebuy decisions are made either individually or through an informal group, perhaps the purchasing agent consulting one or more individuals within the organization.[15]

3. *New task.* This is a first-time buying situation, involving extensive information search to develop product specifications and identify prospective suppliers. Decisions are usually made by formal groups, with representatives from all departments that will be affected by the purchase.

Type of Organization   The organization's culture, its corporate objectives, and its policies and procedures all influence and direct buying processes. Three factors in organizational structure affect purchase decisions: first, complexity—the extent to which job specialties within the organization differ from each other; second, formalization—the degree of emphasis placed on adhering to standard regulations and procedure; and third, centralization—the extent to which decision-making power is diffused throughout the organization. Research suggests that the initiation of new tasks is more easily accomplished in an atmosphere of high complexity, low formalization, and low centralization. This means that the more complex (and less formal and decentralized) an organization is, the greater the likelihood that purchasing decisions are autonomous, even in new task situations.[16] However, other research has shown that the more formal the organization (as measured by the percentage of the buying process that is formalized in writing), the more people there are in the buying center. That is, the more formal the organization, the greater the likelihood that the purchase decision will be joint rather than autonomous.[17]

Type of Buying Situation   Situational factors that influence decision making include existing economic, climatic, and geographical considerations. Transportation and energy costs, interstate commerce regulations, shortages in raw materials, and labor problems can all affect costs and delivery dates and, consequently, are critical considerations in every organizational purchase. Decisions may be made jointly or by a single individual, depending on the extent of perceived risk resulting from one or more of these situational factors. The greater the perceived risk, the more likely purchase decisions are to be made jointly.[18]

18-1c Roles of Organization Members in the Decision-Making Process

Just as in family and household decisions, different people within an organization play different roles at the various stages of the organizational buying decision process (see Exhibit 18-5). As we have seen, individuals within the organization who interact in making purchasing decisions make up its buying center. Within the buying center, job titles alone are inadequate to identify purchase decision makers. A procurement officer in one organization, for example, may perform the same duties as a purchasing agent or a financial vice president in another. A more useful means of understanding how the buying center operates is to identify individuals according to the roles they play. Knowing who within an organization takes on which role is extremely important for marketers who seek to influence the purchase decision.

There are at least five key roles in the organizational buying center,[19] as summarized in Exhibit 18-6. The five key roles are defined as follows:

1. *Users.* Individuals who actually use the product purchased are **users.** Teachers and students, for example, are users of textbooks purchased by a school system.

2. *Influencers.* Individuals who help establish specifications for usage or purchase are **influencers.** Influencers may or may not be users as well. In the real estate industry, realtors can influence consumers' choices of a range of related services, from mortgages to title insurance and more.

Exhibit 18-5

Roles of Organization Members in the Decision-Making Process

- Users
- Influencers
- Buyers
- Deciders
- Gatekeepers

---

users Individuals who actually use the product purchased. Teachers and students, for example, are users of textbooks that the school system purchases.

influencers Individuals who help establish specifications for usage or purchase. Influencers may or may not be users as well.

	User	Influencer	Buyer	Decider	Gatekeeper
Identification of need	■	■			
Establishing specifications and scheduling the purchase	■	■	■	■	
Identifying buying alternatives	■	■	■		■
Evaluating alternative buying actions	■	■	■		
Selecting the suppliers	■	■	■	■	

Source: From *Organizational Buying Behavior* by Frederick E. Webster, Jr., and Yoram Wind, p. 80. Reprinted by permission of Pearson Education, Inc., Upper Saddle River, NJ.

Exhibit 18-6

Roles of Members of the Buying Center by Decision Stage

buyers Individuals with authority to select suppliers and handle the transaction. In some cases, buyers are responsible only for implementing decisions previously made by users and influencers.

deciders Individuals with the ultimate authority to select vendors. Although buyers may hold formal purchasing power, they are not always involved in the decision.

gatekeepers Individuals responsible for controlling the flow of information into the buying center. Gatekeepers, often purchasing agents, perform the key role of providing salespeople with access to appropriate members of the buying center.

3. *Buyers.* Those with authority to select suppliers and handle the transaction are **buyers.** In some cases, the buyer is responsible only for implementing decisions previously made by users and influencers.

4. *Deciders.* Those with ultimate authority to select vendors are the **deciders.** Although buyers may hold formal purchasing power, they are not always involved in the decision. For example, an engineer might be the decider when the technical requirements are so complex that the buyer is not competent to choose a supplier.

5. *Gatekeepers.* **Gatekeepers** are the people responsible for controlling the flow of information into the buying center. Gatekeepers, often purchasing agents, perform the key role of providing salespeople with access to appropriate members of the buying center. Exhibit 18-7 identifies secretaries as gatekeepers—the kind that keep marketing information and salespeople away from the decision makers. To bypass the secretary and reach the boss, the advertisement suggests advertising in *Barron's*, a publication read by top management.

Exhibit 18-7

As this ad reflects, getting past the gatekeeper(s) can be the toughest part of selling into an organization.

Source: Reprinted by permission of *Barron's.*

Marketplace 18-1

The Changing Role of the Purchasing Agent

As our perception of the buyer-seller relationship has evolved, so has the role of the purchasing agent in organizational buying. Purchasing is no longer perceived as the exclusive domain of the professional buyer. While the purchasing department continues to play a key role in choosing among alternative brands and suppliers, the departments of design and production, research, and administration can also play major roles in purchase decision making. In some companies, purchasing, transportation, traffic, inventory control, and other related areas have been merged into one functional area, the materials management department. A major trend in organizational buying has been the upgrading of purchasing departments and their managers to top management positions. Companies including DuPont, Sperry, and Champion International have promoted their purchasing managers to vice-presidential level. As the field of materials management continues to grow, many professional associations have stepped up their efforts to upgrade and certify the skills of their members by sponsoring seminars and by instituting full courses in purchasing fundamentals.

F A Q

How does a business service company like Federal Express expect to benefit from advertising during sporting events?

The identification of roles within the buying center can, however, be far more complex than this simple list suggests. Even within a single industry, the roles played by members of the decision-making unit vary greatly from one organization to another, and an individual's role might be greater or lesser than is suggested by conventional role designations. In one investigation of the purchasing of radiology equipment by various hospitals, a linking-pin role was identified. This role was played by individuals who exert influence and leadership not only in their own groups but also at higher levels within the organization. The chief radiologist, for example, was found in some cases not only to be head of the radiology department but to be a major influence on financial managers and hospital administrators.[20] In any organization, the individual possessing the greatest amount of relevant information regarding the purchase generally becomes the most influential member of the buying center and, therefore, the most valuable target for sales representatives seeking to establish a liaison with other key personnel.[21] Marketplace 18-1 describes how purchasing has changed over the years from a one-person job (that of the purchasing agent) to the responsibility of the buying center.

Almost as important as knowing who to approach in the buying center is the timing of that approach. Some roles become more influential than others at different stages of the purchase decision cycle. For example, members of the buying center assuming the roles of the user, influencer, buyer, and decider may establish specifications and schedule a purchase very early in the decision cycle. Through prompt identification of the roles each plays, the marketer can effectively target messages designed to influence the specification list and position his or her company as the optimal supplier when the final selection is made.

As we saw in Exhibit 18-6, the roles of members of the buying center differ at each stage of the decision cycle.[22] Identification of product need is usually a decision made by organizational personnel who use the product. The production manager at XYZ manufacturing plant realizes that a duplication unit is on the verge of breaking down and needs to be replaced. In this example, the production manager assumes the role of user and identifies the need for a purchase. At the same time, an XYZ engineer sees a new product report in a trade magazine for a new and improved model of the duplication unit. By providing the buying center with information on the new product, the engineer influences the purchase. Knowing this, marketers of duplication units need to establish ongoing communication not only with the production manager but also with the engineer. CBite 18-2 provides many tidbits about effective business-to-business ads.

CBite 18-2
What Makes a Good Business-Oriented Ad?

To determine what separates good industrial advertising from bad, look at the recommendations of *Business Marketing* magazine's popular "Copy Chasers" column:

1. Create visual magnetism.
2. Select the right audience.
3. Invite the reader into the scene.
4. Promise a reward.
5. Back up promises with specifics.
6. Present the proposition in logical sequences.
7. Talk person-to-person.
8. Make the ad easy to read.
9. Emphasize the service, not the source.
10. Reflect the company's character.

There is an eleventh advertising technique which is, according to Bob Donath, editor of *Business Marketing,* informally one of the Copy Chasers' criteria: the use of dramatic expression, "some unique way of explaining a powerful benefit that is highly salient to the prospect—a headline, an illustration working together to dramatize the idea, and body copy, driving the point home in terms that the reader can identify with—that's what makes superior advertising."

Source: From "Criteria for Ad Effectiveness Listed for Business Marketers" from *Marketing News,* Vol. 20, No. 13, June 20, 1986, p. 19. Reprinted by permission of the American Marketing Association.

Marketing Management—Implications and Actions

Like individual consumers, organizations go through a decision-making process that takes them through the five stages we have examined earlier in this section—needs assessment, information gathering, choice, consumption, and post-purchase evaluation. Because more than one person is involved in the process, however, the dynamics of decision making are complicated by the different roles of each member of the group at each stage of the decision process. Not only do the different roles played by individual group members affect the decision, but their personalities, lifestyles, behavior patterns, and relationships with each other all influence the process and the final outcome. By understanding organizational consumer behavior, marketers are better equipped to target businesses and to influence group decision making. Understanding organizational buying processes helps marketers:

- Market effectively at each stage of the organizational buying process. That is, marketers should realize that each stage of the organizational buying process (identify need, establish purchasing objectives and specifications, obtain technical data, ...) entails different organizational roles assumed by different people within the organization. Each stage requires a different marketing approach directed to a different role within the organization.
- Understand what type of purchase their product is likely to be. Is it a routine order, a procedural purchase, a performance purchase, or a political one? Understanding the type of purchase provides insight for the decision criteria that may be used in the purchase (e.g., reputation, financing, flexibility, past experience, ...).
- Create marketing communication vehicles that address the emotional needs of organizational buyers. Understanding the emotional factors underlying certain decisions (e.g., impress upper management and reduce the risk of error) may allow marketers to create advertising with targeted emotional appeals.
- Identify the ultimate decision maker in a group. Knowing the decision maker may allow marketers to reach that person within the organization with targeted messages to convince him or her that the purchase is "best" for the firm.

diffusion of innovations
The process through which a new product moves from initial introduction to regular purchase and use.

18-2 Diffusion of Innovations

As we have seen throughout the text, consumers do not really buy products, they buy benefits. That is, we make purchases not for the sake of the products themselves, but for the problems they solve, for the needs they satisfy, or for the opportunities they offer. This is most evident with innovations, for the best new products are developed around important consumer benefits and within markets that are large enough to support them.

New products are always possible because the benefits consumers seek are constantly changing as values shift, lifestyles change, and new technologies emerge. Technologies developed for specific fields often usher in an unforeseen variety of new products. Car seat belt restraints and antilock brakes, for example, had their origins in aircraft design. Microchips, a product of the U.S. space program, are now used in everything from digital watches to computers to automobiles. The technology that made VCRs and DVD players possible has also opened a huge market for movie rentals. The photography industry is experiencing dramatic change as people continue to transition from film-based cameras to digital cameras that use chips to store pictures. The latter has also spawned software for transfer of photos to the personal computer, and printing of one's own photos at home is becoming more common. We are also seeing a decrease in manufacturing where wire and cord are needed. First telephones became cordless, then computer mice and keyboards, followed by entire home computer networks. Now, consumer-electronics companies are moving ahead with television sets that will be wireless. The first of these was introduced in late summer 2004. It is the Sharp Wireless Aquos. You simply connect your cable and up to three other sources—DVD, TiVo, etc.—to the Wireless Aquos base station. You can then take the 15-inch LCD screen with you to the kitchen or patio and watch.[23] Although spurred by technology, the adoption of innovations usually represents parallel changes within the culture that make the new products attractive.

Diffusion of innovations is a process through which a new product moves from initial introduction to regular purchase and use.[24] In other words, it is the process of acceptance or adoption of a product by consumers. By understanding innovation diffusion, marketers are able to offer the type of new product that best meets the needs of targeted consumers and promote it in such ways that it is readily accepted by them. Exhibit 18-8 shows the types of innovations, rates of diffusion, and consumer evaluation factors that can be present when innovations enter the market.

18-2a Consumer Evaluation of Innovations

As we learn about and use innovations, whether we are aware of it or not, we go through a process of evaluation. Positive evaluation leads to acceptance and negative evaluation to rejection. We evaluate products in terms of ten key characteristics: type of innovation, relative advantage, compatibility, complexity (simplicity), trialability (divisibility), observability (communicability), value, use, risk, and price.[25] By analyzing innovations in terms of each of these criteria, marketers obtain a clearer picture of the benefits targeted consumers are likely to seek and the ease with which the product is likely to be accepted as compatible with their lifestyles.

Types of Innovation   There are two ways of viewing innovations. First, an innovation is any product that is measurably different from existing goods and services. For instance, when home theater entertainment centers were introduced, they were technically very different from older television sets. In the same way, cellular telephones are different from land-line models, and roller blades are different from roller skates. A second, broader category of innovations includes any product that is perceived as new by target consumers. When Sony first sold its Walkman in the United States, it was considered a new product even though it had been marketed in Japan for years.

Some new products are more readily accepted and adopted by consumers than others. One reason for this is that they require little effort on the part of consumers to incorporate them into their lifestyles. It is useful for marketers to classify each innovation according to the ease with which it can be accepted. Doing so provides insight into the extent to which consumers will need to be educated about the product, the benefits it

offers, its use, and the changes in consumption patterns it may require. Using this perspective, there are three types of innovations: continuous, dynamically continuous, and discontinuous.[26]

When products that are already accepted and used by consumers are modified, and these changes require little or no effort on the part of consumers to modify their behavior in order to use them, these are **continuous innovations.** Adding fluoride to toothpaste, liquid centers to chewing gum, extra vitamins to dry breakfast cereal, or cushioned arch supports to running shoes are examples of continuous innovations.

Dynamically continuous innovations disrupt the consumer's use patterns but still do not radically alter them. Waterbeds, push-button telephones, electric toothbrushes, automatic elevators, and compact discs are all dynamically continuous innovations. As shown in Exhibit 18-9, this also applies to an everyday product that requires the consumer to take an extra step in its use—a digital camera.

Discontinuous innovations necessitate real change in consumption and behavior patterns. Cars, radios, airplanes, and televisions were all discontinuous innovations. More recently, online grocery shopping services, automatic teller machines, and ticketless airline flights have all required radical changes in behavior.

Most technological changes can be described as a substitution of one product for another, one process for another, one material for another, and so forth. Each following technology, if successful, starts slowly, since most people resist the change called for. However, as the competition between the old and new picks up and other competitors enter the marketplace the pace of acceptance will quicken. After the technology spreads, the rate of

continuous innovations When products that are already accepted and used by consumers are modified, and the changes require little or no effort on the part of consumers to modify their behavior to use the products.

dynamically continuous innovations Innovations that disrupt the consumer's use patterns but still do not radically alter them.

discontinuous innovations Innovations that necessitate real change in consumption and behavior patterns.

its growth will begin to slow. In general, new technology often appears before the old technology is accepted by all potential target members. Hence successive technology generations' sales are made up of customers switching from earlier technology, those who pass up the earlier technology for the new, and those who would only adopt the new.[27] New technologies can also be rejected because they do not have the design finesse of existing products, or they are too expensive, or are positioned on unproven marketplace assumptions. Resistance by potential buyers also occurs because of switching costs, the learning needed to switch, and incompatibility.[28]

Logic tells us that in most situations consumer acceptance is more likely with continuous and dynamically continuous innovations than with radically new products. However, determining which of these three categories a new product falls into is not as easy as it may seem. Consumer perceptions complicate any attempt at classifications. For example, with a dynamically continuous innovation like the one in Exhibit 18-9, the behavior modification required may be very slight. Yet if the consumer does not perceive it as such or does not consider it a worthwhile trade-off for additional benefits offered, acceptance may be much slower than anticipated. The challenge for marketers is to determine where along the spectrum of continuous to discontinuous each new product is likely to be in the minds of the targeted group of consumers.

relative advantage
The extent to which consumers in the target market perceive an innovation to be superior in some important way to existing products.

Relative Advantage

The **relative advantage** of an innovation is the extent to which consumers in the target market perceive it to be superior in some important way to existing products. Consumer perception is key, for even if a product is technically superior, if it is not seen as such by the consumer, it is not superior at all. Moreover, an innovation must be recognizably superior according to one or more important (salient) evaluative criteria used by the consumer. When video laser disc players were originally introduced in the 1970s, their success was limited because the video cassette recorder was seen as superior by most potential customers. The VCR allowed consumers to play their own family videos, to record from the television, and to rent a wide selection of movies. All disc players offered was the ability to play a smaller selection of higher-cost purchased or rented movies. In the 1990s, advances in technology allowed for the development of digital video disc (DVD) players that provided much higher quality pictures and sound than was possible with video tape VCR machines. For a number of consumers, this benefit alone outweighed the fact that the DVD players did not record directly from television or other sources. In addition, the widespread availability of rental discs and the increased demand for in-home movie viewing in general contributed to the success of the product. Now DVD player-recorders are available on the market, and consumers can copy and record off the air. As well as demonstrating the importance of consumer perceptions on relative advantage, this example also shows that timing, technology, and cultural trends greatly influence innovation acceptance. See Exhibit 18-10 for a good example of the use of the relative advantage principle.

compatibility The degree to which an innovation fits with the needs, values, and past experiences of the consumer.

Compatibility

Compatibility is the degree to which an innovation fits with the needs, values, and past experiences of the consumer. The success of many brands of toothpaste containing hydrogen peroxide and/or baking soda can be chalked up to high compatibility. Why was this innovation so compatible for consumers? Hydrogen peroxide was traditionally used and widely accepted as an antiseptic. Brushing teeth with baking soda was popular in the 1940s and 1950s. Also, baking soda has long been associated with freshness and has been used in the home to deodorize refrigerators, freezers, carpeting, and drains. The combination of antiseptic and freshening power meshes easily with consumer expectations of toothpaste, and so the brands with these new ingredients were easily accepted. A high level of compatibility existed.

An example of an unsuccessful innovation was the attempted introduction into the United States of a cake mix for which the consumer only had to add water. Because of a perceived need of consumers to be more involved in food preparation, the cake mix was changed to require the addition of eggs and, in some cases, milk. This simple change made the cake mix more compatible with the needs and expectations of the consumer.

complexity The innovation's level of difficulty to understand and use.

Complexity (Simplicity)

What is the innovation's **complexity?** How difficult is it to understand and use an innovation? In general, the more complex the product, the lower

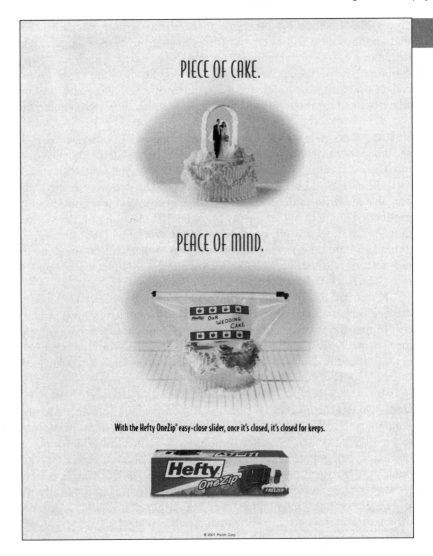

Exhibit 18-10

This Hefty ad shows one significant advantage of using the Hefty OneZip bags.

Source: Reprinted with kind permission from Pactiv Corporation.

the likelihood of acceptance. The personal computer (PC) was originally thought to have the potential for rapid acceptance in the United States, but growth initially was much slower than expected. In response, manufacturers have made the documentation for setting up and operating the systems more "user-friendly." To push the adoption process along, they also offer round-the-clock support lines that owners can call to get help. Further, publishers have produced a great number of simplified "how-to" or "quick-start" books. All these goods and services are making the installation and use of computers simpler, as are technical innovations such as the mouse and icon-driven programs such as Windows. Since the younger generations have only lived in the PC era, and the computer is a natural part of their lives and the culture.

Trialability (Divisibility)   Trialability (**divisibility**) is the degree to which an innovation may be sampled or tried out. Divisibility is the ability to separate the product into units small enough to try out. For example, there are some goods and services that simply cannot be offered on trial. A new hairstyle that requires cutting or shaving is not trialable. We can test-drive cars or test-fly aircraft, but it's difficult to test a refrigerator before purchasing it. The easier it is to try an innovation, the greater the chance it will be tested, which, in turn, increases the probability of adoption.

Observability (Communicability)   If an innovation is often seen in the target market or if it can easily be shown or described by the marketer, it is considered

▶**trialability (divisibility)**
The degree to which an innovation may be sampled or tried out. Divisibility is the ability to separate the product into units small enough to try out.

observability (communicability)
The frequency with which an innovation is seen in the target market or the ease with which a marketer can show or describe the innovation.

value An innovation's benefits compared to the money paid for it. The more benefits (and less cost), the greater the value.

use The extent to which consumers feel they are likely to use the innovation sufficiently to justify its purchase.

risk Consumers' perception of the costs associated with the purchase and use of the innovation. These costs can be economic, psychological, social, physical, or performance-related.

innovators (see p. 565) The first individuals to adopt new products. Typically, they are younger, well educated, with higher incomes and a cosmopolitan outlook and lifestyle. More self-confident than most, they are willing to gather information from a wide variety of sources to evaluate a product. They are less worried about risk than are members of other groups.

early adopters (see p. 565) Individuals who are more sensitive to reference group values and norms than other types of consumers. They tend to be opinion leaders for the product categories in which they are early adopters. They use commercial and personal sources of information extensively in the purchase decision.

observable or communicable. High **observability (communicability)** increases the odds that an innovation will catch on. A homeowner buys a new mulching lawn mower. The neighbor sees it in action and notices that the owner no longer has to stop to dump grass clippings. The neighbor takes a closer look and heads to the hardware store to buy one. A college student who cuts lawns for a number of elderly people in the community sees an advertisement for the same mulching mower and realizes that it could save time.

Value Does an innovation offer **value** for money? In other words, is the benefits package it offers sufficient to justify the price asked? In the late 1970s when in-home VCRs were introduced, a really good machine was about $2,000, and blank videotapes were $10 to $15 each. Few were sold because the value was not felt to be worth the high price. VCRs are available today for under $100, as are the increasingly more common DVD players. Both product types are of higher quality than the first machines on the market and offer many more features. As a result of high perceived value, the DVD players sell very well. Cell phones also are experiencing significant price drops while at the same time offering may new features. Also, cell phone service suppliers have made deeply price-discounted high tech phones a key part of the plans they offer customers.

Perception of value affects not only high-priced products. No matter what the price, the question is always whether the added features of an innovation are worth the extra cost to the consumer. A laundry detergent product in tablet form offered convenience in measurement—just drop two tablets into the machine for each wash. Yet when the product was introduced, acceptance by consumers was not high. The added feature did not justify the slightly higher cost.

Use Do target consumers feel they will use a product sufficiently to justify its purchase? If an innovation does not fit easily into the normal **use** patterns of consumers, it is unlikely to be adopted. When personal computers were first introduced, powerful, high-speed machines were not attractive in most households because people typically used the computer only for word processing, to play games, or to run simple educational programs. However, the explosion of exciting software, high-level games, significantly more powerful and faster machines, and online services has attracted in-home users to more sophisticated machines. Today we are also seeing people able to buy PCs at every level of sophistication at more reasonable prices than in the past.

Risk The level of perceived **risk** associated with an innovation affects its acceptance. As we saw in Chapter 2 (section 2-3b, "Internal and External Information Search"), if the level of economic, psychological, social, physical, or performance risk is perceived to be too high, an innovation will not be readily accepted. In some cases, trial offers lessen concerns about risk. So, too, does special training in product use. Marketers of computer systems to businesses typically offer staff training and support. We are seeing extended warranties for new technologies, and websites and "800" telephone numbers buyers can use for assistance and "troubleshooting." Some retailers offer in-store classes to home computer buyers.

Price The price of the innovation affects its adoption, especially the timing of the adoption. Consumer behavior researchers have provided evidence to show the effect of price on adoption of technological innovations. For example, when products such as camcorders, personal digital assistants, plasma television sets, DVD players, and personal computers first came out, they were expensive. Eventually, the price came down significantly, allowing those who wanted to buy to do so.[29]

18-2b Adopters of Innovations

What kinds of people are open to innovations? Some people are always ready to try something new in certain product and service classes. They are the first to wear the latest fashions, buy the latest audio and video entertainment technology, try out a debit card, or go to a wireless phone as the only one they use. At the other extreme are people who resist change. These are individuals who will accept a new product only if they have no other

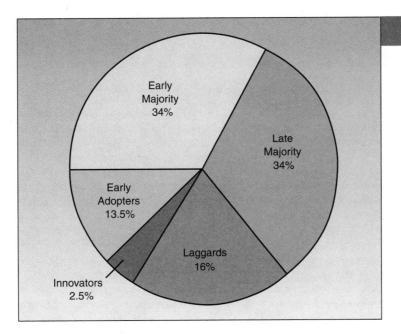

Exhibit 18-11

Adopter Groups

Note that innovators make up a small share of the population. The majority of consumers are early- and late-majority adopters.

Source: Everett M. Rogers, *Diffusion of Innovations,* 4th ed. New York: The Free Press, 1962, 1971, 1983, 1995.

choice. Exhibit 18-11 identifies five adopter groups, classified on the basis of the relative time it takes them to adopt.[30] The exhibit shows the approximate share of consumers thought to be in each category.

1. **Innovators** are the first to adopt new products. Typically, they are younger, well educated, with higher incomes and a cosmopolitan outlook and lifestyle. More self-confident than most, they are willing to gather information from a wide variety of sources in order to evaluate a product. They are less worried about risk than are members of other groups. These individuals are said to have *innate consumer innovativeness,* an inherent innovative personality, predisposition, and cognitive style towards innovations that is evident in their consumption across a variety of product and service classes. The combination of this consumer characteristic with younger age and higher income were found to be related to the purchase and consumption of new consumer electronics products.[31]

2. **Early adopters** are more sensitive to reference group values and norms than are other types of consumers. They tend to be opinion leaders for the product categories in which they are early adopters.[32] They use commercial and personal sources of information extensively in the purchase decision.

3. **Early-majority adopters** wait to see whether a new product will prove to be successful. They watch opinion leaders and follow when ready. They are less educated than innovators or early adopters, with less social mobility.

4. **Late-majority adopters** are typically skeptical of new products. They tend to be older and less educated than the members of other groups. They adopt innovations only because of the social pressure to do so or because of forced choice. Their primary information source is word-of-mouth from relatives, friends, and acquaintances. Advertising and couponing have little effect on this group.

5. **Laggards** dislike change, are suspicious of new products and ideas, and will only accept innovations when forced to so. They feel alienated from a society that they perceive is passing them by. They are typically of low socioeconomic status, and many are seniors.[33]

How quickly an innovation spreads within a culture or a segment within a culture is referred to as the **rate of diffusion.** That is, how much time does it take to achieve acceptance? CBite 18-3 describes how innovation diffusion trickles down from the upper classes of society to the lower classes. Marketplace 18-2 offers interesting insights about ways to enhance the diffusion of technological innovations.

▶**early-majority adopters** Individuals who wait to see whether a new product will prove to be successful. They watch opinion leaders and follow when ready. They are less educated than innovators or early adopters, with less social mobility.

▶**late-majority adopters** Individuals who typically are skeptical of new products. They tend to be older and less educated than are members of other groups. They adopt innovations only because of the social pressure to do so or because of forced choice. Their primary information source is word-of-mouth from relatives, friends, and acquaintances.

▶**laggards** Individuals who dislike change, are suspicious of new products and ideas, and will only accept innovations when forced to so. They feel alienated from a society that they perceive is passing them by. They are typically of low socioeconomic status, and many are seniors.

▶**rate of diffusion** The time it takes to achieve acceptance of an innovation in society.

Marketplace 18-2

Sell High-Tech Products by Exploiting Human Nature

Want to sell tons of your high-tech new product or service? Want to make tons and tons of money? Then learn what your colleagues in some mature industries learned long ago.

People do not buy products and services. They buy potions to make them feel better, even if temporarily. If you try to sell them products or services, you won't get far. But if you try to sell them something that will make them feel more relaxed, more attractive, smarter or richer, well, congratulations. You've just joined the new millionaires' club.

Great technological innovation, even breakthrough technology, is not enough to ensure a new product's successful introduction into mass markets. Often, technological innovation isn't even necessary. To make a high-tech product acceptable to the masses—people like you and me—the product has to give consumers something they want. Some of those things are sex, power, convenience, feeling superior, feeling connected, feeling loved.

That's why we have marketing, the mystical science of figuring out why people behave the way they do so you can make them behave the way you want. Consider the following:

- *They don't want 64 bits. They want control.* At one level, video games are fun and entertaining. At a deeper level, video games allow people, usually teenage boys, to have control over their environment. Young boys develop a chance to feel like the adults they so much want to be. Successful video game developers aren't selling technological superiority—they're selling freedom.

- *I don't want technology convergence. I want to look cool.* I frequently take my family to Hawaii for vacation. What I'd really like is for technology to converge in a device that would show me how to act like a local instead of the profoundly uncool tourist that I am now. What I want is to hang out in Hanalei and look cool, catch a few beach babe wannabes from New Jersey staring longingly in my direction. I'd pay a lot for that. Do I care if that requires a wireless Internet connection and software that automatically updates a database while I'm at the local bar impressing the tourists from Jersey? Do I care if the product requires groundbreaking new technology? Nope. I care about feeling cool, being on the inside. I'll put out big bucks for cool and elitist, but I won't spend nearly as much for code or circuits.

- *People don't want to change. We want to take it easy.* Occasionally, a product will offer a benefit so compelling that consumers will radically alter their behavior to use it. Generally, though, this is rare. Listening to the radio was an extension of talking around the kitchen table. Television watching was an extension of listening to the radio. Video rental was an extension of television watching. Movies on demand are an extension of video rentals. Accessing the web from your TV requires far more energy than we are used to spending in front of a TV; people relate to their televisions in a passive way. Getting people to change will require a compelling answer to the old, "What's in it for me?" question.

CBite 18-3
Innovation Diffusion and Social Class

The trickle-down theory of product diffusion suggests a pattern of adoption that is based on social class. Innovations are first accepted and used by the upper classes and act as symbols of social status. Over time, they find their way into the lives of those lower on the socioeconomic scale. Products that are not initially adopted by the upper classes and, therefore, cannot trickle down, trickle up instead. Products like blue jeans, work boots, and hip-hop music all became popular first among the lower classes. Over time, they gradually entered the mainstream and finally were adopted even by the upper classes. Mass media and marketing communications do a great deal to disseminate product information and so accelerate diffusion.

Source: Thorsten Veblen, *The Theory of the Leisure Class* (New York: Macmillan, 1912).

- *Consumers don't want product features. We want to go home early.* Years ago, I worked for the dominant advanced word processing software company in the world. They were very focused on a new competitor. Unfortunately, they were most concerned with making more bells and whistles for their software than the other guy had on his. They would literally count the number of features listed in the competitive product's brochure and set out to create a longer list! Research indicated that consumers didn't care about features; they wanted to get their jobs done easier and faster. Need I mention that the company that once owned 90% market share no longer exists?

- *We don't want to save money. We want status.* Pricing is an area that surprises engineers. Cheaper is always better. Right? Wrong. Sometimes, though rarely, people prefer to buy the more expensive product, even when everything but price is identical. More common is when consumers assign status to the more expensive option and then rationalize the purchase: "Mercedes-Benz cars are much safer to drive than Lexus, aren't they? And you know, our youngest is only 9."

- *She doesn't want spices. She wants her mother's love.* There is ample research showing that color, shape, typefaces, and so on play a profound role in purchasing behavior. I once worked on a new package for spices that caused a 20% increase in sales in its first year with no marketing support. The background on the new package was a rich forest green, which subconsciously communicated freshness to consumers. In this case, the consumers were primarily women cooking for their families. Freshness conveys many powerful benefits, such as better taste and healthier meals, which suggest the purchaser is a better cook, wife, and mother, and able to gain the approval of her mother—the psychological laddering goes on and on. Did those consumers buy spices or did they just confirm and validate their mothers' values?

Marketers in mature industries have a rich history of exploiting human frailties in their quest to sell more. High-tech product developers must understand that product development is not the last step. Once the product exists, consumers must be made to understand what's in it for them. And we have to be told in a way that makes sense to us. Remember, we consumers don't care how many features your new gizmo has or how it does what you say it can do. We just care what's in it for us. This is all about consumers not buying products and services; they are buying benefits. A discussion of this fact was presented in Chapter 1.

Source: From "Sell High-Tech Products by Exploiting Human Nature" by Dick McCullough from *Marketing News*, February 1, 1999, p. 4. Reprinted by permission of the American Marketing Association.

The five types of adopter groups search for and use information in different ways and are receptive to it in varying degrees. Innovators are the most willing to search for information and to turn to technical experts for advice. They are less likely to rely on mass media or word-of-mouth recommendations in order to try out new products. Early adopters look to the mass media for help with information gathering during the earlier stages of the adoption process.[34] However, as this group moves closer to actual trial and adoption, they begin to rely more on friends and relatives for information and feedback. Early adopters are the group most likely to tell others about products purchased, particularly innovations.[35] Word-of-mouth recommendations, particularly from opinion leaders, are influential among early-majority adopters, late-majority adopters, and laggards.[36]

Of course, the five categories are generalizations, and many exceptions can be found. The categories do, however, provide a means through which we can understand and predict how consumers are likely to respond to innovations. What type of consumer are you? Consider your behavior in the adoption of such goods and services as online access, snowboards, laser disc players, and the latest fashions.

Marketplace 18-3 describes the conflicting motives that consumers experience in adopting technological innovations. Understanding consumers' motivational conflict helps marketers to promote their products in a way that allows consumers to resolve that conflict. For additional tidbits about marketing technological innovations from those who are successful at this task, see Marketplace 18-4.

F A Q

Are online information services ever likely to replace print media?

Marketplace 18-3

Paradoxes of Technology

Professors David Mick and Susan Fournier have studied how consumers use technological devices in their daily lives and have found that there are eight central paradoxes of technological products. These are:

- *Control and chaos:* Technology can help with the regulation of our lives. Technological products can help create order in our lives. In contrast, technological products can also create chaos and disorder. For example, ownership of a car allows a person a certain sense of control to go to places whenever he or she wishes. By the same token, the same car can create chaos in the car owner's life when he or she has a car accident.

- *Freedom and enslavement:* Technological products facilitate independence, but they can lead to more dependence. A person who uses email to communicate with many colleagues and friends feels that email gives her the freedom not to be tied to the office—she can do things and not miss messages. On the other hand, she finds herself enslaved to email and feels compelled to check her email many times a day.

- *New and obsolete:* Technological products help consumers become more efficient in doing things. However, as soon as one buys a new product, it becomes obsolete, requiring the purchase of an upgrade. Many computer software products are readily accepted because they help us in different ways to do different things. However, as soon as we buy them, we find out that newer software will make the version we just bought obsolete.

- *Competence and incompetence:* Technological products are mostly designed to make us more efficient in the way we do things. On the other hand, the same technological products can make us feel inept and incompetent because we can't operate them well. Computers can make us more competent on our jobs but also makes us feel incompetent when we can't get them to perform as expected.

- *Efficiency and inefficiency:* Technological products like computers can help us with many tasks by reducing time and/or effort, but the same devices can lead to inefficiency because we have to spend more time and expend effort to learn how to operate and maintain them.

- *Fulfill and create new needs:* Technological products can satisfy certain needs, but they can create new needs, too. For example, buying a computer to help with typing and processing documents leads a person to take advantage of the Internet. However, getting on the Internet requires an Internet communication device and an Internet service provider. Thus, needs related to the Internet were created by the mere fact of purchasing and using a computer.

- *Assimilation and isolation:* Technological products can facilitate getting people together (e.g., through the use of email and chat rooms). On the other hand, technological products contribute to a sense of social alienation because the same devices get people to move away from people to pay attention to these devices.

- *Engaging and disengaging:* Technological products can be rewarding in the way they get people to be totally absorbed with the activity. However, the same use of these products may lead consumers to disengage from the people they love. For example, teenagers tend to get so engaged with computer games that they forget they have friends and a family.

Source: From "Paradoxes of Technology: Consumer Cognizance, Emotions, and Coping Strategies" by David Glen Mick and Susan Fournier in *Journal of Consumer Research,* Vol. 25, September 1998, pp. 123–143. Copyright © 1998. Reprinted by permission of The University of Chicago Press.

Marketing Management—Implications and Actions

Understanding innovation diffusion helps marketers:

- View innovations in terms of how they will be evaluated by consumers and so emphasize benefits likely to spur acceptance and de-emphasize barriers to acceptance.
- Classify target consumers into one or more of five adopter types and disseminate information to them in ways and through media in which it is likely to be noticed and understood.

Marketplace 18-4

Six Principles for New Product Success

Nine out of ten new products fail within the first twelve months from introduction. The following six rules of thumb can make the difference:

1. *Know what your product stands for, and make its benefits superior.* Don't settle for parity or technical superiority. Find a noticeable benefit consumers care about, and make your product the best there is in delivering it. A cold-water detergent got off to a slow start until marketers understood that cold-water washing is not a benefit, but that color care is. Once they began focusing on superiority of color care, the product was rejuvenated.

2. *Search the globe for ideas.* Innovation is occurring on a global scale on the product, advertising, and promotional fronts. In the case of automatic dishwashing detergents in the early 1990s, the smaller markets of Europe, not the large U.S. market, were the most competitive and innovative in product design and packaging.

3. *Form strategic product alliances.* Look for win-win relationships by associating your product with others of similar superiority or image. Consider this scenario. If a liquid dishwashing detergent eliminates grease best, and if consumers have said grease on plastic is the toughest to clean, then hook up with the foremost plastic kitchenware manufacturer.

4. *Uncover latent consumer insights.* Consumers won't always tell you in specific terms what their biggest problems are. They will, however, show you how much effort they'll expend to get the results they want. For instance, was anyone saying there was a big problem with laundry detergent? No. But observations revealed consumers were using a vast array of additives to help their detergents remove soil. This led to the introduction of detergent with bleach. Again, no one was complaining about color care, but lots of people were relegating some of their favorite clothes to weekend wear because of fading.

5. *Market readiness drives loyalty.* Not only must your marketing strategy be excellent, but your product must not disappoint the hard-won trial user. You can make certain of what you are doing by carrying out target-audience research. When you begin testing the product, make sure that you do this with users. More and more often, marketers are using in-store research to evaluate concepts and packaging, to choose between promotional techniques, and to assess sales potential. Product users, not product tryers, should be the focus.

6. *Reaching your global market as soon as possible wins big.* Being first is important, but getting the idea or the product in as many places as possible as quickly as possible is even more important. There are more similarities among consumers of the world than differences. Take the differences into account, but focus more attention on the similarities. You must also consider using similar elements in your strategy and try to standardize your development steps. For example, when doing marketing research, use the same research process to gather the same core data about the same product regardless of geographic location. This will reduce decision-making time by eliminating the long discussions about whose data are correct. This approach will reveal local nuances of flavor, appearance, use, and culture that are so important to the local success of a new product.

Source: Adapted from Frank Bossu, "A Few Principles Guide New Product Success," *Marketing News,* Vol. 29 (May 8, 1995), p. 11.

Chapter Spotlights

Organizations make purchasing decisions in groups. Just as individual consumers make their way through a decision cycle, so do firms, starting with problem recognition and leading to final purchase and evaluation. The challenge for marketers is to identify which member or members of the firm influence the purchase decision at each stage of the cycle.

1. The organizational consumption unit. Like household purchases, organizational decisions are made by groups of people working together to satisfy common needs. Decisions can be made autonomously, perhaps by a purchasing agent, or by consensus, as through a buying center.

2. Organizational decision making. There are several stages in the organizational buying decision cycle, the most important of which is the evaluation and selection of vendors. By understanding the various product and emotional criteria organizations use to compare vendors, marketers can better position themselves to win the selection process.

3. Roles of organization members. Although some types of organizational decisions—mostly rebuys and modified rebuys—are made by individuals, the majority of high-investment, new-task decisions are made by groups and are influenced by any number of departments within the organization. By knowing the various roles played by members of the organization's buying center, marketers can deliver the right communications, with the right product information, to the right decision influencer, at the right time.

4. Innovations and innovation diffusion. Any product perceived as new by its target market or as measurably different from existing products is an innovation. There are three types: continuous, dynamically continuous, and discontinuous innovations. The greater the need for behavior modification on the part of the consumer, the less continuous the innovation.

5. Consumer evaluation of innovations. The rate of acceptance of innovations by target consumers depends upon nine characteristics: relative advantage, compatibility, complexity, trialability, observability, value, use, risk, and price.

6. Adopters of innovations. There are five adopter categories, namely, innovators, early adopters, early majority, late majority, and laggards. These groups adopt at different rates and also use different sources to different degrees as they gather information about new products.

Key Terms

buyers (p. 557)
buying center (p. 555)
compatibility (p. 562)
complexity (p. 563)
continuous innovations (p. 561)
deciders (p. 557)
decision cycle (p. 549)
diffusion of innovations (p. 560)
discontinuous innovations (p. 561)
dynamically continuous innovations (p. 561)
early adopters (p. 565)
early-majority adopters (p. 565)

gatekeepers (p. 557)
influencers (p. 556)
innovators (p. 565)
laggards (p. 565)
late-majority adopters (p. 565)
modified rebuy (p. 556)
new task decisions (p. 551)
observability (communicability) (p. 564)
performance purchases (p. 551)
political decisions (p. 551)
procedural purchases (p. 551)
rate of diffusion (p. 565)

relative advantage (p. 562)
risk (p. 564)
routine decisions (p. 551)
straight rebuy (p. 555)
supplier benevolence (p. 554)
supplier reliability (p. 554)
trialability (divisibility) (p. 563)
use (p. 564)
users (p. 556)
value (p. 564)
vendor stratification (p. 555)

Review Questions

Note: You can find the correct answers to these questions by taking the quiz and then submitting your answers in the Online Edition. The program will automatically score your submission. If you miss a question, the program will provide the correct answer, a rationale for the answer, and the section number in the chapter where the topic is discussed.

1. The evaluation criteria in vendor selection can be divided into two groups: product criteria and _____ criteria.
    a. service
    b. emotional
    c. relationship
    d. working terms

2. A _____ type of purchase comes about because product specifications or supplier suitability have changed, necessitating information search and vendor evaluation.
    a. straight rebuy
    b. new task
    c. modified rebuy
    d. routinized rebuy

3. Bill Gomez is responsible for controlling the flow of information into the buying center. Bill is classified as a
    a. gatekeeper.
    b. buyer.
    c. decider.
    d. influencer.

4. Discontinuous innovations necessitate real change in _____ and _____ patterns.
    a. consumption, storage
    b. behavior, storage
    c. behavior, frequency of use
    d. consumption, behavior

5. Dynamically continuous innovations disrupt the consumer's use patterns but still do not
    a. cause the consumer to reject them.
    b. radically alter them.
    c. cause the consumer to switch brands.
    d. necessitate deleting the product.

6. Compatibility is the degree to which an innovation fits with the needs, past experiences, and _____ of the consumer.
   a. values
   b. price range
   c. outlet suitability
   d. ease of shopping

7. Judy LaBlanc feels that products should possess trialability to make product selection more user friendly. This has to do with the degree to which an innovation may be
   a. taken home for a trial period.
   b. guaranteed for a longer trial period.
   c. sampled or tried out.
   d. none of the above.

8. _____ watch opinion leaders and follow when ready.
   a. Early-majority adopters
   b. Innovators
   c. Early adopters
   d. Late-majority adopters

9. Henry and Emma only accept innovations when forced to do so. They are
   a. innovators.
   b. laggards.
   c. early adopters.
   d. late-majority adopters.

10. Konnie is very willing to search for information and to turn to technical experts for advice. She is
    a. an early innovator.
    b. a preinnovator.
    c. an early adopter.
    d. an innovator.

Team Talk

1. In recent years, competing long-distance telephone services have run ads in which corporate buyers are told that the service they purchased has put their jobs in jeopardy. Discuss this marketing strategy and how it seeks to influence organizational buying behavior.

2. Discuss whether you feel gatekeepers serve a positive or negative function in the organizational buying process.

3. Discuss whether and/or why reciprocity is unethical.

4. We discussed nine characteristics consumers use to evaluate the potential of innovations. Identify any two innovations that have been introduced in the past two years. How do these rate on each of the characteristics?

5. Do you know someone who you think is an innovator? What is it about his or her behavior as a consumer that makes you think so? Do you know someone you would classify as a laggard? What characteristics or behaviors of this person make you think this?

Workshops

Research Workshop

Background

The Flimsor Telecommunications Company is in the business of marketing the latest video teleconferencing equipment to the corporate world. The latest technology involves teleconferencing through the Internet. Doing so allows all the parties involved to transmit video as well as data in the form of spreadsheets and databases as well as other typed documents and exhibits. The purchase of this equipment requires an appeal to the corporate executives. The objectives of this workshop are to design a research method for uncovering the relevant organizational issues.

Methodology

The marketing director of Flimsor wants a research questionnaire that can be used to identify organizational influences likely to affect the purchase of the latest technology. It should be brief. Also, it is to be administered separately to corporate executives at a trade show involving information technology.

To the Marketplace

Design this questionnaire and the method for implementing it. Decide how you should intercept and convince corporate executives to complete the brief survey. Should the corporate executives be interviewed on the spot while they are walking through the exhibits? Should the questionnaire be distributed through the registration

packets of all trade show registrants? A drop-off box can be placed in a central location within the facility, and respondents could be instructed to complete the survey and place it in the drop-off box. What incentive would you give the trade show registrants to complete the questionnaire?

Creative Workshop

Background

Your advertising agency has landed the account of a major manufacturer of restaurant stoves. The objective of this workshop is to develop ads that appeal to different members of target business buying centers.

Methodology

Your assignment is to create three alternate advertising campaigns to run in trade journals read by owners and managers of restaurants and hotel kitchens. Consult the list of evaluation criteria for selecting suppliers in Exhibit 18-2 to determine the basis of your appeals. Your campaigns should each suggest a theme, the direction of the body copy, and the type of illustrations to be used.

To the Marketplace

Write a one-page memo to the account executive who will present your ideas to the client, explaining which campaign you believe to be the strongest and why.

Managerial Workshop 1

Background

This workshop is designed to help you better understand how innovations are positioned and evaluated. The objectives are to identify an innovation currently being promoted, to assess it on the basis of the innovation evaluation criteria given in the text, and to identify the target market.

Methodology

Find a magazine advertisement or a television commercial for a new product that could be classified as either discontinuous or dynamically continuous. Cut out and mount the advertisement or make a copy of the commercial. Considering both the message and the medium, decide on and describe the intended target market for the advertisement or commercial. Assess how the marketer has positioned the product in terms of relative advantage, compatibility, complexity, trialability, and observability.

To the Marketplace

What would you do differently in your advertising to better position the product for the target market? Consider the current advertising, your assessment of the type of innovation, and the performance of the product in terms of the five characteristics identified.

Managerial Workshop 2

Background

You are a store manager of a new retail outlet for Office Software, Inc., both a manufacturing company and a national retailer specializing in the development and marketing of a variety of office management software. Examples include software for database management, spreadsheet, word processing, web-page design, Internet access, email communications, teleconferencing through the Internet, graphics and design software, software to manage sales, financial and bookkeeping software, product design software, market research design software, and statistical software. The objective of this workshop is to develop a method for training sales staff to present the product line to small business owners.

Methodology

Prepare a strategy that outlines a scenario or script that salespeople should use to guide them with the communication and interaction with the small business owners. The goal is to help small business owners buy the right software to manage their operations efficiently.

To the Marketplace

Set up a role-playing interview between a salesperson and a customer that covers this scenario or script.

Notes

1. John A. Hoard, *Consumer Behavior in Marketing Strategy* (Englewood Cliffs, NJ: Prentice Hall), p. 201.
2. B. C. Ames and J. D. Hlavacek, *Managing Marketing for Industrial Firms* (New York: Random House, 1984), p. 22.
3. Lowell E. Crow and Jay D. Lindquist, "The Impact of Decision Type on the Number of Acceptable and Biddable Vendors," in Kenneth D. Bahn, ed., *Developments in Marketing Science*, Vol. 11, (Blacksburg, VA: Academy of Marketing Science 1988), pp. 508–512.
4. Donald R. Lehmann and John O'Shaughnessy, "Differences in Attribute Importance for Different Industrial Products," *Journal of Marketing*, Vol. 38 (April 1974), pp. 36–42.
5. Philip Kotler and Ronald E. Turner, *Marketing Management: Analysis, Planning, and Control*, Canadian 4th ed. (Scarborough, Ont.: Prentice-Hall Canada, 1981), p. 188.
6. Lehmann and O'Shaughnessy, "Differences in Attribute Importance for Different Industrial Products."
7. Ernest Dichter, "Emotion: The Third Ear and Industrial Sales," *Industrial Marketing* (July 1980), p. 81.
8. Monroe M. Bird and Wayne C. Sheppard, "Reciprocity in Industrial Buying and Selling: A Study of Attitudes," *Journal of Purchasing*, Vol. 9 (November 1973), pp. 26–35.
9. Ibid.
10. Fred Selnes and Kjell Gonhaug, "Effects of Supplier Reliability and Benevolence in Business Marketing," *Journal of Business Research*, Vol. 49 (September 2000), pp. 259–271.
11. Rohit Deshpande and Frederick E. Webster, Jr., "Corporate Culture, Customer Orientation, and Innovativeness in Japanese Firms: A Quadrad Analysis," *Journal of Marketing*, Vol. 57 (January 1993), pp. 23–37.
12. Thomas L. Baker, Penny M. Simpson, and Judy A. Siguaw, "The Impact of Suppliers' Perceptions of Reseller Market Orientation on Key Relationship Constructs," *Journal of the Academy of Marketing Science*, Vol. 27 (Winter 1999), pp. 50–57.
13. Michael J. Dorsch, Scott R. Swanson, and Scott W. Kelly, "The Role of Relationship Quality in the Stratification of Vendors as Perceived by Customers," *Journal of the Academy of Marketing Science*, Vol. 26 (Spring 1999), pp. 128–142.
14. Ajay Kohli, "Determinants of Influence in Organizational Buying: A Contingency Approach," *Journal of Marketing*, Vol. 53 (July 1989), pp. 50–56.
15. Jagdish N. Sheth, "A Model of Industrial Buyer Behavior," *Journal of Marketing*, Vol. 37 (October 1973), pp. 47–60; Peter Doyle, Arch G. Woodside, and Paul Michell, "Organizational Buying in New Task and Rebuy Situations," *Industrial Marketing Management*, Vol. 8 (1979), pp. 7–11.
16. Kjell Gonhaug, "Autonomous Versus Joint Decisions in Organizational Buying," *Industrial Marketing Management*, Vol. 4 (1975), pp. 265–271.
17. Wesley J. Johnston and Thomas V. Bonoma, "The Buying Center: Structure and Interaction Patterns," *Journal of Marketing*, Vol. 45 (Summer 1981), pp. 73–156.
18. Sheth, "A Model of Industrial Buyer Behavior"; also the following study provided results consistent with the notion that there is more perceived risk in new task decisions that entail a larger decision group: Lowell E. Crow and Jay D. Lindquist, "Impact of Organizational and Buyer Characteristics on the Buying Center," *Industrial Marketing Management*, Vol. 14 (1985), pp. 49–58.
19. Frederick E. Webster, Jr., and Yoram Wind, *Organizational Buying Behavior* (Englewood Cliffs, NJ: Prentice-Hall, 1972), p. 80.
20. Yoram Wind and Thomas S. Robertson, "The Linking Pin Role of the Organizational Buying Center," *Journal of Business Research*, Vol. 10 (1982), pp. 169–184.
21. Robert E. Krapfel, Jr., "An Extended Interpersonal Influence Model of Organizational Buying Behavior," *Journal of Business Research*, Vol. 10 (June 1982), pp. 77–157.
22. Webster and Wind, *Organizational Buying Behavior*.

23. Jay Greene, "Now Your TV Can Go Wireless, Too," *Business Week*, (August 9, 2004), p. 17.

24. John H. Antil, "New Product or Service Adoption," *Journal of Consumer Marketing*, Vol. 5 (Spring 1988), pp. 5–16.

25. The first five characteristics are suggested by Everett M. Rogers and F. Floyd Shoemaker, *Communication of Innovations*, 2nd ed. (New York: The Free Press, 1971). The final three characteristics are suggested by S. Ram and Jagdish N. Sheth, "Consumer Resistance to Innovations: The Marketing Problem and Its Solutions," *Journal of Consumer Marketing*, Vol. 6 (Spring 1989), pp. 5–14. More recently, Boyd and Mason categorized the "extra-brand attributes" into three major categories—product, firm, and market related. Product-related attributes include key benefits, variety, complexity, switching cost, relative advantage, perceived risk, price range/trends, feasibility, observability, future enhancements, and media reviews. Firm-related attributes include reputation, size, age, compatibility of innovation with other lines of firm, and image. Market-related factors include number of firms, supporting products/services, advertising expenditures, competition, values/norms of the social system, industry standardization, alternatives, distribution system, future sales expected, number sold to date, and aggregate of firm-related attributes. The reference of that article is: Thomas C. Boyd and Charlotte H. Mason, "The Link between Attractiveness of 'Extrabrand' Attributes and the Adoption of Innovations," *Journal of the Academy of Marketing Science*, Vol. 27 (Summer 1999), pp. 306–319.

26. Thomas S. Robertson, "The Process of Innovation and the Diffusion of Innovation," *Journal of Marketing*, Vol. 31 (January 1967), pp. 14–19.

27. Jae H. Pae and Donald R. Lehmann, "Multigeneration Innovation Diffusion: The Impact of Intergeneration Time," *Journal of the Academy of Marketing Science*, Vol. 31 (Winter 2003), pp. 36–45.

28. John A. Norton and Frank Bass, "Evolution of Technological Generations: The Law of Capture," *Sloan Management Review*, Vol. 33 (Winter 1992), pp. 66–77.

29. Wagner A. Kamakura and Siva K. Balasubramanian, "Long-Term View of the Diffusion of Durables," *International Journal of Research in Marketing*, Vol. 5, pp. 1–13.

30. Everett M. Rogers, *Diffusion of Innovation*, 3rd ed. (New York: The Free Press, 1983).

31. Subin Im, Barry L. Bayus, and Charlotte H. Mason, "An Empirical Study of Innate Consumer Innovativeness, Personal Characteristics, and New-product Adoption Behavior," *Journal of the Academy of Marketing Science*, Vol. 31 (Winter 2003), pp. 61–73.

32. Thomas S. Robertson, "Determinants of Innovative Behavior," in Reed Moyer, ed. *Winter Conference of the American Marketing Association*, No. 26 (Chicago: American Marketing Association, 1967), pp. 328–332.

33. Ibid.

34. See James F. Engel, Robert J. Kegerreis, and Roger D. Blackwell, "Word-of-Mouth Communication by the Innovator," *Journal of Marketing*, Vol. 33 (July 1969), pp. 15–19; Jagdish N. Sheth, "Word-of-Mouth in Low-Risk Innovation," *Journal of Advertising Research*, Vol. 11 (June 1971), pp. 15–18; H. David Stratton and James R. Lumpkin, "Information Sources Used by Elderly Health Care Product Adopters," *Journal of Advertising Research*, Vol. 32 (July–August 1992), pp. 20–30.

35. Zarrel V. Lambert, "Perceptual Patterns, Information Handling and Innovativeness," *Journal of Marketing Research*, Vol. 9 (November 1972), pp. 427–431.

36. Geoffrey A. Moore, *Crossing the Chasm* (New York: Harper Business, 1991); Geoffrey A. Moore, *Inside the Tornado* (New York: Harper Business, 1995).

Conducting Research

This chapter is about shopper/buyer/consumer research. The information obtained from this research is used to answer a host of research questions that guide marketing decision making as well as public policy decisions.

The typical marketing research project involves the following steps: (1) identifying the research problem or opportunity, (2) developing the research questions, (3) selecting the shopper/buyer/consumer behavior model to guide the research, (4) selecting the research design, (5) selecting the data collection method, (6) selecting the sampling method and sample size, (7) developing the research instruments, (8) collecting data, (9) analyzing the data, and (10) interpreting the data and writing follow-up reports. The vast majority of marketing research textbooks cover the latter six steps in some detail. However, from the vantage point of the study of shopper/buyer/consumer behavior, the student needs to fully understand and appreciate the first four steps of the research process. These steps interface significantly with the study of shopper/ buyer/ consumer behavior. To reiterate, these steps are:

1. Identifying the research problem or opportunity,
2. Developing the research questions,
3. Selecting the shopper/buyer/consumer behavior model to guide the research,
4. Selecting the research design.

Since the remaining steps are well covered in the marketing research textbooks, we will not devote any time and attention to them. Students interested in knowing more about steps 5–10 are encouraged to take a course in marketing research and/or consult a marketing research text.

19-1 Identifying the Research Problem or Opportunity

Consider the following case. Compaq Computer Corp. and preschool toy giant Fisher-Price, Inc., have created a joint venture to develop a new product line. This product line allows consumers to turn their home PCs into toys for preschoolers. There are 18 million U.S. families with children under the age of seven. The idea is to get many of these fam-

CHAPTER
SPOTLIGHTS

1 Identifying research problems or opportunities

2 The development of research questions

3 The selection of shopper/buyer/consumer behavior models to guide the research

4 The selection of a suitable research design (survey, experimental, and qualitative)

ilies to buy computer attachments such as an oversized keyboard and car-like controls to make the PC appealing to preschoolers. This hardware comes with a variety of software programs that involve both learning and adventure—exciting stuff for the kids.

For this joint venture between Compaq and Fisher-Price to be successful, much research is needed to guide marketing decision making. The marketing manager assigned to work on this project has to make product development decisions, pricing decisions, distribution decisions, as well as promotion decisions. The research problem or opportunity here is related to these decisions. To make those decisions, the first step is to specify information requirements. In other words, to make product development (pricing, distribution, and promotion) decisions, what information does the marketing manager need? Once the **information needs** are specified, the next step is to convert the needed information into **research questions.**

Identifying the research problem or opportunity is very important in that it initiates the marketing research process. A good definition of the research problem or opportunity directs the research process to collect and analyze consumer data for marketing decision making.

19-2 Developing the Research Questions

Returning to the Compaq/Fisher-Price case, we can articulate a set of research questions such as:

- Are preschoolers happy with the available computers on the market used for learning? For games and entertainment?

- If they are unhappy with the computers used for learning, then what are the sources of their dissatisfaction? If they are unhappy with the computers used for games and entertainment, then, again, what are the sources of their dissatisfaction?

- How will preschoolers perceive a newly designed computer attachment made to assist learning? To assist in games and entertainment? How will they perceive it in relation to competitor products such as computer attachments made by Packard Bell, IBM, and Microsoft?

- Will the preschoolers prefer the Compaq/Fisher-price brand over competitor brands?

- In what situations or on what occasions do families buy computer attachments? For example, are computer attachments typically bought as birthday gifts by parents?

- Who in the family is likely to recognize a computer attachment as a potential birthday gift? Father? Mother? Older siblings? Grandparents? Who in the family is most likely to gather information about computer attachments? Who is likely to make the purchase decision? Who is likely to order the product?

- How should the computer attachment be designed to be most attractive for preschoolers? Colors? Shapes? Bells and whistles?

These are all research questions that need to be addressed in some form to help the marketing manager of Compaq/Fisher-Price develop the marketing plan and implement its recommendations (see Exhibit 19-1). Answering these research questions is the heart of the study of shopper, buyer, and consumer behavior. Marketing managers use shopper/buyer/consumer models to assist them in guiding the research endeavor. We will see how this is done in the next section.

19-3 Selecting a Shopper/Buyer/Consumer Behavior Model to Guide the Research

To conduct effective shopper/buyer/consumer research, the researcher first and foremost attempts to choose the shopper/buyer/consumer behavior model that can best address the research questions. All the conceptual models we reviewed throughout the book are candidate models guiding the research process. Attempting to match the research question

> **information needs**
> Information that marketing managers desire to have to help them make decisions about such things as market selection, product development, pricing, distribution and logistics, and marketing communications.

> **research questions**
> Information needs are translated into research questions, which are much more specific in that they involve a set of specific questions designed to guide the research process.

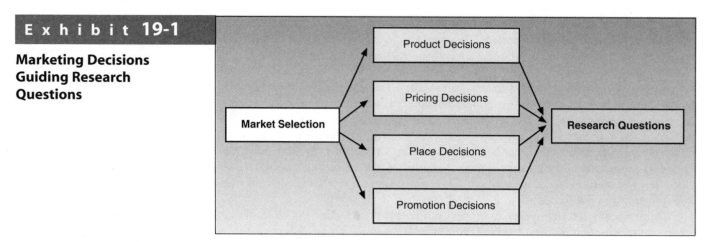

with an appropriate model requires the marketing practitioner to become familiar with the many models of shopper/buyer/consumer behavior. This matching process of research questions with an appropriate model is key to effective research. Let us go through the research questions pertaining to the Compaq/Fisher-Price situation and see what models match these research questions.

- Are preschoolers happy with the available computers on the market used for learning? For games and entertainment?

- If they are unhappy with the computers used for learning, then what are the sources of their dissatisfaction? If they are unhappy with the computers used for games and entertainment, then, again, what are the sources of their dissatisfaction?

These research questions can be addressed with the help of consumer satisfaction/dissatisfaction models. We described a number of these models in Chapter 4 (Consumption and Post-purchase Behavior). For example, in section 4-2b (Relationship between Expectation and Satisfaction) we described a model commonly referred to as *expectancy confirmation/disconfirmation*. This model posits that consumers experience positive feelings when the product performs better than expected (positive disconfirmation); they feel satisfied when the product matches their expectations (confirmation); and they feel negative about the product when it fails to meet their expectations (negative disconfirmation).

Another model of consumer satisfaction deals with types of expectation (ideal, equitable, and expected performance) and how different types of expectation are involved with the experience of positive and negative affect toward the product after consumption. In other words, consumers do not have just one type of expectation regarding product performance. Pre-schoolers may have a vision of their ideal product, perhaps an ideal computer that does wonderful things to help them learn and play games, and it may be that this vision was formed watching science fiction shows. If so, they may compare the computer equipment they have now to that ideal vision (ideal expectation). Doing so should make them feel dissatisfied with the computer they currently use. Equitable expectations tend to generate feelings of fairness or lack of fairness. For example, a preschooler spends some time with a friend at his friend's home. His friend has a fancy computer that is loaded with learning software and games. The computer keyboard and accessories allow the user to do all kinds of neat things. The preschooler compares his own computer with his friend's and quickly realizes that his computer is nowhere near as fancy as his friend's. He feels that it is not fair that his friend has so much better a computer than he does. These feelings of inequity translate to feelings of dissatisfaction with his computer.

Marketplace 19-1 shows consumer satisfaction ratings of specific industry sectors. This is a well accepted and popular measure that many Fortune 500 firms have used to track customer satisfaction.

Another model, described in Chapter 4, section 4-2c (Relationship between Performance and Satisfaction), deals with the distinction between objective and affective performance. This model asserts that consumers have objective or functional expectations

Marketplace 19-1

ACSI's Scores in Relation to E-Commerce

The University of Michigan conducts an annual poll to measure customer satisfaction in relation to major brands. It is called the American Customer Satisfaction Index (ACSI). Recently, they have reported scores related to e-retailers in comparison to e-travel services. The data show that online travel services are lagging compared with e-retailers. E-retail earned an aggregate of 84 points (100-point scale) for 2003, up 1.2 percent from 2002. In contrast, online auctions had a customer satisfaction score of 78 points (up 1.3 percent from 77), travel had a score of 77 points (same as 2002), and brokerages had a score of 76 points (up 4.1 percent from 73). Overall, e-commerce had a healthy growth over 2002, up 4.1 percent to 80.8. This figure is the best aggregate customer satisfaction score ever recorded.

Amazon.com did very well in relation to all other e-retailers as well as all e-travel services. It rated 88 in both 2002 and 2003. The list that follows gives you details of the major e-retailers and e-travel services in relation to 2002 and 2003.

**American Customer Satisfaction Index
Year-to-Year Comparison**

Online Brand	2002	2003	% Change
E-retailers	83	84	1.2%
Amazon.com	88	88	0
Barnesandnoble.com	87	86	−1.1
All others	82	83	1.2
Buy.com	80	80	0
1-800-Flowers.com	78	76	−2.6
E-travel services	77	77	0
Expedia	80	78	−2.5
All others	77	77	0
Orbitz	76	77	1.3
Travelocity.com	76	76	0

Source: Adapted from Susan Posnock, "Customer Satisfaction Up Online," *American Demographics,* April 2004, p. 16.

regarding the performance of a product, and when these expectations are unmet, consumers feel dissatisfied. However, equal to the objective or functional expectations are affective or emotional expectations that many people are not aware of. For example, preschoolers are not likely to have objective or functional expectations regarding computers, learning, and entertainment. Their expectations are more likely to be affective or emotional in nature. They may be based on style and color of the equipment. Style and color are affective-based expectations. In contrast, expectations relating to computer memory and speed are functional-type expectations.

Using any of these three models or possibly a combination of them (see Exhibit 19-2) should help guide the research process. How? In this case, the researcher has to determine all the possible sources of dissatisfaction in relation to how preschoolers use computers for learning (for games and entertainment). Examples of sources of dissatisfaction may include:

- The letters and numbers on the keyboard are too small,
- The mouse is very difficult to control,

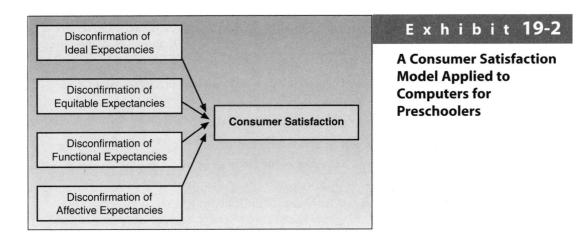

E x h i b i t 19-2

A Consumer Satisfaction Model Applied to Computers for Preschoolers

- It is not easy to figure out how to do basic editing functions such as shifting to uppercase and erasing,
- The style is boring,
- The color is not exciting,
- The computer crashes when the user attempts more than one application, and
- The computer is too slow.

The expectancy confirmation/disconfirmation model guides researcher to focus on sources of dissatisfaction arising from expectancy disconfirmation experiences. That is, the researcher has to capture preschoolers' dissatisfaction with computer features (the letters on the keyboard are too small, the mouse is very difficult to control, can't figure out how to do basic editing functions such as shifting to uppercase and erasing, etc.) *in relation to their expectations.* The researcher has to find out what their precise expectations are regarding the size of letters and numbers on the keyboard. What is a preschooler's idea of mouse control? What are preschoolers' expectations regarding basic editing functions? What are their expectations concerning the style of the computer? What are their expectations regarding color? And so on.

The ideal, equitable, and expected model of consumer satisfaction leads the researcher to capture preschoolers' ideal and equitable expectations. For example, in relation to the letters and numbers on the keyboard, the researcher probes to find out what preschoolers' ideal form of keyboard is in terms of size of the letters and numbers on the keyboard, a vision of a keyboard that may have originated in science fiction shows.

The objective and affective performance model of consumer satisfaction leads the researcher to realize that preschoolers may judge the performance of computers not as much on their functional features (e.g., memory and speed) but more on their affective features (e.g., style and color). Knowing this, the researcher probes to better understand these affective features and how preschoolers judge them.

Now let us turn to the next research questions and see how the study of shopper, buyer, and consumer behavior helps guide the research process. The questions are as follows:

- How will preschoolers perceive a newly designed computer attachment made to assist learning? To assist in games and entertainment? How will they perceive it in relation to competitor products such as computer attachments made by Packard Bell, IBM, and Microsoft?
- Will the preschoolers prefer the Compaq/Fisher-price brand over competitor brands?

shopper/buyer/consumer behavior models Concepts and theories about how shoppers, buyers, and consumers perceive and evaluate goods and services in the marketplace and act accordingly.

What are the **shopper/buyer/consumer behavior models** that can help guide the research to answer the above questions? In Chapter 9, we described several attitude models, including the functional theory of attitude (section 9-2a), the Fishbein model (section 9-2b), and the belief-importance model (section 9-2c). These models are designed to help the researcher map out the psychological connection between product attributes and their effect on brand attitude and preference. In light of the fact that the two research questions deal with brand preference more than brand attitude, we should use the belief-importance model. This model maps out the determinants of brand preference in relation to a set of alternative brands in the minds of preschoolers. The model leads the researcher to do several things. First, the researcher has to flesh out all the product attributes that may affect brand preference. These include the following:

- The size of letters and numbers on the keyboard,
- User's control of the mouse,
- User's control of a joystick,
- The size of the screen,
- The color of the computer,
- The shape and style of the computer,
- Relative ease or difficulty in typing,
- Relative ease or difficulty in drawing,

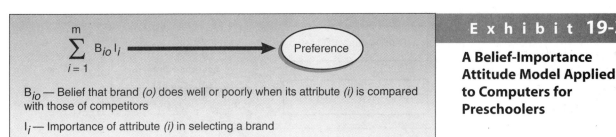

- Variety of software games embedded in the computer, and
- Variety of learning and educational software embedded in the computer.

Now suppose that Compaq/Fisher-Price came up with a new computer to compete directly with other computers made by Packard Bell, IBM, and Microsoft. The belief-importance model guides the researcher to develop a survey questionnaire containing belief measures in relation to Compaq/Fisher-Price, Packard Bell, IBM, and Microsoft in relation to every product attribute listed above. A sample of preschoolers is selected for the study, and these kids are asked to rate their perception of each computer with respect to each and every product attribute (the size of letters and numbers on the keyboard, user's control of the mouse, etc.). After getting the belief ratings, the study respondents are asked to rate the importance of all of the product attributes (see the Reebok, Nike, and Asahi example in section 9-2c). The resulting data should allow the researcher to see how the new Compaq/Fisher-Price computer stacks up against Packard Bell, IBM, and Microsoft in the minds of the preschoolers who sampled it. The goal is to ensure that the new computer is perceived as better than its competitors along important product features as defined by the preschoolers, leading the preschoolers to express a greater preference for the Compaq/Fisher-Price computer over those of Packard Bell, IBM, and Microsoft. This research should reveal whether the new computer was successful in generating those beliefs, paving the way to a higher brand preference (see Exhibit 19-3).

The next research questions are the following:

- In what situations or occasions do families buy computer attachments? For example, are computer attachments typically bought as birthday gifts by parents?
- Who in the family is likely to recognize a computer attachment as a potential birthday gift? Father? Mother? Older siblings? Grandparents? Who in the family is most likely to gather information about computer attachments? Who is likely to make the purchase decision? Who is likely to order the product?

What shopper/buyer/consumer behavior model can assist in designing a study to answer these questions? We turn to Chapter 15 (Household and Family Influences), where we described a model dealing with roles of family/household members at each stage in the decision process (section 15-3e). The model asserts that family members tend to assume different roles throughout the consumer decision process—product need recognition, information search, alternative evaluation and choice, and consumption and post-purchase evaluation. For example, preschoolers may ask for the Compaq/Fisher-Price computer if they see it in a television commercial. Perhaps their parents or grandparents will realize that this computer would make a great birthday gift if they see it displayed in a toy store.

Who is most likely to gather information about the Compaq/Fisher-Price computer and its rivals (Packard Bell, IBM, and Microsoft)? Would that role be assumed by one of the parents or grandparents? If so, who in particular? Could it be the grandfather? Who is likely to evaluate the alternatives and make the choice? Who is likely to make the purchase? And so on. Knowing who in the family is most likely to be involved in each stage of the consumer decision process should help the marketing manager target the right person within the family with appropriate information. Thus, the family roles model should help the researcher by guiding him or her to select a sample of families with preschoolers and design a questionnaire to find out who within the family is most likely to assume which

E x h i b i t 19-4

A Role Model in Family Decision Making Applied to Computers for Preschool Families

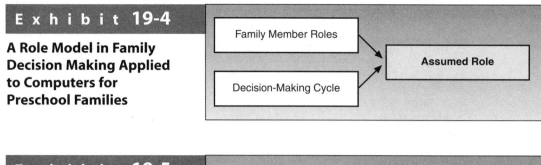

E x h i b i t 19-5

A Sensory Perception Model Applied to Computers for Preschool Families

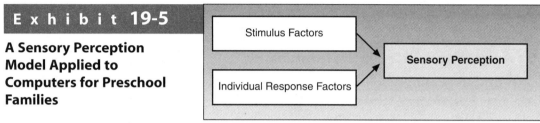

role in product need recognition, information search, alternative evaluation and choice, and consumption and post-purchase evaluation (see Exhibit 19-4).

The next research question was phrased as follows:

- How should the computer attachment be designed to be most attractive for preschoolers? Colors? Shapes? Bells and whistles?

Research should be conducted to find out what shape, color, style, texture, and other visual features of the computer are most attractive for preschoolers. To assist with this research, the sensory perception model described in Chapter 7 (Memory, Learning, and Perception) can be a suitable model. The model is described in section 7-3a. It describes examples of stimulus and individual response factors affecting sensory perception. Stimulus factors related to computer design involve visual cues (color, shape, size, etc.), aural cues (tempo, pitch, music, etc.), and olfactory cues (odors, scent, etc.). The model describes the importance of sensory congruity among the stimulus cues and how consumers' responses to these cues are dependent on consumers' sensory acuity, sensory preferences, and expectations. This means that the researcher has to experiment with a variety of design configurations to uncover the most preferred design. The researcher also has to measure preschoolers' sensory acuity, preferences, and expectation in relation to each of the stimulus factors to help select the most effective design elements. See Exhibit 19-5.

19-4 Selecting the Research Design

Once a shopper/buyer/consumer behavior model is selected to guide the research process, the researcher has to make a decision about the **research design.** There are three types of research designs typically employed in shopper/buyer/consumer research, namely survey, experimental, and qualitative research. **Survey research** involves the construction of a questionnaire, which is then used to collect data using mail, telephone interviews, mall intercepts, email, the Internet, or another appropriate method. Let us use some of the research questions identified earlier as examples:

- In what situations or on what occasions do families buy computer attachments? For example, are computer attachments typically bought as birthday gifts by parents?

- Who in the family likely to recognize the opportunity of a computer attachment as a potential for a birthday gift? Father? Mother? Older siblings? Grandparents? Who in the family is most likely to gather information about computer attachments? Who is likely to make the purchase decision? Who is likely to order the product?

research design Three different approaches to conducting research, namely exploratory research, descriptive research, and hypothesis-testing research.

survey research Research involving the construction of a questionnaire, which is then used to collect data using such methods as mail, telephone interviews, mall intercepts, email, or the Internet.

We decided to use a model dealing with roles of family/household members at each stage in the decision process (Chapter 15, section 15-3e). The model asserts that family members tend to assume different roles throughout the consumer decision process—product need recognition, information search, alternative evaluation and choice, and consumption and post-purchase evaluation. A survey study may be the best research design for this situation. The sample of people we would talk to would be families with preschoolers. The data collection method may be personal interviews in the homes of the sample families. A survey questionnaire would be designed to capture different family member responses to questions concerning who in the family is most likely to recognize the Compaq/Fisher-Price computer as a gift opportunity, who is most likely to gather information about the alternative computer brands, who is most likely evaluate the alternative brands, and so on.

In contrast, **experimental research** involves setting up a situation in which one or more variables are manipulated (e.g., price and message appeal) and the effects of this manipulation are observed on a selected shopper/buyer/consumer behavioral phenomenon (e.g., brand preference, brand choice, consumer satisfaction). The objective is to find cause and effect. For example, if you experiment with different potential prices, what will happen to shoppers' intentions to buy the product? The last group of research questions concerning the product design seems to lend itself to an experimental design. Here again are the questions and the shopper/buyer/consumer behavior model used to guide the research:

- How should the computer attachment be designed to be most attractive for preschoolers? Colors? Shapes? Bells and whistles?

We selected the model described in Chapter 7, section 7-3a, dealing with sensory perception. The model focuses on stimulus and individual response factors affecting sensory perception. In this case, an experiment can be designed to test the various effects of combination of stimulus cues such as color, shape, size, startup music, scent, and texture. A sample of preschoolers would be given various configurations of the computer involving the various stimulus cues and asked to express how much they like the design.

An example of experimentation in the marketplace has to do with gathering product selection information from shoppers as they check out at the store. Data scanning equipment at many retail establishments now allow marketing researchers to conduct real-time experiments, called "market tests." Just swipe the card at the checkout register and the consumer gets a discount on the purchased item. The consumer saves money and the store builds a record that lets it know how shoppers respond to changes in their marketing program. For example, a store might conduct a market test of two promotional campaigns and compare their effectiveness. One campaign may be conducted at certain stores, while another campaign happens at other stores. The marketing researcher looks at actual purchases of those consumers who use their discount cards and compare the effectiveness of the two promotional campaigns.

Qualitative research (sometimes referred to as **idiographic research, interpretive research,** or **exploratory research**), on the other hand, involves collecting data from a small sample (typically a sample chosen using a "convenience" method that is not necessarily representative of the population at large) using data collection methods that do not produce "quantitative data." Focus groups, in-depth personal interviews, and projective techniques are examples of such data collection techniques. Qualitative data is rich in meaning (e.g., a personal shopping diary) and does not easily lend itself to analysis using inferential statistics (the kind of statistical analysis that tests whether relationships between variables of differences between groups are significant at some confidence level). The data are grouped into similar answer types that allow the researcher to capture themes or key ideas.

Here again are the research questions selected to guide the research process:

- How will preschoolers perceive a newly designed computer attachment made to assist learning? To assist in games and entertainment? How will they perceive it in

---

experimental research
Research involving setting up a situation in which one or more variables are manipulated (e.g., price and message appeal) and the effects of this manipulation are observed on a selected shopper/buyer/ consumer behavioral phenomenon (e.g., brand preference, brand choice, consumer satisfaction). This is a research process to test cause and effect.

qualitative research
Research involving collecting data from a small sample (where data is typically gathered using a convenience sampling method that is not necessarily representative of the population at large) using data collection methods that do not produce quantitative data. Focus groups, in-depth personal interviews, and projective techniques are examples of methods that produce qualitative data. Qualitative data is rich in meaning (e.g., a personal shopping diary) that does not easily lend itself to analysis using inferential statistics. The data are interpreted by capturing themes (or key ideas) and categorized as such.

idiographic research or **interpretive research** or **exploratory research**
The kind of research designed to generate hypotheses. It is not considered to be definitive as in quantitative research (correlational or experimental research). For examples of this type of research, see **qualitative research.**

Marketplace 19-2

Visual Ethnography: A Research Tool Used by Cultural Anthropologists

Visual ethnography, a form of anthropological research, looks at the consumer in his or her natural habitat. That could be in the home or place of work—settings or situations involving the use of goods and services. The method involves using video and engaging the subject within a natural setting. Consumers in a familiar environment are more likely to be less self-conscious, and their responses may approximate their real consumer behavior. In contrast, a consumer stopped in a mall and asked to answer questions, or fill out a survey, is less likely to offer time and real information than will consumers who open up their homes to the researcher.

The visual ethnographer listens to what consumers have to say in their natural surroundings and also observes what they are doing. The method provides more information about emotions, motivations, and underlying beliefs and values. People have a hard time disclosing their inner self, but they may feel more comfortable doing so in their natural environment with a researcher who has a "human" touch. Therefore, this method serves to humanize the research. It offers a live picture of who these consumers are and what they do, not simply numbers.

Source: Adapted from American Demographics, "Futurespeak: Solutions for Evolving Consumer Needs," *American Demographics,* April 2004, p. 44.

relation to competitor products such as computer attachments made by Packard Bell, IBM, and Microsoft?

- Will the preschoolers prefer the Compaq/Fisher-price brand over competitor brands?

We selected the belief-importance model (Chapter 9, section 9-2c) as the conceptual model guiding the necessary research. Before applying the belief-importance model, we talked about the need to flesh out all the product attributes that may affect brand preference. We described examples of these attributes as:

- The size of letters and numbers on the keyboard,
- User's control of the mouse,
- User's control of a joystick,
- The size of the screen,
- The color of the computer,
- The shape and style of the computer,
- Relative ease or difficulty in typing,
- Relative ease or difficulty in drawing,
- Variety of software games embedded in the computer, and
- Variety of learning and educational software embedded in the computer.

This list of product attributes can be easily obtained using qualitative research. In this case, a reasonable qualitative design could be a series of in-depth interviews with perhaps 10 to 15 preschoolers. The in-depth interviews would probe preschoolers' likes and dislikes about various computers used for learning and games. The interviews would be taped and the content analyzed for references concerning product attributes that are liked and disliked. Those references would then be categorized and a list of product attributes would be generated.

Marketplaces 19-2 and 19-3 describe research methods employed by marketing researchers Specifically, Marketplace 19-2 describes visual ethnography—a research tool used by marketing researchers who conduct research from a cultural anthropological perspective. Marketplace 19-3 describes how marketing researchers use focus groups; it also explains why this particular research tool has gained popularity over the years.

Marketplace 19-3

Focus Groups: How They Are Becoming So Popular

Marketers are heavy users of focus groups. In 2001, companies spent $1.1 billion on qualitative research, most of this in the form of focus groups. Target, the Minneapolis-based discount retailer, wanted to launch a product line aimed at college-bound students. Target hired the San Mateo, California-based research firm Jump Associates to conduct a series of focus groups using college-bound students. The research enabled the marketing people at Target to hear firsthand from college-bound students about their shopping needs and concerns.

The research firm sponsored a series of "game nights" at high school grads' homes, inviting incoming college freshman as well as students with a year of experience in dorm living. Jump devised a board game that involved issues associated with going to college. The game naturally led to informal conversations and questions about college life. Jump researchers as well as Target marketing people were on the sidelines to observe, while a video camera recoded the sessions.

Based on the research, Target was able to offer a product line designed for college freshman. Product examples include Kitchen in a Box (basic accoutrements for a budding college cook), Bath in a Box (an extra-large bath towel to preserve modesty on the trek to and from the shower, and Laundry Bag (a laundry bag with instructions on how to actually do the laundry printed on the bag). That product line was successful in the sense that it increased sales at Target stores by a significant margin.

The heart of the focus group is the interview, but recruiting the subjects is equally important. The goal is to recruit subjects who are highly representative of the targeted population. For example, Roper ASW in New York City recruits a consumer segment it calls "the Influentials"—people who have significant word-of-mouth clout. Roper ASW uses its knowledge of this segment to help its clients recruit candidates for focus groups. Once consumers are recruited, the moderator plans the interview strategy. Effective moderators tend to downplay the marketing agenda and acknowledge the importance of the environment. In doing so, respondents are likely to share their feelings uninhibited if they feel comfortable in the focus group environment. Focus groups environments are designed to mimic the real environment such as a kitchen, a playroom, or a bar. Of course, there is one-way mirror and videotaping equipment, usually placed in inconspicuous places in the room.

Source: Adapted from Alison Stein Wellner, "The New Science of Focus Groups," *American Demographics,* March 2003, pp. 29–33.

Chapter Spotlights

This chapter described how marketing researchers conduct research guided by shopper/buyer/consumer behavior models. The information obtained from this research is used to answer a host of research questions guiding marketing decision making as well as public policy.

1. Identifying research problems or opportunities. Identification of the research problem or opportunity initiates the marketing research process. A good definition of the research problem or opportunity directs the research process to collect and analyze consumer data for marketing decision making.

2. The development of research questions. We showed how research questions are formulated based on problems recognized and marketing decision making. That is, the marketing manager identifies information needs to assist in making decisions about such things as market selection, product development, pricing, distribution and logistics, and marketing communications. Information needs are translated into research questions.

3. The selection of shopper/buyer/consumer behavior models to guide the research. When conducting research necessary to provide answers for the research questions, the marketing researcher selects a suitable shopper/buyer/consumer behavior model as a guide. We provided a number of examples to illustrate this process.

4. The selection of a suitable research design (survey, experimental, and qualitative). Once the shopper/buyer/consumer behavior model is selected, the next step is to determine the research design. We described three types of research designs: survey, experimental, and qualitative research. Survey research involves the construction of a questionnaire, which is then used to collect data using such methods as mail, telephone interviews, mall intercepts, email, or the Internet. In contrast, experimental research involves setting up a situation in which one or more variables are manipulated (e.g., price and message appeal) and the effects of this manipulation are observed on a selected shopper/buyer/consumer behavioral phenomenon (e.g., brand preference, brand choice, consumer satisfaction). This is a research process to test cause and effect. Qualitative research, on the other hand, involves collecting data from a small sample (where data is typically gathered using a convenience sampling method that is not necessarily representative of the population at large) using data collection methods that do not produce "quantitative data." Focus groups, in-depth personal interviews, and projective techniques are examples of methods that produce "qualitative" data. Qualitative data is rich in meaning (e.g., a personal shopping diary) that does not easily lend itself to analysis using inferential statistics. The data are interpreted by capturing themes (or key ideas) and categorized as such.

Key Terms

experimental research (p. 581)
exploratory research (p. 581)
idiographic research (p. 581)
information needs (p. 575)

interpretive research (p. 581)
qualitative research (p. 581)
research design (p. 580)
research questions (p. 575)

shopper/buyer/consumer behavior
   models (p. 578)
survey research (p. 580)

Review Questions

Note: You can find the correct answers to these questions by taking the quiz and then submitting your answers in the Online Edition. The program will automatically score your submission. If you miss a question, the program will provide the correct answer, a rationale for the answer, and the section number in the chapter where the topic is discussed.

1. The first step of marketing research is to
   a. identify the research problem or opportunity.
   b. select the shopper/buyer/consumer behavior model to guide the research.
   c. select the research design.
   d. select the data collection method.

2. Research questions are guided by
   a. market selection decisions.
   b. product development decisions.
   c. pricing decisions.
   d. all of the above.

3. What is the difference between information needs and research questions?
   a. Information needs are more abstract than research questions.
   b. Information needs are directly deduced from marketing decisions.
   c. Research questions are directly deduced from information needs.
   d. All of the above.

4. Important marketing research steps that mostly pertain to the study of shopper, buyer, and consumer behavior are
   a. Developing the research questions, selecting the shopper/buyer/consumer behavior model to guide the research, and selecting the research design.
   b. Developing the research questions, selecting the data collection method, and selecting the research design.
   c. Developing the research questions, developing the research instruments, and collecting the data.
   d. Selecting the shopper/buyer/consumer behavior model to guide the research, selecting the research design, and analyzing the data..

5. What does selecting a suitable shopper/buyer/consumer behavior model to guide the research process mean?
   a. The model helps interpret the data.
   b. The model helps generate specific hypotheses related to the research questions.
   c. The model helps with the selection of the research design.
   d. None of the above.

6. What are the three types of research design?
   a. survey, experimental, and exploratory
   b. nomothetic, idiographic, and exploratory
   c. quantitative, qualitative, and correlational
   d. none of the above

7. Survey research involves
   a. the construction of a questionnaire.
   b. collecting qualitative data.
   c. conducting an experiment.
   d. conducting a focus group.

8. Experimental research involves
   a. the construction of a questionnaire.
   b. collecting qualitative data.
   c. the manipulation of one or more variables.
   d. collecting quantitative data.

9. Exploratory research involves
   a. collecting qualitative data.
   b. the use of convenient samples.
   c. using small samples.
   d. all of the above.

10. Idiographic research involves
    a. the construction of a questionnaire.
    b. conducting an experiment.
    c. collecting qualitative data.
    d. the manipulation of one or more variables.

Team Talk

1. Your team is working for Ford. Ford wants to target young drivers, ages 16–18, and the company wants to design a new car for this target market. Research is to be conducted to identify automobile characteristics that would be highly appealing to that target market. What shopper/buyer/consumer behavior model would you use to assist in this research? Discuss this with your teammates and justify your model selection in the best way you can.

2. Your team is hired by the owner of a local restaurant. The owner wants to make changes to the restaurant to increase patronage. She thinks marketing research is a good idea to help identify possible changes. What shopper/buyer/consumer behavior model would you use to guide this research? Discuss your choice.

3. The owner of a local clothing boutique hires your team. He is convinced that targeting career women who are somewhat overweight may be the way to develop the business. The owner needs help with developing an ad campaign involving local television, radio, and newspaper. He does not know what images, symbols, and messages to use in the ad campaign. Discuss with your team how research could be conducted to identify those images, symbols, and messages. What shopper/buyer/consumer behavior model can be used to guide this research? Discuss your choice.

4. Your team is asked to consult on the marketing of a new software package that is targeted to the leaders of professional associations. The goal of this software is to allow association secretaries to process membership applications, conference registrations, and order publications, all on the Internet. Doing this would result in a reduction of paperwork processing and save considerable money. How would your team advise the software developer to market this innovation? What information needs do you have? What are the research questions? Discuss your decisions.

5. Using the Question 4 example, have the team discuss potential shopper/buyer/consumer behavior models that can be used to answer the following question: How will executive directors of professional associations likely evaluate the new software? What decision criteria are they most likely to use?

6. Examine the diffusion of innovation model described in Chapter 18, section 18-2c. Suppose your team decides to use this particular model to answer the following research question: How will executive directors of professional associations likely evaluate the new software described in Question 4? What research design can be used for this kind of research? Discuss your answers.

7. Examine the model described in Chapter 18, section 18-1c (Roles of Organization Members in the Decision-making Process). Suppose your team decides to use this particular model to answer the following research questions: Who in the professional association is most likely to identify the need for the new software described in Question 4? Who is most likely to establish specifications? Who is most likely to make the purchase? Who is most likely to identify buying alternatives? Who is most likely to evaluate alternative buying actions? Who is most likely select the supplier? Have your group discuss a plan of study to answer these questions.

8. Your team is hired to provide advice on how to deal with shoplifting in a franchise sporting goods store. The marketing manager wants to find ways to discourage shoppers from shoplifting. His idea is to put up signs throughout the store counter arguing against the mental justifications shoplifters commonly use to sustain their illicit practice. What shopper/buyer/consumer behavior model can be used to conduct research to identify methods? Discuss your choice.

Workshops

Research Workshop

A new bank is getting ready to open its doors in your community. This bank is different from other banks in the sense that it is community based—it is not part of a statewide or national banking franchise. It is somewhat like a credit union with the notable difference that the shareholders are community residents instead of employees of certain organizations. However, before setting a date to begin doing business, the bank wants to conduct research to answer the following question: Should the bank target a certain segment of the community? If so, what segment?

Plan a shopper/buyer/consumer behavior study that can effectively address this question.

Creative Workshop

Suppose the segment chosen for targeting is "committed community residents." These people are long-time residents of the community. Their extended family resides in the same community. That is, they have roots in the community. They identify with the community and feel that this place is their home, and it is the home of their grandparents, parents, children, and possibly grandchildren. Their family and kin have invested in many ways in the community. They have made financial contributions to local churches and community organizations, they have volunteered to help in those organizations, and so on.

Your task is to develop a study that can guide the promotion campaign for the community bank. What shopper/buyer/consumer behavior model would you use to help you formulate the promotion campaign? Once you select a model and justify its selection, go ahead and plan a study using that model.

Managerial Workshop

Still focusing on targeting the committed community residents, how would you go about designing the interior of the bank to appeal to that segment? What shopper/buyer/consumer behavior model would you use to help you plan a study that focuses on the interior design of the bank? Develop a plan for this study in the best way you can.

Ben & Jerry's

By M. Joseph Sirgy

A-1 The Company in General

Ben & Jerry's (http://www.benjerry.com) is a top maker of super-premium ice cream. The company was bought by consumer products giant Unilever (http:// www.unilever.com) in 2000. It sells ice cream, ice-cream novelties, and frozen yogurt with names such as Phish Food and Cherry Garcia. It also franchises or owns more than 230 Ben & Jerry's "scoop shops." Ben & Jerry's donates $1.1 million of pretax profits to philanthropic causes. Its markets include the U.S., Canada, Mexico, and Europe. Co-founders Ben Cohen and Jerry Greenfield created the company in 1978 in a renovated gas station in Burlington, Vermont.

A-2 Company Image

Ben & Jerry's Homemade, Inc. has an image of being independent, earthy, and hippie-like, an image ascribable to the company's founders, Ben Cohen and Jerry Greenfield. Over the years, Ben and Jerry made their brand of ice cream stand out by developing goofy flavor names (occasionally linked to their favorite musicians such as Jerry Garcia and Phish) and their stance on the environment.

A-3 Promoting the Environmental Cause

Now the company has been sold to Unilever, but the environmentalism cause remains linked with the brand name. For example, the most recent cause-related tie-in has been with the Dave Matthews Band. Matthews has put his own "green" philosophy on the new flavor, One Sweet Whirled, a play off his song "One Sweet World." The promotion campaign encourages the reduction of greenhouse gases. Marketers at Ben & Jerry's have held One Sweet World Interactive Events at Matthews' concert venues, offering tastes of the new product and giving information about how to help reduce global warming. The same information can be found on their website (www.onesweetwhirled.com). At the retail level, Ben & Jerry's is setting up "action stations" to encourage people to become active in the environmentalism movement. Portion of the sales go to a consortium called Save Our Environment, to green non-government organizations (NGOs) such as the Sierra Club (www.sierraclub.org) and to the World Wildlife Federation (www.wwf.org). To know more about the consortium, visit their website at www.SaveOurEnvironment.org.

It seems that Ben & Jerry's is countering the Bush administration's stance on the environment. The Bush administration has failed to sign the Kyoto Treaty, which puts pressure on governments to take measures to reduce toxic gas emissions. The same administration also has pushed hard to open the Alaskan National Wildlife Refuge to oil drilling, despite the fact that the majority of Americans want a cleaner and safer environment. According to a Gallup poll, 60 percent of Americans favor energy conservation, 72 percent support tougher auto emissions standards, 83 percent favor higher standards for corporate pollution, and 82 percent want tougher enforcement of environmental laws.[1]

A-4 Effectiveness of the Promotion Campaign

Who buys Ben & Jerry's One Sweet Whirled brand of ice cream? Most young adults and the baby boomers! This ice cream is essentially flavored with caramel, coffee, and marshmallow. American Demographics (www.demographics.com) reporter Matthew Grimm believes that Ben & Jerry's environmentalism campaign is not making much of a dent because the message is not reaching mainstream America.[2] He reports the results of a survey of the Gallup organization that tracked American consciousness of global warming, which indicated that consciousness of global warming rose from a low of 24 percent in 1997 to a high of 40 percent in 2000, but then fell to 29 percent in 2002. September 11 and the economic recession have made environmental issues an even lower priority since that time.

A-5 Using Music to Help Provide Aid Relief in Sudan

Jesse Brenner, a 23-year-old senior at Wesleyan University, studied abroad in Botswana in 2003 and came back to the U.S. determined to help people caught in the escalating ethnic violence in Darfur, Sudan. Brenner, with his friend Eric Herman, started Modiba Records, involving African music. The *Afrobeat Sudan Aid Project (ASAP)* is the label's first release, a compilation of African-beat music with 100% of the proceeds going to Kebkayiah Smallholders Charitable Society, a community group that helps the Sudanese find food and shelter.

Brenner approached Ben Cohen for startup funds. Cohen fronted Modiba the cash needed for production and legal costs (about $10,000), while Brenner secured the African artists through connections from his semester abroad and New York-based music organization Afropop Worldwide.

Then, iTunes, Apple's (http://www.apple.com) successful Internet music store, signed on as a pro-bono distributor. In one week right after the launch (in early December 2004), *ASAP* had already cracked the iTunes top 30 albums chart, sharing space with the likes of Shania Twain and U2.[3]

A-6 Other Elements of the Marketing Mix

The company is implementing what they preach to others. The company is evaluating its refrigeration systems to reduce CO_2 emissions; they are looking at alternative energy sources; and they encourage their own employees to buy and consume products in ways that can reduce CO_2 emissions.

Discussion Questions

1. One of the important consumer rights is the right to a healthful environment. Ben & Jerry's is a company that advocates sustainable consumption. How does it do this? Read the section on Consumer Rights in Chapter 16 and discuss your answer as it relates to the section.

2. Do you believe that business should be involved in advocating causes like sustainable consumption? How do you feel about cause-related marketing in general? Read chapters 16 and 17 and discuss your answer.

3. Do you believe that the Ben & Jerry's cause-related marketing campaigns are successful? Evaluate the campaign using the principles specified in the Communication and Persuasion chapter (Chapter 10).

Notes

1. Grimm, Matthews (2002). "Earthy Crunch," *American Demographics* (June), pp. 46–47. Newton, Well (2004). "Ben & Jerry's," Hoover's (http://www.hoovers.com/global/hoov.index.xhtml?pageid=10637&Editor=Nell+Newton&CoShortName=Ben+&+Jerry's+Homemade+Inc.&COID=12763).
2. Ibid.
3. Kurtz, Rod (2004). "A Startup's Songs for Africa: with Help from Ben & Jerry's Ben and Apple's iTunes, Two College Kids Use the Continent's Music to Aid Relief Efforts in Darfur, Sudan," *BusinessWeek*, December 2, 2004.

Bavarian Motor Works (BMW)

By Matt Crumley, Dana Lascu, Lisa Yers, Pascal Ontijd, Taylor Roberts, Kerrie Robinson, and Sean Wygovsky

Bavarian Motor Works, or BMW (http://www.bmw.com), is a leading global manufacturer of luxury automobiles. A high-priced, high-performance automobile, the BMW has long been a status product for consumers worldwide. Known as the "Beemer" to consumers in the United States and the "BMW" (pronounced Beh Em Veh) to most consumers in continental Europe, this automobile is a legend of style and class. One of BMW's greatest challenges is retaining its leadership position in the luxury automobile market—a challenge that has been recently compounded by the company's decision to diversify into the lower-priced automobile market. Recently, in one of its most daring moves, BMW successfully launched the MINI—a very non–BMW-like automobile, the progeny of BMW's ill-fated relationship with the British Rover group, known as the most beloved British car.

B-1 The Automobile Industry

The boom in the global economy in the late 1990s, coupled with increased consumer confidence, led to high growth in the automobile industry. Vehicle manufacturers were under pressure as never before to increase production, and the globalization of the industry posed further challenges with long-term structural changes for the industry:

1. Mergers and other strategic alliances led to a diminishing pool of independent manufacturers remaining in the industry.[1] Ford (http://www.ford.com) and DaimlerChrysler (http://www.daimlerchrysler.com) are likely to acquire additional companies, leading to the 2001 projection that by 2005, there would be fewer than ten international players in the automobile market.[2]

2. The Internet is also changing many aspects of the automobile industry. Consumers increasingly use it to research features, specifications, styles, and designs of numerous makes and models. Most importantly, consumers can use independent sources to precisely assess dealer profit and bargain successfully on price, adding to the downward pressure on price that the industry is experiencing. In addition, many websites offer detailed information about specific models, and it is predicted that consumers will eventually be able to circumvent dealerships and order automobiles from manufacturers via the Internet.[3] According to J. D. Power and Associates (http://jdpower.com), 62 percent of new automobile buyers surveyed in 2001 in the United States logged on to the Internet for information on their prospective purchases.[4]

3. Finally, there is a rising trend of automakers establishing a niche in the marketplace. These automakers are relying on new categories of vehicles that will expand the overall market. Chrysler's (http://www.chrysler.com) PT Cruiser sedan has proven to be especially popular, with demand exceeding supply.[5]

In the United States alone, sales of new cars and light trucks reached a record level of 17.4 million units in 2000—an increase of 500,000 units over the previous year's sales of 16.9 million automobiles.[6] The U.S. automobile market is the largest in the world for passenger vehicles.[7] However, with the downturn of the economy in 2001, sales volume fell 2.5 percent, to 16.92 million vehicles.[8] Globally, sales of new vehicles worldwide have also been projected to grow from 50.6 million units in 1998 to 57.2 million in 2005.[9] In Europe, automobile sales for 2001 surpassed the 14.7 million units recorded in 2000.[10]

B-2 The Company

Karl Rapp created BMW in 1913 as an aircraft engine design shop just outside Munich, the capital of the state of Bavaria, Germany. The name of the shop was Bayerische Motoren Werke (Bavarian Motor Works). At the end of World War I, German aircraft production declined drastically, and the company began producing railway brakes. BMW made its first motorcycle in 1923, and the company began making automobiles in 1928 after purchasing a small automobile manufacturing company. Larger automobiles were added to the product line in 1933, but in 1941 the company stopped automobile production to produce aircraft for the German air force. Following World War II, the production of automobiles and motorcycles resumed. Over the remainder of the decade, the company expanded through acquisitions, and, in 1986, it began producing luxury vehicles. Sales rose. In 1992, BMW outsold Mercedes in Europe for the first time ever.[11]

Currently, the BMW headquarters constitute a Munich landmark, reigning in its imposing three-cylinder building just outside the Middle Ring (the Middle Beltway) as the city's tallest structure.

BMW Group products are currently in greater demand worldwide than ever before. The fiscal year for 2000 held the record for deliveries, sales, and profits, with net income recorded at $966.1 million.[12] BMW pursues a premium brand strategy and concentrates on markets with above-average growth potential and high margins; with this strategy, BMW sales rose an additional 7 percent in 2001, and sales are expected to grow at a faster pace than the overall market because consumers who typically purchase luxury cars are not affected as much by recession.[13]

B-3 Communicating Excellence at BMW

BMW developed the Herbert Quandt Foundation to promote the company's social involvement. The Herbert Quandt Foundation fosters national and international dialogue and mutual understanding between business, politics, and society. In addition, the foundation organizes a range of important events to bring together the leaders of industry and society. BMW focuses on environmental sustainability, understanding that oil is a limited resource and other forms of energy need to be explored. BMW is currently introducing a new 7 Series powered by hydrogen, and the company continues to use much of its research and development resources to explore solar-powered alternatives. But BMW's social consciousness goes beyond the environment. In addition to just traffic safety, BMW focuses on social development issues such as intercultural learning, sponsorship of gifted students, and other educational programs.[14]

In addition to its foundation, BMW spreads the word of its excellence in other forums. It is present at the North American International Auto Show in Detroit and the Frankfurt Auto Show. It also sponsors the BMW International Open, one of the most important golf tournaments, and the BMW Golf Cup International. It is also a presence in the Formula 1 Racing circuit.

BMW has national websites in Austria, Belgium, Czech Republic, Denmark, Ireland, Estonia, Finland, France, Germany, Greece, Great Britain, Hungary, Italy, Lithuania, Netherlands, Norway, Portugal, Russia, Sweden, Switzerland, Spain, and the Ukraine. Also, it covers nineteen countries in the Americas, three in the Middle East, nine in Asia, and in South Africa, Australia, and New Zealand. Its website offers insights into its long-standing tradition of innovation and quality. One of its sites, www.bmwfilms.com, offers a display of quality in the form of five different short films with action-packed mini plots. Its automobiles are placed in James Bond movies, and its "Ultimate Driving" message is widely known.

BMW offers zero-percent financing and reasonable leasing structures to penetrate the lower income market. Also, it prides itself on continuous customer service with credit, personal banking, credit cards, and insurance.[15] BMW also offers a protection plan, certification, and roadside assistance on all new and used BMW automobiles for most consumers in developed countries. Finally, BMW facilitates buying by offering a program that allows the buyer to customize his or her own car on the website and have it delivered without the buyer even leaving home.

B-4 The BMW Driver

Although BMW has many different types of consumers, a certain type of person tends to purchase its vehicles: upper middle class and upper class professional males. BMW has recently seen an increase in its female customers.[16] Baby boomers are the primary consumers, as they tend to have the most money to spend. In fact, consumers aged 35–44 account for more new vehicle sales dollars than any other group.[17] Over the years, BMW has sought to target young professionals who are well-educated, usually college graduates.[18] Recently, however, BMW has widened its target market. It now caters to single, male executives, to families with children, and to older couples.[19] Also, with the addition of the 3 Series, it is attempting to attract the "20-something" generation.

BMW's superior design and quality attract consumers who are very safety conscious but who are also seeking the status of owning a BMW. BMW's sleek styling also attracts consumers who are style conscious. With the introduction of the 3 Series, a more affordable automobile, BMW has seen a decrease in the average age of its consumers.[20]

B-5 All Things BMW

The company offers a full line of automobiles for a large variety of luxury market segments: It produces sports cars, family cars, performance machines, and a variety of non-car products. BMW's introductory automobile is a BMW 3 Series. The company has a 5 Series targeted at the mid-luxury market and offers a 7 Series for the high-end luxury automobile buyer. BMW also offers sports cars, SUVs, and other vehicles.

The 3 Series BMW, its introductory automobile, is offered as a sedan, coupe, convertible, touring car, and a compact, with 4–8 cylinders and a choice of gas or diesel fuel. Safety is also a key concern in any BMW car, and the 3 Series BMWs have a variety of safety features, including special headlight adjustments, multiple airbags, and special braking systems.[21] [The manufacturer's suggested retail price (MSRP) for these cars ranges from $27,100 to $42,400.[22] A typical 3 Series BMW could be considered a 325 Series four-door vehicle. The price tag of this car usually runs $27,100. The BMW has as standard features a 2.5L, 6-cylinder, and 184-horsepower engine with a 5-speed transmission, ABS brakes, front and rear antiroll bars, a multilink suspension, rack and pinion steering, front- and rear-vented brakes, sixteen-inch alloy rims, and a full-size spare. Standard safety features include side impact bars, driving lights, a full gauge panel, multiple airbags, and a security system.[23]

The BMW 5 Series is its mid-price offering. A sedan and a touring car are the options available in the 5 Series. These vehicles are also offered in a 4-cylinder engine with a choice of fuel consumption. Safety and design are enhanced for this series. The sophisticated safety system includes crumple zones, airbags, and tire pressure controls, among others.[24] MSRP ranges from $35,950 to $39,450.[25]

The top-of-the-line BMW is the 7 Series. This high-end vehicle is available in an 8-cylinder, 6-speed transmission. Safety and the ultimate in luxury are the key components in this vehicle. The car comes with a very sophisticated safety system that utilizes fourteen sensors to maintain safety and comfort.[26] MSRP for this automobile ranges from $67,850 to $71,850.[27]

BMW also offers a variety of additional vehicles such as sports cars and sports utility vehicles (SUVs). The BMW Z3 is its sports car. The automobile is available in a coupe or roadster with a 4- or 6-cylinder engine. Safety features include impact safety absorbers, electronic ignition immobilizer, and smart airbags.[28] MSRP ranges from $31,300 to $37,900 for this BMW.[29] The X5 is the BMW performance SUV, available in the normal X5 and the X5 4.6is. The normal X5 comes with a 6-cylinder engine, while the X5 4.6 is available with a powerful 8-cylinder engine. Safety features include a high-impact body shell, head and side airbags, and a sophisticated braking system.[30] The MSRP ranges from $38,900 to $66,200.[31] The BMW Z8 is the ultimate in driving performance, offering the highest quality and performance of any of BMW's products. The car comes with an electronic-start 8-cylinder engine that is completely electronically controlled. This BMW is a high-performance computer-run car.[32] The MSRP for this car is around $130,000.[33]

BMW also produces M Series stock vehicles with "muscle" as the main function. These high-performance machines are made especially for those individuals searching for very high performance, safety, and design. Suspension, wheels, brakes, exhaust, and engine components are all modified to increase performance to its highest level. The M series is available as an M3 coupe, M3 convertible, M5 sedan, M coupe, or an M roadster.[34] MSRP for these driving machines range from $44,900 to $69,990.[35]

BMW also has an array of other products introduced in an attempt to decrease the cyclical aspect of automobile retailing and increase diversification. BMW offers eleven different types of motorcycles that are used for a variety of purposes, including touring, racing, street, and off-road use. Prices range from $8,000 upward to $30,000. BMW also offers a full line of motorcycle and car apparel and accessories. Clothes, bikes, and other similar products are all offered by the company.[36]

The automobile manufacturer also offers financial services, BMW driver training, BMW international Direct and Corporate Sales, BMW ASSIST, and sponsorships. The company makes information available such as split-screen maps, digital road maps, and drivers' assistance programs. BMW also produces a C1, similar to a covered motorcycle, which is used in crowded cities to move in tight places. It is also involved in the comeback of the MINI as it reaches for world markets.[37]

B-6 Competition within the Luxury Automobile Segment

According to numerous websites,[38] comparing luxury automobiles with prices between $40,000 to $60,000 reveals that the BMW 5 Series lives up to the slogan "the ultimate driving machine"—it is spacious, comfortable, responsive, powerful, and safe, though its options are very expensive. In comparison, the Mercedes E class is more fuel efficient than the BMW; it is large, comfortable, among the safest in the automobile industry; and it handles well although not in snow. The Lexus GS is also more fuel efficient than the BMW; it is comfortable, reliable, and quite luxurious; and it fits its slogan, "Passionate pursuit of perfection." It has rear-wheel drive, which needs getting used to, and its options are also expensive.

For automobiles with a price range from $30,000 to $40,000, the BMW 3 Series is very responsive; it accelerates quickly, brakes well, and has smooth steering, but it also has rear-wheel drive, which may pose a challenge, and it is quite loud. The Mercedes C (http://www.mercedes.com) class is less fuel efficient, but it provides a safe and quiet ride. The Lexus ES (http://www.lexus.com) has a firm front-wheel drive; it is luxurious, spacious, and reliable, but its extra options are expensive.

In terms of market performance, BMW's sales rose 15 percent through November 2001, vaulting it into second place among luxury automobiles in the United States. BMW sales jumped over Mercedes-Benz, which held the third spot in 2002. Mercedes-Benz has been slumping since 1998, when the company completed its merger with Chrysler, forming DaimlerChrysler. Toyota Motor Corporation's Lexus held the number-one slot in the U.S. market in 2002.[39] There is fierce competition among the luxury automobile makers, and focusing on such factors as customer service, price, and new product innovations will help BMW outperform its competitors.

B-7 Targeting to Lower-Price Segments: The MINI and the Certified Pre-Owned BMWs

B-7a A Truly Unique Car: "The MINI puts a smile on your face."

With the March 2002 introduction of the MINI to the United States, BMW hopes to gain a share of the small and compact car market. Targeting a high-tech and high-style consumer, the MINI features heated mirrors, a computer navigation system, an air-conditioned glove box, rain-sensing windshield wipers, and an eight-speaker premium stereo.[40] The very "Euro-looking" MINI also features bright, flashy colors and a hard top that is of a different color. The wide range of colors and options gives each owner the opportunity to personalize it.

The BMW Group's 2000 Annual Report states, "Through the MINI brand, the BMW Group will further enhance its appeal to young and modern customers. With its emotional character, the MINI is tailored precisely to these target groups and meets the growing demand for premium offers also in the small car segment."[41] The MINI has fared well in Europe. The drivers, typically young, urban, and trendy, find the MINI easy to drive and park in congested cities and appreciate the high kilometer to gasoline liter ratio.[42] The MINI is quite small, under 12 feet long, and 4 feet 7 inches tall; with its doors open, it is wider than it is long.[43] BMW hopes to lure the same segment that Volkswagen did so successfully with its new Beetle.[44]

BMW hopes not only to woo new customers, but also to bring back current owners of the larger BMW cars. The Annual Report states, "The MINI will give BMW Group an excellent position in the small car segment in the future, especially as a MINI is the ideal second or third car for the BMW driver and other customers in existing BMW segments."[45] The price is right for many consumers at $16,850 to $19,850, less than half the price of the standard size BMW.[46]

BMW sells the MINI through MINI franchises, which do not carry the BMW name; any dealers that are approved to carry the MINI have to provide separate facilities for the automobiles.[47] In addition, the car itself will not show the BMW logo but will have a separate MINI logo.

B-7b Problems with the MINI

In an effort to reach bargain-conscious consumers, BMW provides the MINI at an exceptionally low price. Serious concerns have been raised about the quality of the MINI and the fact that it is associated with the BMW name. Brand name dilution may be a serious future concern. BMW owners typically desire luxury and status; however, with the MINI being so price competitive, it is possible that many who cannot afford to purchase a BMW will purchase a MINI to be a part of the BMW family of cars. On the other hand, "as a luxury brand, if you lower your price range, it gets more risky," says Wendelin Wiedeking, president and chief executive of Porsche AG. "Exclusivity is very much related to price."[48]

More problems with the MINI have arisen in the company's international markets. A recall of 500 MINIs took place after workers noticed sparks while fueling vehicles.[49] More than 6,500 vehicles were retrofitted in order to correct the problem, costing BMW more than $508,000.[50] These types of setbacks have the potential to inflict damage to a prestigious brand name. "People are watching the MINI launch very carefully," said John Lawson, an analyst at Schroder Salomon Smith Barney. "They need to be convinced that the MINI will be a high-quality product and will be sensitive to anything that suggests it is not."[51]

B-7c The Certified Pre-Owned BMWs

In 2002, BMW focused its advertising efforts on its Certified Pre-Owned vehicles. The Certified Pre-Owned BMW is given a warranty and a series of checks in order to be classified as Certified. With this new push toward selling used cars, BMW might again be risking a dilution of brand image with luxury-conscious consumers. Making the BMW name a more affordable prospect to more segments of the population may reduce the prestige and luxury appeal of a BMW. In addition, continuous advertising of a pre-owned vehicle can lessen the brand name in the eyes of prestige-conscious consumers.

Discussion Questions

1. As you analyze this case, focus on segmentation and the targeting strategy used by BMW in marketing the MINI and the Certified Pre-Owned BMW.
2. How is the BMW positioned in the consumer's mind? Describe the typical BMW driver, using psychographic and demographic variables for the description. What leisure activities does this driver engage in? What are the driver's hobbies? What magazines does this driver subscribe to?
3. What strategy suggestions would you offer to BMW to ensure that the MINI and the Certified Pre-Owned BMW do not dilute the BMW brand?

Notes

1. "Worldwide Automotive Database and Forecasts," *International*, London, Second Quarter 2000, pp. 165–271.
2. "Passenger Cars, ATVs, RVs and Pick-ups in the USA (July 2001)," www.euromonitor.com.
3. Ibid.
4. "Autos & Auto Parts Industry Survey," *Standard & Poor's*, December 27, 2001.
5. Ibid.
6. "Passenger Cars, ATVs, RVs and Pick-ups in the USA (July 2001)," www.euromonitor.com.
7. "Autos & Auto Parts Industry Survey," *Standard & Poor's*, December 27, 2001.
8. Ibid.
9. "World Vehicle Industry Prospects to 2005," *Motor Business International*, London, Third Quarter 1999, pp. 88–100.
10. Michael Robinet, "The Mixed Scene in Europe," *Automotive Design & Production*, Cincinnati, February 2002, Vol. 114, No. 2, pp. 24–25.
11. www.hoovers.com.
12. Ibid.
13. Beth Reigber, "Companies: BMW Says Sales," *The Wall Street Journal Europe*, January 29, 2002.
14. More information about the Herbert Quandt Foundation can be found at www.herbertquandtstiftung.com.
15. A complete list of financial services can be found at http://www.bmw-financialservices.com/international/index.html.
16. "Passenger Cars, ATVs, RVs and Pick-ups in the USA (July 2001)," www.euromonitor.com.
17. Ibid.
18. "BMW" Encyclopedia of Major Marketing Campaigns.
19. Ibid.
20. "Passenger Cars, ATVs, RVs and Pick-ups in the USA (July 2001)" www.euromonitor.com.
21. www.carsDirect.com, Research Center, February 25, 2002.
22. www.bmw.com, Products, February 25, 2002.
23. www.carsDirect.com, Compare Vehicles, February 25, 2002.
24. www.bmw.com, Products, February 25, 2002.
25. www.carsDirect.com, Research Center, February 25, 2002.
26. www.bmw.com, Products, February 25, 2002.
27. www.carsDirect.com, Research Center, February 25, 2002.
28. www.bmw.com, Products, February 25, 2002.
29. www.carsDirect.com, Research Center, February 25, 2002.
30. www.bmw.com, Products, February 25, 2002.
31. www.carsDirect.com, Research Center, February 25, 2002.
32. www.bmw.com, Products, February 25, 2002.
33. www.carsDirect.com, Research Center, February 25, 2002.
34. www.bmw.com, Products, February 25, 2002.
35. www.carsDirect.com, Research Center, February 25, 2002.
36. www.bmw.com, Products, February 25, 2002.
37. Ibid.
38. Information is taken from the following web pages: www.epinions.com, www.caranddriver.com, www.newcartestdrive.com, www.auto.com, www.edmunds.com, and www.autoweb.com.
39. Bill Koenig and Jeff Green, "High-end Cars," December 11, 2001.
40. Gregory White, "High Style in a Tiny Package," *The Wall Street Journal*, October 17, 2001.
41. BMW Group AG, 2000 Annual Report.
42. White, "High Style in a Tiny Package," October 17, 2001.
43. Ibid.
44. Terry Box, "Got Your Eye on a MINI?" The Dallas Morning News, January 26, 2002.
45. BMW Group AG, 2000 Annual Report.
46. Box, "Got Your Eye on a MINI?" January 26, 2002.
47. Ibid.
48. White, "High Style in a Tiny Package," October 17, 2001.
49. Suzanne Kapner, "BMW Faces Setback with Its Entry into Small Car Market," *The New York Times*, September 4, 2001.
50. Ibid.
51. Ibid.

Campina

By Dana Lascu[1]

Campina (http://www.campina.com) is one of the leading dairy companies in the world and one of the few that produces only dairy products. A European company that remains close to its Dutch roots, Campina's image evokes picturesque Dutch cow pastures and healthy lifestyles. The company's history can be traced to Southern Holland in the Eindhoven area; a dairy cooperative with the name "De Kempen" was created in 1947 and used the brand name "Campina." In 1964 the cooperative merged with another cooperative in the Weert region in Holland and formed Campina (named after a regional moor—its meaning is "from the land"). After several consecutive mergers—more recently, with Melkunie Holland—Campina Melkunie (or Campina, as it is informally known) became the largest dairy cooperative in the Netherlands.

In the Netherlands alone, Campina boasts 7,500 member dairy farmers. The farmers own the cooperative: Campina must buy all the milk the farmers produce, while the farmers must finance the cooperative and, in return, the farmers obtain a yield of the products sold. Campina itself is a nonprofit organization. Member farmers receive all the company profits. They have voting rights in the company that are proportional to the amount of milk they deliver, and they are represented by the Members' Council, the highest managerial body of the cooperative.

The separation between Campina, the operating company, and its cooperatives is evident: Campina is headquartered in Zaltbommel, in an industrial park in Southern Holland, while the dairies are located close to the consumers they serve, in different areas of the country.

C-1 Industry Trends

Consolidation is a dominant trend of the dairy industry. The number of dairy companies is falling, and the production capacity of those that remain is increasing and becoming more efficient.[2] Despite the bad news, there are still companies that exist successfully in the $100 million to $200 million range of sales, surviving through a mix of ingenuity and innovation.[3]

The European Union remains the world's top dairy producer, manufacturer, and trader of dairy products. Of the world's top twenty-five dairy organizations, fourteen have their headquarters in Europe.[4] Because the EU is a mature dairy market, the emphasis is on value growth and processing milk into products with high added value.[5] As such, Campina's strategy and general mission, "adding value to milk," fits well with this trend.

The degree of concentration varies significantly, however, from region to region. In Scandinavia and the Netherlands, a handful of major cooperatives dominate. In Greece, there are more than 1,000 dairy businesses, of which more than 700 make cheese. In Germany, the industry has changed from numerous small, localized firms to most milk processors either collapsing or merging. In France, the top five dairy businesses control 55 percent of milk production. And in Scandinavia, the major players wield even more control: in Denmark, MD Foods (http://www.mdfoods.dk) and Klover Maelk control 95 percent of milk production, and in Sweden, Arla (http://www.arlafoods.com) handles 80 percent.[6]

Another important trend is the focus on convenience (a packaging issue) and on value-added nutrition for functional foods (a product ingredient issue). Changes include creating new packaging and unique containers for innovative products. For example, German-based Schwalbchen Molkerei (http://www.schwaelbchen-molkerei.de) has debuted Go! Banana, the first milk-energy drink made from fresh milk and real, pureed bananas, packaged in 330-ml Tetra Prisma cartons with fluted sides. Spain's Pascual Dairy (http://www.lechepascual.es) offers milk-based energy drink Bio Frutas in two flavors: Tropical and Mediterranean. German milk processor Immergut (http://www.immergutrocken.de) has introduced Drinkfit Choco Plus, a vitamin-fortified, chocolate-flavored milk, in the same carton. The United Kingdom company Miller (http://www.miller.co.uk) offers dual-compartment, side-by-side containers of refrigerated yogurt, while a new drinkable fruit yogurt from Nestle SA (http://www.nestle.com) debuted in the United Kingdom under the name Squizzos, sporting Disney Jungle Book characters in a triangular-shaped package that is easy to tear, squeeze, and drink.[7]

Cheese is also presented in innovative packaging. Baars, a subsidiary of the BolsWessanen Group, a United Kingdom Dutch company, launched a smooth, flavorful medium/mature cheddar cheese, named Maidwell, that does not crumble; it is sold in an attractive, innovative, clear-plastic, resealable pack. Rumblers, a convenient all-in-one breakfast product manufactured by Ennis Foods Ltd., United Kingdom, is also available in an innovative package that holds cereal and fresh, semiskimmed milk separately, all in one pack.[8]

Functional ingredients (health foods or ingredients that enhance the nutritional value of products) represent yet another important trend in the dairy industry: Dairy products represent the most important sector, accounting for 65 percent of sales in a sector that is very buoyant, given the consumer interest in health and diet.[9] The leading companies in Europe in this domain are Campina Melkunie (Netherlands), Nestle (Switzerland), and Danone (France) (http://www.danone.com).[10] Worldwide, Japan leads in the functional foods trend and is the only country with a regulatory policy on such foods, FOSHU (Foods for Specified Health Use).[11] There is a tradition of lactic acid bacteria culture drinks and yogurts in Japan, and many of these fermented drinks and yogurts contain other functional ingredients, such as oligofructose, calcium, and DHA, which is a polyunsaturated fatty acid derived from fish oil that is said to improve learning, lower blood pressure, help prevent cancer, and lower serum cholesterol.[12] And from Dairy Gold, Australia, comes Vaalia Passionfruit Smoothie, a low-fat milk-based drink containing 25 percent fruit juice, acidophilus and bifidus cultures, and insulin.[13]

C-2 Meeting Competitive Challenges at Campina: Adopting a Market Orientation

Historically, milk production has been supply driven, and excess milk was used to produce cheese and powder milk; this strategy led to excess cheese/commodities on the market and the need for subsidies. Campina initiated a change in this practice. In the past fifteen years, the company has been demand driven: Farmers are assigned production quotas that they are not allowed to exceed.

In other attempts to adopt a market orientation, Campina decided to eliminate all milk powder production because milk powder is a low-margin commodity. Instead, the company is focusing on building the brand to ensure recognition by consumers as a value offering and as a quality brand name.

According to R. J. Steetskamp, Director of Strategic Business Development at Campina, the company examines consumer behavior to determine where to fit Campina products in consumers' lives. As such, Campina offers four categories of products:

1. **Indulgence products.** This category constitutes an important growth area for the company. Campina produces numerous milk-based desserts, with the exception of ice cream—primarily due to the product's seasonality and the logistics strategies involved in the transportation and storage of ice cream, which differ from those for the rest of the company's offerings.

2. **Daily essentials.** This category includes Campina products that shoppers purchase routinely, such as milk, buttermilk, yogurt, coffee cream, butter, cheese, and others. Campina, using a strategy employed by all its competitors, also sells daily essentials under dealer (store) brands, rather than under its own brand name. For example, in Holland, it sells milk, plain yogurt, butter, Gouda cheese, and vla (chocolate or vanilla custard) under the Albert Heijn brand name. Albert Heijn is a dominant, quality supermarket chain in Holland that is owned by Royal Ahold—a large conglomerate that also owns supermarket chains in the United States (BI-LO, Giant, and Stop & Shop). The company also sells daily essentials under dealer brands in Germany.

3. **Functional products.** According to Mr. Steetskamp, this product category needs to be further explored and defined by the company. In this category are health foods and other milk-based nutritional supplements sold to consumers. DMV International is a Campina division that is present all over the world; it produces pharmaceutical products, food ingredients, and ingredients used to enhance the nutrition of consumers and their pets, such as proteins and powders with different functions. All these products are milk-based, and many of them are well known. For example, Lactoval is a popular calcium supplement.

4. **Ingredients (food and pharmaceutical ingredients).** This product category is targeted at other food product manufacturers, rather than at the individual consumers. The primary purpose of the food and pharmaceutical ingredients is to enhance the quality, taste, texture, and/or nutritive content of the products manufactured by Campina's clients. The company's Creamy Creation unit specializes in blending dairy and alcohol to make various cream liqueurs, leading to both healthy and indulgent drinks. In this category fall meal replacement drinks and high protein drinks as well. With this category, Campina becomes a supplier to other manufacturers, rather than a product manufacturer distributing to supermarkets.

C-3 International Expansion at Campina

One of the most important undertakings at Campina in the last decade was to expand beyond the Netherlands. In its first expansion effort, the company bought Belgium's Comelco, another dairy cooperative. In Belgium, the company boasts the Joyvalle dairy products and milk brand and the Passendale, Père Joseph, and Wynendale cheese brands, all marketed under the Campina umbrella brand.

Campina expanded into Germany, purchasing a number of cooperatives, including Sudmilch (Southern Germany), Tuffi (Western Germany), and Emzett (Berlin). In Germany, its primary brand is Landliebe; here, the company sells Landliebe milk, cream, yogurts (seasonal, fruit, plain, and in different types of containers); different types of puddings including rice pudding, ice cream, cheese, and qwark (a traditional creamy cheese) plain or with fruit; yogurt drinks (with fruit flavors such as banana, cherry, lemon, peach, and orange); and different milk drinks with flavors such as vanilla and chocolate. The company also offers products such as coffee machines, cups, spoons, and others for purchase online at its site, www.landliebe-online.de. According to R. J. Steetskamp, the Campina name will be used as the umbrella brand for all the company products; the name comes from the Latin "from the land," and it is easily pronounced in all the different languages in Europe, the brand's target market. The only brands that will not be brought under the Campina umbrella brand, according to Mr. Steetskamp, are the Mona brand in the Netherlands and the Landliebe brand in Germany, because both have high brand franchise with consumers in their respective countries. Interestingly, the Landliebe brand name is close in meaning to Campina, both making reference to the land.

As a result of these acquisitions and mergers, according to Mr. Steetskamp, Campina is the market leader in Holland, Germany, and Belgium. As the company website states, "Campina is a household name in the Netherlands, Belgium and Germany."[14]

Campina has further expanded, with its own subsidiaries in the United Kingdom, Spain, Poland, and Russia, where it ultimately plans to use the Campina brand name (the Campina Fruttis brand is one of the most popular fruit yogurt brands in Russia).

Discussion Questions

1. One can argue that the consumption of dairy products is related to certain lifestyles. Develop your own lifestyle typology directly related to dairy products, and attempt to identify constellations of dairy products that correspond to each lifestyle segment.

2. In the U.S., the use of dairy products is likely to differ significantly by subcultures. Explain why, and provide examples.

3. Campina is expanding into new markets in different countries. It is essential to conduct consumer research in each country to adapt selected dairy products to the taste of the local culture. Describe a typical taste test conducted in the context of a specific local culture.

Notes

1. Case designed with input from Anne Carson, Todd Fowler, Kim Hribar, Liz Manera, and Brian Thoms.
2. Sarah McRitchie, "Europe Shrinks to Expand," *Dairy Foods,* January 1999, Vol. 100, No. 1, pp. 75–79.
3. Gerry Clark and Dave Fusaro, "Survival of the Smallest," *Dairy Foods,* August 1999, Vol. 100, No. 8, pp. 48–55.
4. Ibid.
5. Ibid.
6. McRitchie, "Europe Shrinks to Expand," pp. 75–79.
7. Ibid.
8. Ibid.
9. Ibid.
10. Ibid.
11. Donna Gorski Berry, "Global Dairy Food Trends," *Dairy Foods,* October 1998, Vol. 99, No. 10, pp. 32–37.
12. Ibid.
13. Ibid.
14. www.campina-melkunie.nl.

Royal Philips Electronics

**By Christianne Goldman, Ryan Ganley,
Dana Lascu, Leslie Ramich, and Akshay Patil**

D-1 Background

Royal Philips (http://www.philips.co.uk) is the world's third-largest consumer electronics firm, following market leaders Matsushita (www.mei.co.jp) and Sony (www.sony.com). The Philips brands include Philips, Norelco, Marantz, and Magnavox. The company was established in 1891 in Eindhoven, in the Southern region of the Netherlands, primarily as a manufacturer of incandescent lamps and other electrical products. The company first produced carbon-filament lamps and, by the turn of the century, it had become one of the largest producers in Europe. Later, the company diversified into many other areas, such as electronics, small appliances, lighting, semiconductors, medical systems, and domestic care products, among others. The company headquarters moved to Amsterdam in the 1980s, but its lighting division continues to occupy the center of Eindhoven.

Around the early 1900s, Philips started to diversify its offerings to radio valves and X-ray equipment, and later to television. Later in the century, Philips developed the electric shaver and invented the rotary heads, which led to the development of the Philipshave electric shaver. Philips also made major contributions in the development of television pictures, its research work leading to the development of the Plumbicon television camera tube, which offered a better picture quality. It introduced the compact audio-cassette in 1963 and produced its first integrated circuits in 1965. In the 1970s, its research in lighting contributed to the development of the PL and SL energy-saving lamps. More recent Philips innovations are the LaserVision optical disc, the compact disc, and optical telecommunication systems.[1]

Philips expanded in the 1970s and 1980s, acquiring Magnavox (1974) and Signetics (1975), the television business of GTE Sylvania (1981), and the lamps division of Westinghouse (1983). Currently, Philips operates in more than sixty countries, with more than 186,000 employees, and is the market leader in many regions for a number of product categories—for example, lighting, shavers, and LCD displays.[2]

In the 1990s, Philips carried out a major restructuring program and changed from highly localized production to globalized production; this change translated into a more efficient concentration of manufacturing—from more than 100 manufacturing sites to 36, and to 14 sites for production, including Juarez and Manaus in Latin America; Bruges, Dreux, and Hasselt in Western Europe;

Kwidzyn, Szekesfehervar, and Szombathelv in Eastern Europe; and Beijing, Suhzou, Shenzen, and Chungli (all in China) in Asia.

Another important change was the appointment of Gerard Kleisterlee as president of Philips and chairman of the Board of Management in 2001. Kleisterlee has been seen as a product of his Philips background, following a traditional Philips career path that had been embraced by company employees until the 1980s. He was trained locally, at the Eindhoven Technical University, in electronic engineering, and he has worked with the company for three decades. According to Martien Groenewegen, former research and development engineer with Philips, Kleisterlee is perceived by present and former employees as taking the company back to its original path to success. In fact, in a recent interview, Kleisterlee mentioned that the company is presently concentrating on its initial core activities with a focus on its key areas of profitability; this is a different type of restructuring from earlier attempts, when the company pursued "wrong activities."[3] Mr. Groenewegen contends that the perception among employees and the industry is that Philips, under Kleisterlee's leadership, will have a strong product orientation and that it will support an environment in which product innovation will constitute a primary focus of the company. That has been, historically, Philips' proven path to success.

D-2 Philips' Offerings

Philips offers consumer products, such as communications products (cordless phones, mobile phones, fax machines), electronics (Flat TV, Real Flat TV, digital TV, projection TV, professional TV, DVD players and recorders, Super Audio CD, VCRs, satellite receivers, CD recorders/players, home theater systems, Internet audio players, shelf systems, portable radios, clock radios, PC monitors, multimedia projectors, PC cameras, PC audio, CD rewriteable drives, DVD drives, among others); home and body care products (vacuum cleaners, irons, kitchen appliances, shavers, oral healthcare products), and lighting products. Its professional products include connectivity, lighting, medical systems (such as magnetic resonance imaging, ultrasound equipment, X-rays), semiconductors, and other products, such as security systems, manufacturing technologies, automotive products, broadband networks, and so on.

D-3 The Competition

Among Philips' competitors are Matsushita, Sony, Hitachi, and Thomson (http://thomson.net/EN/home). Matsushita Electric Industrial is the world's number-one consumer electronics firm. In North America, Matsushita makes consumer, commercial, and industrial electronics (from jukeboxes to flat-screen TVs) under the Panasonic, Technics, and Quasar brands. Matsushita sells consumer products (which account for 40 percent of sales) such as VCRs, CD and DVD players, TVs, and home appliances. It also sells computers, telephones, industrial equipment (welding and vending machines, medical equipment, car navigation equipment), and components such as batteries, semiconductors, and electric motors. The Matsushita group includes about 320 operating units in more than forty-five countries. Its products are sold worldwide, but Asia accounts for more than 70 percent of sales.[4]

Sony is another competitor. Their PlayStation home video game systems account for nearly 10 percent of the company's electronics and entertainment sales. Sony, the world's second-largest consumer electronics firm after Matsushita, also makes several other products, including semiconductors, DVD players, batteries, cameras, MiniDisc and Walkman stereo systems, computer monitors, and flat-screen TVs. The company's TVs, VCRs, stereos, and other consumer electronics account for more than 65 percent of sales. Sony's entertainment assets include Columbia TriStar (movies and television shows) and record labels Columbia and Epic. The company also operates insurance and finance businesses.[5]

Hitachi (www.hitachi.com), another large player in the consumer electronics industry, is a leading manufacturer of both electronics components and industrial equipment. The company manufactures mainframes, semiconductors, workstations, elevators and escalators, power plant equipment, and also metals, wire, and cable. Hitachi produces consumer goods, such as audio and video equipment, refrigerators, and washing machines. Similarly to Philips, Hitachi is focusing on developing Internet-related businesses and expanding its information technology units, which account for more than 30 percent of sales.[6]

Finally, Thomson Multimedia is another major competitor and leading manufacturer of consumer electronics (which account for nearly 80 percent of sales), including TVs, video cameras, telephones, audio products, DVD players, and professional video equipment. Thomson Multimedia also produces displays and TV components. Its products, which are sold in more than one hundred countries, include brands such as RCA in the United States and Thomson in Europe. Almost 60 percent of the company's sales are in the U.S.[7]

D-4 Philips' Brand Image

Philips' primary mission is to "continually enhance people's lives through technology and innovation."[8] This philosophy is also reflected in its tagline, "Let's make things better," launched in 1995.[9] Philips focuses on the multisensory impact of its products and their power to create memories and spur emotions to touch people's lives on a very personal level; Philips also aspires to be the world's leading eco-efficient company in electronics and lighting.[10]

While Philips is a household name in European markets, the company continues to struggle to spread brand awareness in the United States. As recently as 1996, the Philips brand was virtually unknown in the United States, compared with competitors Sony and RCA; the brand was associated with milk of magnesia, petroleum, or screwdrivers.[11] After spending millions to build brand awareness, Philips has successfully achieved recognition among consumers in the U.S. as a brand that makes exciting products that improve people's lives. In 1998, for example, Philips spent $100 million in advertising, sponsorships, movie tie-ins, and retail promotions worldwide to boost brand awareness.[12] In the same year, Philips embarked on its Star campaign in an attempt to create a more human, imaginative, and seductive brand image. Using

dynamic state-of-the-art products, the Philips campaign was able to reach consumers on a very personal level, thus gaining their trust, loyalty, and brand preference. The campaign resonated very well with its target market: well-educated, independent, and carefree consumers.[13]

Another venue for communicating with its target market is Philips' five-year sponsorship of the U.S. Soccer Federation as of June 2001. This sponsorship is also expected to help Philips reach more of its young target consumers and more female consumers. Philips thus has 30-second air spots on ABC and ESPN during soccer broadcasts, as well as a presence on stadium billboards and logo visibility on all training kits, and the Philips' branded goal cameras are highly visible.[14]

Apart from the need to generate awareness in the U.S. markets, Philips also recognizes the need for consolidation and consistency across all of its marketing communications worldwide. To this end, Philips awarded its $600 million account in media buying and planning to the Aegis Group's Carat International.[15] With Carat's help, Philips is attempting to

- Create a consistent brand experience that will give all products a shared look and feel and will demonstrate a deep understanding of the customer,[16]

- Become more consumer-focused and more brand-centric in its marketing efforts, expanding beyond its traditional television and print communications to direct marketing and more unconventional media,

- Create a total marketing package, which will resonate well with the U.S. consumer and therefore lead to increased U.S. sales,[17] and

- Engage in extensive direct marketing and Internet marketing; this is especially possible given Philips' alliance with AOL Time Warner.[18]

Discussion Questions

1. As stated in the case, Philips' primary mission is to "continually enhance people's lives through technology and innovation." The company's slogan is "Let's make things better." Philips focuses on the multisensory impact of its products and their power to create memories and spur emotions to touch people's lives on a very personal level; Philips also aspires to be the world's leading eco-efficient company in electronics and lighting. Suppose you are hired as a marketing researcher by Philips USA, and you are asked to develop a consumer measure that can capture Philips' brand image among U.S. consumers. Develop a proposal for such a measure.

2. Philips tries hard to demonstrate that it is a company that tries its best to develop products that improves people's lives. The focus is on quality of life. As a consumer researcher well-versed in consumer behavior, can you propose a measure for Philips that can allow them to measure and monitor the extent to which their products enhance the quality of life?

3. Philips has launched an aggressive promotion campaign in the U.S., spending many millions of dollars in advertising, sponsorships, movie tie-ins, and retail promotions. Assume that you are part of the marketing research team hired by Philips to gauge the level of effectiveness of the promotion campaign. Suggest possible concepts and measures to help the team collect data that test the level of effectiveness of the campaign.

Notes

1. Material available at www.philips.com.
2. www.philips.com.
3. Bill Griffeth, *Philips Electronics—CHM & CEO—Interview,* Dow Jones Business Video, January 9, 2002, p. 1.
4. Hoover's Online, www.hoover.com, February 19, 2002.
5. Ibid.
6. Ibid.
7. Ibid.
8. Jennifer B. Simes, "Philippines a Key Hub, Says Philips," *Computerworld Philippines,* Dow Jones Interactive, December 10, 2001, p. 1.
9. "Brand Building," www.philips.com, p. 1.
10. "A Serious Responsibility," www.philips.com, p. 1.
11. Michael McCarthy, "Philips Can't Lose with Puppies, Beatles," *USA Today,* www.usatoday.com, January 15, 2001, p. 2.
12. Tobi Elkin, "Building a Brand," *Vision Magazine,* www.ce.org/, July/August 1999, pp. 1–2.
13. See "Owning the Right Image," www.news.philips.com, p. 1, for a more extensive analysis of the Philips communication strategy.
14. Tobi Elkin, "Philips to Sponsor U.S. Soccer Games," Adage.com, www.adage.com, June 19, 2001, p. 1.
15. Tobi Elkin and Richard Linnett, "Media Moves Up," *Advertising Age,* ABI Inform, July 9, 2001, p. 2.
16. Message from the President, Annual Report 2001, www.philips.com, p. 2.
17. Elkin and Linnett, "Media Moves Up," p. 3.
18. Philips Mainstream Consumer Electronics Powerpoint presentation, www.philips.com.

Hilton Sorrento Palace

CASE

E

By Dana-Nicoleta Lascu

Two hours south of Rome, to Naples, by the Eurostar, the Italian high-speed train, and an additional hour west along the Bay of Naples via the Circumvesuviana regional railway is the town of Sorrento. The Hilton Sorrento Palace (http://www.sorrento.hilton.com) reigns high among the hills of Sorrento, overlooking Mount Vesuvius, the now dormant volcano (since 1944), which buried the towns of Pompeii and Herculaneum in the year 79 A.D.

Sorrento is a small resort town, well known throughout Europe, an ideal vacation destination for its picturesque location and mild weather. A favorite of British travelers, the town of Sorrento has 10,000 beds, according to Mr. Ziad Tantawi, director of business development at the Hilton Sorrento Palace. The Hilton Sorrento Palace is the largest of all hotels in the small resort town, with 383 rooms. Owned by the Sorrento Palace Gruppo, its owner since its year of construction (1981), the hotel became part of the Hilton chain in May 2001 and is now under Hilton management. One of the few hotels open in the winter in Sorrento, the Sorrento Palace boasts an average occupancy rate of 60 percent, with an average occupancy of 30 percent from November to March and more than 85 percent from May to October.[1]

The Hilton Sorrento Palace faces competition from bed and breakfasts. These family-run lodges are very popular because they are competitively priced at or below the room rates of leading hotels in the area. Most bed and breakfast accommodations are open year round. Sorrento is also a popular destination for cruise lines during the summer months. For cruise ship passengers, Sorrento offers easy access to the ruins of Pompeii, Mount Vesuvius, and the Isle of Capri. Overall, prices for cruise ships are higher than that of hotels, but cruise packages include meals and entertainment, as well as airfare to Italy.

Other local hotels compete directly with the Sorrento Hilton. The historic Europa Palace Grand Hotel (www.europapalace.com), for example, offers close views of the Bay of Naples and the cliffs of Sorrento.

E-1 The Hotel Offerings

The four-star Hilton Sorrento Palace is situated on a hill overlooking the town of Sorrento and the Bay of Naples, a short walk from downtown's busy tourist markets. Surrounded by residences and lemon and orange groves, the hotel is modern and elegant. One of its restaurants, L'Argumento, is situated amidst blooming cannas and orange and lemon trees. Another, Le Ginestre, has frescoes and elegant columns, and an indoor pool with a lush painted background. Its other four restaurants abound in blooming bougainvillea and oleander and have a splendid view of the Bay of Naples and Mount Vesuvius. The indoor lounge has excellent performers scheduled every evening and boasts a view of the city and the bay.

The executive lounge is situated on the top floor of the hotel and has a splendid view of the bay and town. It also boasts a swimming pool at the highest altitude in the region. The lounge serves complimentary food and drinks to executive guests and to gold- and diamond-level Hilton Honors members.

The hotel has a total of six outdoor swimming pools of different depths, flowing into each other, a tennis court, and a relatively well-equipped fitness center. Among the services offered at the hotel pool is the Hilton Kids Club: Every day, from 10 to 12 and from 2 to 4 in the afternoon, the Hilton kids can enjoy entertainment by the pool ("uno spazio giochi per bambini").

E-2 Marketing Strategies

The hotel's targeting strategies focus primarily on meetings: Its meeting space is one of the largest in Europe. The Centro Congressi (congress center) has a full range of rooms for conferences and conventions of any type or size, from the 1,700-seat auditorium to smaller rooms, a 2,300-square meter exhibition space, a banquet facility that can accommodate 1,000 people, and a parking facility that can accommodate 300 automobiles. In addition, the Centro also offers conference interpreting systems (six conference interpreting booths) and audiovisual presentation equipment, including a megascreen, making it an ideal venue for international events. About 65 percent of all hotel guests are conference participants. Hilton's sales offices in Italy (Milan) and overseas (in Germany, the United Kingdom, France, Sweden, and the Emirate of Dubai) are responsible for conference sales.

Tour operators constitute a second target group, accounting for 25 percent of the hotel's business. Their demand is highest in the months of July and August, when demand exceeds supply—Sorrento's location on the bay and up a steep hill does not allow for space that could accommodate additional hotels. Only 10 percent of the hotel's business comes from individual bookings, Internet bookings, and telephone bookings.

The Sorrento Palace's main target market is Italy. In addition, the hotel also actively targets groups from the United Kingdom, Germany, Belgium, France, and Japan—in that order, according to Mr. Tantawi. Visitors from the United States constituted an important presence at the hotel, particularly in the summer, in organized tours; however, since the terrorist attacks of September 11, 2001, demand has fallen sharply.

Mr. Tantawi would like to direct the hotel's marketing strategies to the United States. In particular, he would like to increase conference attendance at the hotel, as well as the number of tour groups and individual tourists in the off-season (November to March). At present, the hotel draws guests primarily from Italy and the United Kingdom. However, because European economies tend to follow a similar cycle, it is preferable for the hotel to diversify to other markets. Recently, the hotel has made extensive marketing attempts aimed at Japanese tour groups, with great success. Mr. Tantawi would like to find a way to bring in more tourists from the United States—especially conferences and tour groups.

Discussion Questions

1. Visit the website of Hilton Sorrento Palace at www.sorrento.hilton.com. Click on "Take a Tour of Our Hotel" and then click on the Photo Gallery. There will be images under Welcome, Accommodations, Meeting & Events, and Restaurants & Lounges. There should be a verbal description of each image, too. Your task is to evaluate the effectiveness of these images in the context of the hotel's overall website.

2. An important difference between the Hilton Sorrento Palace and other Hilton and competing hospitality properties is the reliance on the conference segment. How should the hotel market more effectively to this particular market segment through its website?

Note

1. Interview with Mr. Ziad Tantawi, Director of Business Development.

AvtoVAZ

**By Dana Lascu, Maria Vornovitsky,
and Ramil Zeliatdinov**

AvtoVAZ (http://www.gm-avtovaz.com/ru/index.php), or Automobile Factory of the Volga Region, also known as VAZ, was created in 1966 by the Soviet government. The government had as a goal to create a venue for the mass production of affordable automobiles for the Soviet consumer. The company was built by transplanting a defunct Fiat assembly plant from Italy to Togliatti, a small industrial town on the Volga River shores.

F-1 AvtoVAZ in the Soviet Era

AvtoVAZ's first car, the Zhiguli (better known in the West as the Lada), was built based on the Fiat 124, an automobile produced in Italy twenty years earlier. This first Lada was produced on April 19, 1970, and quickly became Russia's most popular passenger automobile.[1] Its first model was the VAZ 2101, which was endearingly called "kopeika" (the penny). It was considered to be of very high quality, and many of these models can still be seen on the road today. Russians were so infatuated with this automobile that there was a movie made titled *Kopeika,* dedicated to this automobile, illustrating the life of the car and its owners.

Over the years, the factory began to gain popularity as it strove to "supply Russian citizens with cars especially made for the tough Russian climate and harsh road conditions."[2] During the Soviet era, AvtoVAZ quickly grew and expanded its production of the Lada. It later introduced the Niva, a new model, in 1977, and the Samara, in the 1980s. These efforts allowed the company to move ahead of other Soviet automobile manufacturers AZLK, producer of the Moskvich, a higher-end automobile, and AvtoGAZ, producer of the Volga, an automobile used primarily for government officials and functions.

F-2 Post-Soviet AvtoVAZ

After 1989, the end of Soviet Communism brought drastic changes to the political and economic environment. In addition to the breakup of the Soviet Union, the drive toward a new market economy placed substantial pressure on the old state-owned enterprises. AvtoVAZ needed to implement important changes in order to continue to compete in the new transition economy and to operate successfully in an unstable economic environment. The company privatized immediately after the fall of Communism—it was the first automobile company in post-Soviet Russia to adapt to a market environment[3]—and promptly lost its former government pro-

tection. It also became a target of corruption and mismanagement. At first, the Yeltsin government turned a blind eye to conflicts of interest and theft by corporate managers to win support for policies such as privatization. Today, Russia and AvtoVAZ are paying the price: Companies are held hostage by networks that rob the government of tax revenues, soak up cash needed for industrial modernization, and fuel organized crime.[4]

In 1989, Boris A. Berezovsky, a management-systems consultant to AvtoVAZ, organized a nationwide car-dealership chain that would later bring him vast wealth; he persuaded AvtoVAZ chief executive Vladimir Kadannikov to supply him with automobiles without up-front payment. As hyperinflation raged in the early 1990s, Berezovsky earned billions of rubles, partly by delaying payments for AvtoVAZ cars.[5] When the company privatized, in 1993,[6] Kadannikov and Berezovsky set up a company, called the All-Russian Automobile Alliance, which gradually amassed a 34 percent stake in AvtoVAZ. Other AvtoVAZ managers and employees own 35 percent of the company, and Automotive Finance Corp., an affiliate headed by Kadannikov, holds an estimated 19 percent.[7]

Subsequently, trading companies mushroomed around AvtoVAZ, taking advantage of its need for parts and its poor distribution network. The companies swapped components for cars—straight from the factory—at prices as much as 30 percent below market value. Many traders took cars without prepaying, often waiting months before settling. By late 1996, some 300 trading companies were operating with AvtoVAZ. While they raked in millions of dollars in profits, they also owed AvtoVAZ $1.2 billion, about 35 percent of annual sales, for cars delivered to dealers.[8] Furthermore, organized crime became involved in AvtoVAZ, requiring payments equivalent to $100 per automobile to ensure safe delivery. The late 1990s, however, announced a new period for AvtoVAZ, one in which the company was forced to address these irregularities. These changes, along with a slowdown in rampant inflation, have helped the company turn around and have enabled it to explore new growth options through joint ventures.

F-3 AvtoVAZ Today

Currently, AvtoVAZ has a substantial part of the Russian automobile market. A high percentage of automobiles on Russian roads (70.31 percent, or 960,000 automobiles) are produced by AvtoVAZ, while only 13.02 percent are produced by its largest Russian competitor, AvtoGAZ. In provincial Russia, there are primarily just two makes of automobiles: the Zhiguli, by AvtoVAZ, which has about 60 percent of the market share, and the Volga, by AvtoGAZ.[9] AvtoVAZ exports more than 98,000 automobiles yearly.[10]

Even though AvtoVAZ operates less efficiently than its foreign competitors (it builds an automobile in 320 hours, whereas it takes an average of 28 hours to build an automobile at a typical European plant[11]), it is a perfect fit with the budget and aptitudes of the Russian consumer. AvtoVAZ touts itself as "optimal for the Russian market relationship between price and quality."[12]

Indeed, Russian automobile buyers spend an average price of $5,000 to $6,000 for a new Lada and have an interesting relationship to the automobile. For example, VAZ owners hardly ever use official dealer automobile services; instead, they prefer to use private garages, with self-taught mechanics. Russian automobile buyers are practical: They do not expect the automobile to function perfectly right off the assembly line; the automobile's performance problems are addressed by the private garages at a reasonable fee. Russians expect their brand-new Ladas to have some sort of defect; it is recommended that buyers take the car for tuning as soon as it is bought. The tuning typically consists of a complete change of transmission, some modification of the battery, and a complete change of brakes and tires.[13]

Russian buyers are not too concerned about design—their main consideration is price. Russians also make practical choices when it comes to automobile options: They prefer metallic color, which lasts longer; metal protection for the bottom of the car against winter damage; and rubber mats so that they do not have to vacuum the automobile often. Russian drivers value Ladas for their simplicity, which allows them to fix the automobile themselves; for their durability in withstanding tough climate and road conditions; and for their small size, which makes driving and parking in cities easier.[14]

AvtoVAZ is planning to introduce a new model, the Kalina, a cheaper car than the Lada; it will sell for about $4,000. However, the company has had difficulty raising the funds to develop the new car.[15]

F-4 VAZ Competitors

In spite of the popularity of its Lada model, AvtoVAZ is rapidly losing market share to foreign competitors. Used automobiles from Europe, especially from Germany, compete directly with the VAZ automobiles, and especially with its latest models—the 2110, 2111, and 2112. German automobiles continue to function without needing any repairs after four years of operation. In fact, without duties on imports of up to 100 percent, Russian automakers would be out of business. Even with the duties, more than 400,000 automobiles are imported yearly.[16] But important drawbacks to importing foreign cars are parts, which are expensive, and service; moreover, neither exists outside Moscow and St. Petersburg.[17]

Competitors such as Daewoo Corporation (Korea) (www.daewoo.com) and Skoda (Czech Republic) (www.skoda-auto.com) are also assembling cars in Russia,[18] creating additional competition for AvtoVAZ. General Motors and Ford are trying to set up assembly operations: GM to make 50,000 Chevy Blazers a year in Tatarstan, 700 miles from Moscow, and Ford to assemble 6,000 cars and vans near Minsk.[19]

Among Russian competitors, the worst of the local carmakers, AZLK (making the Moskvich) and truck maker ZIL, have practically shut down. The viable Russian competitors, truck maker Kamaz and GAZ, have seen production pick up in the past few years. The GAZ (Gorky Auto Works) factory complex was built in Gorky—known today as Nizhny Novgorod—in the 1930s, with help from Henry Ford. GAZ has a huge plant, with a capacity for 400,000-plus vehicles, including 300,000 medium-size trucks targeted to the military, agriculture, and industrial markets. GAZ has also created a light truck, the Gazelle, targeted toward Russia's new small businesses. The GAZ passenger car is the Volga, targeted initially for government use, which maintains its 1970s looks.[20] As the company is changing its focus from production to profits as its principle, the price of the Volga has been raised, which ultimately has hurt sales (its price is now close to that of many foreign automobiles); consequently, spare capacity was switched to making the more profitable light trucks and minibuses.[21]

Soviet planners decided to build the largest truck factory in the world: They built the Kamaz plant along the Kama River in Tatarstan, near the Urals. Kamaz covers 50 square kilometers with foundries, an engine plant, and an assembly line theoretically capable of producing 150,000 big trucks a year. (For comparison, the entire U.S. heavy truck market is about 150,000 in a normal year.) The fall of Communism led to a plummeting production, and the company was ripe for restructuring; costs were cut so that Kamaz would produce just 25,000 to 35,000 units a year, and the firm Deloitte & Touche was hired to keep the books and suggest improvements. The firm Kohlberg Kravis Roberts agreed to raise $3.5 billion over six years in exchange for 49 percent of Kamaz; the money was used to develop a new 25-ton truck for the oil and timber industries—a tractor trailer capable of competing with the best from abroad, with a diesel engine from Cummins (of the U.S.), a transmission from ZF (of Germany), and a cab from DAF (of the Netherlands)—and a light truck to challenge the Gazelle. Kamaz is also moving into passenger cars, with a microcar, the 30-hp Oka, which sells for $3,500. Kamaz loses $1,000 or so per automobile, but its goal is to be profitable at 50,000 units.[22]

The last of the still-healthy Russian carmakers is UAZ. It makes off-road utility vehicles and small buses, for a total of 93,000 yearly. Its designs date back to the 1970s. The company has limited working capital.[23]

F-5 The AvtoVAZ—GM Joint Venture

General Motors and the European Bank for Reconstruction and Development, whose mission is to finance economic development projects in Eastern Europe, have created a new opportunity for AvtoVAZ: a $340 million joint venture to manufacture off-road vehicles in Togliatti. GM owns a 41.5 percent stake in the joint venture and invested $100 million; EBRD has a 17 percent stake, has invested $40 million, and is lending an additional $100 million; and AvtoVAZ contributed manufacturing facilities and intellectual property valued at $100 million, for a 41.5 percent stake. The new company produces the new GM-branded Niva, aiming for a maximum yearly output of 75,000 vehicles, of which more than half are built for export.[24] The new Niva is sold in Western Europe and to markets in Africa, Asia, Latin America, and the Middle East, where the old Niva was popular.[25] In Germany, the Niva will be equipped with engines from Adam Opel.[26]

The joint venture is attempting to maintain the price of the new cars below $10,000 (still beyond the reach of most Russian automobile buyers), but this requires dependence on domestic components; and lack of these in sufficient volumes and at required quality levels have previously set back plans by Ford (U.S.) and Fiat (Italy) to produce for the Russian market.[27]

The Niva sport-utility vehicle looks very attractive and has an impressive design. However, Russian consumers, in addition to balking at its price, still perceive it as being of lower quality: The automobile is assembled on the VAZ platform by VAZ workers. Also, the automobile body is produced at VAZ facilities—not at new GM facilities—so the Niva buyers do not expect the finished automobile to be superior or last longer than the Niva ancestor, the VAZ 21213.

Discussion Questions

1. Discuss the positioning strategies of the different competitors in the Russian market.

2. Are Russian owners of AvtoVAZ satisfied with their cars? Discuss.

Notes

1. www.vaz.ru.
2. www.vaz.ru.
3. www.vaz.ru.
4. Carol Matlack, "Anatomy of a Russian Wreck," *Business Week,* September 7, 1998, No. 3594, p. 86b.
5. Ibid.
6. www.vaz.ru.
7. Matlack, "Anatomy of a Russian Wreck," p. 86b.
8. Ibid.
9. Ben Aris, "A Tale of Two Car Companies," *Euromoney,* January 2002, Vol. 393, pp. 24–25.
10. "GM's Russian Partner," *Manufacturing Engineering,* February 2001, Volume 126, No. 2, pp. 20–22.
11. Matlack, "Anatomy of a Russian Wreck," p. 86b.
12. www.vaz.ru.
13. www.avtoreview.ru.
14. www.avtoreview.ru.
15. Aris, "A Tale of Two Car Companies," pp. 24–25.
16. Jerry Flint and Paul Klebnikov, "Would You Want to Drive a Lada?" *Forbes,* August 26, 1996, Vol. 158, No. 5, p. 66.
17. Ibid.
18. Matlack, "Anatomy of a Russian Wreck," p. 86b.
19. Flint and Klebnikov, "Would You Want to Drive a Lada?" p. 66.
20. Ibid.
21. Aris, "A Tale of Two Car Companies," pp. 24–25.
22. Flint and Klebnikov, "Would You Want to Drive a Lada?" p. 66.
23. Ibid.
24. "GM Seals AvtoVAZ Deal," *Country Monitor,* July 16, 2001, Vol. 9, No. 27, p. 8.
25. "GM's Russian Partner," *Manufacturing Engineering,* February 2001, Vol. 126, No. 2, pp. 20–22.
26. "GM Seals AvtoVAZ Deal," *Country Monitor,* p. 8.
27. "Auto Investment," *Country Monitor,* February 19, 2001, Vol. 9, No. 6, p. 2.

Disneyland Resort Paris

By Dana Lascu and Jessica DiTommaso

G-1 The Challenge

Disneyland Resort Paris (http://www.disneylandparis.com) was known as Euro Disney in its first incarnation on the European continent. After its launch in April 1992, many name changes were made with the purpose of distancing the company from bad publicity.[1] After four different name revisions, the Disney Corporation has settled on Disneyland Resort Paris.

The idea of expanding the Disney magic to Europe proved to be a project that involved more attention to marketing than even this advertising giant could handle. Many Europeans did not want the American dreamland to distract their children, economy, and country from their own home-grown successful entertainment. David Koenig, author of *Mouse Tales: A Behind-the-Ears Look at Disneyland,* commented, "To the Parisian intellectuals, Disneyland was a symbol of everything contemptible about America: artificial, unstimulating, crass, crude, for the masses. Yet here was a 5,000-acre Disneyland springing up half an hour from the Louvre."[2]

From the very beginning, the Disney Corporation had the best of intentions for its European operation. After a successful opening of Disneyland Tokyo, the company was ready for its next international challenge. The company believed that locating the theme park in close proximity to Paris, France, would both ensure growth for Disney and offer an opportunity for it to incorporate different European cultures. It envisioned a Discoveryland that incorporated the histories of European countries through its fairytales: Italy for Pinocchio, England for Alice in Wonderland, and France for Sleeping Beauty's chateau.[3]

G-2 Marketing Failure

As Euro Disney, the company failed in many aspects of its marketing strategy:

- Euro Disney failed to target the many different tastes and preferences of a new continent of more than 300 million people; addressing the needs for visitors from dissimilar countries, such as Norway, Denmark, Germany, on one hand, and Spain, Italy, and France, on the other, was a challenge.
  - Disney's admission costs were 30 percent higher than a Disney World ticket in the United States, and the company refused to offer discounts for winter admissions.

- Euro Disney ignored travel lifestyles of Europeans: Europeans are accustomed to taking a few long vacations, rather than the short trips that would better fit with the Disney model.[4] The company also neglected to consider national holidays and traditional breaks when Europeans are more likely to travel.
- Euro Disney's restaurants did not appeal to visitors. Morris Nathanson Design in Rhode Island was responsible for designing the restaurants for Euro Disney. The company designed classic American-style restaurants. American-style restaurants are considered by most Europeans as exotic and unusual; unfortunately, the Europeans did not respond well to this format.[5]
- Euro Disney assumed that all Europeans wanted gourmet meals, which is not the case. While French consumers tend to live a more lavish lifestyle and spend larger amounts for gourmet meals, many other consumers in Europe do not—especially when they have to also spend large amounts on air travel, resorts, and park entrance fees. Meal scheduling was also problematic: the French, for example, are accustomed to having all businesses close down at 12:30 for meal times, but the park's restaurants were not made to accommodate such large influxes for meals, leading to long lines and frustrated visitors.[6] Finally, Euro Disney initially had an alcohol-free policy, which did not fit with local traditions, where wine is an important part of the culture.

G-3 New Strategy

Disney's failed marketing strategy for Euro Disney led to below-average attendance levels and product sales; the park was on the edge of bankruptcy in 1994, with a loss per year of more than a billion dollars.[7] Changing strategies—as well as its name, to Disneyland Resort Paris—has recently led to increased revenues of more than 4 percent, with operating revenues increasing by $32 million to $789 million.[8] Net losses have also decreased from $35.4 million to $27.6 million.[9]

With a full-scale change in the company's marketing direction, Disneyland Resort Paris has been successful in attracting visitors from many countries. Access was a priority for Disney. The company worked on access to the park via the fast train—the TGV; it also worked deals with the EuroStar and Le Shuttle train companies.[10] Disney has worked deals with trains and airlines to reduce prices—a move that ultimately benefited all; the price for transportation to Disney has dropped by 22 percent since the park's opening.[11] In 1992, the Walt Disney Company negotiated with Air France to make Air France the "official" Euro Disney carrier.[12] For visitors from the United Kingdom, British Airways is the preferred carrier of Disneyland Resort, and British Airways Holidays, its tour subsidiary, is the preferred travel partner.[13]

Disney also adapted targeting strategies to individual markets to address the interests and values of different segments of European consumers. It placed representatives around the world with the task of researching specific groups of consumers and creating the best package deals for potential visitors; the new Disney offices were established in London, Frankfurt, Milan, Brussels, Amsterdam, and Madrid.[14] Research results led to the tailoring of package deals that were in line with vacation lifestyles of the different European segments. In addition to the package deals, Disney offered discounts for the winter months and half-price discounts for individuals going to the park after 5:00 P.M.

To better accommodate its guests, Disneyland Paris revised its stringent no-alcohol policy, allowing wine and beer to be served at its restaurants. The resort hotels also lowered their room rates and offered less expensive menu choices in their restaurants.[15] The restaurants created more suitable food options, catering to different regional European tastes, but continued to offer large American-size portions.[16] Crepes and waffles are on the menu of almost every street stand in the park.

Names and accents changed as well. Mickey Mouse and Donald Duck have French accents, and many rides were renamed to appeal to French visitors: in Adventureland, Le Ventre de la Terre (Galleries under the Tree), l'Ile au Tresor (Treasure Island), La Cabane des Robinson (Robinsons' Cabin); in Fantasyland, Le Chateau de la Belle au Bois Dormant (Sleeping Beauty's Castle, rather than Cinderella's Castle at Disney World, United States), Blanche-Neige et les Sept Nains (Snow White and the Seven Dwarfs), Le Carrousel de Lancelot, Le Pays des Contes des Fee (the Country of Fairytales); and in Discoveryland, L'Arcade des Visionnaires, Le Visionarium (a time-travel adventure with Jules Verne), Les Mysteres du Nautilus (Nautilus's Mysteries).

The French-named attractions exist alongside attractions such as Main Street U.S.A., with its Main Street Station, vehicles and horse-drawn streetcars, and Frontierland, with Thunder Mesa River Boat Landing, Legends of the Wild West, Rustler Roundup Shootin' Gallery, and other similar themes. The hotels also have more traditional American themes—New York, Newport Bay, and Sequoia Lodge.

The park also has numerous attractions that appeal to European guests in general, such as Pinocchio's Fantastic Journey, and Cinemas Gaumont, which feature live concerts with performers from around the world.

Along with creating an environment of greater appeal to European visitors, Disney changed the name of its resort to Disneyland Resort Paris. In its advertising strategy, the company decided to focus its efforts on brand building, initially targeting consumers with a new communication strategy implemented by Ogilvy & Mather Direct.[17] Disney changed its advertising, aiming its message at Europeans who did not grow up with Mickey Mouse; in the park's new commercials, parents and grandparents are shown delighting in the happiness of their children and grandchildren.

The advertisements feature "children impatient to depart for and thrilled to arrive at the Magic Kingdom or a grandfather delighted by his grand-daughter's excitement at the prospect of seeing Mickey; or grown-ups sitting tensely before riding on the Space Mountain."[18] The park is also working with Red Cell, a leading Paris-based advertising agency, for all its television campaigns for the park's new attractions.[19]

Disney is capitalizing on its recent European success by offering yet another grand theme park adjacent to Disneyland—the Walt Disney Studios. Disney is attempting to promote Walt Disney Studios in a manner that would not cannibalize attendance at Disneyland Paris.[20] Among its attractions are a Rock'N'Roller Coaster Starring Aerosmith, capitalizing on the U.S. band's success in Europe; Animagique; and Cinemagique. The park is dedicated to the art of cinema, animation, and television, and it focuses on the efforts of many Europeans who made it all possible to bring fantasy to reality.

Discussion Questions

1. How do the values and lifestyles of European consumers differ from those of consumers in the United States? Discuss the Disney failure to address European consumers' preferences based on the respective values and lifestyles.

2. A large proportion of the park's visitors come from Spain and Latin America. How can Disneyland Resort Paris appeal more effectively to this market? Design a new target marketing strategy aimed at the Spanish and Latin American market.

Notes

1. Harriet Marsh, "Variations on a Theme Park," *Marketing*, London, May 2, 1996.
2. David Koenig, Mouse Tales: *A Behind-the-Ears Look at Disneyland.* Irvine, CA: Bonaventure Press, 1994.
3. Ibid.
4. "Euro Disneyland SCA," *International Directory of Company Histories*, Vol. 20, pp. 209–212.
5. Gail Ghetia, "As American as French Fries: Euro Disneyland, When It Opens, Will Feature Typically American Restaurants," *Restaurant Hospitality*, August 1990.
6. "Euro Disneyland SCA," pp. 209–212.
7. "The Kingdom inside a Republic," *The Economist*, April 13, 1996.
8. Juliana Koranteng, "Euro Disney Revenues Rise," *Amusement Business.* August 6, 2001.
9. ——— , "Future May be Bright for Euro Disney," *Amusement Business,* May 21, 2001.
10. "Euro Disneyland SCA," pp. 209–212.
11. Marsh, "Variations on a Theme Park."
12. Ibid.
13. Barbara J. Mays, "French Park Still Negotiating for Airline Partnership," *Travel Weekly*, April 20, 1992.
14. "The Kingdom inside a Republic," *The Economist.*
15. Barbara Rudolph, "Monsieur Mickey: Euro Disneyland Is on Schedule, but with a Distinct French Accent," *Time*, March 25, 1991.
16. Ibid.
17. Marsh, "Variations on a Theme Park."
18. "The Kingdom inside a Republic," *The Economist.*
19. Juliana Koranteng, "Taking It to the Tube: Parc Asterix to Unleash National TV Campaign," *Amusement Business*, February 11, 2002.
20. Koranteng, "Euro Disney Revenues Rise."

AgeLab

By M. Joseph Sirgy

H-1 Aging

The world's population is aging rapidly (see Exhibit 1). The 50+ population is the fastest-growing segment worldwide, and predicted life expectancies are at a historical high. Consider the following statistics and predictions:

- An American turns 50 once every seven seconds.
  - Within the next few years, 50% of the European Union's population will be 65+.
  - By 2030, in Italy, retirees will outnumber active workers.
- By 2050, the median age ·in Thailand will rise to 50.

With advances in medicine, public policy, and technology, people are not only living longer, but many are living better. Today's older adults are more educated and engage in more activities than previous generations, including work, leisure, learning, and other pursuits. The modern face of aging is one that expresses vitality and commands a greater quality of life. We must look at the demands of this population with open minds to new opportunities for innovation. Innovations from government, business, and research created for the older population will ultimately benefit all ages. An aging society is the opportunity to invent the future of healthy, active living.[1]

H-2 The University Research Center

Professor Joseph Coughlin of the AgeLab (http://stuff.mit.edu/afs/athena/dept/agelab) at the Massachusetts Institute of Technology (MIT) is a professor of management and specializes in developing products and services catering to the elderly. AgeLab is a partnership between MIT, industry, and the aging community. Its mission is to engineer innovative solutions of problems that can enhance the quality of life of the elderly.

H-3 Health and Personal Wellness Research Projects

Scientists at AgeLab are developing a lightweight "space suit" for the elderly that can monitor their health and help them move without walkers. The space suit is also designed to protect them from falling by cushioning their fall impact. But one wonders why would the elderly be interested in buying a space suit? Professor Coughlin argues that the baby boomers are now turning elderly. One estimate puts the size of this market at 78 million consumers. Compared to

Exhibit 1

Percent of the Population Age 60 and Over, 2000–2025

	2000	2025
Africa	10.6%	15%
Asia	14.3%	25.3%
Europe	19.8%	28.8%
Former USSR	16.5%	25%
Latin America and Caribbean	7.7%	14.5%
North America	16.5%	25%
Oceania	13.5%	20.7%

its predecessor, the baby boomer generation grew up with high tech products and services. Therefore, a space suit is likely to appeal to the baby boomer generation turned elderly. This is a good example of developing products and services as a direct function of understanding the needs and motives of target consumers.[2]

H-4 Projects Related to Transportation Services

Another example of developing products and services designed to enhance the quality of life of the elderly is public transportation services. The baby boomer generation grew accustomed to driving their own vehicles. But what happens when they can no longer drive? Will they turn to public transportation? If so, is the public transportation system available in the towns and cities where they reside adequate for their needs? How do business marketers and public officials in the many communities throughout the U.S. address this demand? Professor Coughlin believes that transportation is the No. 1 problem that should be addressed with a sense of urgency. The challenge is to provide an alternative solution to the car, especially in the suburbs. The vast majority of people (and, yes, the baby boomers) live in the suburbs and rural areas, which typically do not have public transportation services. One solution is a regional shuttle service. Elderly baby boomers would call this service from their cell phones, personal digital assistants, or cable TV, and have that vehicle pick them up in half an hour. Today, many older adults have to book a ride 24 hours in advance, and today's van services for the elderly are often not reliable. Professor Coughlin estimates that there is a 1 in 5 chance that the van won't show up. This kind of service makes today's elderly feel hostage in their own homes. Going out for a cup of coffee or to visit a friend is a major undertaking full of risks and pains.

H-5 Projects Related to Assisted Living

Consider another problem—falling down and needing assistance. Or perhaps needing assistance getting something down from a shelf or moving something heavy. Today's elderly live with others or in assisted-living communities because they know they can count on others being around when and if they need physical assistance. Professor Coughlin envisions more comprehensive personal emergency response systems. The elderly needing assistance can click on a pendant or wristwatch that taps into a support system. The support system may involve a virtual service collaborator that brings service providers together in a network that may use the Internet as a base. This system would allow companies to offer all kinds of services to the elderly, not only emergency physical assistance but also nutrition with health monitoring and food shopping, among others.

H-6 Projects Related to Shopping

What about shopping at the grocery store and needing to select food items that won't exacerbate health problems such as high blood pressure, diabetes, and other diseases common to the elderly? Can the elderly shop with devices that can assist them in identifying food items that may not adversely affect their health condition? The problems are many, but so are possible solutions. These solutions can be marketed to the elderly by businesses whose mission is to enhance the quality of life of the elderly. For more information about AgeLab and its research, go to http://web.mit.edu/agelab.

Discussion Questions

1. The AgeLab caters to a particular consumer segment—the aging baby boomers. Who are the baby boomers? Please describe them.

2. Product development in the AgeLab is guided by the concept of quality-of-life marketing. Read about this concept in Chapter 17, and describe the concept in some detail. Compare and contrast AgeLab's approach to product development with the traditional marketing approach.

3. Describe the types of innovations launched by the AgeLab (refer to the Diffusion of Innovations section in Chapter 18).

4. Can you predict the rate of diffusion for each of AgeLab's innovations?

Notes

1. AgeLab (http://stuff.mit.edu/afs/athena/dept/agelab).

2. "Futurespeak: Science's Potential to Create New Markets," *American Demographics* (May 2002 issue), p. 49.

S. C. Johnson Company

By M. Joseph Sirgy

I-1 The Company

S. C. Johnson (http://www.scjohnson.com), formerly Johnson Wax, is a private, "family company." It makes and markets a broad array of household goods under the Fantastik, Saran, and Edge brands, among others. Beginning in 1886 as a parquet flooring company, the company earned a reputation for consumer-driven innovation through a product specially formulated to care for parquet floors—Johnson's Prepared Paste Wax. The company passed through five generations of the Johnson family. Today the company has more than 9,500 people in nearly 70 countries.[1]

I-2 Corporate Mission

The corporate mission is stated as follows:

- *Employees*—We believe our fundamental strength lies in our people.
- *Consumers*—We believe in earning the enduring goodwill of the people who use and sell our products and services.
- *General public*—We believe in being a responsible leader in the free market economy.
- *Neighbors and hosts*—We believe in contributing to the well-being of the countries and communities where we conduct business.
- *World community*—We believe in improving international understanding.[2]

Family Values

Family values are the kind of values that promote the propagation of families, family nurturance, and healthy communities. Families are said to make up the basic unit of society, not the individual. Social critics argue that many of our social ills (crime, violence, sexual promiscuity, and rampant materialism) are directly and indirectly related to values that promote the individual self over and above the family. Family values are the kind of cultural values that are high on the American list of ideal cultural values. Politicians tout themselves as standing up for family values. Churches, synagogues, mosques, temples, and other places of worship lay claim to the notion that family values are at the heart of good society, humanity, and the spiritual life. Companies that position themselves as representing family values are successful in creating an aura of trust and commitment. One such company is the S. C. Johnson Company.

I-3 Advertising Campaign

S.C. Johnson has run many advertising campaigns such as those for the Pledge Grab-It mop and Ziploc. One of their ad campaigns touts "family values" in which Mr. Johnson (great grandson of the company's founder and chief executive over the period of its great expansion) emphasizes the fact that the company is not only family-owned but also is dedicated to serving the family. He says, "in many ways taking care of one's home is just like taking care of a family, and we've never lost sight of that."[3]

I-4 Packaging

The company emphasizes the notion that they are a family company by promoting family values not only in their advertising but also in their packaging. The company's name is on the package of every product with a tag identifying S. C. Johnson as "A Family Company." Reinforcing the customers' image of a family company standing up for family values is a good marketing strategy. Matthew Grimm reports that the company's own consumer research showed that 80 percent of Americans considered products from family-owned companies trustworthy, versus 43 percent who say the same of those from publicly traded companies.[4] This image breeds trust, which in turn affects customer loyalty and commitment. More recent research conducted by S .C. Johnson showed that 62 percent of surveyed adults said their trust in large family companies has stayed the same during the recent corporate scandals, while 21 percent said their trust has decreased. Compare these figures with those for public companies. The same survey showed that 33 percent said their trust has remained the same for public companies, while 61 percent said it has declined.[5]

I-5 So?

The moral of this story is that the promise of a good brand is a reflection of the people behind it. Consumers make attributions about the quality of the brand and the company service aspects based on their image of the people behind that brand, especially corporate executives. The more they feel they trust these people, the more they feel the company products and services are of high quality and that the company's representatives can be trusted to deliver on their promises.

Discussion Questions

1. How does S. C. Johnson position itself in the minds of its consumers?

2. Read the discussion pertaining to traditional and emergent American values in Chapter 12. Do you think it is a good idea to promote a company and its product line based on family values in this modern age in the U.S.?

Notes

1. The website of S. C. Johnson Company (http://www.scjohnson.com).

2. Ibid.

3. Grimm, Matthew (2002). "Voice in the Wilderness." *American Demographics* (October), pp. 46–47.

4. Ibid.

5. Ibid.

BlackBerry

By M. Joseph Sirgy

J-1 The Product

A BlackBerry (www.rim.net) is a portable two-way email device, a cigarette pack-sized wireless product with a built-in keyboard that enables users to send and receive text messages. Its larger handheld units include Internet browsing and phone capabilities. The name "BlackBerry" has become almost shorthand for wireless email itself. The addictive little device, introduced in early 1999, defies many of the stereotypes of high tech. The brand has become the industry standard. Every major carrier (e.g., Sprint, T-Mobile, and Nextel) offers a BlackBerry to its customers. The core product is essentially email that is automatically pushed to the BlackBerry as it's going to the desktop. Email can be instantly answered with an intuitive, thumb-operated keyboard.

J-2 The Company

The BlackBerry is produced and marketed by Research in Motion (RIM) Limited (http://www.rim.net). RIM is a designer, manufacturer, and marketer of innovative wireless solutions for the worldwide mobile communications market. BlackBerry is one of RIM's award-winning products. The company is reported to have made $594.6 million in sales in 2004, a 93.9% 1-year sales growth. RIM is located in Waterloo, Ontario, a quiet university town of 99,000 about an hour's drive west of Toronto. The University of Waterloo plays a very strong role in the town and in the business, as RIM is the largest industrial employer of co-op students.

RIM was founded two decades ago to consult and develop technologies like the film bar-code readers that won technical awards. It had 2,223 employees as of December 2004. Everyone wants to work there. The stock price roared from $12.75 to $108 in 2004.

J-3 The People behind the BlackBerry

The brains behind the BlackBerry are the co-chief executives of RIM—Mike Lazaridis and Jim Balsillie. Lazaridis and Balsillie, both in their mid forties, are the quiet men behind the hottest wireless email gadget around. Lazaridis was born in Turkey but grew up in Windsor, Ontario, across the border from Detroit. He later dropped out of college to build an industrial display network for General Motors Corp. Balsillie is a tradesman's son from rural Ontario who was very successful in college and Harvard Business School. Lazaridis' stake in RIM is worth $782 million; Balsillie's stake comes to $674 million.

Lazaridis is a science buff who once won a special award from his public school for checking every science and math book out of the library. "Science is the core of everything, yet we take it for granted," he says. Lazaridis is the mastermind behind the BlackBerry, the inventor, the dreamer, and the engineer. He frequents physics lectures and read books like *Sojourner: An Insider's View of the Mars Pathfinder Mission*. In contrast, Balsillie is the business maven who as a young father mortgaged his house and poured much of his net worth into the company back in 1992. Balsillie is the ultimate corporate strategist, the controller, the negotiator, and the public face of the company.

In an interview with *Business Week* magazine, Lazaridis described how he came about creating the BlackBerry. He said, "We started working with wireless email really early. When I was at university in the early 1980s, I had access to what became the Web. I had an email address from the day I left university, but the addresses were hard. You had to describe the path that you wanted the email to go through—what's called the hops. Nowadays, it's all done automatically. I think the fact that I had a fax number and two email addresses put us ahead of accepted business practices at the time. But I knew there was an opportunity there. We had a LAN in our office. We had the first PCs in town that had disk drives in them in 1984/85. We brought in laser printers when they first came out. As soon as I found an affordable laser printer—at around $5,000—I bought it. In 1987, I went to a trade show and saw a company called DoCoMo. They were talking about a wireless data network they put in Tokyo to monitor Coke's vending machines, so the trucks didn't have to spend so much time driving around the city. The vending machines could call out for stock. I thought, wow, there is value here. Within a few months, I get a call from a company called Cantel that had bought this wireless data system called Mobitex and needed a consultant to come and look at it. I was so personally motivated. I saw there was no competition in this area. We always had this email in our head. One of the first products we did for Ericsson [a cell phone manufacturer and client of BlackBerry's] was send electronic mail over the radio. What excited me was 'push email' and trying to make that work wirelessly. But it was incredibly hard. There were a whole series of innovations we had. What kept driving us was the value. Sure, you can come up with cool stuff, but that's just a dot-comism. Business is about searching for value. It took us years of evolving this and redeveloping it and, at the same time, we were watching the market catch up. We realized these things had value when people were taking these big clunky things home, and we asked why. They said: So I can keep in touch."

Both Lazaridis and Balsillie are building a legacy beyond the BlackBerry. Lazaridis donated about $100 million (Canadian) in stock to start Waterloo's Perimeter Institute for Theoretical Physics. He says, "I've been interested in physics since I was in public school. Just the idea of the energies involved, the different scales—the universe, gravitation, black holes, lasers, quantum mechanics. If you have any active imagination, you can get carried away with this. When I got to university, I noticed that science had gotten so advanced that it lost its apparent relevance to day-to-day life. Without an active investment to make it more relevant, it would almost become like a forgotten art. How many jobs are there really for physicists in the world? Someone struggles through to get his PhD, then post-doc, and then maybe he'll struggle through to get an associate professorship. Yet so much discovery comes from those fundamental physics discoveries. But we didn't understand the connection between physics discoveries and our way of life. The time scales are too long. A business investment cycle is anything under three years. A government cycle is under eight years. Education cycles are generational—10 to 20 years. That's still too short. The stuff we are using today really didn't get commercialized for years. Semiconductors didn't get commercialized until the middle of the last century, but the quantum mechanics that led to the discovery of semiconductors happened around the turn of the last century. That's a 50-year lag. I recognize it's shortening, but the problems are getting harder. You need to understand the cycle, believe in it, and support it. I found myself in a position where I'm able to support it. Philanthropy is important. There are a lot of people in a position to do it who haven't."

Balsillie, in turn, gave $30 million to start the Centre for International Governance Innovation.

J-4 The Consumer Market

RIM launched the BlackBerry in 1999 as an enterprise product, the same time email became critical in the functioning of every organization. If RIM had launched the BlackBerry any earlier, the company would have been trying to sell two things: the value of email and the value of wireless access to that email. The market demand was in place for a wireless email device, and the BlackBerry filled that market niche. "We were the first company to come up with two-way communications devices where you had a thumb keyboard that actually worked," says Lazaridis.

The BlackBerry is marketed to organizations, not individual consumers. Organizations can afford it. Effective communication drives business. Miscommunication or lack of communication costs companies in many ways. The BlackBerry facilitates communication—effective communication. Thus, for most companies, the return on investment in having their employees communicate effectively (using BlackBerries) is very high. Information is disseminated immediately.

The consumer market is exploding. With added features like voice, color screens, and international roaming, the consumer market, which doubled by the end of 2004, to 2 million, could easily continue to grow exponentially. On Apr. 7, 2004, RIM reported that its subscriber base increased by 24%, to almost 1.1 million. The market will continue to grow as RIM tries to make the BlackBerry more affordable. Lazardis says, "We already know the value of BlackBerry. The trick is now to change the value equation so that we have a larger audience for it. We want more people to take advantage of it."

J-5 Competition

The BlackBerry faces competition ranging from pocket PC devices to similar handhelds put out by Good Technology, Inc., which just settled a patent lawsuit with RIM and agreed to pay royalties for using its technology.

J-6 The Business Market

BlackBerry software is licensed to many companies ranging from Microsoft Corp. to PalmSource, Inc. RIM recently signed a deal with Sun Microsystems, Inc., to extend wireless web services to BlackBerry customers. The goal is to enable people to have wireless email whenever and on whatever device they want.

Discussion Questions

1. White-collar professionals are likely to recognize the need to use a BlackBerry. What factors may influence their need recognition? Use your knowledge of these factors to recommend an effective promotion campaign targeting white-collar professionals. Use the product need recognition model described in Chapter 2 to formulate your answer.

2. The user image associated with BlackBerry is that of a white-collar professional. Develop creative ideas that can be used in an advertising campaign directed to that consumer group. Use the self-image congruence model described in Chapter 5 to formulate your suggestions.

3. One way to motivate white-collar professionals to consider adopting the BlackBerry is to heighten their level of involvement with wireless email. Develop creative ideas that can be used in an advertising campaign to heighten white-collar professionals' involvement with wireless email. Use the involvement model described in Chapter 8 to formulate your answer.

Sources: Brady, Diane (2004), "The Brains behind BlackBerry: Research in Motion's Co-CEOs Keep Taking Wireless E-mail to the Next Level," *Business Week,* April 19, 2004. Brady, Diane (2004), "RIM's Lazaridis: 'We're Not a Startup': The BlackBerry Inventor, Wireless Pioneer, and Physics Buff Says, 'We've Passed All the Initiation by Fire to Get to 20 Years Old,'" *Business Week,* April 19, 2004. Lower, Josh (2004), "Research in Motion Limited." *Hoovers* (http://www.hoovers.com/free/co/factsheet. xhtml? COID=59141&cm_ven=PAID&cm_cat=OVR&cm_pla=CO4&cm_ite=rimm).

iPod

By M. Joseph Sirgy

K-1 The Product

The iPod (www.apple.com/ipod) is a portable music player. iPod is designed to do one thing really well—play music. Apple Computers makes iPods. Recently, Apple came up with the new iPod photo ($499 with a 40-gigabyte drive). It looks just like a standard iPod, although it is a little thicker. The color display is much brighter and easier to read than the regular monochrome screen. Also, what is new is the ability to download pictures—from iPhoto on a Macintosh or Adobe (http://www.adobe.com) Photoshop Album on Windows—and display them on the 2-sq.-in. screen.

K-2 Downloading Music

Apple uses a simple 99-cents-per-song formula that the record labels could live with. Also, Apple used brand and advertising to make legal music downloading a hip alternative to illegal file-sharing. Apple's control over its hardware and software created the most elegant, glitch-free music-buying experience for consumers.

K-3 Battery Life

Apple customers have long complained about the iPod's low battery life and its high price. Apple responded by improving the product. On July 19, 2004, it unveiled new models that feature 12 hours of battery life and a starting price of $299, $100 lower than before.

K-4 Accessories

K-4 a Carrying Case

Incase makes a handful of music-player holders, particularly for the iPod mini, including snazzy $30 iPod mini sleeves featuring a "flame" design (http://www.goincase.com). WaterField Designs' iPod case is a $40 ballistic nylon home with a subtle color weave on the side and a flap that covers the device's face (http://www.sfbags.com). The inside of the flap includes a little pocket for the earphones. The iPod has a haute couture wardrobe, too, including Kate Spade's shimmery gold crinkle leather case for the mini, complete with matching carry strap, for $75 (http://www.katespade.com).

K-4 b Speaker

Speakers are used to help the user share music with others. A handful of high-end speaker makers have designed ones that match the iPod's sleek look, starting with Bose's $300 SoundDock (http://www.bose.com). JBL's OnStage is a doughnut-shaped speaker system that nearly matches the Bose in sound quality but costs $100 less (http://www.jbl.com). Altec Lansing's $180 inMotion iM3 speakers are of lesser quality (http://www.alteclansing.com). But unlike the others, they fold up and come with a carrying case. All of the speakers recharge the iPod while it's docked.

K-4c Earphones

The biggest complaint about the iPod is the ill-fitting earphones that come with it. In response, Etymotic Research came out with its $150 white ER-6i earphones that slip inside the ear canal and pump out superior sound (http://www.etymotic.com).

K-4d Car Stereo

A handful of companies have come up with ways to play music from the iPod through a car stereo. Griffin's $35 iTrip fits right on top of the player and sends out music over a free FM radio frequency that you select (http://www.griffintechnology.com). The problem with an FM transmitter, though, is that it is prone to interference in city driving. One solution: Alpine Electronics' KCA-420i, a $100 adapter that plugs iPods directly into Alpine's car stereo units (http://www.alpine-usa.com). Drivers then navigate their iPod tunes using the stereo's controls.

K-5 Consumers

Consumer research has shown that the iPod is perceived by consumers to be an extension of the self. The iPod reflects consumers' favorite tunes. It is also perceived to be a status symbol, just like a fine suit or a designer watch. It serves to enhance consumers' self-esteem.

Casey Neistat, 23, is a self-professed Apple junkie. He is building his filmmaking career with the company's iMac computers and editing software. He usually leaves his Manhattan apartment with an iPod plugged into his ear. When Neistat discovered the digital music player's batteries were irreplaceable and lasted just 18 months, he made a film called *iPod's Dirty Secret* and launched a protest website. Neistat insists that the protest was an act of love: "We made that film because we believe in the brand so much." Apple Computer addressed the problem. Neistat is one of many consumers who are part of the community of Apple consumers—a cult of sorts. The loyal, if sometimes nagging, band of true believers behind Apple's iPod helped the dollar value of the Apple brand jump 23.7%, to $6.9 billion, in 2004.

K-6 The Market

There are 5.7 million iPod players out there. Despite an already dominant position, iPod continues to outgrow the market. In the second quarter in 2004, Apple sold more than 800,000 iPods and by then had already sold over 100 million songs. Apple moved 860,000 iPods during its fiscal third quarter, a performance that helped the company triple its profit to $61 million and boost revenues 30% to $2.01 billion.

The momentum should continue in the months ahead, due in part to savvy marketing deals. Apple made a deal with computer giant Hewlett-Packard (http://www.hp.com) to sell an HP-branded iPod and start loading iTunes software on millions of its home PCs. In July 2004, Motorola (http://www.motorola.com) announced that by early 2005, some of its phones will be capable of storing and playing a handful of songs downloaded from iTunes.

Apple's red-hot iPod music player enjoys roughly a 50% market share. And since the iPod works only with Apple's iTunes Music Store, consumers have made Apple king of the legal download market as well, with more than a 70% share. So far, even giants such as Sony (http://www.sony.com), Wal-Mart Stores (http://www.walmart.com), and Microsoft (http://www.microsoft.com) have failed to make any significant inroads into the market. Yet a smaller rival, RealNetworks (http://www.realnetworks.com) thinks it has found a way to break Apple's lock. As of July 27, 2004, consumers can go to Real's website and download software, dubbed Harmony, that lets them play songs purchased at Real's download store on any portable player they choose—including the iPod. What's more, Real is hoping to license Harmony to other online stores that might also want to sell to iPod users—without Apple's approval. Experts say that Apple may be able to counter Real's move by requiring iPod owners to download a firmware upgrade the next time they try to buy a song from iTunes that would render Harmony useless, much as a security patch resolves a computer virus. Or Apple might inform iPod owners that Apple will no longer honor their warranty if they buy songs from Real or other rival online music stores.

In mid-August, 2004, Sony Corp. rolled out its answer to the iPod music player: the NW-HD1 Network Walkman. This MP-3 player weighs in at less than four ounces, making it slightly smaller than Apple's iPod. Sony claims that its 20-gigabyte Walkman can store 13,000 songs, compared with the 5,000-song capacity of a similarly equipped iPod.

Apple responded immediately, saying that Sony is misleading consumers. Sony's Walkman can cram 13,000 songs onto its player but only by reducing sound quality. Sony fired back, arguing that its superior technology allows it to give consumers more music at comparable quality to the iPod. Compressed music is an issue of quantity vs. quality. Getting a lot of songs onto a player or a PC, or making them small enough to download fast, entails compressing digitized music files. The maker crunches them down by deleting redundant sounds as well as those that humans cannot hear. The industry uses a standard compression measure called bit rate; the lower it is, the smaller the music file and the more you can squeeze onto a PC or music player. The downside of that, however, is that a lower bit rate generally means lower sound quality.

Discussion Questions

1. Can you explain why the iPod diffused in the marketplace in a short period? What factors affected its rapid rate of diffusion? Use the consumer evaluation model described in Chapter 18 to formulate your answer.

2. Can you hypothesize what the demographic and psychographic profiles are of those who first adopted the iPod?

3. What are the values associated with the use of the iPod? Can you use these values to identify points of leverage in developing an advertising campaign targeting the iPod opinion leaders? Use the means-end chain model described in Chapter 6 to identify the values associated with the iPod.

Sources: Brady, Diane, Robert D. Hof, Andy Reinhardt, Moon Ihlwan, Stanley Holmes, and Kerry Capell (2004), "Cult Brands: The *Business Week*/Interbrand Annual Ranking of the World's Most Valuable Brands Shows the Power of Passionate Consumers," *Business Week,* August 2, 2004. Burrows, Peter (2004), "For Apple, Harmony Is Off-Key: RealNetworks' Attempt to Make Its Music Downloads Work on iPods Does Jobs & Co. and Consumers a Disservice—and Should be Thwarted," *Business Week,* July 27, 2004. Edward, Cliff (2004), "In This Corner, the iPod: Sony's Claims for Its New Walkman Have Goaded Apple into a Fight," *Business Week,* July 26, 2004. Greene, Jay (2004), "What Are You Getting Your iPod? With 5.7 Million of Them Out There, Makers of Add-ons Are Vying to Get in on the Action," *Business Week,* December 13, 2004. Wildstrom, Stephan H. (2004), "Playing Music Is Enough, Fellas: The New iPod and Some of Its Rivals Are Trying Too Hard to Show Pictures," *Business Week,* December 20, 2004.

Netflix

By M. Joseph Sirgy

L-1 The Service

Netflix, Inc. (http://www.netflix.com) is an online DVD rental service. Netflix offers a $22-a-month Internet DVD subscription service. Consumers can rent as many movies as they want and keep them as long as they want. There are never any late fees or due dates. Netflix has a wide selection of DVDs and a good search engine to allow consumers to find great movies and other DVDs.

L-2 The Market

There are three benefit segments to the Internet DVD rental service: (1) those seeking better value on DVD rentals, (2) those seeking service providers with a better selection of DVDs, and (3) those who like the convenience of having the rented DVDs delivered to their home.

L-3 Competition

In 2004, Netflix's main rival, Blockbuster, Inc. (http://www.blockbuster.com), unveiled the test site for its own DVD-by-mail service to directly compete with Netflix, which Blockbuster had been vowing to do for years. The Blockbuster rental service costs $20 a month instead of Netflix's $22. Netflix is not worried about Blockbuster. Its CEO is counting on their experience curve to give them a competitive advantage.

Netflix differentiates itself from Wal-Mart (http://www.walmart.com), which also has a DVD-by-mail service, in terms of price. Wal-Mart charges consumers $18.76. At the high end, there is Netflix, for consumers who want value and a quality service. And in the middle, there is Blockbuster.

Analysts estimate that Netflix has five times as many DVD-by-mail subscribers as Wal-Mart Stores, Inc., and an even greater lead on Blockbuster. Netflix has proprietary software that uses factors such as customers' past rentals to help subscribers find movies they like. About half of Netflix's customers rate movies, and its 24 distribution centers let it ship to 80% of American addresses overnight by U.S. mail, compared with two or three days for rivals.

Stand-alone video chains such as Wal-Mart, Best Buy, and Target together have grabbed 29.8% of the $24.7 billion market for video sales and rentals over the last six years or so. They've done it by undercutting the competition on price. They have also proved that movie fans often are more interested in buying DVDs than renting them.

Will Netflix be able to compete against the cable and phone companies who are getting ready to deliver video-on-demand? Netflix is positioning itself to expand into the downloading market by gearing up for electronic delivery in addition to DVD mail delivery, allowing consumers to choose what they want, mixing and matching, on a single subscription. Netflix plans to begin distributing movies digitally in 2005. Consumers can choose to download a movie from a selection of 25,000 movie titles any time. Netflix is focused on downloading to TVs, over the Internet, and on continuing to rent out DVDs. Thus, consumers can get unlimited DVDs and unlimited downloads under one subscription. Nowadays, there is a wide range of companies bringing the Internet to the TV. There are Wi-Fi DVD players emerging. Most consumer electronics over the next several years will have integrated Wi-Fi. Thus, the Internet will be brought to the television.

L-4 The Company's Financial Position

Netflix has been growing at a very rapid rate. In 2003, Netflix had $270 million in revenue. The company estimated that it would make $525–530 million in revenues and about $10.2 net income by the end of 2004. As the year passed, the company raised its 2004 net income target, to between $12.6 million and $22.1 million.

L-5 The Company's Market Position Sales Forecast

Netflix is still by far the leading online DVD rental service, with 2.1 million subscribers and 80% customer growth. The company predicts it will reach 5 million subscribers by 2006.

Discussion Questions

1. Do you have any thoughts regarding the lifestyle of consumers who are attracted to Netflix? Can you hypothesize what their psychographic might be? Explain. Use the lifestyle and psychographic concepts in Chapter 6 to formulate your answer.

2. Let's segment the market for DVD/video rentals by family lifecycle. Identify segments that may find Netflix appealing. Why? Develop ideas for an ad campaign based on your explanation. Use the description of the family lifecycle in Chapter 15 to formulate your answer.

3. Let's focus on two segments—one described as the science buffs, the other as the movie buffs. The science buffs are

consumers who like to watch DVDs/videos about science-related topics—the kind of films typically shown on the Discovery Channel and Public Broadcasting Service (PBS). What are those features about Netflix that might appeal to these different segments? Which segment is likely to be more profitable for Netflix? Explain.

Sources: Mullaney, Timothy J. and Tom Lowry (2004), "Reed Hastings' Script for Netflix," *Business Week,* August 2, 2004. *Business Week* (2004), "Netflix: Moving into Slo-Mo? The Rising Cost of Online Ads Blindsided the Movie Outfit. And Rivals Are Looming," *Business Week,* August 2, 2004. Grover, Ronald (2004), "Hollywood Video's Hot Sequel: Despite Recent Setbacks, Potential Acquirers Like Blockbuster Are Lining Up. But Even a Merged Video Chain Faces Big Challenges," *Business Week,* December 9, 2004.

Nextel

By M. Joseph Sirgy

M-1 The Company

Nextel (http://www.nextel.com), a FORTUNE 200 company based in Reston, Virginia, is a leading provider of fully integrated wireless communications services. It has built the largest guaranteed all-digital wireless network in the country, covering thousands of communities across the United States. Today 95 percent of FORTUNE 500 companies are Nextel customers. Nextel and Nextel Partners, Inc., currently serve 297 of the top 300 U.S. markets, where approximately 259 million people live or work. Nextel is the nation's fifth-largest wireless company.

M-2 Nextel's Competitive Advantage

As the competition chased the booming consumer market over the last few years, Nextel stuck to selling its unique walkie-talkie-like service to business users in industries such as trucking, plumbing, home repair, and construction. This strategy has paid off. It has proven to be a remarkably popular mode of communication and Nextel's main differentiator. Indeed, many analysts credit it with allowing the fifth-largest wireless carrier in the U.S. to enjoy the industry's lowest customer turnover and an average revenue per user of at least $10 more than that received by the other players. Indeed, Nextel grabbed the coveted top spot in the 2004 *Business Week* Info Tech 100 ranking.

Nextel's competitive advantage may soon evaporate. AT&T Wireless (http://www.at&twireless.com), Verizon Wireless (http://www.verizonwireless.com), and Sprint PCS (http://www.sprintpcs.com) introduced competing walkie-talkie-like services in late 2003, and they started refocusing on corporate customers. It will take time for the competition to catch up with Nextel, however. Nextel's decade-old Direct Connect phone, made by Motorola (http://www.motorola.com), links users within a second at the push of a button. That's a convenience construction workers, salespeople, and many others will pay a premium for. Today, competing technologies involve at least a four-second delay to set up a call. On May 4, 2004, Nextel began offering push-to-talk nationally and internationally (instead of just regionally), and other new services are on the way domestically. Late in 2004, Nextel launched several new handsets featuring popular built-in cameras and sleek, small designs. And it continues to expand popular premium wireless-data applications, such as the @Road service, which helps truck-fleet operators locate vehicles through a global positioning satellite system.

Although only 20 percent of its 10.6 million subscribers use wireless data today, they pay more than $90 in revenues a month on average and defect at half the rate of other customers. Analysts predict that by 2010, 5.5 percent of Nextel's revenues per user could come from wireless data, up from 1 percent in 2004.

Nextel is going after new users among the white-collar workforce, government employees, and even young consumers. Government workers—including first responders on the front line in homeland security—are one of its fastest-growing sectors. And Nextel is deciding whether to pursue the 18- to 24-year-old market. By selling Nextel phones via surfer shops and music stores, such as Billabong (http://www.billabong.com) and Wherehouse (http://www.wherehouse.com), Nextel is testing whether it is worth risking its business-oriented brand image to capture the potentially high-margin youth market.

M-3 Boost Mobile

Boost Mobile (http://www.boostmobile.com), a division of Nextel aimed at young subscribers and ethnic groups, is ramping up. Boost Mobile, a prepaid service, added 132,000 customers in the first quarter of 2004, on top of 385,000 customers in all of 2003. In May of 2004, Nextel reported that it had 13 million subscribers.

M-4 The Company's Financial Position

During one of telecom's toughest years, Nextel scored $1.66 billion in profit in 2002. It collects an average of $71 in revenues per subscriber per month, compared with $50 by other carriers—and its 2.1 percent monthly customer-defection rate is the lowest in an industry that averages a 2.6 percent monthly churn.

Operating performance remains impressive. In 2004's first quarter, Nextel added 474,000 subscribers—about 15 percent of the overall industry's total gains in that period. Nextel is gaining market share. Despite the vicious price-cutting that the industry is witnessing, Nextel's income jumped 184 percent, to $591 million, on revenues that were up 31 percent, to $3.1 billion, in the quarter.

M-5 What Lies Ahead

M-5a New Spectrum

Because Nextel uses the same frequencies as police and fire departments, all parties suffer from interference. The Federal Communications Commission (FCC) has been trying for several years to relocate part of Nextel's service to a different wireless spectrum. Doing so should allow Nextel to build a superfast network similar to those being constructed by rivals like Verizon Wireless, the No. 1 U.S. wireless company. On July 8, 2004, the FCC made a decision to allot Nextel valuable new spectrum space (in the 1.9-gigahertz band) to carry its cell-phone service. Under this agreement, Nextel will get the frequency in return for relinquishing some of its existing spectrum to police and fire departments and helping them relocate to the spectrum it is giving up. This upgrade will cost Nextel three times what it had originally offered for relocation. The deal ultimately is expected to cost $3.2 billion. On the bright side, having the new spectrum should allow Nextel to handle more voice calls, provide more advanced data services, and keep up with its rivals in the long run. Without the spectrum swap Nextel is likely to be at a competitive disadvantage due to its spectrum limitations—its existing spectrum did not have enough capacity to support more voice calls and advanced services. Analysts agree that the company's long-term survival now looks to be more assured. Earnings should grow 45 percent this year, to $2.07 per share, on revenues of $12.9 billion.

M-5b New Technologies

Analysts say that a new technology, push-to-talk, or PTT, is likely to create waves in the cellular phone market. With PTT, the user can connect to another party simply by holding down a special button when talking. The feature connects users within a few seconds, vs. 20 to 25 seconds with conventional cell-phone dialing.

Verizon Wireless is charging $20 a month for the service. That price is likely to drop when other carriers enter the market. Building out a PTT service is not that expensive, costing well under $100 million for most carriers, vs. the tens of billions they spent on networks allowing for more voice calls and other data services, such as interactive mobile games, which add only about $2 in extra revenue per user each month.

A Yankee Group (http://www.yankeegroup.com) survey in May 2003 of 2,490 business users and consumers showed that 24 percent of them want the PTT function. That's why Cingular (http://www.cingular.com), AT&T Wireless, and T-Mobile (http://www.t-mobile.com) have got together with equipment vendors Ericsson (http://www.ericsson.com), Nokia (http://www.nokia.com), and privately held Sonim Technologies to standardize the PTT technology. The standard would ensure that different carriers' customers can call each other using PTT. To counter this thrust, Nextel is working with Motorola, the creator of the unique iDen technology its network is based on, and wireless technology powerhouse Qualcomm (http://www.qualcomm.com) on interoperability with technology used by Sprint PCS.

Nextel has another reason to worry. It has not paired up its walkie-talkie service with an instant-messaging-friendly screen, showing which of the users are available at a given time, as Verizon has done. And analysts say that is what will make the improved PTT service the next wireless killer application.

Nextel has some key advantages. Its service is easy and connections are fast. In contrast, a caller on the Verizon network has to wait three to five seconds to connect to the recipient. Then, a delay of several seconds occurs in between each person speaking and the voice actually coming through on the phone. Sonim, says its PPT connection times will eventually be virtually instantaneous, under a second like Nextel's. Another barrier that Nextel's rivals have to overcome is the dearth of PTT-enabled phones, which have a special button and better speaker quality. These rivals will have to find a way to get their customers to upgrade to new phones which come, in the case of Verizon Wireless, at $149.99 a unit for a Motorola V60p phone on a two-year contract.

M-5c Mergers and Acquisitions

Sprint Corp. (http://www.sprint.com) and Nextel announced on Dec. 15, 2004, a $35 billion deal to merge into the third-largest wireless powerhouse. With a market capitalization of $70 billion, the new Reston (Va.)-based Sprint Nextel hopes to gain the competitive advantage it needs to fight the two leading Bell-owned wireless giants—Cingular and Verizon Wireless. Cingular grabbed the No. 1 spot in the wireless market with 47 million subscribers after its October 2004 acquisition of AT&T Wireless. And Verizon Wireless, the No. 2 player, reached its 42-million-users mark. Sprint, a distant third with 20 million customers, and No. 5 Nextel, with 14.5 million, need each other to hold their own. While Sprint has local and long-distance businesses in addition to wireless, it does not have the scale to compete over the long haul with the Bells. And though Nextel has the wireless industry's highest margins, its focus on a unique niche—push-to-talk service to business users—is too narrow to sustain an independent company as the industry consolidates.

The long-term goals may be twofold. First, the deal allows Sprint Nextel to play a pivotal role in the coming convergence between traditional and wireless phones, web access, and video services. As the Bells race against the cable operators to sell consumers everything from voice to data to video, both sides need wireless phone services to sweeten their bundle of offerings. The Bells already own their own wireless companies, not the cable companies. Sprint Nextel can provide a ready-made wireless offering for cable companies. Second, the merger creates a business that can compete against the Bells and cable operators in the market for converged services. The two wireless carriers together own enough airwaves, stretching coast-to-coast, to offer voice, data, and even video over next-generation wireless broadband technology, the WiMax standard.

The two companies seem to complement each other well. Nextel needs Sprint's innovative know-how in creating new wireless data applications in mobile music, video, and games to go after the youth consumer market with its Boost Mobile brand. Sprint can expand in the business market by helping to bolster Nextel's attempt to equip corporate campuses with communications services. Sprint's long-distance networks, along with Nextel's wireless offering, give companies a more complete offering. Nextel uses a special wireless technology that no other carrier uses. Without Sprint, Nextel would have to build an entirely new network to offer customers email and video services that zip along at speeds up to 300 kilobits per second. By using Sprint's digital network, Nextel can save much of the $2 to $3 billion it would otherwise spend to build its own next-generation infrastructure.

Discussion Questions

1. What is the image associated with Nextel? Can you develop a measure that marketing researchers can use to test your hypothesis of that image? Use the concept of brand user image discussed in Chapter 5 in formulating your answer.

2. Nextel is contemplating targeting young adult consumers. Do you think this is a wise move? Explain.

3. Consider a family involving a father, mother, and two teenage kids as the target for an ad campaign. Develop some creative ideas guided by your understanding of consumer behavior that can be developed into actual ads. Use concepts described in Chapter 15 to formulate your answer.

Sources: Kharif, Olga (2003), "Crashing Nextel's Walkie-Talkie Party: Time Will Tell If Copycat Rivals' Push-to-talk Features Measure up to the Original, But It's Certain That Next Year Will See a Fierce Fight for Customers," *Business Week,* September 2, 2003. Kharif, Olga (2004), "Can Nextel Strike Up the Bandwidth? The Wireless Spectrum It Needs May Carry a High Price—and What It Gets Might Not be What It Wants. Dismal Prospects? Maybe Not," *Business Week,* May 17, 2004. Yang, Cathy (2004), "Nextel: Defending a Juicy Niche: Though Its Successful Walkie-Talkie-like Service Will Soon Spawn Copycats, the Wireless Carrier Is Busy Extending Its Lead," *Business Week,* June 23, 2004. Kharif, Olga (2004), "Nextel's Sweet Spectrum Win: The FCC's Award of Key Frequency Space to the Wireless Carrier Should Help it Compete Better—Unless Rivals Get the Deal Overturned," *Business Week,* July 9, 2004. Crockett, Roger O., Catherine Yang, and Tom Lowry (2004), "Why Sprint and Nextel Got Hitched: They Buy Themselves Enough Time and Size to Play with the Big Boys. For Now," *Business Week,* December 27, 2004.

Glossary

A

abstract thinking cultures Those societies whose members are logical thinkers, interested in the principle of cause and effect.

abstraction A process in which concrete attributes of a product are associated with more meaningful aspects to the consumer.

accidental information search A form of pre-purchase search that occurs when a consumer who is not looking for any product or service acquires information as a result of such occurrences as coming across an attractive store display, seeing a persuasive commercial, observing a person using the product, or learning of it from friends.

accretions (cultural accretions) Those things that are added to the natural environment by members of a culture or that have accumulated over time. Both tangible and intangible characteristics of a culture may be evidenced by accretions.

acculturation The process whereby people learn about the ways of a culture foreign to their own.

acquisition self-presentation The motivational tendency to self-monitor in situations where there is chance for social gain, if social risk is involved (for example, telling a lie to gain approval).

action-oriented See *state versus action orientation.*

actual self-congruity The degree of match between the consumer's actual self-image and the brand-user image.

actual self-image How consumers see themselves.

actual state Current state of benefits the consumer enjoys from products or services used or possessed.

addictive or compulsive consumption Consumption that is beyond the control of the consumer. Often acting out of tension, anxiety, depression, or boredom, a compulsive person seeks immediate gratification of needs or desires, no matter how short-lived and no matter how deeply that behavior is regretted afterward.

adjustment The tendency to develop affective responses that lead the consumer to purchase a product or service because this product or service leads to gaining certain rewards and avoiding certain punishments.

advertising substantiation An FTC-developed program that says that companies that make claims about a product's safety, performance, efficacy, quality, or comparative price must provide tests, studies, or other data to support their claims.

affect The way in which we feel in response to marketplace stimuli, such as brands. Unlike belief, affect is emotive rather than cognitive in nature. It results not just from our knowledge of marketplace stimuli but from our evaluation of them. In other words, affect is made up of beliefs, plus the way in which we feel about or evaluate those beliefs.

affect intensity A personality trait describing a tendency to consistently experience emotions with greater strength when exposed to emotionally provocative situations, regardless of whether these emotions are positive or negative.

affective performance A measure of how well the product or service purchased meets the emotional (benefits) expectations (feelings associated with possession and use of product or service) of the buyer.

aggressiveness A personality trait describing a tendency to deal with anxiety by moving against people and offending them.

alternative evaluation The process through which consumers compare and contrast different solutions (products, services, outlets, brands) to the same marketplace problem.

analytic categorization Having the perceived product conform to a set of necessary attributes before it can be put into a certain category.

androgynous Displaying both masculine and feminine characteristics.

androgyny A gender role state where the individual experiences or acts out a blurring of gender roles, not favoring the male or female role.

antecedents In the consumer decision model, proposed causes of certain results (or *consequences*).

approach-approach conflict A situation in which the consumer faces a dilemma of choosing between or among alternatives—or approaches—that seem equally attractive.

approach-avoidance conflict A situation in which the same goal has both positive and negative characteristics.

approaches to time See *time approaches.*

aspirational group A group that a person would like to be part of but to which he or she does not currently or may never belong.

assimilation (theory of) The process whereby ethnic and/or nationality groups lose their customs and traits over time and gradually adopt behaviors, lifestyles, and purchasing habits associated with the dominant culture in which they live.

associative network A system of beliefs organized in memory.

associative thinking cultures Those societies in which connections or associations with people, celebrities, and events impact on the importance of things.

asymmetric effect An imbalance in level of satisfaction. For example, if a consumer experiences a certain level of negative disconfirmation with the performance of a particular product or service attribute, this has a greater impact on the dissatisfaction level than the same level of positive performance of the same attribute would have on the level of satisfaction.

attention to social comparison information A personality trait describing a tendency to compare oneself with others—to pay heed to social comparison information.

attitude-behavior consistency Refers to the extent to which attitude leads to purchase.

attitude toward the act The consumer's attitude toward the act of purchasing a particular brand, expressed by consumer researchers as A_{act}. It is the sum of the consumer's belief strengths in consequences that will result from a purchase and the evaluation weight assigned to each of those consequences.

attitude toward failure The extent to which the consumer would feel bad, given that he or she tries to consume the product and fails to attain the desired goal.

attitude toward the process Involves the consumer's feelings toward the actions necessary in order to consume a product.

attitude toward success The extent to which the consumer would feel good, given that he or she tries to consume the product in question and succeeds in goal attainment.

attribution The process through which people connect events and behavior with causes. This cause-and-effect association can be critical to marketers. Attribution can take three forms: *product perception, self-perception,* and *person perception.*

authoritarian parents Parents who restrict their children's activities and are not nurturing.

authoritative parents Parents who set limits on their children's activities but are nurturing.

autonomic family decision making Decision making in which husband and wife independently make the same type of decision, each doing it about one-half of the time.

avoidance-avoidance conflict A situation in which the consumer faces two negative alternatives.

B

backward conditioning Occurs when the unconditioned stimulus is presented first, followed by the conditioned stimulus.

behavioral intention The behavior component of attitude. Behavioral intention describes attitude not toward a brand but toward brand purchase and, as such, is a far better predictor of behavior than either beliefs or affective responses.

behavior analysis A theory of learning that focuses on how learning can be modified through incentives and offers, counteroffers, and other forms of rewards and punishments.

belief A psychological association between a product or brand and an attribute or feature of that product or brand.

belief-importance model A model that compares affective responses toward competing brands. We each have an evoked set of brands—a list of brands we consider prior to making a decision. The final selection is made only after we evaluate the desirability of each brand according to the same set of attributes.

binary opposition Occurs in a myth when conflicting options are offered—for example, good versus evil or technology versus nature.

bodega A small general store in a Latino-American neighborhood that serves as a popular gathering place for local residents.

body cathexis Satisfaction with a particular physical feature or body part.

body image How people see their bodies, physical selves, and appearance.

brand image An overall vision or position of a brand in the mind of the consumer.

brand personality A framework of human traits that consumers attach to products and services when they position the latter in the marketplace against other products or services; also called "brand image."

brand-user personality or **brand-user image** A mental representation of a brand along value-expressive attributes.

browsing information search A type of pre-purchase search where there is no immediate intent to buy.

buyer The person who completes the marketing transaction through a purchase or other exchange either for himself/herself or another person or group of persons. In the organizational sense, a buyer is the person who purchases goods or services and may or may not be involved in the mechanics of transaction completion.

buyers Individuals with authority to select suppliers and handle the transaction. In some cases, buyers are responsible only for implementing decisions previously made by users and influencers.

buying center Essentially, a committee put together to make a purchase decision. The committee is usually composed of members of several organizational units selected on the basis of expertise or experience with the product to be purchased and includes the purchasing manager.

C

Cable Communications Act The 1984 act that mandates cable companies to disclose to their subscribers any information collected about them, the reason for its collection, how long it will be retained, and who might use it and under what conditions.

categorization The psychological process through which a consumer compares the perception of a product with a mental representation of that product in memory.

centrality of visual product aesthetics The overall level of significance that visual aesthetics hold for a particular consumer in his or her relationships with products.

class consciousness A person's sense of belonging to a certain social class.

classical or **respondent conditioning** Conditioning based on the simple premise that learning results from a relationship between stimulus and response.

cognitive theory An alternative to *behavior analysis* that emphasizes the thinking rather than the doing aspects of learning.

collectivistic culture A culture in which people put the good of others, the groups they belong to, and the society as a whole above their own.

comparative message A message in which the product is compared directly with a competing product in terms of one or more product features.

compatibility The degree to which an innovation fits with the needs, values, and past experiences of the consumer.

compensatory consumer decision rule A decision rule designed to allow for trade-offs among the strengths and weaknesses of alternatives being evaluated. Typically results in a winning choice.

complexity The innovation's level of difficulty to understand and use.

compliance A personality trait describing a tendency to deal with anxiety by moving toward people and complying with their wishes.

compulsive consumption A response to an uncontrollable drive or desire to obtain, use, or experience a feeling, substance, or activity that leads the individual to repetitively engage in behavior that will ultimately cause harm to the individual and/or others.

concept-oriented communication Communication based on individual thought and analysis.

Confucian Dynamic A cultural comparative measure. At the positive end of the Confucian Dynamic scale are such values as persistence, hard work, thrift, shame, and regard for relationships that indicate a future-oriented, dynamic mentality. At the negative end are values indicating a static mentality. They are tied to the present and the past and include "face," reciprocity, and tradition.

conjugal family or **family of procreation** The family formed by marriage.

connectedness A personality trait describing a tendency for some people to perceive themselves as highly connected with others. Contrast with *separateness.*

consanguine family or **family of orientation** The family into which a person is born or into which a person is adopted.

consequences In the consumer decision model, proposed results of certain causes (or *antecedents*).

consequences test The ethics concept that states that ethical marketers consider both the positive and negative potential consequences of their actions, with the intent of providing as many positive consequences as possible for both parties.

consumer The individual who actually uses and/or possesses a product or service.

consumer benefits Those positive factors that the consumer obtains as a result of the possession and/or use of a product or service. See *total product concept.* Tangible benefits are those that are in some sense measurable, whereas intangible benefits are based on the feelings experienced.

"Consumer Bill of Rights" Laws designed to protect consumers from unfair and unjust marketing practices. Specifically, these laws protect the right to be informed, the right to safety, the right to redress, the right to choose, the right to a healthful environment, and the right to privacy.

consumer cheating Examples of consumer cheating (besides shoplifting) include the purchase of goods with the intention of using them for some time and then returning the goods for a full refund.

consumer culture A culture in which a high level of economic development is reflected in a high level of consumption of goods and services by a majority of culture members—a state of macroconsumption.

consumer decision model A theoretical framework used to describe the processes consumers go through before, during, and after making a purchase decision. It is a means of describing a concept, its causes, and its effects. Models provide a framework for analyzing consumer behavior.

consumer decision process The five steps suggested in the Engel, Kollat, and Blackwell (EKB) model—namely, problem or need recognition, information search, alternative evaluation, choice, and outcomes. Consumers do not go through all five steps in all situations.

consumer ethnocentricity An economic form of ethnocentrism. It is based on the consumer's love and concern for his or her own country and the perceived harmful economic impact of importing goods from other nations. Strong consumer ethnocentrists see buying foreign goods as not just an economic issue but also a moral one.

consumer innovativeness A product-specific tendency on the part of consumers to be among the first to purchase new products within specific categories.

consumer involvement The extent to which the audience is motivated to process the message.

consumer motivation The drive to satisfy needs and wants, both physiological and psychological, through the purchase and use of products and services.

Consumer Product Safety Commission (CPSC) The commission established under the 1972 Consumer Product Safety Act that protects the consumer's right to safety in the United States. Three other federal agencies also monitor aspects of product safety: the Federal Trade Commission (FTC) regulates advertising claims related to product safety; the Traffic Safety Administration (TSA) ensures that automobile manufacturers adhere to safety standards and remedy safety defects; and the Food and Drug Administration (FDA) oversees safety issues in food and drug-related products.

consumer sovereignty The situation in which consumers' interests dominate producers' interests. If consumers are accurately informed about quality and price of optional brands, then they can reward producers who develop high-quality products at lower prices. Thus, consumers have clout by exercising their economic votes—that is, the contents of their pocketbooks.

consumption The possession and/or use of goods and services and the benefits they deliver.

consumption episode The set of items consumed belonging to the same event and occurring in temporal proximity.

consumption set The mix of goods and services acquired and used by a person, household, or other group.

consumption situation The physical and social context in which we actually use goods and services purchased.

consumption-specific personality trait A trait that affects the consumer only in situations related to consumption and does not extend its influence into nonconsumption situations.

consumption system A bundle of goods and services that are consumed over time in multiple episodes.

context (cultural context) May be high or low in a culture. A high-context culture is one in which the rules, values, beliefs, and such of the culture are well known by all, and there is little explanation needed for its members. In low-context cultures, the knowledge of the ins and outs of the society is not as widespread, and guidance on the "why's" and "how's" of the culture is needed.

continuous innovations When products that are already accepted and used by consumers are modified, and the changes require little or no effort on the part of consumers to modify their behavior to use the products.

continuous reinforcement A schedule of rewards and punishments that reflects the situation in which every correct response is rewarded and every incorrect one is punished.

contrast effect The reaction that occurs when there is a wide negative disparity between expectations and actual performance, and customers tend to magnify this poor performance.

conventions Those practices tied to the conduct of everyday life in various settings in a culture.

corrective advertising An FTC-developed program that compels marketers to correct wrongful beliefs consumers form about a product as a result of deceptive advertising.

cosmological myth A myth that functions as a way to show that the components of the universe are part of a single whole.

cost per thousand (CPM) A media concept that describes the dollar cost to reach a thousand consumers.

countersegmentation Reducing the number of market segments served from current levels.

country image An image in the mind of most consumers that signals an association between a specific product or service and a country.

coupon proneness A marketplace-specific tendency to use coupons in the purchase of economic goods from retail outlets.

crescive norms Norms that are learned and practiced by members of a social unit but that nonmembers may not readily recognize.

cultural animosity A situation in which the people in one nation have a very strong aversion to (in some cases, bordering on hatred) the people of another country. This is based on very negative historical experiences—the results of war, economics, religious or ethnic discrimination, and the like.

cultural diffusion Occurs when people in one culture are exposed to people and/or ways of another culture, and this exposure begins to change the culture.

cultural relativism When a person views or judges any behavior, value, or norm within its own social and cultural setting.

culture Patterns of values, beliefs, and learned behavior that are held in common and transmitted by the members of any given society.

culture rejection The breaking away from the ways of one's culture that may cause people to follow one of four paths: hedonism, etherealization, search for community, or activism.

customs Behaviors that have lasted over time and are often passed down in the family setting. Examples are gender roles and special family celebrations and traditions.

D

deal proneness A marketplace-specific tendency to seek the best bargain possible in shopping situations.

deciders Individuals with the ultimate authority to select vendors. Although buyers may hold formal purchasing power, they are not always involved in the decision.

decision cycle A sequential process, beginning with the identification of a need within the organization and progressing through the actual receipt and use of the products purchased.

decision heuristics Rules of thumb or shortcuts that allow the consumer to make rapid decisions about which alternative is best.

decision imminence The state in which an imminent decision is present; an imminent decision is one that the consumer expects to make in the very near future.

decision irrevocability The state in which a decision will be irrevocable; an irrevocable decision is one that once made cannot be undone.

demarketing The marketing processes sellers use to reduce the demand for their goods and services. This is usually a result of environmental sensitivity and/or undersupply of their products or services.

desacralization What occurs when the consumer transforms objects, places, people, and events from the sacred to the profane. Sacralization is the reverse action.

desired state The state of benefits that the consumer wishes to enjoy from products or services used or possessed.

detachment A personality trait describing a tendency to deal with anxiety by moving away from people and asserting one's independence.

determinant attributes Those evaluative criteria that have a direct influence on alternative evaluation and final alternative choice.

diffusion of innovations The process through which a new product moves from initial introduction to regular purchase and use.

directed information search A type of pre-purchase search that is purposeful, having a clear and conscious objective, which is to gather information that will help solve a specific problem.

disclosure of interest rate provisions Disclosure required by the 1968 Truth-in-Lending Act, which was enacted to give consumers information on credit terms to help them seek favorable interest rates. Most significantly, the law requires that lenders inform consumers of the actual rate of interest—expressed, for example, as 18 percent per year rather than as a monthly rate of 1.5 percent.

discontinuous innovations Innovations that necessitate real change in consumption and behavior patterns.

discrimination Learning to respond to two similar stimuli differently.

dissociative group A group that individuals avoid or deny connections with.

distraction Anything that pulls the consumer's attention away from the content of a factual message and lessens the message's ability to communicate effectively.

distributive justice When, during the complaint process, equity in terms of settlement versus perceived costs experienced by the person is the issue.

dogmatism A personality trait describing a tendency to be closed-minded, seeing life in terms of black and white.

duty of beneficence The ethics concept that states that the marketer should, if possible, take actions to improve the lives of consumers.

duty of fidelity An ethics concept regarding the promise to remain faithful to contracts, to keep promises, and to tell the truth.

duty of gratitude The ethics concept that states that the marketer owes and should express gratitude to consumers for their transactions.

duty of justice The ethics concept that states that the marketer is obligated to distribute rewards based upon merits.

duty of nonmaleficence The ethics concept that states that the marketer is obligated to do no harm to consumers.

dynamically continuous innovations Innovations that disrupt the consumer's use patterns but still do not radically alter them.

E

early adopters Individuals who are more sensitive to reference group values and norms than other types of consumers. They tend to be opinion leaders for the product categories in which they are early adopters. They use commercial and personal sources of information extensively in the purchase decision.

early-majority adopters Individuals who wait to see whether a new product will prove to be successful. They watch opinion leaders and follow when ready. They are less educated than innovators or early adopters, with less social mobility.

editorial content The topics usually covered in a certain communication medium. Media planners study the editorial content of various media to match products with media.

ego defense The tendency to develop affective responses that lead the consumer to purchase a product or service because this product or service leads to the attainment of personal goals and images.

ego-focused emotional appeals Messages that arouse certain kinds of emotions, such as pride, happiness, frustration, and anger. These emotions are characterized as reflective of an "independent self" and relate to the person as an autonomous individual.

elaboration likelihood A marketing communications model that argues that there are two routes to persuasion—central and peripheral. The central route is a process of attitude change as a direct response to the physical attributes or benefits of the products as processed through the consumer's cognitive faculties. In contrast, the peripheral route to persuasion reflects the processing of emotional appeals. The consumer does not respond to the pros and cons of the product by making a cognitive decision but responds instead to the feelings the message arouses.

e-loyalty Consumer loyalty to an electronic retailer.

Emergency Response Act The 1986 act that amends the Toxic Substances Control Act to require the EPA to develop regulations pertaining to inspections and development of plans to manage asbestos.

emotional appeal A message that reflects certain emotions, such as fear, humor, sex, romance, anger, and nostalgia.

emotions Affective responses that reflect the activation of deep-seated and value-laden beliefs within the consumer.

enacted norms Norms that may be viewed as explicit rules, easily recognized by people inside and outside of the social unit.

enculturation The process of learning one's own culture.

Environmental Protection Agency (EPA) The agency that sets and regulates polices to protect the environment.

erosions (cultural erosions) The "tracks" or "wearing away" or "removals" left behind by past cultures. Both tangible and intangible characteristics of a culture may be evidenced by erosions.

e-tailer A retailer who offers goods and services on the web; also called an electronic retailer.

ethnocentrism The act of viewing one's own culture as better or even superior to others. This may result in judging other cultures by such standards.

evaluative criteria The tangible and/or intangible benefits that consumers use to compare product classes, brands, vendors, and so on.

exemplar A cognition used to classify incoming perceptions to attribute meaning to these perceptions.

expectancy disconfirmation What occurs when realization—actual or perceived performance in terms of possession and/or use of a good or service—does not match expectation; what the consumer thought would happen is not confirmed.

expectation of failure The extent to which the consumer anticipates that he or she will fail in goal attainment, given the consumption of the product.

expectation of success The extent to which the consumer anticipates that he or she will be successful in goal attainment, given the consumption of the product.

experience products Goods and services where the evaluation cost of even the key attributes or benefits is so high that direct experience results in the lowest expenditure of time, money, cognitive effort, and other resources.

experiential or aesthetic needs Needs that are met by products that satisfy sensory expectations.

experimental research Research involving setting up a situation in which one or more variables are manipulated (e.g., price and message appeal) and the effects of this manipulation are observed on a selected shopper/buyer/consumer behavioral phenomenon (e.g., brand preference, brand choice, consumer satisfaction). This is a research process to test cause and effect.

expert Consumers who have extensive prior knowledge and experience with a product or service category.

exploratory research The kind of research designed to generate hypotheses. It is not considered to be definitive as in quantitative research (correlational or experimental research). Other terms for exploratory research are *qualitative research, interpretive research,* and *idiographic research*. For examples of this type of research, see *qualitative research*.

extended dual mediation model A marketing communications model that argues that an audience exposed to an ad reacts to the ad emotionally and that this feeling influences thoughts about the ad, as well as the attitude toward the ad. In turn, both the thoughts about and the attitude toward the ad influence the formation or change of the audience's thoughts about the brand and the attitude toward the brand.

external information search Gathering information from a variety of sources not part of the person's own memory, knowledge, or experience.

externals People who believe that events or outcomes are determined by forces such as luck or fate that are outside their control.

extraversion Part of a personality trait dealing with two polar opposites, namely extraversion-introversion. This personality trait refers to the extent to which people seek stimulation from the environment. Thus, an extravert is likely to be quite sociable and socially active. In contrast, introverts are typically loners—they like to be left alone. They feel uncomfortable in an environment full of people, noise, and things.

F

factual versus emotional appeals The tone of a message or the way in which it appeals to consumers can be either factual or emotional. A factual tone appeals to the consumer's thinking processes and focuses on informational reasons to buy, whereas an emotional tone appeals to feelings.

factual versus evaluative information Factual information in an ad is a logical and verifiable description of tangible product features. In contrast, evaluative information is an emotional, subjective impression of intangible aspects of the product.

Fair Credit Reporting Act The first privacy act, passed by Congress in 1970, which requires credit reporting agencies to notify consumers and supply information on adverse decisions made about them.

family lifecycle (or life stage) A person's position in life based on such demographic factors as his or her age, marital status, presence of children, ages of children, working status (working, receiving government financial assistance, or retired), and survivor status (retired and widowed or single).

fandom Extreme devotion to sports teams and even in non-sport contexts such as the "Trekkies" (*Star Trek* television and movie series devotees).

fear appeal A message communicated to an audience through the use of fear—that is, the message is designed to arouse fear in the audience.

Federal Trade Commission (FTC) The U.S. government body responsible for protecting the consumer's right to be informed. The FTC regulates truth in marketing, which covers deceptive advertising, false advertising claims, mail-order fraud, retail sales fraud, retail credit contracts, and door-to-door sales. The FTC also sets and enforces packaging and labeling policies.

feminine culture A society in which female roles are considered superior to male roles.

Fishbein model A model that directly relates consumer beliefs with affective response. Affective response to a brand is made up of two factors: the strength or weakness of a consumer's beliefs about that brand and its attributes and the consumer's evaluation of or feelings toward those attributes.

flow Motivation experienced when the skills involved in the achievement task match the consumer's skills level.

formal group A group in which there is some sort of structure, and in some cases, for which there are specific membership requirements.

forward conditioning The type of conditioning that occurs when the conditioned stimulus is presented first, followed by the unconditioned stimulus.

frequency A media concept that refers to the number of message exposures generated by a particular media schedule.

functional theory of attitude Attitude toward a product based on four functions: adjustment, ego defense, value expression, and application of prior knowledge.

G

gatekeepers Individuals responsible for controlling the flow of information into the buying center. Gatekeepers, often purchasing agents, perform the key role of providing salespeople with access to appropriate members of the buying center.

gender-role orientation The extent to which men and women see themselves as masculine, feminine, or androgynous.

gender-typed products Products associated with gender types—that is, masculinity and femininity.

generalization The tendency to respond in similar ways to similar stimuli. When a new stimulus is similar to one previously learned, consumers are likely to respond to it in the same way as to the old one. And the more the new stimulus resembles the earlier one, the stronger the response.

generalized self-confidence A personality trait describing a tendency to feel comfortable making decisions.

generally planned purchase A purchase in which a decision is made before visiting a store that an item from a certain product category will be purchased.

general personality trait A trait that invariably affects an individual across a range of situations—both those that are consumption-related and those that are not.

Gestalt principle The processes through which we organize the sensations that play an integral part in human comprehension and interpretation of experience and that demand a higher level of perception beyond the five senses.

green consumers Consumers who are very conscientious about doing the right thing when it comes to protecting the environment.

green marketing The development and selling of products and services that are environmentally friendly.

H

hierarchy of effects Refers to a sequence of cognitive, affective, and conative responses consumers experience in relation to exposure to marketing communication messages.

hierarchy of needs As described by Maslow, a hierarchy of human needs—from the basics of food and shelter to sophisticated psychological desires—the identification and satisfaction of which motivate human growth.

high-context culture See *context (cultural context)*.

high-involvement product, service, or outlet Products, services, or outlets for which the consumer feels it is essential to make the "right" decision to avoid the unpleasant consequences and risks of making a decision that is improper.

Homan's equation The difference between the price we pay for conformity (loss of freedoms, time commitment, financial commitment, etc.) and the rewards obtained for doing so (levels of acceptance, advancement within the group, prestige gained, etc.). This determines for each of us whether we will conform to group expectations and to what extent.

household A group of individuals living together in any dwelling, no matter what the relationships are among the people.

humor appeal A message communicated to an audience through the use of humor—that is, the message is designed to arouse humor in the audience.

I

icons Visual representations of objects, persons, or events.

ideal body image How people would like their bodies to be.

ideal self-congruity The degree of match between the consumer's ideal self-image and the brand-user image.

ideal self-image How consumers would like to see themselves.

ideal social self-congruity The degree of match between the consumer's ideal social self-image and the brand-user image.

ideal social self-image How consumers would like others to see them.

identification with actual self Consumer identification with a source, seeing similarities between that source and the way the consumer perceives himself or herself.

identification with ideal self Consumer identification with a source, seeing similarities between that source and the way the consumer would like himself or herself to be. Marketers achieve consumer identification with ideal self through the use of either popular celebrities or attractive models.

idiographic research The kind of research designed to generate hypotheses. It is not considered to be definitive as in quantitative research (correlational or experimental research). Other terms for idiographic research are *qualitative research, interpretive research,* and *exploratory research.* For examples of this type of research, see *qualitative research.*

implicit versus explicit conclusion In advertisements with implicit conclusions, the outcome or desired response is not boldly stated but rather is left to the consumer to infer. When the outcome is spelled out clearly, the advertisement has an explicit conclusion.

impulsiveness A personality trait describing a tendency to act on the spur of the moment without considering the consequences of one's action.

indexes Easily recognizable properties of an idea.

individualistic culture A society in which members put their personal advancement and welfare ahead of that for other groups, institutions, and the culture as a whole.

influencers Individuals who help establish specifications for usage or purchase. Influencers may or may not be users as well.

informal group A group in which there are no special membership or attendance requirements other than common interests.

information capital Information about product attributes, benefits, and prices learned by a consumer in the past that can still be used in the current situation.

information control The level of control consumers have over what information they are exposed to, how long it will be presented to them, and what information follows.

information disclosure An FTC-developed program that mandates the use of warning labels on several products and their supporting advertising.

information needs Information that marketing managers desire to have to help them make decisions about such things as market selection, product development, pricing, distribution and logistics, and marketing communications.

innovators The first individuals to adopt new products. Typically, they are younger, well educated, with higher incomes and a cosmopolitan outlook and lifestyle. More self-confident than most, they are willing to gather information from a wide variety of sources to evaluate a product. They are less worried about risk than are members of other groups.

instrumental values Personal values that are enduring beliefs that specific modes of conduct or end-states of existence are preferred to other specific modes of conduct or end-states. Specific modes of conduct might be ambition, broad-mindedness, capability, cheerfulness, cleanliness, or helpfulness, among others.

integrated information-response model A marketing communications model that shows that, in making purchase decisions, consumers combine information from marketing communications with information from direct product experience.

intention to try The plan to engage in action, which is motivated by frequency of past trying, social norms toward trying, and attitude toward trying.

interactional justice The perceived justice that has to do with the way customers are treated during the complaint settlement process, including such factors as politeness, interest, truthfulness, and the seller's acceptance of blame.

intermittent reinforcement The use of rewards and punishments on a fairly regular basis.

internal information search Searching no sources other than the consumer's own memory, knowledge, and experience.

internals Individuals who believe they are at least in part responsible for the outcomes of their actions.

interpretive research The kind of research designed to generate hypotheses. It is not considered to be definitive as in quantitative research (correlational or experimental research). Other terms for idiographic research are *qualitative research, idiographic research,* and *exploratory research.* For examples of this type of research, see *qualitative research.*

intervening variables The factors that arise after intention to act in a certain way is determined and that are the causes of change in consumer choice results.

involvement A heightened state of awareness that motivates consumers to seek out, attend to, and think about product information prior to purchase.

J

justice test The ethics concept that states that the responsible marketer avoids marketing actions that damage the well-being of targeted consumers.

L

laddering A method of analyzing means-end chains to reveal how certain goods and services are connected with personal values in the minds of consumers.

laggards Individuals who dislike change, are suspicious of new products and ideas, and will only accept innovations when forced to so. They feel alienated from a society that they perceive is passing them by. They are typically of low socioeconomic status, and many are seniors.

late-majority adopters Individuals who typically are skeptical of new products. They tend to be older and less educated than are members of other groups. They adopt innovations only because of the social pressure to do so or because of forced choice. Their primary information source is word-of-mouth from relatives, friends, and acquaintances.

learn-feel-do hierarchy A simple matrix that attributes consumer choices to information (learn), attitude (feel), and behavior (do) issues.

legal test A test that marketers use to recognize whether an action is ethical and does not violate the law. By becoming familiar with all laws, rules, and regulations governing their industry and its marketing practices, marketers respect the legal rights of consumers.

lifestyle A constellation of individual characteristics that reflect certain behaviors, such as participation in social groups and relationships with significant others, commitment to certain behaviors, and a central life interest, and that may vary according to sociologically relevant variables, such as age, sex, ethnicity, social class, and region, among others.

links See *nodes and links*.

List of Values (LOV) Consists of nine dominant consumer values: self-fulfillment, excitement, sense of accomplishment, self-respect, sense of belonging, being well respected, security, fun and enjoyment, and warm relationships with others.

long-term memory Information that is rehearsed in short-term memory and transmitted to long-term memory, where it is stored for a long time and can be retrieved as needed.

low-context culture See *Context (cultural context)*.

low-involvement learning The situation in which consumers replace old brand perceptions with new beliefs about the product without the mediation effects of brand attitude.

low-involvement product, service, or **outlet** Products, services, or outlets the consumer does not see as important and for which the risks associated with an improper decision are not viewed as high.

loyalty A consumer's feeling of commitment to a product, brand, marketer, or outlet that results in high levels of repeat purchases or visits.

M

market maven A marketplace-specific personality trait describing a tendency to gather information about many kinds of products, places to shop, and other aspects of the marketplace. A market maven also initiates discussions with and responds to others who request product and store information.

marketplace Any location (store, mall, street market, etc.) or medium (by mail, by phone, on the web, etc.) in which a marketing exchange is carried out.

market segmentation The identification of like-minded clusters of consumers who can be expected to behave in similar ways, making similar decisions in the marketplace in similar situations.

masculine culture A society in which male roles are considered superior to female roles.

mass market Consumers in the lower-middle and upper-lower classes.

material artifacts The record of physical items that were part of a culture historically or are in existence in today's society.

materialism The extent to which we regard material goods as important to the overall quality of life. To be materialistic is to measure our self-worth by our external assets and possessions, rather than by other intrinsic characteristics.

meaning-level processing Storage of the meaning of the information, not the "raw" information per se.

means-end chain A cognitive map of a product in the consumer's mind that connects how the consumer perceives the product in terms of concrete attributes and how these concrete attributes are linked to abstract attributes, functional consequences, psychosocial consequences, and instrumental and terminal values.

membership group The group to which a person currently belongs.

mere-possession The concept that simply possessing a brand of a product or service can lead to preference for that brand or for that good or service over other options.

message evidence Information that substantiates product claims.

message execution The combination of strategies through which a message is implemented.

message narrative A message that is communicated in a narrative form—describing the sequence of events that would occur.

message pace How fast or slow a message is presented to an audience in the context of a media vehicle.

message relevance The extent to which the marketing communications message is perceived to be personally relevant to the consumer.

message size or duration The size of an ad in a print medium (measured in column inches and page dimensions) and the duration or length of an ad in other media (for example, a 15-second spot, a 30-second spot, or a 60-second spot).

message tone The emotional versus factual appeal of a message.

metaphysical myth A myth that functions as a guide to the origin of existence.

mobilization (theory of) The process whereby ethnic identification is preserved from one generation to the next through family traditions and the formal teaching of language, religion, and other cultural values within the subculture.

modeling The process through which an individual learns a behavior by observing the behavior of others and the consequences of this behavior.

modified rebuy Similar to a *straight rebuy*, with modifications. Although the customer is happy with the product (and therefore re-orders it), the customer makes modifications to the order based on his or her experience with the product.

mood An affective state that is general and pervasive. Moods are much less intense than emotions.

moral equity The extent to which a situation is perceived by an individual to be fair, just, morally right, and acceptable to one's family.

mores A set of standards for values and behaviors that are considered "morally right."

motivation arousal The sense of drive to action (motivation) a consumer experiences once a problem or need has been recognized. Calling this motive into being is arousal.

motivation to comply The extent to which the consumer considers the possible opinions of significant others when forming an intent to purchase.

motives test The ethics concept that states that marketers should examine the intentions of their actions to ensure that they keep the good of the consumer in mind.

mystery advertising A message designed to arouse a sense of mystery and therefore involve the audience in message processing.

myth A story or fable that reflects important values shared by members of a culture and that is used to teach one or more of these values.

N

need for achievement A personality trait describing a tendency to achieve high scores on performance tasks.

need for affiliation A personality trait describing a tendency to be friendly with others and to establish and maintain social relationships.

need for cognition A personality trait that distinguishes people who have varying needs of thinking. Those high in need for cognition feel the urge to think most of the time. Those low in need for cognition don't like to do much thinking.

need for power A personality trait describing a tendency to seek control of one's environment by influencing people and events.

need for tactile input A tendency for certain consumers to inspect the product by exploring the product's impact, sticking, sliding, slipping, and texture.

neuroticism A personality trait describing a tendency to experience negative affect.

new task decisions Initial purchase decisions based on little or limited prior buying experience.

nodes and links In the context of an associative network, concepts involved in beliefs are nodes that are connected to other nodes through links.

nonanalytic categorization The process by which the consumer classifies a product by focusing on the entire pattern of features in a holistic manner, whereas in analytic categorization the consumer classifies a product by analyzing specific features.

noncompensatory consumer decision rule A decision rule that does not allow for weaknesses in an alternative to be offset by its strengths. Such a rule is used to reduce the number of alternatives to be further evaluated.

normative beliefs The perceived expectation that significant others think the consumer should or should not behave in a certain way (buy the brand).

novice Consumers who have little or no prior knowledge and experience with a product or service category.

O

objective performance A measure of how well a product or service meets all functional (benefits) expectations.

observability (communicability) The frequency with which an innovation is seen in the target market or the ease with which a marketer can show or describe the innovation.

ongoing search Continually observing what is happening in the marketplace, looking for and being open to new information. Ongoing search can occur pre-purchase, after purchase, or both.

operant or instrumental conditioning The process in which the frequency of occurrence of a bit of behavior is modified by the consequences of the behavior.

opinion leadership A product-specific tendency to acquire, store, and communicate information to others about a particular product class.

opportunity recognition A variation of problem recognition. Here, the consumer is apparently completely satisfied with the current actual state. However, an option that is new or not previously known is found. The consumer does not perceive a problem but, rather, perceives an opportunity that leads to a comparison between actual state and desired state.

optimum stimulation level (OSL) A personality trait describing a desire to explore the environment and seek stimulation.

other-focused appeals Messages that arouse emotions such as empathy, peacefulness, indebtedness, and shame, which reflect an "interdependent self." These emotions tend to be associated with others, such as family, friends, co-workers, etc.

P

perceived age The age a person sees himself or herself to be. This is usually younger than a person's chronological age.

perceived concern Consumer perception that the source cares whether or not the consumer complies.

perceived control Consumer perception that the source is able to administer rewards and/or punishments if the consumer does not comply with the message demand.

perceived scrutiny Consumer perception that the source is able to know whether the consumer complied or not.

perceived value Perceptions of trade-off between product benefits (e.g., product quality) and monetary sacrifice.

performance purchases Purchases in which vendors solve technical problems. Examples are photocopy machines and image setters.

permissive parents Parents who are nurturing but do not set restrictions on their children's activities.

person perception A form of mental inference (or attribution) consumers make about the reasons behind the actions of others.

personal (shopping) motives Reasons for shopping that do not relate to the selection of goods and services but are primarily focused on personal feelings, role-playing, diversion, and other related outcomes tied to the shopping experience.

personal values Enduring beliefs that specific modes of conduct or end-states of existence are preferred to other specific modes of conduct or end-states.

personality An individual's response tendencies across situations and over time.

physical (consumption) context The time and place of consumption of a good or service.

political decisions Decisions that involve major capital outlay, such as high-cost medical equipment purchased by a hospital. In political purchases, multiple departments compete for the same funds.

positioning The placement of such things as a product, service, company, or retail outlet in the mind of the consumer. Position is achieved based not upon the benefits possessed alone, but on the way in which consumers perceive such benefits.

post-purchase information search When a consumer who has already made a purchase continues to gather information about his or her choice and/or evaluates other options in the marketplace.

power distance The level of social inequality that exists in a society and how willing members are to accept authority at all levels. High power distance means high social inequality.

pre-purchase information search A search for information made before making a purchase decision. Such searches are classified as directed, browsing, or accidental.

primary reference group The group with which the individual has frequent face-to-face contact and in which members are close-knit.

priming A preliminary presentation of visual or copy information that places a product or service into a category based on type or benefits. This is offered before the target member is exposed to the ad itself.

Privacy Act The 1974 act that applies broader record-keeping restrictions to U.S. government agencies.

private action Dissatisfied customer action with no attempt to obtain redress; it could involve negative word-of-mouth and personal boycott of brands and outlets.

probability theory A theory of learning that treats learning as the formation of habits by examining the person's history of behaviors.

problem recognition A psychological process through which we evaluate the difference between our actual state and our desired state. This is a comparison of our current need or benefits state with what we would like it to be. The greater the "perceived distance" between these two, the more clearly the consumer recognizes a problem or potential need.

procedural justice The perceived justice that is derived from the complaint policies, procedures, and criteria used to make a decision; heavy emphasis is placed by the consumer on timeliness, responsiveness, and convenience.

procedural purchases Purchases that involve products or services that require training, such as accounting information systems.

producer sovereignty The situation in which producers' interests dominate consumers' interests. The opposite of *consumer sovereignty*.

product constellation Certain goods and services that go together, reflecting certain lifestyles.

product disposition The process of reselling, recycling, trashing, repairing, trading, and the like associated with the physical product, its packaging, and its promotional materials when the consumer or marketer no longer perceives the product as useful.

product familiarity The extent to which the consumer is experienced with the product in question.

product labeling An FTC-developed program that mandates labeling on most food products to indicate appropriate product warnings, use-by dates, and nutritional values.

product/service perception A form of mental inference (or attribution) that consumers make about products or services, attributing product or service performance to specific qualities or features.

product-specific involvement A product-specific tendency to feel emotionally involved in a product class.

product-specific self-confidence A product-specific tendency to make decisions about the product category without doubting the effectiveness of one's decisions.

product-specific self-efficacy A product-specific tendency to perceive oneself as being highly capable and competent in the acquisition, use, and disposal of a product class.

profane consumption Consumption of goods or services that is part of everyday life.

protective self-presentation The motivational tendency to self-monitor out of fear of socially adverse reactions from others.

psychographics A term that consumer researchers use to describe consumers in terms of personality traits and concept of self; attitudes toward product classes and toward brands; activities, interests, and opinions; value systems; goods and services consumed; and media use patterns.

psychological myth A myth that functions as a guide to appropriate personal conduct.

public action What occurs when a dissatisfied customer seeks a remedy for the problem at the purchase location or from the manufacturer, by taking legal action, or complaining to groups that represent the interests of consumers, such as the Better Business Bureau, the Federal Trade Commission, or the attorney general of the state in which the customer resides.

purchase-associated cognitive dissonance The state of mind that occurs before the consumer determines whether a product or service is satisfactory. As the consumer makes a commitment to the purchase or selection of the product—in most cases, before use or possession—there is a feeling of uncertainty about whether the right choice is being made.

purchase responsibility The extent to which the audience of a marketing communications message feels responsible in making a purchase decision.

Q

qualitative research Research involving collecting data from a small sample (where data is typically gathered using a convenience sampling method that is not necessarily representative of the population at large) using data collection methods that do not produce quantitative data. Focus groups, in-depth personal interviews, and projective techniques are examples of methods that produce qualitative data. Qualitative data is rich in meaning (e.g., a personal shopping diary) that does not easily lend itself to analysis using inferential statistics. The data are interpreted by capturing themes (or key ideas) and categorized as such.

quality market Consumers in the lower-upper and upper-middle classes.

quality-of-life marketing A movement within marketing thought and practice that guides marketers to seek the best interests of consumers and other publics without damaging the organization's financial health, restricting its growth, or otherwise harming its stakeholders.

R

rate of diffusion The time it takes to achieve acceptance of an innovation in society.

reach The media concept that describes the extent to which messages inserted in certain media vehicles will be exposed to the audience.

recovery expectations Expectations tied to customer beliefs about the level of "reparation" (compensation of the customer for losses produced by the service failure) that is appropriate after a failure.

reference group The group whose perspective an individual takes on in forming values, beliefs, attitudes, opinions, and overt behaviors.

reinforcement schedule A schedule of rewards or punishments used for learning.

relationship marketing Refers to the development of marketing strategies to enhance relationships with customers.

relative advantage The extent to which consumers in the target market perceive an innovation to be superior in some important way to existing products.

research design Three different approaches to conducting research, namely exploratory research, descriptive research, and hypothesis-testing research.

research questions Information needs are translated into research questions, which are much more specific in that they involve a set of specific questions designed to guide the research process.

retail outlet image Image or personality resulting from a mix of functional and psychological attributes of the outlet as perceived by the consumer.

retention The amount of material previously learned that is remembered.

retrieval The consumer's ability to recognize or recall product or service information previously retained in memory.

reverse coded When a measurement item is capturing the concept being measured in the reverse manner—that is, when adding the scores pertaining to all items, the researcher has to reverse code those particular items that are reversed in meaning.

right to be informed The consumer's right to be protected against fraudulent, deceitful, or grossly misleading information, advertising, labeling, or other practices, and to be given the facts he or she needs to make an informed choice.

right to choose The consumer's right to assured access, whenever possible, to a variety of products at competitive prices. In those industries in which competition is not workable, government regulation is substituted to assure satisfactory quality and service at fair prices. The intent here is to discourage monopolies and encourage fair competition. Monopoly restricts choice and, in extreme cases, forces consumers to accept questionable quality and/or high prices. Competition typically motivates marketers to offer improved quality and fair pricing.

right to a healthful environment The consumer's right to have legislation that protects public health in the areas of hazardous waste control, toxic substance control, and safe drinking water programs.

right to privacy The consumer's right to be left alone. Four out of five consumers report that they value their privacy and believe it should be protected by law. Business does not have the right to collect information about consumers to establish detailed profiles about their lives and shopping habits.

right to redress The consumer's right to complain and express grievances about product failure.

right to safety The consumer's right to have several U.S. federal agencies monitor aspects of product quality and safety, both through safety legislation and consumer education campaigns. One consideration in the setting of policies is the extent to which consumers are willing to sacrifice such benefits as low price for improved quality or safety.

rights test The ethics concept that states that responsible marketers ensure that marketing actions do not infringe upon consumer rights, as protected by the "Consumer Bill of Rights." These include the right to information, the right to safety, the right to redress, the right to choose, the right to a healthful environment, and the right to privacy.

rigidity   A personality trait describing a tendency to be inflexible in tastes and preferences.

risk   Consumers' perception of the costs associated with the purchase and use of the innovation. These costs can be economic, psychological, social, physical, or performance-related.

risk perception/risk reduction   A perceptual process and behavior outcomes generated from the perception of risk in the purchase of a product or service.

ritual   A pattern of behavior tied to an event that we consider important in our lives.

ritual artifacts   Those objects needed in order for rituals to be carried out successfully.

ritual consumption   Consumption of goods and services that is tied to specific rituals.

Robinson-Patman Act   Antitrust law designed to protect the consumer's right to choose. In those industries in which competition is not workable, government regulation is substituted to assure satisfactory quality and service at fair prices. The intent here is to discourage monopolies and encourage fair competition. Monopoly restricts choice and, in extreme cases, forces consumers to accept questionable quality and/or high prices. Competition typically motivates marketers to offer improved quality and fair pricing.

routine decisions   Decisions that involve frequently ordered and used products, such as office supplies. No training is needed in the use of such products.

S

sacralization   What occurs when the consumer transforms objects, places, people, and events from the profane to the sacred. Desacralization is the reverse action.

sacred consumption   Consumption that occurs during out-of-the-ordinary situations.

Safe Drinking Water Act Amendment   The 1986 act that authorizes appropriations for and revision of EPA safe drinking water programs.

salience   The relative importance of each evaluative criterion in the alternative evaluation process.

sanctions   A negative action taken by members of the culture when a person acts contrary to norms, mores, customs, or conventions.

satisfaction   A measure of how well a product or service performs compared to consumer expectations.

scrambled merchandising   A wide variety of unrelated product types offered in close proximity to one another in a single retail outlet.

search products   Goods or services for which most essential attributes and benefits can easily be evaluated prior to the purchase. This means that enough information can be found to make an informed buying decision resulting in the best product/brand being chosen.

secondary reference group   The group in which interaction with other members is less frequent than in a primary group situation.

segment bounding   A method of setting conditions whereby consumers qualify or do not qualify as part of a segment. Segments are bounded on descriptors, location, and time.

self-concept   Consumers' perceptions of their own personal identity—their private and public self, their actual and ideal self.

self-consciousness   A personality trait describing a tendency to be keenly aware of oneself in many situations.

self-consistency motive   The motivational tendency that drives people to act in a manner consistent with their actual self-images.

self-esteem   A personality trait describing the extent to which the actual self is congruent with the ideal self. People whose actual self falls very short of their ideal self are characterized as low in self-esteem. Conversely, those whose actual self is close to their ideal self are characterized as high in self-esteem.

self-esteem motive   The motivational tendency that drives people to act in a manner consistent with their ideal self-images.

self-image   A configuration of beliefs about the self.

self-image congruence   The degree of match between the consumer's self-image (actual, ideal, social, or ideal social self-image) and the brand-user image.

self-monitoring   A personality trait describing a tendency to adapt to different situations and so manage the impressions made on others.

self-perception   A form of mental inference (or attribution) in which consumers attribute their own behavior, such as the purchase of a brand, as reflecting their preference for that brand.

self-reference   Messages that speak directly to the consumer, making the advertisement seem particularly relevant to the consumer's personal situation.

semiotics   The study of signs and their meanings.

sensory memory   That part of the brain that captures information when it first enters the brain. The information may register as little more than a sensation and may last for only fractions of a second.

sensory perception   Perception governed by the five senses—sight, sound, smell, touch, and taste. Sensory perception focuses on specific attributes of a product or service and how these attributes are understood and ultimately evaluated by consumers.

separateness   A personality trait describing a tendency for some people to perceive themselves as individuals, separated from others. Contrast with *connectedness*.

sets   Groups used to limit external search and alternative evaluation. The types include (1) universal—the group of brands or retail outlets to which the consumer has reasonable access whether aware of them or not, (2) retrieval—the group of which a person has front-of-mind awareness, (3) consideration (evoked, relevant)—all of the brands or outlets of which a person has front-of-mind awareness and that the consumer accepts as the set from among which a choice will likely be made.

sex appeal   A message communicated to an audience through the use of sex—that is, the message is designed to arouse sexual excitement in the audience.

shaping   A form of operant conditioning in which consumers are gradually trained to produce a desired response. Behavior is reinforced or punished until it approximates more and more closely the response ultimately desired.

Sherman Act   Antitrust law designed to protect the consumer's right to choose. In those industries in which competition is not workable, government regulation is substituted to assure satisfactory quality and service at fair prices. The intent here is to discourage monopolies and encourage fair competition. Monopoly restricts choice and, in extreme cases, forces consumers to accept questionable quality and/or high prices. Competition typically motivates marketers to offer improved quality and fair pricing.

shoplifting   The act of taking goods from retail stores without paying for them at the cashier or checkout stand.

shopper   The person who gathers information in the marketplace about products and/or services in preparation for making or recommending a choice from among them.

shopper/buyer/consumer behavior models   Concepts and theories about how shoppers, buyers, and consumers perceive and evaluate goods and services in the marketplace and act accordingly.

shopping orientation   A consumer's style or way of shopping. Both feelings about shopping and actual shopping procedures come into play.

short-term memory   The part of the brain that analyzes the information from sensory memory and assigns meaning to the information.

skill capital   The amount of skill a consumer brings to a search. Consumers who have learned how to search from past experience will enjoy lower search costs, and the amount of information gathered will also be higher.

social approval motive The motivational tendency that drives people to act in a manner consistent with their ideal social self-images.

social class A status hierarchy by which groups and individuals are classified on the basis of esteem and prestige.

social consistency motive The motivational tendency that drives people to act in a manner consistent with their social self-images.

social (consumption) context The presence of others when consumption occurs.

socialization The process through which we strive to acquire the characteristic ways of behaving in accordance with the values, norms, and attitudes of the social unit of which we are a part.

social judgment theory The theory that states that people attribute meaning to incoming information by matching this information to a mental category or referent. This matching process is characterized as involving two regions—one called the assimilation region and the other called the contrast region. The assimilation region is the area around the referent in which the incoming information is categorized as similar to that referent. The contrast region is the area in which the incoming information is categorized as different from the referent.

social norm Any rule of behavior for meeting societal (group) expectations.

social norms toward trying The extent to which the consumer thinks that others expect him or her to try to engage in the consumption act in question.

social pressure Influence over purchase decisions coming from significant others such as friends, parents, relatives, and associates.

social self-congruity The degree of match between the consumer's social self-image and the brand-user image.

social self-image How consumers believe others see them.

social (shopping) motives These reasons for shopping are based on the desire to have social experiences outside of the home, including interactions with others.

sociological myth A myth that functions to provide clues to the social code of a culture.

socio-oriented communication Communication characterized by harmony, pleasant social interactions and cohesiveness, and avoidance of conflict and controversy.

source attractiveness Refers to the audience perception of the source (communicator) as being physically attractive.

source congruity The extent to which a celebrity who endorses a brand has characteristics that match the brand attributes.

source credibility Perception by the target audience that a source has the knowledge, skill, or experience related to the product or service promoted and that the source is objective and trustworthy.

source power The different kinds of power that consumers perceive communicators as having.

special obligations test The ethics concept that states that marketers should consider any special obligations peculiar to their industry.

specifically planned purchase A purchase in which the item and even the brand are decided before the consumer visits a store or investigates other outlet options.

state approach to personality A method of studying personality involving studying how the whole person (all of his or her traits) affects behavior. The study focuses on one person at a time.

state versus action orientation A personality trait in which some people have a tendency to act readily without hesitation (action-oriented), whereas others hesitate and procrastinate in taking action (state-oriented).

straight rebuy A purchase decision typically determined by post-purchase satisfaction. The customer tries a new product. The customer is satisfied with its performance. The customer buys it again.

subculture Any cultural patterning that preserves important features of the dominant society but provides for values, norms, and behaviors of its own.

subjective norm Our perception of what other people think we should do with respect to a certain behavior, such as a brand purchase.

substitute purchase A purchase in which a consumer switches from a specifically or generally planned item to an altogether different one for purchase.

subtle persuasion The attempt to persuade the audience without being overt about the motive to persuade.

Superfund Amendments and Reauthorization Act The 1986 act that authorizes appropriations for the EPA Hazardous Substance Response Trust Fund program to charge violators and to clean up hazardous waste sites.

supplier benevolence A perceived willingness of the supplier to behave in a way that benefits the interest of both parties in the relationship (for example, willingness to support the customer if the environment causes changes, consideration of the customer's welfare when making important decisions, responding with understanding when problems arise, consideration of how future decisions and actions will affect the customer, and dependable support on things that are important to the customer).

supplier reliability The supplier's ability to keep a promise (for example, ability to deliver according to contract, provision of enough and relevant information, trust in provided information, and trustworthiness of supplier).

surface-level processing Storage of information as is, without analysis of its meaning.

surrogate shopper A person, firm, or other entity engaged and paid by the consumer or other interested party on behalf of the consumer to make or facilitate a product or service selection decision on behalf of that consumer.

survey research Research involving the construction of a questionnaire, which is then used to collect data using such methods as mail, telephone interviews, mall intercepts, email, or the Internet.

symbolic consumption The process through which consumers—on the basis of symbols—buy, consume, and dispose of products.

symbols Learned associations between a signifier and a signified to communicate ideas.

syncratic family decision making Decision making that husband and wife share.

T

technology anxiety The fear, apprehension, and hope consumers feel when they consider using or actually use computer technology.

terminal values Personal values that are enduring beliefs that specific modes of conduct or end-states of existence, if enacted over time, lead to desirable end-states or terminal values (end-states of existence that are preferred over other end-states). Terminal values might be a comfortable life, a sense of accomplishment, a world at peace, or racial equality.

theory of reasoned action The theory that states that behavior is a direct result of intention. Particularly with planned purchases, and even with impulse purchases, we buy only after we have formed an intention to do so. Two factors are involved in behavioral intention: attitude toward an act and subjective norm.

theory of trying The theory designed to predict consumption behavior rather than buying behavior. According to the theory of trying, the intensity of an attempt to consume a product can be predicted by intention to try, frequency of past trying, and recency of past trying.

time activity level A measure of whether consumers are more comfortable doing one thing during a clock block of time, called monochronic behavior, or more comfortable doing two or more things at a time, named polychronic behavior. Monochrons are persons who are monochronic, and polychrons are those who are polychronic.

time approaches (approaches to time) Related to the issues and assumptions used in discussing and thinking about time. The approaches are economic, sociocultural, psychological, measurement, and physiological.

time orientation A person's perception of the importance of the past, present, or future in his or her life. Individuals see past, present, and future as either short-term (immediate), intermediate, or long-term (extended).

time personality Can be identified for persons, household units, organizations, institutions, and cultures, and is based on their use of a variety of time styles.

time processing methods Tied to time flow and, in some cases, time value. The three types are (1) ribbon, linear, linear separable, or economic; (2) procedural; and (3) circular or cyclical time.

time styles The building blocks of time personality that tentatively consist of approaches to time, time orientation, activity level, and time processing.

timing of measurement A concept that helps us understand why a consumer's expression of an attitude toward a product (or service) is sometimes different from their actual purchase. That is, when people are surveyed and indicate a positive attitude toward a product (or service), yet they end up purchasing a different product or service. The timing of measurement is one factor that explains this discrepancy—the more time that lapses between the attitude survey and the observed purchase behavior, the greater the probability of other intervening factors coming into play and changing the consumer's attitude toward the product (or service).

tolerance of ambiguity A personality trait describing a tendency not to feel bothered by situations in which the person lacks information to guide action.

total product concept A concept that involves four types of benefits: a basic core, an accessory ring, a psychological ring, and time. The basic core of a product is the bundle of utilitarian benefits purchased. Accessory benefits include those not directly paid for, yet received. Benefits that result from the consumer's feelings associated with the possession and/or use of a product make up the psychological ring. The fourth element is time. Everything we purchase either saves time or takes time from us, and in each case, this may be perceived as good or bad.

trait approach to personality The method of studying personality involving studying how one personality trait affects behavior. The study focuses on one trait at a time across many people.

trialability (divisibility) The degree to which an innovation may be sampled or tried out. Divisibility is the ability to separate the product into units small enough to try out.

trivial attribute An irrelevant or unneeded criterion that affects the consumer's evaluation of a product or service alternative.

U

U-commerce (Uber-commerce) This new view of what global commerce is becoming flows out of the hyper-networking of computers on the world stage. The network is described as having four characteristics: (1) ubiquity, (2) universality, (3) uniqueness, and (4) unison.

uncertainty avoidance The willingness of the members of a society to accept ambiguity and uncertainty.

underclass People who are on welfare, not regularly employed, poverty-stricken, lacking in education, or employed in very low-paying, menial jobs.

unit pricing An FTC-developed program that says that retailers must provide consumers with two prices for every packaged goods item: the price per package and the price per unit of measure. The goal is to allow consumers to make value comparisons among products and package sizes.

unplanned purchase When consumers buy, for whatever reasons, an item that is not on a written or mental shopping list.

use The extent to which consumers feel they are likely to use the innovation sufficiently to justify its purchase.

users Individuals who actually use the product purchased. Teachers and students, for example, are users of textbooks that the school system purchases.

utilitarian or functional needs Needs that are met by products that help consumers remove or avoid problems.

utilitarian test The ethics concept that states that responsible marketers consider all alternative actions and their potential benefits to consumers before making marketing decisions.

V

value An innovation's benefits compared to the money paid for it. The more benefits (and less cost), the greater the value.

value consciousness A marketplace-specific tendency to consider the value (both costs and benefits) of the product in the purchase of economic goods.

value expression The concept that an attitude can serve to express a person's values. For example, buying a hybrid car may express the buyer's values related to environmentalism.

value-expressive or symbolic needs Needs that are met by products that help consumers express their own self-images.

vendor stratification What occurs when many customers in highly competitive markets stratify vendors and develop what is known in business-to-business purchasing as "preferred supplier programs." Vendors are rated according to criteria related to relationship quality. Thus, a cumulative set of customer experiences with the company's vendors provides a basis from which to rank the vendors.

Brand Index

Note: Page numbers in *italics* indicate exhibits; page numbers followed by an italic *n* indicate material in footnotes or endnotes.

Name Index

Note: Page numbers in *italics* indicate exhibits; page numbers followed by an italic *n* indicate material in footnotes or endnotes.

Subject Index

Note: Page numbers in *italics* indicate exhibits; page numbers followed by an italic *n* indicate material in footnotes or endnotes.